	DATE DUE		

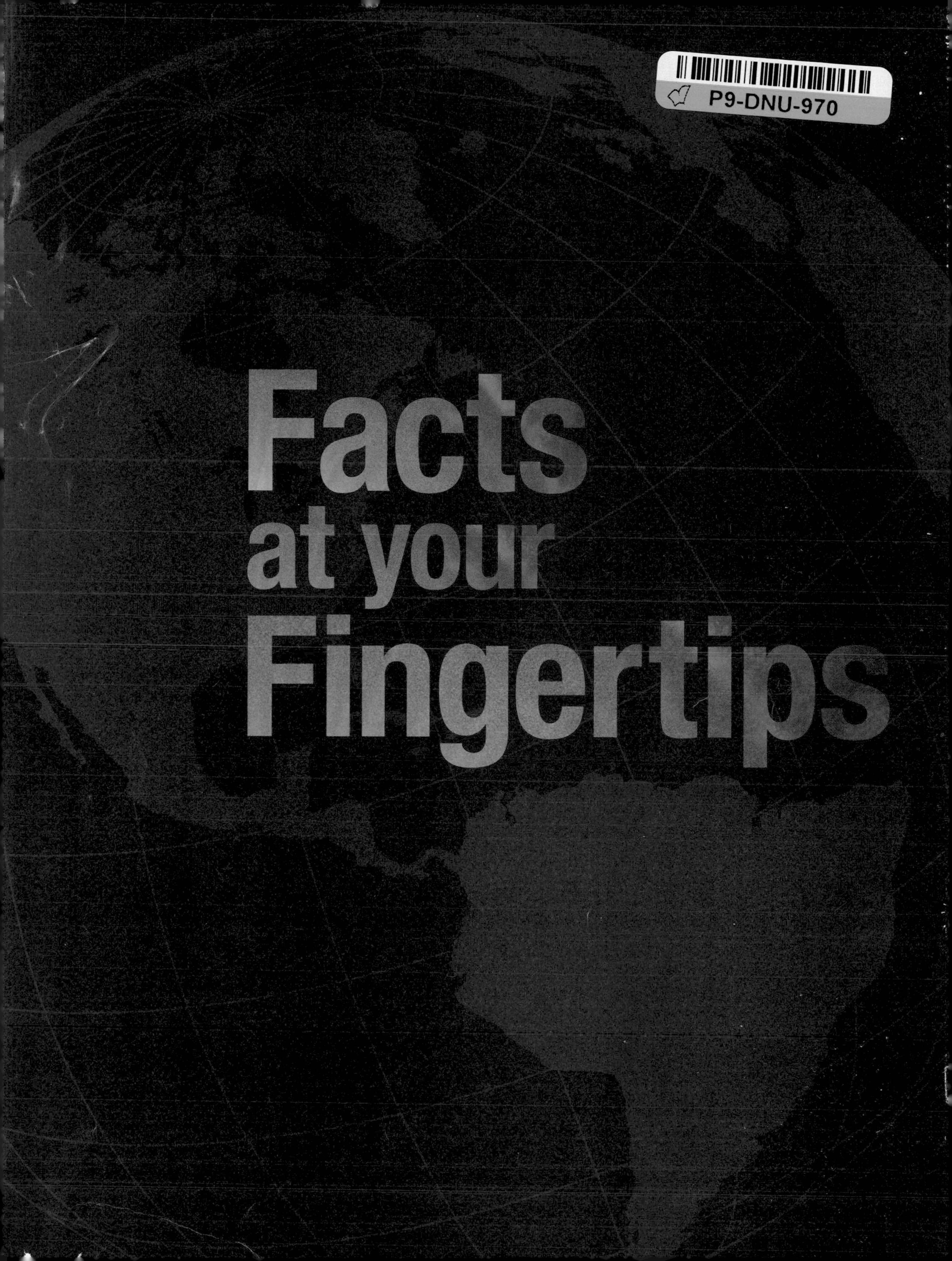

Facts at your Fingertips

Facts at your Fingertips

Reader's Digest
THE READER'S DIGEST ASSOCIATION , INC.
PLEASANTVILLE, NEW YORK / MONTREAL

at your
tips

FACTS AT YOUR FINGERTIPS

North American Edition produced by
NOVA GRAPHIC SERVICES, Jamison, PA
President David Davenport
Editorial Director Robin C. Bonner
Copyeditor Linnea Hermanson
Proofreaders Margo McMahon, Linnea Hermanson
Composition Manager Steve Magnin
Compositor Linda Magnin

READER'S DIGEST PROJECT STAFF
Senior Editor Don Earnest
Senior Design Director Elizabeth Tunnicliffe
Production Technology Manager Douglas A. Croll
Manufacturing Manager John L. Cassidy

READER'S DIGEST HOME AND HEALTH BOOKS
Editor in Chief Neil Wertheimer
Art Director Michele Laseau
Managing Editor Suzanne Beason

Vice President and General Manager Keira Krausz
Marketing Director Dawn Nelson

CANADIAN PROJECT STAFF
Project Editor Robert Ronald

Books and Home Entertainment
Vice President Deirdre Gilbert
Art Director John McGuffie

THE READER'S DIGEST ASSOCIATION, INC.
Editor in Chief and President, Reader's Digest North America Eric W. Schrier

Library of Congress Cataloging in Publication Data
Facts at your fingertips / Reader's Digest.
p. cm.
Includes index.
ISBN 0-7621-0471-6
1. Handbooks, vade-mecums, etc. I. Reader's Digest Association.

AG106.F33 2003
031.02--dc2 2003043240

Address any comments about *Facts at your Fingertips* to:
Editor in Chief
Reader's Digest Home and Health Books
Reader's Digest Road
Pleasantville, NY 10570-7000

To order additional copies of *Facts at Your Fingertips*, call 1-800-846-2100.

For more Reader's Digest products and information, visit our Web site at: rd.com
In Canada: **readersdigest.ca**

UK 1050/IC

Printed in the United States of America
3 5 7 9 10 8 6 4 2

Original edition was created by
TOUCAN BOOKS LTD, London
for the Reader's Digest Association

Contributing authors Sarah Angliss, Julia Bruce, Thomas Cussans, Mike Flynn, Richard German, Robin Hosie, Antony Mason, Nigel Rodgers, Carmine Ruggiero, Elizabeth Taylor, Helen Varley, Christine Vincent, John Wright, Michael Wright

Managing editors Helen Douglas-Cooper, Andrew Kerr-Jarrett, Robert Sackville West

Editors Alison Bravington, Liz Clasen, Celia Coyne, Finny Fox-Davies, Daniel Gilpin, Simon Hall, Jane Hutchings, Justine Johnstone, Cécile Landau, Marion Moisy, Alison Moss, Charlotte Rundall, Simon Tuite, Richard Walker, Susan Watt, Michael Wright

Researcher Michael Paterson

Picture researchers Sandra Assersohn, Christine Vincent, Caroline Wood

Consultants Dominic Alexander, Sarah Angliss, Jock Boyd, David Burnie, Brian Candy, Joan Candy, Alison Ewington, Nigel Hawkes, David Kynaston, Frank Meddens, Colin Uttley

Proofreaders Roy Butcher, Ken Vickery

Indexer Laura Hicks

Design Bradbury and Williams

Toucan Books would also like to thank the following for their assistance in the preparation of this book: Ian Barnett, Central School of Ballet, London, Janet Guggenheim, John Meek, Alice Palmer, Stevie Williams

ORIGINAL READER'S DIGEST PROJECT STAFF
Project Editor Jonathan Bastable
Art Editor Julie Bennett
Editorial Assistants Rachel Weaver, Liz Edwards
Proofreader Barry Gage

About this book

Facts at your Fingertips is a distillation of the most asked questions and most useful facts about the world. It is a book that extracts the essence of knowledge from mountains of information. It is the first place to check before you turn on your computer or go to the library, because nine times out of ten it will save you the trouble.

Understanding **Facts at your Fingertips'** structure is the first step to getting the most out of it. There are nine chapters, each covering a different area of knowledge:

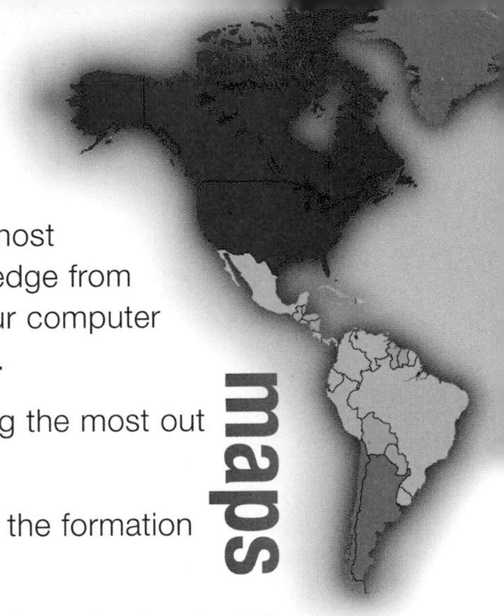

- **The Universe and our planet** looks at the birth and growth of the Cosmos, the formation of the Earth, and Earth's geographical character.

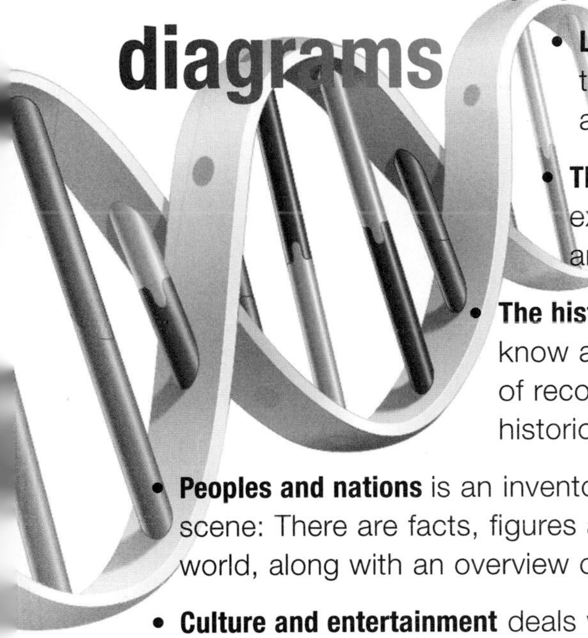

- **Life on Earth** focuses on the origins of plants and animals. It traces the development of life and looks at the variety of modern life forms and their classification.
- **The human body** focuses on our own highly successful species and examines in detail how our bodies function, how they can go wrong, and what they are physically capable of.
- **The history of mankind** chronicles what we know about our past, from the first glimmer of recorded history to the most recent historic events.
- **Peoples and nations** is an inventory of the present-day geopolitical scene: There are facts, figures and maps for every country in the world, along with an overview of international organizations.
- **Culture and entertainment** deals with all the achievements of the human spirit and intellect: religion, philosophy, psychology, literature, art, music, sports and cinema.
- **The global economy** looks at the world's natural resources, finance, trade, agriculture, transportation and communications.
- **Science and invention** gives the facts about technology, medicine and the pure sciences.
- **Ready reference** provides useful lists, statistics and conversion tables.

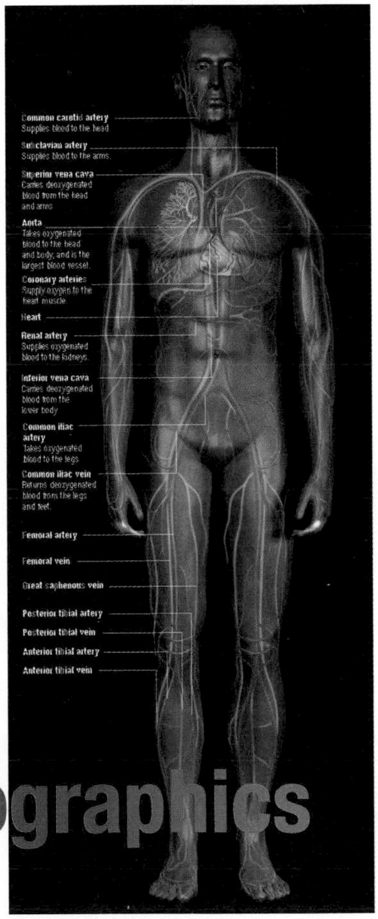

Turn to **Facts at your Fingertips** whenever you have a factual question of any kind. Once you have taken it off the shelf, the answer is within your grasp.

—The Editors

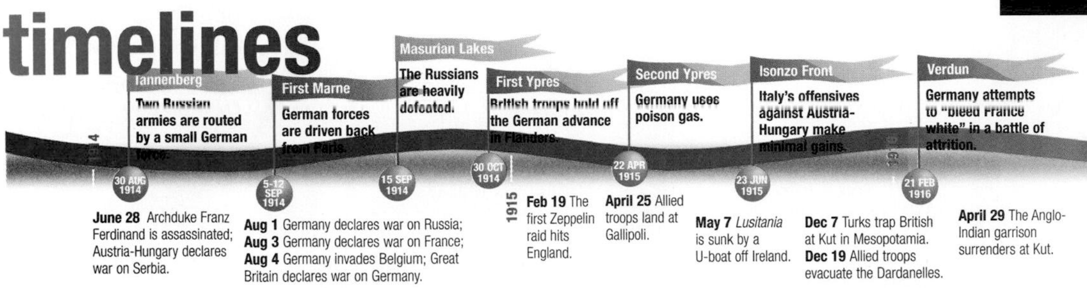

Contents

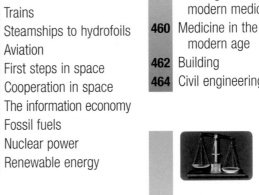

The Universe and our planet

The Universe and our planet

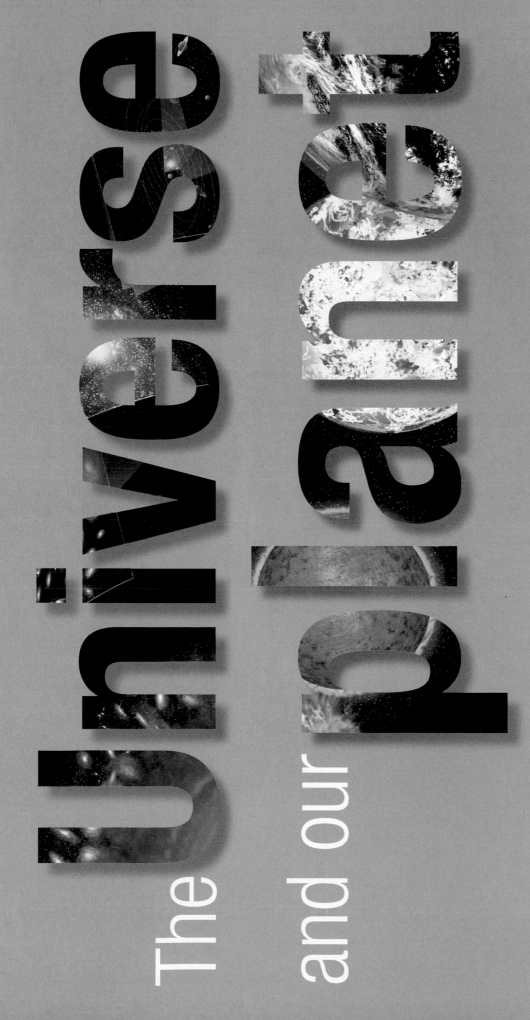

The Earth was created from an immense cloud of dust particles and gas circling a newly formed star – our Sun. It became the fifth-largest planet in the Solar System and, as far as we know, the only body in the Solar System to support life. The Earth orbits the Sun and rotates on its own tilted axis, producing the cycles of seasons and day and night.

1 A cold, dark beginning The Earth and other planets were created 4.6 billion years ago from a cloud of gas and dust swirling around the embryonic Sun. The Earth formed as particles of dust collided and merged. The Sun was much smaller and dimmer than it is today, and the early Solar System was dark and cold.

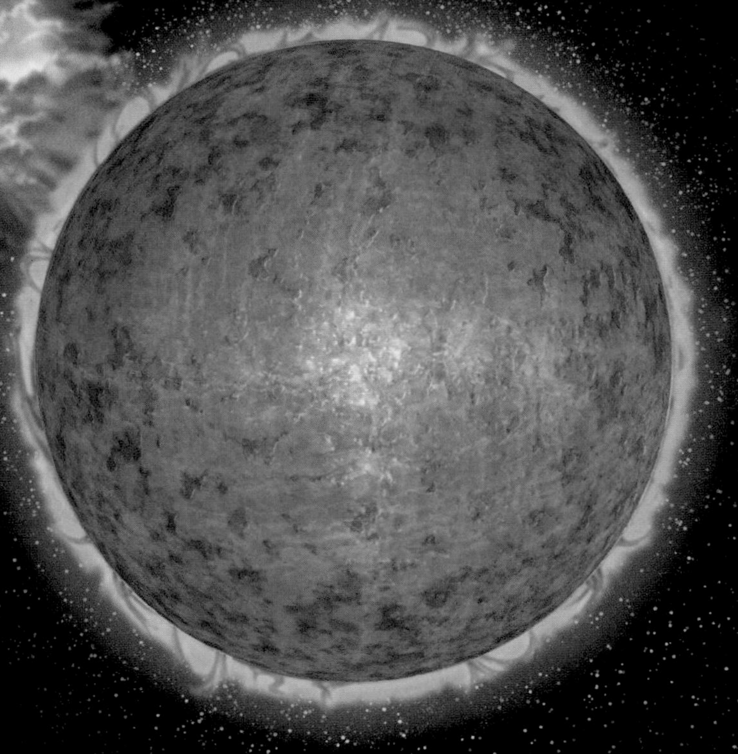

2 Melting pot From 4.6 to 4.2 billion years ago, gravity compacted the Earth's interior, and decomposing radioactive elements caused it to melt. Iron sank to form the core, leaving lighter materials to make up the mantle.

THE FORMATION OF OUR WORLD

The Earth was formed in stages over billions of years. Since its creation it has been in a constant state of flux. Its temperature, atmosphere and geography have all altered dramatically, and it continues to change.

Earth statistics

Total surface area	509 600 000 km^2 (197 000 000 sq miles)
Land area	29 percent, 148 000 000 km^2 (57 000 000 sq miles)
Speed of rotation	1674 km/h (1040 mph)
Orbit speed around the Sun	107 180 km/h (66 600 mph)
Inclination of axis	23.44 degrees

EFFECTS OF THE EARTH'S POSITION, TILT AND ROTATION

The most obvious effect of the Earth's movements is the cycle of day and night, but its tilt and position also account for day length and seasons.

The seasons Earth's axis of rotation tilts at about 23 degrees from the vertical. This means that during the northern summer (southern winter), the Northern Hemisphere is tilted toward the Sun and the Southern Hemisphere away from it. This is enough to account for the temperature differences between summer and winter. In the northern winter (southern summer) the position is reversed. During summer, the Sun rises higher in the sky than in winter, and the time from sunrise to sunset (a solar day) is longer.

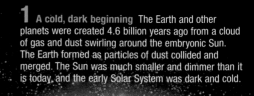

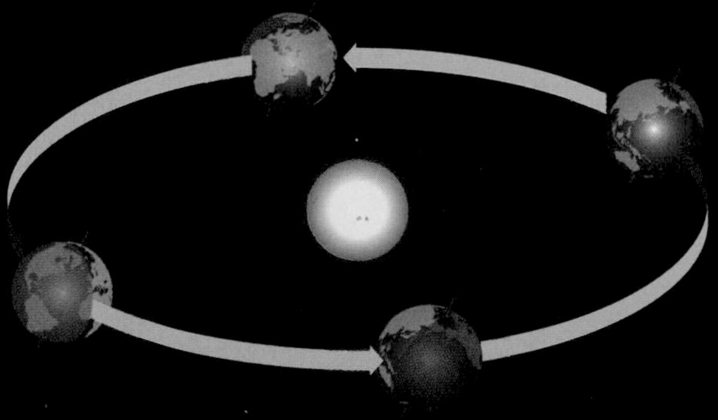

Day and night The Earth rotates on its axis roughly once every 24 hours as it orbits the Sun. Because it tilts as it orbits, days and nights are unequal in length, except at the spring and fall equinoxes.

Equinoxes There are two days each year when neither the Northern nor Southern Hemisphere is inclined toward the Sun. On these days, night and day are of equal length all over the world. They occur around March 21 (vernal equinox) and September 22 (autumnal equinox).

Solstices These are the longest and shortest days in the year, that is, the day with the greatest amount of daylight and the day with the least daylight. In the Northern Hemisphere, the summer solstice is on or around June 21, and the winter solstice is on or around December 21. The opposite is true in the Southern Hemisphere.

Climate zones Latitudes near the Equator are roughly the same distance from the Sun throughout the year and therefore experience little temperature variation. Because the Earth tilts, variation in temperature increases with latitude, and the poles experience the greatest contrast, having 24 hours of sunlight daily at the height of summer and 24 hours of darkness in midwinter. This is a major determining factor of climatic zones. Tropical and subtropical climates near the Equator are uniformly warm; the temperate climates of higher latitudes have greater seasonal variation, and the far north and south experience extreme winter cold.

Midnight sun The Sun does not dip below the horizon in midsummer at the poles, so there is daylight throughout the night.

4 Toward the modern world As the oxygen in the atmosphere built up, a protective layer of ozone formed, blocking ultraviolet radiation from the Sun and making the surface waters of the oceans safe for complex organisms to evolve. By 400 million years ago, the colonization of land by plants and animals was well under way and the planet was beginning to resemble the Earth we know today.

see also

20-21 **The planets**
48-49 **Weather**
52-53 **The ages of life on Earth**

3 The surface cools Between 4.2 and 3.8 billion years ago, the Earth's surface cooled and the crust formed. Bombardment by icy comets provided water which, supplemented by water vapor that billowed out from volcanoes, slowly filled the seas. As this period ended, bombardment ceased, and the first life appeared in the seas. Cyanobacteria used the Sun's energy and carbon dioxide to produce food and expelled oxygen as a waste product, which gradually accumulated in the young atmosphere.

The Universe

From the big bang to the present – a 15 billion year journey through time and space

Fifteen billion years ago our Universe did not exist. It came into being in a cosmic explosion, the big bang, expanding from nothing to 2 billion billion km (1.25 billion billion miles) wide in a single second, and it is still expanding today. At present, scientists can only speculate about why the big bang occurred, but we are beginning to understand what happened in the first few moments.

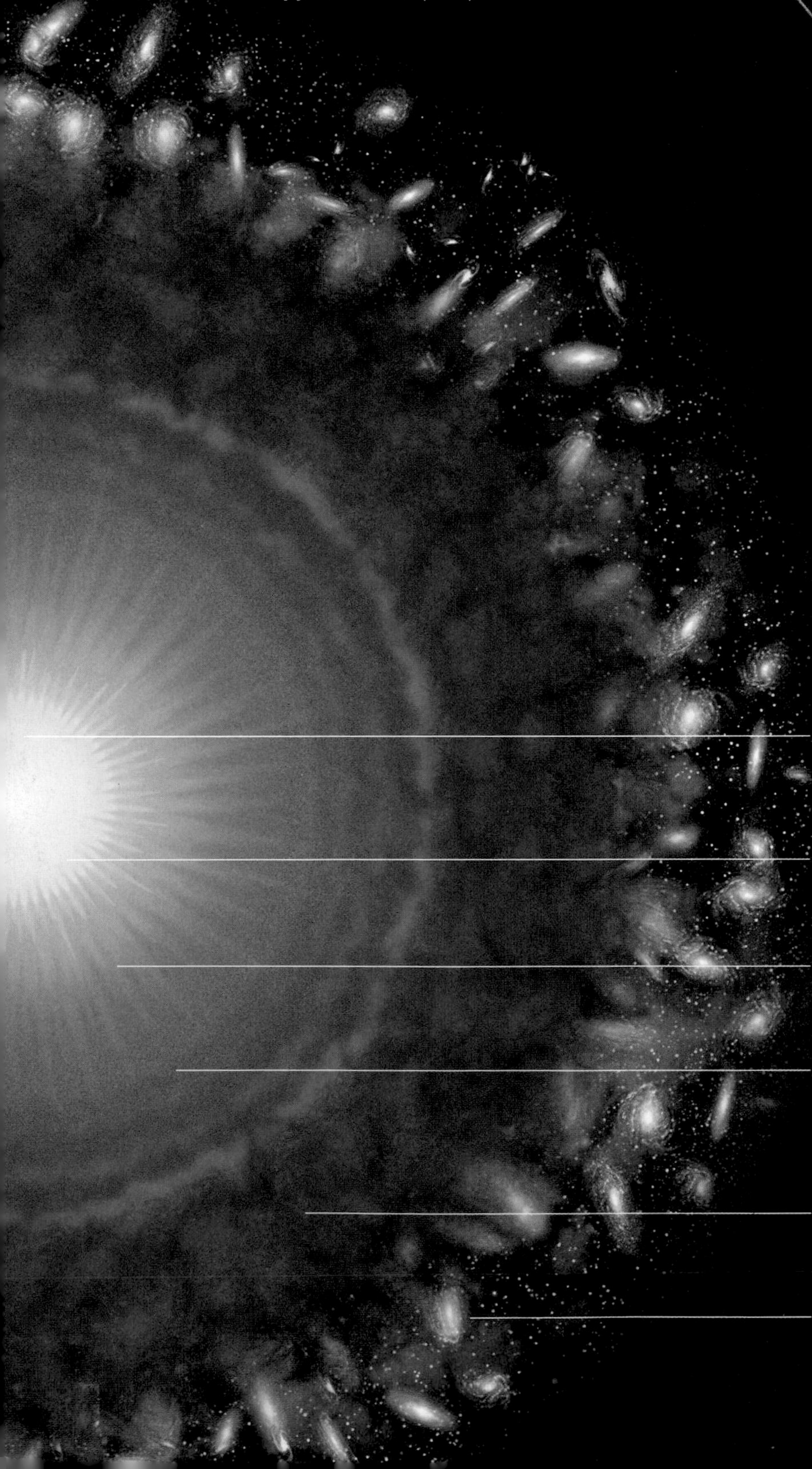

1 The Local Group There are billions of galaxies in the Universe, each containing billions of stars. Galaxies typically cluster together. Our Galaxy is one of about 30 in a cluster known as the Local Group. One of the nearest galaxies to ours is Andromeda, 2.2 million light years away.

EARLY EVOLUTION OF THE UNIVERSE

Within a second after the big bang, the building blocks of all matter were created, but it took another 2 billion years before the first stars and galaxies started to form.

After 1 millionth of a trillionth of a trillionth of a second (10^{-43} secs) The temperature of the infant Universe is 100 000 billion billion billion°C. The Universe expands rapidly and fills with radiation, mostly in the form of light and heat. Gravity appears as a distinct force.

After 10 000 trillionths of a trillionth of a second (10^{-32} seconds) Expansion slows down. Quarks, the smallest known particles, appear and start to combine to create larger subatomic particles.

After 10 millionths of a second (10^{-5} seconds) Subatomic particles combine to form protons and neutrons, the two components of the nuclei of atoms.

After 100 seconds The temperature drops to 1 billion°C. Space is now filled with protons, neutrons, and electrons; the three particles that make up atoms. Over the next 32 000 years, protons and neutrons react with background radiation to combine and form nuclei of hydrogen and helium – the two simplest chemical elements.

After 1 billion years The Universe becomes transparent and its temperature drops to about 4000°C, low enough for complete atoms to form. These are pulled together by gravity, creating clumps of matter.

After 2 billion years The first stars and galaxies begin to condense from clouds of gaseous hydrogen and helium.

Measuring space

Distances in space are so vast that miles are too small to express them. Instead, units such as the light year, astronomical unit, and parsec are used.

- **Light year** This is the distance traveled by light in a year (9461 billion km/5880 billion miles). Light from Proxima Centauri, our closest star after the Sun, takes 4.2 years to reach Earth, so Proxima Centauri is 4.2 light years away.
- **Astronomical unit** This smaller unit of measurement is the average distance of the Earth from the Sun (153 million km/95 million miles).
- **Parsec** 3.26 light years. It is used for measuring star distances.

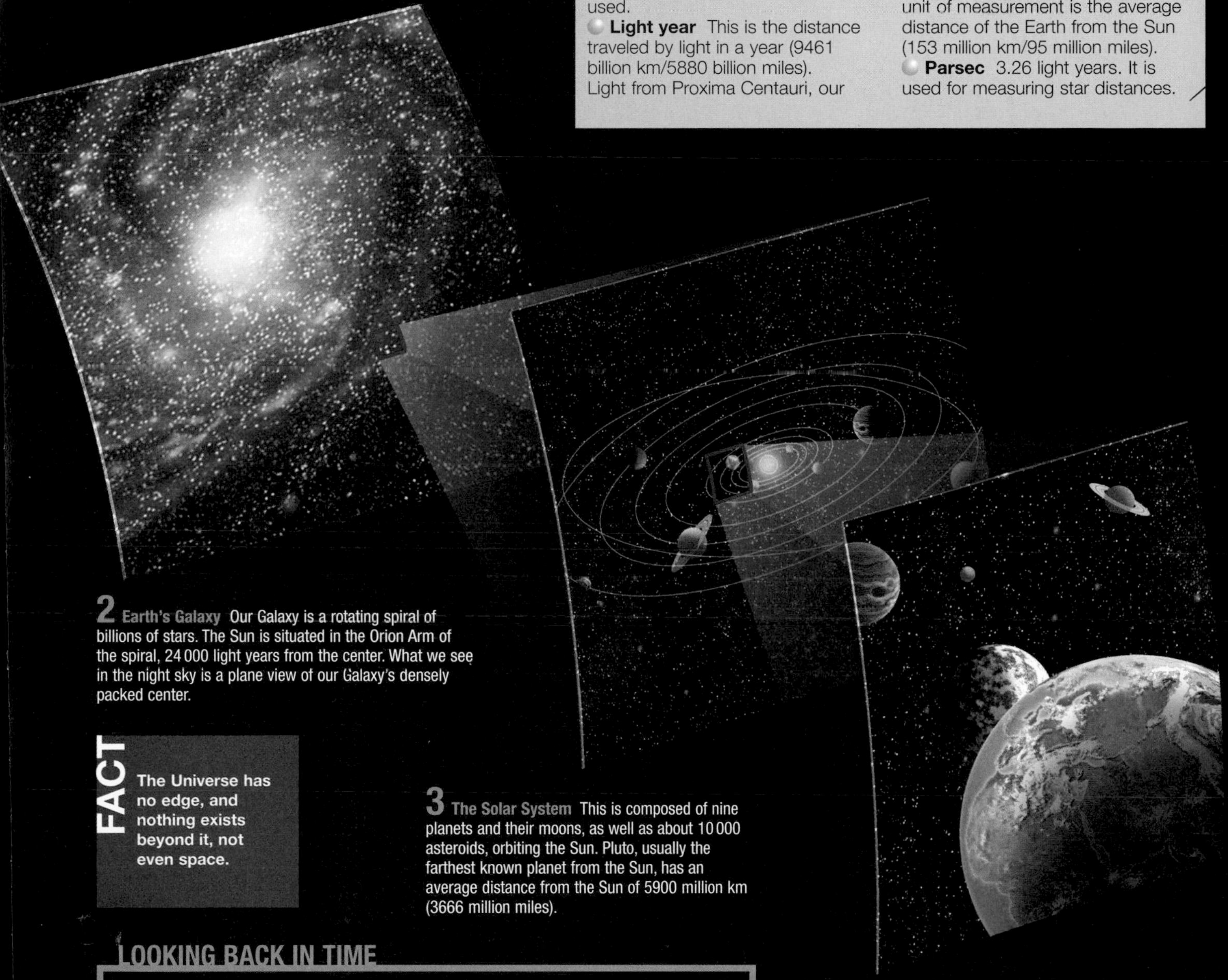

2 Earth's Galaxy Our Galaxy is a rotating spiral of billions of stars. The Sun is situated in the Orion Arm of the spiral, 24 000 light years from the center. What we see in the night sky is a plane view of our Galaxy's densely packed center.

3 The Solar System This is composed of nine planets and their moons, as well as about 10 000 asteroids, orbiting the Sun. Pluto, usually the farthest known planet from the Sun, has an average distance from the Sun of 5900 million km (3666 million miles).

4 The Earth Our planet and its moon orbit the Sun at an average distance of 150 million km (93 million miles). The Earth is the third planet from the Sun.

FACT

The Universe has no edge, and nothing exists beyond it, not even space.

LOOKING BACK IN TIME

How do we know what happened billions of years ago? Simply put, we can see it. Looking across the vast distances to stars, space and time become impossible to separate. We can only see objects when the light from them reaches us. The farther away an object is, the longer it takes. For instance, it takes eight years for the light from the brightest star, Sirius, to travel to Earth, so we are actually looking at it as it was eight years ago. With more distant objects we are looking even farther back in time. It takes the light from the Virgo Cluster 50 million years to reach us, so we are looking at it as it was long before human beings even existed.

Stellar objects emit other types of radiation, such as radio waves, as well as light. These can be detected by specialized telescopes, and the data they provide helps to build up a fuller picture of the Universe.

At the moment, the farthest galaxies that we can perceive are 13 billion light years away, only 2 billion years after the big bang. In theory, if we could see far enough we should be able to see right to the beginning of the Universe.

Big Bang

The term big bang was facetiously coined by the astronomer Fred Hoyle, who did not believe in the theory. He considered it a return to an almost biblical version of creation.

see also

14-15 **Galaxies**
16-17 **Stars**
18-19 **The Sun**
20-21 **The planets**

Galaxies

Clusters of stars held together by gravity

Stars are not distributed evenly throughout the Universe; they clump together in galaxies. In turn, galaxies group together in clusters and superclusters. Although stars appear closely packed in galaxies, they are separated by vast distances. If our Sun were the size of a grain of sand, its nearest star neighbor would be 6 km (4 miles) away.

Measuring magnitude

There are two methods for measuring the magnitude, or brightness, of a star.

- **Apparent, or visual, magnitude** is the brightness of a star as it appears from Earth. A very bright star is magnitude one, and a barely visible one is magnitude six. Apparent magnitude does not take a star's distance from Earth into account. Because something farther way looks fainter than something closer, apparent magnitude is not appropriate for making comparisons between stars.
- **Absolute magnitude** is defined as the apparent magnitude that a star would have if viewed from a standard distance of 32.6 light years (10 parsecs). This standardized measurement allows the true brightness of stars to be compared.

GALAXY TYPES

Galaxies are classified by shape. There are three main types:

Spiral About 30 percent of galaxies are believed to be spiral. There are two kinds. **Normal spirals** are pinwheel-shaped with a central bulge and spiral arms. **Barred spirals** (left) have an elongated central region and protruding arms.

Elliptical Most galaxies are thought to be this shape, a stretched sphere. They range from the virtually spherical to almost flattened. M87 in Virgo is an example

Irregular Many galaxies have an ill-defined structure with no definite outline. The Magellanic Cloud in our Local Cluster is an example of an irregular galaxy.

The Milky Way

Our Galaxy consists of at least 200 billion stars and their planets, grouped into a flattened disk with spiral arms and a bulge at its center. Looking up from Earth along the plane of this disk, the Galaxy appears as a luminous band of stars and glowing gas – the Milky Way – spanning the sky. The whole Galaxy is sometimes referred to as the Milky Way Galaxy, but, strictly speaking, the term refers to the luminous band of stars visible from Earth.

FACT

Using the Hubble Space Telescope, researchers have found 600 stars adrift in space between the Virgo Cluster galaxies.

Neighbor The Andromeda galaxy, photographed here from Earth, is our nearest galaxy neighbor. There are no external images of our own galaxy as nothing man-made has ever traveled beyond it.

GALAXY FEATURES

Black holes The name given to immeasurably dense collapsed stars with such a strong gravitational pull that nothing, not even light, can escape from them. The size of black holes is dependent upon the mass of the collapsed star. Because they are invisible, no black hole has been detected directly. Their existence can only be inferred from the effect they have on other objects.

Quasars These are cores of very active distant galaxies, possibly with black holes at their centers. They are point sources of radio waves. Because they are so distant, light from them has taken a long time to reach us. When we look at a quasar, we are looking at a galaxy in a very early stage of its evolution.

Colliding galaxies If galaxies move close enough for their gravitational fields to affect each other, the structure of one or both galaxies can alter radically. They may collide and even merge. The closest colliding galaxies to us are NGC 4038 and 4039, known as the Antennae. They are just 80 light years apart and streams of material from them are already converging. Eventually the two systems will merge.

Dark matter Also known as missing mass, this is matter that cannot be seen directly, because it emits little or no radiation. Its presence can be inferred from the effect it has on other bodies. Its gravitational force explains the rotation speeds of galaxies and the fact that they tend to group together into clusters. It has been estimated that as much as 90 percent of the matter in the Universe is dark matter, in the form of particles left over from the big bang.

EARTH'S GALAXY FACTS

- It rotates around its center, and the Sun takes 225 million years to complete one rotation.
- It is 100 000 light years in diameter.
- The central bulge is 10 000 light years across and 20 000 light years thick. It contains only old stars.
- The disk formed by the spiral arms is 3000 light years thick.
- The Sun lies 30 000 light years from the center of the Galaxy, in the Orion Arm.
- The center of the Galaxy is Sagittarius A – a source of powerful radio waves that could be a black hole.

see also
12-13 **The Universe**
16-17 **Stars**
18-19 **The Sun**

It is impossible to estimate how many stars there are in the Universe. There are thought to be about 200 billion stars in our Galaxy alone, although only about 6000 of these are visible with the naked eye from Earth. Stars are fueled by the nuclear fusion of hydrogen atoms. They display a great range of sizes, brightness, color and stages of development, from red giants to white dwarfs, nebulae to supernovae.

LIFE CYCLE OF A STAR

Stars are created in swirling clouds of cosmic dust and gas called nebulae. Within the nebulae strong gravitational forces are at work pulling particles together to form clumps called Bok globules. As gravity pulls the particles closer and closer together temperatures in these spinning masses soar to around 10 000 000°C. Under such extreme conditions, hydrogen nuclei combine creating helium atoms in a process called nuclear fusion. Energy is released and a protostar is born.

Star birth

Protostars condense in clouds of gas and dust called nebulae. They then follow one of four possible life cycles depending on their original mass.

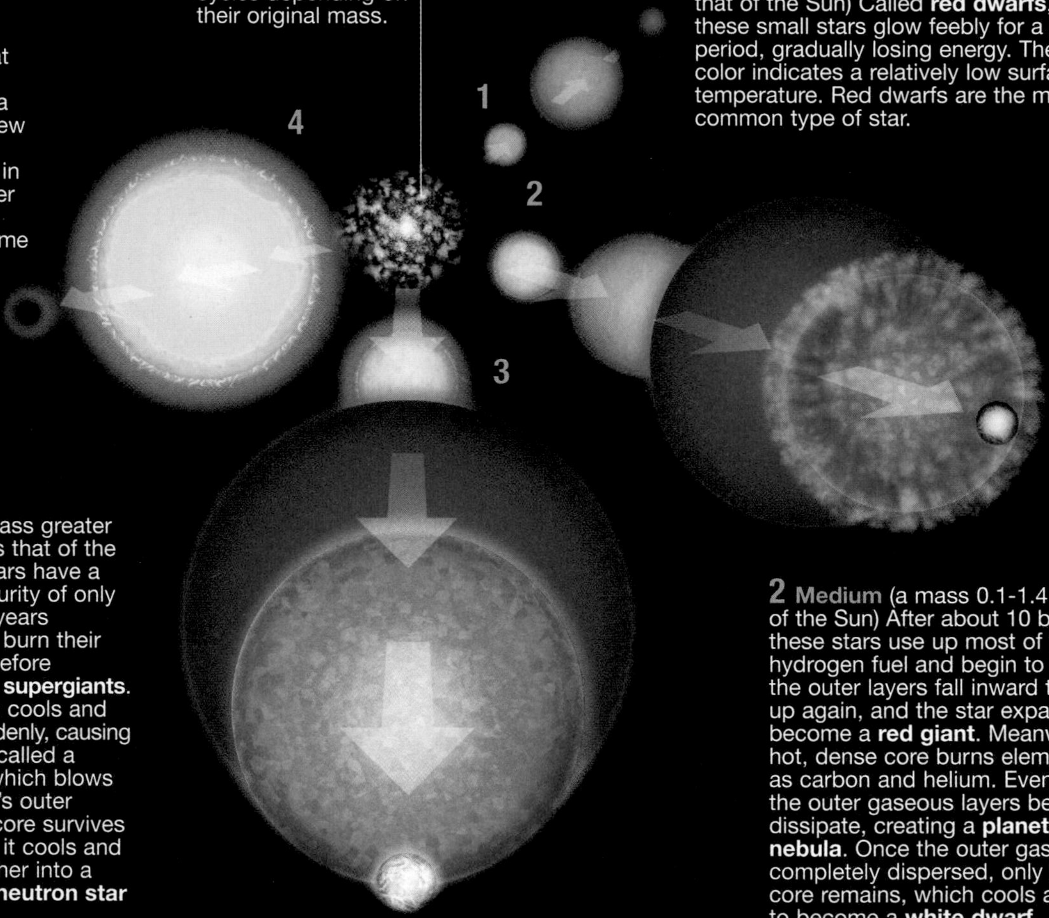

1 Small (a mass less than one-tenth that of the Sun) Called **red dwarfs**, these small stars glow feebly for a long period, gradually losing energy. The red color indicates a relatively low surface temperature. Red dwarfs are the most common type of star.

2 Medium (a mass 0.1-1.4 times that of the Sun) After about 10 billion years, these stars use up most of their hydrogen fuel and begin to cool. As the outer layers fall inward they heat up again, and the star expands to become a **red giant**. Meanwhile the hot, dense core burns elements such as carbon and helium. Eventually, the outer gaseous layers begin to dissipate, creating a **planetary nebula**. Once the outer gases have completely dispersed, only the dense core remains, which cools and shrinks to become a **white dwarf**.

3 Large (a mass greater than 1.4 times that of the Sun) Large stars have a period of maturity of only a few million years because they burn their fuel quickly, before becoming **red supergiants**. The core then cools and contracts suddenly, causing an explosion called a **supernova**, which blows away the star's outer layers. If the core survives the explosion it cools and contracts further into a small, dense **neutron star** or **pulsar**.

4 Supergiant (a mass 100 times that of the Sun) Stars in this category have a life span of only a few million years. They eventually collapse in on themselves under the weight of their own gravity to become **black holes**.

Why stars shine

Stars shine as a consequence of the nuclear fusion of hydrogen into helium that is constantly taking place in their cores. These reactions release energy in the form of heat and light. The Sun converts 600 million metric tons of hydrogen into helium every second, with a resultant loss of 4 million metric tons in mass.

Stellar variations

Variable and double stars are notable star types.
Double stars are either
a. two stars in close proximity moving around a common center (also called binary stars), e.g. Mizar, or
b. two stars far away from each other, but which appear close because they lie in the same direction when viewed from Earth.
Variable stars appear to vary in brightness over time.

CLASSIFYING THE STARS

To tell a star's type and lifecycle stage, astronomers use a graph called a Hertzsprung-Russell diagram. A star's position is worked out by plotting its brightness against its temperature, deduced from the color of the light that the star emits. Young, hot stars tend to be blue, and older, cooler stars are usually red or orange. The star is classified according to the area of the graph in which it falls.

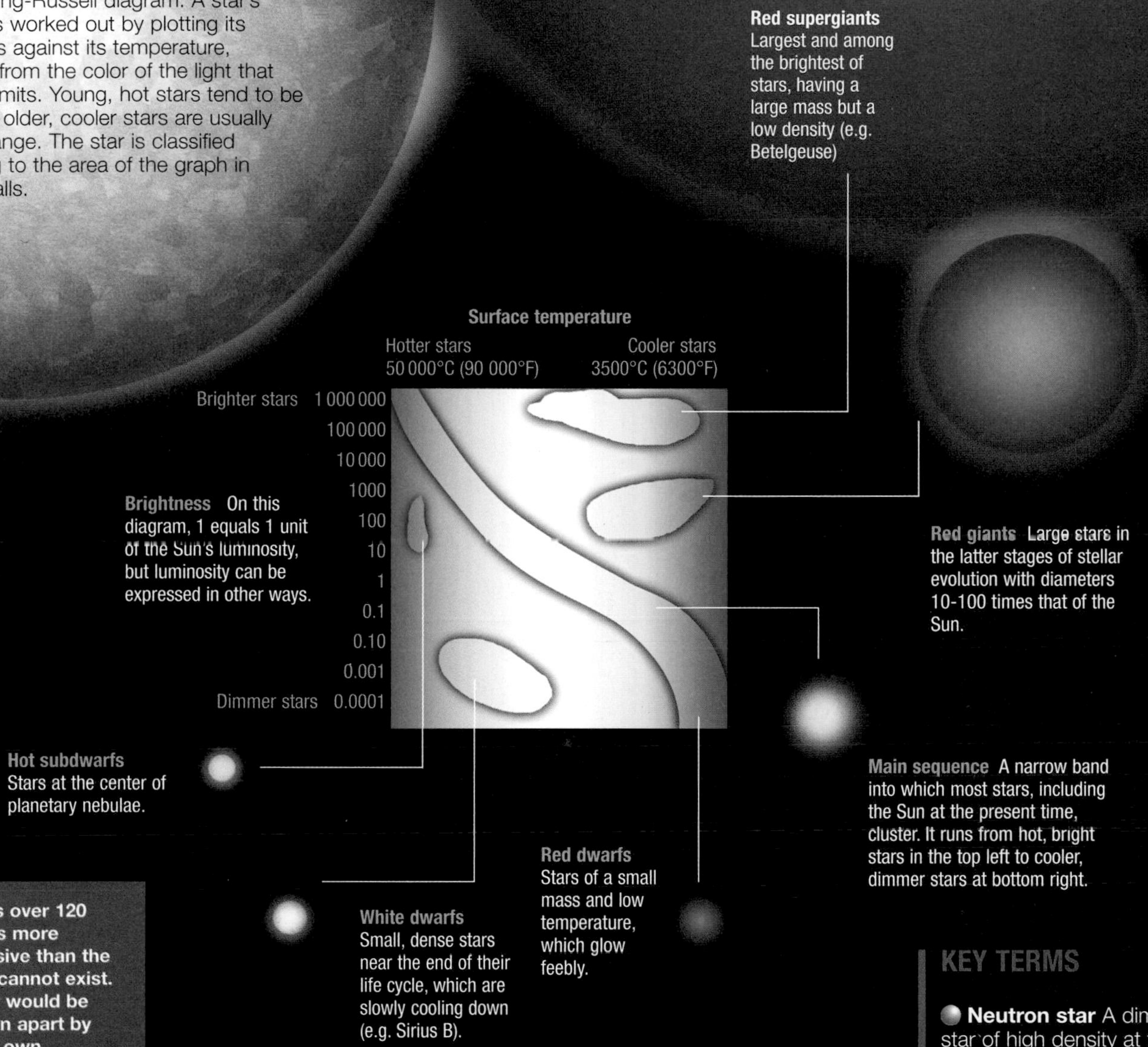

Red supergiants Largest and among the brightest of stars, having a large mass but a low density (e.g. Betelgeuse)
Surface temperature
Hotter stars 50 000°C (90 000°F)
Cooler stars 3500°C (6300°F)
Brighter stars 1 000 000
100 000
10 000
1000
100
10
1
0.1
0.10
0.001
Dimmer stars 0.0001
Brightness On this diagram, 1 equals 1 unit of the Sun's luminosity, but luminosity can be expressed in other ways.
Red giants Large stars in the latter stages of stellar evolution with diameters 10-100 times that of the Sun.
Hot subdwarfs Stars at the center of planetary nebulae.
Main sequence A narrow band into which most stars, including the Sun at the present time, cluster. It runs from hot, bright stars in the top left to cooler, dimmer stars at bottom right.
Red dwarfs Stars of a small mass and low temperature, which glow feebly.
White dwarfs Small, dense stars near the end of their life cycle, which are slowly cooling down (e.g. Sirius B).

FACT

Stars over 120 times more massive than the Sun cannot exist. They would be blown apart by their own radiation.

KEY TERMS

- **Neutron star** A dim star of high density at the end of its life cycle composed predominantly or entirely of neutrons.
- **Pulsars** Probably rotating neutron stars, emitting intermittent radio signals.
- **Light year** The distance traveled by light in one year (9460 billion km/5900 billion miles).
- **Black hole** A collapsed star with such high gravity that not even light can escape from it.

BRIGHTEST STARS SEEN FROM EARTH

A star's brightness is affected by distance. A close dim star might appear brighter than a distant bright star. The lower the figure, the brighter the star.

Star	Constellation	Brightness (apparent magnitude)
Sirius	Canis Major	-1.46
Canopus	Carina	-0.72
Arcturus	Boötes	-0.04
Rigil Kentaurus	Orion	0.02
Vega	Lyra	0.03
Capella	Auriga	0.08
Rigel	Orion	0.12
Procyon	Canis Minor	0.38
Betelgeuse	Orion	0.50

STARS CLOSEST TO EARTH

Star	Distance
Sun	149 600 000 km (93 000 000 miles)
Proxima Centauri	4.24 light years
Alpha Centauri A	4.34
Alpha Centauri B	4.34
Barnard's Star	5.97
Wolf 359	7.8
Lalande 21185	8.19
UV Ceti A	8.55
UV Ceti B	8.55
Sirius A	8.68

see also
12-13 **The Universe**
14-15 **Galaxies**
18-19 **The Sun**
472-73 **The night sky**

The Sun is a mature, medium-sized star that formed from a collapsing cloud of gas about 4.6 billion years ago. It burns 700 million metric tons of hydrogen in its core every second and converts about 5 million metric tons a second into pure energy. In about 5 billion years, when this fuel begins to run low, the Sun will expand into a red giant and engulf the inner planets – including the Earth.

SUN STATISTICS

Age	4. 6 billion years +
Life span	About 13 billion years
Diameter	1 392 000 km (865 000 miles)
Composition by mass	71% hydrogen 27% helium 2% heavier gases
Temperature at core	15 million °C
Surface temperature	5500 °C (4930°F)
Rotation period	25–36 days
Distance from Earth	149 597 893 km (92 970 000 miles) 1 astronomical unit
Time for sunlight to reach Earth	8.3 minutes
Surface gravity	38 times that of Earth

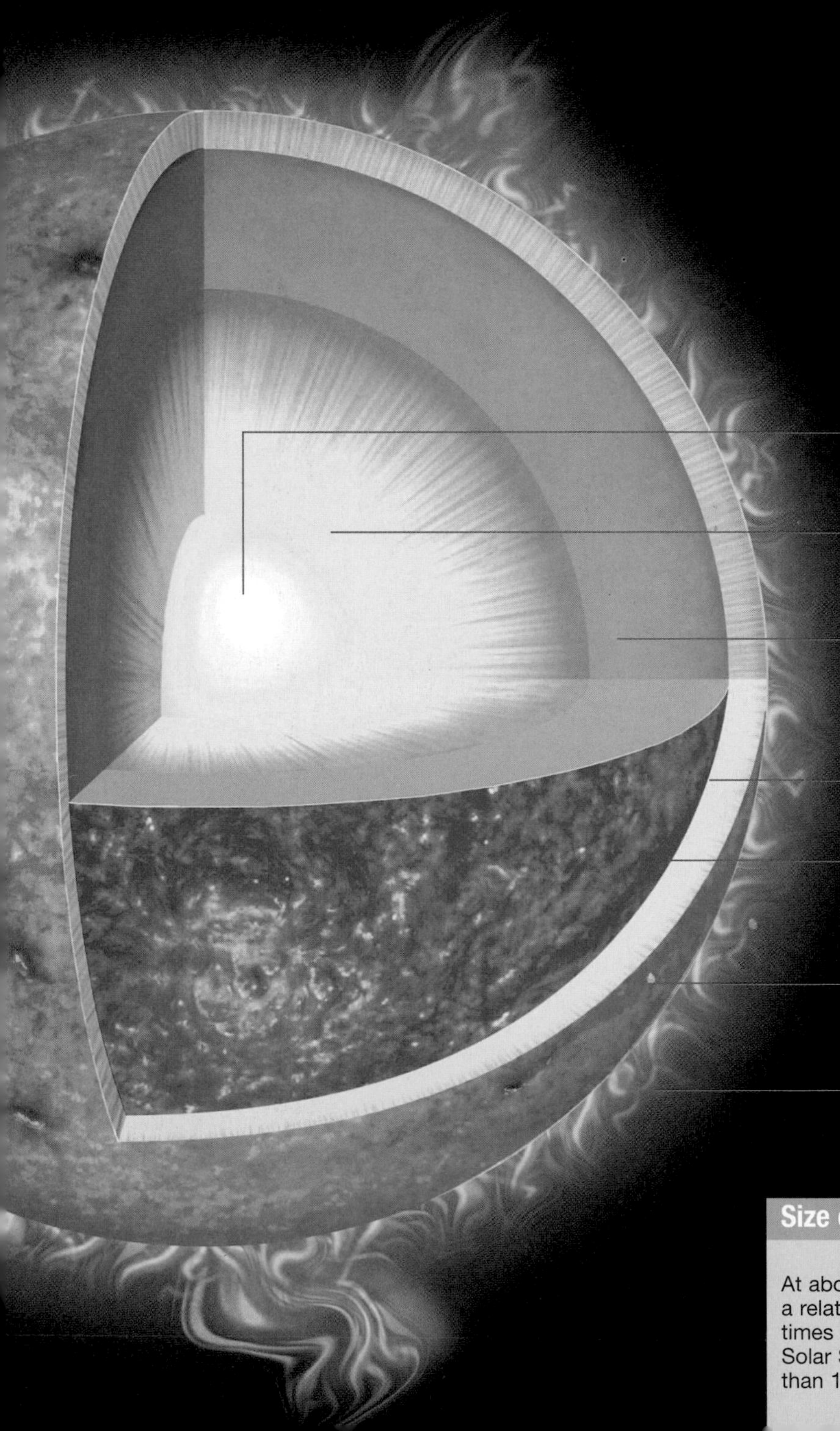

SOLAR STRUCTURE

Interior

Core Diameter 450 000 km (280 000 miles). Temperature 15 million °C. Here the thermonuclear fusion of hydrogen, which forms helium, produces the Sun's energy.

Radiative layer Extends to 70 percent of the Sun's radius. Temperature ranges from 2 million to 7 million °C. Heat energy generated by the core is carried outwards by radiation.

Convective layer 200 000 km (125 000 miles) deep. Temperature ranges from 5500 to 2 million °C. Heat energy is carried upwards by streams of gas.

Atmosphere

Photosphere 300–500 km (200–300 miles) deep. Temperature 4500–7600°C (8100–13 700°F). Bright surface of the Sun, which emits most of its energy as light and heat.

Chromosphere 2000–3000 km (1200–1900 miles) deep. Temperature 4000–50 000°C (7200–90 000°F). Visible as a distinct pink layer during solar eclipses. Characterized by flamelike protrusions of gas.

Corona Constantly changing halo of plumes and loops of very hot gases up to 1.6 million km (1 million miles) thick. Temperature 2 million °C. Visible to the naked eye only during total eclipses.

Solar wind Continuous stream of X-rays, gamma rays, protons and electrons flowing into space at 3 million km/h (2 million mph). Higher speed streams emanate from holes in the corona.

Size of the Sun

At about 1.4 million km (864 000 miles) in diameter, the Sun is a relatively small star. The red giant Betelgeuse is hundreds of times larger. Even so, the Sun dwarfs the other objects in the Solar System. It is 109 times wider than the Earth, and more than 1 million Earth-sized planets could fit inside it.

SURFACE ACTIVITY

Sunspots

- These dark patches often appear as pairs or groups on the Sun's surface, usually around the Sun's equator.
- In these regions, the magnetic field of the Sun is stonger.
- Sunspots last from one hour to six months, depending on size, with larger ones being longer-lived.
- Diameters vary from 300 km (186 miles) to 100 000 km (62 150 miles).

Solar flares

- Solar flares are violent, short-lived bursts of magnetic energy that emit radiation and charged particles into space.
- Flares occur in the chromosphere and lower corona.
- They typically last 20 minutes, but the longest observed lasted for 13 hours on August 16, 1989.

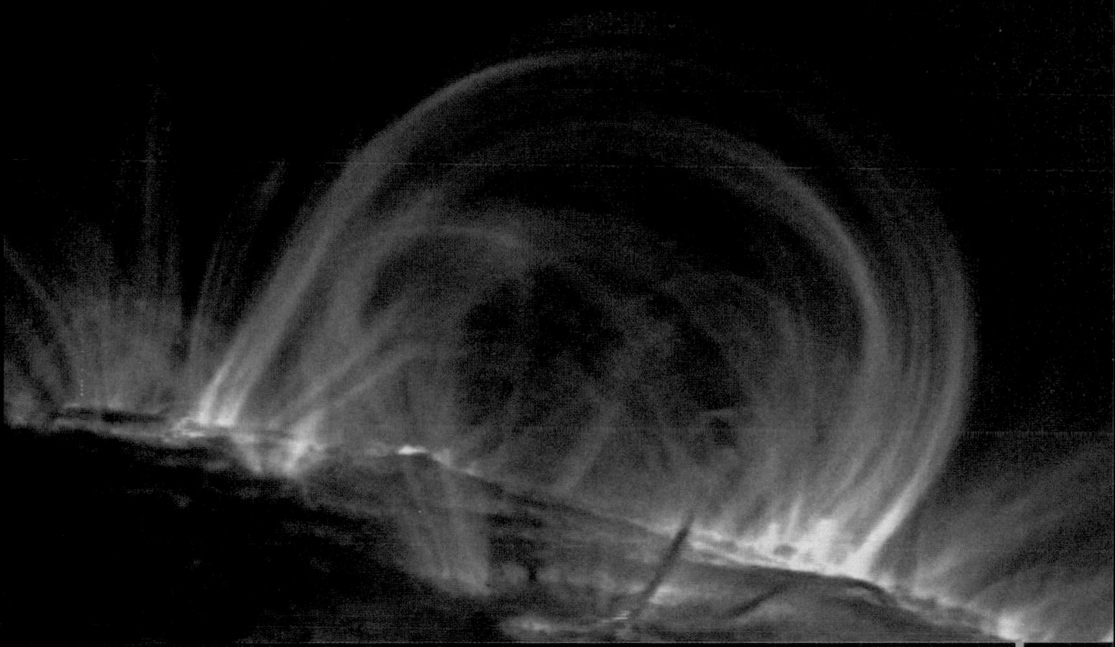

Prominences An arch of relatively cool, charged gases erupts from the Sun's surface. Sometimes the gases escape into space.

Prominences

- These cool, dense, flamelike clouds in the upper chromosphere and lower corona, form massive arches or loops.
- They are supported by magnetic fields, which give them their characteristic arched appearance.
- Prominences are most common during the peak of the solar cycle.
- Quiescent prominences are usually arch-shaped and change little. They are concentrated at the poles, can be tens of thousands of miles high and tend to be long-lived, lasting several months.
- Active prominences display rapid motion and are usually concentrated near the equator. They are associated with sunspots and last a few days.

Faculae

- Faculae are temporary bright patches on the surface of the Sun.
- They are sites of strong magnetic fields and are slightly hotter than the Sun's normal surface temperature.
- Faculae often appear before the formation of sunspots and persist for several days after the sunspots have disappeared.
- They also occur near the Sun's poles.

Solar cycles

The level of the Sun's activity varies, following a fairly regular cycle of about 11 years, thought to be caused by magnetic fields slowing the flow of heat from the Sun's core to the surface. The most obvious indicator of solar cycles is the number of sunspots, cooler areas visible as dark depressions in the photosphere (right), that are visible on the Sun's surface. During a cycle, sunspots appear, grow in number, then gradually die away. During a solar cycle, there is an increase in flares and a stronger solar wind.

Solar cycles have a marked effect on the Earth. The increase in flares and the solar wind means that more charged particles from the Sun reach the Earth at these times. They intensify the effects of the northern and southern lights (aurora borealis and aurora australis). Charged solar particles can also interfere with radio signals and cause surges in power lines, sometimes resulting in blackouts.

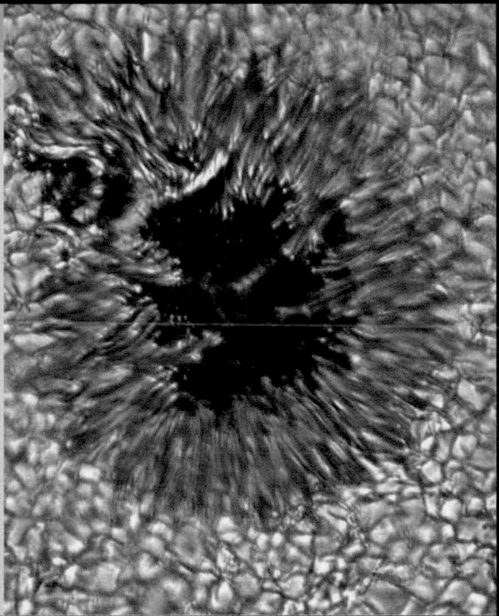

FACT It takes 10 million years for heat generated in the Sun's core to reach its outer layer, the photosphere.

see also
14-15 Galaxies
16-17 Stars
20-21 The planets
46-47 Earth's atmosphere

The planets

Nine planets and their satellites orbit the Sun

The word planet comes from the Greek for "wanderer," because seen from Earth, the planets appear to move across the sky in an erratic way. In fact, the planets all circle the Sun in the same direction, and in a similar plane, and each spins on its axis as it orbits. More than 100 moons orbit the nine planets, and each planet has evolved differently, according to its composition and distance from the Sun.

Formation of the planets Five billion years ago, a new star, the Sun, was surrounded by a swirling disk of gas and dust. Heavier elements were pulled together to form the inner, rocky or "terrestrial" planets – Mercury, Venus, Earth and Mars. Lighter elements, such as hydrogen and helium, were swept up into the outer gaseous giants Jupiter, Saturn, Uranus and Neptune. Tiny Pluto, on the outer edge of the Solar System, is probably an asteroid caught in orbit round the Sun.

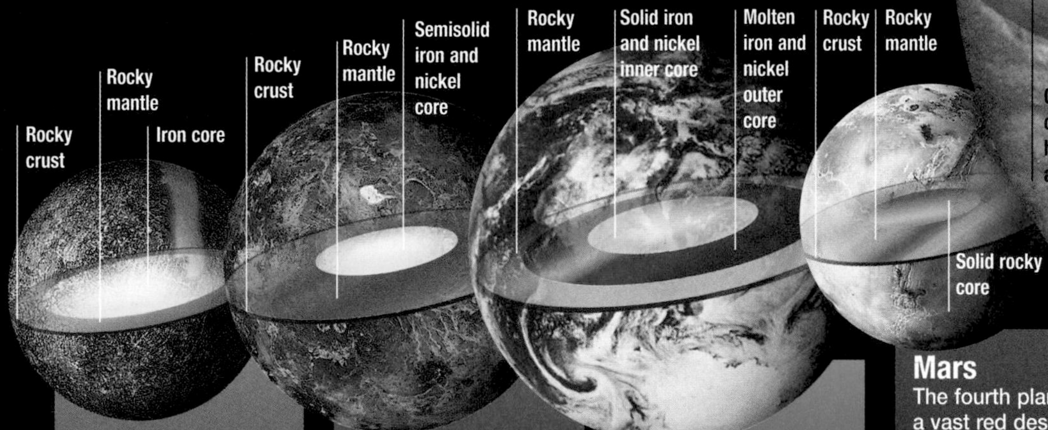

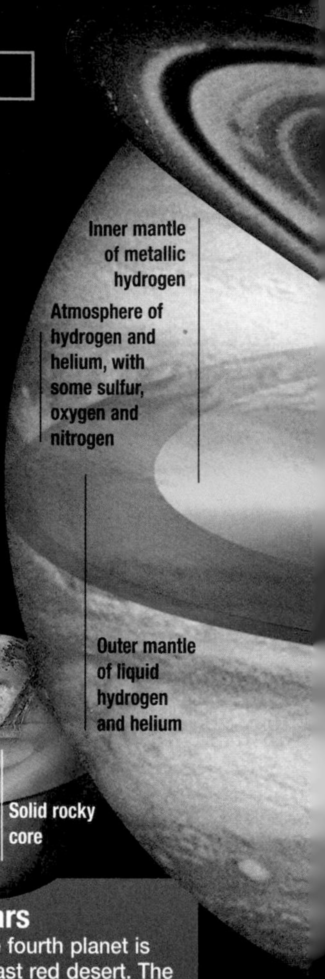

Mercury

Mercury is the closest planet to the Sun. Its surface is scarred and pitted by meteorite impacts. It has almost no atmosphere, so it is scorching during the day and freezing at night. It is visible to the naked eye.

Venus

The rocky surface of Venus is marked by volcanoes, rifts, and solidified lava flows. The atmosphere is rich in carbon dioxide. Atmospheric pressure on the surface is 90 times that of Earth.

Earth

Earth is unique in the Solar System in having liquid water on the surface and in being the only planet known to be geologically active. It is also the only place in the Universe known to support life.

Mars

The fourth planet is a vast red desert. The barren wastes of Mars have been eroded by ferocious winds and are dotted with large volcanoes and impact craters. The atmosphere of Mars consists mainly of carbon dioxide. Its day length is similar to Earth's.

	Mercury	Venus	Earth	Mars
Minimum distance from Sun	45 900 000 km (28 520 000 miles)	107 400 000 km (66 740 000 miles)	147 000 000 km (91 340 000 miles)	206 700 000 km (128 440 000 miles)
Maximum distance from Sun	69 700 000 km (43 300 000 miles)	109 000 000 km (67 730 000 miles)	152 000 000 km (94 450 000 miles)	249 000 000 km (154 730 000 miles)
Diameter at equator	4878 km (3031 miles)	12 104 km (7521 miles)	12 756 km (7926 miles)	6794 km (4222 miles)
Mass relative to Earth	0.055	0.815	1	0.11
Period of orbit round Sun	87.97 days	224.7 days	365.3 days	687 days
Spin period	58 days 15 h 36 min	243 days 3 h 50 min	23 hours 56 min	24 hours 37 min
Temperature at surface	660°F day/–274°F night	480°C (866°F) average	22°C (72°F) average	–63°C (–81°F) average
Known moons	None	None	1	2
Names of main moons			Moon	Phobos, Deimos

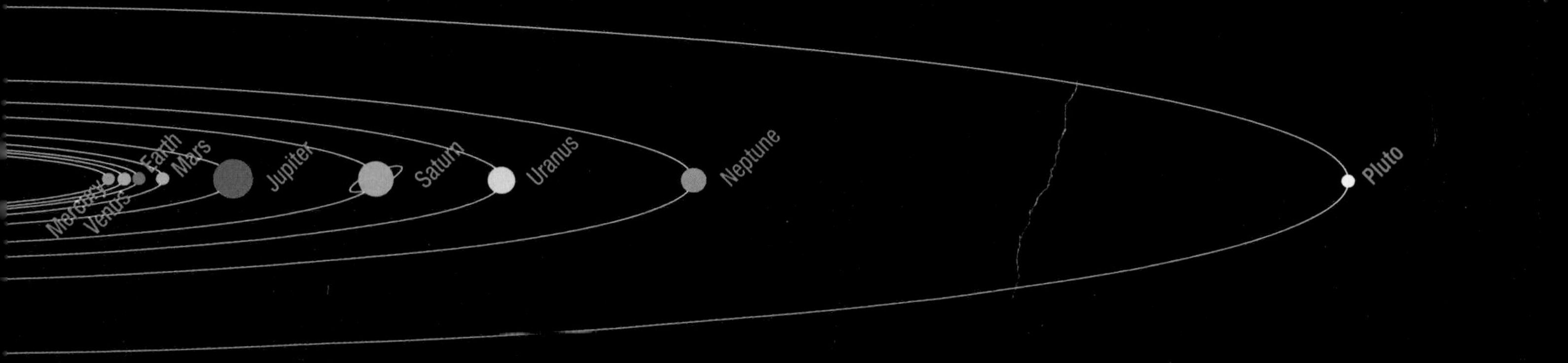

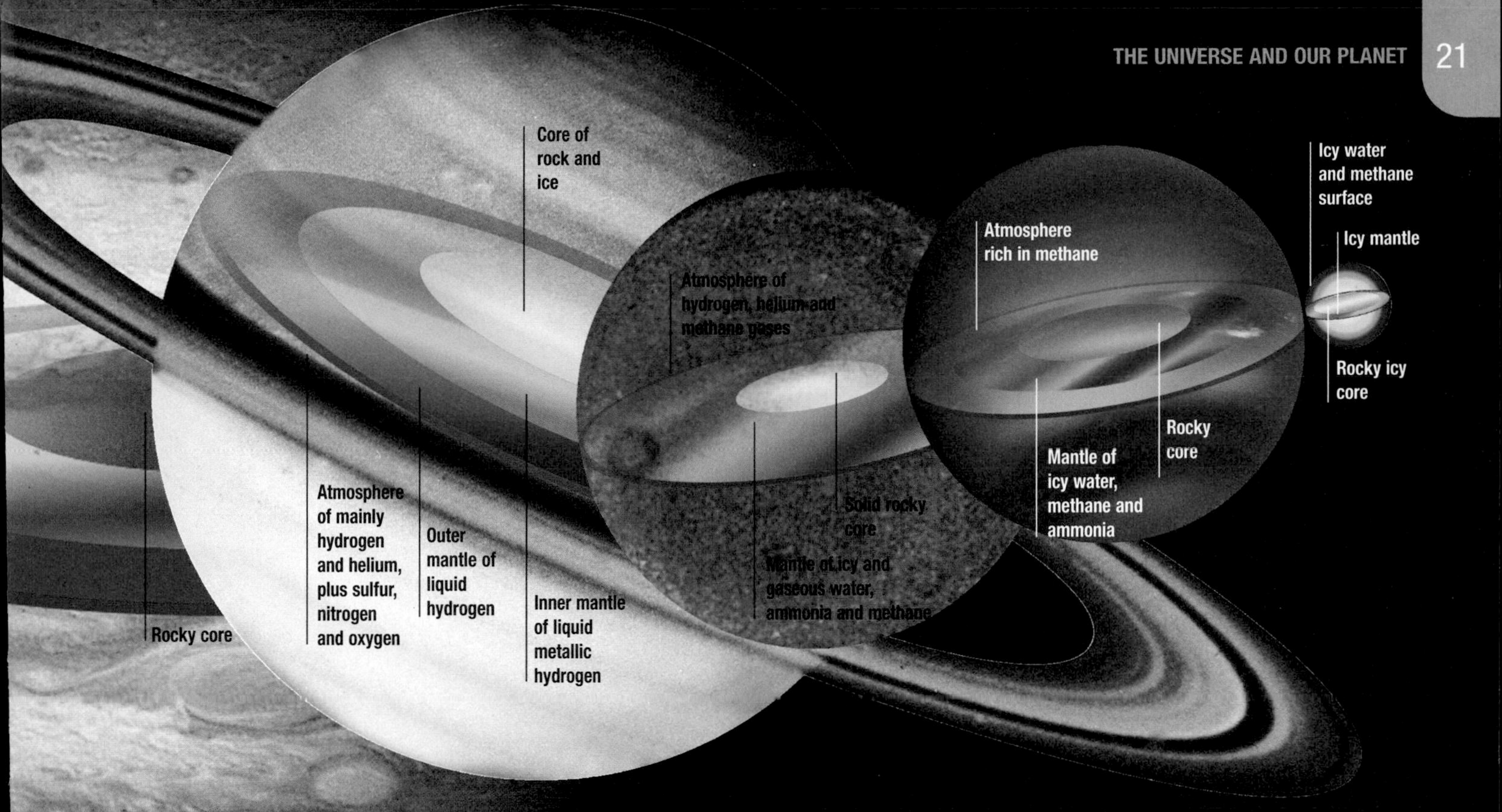

Jupiter

Jupiter is the largest planet. Its atmosphere is composed mainly of hydrogen and helium. High pressure in the lower regions has compressed the hydrogen into liquid and metallic layers around the rocky core. Surface spots and markings are actually atmospheric storms.

Saturn

Saturn is a globe of gases similar in composition to Jupiter. It rotates so fast that it bulges in the middle and is flattened at the poles. Saturn's rings consist of tens of thousands of subdivisions made up of ice particles. Fast winds whip around the planet's equator.

Uranus

The planet Uranus was discovered in 1781. Its atmosphere consists of hydrogen, helium and methane. Unique in the Solar System, its axis of rotation coincides with the orbital plane – it spins on its side – possibly as a result of an ancient collision with a comet.

Neptune

The planet Neptune was discovered in 1846, although it may have been spotted by Galileo in 1613. It has a methane-rich atmosphere that becomes liquid and then metallic toward the center. It has an almost circular (rather than elliptical) orbit. Faint rings are visible.

Pluto

Pluto was discovered in 1930, and there is still some question as to whether it qualifies as a planet at all. The surface is a solid landscape of frozen methane, and the atmosphere is very thin. Pluto has an erratic orbit that at times brings it inside Neptune's orbit.

Jupiter	Saturn	Uranus	Neptune	Pluto
741 000 000 km (460 000 000 miles)	1 352 600 000 km (840 505 640 miles)	2 735 300 000 km (1 703 443 820 miles)	4 444 450 000 km (2 761 781 230 miles)	4 434 990 000 km (2 755 902 786 miles)
816 000 000 km (507 000 000 miles)	1 507 000 000 km (936 000 000 miles)	3 004 000 000 km (1867 000 000 miles)	4 545 670 000 km (2 824 679 338 miles)	7 304 330 000 km (4538 910 662 miles)
142 800 km (88 736 miles)	119 900 km (74 506 miles)	51 108 km (31 764 miles)	49 493 km (30 755 miles)	2390 km (1485 miles)
317.9	95.2	14.5	17.2	0.002
11 years 314 days	29 years 168 days	83 years 273 days	164 years 292 days	248 years 197 days
9 hours 55.5 min	10 hours 40 min	17 hours 14 min	17 hours 15 min	6 days 9 hours
–150°C (–238°F) (average)	–180°C (–292°F) (average)	–214°C (–353°F) (average)	–220°C (–369°F) (average)	–230°C (–382°F) (average)
52	30, plus rings	21 confirmed, plus rings	8, plus rings	1
Io, Europa, Ganymede	Titan	Titania, Oberon	Triton	Charon

SOLAR SYSTEM FACTS

- **Fastest mover** Mercury has the highest average orbiting speed at 172 248 km/h (107 030 mph).
- **Hottest place** Venus has the highest surface temperature because of its proximity to the Sun and its heat-trapping, carbon-rich atmosphere.
- **Largest rings** Saturn's rings are 270 000 km (170 000 miles) in diameter.
- **Longest day** Venus rotates backwards on its axis once every 243 days, so a “day” is longer than a “year.”
- **Coldest place** The lowest recorded surface temperature in the Solar System is –235°C (–391°F), on Neptune's moon Triton.
- **Brightest planet** Venus's blanket of cloud reflects about 79 percent of incoming light.
- **Most active satellite** Jupiter's moon Io emits vast clouds of sulfur from vents in its surface.
- **Largest volcano** Olympus Mons, on Mars, is 600 km (375 miles) across and 25 km (15 miles) high.

see also

10-11 **Planet Earth**
18-19 **The Sun**
22-23 **The Moon**
24-25 **Comets and meteorites**

Most of the planets in the Solar System have natural satellites, or moons. Our Moon was probably formed 4.6 billion years ago when debris from a collision between the Earth and a passing asteroid fused together. The Moon's gravity exerts a strong influence on the Earth, causing the tides and, over millions of years, slowing the spin of the Earth, lengthening the day.

THE FACE OF THE MOON

Unlike the Earth, the Moon is not tectonically active; there are no volcanoes or violent earthquakes, just the occasional tremor. Nor is there any running water, rain, snow or wind to erode the landscape. The surface features of the Moon are mainly the result of meteorite impacts.

Two main landscape areas have been identified: the cratered, older highlands and the younger "maria," or "seas." These areas are characterised by a number of features.

Maria Medieval astronomers described the smooth, dark areas visible on the Moon's surface as "seas." They were later given romantic names such as Mare Tranquillitatis (Sea of Tranquillity) and Mare Imbrium (Sea of Showers). We now know that they do not contain water. These areas, which cover 16 percent of the Moon's surface, are the result of meteorite impacts on its surface soon after its formation. The force of the impacts cracked the surface, causing lava to flow out. The cooled and solidified lava flows formed the smooth areas.

Craters Found all over the surface of the Moon, craters are the result of bombardment by meteorites, mainly between 500 million and 700 million years after the Moon's formation.

Mountains At the same time as the maria were being formed, the meteorite bombardment also formed mountain ranges, such as the lunar Apennines that border the Mare Imbrium.

Domes These circular, shallow-sided raised areas, often with central pits, are associated with maria. They are thought to be extinct volcanic vents, similar to shield volcanoes found on Earth.

Rays Rays are formed by material ejected from impact craters.

Moon dust A steady rain of minor debris from space has eroded the surface, leaving the Moon covered in a light layer of dust.

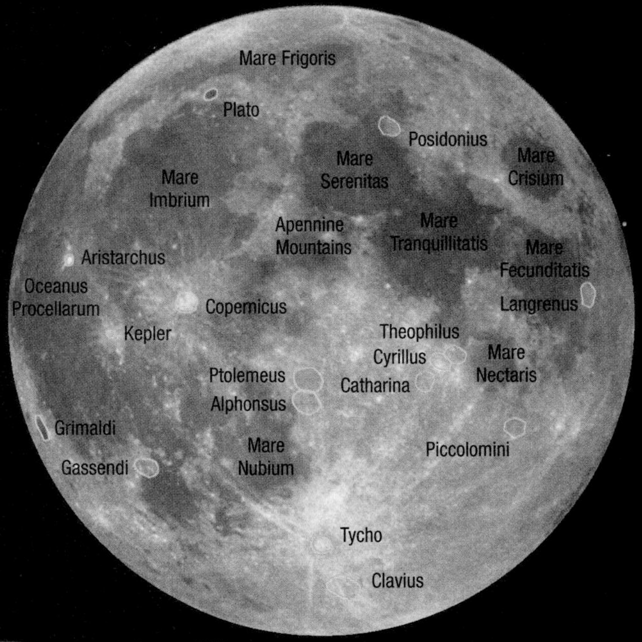

Moon statistics

Average distance from Earth (center to center)	384 400 km (238 828 miles)
Time to orbit Earth	27.32 days
Time to spin once on axis	27.32 days
Interval between new moons	29 days 12 hrs 44 mins 3 secs
Average orbital velocity	3680 km/h (2286 mph)
Average diameter	3476.6 km (2160 miles)
Density (water = 1)	3.34
Volume (Earth = 1)	0.02
Surface gravity (Earth = 1)	0.165

DARK SIDE OF THE MOON

Gravitational forces between the Earth and the Moon keep them in synchronous rotation. That is, the time the Moon takes to spin once on its axis is the same as it takes to orbit the Earth, so the same side of the Moon always faces us. The far or "dark" side was a mystery until October 1959, when the Soviet spacecraft Luna 3 sent back images of it. These revealed that it is more cratered than the near side and has only one mare. The lack of maria probably results from the crust being thicker on the far side and therefore not cracking and releasing lava when hit by meteorites.

Moon composition

More than 2000 samples of Moon rock have been collected and brought back to Earth. These indicate that there are many rock types on the Moon, but they can be broadly divided into two categories: basaltic volcanic rocks associated with the maria, and aluminium and calcium-rich rocks, relics of the Moon's earlier history.

Recent probes indicate that there may be frozen water at the Moon's poles. If it could be melted, it could help to support life on a permanent lunar space station.

FACT

The Moon is moving away from the Earth at a rate of about 4 cm (1 1/2 in.) a year.

THE TIDES

The daily rise and fall of the oceans results from the interplay of the gravitational forces of Earth, Moon and Sun.

The Moon pulls on the oceans on the side of the Earth facing it, causing a bulge – high tide. The solid Earth on the opposite side is also pulled toward the Moon, and away from the oceans, which are also flung outward by the Earth's spin, causing an equivalent high tide on the other side. Low tides occur where water has been drawn away.

The Sun also has a gravitational effect on the Earth. When it is in line with the Moon, at the time of the new and full moons, they act together to create particularly high tides (spring tides). When the Moon and Sun lie at right angles, at the time of the half moon, they work against each other, resulting in low tides (neap tides).

The tidal range in any place is also affected by the shape of the coastline and depth of water. The height between high and low tides along open coastline can be as much as 61 m (20 ft), and in restricted narrow bays, it can be up to 15 m (50 ft). In the open ocean it is rarely more than 60 m (2 ft).

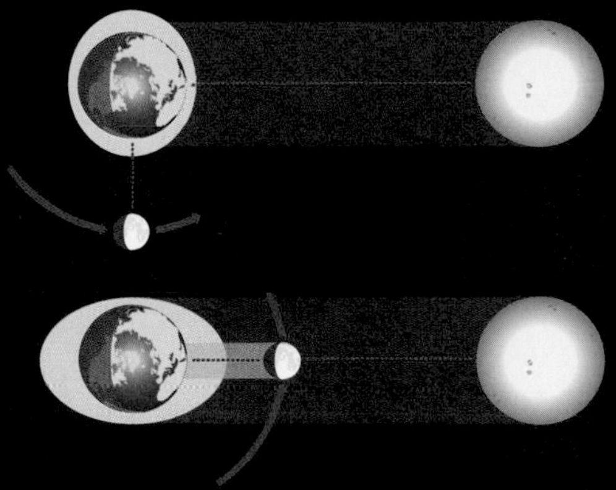

Spring and neap tides In the top diagram the Moon and Sun are pulling at right angles, resulting in low (neap) tides. Below, the Sun and Moon are in line, their combined gravity creating high (spring) tides.

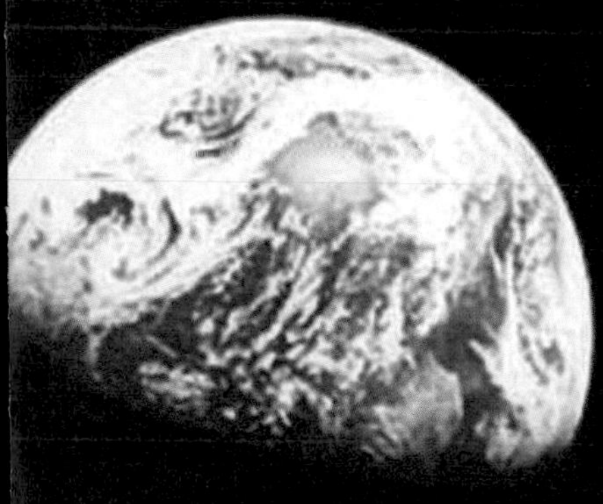

Earthrise as first seen on the Apollo 8 mission in 1968. From the Moon, the Earth is seen to rise and set, just as we can see the Moon rising and setting from the Earth.

PHASES OF THE MOON

From Earth we only see the side of the Moon that is reflecting light from the Sun. As the Moon circles the Earth every month, we see different amounts of its illuminated face, which gives the impression that the Moon changes shape. These phases range from the new moon, when none of it is visible from Earth, to the full moon, when the entire face is lit. In this diagram, the small moons show how the Sun's light shines onto the Moon, and the large moons show how it appears from the Earth throughout the month.

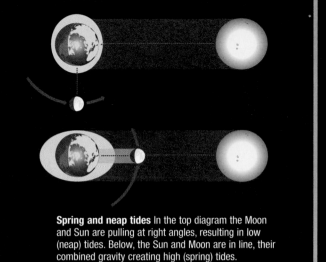

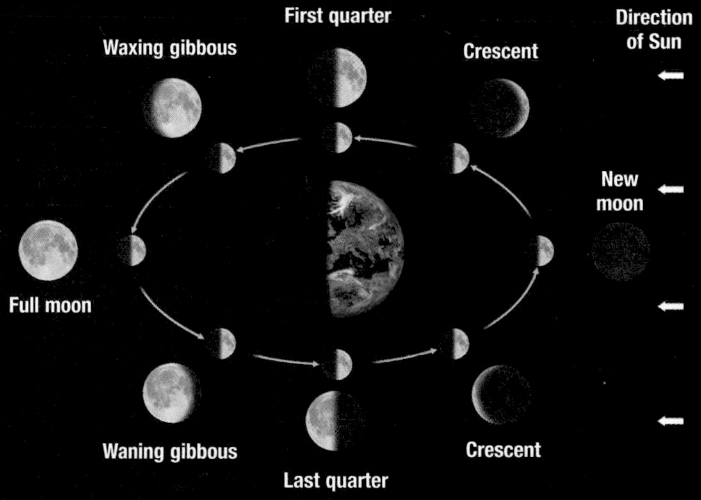

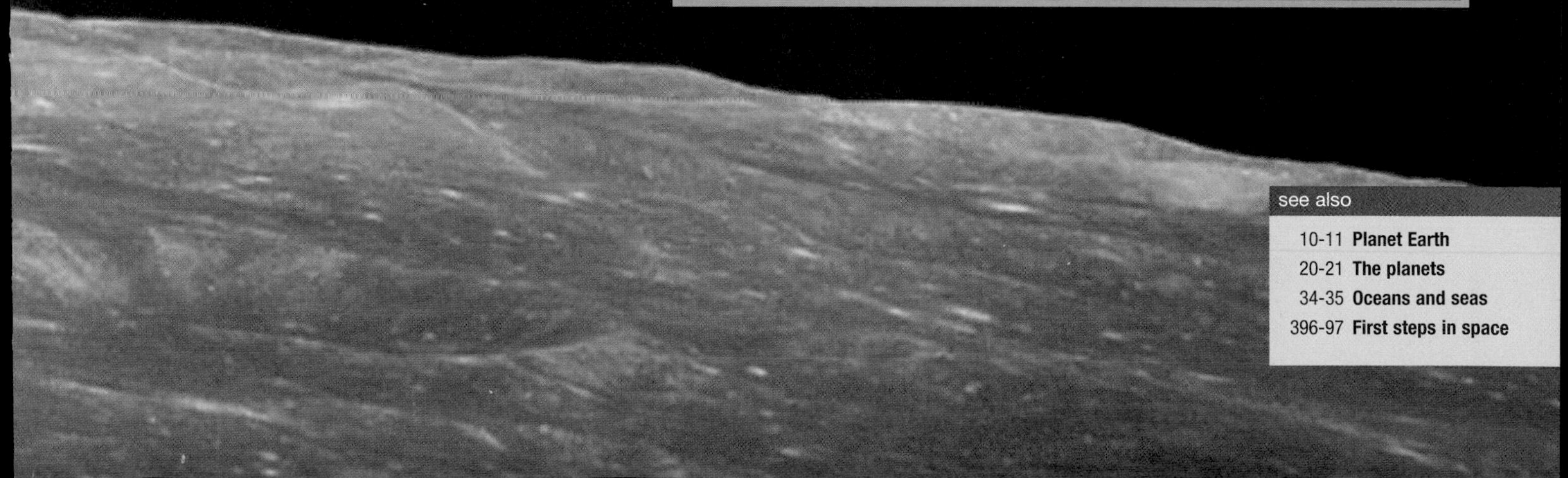

see also
10-11 **Planet Earth**
20-21 **The planets**
34-35 **Oceans and seas**
396-97 **First steps in space**

Comets and meteorites ▶

The Solar System is littered with solid debris left over from the formation of the planets. Comets and asteroids orbit the Sun, while meteors are fragments that enter Earth's atmosphere and burn up. Large fragments that hit the ground are called meteorites.

COMETS

Comets are like large, dirty snowballs, a few miles in diameter, made up of rocks and dust held together by ice and frozen gas. They originate in distant regions of the Solar System past Pluto. Occasionally, the gravity of a passing star nudges a comet from these outer reaches into the inner Solar System, leaving it in elliptical orbit around the Sun.

A comet emits no light of its own, so for most of its orbit it is invisible. When it passes close to the Sun and its crust begins to melt, it produces a glowing cloud of gas and dust, the coma. Luminous gas tails can also be seen on most comets, pointing away from the Sun because they are deflected by the solar wind.

Some comets have orbits that frequently bring them close to the Sun, and they are visible from Earth. Halley's comet is one such, with a return period of about 76 years. Every time they pass close to the Sun comets lose material, until they eventually disappear.

Well-known comets

Name	Discovered	Return period (years)
Halley	239 B.C.	76
Tycho	1577	Not known
Kirch (Newton)	1680	8814
Encke	1786	3.3
Tuttle	1790	13.7
Great Comet	1843	512.6
Donati	1858	1950
Swift–Tuttle	1872	125
Wolf	1884	8.4
Daylight Comet	1910	Not known
Schwassmann–Wachmann 1	1927	15
Arend–Roland	1957	Not known
Seki–Lines	1962	Not known
Kohoutek	1973	75 000
West	1975	500 000
Shoemaker–Levy 9	1992	None – crashed into Jupiter in 1992
Hale–Bopp	1995	18 000

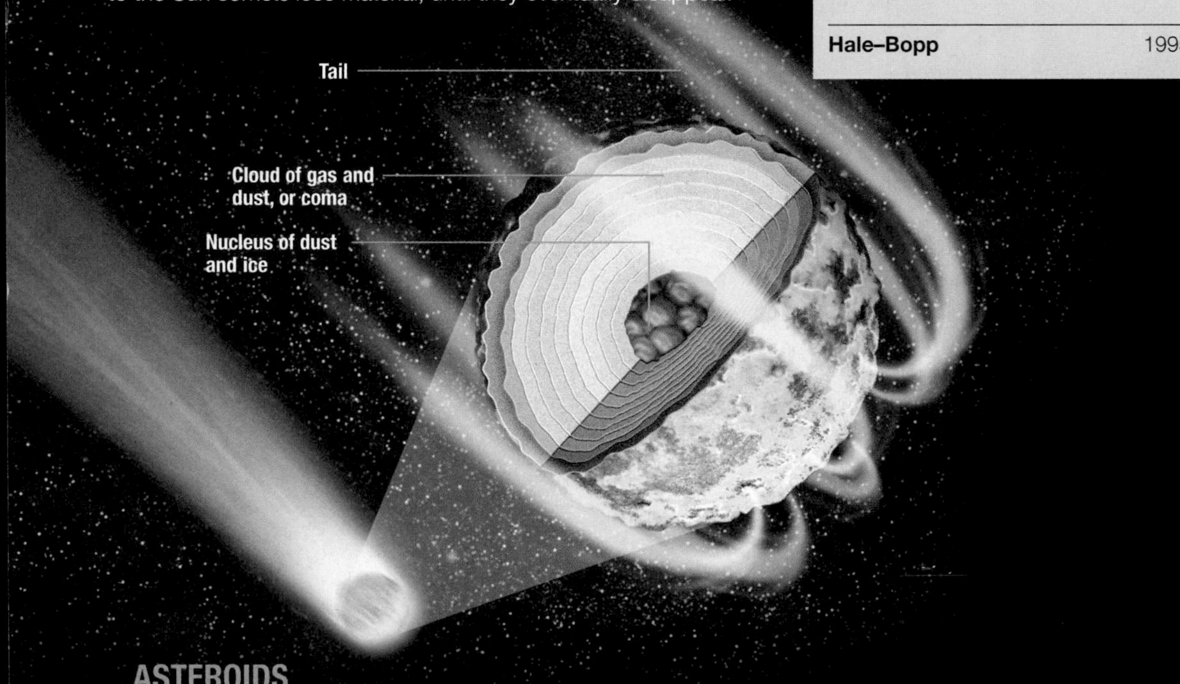

COMET FACTS

- About 900 comets are currently known.
- About 25 comets are seen from Earth through telescopes every year.
- The tail of a comet can be up to 300 million km (200 million miles) long.
- Comets travel at speeds of up to 20 km/s (12 miles/s).
- The coma of a comet can be larger than the Sun.

ASTEROIDS

Asteroids, or minor planets, are rocky or metallic bodies found unevenly distributed in the Asteroid Belt between Mars and Jupiter, shown here as a blue band. They are thought to be material that failed to form a planet because of the gravitational pull of Jupiter. There are at least 1 million asteroids in the Solar System. They range in size from 10 m (35 ft) to about 900 km (560 miles) in diameter. The largest are roughly spherical and have a similar structure to planets. One, Ida, has a satellite.

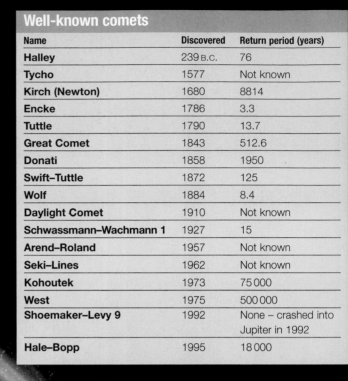

Major asteroids

The ten largest known asteroids (with their diameters) are

Ceres	940 km (584 miles)
Pallas	580 km (360 miles)
Vesta	576 km (358 miles)
Hygeia	430 km (267 miles)
Interamnia	338 km (210 miles)
Juno	288 km (180 miles)
Psyche	248 km (154 miles)
Thule	130 km (80 miles)
Astraea	120 km (75 miles)
Feronia	96 km (60 miles)

METEOR SHOWERS

When small fragments of natural space debris (meteoroids) enter the Earth's atmosphere, they burn up. The result is a bright streak of light in the sky, known as a meteor or shooting star. Meteoroids are about the size of a grain of sand, and an estimated 100 million a day zip through the thin air at up to 209 200 km/h (130 000 mph), 65 km (40 miles) above the Earth's surface. Dust trails from comets cause regular meteor showers.

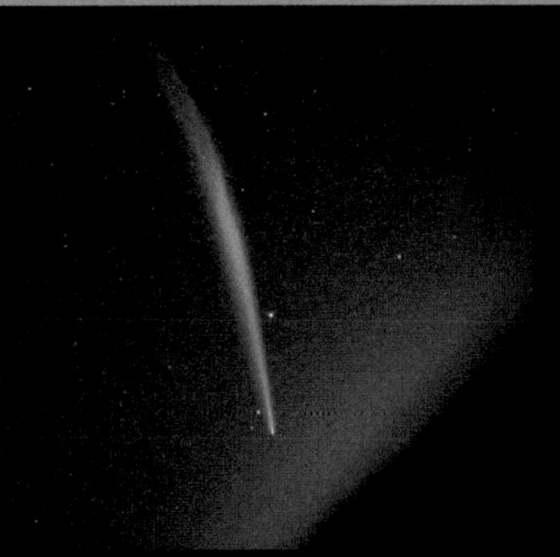

Shooting star A meteor arches through the sky, its gas tail deflected away from the Sun by the solar wind.

Regular meteor showers caused by the Earth passing through comet trail debris.

Quadrantids	(1-6 Jan)
Lyrids	(19-25 April)
Alpha-Scorpiids	(20 April-19 May)
Eta Aquariids	(1-8 May)
Delta Aquariids	(15 July-20 Aug)
Perseids	(27 July-17 Aug)
Orionids 1	(5-25 Oct)
Taurids	(25 Oct-25 Nov)
Leonids	(14-20 Nov)
Geminids	(8-14 Dec)
Ursids	(19-24 Dec)

METEORITES

Meteorites are pieces of rocky or metallic space debris that actually collide with the Earth. There are three recognized types.

- **Stony meteorites**: rocky with small amounts of nickel and iron. Most meteorites are of this type, but because they are difficult to tell from terrestrial rocks, they often go unnoticed.
- **Iron meteorites**: mainly iron and nickel, thought to originate in the cores of asteroids. They account for about 4 percent of known meteorite falls. The largest known meteorites are of this type.
- **Stony-iron meteorites**: approximately 50 percent nickel and iron and 50 percent rock. Also thought to originate in asteroids. They account for about 1 percent of known meteorite falls.

TEN HEAVIEST METEORITES

The heaviest known meteorites were found at:

Hoba West, Namibia	(60 metric tons)
Ahnighito, West Greenland	(34 metric tons)
Bacuberito, Mexico	(27 metric tons)
Mbosi, Tanzania	(26 metric tons)
Agpalik, W. Greenland	(21 metric tons)
Armanty, Outer Mongolia	(20 metric tons)
Chupaderos, Mexico	(14 metric tons)
Willamette, Oregon	(14 metric tons)
Campo del Cielo, Argentina	(13 metric tons)
Mundrabilla, Western Australia	(12 metric tons)

METEORITE FACTS

- About 1 metric ton of meteorites hits the Earth every day; most of them are very small and go unnoticed.
- Meteorites hurtle through the atmosphere at speeds of 32-95 km/s (20-60 miles/s)
- No person is known to have been killed by a meteorite.

Wolf Creek Crater A meteorite weighing more than 50,000 metric tons formed this crater in Australia.

Meteorite craters

Most meteorites are destroyed on impact, but large meteorites may leave behind craters, which give some idea of their size.

Name	Discovered	Diameter
Meteor Crater, Arizona	1871	1265 m (4150 ft)
Wolf Creek, Australia	1947	675 m (2200 ft)
Boxhole, Australia	1937	175 m (574 ft)
Odessa, Texas	1921	170 m (558 ft)
Oesal, Estonia	1927	100 m (328 ft)
Waqer, Arabia	1932	100 m (328 ft)

see also
10-11 **Planet Earth**
20-21 **The planets**
46-47 **Earth's atmosphere**

Structure of the Earth

Processes within the Earth drive plate tectonics

The Earth is made up of concentric layers – the core, mantle, and crust – each with its own distinctive physical and chemical characteristics. These layers are not homogeneous: The variations within them explain the existence of such phenomena as continental drift, volcanoes, earthquakes, and the Earth's magnetic field.

INSIDE THE EARTH

Our deepest drilling has failed to penetrate beyond the Earth's crust, so information about our planet's internal structure has to be gleaned from a variety of other sources. These include the behavior of earthquake waves as they pass through the Earth; the composition of meteorites, which are remnants of other planetary material; and the chemistry of rare mantle rocks occasionally found at the surface. This evidence combines to give us a picture of an Earth composed of four distinct concentric layers.

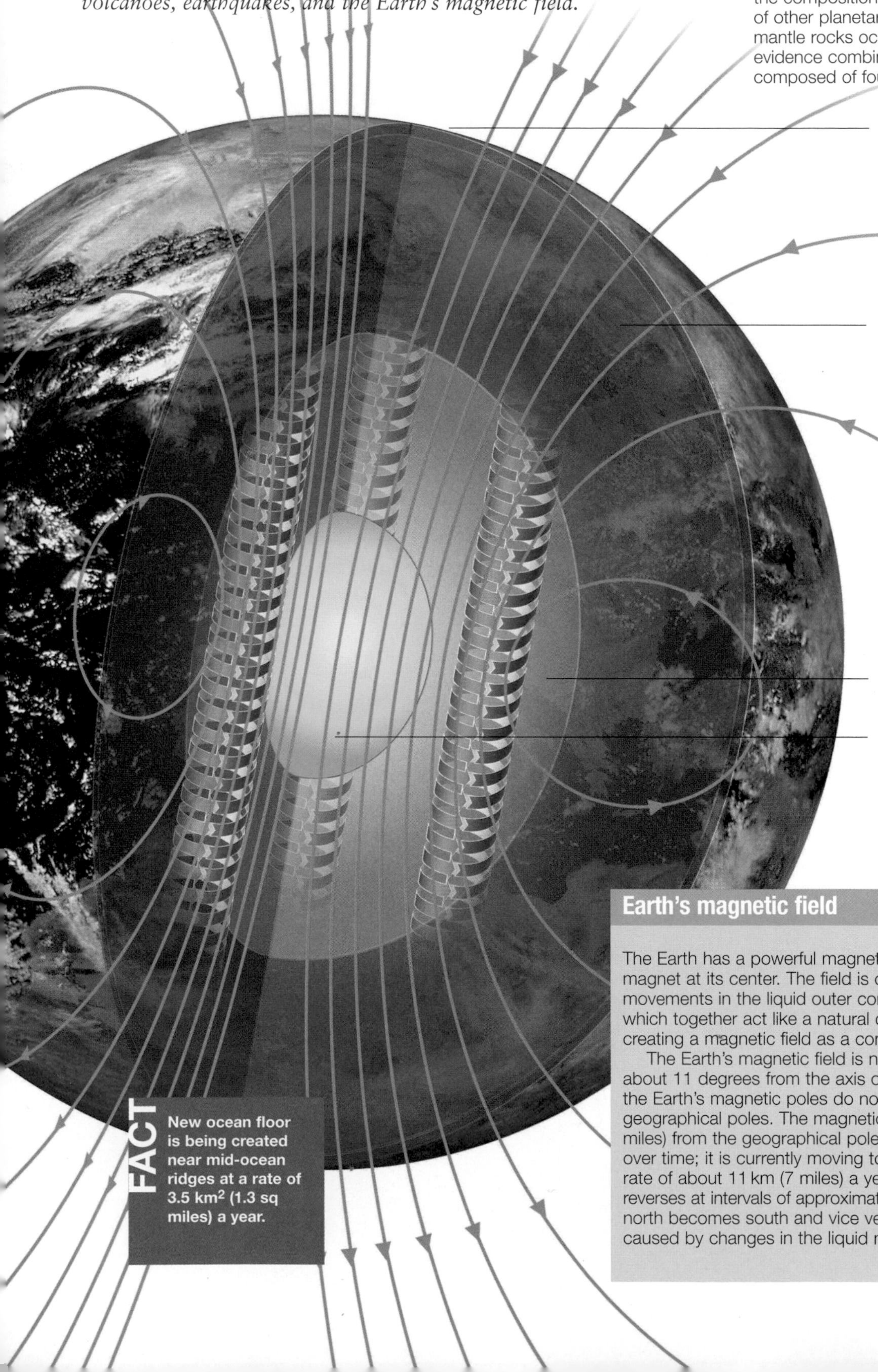

Crust Solid outer layer ranges in thickness from a minimum of 5 km (3 miles) beneath the oceans to a maximum of 80 km (50 miles) under the highest mountain ranges. Two types of crust exist: young, thin, dense basaltic oceanic crust comprising 65 percent of the Earth's surface; and older, thicker, less dense continental crust, comprising 35 percent of the Earth's surface.

Mantle A mainly solid layer 2900 km (1800 miles) thick. Average density 3-4.5 times that of water. Temperature 700-1800°C (1300-3300°F). Composed largely of a dense rock called garnet peridotite. Convection currents in a partially melted zone at the top of the mantle provide the driving force for continental drift. Although solid, the rest of the mantle also moves in slow currents.

Core Begins at a depth of 2900 km (1800 miles). Total diameter 6900 km (4300 miles). Composed predominantly of iron with some nickel and a small amount of a lighter element – probably sulfur.
The core is divided into two parts.

Outer core A liquid layer 2100 km (1300 miles) thick.

Inner core A solid layer 2700 km (1700 miles) in diameter, thought to rotate at a different speed from the rest of the Earth. Temperature in the center is estimated at 4000-5000°C (7200-9000°F).

Earth's magnetic field

The Earth has a powerful magnetic field, as if there were a giant bar magnet at its center. The field is created by interactions between movements in the liquid outer core and the rotation of the Earth, which together act like a natural dynamo, generating electricity and creating a magnetic field as a consequence.

The Earth's magnetic field is not fixed. At present, it is angled at about 11 degrees from the axis on which the planet spins, so that the Earth's magnetic poles do not coincide exactly with its geographical poles. The magnetic north pole is about 850 km (530 miles) from the geographical pole. This position changes slightly over time; it is currently moving toward the geographical pole at a rate of about 11 km (7 miles) a year. The polarity of the field also reverses at intervals of approximately 1 million years so that magnetic north becomes south and vice versa. These reversals are probably caused by changes in the liquid movements of the outer core.

FACT

New ocean floor is being created near mid-ocean ridges at a rate of 3.5 km^2 (1.3 sq miles) a year.

PLATE TECTONICS

The Earth's crust and upper mantle (together called the lithosphere) are divided into rigid interlocking segments, or plates, which are in constant motion in relation to each other. Their movement is driven by convection currents in the mantle. The plates carry the continents and underlie the oceans, although their boundaries do not necessarily coincide with continent margins. Plates are created or destroyed along constructive and convergent boundaries.

Constructive boundaries These occur at mid-ocean ridges. Upwelling magma drives the plates apart, adding new material along their edges in the process. The Mid-Atlantic Ridge is a major example. Plates at mid-ocean ridges can move apart at a rate of 15 cm (6 in.) a year.

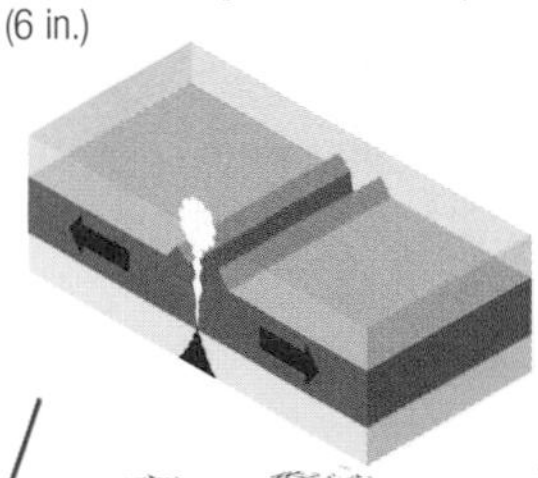

Conservative boundaries Two plates slide past each other along a transform fault and are neither created nor destroyed. They are characterized by earthquake activity. California's San Andreas Fault is an example of a conservative plate boundary.

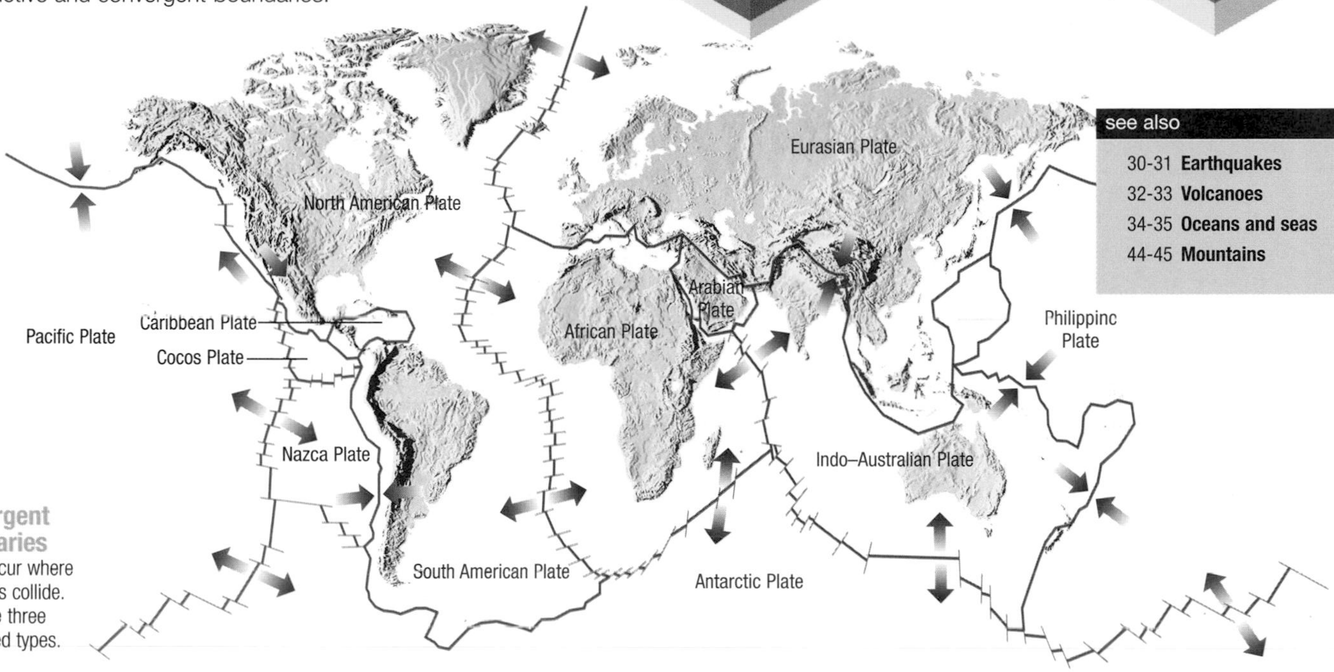

see also
30-31 **Earthquakes**
32-33 **Volcanoes**
34-35 **Oceans and seas**
44-45 **Mountains**

Convergent boundaries These occur where two plates collide. There are three recognized types.

Oceanic/continental Dense oceanic crust sinks beneath continental crust and into the mantle, where it melts, causing volcanoes and earthquakes. Sediments on the edge of the plates are folded and thrust up. The Andes are an example of this type of boundary.

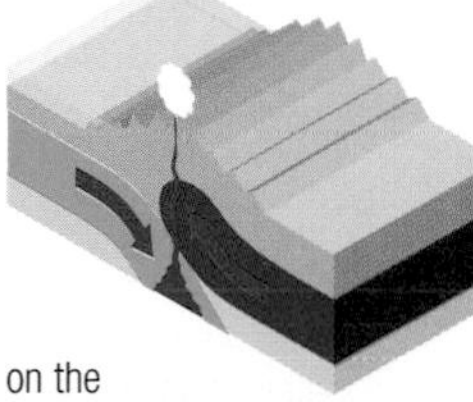

Continental/continental Plates carrying continents or islands collide. The margins of both plates are forced upward, causing earthquakes, volcanism, and major fold-mountain regions. The Himalayas are the result of a collision between plates carrying Asia and India.

Oceanic/oceanic One oceanic plate is forced under the other. Rising magma from melting of the descending plate creates a volcanic island arc, such as Japan or the Aleutians.

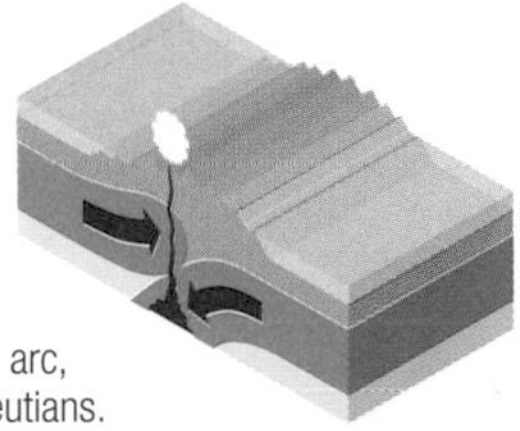

A shifting world

The position of continents is not fixed. Over geological time they have been created and destroyed, come together and moved apart. The maps below show how the present continents have come into being and how they might be positioned in the future.

250 million years ago The continents were joined together into one large landmass called Pangaea, from the Greek meaning "all lands."

135 million years ago Pangaea split into Laurasia in the north (North America and Eurasia) and Gondwanaland in the south (Africa, South America, Australia, India and Antarctica).

Today The Atlantic is widening, and a new constructive plate boundary appears to be forming along Africa's Rift Valley, but this might not happen.

The future If current movements continue, the Atlantic will widen, Africa will collide with Europe, Australia will collide with Southeast Asia, and California will slide north to Alaska.

From the formation of the planet right up to the present day, the Earth's long history is recorded in its rocks. Geology can reveal a range of information about past environments, for instance where deserts, volcanoes, seas and forests once existed. It can also tell us about the position of past continents and how old they are. Rocks are constantly being created and destroyed by erosion, deposition, volcanism, and mountain building.

Quantities of main elements in the Earth's crust

Element	%	Element	%
Oxygen (O)	45.0	Magnesium (Mg)	2.8
Silicon (Si)	27.0	Sodium (Na)	2.3
Aluminium (Al)	8.0	Potassium (K)	1.7
Iron (Fe)	5.8	Hydrogen (H)	1.5
Calcium (Ca)	4.7	Titanium (Ti)	0.6

CATEGORIES OF ROCK

Rocks are aggregates of minerals or organic matter, either consolidated or loose. Thus, in geological terms, sand and gravel are technically rocks, as are more familiar examples such as marble, sandstone and granite. Minerals are naturally occurring inorganic substances such as quartz and calcite.

Geologists divide rock into categories related to how the rock was formed. The three main categories are:

- **Igneous**
- **Sedimentary**
- **Metamorphic**

Sedimentary rocks are formed by the accumulation and cementation of mud, silt or sand derived from the breakdown of preexisting rocks, and from organic material such as trees or shells. Deposits precipitated from water, for instance rock salt, are also included. Sedimentary rocks represent less than 5 percent of the Earth's crust but 75 percent of its land surface.
Appearance Usually composed of fragments cemented together by calcite, quartz, or other minerals. Sedimentary rock outcrops often have a layered appearance; the layers represent successive periods of sediment deposition. Many sedimentary rocks contain fossils – preserved organic remains. Some limestones are composed entirely of cemented shell fragments.
Examples Sandstone, limestone, rock salt and peat.

Ironstone (Hamersley Range, Pilbara Region, Western Australia) This sedimentary rock clearly shows depositional layering. It is cemented by iron compounds, which give it its distinctive red color.

Igneous rocks were once molten; they include lavas, such as basalts, expelled by volcanoes, and rocks such as granites that originated as hot liquids deep in the Earth's crust. The first surface rocks created after the formation of the Earth were igneous. Today igneous rocks represent 95 percent of the Earth's crust.
Appearance Igneous rocks are usually very hard. They are made up of crystals of different minerals such as quartz and feldspar. In some rocks, for example granite, the crystals are very large and can be clearly seen. In contrast, the crystals in lavas tend to be small and are difficult to see with the naked eye. Igneous rock faces are uniform in appearance. They are not normally layered, although they may be cracked or have patchy coloration.
Examples Granite, basalt, andesite and obsidian.

Granite outcrop (Joshua Tree National Park, California) This outcrop shows the characteristic manner in which igneous granite weathers and erodes into rounded blocks and boulders.

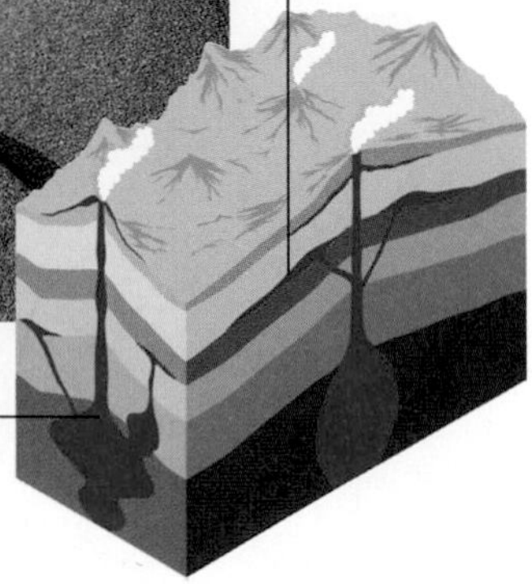

Sill Magma intrudes into horizontal fractures in the rock, then cools and hardens.

Magma chamber Molten rock store deep underground.

A marble quarry (Greece) Marble is metamorphosed limestone that has recrystallized under heat and pressure.

see also
26-27 **Structure of the Earth**
32-33 **Volcanoes**

Heat Volcanic activity and magma alter surrounding rock.

Faulting and folding Existing rock layers are crushed and compressed.

Metamorphic rocks are igneous or sedimentary rocks that have been altered by heat, pressure, or both, either because they have been buried and folded deep in the crust or because they have come into contact with molten igneous rock. Metamorphism can result in the formation of completely new minerals. It can also destroy original structures such as sedimentary layering or fossils. Intense pressure can cause the realignment of minerals, forming new layers. About 1 percent of rocks in the crust are metamorphic.
Appearance Metamorphic rocks are usually crystalline and often show layering.
Examples Marble, gneiss, schist, slate and coal.

Sedimentary environment Deposits build up in coastal waters.

Layering Older layers of sediment become compressed by the buildup of new layers overlying them.

The oldest rocks on Earth

The oldest known rocks date back to the early formation of the Earth's crust. Originally igneous, they have changed over time into metamorphic rocks.

- **Gneisses** at Isua in Greenland dated at 3.8 billion years old.
- **Eclogites** from Roberts Victor Mine in South Africa dated at 4 billion years.
- **Zircon** (a mineral), found in Australia, eroded from its original rock, dated at 4.2 billion years.

THE ROCK CYCLE

The rocks of the Earth's crust are constantly being created, worn down, and redeposited in a slow cycle.

Sedimentary and igneous rocks can undergo metamorphism, or complete melting back into magma.

Volcanic activity Formation of igneous rock from molten lava and magma.

Weathering and erosion Exposed rock is broken down by heat, frost, rain, ice, wind, running water and plant roots.

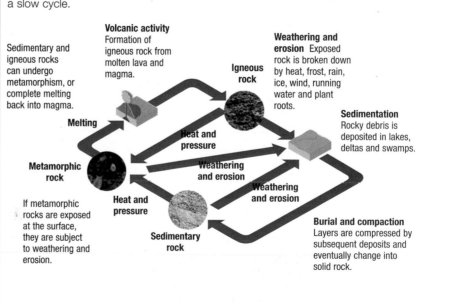

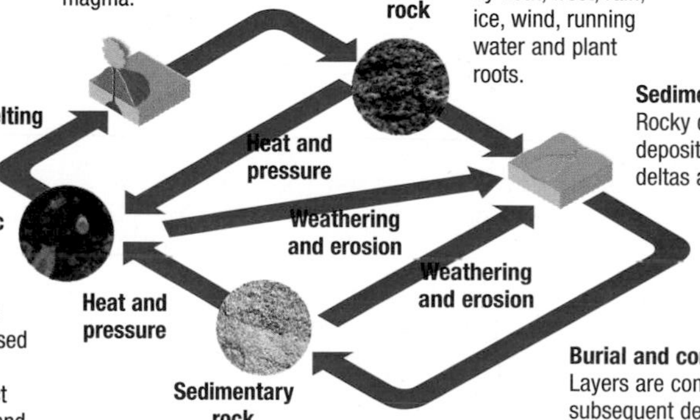

Sedimentation Rocky debris is deposited in lakes, deltas and swamps.

If metamorphic rocks are exposed at the surface, they are subject to weathering and erosion.

Burial and compaction Layers are compressed by subsequent deposits and eventually change into solid rock.

Earthquakes are natural phenomena caused by sudden movements within the Earth's crust. These movements release stresses that have built up in rock because of movement of the interlocking tectonic plates that make up the Earth's crust. Most earthquakes are so small or occur at such depth (greater than 300 km or 200 miles), that they are not felt at the surface.

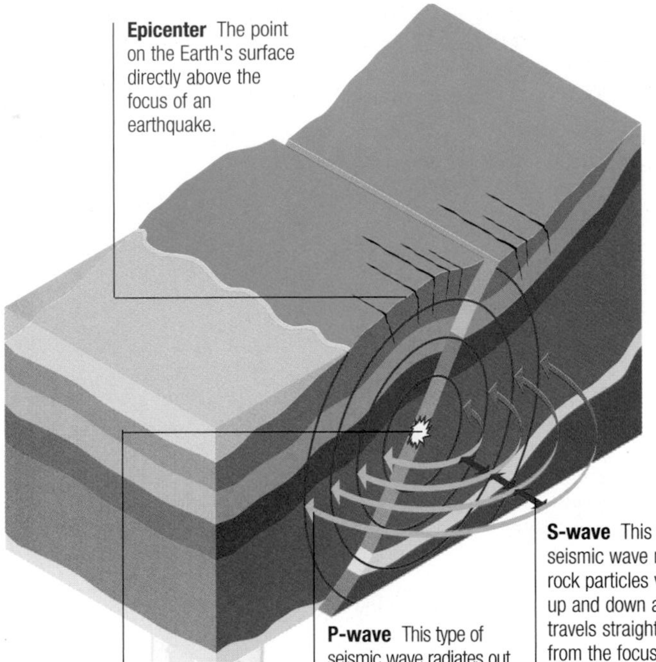
Epicenter The point on the Earth's surface directly above the focus of an earthquake.
Focus The point where an earthquake originates.
P-wave This type of seismic wave radiates out from the focus, pushing and pulling at rock particles as it goes. P-waves are the fastest-moving type and are the first to be picked up by earthquake monitoring stations.
S-wave This type of seismic wave makes rock particles vibrate up and down as it travels straight out from the focus.

HOW EARTHQUAKES HAPPEN

Rocks do not bend or break easily and tend to absorb strains and stresses. But there comes a point when they will give way, breaking or moving along fault lines (preexisting cracks) and releasing energy in the form of seismic waves, which vibrate through the surrounding rock and any structures, such as buildings, on the surface. Most earthquakes occur at boundaries between the plates of the Earth's crust. Here, friction is produced as the plates move relative to each other, and strain builds up prior to its release as an earthquake.

Earthquakes can also be initiated by volcanoes, meteorite impacts, and by human activities such as bomb explosions, the filling of reservoirs, and the injection of fluids into wells for oil recovery. Unlike earthquakes that occur at faults, these are the result of the sudden input of energy, which imposes an immediate stress on the rocks.

Earthquakes are classified by their depth of origin.

- **Shallow** – less than 70 km (40 miles)
- **Intermediate** – 70-300 km (40-186 miles)
- **Deep** – greater than 300 km (186 miles)

MEASURING EARTHQUAKES

There are two ways to measure earthquake size: **magnitude**, based on instrumental readings of the amount of energy an earthquake releases, and **intensity**, based on the effect an earthquake has. These are measured on different scales.

The **Richter scale** was developed in 1935 by Charles F. Richter as a way to compare the magnitude of earthquakes.

- Magnitude is obtained from recordings of earth movements during earthquakes, made on machines called seismographs.
- Each whole number on the Richter scale represents a release of energy 31 times greater than the previous whole number point. The scale has no upper limit, but the greatest earthquake ever recorded measured 9.5.

The **Modified Mercalli scale**, developed in the 1930s, is used to assess intensity. It grades earthquakes on a scale of I–XII depending on their effects.

I–II	Barely felt, generally not recognized as an earthquake.
III–IV	Often felt, no damage.
V–VI	Felt widely, objects moved, slight damage.
VII	Damage to poorly constructed buildings.
VIII	Damage to well-constructed buildings.
IX–X	Landslides, wholesale destruction.
XI	Total damage, visible ground movement.
XII	Total damage over large area, objects thrown into air.

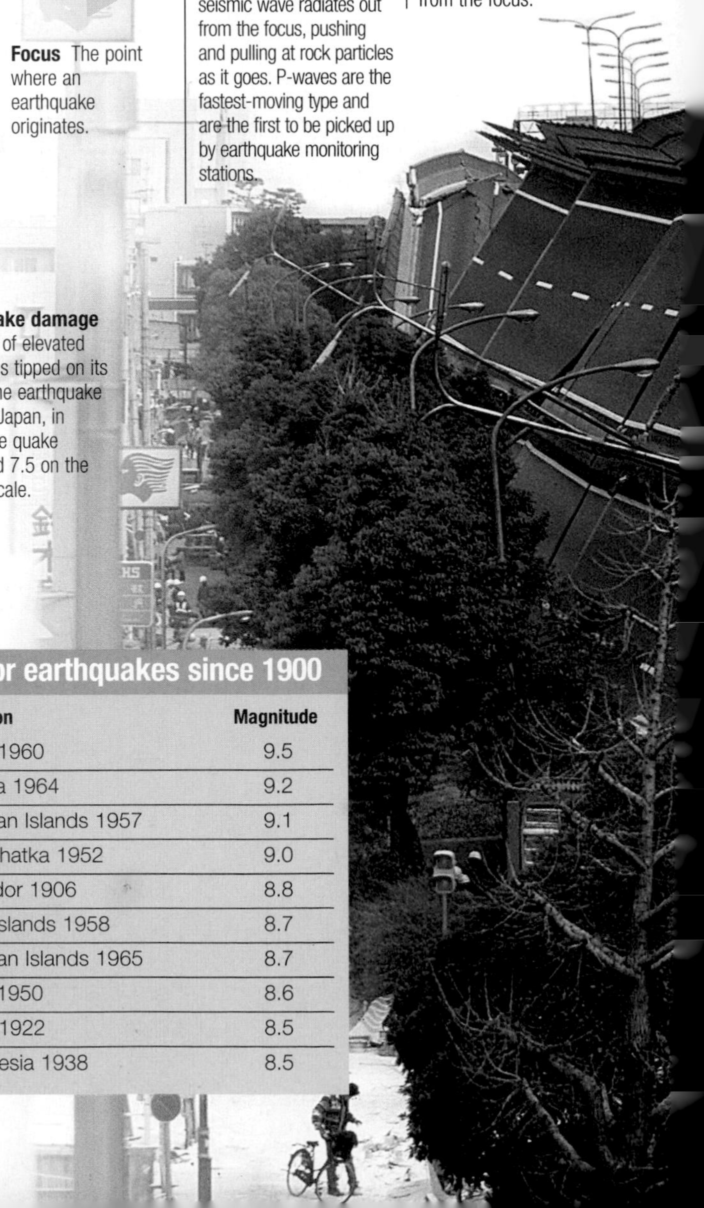

Earthquake damage A stretch of elevated highway is tipped on its side by the earthquake in Kobe, Japan, in 1995. The quake measured 7.5 on the Richter scale.

Major earthquakes since 1900

Location	Magnitude
Chile 1960	9.5
Alaska 1964	9.2
Aleutian Islands 1957	9.1
Kamchatka 1952	9.0
Ecuador 1906	8.8
Kuril Islands 1958	8.7
Aleutian Islands 1965	8.7
India 1950	8.6
Chile 1922	8.5
Indonesia 1938	8.5

TSUNAMIS

Tsunamis are giant ocean waves. The most common causes are submarine earthquakes that shift a significant area of sea floor up or down, displacing millions of cubic tons of water. Traveling outward from the displacement, the water builds into a large, destructive wave when it reaches shallow coastal waters. The sudden introduction of a large amount of material into the ocean by an erupting submarine volcano or the sudden downward slide of ocean-floor sediments or a landslide into water from a cliff or collapsing volcano has a similar effect. Tsunamis are relatively common in the earthquake-prone region around Japan, and the word "tsunami" is Japanese for "port wave."

Tsunamis have nothing to do with tides, but they can be exacerbated by local tidal conditions.

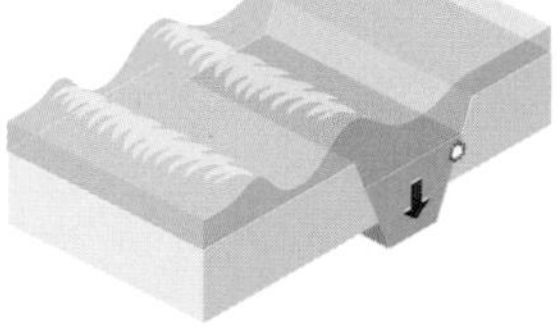

Underwater earthquake Movement of the seabed causes the displacement of a large block of water.

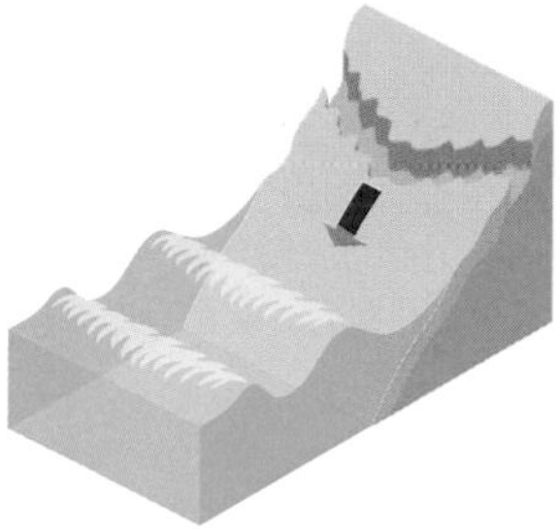

Landslide The sudden collapse of a cliff into the sea triggers a wave.

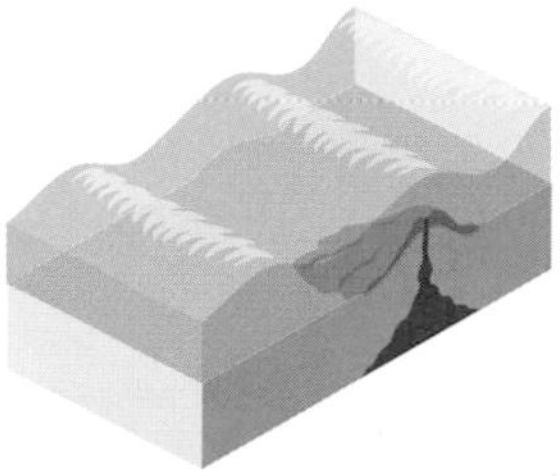

Underwater volcano An extensive lava flow from a submarine eruption displaces a large water volume.

FACTS

- About 500,000 detectable earthquakes occur worldwide every year; one-fifth can be felt.
- Ninety percent of earthquakes occur along plate boundaries.
- There are about 8000 microearthquakes every day. These have a magnitude of 2 or less and are not commonly felt, although they are recorded by sensitive seismographs.
- About 7000 shocks a year of magnitude 4 or greater are recorded worldwide.
- On average, one earthquake of magnitude 8 or higher occurs somewhere in the world every 12 months.

FACT About 70 percent of the world's earthquakes occur around the edge of the Pacific ocean: the "Ring of Fire."

see also
26-27 **Structure of the Earth**
34-35 **Oceans and seas**

Volcanoes are naturally occurring vents or fissures in the Earth's surface through which molten, gaseous or solid material is ejected. They occur mainly along plate boundaries. There are more than 1500 active volcanoes in the world today. Volcanic ash, circulating in the upper atmosphere, can cause temporary changes in global weather.

TYPES OF VOLCANO

Most volcanoes are one of four major shapes. The shape depends on factors that include age and type of eruption.

Shield volcanoes Large with broad summit areas and gently sloping sides, formed from very runny basaltic lava flows. Some of the largest volcanoes in the world are shield volcanoes – the island of Hawaii is made up of five coalesced shield volcanoes of successively younger ages.

Lava domes Formed by the slow release of extremely thick lava. Domes can be solitary, form in clusters, grow in existing craters, or appear along the flanks of volcanic cones. A dome has been growing slowly within the crater of Mount St. Helens since its eruption in 1980.

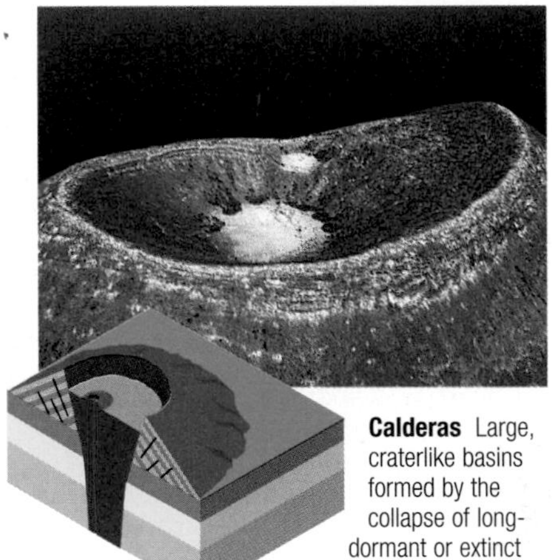

Calderas Large, craterlike basins formed by the collapse of long-dormant or extinct volcanoes. Some calderas, such as Krakatoa in Indonesia, are the result of cataclysmic explosions that destroy the erupting volcano. Others result from the collapse of the cone once the magma chamber below has emptied and can no longer support it.

Composite or stratovolcanic cones The classic volcanic cone is built up by multiple eruptions of lava and ash over hundreds or thousands of years. Composite cones can grow to great heights, and comprise 60 percent of the Earth's individual volcanoes. Examples include Mount Fuji in Japan and Mount Rainier in the US.

Life history of a volcano

- **Eruptive stage** Violent phase with continuous or periodic eruption of lavas, gases or solid material. This may be short or long-lived. Paricutin, Mexico, was in eruption for 9 years. Stromboli, Italy, has been in eruption for over 2000 years.
- **Fumarolic stage** For a long period after it has ceased to erupt, a volcano continues to emit acid gases and vapor.
- **Cooling stage** The ground still contains latent heat, which can heat ground water to form hot springs. Examples include the geysers and hot springs of Yellowstone National Park and of North Island, New Zealand.
- **Dormancy and extinction** The last traces of volcanic heat disappear and the volcano gradually reduces through erosion. As the magma beneath the volcano cools and contracts, the cone might collapse, forming a caldera. Finally, erosion might completely eradicate the volcano or leave only the harder rock in the vent, now called a volcanic pipe. Examples of volcanoes that have become inactive in recent geological time include Mount Shasta in California and Mount Hood in Oregon.

Inside a volcano

The diagram below shows the major features of a composite volcano.

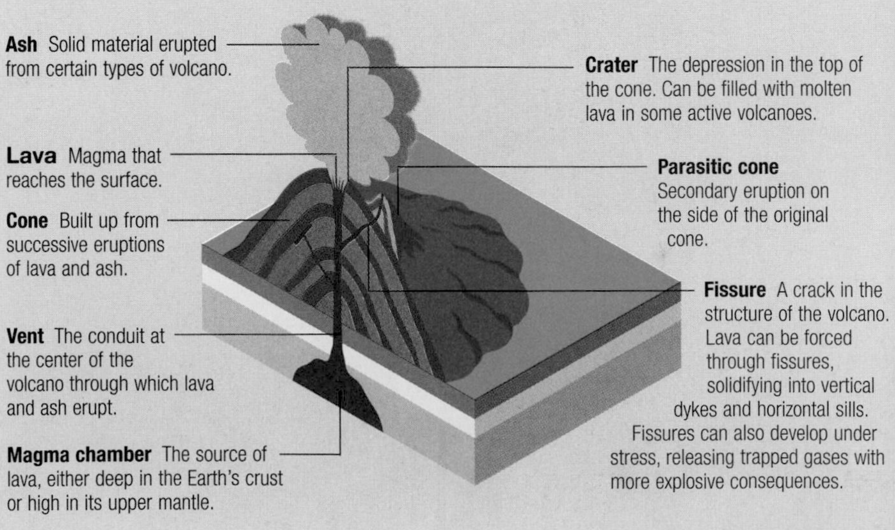

Ash Solid material erupted from certain types of volcano.
Crater The depression in the top of the cone. Can be filled with molten lava in some active volcanoes.
Lava Magma that reaches the surface.
Parasitic cone Secondary eruption on the side of the original cone.
Cone Built up from successive eruptions of lava and ash.
Fissure A crack in the structure of the volcano. Lava can be forced through fissures, solidifying into vertical dykes and horizontal sills. Fissures can also develop under stress, releasing trapped gases with more explosive consequences.
Vent The conduit at the center of the volcano through which lava and ash erupt.
Magma chamber The source of lava, either deep in the Earth's crust or high in its upper mantle.

Volcanic Explosivity Index

The Volcanic Explosivity Index (VEI) is used to judge the size of an eruption. It is based on a number of observations, including the volume and height of material erupted. In the geological past, there have been infrequent supervolcanoes, much larger than anything witnessed in the historic past. The most recent was in North America (Yellowstone National Park area) about 2 million years ago.

VEI	Eruption type	Plume height	Volume	Occurrence
0	**nonexplosive**	100 m	1000 m^3	Every day
1	**gentle**	100-1000 m	10 000 m^3	Every day
2	**explosive**	1-5 km	1 million m^3	Every week or so
3	**severe**	3-15 km	10 million m^3	Every year or so
4	**cataclysmic**	10-25 km	100 million m^3	Every few decades
5	**paroxysmal**	25 km	1 km^3	About once a century
6	**colossal**	25 km	10 km^3	Every few centuries
7	**supercolossal**	25 km	100 km^3	Every few 1000 years
8	**megacolossal**	25 km	1000 km^3	Every few 100 000 years

Where volcanoes occur

The great majority of volcanoes are concentrated along the boundaries of tectonic plates.

At constructive boundaries, such as mid-ocean ridges, where plates are moving apart, lava erupts from the upper mantle.

At convergent boundaries, where one plate plunges beneath the other, material on the upper surface of the sinking plate is dragged down until it reaches a depth where it becomes molten. Because it is less dense than the surrounding solid rock, it rises up to erupt at the surface.

Volcanoes also occur above "hot spots" created by uprising plumes of hot material in the mantle. As the plate moves slowly over a hot spot, a chain – or arc – of volcanic islands, such as Hawaii, is produced.

Mount Hekla, Iceland Iceland straddles the Mid-Atlantic Ridge, an active constructive plate margin, and was created by the buildup of basalt eruptions from submarine volcanoes.

see also

26-27 **Structure of the Earth**
38-39 **Lakes**
44-45 **Mountains**

Oceans and seas

The salt water that covers most of our planet

Oceans are large, deep, open expanses of water, whereas seas are shallower and partly encircled by land. Both oceans and seas are composed of salt water. Taken together, the five oceans (Pacific, Atlantic, Indian, Southern and Arctic) contain 97 percent of all the water on the Earth and cover about 71 percent of its surface.

OCEAN PROFILES

The oceans form one vast, continuous area of water dotted with continents and islands. They are in a state of slow but unremitting change, expanding or contracting as the relative positions of the continents change. The longest mountain range on the planet is the mid-ocean ridge beneath the Atlantic, stretching 50 000 km (30 000 miles) from the Arctic to the South Atlantic, where it divides, one branch extending into the Pacific, the other stretching across the Indian Ocean.

	Pacific Ocean	Atlantic Ocean
	The Pacific is by far the largest ocean, being twice the size of the Atlantic. It covers about a third of the Earth's surface and contains more than half the water on the planet.	The second-largest ocean, the Atlantic is widening at a rate of 2-4 cm ($3/4$-$1\,1/2$ in.) per year along the Mid-Atlantic Ridge.
Area	180 000 000 km^2 (70 000 000 sq miles)	106 000 000 km^2 (40 000 000 sq miles)
Volume	724 000 000 km^3 (173 000 000 cu miles)	354 000 000 km^3 (85 000 000 cu miles)
Average depth	3940 m (12 930 ft)	3310 m (10 860 ft)
Deepest point	Mariana Trench, 10 920 m (35 826 ft)	8648 m (28 374 ft)
Widest point	17 700 km (11 000 miles)	9600 km (5965 miles)
Features	**East Pacific Rise** A range of underwater mountains along a spreading ridge; 2000-3000 m (6500-9800 ft) high, they lie 3300 m (10 800 ft) below the surface. **Volcanic islands** Hundreds of volcanic islands are scattered across the Pacific; many are inhabited. **Great Barrier Reef** The world's largest living structure is situated in the Pacific, off the coast of Australia.	**Mid-Atlantic Ridge** A spine of submarine volcanic features running roughly north to south marking a constructive plate boundary. The ridge is up to 4000 m (13 123 ft) high. **Sargasso Sea** An area of calm water in the western North Atlantic. The water surface is covered by green–brown *Sargassum* seaweed.

On the ocean floor

The ocean floor is divided into the **continental shelf**, the gently sloping margin extending seaward from the shore, and the **continental slope**, where the shelf ends and plunges steeply to the **ocean basin floor**, where the following can be found.

- **Abyssal plains** Flat, featureless expanses of ocean floor at depths of 4000-6000 m (13 000-19 500 ft).
- **Spreading ridges** Places where two plates of the Earth's crust are moving apart. New crust forms in these regions.
- **Fracture zones** Cracks in the oceanic crust at right angles to spreading ridges.
- **Seamounts** Volcanic cone-shaped or flat-topped underwater mountains.
- **Trenches** Deep valleys where one crustal plate slides under another.

FACTS AND FIGURES

- **Total length of world's coastlines** 504 000 km (312 000 miles)
- **Warmest sea** Persian Gulf
- **Saltiest sea** Red Sea
- **Deepest trench** Mariana Trench (Pacific Ocean) 10 920 m (35 826 ft) below sea level. At 8863 m (29 029 ft), Mount Everest could be completely sunk in the Mariana Trench.
- **Longest trench** Aleutian Trench (Pacific Ocean) 1700 km (1055 miles)
- **Highest seamount** Great Meteor Tablemount (North Atlantic) 4000 m (13 123 ft) high

SEAS

Seas are subdivisions of oceans, especially where the oceans are partly bounded by land. Seas are always salt water. Large landlocked bodies of salt water such as the Dead and Caspian Seas should be classified as lakes.

- **Coral Sea** 4 791 000 km^2 (1 850 000 sq miles). Part of the Pacific Ocean, lying between Australia and New Caledonia.
- **China Sea** Part of the Pacific Ocean, it has two areas: the East China Sea, 13 248 000 km^2 (481 850 sq miles); and the South China Sea, 2 318 000 km^2 (894 980 sq miles).
- **Caribbean Sea** 2 640 000 km^2 (1 019 000 sq miles) Part of the Atlantic Ocean containing many islands.
- **Mediterranean Sea** 2 516 999 km^2 (971 000 sq miles) An almost landlocked and tideless body of water. In 50 million years, if present plate motions continue to force Africa north, the Mediterranean will probably close up altogether.
- **Bering Sea** 2 270 000 km^2 (880 000 sq miles) Part of the northern North Pacific, lying between Alaska and Kamchatka, the Bering Sea is often frozen for several months during the winter.
- **Sea of Okhotsk** 1 528 000 km^2 (589 961 sq miles) An extension of the northwest North Pacific, off the eastern coast of Russia.
- **Sea of Japan** 1 008 8000 km^2 (389 200 sq miles) Part of the North Pacific, between Japan, Korea and Russia.
- **Andaman Sea** 777 000 km^2 (297 572 sq miles) Part of the Indian Ocean, lying between the Andaman Islands and Thailand.

Indian Ocean

The Indian Ocean comprises about a fifth of the total area covered by seawater. It is the third-largest ocean.

Southern Ocean

Includes all water lying south of latitude 55°S and is the fourth-largest ocean. In winter, more than half the surface is covered by ice.

Arctic Ocean

The smallest and shallowest ocean, containing just 1 percent of the Earth's saltwater. A thick sheet of ice covers it for most of the year.

Indian Ocean	Southern Ocean	Arctic Ocean
75 000 000 km² (29 000 000 sq miles)	35 000 000 km² (13 500 000 sq miles)	14 090 000 km² (5 440 000 sq miles)
292 000 000 km³ (70 000 000 cu miles)	Unknown	17 000 km³ (4100 cu miles)
3840 m (12 600 ft)	Unknown	1205 m (3950 ft)
Java Trench, 7450 m (24 442 ft)	4500 m (14 765 ft)	Pole Abyssal Plain, 5450 m (17 880 ft)
Not applicable	Not applicable	Not applicable
Mid-Indian Ocean Ridge This stretches from the Red Sea in the north almost to the southern limit of the Indian Ocean. **Ninety East Ridge** A major feature stretching 2735 km (1700 miles). **Red Sea** 453 000 km² (175 000 sq miles). Lies over a spreading ridge and has been widening for the last 25 million years.	Information about the remote Southern Ocean is incomplete because Antarctic ice extends seaward hundreds of miles from the continent and observations from the ice-covered regions are sparse.	**Arctic Mid-Ocean Ridge** An extension of the Mid Atlantic Ridge; actively spreading.

see also

22-23 **The Moon**

26-27 **Structure of the Earth**

40-41 **Islands in the sea**

OCEAN CURRENTS

Ocean currents can be divided into surface (warm) and deep water (cold).

Surface currents Driven by the wind, surface currents can be up to 80 km (50 miles) wide and move at speeds of up to 220 km (136 miles) per day in roughly circular patterns called gyres. There are two gyres in the Northern Hemisphere (clockwise) and three in the Southern Hemisphere (counterclockwise). Water is warmed at the Equator, and this heat is transported by the currents toward the poles.

Deep-water currents Changes in water density create deep-water currents. The colder and saltier the water, the greater its density. Water is at its coldest and saltiest near the poles, where it sinks to the ocean floor. It spreads slowly toward the Equator at a rate of a few meters a day, and warmer water flows in to take its place.

■ **Surface currents** **1** West Australia Current; **2** North Pacific Current; **3** North Equatorial Current; **4** Equatorial Counter Current; **5** South Equatorial Current; **6** East Australia Current; **7** Florida Current; **8** Gulf Stream; **9** North Atlantic Drift; **10** North Equatorial Current; **11** Guinea Current; **12** Brazil Current; **13** Agulhas Current; **14** Somali Current.

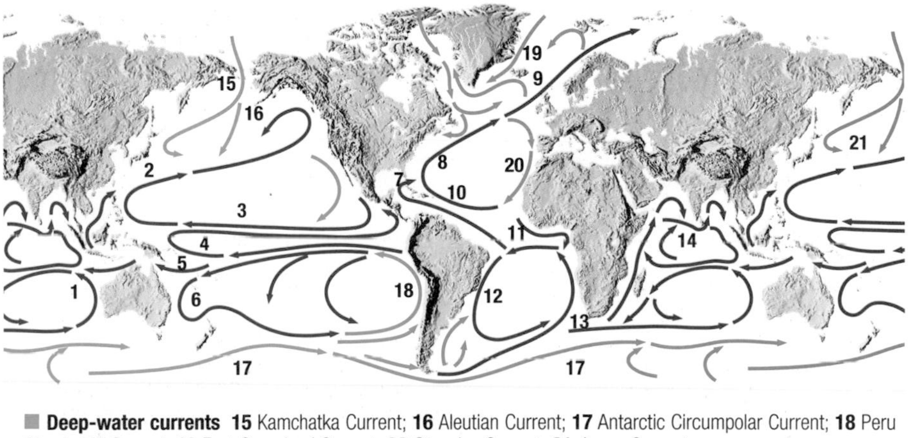

■ **Deep-water currents** **15** Kamchatka Current; **16** Aleutian Current; **17** Antarctic Circumpolar Current; **18** Peru (Humboldt) Current; **19** East Greenland Current; **20** Canaries Current; **21** Japan Current.

Rivers are a vital element in the Earth's water cycle, transporting water that falls as rain or snow back to the sea. In the process, rivers irrigate the land and provide a rich habitat for wildlife. With the exception of the frozen polar regions, rivers exist everywhere on the Earth's land surface. They can even be found in the driest deserts, although their flow may be intermittent.

RIVER FORMATION

Water finds its own level, and surface water tends to channel along depressions and hollows and make its way, under the influence of gravity, downhill to the sea. Rivers form when small channels combine to become a major feature. Rivers have their origins in high ground and tend to be small but fast-flowing near their sources, gradually growing larger, wider and slower-flowing farther down their length as tributaries join them and they approach the sea.

Rivers have three main stages. In the first stage, young rivers carve downward, forming characteristic V-shaped valleys and picking up rocky debris in the process. Waterfalls and rapids are common features of young rivers. In the second stage, rivers slow and begin to deposit material, at the same time eroding the river channel. Flood plains develop along second-stage rivers, and they begin to meander. In the final stage, they flow sluggishly, and meanderings become more pronounced. Remaining sediment is deposited in an estuary or delta.

Deltas

Some rivers form deltas where they meet the sea. As water enters the sea, it suddenly loses speed and deposits any suspended particles of sand or mud (sediment) that it was carrying. Over time, these particles may build up until they block the river. The river then divides and flows to either side of the blockage, each new stream forming its own banks. As division continues, a delta is formed. There are two types of delta: Fan-shaped deltas are called arcuate deltas – e.g., the Nile. Lobe-shaped deltas are called bird-foot deltas – e.g., the Mississippi.

Fan delta The Nile delta is a classic fan shape. The Nile splits into several channels far inland, and these deposit the sediment in the delta area. Strong wave action in the Mediterranean redistributes the sediment along the delta front.

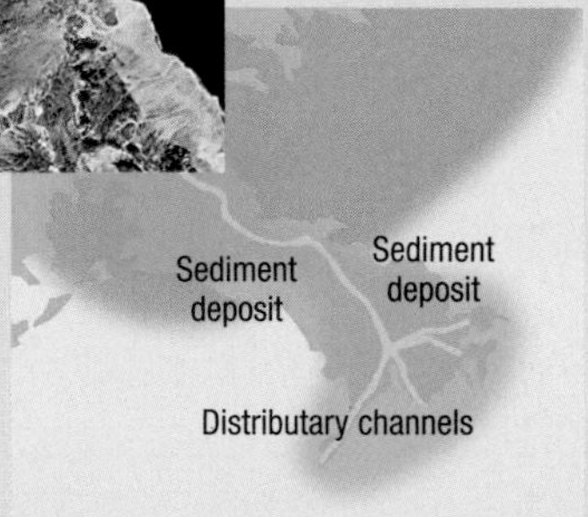

Lobe delta The Mississippi has a lobe, or bird-foot, delta. A small number of major channels carry sediment out to sea, extending the delta in a characteristic tongue shape.

THE WORLD'S LONGEST RIVERS

1 Nile

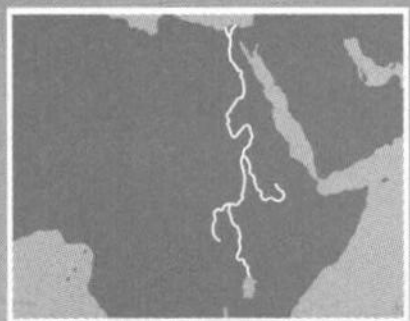

The Nile is the world's longest river; it has the third-largest drainage basin (area of land drained). Its volume of water is relatively small because much of the area it drains is so dry.

Location: NE Africa
Length: 6700 km (4100 miles)
Drainage basin: 3.3 million km^2 (1.3 million sq miles)
Source: East African Rift Valley (White Nile); Ethiopian Highlands (Blue Nile)
Major tributaries: None
Flows into: Mediterranean

2 Amazon

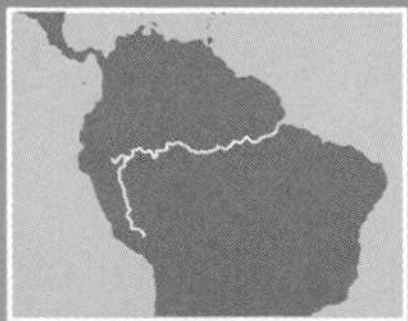

The world's second-longest river; and arguably the longest, depending on which channel in its delta it is measured from. It has the largest drainage basin.

Location: South America
Length: 6400 km (4000 miles)
Drainage basin: 7 million km^2 (2.7 million sq miles)
Source: Eastern flanks of the Andes mountain range
Major tributaries: Negro, Japura, Putumayo, Napo, Ucayali, Jurua and Purus
Flows into: Atlantic Ocean

3 Chiang Jiang

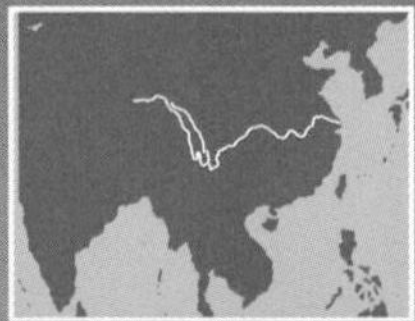

The Chiang Jiang begins in Tibet, where it is fed by melting snow. It is Asia's largest river, and the world's deepest. In places, floods have caused the river to rise by up to 50 m (170 ft).

Location: East Asia
Length: 6300 km (4000 miles)
Drainage basin: 1.8 million km^2 (0.7 million sq miles)
Source: Tibetan plateau
Major tributaries: Gan, Han, Jialing and Litang
Flows into: East China Sea

4 Mississippi

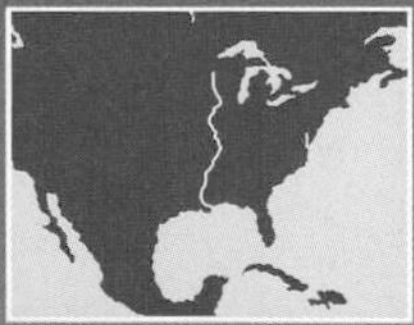

The Mississippi divides the US in two. The word Mississippi derives from Algonquin, a Native American language, and means "father of waters."

Location: North America
Length: 6000 km (3700 miles)
Drainage basin: 3.2 million km^2 (1.2 million sq miles)
Source: Lake Itasca, Minnesota
Major tributaries: Missouri and Arkansas
Flows into: Gulf of Mexico

5 Yenisei

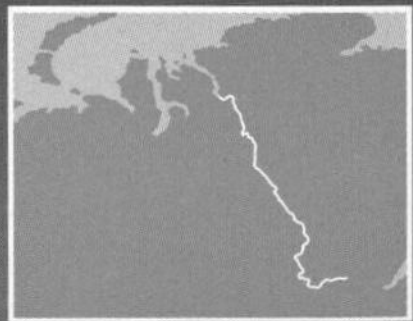

The Yenisei drains an area of Siberia almost as large as that in the US drained by the Mississippi. In places it reaches a width of 40 km (25 miles). It is frozen throughout winter.

Location: Russia
Length: 5540 km (3442 miles)
Drainage basin: 2.5 million km^2 (1 million sq miles)
Source: Lake Baikal
Major tributaries: Angara and Nizhnaya Tunguska
Flows into: Kara Sea (Arctic Ocean)

FACT The world's rivers contain only 0.0001 percent of the Earth's total water.

WATERFALLS

Within a river's lifetime, a waterfall is a temporary feature that is eventually worn away. Waterfalls are divided into three types:

- **Cataract** A high fall over which large volumes pass.
- **Cascade** Low in height and less steep than cataracts. The term also describes a series of small falls along a river.
- **Rapids** An increase in channel steepness causes turbulent flow and white water.

Waterfalls form for one of four main reasons:

- **Change in rock type** When a river passes from harder to softer rock, it erodes the softer rock more quickly, creating a drop.
- **Change in topography** Raised blocks such as lava flows and land uplifted by faults create platforms.
- **Glaciation** Waterfalls drop from hanging valleys left high on a valley side after the glacier ice has melted.
- **Drop in sea level** The river has to cut down along its channel, causing a sharp change of gradient.

The world's highest waterfall Angel Falls drops 979 m (3212 ft) in total.

FACTS

- **Waterfall with the largest volume:** Stanley (Boyoma) Zaire, has a flow of 17 000 m^3 (600 900 ft^3) per second.
- **Widest waterfall:** Chutes de Khone (Khone Falls), Mekong River in Laos is 10.8 km (6 3/4 miles) wide. The volume of water passing over it has been estimated at 11 600 m^3 (410 000 ft^3) per second, although its height is only 70 m (230 ft).
- **Highest waterfall in Europe:** Utigård, Nesdale, Norway, is 800 m (2625 ft) high.

Other major rivers

Murray (Australia)
3800 km (2300 miles)
Australia's longest river.

Volga (Russia)
3700 km (2300 miles)
The longest river in Europe.

Danube (Europe)
2800 km (1800 miles)
The only east-flowing river in Europe.

Rhine (Europe)
1300 km (800 miles)
The longest river in western Europe.

see also
38-39 **Lakes**
42-43 **Glaciers**
44-45 **Mountains**

6 Huang He

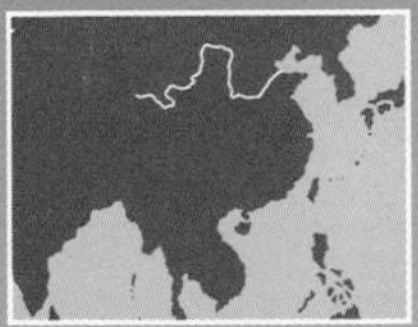

The Huang He (Yellow River) runs eastward from Tibet, over the North China Plain. It deposits an estimated 1.4 billion metric tons of sediment at its mouth each year, making its delta the fastest growing in the world, increasing by 2 km (1 mile) each year.

Location: China
Length: 5464 km (3400 miles)
Drainage basin: 750 000 km^2 (300 000 sq miles)
Source: Tibetan plateau
Major tributaries: Wei and Fen
Flows into: Yellow Sea

7 Ob

The Ob originates in the Altai mountains, where Russia, Mongolia and China meet. It snakes through western Siberia before meeting the Irtysh about 500 km (300 miles) east of the Ural mountains.

Location: Russia
Length: 5410 km (3362 miles)
Drainage basin: 2.9 million km^2 (1.1 million sq miles)
Source: Altai mountains
Major tributaries: Irtysh, Chulym, Biya and Katun
Flows into: Arctic Ocean

8 Congo

The Congo drains west Central Africa's rain forests, and is the world's second-largest river by volume of water after the Amazon. It flows north then west in an arc.

Location: West/Central Africa
Length: 4700 km (2900 miles)
Drainage basin: 3.5 million km^2 (1.3 million sq miles)
Source: Hills of northern Zambia
Major tributaries: Lualaba, Lomami and Aruwimi
Flows into: Atlantic Ocean

9 Amur

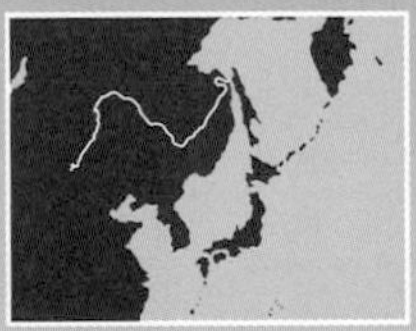

The Amur is one of Asia's principal waterways. It rises along the border of Siberia and Manchuria. For about 1600 km (1000 miles), it forms the border between Russia and China, where it is known as the Heilong.

Location: Russia and China
Length: 4400 km (2734 miles)
Drainage basin: Unknown
Source: Yablonovy Mountains, southern Siberia
Major tributaries: Shilka, Songhu and Argun
Flows into: Sea of Okhotsk

10 Lena

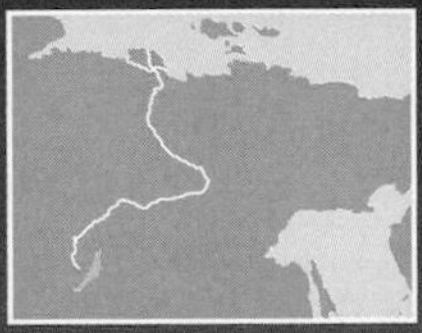

The Lena starts life close to the source of the Yenisei. But whereas the Yenisei heads northeast, the Lena flows northwest, ending in a 400 km (250 mile) wide delta.

Location: Russia
Length: 4400 km (2734 miles)
Drainage basin: Unknown
Source: Mountains around Lake Baikal
Major tributaries: Vilyui, Vitim and Chara
Flows into: Laptev Sea (Arctic Ocean)

A lake is any large body of water, either fresh or salt water, that is completely surrounded by land. Many so-called seas, such as the Sea of Galilee and the Dead Sea, are technically lakes. Lakes become more common at higher latitudes because there is less evaporation in these colder climates.

LAKE FORMATION

Lake basins are formed by a variety of Earth's processes.

- Tectonic forces in the Earth's crust cause rock-folding, subsidence, and faulting, creating large depressions where water collects.
- Landslides, mud flows, lava flows and glacial debris block valleys, which slowly fill with water.
- Glaciers scour depressions out of the bedrock.
- Violent volcanic eruptions and collapsed cones produce volcanic craters deep enough for a lake to form.
- River meanders are cut off to form oxbow lakes.

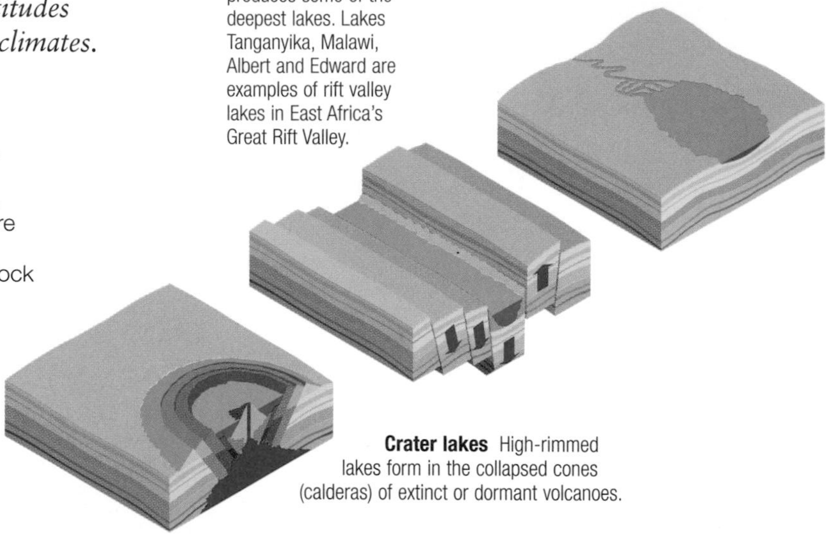

Folds Downfolded rocks create depressions in which lake water can collect.

Rift lakes Blocks of land sink along faults. Faulting produces some of the deepest lakes. Lakes Tanganyika, Malawi, Albert and Edward are examples of rift valley lakes in East Africa's Great Rift Valley.

Crater lakes High-rimmed lakes form in the collapsed cones (calderas) of extinct or dormant volcanoes.

THE WORLD'S LARGEST LAKES

1 Caspian Sea

The Caspian Sea is fed by the Volga River. It is linked to the Baltic, White and Black seas. The Caspian Sea has no outlets and has become salty over the millennia. It lies 28 m (92 ft) below sea level.

Location: Southeastern Europe/southwestern Asia
Area: 370 998 k m^2 (143 243 sq miles)
Maximum depth: 995 m (3264 ft)
Length: 1200 km (746 miles)

2 Lake Superior

Lake Superior is the biggest and westernmost of North America's Great Lakes. Much of its northern shoreline is in Ontario, Canada. The rest is shared among Michigan, Wisconsin and Minnesota.

Location: North America
Area: 82 100 km^2 (31 700 sq miles)
Maximum depth: 405 m (1330 ft)
Length: 560 km (350 miles)

3 Lake Victoria

Lake Victoria is Africa's largest lake. Its surface is 130 m (3720 ft) above sea level. The main river running into Lake Victoria is the Kagera. At its northern end, Lake Victoria drains into the Nile River.

Location: East Central Africa
Area: 69 490 km^2 (26 830 sq miles)
Maximum depth: 85m (279ft)
Length: 337 km (209 miles)

4 Lake Huron

The second-largest of the Great Lakes, Lake Huron receives the waters of Lake Superior and Lake Michigan and drains into Lake Erie. Like Lake Superior, it has shores in both Canada and the US.

Location: North America
Area: (including arms such as Georgian Bay and Saginaw Bay) 59 600 km^2 (23 000 sq miles)
Maximum depth: 229 m (750 ft)
Length: 332 km (206 miles)

5 Lake Michigan

Lake Michigan is North America's third-largest lake. It is contained entirely within the US but is shared among the states of Wisconsin, Michigan, Indiana and Illinois.

Location: North Central United States
Area: 57 800 k m^2 (22 300 sq miles)
Maximum depth: 281 m (923 ft)
Length: 494 km (307 miles)

Lake life cycles Lakes are fed by rain, meltwater and ground water via springs, streams and rivers. Some lakes are permanent features; others are more short-lived. They may evaporate as the climate becomes more arid or fill up with sediment, leaving a bog or swamp in their place. In arid regions, lakes rise and fall with the seasons and sometimes dry up for long periods. In some lakes in which there is no outflow, substances dissolved in the water become concentrated. These salt or soda lakes can be rich in salts, sulfates and carbonates. If there is a lot of water evaporation, these minerals can form solid deposits.

Salt lake Talah Lake in Chile's Atacama Desert is rich in dissolved solids, and a salt rim forms where the lake waters have evaporated under the arid conditions.

OTHER LARGE LAKES

South America	Km²	Sq miles
Maracaibo, Venezuela	13 300	5150
Titicaca, Peru-Bolivia	8300	3200
Poopó, Bolivia	2600	1000
Buenos Aires, Chile–Argentina	2240	865
Chiquita, Argentina	1850	714
Europe		
Vänern, Sweden	5585	2156
Iso Saimaa, Finland	4377	1690
Vättern, Sweden	1912	738
Sevan, Armenia	1360	525
Mälaren, Sweden	1140	440
Inari, Finland	1102	425
Australasia		
Eyre, South Australia*	9300	3600
Torrens, South Australia*	5776	2230
Gairdner, South Australia*	4780	1845
Frome, South Australia*	2400	900
Amadeus, NT, Australia*	880	340
Taupo, North Island, NZ	606	234

* *Usually dry*

Alpine glacial lakes

There are 11 major lakes fringing the Alps: Geneva, Maggiore, Lugano, Como, Garda, Neuchâtel, Luzern, Zürich, Constance, Attersee and Chiemsee.

During the last Ice Age, glaciers carved a way through the mountains, deepening valleys and depositing debris.

At the end of the Ice Age, the glaciers melted. Water filled the valleys and was dammed by rocky debris.

Artificial lakes

Many of the world's lakes have been created artificially by the damming of rivers. Lake Nasser, behind the Aswan dam on the Nile River, is an example. It is 480 km (300 miles) long and about 14 percent of its water evaporates, reducing the volume of the Nile downstream. The area was the site of the ancient temples of Abu Simbel; these temples were moved to preserve them.

FACTS

- **Greatest volume of fresh water** Lake Baikal holds a fifth of the Earth's fresh surface water, approximately 22 995 km³ (5517 cu miles).
- **Unique ecology** Lake Baikal contains 1000 unique species.
- **Highest navigable** Lake Titicaca (southeastern Peru and western Bolivia) is 3810 m (12 500 ft) above sea level. It is also 196 km (122 miles) long, and has an average width of 56 km (35 miles).

6 Lake Tanganyika

Lake Tanganyika is Africa's second-largest lake in area and the second-deepest in the world. It is drained by the Lukunga River, which flows into the Zaire.

Location: East Central Africa
Area: 32 900 km² (12 700 sq miles)
Maximum depth: 1435 m (4702 ft)
Length: 680 km (420 miles)

7 Aral Sea

The Aral Sea is the second-largest saltwater lake on the planet. In 1960, it was the world's fourth-largest lake overall, but diversion of its feeder rivers for crop irrigation has since caused it to shrink dramatically. Today, its volume is less than one fifth what it once was.

Location: Central Asia, in southwestern Kazakhstan and northwestern Uzbekistan
Area: 32 370 km² (12 500 sq miles)
Maximum depth: 54 m (177 ft)
Length: 270 km (168 miles)

8 Great Bear Lake

Great Bear Lake is the largest lake entirely within Canada. It lies near the northern coast and straddles the Arctic Circle, making it one of the world's northernmost lakes.

Location: Northwest Territories, northwestern Canada
Area: 31 790 km² (12 270 sq miles)
Maximum depth: 396 m (1299 ft)
Length: 300 km (186 miles)

9 Lake Baikal

Lake Baikal is by far the deepest lake in the world. Its waters reach depths of over 1.5 km (1 mile) in places. It is fed by the Selenga, Barguzin and Verkhnaya Angara rivers and more than 300 mountain streams.

Location: Southern Siberia
Area: 31 500 km² (12 200 sq miles)
Maximum depth: 1620 m (5315 ft)
Length: 636 km (395 miles)

10 Lake Malawi

Lake Malawi, also known as Lake Nyasa, lies southeast of Lake Tanganyika along eastern Africa's Great Rift Valley.

Location: Malawi–Mozambique–Tanzania
Area: 29 604 km² (11 430 sq miles)
Maximum depth: 695 m (2280 ft)
Length: 627 km (390 miles)

Crater Lake, Oregon, formed in a caldera created by the collapse of Mount Mazama volcano over 6000 years ago.

Glacial lake Loch Coruisk in the Scottish Highlands fills a valley scoured out by a glacier during the last glaciation.

see also

26-27 **Structure of the Earth**
32-33 **Volcanoes**
36-37 **Rivers**
42-43 **Glaciers**

Islands form in various ways. Chunks can shear off the continents and be carried into the sea on oceanic plates: These fragments are what constitute the world's biggest islands. Submarine volcanism creates islands and island chains such as Iceland and Hawaii, and coral grows in shallow waters and can eventually make dry land. Islands are constantly born and destroyed as sea level fluctuates.

FACT The isle of Surtsey near Iceland was born violently in 1963, when a volcanic eruption broke the surface of the North Sea.

The world's largest islands

The biggest islands are not volcanic: They are all tracts of land that have broken away from a continental landmass. One, Australia, is so large that it is not classified as an island at all – it is a continent in its own right. These satellite images show the world's ten largest islands to scale.

1 In 1835, Charles Darwin was the first to guess that the round coral atolls of tropical waters had built up on the remnants of once live volcanoes.

2 As a volcano sinks, a coral reef grows on its submerged sides, just beneath the surface. This is called a fringing reef. What is left of the volcano is colonized by vegetation.

3 The dead volcano all but disappears, but the shape of the new coral islands reflects the conical form of the sunken mountain.

Key terms

Atoll A ring of coral islands enclosing a lagoon, formed on a sunken volcano.
Islet A small island.
Key A low-lying island, usually in the Caribbean Sea.
Crannog An artificial island made for habitation by a hermit.
Reef A ridge of coral at or near the surface of the sea.
Archipelago A string or group of islands.

MADAGASCAR: A NOAH'S ARK

Many of the species on Madagascar are unique to the island. After it broke away from the African mainland, the animals on the island took their own evolutionary path. One of the strangest living things on Madagascar, also found on mainland Africa, is the baobab (left), a giant water-filled sponge of a tree which deflates like a balloon when toppled.

Cities of coral The Great Barrier Reef in Australia, the world's largest collection of coral reefs, stretches 2027 km (1260 miles) and has built up over the millennia to more than 300 m (984 ft) high. Some coral islands grow up from the sea floor, without being anchored on a dead volcano or submerged mountain. Corals can only survive in shallow water, so these islands have built up as the sea level has risen.

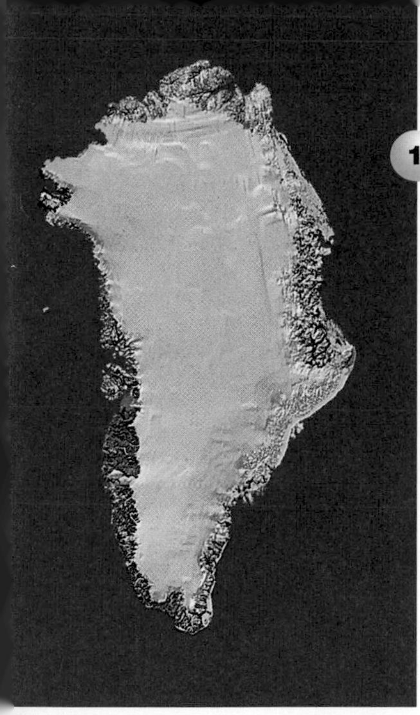

1 Greenland North Atlantic
Area: 2 175 600 km² (839 780 sq miles). About 85 percent of Greenland is covered by ice. The ice is 3 km (2 miles) thick in places and accounts for 10 percent of the world's fresh water.

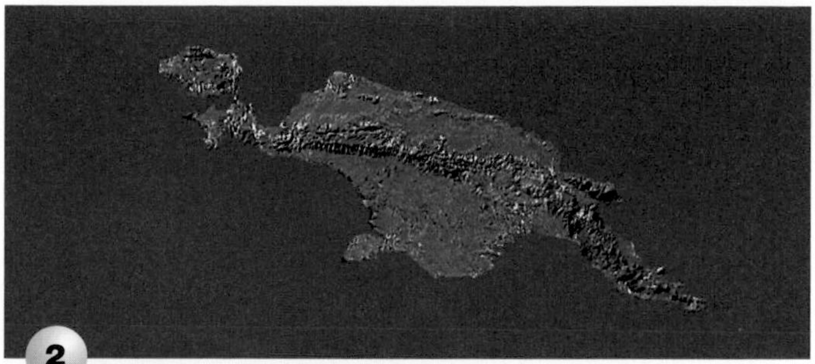

2 New Guinea Australasia Area: 808 510 km² (312 085 sq miles). Natural extremes make New Guinea one of the most dangerous islands on Earth. Volcanoes dot its mountain backbone, and tsunamis are a common occurrence along its coast.

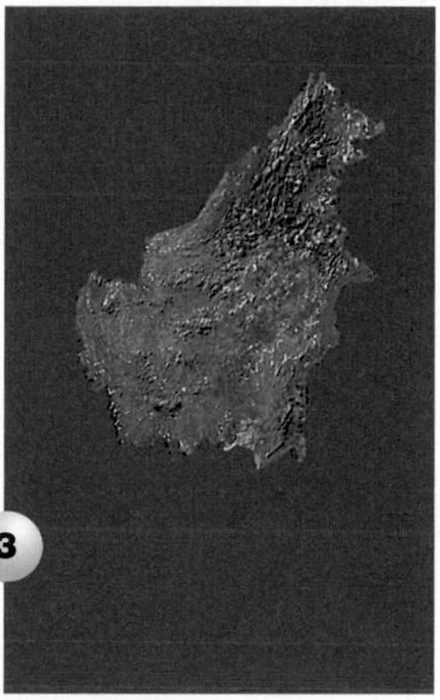

3 Borneo South China Sea
Area: 757 050 km² (292 220 sq miles). It has the world's largest cave, the Sarawak Chamber, which is 300 m (990 ft) long.

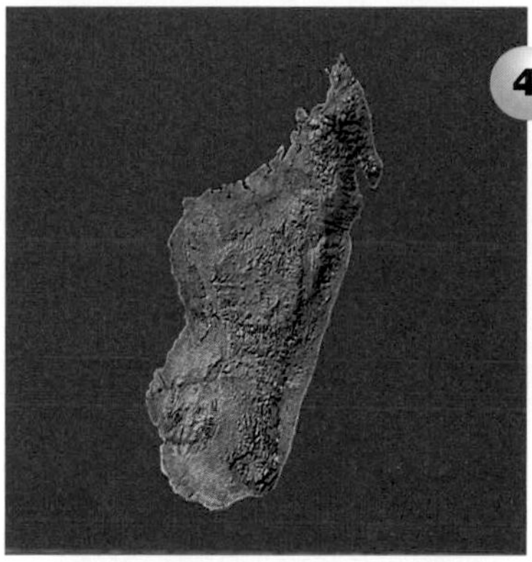

4 Madagascar
Indian Ocean
Area: 594 100 km² (229 322 sq miles). Madagascar has evolved unique flora and fauna in isolation from the African mainland.

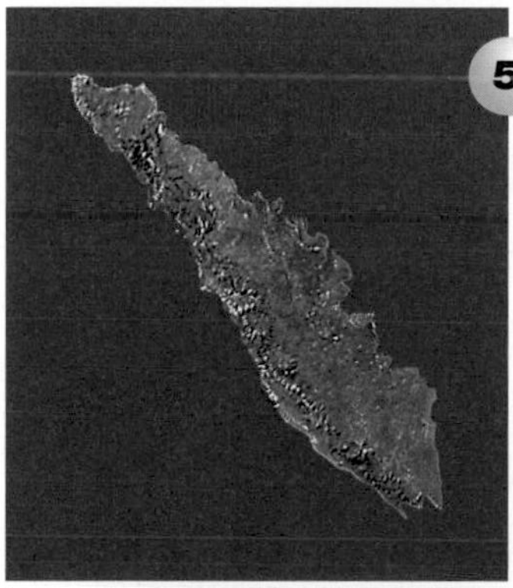

5 Sumatra
Indian Ocean
Area: 524 100 km² (202 300 sq miles). Sumatra's Lake Toba is a vast crater of 1166 km² (450 sq miles), formed when a volcano exploded about 60 000 years ago.

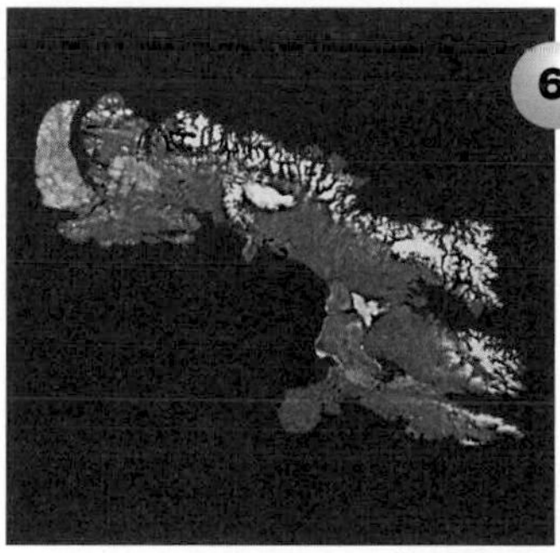

6 Baffin Island
Canadian Arctic
Area: 476 070 km² (183 760 sq miles). Baffin is the largest island of the Canadian Arctic archipelago.

7 Honshu Sea of Japan
Area: 230 455 km² (88 955 sq miles). Honshu contains the world's largest urban mass, Tokyo–Yokohama.

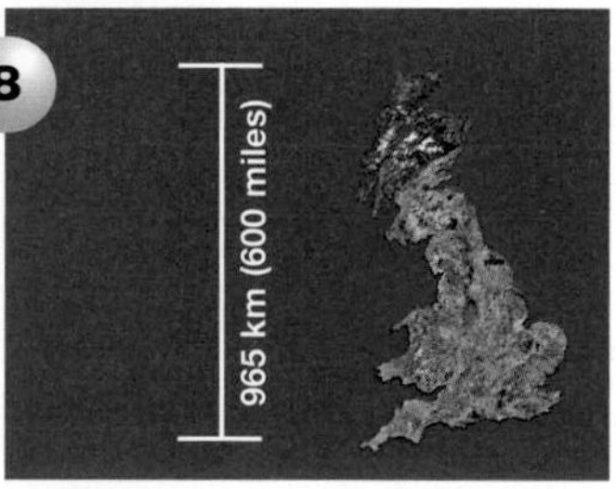

8 Great Britain North Atlantic
Area: 229 870 km² (88 730 sq miles). Britain occupies 1/1000 of the Earth's surface, but has 1/100 of its population.

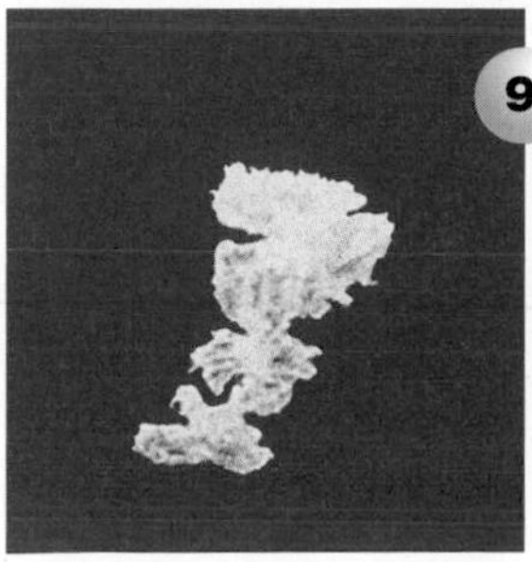

9 Ellesmere Island
Canadian Arctic
Area: 212 690 km² (82 100 sq miles). An ice shelf on the northern coast produces raft-like ice islands, which have been used as floating research stations.

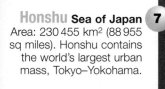

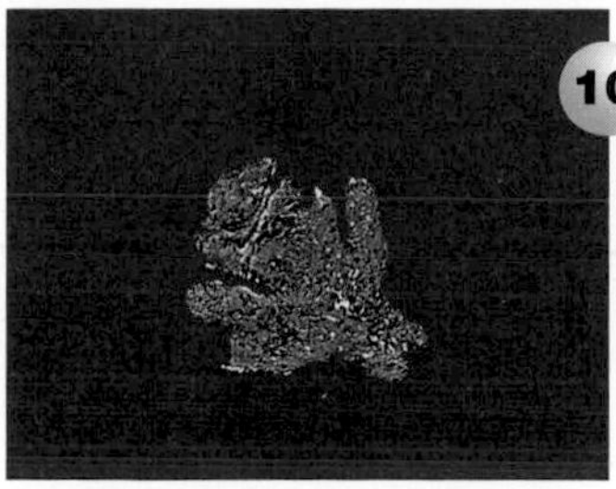

10 Victoria Island
Canadian Arctic
Area: 212 200 km² (81 910 sq miles). The third-largest island of the Canadian Arctic archipelago, Victoria Island was not explored by Europeans until 1851.

see also

26-27 **Structure of the Earth**
32-33 **Volcanoes**
34-35 **Oceans and seas**

Glaciers are made up of fallen snow that compresses into large, thickened ice masses. Eventually they become so heavy that they move very slowly downhill. Some glaciers are as small as football fields, and others grow to be more than 160 km (100 miles) long. They occur where snowfall in winter exceeds melting in summer, conditions that presently prevail only in high mountain areas and polar regions.

LONGEST GLACIERS

The lengths of the world's largest glaciers are represented on this diagram by the blue blocks.

Lambert–Fisher 515 km (320 miles)
Arctic Institute 418 km (260 miles)
Nimrod–Lennox–King 290 km (180 miles)
Denman 241 km (150 miles)
Beardmore 225 km (140 miles)
Recovery 225 km (140 miles)
Slessor 185 km (115 miles)
Petermanns 200 km (124 miles)
Humboldt 114 km (71 miles)
Novaya Zemlya 418 km (260 miles)
Siachen 70 km (44 miles)
Tasman 27 km (17 miles)
Franz Joseph 11 km (7 miles)
Bering (Alaska) 204 km (126 miles)
Hubbard (Alaska) 146 km (91 miles)
Aletsch 35 km (22 miles)
Fedchenko 77 km (48 miles)
Langjökull 64 km (40 miles)
Jostedals 75 km (45 miles)
Antarctica
Greenland
Russia
India/Pakistan
New Zealand
US
Switzerland
Tajikistan
Iceland
Norway

HOW AND WHY GLACIERS FORM

- Glaciers form when snow remains in one location long enough to turn into ice.
- Each year, new layers of snow bury and compress the previous layers.
- Glaciers are constantly added to by snowfall along their upper reaches. Once the compressed ice reaches a critical thickness, about 8 m (25 ft), it becomes so heavy that it starts to move under the influence of gravity.
- The ends (snouts) of glaciers periodically retreat or advance, depending on the balance between snow accumulation and ice melting and evaporation.
- Glacier retreats and advances are usually very slow occurrences, noticeable only over long periods of time. However, glaciers can retreat rapidly with movement visible over a few months. Alternatively, they may surge forward several meters a day for weeks or even months.

Features of a glacier Glaciers originate in high mountain snowfields and move down valleys. Rocks and other debris from the valley sides and floor become frozen into the glacier and are carried along by it.

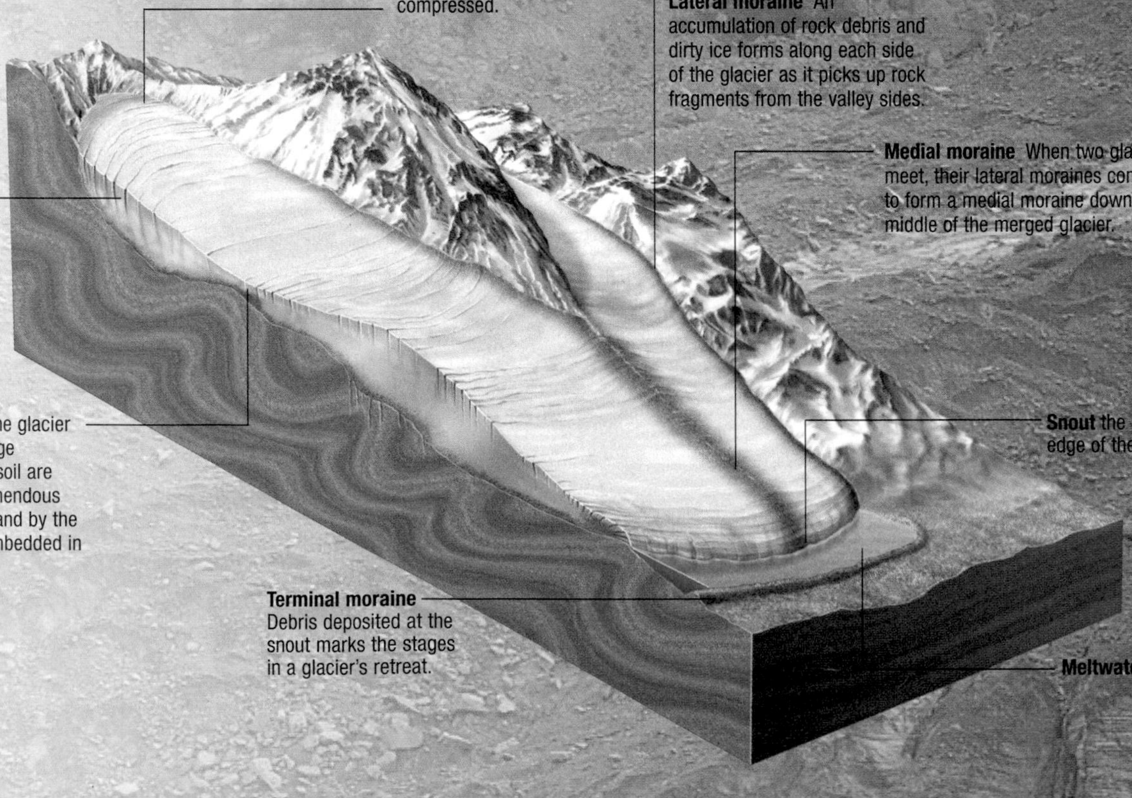
Accumulation zone Snow builds up in the upper reaches of a mountain and becomes frozen and compressed.
Lateral moraine An accumulation of rock debris and dirty ice forms along each side of the glacier as it picks up rock fragments from the valley sides.
Medial moraine When two glaciers meet, their lateral moraines combine to form a medial moraine down the middle of the merged glacier.
Crevasses Giant cracks form as a result of stresses that build up within the moving mass of ice.
Snout the leading edge of the glacier.
Valley floor Where the glacier meets the ground, large amounts of rock and soil are ground up by the tremendous weight of the glacier and by the rocks that become embedded in its lower surface.
Terminal moraine Debris deposited at the snout marks the stages in a glacier's retreat.
Meltwater

Sea of Ice Mer De Glace, near Chamonix, France, is the second-largest glacier in the Alps. Nearly 14.5 km (9 miles) long and 1.6 km (1 mile) wide, at points it is almost 200 m deep. The ice moves by as much as 70 meters (230 ft) each year. The crescent-shaped flow marks show that the ice is moving faster at the center of the glacier.

Key terms

- **Arete** A jagged, narrow ridge between two glaciers.
- **Cirque** A bowl-shaped hollow caused by a glacier eroding into a mountainside.
- **Drumlin** A teardrop-shaped hill formed from till deposited by a receding glacier. Drumlins run parallel to a glacier's flow.
- **Erratic block** A large rock picked up by a glacier and deposited, often a great distance away, when the glacier melted.
- **Fjord** A long, deep, narrow coastal valley, originally carved out by a glacier, that filled with sea water after the glacier had melted.
- **Glaciated valley** A trough-shaped, often steep-sided valley formed by glacial action. Examples can be seen in the English Lake District and Yosemite National Park.
- **Till or boulder clay** The material – ranging from house-sized boulders to clay particles – laid down as an unsorted deposit when a glacier melts.

see also

36-37 **Rivers**
38-39 **Lakes**
44-45 **Mountains**

A mountain is any landmass that stands significantly above its surroundings. The distinction between a mountain and a hill is arbitrary; it is not defined by any internationally accepted measurement.

MOUNTAIN FORMATION

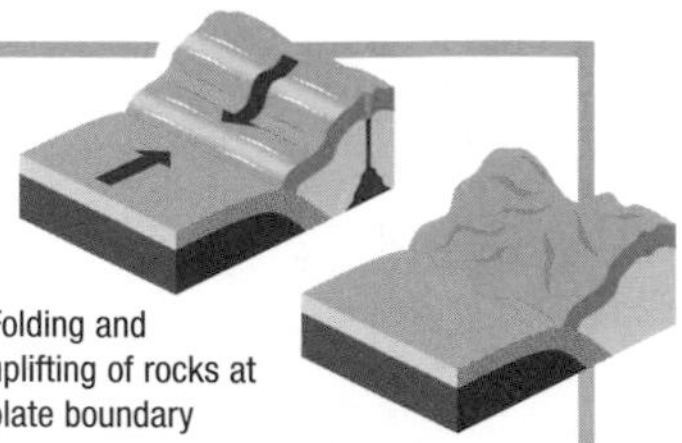

Folding and uplifting of rocks at plate boundary

Uplifted rock is eroded

Mountains are categorized according to how they formed.

- **Fold mountains** The majority of mountains are created when tectonic plates collide, causing folding and uplifting of rocks along the plate boundaries, a process called orogenesis. The uplifted land is then eroded into peaks and valleys. Examples: Himalayas, Andes and Alps.
- **Volcanoes** Many volcanoes create a cone of erupted material: ash, lava or both. Such cones can reach great heights. Mount Erebus, an active volcano in Antarctica, is 4032 m (13 200 ft) high. Examples: Kilimanjaro, Tanzania; Mount St. Helens, US.
- **Erosional mountains** These form from high ground that has been deeply eroded, for instance by rivers. Examples: Blue Mountains, Australia; Table Mountain, Cape Town, South Africa.
- **Island mountains** These are isolated hills that remain after erosion has worn away the surrounding land. Examples: Uluru (Ayers Rock), Australia; the pinnacles of the Metéora, Spain.

Highest mountains on each continent

Mountains exist on all the world's continents, but some continents are flatter than others. No new mountain ranges have been created in Australia for millions of years, and its surface has undergone much erosion, whereas the Alps and the Himalayas formed as recently as 10 million years ago.

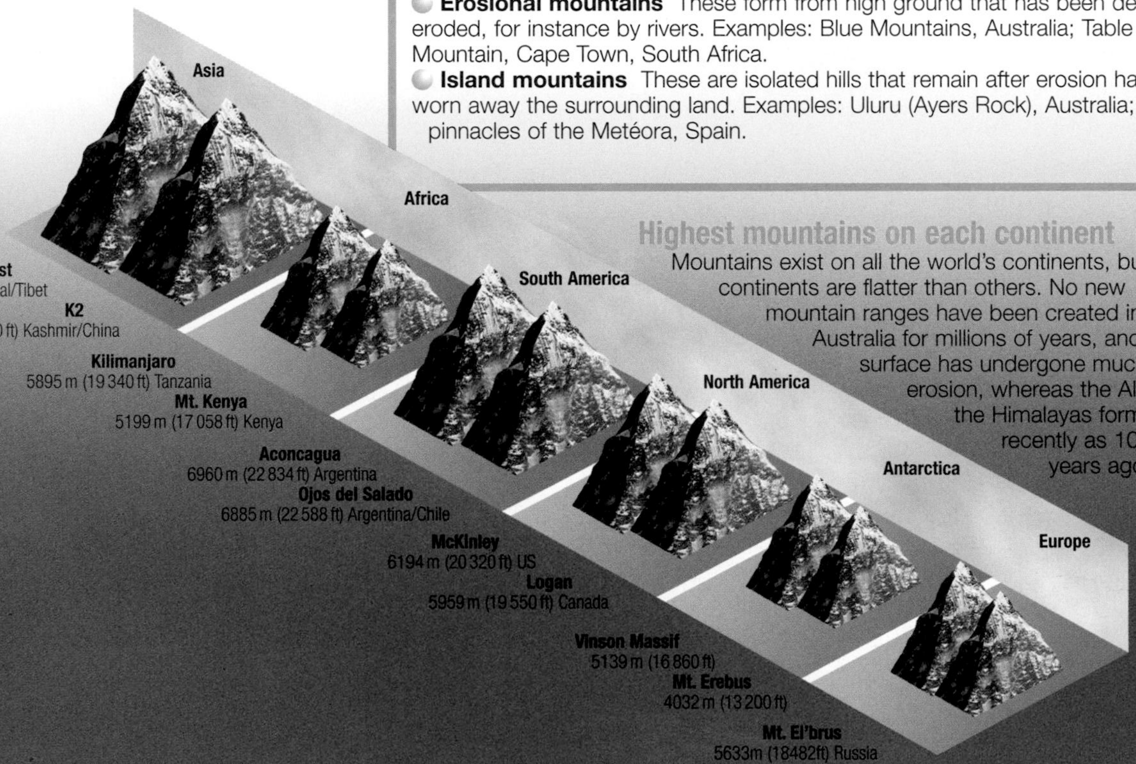

Mount Everest The world's highest mountain above sea level dominates the Himalayas, a range of young-fold mountains created when India collided with Asia. Everest's pyramidal shape is the result of erosion by glaciers.

FACT The Himalayas (including the Karakorams) contain 96 of the world's 100 tallest mountains.

Mountains and ranges of the world

LONGEST MOUNTAIN RANGES

1. **Andes** South America 7242 km (4500 miles)
2. **Rockies** North America 6035 km (3750 miles)
3. **Himalaya/Karakoram/Hindu Kush** Asia 3862 km (2400 miles)
4. **Great Dividing Range** Australia 3651 km (2250 miles)
5. **Brazilian East Coast Range** Brazil 3058 km (1900 miles)
6. **Sumatran Range** Java 2897 km (1800 miles)
7. **Tien Shan** China 2253 km (1400 miles)
8. **Eastern Ghats** India 2092 km (1300 miles)

HIGHEST RANGES (Maximum height above sea level)
Himalaya/Karakoram/Hindu Kush 8848 m (29 028 ft)
Andes up to 6959 m (22 864 ft)
Alaska Range up to 6194 m (20 321 ft)

OTHER MOUNTAINS AND RANGES
Alps Europe 1207 km (750 miles) long.
Mt. McKinley Alaska 6194 m (20 321 ft).
Mauna Kea Hawaii 10 206 m (33 484 ft) from seabed.
Mount Fuji Japan 3798 m (12 460 ft). A young volcano.

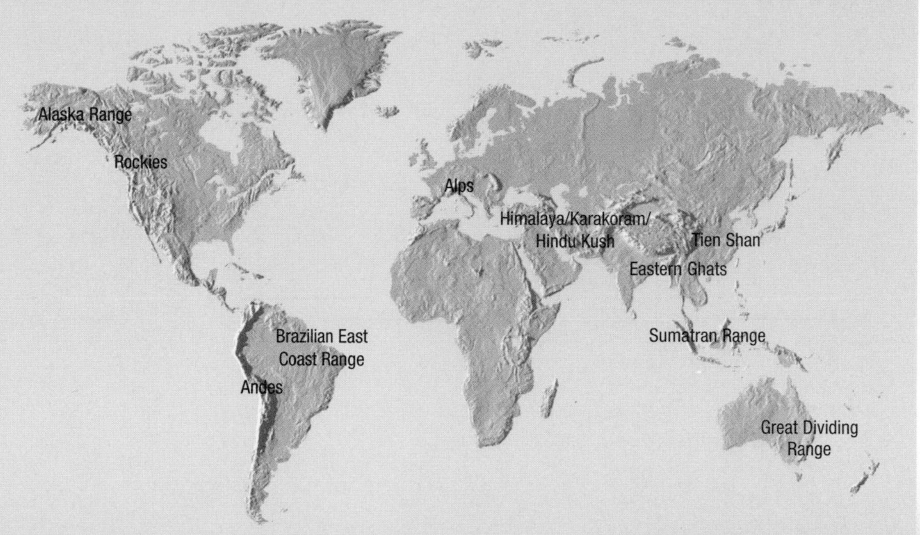

Erosion

With the exception of recently formed volcanoes, the appearance of a mountain or range results almost entirely from the effects of erosion. The jagged ridges and pointed peaks that we commonly associate with mountain ranges have been formed by the powerful erosive action of glaciers. Even near the equator, high mountains are snow-capped and susceptible to glaciation. Mounts Kenya and Kilimanjaro in east Africa are old volcanoes whose peaks have been sculpted by ice. Other mountains, such as Australia's Blue Mountains, are formed when horizontal rocks forming high ground are cut through by rivers.

Rock type is another factor in determining the shape of mountains. The soft mudstone of Italy's Dolomites, for example, erodes more easily than the overlying limestone layers. The undercut limestone eventually collapses, forming steep cliffs.

The French Alps Glacial action has produced jagged peaks and ridges.

The Dolomites, Italy The magnesium-rich limestone (called dolomite) typical of the area has eroded into pinnacles and cliffs.

see also

26-27 **Structure of the Earth**
32-33 **Volcanoes**
36-37 **Rivers**
42-43 **Glaciers**

Earth's atmosphere

Our planet's cushion of air

The atmosphere is an envelope of air kept near the Earth by gravity. It absorbs energy from the Sun, recycles water and other chemicals, and works with electrical and magnetic forces to provide a moderate climate and so supports life on Earth. It also shields us from high-energy radiation and the vacuum of space.

LAYERS OF THE ATMOSPHERE

The atmosphere extends more than 600 km (370 miles) out from the Earth's surface. Four distinct main layers have been identified, and each layer has particular chemical, physical and temperature characteristics. At the edge of the atmosphere is a boundary layer, the exosphere, a region of hydrogen and helium that gradually merges into space.

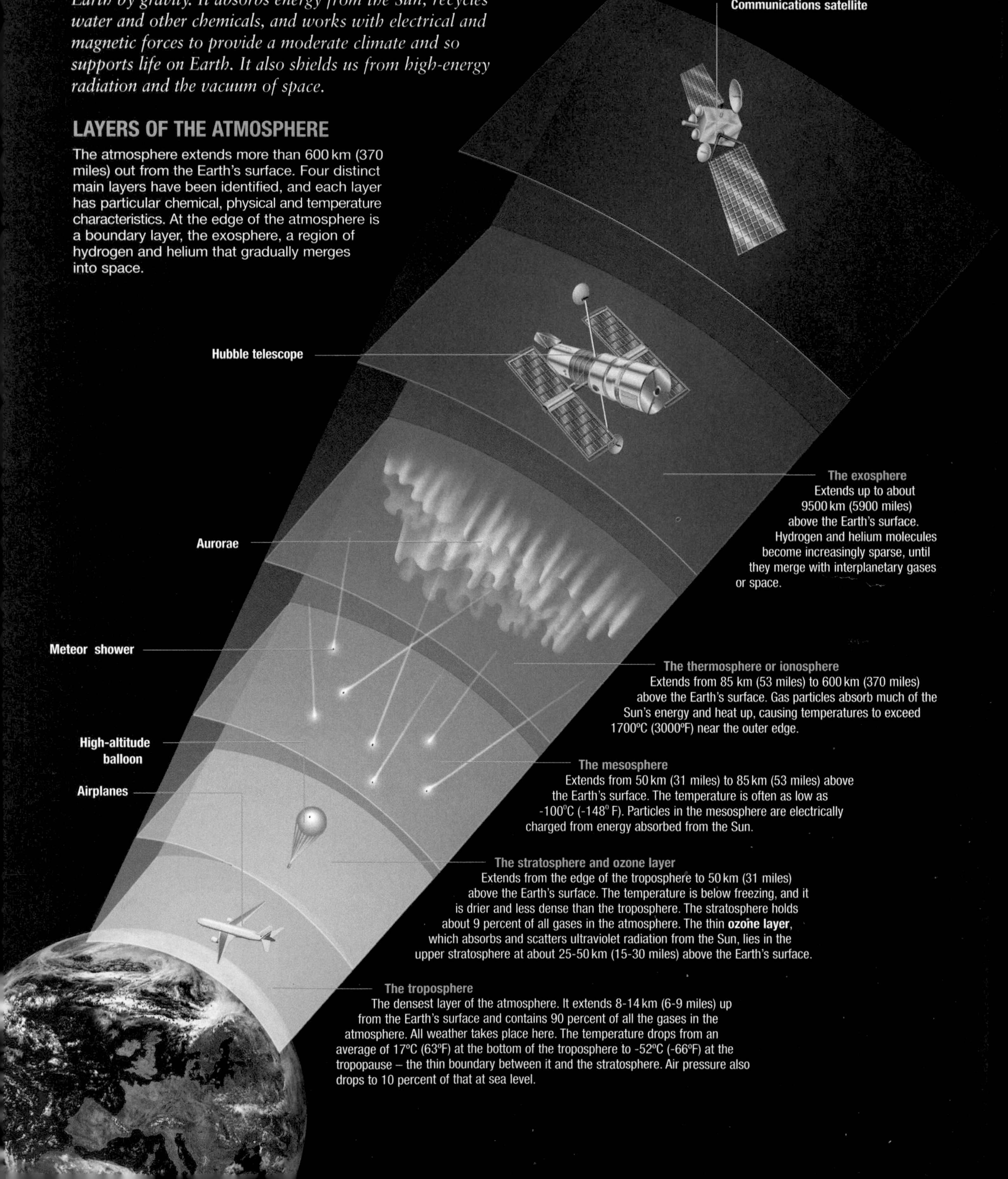

The exosphere
Extends up to about 9500 km (5900 miles) above the Earth's surface. Hydrogen and helium molecules become increasingly sparse, until they merge with interplanetary gases or space.

The thermosphere or ionosphere
Extends from 85 km (53 miles) to 600 km (370 miles) above the Earth's surface. Gas particles absorb much of the Sun's energy and heat up, causing temperatures to exceed 1700°C (3000°F) near the outer edge.

The mesosphere
Extends from 50 km (31 miles) to 85 km (53 miles) above the Earth's surface. The temperature is often as low as -100°C (-148° F). Particles in the mesosphere are electrically charged from energy absorbed from the Sun.

The stratosphere and ozone layer
Extends from the edge of the troposphere to 50 km (31 miles) above the Earth's surface. The temperature is below freezing, and it is drier and less dense than the troposphere. The stratosphere holds about 9 percent of all gases in the atmosphere. The thin **ozone layer**, which absorbs and scatters ultraviolet radiation from the Sun, lies in the upper stratosphere at about 25-50 km (15-30 miles) above the Earth's surface.

The troposphere
The densest layer of the atmosphere. It extends 8-14 km (6-9 miles) up from the Earth's surface and contains 90 percent of all the gases in the atmosphere. All weather takes place here. The temperature drops from an average of 17°C (63°F) at the bottom of the troposphere to -52°C (-66°F) at the tropopause – the thin boundary between it and the stratosphere. Air pressure also drops to 10 percent of that at sea level.

Atmospheric effects visible from Earth

The Aurorae The aurora borealis in the Northern Hemisphere and the aurora australis in the Southern Hemisphere are light phenomena visible in the night sky at higher latitudes. They occur when high-speed particles emitted by the Sun enter the Earth's thermosphere and are channeled around the magnetic poles. Here they excite air molecules, causing them to release light – usually green or red. Spectacular arcs, curtains and streamers are created by the movements of the excited air molecules along lines of the Earth's magnetic field. Aurorae are more common during sunspot activity because more solar particles are released at these times.

Rainbows Rainbows are produced when sunlight is refracted through raindrops, splitting it into the seven component colors of white light. All rainbows are part of a perfect circle. Entire circular rainbows are visible only from aircraft and are called "glories."

Solar and lunar halos These are created by light from the Sun or Moon passing through ice crystals high in the sky.

Parhelia Also called sundogs or mock suns, parhelia are partial halos or bright spots that appear on either side of the Sun from light reflecting off ice crystals in high cirrostratus clouds.

Sun pillars These are streaks of light rising from the Sun at sunrise or sunset, caused by the reflection of light by ice crystals in high clouds.

Aurora effect The aurora borealis lights up the Northern Hemisphere night sky.

GREENHOUSE EFFECT AND GLOBAL WARMING

The greenhouse effect is a natural phenomenon that helps to heat the Earth's surface. The process is so named because it is very much like the warming effect found in greenhouses. The Earth's atmosphere acts like the greenhouse glass, which the Sun's rays penetrate to warm the Earth's surface. Some heat is reflected back from the surface and much of it escapes into space. However, some is absorbed by naturally occurring atmospheric gases, such as carbon dioxide and methane. An increase in these greenhouse gases in the atmosphere means an increase in the amount of heat trapped, resulting in a rise in the Earth's temperature – the phenomenon known as global warming. Scientists fear that human activities such as the burning of fossil fuels are increasing the level of greenhouse gases and therefore global warming. There is speculation that this will lead to sudden changes in weather patterns and rising sea levels as the polar ice caps start to melt.

Normal conditions The Earth's surface reflects heat from the Sun. Some of this escapes through the atmosphere into space.

Global warming When greenhouse gases build up in the atmosphere, they absorb reflected heat, stopping its escape back into space.

The ozone layer

Ozone (O_3) is a gas composed of three atoms of oxygen combined. It is created when ultraviolet radiation (part of sunlight) strikes the stratosphere, splitting oxygen molecules (O_2) into two atoms of oxygen (O). These oxygen atoms quickly combine with ordinary oxygen molecules to form ozone. The ozone layer absorbs ultraviolet radiation, shielding the Earth from its harmful effects, which include inducing skin cancer.

What is the ozone hole? An area of the ozone layer centered over Antarctica has thinned to about 30 percent of normal levels, allowing more ultraviolet radiation to reach the surface of the Earth. Seasonal fluctuations in ozone levels are natural, but man-made chemicals such as chlorofluorocarbons (CFCs) have made the hole bigger as they react with ozone and destroy it. These reactions occur in stratospheric clouds, found only in polar regions, where the effect is concentrated. Depletion is greater over the South Pole where there are more stratospheric clouds.

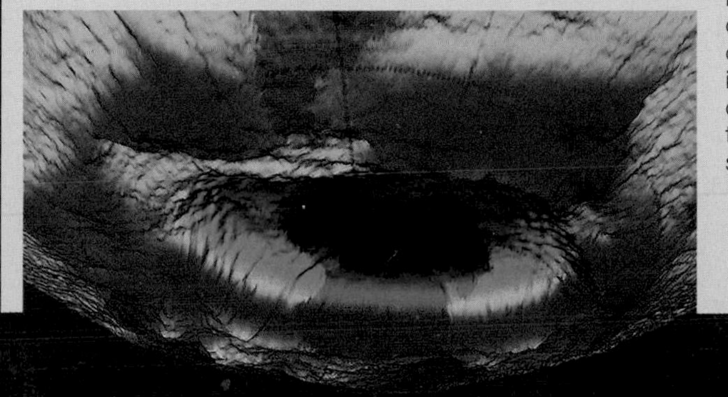

Ozone hole The hole in the ozone layer over the Antarctic shows up as a blue circle in this image created from data collected from space.

FACT

The atmosphere is composed mainly of nitrogen – 78 percent. Only 21 percent is oxygen.

see also

10-11 **Planet Earth**
18-19 **The Sun**
24-25 **Comets and meteorites**
48-49 **Weather**

Weather occurs in the troposphere, the layer of the atmosphere next to the Earth. It is the sum total of several physical conditions, including temperature, wind speed and direction, atmospheric pressure, precipitation and humidity, as they occur in any one place or region at any one time. The Earth's weather is a highly unpredictable system in constant flux.

WHAT MAKES WEATHER HAPPEN?

Atmospheric pressure is the key to explaining overall weather conditions. It can be defined as the downward force exerted by the atmosphere at any given point on the Earth, and it is extremely variable. Low atmospheric pressure gives rise to unsettled weather. In a low-pressure region, air rises and cools. Water vapor in the air condenses and clouds form – in the same way that warm air forms condensation on a cold window – and rain often results. High atmospheric pressure brings settled weather. Air is compressed by the high pressure and warms up, no clouds form, and there are often clear skies. Wind is also controlled by air pressure because air tends to flow from a high-pressure area into a low-pressure area.

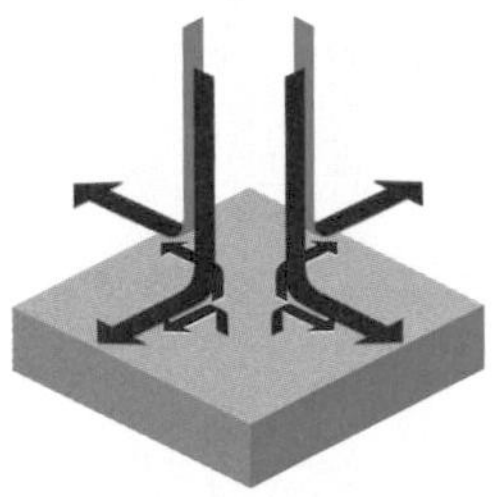

High atmospheric pressure Cold air slowly descends. As it falls, it is compressed and warms up and generally brings warm, settled weather.

Low atmospheric pressure Air slowly rises and cools. Water in the air condenses, creating clouds and unsettled weather.

Wind Wind blows from areas of high pressure to areas of low pressure. When the Sun warms an area of air at the Earth's surface, that air expands, gets lighter and rises. Rising air exerts less pressure than static or falling air, so this is an area of low pressure. Cooler, heavier air from a high-pressure area flows in to fill the void left by the warmer air, creating wind. The closer the high-pressure area is to the low-pressure area, or the greater the difference in pressure or temperature between the two areas, the faster the wind blows.

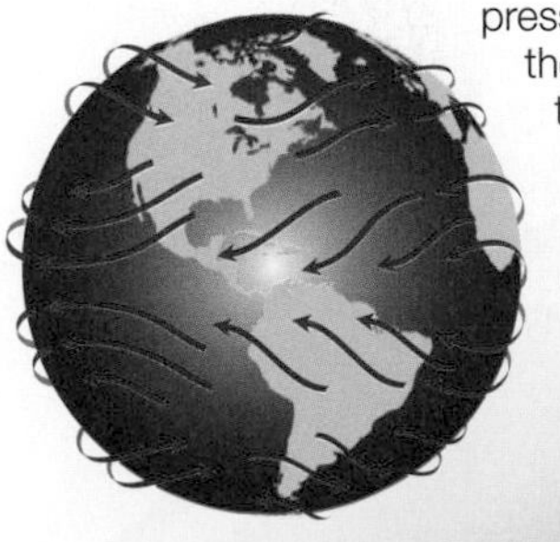

Prevailing wind patterns Trade winds, Westerlies and Easterlies, blow in bands across the globe.

Rain Rising warm air carries water vapor high into the sky, where it cools, forming water droplets around dust particles in the air. These drops freeze into ice crystals, and when they become heavy enough, they begin to fall. On meeting warmer air on the way down, the ice crystals melt to form raindrops.

Snow Snowflakes form when water vapor freezes into ice crystals in cold clouds. The ice crystals attract cooled water droplets and grow in size. Eventually they become heavy enough to fall, and if the air is cold enough, they fall all the way to the Earth as snow, without melting.

Snowflake shape This depends on the temperature of the air. When water freezes, its molecules, each made up of two hydrogen atoms and one oxygen atom, join together in hexagonal patterns, which is why snowflakes are always six-sided. In colder air, several may join up and freeze together to form snowflakes that are needle- or rod-shaped.

Thunder and lightning When cold air and warm air meet, the cold air sinks and moves under the warm air, forcing it to rise rapidly. The rising air takes water vapor with it, which quickly cools and condenses, forming cumulonimbus clouds, sometimes called thunderheads. As the water vapor condenses, heat is released, which pushes the air even higher. Water droplets and ice particles crash together, resulting in a separation of electrical charges in the cloud: Positively charged particles move to the top and negatively charged particles move to the bottom. The difference between the two builds up until an electrical discharge – lightning – takes place between the negative charge in the cloud and the positively charged ground or prominent objects such as tall trees or buildings. This is followed by a return discharge from the ground back up to the cloud. The second discharge is visible as a lightning flash. Thunder is a side effect of lightning. The lightning flash superheats the air around it, causing it to expand faster than the speed of sound, 1238 km/h (769 mph), causing a loud sonic boom, or thunder.

Beaufort scale

Wind strength can be estimated by comparing the wind's effects against the internationally recognized Beaufort scale.

Force	Effects
0	Smoke rises straight up; no motion.
1	Smoke drifts slowly; leaves barely move.
2	Drifting smoke clearly indicates wind direction.
3	Gentle winds. Leaves rustle; wind felt on face.
4	Moderate winds. Leaves in constant motion; dust blows.
5	Small trees sway; paper blows away.
6	Strong winds. Large branches sway.
7	Whole trees sway.
8	Gales. Tree twigs break; hard to walk.
9	Branches break; roof tiles blown off.
10	Small trees uprooted; roofs damaged.
11	Violent storms. Widespread building damage.
12	Hurricane winds. Severe destruction.

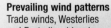

Background: Tornado in Caldwell, Kansas, on March 13, 1990.

Hurricanes Revolving storms in areas of extreme low pressure with winds that exceed 119 km/h (74 mph or 64 knots) are called hurricanes. They rotate counterclockwise in the Northern Hemisphere and clockwise in the Southern Hemisphere. Hurricanes are called by different names in different parts of the world: cyclones in the Indian Ocean, southeast Pacific and Australia; typhoons in the northeast Pacific and on the Asian mainland; and hurricanes in the US and Caribbean. There are, on average, over 120 of these tropical cyclonic storms around the world every year.

Tornadoes These are small-scale but very strong whirlwinds, or twisters, common in the United States. Tornadoes can develop in low-pressure weather systems. In the strongest thunderstorms, the lower part of a thunder cloud may start spinning. If this spinning air reaches the ground, it becomes a tornado. Tornadoes are normally no more than 400 m (1/4 mile) across, but they can be very destructive. They travel at between 30 and 60 km/h (20-40 mph), and winds at the center can rotate at almost 300 km/h (200 mph). Heavy rain and thunder usually accompany tornadoes.

El Niño

The phenomenon known as El Niño is a periodic reversal of Pacific Ocean currents that affects global weather conditions.

- **In a normal year,** warm water in the Pacific flows west toward Australia and Indonesia. There it evaporates quickly, creating storm clouds over Australia. Warm water off the South American coast is replaced by cold, nutrient-rich water coming up the coast from Antarctica, creating good fishing grounds.
- **In an El Niño year,** the winds and currents that hold warm water in place off Australia weaken. The warm water flows back east toward Peru and spreads out along the coast of the Americas. Here it evaporates and creates rain clouds and thunderstorms. Rain fails to materialize in Australia, causing drought. The thunderstorms drive warm humid air high into the atmosphere, where it interferes with the normal currents of air circulation, causing extreme and unpredictable weather conditions as far away as Europe.

A normal year Warm surface currents in the Pacific Ocean flow west and bring rain to Australia.

An El Niño year Warm surface currents in the Pacific reverse, causing storms in America and drought in Australia.

Clouds Clouds form when air rises and the water vapor contained within it cools and condenses, turning into water or ice. The following factors can cause air to rise:

- Heating from areas of ground warmed by the Sun.
- Interaction between weather fronts: the boundaries between large air masses. A cold front brings in cold air behind it and pushes under warm air, forcing it to rise; a warm front brings in warm air, which slides over cold air.
- Mountains: When winds blow against mountains, air is forced upward.

Cirrus High wispy clouds consisting of ice occurring in fair weather.

Cumulus Puffy mid-level white clouds consisting of water and ice, usually associated with fair weather.

Cumulonimbus (thunderheads) Dark, puffy clouds consisting of water. They often produce thunderstorms.

Stratus Flat, low clouds consisting of water droplets. They sometimes produce light rain or drizzle. Fog is very low-lying stratus cloud.

Nimbostratus Thick, dark, low-level clouds consisting of water droplets. They can produce rain or drizzle.

see also

10-11 **Planet Earth**

46-47 **Earth's atmosphere**

Life on Earth

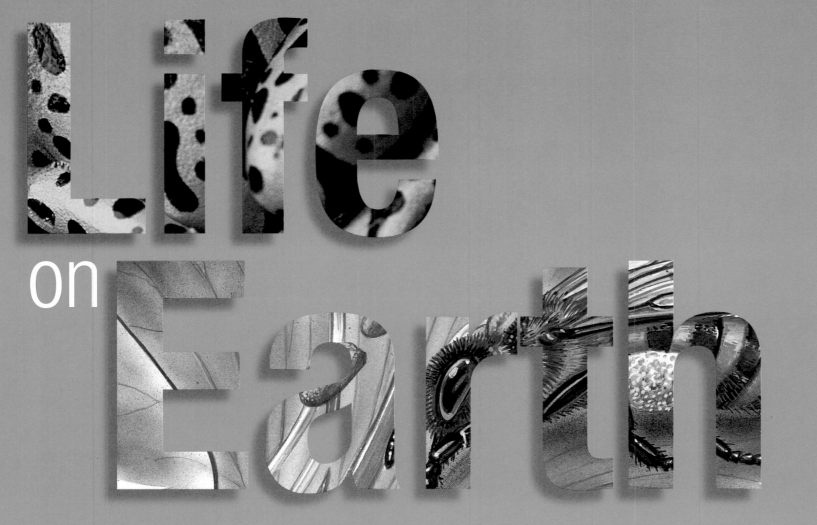

Life on Earth

The ages of life on Earth

The 4.6 billion-year story of life

Geologists break down the 4.6 billion years of the Earth's history into a hierarchy of time intervals based on major changes in rock formation. The largest intervals – the Paleozoic, Mesozoic and Cenozoic – are called eras. These are subdivided into periods, such as the Jurassic. Periods are further divided into epochs, such as the Oligocene.

Precambrian

4.6 billion years ago
The **Earth is formed**.

4.5 billion years ago
The **Moon is formed**.

Fossil bacteria

3.8 billion years ago
First life appears. It consists of primitive single-celled organisms.

3.3 billion years ago
Cyanobacteria, or blue-green algae, appear. These are single-celled organisms able to harness energy from sunlight by photosynthesis.

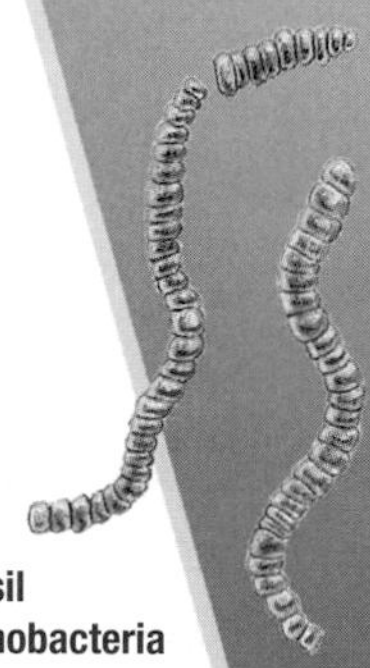

Fossil cyanobacteria

2.1 billion years ago
The **first single-celled organisms with a nucleus** appear.

720 million years ago
The **first multicellular animals** appear.

Paleozoic

Cambrian
550-505 million years ago

Trilobites and other marine animals with hard shells appear. Cambrian rocks are the first to contain an abundance of fossils.

Ordovician
505-438 million years ago

The **first fishes** appear, along with the first corals. The fishes are the first vertebrates.

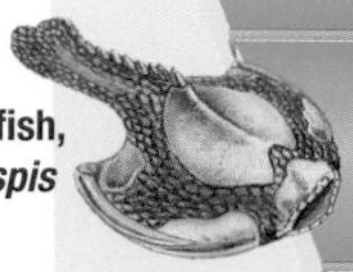

Jawless fish, *Drepanaspis*

Silurian
438-408 million years ago

The **first land plants and first jawed fishes** appear.

Devonian
408-360 million years ago

Land plants and fishes diversify. The **first insects and amphibians** appear.

Carboniferous
360-286 million years ago

Amphibians and fishes diversify. **The first reptiles** appear. Dominant land plants include club mosses.

Club mosses

Permian
286-245 million years ago

Reptiles diversify. Seed-bearing plants establish themselves. At the end of the Permian, the trilobites become extinct.

Mesozoic

***Coelophysis* dinosaur**

Triassic
245-208 million years ago

Early dinosaurs appear.

Jurassic
208-144 million years ago

Dinosaurs flourish. Primitive mammals and birds appear.

Quetzalcoatlus

Cretaceous
144-65 million years ago

Flowering plants develop. **First placental mammals** appear. Flying reptiles include the giant *Quetzalcoatlus*.

At the end of the Cretaceous, **a mass extinction includes the disappearance of the dinosaurs**.

Cenozoic

Paleozoic

Mesozoic

Cenozoic

Divisions of geological time

Precambrian	4.6 billion-550 million years ago
Paleozoic (ancient life)	550-245 million years ago
Mesozoic (middle life)	245-65 million years ago
Cenozoic (recent life)	65 million years ago to present

Cenozoic:
Tertiary period
65-1.8 million years ago

Tertiary

Paleocene
65-57 million years ago

The **first large mammals emerge**.

Tertiary

Early horses, camels, rodents, elephants and monkeys appear, along with the first bats and whales. The 33-metric-ton leaf-eating *Indricotherium* is the largest land mammal ever.

Birds and flowering plants diversify.

Eocene
57-34 million years ago

Indricotherium

Tertiary

Aegyptopithecus, a cat-sized primate, is believed to be **an ancestor of modern man**.

Oligocene
34-23 million years ago

Tertiary

Amebelodon

Miocene
23-5 million years ago

Early apes, dogs and bears appear. **Large browsing mammals flourish**. These include *Amebelodon*, equipped with huge tusks for gouging out water plants.

"Upright man,"
Homo erectus

The **australopithecines, upright-walking hominids**, appear and diversify.

Pliocene
5-1.8 million years ago

Homo habilis, *Homo erectus* and finally ***Homo sapiens*, early modern man,** emerge in Africa.

Pleistocene
1.8 million-10 000 years ago

Cenozoic:
Quaternary period
1.8 million years ago to present

Quaternary

Holocene
10 000 years ago to present

TIMESCALE OF LIFE

If the 4.6 billion years since the Earth's formation were crammed into the thousand years from A.D. 1000 to the eve of 2000, it would yield the following dates:

1000 Formation of the Earth.
1173 First life appears.
1543 First single-celled organisms with a nucleus appear.
1843 Multicellular animals appear.
1891 The first land plants appear.
1950s to mid-80s The age of the dinosaurs.
Mid-December 1999 Early modern man, *Homo sapiens*, appears.
Around December 22, 1999 The emergence of modern man, *Homo sapiens sapiens.*

FOSSILS

The story of life's evolution on Earth is written in the fossil evidence. Fossils are the remains or traces of living organisms preserved in rock. They include footprints and chemical remains as well as petrified bones and shells. The oldest known fossils date back 3.5 billion years; they are of bacteria and were discovered in the Barberton Greenstone Belt in southern Africa, in 1996.

Conditions conducive to fossilization are very specific; the majority of living things do not become fossilized after death. The fossil record is not complete; it gives only an occasional glimpse of the life forms that existed in the past.

How fossils form

- To become fossilized, organic remains need to be buried quickly by sediment to prevent them from decaying or being destroyed. Therefore, fossilization is most likely in an environment where rapid sedimentation is taking place, such as a sea, lake or swamp.
- Once buried, the remains may dissolve, leaving a mold of the original form in the surrounding sediment. In some cases, new minerals crystallize in the space, creating a "cast" of the organism.
- Alternatively, hard parts, such as shell or bone, may become mineralized, or petrified – that is, replaced, molecule by molecule, by mineral-rich solutions in the sediment: They become rock.
- Sometimes soft parts of animals or plants are preserved in very fine sediment or by carbonization. This happens when the oxygen and hydrogen in organic remains dissolve, leaving only a carbon film on the rock in the shape of the original animal or plant.

Preserved in rock Buried plant or animal remains, such as these 40 million-year-old *Knightia alta* fish, leave an impression in the rock or even become rock themselves.

Evolution is the idea that living things change from generation to generation, with features that favor survival tending to be passed down. Over millennia, inherited features amplify and diverge, creating the huge variety of species alive today. Evolutionary theory, as first postulated by Charles Darwin and others in the 1850s, has had an influence far beyond the bounds of science.

EVOLUTION – A BIOLOGICAL ARMS RACE

To understand how evolution works, imagine a bird that eats nothing but one species of beetle; imagine also that this beetle lives in burrows that it digs deep into the ground.

To eat, the bird must stick its beak down the long, thin burrows. Birds with the longest, thinnest beaks are more likely to survive and breed than birds with shorter, fatter beaks. Therefore, most birds in the next generation will have the genes for a long thin beak.

Meanwhile, beetles with a natural predisposition to burrow deep are less likely to be eaten. Consequently, the genes that bestow this ability are more likely to be found in the next generation of beetles.

Passing on the improvement The result is that over hundreds of generations the birds' beaks will become longer and thinner, and the beetles will tunnel even farther from their reach. It might look like the bird's beak is designed to catch beetles, and that the beetles have a strategy to avoid the birds. This is an illusion, created by natural weighting in favor of one feature in both animals.

This bias is what Darwin called "natural selection." Nature "selects" the birds with longer beaks and the deep-digging beetles and so ensures that the biological arms race goes on.

Divergent evolution

Divergent evolution (also known as adaptive radiation) is the process by which several species evolve from a single common ancestral species.

Divergent evolution at work The many species of finch living on the Galápagos Islands off Ecuador in South America are a famous example of divergent evolution – Darwin's study of these birds contributed to his formulation of a theory of evolution. The original population consisted of a few birds of one species blown in from mainland South America. These birds strayed and spread across the islands, where new populations adapted to the different types of food and different types of environment. Distinct new species of finch gradually evolved, displaying the different beak shapes favored for each food type.

NATURAL SELECTION AT WORK

Although evolution is usually a long-term process, it can sometimes be observed in action. Britain's peppered moth, for example, altered its appearance over a relatively short period in response to changing environmental conditions caused by the Industrial Revolution.

Before industrialization, all peppered moths were a mottled gray, camouflaging them against the lichen-covered trees on which they lived. But in the 1850s, a darker variety was found in Manchester, where pollution had been killing tree lichens and blackening the tree bark. Under these circumstances, the darker moth was better camouflaged than the mottled one, and it soon spread widely throughout industrial England.

Both types exist today and are still the same species, but one or the other does better in different areas.

Changing with the times In an environment blackened by soot, the darker form of peppered moth (above) was better adapted to survive.

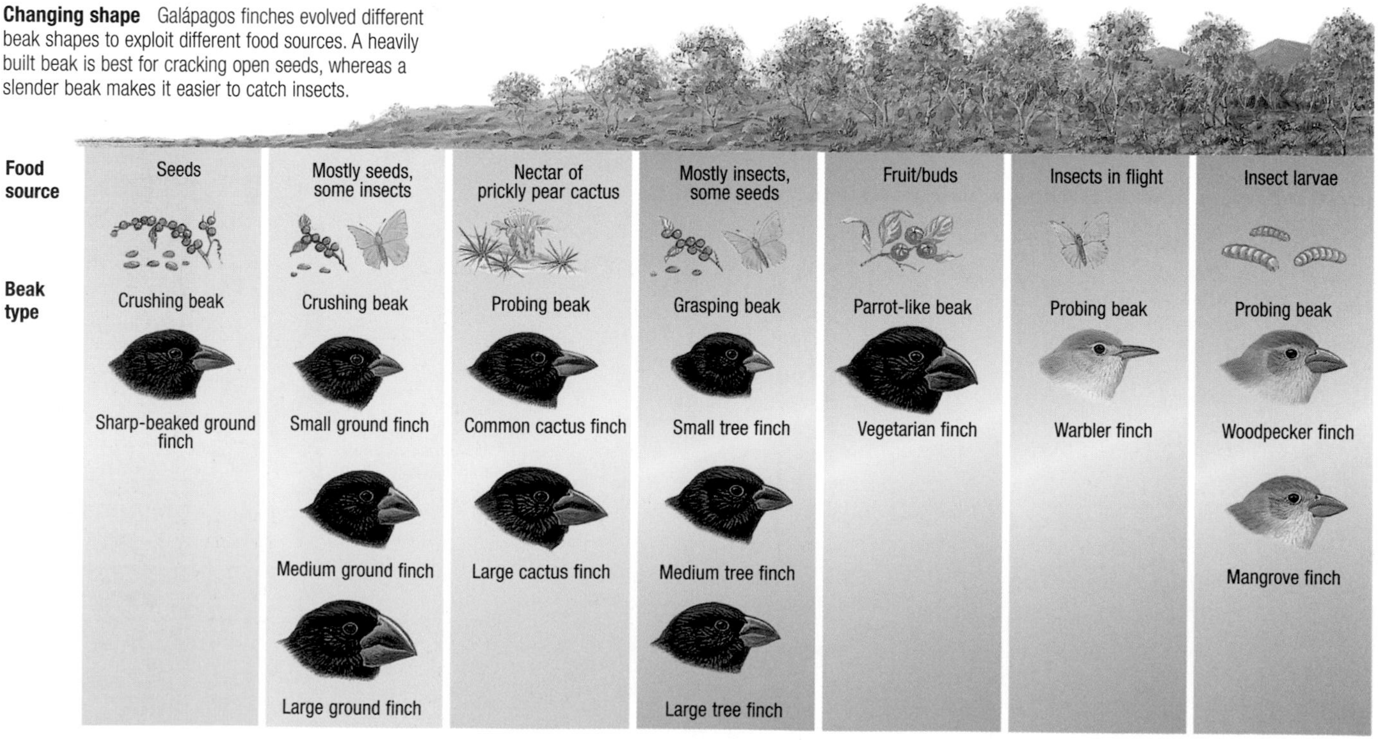

Changing shape Galápagos finches evolved different beak shapes to exploit different food sources. A heavily built beak is best for cracking open seeds, whereas a slender beak makes it easier to catch insects.

Main extinctions: the big five

Sudden environmental change in the past has led to mass extinctions. Scientists have identified five major events:

1 **End of the Ordovician**
(438 million years ago)
Global cooling led to the extinction of 70 percent of marine life.

2 **Late Devonian**
(365 million years ago)
A sharp drop in sea level led to the extinction of many marine invertebrates and most fishes.

3 **End of the Permian**
(245 million years ago)
Formation of the Pangaea supercontinent and a drop in sea level caused a 96 percent extinction of marine species.

4 **End of the Triassic**
(208 million years ago)
Sea level drop led to the extinction of 40 percent of all species.

5 **Cretaceous-Tertiary**
(65 million years ago)
A meteorite impact and high volcanic activity resulted in the extinction of 70 percent of animal species, including the dinosaurs.

We may be experiencing a mass extinction now as a result of human activities. If current rates of extinction continue, we can expect half of the world's known species to have disappeared by the end of the 21st century.

Taking to the air Wings have evolved more than once in the history of life on Earth but not always in the same way. The skeletal structures supporting the wings of birds and bats, for instance, are completely different.

Convergent evolution Sometimes similar features evolve in completely unrelated species. This convergent evolution happens when the two species evolve a solution to the same problem of lifestyle or environment. More often than not, the anatomy underlying these features is different in each species.

Convergent evolution at work The wings of bats and birds are an example of convergent evolution. They are superficially similar – because any flying animal will need to be equipped with something resembling a set of wings – but the underlying structure is very different: Bats' wings are supported by elongated finger bones; birds' are not. Another example is the shape of sharks and dolphins. Although completely unrelated, both have fins and gently curving streamlined bodies adapted for an aquatic lifestyle.

see also
52-53 **Ages of life on Earth**
68-71 **Dinosaurs**
314-15 **Scientific thinkers**
436-39 **Biology**

How new species emerge

Members of the same species can mate and produce fertile offspring. If part of a population becomes isolated in a way that prevents it from breeding with the rest and the two groups then experience different living conditions, they will be driven by natural selection to evolve in different ways. Eventually, the genetic differences between the two groups will become so great that even if they come together again, they will not be able to interbreed – two distinct species will have evolved.

KEY TERMS

- **Darwinism** The theory that natural selection is the mechanism of evolution.
- **Evolution** A change in the genetic composition of a population over time.
- **Fitness** The ability of an organism to survive and reproduce; it is a measure of reproductive success.
- **Natural selection** The tendency for useful variations to be preserved through generations.
- **Neo-Darwinism** The application of modern genetic knowledge to Darwin's theory.
- **Population** A group of interbreeding individuals that occupies a defined geographical region, such as a particular species of fish in a lake.
- **Speciation** The development of new species, which occurs when different populations of the same species evolve along different lines and under the influence of different environmental conditions.
- **Survival of the fittest** A term coined by the 19th-century English philosopher Herbert Spencer to describe the survival of those organisms that are best fitted to exist in their environment.

The recipe for the origins of life is unknown, but likely ingredients were methane, carbon dioxide, ammonia and water in the atmosphere and seas of the young Earth. The action of ultraviolet radiation or lightning could have combined these chemicals into amino acids, the building blocks of protein – and so of all living things.

WHAT IS LIFE?

Anything alive rather than dead or inanimate, will
- **metabolize** – carry out chemical processes involved in producing energy or eliminating waste, for example.
- **grow** and develop.
- **respond to stimuli** such as light or heat.
- **reproduce** either sexually or asexually.

The simplest forms of life are single cells, which have
- **cell membranes** to insulate them from the environment and to allow the selective flow of chemicals into and out of each cell.
- **the ability to harness** or produce energy.
- **genetic material** to allow them to reproduce.

More than 4.5 billion years ago
The Earth's thin surface crust is hot and unstable. It is wracked by volcanoes and earthquakes and bombarded by meteorites. The atmosphere contains no oxygen; it is composed mainly of hydrogen and small amounts of the gases helium, krypton and xenon.

4.5 billion years ago
According to one theory, a large rocky body collides with the Earth, stripping away the first-generation atmosphere and triggering further volcanism. The Moon is formed from debris from the collision.

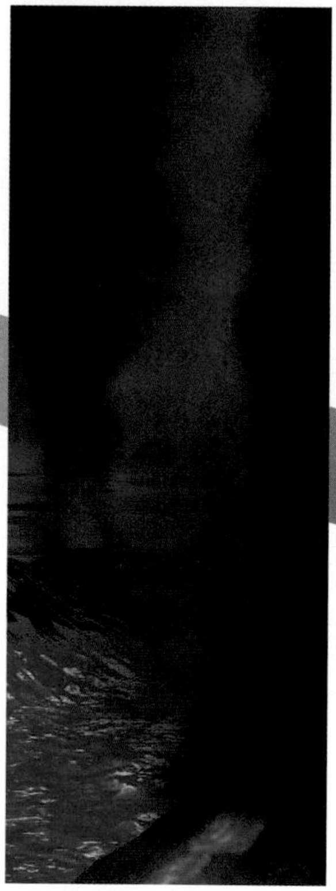

4.35 billion years ago
Volcanic gases and water vapor released by the collision create a new, hydrogen-rich atmosphere.

3.8 billion years ago
The first life forms appear, probably around volcanic vents on the ocean bed and in hydrothermal pools, where there is a good supply of minerals and warmth. They consist of single-celled archaebacteria. These have a very simple cell structure, with no nucleus, and can exist without oxygen. These organisms may have used hydrogen sulfide from the volcanic vents as their energy source.

Life in a test tube

Life may have been formed in conditions of either extreme heat or extreme cold. Laboratory experiments have provided evidence for both theories.

Extreme heat In 1953, American scientists Stanley Miller and Harold Urey passed an electrical current to simulate lightning through a cocktail of compounds thought to be present in the early Earth's atmosphere and seas. Amino acids, the basis of protein, were among the new substances formed.
Extreme cold In the 1960s, another American, Leslie Orville, froze a similar mix of chemicals. A constituent compound of DNA was created, suggesting that life might have evolved during one of several ice ages that occurred in the millions of years of Earth's early history.

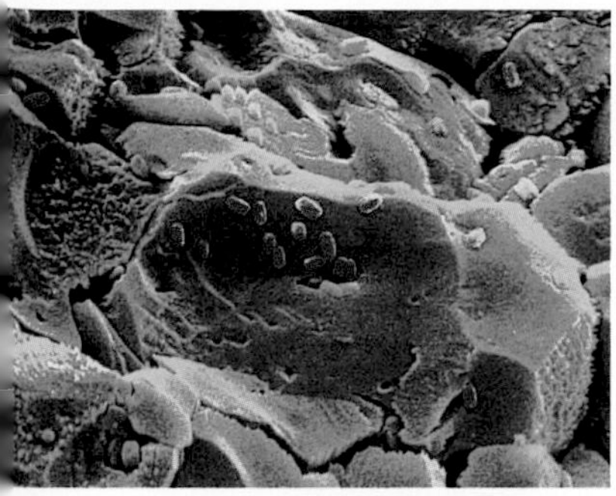

Earliest fossils The evolution of living forms from organic chemicals occurred remarkably soon after the formation of the Earth. Among the oldest evidence of life on Earth are 3.5 billion-year-old bacteria fossils (shown on the left in a computer-enhanced image). Evidence suggests that life began a mere 700 million years after the planet's formation.

3.5 billion years ago

Some organisms can now produce chlorophyll, which allows them to create energy by photosynthesis. These cyanobacteria – or blue-green algae – spread in watery environments across the surface of the Earth. Over time, excess oxygen released by the cyanobacteria starts to accumulate in the Earth's atmosphere.

2.1 billion years ago

Amounts of atmospheric oxygen are about 1 percent of current levels, enough to support the development of organisms that respire – that is, use oxygen to fuel their metabolic processes. A layer of ozone, created by the combination of oxygen molecules, starts to form in the upper atmosphere. Cells with nuclei – called eukaryotes – appear.

The coming of the nucleus

The earliest life forms were single cells with no nuclei, known as prokaryotes. As life evolved, different parts of the cell took on specific, specialized functions – for instance, respiration – with genetic material becoming focused in one area called the nucleus and bound by a membrane. Cells with nuclei are described as eukaryotic. They are more organized than the prokaryotic cells that gave them the potential to evolve into more complex life forms. All multicellular life is eukaryotic, and all bacteria are prokaryotic.

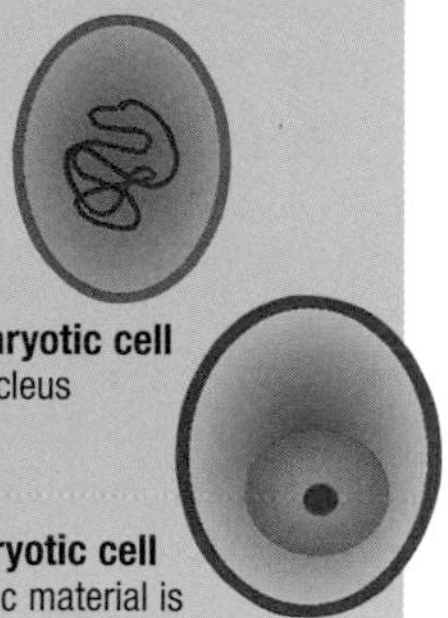

Prokaryotic cell
No nucleus

Eukaryotic cell
Genetic material is contained within a nucleus

720 million years ago

Some eukaryotic cells begin to live in groups. Over time, cells in these colonies take on specialized roles, such as respiration, for the colony until they become inter-dependent and can no longer exist singly. They are now part of a multicellular organism. New species are evolving, including, by 600 million years ago, the first to have hard exoskeletal parts.

420 million years ago

Oxygen in the atmosphere has increased to about 10 percent of current levels and continues to rise over the next 100 million years. The ozone layer thickens, acting as a filter for ultraviolet rays from the Sun, which are harmful to life. This makes the land surface of the Earth habitable. The first land plants appear.

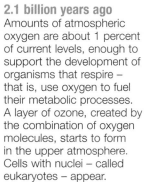

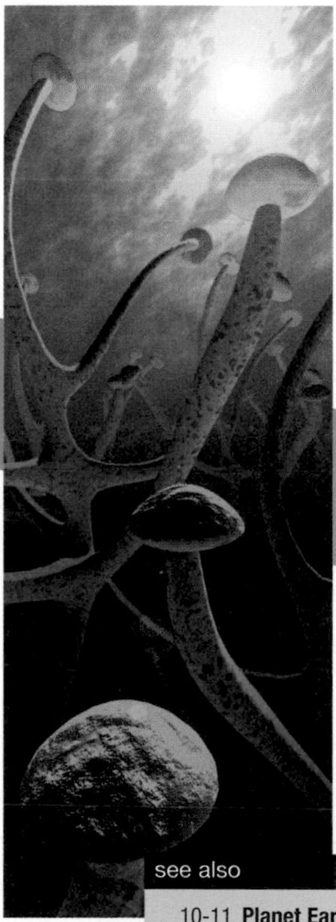

Stromatolites Rounded structures formed by mats of cyanobacteria (blue-green algae) are the most common fossil evidence of early life. These modern stromatolites (left) were found in Australia.

see also
10-11 **Planet Earth**
46-47 **Earth's atmosphere**

The plant kingdom ▶ The classification of the Earth's vegetation

Plant life is enormously varied. It ranges from single, microscopic cells to the largest living things on Earth – California's giant sequoias. Vegetation can be found in almost all of the Earth's environments, and it is this immense diversity that is the key to its success. Plants can also live to a great age – there are 4600-year-old bristlecone pines in the Rocky Mountains of North America.

Early blossom Magnolias were some of the first flowering plants to evolve.

GREEN ALGAE

Chlorophytes
40 000 species

Key features:

- Range from single-cell to multicellular species.
- Contain chlorophyll, so can carry out photosynthesis (see page 60).
- Produce 70 percent of all oxygen released into the atmosphere by photosynthesis.
- Live in water or a moist environment.
- Reproduce both asexually and sexually (see page 61).

LIVERWORTS, HORNWORTS AND MOSSES

Bryophytes
29 000 species

Key features:

- The simplest land plants.
- Do not possess vascular tissue (see page 60).
- Lack real roots and leaves.
- Small and low to the ground; some grow on other plants.
- Rely on surrounding moisture for water.
- Can live only in damp places.
- Reproduce via spores.

FERNS, CLUB MOSSES AND HORSETAILS

Pteridophytes
13 000 species

Key features:

- Descended directly from the simplest land plants.
- Are vascular plants.
- Possess roots.
- Ferns have special leaves called fronds.
- Require damp conditions for reproduction but not as reliant on surface water as liverworts and mosses.
- Reproduce via spores.

CONE-BEARING PLANTS

Gymnosperms
936 species

Key features:

- Possess a complex vascular system (see page 60).
- Have an extensive root system.
- Pollinated by the wind (see page 61).
- Reproduce via seeds.
- Seeds usually produced in a cone-like structure.
- Do not produce flowers or fruits.

FLOWERING PLANTS

Angiosperms
250 000 species

Key features:

- Are the most successful group of plants ever.
- Are found in almost any kind of environment.
- Possess great variation in size, form and structure.
- Have a complex vascular system (see page 60).
- Produce flowers.
- Pollinated by animals, wind and water (see page 61).
- Reproduce via seeds.
- Seeds grow inside an ovary, which swells to become a fruit.

Cones

Conifers produce cones that develop from the female sexual organs after pollination in the same way as fruits, nuts, and seed heads develop from the flowers of flowering plants. Cones protect the pollinated (fertilized) female sex cells while they develop into seeds. When the seeds are mature and conditions are right for their dispersal, the cone opens to release them. Cone-bearing plants are an ancient group, and cones themselves have changed little in the hundreds of millions of years since they first made their appearance – a tribute to their successful design.

Wide open This Scotch pine (*Pinus silvestris*) cone has shed its seeds.

Shut tight This giant fir (*Abies grandis*) cone is closed with its seeds held inside.

Ancient design The cone of the monkey puzzle tree (*Araucaria araucaria*) has remained unchanged since the Jurassic period.

Flowering plants are divided into two groups depending on how many seed leaves (*cotyledons*) they produce. The seed leaf is a structure in the plant's embryo, which in many species acts as a food store for the embryo and often appears above ground as the sprouting seed's first leaves.

ONE SEED LEAF

Monocotyledons
About 50 000 species

- Seeds produce one seed leaf on germination.
- Leaves have veins running in parallel along their length.
- Vascular tissue is scattered randomly throughout the stem.
- Includes lilies, grasses and many related cereal crops, and among trees, the fruit-bearing palms.

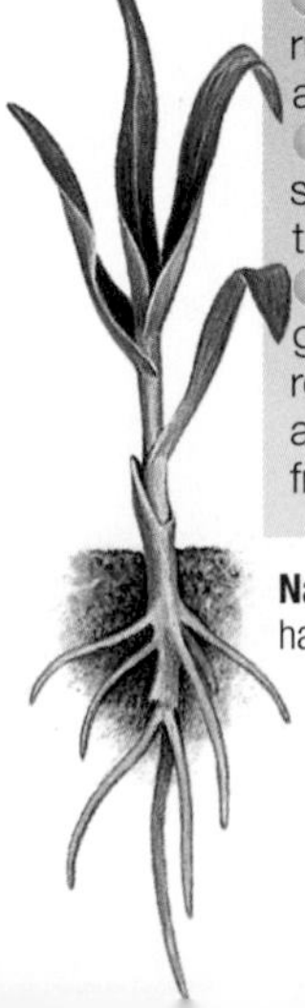

Narrow leaf Monocotyledons have blade-shaped leaves.

TWO SEED LEAVES

Dicotyledons
About 200 000 species

- Seeds produce two seed leaves on germination.
- Generally more complex than monocotyledons.
- Veins spread net-like across their leaves.
- Vascular tissue is arranged in an orderly ring around the stem.
- Includes most flowering plants and many hardwood trees, such as oaks, limes and beeches.

Broad leaf The leaves of dicotyledons (right) are wide with rounded edges.

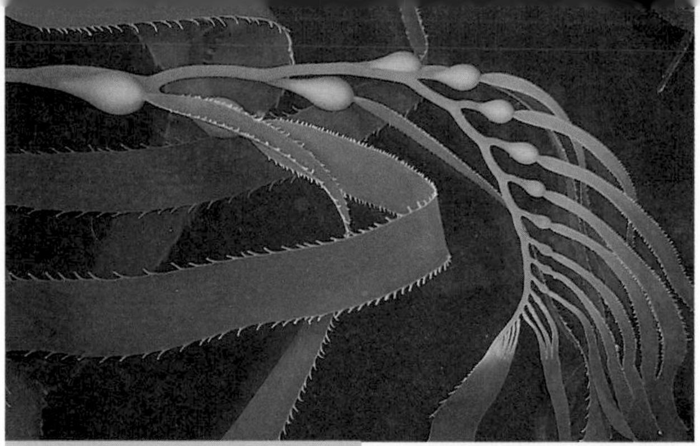

Longest seaweed
Pacific giant kelp *(Macrocystis pyrifera)* is the world's biggest seaweed. It has fronds that can grow up to 60 m (196 ft) long. They can reach this length in just one year, making this plant of coastal waters the fastest-growing form of marine life.

Largest seed
The rare coco de mer palm *(Lodoicea maldivica)*, produces the biggest seeds of any living plant. Each one weighs up to 20 kg (44 lb) and takes about ten years to ripen. In the past, sailors thought that such seeds grew at the bottom of the sea. In fact, the palm grows in the Seychelles in the Indian Ocean.

Widest flower
The widest single flowers grow on the Rafflesia plant *(Rafflesia arnoldii)*, which lives in the rain forests of Southeast Asia. They are about 91 cm (3 ft) across and weigh up to 7 kg (15 lb). To attract flies – as pollinators – they give off a foul smell, reminiscent of rotting meat.

Tallest flower
The tallest single flower belongs to the Titan arum *(Amorphophallus titanum)* from Sumatra. Up to 2.6 m (9 ft) high, it stinks of rotting fish, which attracts the insects that help to pollinate it. The flower grows at a rate of more than an inch a day and collapses two days after reaching its full size.

Tallest flowerhead
The flowers of some plants grow in clusters called flowerheads. The tallest flowerhead is found on the giant puya *(Puya raimondii)* from Bolivia. It can be over 10 m (33 ft) tall and contain up to 8000 separate flowers. Puya plants live for about 150 years before growing this flowerhead, and then they die.

see also

60-61 **How plants live**
436-39 **Biology**

Plants need light, water and the right soil and temperature conditions to thrive. Light and warmth are provided by the Sun, whose energy is also utilized to make food by photosynthesis. Water, along with essential nutrients and minerals such as nitrogen, potassium and magnesium, is obtained from the soil through the roots. Water is also used in photosynthesis and creates a buildup of pressure, called turgor pressure, within a plant's cells. Without this, the cell walls would collapse, and the plant would wilt and eventually die.

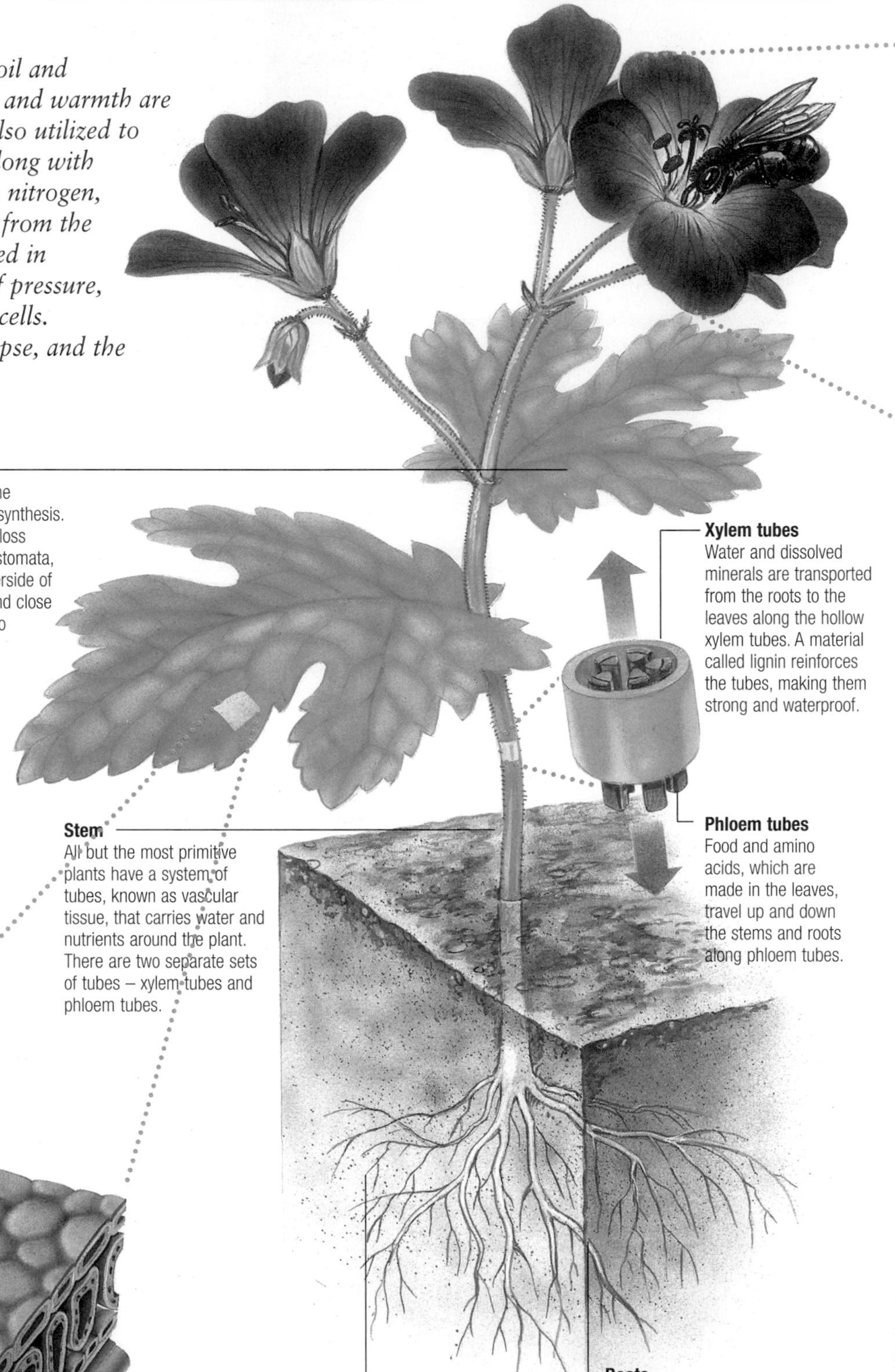

Leaves
Leaves contain most of the chlorophyll used in photosynthesis. They also regulate water loss through openings called stomata, found mainly on the underside of the leaf. Stomata open and close in response to the need to release or retain water.

Stem
All but the most primitive plants have a system of tubes, known as vascular tissue, that carries water and nutrients around the plant. There are two separate sets of tubes – xylem tubes and phloem tubes.

Xylem tubes
Water and dissolved minerals are transported from the roots to the leaves along the hollow xylem tubes. A material called lignin reinforces the tubes, making them strong and waterproof.

Phloem tubes
Food and amino acids, which are made in the leaves, travel up and down the stems and roots along phloem tubes.

Nodules
Some plants have knotlike protuberances on their roots containing bacteria that can absorb and convert (fix) atmospheric nitrogen into ammonia (NH_3), which the plant then uses to make nitrates and amino acids.

Roots
A network of roots anchors the plant in the ground. Roots also absorb water and essential minerals from the soil and can store nutrients. They vary greatly in size and number, depending on the size of a plant and the conditions under which it grows.

PHOTOSYNTHESIS

Photosynthesis is the process by which plants use the Sun's energy to combine simple substances, present all around them, into food.

The key to this process is the green pigment chlorophyll. This substance is found in chloroplasts – tiny structures in a plant's leaves. It absorbs the light energy from the Sun, which is then used to combine water from the soil and carbon dioxide from the air to produce a sugary food called glucose. Oxygen is released into the atmosphere as a by-product. Nearly all atmospheric oxygen – upon which most animal life on Earth depends – is created by photosynthesis.

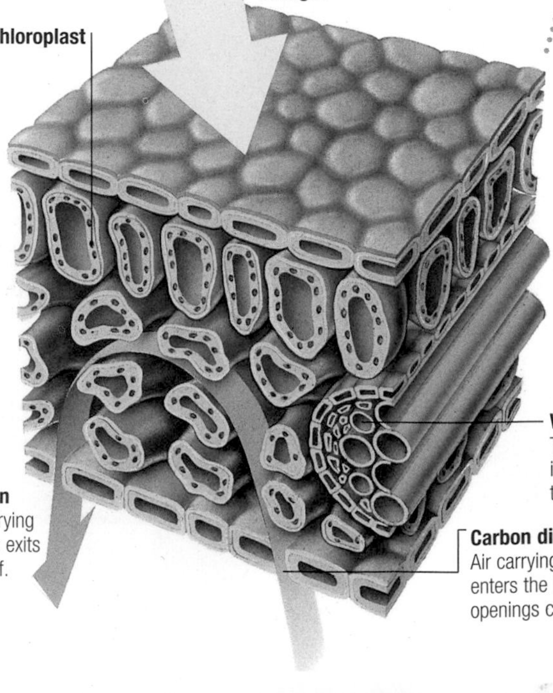

Energy from sunlight

Chloroplast

Water
This is drawn into the leaf through its veins.

Oxygen
Air carrying oxygen exits the leaf.

Carbon dioxide
Air carrying carbon dioxide enters the leaf through openings called stomata.

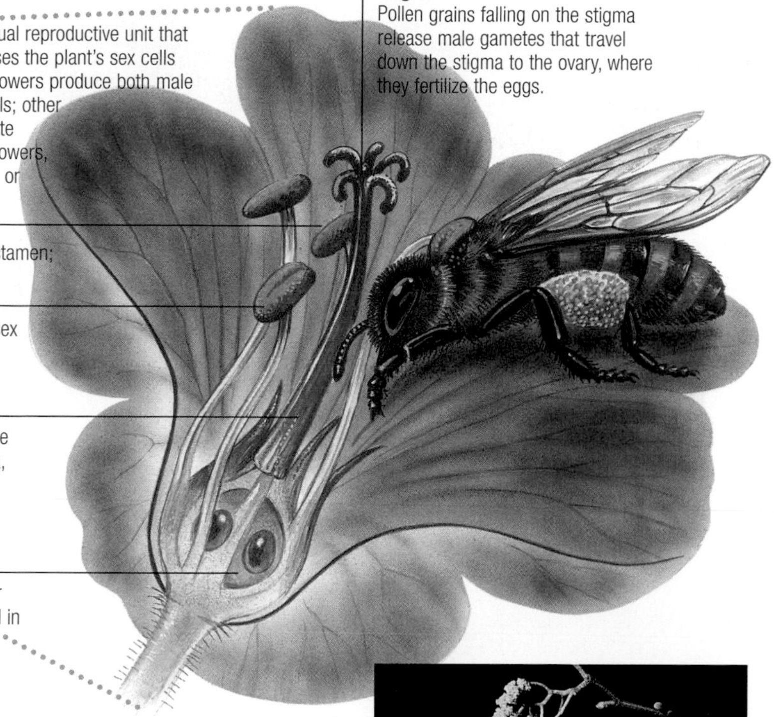

Flower
A flower is the sexual reproductive unit that produces and houses the plant's sex cells (gametes). Some flowers produce both male and female sex cells; other plants have separate male and female flowers, either on the same or different plants.

Anthers
Upper part of the stamen; produces pollen.

Pollen
Male gametes or sex cells are found in pollen grains.

Style
Stalk supporting the stigma. The stigma, style and ovary together are called the carpel.

Ovary
Female gametes or egg cells are found in the ovary.

Stigma
Pollen grains falling on the stigma release male gametes that travel down the stigma to the ovary, where they fertilize the eggs.

SEED DISPERSAL

Once fertilization has taken place, seeds are produced. These new seeds need to move away from the parent plant both to find space to germinate and grow and to help to colonize new areas. A number of agents help to achieve this.

Wind Light seeds with feathery parachutes, such as the dandelion, catch the wind and can be carried long distances. Seeds with "wings" and airfoils, such as sycamore (right) and lime, rotate in the air and ride the wind like tiny aircraft.

Animals Seeds with hooks, such as burdock (right), cling to animals' coats and get carried off. The seeds in fruits eaten by animals usually pass unharmed through their digestive systems. By the time they emerge, they will usually have traveled some distance from the parent plant.

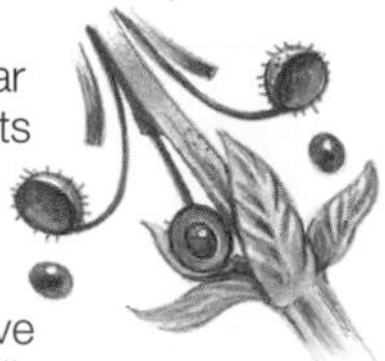

Explosive mechanisms Some seedpods are designed to explode when mature, scattering the seeds far and wide. Broom (right) sheds its seeds in this way.

"Pepper pot" mechanisms Plants, such as the poppy, have seedpods that are perforated like a pepper pot. Seeds sprinkle from them as they sway in the wind.

Water Plants living by water can use currents or tides to distribute seeds. Such seeds must float and be waterproof. Coconuts, for instance, are carried from beach to beach by the sea.

POLLINATION

When pollen is transferred from the anthers to the stigma, an outgrowth from the pollen grain passes down through the style to the ovary. Male gametes travel down the tube to fertilize the egg cells within the ovary. Self-pollination occurs when the pollen is from the same plant; cross-pollination occurs when the pollen is from a different plant.

Species that have male and female flowers on separate plants can only ever be cross-pollinated. Some flowers having both male and female parts can be self- or cross-pollinated, but others have mechanisms that prevent self-pollination.

Pollen is usually carried by the wind or by animals, such as bees.

By wind Wind-blown pollen tends to be very smooth and light to increase buoyancy in the air. Most grasses rely on the wind to transport their pollen, as do many trees.

By animals This is a more reliable and targeted method. It also encourages cross-fertilization, which helps to increase the genetic variety of a species. Animal pollinators are usually invertebrates or small mammals. This pollen is commonly large, with a rough surface to help it cling to the pollinator's body. Pollen is picked up and deposited as the animal visits successive flowers. Flowers attract potential pollinators by color, shape, scent and the promise of nectar.

Windblown The male flowers, or catkins, of hazel bushes use the wind to spread their pollen.

see also
436-39 **Biology**

Plants of arid areas

Plants that live in dry places often develop long roots to reach water deep in the ground. They also need to conserve water once they have it. Water vapor is lost through microscopic pores in the leaves called stomata, which open and close to control this loss, a process called transpiration. To limit transpiration, plants in arid conditions often have one or more of the following features:

- **Fewer stomata**, which limits the amount of water that can be lost.
- **Stomata that close** during the day and open at night, when there is no drying effect from the Sun.
- **A waxy cuticle** on the leaf surface, which helps to reduce water loss.
- **No leaves** – leafless plants such as cacti have a smaller surface area from which transpiration can take place.
- **Fleshy stems and leaves** – cacti and succulents store water in this way.

Dry area plants with leathery, hard or spiny leaves, adaptations to low-nutrient soils, include Australian Banksias, eucalyptus and acacias. They are slow-growing and often resistant to fire.

Desert beauty The prickly pear has a whole range of water-retaining features.

The first organized life, simple bacteria consisting of single cells without nuclei, would eventually give rise to all life on Earth. But it was only with the evolution of eukaryotes – cells with nuclei – around 2.1 billion years ago, that the evolution of multicellular life finally became possible.

One cell engulfs another

As multicellular life evolved from the first eukaryotic cells, the cells themselves became increasingly complex. Larger eukaryotic cells developed mutually beneficial relationships with other, smaller ones, eventually incorporating them. The smaller cells could now perform useful functions, such as respiration and photosynthesis, for their hosts. Over time, the engulfed cells lost their autonomy and became specialized parts of the host cell – its organelles. Chloroplasts (see page 60) and mitochondria are cell organelles.

The origin of sexual reproduction

Without the emergence of eukaryotic cells, there would have been no sex. Packaging genetic information into one specialized part of a cell – the nucleus – made sexual reproduction possible. Unlike asexual reproduction, which creates only offspring that are genetically identical to the parent, sexual reproduction combines genetic material from two individuals, allowing for an infinite number of combinations. Genetically varied populations can evolve much faster than those that are not. The rapid evolution of life forms after the arrival of eukaryotes illustrates this. During the approximately 1.5 billion years when only prokaryotic cells existed, the most developed life forms were bacteria. But in the 1 billion years since eukaryotic cells appeared, there has been an explosion of multicellular life.

PRECAMBRIAN

2.1 billion years ago
Eukaryotes, cells with nuclei containing their genetic information, first appear.

800 million years ago
Single-celled animals (protozoans) first appear in the fossil record.

720 million years ago
Multicellular animals (metazoans) are thought to have evolved, although there is no fossil evidence from this date. Scientists using the molecular clock theory (see box opposite) estimate that they would have originated around this time.

680 million years ago
The **earliest fossil evidence of multicellular animals** dates from this time. Examples are impressions of soft-bodied animals found in the Ediacara Hills of South Australia in the 1940s. Some are unrelated to modern life, but some resemble the worms and arthropods of today.

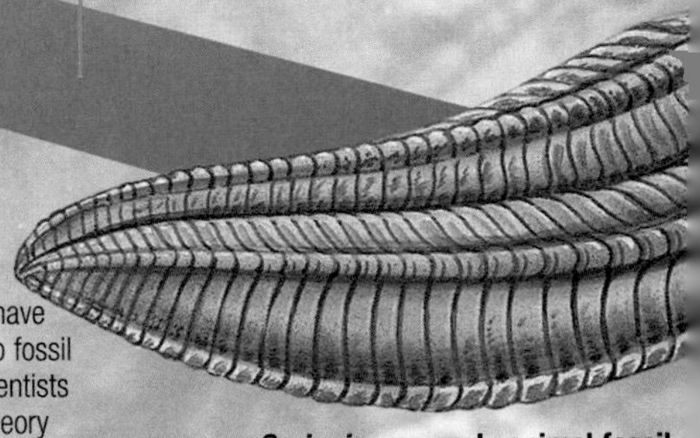

***Spriggina*, an early animal fossil** from the Ediacara Hills. Scientists are unsure what kind of animal *Spriggina* was. Some believe that it was an ancestral arthropod; others think that it was part of a group that led to segmented worms.

THE CAMBRIAN EXPLOSION

What happened?

- 550 million years ago, life on Earth underwent a huge expansion.
- 70 new animal phyla appeared, including 30 that still exist.
- 470 new animal families appeared.
- A wide range of animal forms was created.
- Basic forms of all animals alive today were established. Only improvements and variations have occurred since.

Why did it happen?

Scientists have put forward a number of possible explanations. The truth may be a combination of them.

Continental break-up At the end of the Precambrian era, a giant supercontinent called Rodinia began to break up. This involved underwater volcanic activity, which pumped minerals into the sea and raised sea levels. Higher sea levels drowned most of the land, creating shallow, mineral-rich seas separated by deep ocean troughs: new environments for rapidly evolving life forms to exploit. Never before or since in the history of the Earth has such an unbounded ecological opportunity been available.

After the freeze The creation of the supercontinent Rodinia in the Precambrian was accompanied by a severe ice age, causing a mass extinction of primitive life. Explosions of new life tend to follow mass extinctions, and the eventual warming of the Earth at the end of the Precambrian heralded the appearance of the first multicellular animals about 720 million years ago. Because multicellular life allows for the development of diversity, the rapid evolution of new species was inevitable. Competition for mates, living space and food fueled the evolution of new species through natural selection.

Slow, fast, slow When life first moves into a new environment, population growth is usually slow because only a small number of individuals is reproducing. As numbers increase, so the rate of growth increases until the available space is full. Further expansion is then impossible, and the rate of growth slows down until the population reaches a sustainable level. Any colonization of a new environment, if unrestrained by external factors, will conform to this pattern. Some scientists argue that this model is true of the Cambrian explosion. The evolution of multicellular life in a world full of ecological niches waiting to be filled would inevitably show a slow initial increase, followed by an explosion of new life forms. The only explanation needed for the Cambrian explosion is the existence of an empty environment to fill, and life forms with the evolutionary potential to fill it.

THE TRILOBITES

Trilobites are one of the largest and most diverse groups of extinct animals to appear during the Cambrian life explosion. About 15 000 species are known. Trilobites were arthropods, like today's crabs, insects, and spiders. They scavenged along the seabed and evolved a variety of shapes and sizes. Tiny *Agnostus*, for example, was just 7 mm (1/4 in.) long, whereas later species, such as *Isotelus*, grew to up to 70 cm (28 in.).

Trilobite means "three lobes" because the bodies of many species had a threefold division, with a raised central portion down the back flanked by a flatter portion on either side. They had a hard outer casing, or exoskeleton, and many pairs of legs. The exoskeleton was vital to the development of multicellular life. It provided a protective framework on which an animal could grow and allowed for an increase in cell number and type. Cell specialization made adaptation to a wide range of conditions possible.

The trilobites were highly successful and thrived until the end of the Permian, when they succumbed to a mass extinction that wiped out 96 percent of all marine life.

Visually arresting Unusual for trilobites, this Russian species, *Neoasaphus*, has eyes raised on stalks to watch for danger above the loose debris or algal growth of the shallow seabed.

The Burgess Shale – a fossil portrait

In 1909, Charles Doolittle Walcott discovered some extremely well-preserved fossils in a formation called the Burgess Shale in British Columbia, Canada. Doolittle, an American paleontologist, found 140 different species that he estimated to be about 530 million years old. They included some of the first creatures known to have had hard body parts and 20 species for which no earlier evidence has ever been found.

The Burgess Shale fossils are a scientific treasure trove. The fossilizing conditions were so good that even internal organs and soft-bodied animals were preserved, offering unique clues about the nature of animal evolution.

The fossils also give a snapshot of a marine community just after the explosion of new life in the Cambrian and provide the oldest evidence of a group of interacting species.

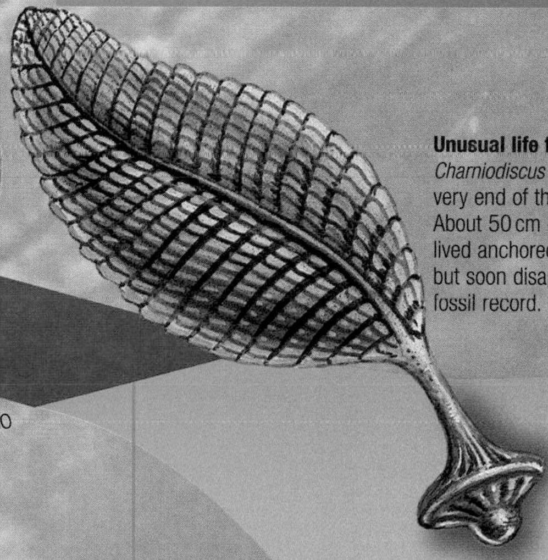

Unusual life forms *Charniodiscus* appeared at the very end of the Precambrian. About 50 cm (20 in.) long, it lived anchored to the seabed but soon disappears from the fossil record.

Ancient arthropod This well-preserved fossil of a lobsterlike creature is from the Burgess Shale.

550

CAMBRIAN

550 million years ago
Cambrian explosion
All known phyla emerge at this time including arthropods, flatworms, mollusks, chordates, and sponges.

Molecular clocks

The fossil record is often incomplete, so scientists have devised other ways of ascertaining when particular species are likely to have first appeared on Earth. One of these is the use of molecular evidence from the study of proteins, organic compounds found in all living species.

Proteins are made up of amino acids. In the 1960s, it was found that different species have different amino acid sequences for the same protein. It was concluded that the number of differences was proportional to the time since those different species evolved from a common ancestor. The longer a species has existed, therefore, the more differences, or mutations, there will have been. Mutation rates are then used to estimate when species evolved.

see also
28-29 **Geology of the Earth**
52-53 **Ages of life on Earth**
54-55 **Evolution explained**

The age of the fishes

The first creatures with an internal skeleton emerge and diversify

Fishes hold a crucial place in the history of animal evolution. They evolved from chordates, animals with a stiffened rod running along their bodies, to become the first true vertebrates – animals with backbones. All other vertebrate groups – amphibians, reptiles, birds, and mammals – including humans – ultimately emerged from fishes.

CAMBRIAN

505

530-525 million years ago
The earliest known chordate appears. At 4 cm (1 1/2 in.) long, *Pikaia gracilens* has a head, notochord (primitive backbone) and fishlike muscles. *Pikaia*'s relationship to the conodonts is uncertain.

More than 515 million years ago
Conodonts, small eel-like chordates, emerge. They have fishlike muscles and are possible ancestors of the fishes.

500 million years ago
The first true fishes, Agnathans, appear. The jawless Agnathans show great diversity and colonize both salt water and fresh. Their descendants – hagfish and lampreys – still exist. Other key features of Agnathans include the following.

- They had cartilage skeletons.
- They had bony external plates.
- They were filter feeders that combined their gills as a breathing and filter-feeding mechanism.
- They did not have fins.

440-400 million years ago
First jawed fishes emerge. The earliest forms are Acanthodians, which probably evolve in the sea, but soon colonize fresh water too. Having jaws lets them become active predators – see the box "The benefit of jaws." Other key features of Acanthodians include the following.

- They had fins.
- They used their gills to breathe but no longer used them for filter feeding.
- They had an enlarged gut to digest larger food.

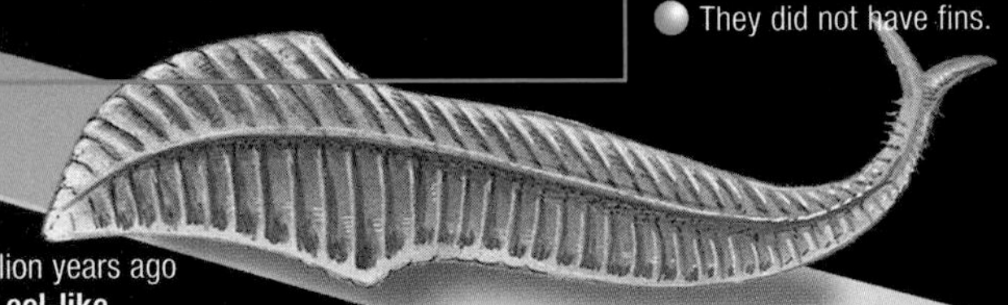

First forerunner *Pikaia* is the earliest creature known to have possessed a spinal rod.

ORDOVICIAN

435

SILURIAN

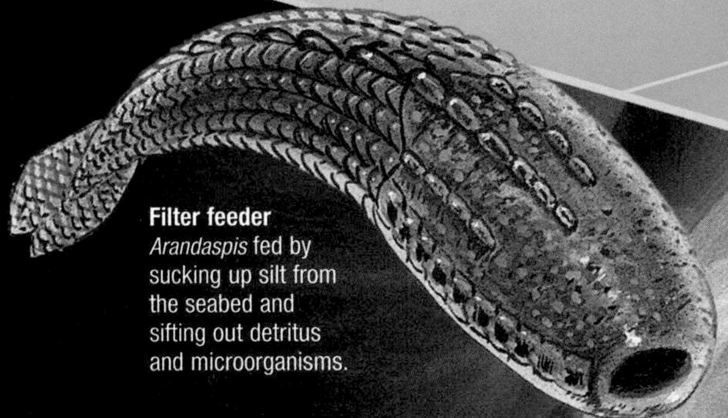

Filter feeder
Arandaspis fed by sucking up silt from the seabed and sifting out detritus and microorganisms.

The evolution of gills

Gills are the organs that most aquatic animals use to obtain oxygen from the surrounding water. The first gills appeared in sea-living invertebrates. If under a certain size, these creatures got enough oxygen from the water by simple exchange through their body surfaces. As they became bigger, they had to increase their surface areas by infolding areas of the body: In this way they could absorb more oxygen. Over millions of years of evolution, these folded areas developed an increased blood supply and became gills. By the time fishes appeared, gills were already complex internal organs. Later, their efficiency was improved by the fish pumping water over them (left), much as we pump air over our lungs when we breathe. The total surface area of the gills of any fish far exceeds that of its outer body surface.

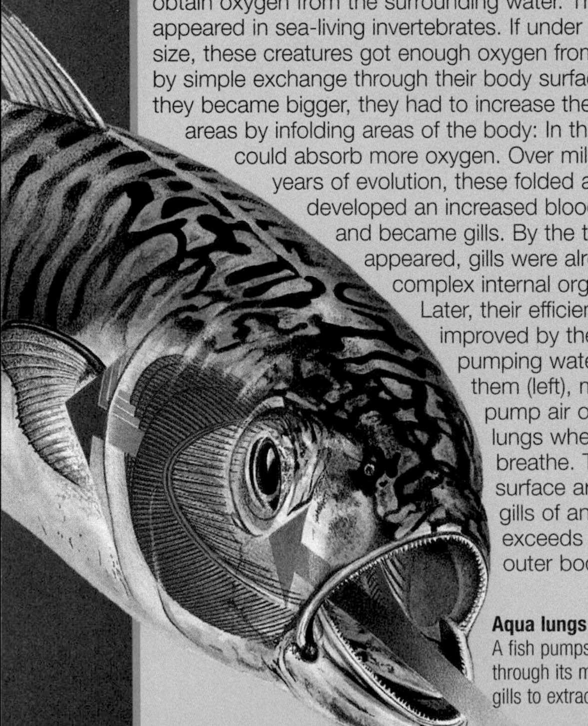

Aqua lungs
A fish pumps water through its mouth over its gills to extract oxygen.

HAVING A BACKBONE

All animals with flexible spinal rods along their bodies during some stage of their development are known as chordates. Scientists place them in a large group, or phylum, called the Chordata. In vertebrates, this spinal rod has evolved into a true backbone made up of distinct bones, called vertebrae, which are linked together. Exactly how the spinal rod, or notochord, originated, is still unknown, but its appearance, along with attached muscles down the back, was a major step in animal evolution. It has a number of advantages.

- It makes movement more efficient.
- It provides support for the shoulder and pelvic girdles – the attachment sites of various limbs and appendages.
- It protects the dorsal (spinal) nerve cord, allowing the nervous system to develop and become more sophisticated.

Jawed fishes

Acanthodians
Earliest jawed fishes

- Resembled modern sharks.
- Evolved in the sea at the beginning of the Silurian Period.
- Later moved into fresh water.

Placoderms
Heavily armored marine fishes

- Emerged in the early Devonian.
- Short-lived group died out in the early Carboniferous.

Osteicthyans
Include the majority of modern fishes

- Emerged in the early Devonian Period.
- Skeletons made of bone.
- 20 000 modern species (half of all vertebrates).

Lobe-finned fishes (*Sarcopterygians*)
Seven species survive today: six lungfish and the coelacanth

- Fleshy, lobe-shaped fins supported by bones and rays. Muscles in the fins.
- Amphibians evolved from this group.

Ray-finned fishes (*Actinopterygians*)
Earliest group of bony fishes to appear

- Bony spines, known as rays, support the fins. No muscles in the fins.
- Evolved into the huge range of modern freshwater and sea fishes, from salmon to sea horses, sturgeon to plaice.

Chondrichthyans
Include sharks, skates and rays

- Emerged in the early Devonian.
- Skeletons made of cartilage.
- Teeth and body scales replaced throughout life.

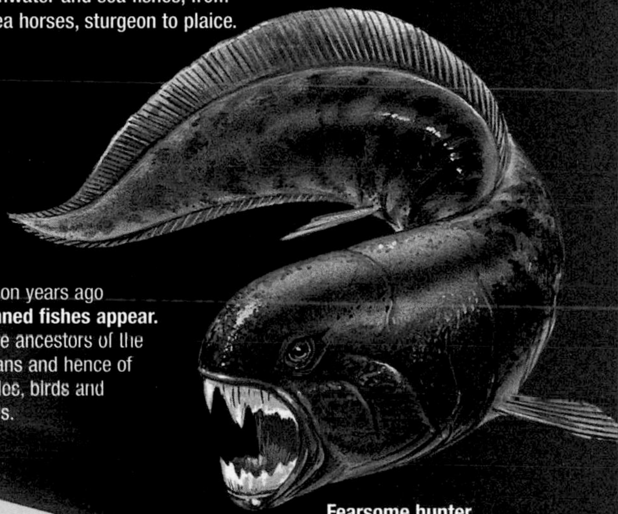

Fearsome hunter Placoderm *Dunkleosteus* reached 6 m (20 ft) long.

SILURIAN 408 DEVONIAN 360

390 million years ago (early Devonian) **New groups of jawed fishes emerge,** including sharks, skates and rays. Early kinds of bony fishes, the group that includes most modern fishes, appear.

380 million years ago **Lobe-finned fishes appear.** These are ancestors of the amphibians and hence of the reptiles, birds and mammals.

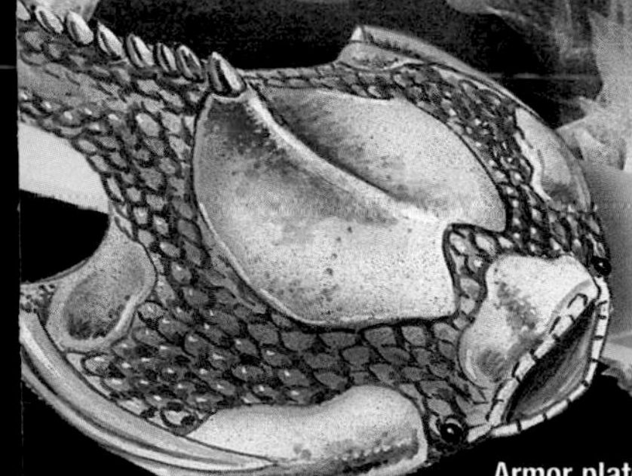

Armor plated *Drepanaspis* was a jawless fish well protected from attack.

420 million years ago **Life starts to move from salt water into fresh water.** Giant invertebrates called Eurypterids, or sea scorpions, often nearly 2 m (7 ft) long, are the first predators to venture into fresh water. They are soon followed by jawed fishes that compete with them for food.

THE BENEFIT OF JAWS

Jaws probably evolved from the first pair of gill supports, located in jawless fishes just behind the mouth (above), and teeth developed from skin lining the mouth. It was a crucial development. Jaws enabled fish to move up a level in the food chain from passive filter feeding on detritus to actively pursuing and seizing prey. As a result, jawed fishes soon diversified in diet and lifestyle. Part of the digestive system enlarged to digest the larger food being eaten, and the fish themselves grew bigger.

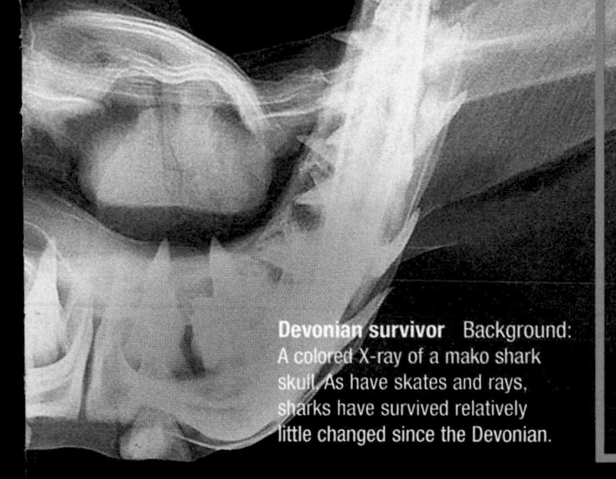

Devonian survivor Background: A colored X-ray of a mako shark skull. As have skates and rays, sharks have survived relatively little changed since the Devonian.

see also
52-53 **Ages of life on Earth**
54-55 **Evolution explained**
80-83 **Fishes**

The move to land ▶ Animals finally leave the water

The first animals to colonize dry land were not air-breathing fish or early amphibians, but myriapods, the ancestors of centipedes and millipedes. The oldest-known tracks of these ancient arthropods were found in fossilized sediments in northern England. They suggest that the earliest dry-land pioneers did not come from the sea, but from fresh water. The first tetrapods (vertebrates with four limbs), including amphibians and reptiles, did not evolve until nearly 100 million years later.

Coelacanth

The coelacanth belongs to a group of lobe-finned fishes that had been presumed extinct since the end of the Cretaceous period, about 65 million years ago. Then a living specimen caught in the Indian Ocean in 1938 was identified by a South African scientist. Local fishermen were astounded at the interest in this find. They had apparently been catching it for years but discarding it because it was not good to eat. Since this first identification, about 200 specimens have been caught off the Comoros Islands. To ensure the species' survival, fisherman are now urged to release any coelacanths they catch.

The coelacanth belongs to the same group of fishes that evolved into amphibians.

500 million years ago
Plants begin to colonize the land.

505

460-440 million years ago
Invertebrates move from fresh water onto land. Myriapods and spiders are the earliest types found in the fossil record.

ORDOVICIAN

438

SILURIAN

377 million years ago
***Panderichthys*, a likely precursor of true amphibians, appears.** It is a fish with amphibian-like skull and ribs and paired muscular fins that could have been the starting point for the evolution of legs.

408

DEVONIAN

363 million years ago
Invertebrates diversify. Flightless insects evolve.

The first amphibians evolve from a group of lobe-finned freshwater fishes called the Rhipidistians. They include *Acanthostega*, which was 60 cm (2 ft) long and had limbs adapted for scrambling through dense swamp vegetation.

KEY TERMS

- **Amphibians**
These tetrapods require water for part of their life cycle. They lay eggs in water, and their larvae are aquatic and breathe using gills. The larvae metamorphose into land-dwelling adults that breathe using lungs. Amphibians were the first land-dwelling vertebrates.
- **Arthropods**
These invertebrates have jointed limbs and a hard protective and supportive outer skeleton. Crustaceans, insects, arachnids, millipedes and centipedes (myriapods) are all examples of arthropods.
- **Lobe-finned fish**
This group of fish with fleshy fins gave rise to tetrapods. Lungfish and coelacanths are living examples.
- **Reptiles**
These were the first vertebrates to live entirely on land. Adaptations to land-dwelling include watertight skin and air-breathing lungs.
- **Tetrapods**
These are vertebrates with four limbs. All amphibians, reptiles, birds, and mammals are tetrapods. Their limbs are all based on the same five-digit pattern – pentadactyl limbs (Greek for five fingers).

First steps These 460 million-year-old fossilized tracks from England's Lake District are the earliest evidence of animal life on land.

ADAPTING TO LIFE ON LAND

The land was an untapped source of food, but in order to exploit this, the first land colonizers had to overcome a number of problems and dangers, including

- **Water loss** – amphibians need to keep their skin moist to avoid drying out.
- **Reproduction** – fish and amphibians need an aquatic environment to lay eggs and to support their young.
- The **full force of gravity** – in water, animals do not have to carry their whole weight; in air they do.

The first land-dwellers developed different strategies to cope with these factors. Arthropods developed a hard exoskeleton that protected them from drying out and supported their weight.

Amphibians evolved lungs and limbs so that they could breathe and move on land. They still returned to water to breed. Reptiles' scales and self-contained eggs, which provided a sealed aquatic environment for the developing fetus, allowed them to become the first entirely terrestrial vertebrates.

FACT

Flood plains along the edges of rivers were the first areas of land to be colonized by plants.

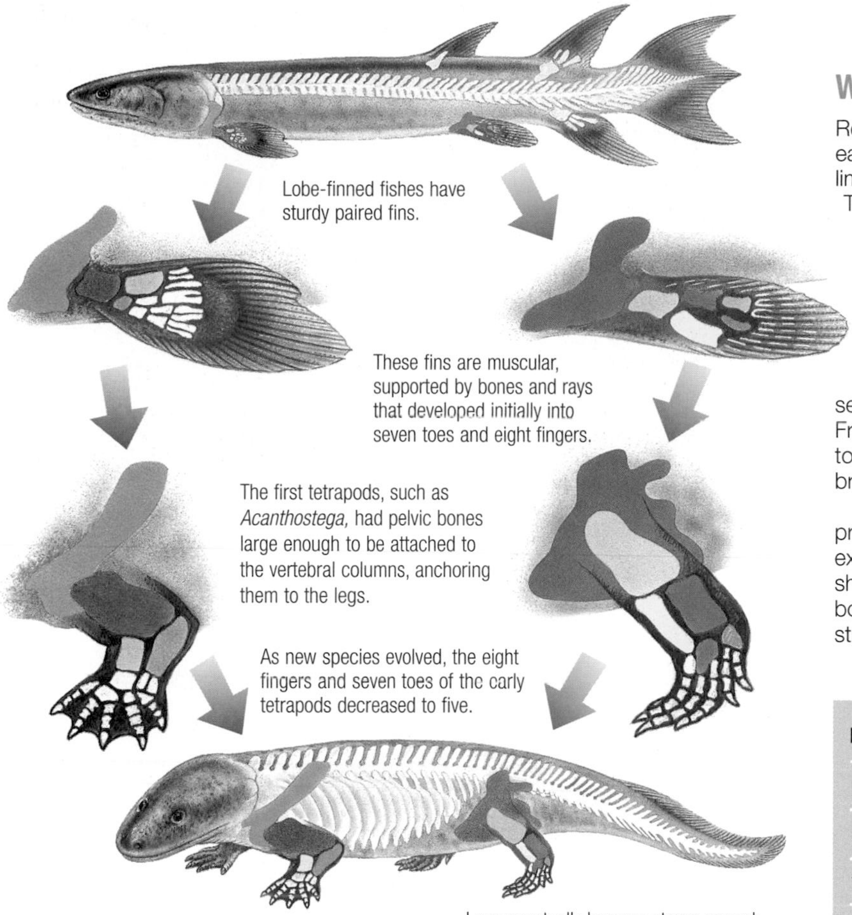

Lobe-finned fishes have sturdy paired fins.
These fins are muscular, supported by bones and rays that developed initially into seven toes and eight fingers.
The first tetrapods, such as *Acanthostega,* had pelvic bones large enough to be attached to the vertebral columns, anchoring them to the legs.
As new species evolved, the eight fingers and seven toes of the early tetrapods decreased to five.
Legs eventually became strong enough for true walking.

WHY DID LEGS EVOLVE?

Recent work on Devonian *Acanthostega*, one of the earliest tetrapods, indicates that the development of four limbs was not initially an adaptation for walking on land. These creatures were still better adapted for life in water than for life on dry land. They lived in bayou-like swamps and breathed like fish. Their spine and ribs could not support their internal organs, and their four limbs were too weak to walk with.

So what purpose did the four protolimbs serve? It is thought that they were initially simply a specialized fin, which helped the animal to maneuver under water in search of food through the dead vegetation of the swamps. From these beginnings, their descendants may have started to use their limbs to move briefly onto land, either for breeding or as an escape route from predators.

The narrow-based fins of the lobe-finned fishes were ideal precursors of limbs. The paired fins of *Panderichthys*, for example, were supported by a single bone that joined the shoulder and hip girdles. At the other end were two wrist bones and the rays that supported the fin. This was a much stronger arrangement than that of the ray-finned fish.

Main structural differences between fish and tetrapods.

Fish	Tetrapod
Flexible backbone	More rigid backbone
Thin ribs	Sturdy ribs
Shoulder girdle poorly developed and attached to skull; unable to bear weight.	Well-developed shoulder girdle, separate from skull; weight-bearing.
Pelvic girdle poorly developed; unable to bear weight.	Pelvic girdle well developed; weight-bearing. Pelvis fused to vertebrae.
Limb bones short	Limb bones longer, joints stronger and more flexible.
No digits	Toed and fingered limbs modified for walking, jumping, climbing, flying and grasping.

360 million years ago
Winged insects, including giant dragonflies, appear, as do scorpions, worms and snails. Amphibians diversify into about 20 families.

310 million years ago
The lizardlike *Hylonomus* – found in Nova Scotia – is one of the earliest reptiles. Just 20 cm (8 in.) long, it is an active land animal with strong jaws. Its remains were discovered in hollow trunks, where it may have sheltered or looked for food.

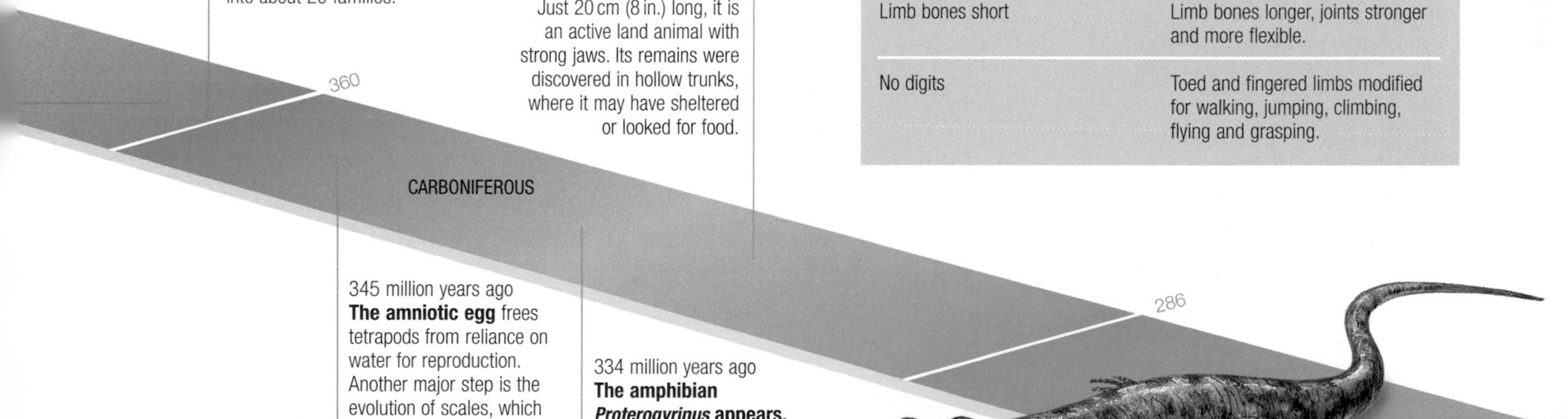

345 million years ago
The amniotic egg frees tetrapods from reliance on water for reproduction. Another major step is the evolution of scales, which decrease water loss through the skin.

334 million years ago
The amphibian *Proterogyrinus* appears. It is large – 1 m (3 ft) long – and walks competently on land. It feeds on fish and land invertebrates and is a reptile ancestor.

Living at the same time, the 25 cm (10 in.) *Eucritta melanolimnites* (literally "the creature from the black lagoon") combines amphibian and reptilian features. It may be capable of walking.

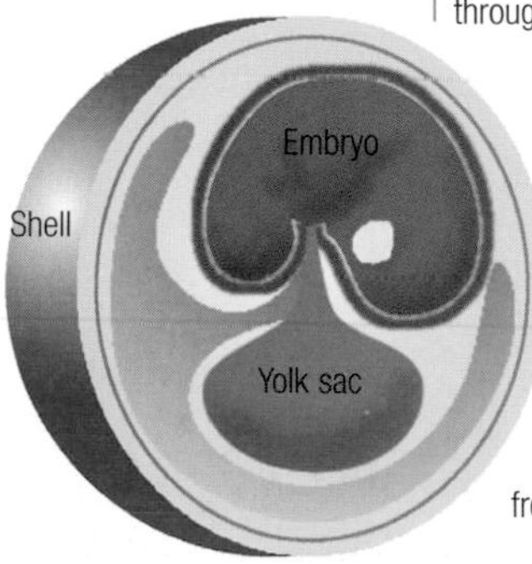

Life preserver
An amniotic egg has an impervious shell, which protects the embryo inside from the environment.

New kind of hunter
Early reptile *Hylonomus* fed on land invertebrates.

see also
52-53 **Ages of life on Earth**
54-55 **Evolution explained**
84-85 **Amphibians**
86-87 **Reptiles**

The rise of the dinosaurs

The age of the "terrible lizards"

The first dinosaurs were small two-legged carnivores that lived about 228 million years ago. They later evolved into many different groups, including the herbivorous giants such as Apatosaurus. *The dinosaurs dominated the Earth for 155 million years, making them an extremely successful animal group. If that reign had been 1 month, then by comparison, the time that modern humans have existed would be just 1 minute.*

Nesting and hatching

Dinosaurs, like most reptiles, laid eggs, although a few species with wide pelvises may have given birth to live young. The largest eggs known would have weighed about 10 kg (22 lb); the smallest weighed just 400 g (14 oz). Some dinosaurs, such as the 3.6 m (12 ft) long *Troodon*, nested in colonies. Some protected their eggs until they hatched, and a few may have fed and cared for their young as they grew. Most hatchlings would have been mobile almost from birth and would not have stayed in the nest for any appreciable time.

Eggs in stone Fossilized eggs of the dinosaur *Oviraptor* found in the Gobi Desert.

1 CHASMATOSAURUS
Dinosaur precursor
Chasmatosaurus was one of the first known archosaurs. Resembling a long-legged crocodile, *Chasmatosaurus* was a carnivorous, predominantly water-dwelling creature, although it could walk on land with a lizardlike gait.
Size: 2 m (7 ft) long
Where found: South Africa and China

3 PETEINOSAURUS
This small pterosaur (flying reptile) was one of the first vertebrates to fly, rather than simply glide. Its skeleton was very light and its wings stretched from an elongated finger to its foot. *Peteinosaurus* had small sharp teeth and was probably insectivorous, catching its prey in flight.
Wingspan: 60 cm (2 ft)
Where found: Cene, northern Italy

4 COELOPHYSIS
This dinosaur was a small, slender hunter. Fossil finds have shown evidence of herding and cannibalism.
Size: 0.6-3 m (2-10 ft) long
Where found: Arizona and New Mexico

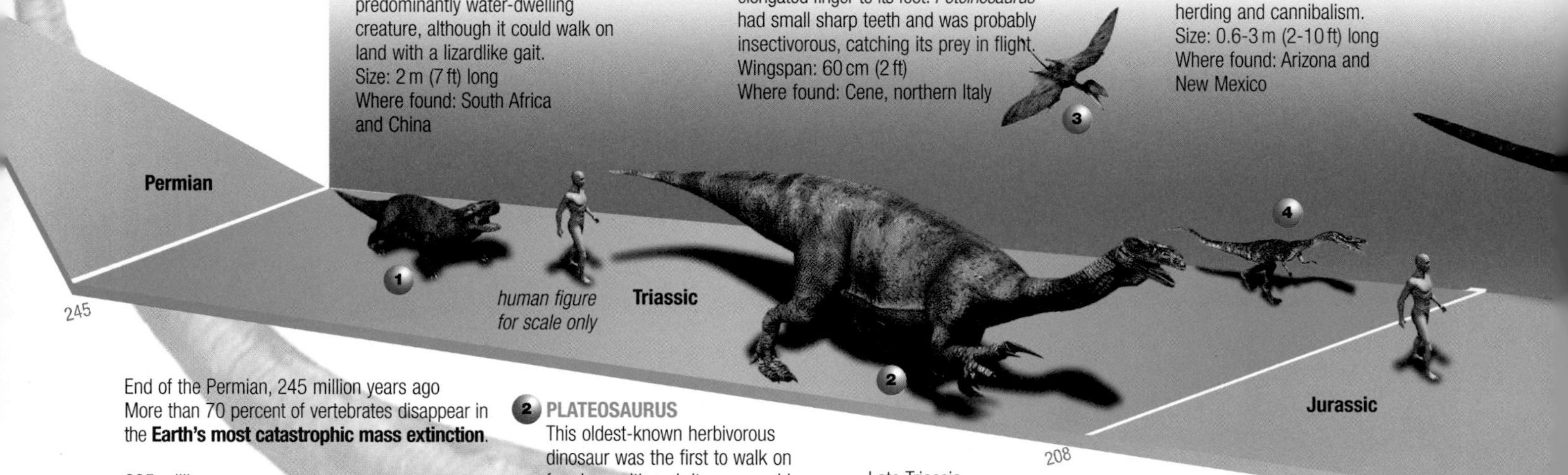

End of the Permian, 245 million years ago
More than 70 percent of vertebrates disappear in the **Earth's most catastrophic mass extinction**.

235 million years ago
Several distinct **reptile groups have evolved**, including the archosaurs ("ruling reptiles").

228 million years ago
The earliest-known dinosaurs, *Eoraptor* and *Herrerasaurus*, **have appeared**.

2 PLATEOSAURUS
This oldest-known herbivorous dinosaur was the first to walk on four legs, although it was capable of rearing up on two. It was also the first dinosaur to weigh over a ton and (with *Coelophysis*) the first known to live in herds.
Size: Up to 11 m (35 ft) long
Where found: Europe

Late Triassic
The **first mammals evolve** from mammal-like reptiles.

Walking tall

The key to the dinosaurs' success lay in an efficient new way of walking. Their immediate ancestors were the meat-eating archosaurs, some of which developed a semisprawling stance. They were able to run for short distances with almost straight legs, much as crocodiles do today. These gave rise to small, two-legged archosaurs, such as *Lagosuchus*; it was from these that the dinosaurs evolved.

Upright advantage The oldest-known dinosaurs, *Eoraptor* and *Herrerasaurus*, were small carnivores and lived about 228 million years ago. Like *Lagosuchus* they walked on two legs, but they had a more upright stance, with straight legs tucked under their bodies. This freed their front legs for other uses such as grasping and clawing. Thus the early dinosaurs had a huge advantage over other reptile groups: The improved stance meant they were quicker, and their legs could support more weight, allowing them to grow bigger.

Back to four legs Later, many of the biggest dinosaurs, such as the sauropods, moved around on four legs because they needed the extra support for their enormous bulk. They were plant eaters, so they did not need to chase after prey or use their front limbs to grasp and tear it up. Some, such as *Plateosaurus*, could rear up on their hind legs to reach food in the treetops or escape quickly if in danger.

Sprawling stance *Hylonomus* first reptile

Semisprawling stance *Chasmatosaurus* archosaur precursor to dinosaurs

Erect stance *Deinonychus* dinosaur predator

Vertebrate family tree
From their origins as amphibians in the late Devonian, land-living vertebrates diversified into many different groups. Some, such as the dinosaurs and plesiosaurs, appeared and after many million years, became extinct. Others, such as mammals, birds, crocodiles and snakes, still survive.

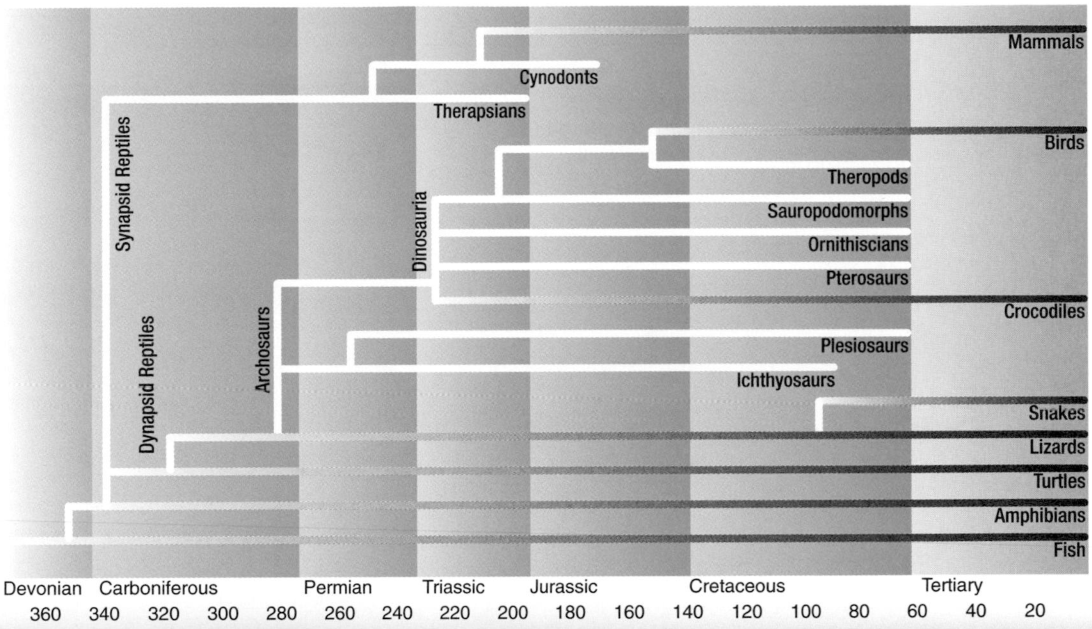

5 RHAMPHORHYNCHUS
Rhamphorhynchus was a common pterosaur of the Jurassic period, with a long tail ending in a diamond-shaped rudder. A fish-eater, it dragged its lower jaw through the water to catch its prey on its sharp teeth.
Wingspan: Up to 1.8 m (6 ft)
Where found: UK, Germany and Tanzania

6 MEGALOSAURUS
This large carnivore was one of the most prevalent predators in Europe during the Jurassic.
Size: 12 m (40 ft) long
Where found: UK

7 APATOSAURUS
More commonly known as *Brontosaurus*, meaning "thunder lizard," *Apatosaurus* was a giant herbivore. It "raked" leaves off trees with its gapped, peglike teeth, and, despite its huge bulk, it could rise up on its hind legs to reach the highest vegetation. It may also have used this ability to crash down on predators such as *Allosaurus*.
Size: Up to 21 m (70 ft) long and weighing up to 33 metric tons.
Where found: North America

8 STEGOSAURUS
The diamond-shaped plates arranged alternately in two rows down *Stegosaurus*' back present something of a mystery. What was their function? They could have been for protection, signaling or temperature regulation. *Stegosaurus* had one of the smallest brains in relation to body size of any dinosaur.
Size: Up to 9 m (30 ft) long.
Where found: US

9 CAMARASAURUS
This large herbivore roamed in herds, possibly making long migrations in search of food. Piles of polished stones preserved in the same rocks as *Camarasaurus* fossil remains suggest that, like some modern birds, *Camarasaurus* swallowed stones to aid the grinding of tough vegetable foods in the stomach. Prominent nasal openings on the top of the head may also have acted as a cooling device for the brain.
Size: Up to 18 m (59 ft) long
Where found: North America

10 COMPSOGNATHUS
The smallest of the dinosaurs, *Compsognathus* was a swift, two-legged hunter. It had hollow bones and probably weighed only about 3.6 kg (8 lb). Its long tail would have helped balance while running.
Size: 60 cm (2 ft) long
Where found: Germany and France

Compsognathus (shown here at actual size)

see also
52-53 **Ages of life on Earth**
54-55 **Evolution explained**
86-87 **Reptiles**

The Cretaceous period saw the emergence of new types of dinosaur, such as the three-horned Triceratops. *By the late Cretaceous, however, the dinosaurs' supremacy was waning, and their fate was finally sealed when an ecological disaster culminated in mass extinction.*

ARCHAEOPTERYX
Fossils of *Archaeopteryx,* the world's first bird, were found preserved in exceptional detail in the limestone of Solnhofen, Germany. They show an animal the size of a crow with both dinosaur and bird features, and they provide the clearest evidence that birds evolved from dinosaurs. *Archaeopteryx* – meaning "ancient wing" – had teeth, bony tails and claws on their wings (dinosaur features), as well as wishbones and feathers (birdlike features).

Taking to the air

The ability to glide evolved for reptiles five separate times between the Permian and the Jurassic, but only one group, the pterosaurs, were capable of sustained flight achieved by flapping their wings.

Pterosaur aeronautics Pterosaurs flew on wings formed from flaps of flexible skin, like those of bats. Like dinosaurs, the pterosaurs evolved into a wide range of sizes. The smallest were no bigger than pigeons, whereas the largest, the giant *Quetzalcoatlus* of the late Cretaceous period, had a wingspan of approximately 12 m (40 ft). Also like the dinosaurs, pterosaurs declined during the late Cretaceous, and none survived the mass extinction 65 million years ago.

Last link Birds did not evolve from the earlier flying or gliding reptiles. The fossil record strongly points toward them evolving from small carnivorous dinosaurs in the late Jurassic and coexisting with pterosaurs for 70 million years. Most scientists believe that modern birds are the closest living link to the dinosaurs.

11 POLACANTHUS
Polacanthus was a squat, armored herbivore related to the ankylosaurs and stegosaurs and characterized by bony spikes on its flanks. It has been difficult to reconstruct the appearance of *Polacanthus* because only its hind legs and some body armor have ever been found. Some experts believe it is actually the same animal as *Hylaeosaurus*.
Size: 4 m (13 ft) long
Where found: UK

12 IGUANODON
Iguanodon was bipedal but probably also walked on all fours. One of its characteristic features was a thumb spike, which it may have used as a weapon in self-defense or in mating disputes.
Size: Up to 10 m (33 ft) long
Where found: UK, Europe, and the US

13 DEINONYCHUS
A fast and agile predator, *Deinonychus* was built to hunt and kill. It was two-legged and lightweight, with shearing teeth that curved backward. Its powerful hind legs were each armed with a large, sharp, slashing claw on its second toe – *Deinonychus* means "terrible claw." Its long tail, stiffened with bony rods, helped it maintain its balance when attacking its prey.
Size: 3-4 m (10-13 ft) long
Where found: North America

14 PTERODACTYLUS
With its long neck, short tail and much elongated fourth finger, which supported its wing, *Pterodactylus* was a typical Cretaceous pterosaur. It preyed predominantly on fish and had long, narrow jaws and sharp teeth.
Wingspan: up to 75 cm (2 ft 5 in.)
Where found: Africa, Europe, and the UK

15 ICHTHYOSAUR
Ichthyosaurs were the reptile equivalent of dolphins. They hunted fish and free-swimming mollusks, such as ammonites and belemnites. Ichthyosaurs gave birth to live young.
Size: Up to 9 m (30 ft) long
Where found: UK, Europe and North and South America.

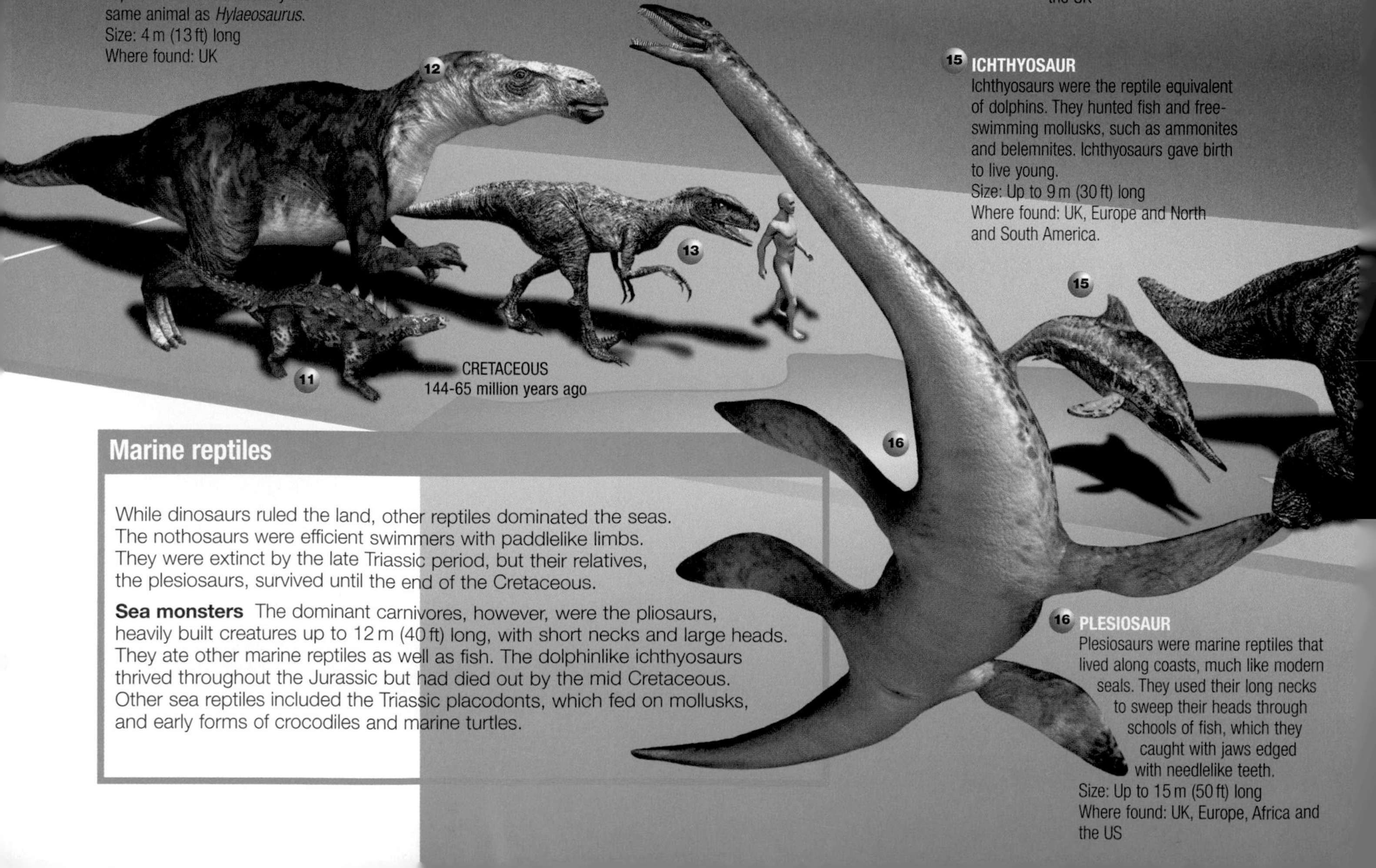

Marine reptiles

While dinosaurs ruled the land, other reptiles dominated the seas. The nothosaurs were efficient swimmers with paddlelike limbs. They were extinct by the late Triassic period, but their relatives, the plesiosaurs, survived until the end of the Cretaceous.

Sea monsters The dominant carnivores, however, were the pliosaurs, heavily built creatures up to 12 m (40 ft) long, with short necks and large heads. They ate other marine reptiles as well as fish. The dolphinlike ichthyosaurs thrived throughout the Jurassic but had died out by the mid Cretaceous. Other sea reptiles included the Triassic placodonts, which fed on mollusks, and early forms of crocodiles and marine turtles.

16 PLESIOSAUR
Plesiosaurs were marine reptiles that lived along coasts, much like modern seals. They used their long necks to sweep their heads through schools of fish, which they caught with jaws edged with needlelike teeth.
Size: Up to 15 m (50 ft) long
Where found: UK, Europe, Africa and the US

21 QUETZALCOATLUS
The largest flying creature of all time, *Quetzalcoatlus* was one of the last pterosaurs, and it became extinct at the end of the Cretaceous period. *Quetzalcoatlus* probably used its vast wings to glide long distances on rising heat. Some scientists believe it ate carrion, using its long neck and toothless jaws to probe deep inside carcasses. Others think it fed on fish or shellfish.
Wingspan: 12 m (40 ft)
Where found: US

19 SAUROLOPHUS
One of the larger duck-billed dinosaurs, *Saurolophus* had a bony crest and an inflatable bag of skin on its snout, which it used to produce bellowing sounds. A communal herbivore, *Saurolophus* may have used alarm calls to alert the herd to the presence of predators.
Size: 9-12 m (30-40 ft) long
Where found: North America and Asia

20 TYRANNOSAURUS REX
T. rex was one of the largest known carnivorous dinosaurs and by far the biggest still in existence at the end of the Cretaceous period. *Tyrannosaurus rex* means "king of the tyrant reptiles," an apt description of a beast with a 1.5 m (5 ft) long head and a mouth filled with 15 cm (6 in.) long serrated teeth. *T. rex* also had a powerful tail and hind limbs, but its forelimbs were tiny.
Size: 13 m (43 ft) long
Where found: US

WHY DID THE DINOSAURS DIE OUT?

The dinosaurs were one group among many that perished in a mass extinction 65 million years ago. The cause of this extinction has been the subject of much debate.

Two theories are currently favored.

Meteorite impact There is strong evidence that a large meteorite hit the Earth near what today is the Yucatán Peninsula of Mexico. Geologists estimate that the meteorite was about 10 km (6 miles) across and that it shattered and melted the Earth's crust to a depth of almost 30 km (20 miles).

The effects of the impact would have been catastrophic, throwing up millions of metric tons of dust into the atmosphere, blocking out the sun, and drastically reducing temperatures around the globe. Another consequence would have been the release of sulfur into the atmosphere. This would have combined with water vapor to create corrosive acid rain, turning the world's seas and oceans into acid baths.

Volcanic activity The effect of the meteorite impact was compounded by a simultaneous event happening on the other side of the world in what is now India. For 2 to 3 million years at the end of the Cretaceous and the beginning of the Tertiary, this large area was subject to violent volcanic activity. Carbon dioxide and volcanic dust released by the volcanism would also have caused acid rain and adversely affected the climate. In addition, there is a theory that the element selenium, released by the volcanoes, was poisonous to dinosaurs.

Who survived and why? There seems to be little pattern to the species that died out and those that survived. Dinosaurs succumbed, but crocodiles and many other reptiles survived; birds and marsupial mammals suffered, but placental mammals escaped; simple plants coped better than flowering plants.

One factor is noticeable, however: All land creatures weighing more than about 25 kg (55 lb) were wiped out. The reasons for this are unclear but the currently favored theory is that the warm-blooded, nocturnal, and often burrow-dwelling mammals – which also happened to be small – were better equipped for survival in the cooled climatic conditions of the time than many other groups, particularly large, possibly cold-blooded dinosaurs, who could not control their body temperature as effectively as the mammals.

17 TRICERATOPS
The herbivorous *Triceratops* was one of the last dinosaurs to live on Earth. It had a bony frill on the skull to intimidate predators and protect its neck region, and three facial horns – the name *Triceratops* means "three-horn face."
Size: Up to 9 m (30 ft) long
Where found: US

18 STEGOCERAS
Stegoceras had a thick domed skull, suggesting that head-butting was an important part of its lifestyle, either as defense or more likely as a mating display ritual. This herbivore probably lived in herds.
Size: 2 m (6 ft 6 in.) long
Where found: North America

see also
24-25 **Comets and meteorites**
32-33 **Volcanoes**
88-95 **Birds**

It is hard to pinpoint when mammals evolved because mammalian characteristics, such as fur and lactation, are not easily fossilized and so are lost to the fossil record. Mammalian teeth patterns, however, have been found in some reptile fossils from the late Permian. Called mammal-like reptiles, it is likely that these were the ancestors of true mammals. When the dinosaurs became extinct, mammals moved into the niches they had left vacant.

WHY DID MAMMALS FLOURISH?

Tens of thousands of mammal species evolved in the 65 million years after the Cretaceous/Tertiary mass extinction. A large number of these were herbivores, which grazed on the flowering plants, particularly grasses, which were also spreading and diversifying. Warm-bloodedness gave the mammals a particular advantage: They could regulate their own body temperature and therefore thrive in a wide range of temperatures and environments. They also had the intelligence to survive and flourish in rapidly changing conditions. The mammals did not displace the dinosaurs, they simply diversified to fill the niches left empty after their extinction.

280-245 million years ago
Mammal-like reptiles appear. They have mammalian features, such as incisors, canines and molars.

230 million years ago
Cynodonts, such as *Thrinaxodon*, **appear**.

First true mammals appear. All known forms at this time are shrew-sized insectivores.

208-144 million years ago
Mammals remain small, nocturnal creatures throughout the Jurassic, evolving such attributes as warm-bloodedness, giving birth to live young and feeding their young on milk.

100-75 million years ago
Marsupial mammals appear in South America, then spread across the entire supercontinent of Gondwanaland and consisting of Australia, Antarctica, India, Africa and South America.

100 million years ago
Monotreme mammals appear in Australia.

Late Jurassic
Multituberculate mammals appear.

PERMIAN 245 TRIASSIC 208 JURASSIC 144 CRETACEOUS

MEGAZOSTRODON
This tiny creature, one of the earliest-known mammals, was just 13 cm (5 in.) long. It fed on insects and was probably nocturnal. *Megazostrodon* may have laid eggs, like today's platypuses and echidnas. It lived from the late Triassic until the early Jurassic.

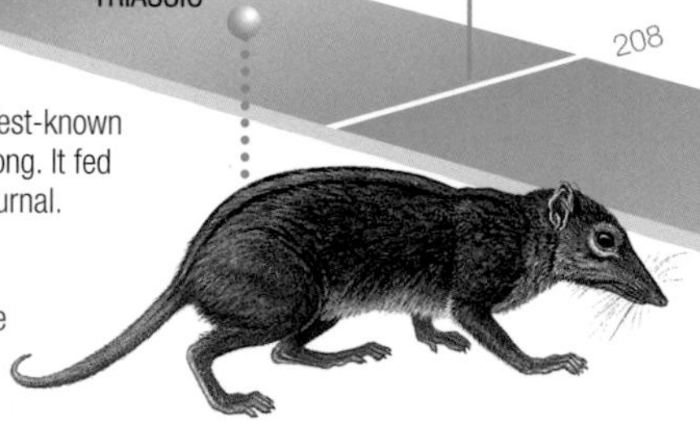

Returning to the sea

Whales, dolphins and porpoises are the only mammals completely adapted to living their entire lives in the sea, yet they evolved from land-dwelling ancestors.

There is evidence, based on its teeth, that the earliest-known whale, the 54-million-year-old *Pakicetus*, descended from a flesh-eating ancestor of hoofed mammals, such as *Pachyaena*. The early whales were not well adapted to aquatic living and probably spent a lot of time on land, moving around on paddle-shaped limbs. Today's whales, including the baleen whales, evolved from the primitive toothed whales, such as *Pakicetus*.

Another group of mammals that took to life in the sea was the sirenians, or sea cows. Unlike whales, the sirenians are herbivores. DNA studies indicate that they share an ancestor with elephants.

The four kinds of mammals

By the end of the Cretaceous, four mammal groups existed.

1. **Placentals** Mammals that produce fully developed live young nurtured on milk. Currently the largest group.
2. **Marsupials** Mammals that produce immature young, generally nurtured in a pouch after birth.
3. **Monotremes** Egg-laying mammals that probably evolved completely separately from other mammals. They were mostly confined to Australia, although some fossils have also been found in South America. The duck-billed platypus and the echidna are modern examples.
4. **Multituberculates** Rodentlike herbivores so called because their teeth had ridges (tubercles) on the biting surface. Like marsupials, they produced immature young.

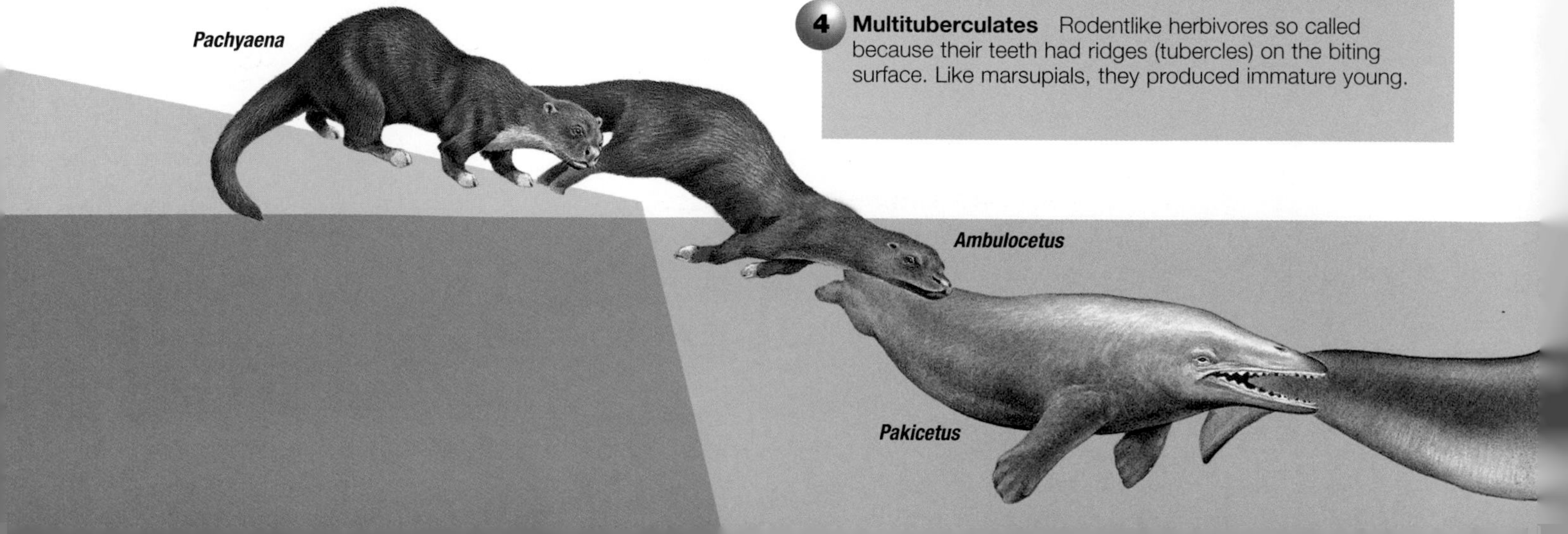

INDRICOTHERIUM
Indricotherium was the largest land mammal that ever lived. At 8 m (26 ft) long, it dwarfed even the greatest mammoths. It is an ancestor of the rhinoceros and weighed an estimated 33.5 metric tons. It had a flexible upper lip that enabled it to feed on leaves much like a modern giraffe.

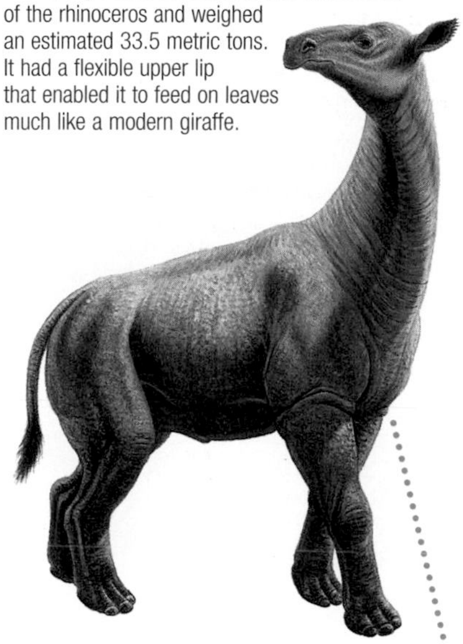

How elephants evolved

Today, there are two varieties of elephant, the African and Indian, but since elephants first appeared, more than 160 species have existed. They originated in North Africa in the Eocene period. The earliest types, such as *Moeritherium*, were pig-sized and looked very little like their modern counterparts, with no trunk or tusks. These features evolved in the Miocene period as adaptations to help the animals to reach food and later became important in communication. Elephants became larger through the Miocene and Pliocene periods, probably as a protection from predators. By the start of the Pleistocene period, some had surpassed even today's African elephant in size. The steppe mammoth (*Mammathus trogontherii*) was 4.6 m (15 ft) tall at the shoulder. Elephants existed in Europe, and the Americas, as well as in Africa and Asia.

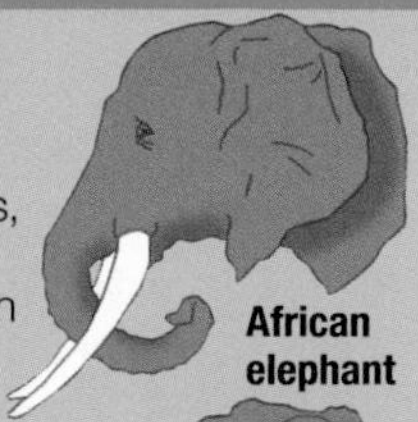

African elephant

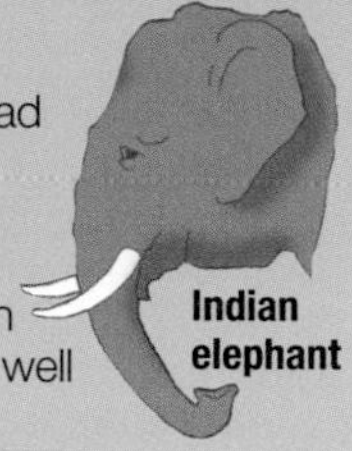

Indian elephant

AMEBELODON
Standing 3 m (10 ft) tall, *Amebelodon* had two adjacent flattened tusks projecting 1 m (3 ft) beyond its lower jaw, forming a shovel-like cutting edge. It probably used this, along with its trunk, to gouge out and grab hold of water plants, its main food, from river bottoms. It lived in North America.

SMILODON
The archetypal "saber-toothed" cat, *Smilodon* was a powerfully built predator with 18 cm (7 in.) long serrated canine teeth. *Smilodon*'s jaw could open 120 degrees to accommodate driving these dagger-like teeth into its prey. It lived in North and South America.

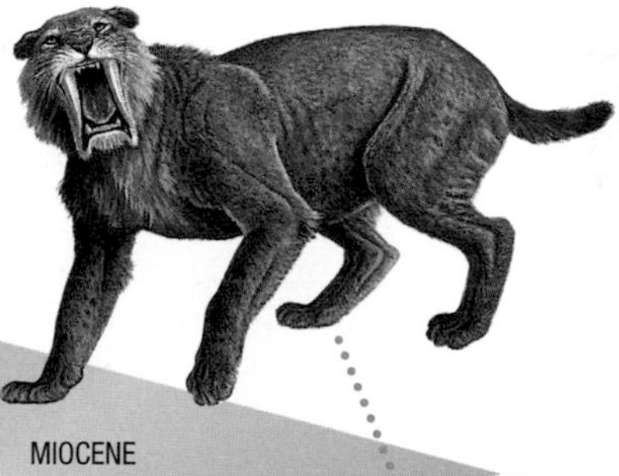

70 million years ago **Placental mammals evolve** in Asia.

65 million years ago **Mass extinction brings the end of the dinosaurs** and many other animal groups.

57-34 million years ago **Whales, sea cows, horses, camels, primates, ruminants, rodents and elephants appear.** Australia and South America evolve many new marsupial forms.

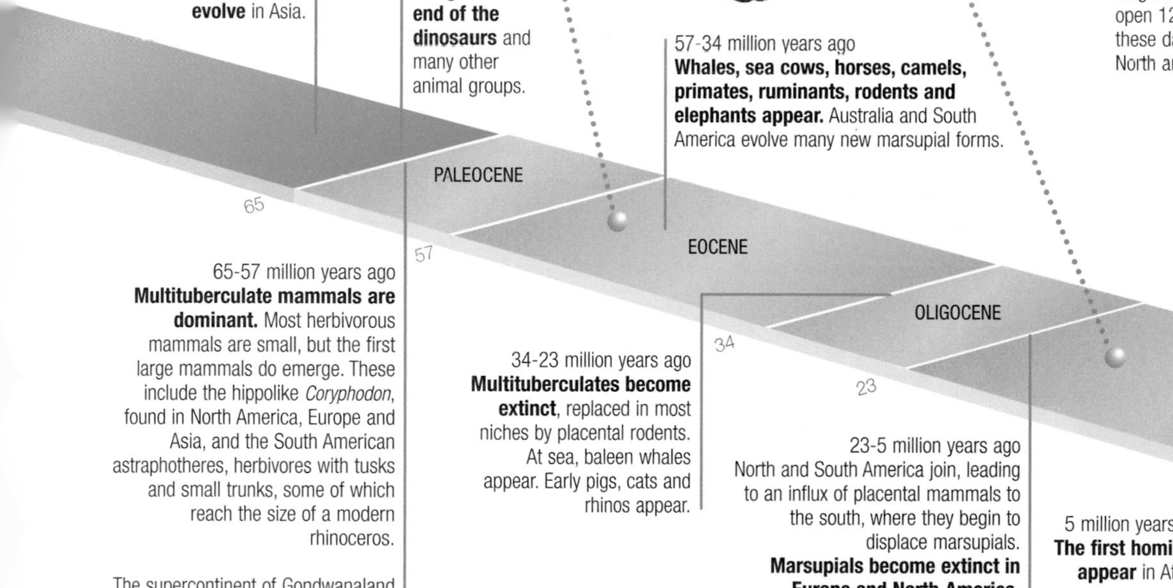

65-57 million years ago **Multituberculate mammals are dominant.** Most herbivorous mammals are small, but the first large mammals do emerge. These include the hippolike *Coryphodon*, found in North America, Europe and Asia, and the South American astraphotheres, herbivores with tusks and small trunks, some of which reach the size of a modern rhinoceros.

The supercontinent of Gondwanaland begins to break up.

34-23 million years ago **Multituberculates become extinct**, replaced in most niches by placental rodents. At sea, baleen whales appear. Early pigs, cats and rhinos appear.

23-5 million years ago North and South America join, leading to an influx of placental mammals to the south, where they begin to displace marsupials. **Marsupials become extinct in Europe and North America.**

Worldwide, grasslands spread, leading to the evolution of new, faster-running species in many mammal families.

5 million years ago **The first hominids appear** in Africa.

1.8 million years ago ***Homo habilis***, the first known member of genus *Homo*, appears.

120 000 years ago **Modern humans emerge.**

Minke whale (*Balaenoptera acutorostrata*)

Aetiocetus

see also

52-53 **Ages of life on Earth**
54-55 **Evolution explained**
98-103 **Mammals**
106-9 **Human evolution**

With more than 1.5 million named species, the animal kingdom is the largest and most diverse group of living things on Earth. More than a million of these are insects. Only multicellular organisms are now defined as belonging to the animal kingdom, but there is also a host of one-celled organisms, the protozoa, that share many animal features.

WHAT IS AN ANIMAL?

All animals, like all plants, have cells with nuclei. Animals generally differ from plants in that they:

- **are mobile** during some part of their life cycle.
- **cannot manufacture their own food** but need to consume organic matter produced by other living things.
- **have cells** without rigid cell walls.
- **have sensory organs** and some sort of nervous system with a central coordinating point (the brain) to control movements and body functions.
- **do not have** specific growing points; growth takes place throughout the body and generally ceases at adulthood.

How cells arrange themselves

The simplest multicellular animals – the sponges – are little more than collections of individual cells joined randomly together. Liquidize a sponge and eventually it will recover, because its cells simply rearrange themselves. Sponges do have specialized cells, but these do not combine to form specific organized structures. In all other animals, cells arrange themselves in more complex ways to form tissues and organs.

Double bud

Jellyfishes, hydras and sea anemones are some of the simplest animals with specialized structures. As embryos, they consist of two layers: an outer layer from which the outer body wall forms and an inner layer from which specific organs, such as the stomach, develop. This development from two layers has led to them being called diploblastic animals (from the Greek, meaning "double bud").

Triple bud

All other animals, from flatworms to humans, are triploblastic ("triple bud"), with three layers as embryos. The additional middle layer develops into complex organs and organ systems.

Simplest structure Sponges have no organs

All creatures great and small
Animals have colonized virtually every environment on Earth, from mountain peaks to the depths of the oceans. This has led to the evolution of an incredible variety of body shapes and life strategies to cope with the conditions those environments impose.

FACT The longest-known worm is the boot-lace worm *(Lineus longissimus)*. A specimen found in 1864 was more than 55 m (180 ft) long.

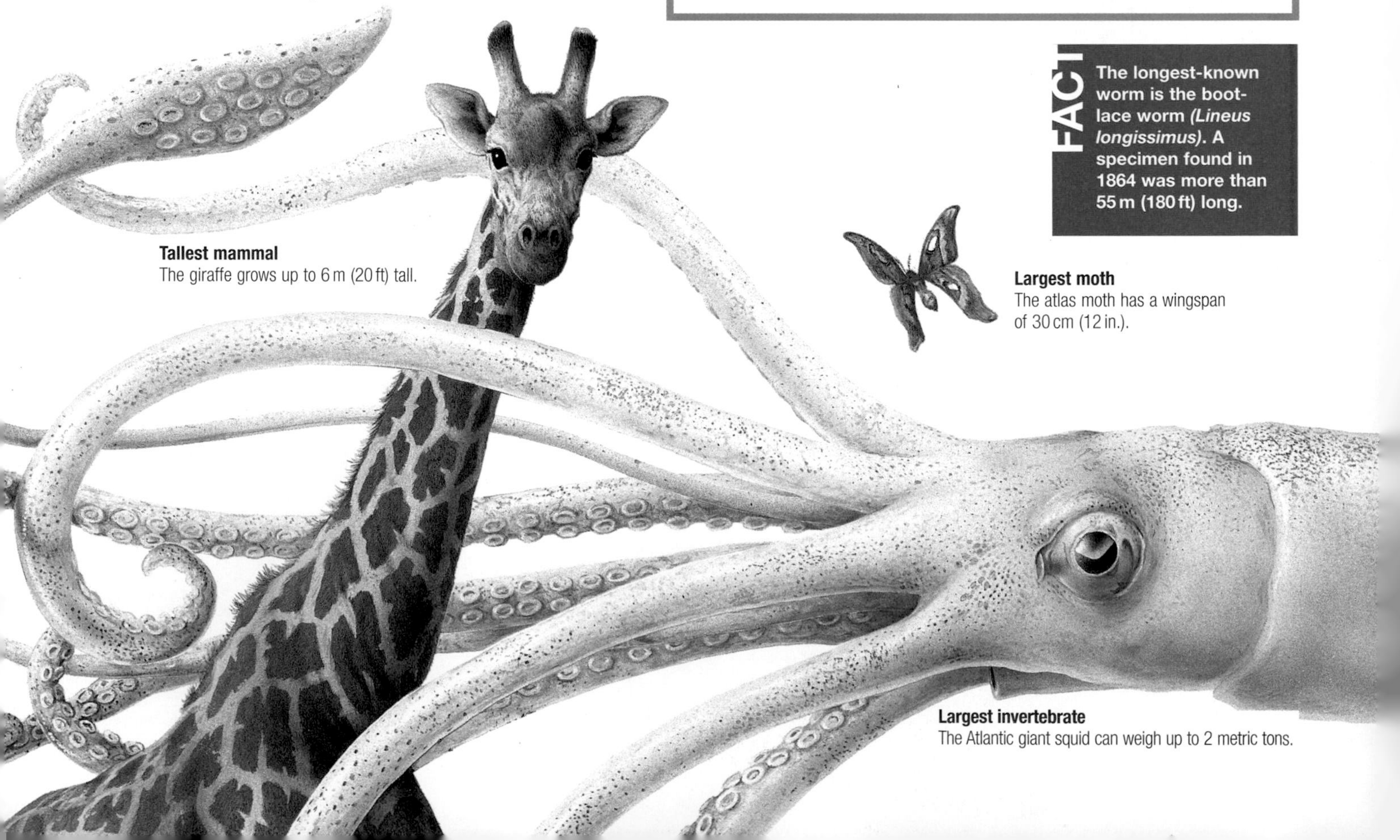

Tallest mammal
The giraffe grows up to 6 m (20 ft) tall.

Largest moth
The atlas moth has a wingspan of 30 cm (12 in.).

Largest invertebrate
The Atlantic giant squid can weigh up to 2 metric tons.

Classification of animal life Taxonomists classify all living things by placing them into a hierarchy of groups based on shared characteristics, such as the possession of a backbone or the suckling of young. This diagram takes you through the classification of a tiger from the largest group, Phylum, down to the smallest, Species.

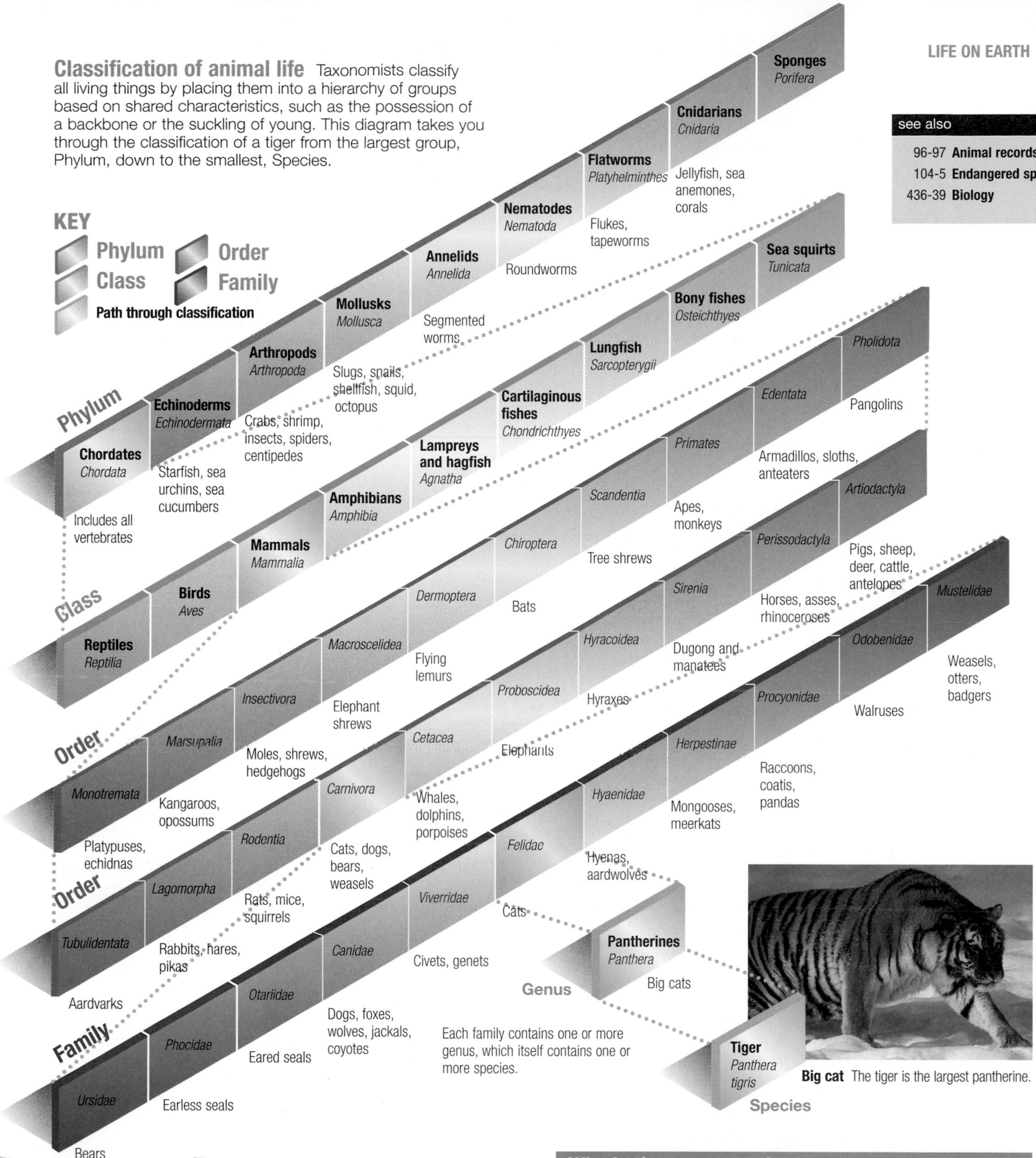

Big cat The tiger is the largest pantherine.

see also
96-97 **Animal records**
104-5 **Endangered species**
436-39 **Biology**

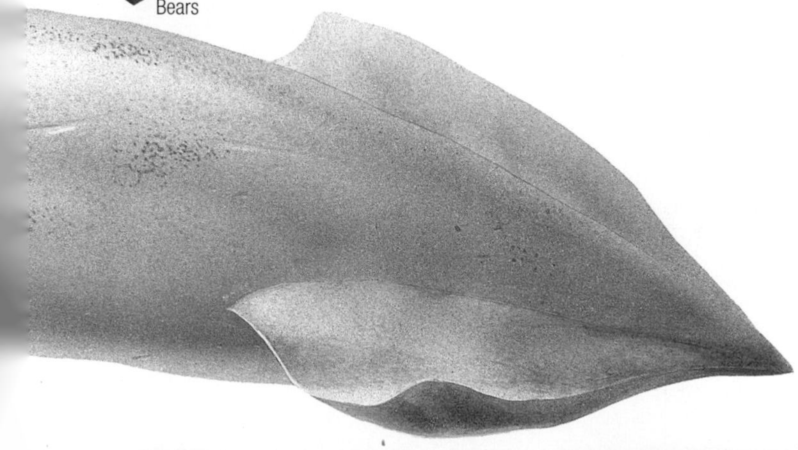

Why Latin names are important

Puma, cougar and mountain lion are three common names for one animal, and that is only in one language. The potential for confusion is limitless. In the 18th century, a Swedish doctor and naturalist, Carolus Linnaeus, established a naming system to avoid such confusion. His system gives every living organism (not just animals) a unique two-word name in Latin. The first name placed it in a group, or genus, of similar organisms, for example, *Homo*. The second designated its species, for example, *sapiens*. More than 200 years later, Linnaeus's naming system is still in use.

Mollusks and arthropods

Two branches of the invertebrate family tree

Mollusks and arthropods are two major groups of invertebrates, animals without backbones. Invertebrates comprise 95 percent of all animal species. All are soft-bodied but some have a hard outer skeleton, called an exoskeleton, which serves as both an anchor point for muscles and as protection for the rest of the body.

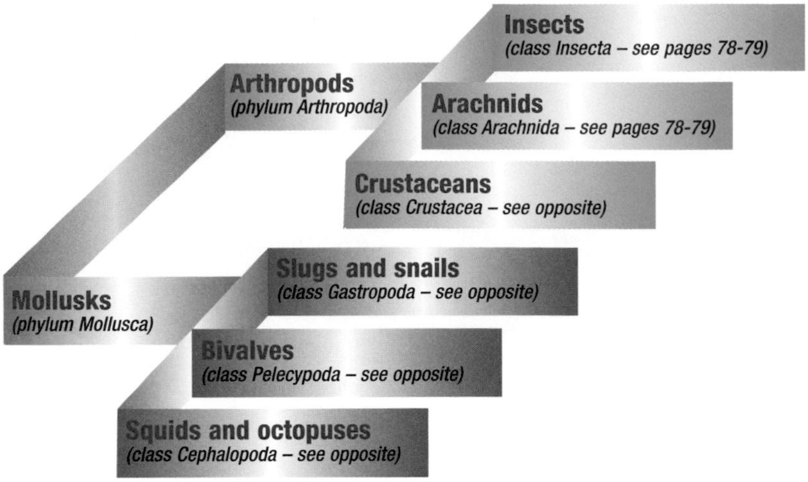

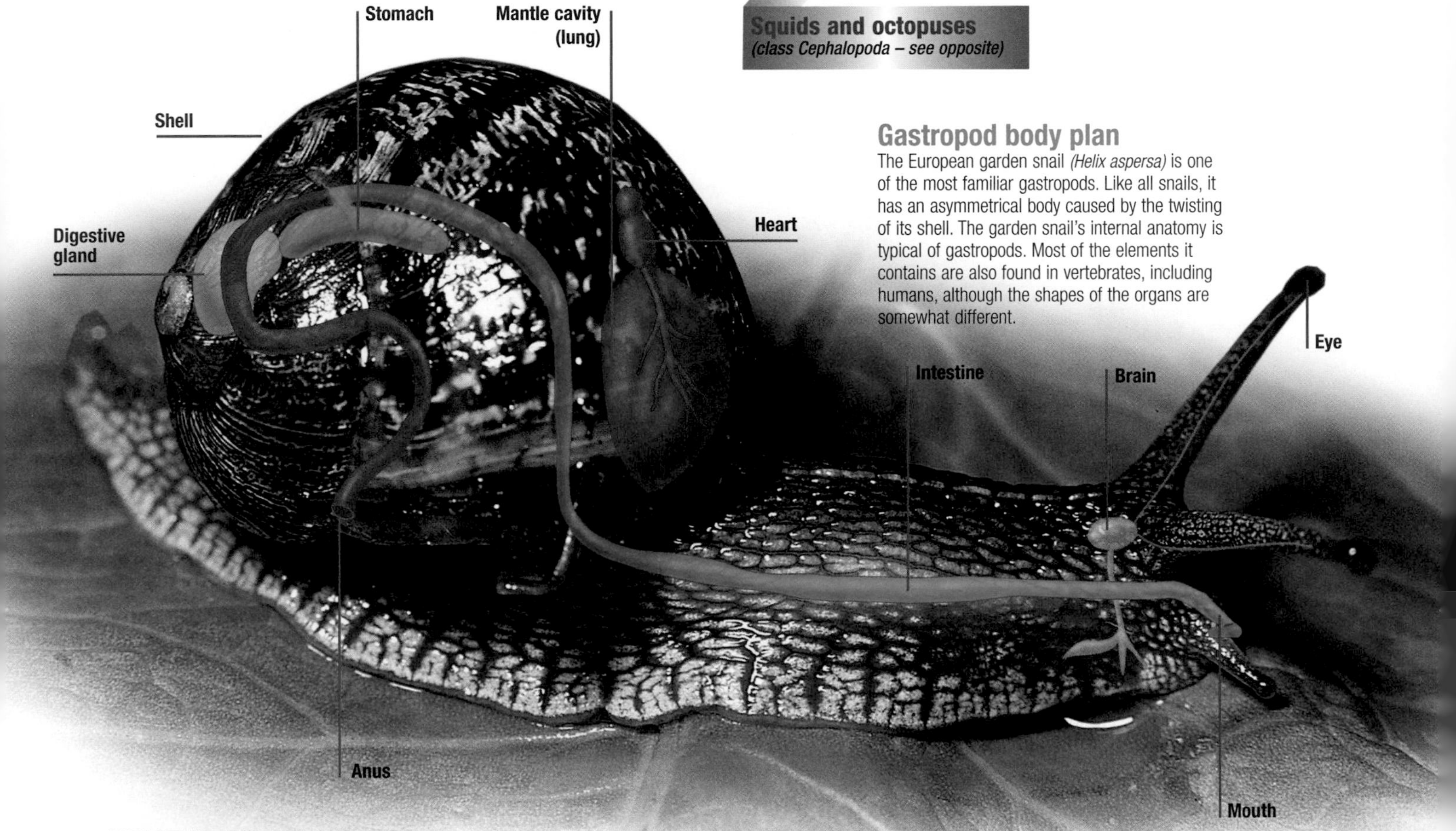

Gastropod body plan

The European garden snail *(Helix aspersa)* is one of the most familiar gastropods. Like all snails, it has an asymmetrical body caused by the twisting of its shell. The garden snail's internal anatomy is typical of gastropods. Most of the elements it contains are also found in vertebrates, including humans, although the shapes of the organs are somewhat different.

WHAT IS AN ARTHROPOD?

Body shell All arthropods have a hard, jointed outer skeleton usually made of chitin – a fibrous organic compound.

- Arthropod means "jointed foot." Arthropods have multiple pairs of flexible, **jointed legs**.
- They have **segmented bodies**, encased in a hard outer skeleton called the cuticle or exoskeleton.
- In order to grow, they **periodically shed and replace their exoskeletons**. This process is called ecdysis.

WHAT IS A MOLLUSK?

- Mollusks are **soft-bodied invertebrates**, but many are covered by a hard shell generated by a fold of skin called the mantle. Squids, octopuses and cuttlefish have some hard internal structures, such as cuttlebone.
- Mollusks are **cold-blooded and produce eggs**.
- The body of a mollusk is made of **three parts**: the head; the central mass containing the vital organs, such as the stomach; and a muscular foot or other means of locomotion.
- Most mollusks **live in the sea**, but a few live in fresh water, and the majority of slugs and snails live on land.

SLUGS AND SNAILS

Gastropods
About 50 000 species

Where they live:
Sea water, fresh water and damp environments on land

Key features:

- Land snails and slugs have a flat, muscular foot on which they glide across the ground – the name gastropod means "belly-footed." In sea-living gastropods, the foot is often smaller.
- Snails have a single shell in a spiral or semispiral form. Slugs and sea slugs (or nudibranchs) have no shell.
- Most land snails and some freshwater ones have eyes on stalks.

Species:
Common limpet *(Patella vulgata)*
Common periwinkle *(Littorina littorea)*
Gray slug *(Lireak maximus)*
Four-colored sea slug *(Chromodoris quadricolor)*

BIVALVES

Pelecypods
About 8000 species

Where they live:
Salt and fresh water

Key features:

- Their bodies are encased by two hinged shells (or valves).
- They feed and breathe by drawing water between the valves and over large gills, which extract both oxygen and food particles.
- Most have separate sexes, but some can be both male and female, alternating between sexes according to surrounding water temperature.
- They have a "foot" that can be pushed out and pulled in to help them to move around.
- Some are free swimming; others burrow in sand, mud or rock.

Species:
Blue mussel *(Mytilus edulis)*
Common cockle *(Cardium edule)*
Common European oyster *(Ostrea edulis)*
Common fingernail clam *(Pisidium casertanum)*
Pilgrim's scallop *(Pecten jacobaeus)*
Shipworm *(Teredo navalis)*
Small razor shell *(Ensis ensis)*
Swan mussel *(Anodonta cygnaea)*
Varied scallop *(Chlamys varius)*

SQUIDS AND OCTOPUSES

Cephalopods
About 750 species

Where they live:
Temperate and tropical seas

Key features:

- Their bodies are soft, with no shell and either eight (octopuses) or ten (cuttlefish and squids) arms, each equipped with rows of suckers.
- Two of the arms of squids and cuttlefish are long, retractile tentacles, used to catch prey. Octopuses use all their arms for this purpose.
- All can move at speed by using a siphon effect to produce a jet of water.
- When frightened, most species release clouds of ink to cover their escape.

Species:
Atlantic giant squid *(Architeuthis dux)*
Chambered nautilus *(Nautilus pompilius)*
Common cuttlefish *(Sepia officinalis)*
Common octopus *(Octopus vulgaris)*
Common squid *(Loligo loligo)*
Dwarf squid *(Alloteuthis subulata)*
Giant octopus *(Octopus apollyon)*
Jewelled squid *(Lycoteuthis diadema)*
North American squid *(Loligo pealei)*
Short-finned squid *(Illex illecebrosus)*

CRABS, SHRIMP, PRAWNS AND LOBSTERS

Crustaceans
About 30 000 species

Where they live:
Salt and fresh water; moist places on land

Key features:

- Their heads have two pairs of antennae.
- They are protected by hard exoskeletons, made of protein and a horny substance called chitin.
- Appendages on each section of exoskeleton have modified to act as feelers, mouth parts, legs and paddle-like swimmerets.
- Pass through a larval stage before growing into their adult form.

Species:
American spiny lobster *(Panulirus argus)*
Brine shrimp *(Artemia sacina)*
Common prawn *(Palaemon serratus)*
Dromid crab *(Dromia vulgaris)*
Edible crab *(Cancer pagurus)*
Goose barnacle *(Lepas anatifera)*
King lobster *(Nephrops norvegicus)*
Krill *(Euphausia superba)*
Mantis shrimp *(Squilla empusa)*
Robber crab *(Birgus latro)*
Rock barnacle *(Balanus balanoides)*
Sapphire shrimp *(Sapphirina fulgens)*
Slipper lobster *(Scyllarus arctus)*

see also
74-75 **Animal kingdom**
96-97 **Animal records**
104-5 **Endangered species**

FACTS AND FIGURES

- The giant clam *(Tridacna gigas)* is the largest bivalve on Earth. Found in coral reefs in the Indian and Pacific Oceans, its shell grows up to 1.4 m (4 ft 6 in.) across.
- The sea snail *Bitium*, found off China, is one of the smallest mollusks, measuring less than 1 mm (1/32 in.) long.
- The heaviest crustacean is the North Atlantic lobster *(Homarus americanus)*. One specimen caught in 1977 weighed over 20 kg (44 lb).
- The Pacific giant octopus *(Octopus dofleini)* is the world's largest, with an average armspan of 2.5 m (8 ft 2 in.).

How pearls form
Oysters and some other mollusks create pearls in response to irritated body tissue caused by a grain of sand or other foreign object. The animal isolates the offending object by covering it with a smooth substance called nacre, creating the pearl.

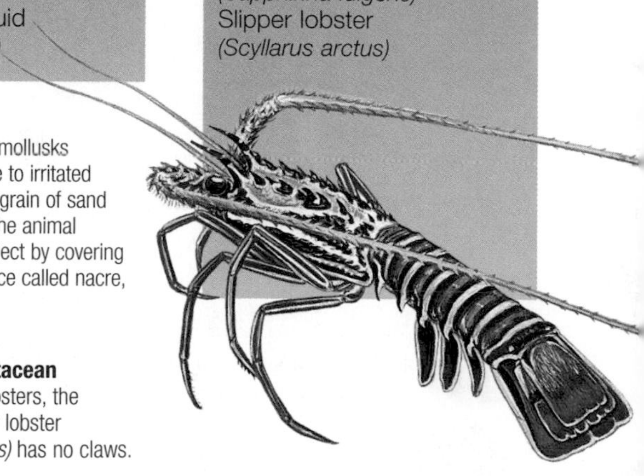

Atypical crustacean
Unlike other lobsters, the American spiny lobster *(Panulirus argus)* has no claws.

Arachnids and insects are arthropods. Like all arthropods, they have bodies that are symmetrical, segmented and covered with a hard exoskeleton. All arachnids and insects breathe air, even those that spend most of their lives under water. Arachnids breathe by means of simple lungs; insects breathe by using a system of air sacs and tubules connected to holes in the exoskeleton.

Sting in the tail
Scorpions catch most of their prey using their pincers alone. The poisonous sting that they carry on their tail is used almost exclusively in self-defense.

WHAT IS AN ARACHNID?

- **Arachnids** include spiders, scorpions, daddy long legs, ticks and mites.
- Their bodies are divided into **two sections**: a fused head and thorax (prosoma) and an abdomen.
- They have **four pairs of jointed legs** attached to the prosoma.
- **Two further pairs of appendages** are attached to the prosoma: the chelicerae, which hold the fangs and are generally adapted for grasping, and the pedipalps, sometimes used as feelers, sometimes equipped (as on a scorpion) with pincers.
- Unlike insects, **arachnids lack antennae and wings**.
- Arachnids are **carnivorous**, except for some plant-eating mites.

SPIDERS

Aranae
About 30 000 species

Where they live:
On land worldwide except the poles; some freshwater habitats

Key features:
- They have eight legs and up to eight eyes.
- They have special silk-producing glands. The silk is forced through structures called spinnerets.
- The female is always larger than the male.

Species:
Ant spider *(Myrmarchne formicaria)*
Black widow *(Latrodectus mactans)*
Cardinal spider *(Tegenaria parietina)*
Common garden spider *(Araneus diadematus)*
European tarantula *(Lycosa tarentula)*
Garden spider *(Araneus diadmatus)*
Goliath bird-eating spider *(Theraphosa leblondi)*
House spider *(Tegenaria domestica)*
Money spider (genus *Dismodicus*, several species)
Sydney funnel-web spider *(Atrax robustus)*
Wasp spider *(Ariope bruennichi)*
Water spider *(Argyroneta aquatica)*
Wolf spider *(Lycosa narbonensis)*
Zebra spider *(Salticus scenicus)*

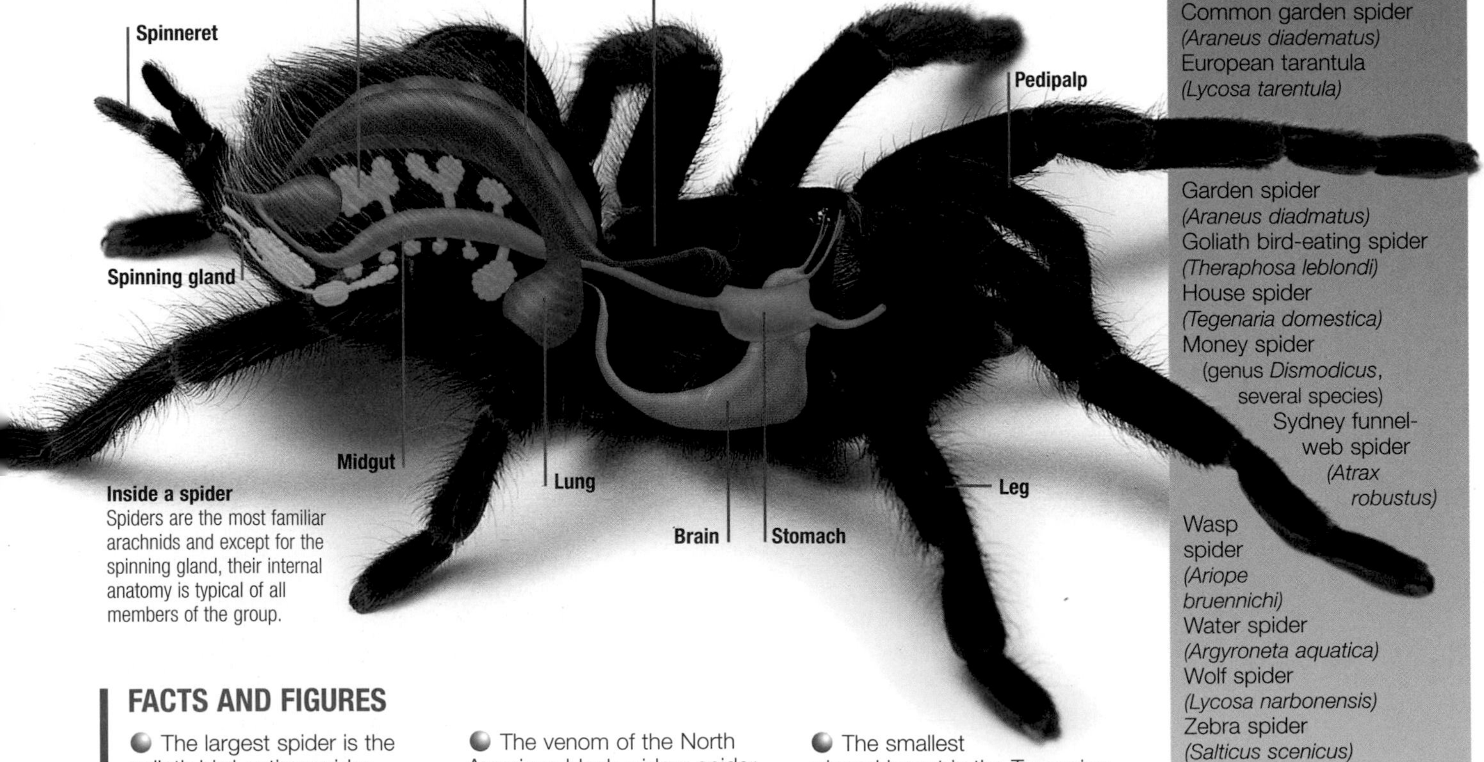

Inside a spider
Spiders are the most familiar arachnids and except for the spinning gland, their internal anatomy is typical of all members of the group.

FACTS AND FIGURES

- The largest spider is the goliath bird-eating spider *(Theraphosa leblondi)* from South America. Its legs can span more than 28 cm (11 in.).
- The insect with the longest recorded life span is the splendor beetle *(Buprestis aurulenta)* at 47 years.
- The venom of the North American black widow spider *(Latrodectus mactans)* is 15 times more potent than that of a rattlesnake.
- Spider silk is stronger than any other known fiber, natural or artificial, of equivalent thickness.
- The smallest winged insect is the Tanzanian parasitic wasp *(Caraphractus cinctus)*. It has a wingspan of just 0.2 mm (0.008 in.).
- The loudest insect is the African cicada *(Brevisana brevis)*. At 107 decibels, it is almost as loud as a road drill.

FACT
More than a million species of insects are known. Thousands more are discovered every year.

see also
74-75 **Animal kingdom**
96-97 **Animal records**
104-5 **Endangered species**

BEETLES AND WEEVILS

Coleoptera
More than 370 000 species

Where they live:
Land and freshwater habitats worldwide except the poles

Key features:
- Beetles and weevils form the largest insect order and account for more than a quarter of all the species in the animal kingdom.
- They have hard, leathery forewings called elytra, which fold down to protect the hind wings.

Species:
Cockchafer *(Melolontha melolontha)*
Colorado beetle *(Leptinotarsa decemlineata)*
Deathwatch beetle *(Xestobium rufoulllosum)*
Glowworm *(Lampyris noctiluca)*
Grain weevil *(Sitophilus granarius)*
Goliath beetle *(Goliathus giganteus)*
Great diving beetle *(Dystiscus marginalis)*
Two-spot ladybird *(Adalia bipunctata)*

FLIES

Diptera
About 90 000 species

Where they live:
On land and in the air worldwide except the poles

Key features:
- Flies have antennae, compound eyes and one pair of wings.
- They have a pair of modified wings, called halteres, used for balance.
- They produce legless larvae called maggots.
- They are the main insect carriers of human diseases, including malaria, sleeping sickness and yellow fever.

Species:
Bluebottle *(Calliphora vomitoria)*
Crane fly (daddy longlegs) *(Tipula maxima)*
Horse fly *(Tabanus bromius)*
House fly *(Musca domestica)*
Mosquito (family Culicidae, many genera and species)
Robber fly *(Asilus crabroniformis)*
Tsetse fly (genus *Glossina*, many species)

BEES, WASPS AND ANTS

Hymenoptera
More than 120 000 species

Where they live:
On land and in the air worldwide except the poles

Key features:
- Bees and wasps possess two pairs of wings.
- The first segment of the abdomen is constricted to form a waist.
- Bees and wasps have a poisonous sting.
- Many species have complex social structures.

Species:
Army ant (genus *Eciton*, several species)
Common wasp *(Vespula vulgaris)*
Garden bumblebee *(Bombus hortorum)*
Giant hornet *(Vespa crabo)*
Honey bee *(Apis mollifera)*
Leafcutter ant (genus *Atta*, several species)
Leafcutter bee *(Megachile centuncularis)*
Oak apple wasp *(Biorrhiza pallida)*
Tawny mining bee *(Andrena fulva)*
Wood ant *(Formica rufa)*

BUTTERFLIES AND MOTHS

Lepidoptera
About 150 000 species

Where they live:
On land and in the air worldwide except the poles

Key features:
- They pass through a four-stage life cycle: egg, larva (caterpillar), pupa or chrysalis and adult.
- Butterflies are active by day and most moths by night.
- Butterfly antennae are shaped like clubs; moths' antennae are plumed or feathery.
- The adults have long, coiled tongues, which they use to feed on nectar.

Species:
Atlas moth *(Attacus atlas)*
Clothes moth *(Tineola bisselliella)*
Common snout butterfly *(Libytheana bachmanii)*
Death's-head hawkmoth *(Acherontia atropos)*
Garden tiger moth *(Arctia caja)*
Gypsy moth *(Porthetria dispar)*
Hummingbird hawkmoth *(Macroglossum stellatarum)*
Large cabbage white *(Pieris brassicae)*
Monarch butterfly *(Danaus plexippus)*
Painted lady *(Cynthia cardui)*
Queen Alexandra's birdwing butterfly *(Ornithoptera alexandrae)*
Red admiral *(Vanessa atalanta)*

WHAT IS AN INSECT?

- Adult insects' bodies are divided into **three sections**: the head, the thorax and the abdomen.
- They have **antennae or "feelers"** attached to their heads.
- They have **three pairs of legs** attached to the thorax and (usually) two pairs of wings.
- They almost all lay eggs and **go through one or more larval stages** before becoming adults. As larvae, they often look very different from the adults.

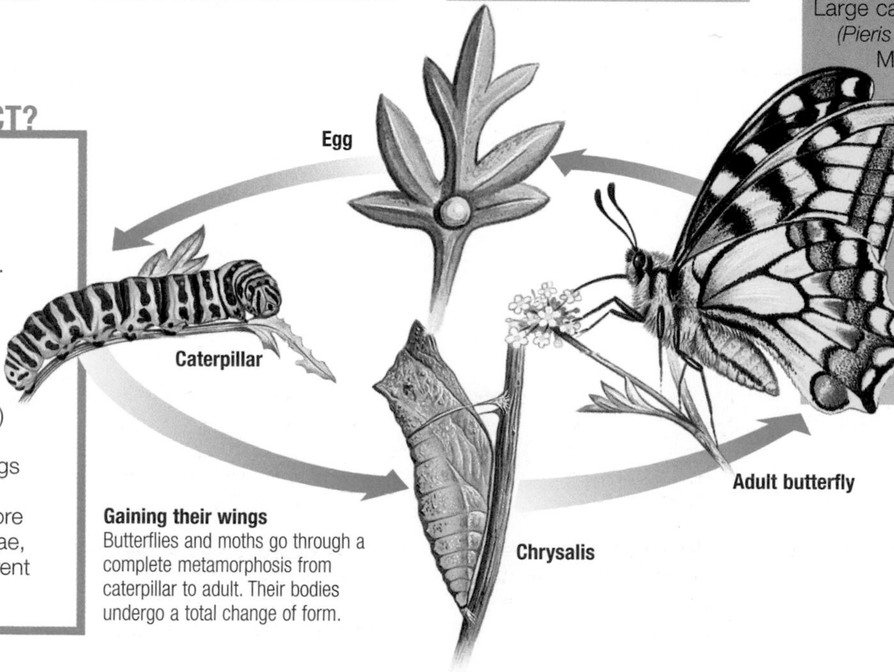

Gaining their wings
Butterflies and moths go through a complete metamorphosis from caterpillar to adult. Their bodies undergo a total change of form.

Fish have evolved and adapted to virtually all the fresh and saltwater habitats of the world. They range in size from the marine dwarf goby found in the Chagos Archipelago of the Indian Ocean, measuring less than 10 mm (1/2 in.) from tip to tail, to the whale shark, which reaches lengths of nearly 20 m (65 ft). Fish make up the largest group of vertebrates, with about 25 000 known species.

WHAT IS A FISH?

- Fish are **cold-blooded vertebrates** found in seas, oceans and fresh waters.
- All fish, apart from lungfish, breathe using **gills**.
- They move through water with the aid of **fins**.
- In most cases, their skins are covered with **scales**.

CLASSIFYING FISH

Modern fish can be broadly grouped into four divisions.

Lampreys and hagfish These belong to the superclass Agnatha, meaning "without jaws." They are primitive, eellike creatures (see right) with rounded mouths that are not articulated into jaws. They do have teeth, however. Other characteristics include smooth, scaleless, slimy skin and single, or unpaired, fins.

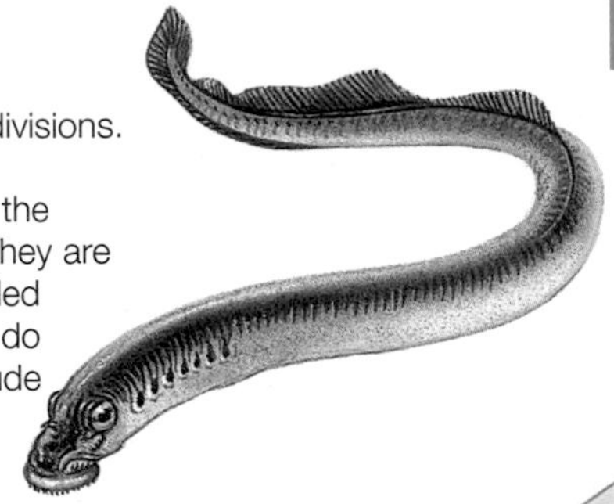

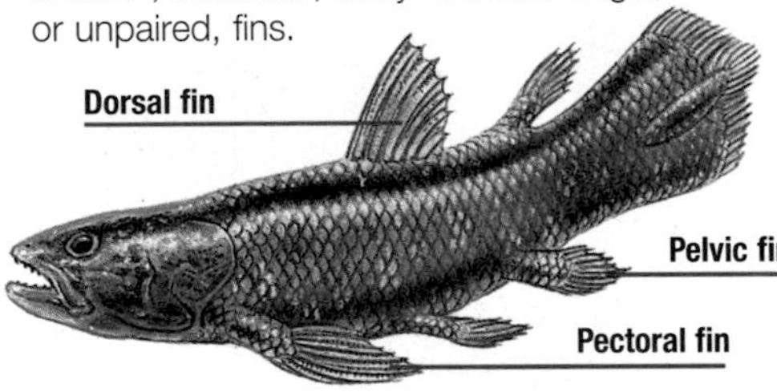

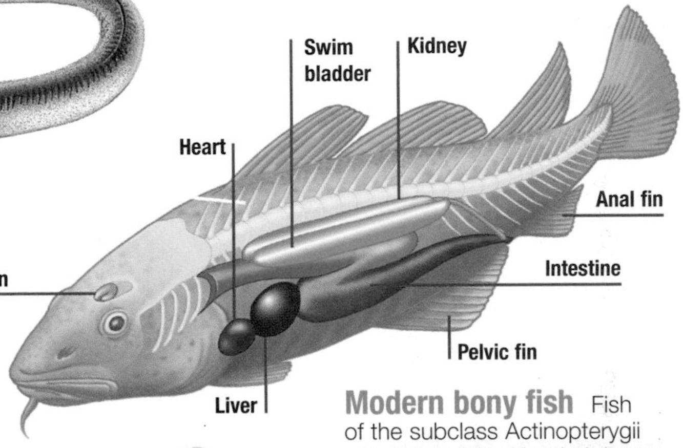

Primitive bony fish Most fish of the subclass Sarcopterygii have become extinct, but a few, such as the coelacanth (above), remain. Strictly speaking, they are not bony fish at all, because many parts of the skeleton are made of cartilage. The head, however, is usually formed from a mosaic of tiny bones. The flexible spine has no vertebrae.

Cartilaginous fish The class Chondrichthyes includes sharks (below), rays, skates and dogfish. They have skeletons made entirely of cartilage. They have jaws (and teeth), and their skin is covered in scales. Once fully grown, the teeth and scales cease to develop but are replaced as they wear out.

Modern bony fish Fish of the subclass Actinopterygii are distinguished by their bony skeletons. Features typical of this class include thin scales on the skin, paired pelvic and pectoral fins, a simple, flaplike covering over the gills, and a swim bladder – a variable-buoyancy device that allows the fish to float at different depths.

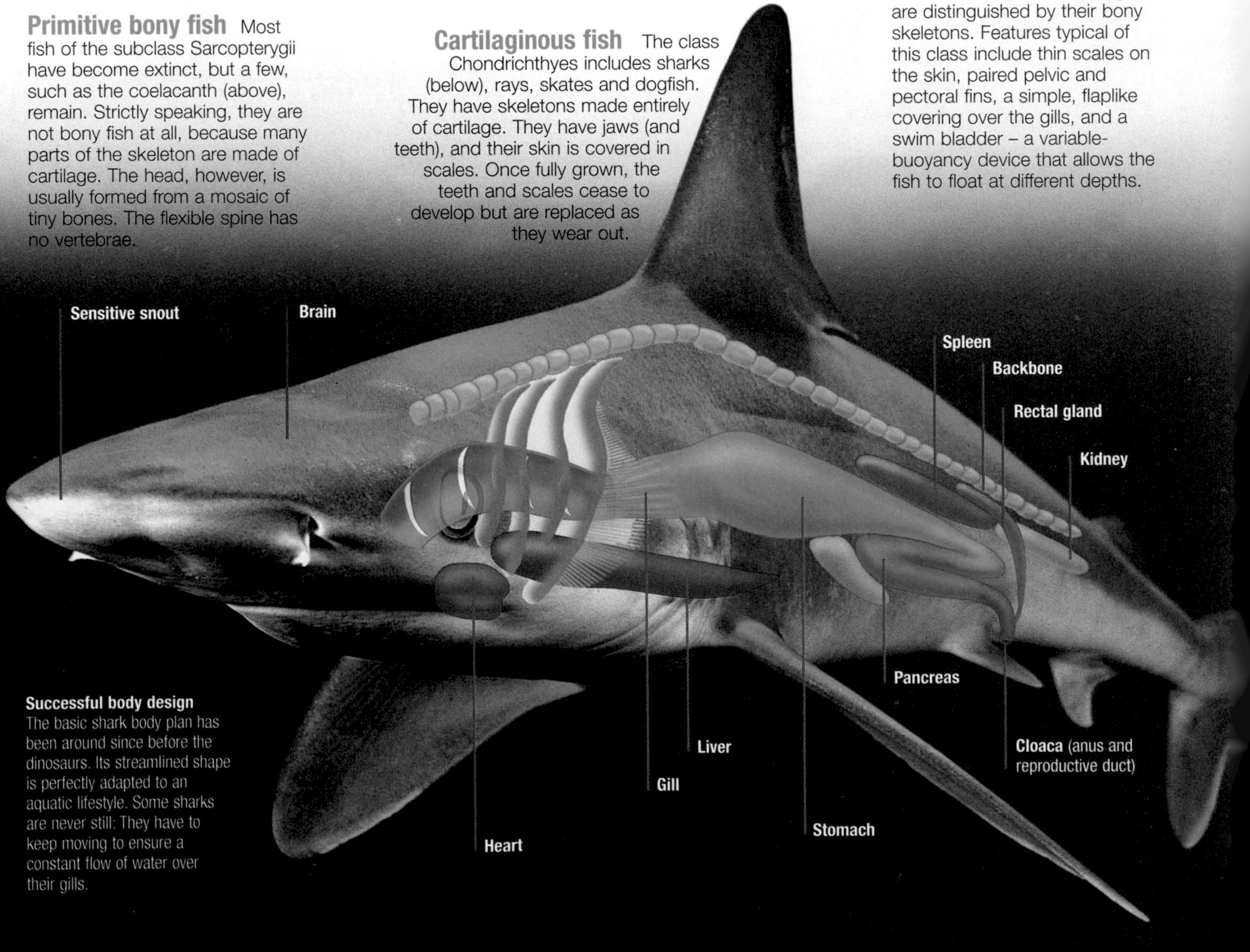

Successful body design
The basic shark body plan has been around since before the dinosaurs. Its streamlined shape is perfectly adapted to an aquatic lifestyle. Some sharks are never still: They have to keep moving to ensure a constant flow of water over their gills.

see also
64-65 **Age of the fishes**
74-75 **Animal kingdom**
96-97 **Animal records**

SHARKS

Pleurotremata
More than 350 species

Where they live:
Seas and oceans worldwide; some rivers

Key features:

- These cartilaginous fish have streamlined bodies and muscular tails, which they use to propel themselves through water.
- They have grayish skins, high dorsal fins and five to seven pairs of gill slits.
- Their excellent sense of smell and specialized cells on their head are for short-range detection of electricity produced by the muscles of prey.
- Sharks have changed little in 400 million years.
- They are mostly saltwater fish, although a few spend much of their lives in fresh water.

Species:
Basking shark *(Cerorhinus maximus)*
Bull shark *(Carcharhinus leucas)*
Common hammerhead shark *(Sphyrna Zygaena)*
Fierce shark *(Carcharias ferox)*
Frilled shark *(Chlamydoselachus anguineus)*
Great white shark *(Carcharodon carcharias)*
Lesser spotted dogfish *(Scyliorhinus canicula)*
Mako shark *(Isurus oxyrinchus)*
Nurse shark *(Gingkymostoma cirratum)*
Thresher shark *(Alopias vulpinus)*
Tiger shark *(Galeocardo cuvieri)*
Whale shark *(Rhincodon typus)*
Wobbegong shark *(Orectolobus maculatus)*
Zebra shark *(Stegotoma fasciatum)*

SKATES, RAYS AND RABBITFISH

Rajiformes
More than 400 species

Where they live:
Temperate and tropical seas; some rivers

Key features:

- They are cartilaginous fish with flattened bodies, enlarged winglike pectoral fins and long, tapering tails.
- They are mostly bottom-dwellers, feeding with blunt, crushing teeth on invertebrates and other fish. Some open-water species eat plankton – tiny plants and animals in the upper layers of the sea.
- The gill openings are on the underside of the body, as is the mouth in bottom-feeders.

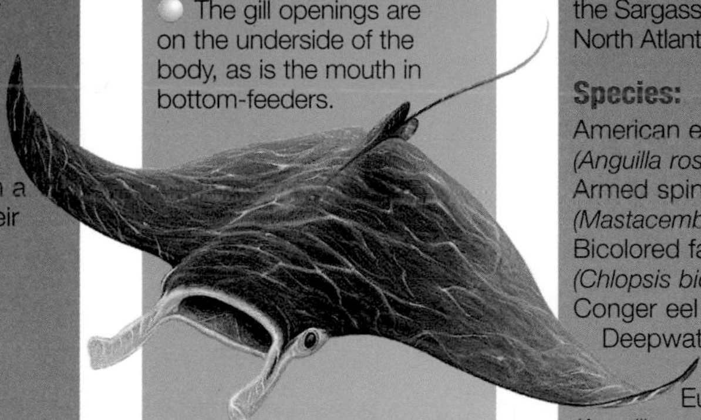

Water wings The manta ray *(Manta birostris)* "flies" through its native tropical waters by flapping its large pectoral fins. With a maximum length of 5 m (16 ft), it is the biggest of the rays.

Species:
Common skate *(Raja batis)*
Common stingray *(Dasyatis pastinaca)*
Eyed electric ray *(Torpedo torpedo)*
Great toothed sawfish *(Pristis microdon)*
Guitar fish *(Rhinosatos productus)*
Manta ray *(Manta birostris)*
Rabbitfish *(Chimaera monstrosa)*

EELS

Anguilliformes
More than 500 species

Where they live:
From coral reefs to the deep sea; also fresh waters

Key features:

- These are snakelike bony fish with elongated dorsal and anal fins and no scales.
- Eels feed on fish and invertebrates.
- Freshwater eels *(Anguilla)* breed at sea, often migrating long distances from their home waters. European and North American freshwater eels, for example, breed in the Sargasso Sea of the North Atlantic.

Species:
American eel *(Anguilla rostrata)*
Armed spiny eel *(Mastacembalus armatus)*
Bicolored false moray eel *(Chlopsis bicolor)*
Conger eel *(Conger conger)*
Deepwater eel *(Cyema atrum)*
European eel *(Anguilla anguilla)*
Giant moray eel *(Gymnothorax javanicus)*
Gray's cutthroat eel *(Synaphobranchus pinnatus)*
Gulper eel *(Eurypharynx pelecanoides)*
Japanese eel *(Anguilla japonica)*
Moray eel *(Muraena helena)*
Pelican-fish eel *(Saccopharynx ampullaceus)*
Snake eel *(Ophichthys gomesii)*
Yellow garden eel *(Heteroconger luteolus)*
Zebra moray eel *(Echidna zebra)*

HERRING AND PILCHARDS

Clupeiformes
More than 400 species

Where they live:
Shallow waters of seas worldwide; some lakes and rivers

Key features:

- These are silvered greenish blue colored fish.
- They swim close to the surface of the water to feed on plankton.
- Herring travel in schools, which can be several miles in length and width.
- They include many species that are important to humans for food.

Species:
Anchovy *(Engraulis encrasiolus)*
Atlantic herring *(Clupea harengus)*
Atlantic menhaden *(Brevoorta tyrannus)*
Australian sardine *(Sardinops neo-pilcharus)*
Denticiptoid herring *(Denticeps clupeoides)*
Japanese sardine *(Sardinops melanosticta)*
Pacific herring *(Clupea pallasii)*
Pilchard *(Sardina pilchardus)*
Shad *(Alosa alosa)*
South African sardine *(Sardinops ocellata)*
South American sardine *(Sardinops sagax)*
Sprat *(Sprattus sprattus)*

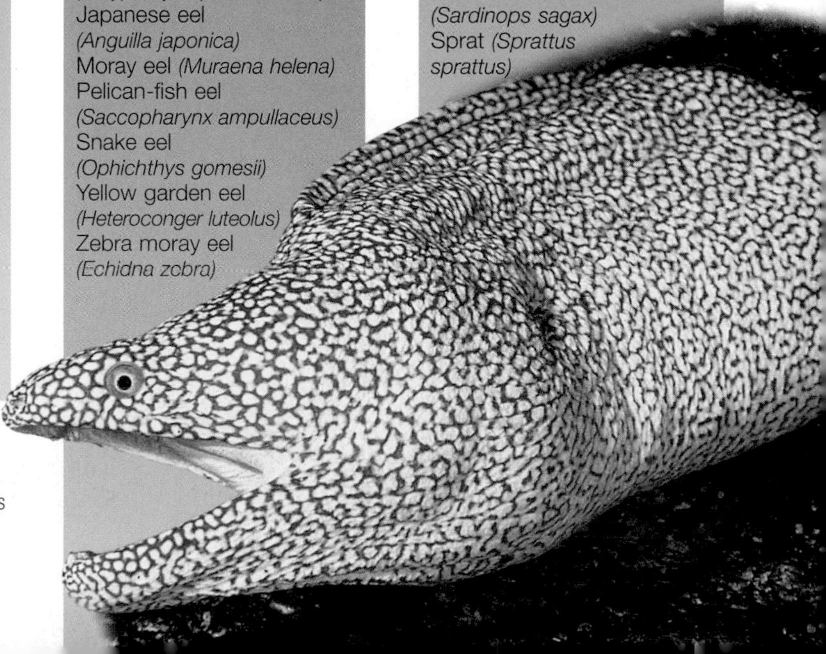

Hidden hunter
Moray eels are found in temperate waters but are most common on coral reefs in the tropics. They hide in crevices and seize fish that swim into reach.

The varied inhabitants of the world's waters

SALMON, TROUT, PIKE AND SMELT

Salmoniformes
About 1000 species

Where they live:
Northern Hemisphere; open ocean, coastal waters, rivers and lakes

Key features:
- Salmon and trout have wide mouths and powerful teeth. Pike and smelt have narrow, pointed heads with sharp teeth.
- All are born in fresh water; salmon migrate to the sea when two years old.
- In the wild, salmon, trout and smelt return to their place of birth to spawn (spawning season runs from September to January).

Species:
Arctic char
(Salvelinus alpinus)
Atlantic salmon *(Salmo salar)*
Dog salmon
(Oncorhynchus keta)
European brown trout
(Salmo trutta)
European smelt
(Osmerus eperlanus)
Grayling
(Thymallus thymallus)
Longnose lancet fish
(Alepisaurus ferox)
Pacific lancet fish
(Alepisaurus borealis)
Pike *(Esox lucius)*
Pink salmon
(Oncorhynchus gorbuscha)
Rainbow trout
(Salmo gairdneri)
River trout
(Salmo trutta fario)
Silver salmon
(Oncorhynchus kitsutch)
Sockeye salmon
(Oncorhynsus nerka)

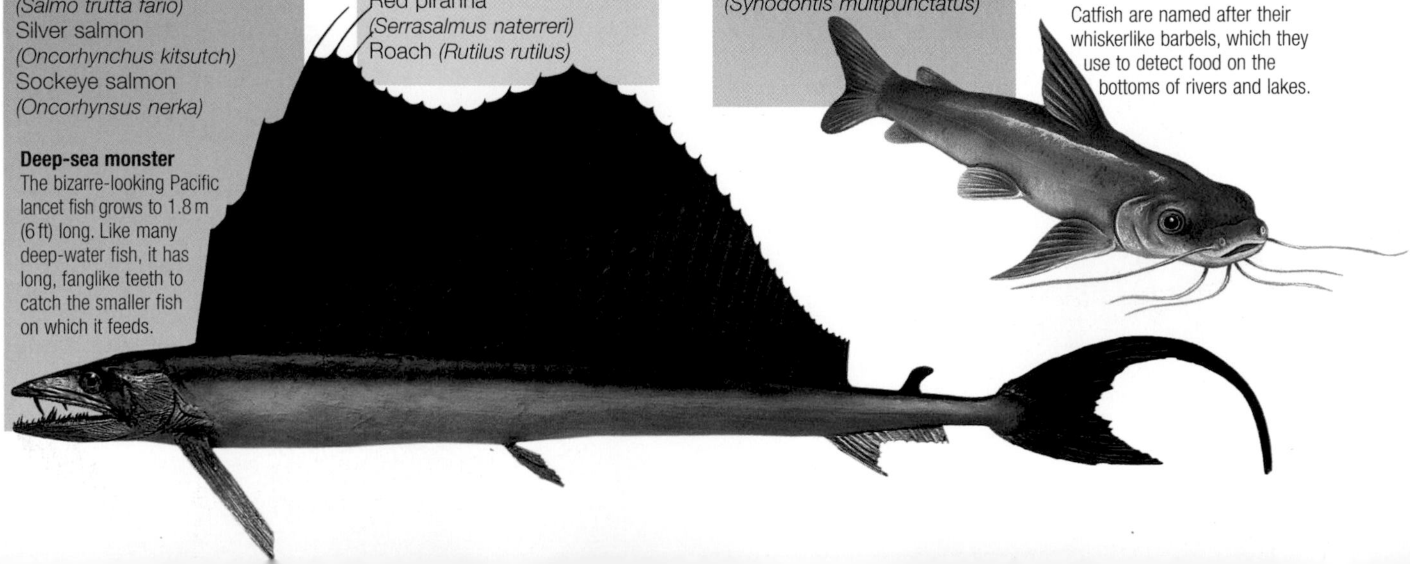

Deep-sea monster
The bizarre-looking Pacific lancet fish grows to 1.8 m (6 ft) long. Like many deep-water fish, it has long, fanglike teeth to catch the smaller fish on which it feeds.

CARP AND CHARACHINS

Cypriniformes
About 3500 species

Where they live:
In fresh water worldwide except Antarctica

Key features:
- They are omnivorous and carnivorous freshwater fish with elongated bodies.
- They have long dorsal fins.
- Some species hibernate in the mud at the bottom of rivers and streams.

Piranha!
South America's red piranha is known as a dangerous meat-eater, but many of the 50 piranha species eat seeds and fruit that have fallen into the water.

Species:
Bitterling *(Rhodeus sericeus)*
Clown loach
(Botia macracantha)
Common carp
(Cyprinus carpio)
Goldfish *(Carassius auratus)*
Minnow *(Phoxinus phoxinus)*
Neon tetra
(Pracherodon innesi)
Red piranha
(Serrasalmus naterreri)
Roach *(Rutilus rutilus)*

CATFISH

Siluriformes
More than 2500 species

Where they live:
Lakes and rivers worldwide; also tropical coastal waters

Key features:
- Catfish are secretive, bottom-dwelling scavengers and hunters and are mostly nocturnal.
- Their bodies are scaleless or covered in bony plates arranged in rows.
- They have broad, flat heads; thick bodies; and long, sensitive barbels (feelers).
- The upper jaw functions mostly as a point for the attachment of barbels.

Species:
Brown bullhead catfish
(Ictalurus nebolosus)
Channel catfish
(Ictalurus punctatus)
Crucifix catfish *(Arius proops)*
East European giant catfish
(Silurus glanic)
Electric eel
(Electrophorus electricus)
European wels
(Silurus glanis)
Giant catfish
(Pangasianodon gigas)
Glass catfish
(Kryptopterus bicirrhis)
Striped dwarf catfish
(Mystus vittatus)
Sucking catfish
(Bagarius bagarius)
Upside-down catfish
(Synodontis multipunctatus)

COD

Gadiformes
About 800 species

Where they live:
Northern Hemisphere; mostly cold sea water but also lakes and rivers

Key features:
- Cod have two anal fins, three dorsal fins, and at least one barbel on the lower jaw.
- They are spotted brown to gray in color and white underneath.
- They are carnivorous.
- They grow to 1.8 m (6 ft) long.
- They include several species that are important to humans as food.

Species:
Arctic Greenland cod
(Arctogadus glacialis)
Atlantic cod *(Gadus morhua)*
Atlantic tomcod
(Microgadus tomcod)
Burbot *(Lota lota)*
Common ling *(Molva molva)*
East Siberia cod
(Arctogadus borisovi)
Greenland cod *(Gadus ogac)*
Haddock
(Melanogramus aeglifinus)
Hake *(Merluccius merluccius)*
Pacific cod
(Gadus macrophalus)
Pacific tomcod
(Microgadus proxismus)
Whiting *(Merlangius merlangus)*

Fish whiskers
Catfish are named after their whiskerlike barbels, which they use to detect food on the bottoms of rivers and lakes.

see also
74-75 **Animal kingdom**
96-97 **Animal records**
104-5 **Endangered species**

SILVERSIDES

Atheriniformes
About 200 species

Where they live:
Fresh, coastal and ocean waters of warm and temperate regions

Key features:
- Small fish with slim bodies and a silver band on each side.
- Two pectoral fins.
- Live in large schools.
- Most lay eggs inside aquatic plants.

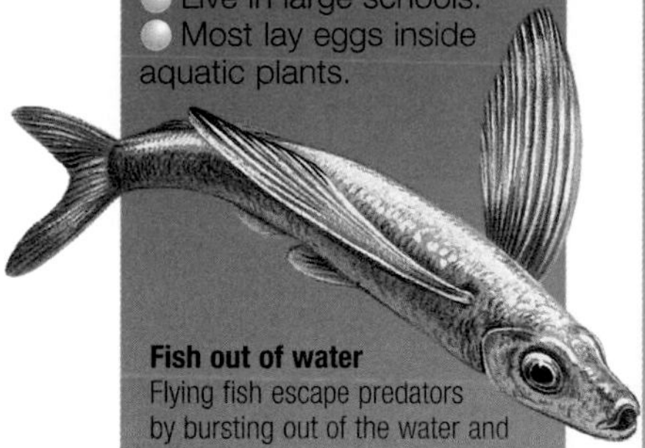

Fish out of water Flying fish escape predators by bursting out of the water and gliding through the air on their winglike pectoral (shoulder) fins.

Species:
Atlantic flying fish *(Cypselurus melanurus)*
California grunion *(Leuresthes tenuis)*
Guppy *(Lebistes reticulatus)*
Houndfish *(Tylosurus crocodilus)*
Jacksmelt silverside *(Atherinopsis californiensis)*
Sardine silverside *(Hubbsiella sardina)*

STICKLEBACKS, PIPEFISH AND SEA HORSES

Gasterosteiformes
About 220 species

Where they live:
Coastal waters, lakes and rivers in temperate and tropical regions

Key features:
- Sticklebacks have a row of spines along their backs in place of a dorsal fin.
- Pipefish and sea horses have horselike heads. Sea horses swim in a vertical position with the aid of an undulating dorsal fin. Most pipefish swim in a horizontal position.
- Males of all species are closely involved in the rearing of young. Male pipefish and sea horses have a brood pouch in which the young hatch.

Species:
Black-spotted stickleback *(Gasterosteus wheatlandi)*
Common Atlantic pipefish *(Syngnathus fuscus)*
Common sea horse *(Hippocampus guttulatus)*
Dwarf sea horse *(Hippocampus zosterae)*
Leafy seadragon *(Phycodurus eques)*
Nine-spined stickleback *(Pungitius pungitius)*
North American freshwater sickleback *(Culaea inconstans)*
Spotted sea horse *(Hippocampus kuda)*
Three-spined stickleback *(Gasterosteus aculeatus)*
Tiger pipefish *(Filicampus tigris)*

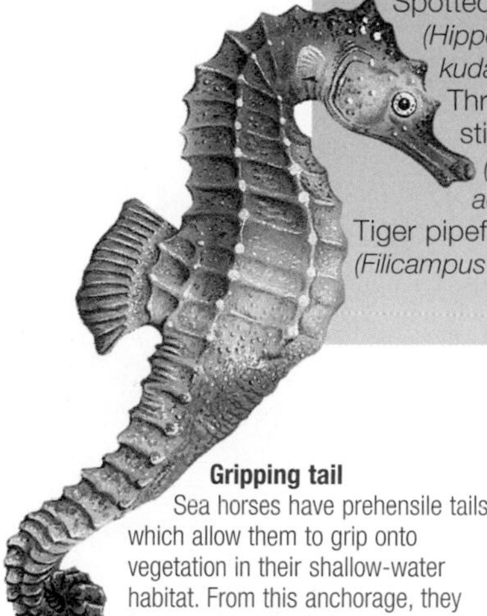

Gripping tail Sea horses have prehensile tails, which allow them to grip onto vegetation in their shallow-water habitat. From this anchorage, they feed on tiny animals by sucking them into their mouths.

PERCH AND PERCHLIKE FISHES

Perciformes
More than 6000 species

Where they live:
Worldwide, in fresh water, seas and oceans

Key features:
- Most have spines on the dorsal, anal and pelvic fins.
- This is by far the largest group of fishes, with about 150 different families in all.
- They include many food and game fishes, such as tuna, mackerel, marlin, swordfish and sea bass.

Popular pets Angelfishes and other members of this group are prized for their colorful appearance.

Families:
Angelfishes (Pomacanthidae)
Barracudas (Sphyraenidae)
Blennies (Blennioidei, several families)
Cichlids (Cichlidae)
Gobies (Gobiidae)
Icefishes (Chaenichthyidae)
Marlins (Istiophoridae)
Mudskippers (Periophthalmidae)
Mullets (Mugilidae)
Parrotfishes (Scaridae)
Perches (Percidae)
Sea bass (Serranidae)
Tunas and mackerels (Scombridae)
Wrasses (Labridae)

FLATFISH

Pleuronectiformes
About 500 species

Where they live:
All seas, especially those in warm and temperate regions

Key features:
- Flatfish have a flattened body, fringed with dorsal and anal fins.
- During the larval stage, one eye moves to join the other on the same side of the head.
- They lurk on the bottom of sandy or muddy coastal waters with their upper surfaces colored to blend with the surroundings.
- They are carnivorous and bony. Most lie in wait for prey.

Species:
Atlantic halibut *(Hippoglossus hippoglossus)*
Black-sea turbot *(Scophthalmus maeoticus)*
Brill turbot *(Scophthalmus rhombus)*
California halibut *(Parlichthys californicus)*
Common sole *(Solea solea)*
Dab *(Limanda limanda)*
Hogchoker *(Trinectes maculatus)*
Norwegian topknot *(Phrynorhombus norvegicus)*
Peacock flounder *(Bothus lunatus)*
Plaice *(Pleuronectes platessa)*
Smallmouth flounder *(Paralichthys dentatus)*
Summer flounder *(Paralichtys dentatus)*
Turbot *(Scophthalmus maximus)*
Winter flounder *(Pseudopleuronectes americanus)*

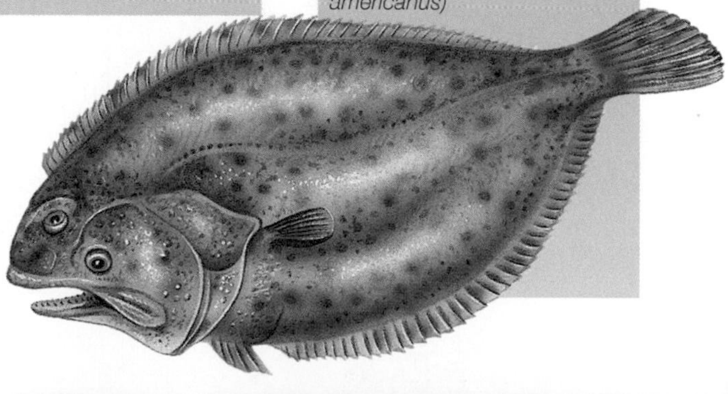

Level-headed The strangely distorted head of the flatfish shows that it evolved from a round-bodied ancestor.

Most amphibians have two distinct phases to their lives. They start off as water-dwellers and then pass through a complete change in their physical form as they are transformed into land-dwelling adults. During this metamorphosis, they slowly change shape, growing legs and replacing their gills with air-breathing lungs.

WHAT IS AN AMPHIBIAN?

- Adult amphibians are **air-breathing, egg-laying, cold-blooded** vertebrates.
- **Although born in water**, most spend the majority of their adult lives on land.
- Many amphibians **hibernate** during the winter months.
- Most are **nocturnal**.

1 Eggs are laid in water in early spring.
2 After two weeks, tadpoles emerge.
3 Feathery external gills are clearly visible.
4 Hind legs appear about three weeks after hatching.
5 Front limbs develop at about four to five weeks old.
6 By five to six weeks, lungs have replaced gills. Soon the tail will disappear.
heart
stomach
lung
intestine
cloaca

LIFE CYCLE OF A FROG

Frogs spend most of their adult lives on dry land, but nearly all species return to the water to breed.

- The male approaches the female from behind, holding her around the body while she releases her eggs, called spawn, into the water.
- Protective jelly surrounding the eggs swells on contact with the water, and the eggs, often in groups of several thousand, float just below the surface, where they are fertilized by sperm released into the water by the male.
- After about two weeks, the eggs hatch into tadpoles, which feed on algae and weeds in the water. They breathe by means of external gills for the next few weeks.
- Gradually, the frog's limbs begin to take shape and the tail shrinks.
- By the time it is six weeks old, the young frog is fully formed and ready to leave the water. Its gills have been replaced by internal lungs and its tail has disappeared. At this stage, it will switch from a vegetarian diet to a diet of insects and will live out the rest of its life near the water's edge.

Typical amphibian Most amphibians have a life cycle similar to that of the common frog (*Rana temporaria*, left). Nearly all species, regardless of their final adult form, start life as legless, fishlike tadpoles. Common frogs are found all over Europe and Asia. Their coloration and markings are very variable.

Poisonous frogs

The tropical forests of Central and South America are home to tiny frogs barely 5 cm (2 in.) long. The skin glands of these colorful creatures produce a poison so toxic that the indigenous tribes of Colombia use it to coat their arrowheads – hence the name arrow-poison frogs.

Unlike most frogs, the approximately 100 arrow-poison species are active during the day. They can afford to be obvious because their gaudy skins warn any would-be attacker to leave them alone or risk being poisoned. Safe from most aggressors, they move around the forest floor looking for ants, their staple diet. Some also possess sticky pads on their fingers and toes, which help them climb plants and trees in search of food.

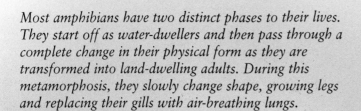

Pretty deadly Even touching Costa Rica's strawberry arrow-poison frog *(Dendrobates pumilio)* can prove fatal.

FACTS AND FIGURES

- The largest amphibian is the Chinese giant salamander *(Andrias davidianus)*, which grows to about 1.8 m (6 ft) in length and weighs about 60 kg (132 lbs).
- The smallest amphibian is the Cuban frog *(Sminthillus limbatus)*, which is just 8.5 mm (3/8 in.) long.
- The rarest amphibian is the painted frog *(Discoglossus nigriventer)*, a native of Israel. Only five of them have been sighted since it was first discovered in 1940.

NEWTS AND SALAMANDERS

Urodela
About 360 species

Where they live:
Temperate regions, mostly north of the Equator.

Key features:
- They have short legs and long bodies.
- They feed off small worms and insects.
- Their skins are smooth or warty and are never covered in scales.
- They move by wriggling from side to side in an S-shaped pattern.
- They tend to stay hidden in damp places.

Species:
Alpine newt *(Triturus alpestris)*
Axolotl *(Ambystoma mexicanum)*
Congo eel *(Amphiuma tridactylum)*
European fire salamander *(Salamandra salamandra)*
Hellbender *(Cryptobranchus alleganiensis)*
Japanese giant salamander *(Megalobatrachus japonicus)*
Marbled newt *(Triturus marmoratus)*
Mudpuppy *(Necturus maculosis)*
Siren *(genus Sirenidae, three species)*

FROGS AND TOADS

Anura
About 3500 species

Where they live:
Most temperate and some tropical regions.

Key features:
- Their bodies tend to be squat and short.
- Their powerful rear legs are well adapted for jumping.
- Their skins are moist and feet webbed.
- Their long, extensible tongues are used for catching prey.

Species:
Asiatic climbing toad *(Pedostibes hosii)*
Bullfrog *(Rana catesbeiana)*
Common frog *(Rana temporaria)*
Edible frog *(Rana esculenta)*
Eurasian midwife toad *(Alytes obstetricians)*
Giant aquatic frog *(Telematobius culeus)*
Grass frog *(Limonaoedus ocularis)*
Leopard toad *(Bufo pardalis)*
Ornate horned toad *(Ceratophrys ornata)*

CAECILIANS

Gymnophiona
About 200 species

Where they live:
Tropical and subtropical regions.

Key features:
- They have no limbs.
- They spend most of their time underground.
- Much of their time is spent burrowing for their staple diet of termites and earthworms.
- Their skins are grooved, giving the impression of being segmented.
- They are rarely observed, so many have no common name.

Species:
Basilan caecilian *(Icythyophis gladulosus)*
Cameroon caecilian *(Geotrypetes seraphini)*
Ceylonese caecilian *(Icythyophis glutinosus)*
Koatao caecilian *(Icythyophis kohtaonsis)*
Lafrentz caecilian *(Dermophis oaxacae)*
Dermophis mexicanus
Icythyophis kohtaoensis
Typhlonectes natans

see also
66-67 **The move to land**
74-75 **Animal kingdom**
96-97 **Animal records**

Giant tadpole The pale pink axolotl *(Ambystoma mexicanum)* never really grows up. It acquires four legs and can breed but remains water-based, never losing its gills. Few survive in the wild today. Their only natural habitat is in lakes around Mexico City.

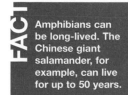

Secretive lifestyle The South American caecilian *(Siphonops annulatus)* spends most of its time burrowing underground, looking for food.

Breathable skin

The largest family of salamanders, the lungless salamanders, breathe through their skin rather than through lungs. A thin moist membrane, the epithelium, covers their skin surface and lines their mouths. Just below it is a network of tiny blood vessels. Oxygen dissolves in the moisture of the epithelium and passes through the thin membrane into the blood. At the same time, waste gases, such as carbon dioxide, pass out in the opposite direction. This process requires continuous moisture, so animals with breathable skin tend to live in damp places.

FACT
Amphibians can be long-lived. The Chinese giant salamander, for example, can live for up to 50 years.

Reptiles live in most warm and temperate regions. They thrive in the tropics, where the greatest variety and abundance of them is found. As cold-blooded creatures, reptiles are entirely dependent on heat transferred from the surrounding air in order to maintain bodily functions. Many species are excellent climbers, aided by claws – or scales equipped with minute hooks – and strong tails that can be used to cling onto branches.

WHAT IS A REPTILE?

- Reptiles are **cold-blooded air-breathing** vertebrates.
- Reptiles **lay yolk-filled eggs with hard shells**, enabling reproduction to take place on land.
- They have **scales** rather than feathers or hair.
- Their **skin is dry**, with few, if any, glands.
- With the exception of snakes, they **move around on four legs**, which project from the side of the body.
- Members of the order Squamata, **lizards and snakes, shed their skins** at intervals.

Flexible jaws A snake can devour prey up to three times its size in one gulp. Highly elastic joints in its jaws and between skull bones allow it to open its mouth remarkably wide. The maxillary bone, which holds the top fangs, swings forward when the mouth opens. Once in the stomach, the victim's body is rapidly broken down by powerful enzymes that can dissolve hair, feathers and even bone.

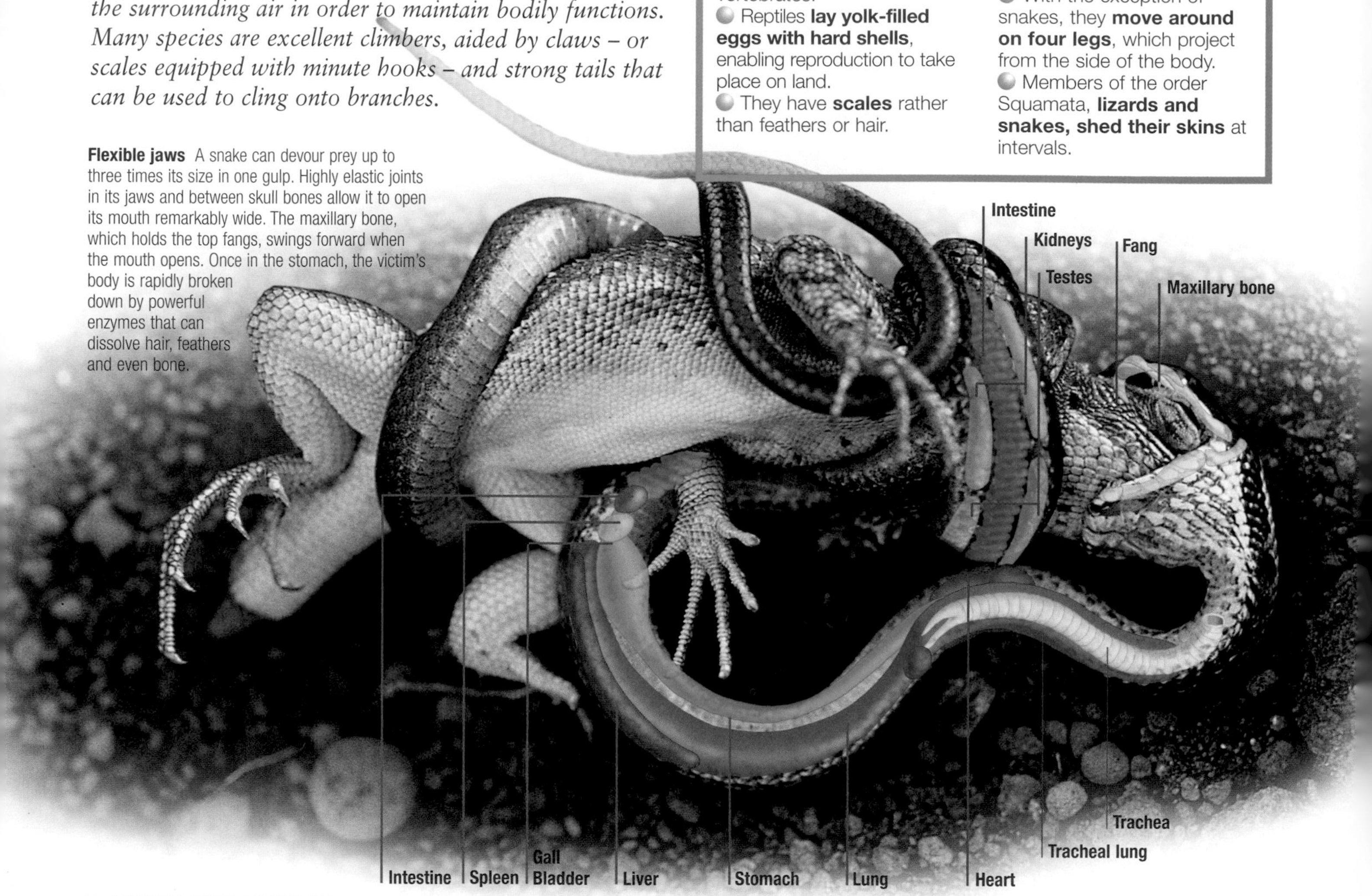

FACTS AND FIGURES

- Reptiles come in a large variety of sizes. They range in length from a 3 cm (1¼ in.) gecko *(Sphaerodactylus parthenopion)*, found in the British Virgin Islands, to the anaconda *(Eunectes murinus)*, a snake native to South America, which can grow to 9 m (29 ft) or longer.
- The heaviest reptile is the marine leatherback turtle *(Dermochelys coriacea)*. It can weigh over 700 kg (0.8 metric tons).
- Dinosaurs, pterosaurs and ichthyosaurs were all reptiles.
- Mammals and birds are both descended from reptiles.

A living fossil?

The tuatara is the sole survivor of the sphenodontid group of reptiles, which appeared about 225 million years ago. It is found only on a few islands off the coast of New Zealand. About 70 cm (28 in.) long, tuataras outwardly resemble lizards, but their skulls and teeth show marked differences. They are nocturnal, emerging at dusk to feed on insects, small animals and birds' eggs. Some live to be 100 years old.

The world's most dangerous snakes

The most dangerous snakes, when attacking their victims, inject venom through grooves or hollows in their fangs. The fangs act like hypodermic needles, which puncture the flesh of the victim when the snake strikes, introducing the poison into the prey's bloodstream.

Mambas These snakes are common in the countries of sub-Saharan Africa. They are among the fastest and most aggressive of all snakes. Their speed of attack is so great that they can pluck a bird out of the sky and kill it with an injection of venom almost before it has hit the ground.

Cobras These are found in Asia and Africa. The spitting cobra has the most fearsome reputation because it can spit blinding venom into the eyes of its victim from a range of nearly 3 m (10 ft).

Coral snakes The toxic venom of the relatively small coral snakes of the Americas is very powerful. Would-be predators are warned of the potential danger by the snakes' distinctive coloring of red, black, yellow and white bands.

see also
66-67 **The move to land**
68-71 **Dinosaurs**
74-75 **Animal kingdom**
96-97 **Animal records**

SNAKES

Serpentes
More than 2300 species

Where they live:
Most tropical and temperate zones

Key features:

- Snakes' vision is limited but attuned to movement.
- Their hearing is restricted to ground vibrations, but their sense of touch is acute.
- They have a sense of smell and can pick up airborne particles for analysis using the tongue.
- Some species have a pit between eye and nostril that is sensitive to infrared radiation so they can detect warm-blooded creatures in the dark.

Species:
Anaconda *(Eunectes murinus)*
Common king snake *(Lampropeltis getulus)*
King cobra *(Ophiophagus hannah)*
Madagascar boa constrictor *(Sanzinia madagascariensis)*
Reticulate python *(Python reticulatus)*
Rock python *(Python sebae)*
Royal python *(Python regius)*
Sidewinder *(Crotalus cerastes)*
Spitting cobra *(Naja nigricollis)*
Western diamondback rattlesnake *(Crotalus adamanteus)*

LIZARDS

Lacertilia
More than 3700 species

Where they live:
Worldwide, but mostly in the tropics

Key features:

- Lizards have ear drums and movable eyelids.
- They lay leathery-shelled eggs in a nest.
- Most are small to medium-sized. Exceptions include monitor lizards, such as the Komodo dragon, which can be over 2 m (7 ft) long.
- They chiefly eat insects or vegetation.
- Most have four legs, but some, such as the European slowworm, have none, like snakes.
- Many can shed their tails if attacked; they regrow.

Species:
Common lizard *(Lacerta vivipara)*
Emerald lizard *(Lacerta viridis)*
Frilled lizard *(Chlamydosaurus kingi)*
Fringe-toed lizard *(Acanthodactylus erythrurus)*
Jeweled lizard *(Lacerta lepida)*
Komodo dragon *(Varanus komodoensis)*
Sand lizard *(Lacerta agilis)*
Schreiber's lizard *(Lacerta schreiberi)*
Slowworm *(Anguis fragilis)*
Stehlin's lizard *(Lacerta stehlinii)*
Wall lizard *(Lacerta muralis)*

Walking on water The broad feet and long, scale-fringed toes of the basilisk lizard *(Basiliscus plumiformes)* mean that it can sprint on the surface of water to escape from predators. This ability has led to it acquiring a further name – the Jesus Christ lizard.

TURTLES AND TORTOISES

Chelonia
About 270 species

Where they live:
Southeast Europe, west Asia, North Africa, Americas, Australia and oceans

Key features:

- Their bodies are protected by a hard shell.
- Their heads and limbs can be withdrawn into the shell when under attack.
- The shell of a turtle is lighter and more streamlined than that of a land tortoise.
- Land tortoises are herbivores.
- Marine turtles are herbivores; freshwater turtles are carnivores.
- Turtles can lay up to 200 eggs at a time.

Deep-sea diver Like all marine turtles, the green turtle *(Chelonia mydas)* spends most of its life under water, where it can hold its breath for over 30 minutes. Flat legs act like flippers, pushing it along.

Species:
African spurred tortoise *(Testudo sulcata)*
Giant leathery turtle *(Dermochelys coriacea)*
Green turtle *(Chelonia mydas)*
Hawksbill turtle *(Eretmochelys imbricata)*
Loggerhead turtle *(Caretta caretta)*
Red-legged tortoise *(Testudo denticulata)*
Snapping turtle *(Chelydra serpentina)*
Spur-thighed tortoise *(Testudo graeca)*
Starred tortoise *(Testudo elegans)*
Stinkpot *(Sternotherus odoratus)*

CROCODILES AND ALLIGATORS

Crocodylia
22 species

Where they live:
Near freshwater shores in warmer regions

Key features:

- They have a lizardlike shape with armored skin made from large, strong, partially ossified (bony) plates.
- Their teeth are situated in deep hollows (known as alveoli) in the jaw.
- They move through the water by swishing their tails in a side-to-side motion.
- Adults feed on fish and turtles; the young feed on insects, worms and tiny fish.
- They are the largest modern reptiles. Male saltwater crocodiles, from tropical Asia and the Pacific, grow to about 3.2 m (10 ft 6 in.) long – and in some cases to more than twice that length.

Species:
American alligator *(Alligator mississippiensis)*
Australian crocodile *(Crocodylus johnsoni)*
Cuban crocodile *(Crocodylus rhombifer)*
Gavial *(Gavialis gangeticus)*
Mugger crocodile *(Crocodylus palustris)*
Nile crocodile *(Crocodylus niloticus)*
Saltwater crocodile *(Crocodylus porosus)*
Spectacled caiman *(Caiman crocodilus)*

Crocodile – teeth visible on both jaws

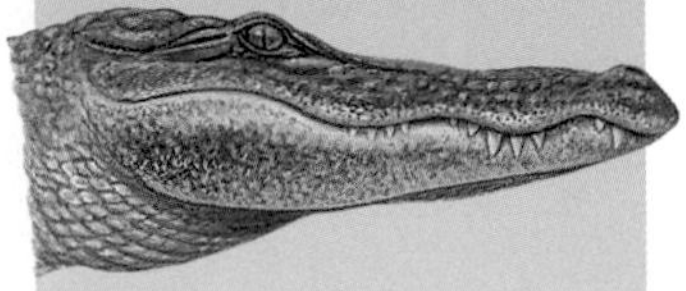

Alligator – only upper teeth visible

Feathers are the one characteristic that separates birds from all other creatures. Feathers serve the dual function of aiding flight and helping to regulate body temperature. Birds have the most acute color vision in the animal kingdom and are capable of distinguishing many more hues than humans can. Most birds restrict their activities to the hours of daylight, when they can fully take advantage of this sense.

WHAT IS A BIRD?

- A bird has **feathers and a bill**, but no teeth.
- Birds are **warm-blooded, air-breathing, two-legged** vertebrates.
- They communicate by means of **visual display or sound**.
- Birds' **eyesight is usually acute**, but their sense of smell is poor.
- **Almost all birds can fly.** They have streamlined bodies, highly adapted forelimbs (wings) and hollow bones.

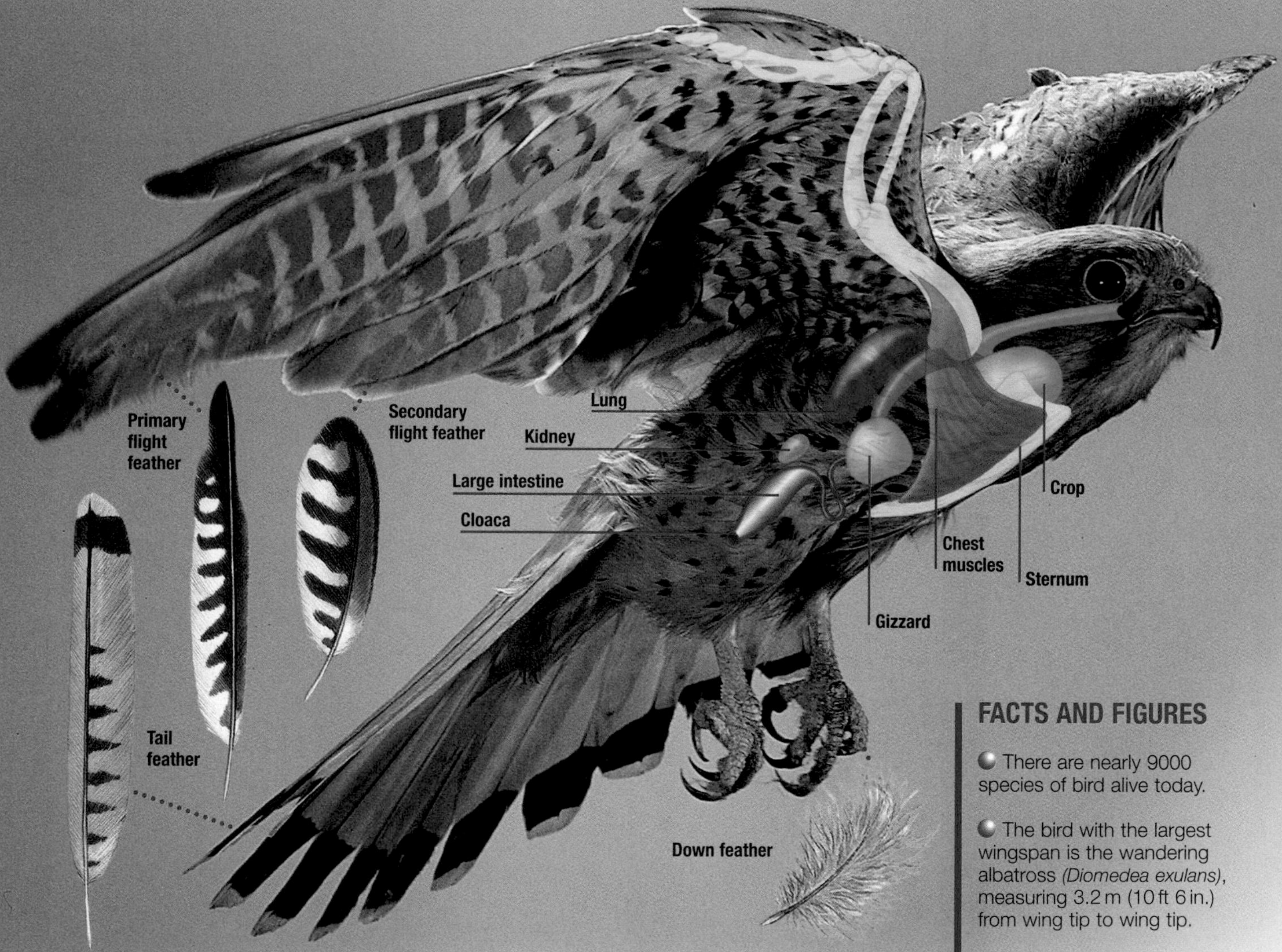

Every flight feather has a central shaft with a series of barbs sprouting from it. These barbs are linked by tiny hooks, giving the feather its solid appearance. The flight feathers give the wing an unbroken surface to push against the air in flight. Down feathers, which insulate the bird, are distinguished by their lack of interlocking hooks.

How birds fly

Birds can fly because air provides resistance to flapping wings in much the same way as water provides resistance against a boat's oars. The down-stroke of the wings provides lift. For every downward and backward movement of the wings, there is a corresponding upward and forward movement of the bird itself. The whole wing surface pushes against the air just as the blade of an oar pushes against the water. On the return stroke, the wing is tilted so that its thin leading edge can slice through the air with least resistance. Birds require strong chest muscles, anchored to a large sternum, to power their wings.

FACTS AND FIGURES

- There are nearly 9000 species of bird alive today.
- The bird with the largest wingspan is the wandering albatross *(Diomedea exulans)*, measuring 3.2 m (10 ft 6 in.) from wing tip to wing tip.
- The bee hummingbird *(Mellisuga helenae)* has the smallest wingspan of any bird at 5.5 cm (2¼ in.).
- Birds exist on every continent. The emperor penguin *(Aptenodytes forsteri)* spends the winter in Antarctica; it is the only vertebrate to do so.
- More than 1000 extinct species of bird have been identified from fossils.

see also

70-71 **Last days of the dinosaurs**

74-75 **Animal kingdom**

96-97 **Animal records**

OSTRICH

Struthioniformes
1 species

Where it lives:

Open grasslands and semidesert regions in Africa

Key features:

- It is flightless.
- It has a long, flexible neck, small head and ducklike bill.
- It is a fast runner, capable of sprinting at up to 65 km/h (40 mph).
- It has long, powerful legs with two toes on each foot.
- The male is black and white with a large, white plume of tail feathers. The female is a drab brown.

Species:

Ostrich *(Struthio camelus)*

Giant egg The ostrich has the largest egg (below) of any living bird, weighing an average 1.7 kg (3 lb 12 oz), the equivalent of about two dozen hen's eggs. Its shell, although only 1.5 mm (1/16 in.) thick, is strong enough to support a 127 kg (280 lb) man.

FACT The unfertilized egg of the African ostrich is the largest single animal cell in the world.

RHEAS

Rheiformes
2 species

Where they live:

The open plains of South America

Key features:

- They are flightless.
- They are smaller than the ostrich or emu.
- Their heads and necks are feathered.
- They have three toes on each foot.

Species:

Common rhea *(Rhea americana)*
Lesser rhea *(Pterocnemia pennata)*

On the run The common rhea (above) – like its African and Australian counterparts, the ostrich and emu – can reach impressive speeds. Its long legs double as a defensive weapon – they can deliver a powerful kick.

EMUS AND CASSOWARIES

Casuariiformes
4 species

Where they live:

Deserts, plains and forests in Australia and New Guinea

Key features:

- They are flightless.
- They reach 2 m (7 ft) tall.
- The emu has dark brown plumage, with naked blue spots on each side of the neck.
- The female emu has a sac in her throat, enabling her to emit a loud booming note.
- Cassowaries have bare heads with a horny helmetlike casque on top. Their plumage is black.
- Both the emu and cassowaries have three toes on each foot.

Species:

Emu *(Dromaius novaehollandiae)*
Common cassowary *(Casuarius casuarius)*
Dwarf cassowary *(Casuarius bennetti)*
Single-wattled cassowary *(Casuarius unappendiculatus)*

KIWIS

Apterygiformes
3 species

Where they live:

Forests in New Zealand

Key features:

- Kiwis are flightless.
- They have long, hairlike brown plumage.
- They are nocturnal.
- They have weak eyes, but well-developed senses of hearing and smell.
- They have long bills, which they use to probe the soil for worms and insects.
- They lay the largest eggs in proportion to body size of any bird, equal to a quarter of the female's total weight.

Species:

Common kiwi *(Apteryx australis)*
Little gray kiwi *(Apteryx owenii)*
Rotaroa kiwi *(Apteryx hastii)*

Why birds have different bills

The shape of birds' bills are directly related to their main food type. Birds of prey have hooked bills, which are ideal for tearing apart the flesh of their victims. By contrast, the long, straight bills of many wading birds are fitted for finding and removing food from mud and wet sand; the curved end of the avocet's bill is an adaptation from this shape for snapping up tiny creatures from shallow water. One of the strangest bills of any bird is that of the skimmer. This fish-eater hunts by flying low over water with the bottom half of its bill trawling through the surface. As soon as it makes contact with prey, the bill snaps shut.

Other features of birds' bills can be explained by different factors. Color, for instance, helps in species recognition and in some cases as an indicator of fitness as a mate. The bills of puffins are bright only during the breeding season; in fall and winter they become dull and gray. Other factors affect color, too. The red spot on a herring gull's bill prompts their chicks to peck at it, which in turn stimulates the parent to regurgitate food for them.

Avocet

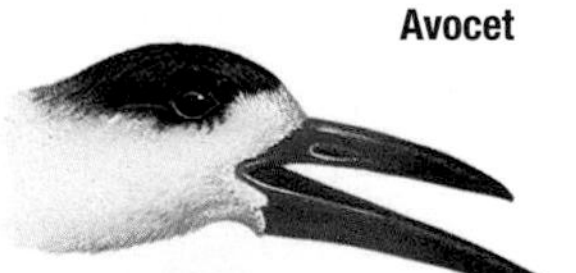

Skimmer

Puffin

Herring gull

From flightless ice-dwellers to hawk-eyed hunters

PENGUINS

Sphenisciformes
18 species

Where they live:
Coastal and open ocean waters in the Southern Hemisphere

Key features:
- Penguins are flightless; their wings are modified to serve as flippers.
- They have short, stiff, closely packed feathers.
- They feed on fish, squid and free-swimming crustaceans, such as krill.
- They breed on coasts from Antarctica to the Galapagos Islands, often in colonies with thousands of pairs.

Species:
Adelie penguin
(Pygoscelis adeliae)
Chinstrap penguin
(Pygoscelis antarctica)
Crested penguin
(Eudyptes pachyrhynchus)
Emperor penguin
(Aptenodytes forsteri)
Gentoo penguin
(Pygoscelis papua)
Jackass penguin
(Speniscus demersus)
King penguin
(Aptenodytes patagonica)
Little penguin
(Eudyptula minor)
Magellanic penguin
(Speniscus magellanicus)
Rockhopper penguin
(Eudyptes crestatus)

Special adaptations As with all other penguins, the feet of the crested penguin are positioned at the rear of their bodies to aid swimming. On land, this leads them to walk upright. Their wings have become adapted as paddles for swimming; the wing bones have fused together to help to stiffen these flippers.

DIVERS

Gaviiformes
4 species

Where they live:
Cold lakes and coastal waters in the Northern Hemisphere

Key features:
- Divers feed on fish, crustaceans and insects.
- Their legs are set far back on their bodies.
- They have webbed feet.
- Their bodies are streamlined for diving.
- They are able to dive to depths of 60 m (200 ft).
- They are also known as loons.

Species:
Black-throated diver
(Gavia arctica)
Great northern diver or common loon
(Gavia immer)
Red-throated diver
(Gavia stellata)
White-billed diver
(Gavia adamsii)

Born water dwellers
Divers, such as this red-throated diver, are so well adapted to life in the water that they actually have great difficulty moving about on land. Their feet are so far back on their bodies that they can only toboggan along on their bellies. In consequence, all nest very close to the water.

GREBES

Podicipediformes
About 20 species

Where they live:
Lakes, rivers and coastal waters in temperate regions

Key features:
- Grebes are weak fliers.
- They do not have webbed feet but instead have horny flaps on their toes to increase their surface areas to help in swimming.
- They feed on small fish and other aquatic animals.
- Many perform elaborate courtship "dances."
- Grebes build floating nests on open water or among reeds.

Species:
Black-throated grebe
(Podiceps novaehollandiae)
Great crested grebe
(Podiceps cristatus)
Great grebe
(Podiceps major)
Hoary-headed grebe
(Podiceps poliocephalus)
Least grebe
(Podiceps dominicus)
Little grebe
(Podiceps ruficollis)
Pied-billed grebe
(Podilymbus podiceps)
Red-necked grebe
(Podiceps griseigena)
Silver grebe
(Podiceps occipitalis)
Western grebe
(Aechmophorus occidentalis)

Dressed to impress In common with all grebes, the great crested grebe is more colorful in the breeding season than during the rest of the year. Once fall arrives and nesting is over, it molts its bright headdress.

ALBATROSSES, PETRELS AND FULMARS

Procellariiformes
More than 100 species

Where they live:
Oceans and coastlines worldwide

Key features:

Ocean glider
The northern fulmar looks like a seagull but is distinguished by its long, straight wings and single tubular nostril. It nests on cliffs across the Northern Hemisphere.

- All have hooked bills with a single tubular nostril running along the top and opening near the end.
- They have webbed feet.
- They visit land only to breed.
- They feed on fish, squid or carrion from on or near the water's surface.

Species:
Black-footed albatross
(Diomedea nigripes)
Fulmar prion
(Pacyptila crassirostris)
Northern fulmar
(Fulmarus glacialis)
Royal albatross
(Diomedea epomophora)
Short-tailed albatross
(Diomedea albatrus)
Short-tailed shearwater
(Puffinus tenuirostris)
Shy albatross
(Diomedea cauta)
Southern fulmar
(Fulmarus glacialoides)
Southern giant petrel
(Macronectes gigantus)
Steller's albatross
(Diomedea albatrus)
Wandering albatross
(Diomedea exulans)
Waved albatross
(Diomedea irrorata)

see also
74-75 **Animal kingdom**
96-97 **Animal records**
104-5 **Endangered species**

PELICANS AND GANNETS

Pelecaniformes
About 60 species

Where they live:
Worldwide, except the interiors of continents and the poles

Key features:
- All of its members have webbing between all four toes of their feet – not just three toes, as in other birds with webbed feet.
- They are all fish-eaters. Some obtain their food by diving from the air, some by diving from the water's surface. Frigate birds steal food from other sea birds.
- This group also includes cormorants, boobies, frigate birds, tropic birds and darters (or snakebirds).

Air raider The brown pelican hunts by plunging at fish headfirst from the air. In this respect, it is unique among pelicans; all other species fish from the water's surface.

Species:
American darter or snakebird *(Anhinga anhinga)*
Blue-footed booby *(Sula nebouxii)*
Great cormorant *(Phalacrocorax carbo)*
Great white pelican *(Pelecanus onocrotalus)*
Magnificent frigate bird *(Fregata magnificens)*
Northern gannet *(Morus bassanus)*
Red-billed tropic bird *(Phaeton aethereus)*
Spot-billed pelican *(Pelecanus philippensis)*

HERONS, STORKS AND FLAMINGOES

Ciconiiformes
About 120 species

Where they live:
Freshwater and coastal habitats worldwide, except the poles

Key features:
- They are water birds with long legs and necks.
- Most feed on fish and other small aquatic creatures. Some storks prefer drier environments and feed on small land animals, such as frogs and insects.
- This group also includes ibises, spoonbills, egrets and bitterns.

Species:
African open-billed stork *(Anastromus lamelligerus)*
Cattle egret *(Bubulcus ibis)*
Eurasian bittern *(Botaurus stellaris)*
Goliath heron *(Ardea goliath)*
Greater flamingo *(Phoenicopterus ruber)*
Grey heron *(Ardea cinerea)*
Marabou stork *(Leptoptilos crumeniferus)*
Painted stork *(Mycteria leucocephala)*
Scarlet ibis *(Eudocimus ruber)*
Snowy egret *(Egretta thula)*
White spoonbill *(Platalea leucorodia)*
White stork *(Ciconia ciconia)*
Wood stork *(Mycteria americana)*

Stilt walker The long, slender legs of herons enable them to creep through shallow water without alerting their prey.

DUCKS, GEESE AND SWANS

Anseriformes
More than 150 species

Where they live:
Worldwide, except for the Antarctic

Key features:
- They have plump bodies, short legs and webbed feet.
- They have an oil gland near the base of the tail. The bird pecks at the gland, then transfers the oil to its feathers to waterproof them.
- They line their nests with down. Almost all nest on the ground.
- The members of this group are commonly known as waterfowl.

Species:
Bean goose *(Anser fabalis)*
Black swan *(Cygnus atratus)*
Canada goose *(Branta canadensis)*
Common eider duck *(Somateria mollissima)*
Mallard duck *(Anas platyrhynchos)*
Mandarin duck *(Aix galericulata)*
Mute swan *(Cygnus olor)*
Red-breasted merganser *(Mergus serrator)*
Snow goose *(Anser coerulescens)*
Swan goose *(Anser cygonides)*

BIRDS OF PREY

Falconiformes
About 280 species

Where they live:
Worldwide, except for the Antarctic

Key features:
- All are carnivorous and have hooked beaks and powerful claws.
- They have extremely sharp eyesight and are active during the day.
- They have long wings in relation to their body size.
- This group includes eagles, buzzards, harriers, condors, falcons, kestrels, hawks, kites and vultures.

Species:
Andean condor *(Vultur gryphus)*
Bald eagle *(Haliaeetus leucocephalus)*
Black kite *(Milvus migrans)*
Common kestrel *(Falco tinnunculus)*
Crested caracara *(Polyborus plancus)*
Eurasian buzzard *(Buteo buteo)*
Hen harrier *(Circus cyaneus)*
Osprey *(Pandion haliaetus)*
Peregrine falcon *(Falco peregrinus)*
Secretary bird *(Sagittarius serpentarius)*
Turkey vulture *(Cathartes aura)*

Eagle-eyed The white-bellied sea eagle grabs fish from near the surface. Like all birds of prey, it has sharp eyes and a strongly hooked bill.

A diversity of forms, colors and lifestyles

PHEASANTS, GROUSE AND TURKEYS

Galliformes
More than 230 species

Where they live:
Worldwide, except for Antarctica

Key features:

- They are heavy-bodied and weak fliers.
- They spend most of their time on the ground, where they forage for seeds, worms and insects.
- The red jungle fowl is the ancestor of the domestic chicken.
- This group includes quails, peacocks, guinea fowl, partridges and curassows. Its members are often called game birds or fowl.

Species:

Black grouse *(Lyrurus tetrix)*
California quail *(Callipepla californica)*
Capercaillie *(Petrao urogallus)*
Common pheasant *(Phasianus colchicus)*
Common quail *(Coturnix coturnix)*
Great argus pheasant *(Argusianus argus)*
Great curassow *(Crax rubra)*
Greater prairie chicken *(Tympanuchus cupido)*
Grey partridge *(Perdix perdix)*
Helmeted guinea fowl *(Numidia meleagris)*
Himalayan snowcock *(Tetroagallus himalayensis)*
Mallee fowl *(Leipoa ocellata)*
Peacock *(Pavo cristatus)*
Red grouse *(Lagopus scoticus)*
Red jungle fowl *(Gallus gallus)*
Wild turkey *(Meleagris gallopavo)*

Prepared for winter The willow grouse is adapted to survive in the frozen north. Its plump body and feathered feet help it to retain heat, and, in winter, it turns almost completely white.

CRANES, RAILS AND BUSTARDS

Gruiformes
About 200 species

Where they live:
Worldwide, except the poles

Key features:

- These birds live in a range of habitats, from wetlands to dry plains.
- They are all omnivores that nest on the ground.
- Cranes and bustards have long necks and legs. Rails are more round-bodied with shorter necks and legs.
- Cranes fly with their necks straight out and legs trailing behind them. Rails are weak fliers. Bustards, although strong fliers, prefer to run from danger.

Weighty flier
At weights of up to 18 kg (40 lb), the great bustard is one of the world's heaviest flying birds.

Species:

Black-necked crane *(Grus nigricollis)*
Common coot *(Fulica atra)*
Common crane *(Grus grus)*
Common moorhen *(Gallinula chloropus)*
Great bustard *(Otis tarda)*
Hooded crane *(Grus monacha)*
Little bustard *(Otis tetrax)*
Sandhill crane *(Grus candensis)*
Takahe *(Porpyrio mantelli)*
Water rail *(Rallus aquaticus)*
Whooping crane *(Grus americana)*

WADERS, AUKS, SKUAS AND GULLS

Charadriiformes
More than 300 species

Where they live:
Worldwide, in freshwater and saltwater habitats

Key features:

- Gulls, terns, skuas and auks (including guillemots, puffins and razorbills) have webbed feet; waders do not.
- Gulls, terns, skuas and auks all eat fish. Waders feed on invertebrates.
- Most waders have long legs and long, narrow bills for probing mud or sand in search of food.
- Almost all species are migratory.
- Waders include avocets, oystercatchers, jacanas, plovers, sandpipers, stilts and turnstones.

Species:

Arctic skua *(Stercorarius parasiticus)*
Arctic tern *(Sterna paradisea)*
Atlantic puffin *(Fratercula arctica)*
Black skimmer *(Rhyncops niger)*
Black-winged stilt *(Himantopus himantopus)*
Comb-crested jacana *(Irediparra gallinacea)*
Common guillemot *(Uria aalge)*
Common gull *(Larus canus)*
Common snipe *(Gallinago gallinago)*
Eurasian curlew *(Numenius araquata)*
Eurasian oystercatcher *(Haematopus ostralegus)*
Herring gull *(Larus argentatus)*
Killdeer *(Charadrius vociferus)*
Kittiwake *(Rissa tridactyla)*
Little auk *(Alle alle)*
Northern lapwing *(Vanellus vanellus)*
Pacific gull *(Larus pacificus)*
Pied avocet *(Recurvirostra avosetta)*
Razorbill *(Alca torda)*
Red-necked phalarope *(Phalaropus lobatus)*
Ruff *(Philomachus pugnax)*

PIGEONS AND DOVES

Columbiformes
About 300 species

Where they live:
Worldwide, except the poles

Key features:

- Pigeons and doves are plump-bodied birds, with short necks, small heads and slim, rounded bills.
- They eat fruit and seeds.
- They are strong fliers.
- The eggs are incubated by both parents.
- They produce a nutritive liquid (pigeon's milk) from the lining of the crop to feed the young. Flamingoes are the only other birds known to do this.
- This group contains many island species, including the now-extinct dodo *(Raphus cucullatus)* of Mauritius.

Fabulous feathers Doves from temperate zones tend to have fairly dull plumage but those from the tropics can have brilliant colors.

Species:

Collared dove *(Streptopelia decaocto)*
Dusky dove *(Streptopelia lugens)*
Red-necked pigeon *(Columba squamosa)*
Spotted pigeon *(Columba maculosa)*
Superb fruit dove *(Ptilinopus superbus)*
Turtledove *(Streptopelia turtur)*
Victoria crowned pigeon *(Goura victoria)*
Wood pigeon *(Columba palumbus)*

see also

74-75 **Animal kingdom**
96-97 **Animal records**
104-5 **Endangered species**

PARROTS

Psittaciformes
About 300 species

Where they live

The tropics and some temperate areas of the Southern Hemisphere

Key features:

Pretty polly The scarlet macaw is one of the most familiar parrots, but, like many members of this family, it is threatened by demand from the pet trade.

- This group includes some of the world's most brightly colored birds.
- They have powerful, hooked bills, the top half of which is connected to the skull by a hingelike joint.
- Two of their toes point forward and two point backward.
- They feed primarily on fruit, seeds and nuts.
- Many species fly in large flocks, calling noisily to one another.
- All but a few species nest in holes in trees.

Species:

African gray parrot
(Psittacus erithacus)
Budgerigar
(Melopsittacus undulatus)
Galah *(Cactua rosicapilla)*
Kakapo
(Strigops habroptilus)
Kea *(Nestor notabilis)*
Rainbow lorikeet
(Trichoglossus haematodus)
Sulfur-crested cockatoo
(Cacatua galerita)

CUCKOOS AND TURACOS

Cuculiformes
About 150 species

Where they live:

Temperate and tropical regions worldwide

Key features:

- All members of this group have slim bodies, strong legs and long tails.
- Cuckoos are generally gray or brown. Turacos are very brightly colored.
- Cuckoos are famous for laying their eggs in other birds' nests but in fact, less than half of all cuckoo species do this.
- Most cuckoos are insectivores, but road-runners also feed on lizards and snakes. Turacos are fruit-eaters.

Species:

Black and white cuckoo
(Clamator jacobinus)
Common cuckoo
(Cuculus canorus)
Drongo cuckoo
(Surniculus lugubris)
Great blue turaco
(Corythaeola cristata)
Greater roadrunner
(Geococcyx californiana)
Great spotted cuckoo
(Clamator glandarius)
Hoatzin
(Opisthocomus hoatzin)
Knysa turaco
(Tauraco corythaix)
Lesser roadrunner
(Geococcyx velox)
Squirrel cuckoo
(Piaya cayana)
Striped cuckoo
(Tapera naevia)

Down to earth The greater roadrunner is a cuckoo that has taken to life on the ground. It uses its long tail as a counterweight to make sharp turns as it sprints after prey.

OWLS

Strigiformes
About 130 species

Where they live:

Worldwide, except for Antarctica

Key features:

- Owls are nocturnal and carnivorous.
- They have hooked beaks and powerful feet equipped with sharp talons.
- Their plumage is soft to muffle the sound of their flight from prey.
- They have sharp hearing and large, forward-facing eyes to pinpoint prey in almost total darkness.
- They can turn their heads all the way around to look behind themselves without moving their bodies.

Species:

Barn owl *(Tyto alba)*
Buffy fish owl
(Ketupa ketupa)
Burrowing owl
(Athene cunicularia)
Dusky eagle owl
(Bubo coromandus)
Elf owl *(Micrathene whitneyi)*
Great grey owl
(Strix nebulosa)
Snowy owl
(Nyctea scandiaca)
Tawny owl *(Strix aluco)*
White-fronted scops owl
(Otus sagittatus)

NIGHTJARS

Caprimulgiformes
More than 80 species

Where they live:

Worldwide, except the poles

Key features:

- Nightjars are nocturnal or active during twilight.
- They feed on insects caught while in flight.
- They have long, pointed wings and tiny feet.
- They are all extremely well camouflaged.
- This group also contains the frogmouths of Southeast Asia and Australia. Frogmouths look similar to nightjars. They are also nocturnal but catch their food on the ground.

Vanishing act Nightjars spend the daylight hours resting perfectly still. Their camouflage is so good that they are rarely seen.

Species:

Common nighthawk
(Chordeiles minor)
Dusky nightjar
(Veles binotatus)
European nightjar
(Caprimulgus europaeus)
Greater eared nightjar
(Eurostopodus macrotis)
Oilbird *(Steatornis caripensis)*
Sickle-winged nightjar
(Eleothreptus anomalus)
Spotted nightjar
(Eurostopodus guttatus)
Tawny frogmouth
(Podargus strigoides)

From specialist feeders to the most diverse group of birds in the world

SWIFTS AND HUMMINGBIRDS

Apodiformes
About 440 species

Where they live:
Tropical and temperate regions worldwide

Key features:

- All of these birds are small. Hummingbirds include the smallest birds on Earth.
- Swifts hunt flying insects and spend more time in the air than any other kind of bird. They even sleep on the wing.
- Hummingbirds' fast wing-beat enables them to hover in front of the flowers from which they feed.

Species:
Alpine swifts *(Apus melba)*
Bee hummingbird *(Calypte helenae)*
Blue-fronted lancebill *(Doryfera johanne)*
Eurasian swift *(Apus apus)*
Giant hummingbird *(Patagonia gigas)*
Great dusky swift *(Cypseloides senex)*
Hairy hermit *(Glaucis hirsuta)*
Pallid swift *(Apus pallidus)*
Sooty barbthroat *(Threnetes niger)*
Spot-fronted swift *(Cypseloides cherriei)*
Tooth-billed hummingbird *(Androdon aequatorialis)*

TROGONS

Trogoniformes
About 35 species

Where they live:
Tropical forests of Africa, Asia and the Americas

Key features:

- Most trogons eat insects caught in flight but some are fruit-eaters.
- They have brilliantly colored plumage.
- Two of their four toes point backward.

Species:
Mountain trogon *(Trogon mexicanus)*
Resplendent quetzal *(Pharomachrus mocinno)*

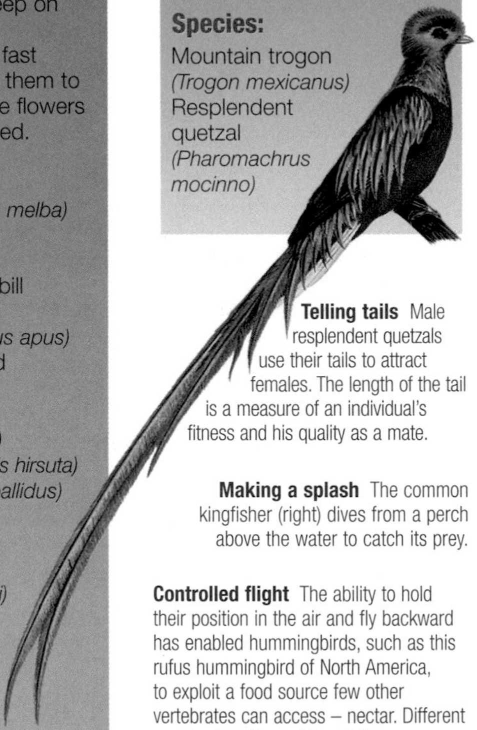

Telling tails Male resplendent quetzals use their tails to attract females. The length of the tail is a measure of an individual's fitness and his quality as a mate.

Making a splash The common kingfisher (right) dives from a perch above the water to catch its prey.

Controlled flight The ability to hold their position in the air and fly backward has enabled hummingbirds, such as this rufus hummingbird of North America, to exploit a food source few other vertebrates can access – nectar. Different species feed from different flowers.

KINGFISHERS AND HORNBILLS

Coraciiformes
About 190 species

Where they live:
Worldwide in temperate and tropical regions

Key features:

- This group also includes bee-eaters, rollers, hoopoes and todies.
- Most members have brightly colored plumage.
- They are all carnivorous except for hornbills, which also eat fruit.
- Kingfishers have big heads and daggerlike bills.
- Hornbills have massive, curved bills.

Species:
Abyssinian roller *(Coracias abyssinica)*
Amazon kingfisher *(Chloroceryle amazona)*
Belted kingfisher *(Megaceryle alcyon)*
Common bee-eater *(Merops apiaster)*

Common kingfisher *(Alcedo atthis)*
Great Indian hornbill *(Buceros bicornis)*
Green kingfisher *(Chloroceryle americana)*
Helmeted hornbill *(Rhinoplax vigil)*
Hoopoe *(Upupa epops)*
Jamaican tody *(Todus todus)*
Kookaburra *(Dacelo novaeguineae)*
Little kingfisher *(Ceyx pusillus)*
Malachite kingfisher *(Alcedo cristata)*

WOODPECKERS AND TOUCANS

Piciformes
About 400 species

Where they live:
Worldwide, except Australia and Antarctica

Key features:

- All of this group, which includes honeyguides, jacamars, barbets and puffbirds, are tree-dwellers that spend most of their lives alone.
- They all have two toes that point forward and two that point backward.
- Woodpeckers hammer at trees for grubs to eat, using straight, pointed bills.
- Toucans eat mostly fruit, and have large, brightly colored bills to reach for their food.

Firm grip A woodpecker grips with its strong, clawed feet and uses its stiff tail for support. It uses its beak to enlarge natural holes in trees to make its nest.

Species:
Black-spotted barbet *(Capito niger)*
Black woodpecker *(Dryocopus martius)*
Collared puffbird *(Bucco capensis)*
Greater honey guide *(Indicator indicator)*
Green aracari *(Pteroglossus viridis)*
Green woodpecker *(Picus viridis)*
Lettered toucan *(Pteroglossus inscriptus)*
Northern flicker *(Colaptes auratus)*
Paradise jacamar *(Galbula dea)*
Toco toucan *(Rhamphastos toco)*
Wryneck *(Jynx torquilla)*

PERCHING BIRDS

Passeriformes
About 5400 species

Where they live:
Worldwide, except the poles

Key features:
- This group includes about 60 percent of all living bird species.
- The vast majority are small birds, less than 25 cm (10 in.) long.
- They have toes adapted for grasping twigs or branches. The toes can lock into place, enabling these birds to sleep while perching.
- They are all land birds, although some species fly over seas and oceans during migration.

THE ASCENDANCY OF PERCHING BIRDS

Perching birds make up the great majority of the birds on the planet. They include all of the so-called "songbirds," such as finches, starlings and warblers, as well as the crows, swallows and more exotic species such as birds of paradise.

Perching birds are considered to be the most highly evolved of all the birds. They have three toes that point forward and one that points backward, enabling them to grip twigs and exploit scrubland and wooded habitats. Their generally small size has led to their success in many grassland habitats, particularly reed beds and marshes, as well.

Perching birds prosper even where perches are totally unavailable. From the snow buntings of the Arctic to the sand larks and trumpeter finches of the Sahara desert, they survive on amounts of food too small or widely scattered to sustain larger or less mobile species.

Of all the perching birds alive today, more than three quarters are songbirds, or "oscines." They are separated from the more primitive "suboscine" perching birds by their more highly developed vocal organ, or syrinx, which can produce the uninterrupted stream of song characteristic of this group.

The earliest-known fossils of perching birds date from about 40 million years ago, although scientists believe that the group has existed since the Cretaceous period. Their global domination is more recent. In the early Miocene period, 25 million years ago, the group underwent an adaptive explosion that paralleled the spread of grasslands caused by global climatic change.

About 3 million years ago, a second adaptive explosion began, leading to a huge increase in the number of species. The trigger for this is unclear, although environmental change may again be a factor because it occurred during a period of four major cycles of glaciation.

see also
74-75 **Animal kingdom**
96-97 **Animal records**
104-5 **Endangered species**

Families:
Perching birds divide into more than 50 families:
Accentors (Prunellidae)
American orioles (Icteridae)
Ant pipits (Conopophagidae)
Antbirds (Formicariidae)
Australian tree creepers (Climacteridae)
Birds of paradise (Pardisaeidae)
Bowerbirds and catbirds (Ptilonorhynchidae)
Broadbills (Eurylaimidae)
Bulbuls (Pycnonotidae)
Cotingas (Cotingidae)
Crows, magpies and jays (Corvidae)
Cuckoo-shrikes (Campephagidae)
Dippers (Cinclidae)
Drongos (Dicruridae)
Finches (Fringillidae)
Flowerpeckers (Dicaeidae)
Flycatchers, thrushes and warblers (Muscicapidae)
Hawaiian honeycreepers (Drepanididae)
Honeyeaters (Meliphagidae)
Larks (Alaudidae)
Leafbirds (Irenidae)
Lyrebirds (Menuridae)
Manakins (Pipridae)
Mockingbirds (Mimidae)
New Zealand wrens (Xenticidae)
Nuthatches (Sittidae)
Orioles (Orioidae)
Ovenbirds (Furnaridae)
Pittas (Pittidae)
Plantcutters (Phytotomidae)
Scrub birds (Atrichornithidae)
Sharpbills (Oxyruncidae)
Shrikes (Laniidae)
Song-shrikes (Cracticidae)
Sparrows and weavers (Ploceidae)
Starlings (Sturnidae)
Sunbirds (Nectariniidae)
Swallows and martins (Hirundinidae)
Tanagers, cardinals, sugar birds and buntings (Emberlzidae)
Tapaculos (Rhinocryptidae)
Tits and chickadees (Paridae)
Tree-creepers (Certhiidae)
Tyrant flycatchers (Tyrannidae)
Vireos (Vireonidae)
Wagtails and pipits (Motacillidae)
Wattlebirds (Callaeidae)
Waxwings and palmchats (Bombycillidae)
Weaver-finches (Estrildidae)
White-eyes (Zosteropidae)
Woodcreepers (Dendrocoplapidae)
Wood swallows (Artamidae)
Wood warblers (Parulidae)
Wrens (Troglodytidae)

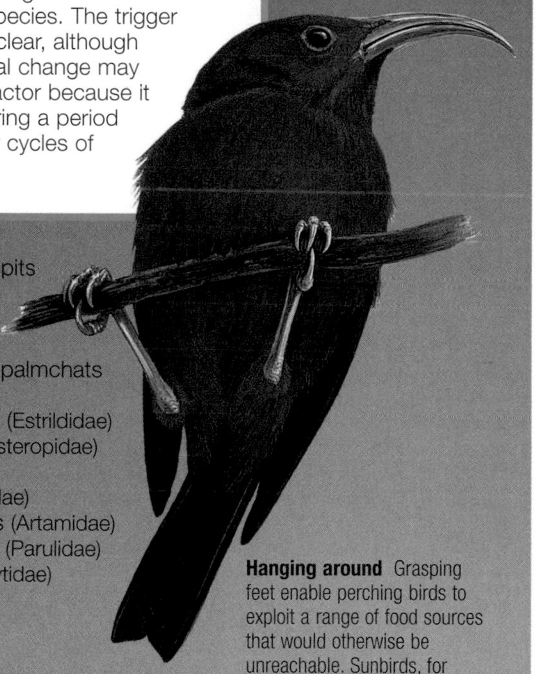

Hanging around Grasping feet enable perching birds to exploit a range of food sources that would otherwise be unreachable. Sunbirds, for example, probe into flowers for nectar from their vantage points of twigs and stems, which they grip with their opposing claws.

Common colonizer House sparrows have exploited human settlements across the globe for food and nesting sites. However, this successful little bird is becoming less common in some areas.

Animals have developed abilities that allow them to live even in the most extreme conditions. The emperor penguin (Aptenodytes forsteri), *for example, can breed in the severe Antarctic winter. Males are able to incubate their single egg with external temperatures as low as –60°C (–76°F), surviving solely on fat reserves in the body for 62 to 67 days without a break.*

ACUTE SENSES

Most complicated song
Male humpback whales *(Megaptera novaeangliae)* have the world's longest, most complicated songs. Each can last over 30 minutes and can be heard by other whales up to 160 km (100 miles) away.

Loudest sound
The low-frequency pulses that fin whales *(Balaenoptera physalus)* and blue whales *(Balaenoptera musculus)* make in order to communicate with each other have been measured at up to 188 decibels – the loudest sound emitted from a living source.

Best sense of smell
Sharks have more highly developed scent organs and a better sense of smell than any other fish. They can detect as little as one part of mammalian blood in 100 million parts of water.

Sharpest hearing
Ultrasonic echolocation gives bats the most acute hearing of any terrestrial animal. Most species can hear frequencies up to about 80 kHz, although some are able to detect sound at 250 kHz. The human limit is only about 20 kHz.

LARGEST

Land animal
The largest land animal is the African bush elephant *(Loxodonta africana africana)*. The biggest recorded specimen is thought to have weighed 12 metric tons.

Land carnivore
The Kodiak bear is the largest land carnivore. Members of this race of brown bear *(Ursus arctos)* can weigh more than half a ton and stand 3.7 m (12 ft) tall.

Carnivore
The largest animal that actively hunts prey is the sperm whale *(Physeter macrocephalus)*. It can be 26 m (85 ft) long and weigh up to 50 metric tons.

Fish
The whale shark *(Rhincodon typus)* reaches lengths of 12 m (40 ft). It is a filter feeder, using its gills to strain crustaceans and fish out of the water.

Reptile
The saltwater crocodile (*Crocodylus porosus*, below) from Asia and the Pacific is the largest living reptile, at about 6 m (20 ft) long and weighing up to 1.5 metric tons. The longest is Southeast Asia's reticulated python *(Python reticulatus)*, which can be 10 m (33 ft) long.

Bird
The largest living bird is the ostrich *(Struthio camelus)*, which can grow to 2.7 m (8 ft 10 in.) tall.

Mammal
The blue whale *(Balaenoptera musculus)* is the biggest living mammal and probably the largest animal ever. The heaviest specimen ever recorded weighed 190 metric tons, whereas the longest measured 33.5 m (110 ft).

SMALLEST

Bird
The world's smallest bird is the bee hummingbird (*Mellisuga helenae*, shown life-size above) from Cuba. Adult males are 5.5 cm (2 1/4 in.) long and weigh 1.6 g (0.056 oz).

Fish
The smallest fish and smallest known vertebrate is the dwarf goby *(Trimmatom nanus)*. It lives in the Indian Ocean and has an average length of 8 mm (5/16 in.).

Mammal
The smallest mammal is the bumblebee bat *(Craseonycteris thonglongyai)* from Thailand. It weighs just 1.7-2 g (0.06-0.07 oz) and is only 2.8-3.3 cm (1 1/8-1 1/3 in.) long.

Most shocking animal
The electric eel or paroque *(Electrophorus electricus)*, from northern South America, can release a shock of up to 650 volts to immobilize and kill prey – strong enough to stun an adult human.

Fastest insect runners
Cockroaches can run at up to 5 km/h (3 mph), the fastest land speed in the insect world. This is amazingly fast. Scaled to human size, it would be like running at 320 km/h (200 mph).

Fastest land animal
The cheetah *(Acinonyx jubatus)* can move faster than any other creature on dry land. In three seconds, from a standing start, it can reach a speed of about 96 km/h (60 mph).

Most fertile animal
With no predators and unlimited food, one cabbage aphid *(Brevicoryne brassicae)* could create an 822 million metric ton mass of offspring every year – three times the weight of the human population.

Longest hibernation
Marmots can hibernate for nine months a year, so they may spend 75 percent of their lives in deep sleep. Sloths, opossums and armadillos spend up to 80 percent of their lives asleep or dozing.

Longest insect
The world's longest insect is *Pharnacia kirbyi*, a stick insect from Borneo. Its body is up to 33 cm (13 in.) long, and its 54.6 cm ($21\frac{1}{2}$ in.) legs are so long that they can get tangled when it sheds its skin.

Longest-lived animal
Giant tortoises can live longer than any other land animal. One on Tonga was said to be 193 when it died in 1966. The oldest verified age is 152, for a specimen that died in Mauritius in 1918.

Longest pregnancy
Gestation periods of up to 38 months have been recorded among Alpine salamanders *(Salamandra atra)* in southern Europe. One or two young are born within a few hours of each other.

Longest migration
Every year the Arctic tern *(Sterna paradisaea)* flies 40 000 km (25 000 miles) from the Southern Ocean to its Arctic breeding ground and back. In 25 years, this equals a return-trip to the Moon.

Most legs
Centipedes and millipedes have more legs than any other animal. The record number of legs counted on a centipede is 354; millipedes have been recorded to have about 700 legs each.

Greediest animal
The larva of the polyphemus moth *(Antheraea polyphemus)* consumes 86 000 times its birthweight in its first 56 days. This is equal to a 3.17 kg (7 lb) human baby taking in 273 metric tons of food.

Most poisonous animal
Arrow-poison frogs, like the yellow-banded one (*Dendrobates leucomelas*, above), secrete some of the deadliest biological toxins in the world. The most lethal poisons are found in the skin of the golden arrow-poison frog *(Phyllobates terribilis)*, native to the jungles of South and Central America.

see also

74-75 **Animal kingdom**
104-5 **Endangered species**

There are three groups of living mammals: placentals, marsupials and monotremes. In placental mammals, such as humans, the young develop inside the mother's body. Marsupials – kangaroos, koalas and the like – give birth to immature young who develop further in the mother's pouch. Monotremes, such as the platypus, are the oldest and most primitive mammals, giving birth to young who hatch from eggs outside the mother's body.

WHAT IS A MAMMAL?

- Mammals are **warm-blooded** vertebrates.
- They have **mammary glands** that produce milk so that the newly born have an immediate food supply.
- With the exception of mature whales, dolphins and porpoises, they have **hair** on their bodies, which helps to maintain a stable body temperature.
- They have a **middle ear**, containing three small bones that modify and transmit sound waves to the inner ear.
- They have **seven vertebrae in the neck**.

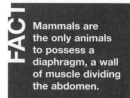

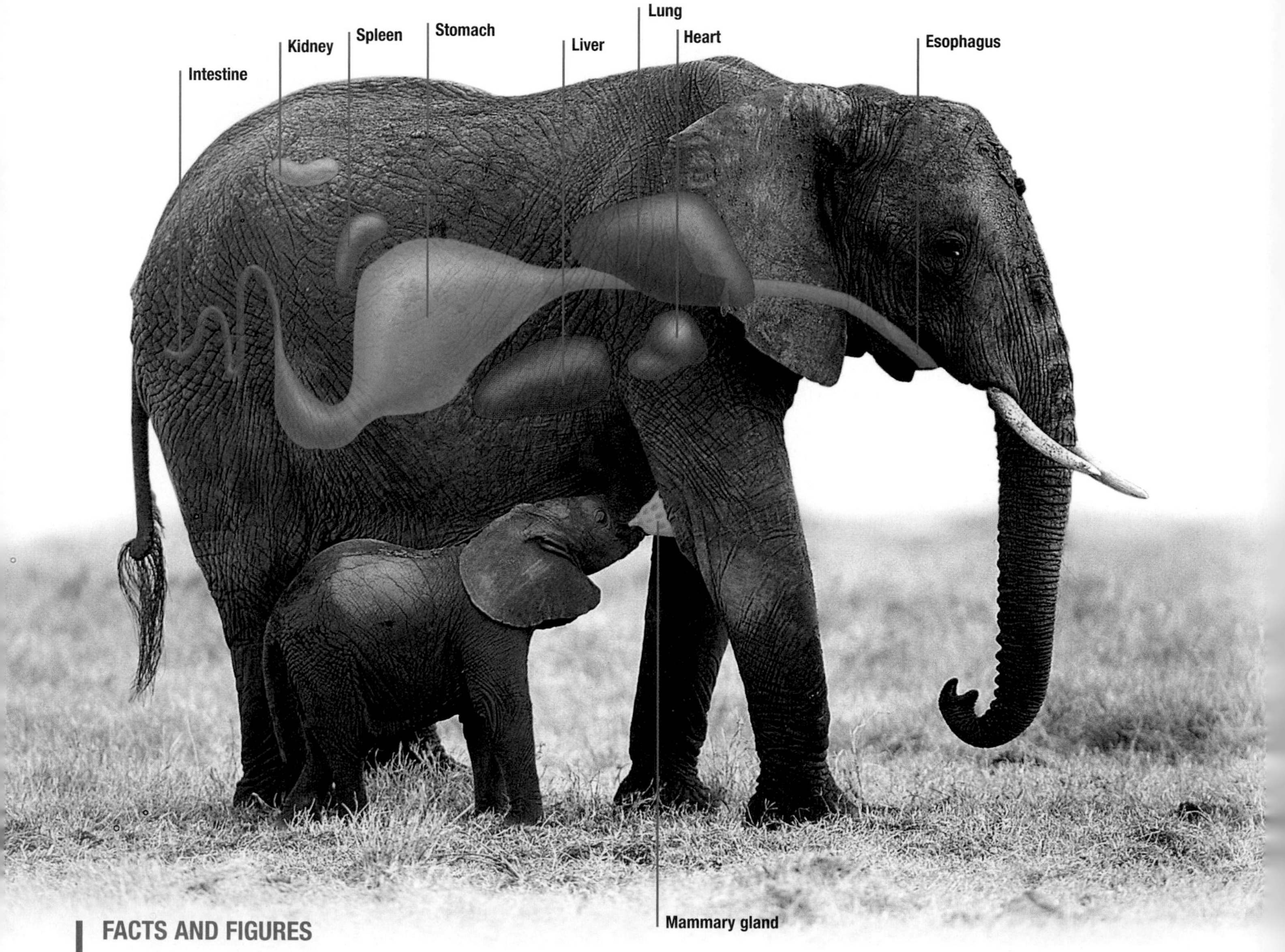

FACTS AND FIGURES

- There are more than 4000 species of mammal.
- The smallest land mammal is the pygmy or Savi's shrew *(Suncus etruscus)*. Its body is just 4-5 cm (1½-2 in.) long. It can creep into holes made by large earthworms.
- Nearly a quarter of all mammals can fly. Bats make up 23 percent of known mammal species.
- No two zebras have exactly the same pattern of stripes and no two giraffes have the same pattern of spots.

FACT **Mammals are the only animals to possess a diaphragm, a wall of muscle dividing the abdomen.**

PLATYPUSES AND ECHIDNAS

Monotremata
3 species

Where they live:
Australia and New Guinea

Key features:

- Monotremes are the most primitive mammals.
- They are the only mammals that lay eggs. Like other mammals, however, they have mammary glands and hair.
- There are three living species, two echidnas and the platypus.
- Echidnas have long, sticky tongues and powerful, short limbs fitted with claws for catching and eating ants.

Families:
Echidnas (Tachyglossidae)
Platypus (Ornithorhynchidae)

Spineless A baby short-nose echidna *(Tachyglossus aculeatus)* lacks the distinctive spiny coat that will help to protect it as an adult.

KANGAROOS, OPOSSUMS AND KOALAS

Marsupialia.
About 250 species

Where they live:
Australia, New Guinea and the Americas

Key features:

- Marsupials have relatively small brains.
- The young are born tiny and immature. In most species, females carry their young in a pouch for several weeks after their birth.
- Marsupial mothers can nurture three generations of young at once: one in utero, one in the pouch and one approaching independence.

Families:
Bandicoots (Peramelidae)
Kangaroos and wallabies (Macropodidae)
Marsupial anteaters (Myrmecobiidae)
Marsupial cats and mice (Dasyuridae)
Marsupial moles (Notorycidae)
Opossums (Didelphidae)
Phalangers and possums (Phalangeridae)
Rat opossums (Caenolestidae)
Wombats (Vombatidae)

SHREWS, MOLES AND HEDGEHOGS

Insectivora
Nearly 400 species

Where they live:
Worldwide, except poles and Australia

Key features:

- They are insect-eaters – hence their name, insectivores.
- They are small, with narrow snouts and sharp, simple teeth.
- They have poor eyesight, but a good sense of smell.
- Many are nocturnal.

Families:
Golden moles (Chrysochloridae)
Hedgehogs (Erinaceidae)
Moles (Talpidae)
Otter shrews (Potamogalidae)
Shrews (Soricidae)
Solenodons (Solenodontidae)
Tenrecs (Tenrecidae)

ELEPHANT SHREWS

Macroscelidea
12 species

Where they live:
Africa

Key features:

- They are ratlike, with long sensitive snouts.
- They eat insects, eggs, and small mammals.
- They used to be included in the Insectivora, but are no longer believed to be closely related to "true" shrews.

Family:
Elephant shrews (Macroscelididae)

Leaps and bounds Although they usually scuttle around on all fours at the first sign of danger, elephant shrews can rear up on their long, slender hind limbs and bound off at great speed. When doing this, they resemble miniature kangaroos.

see also
72-73 **Rise of the mammals**
74-75 **Animal kingdom**
104-5 **Endangered species**

Placentals versus marsupials

During the Cretaceous period, marsupials were the dominant mammals and coexisted with placentals by exploiting different food sources. However, where placental mammals have been introduced into marsupial populations, the marsupials have tended to lose out. This is not always the case. Despite competition from placentals, many Australian marsupial species still flourish.

Placentals	Marsupials
Generally have larger brains	Generally have smaller brains
Can regulate temperature well	Can become torpid in extreme cold
Large placenta – uses up a lot of energy	Small placenta – conserves energy
Mature young at birth	Immature young at birth
Birth can be difficult – mother and offspring vulnerable	Birth easy – young then protected in pouch until sufficiently mature

Reaching safety The sole aim of a newly born kangaroo, known as a joey, is to crawl into the security of its mother's pouch, where it latches onto one of her teats and suckles.

Gliders and flyers, swingers and diggers

FLYING LEMURS

Dermoptera
2 species

Where they live:
Southeast Asia

Key features:

- They can glide more than 120 m (400 ft) at a time on flaps of skin that extend along each side of the body from neck to forelimb to hind limb and tail.
- They hang upside down when resting.
- They feed on buds and leaves.

Family:
Flying lemurs or colugos (Dermopteridea)

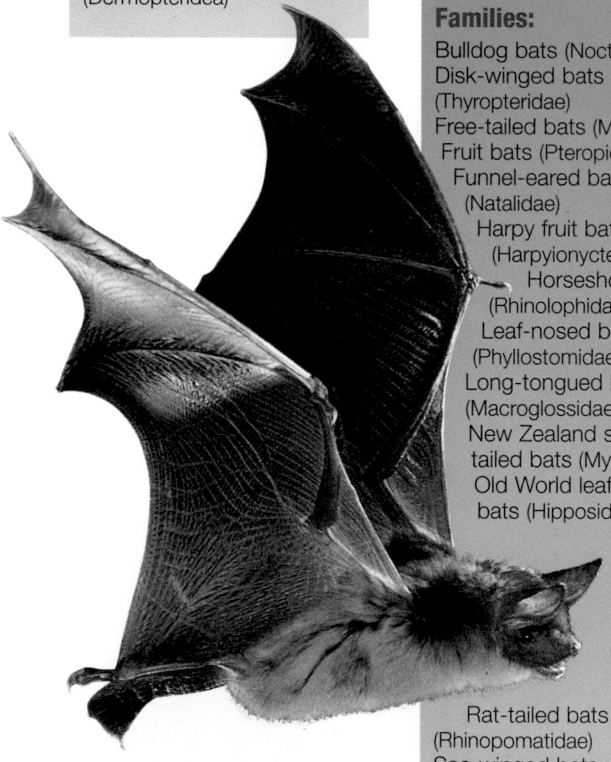

Annual migration The large mouse-eared bat *(Myotis myotis)* migrates between its summer and winter homes, frequently covering distances of over 260 km (160 miles). It is rarely seen in the colder months, when it hibernates in caves.

BATS

Chiroptera
Nearly 1000 species

Where they live:
Most temperate and tropical regions

Key features:

- Bats are nocturnal.
- They eat fruit or insects – also nectar, small animals and blood.
- Insectivorous bats use echolocation to find prey.
- They are the only true fliers (as opposed to gliders) among mammals.
- Their wings are an extension of the skin, supported between forelimb, hind limb and tail.

Families:
Bulldog bats (Noctilionidae)
Disk-winged bats (Thyropteridae)
Free-tailed bats (Molossidae)
Fruit bats (Pteropidae)
Funnel-eared bats (Natalidae)
Harpy fruit bats (Harpyionycteridae)
Horseshoe bats (Rhinolophidae)
Leaf-nosed bats (Phyllostomidae)
Long-tongued bats (Macroglossidae)
New Zealand short-tailed bats (Mystacindae)
Old World leaf-nosed bats (Hipposideridae)
Rat-tailed bats (Rhinopomatidae)
Sac-winged bats (Emballonuridae)
Slit-faced bats (Nycteridae)
Smokey bats (Furipteridae)
Sucker-footed bats (Myzopodidae)
Vampire bats (Desmontidae)
Vespertilionid bats (Vespertilionidae)

TREE SHREWS

Scandentia
About 20 species

Where they live:
Tropical forests of Asia

Key features:

- They are squirrel-like, with long noses.
- They eat insects, fruit and seeds.
- They have good hearing and vision.
- They are about 45 cm (18 in.) long, including their tails.
- They are sometimes classed as small, primitive primates.

Family:
Tree shrews (Tupaiidae)

PROSIMIANS, MONKEYS AND APES

Primates
About 230 species

Where they live:
Mostly in tropical and subtropical regions. Man lives everywhere.

Key features:

- Their eyes face forward.
- They have grasping hands and feet, some with opposable thumbs.
- They have flat nails rather than claws.
- They are adapted for climbing.
- Two mammary glands on the chest.
- Brain size increased in advanced species.
- In more advanced primates, the face is naked or bearded, and the snout tends to be shorter than in prosimians such as lemurs, lorises and tarsiers.

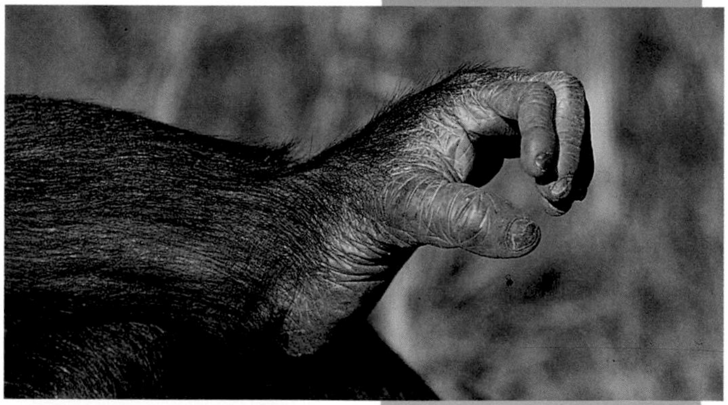

Getting a grip Most primates, such as the chimpanzee *(Pan troglodytes)*, have feet and hands with opposable thumbs, which can be placed opposite the other digits. This allows primates to get a firm grip on the branches of the trees in which they live. The increased dexterity that an opposable thumb brings has allowed man to evolve complex tool-making skills.

Families:
Aye-ayes (Daubentoniidae)
Gibbons (Hylobatidae)
Great apes (Pongidae)
Indri and sifakas (Indriidae)
Lemurs (Lemuridae)
Lorises, pottos and bushbabies (Lorisidae)
Man (Hominidae)
New World monkeys and marmosets (Cebidae)
Old World monkeys (Cercopithecidae)
Spider monkeys, howler monkeys and sakis (Atelidae)
Tarsiers (Tarsiidae)

see also
74-75 **Animal kingdom**
96-97 **Animal records**
104-5 **Endangered species**

ARMADILLOS, SLOTHS AND ANTEATERS

Edentata
30 species

Where they live:
South America

Key features:

- They have long snouts and long, sticky tongues.
- Teeth are small or absent.
- Their backbones are reinforced, making them strong diggers when they excavate ant hills for food.
- They have a well-developed sense of smell.
- They have the most primitive brains of any New World mammals.

Families:
Anteaters (Myrmecophagidae)
Armadillos (Dasyodidae)
Sloths (Bradypodidae)

Slow mover By day the three-toed sloth *(Bradypus tridactylus)* hangs from a branch by its long, curved claws. Even after sunset, it moves only a few yards in search of food.

PANGOLINS

Pholidota
7 species

Where they live:
Africa and Southeast Asia

Key features:

- They have a long, prehensile tail.
- They are nocturnal.
- They are covered with overlapping horny scales.
- They feed on ants and termites.
- They are toothless but have a long, sticky tongue and strong claws.

Family:
Pangolins (Manidae)

Suit of armor Thick overlapping scales cover almost the entire body of the tree pangolin *(Manis tricuspis)*. If attacked, it curls up, leaving the cutting edge of its scales to inflict damage on the attacker.

AARDVARKS

Tubulidentata
1 species

Where they live:
Central and Southern Africa

Key features:

- They have a long snout, large ears and thick tail.
- They feed entirely on termites and ants.
- They use strong claws to break open mounds of termites, which they lap up with a long, sticky tongue.
- They live on grasslands and in open forests.
- They are nocturnal, sleeping in deep burrows by day.

Family:
Aardvark (Orycteropidae)

RABBITS, HARES AND PIKAS

Lagomorpha
About 65 species

Where they live:
All continents, except Antarctica

Key features:

- They are ground-dwelling herbivores.
- At the front of the mouth, they have an extra pair of chisel-shaped upper and lower incisor teeth for cutting through plant stems.
- They have sharp eyesight and hearing, which enable them to escape in good time from potential predators.

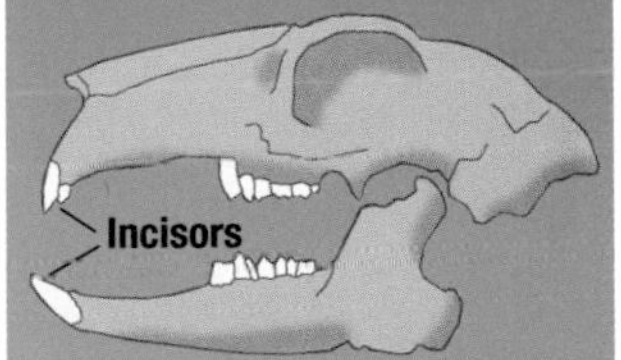

Families:
Rabbits and hares (Leporidae)
Pikas (Ochotonidae)

Mountain-dweller The northern pika *(Ochotona princeps)*, a relative of rabbits and hares, lives in large colonies, mostly high up in remote, rocky parts of northwestern North America.

Feeding machine Having ripped open its prey's home with its long front claws, the giant anteater *(Myrmecophaga tridactyla)*, sweeps the insects into its mouth with its sticky tongue.

Water-dwellers, grassland grazers and meat-eaters

RATS AND MICE

Rodentia
More than 1800 species

Where they live:
Worldwide, except polar regions

Key features:

- Known collectively as rodents, the group also includes beavers, squirrels and guinea pigs.
- They are mostly herbivorous.
- They have chisel-like incisor teeth for gnawing. These teeth never stop growing and stay sharp.

Families:

African mole rats and bamboo rats (Rhizomyidae)
Beavers (Castoridae)
Birch and jumping mice (Zapodidae)
Cane rats (Thryonomyidae)
Capybaras (Hydrochoeridae)
Chinchilla rats (Abrocomidae)
Chinchillas and viscachas (Chinchillidae)
Dormice (Gliridae)
Field mice, deer mice, voles, lemmings and muskrats (Cricetidae)
Guinea pigs, cavies and maras (Caviidae)
Hutias and coypus (Capromyidae)
Jerboas (Dipodidae)
Mole rats (Spalacidae)
New World porcupines (Erethizontidae)
Old World porcupines (Hystricidae)
Old World rats and mice (Muridae)
Pacaranas (Dinomyidae)
Pacas and agoutis (Dasyproctidae)
Pocket gophers (Geomyidae)
Pocket mice, kangaroo rats and mice (Heteromydae)
Rock rats and dassie rats (Petromuridae)
Spiny rats (Echimyidae)
Squirrels, chipmunks and marmots (Sciuridae)
Tuco-tucos (Ctenomyidae)

WHALES, DOLPHINS AND PORPOISES

Cetacea
About 80 species

Where they live:
All oceans and some rivers

Key features:

- These are marine mammals.
- Known collectively as cetaceans, they divide into two groups: toothed whales and baleen whales.
- Baleen whales (gray, humpback, right and rorqual whales) have no teeth. Instead, they have plates of stiff, hairlike material (whalebone) that filter out plankton.
- Toothed whales, as well as dolphins and porpoises, hunt down their prey.
- They have nasal openings (blowholes) at the top of the head but no external ears and almost no hair.
- Highly social, they communicate using a large repertoire of noises.

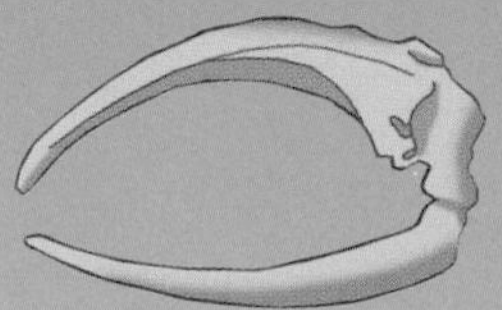

The arched upper jaw of a baleen whale allows space for the baleen plates, which hang down from it.

Families:

Beaked whales (Hyperoodontidae)
Dolphins and killer whales (Delphinidae)
Grey whale (Eschrichtiidae)
Long-snouted dolphins (Stenidae)
Narwhal and beluga whales (Monodontidae)
Porpoises (Phocoenidae)
Right whales (Balaenidae)
River dolphins (Platanistidae)
Rorquals and humpback whales (Balaenopteridae)
Sperm whales (Physeteridae)

CATS, DOGS AND BEARS

Carnivora
270 species

Where they live:
Worldwide, including the Arctic and Antarctic

Key features:

- Known collectively as carnivores, they also include foxes, wolves, hyenas, otters, skunks, seals and walruses.
- They are mostly predatory meat-eaters, though many canids (dogs, foxes, jackals and wolves) are omnivorous, and the giant panda is almost entirely herbivorous.
- Their large, pointed canine teeth are good for stabbing.
- Many have specialized carnassial teeth for shearing through meat.
- Their brains are usually large in relation to body size.

Families:

Bears and giant panda (Ursidae)
Cats (Felidae)
Civets and genets (Viverridae)
Dogs, foxes, jackals and wolves (Canidae)
Eared seals (Otariidae)
Earless seals (Phocidae)
Hyenas and aardwolves (Hyaenidae)
Mongooses and meerkats (Herpestinae)
Raccoons, coatis and lesser panda (Procyonidae)
Walrus (Odobenidae)
Weasels, badgers, skunks and otters (Mustelidae)

ELEPHANTS

Proboscidea
2 species

Where they live:
Sub-Saharan Africa, India, Sri Lanka, Southeast Asia

Key features:

- They are the largest of living land mammals: Adults weigh 6 metric tons and more.
- They are herbivores. An adult male eats up to 180 kg (400 lb) of herbage a day.
- They have a long boneless trunk – a combination of upper lips, palate and nostrils. Tusks are elongated upper incisors.
- In prehistoric times, there were about 300 species; now only two survive.
- The African elephant *(Loxodonta africana)* is bigger than the Asian elephant *(Elephas maximus)*, with noticeably larger ears.

Family:

Elephants (Elephantidae)

Status symbols The tusks of a bull walrus *(Odobenus rosmarus)* can be up to 90 cm (35 in.) long. They are used in courtship disputes and displays to help to attract a mate.

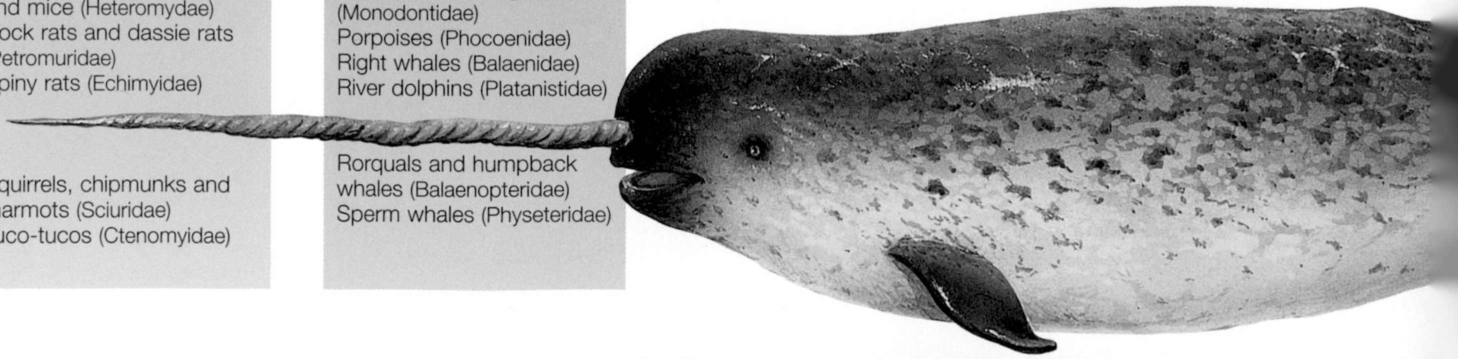

HYRAXES

Hyracoidea
7 species

Where they live:
Africa, Arabia, Syria

Key features:
- They have a small, compact, rabbit-sized body.
- They have no visible tail.
- Their front feet have four hoof-like toes; their hind feet have three toes and one grooming claw.
- They have two-chambered stomach for digesting diet of vegetation.

Family:
Hyraxes (Procaviidae)

DUGONG AND MANATEES

Sirenia
4 species

Where they live:
Tropical coastal waters and adjacent rivers of western Atlantic, Pacific and Indian oceans

Key features:
- They are marine mammals, which live almost continuously submerged.
- They are known collectively as sirenians.
- They are herbivores, browsing on marine plant life.
- They have complex three-chambered stomachs.
- They are placid, slow and defenseless.

Families:
Dugong (Dugongidae)
Manatees (Trichechidae)

HORSES, ASSES AND RHINOCEROSES

Perissodactyla
15 species

Where they live:
Tropical America, eastern and Southern Africa, southern Asia

Key features:
- The group also includes zebras and tapirs.
- They are large herbivores. Grass is an important part of their diet.
- They possess one or three hoofed toes on each hind foot.
- The most primitive of the perissodactyls are the tapirs, which probably resemble the common ancestor of the order.

Families:
Horses, asses and zebras (Equidae)
Tapirs (Tapiridae)
Rhinoceroses (Rhinocerotidae)

PIGS, GOATS, SHEEP AND CATTLE

Artiodactyla
150 species

Where they live:
All continents, except Antarctica

Key features:
- This group also includes giraffes, deer and camels.
- They are frequently described as "cloven-hoofed" because hoofs are divided in two. In fact, each cloven hoof consists of two hoofed toes.
- These herbivores often graze in large herds on grasslands.
- Their stomachs and intestines are specially adapted for digesting the large quantities of cellulose found in plants.
- Many have horns or antlers.

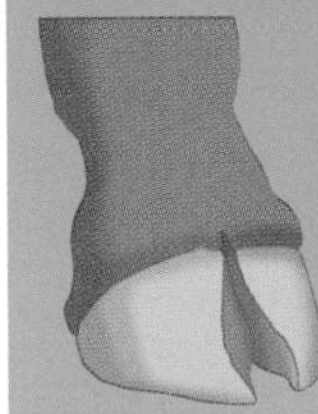

The two surviving toes form the "cloven hoof" of many artiodactyls.

Families:
Camels and lamoids (Camelidae)
Cattle, sheep, goats and antelopes (Bovidae)
Chevrotains (Tragulidae)
Deer (Cervidae)
Giraffes and okapi (Giraffidae)
Hippopotamuses (Hippopotamidae)
Peccaries (Tayassuidae)
Pigs (Suidae)
Pronghorn (Antilocapridae)

see also
74-75 **Animal kingdom**
96-97 **Animal records**
104-5 **Endangered species**

Lone swimmer Unlike the more gregarious dugong of the Indian and Pacific oceans, the West Indian manatee *(Trichechus manatus)* is a solitary creature, living in tropical waters of the western Atlantic.

Hidden herbivore The Malayan tapir *(Tapirus indicus)* is a nocturnal creature living in the densest parts of the forests of Southeast Asia. Man's destruction of its habitat is threatening this elusive species with extinction.

Well armed The tusk of the Arctic narwhal *(Monodon monoceros)* is in fact a modified tooth, growing out from the upper jaw. Up to 3 m (10 ft) long, it is found only in the male.

Safefy in numbers The saiga antelope *(Saiga tatarica)* grazes in large herds on the grassy steppes of Russian and Central Asia.

Extinction is a natural process: 95 percent of all species that have ever lived, from Tyrannosaurus rex *to Neanderthal man, are long since dead and gone. But hundreds of species disappeared in the 20th century because of humankind's unprecedented gift for destruction. These are some of the species that are unlikely to live long into the third millennium.*

Shrinking home The golden bamboo lemur was only discovered in 1987. Its habitat is a single small patch of rain forest in eastern Madagascar, which has been eroded by slash-and-burn agriculture. Its total population is estimated at 1000. There are currently five golden bamboo lemurs in captivity.

Quantifying the dangers

The factors affecting an animal's chances of survival are varied and complex. They include many immeasurable things such as its "cuddly" appeal. Any timeline for endangered species is therefore misleading. It is impossible to say when one near-extinct species is closer to oblivion than another.

It is not unknown for species to recover unexpectedly. Some benefit from captive breeding programs that replenish their numbers.

Dying breed This thylacine, or Tasmanian tiger (left), was shot dead in 1930. The last known thylacine died in 1936, and the species was declared extinct in 1986. There have, however, been unconfirmed sightings since. Thousands of species die out every year – most of them in the rain forests, where we are losing species new to science before they have even been named.

WHY SPECIES DIE OUT

The golden toad of Costa Rica (right, pictured in captivity) is one of many species threatened by loss of habitat. No one has seen five in the same place for decades, and it has not been seen at all since 1989. Some species are in natural decline, but the three main threats to species are all the result of human activity: hunting, pollution and the destruction of habitat, in particular rain forest, which is exploited for timber or cleared for farm land.

Biting the bullet

The main cause of the decline of the California condor is lead poisoning, the result of eating shotgun pellets in carrion. It became extinct in the wild in 1987, when the last one was captured. Since then, captive-bred condors have been released into the wild. They were carefully numbered (see right), and seven are known to have survived.

Passenger pigeon

THE RISING TIDE OF EXTINCTION

Man annihilated about 30 species in the 17th century and about the same number again in the 18th. Approximately 100 were destroyed in the 19th century and hundreds more in the 20th. This list names a few of the animals that are now gone with the exact year of extinction, where known.

1600s
- **Aurochs (1627)**
- **Malagasy elephant bird**
- **Malagasy giant lemur**
- **Dodo (1662)**

1700s
- **Blue antelope (1799)**
- **Leguat's waterhen**
- **Mauritian giant tortoise**
- **Steller's sea cow (1768)**

1800s
- **Great auk (1844)**
- **Burchell's zebra (1883)**
- **Spectacled cormorant (c. 1850)**
- **Labrador duck (1875)**
- **Oregon bison (c. 1800)**
- **Rat kangaroo**
- **Hare-lipped suckerfish (1893)**
- **Falklands fox (1876)**

1900s
- **Passenger pigeon (1914)**
- **Palestinian painted frog (1956)**
- **Golden bandicoot**
- **Mount Glorious torrent frog**
- **Lesser bilby**
- **Syrian wild ass (1928)**
- **Bali tiger (1937)**
- **Japanese wolf (1905)**
- **Barbary lion (1922)**
- **Pig-footed bandicoot (1925)**
- **Schomburgk's deer**
- **Platypus frog**
- **Martinique muskrat (1902)**
- **Texas red wolf (1970)**
- **Badlands bighorn sheep (1905)**

Dodo

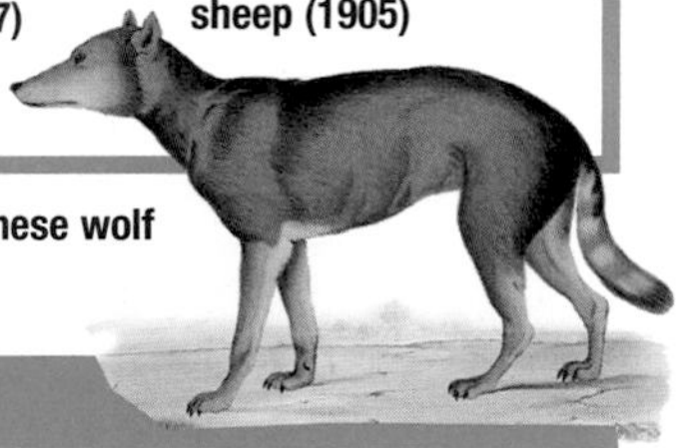
Japanese wolf

Among the rarest of all

Fish and amphibians
- Chinese paddle fish
- Baltic sturgeon
- Barnard's rock catfish
- Red-finned blue-eye
- Aruba Island Ellinopygosteos
- Asprete
- Dwarf pygmy goby
- Ganges shark
- Large-tooth sawfish
- Golden toad

Mammals
- Mediterranean monk seal
- Changjiang dolphin
- Scimitar-horned oryx
- Northern hairy-nosed wombat
- Ethiopian wolf
- Pygmy hog
- Kouprey
- Javan rhinoceros
- Golden bamboo lemur

Birds
- Spix's macaw
- California condor
- Kauai oo
- Bali starling
- Eskimo curlew
- Madagascar fish-eagle
- Amsterdam albatross
- Mauritius parakeet
- Mauritius kestrel
- Pink pigeon

Insects
- Pygmy hog-sucking louse
- Delta green ground beetle
- Cromwell chafer
- St. Helena earwig
- Queen Alexandra's birdwing butterfly
- Sri Lankan relict ant
- Frey's damselfly
- Torreya pygmy grasshopper

Reptiles
- Chinese alligator
- Orinoco crocodile
- Jamaican iguana
- Cayman Island ground iguana
- Aruba Island rattlesnake
- Kemp's Ridley sea turtle
- Painted terrapin
- St. Vincent blacksnake
- Dahl's toad-headed turtle

Drowned out Kemp's Ridley sea turtle nests only at Ranch Nuevo on the Gulf of Mexico. Fifty years ago 42 000 females were counted in a single day; now only a few hundred remain. The turtles are at risk from fishermen, because they drown when they become entangled in fishing nets.

FACT No crustacean is yet known to have become extinct as a result of human activity.

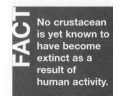

Fragile beauty Every fall, monarch butterflies migrate from their breeding grounds in northeastern North America to forests in the mountains of central Mexico. Logging, however, is threatening these wintering sites, which are vital to their survival. Migrating monarch butterflies are now recognized as an endangered species.

Dying by numbers

At the most recent count, the number of species officially listed as endangered was 5205. Indonesia, China and Brazil have the greatest number of endangered species. This list shows the percentage of threatened animals worldwide:

11 percent of birds
20 percent of reptiles
25 percent of mammals
25 percent of amphibians
34 percent of fishes

see also
74-75 **Animal kingdom**
96-97 **Animal records**

The ancestors of man

Homo sapiens is the only representative of the hominid family alive today, but about 1-2 million years ago, several hominid species coexisted. Because the study of early man has been done largely through the fossil record – which is incomplete – it is not clear how these species were related. Much of what has been inferred is conjectural, although recent techniques, such as comparative biochemistry, have helped to fill in the gaps.

WHAT IS A HOMINID?

- A hominid is **a primate**. The other primates are prosimians, monkeys, gorillas, chimpanzees and orangutangs.
- It is **bipedal**, that is, two-footed, and therefore can **walk upright**.
- It has a relatively **large brain**.

There are two confirmed genera of hominids: *Australopithecus* and *Homo*. The genus *Ardipithecus* may eventually be classified as the earliest-known hominid.

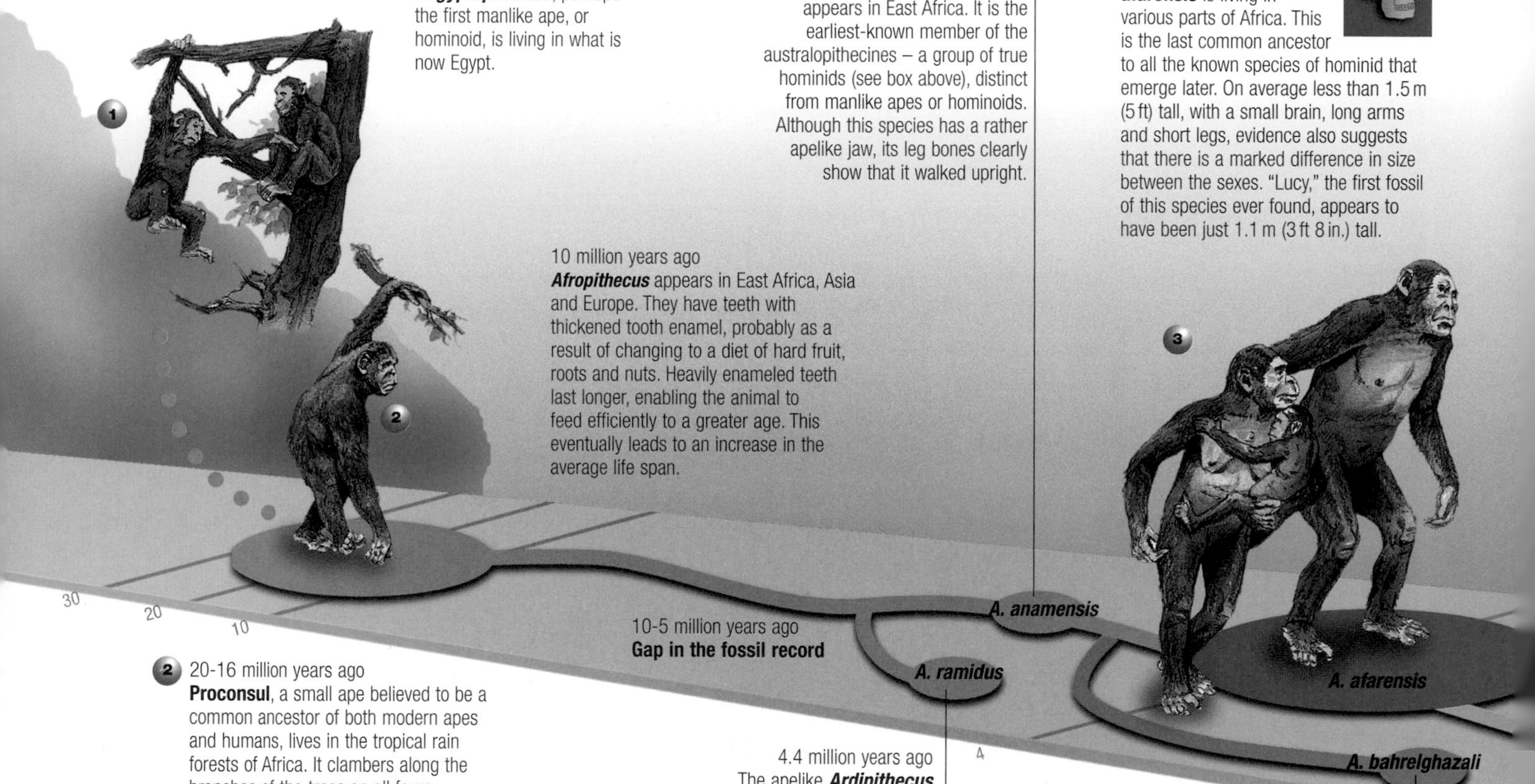

1 30 million years ago
Aegyptopithecus, perhaps the first manlike ape, or hominoid, is living in what is now Egypt.

2 20-16 million years ago
Proconsul, a small ape believed to be a common ancestor of both modern apes and humans, lives in the tropical rain forests of Africa. It clambers along the branches of the trees on all fours.

10 million years ago
Afropithecus appears in East Africa, Asia and Europe. They have teeth with thickened tooth enamel, probably as a result of changing to a diet of hard fruit, roots and nuts. Heavily enameled teeth last longer, enabling the animal to feed efficiently to a greater age. This eventually leads to an increase in the average life span.

10-5 million years ago
Gap in the fossil record

4.4 million years ago
The apelike ***Ardipithecus ramidus*** lives in the area now known as Ethiopia. It probably walks upright on two legs, leading some experts to class it as the first true hominid.

4.2-3.9 million years ago
Australopithecus anamensis appears in East Africa. It is the earliest-known member of the australopithecines – a group of true hominids (see box above), distinct from manlike apes or hominoids. Although this species has a rather apelike jaw, its leg bones clearly show that it walked upright.

3 4-3 million years ago
Australopithecus afarensis is living in various parts of Africa. This is the last common ancestor to all the known species of hominid that emerge later. On average less than 1.5 m (5 ft) tall, with a small brain, long arms and short legs, evidence also suggests that there is a marked difference in size between the sexes. "Lucy," the first fossil of this species ever found, appears to have been just 1.1 m (3 ft 8 in.) tall.

3.5-3 million years ago
Australopithecus bahrelghazali appears in Africa. It is similar to *Australopithecus afarensis*, but with a less apelike jaw.

Two legs good . . .

Becoming bipedal – walking upright on two legs – played a key role in the evolution of human intelligence. There are two major reasons for this. First, bipedalism requires greater coordination, leading to a more developed nervous system and larger brain. Second, it frees the hands for carrying and manipulation. The consequent development of manipulative skills, such as those required for toolmaking, also encourages brain development.

Being upright has other advantages. It increases height, which is useful for spying prey and predators in the open savannah. It also helps to keep the body cool, by raising it up, away from the hot ground and closer to cooling air currents above. It also minimizes the body area being exposed to the heating effect of strong sunlight.

Standing tall Humans are not alone in walking upright. Occasionally, apes do too but less efficiently. Their anatomy is not as well adapted to being bipedal as that of humans. There are disadvantages to being upright. Bipeds cannot run as fast as quadrupeds, and the extra wear and tear bipedalism places on the hips, back and knees can lead to disabilities.

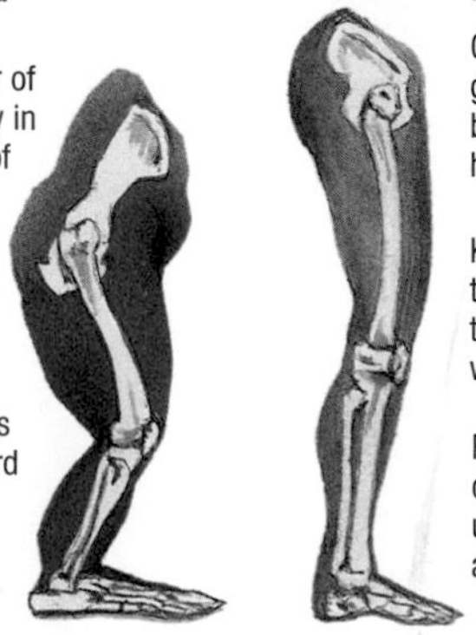

The invention of human society

All primates lead complex social lives, so being socially adept is often more important than appearance or physical prowess. Developing the necessary social skills makes intense intellectual demands, which has helped to develop primate, and particularly human, intelligence.

Features of the development of human social organization

- Larger brains and changes in the voice box lead to greater manipulative abilities and the development of speech.
- Use of fire allows groups to stay in one place, at least temporarily, because it provides warmth and protection.
- Manufacture and use of tools increase food-gathering efficiency.
- Complex communication skills, both verbal and visual, allow for cooperation to find food.
- Sharing of food leads to communal living and social organization.
- Labor divides by gender: The males hunt together; the females educate the children.
- Immature young and a long infancy and childhood create the need for parental supervision and encourages the formation of groups to share childrearing.
- Communal living, increased security and complex communication skills lead to the emergence of culture, such as art, spiritual belief and ritual.
- Long childhood allows time for individuals to acquire the culture of their social group.

5 2-1.5 million years ago
Australopithecus robustus is living in Southern Africa. Large and strong, it has a broad face with powerful jaws and big molar teeth, indicating that it mainly eats plants. Some fossils show a prominent brow ridge.

6 2-1 million years ago
Homo habilis is present in East Africa, living alongside the australopithecines, but unlike them, he was a toolmaker and also had a larger brain.

1.8 million years ago
Homo rudolfensis, living in East Africa, is a close relative of ***Homo habilis***.

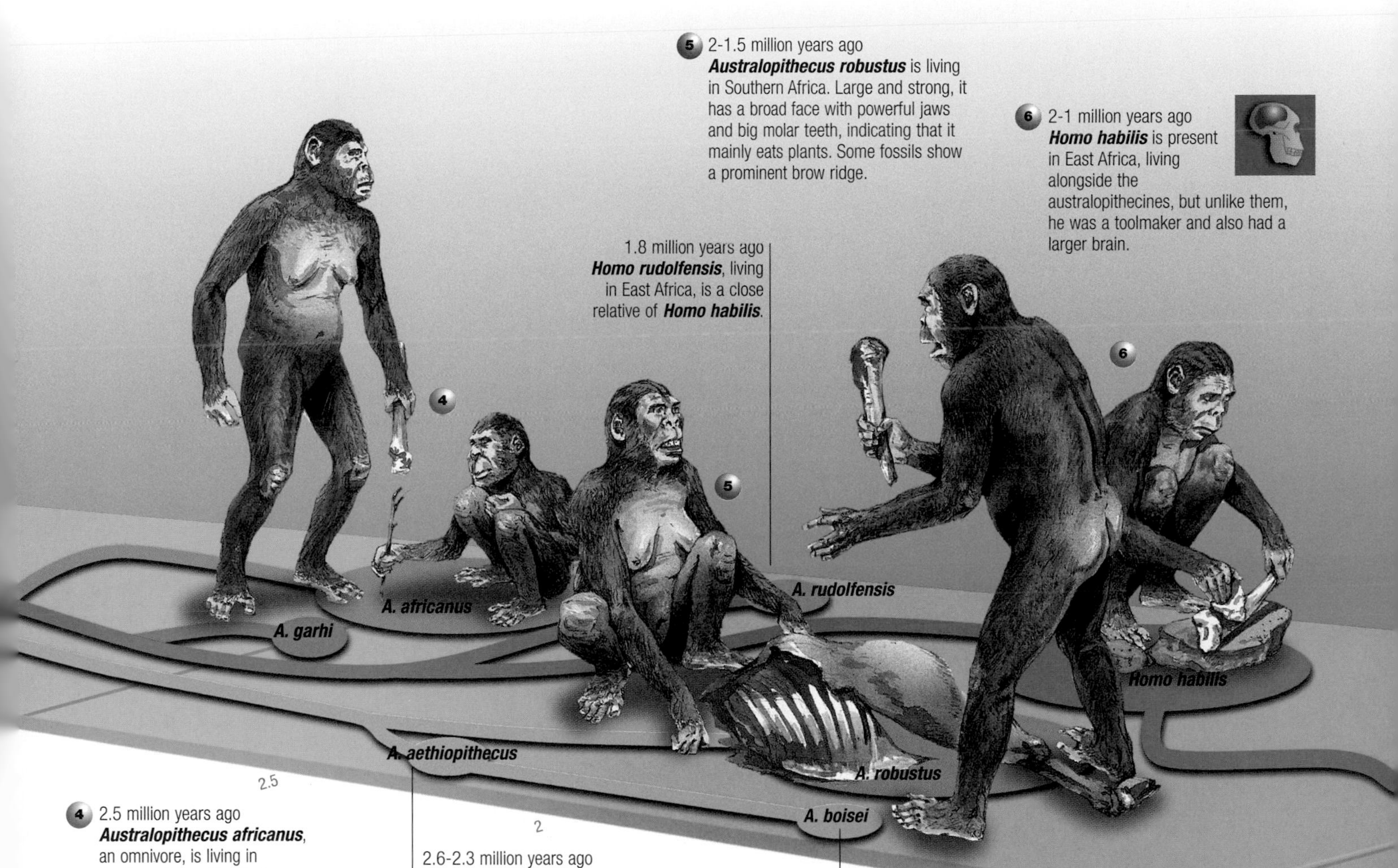

4 2.5 million years ago
Australopithecus africanus, an omnivore, is living in Southern Africa. The first hominid fossil ever unearthed, in Africa in 1924, was an *Australopithecus africanus* child, known as the "Taung child" named after the place where it was found.

2.6-2.3 million years ago
Australopithecus aethiopithecus is found in East Africa. A herbivore, it has very large molar teeth for grinding up plant matter efficiently and a distinct bony crest on the forehead.

2.5 million years ago
By now, a new genus, ***Homo***, has branched off from the hominid family tree. It will live alongside *Australopithecus* for 1.5 million years. The main physical differences between *Homo* and *Australopithecus* are *Homo*'s

- increased brain size
- finer jaw with smaller teeth
- repositioned voice box, which will eventually make speech possible.

2.3-1.4 million years ago
The heavy-boned ***Australopithecus boisei*** is living in East Africa. It has a heavy brow ridge, and huge molar teeth, which suggest that it is predominantly a plant-eater. Males are much larger and heavier than females.

1 million years ago
By this point, the **australopithecines have become extinct**.

see also

54-55 **Evolution explained**
72-73 **Rise of the mammals**
108-9 **Emergence of man**

For 200 000 years, the dominant human species in Europe and Asia was Homo neanderthalensis. *The Neanderthals were short and stocky, lived in sophisticated social groups and had larger brains than modern man. Yet about 30 000 years ago they were ousted from their dominant position and driven to extinction by new arrivals from Africa –* Homo sapiens.

NEANDERTHAL MAN

Neanderthals appeared in Europe about 250 000 years ago – the name comes from the Neander Valley, near Dusseldorf, Germany, where remains were first found in 1856. There is ample evidence to suggest that the Neanderthals were cultural beings. Skilfully wrought stone tools and jewelry have been found. Graves show that they buried

700 000 years ago
Homo heidelbergensis evolves from *Homo erectus* populations in Africa and Europe. He is tall – over 1.8 m (6 ft) – with a powerful anatomy and a large brain. Other key features:
- He can control fire.
- He is capable of more competent speech than *Homo erectus*.
- He makes a wider range of stone tools than *Homo erectus*, including hand axes, cleavers and butchering tools.

600 000 years ago
The Earth's climate starts to fluctuate dramatically, resulting in a **series of ice ages**. Surviving these climatic extremes requires flexible and resourceful behavior. Thus natural selection will favor the more intelligent, resourceful, larger-brained individuals.

9 200 000-140 000 years ago
Homo sapiens evolves in sub-Saharan Africa. He is lighter-built than *Homo neanderthalensis*, but his level of culture and technology is similar.
Other key features:
- He is capable of complex speech.
- He uses fire for cooking, as well as for smoking and drying meat to preserve it.
- He wears a wide range of clothing.

c. 120 000 years ago
Homo sapiens sapiens (modern man) evolves.

100 000 years ago
Homo sapiens sapiens starts to spread from Africa into Europe and Asia, where he lives alongside *Homo. neanderthalensis*.

7 1.8 million-300 000 years ago
Homo erectus originates in Africa, gradually migrating into Europe and Asia. He has a larger brain than *Homo habilis*.
Other key features:
- He is a toolmaker, producing scrapers, axes and cleavers.
- He is a meat-eater so probably has a more nutritious diet than earlier hominids, which helps brain development.
- Remains suggest he was capable of rudimentary speech.
- There is some evidence that he used fire.
- He is well adapted to cope with big variations in climate.

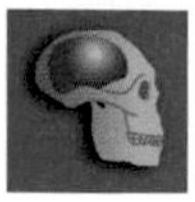

8 250 000-30 000 years ago
Homo neanderthalensis is living in Europe and Asia. He is stockier and shorter than modern humans – about 1.68 m (5 ft 6 in.) tall – but has a bigger brain.
Other key features:
- His anatomy implies that he uses complex speech.
- He shows evidence of cultural development in terms of art and spiritual belief.
- He uses fire for heating and possibly cooking.
- He wears clothes made from hide and fur, and also uses jewelry.

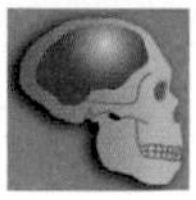

10 30 000 years ago
Homo sapiens sapiens is now the only species of the genus *Homo*. The rapid cultural and technological development from primitive man to modern man in just 30 000 years has made *Homo sapiens sapiens* the dominant species on Earth.

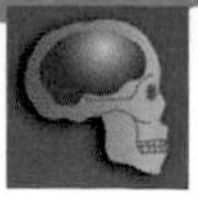

their dead with some ceremony. Skeletons with serious but healed injuries and advanced arthritis indicate that they cared for their old and infirm. They also used fire – vital for survival in the cold climate of the period.

So why did these strong, intelligent hominids die out about 30 000 years ago? The most likely theory is that they were simply outclassed by the more adaptable *Homo sapiens sapiens* – also known as "Cro-Magnon man," named after the place in the Dordogne, France, where they were first found.

Beneath the skin A marked brow ridge, low forehead and receding lower jaw distinguish the Neanderthal skull (above left) from the Cro-Magnon (above, right).

The rise of *Homo sapiens* Cro-Magnon man started moving into Europe from Africa about 100 000 years ago, initially living alongside the Neanderthals. Then, about 40 000 years ago, Cro-Magnon culture advanced rapidly, enabling them eventually to displace their less adaptable Neanderthal neighbors.

Two main theories have been put forward to explain the evolution of *Homo sapiens*. The "Candelabra" – a reference to different branches of *Homo* evolution – theory says that they developed simultaneously from populations of different *Homo* species in Asia, Europe and Africa. The more favored "Out of Africa" theory postulates that they evolved from a single African stock and began to spread to the rest of the world just 100 000 years ago.

DNA analysis of Neanderthal remains shows that they cannot be the ancestors of modern man. Other DNA research (see Mitochondrial Eve, right) indicates that everyone alive today is descended from a human population living in Africa 140 000 to 200 000 years ago.

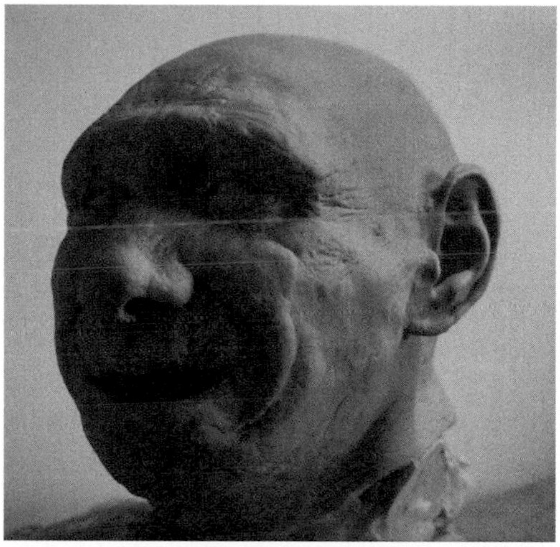

Face from the past This reconstruction, based on a skull found at Monte Circeo in Italy, shows that the Neanderthal face was not completely dissimilar from ours.

Mitochondrial Eve

In 1986 researchers at the University of California concluded that all humans were descended from a single woman who lived in Africa about 200 000 years ago. They based this on analysis of DNA taken from the mitochondria, specific parts of the human cell. This DNA differs from DNA in the cell nucleus and it passes only through the female line. It mutates at a very rapid but steady rate. By comparing the mitochondrial DNA of women from various ethnic groups, they could estimate how long it took for each group to diverge from a common ancestor. In effect, they constructed a family tree for mankind, at the base of which was the Mitochondrial Eve, everyone's 10 000th great grandmother. This doesn't mean that she was the only woman in existence but that it is her lineage that has survived to the present day.

see also

54-55 **Evolution explained**

72-73 **Rise of the mammals**

Origins of race

Despite physical differences among the ethnic groups that make up the species *Homo sapiens*, all modern humans are remarkably similar genetically.

Several theories have been proposed to explain the origin of race. The Candelabra theory of evolution proposed that Asians, Australian Aborigines and modern Africans, among others, emerged from *Homo erectus* populations, and white people evolved from European Neanderthals. Recent research has disproved this theory.

The categorization of humans by race is now seen as having little meaning. The physical differences on which we base "race" are essentially minor adaptations to environmental conditions. Narrow, prominent noses, for example, are advantageous in a cold climate, because they are better at warming chilly air as it enters the body. Skin color corresponds largely to latitude. In hot, tropical regions, high levels of the dark pigment melanin protect the skin from the harmful effects of strong sunlight. Skin color is no more significant genetically than the difference between a black cat and a tabby.

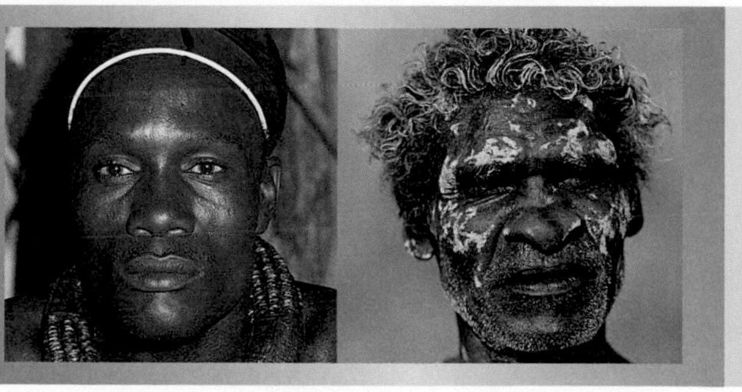

The human body

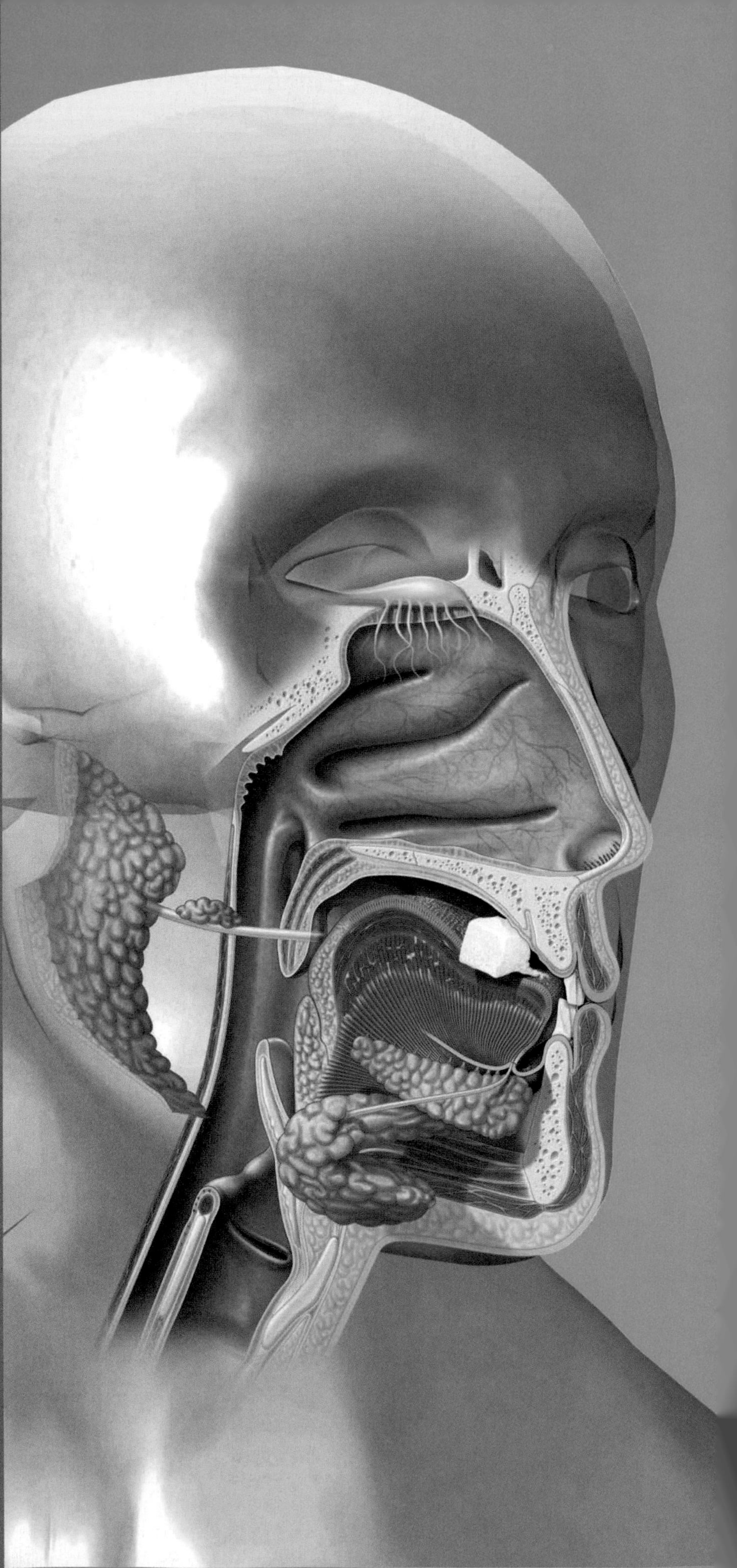

The human body

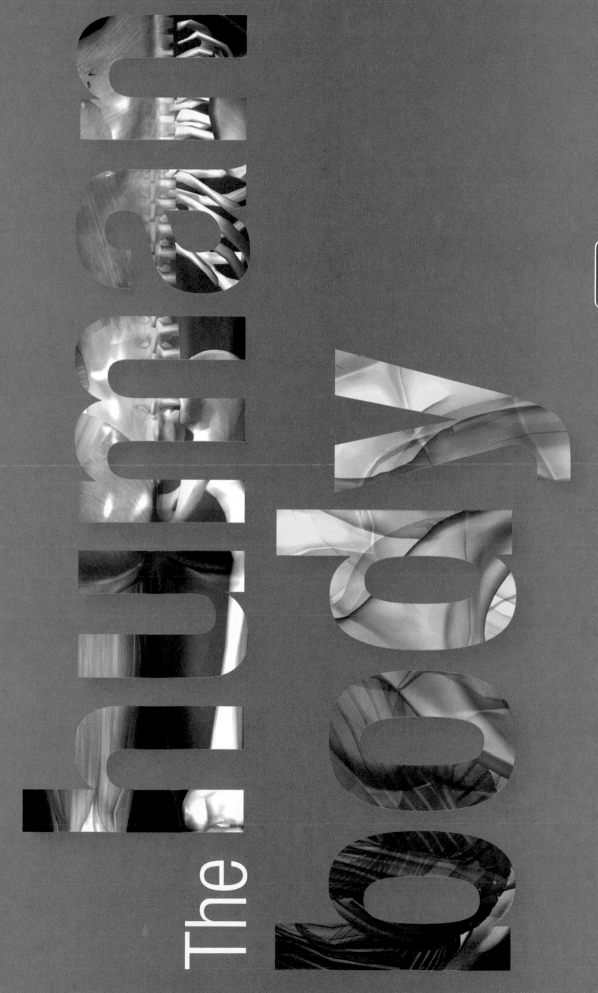

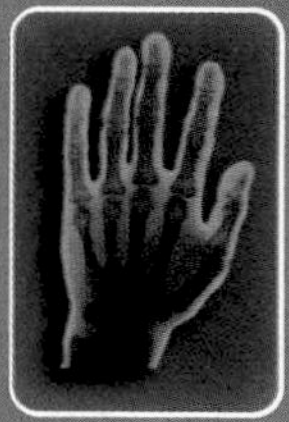

The adult skeleton provides the body's internal scaffolding: It is made up of 206 bones and accounts for one fifth of the body's total weight. Muscles control movement throughout the body, including automatic actions such as heartbeat, movement of the digestive system and blinking. Muscles make up over half of the body's total weight.

THE SKELETON

The skeleton supports the body, protects internal organs, and allows a wide variety of movement. Most bones are connected by ligaments to form flexible joints.

Cartilage A type of connective tissue, cartilage forms shock-absorbing disks between vertebrae, gives elasticity and strength to the knee joint and surrounds the end of every long bone where it meets other bones to form a joint. It also joins the ribs to the breastbone.

MUSCLES

There are three kinds of muscle. Striped muscle, so called because of its striated appearance under the microscope, makes up the majority. It contracts in response to messages from the brain. Smooth muscle is not under conscious control. It controls the digestive, urinary, reproductive and circulatory systems and such unconscious responses as adjusting the iris in the eye. Cardiac muscle is found only in the heart and is unique in being able to contract rhythmically and continuously.

THE SPINE

An adult's spine consists of 26 bones called vertebrae. It is divided into four sections.

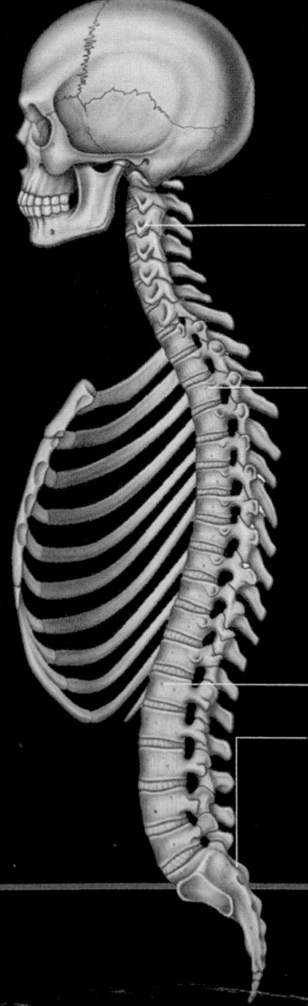
Cervical vertebrae The top seven bones of the spine in the neck.
Thoracic vertebrae These 12 vertebrae are attached to the ribs.
Lumbar vertebrae Five more vertebrae are below the ribs.
Sacrum and coccyx The sacrum is made of five vertebrae and the coccyx of four. In adults, the vertebrae are fused together.

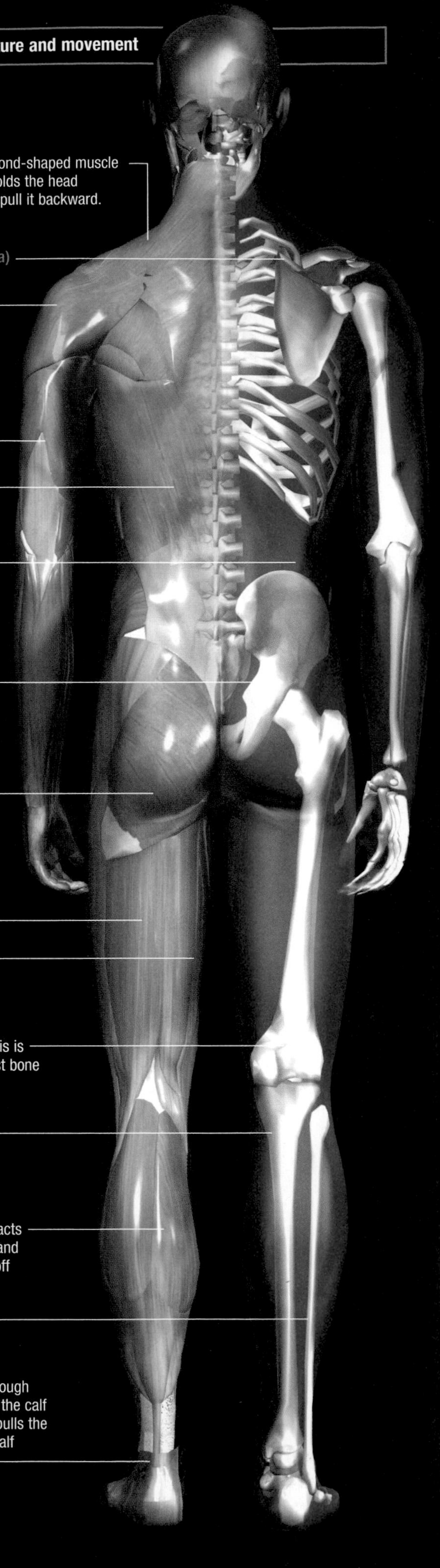
Trapezius A large, diamond-shaped muscle in the upper back, this holds the head straight and contracts to pull it backward.
Shoulder blade (scapula)
Shoulder deltoid This raises the arm outward from the body.
Triceps This contracts to straighten the arm.
Latissimus dorsi This large back muscle holds the body upright.
Ribs These protect internal organs and the chest cavity.
Hip (ilium) Outer part of the pelvic girdle.
Gluteus maximus This is the largest muscle in the body.
Hamstring muscles These contract to bend the leg at the knee.
Adductor muscles These contract to pull the leg inward.
Thigh bone (femur) This is the longest and strongest bone in the body.
Shinbone (tibia) This is the major load-bearing bone of the lower leg.
Calf muscle This contracts to pull the heel upward and lift the back of the foot off the ground.
Fibula The smaller of the two lower leg bones.
Achilles' tendon This tough cord links the bottom of the calf muscle to the heel and pulls the heel upward when the calf muscle contracts.

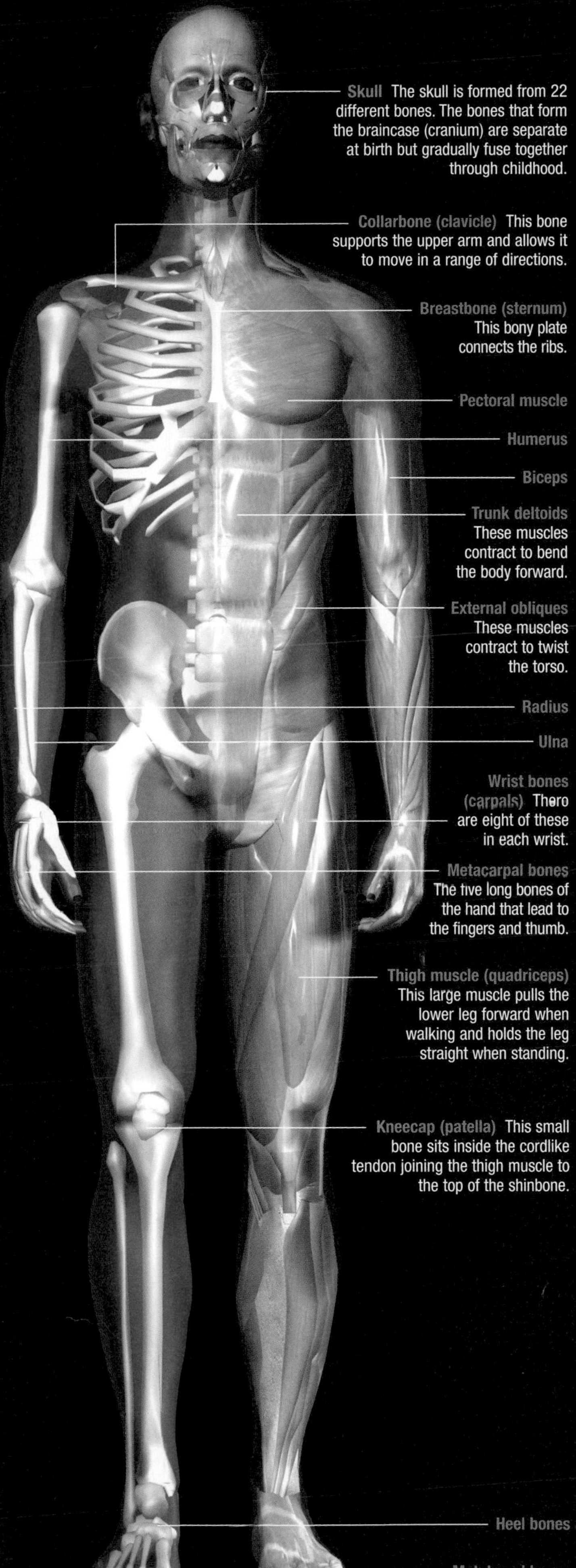
Skull The skull is formed from 22 different bones. The bones that form the braincase (cranium) are separate at birth but gradually fuse together through childhood.
Collarbone (clavicle) This bone supports the upper arm and allows it to move in a range of directions.
Breastbone (sternum) This bony plate connects the ribs.
Pectoral muscle
Humerus
Biceps
Trunk deltoids These muscles contract to bend the body forward.
External obliques These muscles contract to twist the torso.
Radius
Ulna
Wrist bones (carpals) There are eight of these in each wrist.
Metacarpal bones The five long bones of the hand that lead to the fingers and thumb.
Thigh muscle (quadriceps) This large muscle pulls the lower leg forward when walking and holds the leg straight when standing.
Kneecap (patella) This small bone sits inside the cordlike tendon joining the thigh muscle to the top of the shinbone.
Heel bones

HOW DO MUSCLES WORK?

Muscles produce movement by contracting and are arranged in opposing pairs or groups. The illustration shows one of these pairs. To raise the forearm, the biceps at the front of the upper arm contract and shorten while the triceps at the back relax and lengthen. To lower the forearm, the actions of these muscles are reversed. The biceps are stronger than the triceps because raising the arm works against the pull of gravity.

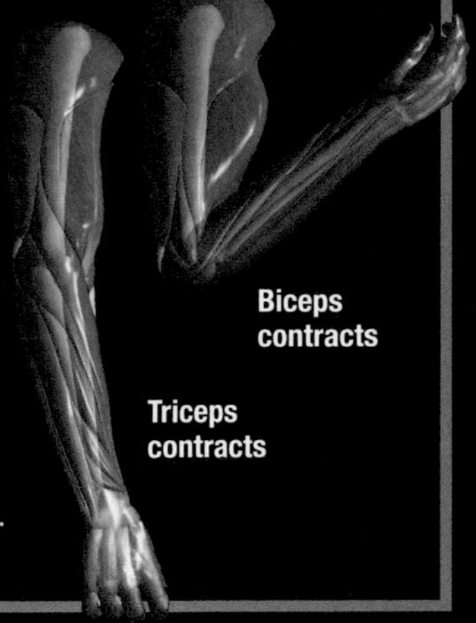
Biceps contracts
Triceps contracts

Joints between bones

There are two categories of joints.
Fixed joints Places where bones become fused together and there is little or no movement, such as in the skull.
Synovial joints Lubricated joints that allow free movement.

The six types of synovial joint

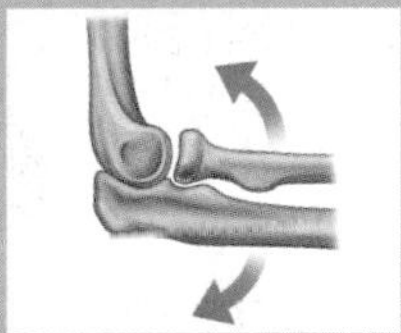

Hinge Movement occurs in one plane only, such as at the elbow. Round end of one bone fits the scooped end of other.

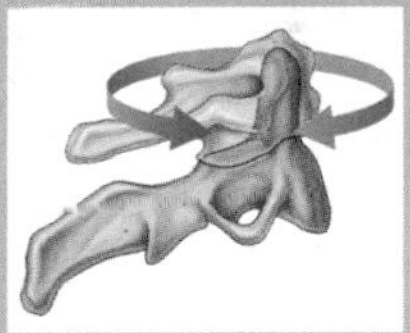

Pivot A projection from one bone turns within a ring-shaped socket on another, such as in vertebrae.

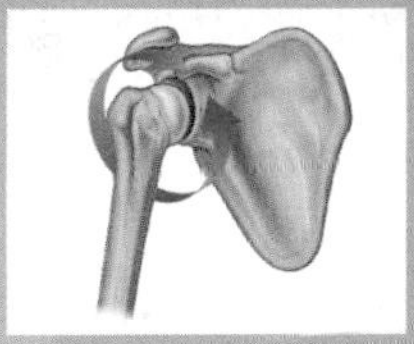

Ball and socket Circular movement such as at the hip. Close fit of ball-ended bone into rounded socket.

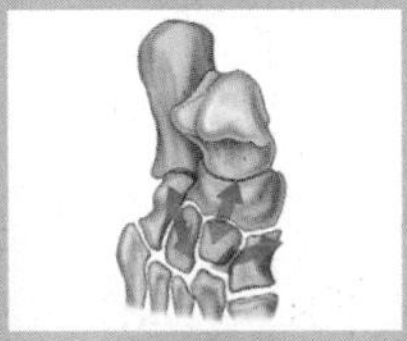

Gliding The flat surfaces of bones slide over each other. Gliding joints occur in the foot.

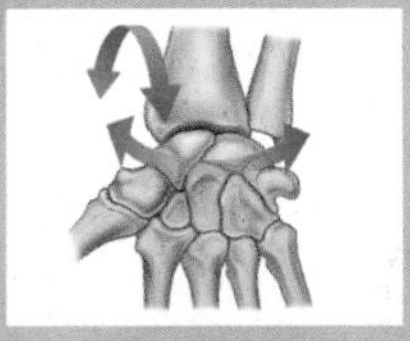

Ellipsoidal The egg-shaped end of one bone fits into the elliptical cavity of another, such as at the wrist.

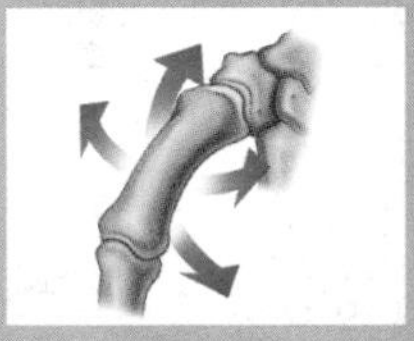

Saddle This kind of joint occurs at the base of the thumb. It allows for limited movement in two planes.

All the bones in the body

There are four classes of bone: long bones (limbs), short bones (wrists and ankles), flat bones (skull) and irregular bones (face, vertebrae). The bones of the hands and feet constitute half the total number of bones in the body.

Skull	22	Pectoral girdle	4
Ears	6	Hip bones	2
Vertebrae	26	Arms (2 x 30)	60
Vertebral ribs	24	Legs (2 x 29)	58
Sternum	3		
Throat	1	**Total**	**206**

see also
114-15 **The brain and nerves**
118 **Glands and hormones**

The brain and nerves

The brain and nervous system control our perceptions, thoughts and voluntary actions and also most of the body's internal processes. The brain is contained within the hard bones of the skull and is cushioned against injury by surrounding membranes, and the spinal cord – the central pathway of the nervous system – runs through a channel within the tough vertebrae of the spine.

THE BRAIN

There are three major areas in the brain: the cerebrum, the cerebellum and the brain stem.

The cerebrum is the largest part of the brain and is associated with conscious activities and intelligence. It is divided into two hemispheres and consists of gray matter (neuron cells) and white matter (nerve fibers).

The brain is wrapped in three separate membranes. The space between these membranes contains fluid, which allows the brain to float and thus insulates it from blows to the head. The same membranes extend over the spinal cord.

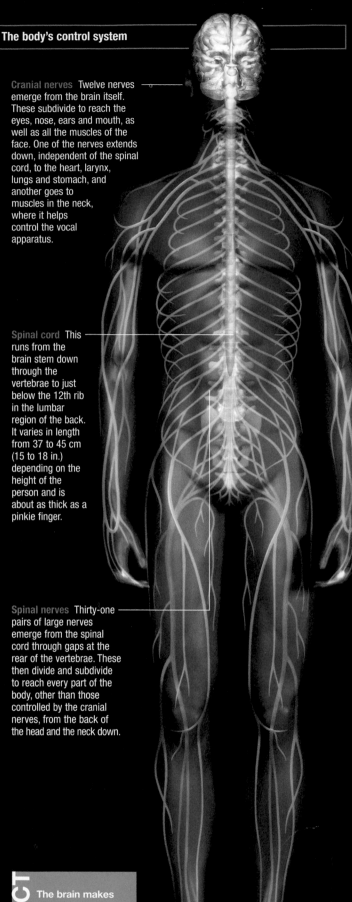

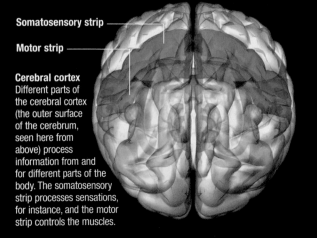

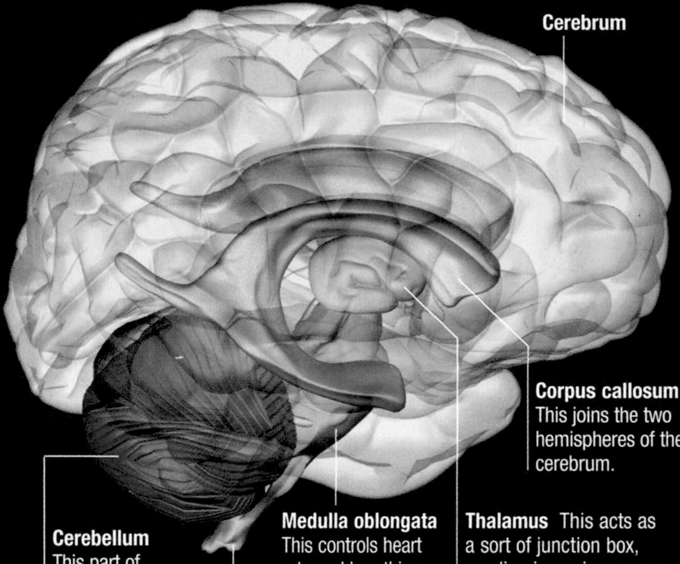

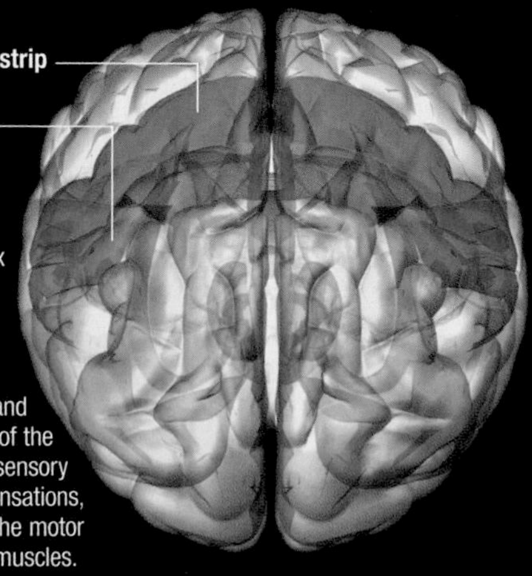

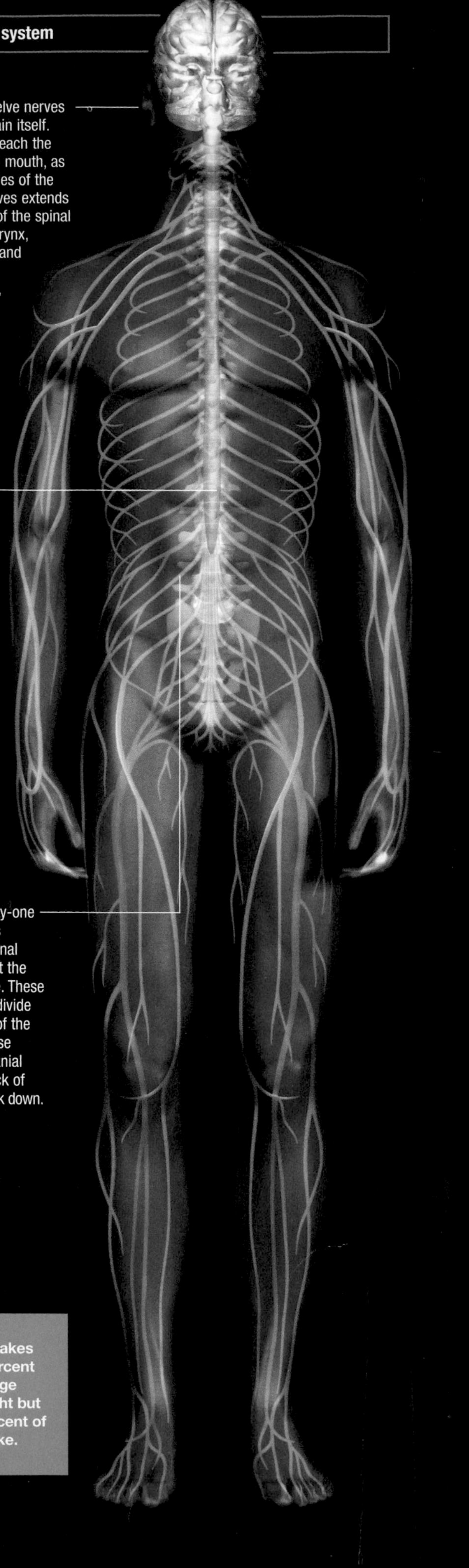

Medulla oblongata This controls heart rate and breathing.
Thalamus This acts as a sort of junction box, sending incoming nerve impulses to different areas of the brain.

Somatosensory strip
Motor strip
Cerebral cortex Different parts of the cerebral cortex (the outer surface of the cerebrum, seen here from above) process information from and for different parts of the body. The somatosensory strip processes sensations, for instance, and the motor strip controls the muscles.

Cranial nerves Twelve nerves emerge from the brain itself. These subdivide to reach the eyes, nose, ears and mouth, as well as all the muscles of the face. One of the nerves extends down, independent of the spinal cord, to the heart, larynx, lungs and stomach, and another goes to muscles in the neck, where it helps control the vocal apparatus.
Spinal cord This runs from the brain stem down through the vertebrae to just below the 12th rib in the lumbar region of the back. It varies in length from 37 to 45 cm (15 to 18 in.) depending on the height of the person and is about as thick as a pinkie finger.
Spinal nerves Thirty-one pairs of large nerves emerge from the spinal cord through gaps at the rear of the vertebrae. These then divide and subdivide to reach every part of the body, other than those controlled by the cranial nerves, from the back of the head and the neck down.

FACT

The brain makes up just 2 percent of the average adult's weight but uses 20 percent of oxygen intake.

THE NERVOUS SYSTEM

A network of nerves extends throughout our bodies, carrying sensory information to the brain and instructions from it. The brain and the spinal cord together form the central nervous system (CNS); the rest of the network is known as the peripheral nervous system (PNS).

The spinal cord

The spinal cord is an extension of the brain and is formed from the same gray and white matter, although it is organized differently from that in the bra[redacted] with the gray matter on the inside and the white ma[redacted]r on the outside.

The spinal cord channels nerve signals from every part of the body to the brain and carries messages back again. It is more than just a connecting cable, however. Many nerve signals, including most reflex actions, are processed in the spinal cord itself. By bypassing the brain in this way, response times become much faster, enabling the body to react to potential danger extremely quickly. The knee-jerk reaction is the best-known reflex, but others include the instant removal of a hand from a hot object. It is only after the hand has been removed that the brain registers what has happened and we feel pain.

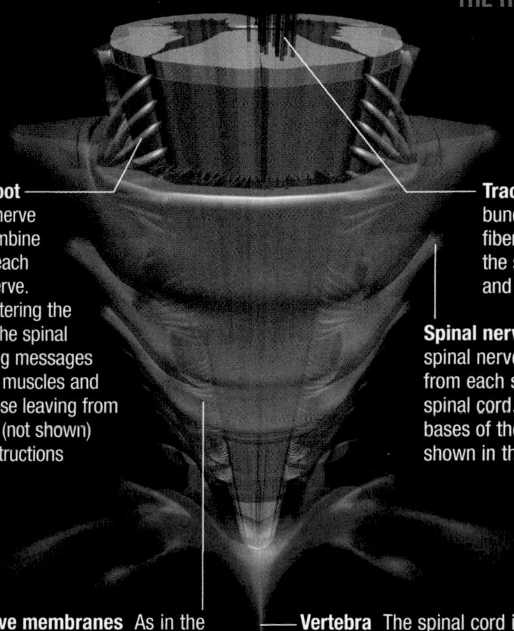

Nerve root Several nerve roots combine to form each spinal nerve. Roots entering the back of the spinal cord bring messages from the muscles and skin. Those leaving from the front (not shown) carry instructions to them.
Tracts These bundles of nerve fibers run through the spinal cord to and from the brain.
Spinal nerve Thirty-one spinal nerves emerge from each side of the spinal cord. Only the bases of the nerves are shown in this illustration.
Protective membranes As in the brain, the nerve tissue of the spinal cord is encased by three separate fluid-filled membranes.
Vertebra The spinal cord is encased by the bones of the spine, or vertebrae, which protect it from damage. The back of one vertebra is shown here.

NERVE STRUCTURE

The nerve cell, or neuron, is the fundamental unit in the nervous system. Each neuron has a cell body with a [redacted]eus and the metabolic structures [redacted]ound in other kinds of cell. Extending from the cell body is a nerve cell fiber, or axon, which carries signals to other cells. Axons are microscopically thin, but some can be up to 1 m (39 in.) long, for example the ones that extend from the spinal cord to the fingertips. They are encased in sheaths of the protein myelin, which insulate them and help increase the speed at which they carry nerve impulses.

Neurons do not connect with each other directly. Information is passed from one to another at an interface called a synapse. Here, a chemical substance called a neurotransmitter is released and carries the impulses across the gap to a branching dendrite from another neuron. Each axon may end in several synapses, enabling it to link with more than one other neuron.

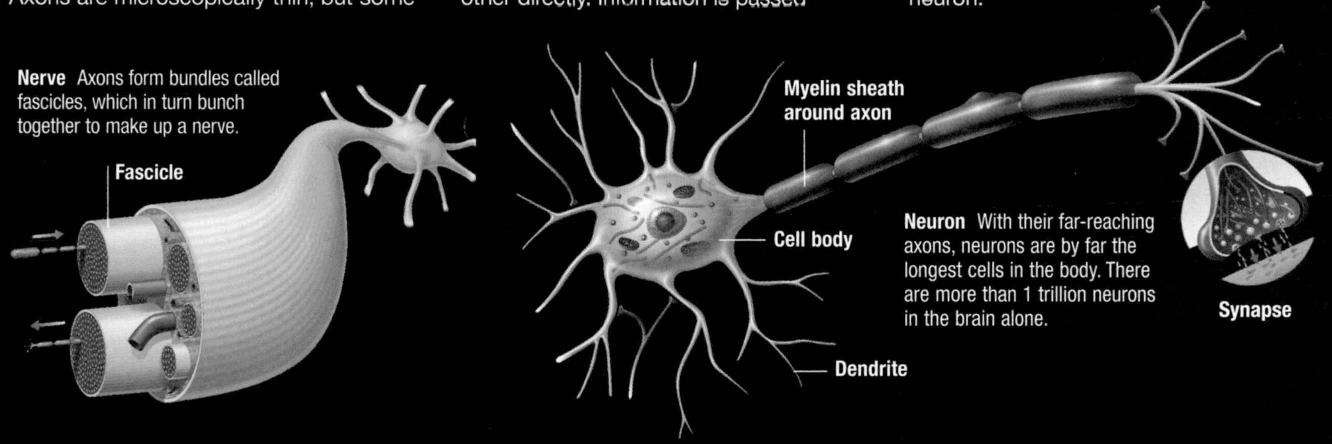

Nerve Axons form bundles called fascicles, which in turn bunch together to make up a nerve.
Fascicle
Myelin sheath around axon
Cell body
Neuron With their far-reaching axons, neurons are by far the longest cells in the body. There are more than 1 trillion neurons in the brain alone.
Synapse
Dendrite

Different types of nerve cell

There are three types of nerve cell or neuron.

Sensory neurons Carry information from sensory receptors to the central nervous system (CNS).

Motor neurons Carry information from the CNS to the organs and muscles.

Association neurons Found only in the CNS, these link sensory and motor nerves and transport incoming messages to the brain, where they are interpreted and the appropriate instructions are sent out.

FACTS AND FIGURES

- The brain has about 1 trillion nerve cells.
- Signals travel along nerves at up to 360 km/h (225 mph): A message sent from head to toe arrives in about 1/50 of a second.
- The left hemisphere of the brain controls the right side of the body and vice-versa. About 90 percent of the human population is right-handed, which means that the left hemispheres of their brains are dominant.
- The average adult male brain weighs 1.4 kg (3 lb); the average adult female brain 1.25 kg (2 3/4 lb).
- The mass of brain tissue reaches a maximum at age 20 and decreases thereafter.
- The spinal cord stops growing when a child reaches four years old. After that, only the spinal nerves continue to grow.

see also
124 **Sight**
125 **Hearing and balance**
132-33 **The seven ages**

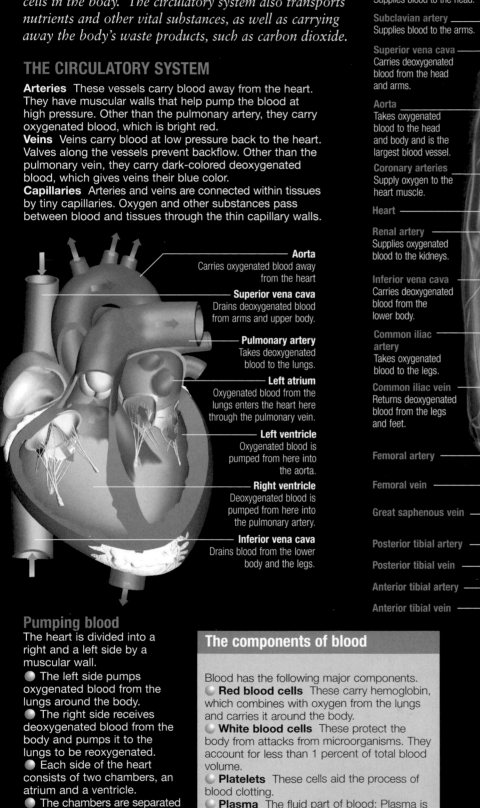

Every cell in the body needs oxygen to function. Oxygen from the air passes into the bloodstream from the lungs. Oxygenated blood is then pumped by the heart to all the cells in the body. The circulatory system also transports nutrients and other vital substances, as well as carrying away the body's waste products, such as carbon dioxide.

THE CIRCULATORY SYSTEM

Arteries These vessels carry blood away from the heart. They have muscular walls that help pump the blood at high pressure. Other than the pulmonary artery, they carry oxygenated blood, which is bright red.
Veins Veins carry blood at low pressure back to the heart. Valves along the vessels prevent backflow. Other than the pulmonary vein, they carry dark-colored deoxygenated blood, which gives veins their blue color.
Capillaries Arteries and veins are connected within tissues by tiny capillaries. Oxygen and other substances pass between blood and tissues through the thin capillary walls.

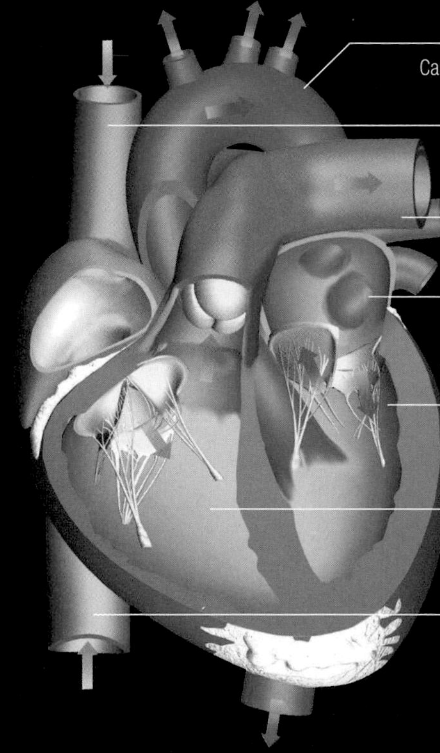
Aorta
Carries oxygenated blood away from the heart
Superior vena cava
Drains deoxygenated blood from arms and upper body.
Pulmonary artery
Takes deoxygenated blood to the lungs.
Left atrium
Oxygenated blood from the lungs enters the heart here through the pulmonary vein.
Left ventricle
Oxygenated blood is pumped from here into the aorta.
Right ventricle
Deoxygenated blood is pumped from here into the pulmonary artery.
Inferior vena cava
Drains blood from the lower body and the legs.

Pumping blood

The heart is divided into a right and a left side by a muscular wall.

- The left side pumps oxygenated blood from the lungs around the body.
- The right side receives deoxygenated blood from the body and pumps it to the lungs to be reoxygenated.
- Each side of the heart consists of two chambers, an atrium and a ventricle.
- The chambers are separated by valves, which open to let blood through and then close to prevent it flowing backward.

The components of blood

Blood has the following major components.

- **Red blood cells** These carry hemoglobin, which combines with oxygen from the lungs and carries it around the body.
- **White blood cells** These protect the body from attacks from microorganisms. They account for less than 1 percent of total blood volume.
- **Platelets** These cells aid the process of blood clotting.
- **Plasma** The fluid part of blood: Plasma is 90 percent water. It carries glucose and vitamins, among other substances.

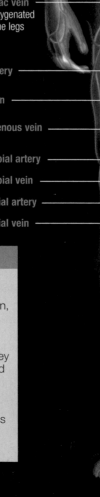

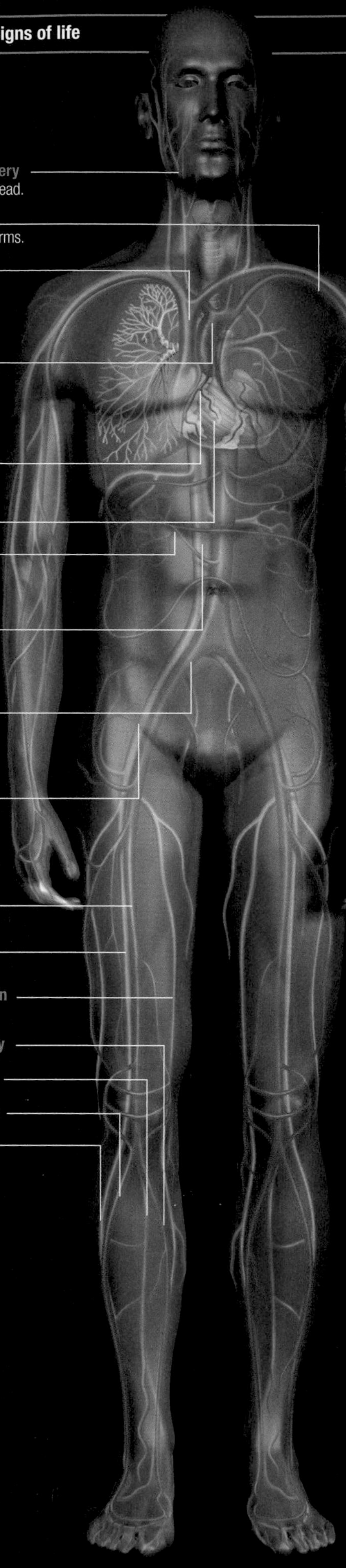
Common carotid artery
Supplies blood to the head.
Subclavian artery
Supplies blood to the arms.
Superior vena cava
Carries deoxygenated blood from the head and arms.
Aorta
Takes oxygenated blood to the head and body and is the largest blood vessel.
Coronary arteries
Supply oxygen to the heart muscle.
Heart
Renal artery
Supplies oxygenated blood to the kidneys.
Inferior vena cava
Carries deoxygenated blood from the lower body.
Common iliac artery
Takes oxygenated blood to the legs.
Common iliac vein
Returns deoxygenated blood from the legs and feet.
Femoral artery
Femoral vein
Great saphenous vein
Posterior tibial artery
Posterior tibial vein
Anterior tibial artery
Anterior tibial vein

THE RESPIRATORY SYSTEM

Respiration is the biochemical process that releases energy from food within the cells of the body. This process is fueled by oxygen from the air that is drawn into the lungs by the movement of the diaphragm. The system also expels the by-products of respiration, water and carbon dioxide.

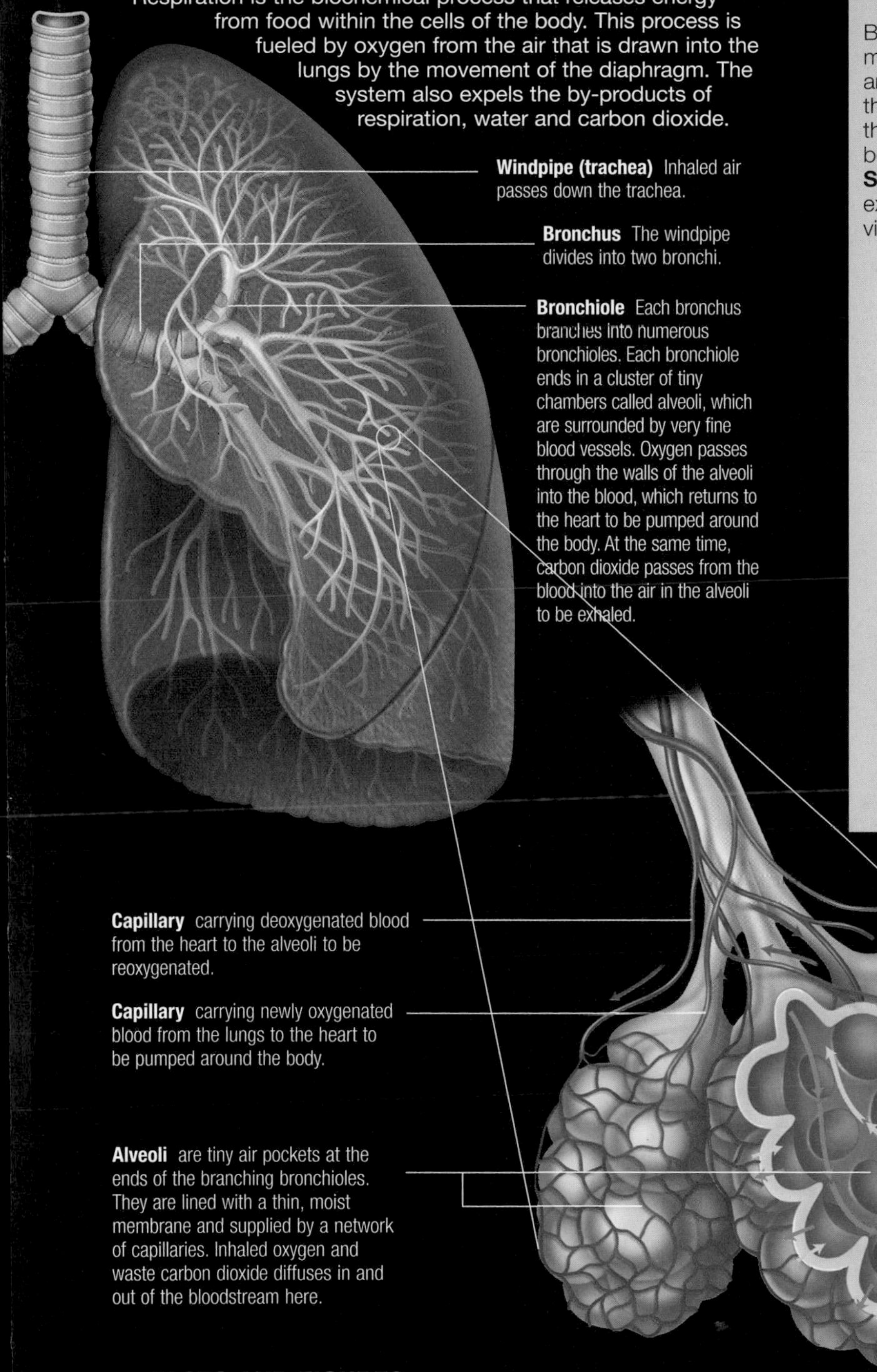
Windpipe (trachea) Inhaled air passes down the trachea.
Bronchus The windpipe divides into two bronchi.
Bronchiole Each bronchus branches into numerous bronchioles. Each bronchiole ends in a cluster of tiny chambers called alveoli, which are surrounded by very fine blood vessels. Oxygen passes through the walls of the alveoli into the blood, which returns to the heart to be pumped around the body. At the same time, carbon dioxide passes from the blood into the air in the alveoli to be exhaled.
Capillary carrying deoxygenated blood from the heart to the alveoli to be reoxygenated.
Capillary carrying newly oxygenated blood from the lungs to the heart to be pumped around the body.
Alveoli are tiny air pockets at the ends of the branching bronchioles. They are lined with a thin, moist membrane and supplied by a network of capillaries. Inhaled oxygen and waste carbon dioxide diffuses in and out of the bloodstream here.

The mechanics of breathing

Breathing is controlled by the diaphragm, a sheet of muscle that lies between the chest and abdominal cavities, and by the intercostal muscles between the ribs. Together, these cause the chest cavity to expand and contract, and the resulting difference in pressure inside and outside the body sucks air into the lungs, then forces it out.

Speech The vocal cords of the larynx vibrate as air expelled from the lungs flows between them. These vibrations produce sounds that we can control.

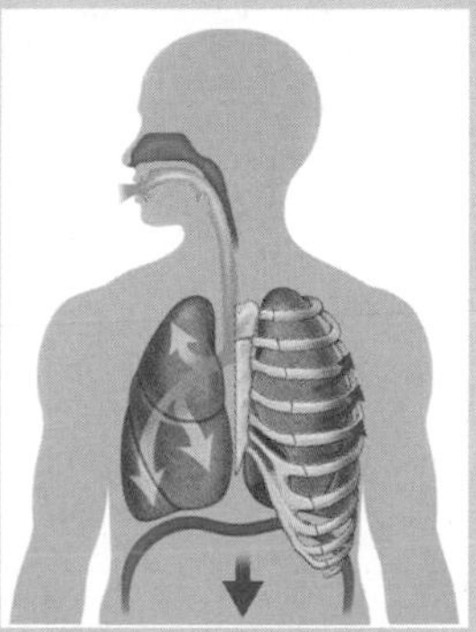

Inhalation The diaphragm contracts and flattens, increasing the volume of the chest cavity, while contraction of the intercostal muscles pulls the ribs upward and outward. Internal pressure decreases, and air is drawn in.

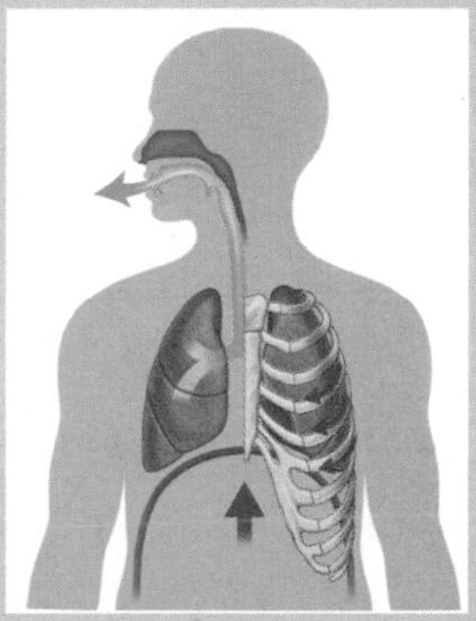

Exhalation The diaphragm relaxes upward, reducing the volume of the chest cavity. As the intercostal muscles relax, the ribs move downward and inward. Internal pressure increases, and air is pushed out.

FACT The combined length of all the arteries, veins and capillaries in the human body is about 150 000 km (93 000 miles).

FACTS AND FIGURES

The heart

- The muscles of the heart contract 100 000 times a day.

Blood

- Red blood cells survive for about 80-120 days. They are replaced by new red blood cells produced in the bone marrow at the rate of 2.5 billion a day.
- On average, blood takes 1 minute to go through the circulatory system once.
- When the oxygen supply in the body is low, the kidneys instruct the bone marrow to make more red blood cells.
- Blood accounts for about 8 percent of a person's total body weight.
- A single drop of blood contains about 250 million red cells and more than 300 000 white cells.
- An adult human contains 5 liters (10.5 pints) of blood.

The respiratory system

- On average, we breathe 18 times per minute.
- We breathe more than 25 000 times a day, inhaling about 14 200 liters (3124 gallons) of air.
- Lungs are not the same shape or size. The right lung is broader and has three lobes. The left has only two lobes.
- Inhaled air is 21 percent oxygen; exhaled air is 16 percent oxygen.

see also
118 **Glands and hormones**
119 **The immune system**

Glands and hormones

Instruction through chemicals

Glands are groups of cells, and some, known as endocrine glands, produce chemicals called hormones. They are scattered around the body and collectively make up the endocrine system. Each hormone acts on a specific target: Some trigger other glands; others regulate the way organs work. Unlike the nervous system, which sends instant messages demanding immediate action, most hormones take effect slowly.

THE ENDOCRINE SYSTEM

Most endocrine glands work by secreting hormones into the blood, which transports them to their target. Others secrete hormones directly into their target via a duct. Endocrine glands are controlled by an area of the brain called the hypothalamus. Hormones are very specific; they affect only their own target cells. They are broken down slowly after release.

Major endocrine glands and hormones

Hormone	Target	Functions
Pituitary gland		
Adrenocorticotropic	Adrenal glands	Influences body's response to stress; controls use of nutrients.
Antidiuretic	Kidneys	Regulates production of urine; helps constrict small arteries.
Thyroid-stimulating hormone	Thyroid gland	Stimulates thyroid gland; influences metabolism, circulation and growth.
Growth hormone	Muscle and bone	Stimulates growth and metabolism.
Pineal gland		
Melatonin	Hypothalamus	Affects body temperature, sleep and appetite.
Thyroid gland		
Thyroid hormones	Most cells	Increase metabolic rate; control growth.
Adrenal glands		
Epinephrine and norepinephrine	Circulatory system and muscles	Increases metabolic rate, heart rate and blood flow to muscles.
Pancreas		
Insulin and glucagon	Liver, fatty tissue and muscles	Regulates level of glucose in blood.
Ovaries		
Estrogen and progesterone	Sex organs and other tissues	Influences development of female sex organs and sexual characteristics; controls the menstrual cycle.
Testes		
Testosterone	Sex organs and other tissues	Influences development of male sex organs and sexual characteristics.

Control system Hormone secretion works through a feedback system that ensures the right amount of a hormone is available when it is needed. The system works in two ways.

- **Negative feedback** If the concentration of a hormone is too high, the excess in the blood acts as an indicator to the secreting gland to reduce production.
- **Positive feedback** Some glands are stimulated into increased production of a hormone when the level in the blood is already high. Oxytocin, which is released by the pituitary gland to stimulate uterine contractions during childbirth, works in this way.

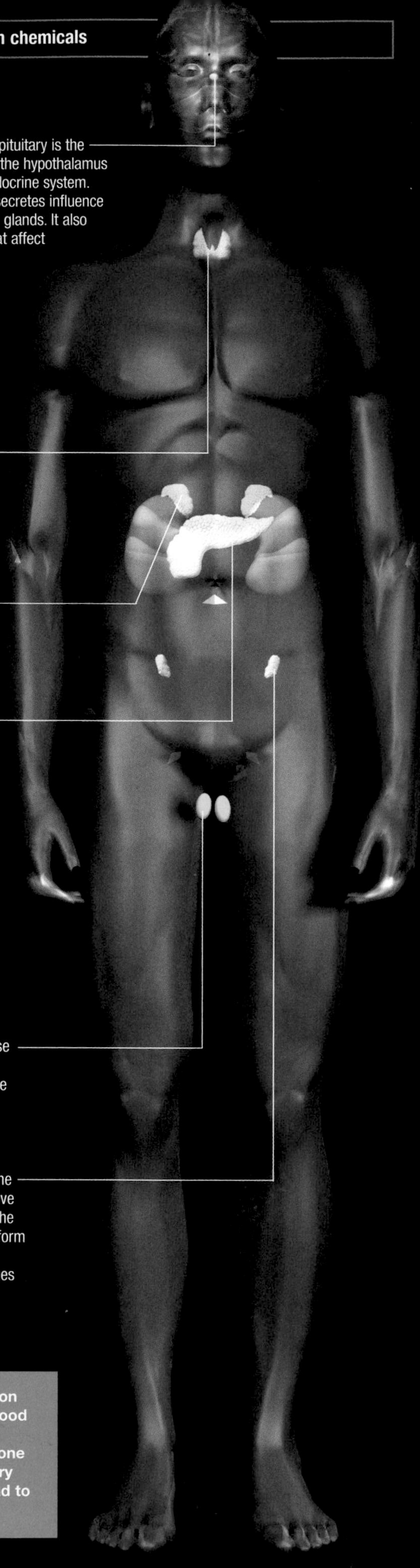

Pituitary gland The pituitary is the intermediary between the hypothalamus and the rest of the endocrine system. The hormones that it secretes influence all the other endocrine glands. It also secretes hormones that affect tissues and organs.
Pineal gland (Not shown) The function of this small gland at the back of the brain is not known.
Thyroid gland Larger in women than men, this gland sometimes increases in size during menstruation.
Adrenal gland The body has two adrenal glands, one above each kidney.
Pancreas This gland has two vital functions: the formation of pancreatic juice, which is the most important of the digestive juices, and the production of insulin and glucagon, which control blood sugar levels. Insufficient production of insulin leads to diabetes.
Testes In males, these two glands begin producing testosterone at between 9 and 14 years old, leading to the onset of puberty.
Ovaries In females, the ovaries sit slightly above and on either side of the bladder. They start to form eggs and produce sex hormones between ages 8 and 13.

FACT Overproduction during childhood of the human growth hormone by the pituitary gland can lead to gigantism.

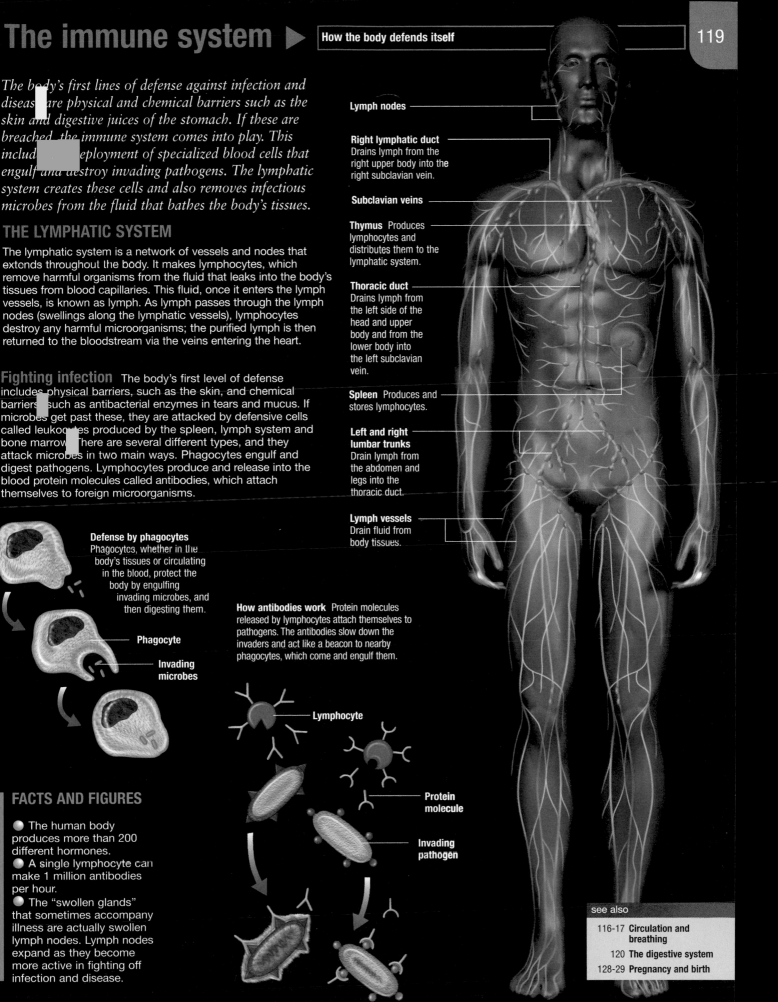

The b[redacted]y's first lines of defense against infection and diseas[redacted]are physical and chemical barriers such as the skin a[redacted]d digestive juices of the stomach. If these are breached, the immune system comes into play. This includ[redacted]eployment of specialized blood cells that engulf [redacted]estroy invading pathogens. The lymphatic system creates these cells and also removes infectious microbes from the fluid that bathes the body's tissues.

THE LYMPHATIC SYSTEM

The lymphatic system is a network of vessels and nodes that extends throughout the body. It makes lymphocytes, which remove harmful organisms from the fluid that leaks into the body's tissues from blood capillaries. This fluid, once it enters the lymph vessels, is known as lymph. As lymph passes through the lymph nodes (swellings along the lymphatic vessels), lymphocytes destroy any harmful microorganisms; the purified lymph is then returned to the bloodstream via the veins entering the heart.

Fighting infection The body's first level of defense includes physical barriers, such as the skin, and chemical barriers[redacted]such as antibacterial enzymes in tears and mucus. If microb[redacted] get past these, they are attacked by defensive cells called leukocytes produced by the spleen, lymph system and bone marrow[redacted]here are several different types, and they attack micro[redacted]s in two main ways. Phagocytes engulf and digest pathogens. Lymphocytes produce and release into the blood protein molecules called antibodies, which attach themselves to foreign microorganisms.

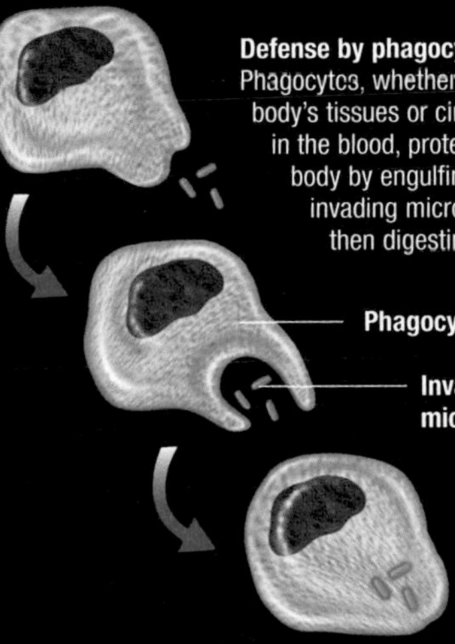
Phagocyte
Invading microbes

Defense by phagocytes Phagocytes, whether in the body's tissues or circulating in the blood, protect the body by engulfing invading microbes, and then digesting them.

How antibodies work Protein molecules released by lymphocytes attach themselves to pathogens. The antibodies slow down the invaders and act like a beacon to nearby phagocytes, which come and engulf them.

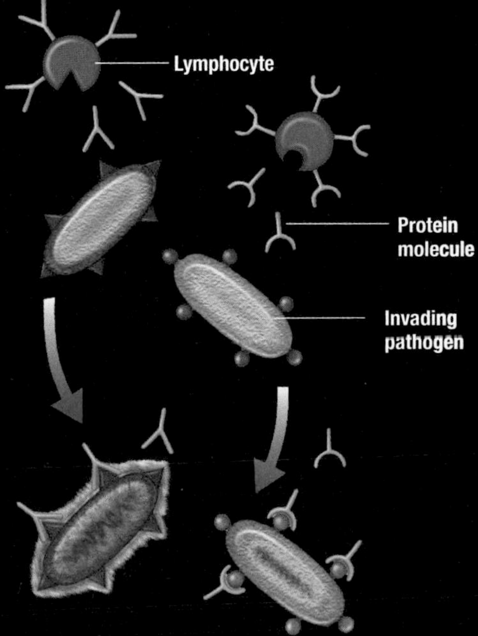
Lymphocyte
Protein molecule
Invading pathogen

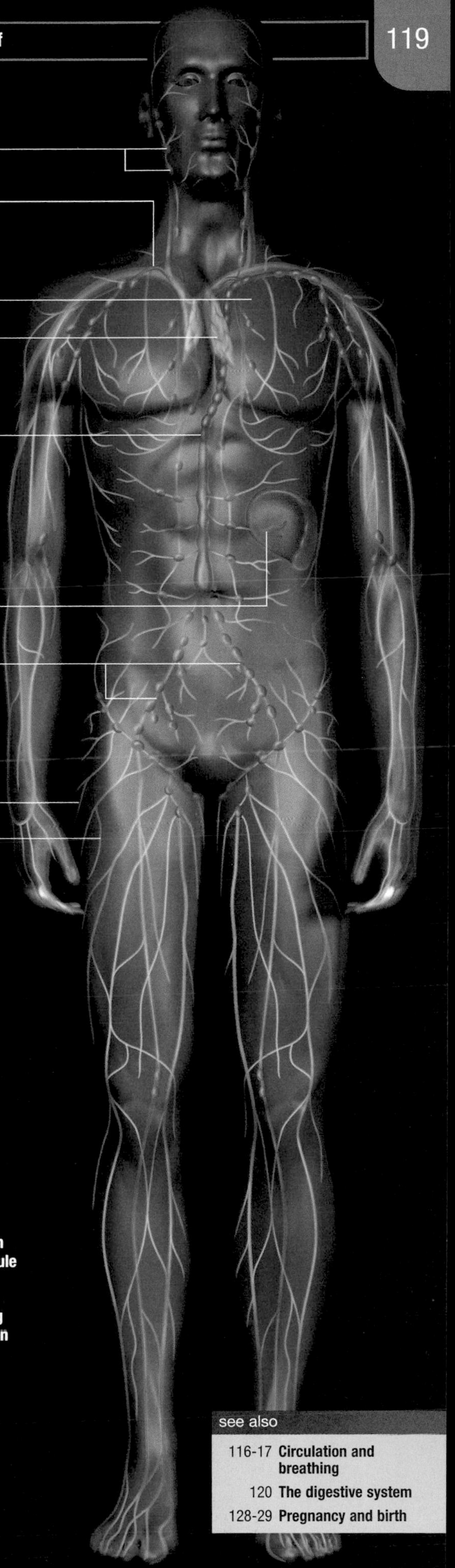
Lymph nodes
Right lymphatic duct Drains lymph from the right upper body into the right subclavian vein.
Subclavian veins
Thymus Produces lymphocytes and distributes them to the lymphatic system.
Thoracic duct Drains lymph from the left side of the head and upper body and from the lower body into the left subclavian vein.
Spleen Produces and stores lymphocytes.
Left and right lumbar trunks Drain lymph from the abdomen and legs into the thoracic duct.
Lymph vessels Drain fluid from body tissues.

FACTS AND FIGURES

- The human body produces more than 200 different hormones.
- A single lymphocyte can make 1 million antibodies per hour.
- The "swollen glands" that sometimes accompany illness are actually swollen lymph nodes. Lymph nodes expand as they become more active in fighting off infection and disease.

see also

116-17 **Circulation and breathing**
120 **The digestive system**
128-29 **Pregnancy and birth**

As soon as food passes our lips, the digestive system begins converting it into essential nutrients. The digestion and absorption of food takes place in the gastrointestinal tract, a tube extending from the mouth to the anus. Muscle action and enzymes break it down into molecules that are absorbed into the bloodstream. The whole process takes about 24 hours.

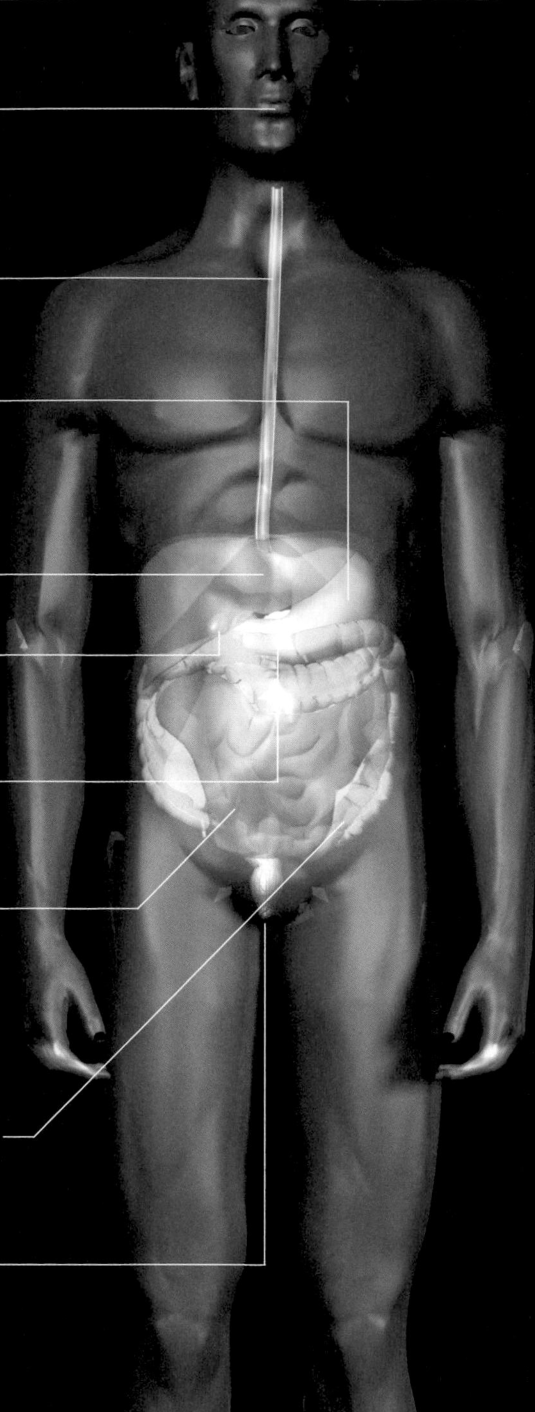

1 Teeth, salivary glands and tongue Teeth grind the food. Saliva softens and lubricates food, and enzymes in the saliva begin the digestion of carbohydrates. The tongue rises and pushes the food to the back of the mouth and down the throat.

2 Esophagus Transports food from the throat to the stomach by means of rhythmic wavelike muscular contractions.

3 Stomach Produces hydrochloric acid and the enzyme pepsin, which break down proteins. The enzyme lipase breaks down fats. The action of the muscular walls blends the food and gastric juices into a watery paste.

4 Liver Produces bile, a thick, green solution that breaks down fats.

5 Gall bladder Bile is stored in this sac. When food is eaten, the amount of bile entering the small intestine increases.

6 Pancreas Secretes enzymes that break down proteins, carbohydrates and fats, and sodium bicarbonate, which neutralizes stomach acid.

7 Small Intestine Secretes enzymes, which, together with bile and pancreatic juice, complete digestion. Most of the nutrients and water needed by the body are absorbed here. Glucose and amino acids are absorbed into the bloodstream. Fatty acids and glycerol enter the lymph stream and are taken to the liver.

8 Colon Muscular movement converts the residue from the small intestine into feces. The progress of waste is slow, to allow the reabsorption of water.

9 Rectum Waste triggers reflex contractions that propel the feces along the anal canal and out of the anus.

Structure of teeth

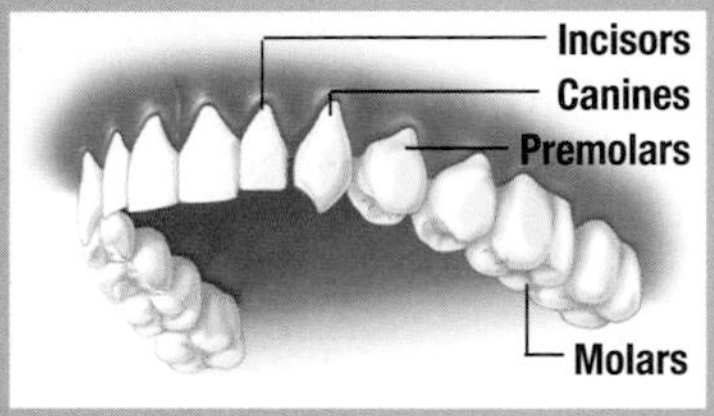

Teeth are embedded in the jawbone and appear as tooth buds by the sixth week of gestation. Humans have two sets of teeth, a temporary (baby) set and a permanent adult set. The 20 baby teeth begin to appear at about six months old. After age six, the already-formed adult teeth push out the baby teeth. Most adults have eight incisors, four canines, eight premolars and twelve molars.

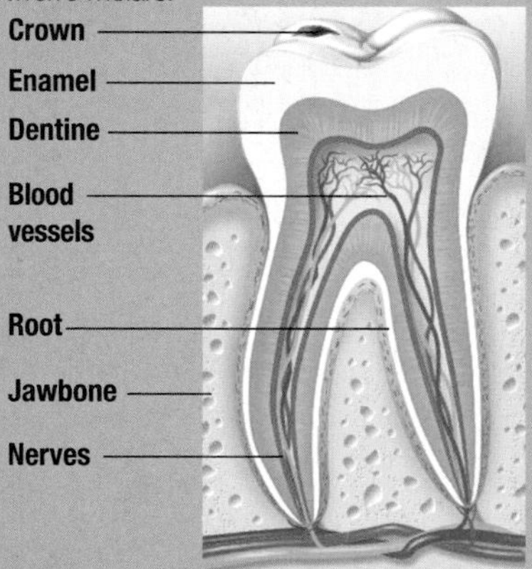

FUNCTIONS OF THE LIVER

The liver is the largest gland in the body. It is a chemical processing plant with several functions.

- **Making bile** Some liver cells make bile, which empties into the small intestine where it helps break down fats.
- **Storing fuel** Blood contains dissolved glucose, a sugar the body uses as fuel. The liver controls the glucose level by converting any surplus into glycogen, which it stores. If the blood glucose level falls, the liver converts glycogen back to glucose.
- **Processing fats** Fats from food are sent to the liver for processing. The liver turns them into a form that the body can use, and it also acts as a fat store.
- **Processing proteins** The liver processes amino acids – chemical units that make up proteins. When amino acids are broken down, they create ammonia, a substance that is poisonous. The liver turns this into urea, which is safely disposed of in urine and sweat.
- **Making blood** In fetuses, the liver makes red blood cells. In children and adults, it stores copper and iron, which are needed to make hemoglobin, blood's oxygen-carrying substance.
- **Cleaning blood** Cells in the liver remove old white blood cells and engulf bacteria and viruses.
- **Storing vitamins** The liver is a major vitamin storage depository, storing vitamins A, B_{12}, D, E and K.
- **Neutralizing toxins** The liver removes substances such as alcohol and drugs from the blood and turns them into safer chemicals.

The urinary system's main functions are to remove waste products from the body, to maintain its water balance and to adjust the concentration of fluids in the blood. The major organs are the two kidneys, which filter waste products out of the blood and reabsorb useful ones. Waste products pass into the bladder and out of the body through the urethra.

THE KIDNEY IN CLOSE-UP

Each kidney contains about 1 million tiny blood filtration units called nephrons, which remove waste products and excess water from the blood to make urine. Tubules carry urine into the renal pelvis, from which it flows to the bladder, where it collects before being expelled.

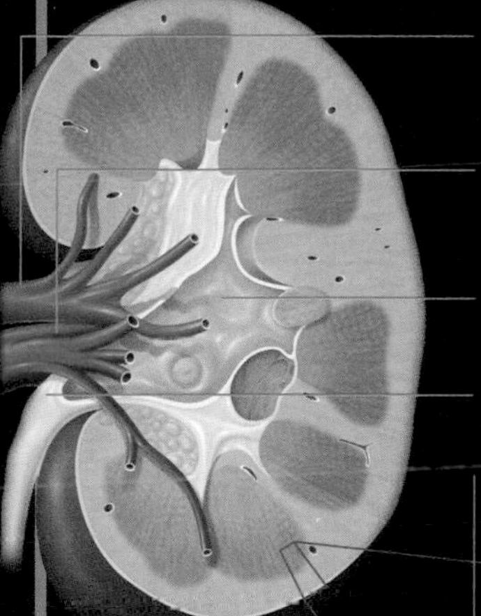
Renal artery Feeds blood to the kidney from the main artery of the body, the aorta.
Renal vein Carries blood from the kidney to the main vein of the body, the vena cava.
Renal pelvis Urine collects here.
Ureter Transports urine from the kidney to the bladder.
Collecting tubule Collects the urine, which consists of waste substances and the remaining water.

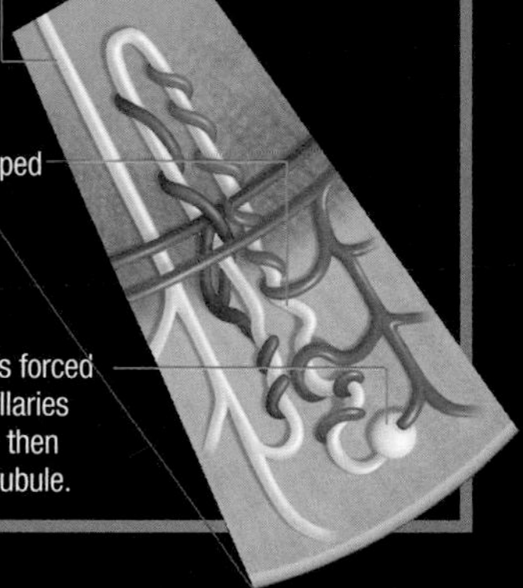
Proximal convoluted tubule Wrapped by capillaries, which reabsorb water, glucose and other vital substances through their walls into the blood.
Bowman's capsule Blood plasma is forced through the thin walls of the tiny capillaries clustered inside this sac. This plasma then passes into the proximal convoluted tubule.

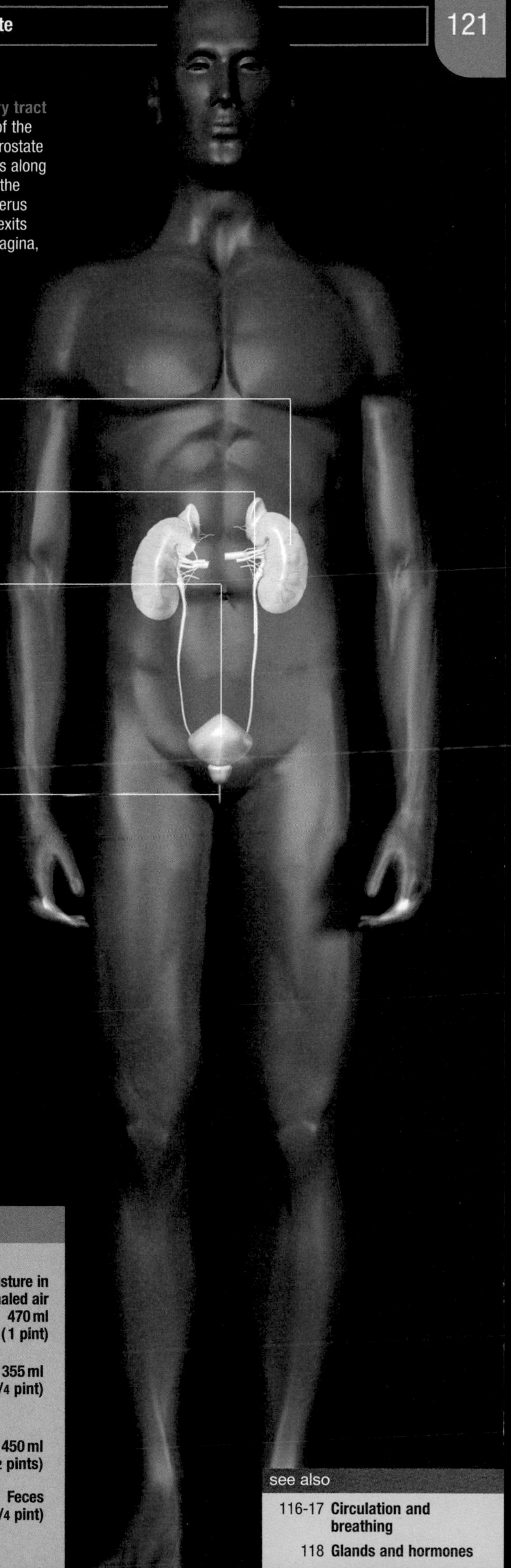
Male and female urinary tract In the male, the bottom of the bladder lies beside the prostate gland. The urethra passes along the penis. In the female, the bladder lies above the uterus and vagina. The urethra exits the body in front of the vagina, within the labial folds.
Kidney Filters urea, uric acid and excess water from the blood.
Ureter Carries urine from the kidney to the bladder.
Bladder A large muscular bag that stores urine. At the exit to the bladder is a circular sphincter muscle that acts as a valve, releasing urine into the urethra when the bladder is full.
Urethra Tube leading from the bladder. Urine passes through it to exit the body.

The importance of water

Water is essential to the body's well-being. As it passes through the kidneys, it dilutes toxins and allows sufficient urine to be produced to keep the body's chemical balance in order. Water is the medium in which all chemical processes occur within the body's metabolism. It is mostly stored in muscle, blood and skin and accounts for 60 percent of an adult's weight.

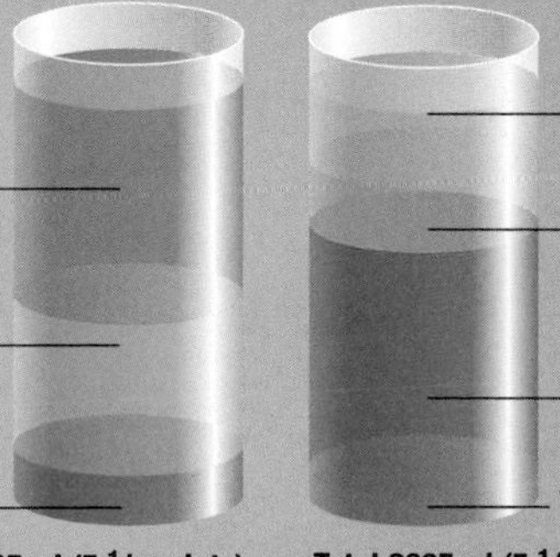
Water in per day
Water out per day
Drink 1240 ml (2 3/5 pints)
Food 890 ml (1 9/10 pints)
Produced by body cells 265 ml (3/5 pint)
Moisture in exhaled air 470 ml (1 pint)
Sweat 355 ml (3/4 pint)
Urine 1450 ml (3 1/2 pints)
Feces 120 ml (1/4 pint)
Total 2395 ml (5 1/10 pints)
Total 2395 ml (5 1/10 pints)

see also
116-17 **Circulation and breathing**
118 **Glands and hormones**

The skin is the largest organ in the body. An adult's skin has a surface area of about 2 m² (21 sq ft). It forms a protective layer, helps temperature regulation, synthesizes vitamin D and contains the nerves that transmit the sensations of touch, pain, heat and cold. Nails and hair are both formed by the skin and are largely made up of dead cells. Nails protect the sensitive fingertips and make it easier to pick up small objects. Hair plays an important role in regulating body temperature.

SKIN STRUCTURE

Skin is made up of two main layers, a thin outer layer, or epidermis, and a thicker foundation layer, or dermis.

- **The epidermis** varies in thickness according to the part of the body it covers (the thickest areas are on the back, the hands and the soles of the feet) and contains no blood vessels. It is constantly regenerated as dead cells on the surface wear away and are replaced by new cells moving up from below.
- **The dermis,** made of fibrous, elastic tissue, contains the touch, pressure and temperature sensory nerves, blood vessels and sweat and sebaceous glands. It also contains about 3 million hair follicles. The dermis includes the many permanent folds that appear on the skin's surface as fingerprint patterns. Beneath the dermis is a layer of fatty tissue, the hypodermis, which provides insulation.

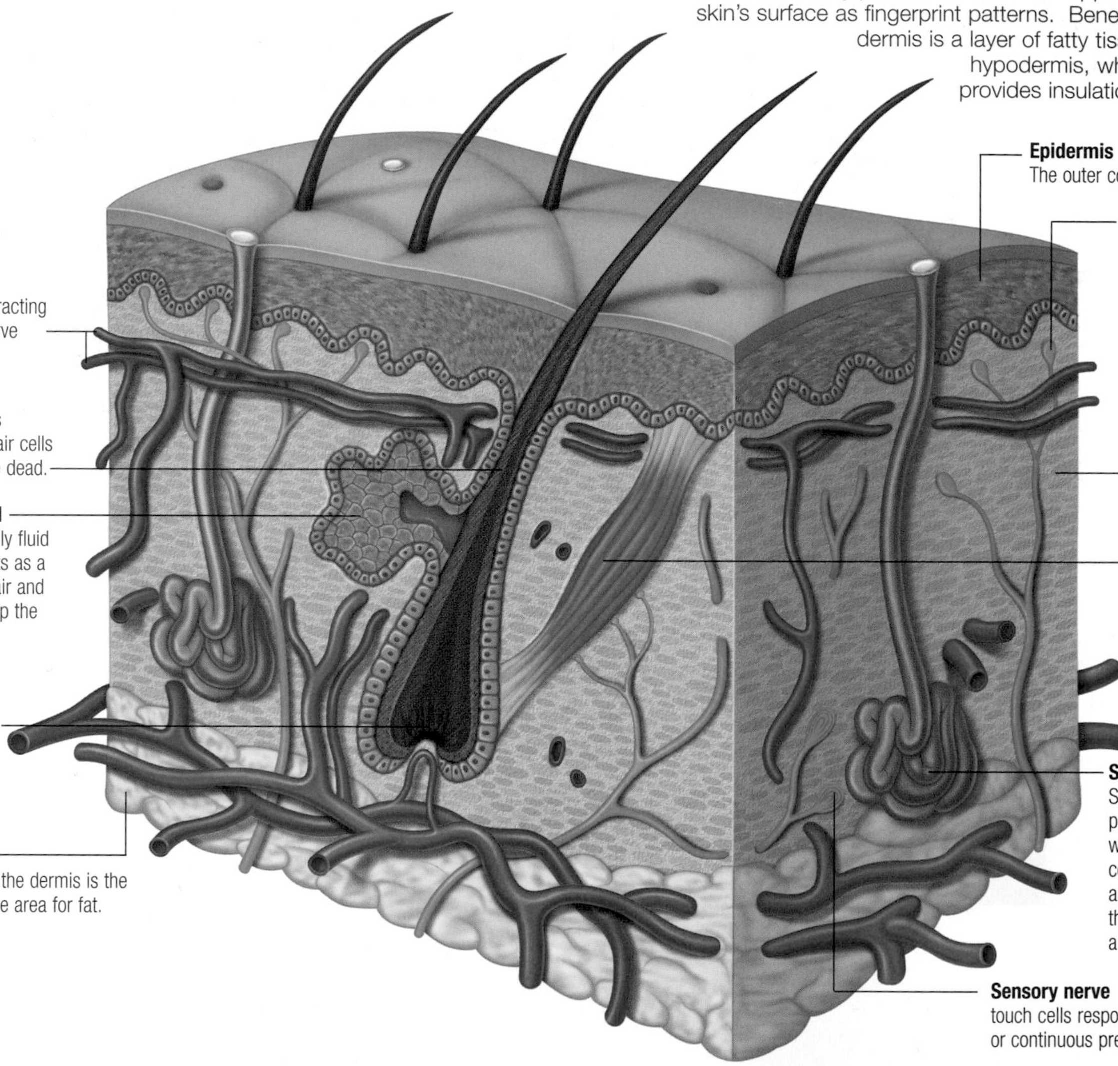

Blood vessels Blood vessels help regulate body temperature by expanding or contracting to dispel or conserve body heat.

Hair shaft New hair growth is constant, but all hair cells above the bulb are dead.

Sebaceous gland This secretes an oily fluid (sebum), which acts as a lubricant for the hair and skin and helps keep the skin supple.

Hair bulb The sac around the bulb and shaft is called the hair follicle.

Hypodermis This layer beneath the dermis is the body's main storage area for fat.

Epidermis The outer covering.

Sensory nerve Nerve cells beneath the epidermis respond to light touch, heat or pain.

Dermis The inner layer.

Hair erector muscle Contracts in response to cold or fear, making hair stand on end.

Sweat gland Sweat is produced within the coiled tubule and reaches the surface via a long duct.

Sensory nerve Deep-set touch cells respond to heavy or continuous pressure.

DAMAGE LIMITATION

When skin is broken, a scab forms to provide a protective cap over the damaged area while it heals. Scabs form from a sticky, fibrous substance called fibrin, which is produced in the blood whenever and wherever a blood vessel is broken. Fibrin meshes together and traps escaping blood cells in a clot, which then dries to become a scab. As a cut or scratch heals from the inside out, the scab moves closer to the surface. Once the damage to the skin has been completely repaired, the scab falls away.

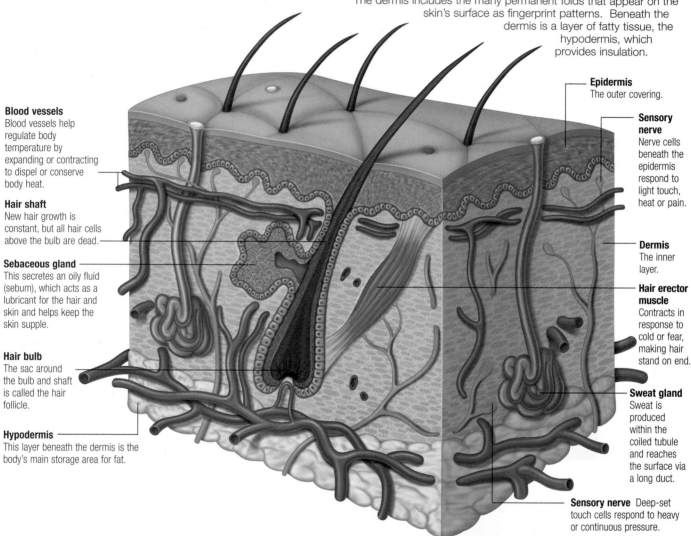

Flaky surface An electron micrograph of the surface of human skin, magnified about 200 times, shows how layers of dead cells peel back and become flakes, which then fall away. Household dust consists largely of these flakes, which are shed at a rate of 4 kg (9 lb) per person per year.

Controlling body temperature

The skin helps to control body temperature in three ways.

- **Perspiration** The evaporation of sweat helps cool the body to maintain a skin temperature of 36.1-37.8°C (97-100°F). This evaporation occurs constantly and imperceptibly. However, body temperature can rise rapidly, through muscular activity or as a result of an increase in the surrounding temperature. When this occurs, the sweat glands can secrete up to 3 liters (6 1/3 pints) of perspiration an hour over a short period.
- **Blood circulation** When body temperature rises, capillaries in the skin widen and the increased blood flow allows more heat to escape. When body temperature drops, the capillaries contract, retaining warmth inside the body.
- **Goose bumps** Hair erector muscles contract and form goose bumps in response to cold. The pits between the bumps hold heat and the erect hairs trap a layer of warmer air against the skin.

SWEAT GLANDS AND PERSPIRATION

Perspiration reaches the surface of the skin through tiny openings (pores) in the epidermis leading from the sweat glands. There are two kinds of sweat gland.

- **Normal sweat glands** Normal (eccrine) sweat glands occur all over the body but are concentrated in large numbers on the soles of the feet and palms of the hands. They secrete a slightly acidic, watery, salty sweat that helps both to regulate body temperature by cooling the skin when it evaporates and to expel small amounts of waste substances.
- **Sexual sweat glands** The sexual (apocrine) glands begin to function at puberty, producing viscous, protein-rich sweat in response to emotional stimuli such as sexual excitement and feelings of fear or anger. They are larger than ordinary sweat glands and occur in the eyelids, in the areola and nipple of the breast, in the armpits and around the anus and external genitalia. The sweat produced by these glands is odorless, but the action of bacteria on it can give it a distinctive smell.

SKIN COLOR

Human skin color ranges from pale pink to dark brown. The variation in color is caused by different amounts of pigments in the cells between the dermis and epidermis. The dark layers in the picture on the right are melanin cells, which give skin a dark color.

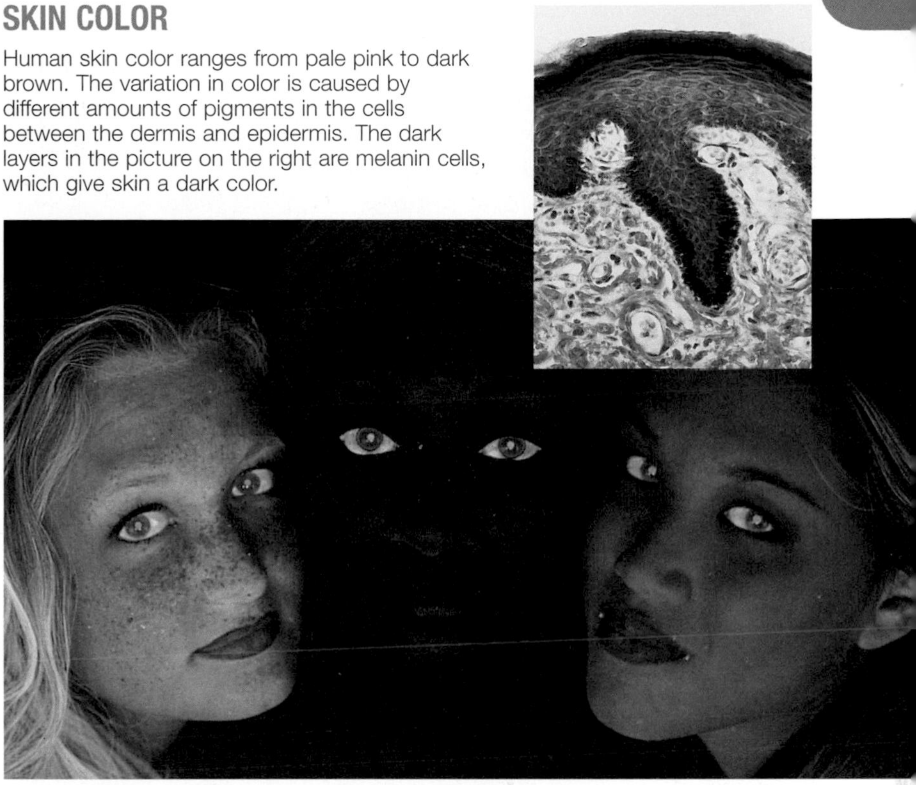

Natural sunblock Ultraviolet (UV) light is potentially very damaging to skin and is present at high levels in strong sunlight. The dark pigment melanin blocks the passage of UV light. This picture was shot under UV light. From left to right, the three women are of European, African and Asian origin. The African skin appears the most violet because it is reflecting the most UV light.

FINGERPRINTS

Patterns of ridges occur in the skin on the inner surfaces of the fingers, thumbs and palms and also on the soles and the lower surface of the toes. Their function is to aid grip. On the fingers and thumbs, these unchanging patterns are known as fingerprints. Each ridge is 0.2-0.4 mm (0.008-0.016 in.) wide, and the patterns are classified by their major features: arches, loops and whorls. Fingerprints are unique to each individual, which is why they are used to help identify suspects in crimes.

FACTS AND FIGURES

- The average person has about 2.5 million sweat glands.
- The palms of the hands have the largest concentration of sweat glands, with up to 500 per cm^2 of skin (3225 per sq in.).
- The body produces more than 1 liter (2 1/10 pints) of sweat every day, even when almost totally inactive.
- The epidermis is 0.1 mm (0.004 in.) thick on the face and 1 mm (0.04 in.) on the soles of the feet.
- There are up to 1 million hairs on the top of the head. Each grows about 0.3 mm (0.01 in.) a day.
- Hair gets its color from the pigments melanin and carotene. Graying is caused by a gradual loss of these pigments and a buildup of air bubbles in the shaft of the hair.
- The average person sheds about 80 hairs a day.
- In one year, fingernails grow 2.5 cm (1 in.). They grow faster in summer than in winter.
- A tan is the result of a buildup of the pigment melanin in response to exposure to ultraviolet light.
- The pigment carotene gives skin a yellowish color.

Nails

Nails develop from the epidermis and are formed from a fibrous protein called keratin. Growth occurs in the nail root beneath the skin of the cuticle. As with hair, only the nail root consists of live cells: Most of it consists of dead cells. The apparent perception of touch in the nails results from the large number of nerves in the nail bed and surrounding skin.

see also
116-17 **Circulation and breathing**
118 **Glands and hormones**
126-27 **Smell, taste and touch**

The eyes contain more than 70 percent of the body's sensory receptors. Changing patterns of light are detected by the eyes and fed as nervous impulses to the brain, which interprets, assesses and reacts to the images it receives. The human eye can operate in a wide range of conditions, rapidly accommodating to low light levels, for instance, as the eye and brain coordinate to make the most of the available information.

ADJUSTING FOR LIGHT

We can see in a wide range of light conditions because the iris contracts or expands to vary the size of the hole (the pupil) at its center. In low light, the pupil widens to allow in as much light as possible; in bright light, it shrinks to prevent from excess light damaging the eye.

◉ **Focusing** Muscles adjust the lens as light passes through it to focus incoming light rays onto the retina, forming an image.

◉ **Nearsightedness (myopia)** The image is focused slightly in front of the retina and is corrected by glasses with concave lenses.

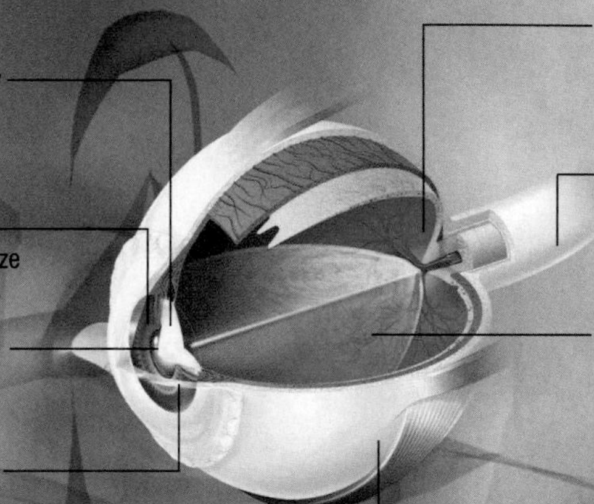

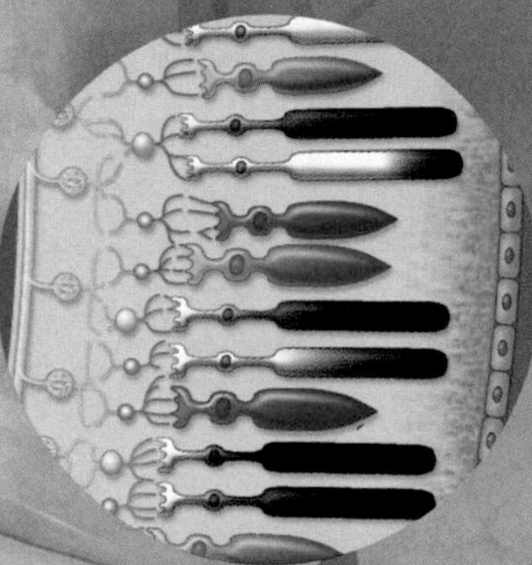

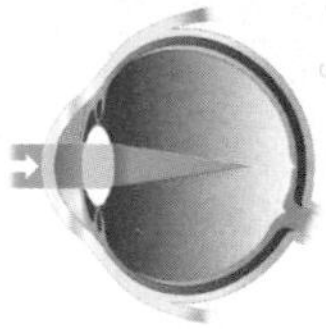

◉ **Farsightedness (hyperopia)** The image is focused slightly behind the retina and is corrected by glasses with convex lenses.

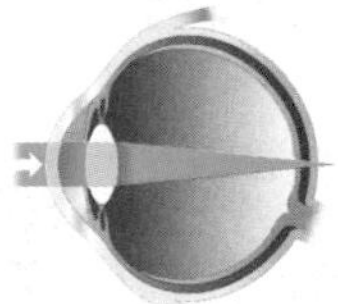

◉ **Astigmatism** The eyeball is not quite spherical, and the eye muscles cannot bring things into sharp focus. It particularly affects close vision and is corrected by glasses with a cylindrical curvature.

Are you color-blind?

Normal color vision needs red, blue and green cone cells to be working perfectly in order to detect all the colors of the spectrum. Some individuals are unable to distinguish between particular colors because certain cone cells are absent or malfunctioning. This condition, called color blindness, is more common among men than women because the genes that lead to it are carried on the X chromosome. An estimated 8 percent of males suffer from color blindness, compared with less than 1 percent of females.

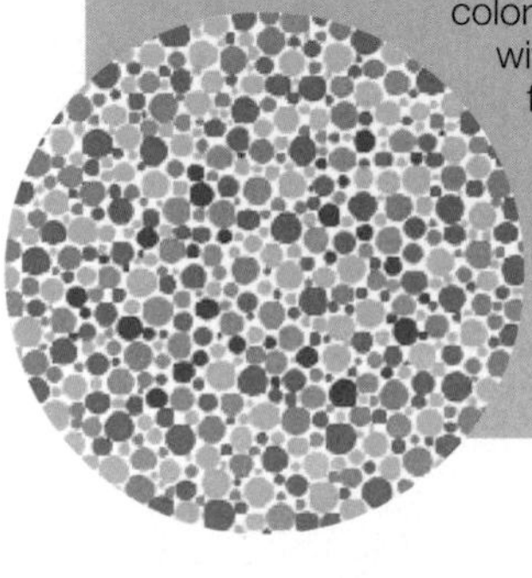

Test yourself
If you cannot detect a number in this pattern of dots, then you are probably color-blind.

THE EYE: OUR WINDOW ON THE WORLD

Each eye sits within a bony socket and is anchored by muscles. Light enters the eye through the transparent cornea, where it is roughly focused and passes via the pupil to a lens. This focuses the light more precisely through the transparent fluid (vitreous humor) that fills the eyeball. It forms an image on a curved screen at the back of the eye called the retina. The retina contains light-sensitive cells called rods and cones. The cones, which respond to particular colors, are clustered in the middle of the retina; the rods, which respond to black and white, are on the periphery. In response to stimulation, the rods and cones produce nervous impulses that are transmitted to the brain via the optic nerve.

Lens This sits directly behind the pupil and provides fine adjustment to focus.

Iris This pigmented muscle controls the size (aperture) of the pupil.

Pupil This is the hole through which light enters the eye.

Cornea This strongly curved window provides most of the eye's focusing power.

Retina The layer at the back of the eye where rods and cones are concentrated.

Optic nerve This is a bundle of about 1 million separate nerve fibers.

Vitreous humor This jellylike transparent fluid fills the eyeball and helps it maintain its spherical shape.

Sclera This tough fibrous layer makes up the white of the eye.

Rods and cones Rods (the longer, darker cells) distinguish between black and white, and are the only receptors active in low light levels. Cones enable us to see colors but require intense light (daylight) to do so.

Protection and mobility

◉ **Eyelids and conjunctiva** The eyelids protect the eye externally. Inside them and extending over the eyeball, a transparent membrane known as the conjunctiva provides extra protection.

◉ **Tears** The cornea must be kept clear for light to enter the eye. Tear fluid (which contains nutrients and protects the eye from bacteria) is washed over the eye by the blinking movements of the eyelids.

◉ **Eye muscles** The eyeball sits in a sling of six muscles suspended in the bony eye socket. These enable the eyeball to swivel in several directions.

FACTS AND FIGURES

◉ For the cells in the retina to function properly, the pattern of light falling on them must keep changing (without change, the cells' nerves cease to fire). The eye makes about 50 tiny flickering movements every second in order for this to happen.
◉ There are about 125 million rod cells and about 7 million cone cells in the retina.
◉ When the light fails, color blindness is experienced by people with normal vision. As evening draws on, we first lose the ability to see red, then orange, yellow and green. Blue is the last color to disappear and the first to reemerge in the morning light.

The ear both detects sound and governs our senses of balance and movement. The eardrum vibrates in response to sound waves in the air and passes these vibrations to the inner ear, where they are converted into nerve impulses. The slightly different wave patterns detected by each ear allow us to sense the direction of sounds. The inner ear's fluid-filled canals are highly sensitive to movement, providing the brain with an instantaneous signal of any change in the head's position.

THE EAR: AN ORGAN IN THREE PARTS

The ear is divided into three sections: the outer, middle and inner ear. The outer ear consists of the auricle or pinna (made of skin and cartilage) and the curved auditory canal. The pinna is shaped to guide sound waves into the ear. The outer part of the auditory canal is lined with fine hairs and glands that secrete wax. The middle ear includes the eardrum (tympanic membrane) stretched across the inner end of the auditory canal. Inside the drum lie three small bones, the hammer (malleus), anvil (incus) and stirrup (stapes), which transmit vibrations to the inner ear. This consists of the spiral cochlea, which converts vibrations into electronic impulses, and the vestibular apparatus, which controls balance. The latter consists of three fluid-filled semicircular canals, which detect movement, and the utricle and saccule, which respond to gravity.

HOW SOUND REACHES THE BRAIN

Cochlea, Anvil, Hammer, Stirrup, Eardrum

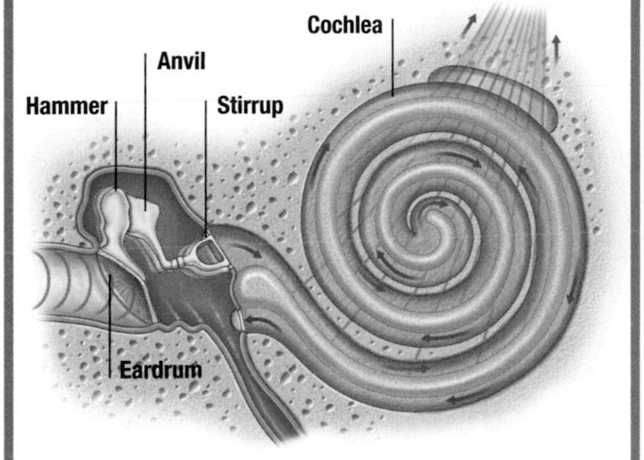

1 Sound waves strike the eardrum and vibrate the hammer, anvil and stirrup bones, which together modify and transfer the vibrations to the inner ear.
2 The fluid-filled chambers within the cochlea carry these vibrations to the corti, a set of membranes spiraling inside it.
3 Tiny hairs along the corti are stimulated by vibrations of different frequencies, converting each into a nervous impulse.
4 These impulses are carried by the vestibulo-cochlear nerve to the temporal lobe of the brain, where they are interpreted as sounds.

Pinna

Semicircular canals These play a vital role in maintaining balance (see box).

Cochlea The part of the ear where sound vibrations are transformed into nerve impulses.

Utricle and saccule Sensitive patches in these chambers detect the position of the head.

Auditory canal

Eardrum This semitransparent membrane vibrates when hit by sound waves. These vibrations are transferred to the cochlea by the hammer, anvil and stirrup bones.

Eustachian tube This leads to the back of the throat and ensures that air pressure remains equal on both sides of the eardrum – a condition vital for the eardrum to function properly.

Maintaining balance

The fluid-filled semicircular canals of the inner ear are fixed at right angles to each other, which means that movement in any direction causes fluid to move in one or more canals. Receptor hair cells in each canal detect this movement and send information to the brain. Hair cells in the utricle and saccule chambers press on one set of receptors when the head is held upright and on others when the head is tilted. Information from these organs helps the brain control eye movements so that an object can be held in view even when the head is moving.

Sixth sense
Balance is the sense we consider least often.

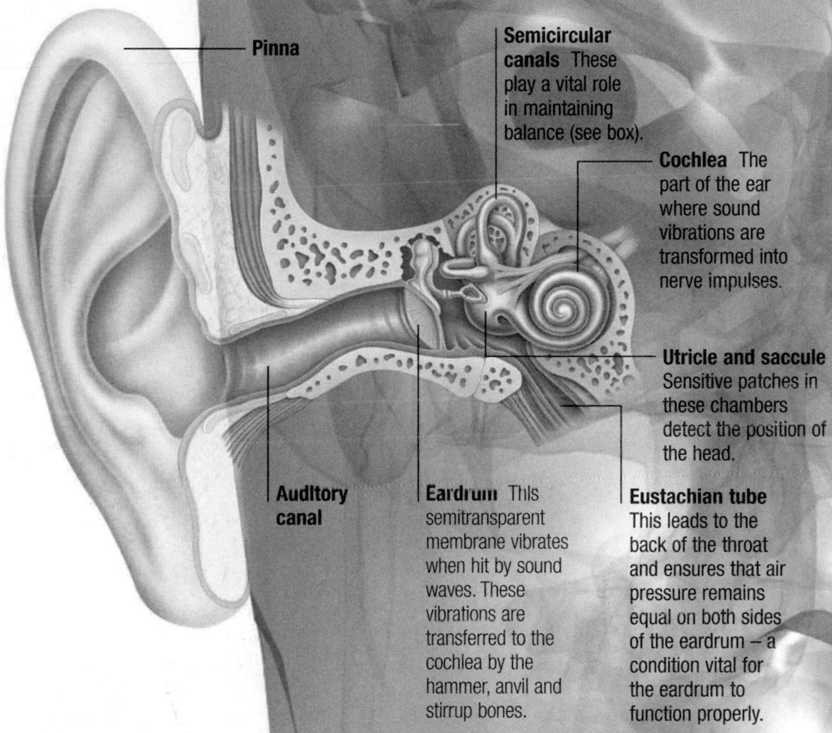

FACTS AND FIGURES

● Most humans can detect sounds pitched between 20 and 20 000 hertz. A rumbling juggernaut produces some sounds lower than 20 hertz, whereas screeching brakes may exceed 20 000 hertz.
● Permanent damage to the ears can be caused by sounds louder than 100 decibels. A jet airplane taking off creates noise ranging upward from 120 decibels in volume.
● The hammer, anvil and stirrup are the smallest bones in the human body.
● The eardrum measures about 8 mm (3/8 in.) across.

see also

114-15 **The brain and nerves**

Odor molecules from myriad sources float freely in the air, and our sense of smell lets us detect the more pungent of these from a distance. Smell also works in tandem with our taste buds to distinguish differences in flavor among foods. The sense of touch provides information that the brain needs to work out other properties of objects, such as their temperature, texture, hardness and weight.

SMELL

Nerve endings inside the nose contain receptor cells that detect chemical molecules in the air. These cells are concentrated in an area about the size of a postage stamp in the nasal cavity on each side of the nose. The receptor cells respond to specific molecules, and the nerves send messages to the brain via the olfactory bulbs.

What is a smell?

Chemicals that evaporate easily into the air, called volatile chemicals, are detected by receptor cells in the nose. Volatile chemicals are produced in different quantities by different substances. Those that produce the largest quantities are the easiest to smell. One of the smelliest substances on Earth is vanilla. It is 1000 times more potent than garlic oil and 15 000 times more potent than lemon peel.

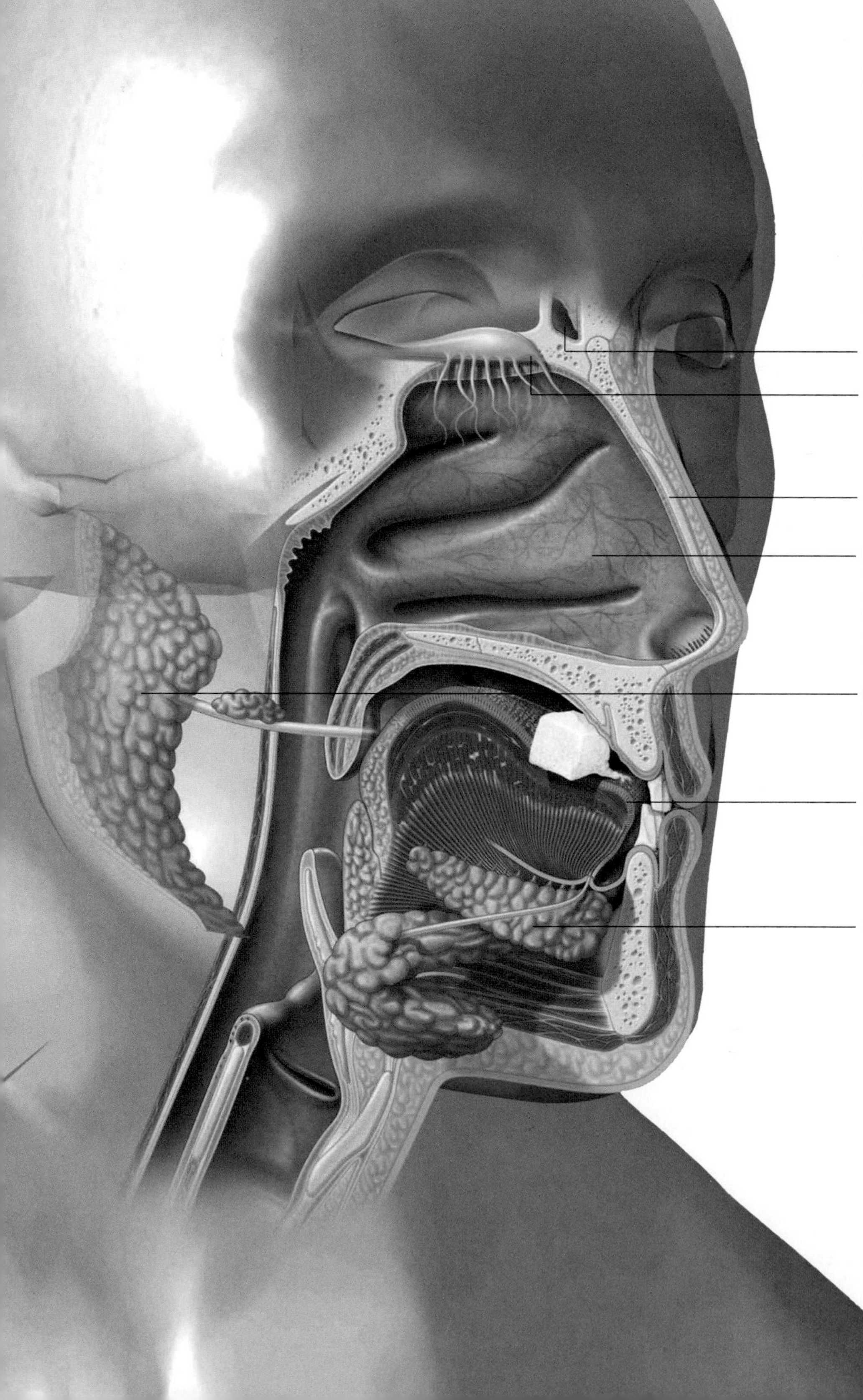

Frontal sinus
Olfactory bulb There are two of these bundles of nervous tissue, one beneath each eye. Nerves project down through the bone of the skull from each into the nasal cavity.
Nasal cartilage This forms the bridge of the nose. It is this cartilage that is damaged if the nose is broken.
Nasal cavity There are two of these large spaces, one for each nostril, lying between the eye sockets and the roof of the mouth. They are separated by a thin layer of cartilage and bone. Beneath a layer of protective mucus, the lining of the nasal cavity is packed with blood vessels to warm incoming air.
Salivary gland Saliva dissolves food chemicals, keeps the mouth moist and lubricates the passage of food down the throat.
Tongue The taste buds are concentrated on the surface of the tongue, which also serves to push food to the back of the mouth for swallowing.
Salivary gland

FACT The tongue is the only muscle in the human body that is attached at just one end.

TASTE

Taste buds are small sense organs concentrated on the tongue, but they also exist in the throat and on the palate. On the tongue, they are found in small projections called papillae, which vary in shape and location. Taste buds are sensitive to four different sensations: bitter, sour, salty and sweet; all the different flavors we recognize are made up of combinations of these four plus odors detected by the nose. Taste receptor cells are stimulated by chemicals in food after it has been dissolved by saliva, and they transmit signals to the brain for interpretation.

Taste areas Rounded (vallate) papillae are situated near the rear of the tongue, ridged (foliate) papillae along the sides, mushroom-shaped (fungiform) papillae on the top surface, and hairlike (filiform) papillae around the tip. Taste buds that respond to the four categories of flavor are concentrated on different parts of the tongue, although some can be stimulated to a lesser degree by one or more of the other main taste categories.

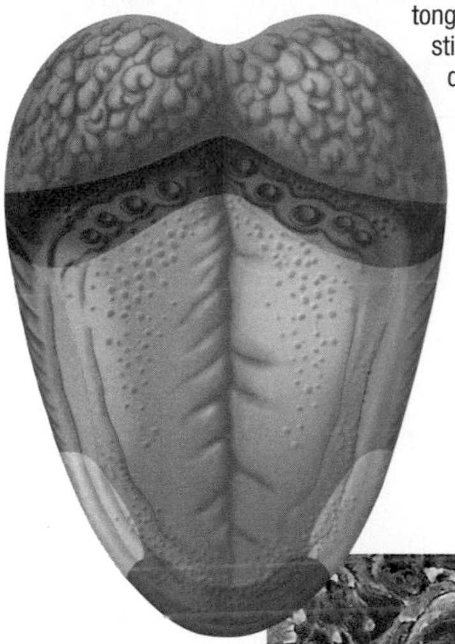

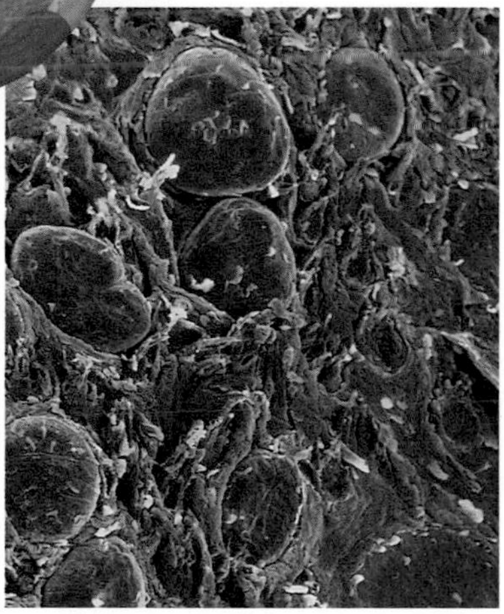

Taste buds In an electron micrograph of the surface of the tongue, fungiform papillae show up as large red areas. A single papilla can contain up to five separate taste buds.

FACTS AND FIGURES

- The 10 000 taste buds on the tongue survive only a few days and are constantly being replaced.
- Democritus, the Greek philosopher who first suggested the presence of atoms, thought that sharp odors were produced by pointed atoms and sweet odors by rounded ones.
- Humans can detect 10 000 different odors. Children can recognize more odors than adults, because the olfactory receptors waste away from birth.
- The nose contains about 50 million smell receptor cells.
- The human fetus has senses of "smell" and "taste." Odors from the mother's food and drink pass to the fetus via the amniotic fluid. At 12 weeks, fetuses begin to swallow amniotic fluid, and monitoring has shown that they prefer sweet flavors.

TOUCH

Human skin is packed with sensory receptors that give the body its sense of touch. Sensory nerves vary in structure, but all react immediately to physical sensations, converting them into nerve impulses to be transmitted to the area of the brain called the thalamus via the central nervous system. Here the impulses are sorted and passed on to the sensory regions of the brain.

Some receptor cells lie close to the surface of the skin and are sensitive to a light touch and heat; others are found at deeper levels and respond to heavy pressure.

Touch receptors are not distributed evenly around the body. The hands, feet and lips have far more than anywhere else. This reflects the importance of touch in these areas, which spend more time in contact with other objects than any other parts of the body.

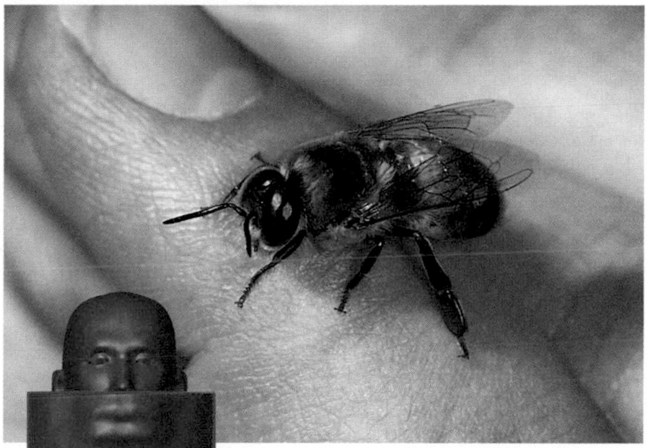

Tiny steps Touch sensors are so concentrated on our hands that we can feel the minute changes in pressure caused by an insect walking over them. By contrast, the same amount of pressure on our backs will elicit almost no response at all. Among other things, touch sensors in our hands enable the brain to tell how hard or soft objects are and how much pressure to exert when holding them or picking them up.

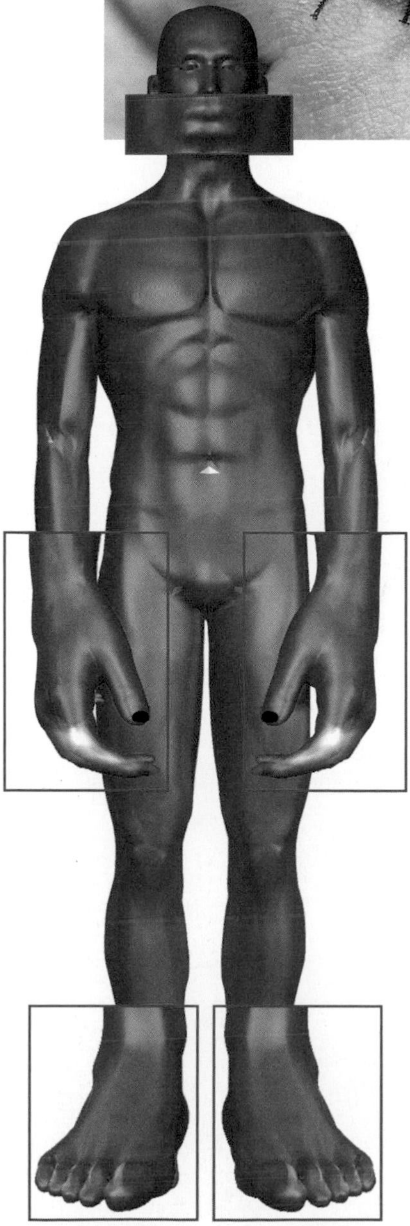

Touch sensitive Our ability to feel objects by touch is amplified in our mouth, hands and feet, which have a greater concentration of touch receptors. This diagram illustrates the proportionately greater sensitivity in these areas.

114-15 **The brain and nerves**
120 **The digestive system**
128-29 **Pregnancy and birth**

During the first eight weeks of a human pregnancy the fertilized egg develops into an embryo. Its cells divide at extraordinary speed, producing clusters that form the emerging organs. Blood vessels begin to form 17 days after conception. Limbs appear as buds by the third week. By the eighth week, the fetus, although only 2.5 cm (1 in.) long, is clearly recognizable as a human being.

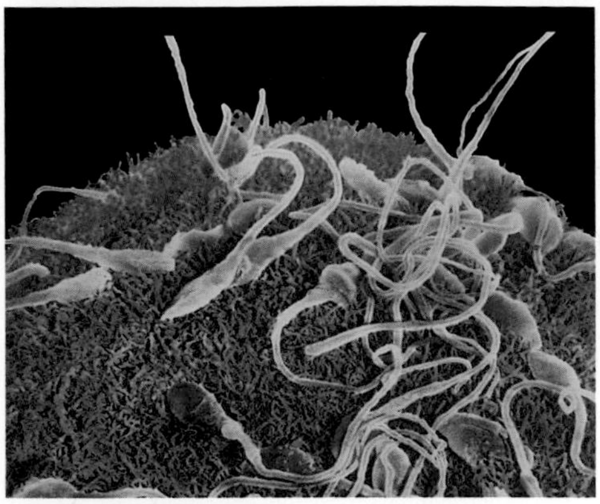

Fighting to fertilize Human sperm cells writhe on the surface of an egg cell (ovum), which dwarfs them. Although only one sperm will gain entry to the egg and fertilize it, it takes many to break down the egg cell's outer coating (by releasing protein-dissolving enzymes) before this can happen.

THE FIRST DAYS AFTER FERTILIZATION

The fertilized egg's rapid development into an embryo occurs mainly within the lining of the uterus – but it actually begins while the egg is still traveling down the Fallopian tube. As well as cells that develop into the embryo (embryoblast cells), the fertilized egg produces trophoblast cells that develop into the placenta, which will supply oxygen and nutrients to the baby from its mother through the umbilical cord and carry away waste products.

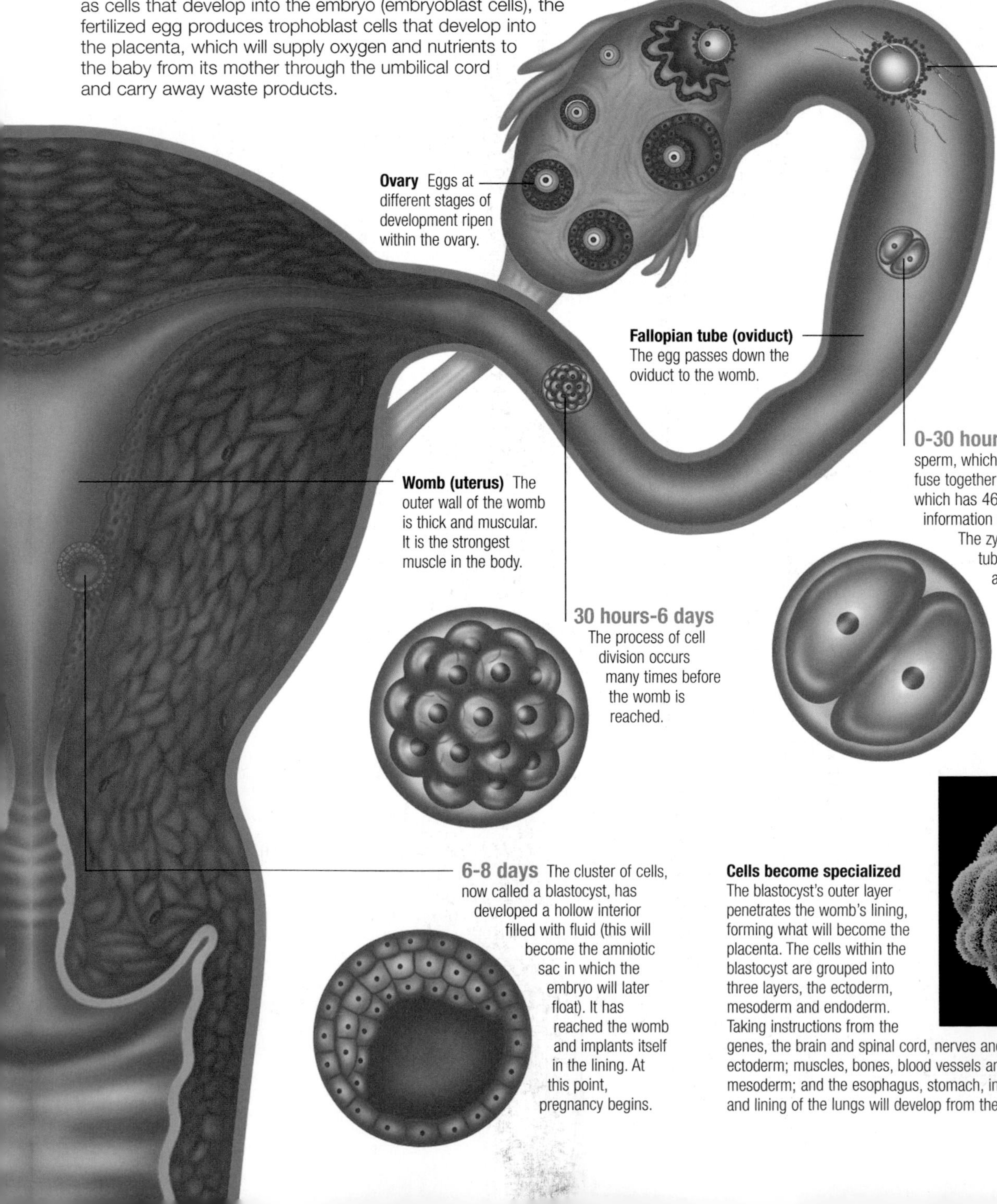

Moment of conception High in the Fallopian tube, a single tadpole-shaped sperm cell penetrates the outer membrane of the ovum and then sheds its body and tail. The head, containing the sperm's nucleus and genetic material, travels to the nucleus of the ovum.

Ovary Eggs at different stages of development ripen within the ovary.

Fallopian tube (oviduct) The egg passes down the oviduct to the womb.

0-30 hours The nuclei of the ovum and sperm, which each contain 23 chromosomes, fuse together to form a single zygote cell, which has 46 chromosomes – all the genetic information required to make a new person. The zygote travels down the Fallopian tube towards the uterus, or womb, and begins to divide, first into two new cells (at 30 hours old), then four, then eight and so on.

Womb (uterus) The outer wall of the womb is thick and muscular. It is the strongest muscle in the body.

30 hours-6 days The process of cell division occurs many times before the womb is reached.

6-8 days The cluster of cells, now called a blastocyst, has developed a hollow interior filled with fluid (this will become the amniotic sac in which the embryo will later float). It has reached the womb and implants itself in the lining. At this point, pregnancy begins.

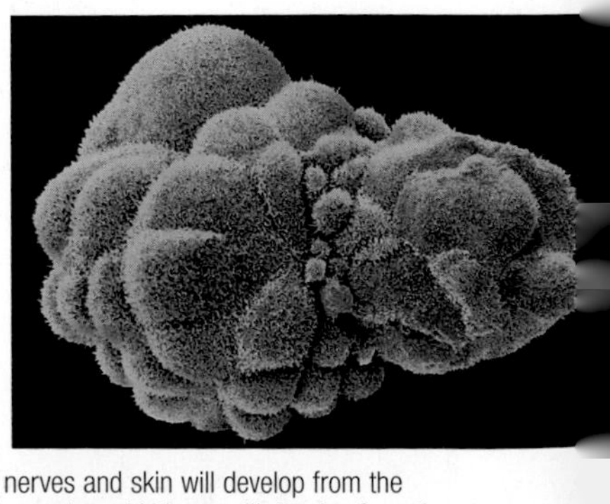

Cells become specialized The blastocyst's outer layer penetrates the womb's lining, forming what will become the placenta. The cells within the blastocyst are grouped into three layers, the ectoderm, mesoderm and endoderm. Taking instructions from the genes, the brain and spinal cord, nerves and skin will develop from the ectoderm; muscles, bones, blood vessels and kidneys will develop from the mesoderm; and the esophagus, stomach, intestine, bladder, pancreas, liver and lining of the lungs will develop from the endoderm.

STAGES OF PREGNANCY

Between eight days and four weeks, the cells of the blastocyst diversify and the organs gradually begin to develop. At four weeks, the blastocyst still does not look recognizably human but is already 80 000 times bigger than the original egg. By the time it is born, the baby will be about a million times bigger again.

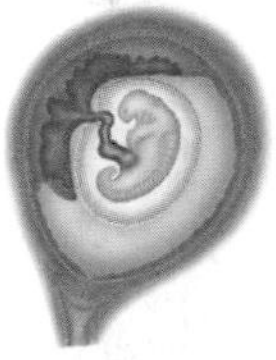

4 weeks The heart has begun to beat. At this point, the embryo is just 5 mm (1/4 in.) long.

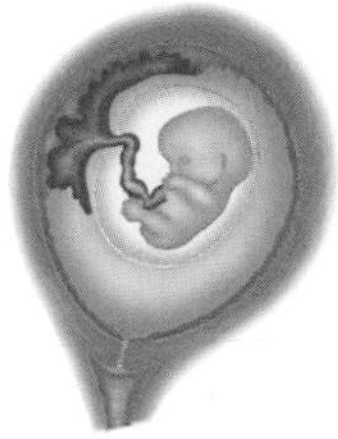

6 weeks The embryo obtains all of its nourishment and oxygen from the placenta and umbilical cord. It now has a simple brain.

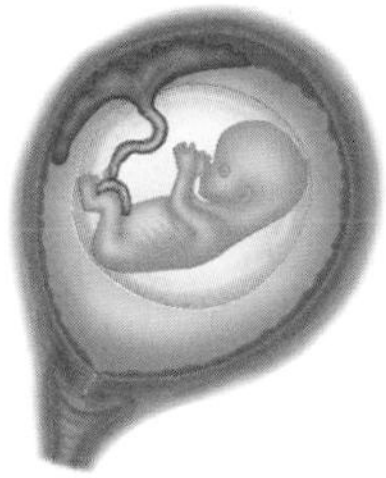

8 weeks Now called a fetus, it has recognizable limbs and measures 2.5 cm (1 in.) long. It starts to move, but this is not yet felt by the mother.

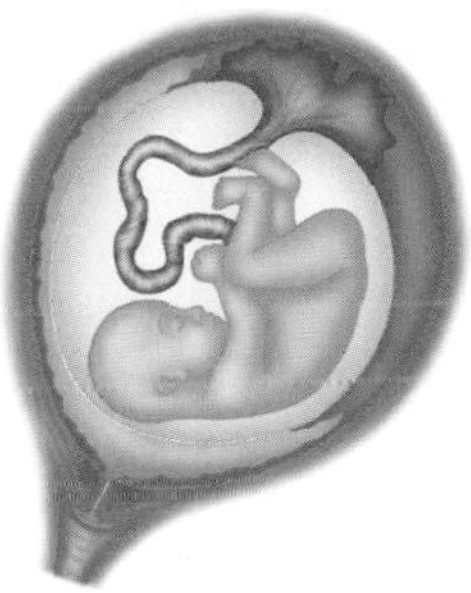

12 weeks Major internal organs have developed, the 32 permanent tooth buds have appeared, and eyelids and the external part of the ears have formed. The external genital organs are similar in both sexes at this stage (it is not possible to distinguish the sex of a baby until the end of the fourth month). Fine downy hair covers the 8-9 cm (3 1/4-3 1/2 in.) long fetus, which is now able to swallow.

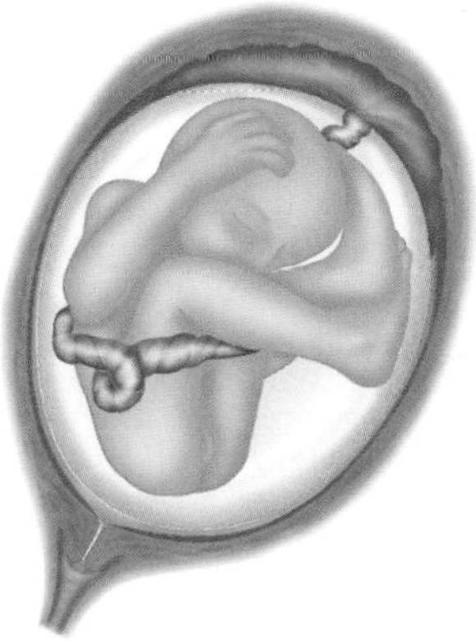

22 weeks All the body systems are established. If born prematurely now, the 15-25 cm (6-10 in.) long baby could survive with medical support.

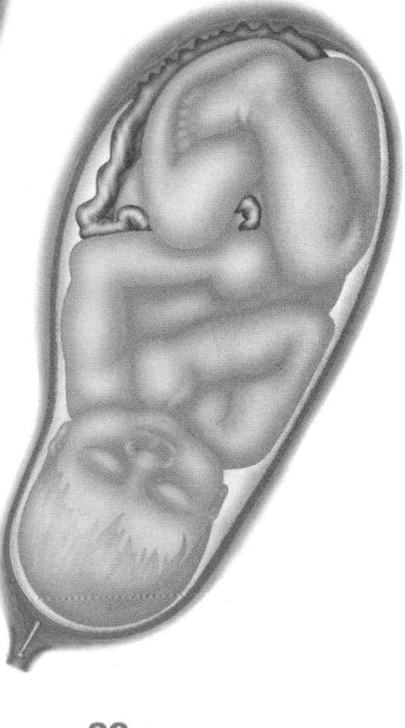

38 weeks The baby is fully formed with its head engaged (positioned downward facing the pelvis), ready to be born.

THE REPRODUCTIVE ORGANS

The female reproductive (sex) organs are inside the body. Every month, one of the ovaries releases an egg (ovum), which travels to the womb (uterus), where an enriched blood supply has developed ready to nourish it. If the egg is not fertilized, it is expelled with the uterine blood, in the menstrual flow (period).

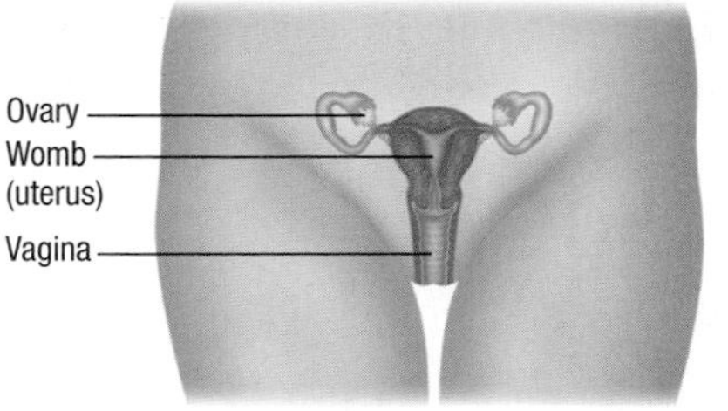

The male sex organs are both inside and outside the body. Sperm formed by the testes mature in about two weeks and are stored in tubes above them. When the is penis erect, sperm moves from these to the urethra, mixing with fluid on the way to form semen. This flows into the penis to be ejected during intercourse.

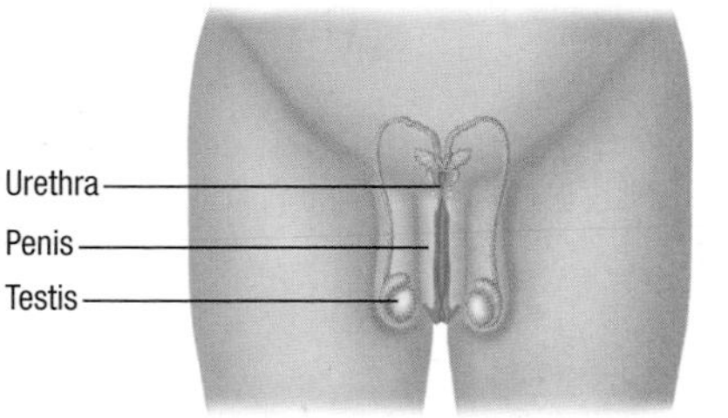

see also

118 **Glands and hormones**

130-31 **Cells and DNA**

438-39 **Inherited characteristics**

Giving birth

Delivery occurs in three stages.

- **First stage** The amniotic sac around the fetus ruptures, and the fluid drains away (the water breaks). The muscles of the womb begin to contract, and the neck of the cervix relaxes and widens (dilates). This stage can take up to 10 hours.
- **Second stage** Contractions occur more frequently. The baby moves down the birth canal (cervix and vagina), emerging head first. The mother pushes with her abdominal muscles to help the baby to be born. This stage may take 2 hours for a first baby.
- **Third stage** The placenta (afterbirth) is expelled. Hormones released during the birth cause the mother's breasts to begin producing colostrum, a rich precursor to milk, almost immediately.

Birth problems

- **Premature baby** A baby born before 37 weeks of pregnancy is not fully developed. It must spend time in an incubator, which helps with breathing and maintains body temperature.
- **Breach baby** The baby is born feet or buttocks first, having failed to turn during pregnancy in order for the head to face the pelvis.
- **Caesarean section** If mother or baby are at risk during natural delivery, an incision is made in the mother's abdomen and the baby is lifted out.

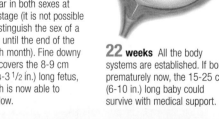

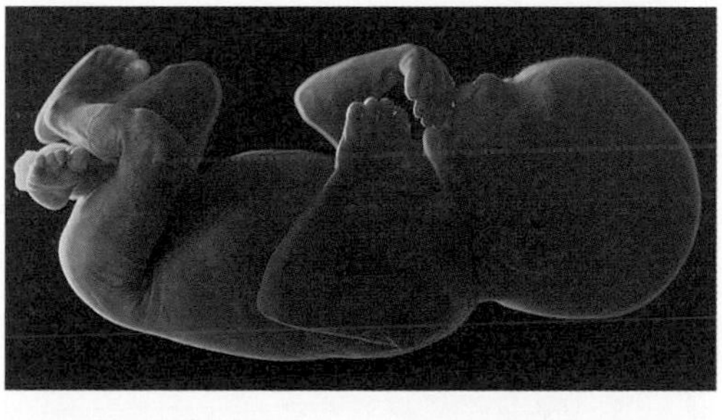

Just over halfway At five months, the fetus looks fully formed. Before birth, however, it will more than double in length and put on thick layers of fat.

Cells are the smallest structural units in the body and are grouped into different types of tissue. All types of cell have a similar internal structure regardless of their function, and most cells have nuclei that contain a substance called DNA, which carries the genetic information that is passed from parent to child. DNA controls not only the distinguishing features of each person but also the way in which individual cells function.

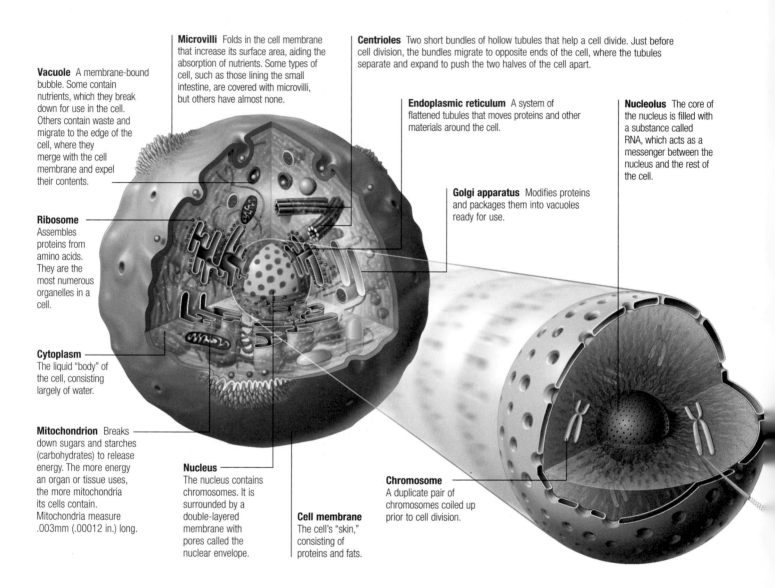

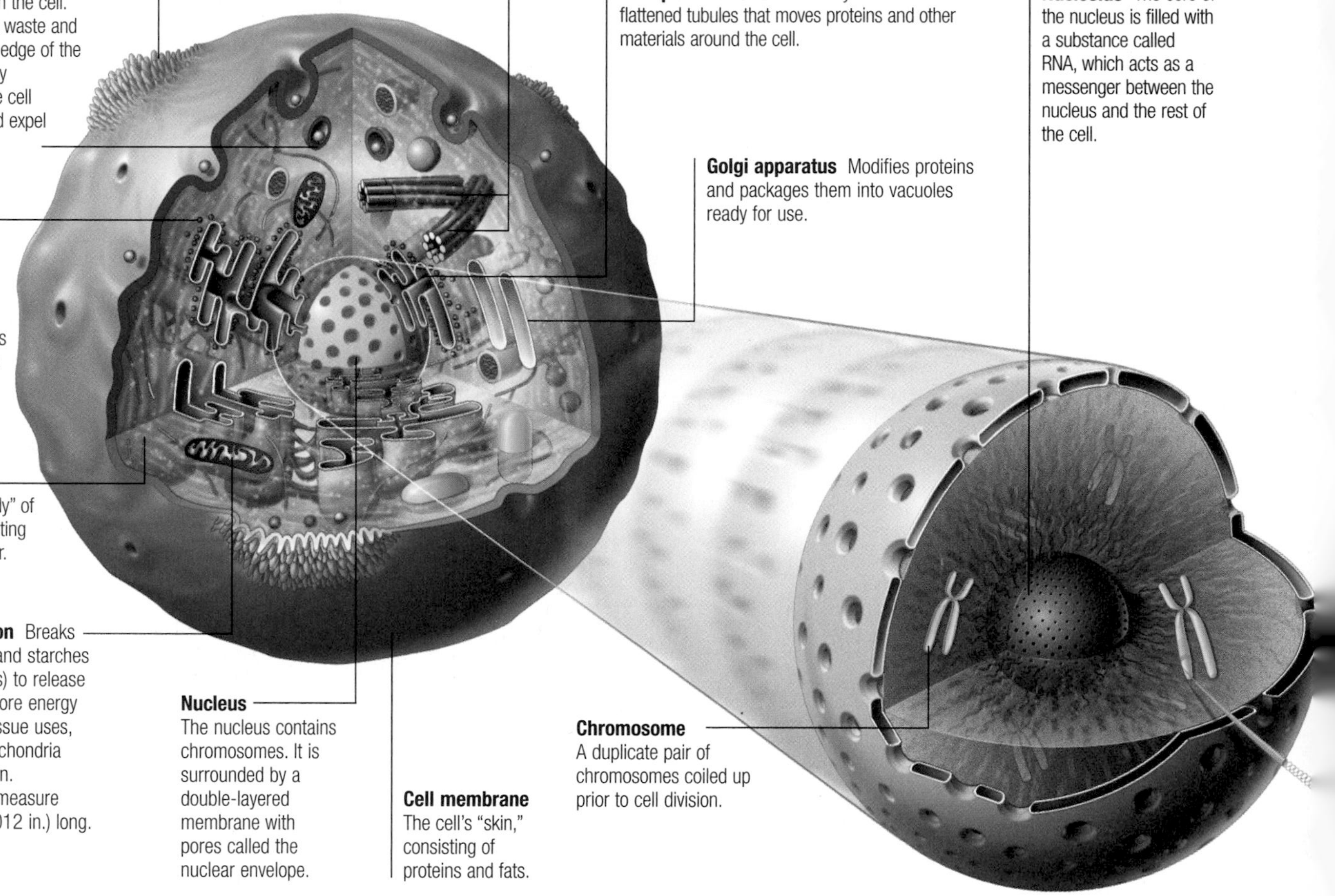

Vacuole A membrane-bound bubble. Some contain nutrients, which they break down for use in the cell. Others contain waste and migrate to the edge of the cell, where they merge with the cell membrane and expel their contents.
Microvilli Folds in the cell membrane that increase its surface area, aiding the absorption of nutrients. Some types of cell, such as those lining the small intestine, are covered with microvilli, but others have almost none.
Centrioles Two short bundles of hollow tubules that help a cell divide. Just before cell division, the bundles migrate to opposite ends of the cell, where the tubules separate and expand to push the two halves of the cell apart.
Endoplasmic reticulum A system of flattened tubules that moves proteins and other materials around the cell.
Nucleolus The core of the nucleus is filled with a substance called RNA, which acts as a messenger between the nucleus and the rest of the cell.
Golgi apparatus Modifies proteins and packages them into vacuoles ready for use.
Ribosome Assembles proteins from amino acids. They are the most numerous organelles in a cell.
Cytoplasm The liquid "body" of the cell, consisting largely of water.
Mitochondrion Breaks down sugars and starches (carbohydrates) to release energy. The more energy an organ or tissue uses, the more mitochondria its cells contain. Mitochondria measure .003mm (.00012 in.) long.
Nucleus The nucleus contains chromosomes. It is surrounded by a double-layered membrane with pores called the nuclear envelope.
Cell membrane The cell's "skin," consisting of proteins and fats.
Chromosome A duplicate pair of chromosomes coiled up prior to cell division.

CELL STRUCTURE AND FUNCTION

All cells consist of an outer membrane enclosing fluid called cytoplasm. Within this are specialized structures, called organelles, that carry out the cell's tasks. At the center of the cell is the nucleus, which contains genetic material (DNA) in the form of chromosomes and acts as the cell's control center. Most cells contain a complete set of genetic instructions, but within each cell, only those needed for its particular function are activated. For example, instructions for making the hormone insulin are present in the DNA of every cell but are only used in cells in the pancreas.

Although most cells contain the same types of organelle, cells are a different shape and size and have differing life spans depending on their function. Fat cells are globular and contain a droplet of fat, whereas nerve cells have long, branching axions for transmitting messages. Some cells are able to change shape. White blood cells, for example, can become long and thin to squeeze through tiny capillaries or send out "arms" to grab and engulf microorganisms.

CHROMOSOMES

Chromosomes are threadlike structures found in the cell nucleus. Each consists of a giant molecule of DNA coiled round a protein core.

Most of the time, chromosomes are unraveled so that their DNA can be easily accessed. Just before a cell divides, chromosomes coil up into bundles fat enough to be seen under a microscope. Each bundle replicates itself, forming two identical versions that link up in an X shape. As the cell divides, each pair of chromosomes splits apart, and one copy is drawn into each new cell. Not long after the new cells separate, the bundled chromosomes unravel again.

All human cells with nuclei have 46 chromosomes, except for sperm and egg cells, which have 23 each. The 46 chromosomes in nonsex cells are copies of the 23 from the mother's egg and the 23 from the father's sperm. The chromosomes in every sex cell are unique (see page 439), so brothers or sisters are never completely alike. Identical twins are the same because they develop from one egg that splits in half after fertilization, the point at which the two sets of parental chromosomes amalgamate in one nucleus.

DNA: WHAT IS IT?

DNA stands for deoxyribonucleic acid, a chemical that exists in all living organisms (and can survive in their remains for thousands of years after death). It carries all the information a cell requires to make the proteins that it needs in order to function. DNA molecules are made up of a series of smaller units consisting of pairs of chemical bases. There are four bases: adenine (A), thymine (T), guanine (G) and cytosine (C). They always pair in the same combinations – adenine to thymine and guanine to cytosine. The order in which the four chemical bases occur along the length of the molecule provides the genetic code. In order to duplicate itself prior to cell division, a DNA molecule splits along its length and each side reproduces the missing half, replicating the entire sequence for use in the new cell.

Genes A gene is a segment of DNA containing the instructions for the formation of one particular protein. The term is also used to describe a section of DNA that determines a specific physical characteristic, such as the gene for blue eyes, or function, such as insulin production.

In order to put the genetic instructions into operation, a substance called RNA (ribonucleic acid) unzips the section of the DNA molecule carrying the gene needed by the cell and makes a copy of one side of it. This RNA copy then travels to the cell's protein-building ribosomes. Amino acids in the ribosomes have chemical markers that enable them to recognize the chemical bases on the RNA copies that arrive from the nucleus, and the appropriate amino acids line up alongside each other. They then bond together to form the protein.

The repeating base-pair units in DNA appear in various different sequences. The order of the base pairs in one molecule of DNA (one chromosome) is known as its genetic code. The combined order in all 46 chromosomes (a complete set of DNA) is known as the genome.

The Human Genome Project

The Human Genome Project was begun in 1990. Its aims are to determine the sequence of all 3 billion base pairs in human DNA and to identify every one of our genes. In February 2001, the first of these objectives was achieved, at least in working draft form. Nine tenths of the sequence has now been determined; a final version should be ready in 2004.

Understanding the human genome could mean an end to hereditary diseases. By comparing the sequence of a healthy person with that of one suffering from a hereditary disease, the mutations responsible could be identified. With that information, gene replacement therapy could not only cure symptoms but prevent the condition from being passed on.

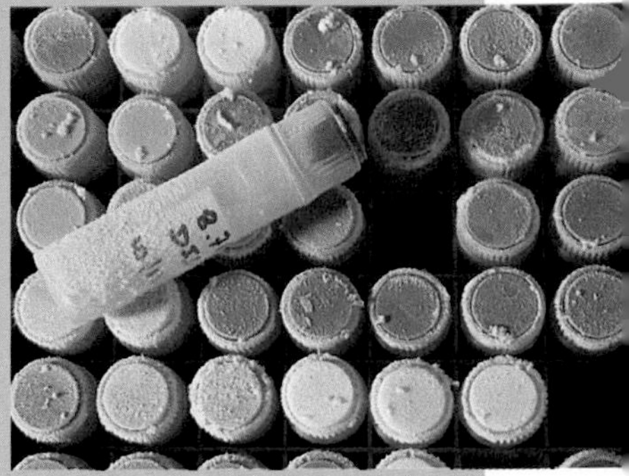

On ice DNA from people with hereditary diseases is stored at a gene bank in France.

FACTS AND FIGURES

- The human body is made up of about 100 trillion cells.
- The largest cell in the human body is the egg cell, or ovum, which can measure up to 0.035 mm (.0013 in.) in diameter.
- Cells lining the mouth usually last for less than three days; they must be replaced at this rate.
- Humans have about 30 000 genes, yet they make up only 3 percent of our DNA; the remaining 97 percent, known as "junk" DNA, apparently does nothing.
- There are no standard genetic differences between people of different races. Indeed, there is often greater variation between individuals of the same race than between those of different races.
- An undamaged tooth can retain stable DNA for thousands of years.
- Bacteria share 20 percent of our genes, mice 90 percent and chimpanzees 99 percent.

DNA unraveled DNA is structured like a spiral ladder (double helix). This illustration shows a molecule of DNA stretched out.

Base pair Chemical bases pair up to form the rungs of the ladder. The order in which the base pairs occur provides the genetic instructions, or code.

Triplet Each triplet of base pairs provides the code for one amino acid, from which proteins are assembled.

Sugar string Each chemical base is attached to a molecule of sugar called deoxyribose. The deoxyribose molecules bond together to form the "supports" of the DNA ladder.

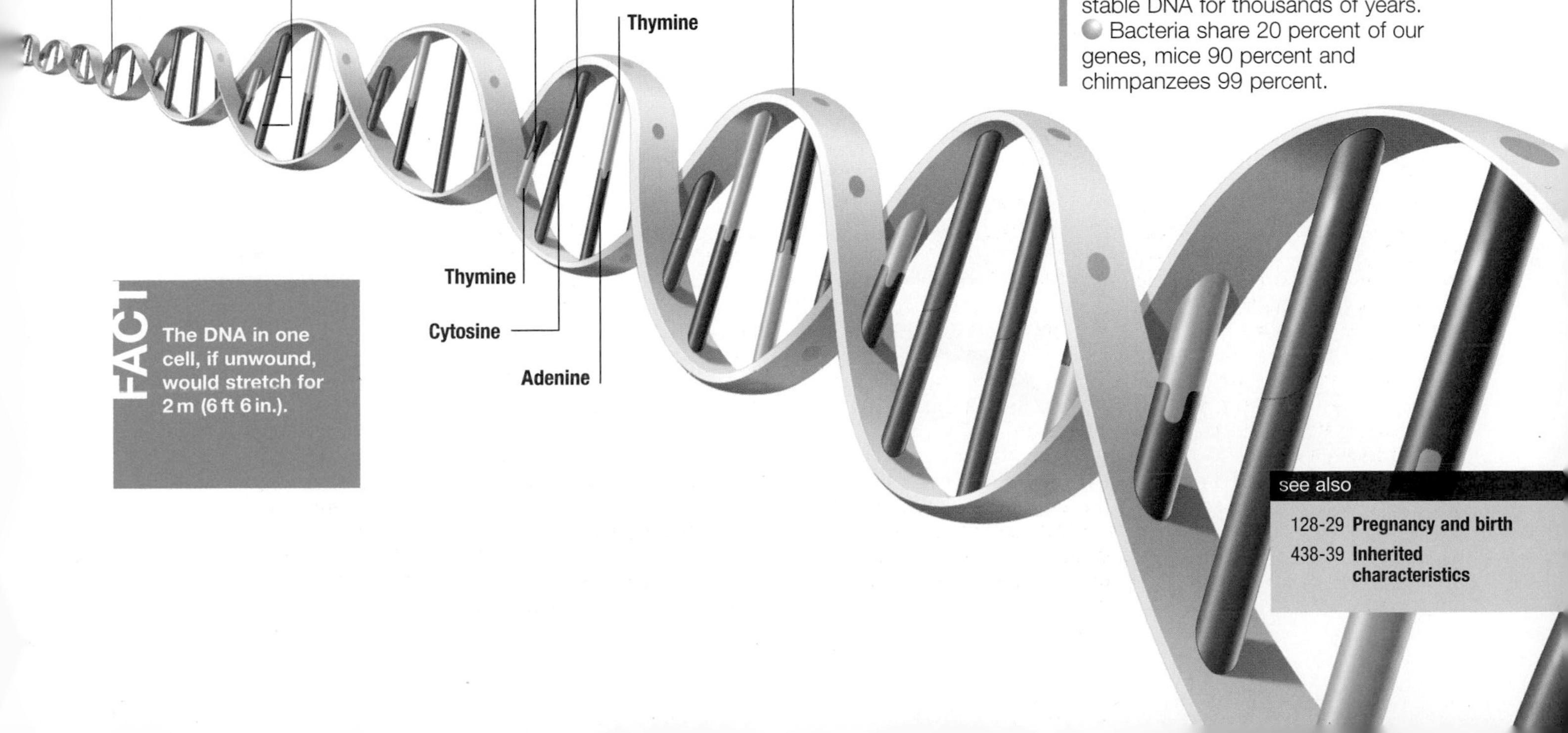

FACT The DNA in one cell, if unwound, would stretch for 2 m (6 ft 6 in.).

see also
128-29 Pregnancy and birth
438-39 Inherited characteristics

The seven ages

William Shakespeare first recognized the seven ages of man, from birth through to death. What he wrote still holds true, but several intervening milestones have since been added to his list. The greatest amount of change in our brains occurs between birth and the age of seven. In that time, we develop from having simple, almost instinctive behavior patterns to a rounded and conscious understanding of the world. Our bodies undergo constant change but alter most noticeably during puberty and as we start to age.

Young achievers

- **Fu Mingxia** of China was just 12 years and 141 days old when she became the women's world platform diving champion.
- **Michael Kearney** became the world's youngest college graduate in 1994 at the age of 10 years and 4 months, when he obtained a degree in anthropology from the University of Alabama.

Birth A newborn baby can see (although not focus clearly) and hear and has primitive reflexes, such as sucking and finger grasping. It can recognize the shape of a human face, and, by three days old, can tell its mother's voice from those of others.

2-6 months During this time, different emotions begin to emerge and become clearly defined. Fear and anger separate and the first signs of satisfaction become apparent. At four months, babies start to recognize objects and by six months have begun to explore the shapes and sizes of things using their mouths.

1-2 years Babies become toddlers and learn to walk. By the time they are two years olld, they can run and kick a ball without overbalancing; they can also string two words (noun and adjective) together. Emotionally, they begin to feel jealousy and guilt. Fear of imaginary monsters and darkness begins.

3-4 years Children move from being able to copy lines and circles to complete letters. Speech becomes more grammatical and sentences become longer. Their sense of balance improves, enabling climbing, jumping and running on tiptoe.

Birth | 2 months | 6 months | 9 months | 1 year | 2 years | 3 years | 4 years

Up to 2 months Babies learn to focus their eyes and smile. The first smiles are just mimicry of adult faces, but babies soon learn that smiling elicits positive responses from others and the process becomes linked with pleasure. During the first eight weeks of life, memory of the existence of objects is limited to 15 seconds.

6-9 months Babies start to focus on facial expressions rather than just facial features, and depth perception improves. During this period, babies realize that hidden objects continue to exist. They learn to sit up and to crawl. The foundations of speech are laid as they go from cooing through babbling to increasingly accurate imitation of adult noises.

9-12 months Most babies utter their first recognizable words and begin to imitate their mother's actions, such as combing hair. Babies can walk with assistance.

2-3 years Children begin to understand the concept of sharing and start to play with others. They increasingly link images of objects with thoughts about them and improve in their ability to classify things.

4-5 years Peers become important to children, and they start to make closer friends. Coordination improves, and they become able to write some letters without needing to copy them. During this period, identification with the parent of the same sex is at its strongest. By five years old, the brain has reached three quarters of its adult size.

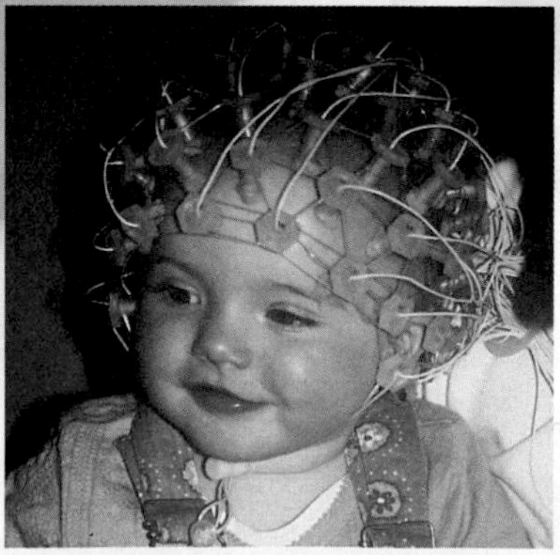

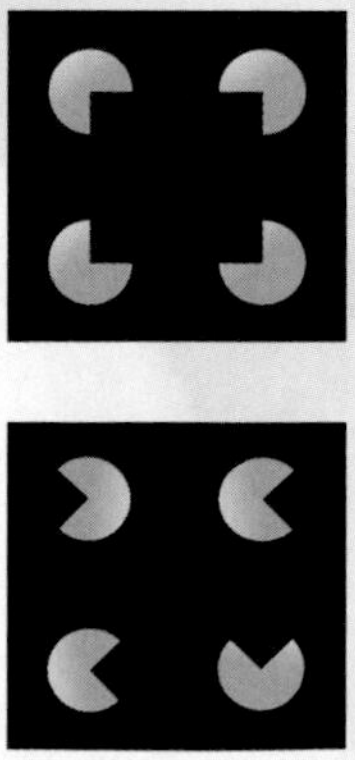

Shape recognition Research into the age at which babies begin to recognize shapes has revealed that at eight months they show more interest in a square shape (top) than in a random collection of elements. At six months they are no more interested in one than the other.

PUBERTY

At puberty, hormones trigger changes in growth and in development of the sex organs, and prepare the body to reproduce. Rapid growth and weight increase occur, as do psychological and emotional changes. These changes start in girls at some point between 9 and 13 years old, and in boys between 10 and 15 years old.

- **Boys** The testes secrete the male hormone testosterone, which is responsible for the growth of facial, body and pubic hair; an increase in muscle bulk; deepening of the voice; growth of the genital organs; and the development of sperm in the testes.

- **Girls** The ovaries secrete the female hormones estrogen and progesterone. These cause breasts to develop, the hips to broaden, and pubic and underarm hair to appear; menstruation begins at about the same time.

Older mom A combination of improved nutrition and health, advances in fertility treatment and medical knowledge is extending the age at which women give birth well into middle age.

Golden oldies

- **Jenny Wood-Allen** completed the 1999 London marathon at age 87.
- **William Baldwin** tightrope-walked across Boulder Canyon in Colorado when he was 82.
- **Jack MacKenzie**, age 77, skied 100 miles to the North Pole.
- **Oscar Swahn**, age 72, won an Olympic silver medal for shooting.
- **Wong Yui Hoi** took up snowboarding in 1995, when he was 75.

5 years · 10 years · 20 years · 30 years · 40 years · 50 years · 60 years · 70 years · 80 years

5-7 years Children can increasingly distinguish between letters. For the first time, their world is dominated by other children rather than by adults, and they learn social roles and their own limits by play. At five, thought is centered on the present, but by seven, concepts of past and future have started to form.

9-15 years Puberty begins, starting with a sudden growth spurt and other physical changes. Girls begin to menstruate about two and a half years after puberty begins.

15-20 years The body reaches its maximum height and the brain is full-sized.

20-30 years The body increases in bulk with extra muscle and fat.

30-40 years Testosterone levels in men begin to fall (from mid-30s).

40-60 years Physiological processes start to decline. By their late 50s, many men have enlarged prostate glands. Thinning of hair occurs in both sexes, as cells that normally produce hair follicle nourishment die. Graying and baldness either begin or accelerate during this period. Menstruation ceases, usually between the ages of 45 and 50, and menopause begins.

60-80 years Vision and hearing deteriorate, skin begins to sag and wrinkles appear. The gradual loss of the protein collagen causes muscles to waste away. The lungs cannot fully inflate or deflate as they lose their elasticity, and bones become less dense and more brittle. The walls of arteries thicken and harden, raising blood pressure, and the risk of heart disease increases.

80 years onward Physiological processes decline further, and the incidence of osteoarthritis greatly increases. The structure of the brain deteriorates, although this is not always accompanied by a reduction in mental ability.

FACTS AND FIGURES

- Jeanne Calment of Arles, France, lived to be 122; hers was the longest human life ever documented. She died in 1997.
- Genes can influence life span. Some citizens of Limone in Italy have inherited a gene mutation that produces increased beneficial cholesterol, reducing the risk of heart disease.
- Gene mutations can quicken the aging process. People suffering from Werner's syndrome carry a mutation that causes them to age prematurely. By their teens, they have the wrinkled skin and gray hair of extreme old age; they succumb to cancers or heart disease and die young.

Up and over Age does not have to be a barrier to an active life, as Californian Carol Johnston proves. At 85 years old, he still competes in pole-vaulting tournaments and holds the world record for his age.

see also

112-13 **Skeleton and muscles**
118 **Glands and hormones**

The history of mankind

The history of mankind

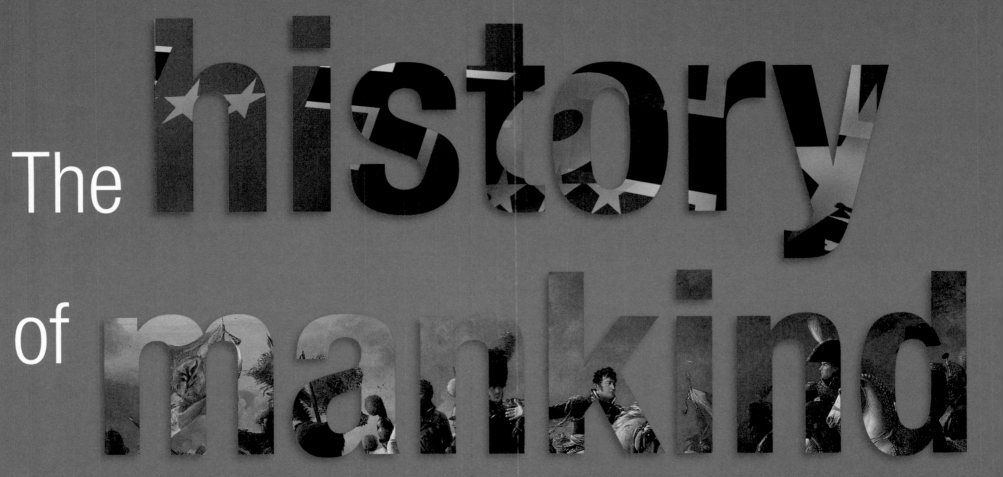

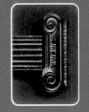

History of the World

From the earliest civilizations to today's world

2500 B.C. | 2000 B.C. | 1500 B.C. | 1000 B.C. | 500 B.C.

Ancient Middle East

- **3500-2500** Sumerian city-states founded
- **2000** Hittites invade Anatolia (Turkey)
- **1750** Babylonian Empire founded
- **c. 1200** Hebrews settle Israel
- **740-612** Assyrian empires dominate Middle East
- **521** Persian Empire extends from Nile River to Indus River

Ancient Egypt

- **c. 2800-2160** Old Kingdom
- **2050-1780** Middle Kingdom
- **1720** Hyksos rule begins
- **1560** New Kingdom founded
- **671-651** Assyrians invade Egypt
- **525** Persians conquer Egypt

India

- **c. 2500** Indus Valley civilization develops
- **c. 1550** Aryans invade Northern India
- **1000-600** Hindu states established
- **c.525** Buddha begins teaching

Ancient Greece

- **c. 2000** Minoan civilization emerges in Crete
- **c. 1900** Mycenaeans settle in Greece
- **c. 1500** Minoan civilization collapses
- **c. 1125** Dorians invade Greece
- **c. 750** First Greek colonies founded

Ancient America

- **c. 2600** Neolithic culture first emerges in Central America
- **c. 1200-c. 400** Olmec culture in Mexico
- **c. 900-c. 400** Chavin culture in Peru

China

- **c. 1600-1050** First Chinese civilization
- **c. 1000-256** "Classical Age"
- **c. 604-531** Life of Lao-Tzu'
- **551-479** Life of Confucius

Africa

- **c. 1000** First Kushite civilization

Rome

- **c. 900** Etruscans settle in Italy
- **753** Rome founded

Byzantium

Japan

Medieval and early modern Europe

Islamic Middle East

Russia

Modern Western civilization

2500 B.C. | 2000 B.C. | 1500 B.C. | 1000 B.C. | 500 B.C.

500 B.C. | 0 | A.D. 500 | A.D. 1000 | A.D. 1500 | A.D. 2000

334-326 Alexander conquers the Middle East

332-330 Alexander conquers Egypt | **30 B.C.** Romans annex Egypt

322-185 Mauryan Empire | **320-480** Gupta Empire of Northern India | **1206-1526** Delhi Sultanate | **1526-1707** Mogul Empire | **1612-1858** British conquest | **1947** Indian independence

469-429 "Golden Age" of Athens | **334-146** Hellenistic age | **146** Romans conquer Greece

A.D. 100-300 Moche and Nazca cultures in Peru | **300-500** Teotihuacan culture in Mexico | **1000-1400** Chimu kingdom in Peru | **1325-1530** Aztec Empire in Mexico | **c. 1438-1533** Inca Empire in Peru | **1530-96** Spanish conquest

221-210 Reign of Qin Shi Huangdi | **304** Hun invasions | **477** Buddhism becomes state religion | **850-900** Rule by warlords | **960-1279** Cultural flowering under Song Dynasty | **1275** Marco Polo reaches Beijing | **1557** Portuguese at Macao | **1839-60** Opium Wars | **1900-1** Boxer Rebellion | **1949** People's Republic

500 B.C.-A.D. 200 Nok civilization in Nigeria | **146** Roman Africa founded | **A.D. 50-400** Empire of Axum | **c. 700** Empire of Ghana emerges | **c. 700-1000** Spread of Islam | **c. 1100-1250** Zimbabwe civilization | **c. 1500** Slave trade begins | **1878** "Scramble for Africa" | **1945** Colonial independence begins to spread

510 Roman Republic founded | **264-146** Punic Wars  | **27 B.C.** Augustus becomes first emperor | **476** Last Western emperor deposed

330 Constantinople founded | **636-838** Arab threat | **867** Orthodox Church breaks with Rome | **1453** Ottomans take Constantinople

c. 300 Yamato clan unifies Japan | **794-1185** Heian period | **1192-1333** Kamakura Shogunate | **1338-1586** Ashikaga Shogunate | **1598-1868** Tokugawa Shogunate | **1941-45** World War II

500 Barbarian kingdoms | **756** Moorish state in Spain | **1095-1272** Crusades | **c. 1300-1600** Renaissance  | **c. 1530-1650** Reformation | **c. 1700-1789** Enlightenment

630-60 Arab conquests | **909-1171** Fatimid Caliphate in Egypt | **c. 1300-1920** Ottoman Empire | **1923** Turkish Republic founded

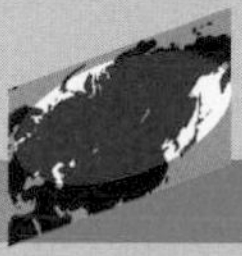
988 Kievan Rus adopts Byzantine Christianity | **1480** Unification of Russia around Muscovy |  **1917** Russian Revolution

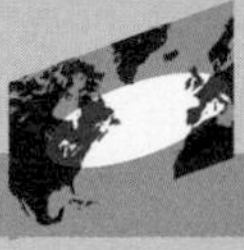
1492 Columbus reaches New World | **1760s** James Watt perfects steam engine | **1776** American Revolution **1789** French Revolution | **1959** Silicon chip invented

500 B.C. | 0 | A.D. 500 | A.D. 1000 | A.D. 1500 | A.D. 2000

The prehistoric world

From human origins to the settlement of all habitable regions

The first modern humans (Homo sapiens sapiens) emerged in Africa 100 000 years ago. Over the next 50 000 years, they colonized much of Asia and Australia before expanding into Europe. New skills were acquired at different rates in different regions, but the landmarks of development followed a similar pattern – from simple stone blades to sophisticated iron jewelry.

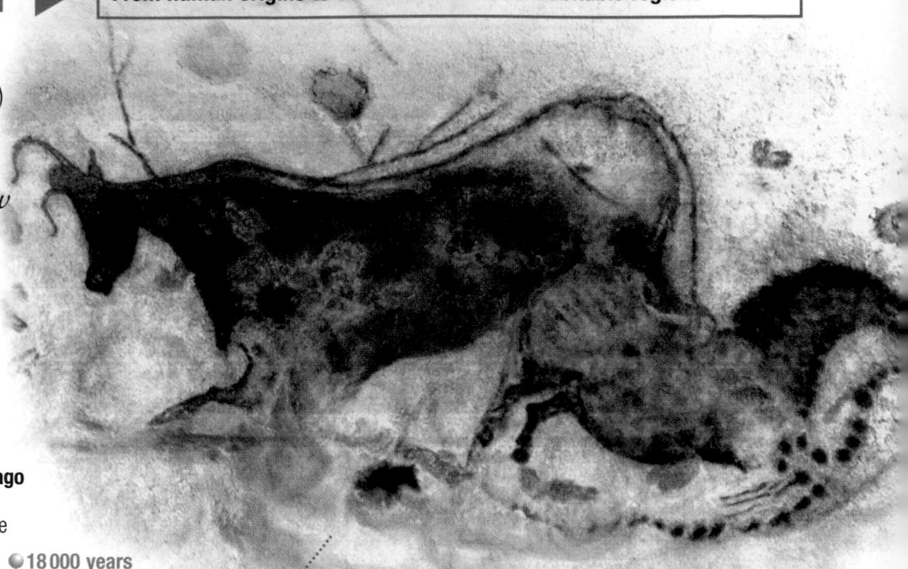

100 000 years ago *Homo sapiens sapiens* emerges from Africa.

50 000 years ago The first humans arrive in Australia.

45 000 years ago The first modern humans migrate into Europe from the Middle East.

40 000 years ago Upper Paleolithic tools begin to appear in Europe.

30 000 years ago The Neanderthals die out, unable to compete with the ancestors of modern humans.

c. 25 000 years ago Female "Venus" figurines are made in Europe.

25 000 ya

20 000 years ago

18 000 years ago The last Ice Age reaches its height.

20 000 years ago Art begins to flourish in Africa and southwest Europe, with rock paintings and carved objects.

15 000 years ago The climate begins to improve, and the ice sheets melt.

15 000 ya

12 000 years ago Animals and plants are domesticated, and the Neolithic Age begins.

11 000 years ago Hunters spread south through the Americas.

10 000 years ago

10 000 years ago (8000 B.C.) The first images of gods are created.

7000 B.C. Copper is first used for tools.

6000 B.C. Irrigation is first practiced in Mesopotamia.

5200 B.C. Farming spreads throughout Europe.

4500 B.C. The world's first-known temple is built at Eridu, Sumer.

4500 B.C.

Cave paintings Paleolithic animal paintings adorn the cave walls at Lascaux, France.

The Stone Age

Upper Paleolithic

40 000-10 000 years ago

Early humans were already expert flint workers by the Upper Paleolithic period. More than 100 distinct tools and weapons have been found at sites in Europe and the Near East. Typical features of Upper Paleolithic cultures include

- Stone spearheads, arrowheads and blades.
- Bone and ivory tools and weapons (fishhooks, needles and spears).
- Jewelry and clothing made of skins sewn using bone needles.
- The ceremonial burial of the dead.
- Cave art and statues.

Stone-age art The "Venus of Willendorf," carved 25 000 years ago, is one of the earliest known sculptures.

Neolithic

About 10 000-3 000 years ago

The later Stone Age saw the development of farming, which replaced hunting and gathering as the primary mode of existence. By the end of the Neolithic, humans had learned to cultivate many crops: wheat and barley in the Near East, corn in Central America, rice in China and potatoes in South America. Farming created surpluses, allowing populations to grow and to establish permanent settlements. Other features of the Neolithic include

- The domestication of animals (by 6000 B.C. in China and Mesopotamia).
- New tools – for example, axes to clear forests and bring new land under cultivation, hoes, sickles and grindstones.
- The use of pottery to store grain.
- The construction of the earliest villages and towns, often surrounded by walls to corral livestock (Jericho and Çatal Hüyük).
- Tombs built of stone.

Stone tools Neolithic craftsmen were expert stone-workers. These hammers and axes date from c. 5000 B.C.

The metal ages

The Bronze Age
From 3000 B.C.

The first experiments with metalworking were made in Iran and Turkey about 9000 years ago. Copper and gold were the first metals to be used for tools and weapons, followed by bronze (an alloy of copper and tin). The Bronze Age featured

- Copper and bronze tools and weapons (spearheads, arrowheads, chisels and saws).
- The practice of trade throughout Europe.
- Early mines and ore extraction methods.
- High standards of craftsmanship (jewelry, statues and decoration).
- The creation of stone alignments.

Bronze shield Bronze Age craftsmen created many finely decorated weapons.

The Iron Age
From 1200 B.C.

Iron was first used long before the Iron Age. The Hittites of Anatolia made iron weapons between 2000 and 1200 B.C. Ironworking spread to Greece in about 1000 B.C. and to northern Europe, Asia and Africa by about 750 B.C. It was brought to Britain by the Celts – members of an Iron Age culture originating in the Austrian Alps. Iron had three advantages over bronze: It gave a sharper, harder-wearing edge; it did not need to be combined with another metal; and supplies were plentiful. It was used for nails, tools, weapons, cooking utensils, jewelry and also for religious articles. The European Iron Age is conventionally said to end with the spread of the Roman Empire. There was no Iron Age in the Americas, where iron was introduced by European colonists.

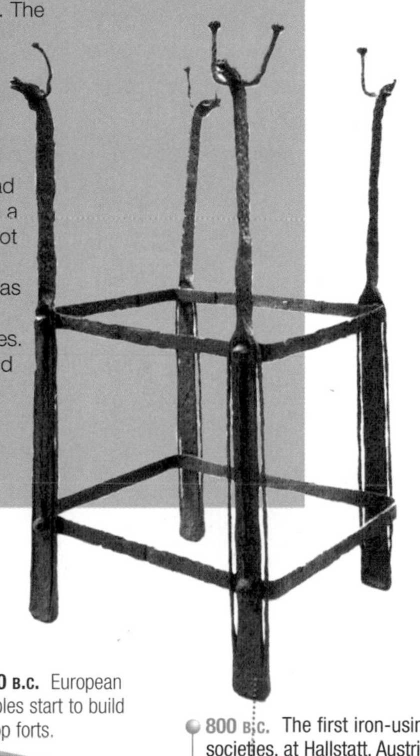

Iron brazier This Iron Age piece has stylized ox-head terminals.

4000 B.C. Amazon pottery is first made in the Americas.

3500 B.C. Early city-states thrive in Mesopotamia, and the first standing stones are raised in Europe.

3000 B.C.

3000 B.C. The Indus Valley civilization emerges. The wheel is in use there and in Mesopotamia.

2686 B.C. Egypt's Old Kingdom begins (and lasts until 2181 B.C.).

2100 B.C. Stonehenge reaches the height of its development.

2000 B.C. The first palaces are built in Crete.

1500 B.C.

1300 B.C. The settlers of the Pacific Ocean islands begin to migrate eastwards to Fiji, Tonga and Samoa.

1200 B.C. Agriculture spreads through North America.

1100 B.C. European peoples start to build hilltop forts.

1000 B.C.

1000 B.C. Agriculture spreads into Central and South America.

800 B.C. The first iron-using societies, at Hallstatt, Austria, herald Europe's Iron Age.

100 B.C.

A.D. 1000 New Zealand is settled by Polynesian seafarers.

Great migrations Modern humans spread slowly throughout the world from their origins in Africa. The South Pacific was the last area settled.

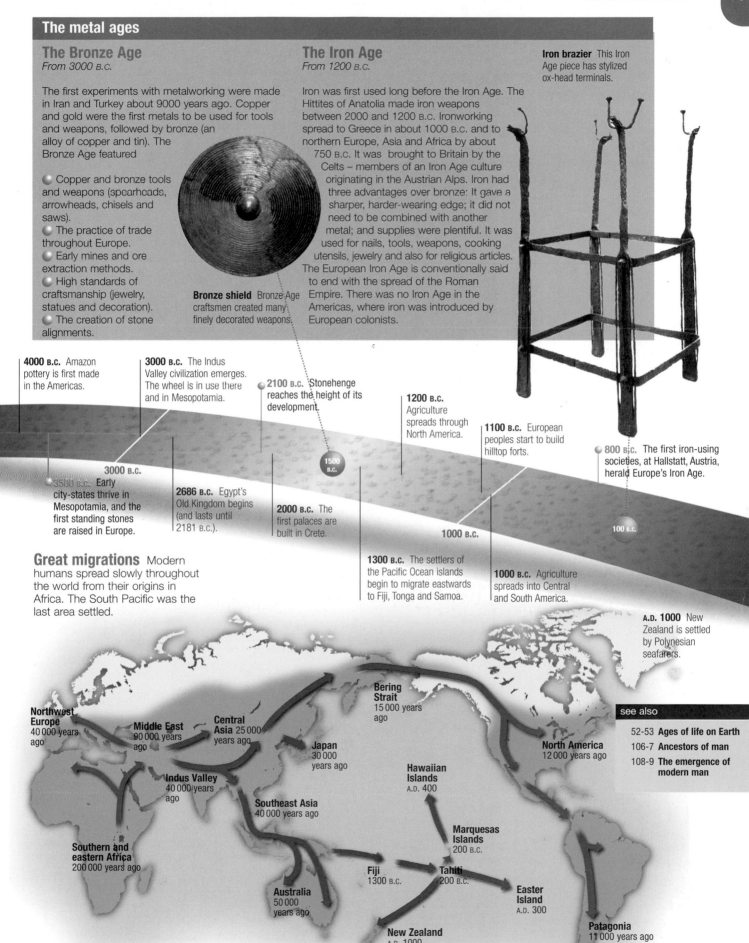

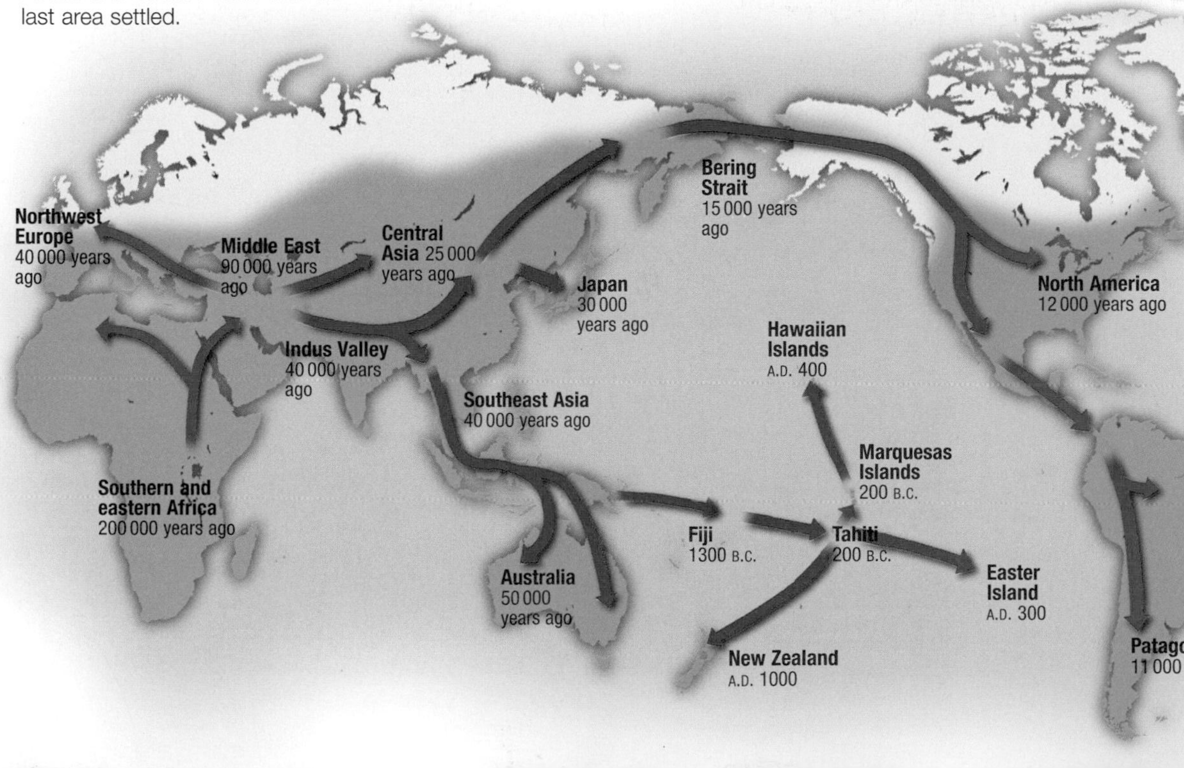

see also

52-53 **Ages of life on Earth**
106-7 **Ancestors of man**
108-9 **The emergence of modern man**

Civilization is closely linked to the rise of cities. Urban life emerged as agriculture started to support artisans, traders, government and organized religion, as well as people living on the land. From about 3000 B.C., cities developed on the banks of the Tigris and Euphrates rivers in Mesopotamia ("Between the Rivers"), part of the "Fertile Crescent." They were independent city–states at first and then parts of empires. At the same time, Egypt grew in power, and the eastern Mediterranean became a crossroads for traders and empire-builders.

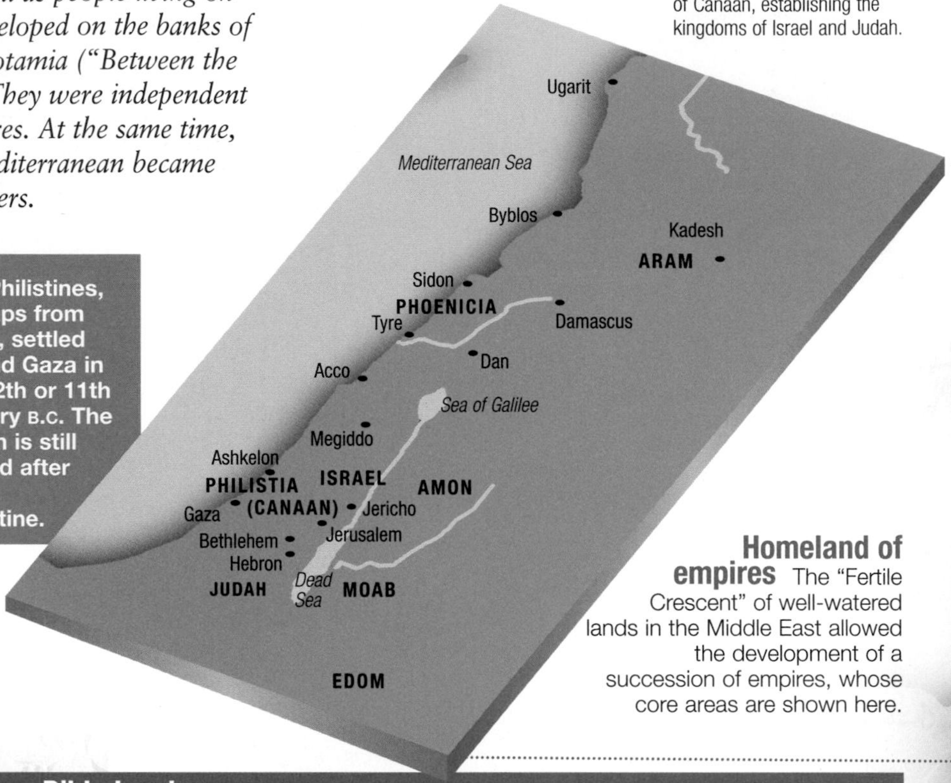

Back to Canaan After the flight from Egypt, the Jews returned to the ancestral land of Canaan, establishing the kingdoms of Israel and Judah.

Homeland of empires The "Fertile Crescent" of well-watered lands in the Middle East allowed the development of a succession of empires, whose core areas are shown here.

Landmarks of civilization

Many of the major developments that we associate with Western civilization first emerged in the Fertile Crescent after 10 000 B.C.

Cities Some of the world's oldest cities such as Jericho, founded c. 8350 B.C., are found in the Middle East. Çatal Hüyük, in Anatolia, was the largest city in the world; it flourished from 6250 to 5400 B.C.

Wheel The wheel started off in Mesopotamia c. 3500 B.C. as a potter's tool. It was used for vehicles after c. 3200 B.C.

Legal systems Hammurabi (*c.*1792-1750 B.C.), king of Babylon, codified the oldest known laws. The Jewish Torah dates from the 4th century B.C.

Writing Around 3300 B.C., the Sumerians developed one of the earliest writing systems, a picture-based script called cuneiform, which was impressed on clay tablets. In about 1100 B.C., the Phoenicians created a sound-based alphabet, which later became the basis of all modern European scripts.

Astronomy The city of Ur was the birthpace of astronomy. By c. 1000 B.C., the Babylonians were predicting lunar eclipses and tracking planets.

Mathematics The number system of Mesopotamia gave us the 60-minute hour and 360-degree circle.

Monotheism Belief in a single all-powerful god was a key feature of Judaism and later of both Christianity and Islam.

FACT The Philistines, perhaps from Crete, settled around Gaza in the 12th or 11th century B.C. The region is still named after them: Palestine.

Bible Lands

The historical story of the Bible begins with Abraham, the first patriarch. The Hebrews, or Israelites, claim descent from his grandson Jacob. After slavery in Egypt and nomadic wandering, they settled in Canaan, clashing with the Philistines. With the decline of the rival Egyptian and Hittite empires, the Israelites founded a powerful kingdom under David. They later suffered defeat by the Assyrians (721 B.C.), captivity in Babylon (c. 586-538 B.C.), and conquest by Alexander (333 B.C.). By the time of Jesus, Palestine was part of the Roman province of Judaea.

Great leaders of the Israelites include

Abraham (c. 1800 B.C.) The founding father of the Hebrew nation, Abraham is said to have migrated to Canaan from Ur about 1800 B.C.

Moses (c. 1200s B.C.) According to the Bible story, Moses led the Hebrews from Egypt and received the Ten Commandments on Mount Sinai.

David (reigned c. 1000-961 B.C.) David founded the Israelite royal dynasty. He became king of Judah and then of Israel, uniting the Israelites. He made Jerusalem his capital.

Solomon (reigned c. 973-922 B.C.) A son of David, Solomon was the greatest king of Israel, famed for his wisdom. He built up Israel's military and trading strength and constructed the first Temple of Jerusalem.

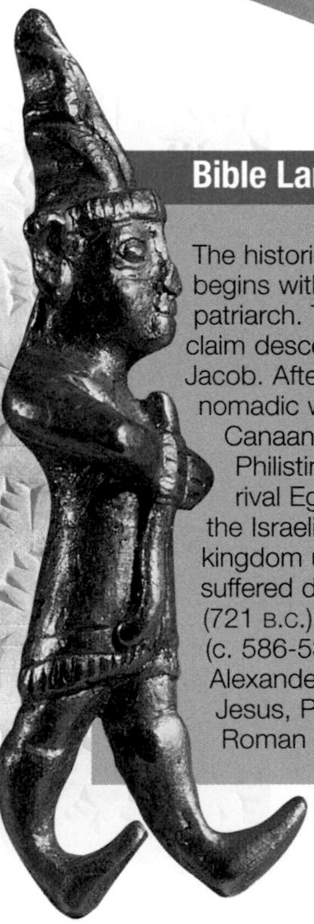

Hittite deity Judaism forbade such representations.

10 000 B.C.

c. 10 000 B.C. The earliest farming occurs north and northeast of the Fertile Crescent.

c. 9000 B.C. Jericho grows into a town of about 2000 people.

c. 8500 B.C. Sheep are domesticated in the Fertile Crescent.

c. 7000 B.C. Copper is first used in toolmaking.

c. 6500 B.C. Çatal Hüyük, Turkey, becomes one of the largest towns of the late Stone Age.

c. 6000 B.C. The development of irrigation permits agriculture to spread beyond river banks.

5000 B.C.

c. 3300 B.C. The earliest cuneiform writing is used in Mesopotamia.

c. 3000 B.C. Major urban centers develop in Mesopotamia.

c. 2350 B.C. Sumer is united as an empire under Sargon of Akkad.

c. 2200 B.C. Rise of Ur, which flourishes as the main city of Sumer for the next two centuries.

2000 B.C.

c. 1800 B.C. Abraham and his family leave Ur for Canaan, as described in the Old Testament.

c. 1300-1250 B.C. The Hebrews leave Egypt. This is known as the Exodus.

1285 B.C. The Egyptians and Hittites clash at Kadesh, near the Sea of Galilee.

The Phoenicians

For several thousand years starting around 3000 B.C., the Phoenicians were expert ship-builders and sailors. They traded around the Mediterranean from their city–states Byblos, Tyre, Sidon and Beirut (in modern Lebanon) and set up coastal colonies including Carthage in North Africa. They were famous for glassware, ivory work and purple dye. Their cities were sacked by Alexander.

Phoenician glassware
An incense bottle from the 3rd-1st centuries B.C.

The Assyrians

Once a subject people of Babylon, the Assyrians emerged as a power in their own right in about 1350 B.C. After 740 B.C., under a succession of strong kings, Assyria won control of most of the area between Egypt and the Persian Gulf. **Ashurbanipal** (reigned c. 668-627 B.C.), who conquered Egypt, created the largest empire the world had known. The Assyrian Empire was ended by the Medes and Chaldeans in 612 B.C.

The Persians

Originally a nomadic tribe, the Persians settled in the Assyrian Empire in about 850 B.C. Under **Cyrus the Great** (d. 529 B.C.) they conquered Babylon and created the Achaemenid Empire, stretching from Egypt to Afghanistan. **Darius I** ("the Great," reigned 521-486 B.C.) consolidated the empire but was defeated by the Greeks at Marathon in 490 B.C. The Persian Empire was conquered by Alexander in 330 B.C.

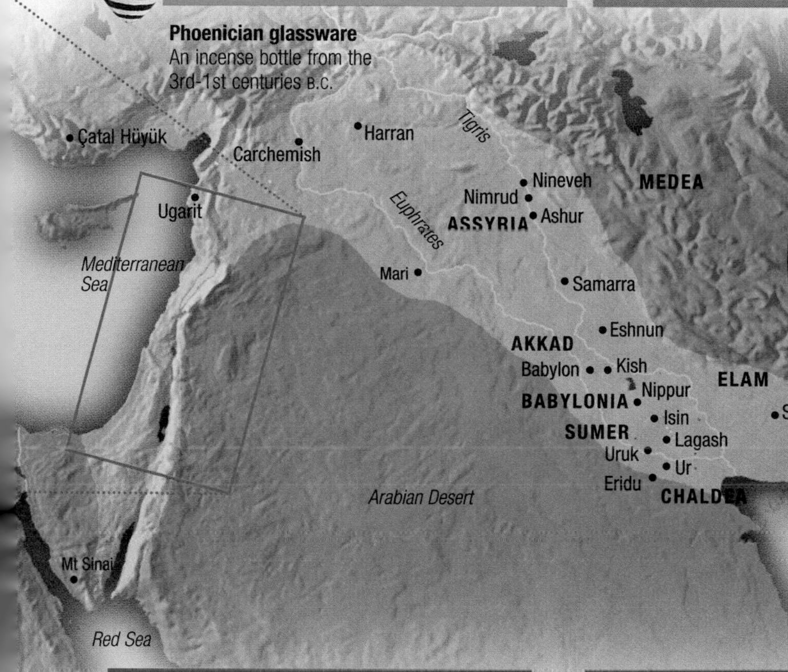

Assyrian warriors
A basalt relief showing charioteers, from the 8th century B.C.

Sacrificial scene
A gold statuette c. 1150 B.C. from Susa, Iran, representing a devotee with a goat.

The Hittites

From about 1700 to 1200 B.C., the northeastern Mediterranean was dominated by the Hittites, who were based in Hattusas (modern Bogazköy). By 1595 B.C., they had expanded as far as Babylon. War with Egypt culminated in the celebrated Battle of **Kadesh** in 1285 B.C., and a treaty was sealed by marriage between a Hittite princess and Pharaoh Ramses II. After 1200 B.C., the Hittites were overrun by the Sea Peoples from Greece and the central Mediterranean.

The Babylonians

Babylon was a leading power by 1750 B.C. The lawmaker **Hammurabi** came to power in 1792 B.C., expanded the empire and brought all Mesopotamia under one rule. Babylon came under Assyrian domination in 721 B.C., but then reemerged as the Chaldean, or neo-Babylonian, Empire under **Nebuchadnezzar II** (reigned c. 604-562 B.C.) – who built the famous Hanging Gardens. The empire fell to Cyrus II of Persia in 539 B.C. and to Alexander in 331 B.C.

The Sumerians

The Sumerians established the world's first real civilization. Their city–states such as Ur, Uruk, Eridu and Kish flourished in southern Mesopotamia (now Iraq) in about 5000 B.C. **Sargon** (c. 2370-2315 B.C.) brought all the cities of southern Mesopotamia under his control to create the Sumerian Empire. It was conquered by the Elamites in about 2000 B.C. and then by the Babylonians and Assyrians.

see also
298-99 **Writing**
440-41 **Archaeology**

c. 1200 B.C. The Sea Peoples spread through the Middle East; the Philistines settle in Canaan.

c. 1000-961 B.C. David extends Israel as far as Palestine and Syria.

1000 B.C.

922 B.C. Jerusalem is sacked by the Egyptians.

c. 922 B.C. Israel and Judah split after the death of King Solomon.

c. 668-627 B.C. The Assyrian Empire reaches its greatest extent but starts to lose military superiority, beginning a period of decline.

605 B.C. Nebuchadnezzar II of Babylon defeats the Egyptians and Assyrians at Carchemish.

586 B.C. Jerusalem is destroyed and 5000 Jews are deported to Babylon (the "Babylonian Captivity").

539 B.C. Cyrus the Great of Persia captures Babylon.

500 B.C.

537 B.C. The Jews return from Babylon and rebuild the Temple in Jerusalem.

333 B.C. Alexander the Great defeats Darius III of Persia at the Battle of the Issus.

331 B.C. Alexander captures Babylon, ensuring the conquest of the Persian Empire.

323 B.C. Alexander dies.

Ancient Egypt

From the Stone Age to the death of Cleopatra

Egypt's civilization flourished on the Nile for 3000 years. Many of its great monuments remain; the best known are the pyramids and the sphinx. Egyptian society was broadly constant over that period: It was itself pyramid-shaped, with the lone figure of the pharaoh at the top and the mass of peasant farmers at the bottom. Society was highly organized, a feat made possible by the invention of writing. It also had a sophisticated theology based on a pantheon of gods and a highly developed mythology.

The Sphinx Sculpted from an outcrop of rock, the Great Sphinx is a portrait of the pharaoh Khafre and stands in front of his pyramid at Giza.

DEATH AND MUMMIES

Not only pharaohs were mummified. The preservation of the body was an important religious ritual for people at all levels of society, as it was believed that the soul returned to the body to take nourishment. The process of mummification took about 70 days, after which the body was released to relatives for burial. The body would be interred with spells from the *Book of the Dead*, which were inscribed on papyri, and with *shabti* (funerary statuettes) to accompany it in the afterlife.

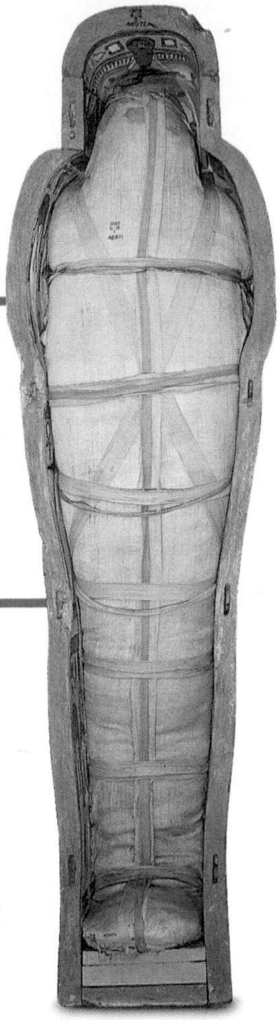

Rulers of the world beyond

Osiris The god of the underworld, Osiris is swaddled like a mummy and carries a scepter and a ceremonial whip.
Horus Horus is the hawk-headed god of the sky, source of royal authority.
Seth God of storms and chaos, Seth hacked Osiris to death and scattered the body parts.
Isis The sister-wife of Osiris, Isis used magic to revive her husband after Seth murdered him.
Taweret Protectress of pregnant women, Taweret has the body of a hippopotamus, with a lion's paws and a crocodile's tail.
Bes Bes is a dwarfish god of the household.
Thoth God of the Moon and of knowledge, Thoth is shown as an ibis or a baboon.
Anubis Anubis is the jackal-headed god of mummification.
Ra The sun-god Ra (right) is often shown with a hawk's head.

The great pharaohs

- **Djoser (2668-2649 B.C.)** Egypt's first pyramid-builder, Djoser, commissioned the step pyramid at Saqqara.
- **Khufu (2589-2566 B.C.)** Khufu built the Great Pyramid of Khufu (Cheops) at Giza.
- **Pepi II (2278-2184 B.C.)** Ascending the throne at six and ruling until he was 100, Pepi had the longest reign known to history.
- **Hatshepsut (1473-1458 B.C.)** For 20 years, Hatshepsut ruled as a female king (Egypt did not then recognize queens). She wore the ritual false beard to defuse antifemale criticism of her reign and is often portrayed in art as a man.
- **Thutmose III (1479-1423 B.C.)** The soldier-pharaoh Tuthmosis extended Egyptian territory to its greatest extent.
- **Akhenaton (1350-1334 B.C.)** With his wife Nefertiti, Akhenaten banned the worship of all gods but Aten, the sun-disk. He built the huge temples at Karnak and Luxor.
- **Tutankhamen (1334-1325 B.C.)** A very minor pharaoh who died in his teens, Tutankhamun is known mainly for his tomb and its fabulous treasures, discovered by Howard Carter in 1922.
- **Ramses II (1279-1212 B.C.)** Ramses built the rock temple at Abu Simbel and raised more monuments than any other pharaoh during his 66-year reign.
- **Cleopatra (51-30 B.C.)** Cleopatra was the lover of Julius Caesar and Mark Antony. Her Egypt was conquered by Rome in 30 B.C., bringing the age of the pharaohs to an end.

Abu Simbel The four colossal seated statues of Ramses II are 20 m (70 ft) high. In the 1960s, they were moved to higher ground to preserve them from the rising waters of Lake Nasser. Abu Simbel is about 250 km (155 miles) south of Philae.

5000 B.C.

c. 5000 B.C. Cattle herders occupy the fertile Sahara.

c. 3100 B.C. Egypt is first unified by King Menes of Upper Egypt.

c. 2630 B.C. The Step Pyramid of Djoser is built at Saqqara.

c. 2600 B.C. The Old Kingdom reaches its zenith, with the 4th Dynasty kings (2613-2498).

c. 2584-2565 B.C. The Great Pyramid of Khufu (Cheops) is built at Giza.

2500 B.C.

c. 2558-2532 B.C. The Pyramid of Khafre (Chephren) and the Sphinx are built at Giza.

2498 B.C. The 5th Dynasty kings (until 2345) adopt the cult of Ra at Heliopolis.

2181-2040 B.C. The First Intermediate Period brings political chaos to Egypt.

2040 B.C. The 11th Dynasty kings reunite Egypt as the Middle Kingdom (until 1782 B.C.).

2000 B.C.

1782 B.C. The decline of royal authority results in the Second Intermediate Period (until 1555 B.C.).

FACT The Alexandrian scientist Eratosthenes proved in the 3rd century B.C. that the world was round. He calculated its girth with 99 percent accuracy.

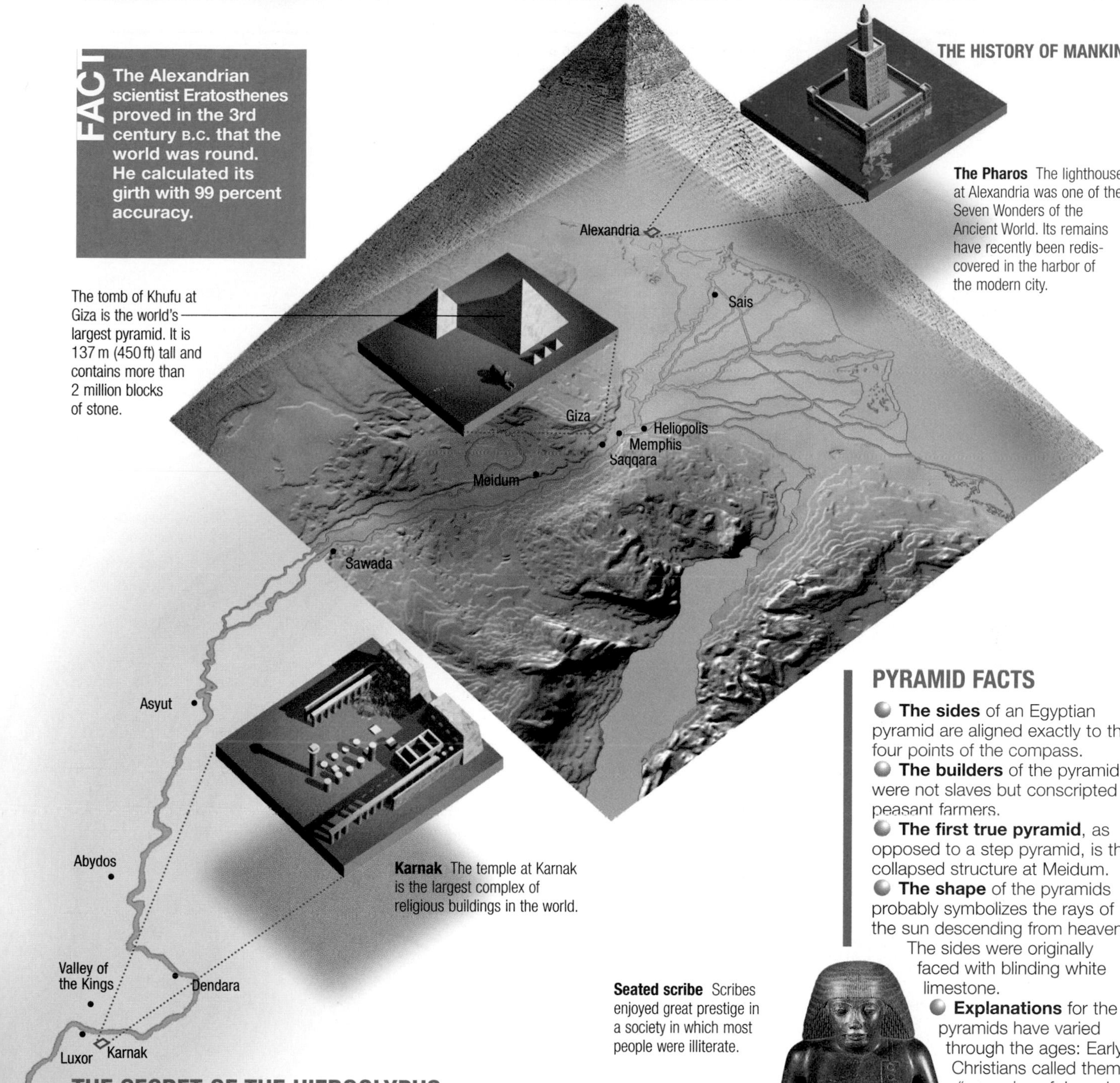

The tomb of Khufu at Giza is the world's largest pyramid. It is 137 m (450 ft) tall and contains more than 2 million blocks of stone.

The Pharos The lighthouse at Alexandria was one of the Seven Wonders of the Ancient World. Its remains have recently been rediscovered in the harbor of the modern city.

Karnak The temple at Karnak is the largest complex of religious buildings in the world.

PYRAMID FACTS

- **The sides** of an Egyptian pyramid are aligned exactly to the four points of the compass.
- **The builders** of the pyramids were not slaves but conscripted peasant farmers.
- **The first true pyramid**, as opposed to a step pyramid, is the collapsed structure at Meidum.
- **The shape** of the pyramids probably symbolizes the rays of the sun descending from heaven. The sides were originally faced with blinding white limestone.
- **Explanations** for the pyramids have varied through the ages: Early Christians called them "granaries of Joseph."
- **No one knows** for sure how the pyramids were built.

Seated scribe Scribes enjoyed great prestige in a society in which most people were illiterate.

THE SECRET OF THE HIEROGLYPHS

The *Book of the Dead*

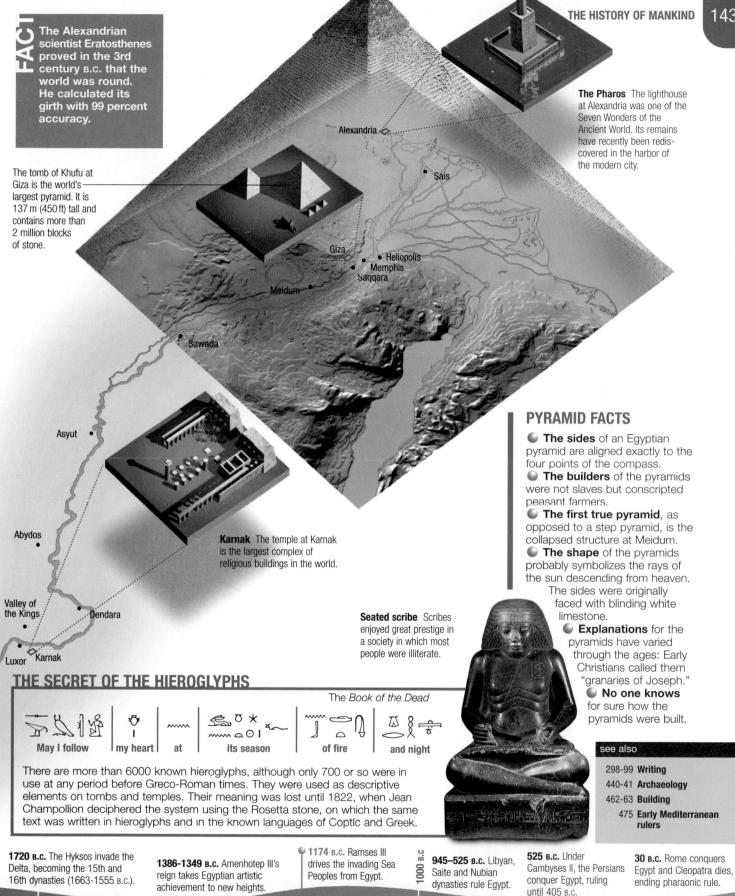

There are more than 6000 known hieroglyphs, although only 700 or so were in use at any period before Greco-Roman times. They were used as descriptive elements on tombs and temples. Their meaning was lost until 1822, when Jean Champollion deciphered the system using the Rosetta stone, on which the same text was written in hieroglyphs and in the known languages of Coptic and Greek.

see also
298-99 **Writing**
440-41 **Archaeology**
462-63 **Building**
475 **Early Mediterranean rulers**

1720 B.C. The Hyksos invade the Delta, becoming the 15th and 16th dynasties (1663-1555 B.C.).

1500 B.C.

1570 B.C. Ahmose drives the Hyksos out of Egypt and creates the New Kingdom (until 1070 B.C.).

1386-1349 B.C. Amenhotep III's reign takes Egyptian artistic achievement to new heights.

1291-1278 B.C. Seti I builds the great Temple of Amun at Karnak and the Temple of Seti at Abydos.

1174 B.C. Ramses III drives the invading Sea Peoples from Egypt.

1069 B.C. Egypt's Third Intermediate Period begins when the high priests of Thebes usurp royal power.

1000 B.C.

945–525 B.C. Libyan, Saite and Nubian dynasties rule Egypt.

525 B.C. Under Cambyses II, the Persians conquer Egypt, ruling until 405 B.C.

500 B.C.

323 B.C. Alexander the Great conquers Egypt; his Ptolemaic successors rule as Egypt's last dynasty.

30 B.C. Rome conquers Egypt and Cleopatra dies, ending pharaonic rule.

Ancient Greece ▶ From the Minoans to the Roman conquest

Many of the essential characteristics of European culture and civilization, including a new sense of individual identity in relation to society, the world and the gods, were forged in ancient Greece. Following the Minoan and Mycenaean civilizations, Greece became a dominant force in the Mediterranean for 400 years, before Alexander the Great briefly created one of the largest empires of the ancient world, spreading Greek (Hellenistic) culture to Egypt and deep into Asia.

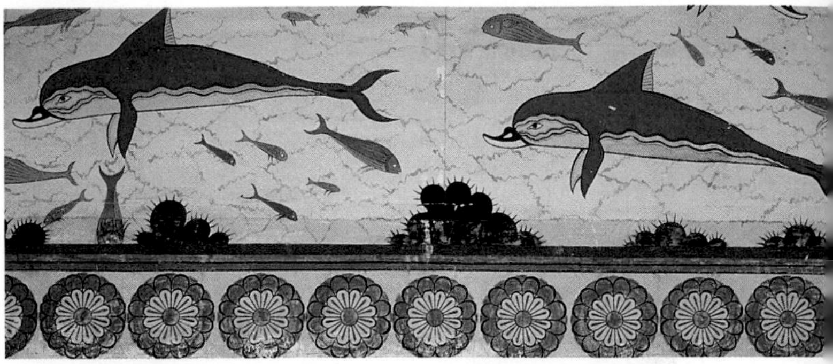

Dolphin fresco from Knossos One of the first Greek cultures to emerge was at Knossos on Crete.

2000 B.C. Minoan palace culture begins on Crete.

1600-1400 B.C. The palace of Minos is built at Knossos.

1500 B.C. (or earlier) A huge eruption of Thera on Santorini island destroys Minoan towns.

c. 1250 B.C. The Greeks destroy Troy, a city in Asia Minor.

c. 1125-1025 B.C. Dorians settle in northern Greece.

c. 1000 B.C. Greeks begin to colonize Asia Minor.

c. 800 B.C. The poet Homer composes the epics *Iliad* and *Odyssey*.

776 B.C. The first Olympic Games are held.

c. 735 B.C. The first Greek colony is founded at Naxos in Sicily.

730 B.C. Sparta becomes a leading power after defeating the Messenians.

c. 508 B.C. Democracy begins to appear in Greek cities.

490 B.C. The Athenians defeat the Persians under Darius at Marathon. This is a turning point in the Persian Wars.

483 B.C. Themistocles builds the Athenian fleet.

480 B.C. The Persians are defeated by the Athenian fleet at Salamis.

2000 B.C. — 1000 B.C. — 500 B.C.

Great Greek leaders

Solon c. 640-560 B.C. The Athenian statesman Solon created a code of moderate laws that became the basis of all Greek and Roman law.

Aristides c. 530-c. 467 B.C. The Athenian general Aristides defeated the Persians at Marathon, Salamis and Plataea. Known as "the Just," he was influential in Athenian politics and in the Delian League against the Persians.

Themistocles c. 525-c. 460 B.C. After the Battle of Marathon, Themistocles encouraged the Athenians to build a navy to ward off Persian invasions. It crushed the Persian fleet at Salamis.

Pericles c. 495-429 B.C. Pericles led Athens c. 460-429 B.C., presiding over the city's golden age of art and culture and its imperial expansion.

Lysander d. 395 B.C. Lysander was a Spartan naval commander whose victory at Aegospotami in 405 B.C. led to Sparta's defeat of Athens.

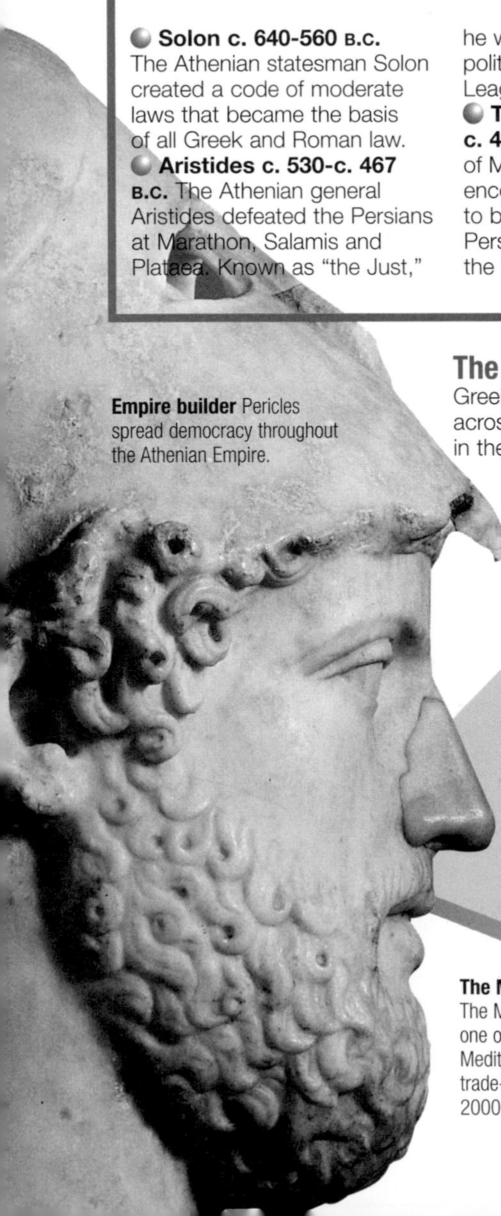

Empire builder Pericles spread democracy throughout the Athenian Empire.

The Greek world

Greek civilization extended across the Aegean to Ionia in the Persian Empire.

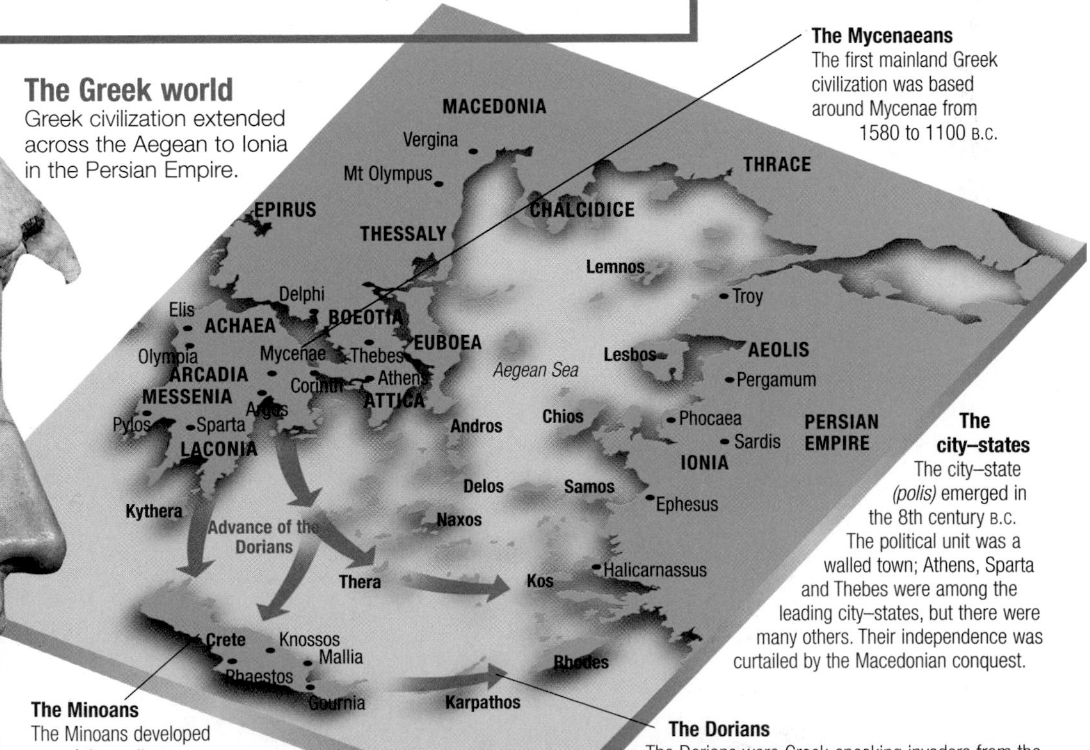

The Mycenaeans The first mainland Greek civilization was based around Mycenae from 1580 to 1100 B.C.

The city–states The city–state *(polis)* emerged in the 8th century B.C. The political unit was a walled town; Athens, Sparta and Thebes were among the leading city–states, but there were many others. Their independence was curtailed by the Macedonian conquest.

The Minoans The Minoans developed one of the earliest Mediterranean civilizations. Their trade-based culture flourished from 2000 to 1450 B.C.

The Dorians The Dorians were Greek-speaking invaders from the north who spread through Greece, Crete and western Asia Minor (Turkey) from 1125 to 1025 B.C. Their Iron Age technology supplanted the Mycenaean Bronze age.

The legacy of Greece

Democracy Rule *(kratos)* by the people *(demos)* was introduced in Athens under Cleisthenes (early 6th century B.C.), replacing the rule of "tyrants." All male citizens had the right to speak and vote at the Assembly.

Philosophy and science Greek thought combined belief in reason with inquiry into the world and how people should live. Socrates (c. 470-399 B.C.), Plato (c. 428-348) and Aristotle (384-322 B.C.) laid the foundations of Western philosophy. Pythagoras (c. 582-c. 507 B.C.), Euclid (lived c. 300 B.C.) and Archimedes (c. 287-212 B.C.) made significant advances in mathematics, science and astronomy.

Athletics and sports Greek sports featured formal competition in running, discus and javelin throwing, wrestling and boxing. There were four large regular meetings, including the Panhellenic Games at Olympia (from 776 B.C.).

Theater Songs and dances at religious festivals were developed into plays beginning about 530 B.C. Tragedies, notably by Aeschylus (c. 525-455 B.C.), Sophocles (c. 496-405 B.C.) and Euripides (c. 485-406 B.C.) dealt with fate; comedies, like those by Aristophanes (c. 448-c. 380 B.C.), offered slapstick humor.

Art and architecture Greek sculpture was influential in Western art until the 19th century, and the calm elegance of Greek architecture is still seen an ideal by some modern architects.

Medicine Hippocrates (c. 460-377 B.C.), the "Father of Medicine," from Kos, developed the first theories of illness and healing based on observation rather than religion.

History Greek authors founded the Western tradition of separating historical events from myth and using evidence from eyewitnesses and visits to historical sites. The great Greek historians were Herodotus (c. 484-420 B.C.), Thucydides (c. 460-396 B.C.) and Xenophon (c. 430-354 B.C.).

Greek achievement (Above) An Athenian doctor at work. (Left) Drunkenness held up for ridicule in figures from Greek comedy.

see also

300-1 **Mythology**
308-9 **Western thought**
316-17 **Western art**
326-27 **Architecture**

478 B.C. Athens forms the Delian League, a Greek alliance against Persia.

479 B.C. The Greek states led by Sparta and Athens defeat the Persians at Plataea, ending the Persian threat.

447 B.C. Work begins on the Parthenon.

431-404 B.C. The Peloponnesian War between Athens and Sparta takes place; Sparta finally prevails.

385 B.C. Plato founds the Academy in Athens.

338 B.C. Philip II of Macedonia becomes the ruler of Greece after defeating the Hellenic League at Chaeronea.

334-326 B.C. Alexander the Great creates an empire stretching from Greece to India.

300 B.C.

323 B.C. Alexander dies in Babylon.

c. 276 B.C. Alexander's empire is split into Antigonid Macedonia, Seleucid Asia and Ptolemaic Egypt.

292-280 B.C. The Colossus of Rhodes is built.

197 B.C. Philip V of Macedonia is defeated by the Romans and loses control of Greece.

146 B.C. The Romans sack Corinth and make Greece a Roman province.

Alexander the Great

Alexander (b. 356 B.C.), son of Philip II and a pupil of **Aristotle**, became king of Macedonia in 336 B.C. By the time he died, little more than a decade later, he had conquered virtually all of the known world east of Greece.

Alexander's campaigns began in 334 B.C., when he invaded the Persian Empire with the largest army ever to leave Greece. He defeated Darius III the following year and was made Pharaoh in Egypt, where he founded the city of **Alexandria**.

Darius raised a huge new army against Alexander. The climactic battle at **Gaugamela** (in modern Iraq) in 331 B.C. was an overwhelming Greek victory. Alexander occupied Babylon and the Persian capitals of **Susa** and **Persepolis**.

In 330 B.C., Alexander's army marched through eastern Persia, founding the cities of **Herat** and **Kandahar** (in modern Afghanistan). They advanced into Sogdiana, where they fought a two-year campaign against King Oxyartes (whose daughter, **Roxana**, Alexander married). Crossing the Hindu Kush mountains, Alexander invaded the Indus Valley in 327 B.C., defeating the powerful rajah **Porus** at the **Hydaspes**. His army finally refused to march farther into India, and Alexander was forced to return to Persia via the southern coast. He died of a fever at age 32 at Babylon in 323 B.C. By 304 B.C., the empire had been divided among his squabbling generals.

Warrior king Alexander fights alongside his troops.

Alexander's route

Alexander's army swept through Central Asia in a series of whirlwind campaigns.

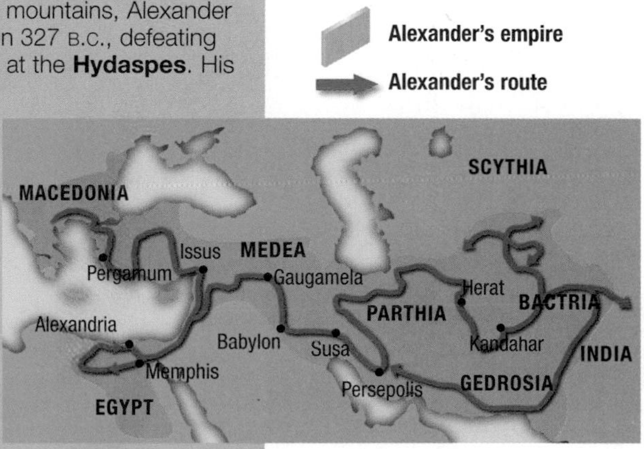

Rome flourished for about 800 years, developing a technically advanced and sophisticated society not seen again in the Western world until the 16th century. The early Roman state was a republic ruled by a senate of leading citizens with elected magistrates or consuls. However, the highly efficient Roman army had carved out a vast territory by the 1st century B.C., and the conquered dominions required the authority of an emperor. Despite frequent mismanagement, Rome sustained the empire for 400 years.

THE LEGACY OF ROME

Law The Roman legal system was codified in 450 B.C. and was regularly modified as the empire grew. Much modern Western law is based on principles established by the Romans.

Building and engineering Roman building was unsurpassed for 1000 years. Architects and engineers extended Greek ideas by developing the arch and the dome (as in the Pantheon in Rome), and through the use of concrete. Roman engineers also created a network of roads throughout the empire. Many of the routes are still in use today.

Towns and cities Many modern European cities (including London, Paris, Cologne and Toledo, Spain) were founded by the Romans.

Preservation of ancient cultures The Romans adopted and preserved much of the best of the cultures they conquered, including Greek traditions of sculpture, learning and literature.

Language and literature Latin remained the universal language of the Christian world until after the Renaissance. It also formed the basis of Romance languages, such as Italian, French, Spanish, Portuguese and Romanian. The great works of Roman literature and history, by writers such as Virgil, Livy, Horace, Ovid, Pliny and Juvenal, provided a major inspiration to the Renaissance.

Christianity Although originally opposed to Christianity, the Roman Empire was mostly Christian by the time it fell. Through its network of churches and monasteries and the universal use of Latin, the Church preserved the traditions of internationalism and learning in Europe long after the collapse of Roman political power.

Roman engineering The Pont du Gard, the finest surviving Roman aqueduct.

Growth of empire Rome gained its first territories outside Italy after the First Punic War against Carthage. The Roman Empire reached its greatest extent in A.D. 117, under Emperor Trajan.

Imperial coins Two gold aureus coins, with the heads of Caligula, emperor from A.D. 37 to 41 (left), and Constantine the Great.

- **753 B.C.** Traditional date for the founding of Rome.
- **510 B.C.** Last Etruscan king, Lucius Tarquin, is expelled from Rome.
- 500 B.C.
- **451-450 B.C.** Codification of Roman law, known as the "Twelve Tables."
- **390 B.C.** Rome is sacked by the Gauls.
- 300 B.C.
- **264-241 B.C.** First Punic War between Rome and Carthage is won by Rome.
- **218 B.C.** Second Punic War begins; Carthaginians under Hannibal invade northern Italy.
- **202 B.C.** Hannibal is finally defeated at Zama, near Carthage, ending the Second Punic War.
- **149-146 B.C.** Rome destroys Carthage in the Third Punic War.
- **130-120 B.C.** Rome annexes parts of Gaul (southern France), Asia Minor (Turkey) and North Africa.
- 100 B.C.
- **72 B.C.** Spartacus's slave revolt is crushed by Pompey and Crassus.
- **58-51 B.C.** Julius Caesar conquers Gaul and raids Britain (55 B.C.).
- **44 B.C.** Julius Caesar is assassinated by the republican senators Brutus and Cassius.

Five reasons why Rome flourished

1. **Efficient, disciplined, professional army** Rome's well-organized army, which had superior weapons technology, outclassed all enemies. Colonies of ex-soldiers also helped maintain security in all the imperial territories.
2. **Excellent communications** Roman ports, roads and aqueducts ensured efficient transport and supply.
3. **Good administration** A single language, an empire-wide legal code and an effective system of territorial governors made it possible to maintain control over large and diverse territories.
4. **Peace and stability** Long periods of relative peace and stability within the empire (the Pax Romana) allowed trade to flourish and a confident, inclusive imperial culture to develop. After A.D. 212, Roman citizenship was granted to all free men in the empire to increase their sense of belonging to the Roman world.
5. **Economic order** The empire's huge and efficient trading network encouraged economic activity, generating tax revenue and both private and civic wealth.

Five reasons why Rome fell

1. **Overstretched defenses** After the crisis of the the 3rd century A.D., the empire lost its ability to dominate beyond its borders.
2. **Oppressive rule** Rather than ruling in cooperation with local rulers, the later emperors attempted to maintain Roman power through force alone.
3. **Internal division** After the splitting of the empire in A.D. 330, the wealthy Eastern Empire increasingly refused to pay for defense of the West.
4. **Taxation** The senatorial class was exempt from taxation, and the centralized tax collection system became oppressive and inefficient.
5. **Barbarian armies** Starting in the 3rd century, the Roman army relied on barbarian soldiers. Germanic tribes were attracted to the empire and settled there in large numbers, eventually becoming a threat to Rome.

Roman rulers

Julius Caesar c. 100-44 B.C. A general, politician and writer, Caesar won military victories in Gaul from 58 to 49 B.C. and made two expeditions to Britain. In 49 B.C., his troops occupied Rome. Because he ruled as a dictator, he was assassinated by republican senators Brutus and Cassius.

Augustus 63 B.C.-A.D. 14 The adopted son of Julius Caesar, Augustus was the first emperor. After Caesar's death, he defeated Brutus and Cassius in 42 B.C. and Mark Antony in 31 B.C. A ruthless politician, he brought peace, security and prosperity after decades of civil war.

Caligula A.D. 12-41 The third emperor (from A.D. 37), Caligula was a mentally unstable and tyrannical ruler. He was killed by the Praetorian Guard (imperial bodyguards).

Claudius 10 B.C.-A.D. 54 Claudius, the fourth emperor (A.D. 41-54), was scholarly and intelligent. He repaired much of Caligula's damage and added Britain to the empire.

Nero c. A.D. 37-68 Emperor from A.D. 54 to 68, Nero was a murderous tyrant. He persecuted the Christians, whom he blamed for the fire that ravaged Rome in A.D. 64.

Trajan c. A.D. 53-117 Trajan ruled from A.D. 98 to 117, bringing the empire to its greatest size.

Hadrian A.D. 76-138 Hadrian ruled from A.D. 117 to 138, during Rome's golden age. He consolidated the empire behind defensible frontiers such as Hadrian's Wall.

Diocletian A.D. 245-31 Diocletian restored order after a period of short-lived emperors. He ruled from A.D. 284 to 305.

Constantine the Great c. A.D. 274-337 Emperor from A.D. 306 to 337, Constantine divided the empire, founded a new capital at Byzantium, and renamed Constantinople (now Istanbul). His Edict of Milan (A.D. 313) proclaimed tolerance of Christianity.

see also
300-1 **Mythology**
326-27 **Architecture**
338-39 **Western literature**
475 **Early Mediterranean rulers**

30 B.C. Octavian becomes the first emperor, taking the name Augustus.

0

A.D. 43 Rome begins the conquest of Britain.

A.D. 64 Rome burns; Nero blames the Christians and begins persecuting them.

A.D. 79 Vesuvius erupts, engulfing Pompeii and Herculaneum.

A.D. 80 The Colosseum is completed in Rome. It seats 50 000 spectators.

A.D. 100

A.D. 98-117 Trajan builds roads, bridges and aqueducts across a vast empire.

A.D. 192-97 Civil war in the Roman Empire.

A.D. 251 Pressure from Goths forces Rome to withdraw from outlying provinces.

A.D. 312-37 After years of fragmentation, the empire is reorganized by Constantine.

A.D. 392 Pagan worship is prohibited in the empire in favor of Christianity.

A.D. 400

A.D. 406 The Vandals, Alans and Sueves invade the Roman Empire.

A.D. 410 Rome is sacked by the Visigoths.

The making of Europe ▶ From the fall of Rome to the Norman Conquest of England

The collapse of the Roman world left a mosaic of competing successor kingdoms in Europe. Many of the Germanic tribes were highly Romanized, had fought for the Romans as mercenaries and had adopted the Christian religion. The changes they brought about were often more evolutionary than sudden. It was a time of turmoil, but out of the turmoil emerged new peoples and powers – and a new stage of European history.

East Anglian kingdom A helmet found at Sutton Hoo is one of many artifacts displaying the wealth of East Anglia in the early 7th century.

Peoples of the Dark Ages

Barbarian tribes helped bring down Rome, but they also preserved and spread many aspects of Roman civilization, including Christianity and the Latin language. As Rome fell apart, local Barbarian rulers increasingly replaced Imperial authority, redrawing the map of Europe. The "Barbarians" included:

- **Angles and Saxons** Pagan tribes from Denmark, including the Angles and Saxons, came to Britain starting in the 5th century, driving local Celtic peoples west. They developed a vernacular literature, and their tongue, Anglo-Saxon, was the forerunner of English. St. Augustine converted them to Christianity in the 7th century.
- **Franks** The Franks were a Germanic people who, in the 5th century, created a kingdom that included large parts of modern France and Germany. By the 8th century, they ruled northern Germany as well.
- **Huns** In the 4th century, nomadic tribes called Huns began to terrorize central and southeastern Europe, forcing migrations and destabilizing Rome. They reached a peak under Attila (434-53), but after 451, they fell into factionalism.
- **Lombards** The Lombards came from the Danube area to occupy much of Italy until defeated by the Franks in 774.
- **Ostrogoths** The "Eastern Goths" settled in the Ukraine but were driven westward by the Huns in 370. Under Theodoric in the 5th century, they came to dominate Italy.
- **Slavs** The Slavs originated south of the Baltic Sea. They were subjugated by the Goths and Huns and spread to the Ukraine, Germany and the Balkans, becoming the ancestors of today's Russians, Ukrainians, Poles and Serbs.
- **Vandals** The Vandals' name is still a byword for destruction. They devastated Spain in 409; the Spanish province Andalusia is named after them. In 429, they invaded North Africa, establishing a capital at Carthage from where they sacked Rome in 455.
- **Visigoths** The "Western Goths" settled within the Roman Empire, contributing to its fall and sacking Rome. They made a kingdom in France and Spain, holding Spanish lands until they were conquered by the Arabs in 711.

Barbarian migrations

Germanic peoples began to migrate toward western Europe in the 1st century B.C. In A.D. 376, the Visigoths crossed the Danube in force, opening the way for a flood of other tribes from the Balkans, Britain and North Africa into Roman lands.

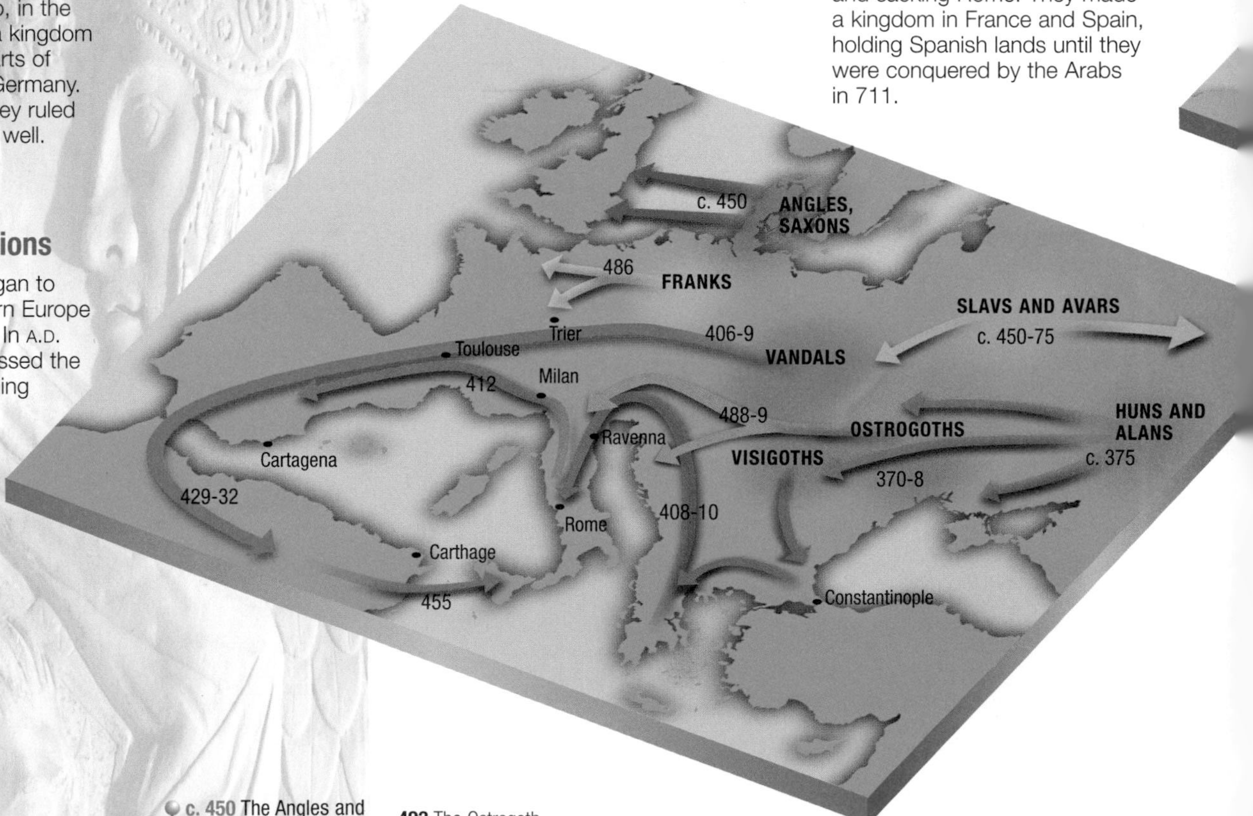

402 The Western Empire moves its court from Milan to Ravenna.

406-7 Vandals invade the Roman Empire.

410 Alaric becomes king of the Visigoths and sacks Rome.

435 St. Patrick takes Christianity to Ireland.

c. 450 The Angles and Saxons begin their conquest of Britain.

476 The last Roman emperor, Romulus Augustulus, is deposed.

493 The Ostrogoth Theodoric the Great becomes king of Italy.

496 Clovis, king of the Franks, converts to Christianity.

507 The Franks defeat the Visigoths, uniting most of France.

533 The Byzantines begin to restore Roman power in Italy.

c. 550 The bubonic plague ravages Europe.

597 St. Augustine of Canterbury begins his mission to England.

VIKINGS

The Vikings were sailors and traders. They emerged from **Norway**, **Denmark** and **Sweden** around the end of the 8th century A.D. and terrorized Europe for more than 200 years. Their first major recorded raid was in 793 on the monastery at **Lindisfarne** in northern England. Their shallow-draft longships could travel far inland on rivers to loot monasteries and capture cattle and slaves. From the mid 9th century, they occupied large areas of England (the **"Danelaw"**), eastern Ireland, western Scotland and Normandy.

Swedish Vikings traveled along the rivers of eastern Europe to the Black Sea, trading with the Arabs and Byzantines. They established ruling dynasties around Kiev and Novgorod. The Norwegian Vikings settled in **Iceland** after 870 and **Greenland** after 982. In c.1000, they set up a short-lived colony in North America. King **Cnut** ("Canute") of Denmark (c. 994-1035) was simultaneously king of Denmark, England and Norway. In the course of the 10th century, the Vikings gradually converted to Christianity.

Viking Europe c. 900

Viking raids of the 8th-10th centuries, assisted by Magyar invasions in the east, broke up the Frankish Empire.

- Viking raids
- Magyar raids
- Frankish kingdoms
- Areas settled by Vikings
- Arab and Moorish states

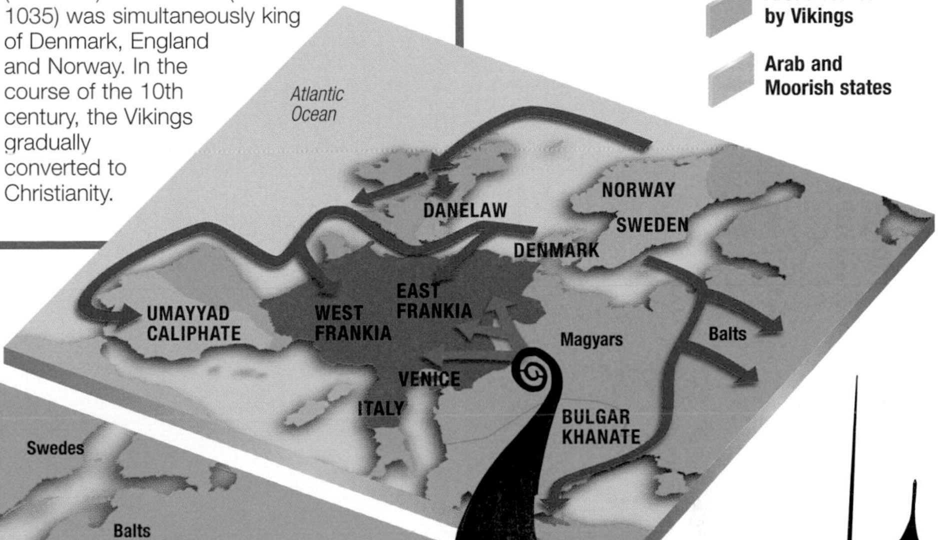

Viking longboat Built for speed, flat-bottomed longboats were ideal for raiding parties.

see also
302-3 World mythology
475 Early Mediterranean rulers
476 European leaders

Europe in 800

Charlemagne's Europe was dominated by the two great Christian empires of the Byzantines and the Franks.

- Frankish Empire
- Byzantine Empire
- Arab and Moorish states

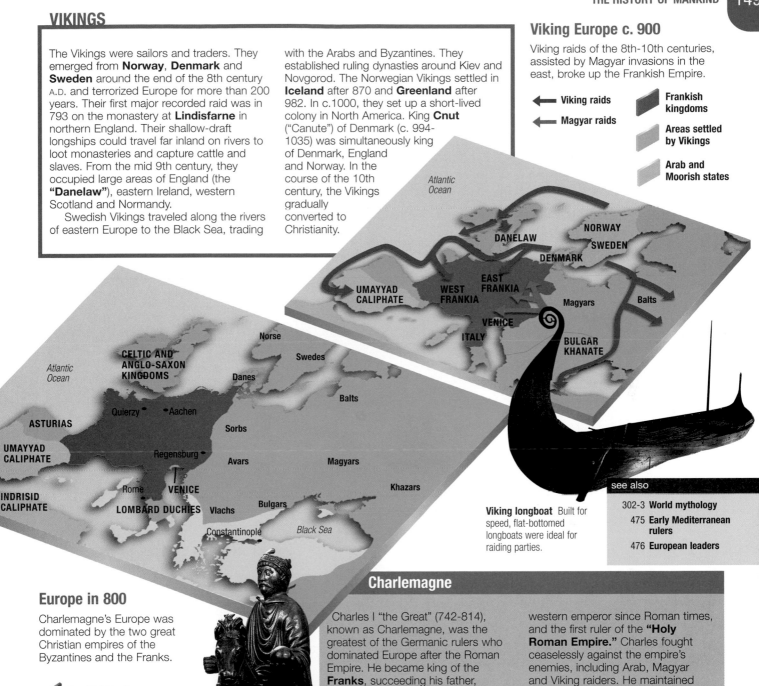

Empire builder Charlemagne doubled the Frankish lands and ruthlessly imposed Christianity.

Charlemagne

Charles I "the Great" (742-814), known as Charlemagne, was the greatest of the Germanic rulers who dominated Europe after the Roman Empire. He became king of the **Franks**, succeeding his father, Pepin III, "the Short," in 768 and aggressively expanded Frankish authority over all the German kingdoms outside England and Scandinavia. On Christmas Day in 800, Pope **Leo III** confirmed Charles' supremacy in Europe by crowning him emperor – the first western emperor since Roman times, and the first ruler of the **"Holy Roman Empire."** Charles fought ceaselessly against the empire's enemies, including Arab, Magyar and Viking raiders. He maintained diplomatic relations with Byzantium, Baghdad and the English kingdoms and presided over a revival of learning known as the **Carolingian Renaissance**. His successors failed to maintain the empire's strong central authority, directly contributing to the rise of **feudalism** in Europe.

700

c. 700 The Lindisfarne Gospels include magnificent Anglo-Saxon illuminated manuscripts.

732 The Franks defeat an Arab invasion near Poitiers, France.

751 Pepin III becomes the first Carolingian king of the Franks.

793 Viking raids begin with an attack on Lindisfarne, Engand.

800 Charlemagne, king of the Franks, is crowned Emperor of the West in Rome.

860 The Kiev Vikings (Rus) attack Constantinople.

865 The Viking "Great Army" invades England.

878 Wessex, led by King Alfred, repulses Danish Vikings at Edington.

900

965 King Harald Bluetooth is baptized, and the Danish Vikings convert to Christianity.

987 Hugh Capet's accession in France marks the end of Carolingian rule.

1000

1000 Christianity is introduced to Sweden, led by King Olaf.

1016 The Normans begin their conquest of southern Italy.

1054 The Eastern Orthodox Church splits from the Roman Church (the "Great Schism").

1066 Duke William of Normandy defeats Harold of England at Hastings.

Within a few years of his crucifixion, Jesus's message spread beyond the Jews and grew into a cult stretching across the Roman Empire. When the empire collapsed, the Western Church preserved much of the learning and traditions of Rome, eventually becoming the dominant force of the medieval world.

ROME'S CHRISTIAN LEGACY

As Roman rule began to fail in Western Europe, the Christian Church took on a political and cultural role as well as a spiritual one. By 600, much of Europe was Christian (see map), because of the activities of early **missionaries** (see below). The Church was now the only major institution to preserve its authority from Roman times and almost the only unifying and civilizing influence in Europe. From the 9th century, its prestige and power were enhanced by association with the **Holy Roman Empire** of Charlemagne and his succesors.

Relations between the popes and Holy Roman emperors deteriorated during the Middle Ages, and the existence of an alternative Roman tradition in the Byzantine east led to the separation of Catholic and **Orthodox** Churches. The split was worsened by the intervention of the **Crusaders** against the Byzantines' Muslim enemies. Factional strife in Rome led to the removal of the papacy to Avignon, France (1309-77), and then to the **Great Schism** (1378-1417), when there were rival popes in Rome and Avignon.

The authority of the pope was restored in the Renaissance but marred by family ambitions, decadence and corruption that helped fuel the **Reformation**.

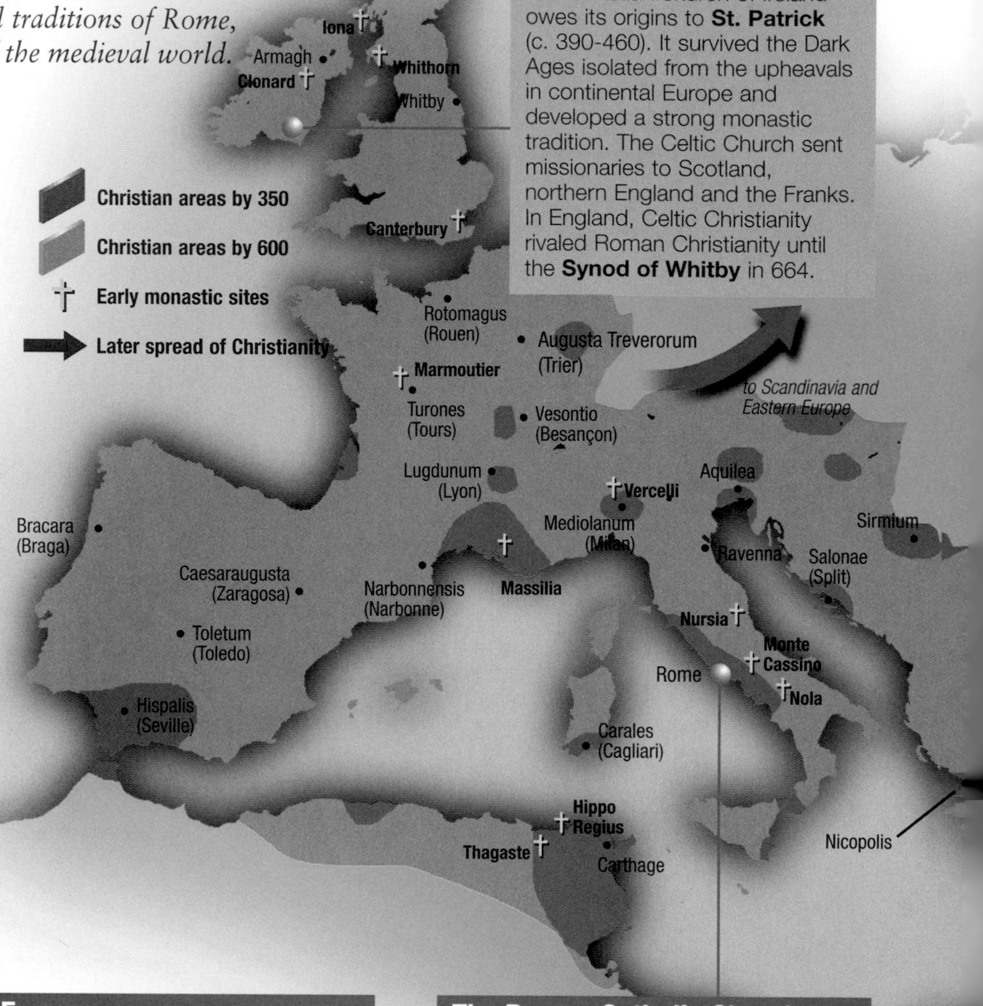

Celtic Church

The Christian church of Ireland owes its origins to **St. Patrick** (c. 390-460). It survived the Dark Ages isolated from the upheavals in continental Europe and developed a strong monastic tradition. The Celtic Church sent missionaries to Scotland, northern England and the Franks. In England, Celtic Christianity rivaled Roman Christianity until the **Synod of Whitby** in 664.

Who's who among the missionaries of Europe

St. Paul (d. c. 67) Paul had the privileges of a Roman citizen. He traveled widely, taking the Christian message to the Aegean islands, Asia Minor, Greece, Italy and possibly Spain.

St. Columba (c. 521-97) Columba was abbot of Iona, which became a center of Celtic Christianity.

St. Columban (c. 540-615) The Irish missionary monk Columban took Christianity to the pagan Franks and established monastic centers of noted asceticism in France and northern Italy.

St. Augustine of Canterbury (d. 605) A Benedictine prior, Augustine was sent by Pope Gregory I to reevangelize Britain in 597. He became the first archbishop of Canterbury.

St. Boniface (675-754). The English-born monk Boniface was called the "Apostle of Germany." Appointed as archbishop of Mainz in 751, he was killed while preaching in Friesland.

The Roman Catholic Church

The Roman Catholic Church was originally geographically equivalent to the Roman Empire of the West. Its leader, the pope, claimed direct succession from **St. Peter** and the right of jurisdiction over the entire Christian world. The organization of the Church, its preservation of the **Latin** language and much Roman learning, its massive cathedral-building program, its sponsorship of the Crusades, its monastic orders and its power and wealth defined the Middle Ages.

c. 4-6 B.C. Jesus of Nazareth is born in Palestine.

0

c. A.D. 23-30 Jesus begins to preach his message publicly.

c. 26-34 Jesus is crucified.

c. 36 The "Christian" message of Jesus begins to spread to non-Jews.

c. 46-57 St. Paul travels across the Mediterranean on his missionary journeys.

c. 64 St. Peter is executed in Rome; the persecution of Christians begins.

100

c. 200 Church leaders assemble Christian writings into the New Testament.

c. 300 The popular Arian doctrine leads to divisions among Christians.

313 The Edict of Milan makes Christianity formally tolerated within the Roman Empire.

325 The Council of Nicaea rejects Arianism as a heresy.

354-430 St. Augustine of Hippo creates a coherent Christian theology.

380 Emperor Theodosius makes Christianity Rome's official religion.

Monastic orders

Withdrawal from society in pursuit of a truly spiritual life was formalized by the creation of monastic communities within the Christian Church. The originators of this formal ("regular") monasticism were St. Basil the Great (c. 330-79) in the East and St. Benedict of Nursia (c. 480-547) in the West. The monastic orders exerted great influence in medieval Europe.

- **Benedictines** St. Benedict's order of monks spread rapidly from its first house at Monte Cassino, Italy (525), to several thousand houses by the 11th century. The Order of **Cluny** (early 10th century on) resulted from the first major reform of the Benedictine order.
- **Carthusians** The austere Carthusian order was founded in 1084 at La Chartreuse by St. Bruno of Cologne.
- **Cistercians** Founded in 1098 by Robert of Molesme at Cîteaux, France, the Cistercian order was based on a strict interpretation of St. Benedict's Rule. It was a prosperous order with large agricultural estates.
- **Franciscans** The Franciscans (Friars Minor) were the first order of friars (mendicant or begging monks), founded in 1209 by St. Francis of Assisi (1182-1226).
- **Dominicans** The Dominican order (Friars Preachers), founded in 1215 by St. Dominic (1170-1221), emphasized public preaching.
- **Augustinians** Augustinian canons flourished from around 1100. Their Rules were based on that of St. Augustine of Hippo.

Franciscan The Gray Friars adopted poverty as a sign of spirituality.

Dominican Many influential scholars and teachers were Black Friars.

Benedictine The Black Monks were the most numerous of all monastic orders.

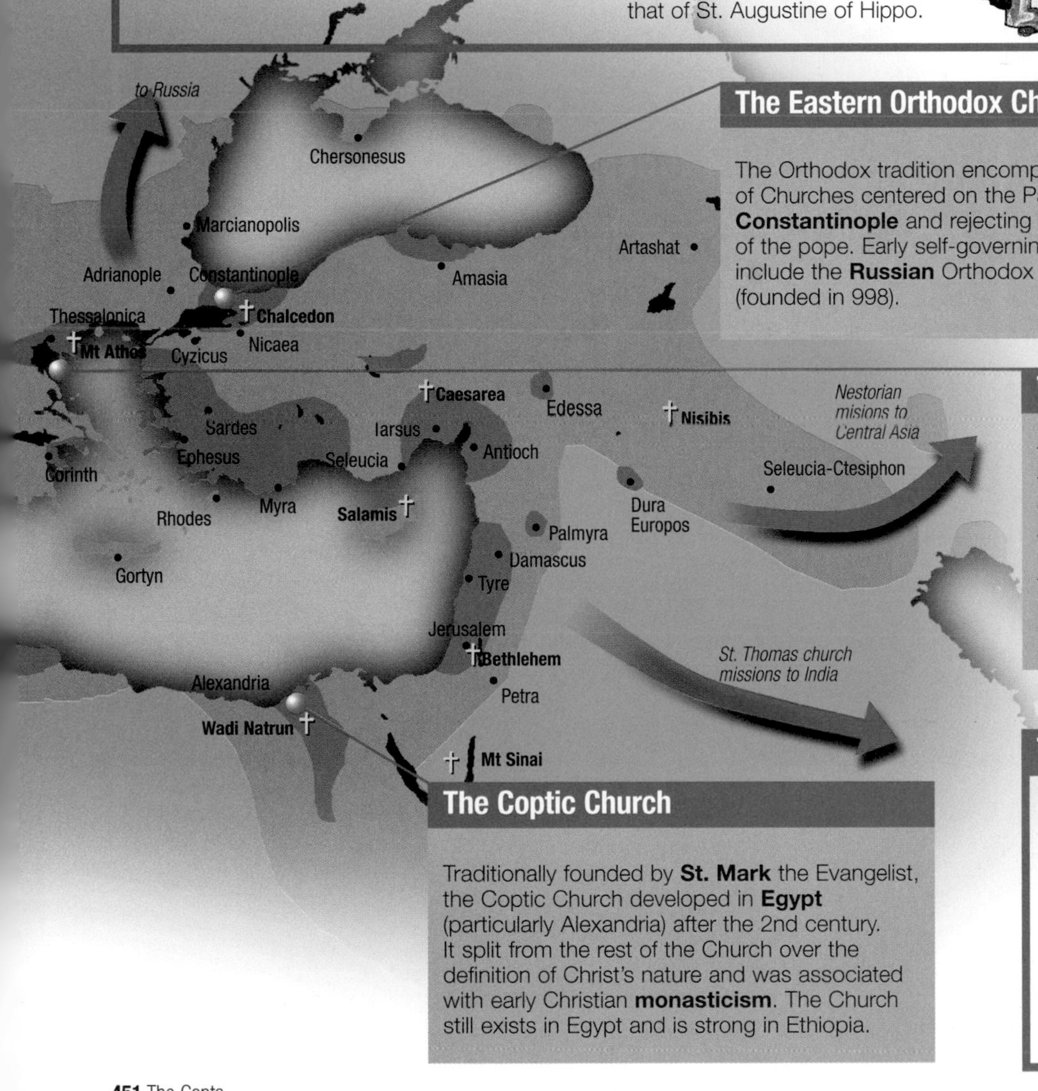

The Eastern Orthodox Church

The Orthodox tradition encompasses a group of Churches centered on the Patriarch of **Constantinople** and rejecting the supremacy of the pope. Early self-governing subdivisions include the **Russian** Orthodox Church (founded in 998).

see also

152-53 **The rise of Islam**
304-5 **Religions**
316-17 **Western art**
476 **European leaders**

The Nestorian Church

The Nestorian church was created by the followers of **Nestorius** (d. 451), bishop of Constantinople. Its basic belief was that Jesus combined distinct human and divine natures. The Nestorians were expelled by the Orthodox Church in 489 and resettled in **Persia**; their missionaries spread to India, Sri Lanka and China.

The Coptic Church

Traditionally founded by **St. Mark** the Evangelist, the Coptic Church developed in **Egypt** (particularly Alexandria) after the 2nd century. It split from the rest of the Church over the definition of Christ's nature and was associated with early Christian **monasticism**. The Church still exists in Egypt and is strong in Ethiopia.

The East–West Schism

Bitter disputes over doctrine and papal authority began to divide the Western and Eastern Churches starting in the 9th century. Mutual excommunications were pronounced by Rome and Constantinople in 1054 (lifted only in 1965). This marked the first great formal separation of the Christian Church – into Roman Catholic in the West and Orthodox in the East.

451 The Copts split from the rest of the Church.

496 Clovis, king of the Franks, converts to Christianity.

500

525 St. Benedict of Nursia founds the first major Western monastery at Monte Cassino, Italy.

596 Pope Gregory sends St. Augustine (later of Canterbury) to England.

800 Charlemagne is crowned Emperor of the West by the pope.

1000

1054 The Eastern Orthodox Church formally parts with the Church of Rome.

1076-7 Pope Gregory VII excommunicates Holy Roman Emperor Henry IV.

1095 Christians conquer the Holy Land in the First Crusade.

1202-4 The Fourth Crusade sacks the Byzantine capital, Constantinople.

1225-74 St. Thomas Aquinas, the greatest theologian of the Middle Ages, lives and writes.

1291 Acre, the last Crusader state, falls to the Muslims.

1453 Constantinople falls to the Ottomans.

1500

The rise of Islam

From the birth of the Prophet to the Ottoman Empire

In A.D. 610, after a series of divine revelations, the Prophet Muhammad founded a religion based on faith in a single god, clear social rules and the promise of an afterlife. Arab conquests quickly spread Islam though Southwest Asia, the Middle East and North Africa. Christian Europe was hostile to Islam but later benefited from the preservation of Greek culture and the scientific and medical knowledge of Arab Muslims.

The Middle East

Islam's expansion beyond Arabia began with the Muslim conquest of Sasanian (Persian) Iraq and Byzantine Syria from 633 to 641. **Jerusalem** was captured in 638 and became the third city of Islam. In 637, Muslim forces defeated the Sasanians at Qadisiya, and by 650 all of Persia was under Islamic rule. The First **Crusade** (1099) established Christian territories in the Middle East, but these were mostly reconquered by Saladin, the **Ayyubid** sultan of Egypt, in 1187. The Middle East was dominated by the Ottoman Empire after 1516.

Spain and Portugal

Visigothic Spain and Portugal were conquered in 711-19 by an Arab and Berber (Moorish) army from North Africa. The Moors took Córdoba, Seville, Malaga, Toledo, Zaragoza and Granada but were defeated by the Franks at Poitiers, France, in 732. The **Umayyad Caliphate of Córdoba** ruled Spain until 1031, followed by the **Almoravids** (1090-1145) and then the **Almohads** (1145-1212). Northern Spain remained Christian and gradually reconquered the south. The last Moorish kingdom, Granada, fell in 1492.

Moorish stronghold A view of the Alhambra, the greatest palace–fortress of Islamic Spain.

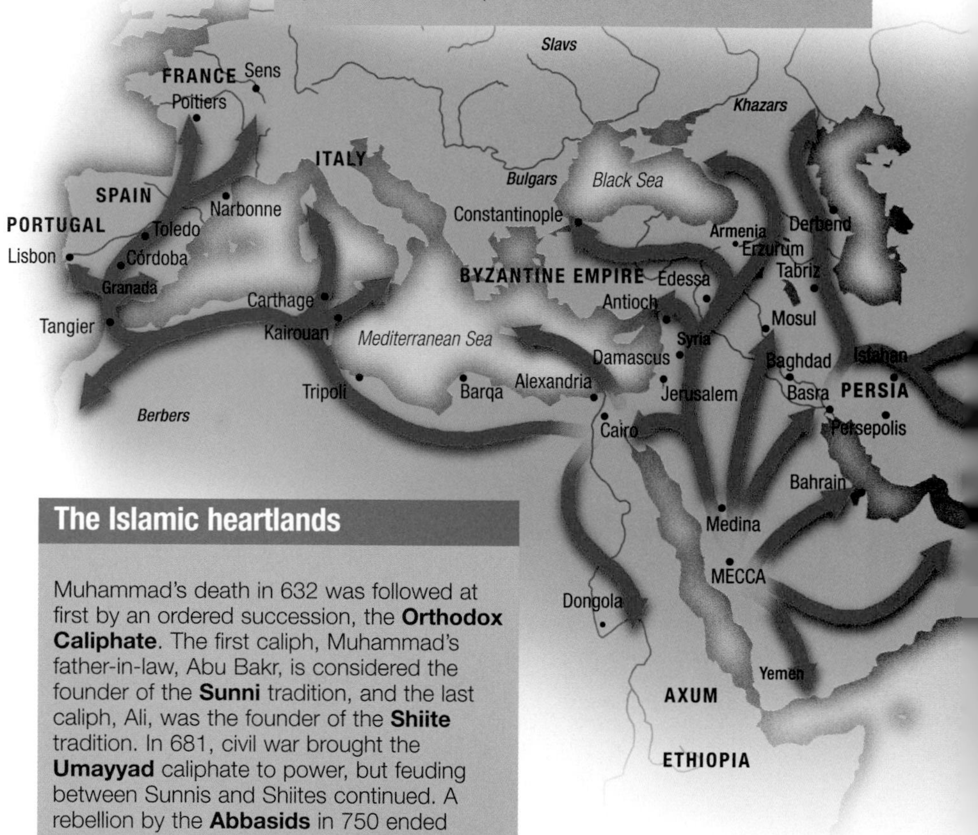

Advance of Islam Islam spread rapidly across the Middle East, North Africa and Persia in the 7th century, as Arab armies overran the Byzantine and Persian empires. Its advance through India and Southeast Asia was much more gradual.

North Africa

Muslim Arab forces under Amr conquered Byzantine Egypt in 639-40 and then advanced westward. By 710, all of North Africa was in Muslim hands. The Berber **Almoravid** dynasty gained control of Morocco and Algeria in 1054 and Spain in 1090, creating an empire spanning the Strait of Gibraltar. From 1147 to 1172, the **Almohad** dynasty supplanted the Almoravids, ruling from Marrakech until 1269.

The Islamic heartlands

Muhammad's death in 632 was followed at first by an ordered succession, the **Orthodox Caliphate**. The first caliph, Muhammad's father-in-law, Abu Bakr, is considered the founder of the **Sunni** tradition, and the last caliph, Ali, was the founder of the **Shiite** tradition. In 681, civil war brought the **Umayyad** caliphate to power, but feuding between Sunnis and Shiites continued. A rebellion by the **Abbasids** in 750 ended Umayyad rule everywhere except Spain and began the political fragmentation of the Islamic world. The Abbasids presided over the greatest age of Islamic culture (including the reign of **Harun ar-Rashid**, from 786 to 809, immortalized by the *Arabian Nights*). However, Persia rebelled under the **Safarids** and **Samanids** in 874, and in 914, Egypt fell to the **Fatimid** caliphate. The authority of the Abbasid caliphs became largely symbolic after Baghdad was captured by the Shiite **Buwayhids** in 950. The Abbasids were finally swept away by the Mongols in 1258.

570 Muhammad is born in Mecca.

600

610 Muhammad experiences revelations of the word of God.

622 Muhammad withdraws to Medina (the Hegira), beginning the Islamic era.

632 Muhammad dies. Abu Bakr becomes his successor (caliph).

634-644 Under Omar, Muslims take Jerusalem and invade Mesopotamia, Asia Minor, Persia and Egypt.

661 The Umayyad dynasty becomes established in Damascus; it rules until 750.

670 Islam advances across North Africa.

700

711 Muslim Arab forces from North Africa invade Spain.

732 Arab armies are heavily defeated by the Franks at Poitiers.

750 The Abbassids defeat the Umayyads and rule the Islamic world until 1258.

762 The Abbassids make Baghdad the Islamic capital.

900

909 The Shiite Fatimids establish an empire in North Africa (until 1171).

Asia Minor and the Balkans

Asia Minor (Turkey) remained the center of Byzantine power during Islam's initial rise; Arab sieges of Constantinople in 670-77 and 716-17 ended in heavy defeats. After 1038, the Muslim **Seljuk Turks** overran much of western Asia and Asia Minor, defeating the Byzantines at Manzikert (in 1071) and resisting the Crusaders. The Seljuk empire was destroyed by the Mongols in 1243. Its successor, the **Ottoman Empire**, expanded rapidly at the expense of the Byzantines (Constantinople fell in 1453, becoming the Ottoman capital). Ottoman forces overran the Middle East, the Balkans and most of North Africa in the 16th century.

Central and southern Asia

The Arab hold on Persia after 650 was brief. From 977 to 1186, the entire region from eastern Persia to northern India fell to the **Ghaznavids** of Afghanistan. The Ghaznavids lost part of their empire to the Seljuks in 1040 and the rest to the **Ghurids** in 1186. In 1206, the Muslim **Sultanate of Delhi** emerged, dominating the Indian subcontinent under the Khalji dynasty by 1321. It was crushed by Tamerlane in 1398 and later destroyed by his descendants, the **Moguls**.

Holy decoration A view of part of the elaborate interior of the Blue Mosque (Sultan Ahmed Mosque) in Istanbul.

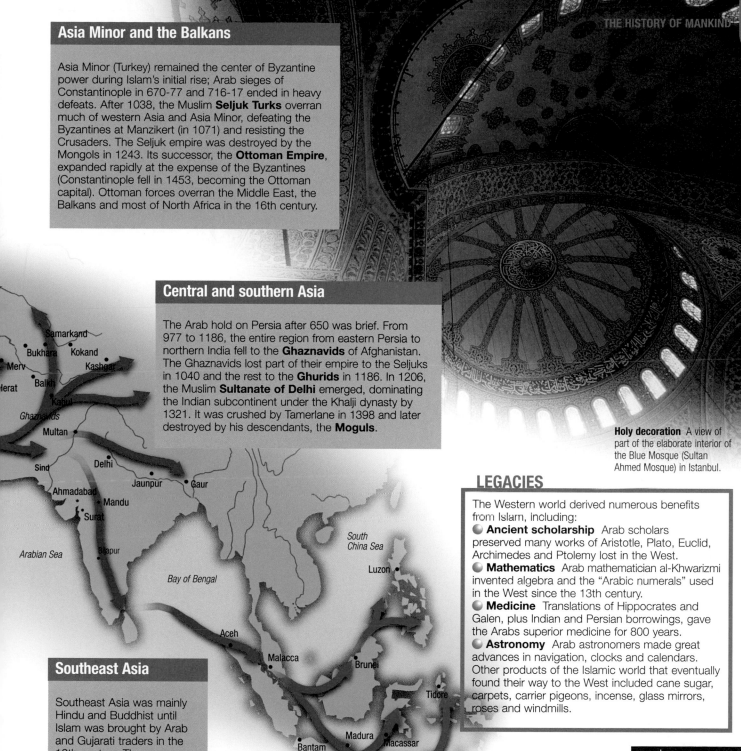

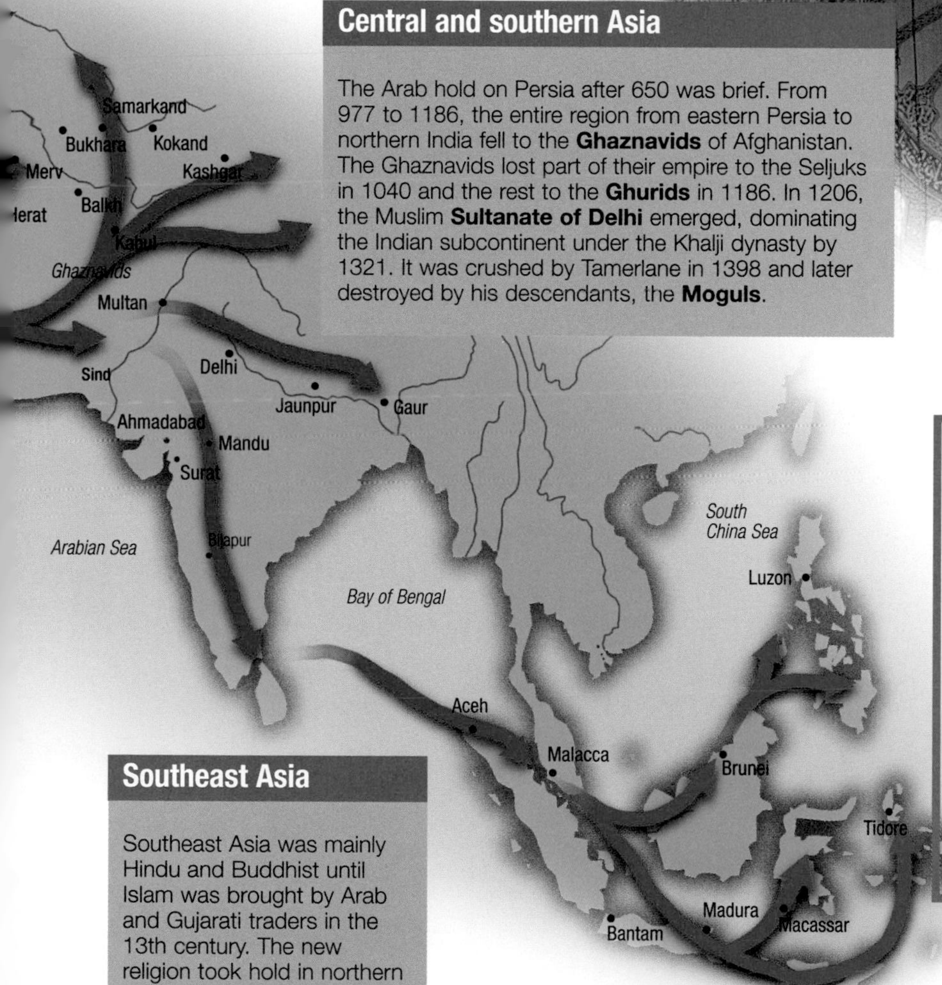

Southeast Asia

Southeast Asia was mainly Hindu and Buddhist until Islam was brought by Arab and Gujarati traders in the 13th century. The new religion took hold in northern Sumatra, Java, the southern Philippines, the Malay peninsula and the Moluccas.

LEGACIES

The Western world derived numerous benefits from Islam, including:

- **Ancient scholarship** Arab scholars preserved many works of Aristotle, Plato, Euclid, Archimedes and Ptolemy lost in the West.
- **Mathematics** Arab mathematician al-Khwarizmi invented algebra and the "Arabic numerals" used in the West since the 13th century.
- **Medicine** Translations of Hippocrates and Galen, plus Indian and Persian borrowings, gave the Arabs superior medicine for 800 years.
- **Astronomy** Arab astronomers made great advances in navigation, clocks and calendars.

Other products of the Islamic world that eventually found their way to the West included cane sugar, carpets, carrier pigeons, incense, glass mirrors, roses and windmills.

see also

150-51 **Christianity**
304-7 **Religions**
476 **European leaders**

1000

1054 The Almoravids begin the conquest of Morocco and Algeria.

1055 The Abbassids are defeated by the Seljuks of Asia Minor.

1085 The Almoravids invade Spain.

1095 First Crusade: Christians attack the Holy Land, taking Jerusalem in 1099.

1147 The Almohads take Marrakech and make it their capital.

1172 The Almohads extend their power through Spain.

1187 The Muslim reconquest of Jerusalem prompts the Third Crusade.

1200

1206 The Sultanate of Delhi is founded (to 1526).

1212 The Almohads begin to retreat from Spain; by 1248, Granada is the only Muslim kingdom in Spain.

1258 The Mongols sack Baghdad, ending Abbassid rule, but in 1260, they are heavily defeated at Ain Jalut.

1299 The Ottoman empire is founded by Osman I, in succession to the Seljuk empire.

1400

1453 The Ottomans capture Constantinople.

1492 Islam is driven out of Europe with the capture of Granada.

Around A.D. 1000, Europe was divided among many monarchs and regional lords whose authority over their territories varied greatly. Trade expanded, towns grew and won autonomy, craftsmen formed guilds and universities were founded. Writers such as Dante and Chaucer produced masterpieces, and massive cathedrals were built to assert belief in the power of the divine order.

Medieval Europe

Europe's states began to achieve something like their modern forms by the late 13th century, as shown here. The Church, trade and education networks, and a common aristocratic culture united Europe.

- English territories
- Aragonese territories
- Venetian territories
- Genoese territories
- Holy Roman Empire

FEUDAL EUROPE

Power in medieval Europe lay with kings and great aristocrats. In many areas – England, for example – all land was said to be held from the king. Some levels of the nobility held **fiefs** (large estates) from the king and aristocrats in return for military service (feudalism). Peasants were sometimes free, but they normally owed a range of rents and services to landholders. Political power was often unstable, and during the chaotic 11th century, the Church drew commoners into "Peace of God" movements, which coerced knights and nobles into regional truces.

Major castles
Lords built castles in order to control their local territory.

Cathedrals
Cathedrals were the most ambitious architectural works of their age.

Trade fairs
Huge annual trade fairs attracted merchants from all over Europe.

Universities
During the 12th century, universities formed and supplanted monasteries as centers of learning.

Hanseatic League
The Hansa was an alliance of north German cities formed in 1241 to protect and promote trading interests abroad. Centering on the Baltic, it included over 70 towns in the late 14th century. The Hansa commanded its own army and navy and had outposts in London, Bruges, Novgorod and Bergen.

St. Andrews
Edinburgh
Carrickfergus
Newcastle
Dublin
York
Limerick
Caernarvon
ENGLAND
Lynn
Norwich
Cambridge
Antwerp
Cologne
Bristol
Oxford
London
Canterbury
Bruges
Louvain
Portchester
Lille
Tournai
Liege
Arras
Mainz
Bayeux
Rouen
Reims
Worms
Mont-St.-Michel
Paris
Heidelberg
Angers
Chartres
Provins
Troyes
Strasbourg
Poitiers
Bourges
Vézelay
Besançon
FRANCE
Cluny
Geneva
Bordeaux
Lyon
Santiago de Compostela
Cahors
Milan
NAVARRE
Toulouse
Genoa
Medina del Campo
Foix
Avignon
GENOA
Burgos
Carcassonne
Beaucaire
Marseille
Zaragoza
PORTUGAL
Salamanca
ARAGON
Barcelona
Corsica
Lisbon
Toledo
CASTILE
Valencia
Córdoba
Sardinia
Seville
EMIRATE OF GRANADA
Cadiz
Granada

1000

1066 William of Normandy defeats Harold II of England at Hastings.

1130 The Normans, led by Roger II, establish a Kingdom of Sicily.

1150 The first paper is made in Europe using an Arab technique.

1170 Thomas Becket is murdered in Canterbury Cathedral.

1215 The Magna Carta establishes customary limits to royal power in England.

Ferdinand III of Castile and León captures Córdoba from the Moors.

1241 The Mongols invade Poland, Hungary and Bohemia, reaching Vienna before withdrawing.

1289 The first use of eyeglasses is recorded.

1299 The Ottoman Empire is founded by Osman I.

c. 1300 Gunpowder is manufactured in Europe for the first time.

1307 Dante begins to write *The Divine Comedy*.

1309 Pope Clement V moves the papacy to Avignon, France (until 1377).

1311 Reims cathedral, a masterpiece of Gothic architecture, is completed.

1300

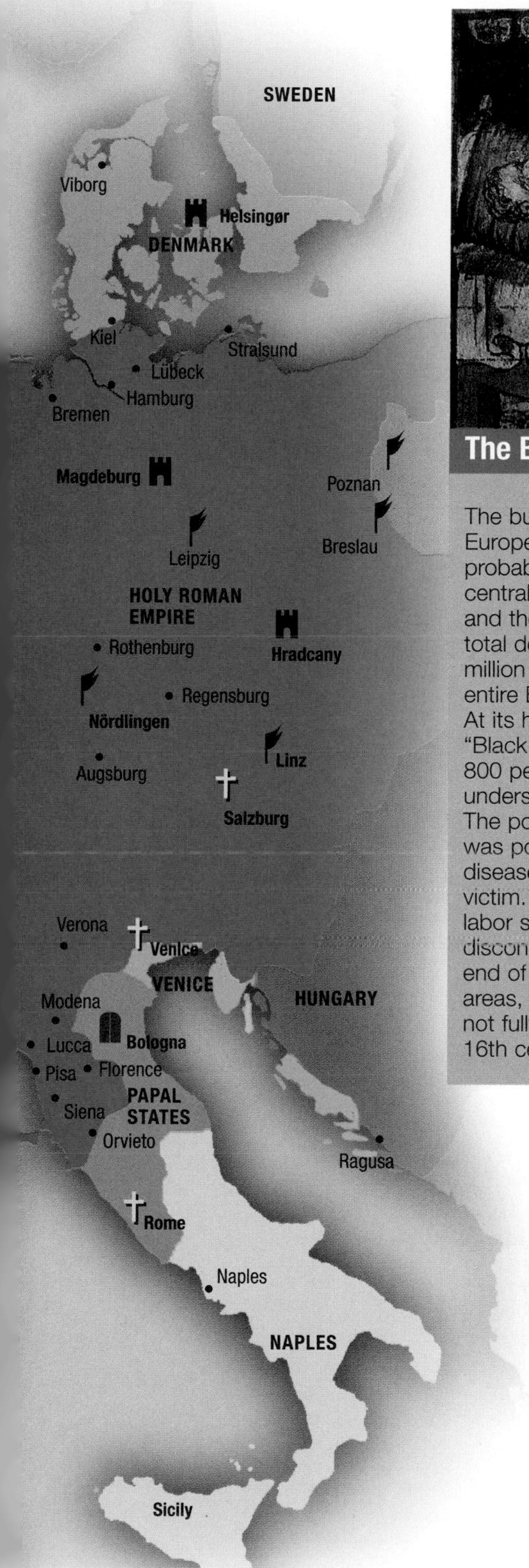

The Black Death

The bubonic plague struck Europe in 1347. It was probably brought from central Asia by black rats and their fleas. By 1351, the total death toll was about 25 million – over a third of the entire European population. At its height in Paris, the "Black Death" claimed about 800 people per day. Medical understanding was limited: The pope's doctor believed it was possible to catch the disease by looking at a victim. The plague caused labor shortages and violent discontent, hastening the end of feudalism. In some areas, population levels did not fully recover until the 16th century.

The Hundred Years' War (1338-1453)

The Hundred Years' War was in fact a series of wars between England and France conducted over 115 years. The main cause was contested territories in France, including Guyenne, Aquitaine, Normandy and Anjou. The war began when Edward III of England asserted a claim to the French throne. The French king retaliated by confiscating Aquitaine, Edward's hereditary fiefdom. English victories followed at **Crécy** (1346) and **Poitiers** (1356), and in 1415, Henry V of England took Normandy after victory at **Agincourt**. Under the Treaty of Troyes (1420), Henry's infant son Henry VI was proclaimed king of France on the death of Charles VI in 1422. **Joan of Arc** persuaded the French heir to claim the crown as Charles VII. Charles's troops gradually evicted English forces from France. The war ended with the French capture of Bordeaux in 1453, leaving Calais as the only English territory in France.

see also

150-51 **Christianity**
152-53 **The rise of Islam**
576 **European leaders**

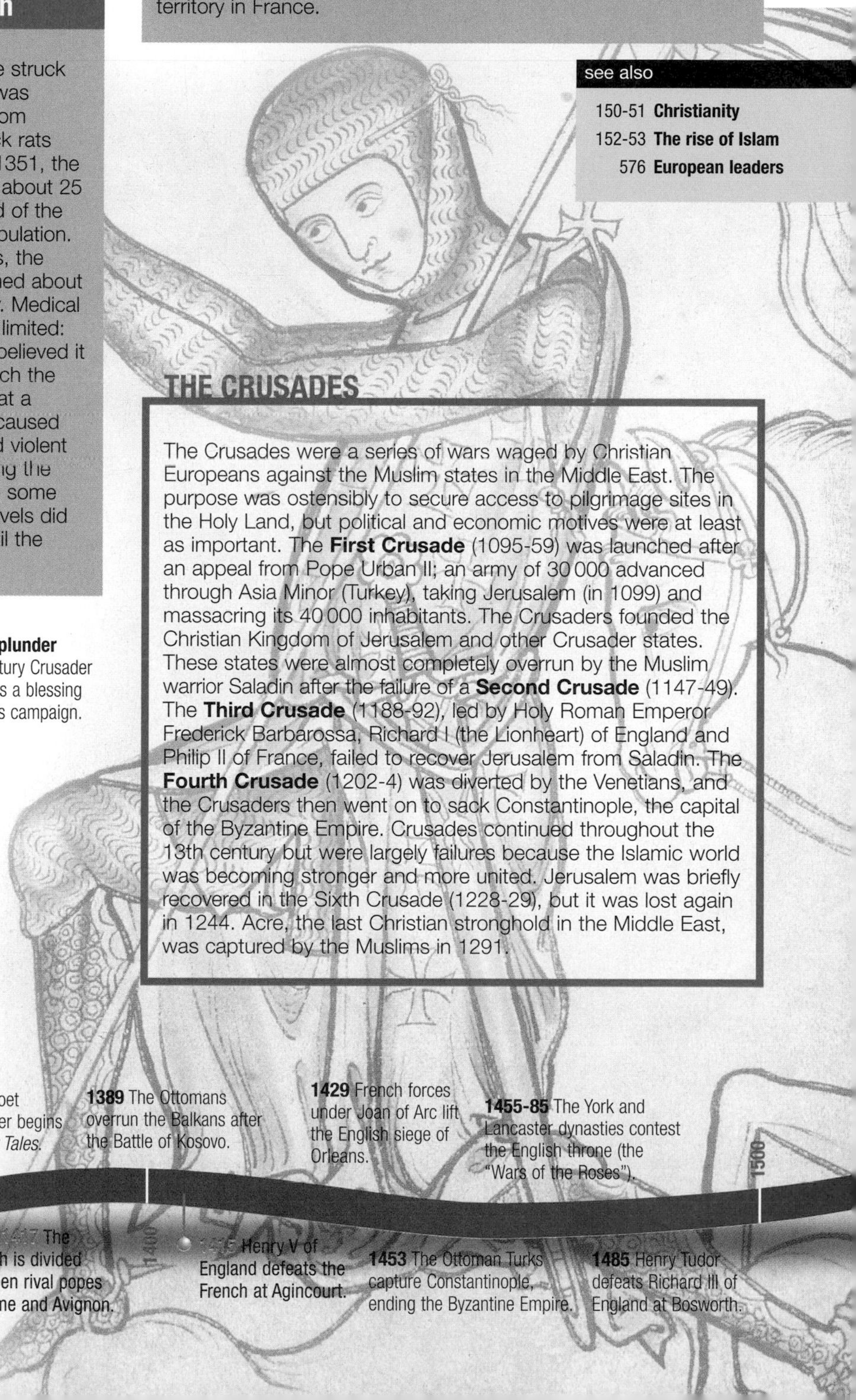

Piety and plunder
A 12th-century Crusader knight seeks a blessing ahead of his campaign.

THE CRUSADES

The Crusades were a series of wars waged by Christian Europeans against the Muslim states in the Middle East. The purpose was ostensibly to secure access to pilgrimage sites in the Holy Land, but political and economic motives were at least as important. The **First Crusade** (1095-59) was launched after an appeal from Pope Urban II; an army of 30 000 advanced through Asia Minor (Turkey), taking Jerusalem (in 1099) and massacring its 40 000 inhabitants. The Crusaders founded the Christian Kingdom of Jerusalem and other Crusader states. These states were almost completely overrun by the Muslim warrior Saladin after the failure of a **Second Crusade** (1147-49). The **Third Crusade** (1188-92), led by Holy Roman Emperor Frederick Barbarossa, Richard I (the Lionheart) of England and Philip II of France, failed to recover Jerusalem from Saladin. The **Fourth Crusade** (1202-4) was diverted by the Venetians, and the Crusaders then went on to sack Constantinople, the capital of the Byzantine Empire. Crusades continued throughout the 13th century but were largely failures because the Islamic world was becoming stronger and more united. Jerusalem was briefly recovered in the Sixth Crusade (1228-29), but it was lost again in 1244. Acre, the last Christian stronghold in the Middle East, was captured by the Muslims in 1291.

1314 Robert Bruce secures Scottish independence by defeating the English at Bannockburn.

1315-19 Famine, floods and a cattle plague devastate much of Western Europe.

1337 Philip VI of France confiscates Guyenne, sparking off the Hundred Years' War.

1348 The Black Death reaches Florence, Paris and London.

1353 English poet Geoffrey Chaucer begins *The Canterbury Tales*.

1378-1417 The Church is divided between rival popes in Rome and Avignon.

1389 The Ottomans overrun the Balkans after the Battle of Kosovo.

1400

1415 Henry V of England defeats the French at Agincourt.

1429 French forces under Joan of Arc lift the English siege of Orleans.

1453 The Ottoman Turks capture Constantinople, ending the Byzantine Empire.

1455-85 The York and Lancaster dynasties contest the English throne (the "Wars of the Roses").

1485 Henry Tudor defeats Richard III of England at Bosworth.

1500

There was a flourishing civilization in the Indus Valley by 2500 B.C. Repeated invasions of India from central Asia brought a succession of empires, influenced at first by Hinduism and Buddhism and then by Islam. The last of these was the Mogul Empire. India's wealth and sophisticated economy continued to attract both trade and military invasion from the east as well as the west – most spectacularly in the form of the British Raj.

The Gupta Empire

The Gupta kings presided over a golden age in which science, philosophy and the arts flourished. Their empire along the Ganges reached its greatest size under **Chandra Gupta II** (reigned 376-401), but it was destroyed at the end of the 5th century by the White Huns.

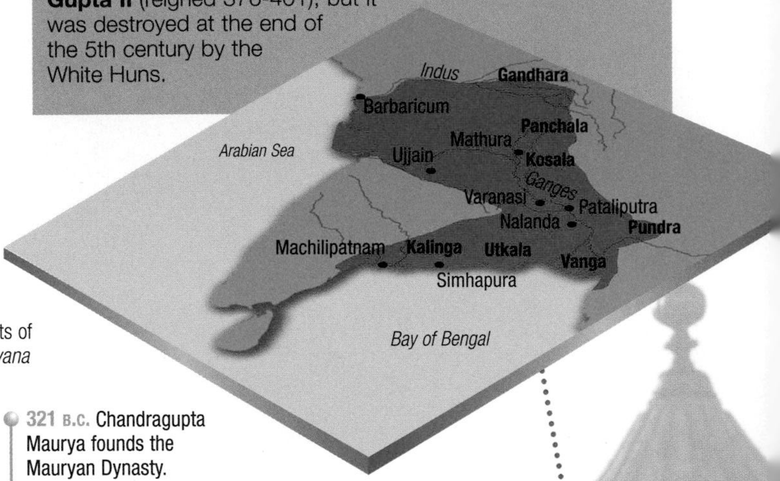

c. 5000 B.C. Farmers in the flood plains of the Indus Valley settle into villages.

c. 2500 B.C. The Indus Valley civilization includes at least five major cities.

c. 1500 B.C. The Indus Valley civilization dies out for unknown reasons.

c. 1500 B.C. Aryans spread from the Indus Valley into the Ganges region and found Hinduism.

563-483 B.C. Siddharta Gautama (the Buddha) lives and teaches in India.

518 B.C. Darius I, king of Persia, conquers the Indus Valley.

c. 500 B.C. Parts of the epic *Ramayana* are written.

500 B.C.

326-325 B.C. Alexander the Great occupies the Indus Valley.

321 B.C. Chandragupta Maurya founds the Mauryan Dynasty.

c. 269-238 B.C. Mauryan control spreads across India under Asoka.

c. 185 B.C. The Mauryans are replaced by the Sunga dynasty.

c. 135-58 B.C. The nomadic Sakas invade northern India.

0

c. A.D. 78-102 The Kushans occupy the Indus Valley and Punjab.

c. 200 The epics *Ramayana* and *Mahabharata* take on their final form.

319 Chandragupta I founds the Gupta Empire on the Ganges.

The Mauryan Empire

The first great empire of the Indian subcontinent developed after the withdrawal of Alexander the Great's armies from the Indus Valley in 325 B.C. Named after **Chandragupta Maurya** (reigned c. 321-297 B.C.), the Mauryan Empire extended across northern India and included modern Pakistan and Afghanistan. It reached its greatest extent and cultural peak under King **Asoka** (reigned c. 269-238 B.C.). Asoka's first experience of military conquest so horrified him that around 263 B.C., he converted to Buddhism and renounced war. He developed a system of government based on Buddhist principles: Rulers were to be responsible for the people's welfare and to behave with respect, tolerance, honesty and compassion – precepts he had inscribed in stone. The empire fragmented after Asoka's death. The last Mauryan emperor was killed in 185 B.C. and replaced by the Hindu Sunga dynasty.

Bodhi tree Buddhist motifs from a shrine of Asoka.

TOP TEMPLES

- **Ajanta caves** The 29 Ajanta caves in northern Maharashtra were carved from solid rock between the 1st century B.C. and the 7th century A.D. They were dwellings and shrines for Buddhist monks and were decorated with fresco paintings and carvings.
- **Khajuraho** The site of 50 Hindu and Jain temples dating mainly from A.D. 950 to 1050, Khajuraho is near Kanpur, in north–central India. The 22 surviving temples are famed for their erotic sculpture.
- **Mahabalipuram** A Hindu religious complex south of Madras, Mahabalipuram was built under the Pallava dynasty in the 7th century A.D. The site includes the remains of the "Seven Pagodas" made of single huge blocks of stone.
- **Taj Mahal** The great masterpiece of Mogul architecture, the Taj Mahal, was built on the River Jumna at Agra in 1632-48. It commemorates the wife of emperor Shah Jahan, Mumtaz-i-Mahal, who died in childbirth in 1629. Designed by a Turkish architect, it is built of white marble and semiprecious stones.

The Cholas and Southeast Asia

Indian influence spread well beyond the subcontinent. Hinduism and Buddhism permeated Southeast Asia from India in the 2nd and 3rd centuries A.D. The Buddhist temple of Borobudur, Java, was built by the Sailendra Empire (c. 750-850), and the Hindu-Buddhist Khmers dominated mainland Southeast Asia from about 900 to 1431. The Cholas, a sea-going Tamil civilization (Tamils are an ethnically distinct south Indian Hindu population), spread Indian influence in a series of expeditions in the 10th and 11th centuries. **Rajaraja I** (reigned A.D. 985-1016) conquered Kerala and northern Ceylon (Sri Lanka); his son **Rajendra** (reigned 1016-44) took Malacca and the Malay Peninsula.

Siva as Lord of the Dance
A Chola bronze from Tamil Nadu in southern India.

c. 335-76 Samudra extends the Gupta Empire to the Indus Valley.

c. 350 The erotic classic *Kamasutra* is written.

c. 480 The White Huns destroy the Gupta Empire.

500

c. 711 Muslim forces from Iraq enter north India.

1000

1081 The Cholas conquer Ceylon (Sri Lanka).

1186 The Ghaznavids lose Lahore to the Afghan Ghurids.

1206 The Muslim Sultanate of Delhi is founded (to 1526).

c. 1321 The Sultanate of Delhi expands to southern India.

1398 The Sultanate of Delhi is crushed by Tamerlane.

1500

1498 Portuguese navigator Vasco da Gama reaches India.

1526 Babur defeats the Sultanate of Delhi at Panipat, founding the Mogul Empire.

1565 The Moguls defeat the Vijayanagar empire of southeast India.

1632 Shah Jahan begins construction of the Taj Mahal.

1700 The British East India Company controls many Indian trading ports.

1746-61 Britain and France compete for control of India.

1803 The Mogul capital Delhi falls to the British East India Company.

1857 The last Mogul emperor is exiled by the British.

The Mogul Empire

Mogul miniature
Shah Jahan with one of his sons, painted in 1615 by Manohar.

The Moguls were a Muslim dynasty of mixed Turkish and Mongol descent founded by the Timurid conqueror **Babur** "the Tiger" (1483-1530). Babur captured Delhi in 1526, and his forces overran most of northern India. The golden age of the Mogul Empire (see map) was under **Akbar** (reigned 1556-1605), whose enlightened court at Fatehpur Sikri promoted religious tolerance and oversaw the greatest achievements of Mogul art and architecture, **Jehangir** (reigned 1605-27) and **Shah Jahan** (1628-58). **Aurangzeb** (1659-1707) extended the empire almost to the southern tip of India, persecuting Sikhs and Hindus and causing widespread internal friction. Religious strife and court rivalries after his reign left the empire vulnerable to British and French aggression. The empire was kept alive in name only by the British until 1857.

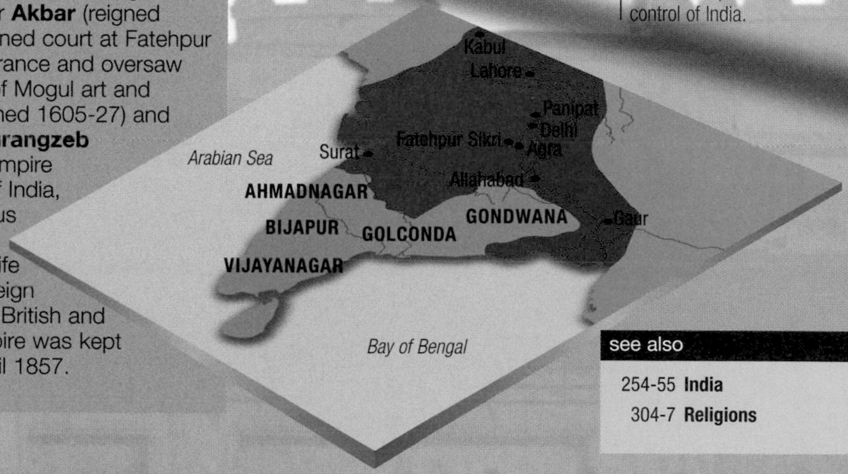

see also
254-55 **India**
304-7 **Religions**

China and Japan

For much of world history, China was the richest and most powerful nation on earth. Until the 19th century, it remained almost entirely self-sufficient, amassing huge national wealth by exporting silk, spices and later porcelain. Japan remained culturally in the shadow of its powerful neighbor for many centuries but was equally insular and self-reliant.

China's ruling dynasties

Political power in China was held by a succession of major dynasties; central control of such a huge nation was possible only because the vast, sophisticated and largely meritocratic Chinese civil service was maintained throughout changes of rule. The chaos that swept China in the "Three Kingdoms" and the "Five Dynasties and Ten Kingdoms" periods emphasized the value of this continuity.

Qin (Ch'in) 221-206 B.C. The Ch'in gave their name to China. Qin Shi Huangdi, the "First Emperor" (reigned 221-210 B.C.), created a strong centralized state with a standardized written language and built much of the Great Wall.

Images of life and afterlife (Above) Life size terracotta warriors, each face unique, from the tomb of emperor Qin Shi Huangdi, c. 210 B.C. (Below) An earthenware tomb guardian figure from the Tang dynasty, A.D. 618-907.

Shang c. 1600-1050 B.C. The Shang rulers controlled most of northern China. Their achievements included writing, a calendar, social classes, bureaucracy, cast bronze, jade carving and pottery.

Zhou c. 1000-256 B.C. The Zhou presided over China's "Classical Age," the era of Confucius (c. 551-479 B.C.), Lao-Zi (c. 604-531 B.C.), iron and the ox-drawn plow.

Han 206 B.C.-A.D. 220 The Han maintained a strong centralized government run on Confucian principles of moderation. They oversaw a period of prosperity and cultural flowering, trading silk with the Roman Empire via the "Silk Route."

Tang A.D. 618-907 The Tang gained control of China from the Sui dynasty, after nearly 400 years of turmoil during the "Three Kingdoms" period. Stability and a cosmopolitan culture stimulated trade, printing developed, and Buddhism spread; poetry hit a golden age around A.D. 70.

China / Japan — 5000 B.C. · 1000 B.C. · 250 B.C. · 0 · 250 · 1000

c. 6000 B.C. Pottery and domesticated animals and plants first appear in China.

c. 551-479 B.C. Life of Confucius.

c. 353 B.C. Work begins on the Great Wall.

c. A.D. 50 Buddhism reaches China.

220-80 The "Three Kingdoms" period of turmoil ends Han rule.

304 The Huns (Xiongnu) invade China.

850-900 Peasant revolts bring local warlord rule to most of China.

979 The Song Dynasty reunites China.

c. 5000-250 B.C. The Neolithic Jomon culture produces pottery and jewelry in Japan.

660 B.C. According to legend, the nation of Japan is founded.

250 B.C.-A.D. 250 Japanese Yayoi culture produces iron and bronze, textiles and rice cultivation.

405 The Yamato court at Nara unifies Japan.

c. 550 Buddhism is introduced to Japan.

900-1100 A purely Japanese culture, script and language emerge.

Japan's turbulent history

The first recognizable states in Japan began to emerge around A.D. 300 within the **Yayoi** culture. Attempts to create a unified and centralized state, however, began in the **Yamato** period (A.D. 300-710). The court was moved from Nara to **Heian** (Kyoto) in 794 to escape growing Buddhist influence over the shogun (emperor). The Heian period, dominated by the powerful **Fujiwara** family, lasted until 1185. The decline of central authority at the end of the period allowed the rise of **feudalism**.

The **Kamakura** shoguns (1185-1333) were effectively dominated by the Minamoto and Hojo families, and Japan repelled two Mongol invasions (1274 and 1281). From 1336 to 1568, Japan was ruled by the **Ashikaga** (or Muromachi) shoguns but suffered from political instability, peasant unrest and civil war, exacerbated by militant "Pure Land" Buddhist monks. From 1467 to 1477, this instability resulted in the **Onin War**, and the century-long Warring States period.

Reunification was effected by **Oda Nobunaga**, **Hideyoshi Toyotomi** and **Tokugawa Ieyasu** between 1568 and 1600. The resulting Tokugawa Shogunate lasted until 1868. Political conservatism was matched by growing **isolationism**, with European traders excluded and Japanese Christians persecuted. Japan's antiforeign policy was finally dropped in the **Meiji** period (1868-1912).

Tea ceremony Ritual taking of tea – thought to have medicinal properties – came to Japan from China in the 13th century.

FACT The indigenous religion of Japan, Shinto, goes back to prehistoric times. It has no founder or sacred text, but many modern Japanese still worship at Shinto shrines.

Artistic achievements in China

Jade Green, white, gray – even blue, red and yellow – jade was imported into China in prehistoric times, mainly from central Asia. It was carved into fine jewelry and ornaments – much sought after because the stone was thought to have powers of healing or even of conferring immortality.

Lacquerware The hard, black resin of the rhus lacquer tree was used for decoration before 400 B.C. Layers of lacquer were applied to a base and then incised and carved to create elaborate scenes and designs. Boxes, dishes, food containers and even whole thrones were lacquered.

Metalwork Cast bronze dates back to c. 2000 B.C. and was often in the form of large ritual vessels used for offerings of food and wine in sacrificial ceremonies.

Painting Exquisite brush and ink painting developed in the Tang period, far outstripping Western art in observation, technique and delicacy. Landscape painting was fully established by the 900s.

Pottery Neolithic earthenware pots show flair for design and very early use of the wheel. Fine modeling is seen, for example, in ceramic horses of the Tang period, decorated with characteristic three-color glaze.

CHINESE FIRSTS

Abacus The abacus was used in China around 500 B.C.

Cast iron The Chinese developed cast iron around 600 B.C.

Gunpowder Explosives were used in fireworks and signals in the Tang period and in weapons during the Song.

Magnetic compass The magnetized needle was first used by Chinese navigators around A.D. 1000.

Paper China produced the world's first paper c. A.D. 105.

Porcelain Hard, fine, white pottery was made in China from about 50 B.C.

Printing The Chinese pioneered printing methods from the 2nd century A.D. Woodblock printing was introduced in the 6th century.

Silk Legend says that silk-weaving began in 2640 B.C.

Song (Sung) 960-1279 The Song oversaw a period of cultural achievement and growing prosperity through expanding trade. Paper currency was developed and widely used; printing helped to spread literacy; and painting, sculpture and philosophy all made important advances.

Yuan (Mongols) 1280-1368 Genghis Khan (c. 1167-1227) united Mongolia, seizing Beijing in 1215 and destroying the Ch'in Empire in north China by 1234. His successor, Kublai Khan, overran the surviving Southern Song Empire in 1268-79 and founded the Yuan dynasty with a capital at Beijing. Popular uprisings drove out the Yuan in 1335-68.

Ming 1368-1644 The Ming dynasty was established by the rebel Zhu Yuanzhang, who reconquered Mongol China in 1368-88. Chinese rule was extended to Korea, Mongolia, Turkistan, Vietnam and Burma. China remained at peace for most of the 15th and 16th centuries.

Ming artistry Flower-motif vase, 16th century.

Qing (Manchu) 1644-1912 The Manchus gained control of China in 1616-52 and created the largest of all Chinese empires. China resisted European influence until the 19th century, when Manchu power began to decline. The last emperor, six-year-old Pu Yi, abdicated in 1912.

1126 Jurzhen tribes invade northern China and establish the Ch'in Empire.

1211 The Mongols overrun the Ch'in Empire.

1275 Marco Polo reaches Beijing.

1300

1405-33 Admiral Zheng He sails to India, the Persian Gulf and East Africa.

1514 The first Portuguese traders reach China.

1500

1542-50 Ming forces defeat two Mongol invasions.

1644 The Manchus (Qing) overthrow the Ming dynasty.

c. 1800 Britain begins to export Indian opium to China.

1899-1901 The anti-Western Boxer Rebellion is defeated.

1912 The Qing are overthrown and a republic is declared.

1900

c. 1100 The *daimyo* (feudal barons) rise to power in Japan.

1274 and 1281 Mongol invasions of Japan are prevented by typhoons.

1467-77 The Onin War ushers in the "Warring States" period in Japan.

1542 The first European traders arrive in Japan.

1582 Hideyoshi Toyotomi begins to unify Japan.

1639 Japan adopts isolationist policies toward the West.

1853 Japan is forced to open its ports to trade.

1905 Japan becomes the dominant power in East Asia.

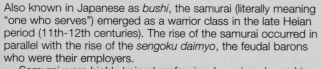

Samurai

Also known in Japanese as *bushi*, the samurai (literally meaning "one who serves") emerged as a warrior class in the late Heian period (11th-12th centuries). The rise of the samurai occurred in parallel with the rise of the *sengoku daimyo*, the feudal barons who were their employers.

Samurai were highly trained professional warriors, bound to their lords by a strict code of loyalty, in much the same way as medieval European knights. For 700 years, samurai dominated Japan as a military elite; their monopoly only came to an end with the creation of a modern imperial army in the 19th century.

see also

258-59 **China**
298-99 **Writing**
304-7 **Religions**
481 **American and world leaders**

The vast scale and natural wealth of Africa are matched by a diversity and richness of culture. From the 1000-year Kingdom of Meroë in southern Egypt to the fabulous wealth of the West African Gold Coast to the mysterious builders of great Zimbabwe, African peoples traded, worshipped and built empires across a vast continent. Arabs arrived in the 7th century, and Europeans in the 15th – first in search of trade and then as settlers, farmers, and adventurers drawn by tales of minerals, gems and gold.

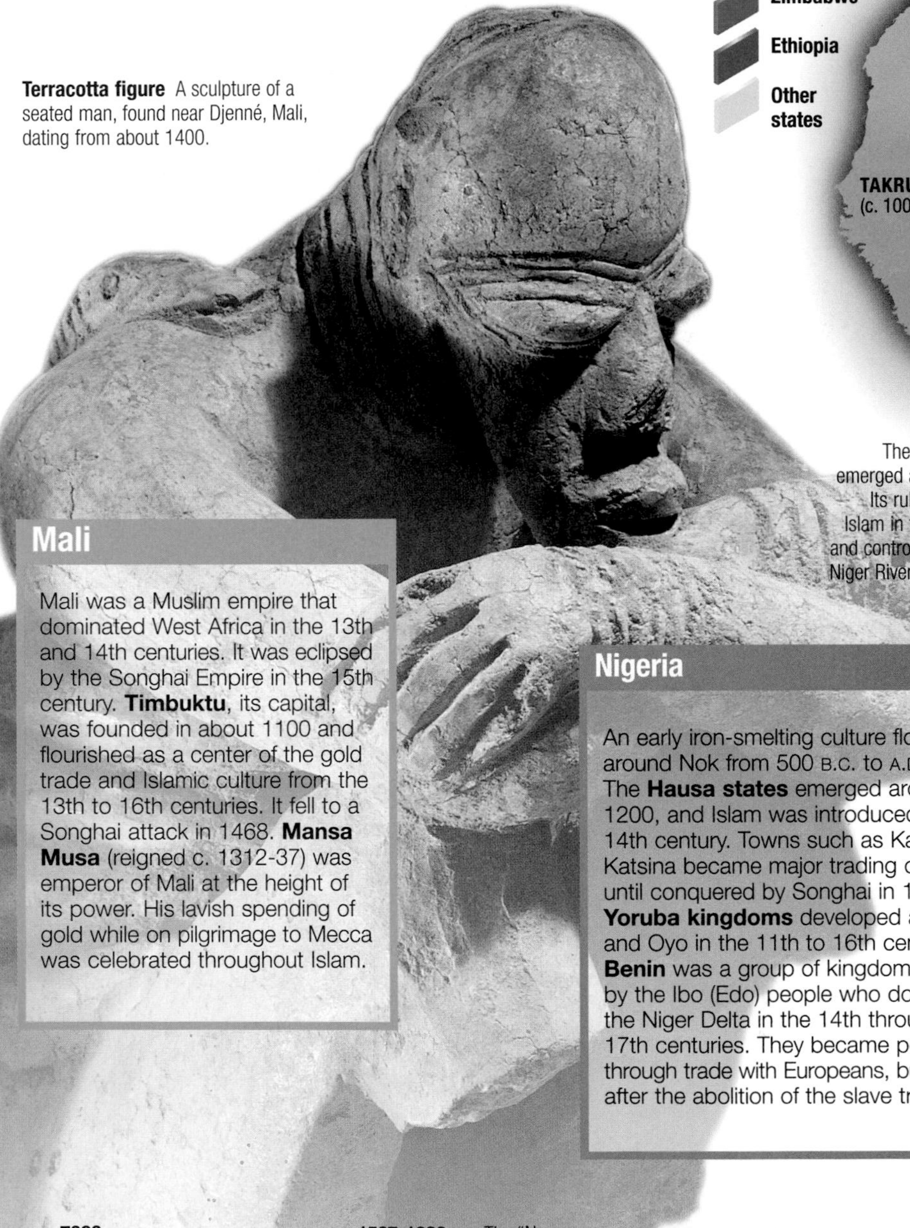

Terracotta figure A sculpture of a seated man, found near Djenné, Mali, dating from about 1400.

African empires

Precolonial Africa saw the rise and fall of a number of states, whose homelands are shown here. Their power was largely based on trade.

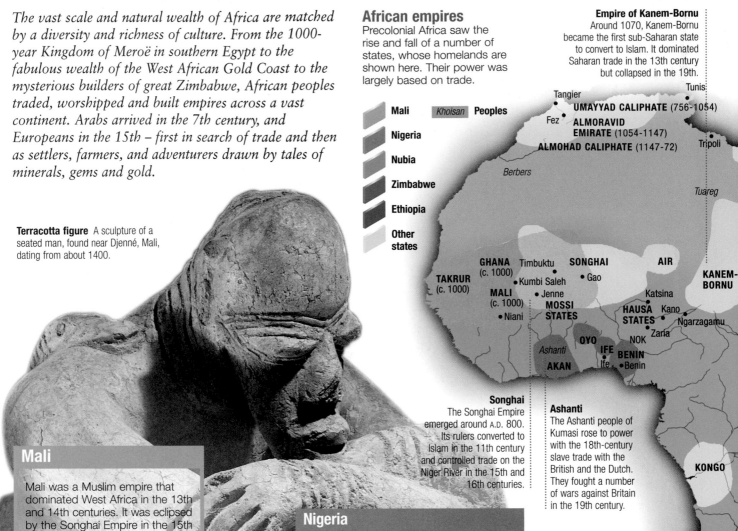

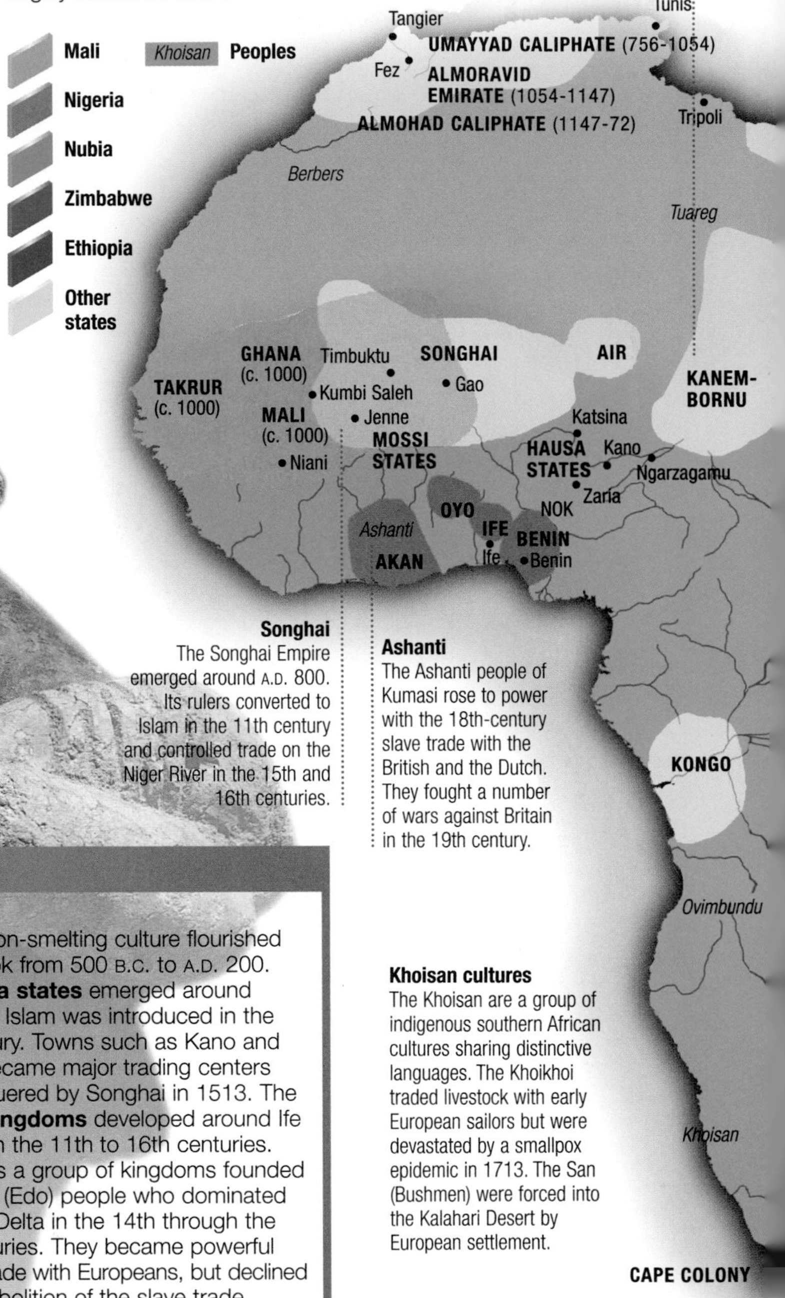

Empire of Kanem-Bornu
Around 1070, Kanem-Bornu became the first sub-Saharan state to convert to Islam. It dominated Saharan trade in the 13th century but collapsed in the 19th.

Songhai
The Songhai Empire emerged around A.D. 800. Its rulers converted to Islam in the 11th century and controlled trade on the Niger River in the 15th and 16th centuries.

Ashanti
The Ashanti people of Kumasi rose to power with the 18th-century slave trade with the British and the Dutch. They fought a number of wars against Britain in the 19th century.

Khoisan cultures
The Khoisan are a group of indigenous southern African cultures sharing distinctive languages. The Khoikhoi traded livestock with early European sailors but were devastated by a smallpox epidemic in 1713. The San (Bushmen) were forced into the Kalahari Desert by European settlement.

Mali

Mali was a Muslim empire that dominated West Africa in the 13th and 14th centuries. It was eclipsed by the Songhai Empire in the 15th century. **Timbuktu**, its capital, was founded in about 1100 and flourished as a center of the gold trade and Islamic culture from the 13th to 16th centuries. It fell to a Songhai attack in 1468. **Mansa Musa** (reigned c. 1312-37) was emperor of Mali at the height of its power. His lavish spending of gold while on pilgrimage to Mecca was celebrated throughout Islam.

Nigeria

An early iron-smelting culture flourished around Nok from 500 B.C. to A.D. 200. The **Hausa states** emerged around 1200, and Islam was introduced in the 14th century. Towns such as Kano and Katsina became major trading centers until conquered by Songhai in 1513. The **Yoruba kingdoms** developed around Ife and Oyo in the 11th to 16th centuries. **Benin** was a group of kingdoms founded by the Ibo (Edo) people who dominated the Niger Delta in the 14th through the 17th centuries. They became powerful through trade with Europeans, but declined after the abolition of the slave trade.

7000 B.C.

c. 7000 B.C. Pastoral farmers inhabit Libya and Algeria.

c. 5000 B.C. Cattle herders occupy the fertile Sahara.

c. 3100 B.C. Egypt is first unified by King Menes.

c. 2584-2465 B.C. The pyramids are built at Giza.

1567-1320 B.C. The "New Kingdom" reigns in Egypt; Napata (Nubia) becomes a major center.

1000 B.C.

590 B.C. The Egyptians sack Napata; Meroë becomes the Nubian capital.

c. 500 B.C.-A.D. 200 The Nok civilization develops in Nigeria.

146 B.C. The Roman province of Africa is established.

0

A.D. 300-400 The kingdom of Axum reaches its height.

c. A.D. 400 The first towns develop in sub-Saharan Africa.

c. 500 Bantu farmers and herders reach South Africa.

642 The Arabs conquer Egypt.

c. 700 Empire of ancient Ghana emerges.

Nubia

Nubia was known as **Kush** to the ancient Egyptians. King Piye of Kush conquered the entire Nile Valley around 732 B.C., founding Egypt's 25th dynasty. The Kingdom of **Meroë** emerged in the 6th century B.C. and survived for almost 1000 years, developing a culture and religion that combined local and Egyptian elements. Nubia became Christian c. A.D. 540, but the north was conquered by Egypt in 652 and the south became part of the Islamic Funj kingdom of Sudan in the 16th century.

Buganda A major trader in slaves and ivory, Buganda became a British protectorate in 1900.

Mythical eagle A carving from Great Zimbabwe (c. A.D. 1200-1400) thought to represent a messenger of the gods.

Ethiopia

Known to ancient Egyptians as **Punt**, Ethiopia was home to the powerful kingdom of **Axum** from the 2nd to 8th centuries A.D. It was the first African kingdom to adopt Christianity (in 321), and became a great stronghold of the Coptic Church – but was isolated by neighboring hostile Islamic states for about 300 years, from 702 on. The **Solomonid** dynasty came to power in 1270. In the 16th century, the reduced kingdom enlisted Portuguese help against Muslim attacks. The last Solomonid emperor, Hailie Selassie, died in 1975.

Ethiopian illumination Christ between Heaven, Hell and the world, from a 10th-century Ethiopian manuscript.

East African Trading States

Traders from Arabia visited East Africa as early as the 8th century A.D. They created coastal settlements such as **Malindi**, **Mombasa** and **Kilwa**, which attracted Arab and Persian migrants starting in the 12th century and became wealthy and independent Islamic city–states. These states traded tools and weapons, textiles, Indian glass beads, Islamic pottery and Chinese porcelain for African ivory, ambergris (for perfumes), tortoiseshell and gold. In 1498, the Portuguese arrived and forced the city–states to pay tribute; they imposed colonial rule after Ottoman attacks in the late 16th century. The **Sultanate of Oman** ousted the Portuguese in the 17th century and took control of much of the coast, overseeing an escalation in the slave trade after 1780. Britain and Germany took colonial control of most of East Africa from the 1880s.

Zimbabwe

Southeastern Africa was occupied by Bantu-speaking farmers in the 5th to 10th centuries A.D. They exported gold and copper to Arab traders on the coast after about 900. The Shona kingdom of the Mwene Mutapa rose to form an empire based on **Great Zimbabwe**, a walled palace complex that flourished from about 1250 to 1450. By the late 15th century, the palace complex was in decline (perhaps because of a shift in the gold trade), but the Mwene Mutapa Empire extended over much of southeastern Africa. Its decline was triggered by Portuguese incursions in the 17th century.

see also

152-53 **The rise of Islam**
178-79 **New nations**
188-89 **End of empire**
272-91 **Africa**

- **c. 700-1000** Islam spreads through northwest Africa.
- **c. 850** Kanem-Bornu develops as a major trading empire.
- **900** Arab merchants settle in East Africa.
- 1000
- **c. 1250** The Mali Empire reaches its height.
- **c. 1300** The empire of Benin develops.
- **c. 1400** Great Zimbabwe is completed.
- **1488** Bartolomeu Dias rounds the Cape of Good Hope.
- 1500
- **c. 1500** The European trade in African slaves begins.
- **1505** The Portuguese sack Kilwa.
- **1546** Songhai destroys the Mali Empire.
- **1652** The Dutch found a colony at the Cape.
- **1698** Omani Arabs evict the Portuguese from East Africa.
- **c. 1700** Ashanti power rises on the Gold Coast (to 1901).
- **1835-39** The Boers trek north from Britain's Cape Colony.
- **1875-1914** European nations divide the continent in the "Scramble for Africa."
- 1900

Ancient America

From the first farmers to the arrival of the Europeans

The people of ancient America developed distinctive civilizations in almost total isolation from the rest of the world. In Mexico, Central America and the Andes, farming peoples created complex urban societies centered on religious cults. Their cultures spread to the hunting and farming societies of North America. All of these cultures were destroyed after the arrival of Europeans in 1492.

Olmecs

The first American civilization emerged around 1200 B.C. on the shores of eastern Mexico. Olmec cities centered on temple platforms and pyramid mounds. Sculptors worked in jade, obsidian, serpentine and – on a monumental scale – basalt. Trading and political influence extended throughout Central America, and Olmec culture formed the basis of most later civilizations of the region: The Aztecs, for instance, adopted Olmec gods. By 400 B.C., the culture had disappeared and the cities were destroyed and abandoned.

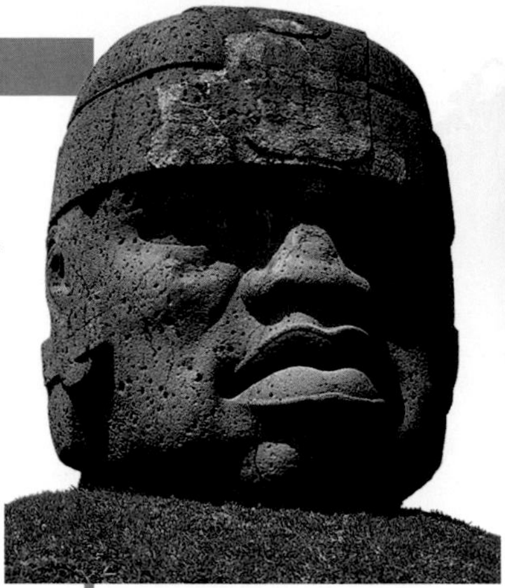

Basalt head The Olmecs made massive stone heads, perhaps of gods, weighing up to 20 metric tons.

Aztecs

The Aztec Empire was founded by the Mexica people in about 1325. They established a capital at **Tenochtitlán** on Lake Texcoco (Mexico City was later built over the site). The Aztecs conquered much of Central America, enforcing huge tribute payments that included human sacrifice. Hernán Cortés reached Tenochtitlán in 1519, and Aztec power was destroyed within 20 years by the conquistadores, supported by rebel subject peoples of the empire.

Tenochtitlán The temple was the center of Aztec life; religious ritual shaped every aspect of existence.

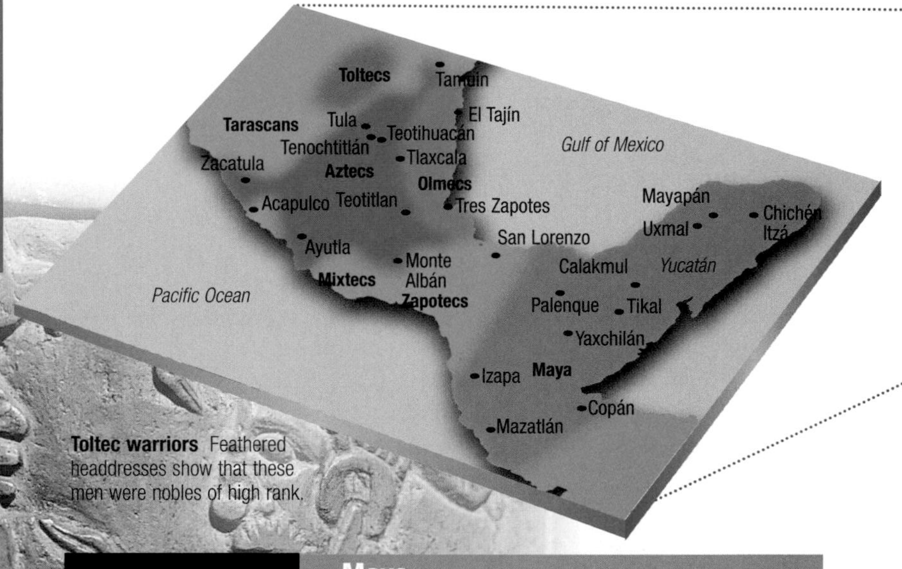

Toltec warriors Feathered headdresses show that these men were nobles of high rank.

Toltecs

Toltec invaders from the north created an empire based around **Tula** (Tollán) across much of Central America after about A.D. 900. The former Maya lands of the Yucatán became the center of a combined Toltec–Maya culture, including the cities **Chichén Itzá** (with its Temple of the Warriors and Castillo pyramid) and **Mayapán**. Toltec influence declined in central Mexico after 1200; the highland regions were taken over by the Mixtecs.

Mayan skill A late-period incense burner.

Maya

Early Mayan culture dates from about 2600 B.C. From around 200 B.C., a temple-based society was organized into city–states (such as **Tikal**). The Maya developed hieroglyphic writing and had an advanced astronomical calendar. Political and trading links were forged with cities of south and central Mexico, and an empire with wide influence was established. The civilization collapsed in about A.D. 750-900 for unknown reasons. "Post-Classic" Maya culture was revived in Yucatán with Toltec support after A.D. 1200 but slid into civil war within 300 years.

5000 B.C.

- **c. 5000 B.C.** Corn farming begins in the highlands of Central America.
- **c. 2500 B.C.** The early Inuit (Eskimo) peoples spread along the ice-bound coasts of North America.
- **c. 1200 B.C.** Olmec culture emerges on the Gulf Coast of Mexico (until c. 400 B.C.).

1000 B.C.

- **c. 900 B.C.** Chavín culture emerges in Peru (until c. 400 B.C.).
- **c. 700 B.C.** The Adena people of the eastern woodlands of North America begin building mounds.
- **c. 100 B.C.** The Hopewell culture replaces the Adena in eastern North America.

0

- **c. A.D. 100** The Moche culture rises in coastal Peru (until c. A.D. 600).
- **c. A.D. 150** Teotihuacán, Mexico, becomes Central America's first true city.
- **c. 400-800** The bow and arrow begin to replace spears in North America.
- **c. 650** Teotihuacán declines for unknown reasons and falls into ruin.
- **c. 750-900** The Maya "Classic" culture collapses; its cities are abandoned.
- **c. 900** The Anasazi of southwest North America develop the first Pueblo settlements.

American empires

The pre-Conquest Americas were home to a range of cultures, including the Aztecs of Mexico and the Incas of Peru.

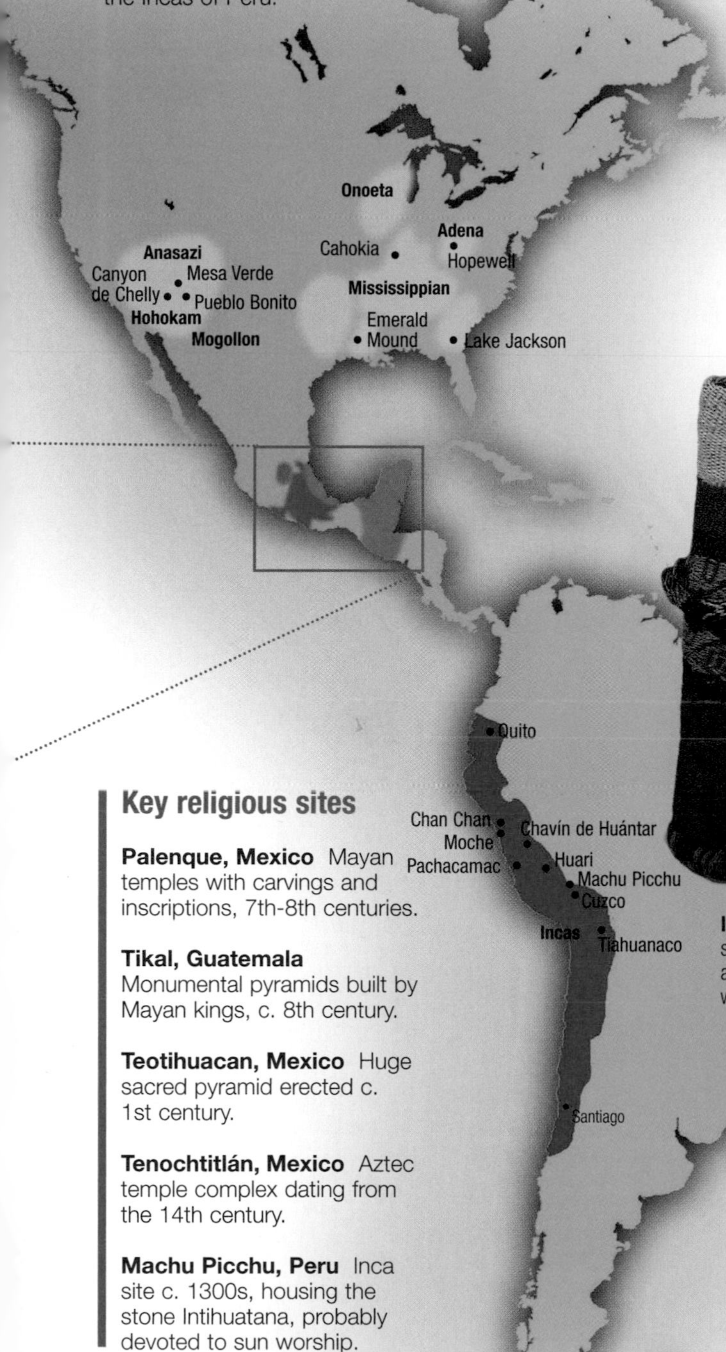

Key religious sites

Palenque, Mexico Mayan temples with carvings and inscriptions, 7th-8th centuries.

Tikal, Guatemala Monumental pyramids built by Mayan kings, c. 8th century.

Teotihuacan, Mexico Huge sacred pyramid erected c. 1st century.

Tenochtitlán, Mexico Aztec temple complex dating from the 14th century.

Machu Picchu, Peru Inca site c. 1300s, housing the stone Intihuatana, probably devoted to sun worship.

North America

Few North American cultures were urban, so little remains of key sites apart from earthworks. The **Adena** and **Hopewell** peoples dominated the Midwest for over 1000 years, from 700 B.C. on, building extensive ritual and burial mounds such as Serpent Mound, Ohio. The **Mississippians** succeeded the Hopewell around A.D. 600, farming corn and beans in the Mississippi valley; the city of Cahokia had a population of 30 000 by A.D. 1050, and they developed the bow and arrow as weapons. The **Anasazi** and **Pueblo** corn-growing cultures emerged in the southwest after A.D. 600, building their distinctive villages of adobe and stone. European settlers destroyed all the native cultures by A.D. 1900.

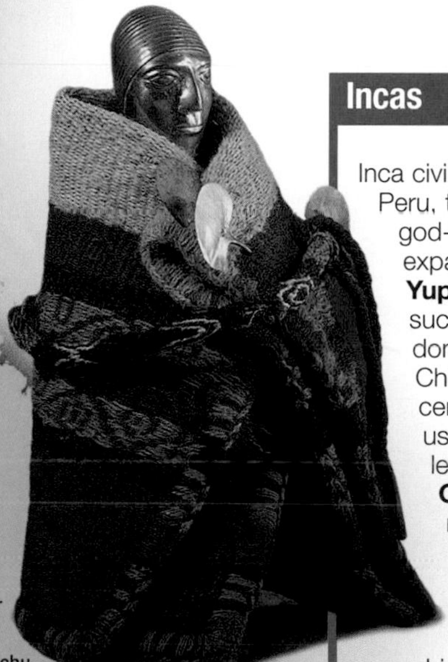

Inca figurine A gold statuette representing a concubine, buried with an Inca emperor.

Incas

Inca civilization emerged in 13th-14th century Peru, tracing its origins to the semilegendary god-king ("Inca") **Manco Capac**. A series of expansionist campaigns by **Pachacuti Inca Yupanqui** (reigned 1438-71) and his successors created an empire that dominated the Andes from Equador to Chile. The Incas developed a strong, centralized administration and imposed the use of their language. A network of roads led to the religious and political capital, **Cuzco**, the "Navel [of the World]," whose massive walls of polygonal cut stone were assembled without mortar. The spectacular **Machu Picchu** was a town and ceremonial center high in the Andes. Inca religion was based on worship of the Sun, and past Inca rulers claimed to be descended from the Sun. The Inca Empire was made vulnerable by a succession dispute after the death of Huayna Capac in 1525. It disintegrated with the invasion of a small force of Spanish conquistadores led by **Francisco Pizarro** in 1532-33. Pizarro executed the Inca claimant **Atahualpa** after helping him depose his half-brother Huáscar. The last Inca dynasty died out in 1572 with the beheading of **Tupac Amaru** by the Spanish at Cuzco.

see also
164-65 **The age of exploration**
196-215 **The Americas**
302-3 **World mythology**

FACT The Aztecs counted using their toes as well as their fingers. As a result, their number system had 20 as its base.

c. 950 The Toltecs emerge as a major military power in Central America.

c. 1000 The Vikings set up a short-lived colony at L'Anse aux Meadows, Newfoundland.

c. 1050 The mound city of Cahokia flourishes in Illinois.

c. 1200 Toltec culture collapses and is replaced by the Mixtecs. The world's largest pyramid is built at Cholula.

c. 1325 Tenochtitlán, capital of the Aztec empire, is founded.

1472 The Inca Empire reaches its zenith in Peru.

1492 Christopher Columbus, in search of Asia, lands in the Bahamas.

1519 Hernán Cortés lands in Mexico. In 1521, he captures Tenochtitlán after a 93-day siege.

1531-33 Francisco Pizarro vanquishes the Incas. Spain rules Peru.

1607 The first permanent European settlement in North America is set up at Jamestown, Virginia.

1625 The native population of Central America falls to 1.25 million, one tenth of the figure for 1500.

1700 The number of European settlers in North America exceeds 250 000.

1890 The massacre of the Sioux at Wounded Knee, South Dakota, marks the final subjugation of the native peoples of the Americas.

1000 | 1500 | 1900

In the 15th century, improvements in shipping and a demand for Far Eastern silks and spices led European navigators to explore new waters. The Portuguese worked around Africa to India and beyond, and Columbus crossed the Atlantic. The whole world was now open to European exploration, trade and settlement.

The great voyages Over a period of 300 years, from Columbus in 1492 to Cook in 1768, European maritime explorers opened up the entire world. Trade empires and then European colonists followed in their wake.

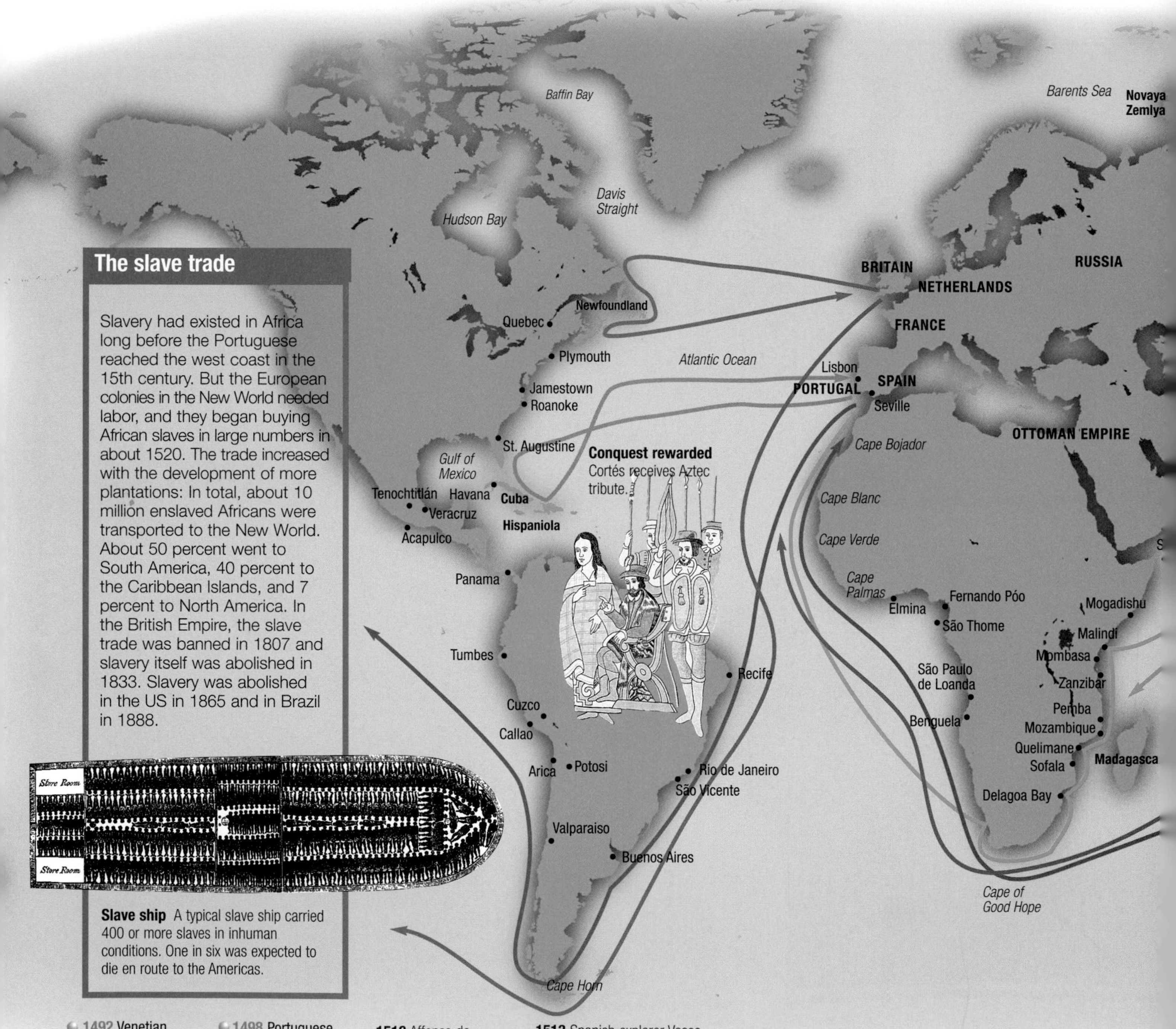

Conquest rewarded Cortés receives Aztec tribute.

The slave trade

Slavery had existed in Africa long before the Portuguese reached the west coast in the 15th century. But the European colonies in the New World needed labor, and they began buying African slaves in large numbers in about 1520. The trade increased with the development of more plantations: In total, about 10 million enslaved Africans were transported to the New World. About 50 percent went to South America, 40 percent to the Caribbean Islands, and 7 percent to North America. In the British Empire, the slave trade was banned in 1807 and slavery itself was abolished in 1833. Slavery was abolished in the US in 1865 and in Brazil in 1888.

Slave ship A typical slave ship carried 400 or more slaves in inhuman conditions. One in six was expected to die en route to the Americas.

1492 Venetian navigator Christopher Columbus, leading a Spanish expedition, lands in the Bahamas.

1497 Genoese navigator John Cabot, leading an English expedition, reaches Newfoundland.

1498 Portuguese navigator Vasco da Gama reaches India by sailing around the Cape of Good Hope.

1500

1500 Pedro Álvares Cabral lands in Brazil. He claims it for Portugal.

1510 Affonso de Albuquerque seizes Goa for Portugal, then captures Malacca (1511).

1512 Portuguese navigator Francisco Serrão explores the Spice Islands (Moluccas).

1513 Spanish explorer Vasco Núñez de Balboa crosses Panama, becoming the first European to see the Pacific Ocean.

1519 Portuguese navigator Ferdinand Magellan's exedition circumnavigates the world.

1535 Jacques Cartier enters the St. Lawrence River, establishing French claims in Canada.

1538-42 Spanish conquistador Hernando de Soto explores Florida and the North American southeast.

1540-42 Spanish explorer Francisco Vásquez de Coronado reaches the Grand Canyon.

Spice and potatoes

One of the aims of European explorers was to gain trading access to spices. These were used in large quantities in Europe to preserve and flavor food and were highly profitable trade items. The explorers found suppliers of cinnamon in Ceylon (Sri Lanka), pepper in Southeast Asia, nutmeg and cloves in the Moluccas (the "Spice Islands") and ginger in China. They also encountered new foods in the Americas: potatoes, corn, tomatoes, turkey, squash, chilies and chocolate. Another profitable new product from the Americas was tobacco.

Cocoa plant A watercolor from a French album, dated 1686, depicts plants of the West Indies.

FACT The accurate calculation of longitude became possible in the 1760s. Before this, navigation had been uncertain for any ship out of sight of land.

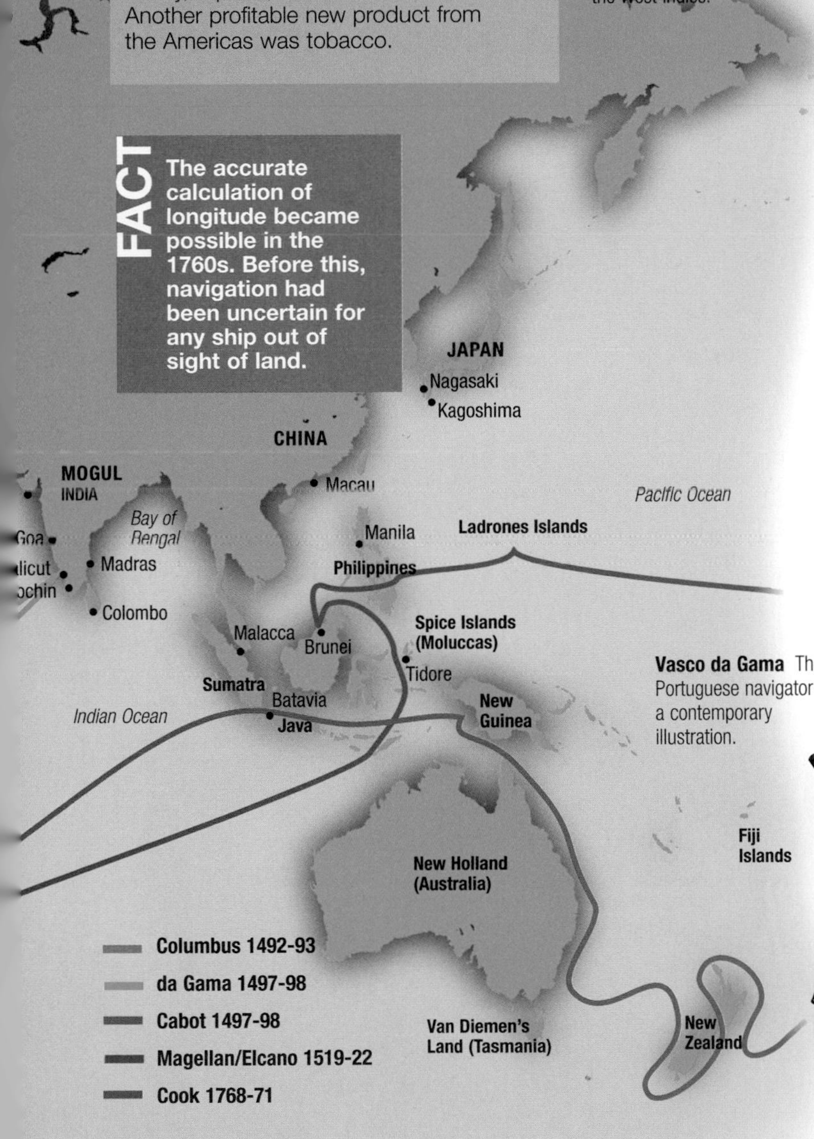

NEW IMPERIAL POWERS

Several European states saw the potential of exploration to increase their economic and political power. The trading empires they created ultimately became the great territorial empires of the 19th century.

Portugal Under the royal patronage of Prince Henry "the Navigator" (1394-1460), Portugal was the pioneer of European maritime exploration. Portuguese navigators opened the sea route to the riches of the Far East, setting up a chain of trading stations including Luanda, Mozambique, Goa, Malacca and Macao. Brazil was at first thought unpromising, but later it became Portugal's most important colonial possession.

Spain The voyages of Christopher Columbus, sponsored by Spain, failed to reach the Far East but led to a huge Spanish Empire in the Americas. Vast quantities of silver from the Potosi mines in Peru were shipped annually to Spain, financing both Spain's political domination of Europe and a boom in Europe's trade with Asia. The Spanish Empire in the Americas and the Philippines proved more durable than Spain's own power.

Netherlands A long war against Spain (1567-1648) encouraged Dutch mariners to attack Spanish and Portuguese colonial possessions. They were outstandingly successful in Southeast Asia, led by the Netherlands East India Company (founded 1602). For most of the 17th century, the Dutch ran the greatest trading empire the world had ever seen, extending from Amsterdam to Cape Town to Japan.

England English colonial expansion began with the settlement of the east coast of North America from 1607 but gathered pace only in the 18th century after a series of wars with the Netherlands. The East India Company (1600-1873) oversaw huge territorial expansion in India, the French were driven out of North America, the Dutch left Africa, and the voyages of James Cook opened up the South Pacific. Only in North America was British expansion checked – and there by the American colonists themselves.

France After the decline of the Dutch Empire, Britain's only serious colonial rival was France. French explorers had created an empire in the interior of North America, and in the early 18th century, French influence in India matched that of Britain. In the Seven Years' War (1756-63), however, Britain systematically overran the French colonial empire.

Vasco da Gama The Portuguese navigator in a contemporary illustration.

see also

156-57 **India**
160-61 **Africa**
162-63 **Ancient America**

1540-43 Spanish conquistador Francisco de Orellana crosses the Andes and sails down the Amazon.

1545-52 Spanish missionary Francis Xavier travels to Goa, Sri Lanka, Japan and China.

1550

1577-80 English navigator Francis Drake makes the second circumnavigation of the globe

1596-97 Dutch navigator Willem Barents dies while seeking a route to Asia via the north of Russia.

1600

1608 Samuel de Champlain founds a French colony at Quebec, Canada.

1610 English navigator Henry Hudson explores Hudson Bay and the Hudson River.

1619 The Dutch found a colony at Batavia (Jakarta) as capital of their East Indies possessions.

1620 The Pilgrims establish a colony at Plymouth Rock, Massachusetts.

1642-44 Dutch navigator Abel Tasman visits Tasmania, New Zealand, New Guinea and Australia.

1650

1679-82 Robert de la Salle claims the entire Mississippi river valley for France.

1768-79 James Cook makes three expeditions to the Pacific, claiming Australia for Britain.

In the 14th century, a new mood of inquiry stirred in Italy and spread across Europe. Inspired by the rediscovery of classical learning, scholars and artists began to reappraise the world. This led to a new confidence in human capabilities and a flowering of the arts. This change was known as the Renaissance, or "Rebirth." It took about 200 years and represents the transition from the medieval world to a modern one.

NORTHERN RENAISSANCE

Around the 14th century, a new outlook, known as **humanism**, emerged in northern Europe, inspired by classical authors and developed by scholars such as Erasmus and Thomas More. Humanism was a secular philosophy, not incompatible with Christianity but rejecting dogma and unquestioning obedience to authority. Its spirit of inquiry turned Europe into the crucible of modern **science** by the 17th century. Technology flowered as well. In the mid-15th century, Johann Gutenberg invented movable type, revolutionizing **printing** and the dissemination of knowledge. Jan van Eyck (1390-1441) developed **oil paints**, increasing the detail, light effects and colors available to artists. Paintings became a commodity, sought after by a new class of wealthy private patrons. Classical themes became increasingly prominent in **architecture**. Skeptical questioning also gave rise to criticism of the Church, but most Renaissance thinkers wanted reform, not the turmoil of the Reformation that followed.

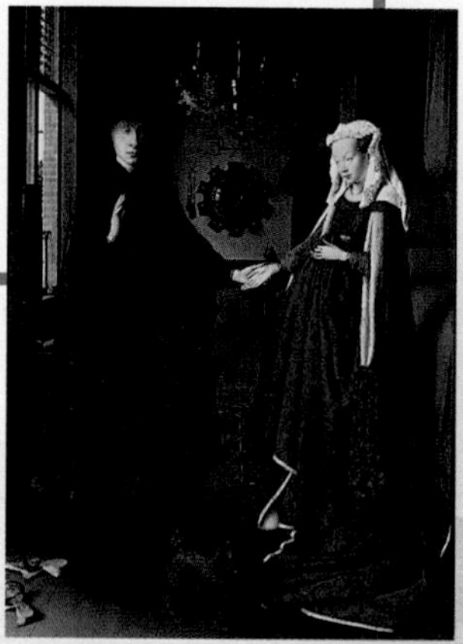

Family snapshot The human scale and colors of bright jewels identify van Eyck's *Arnolfini Portrait* (1434) as a Renaissance work.

SOUTHERN RENAISSANCE

Architects such as Filippo Brunelleschi began studying Roman ruins in the early 15th century, using them as the basis for a **new architecture** that was also championed by artists (classical architecture began to feature in paintings). Architect Andrea **Palladio** (1508-80) created templelike palaces and villas characterized by classical symmetry. From Giotto (c. 1267-1337) on, **painting** was increasingly **naturalistic**, concerned with accurate portrayal of reality rather than with symbolic meaning. Subject matter became more secular in the 15th century, reflecting a new attitude toward the place of mankind in the cosmos. **Sculpture** was strongly influenced by surviving Roman works, and sculptors such as **Donatello** and **Michelangelo** aspired to match classical creativity. Discoveries of key Roman pieces, such as Laocoön in 1506, provided renewed inspiration.

Prosperous and competitive **city-states** (including Florence, Milan and Venice), ruled by sophisticated nobility, cultivated scholars, musicians, painters and architects. Artists were no longer considered simply craftsmen: The anonymity of medieval guilds was slowly replaced by a new **individualism**. In addition, patrons permitted artists (notably Leonardo da Vinci) to indulge in other interests, such as science, engineering, poetry and music. Major advances in **medicine** were permitted by the progressive attitudes of Italian universities, especially regarding human dissection. Flemish physician Andreas **Versalius** (1514-64) published his groundbreaking *On the Structure of the Human Body* (1543) in Italy; it was the first major advance in medical knowledge since Roman times.

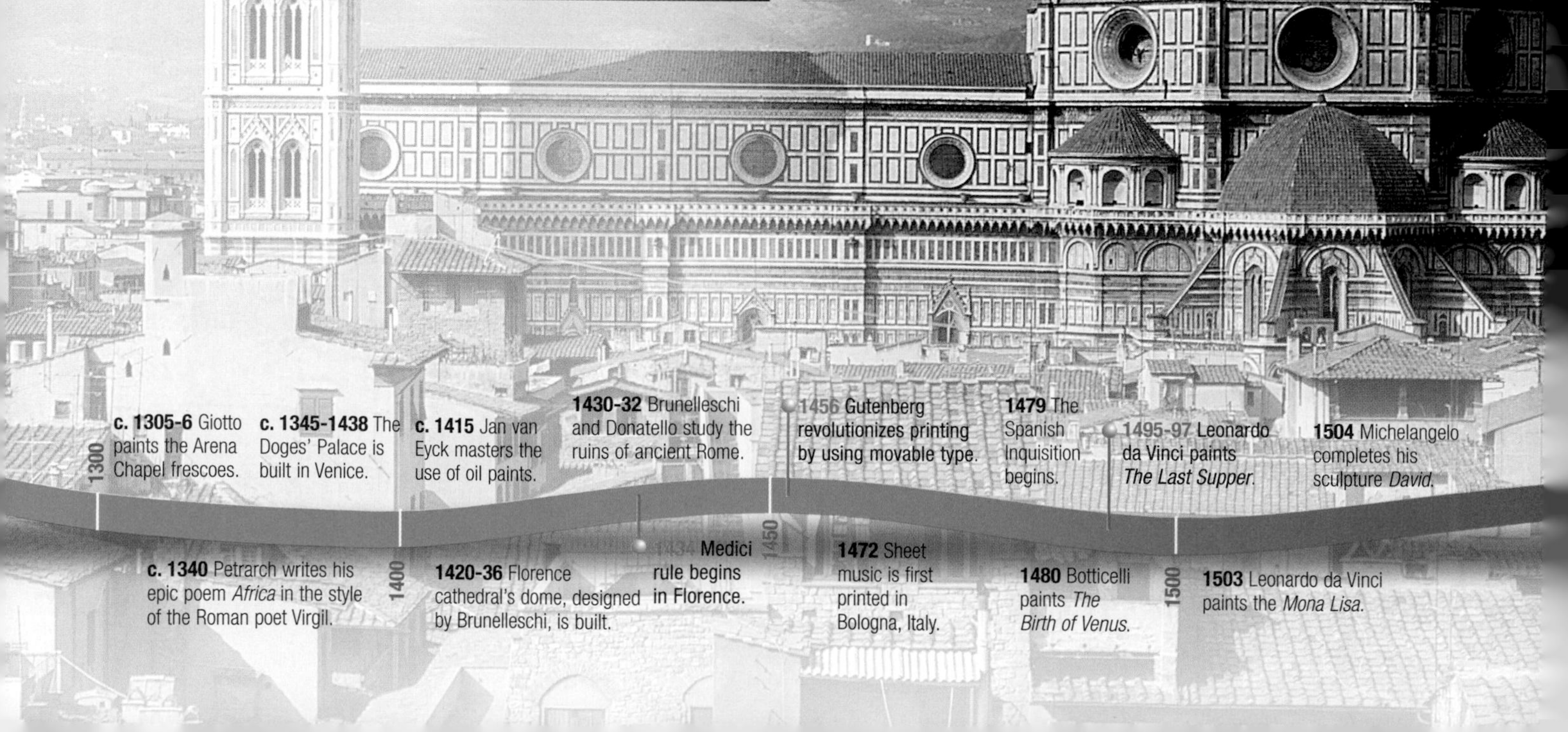

Engineering feat The dome of Florence's cathedral – largest in the world – was the first built without a wooden supporting frame.

1300

c. 1305-6 Giotto paints the Arena Chapel frescoes.

c. 1340 Petrarch writes his epic poem *Africa* in the style of the Roman poet Virgil.

c. 1345-1438 The Doges' Palace is built in Venice.

1400

c. 1415 Jan van Eyck masters the use of oil paints.

1420-36 Florence cathedral's dome, designed by Brunelleschi, is built.

1430-32 Brunelleschi and Donatello study the ruins of ancient Rome.

1434 Medici rule begins in Florence.

1450

1456 Gutenberg revolutionizes printing by using movable type.

1472 Sheet music is first printed in Bologna, Italy.

1479 The Spanish Inquisition begins.

1480 Botticelli paints *The Birth of Venus*.

1495-97 Leonardo da Vinci paints *The Last Supper*.

1500

1503 Leonardo da Vinci paints the *Mona Lisa*.

1504 Michelangelo completes his sculpture *David*.

A new style of painting Ideas about art were transformed in the Renaissance. New methods were developed, new subjects were explored, and the laws of perspective discovered. Technical mastery attained undreamed-of heights. Religious painting began to measure itself by the standards of flesh and blood existence.

The Flagellation Painted in about 1458 for the sacristy of the cathedral of Urbino, Italy, *The Flagellation* by Piero della Francesca (c. 1420-92) is one of the most mysterious of his paintings. The indifference of the three contemporary figures to the scourging of Christ behind them is a striking departure from convention.

- The static attitudes of the figures, their careful poses and the space that separates them are all devices used by the artist to create an effect of calm and grandeur, deliberately recalling the sculpture of the classical past.
- Christ is placed in a realistic, believable world, with ordinary human beings around him. This reflects the Renaissance reassessment of the Christian story and was a way of making the Christian message more immediate to viewers.
- The depiction of Classical architecture (columns and capitals) reflects Renaissance interest in the Greek and Roman past. The Classical setting also expresses the historical nature of the scene.
- The artist's observation of detail, seen here in the fall of cloth rendered by careful shading, is very thorough. The use of light and shade makes an important contribution to the illusion of depth.
- The composition is complex, with two centers of focus that appear almost unrelated – but the viewer's eye is led by the architectural setting from one to the other. Painting in the Middle Ages tended to have far simpler, centralized compositions.
- The use of perspective and foreshortening creates the illusion of depth. This effect distinguishes paintings of the Renaissance from medieval work, but in this painting it is undermined by the exaggerated and overprecise architecture.
- The figures reflect the artist's close observation of anatomy. Painters and sculptors wanted to depict the world naturalistically. With later developments in painting, figures would gradually become more emotional and expressive.

1505 Erasmus publishes *In Praise of Folly.*

1508-12 Michelangelo paints the Sistine Chapel

1510-12 Raphael paints *The School of Athens.*

1513 Machiavelli completes *The Prince.*

1517 Luther initiates the Reformation at Wittenberg, Germany.

1543 Copernicus argues that the Sun is the center of the planetary system.

1550

1551 Palladio designs the Villa Rotunda.

1558 Elizabeth I accedes to the throne of England.

1562 The Wars of Religion break out in France (to 1598).

1582 The Gregorian calendar is introduced in Catholic countries.

c. 1590 The first microscope is made by Hans and Zacharias Jansen.

1600

1600-8 The Flemish painter Rubens works in Italy.

1633 The Inquisition condemns Galileo's belief that the Earth orbits the Sun.

see also

314-15 **Scientific thinkers**

316-19 **Western art**

326-29 **Architecture**

Clash of faiths

Until about 1500, all Christians in Europe belonged to the Roman Catholic Church. Within 50 years, the continent was divided between Catholics and Protestants (who rejected the religious authority of Rome). Hundreds of thousands of people were caught up in the struggle between the two faiths.

Key reformers Pressure for religious change was articulated by a wide range of religious thinkers after Martin Luther. Some, like Luther himself or Henry VIII, sought specific reforms. Others, like Zwingli or Calvin, advocated a radically new spirituality that meant a complete break with the Roman Catholic Church.

Ulrich Zwingli (1484-1531) Zwingli was a Swiss reformer and priest. From about 1517 on, he started to argue that scripture was the only religious authority. He converted the people of Zürich to Protestantism, and his 67 theses on reformation were adopted by Zürich's canton government. He died in battle against the Catholic cantons.

Henry VIII (1491-1547) Henry was king of England from 1509 to 1547. When the pope refused his request for a divorce from Catherine of Aragon, Henry split with Rome and created the (Protestant) Church of England, with himself at its head (1534). He also dissolved England's monasteries (1536-40) and appropriated their property. The resulting religious conflict lasted over 100 years.

John Calvin (1509-64) A French lawyer and theologian, Calvin advocated a strict form of Protestantism based on the idea that every event is planned by God (predestination). He led the city of Geneva from 1536, making it a haven for Europe's Protestants.

John Knox (c. 1513-72) Knox was a founder of the (Protestant) Church of Scotland (1560). He converted to Protestantism in the 1540s and, after being imprisoned by the French for an anti-Catholic conspiracy, became chaplain to Edward VI of England. At the accession of Mary I, a Catholic, he fled to Frankfurt and then Geneva, where he met Calvin. In 1559, he returned to Scotland to lead the reform movement.

Henry IV (1553-1610) Henry was the Huguenot leader and king of France from 1589 to 1610. To protect himself, he twice professed Catholicism but promulgated the Edict of Nantes (1598), granting religious freedoms and bringing peace after the Wars of Religion.

Zwingli Ulrich Zwingli made the Swiss canton of Zürich a Protestant center.

1415 Bohemian John Hus is burned for heresy, triggering the Hussite Wars (1419-34).

1500

1514 The Fuggers, a German banking family, are licensed by Pope Leo X to sell indulgences.

1517 Martin Luther pins his 95 theses to the door of the castle church at Wittenberg.

1521 Luther is excommunicated after writing tracts attacking the papacy and Catholic dogma.

1523 Two Protestants are burned as heretics in the Spanish Netherlands. This is the start of 30 years of persecution.

1525

1528 Henry VIII dismisses Cardinal Wolsey for failing to secure the pope's permission for his divorce.

1534 The Society of Jesus (Jesuits) is founded by Ignatius Loyola. Henry VIII becomes head of the English Church.

1535 Thomas More is executed for refusing to accept Henry VIII as head of the Church of England.

1536-40 Henry VIII closes 800 Catholic monasteries in England.

1541 John Calvin founds a Reformed Church at Geneva.

Martin Luther

Martin Luther (1483-1546) was an Augustinian friar of humble origins. In 1512, he was professor of theology at the University of Wittenberg in Germany. Infuriated by the sale of indulgences (the remission of punishment for a sin), he challenged the Roman Catholic Church to respond to his 95 theses (propositions about the state of the Church) by pinning them to the door of a church in the town in 1517. He sought to restore purity of faith, based on the Gospels, to the Church and called on Germany's ruling princes to take up this Protestant cause. However, he was alarmed by democratic interpretations of his doctrine of the "priesthood of all believers," and therefore emphasized order and obedience within the Church.

Excommunicated in 1521, Luther was summoned to the Diet (parliament) of Worms by Emperor Charles V but refused to retract his beliefs. He married an ex-nun in 1525 and spent the remainder of his life pursuing his cause and creating a translation of the Bible that helped both to spread his ideas and to unify the German language.

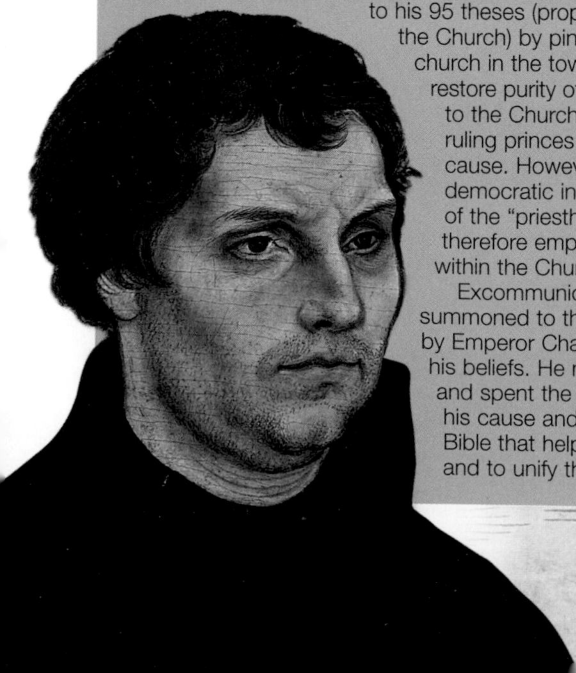

St. Bartholomew's Day Massacre French Huguenots (Protestants) are slaughtered by Catholic troops after rumors of a Protestant plot in 1572.

Reformation criticism of the Church	The responses of the Counter-Reformation
As the Reformation proceeded, political issues became as important as religious arguments in determining Europe's alliances. Nonetheless, Protestantism was rooted in a series of profound criticisms of the Catholic Church.	The Papacy's response to Protestant criticisms was a combination of reform and vigorous defense, spearheaded by the Council of Trent. This "Counter-Reformation" prevented the disintegration of the Church and led to a stricter, reformed Catholicism.
Church corruption Many Christians felt that the opulence of the Renaissance Church was counter to the teaching of the Gospels.	**Baroque style** An even grander artistic style developed in the late 16th century, expressing the Church's renewed confidence.
Lack of biblical authority Renaissance humanism fostered a questioning attitude and drew attention to the gap between practices such as selling indulges and the teachings of Jesus.	**New institutions** The Society of Jesus (Jesuits), founded in 1534, incorporated humanist views into Catholic teaching, making it more appealing to influential lay Christians.
Low caliber of the priesthood Many Christians began to question the caliber and training of priests, the value of their rule of enforced celibacy and ultimately, the claim of the pope to be "Christ's Vicar on Earth."	**New religious orders** The Council of Trent established a new, dynamic preaching order, the Capuchins, to meet the laity's demands for religious instruction. It also set up a program of improved education for priests.
Reliance on unbiblical doctrines Protestants rejected the Church's insistence on the high status and intercessionary powers of Mary, mother of Jesus, and the saints; they also questioned the value of pilgrimages and relics.	**A precise exposition of Catholic doctrine** The Council of Trent's greatest achievement was the clearest definition to date of the beliefs required of all Catholics, including an insistence on all the established sacraments.
Church control of access to the Bible Protestants demanded that the Bible and church services should be made available in languages people spoke. The use of Latin, combined with the Roman Catholic Church's hold on education, gave the Church a monopoly on biblical interpretation, and prevented people hearing the Christian message except through the filter of the Church itself.	**Increased Church control** The reactivation of the Inquisition and the creation of the first "Index of Prohibited Books" tightened the Church's control over the education of its members. A Catholic wishing to read the works of any of the reformers (or of certain lay authors like Machiavelli) was required to obtain specific permission from the Church before doing so.

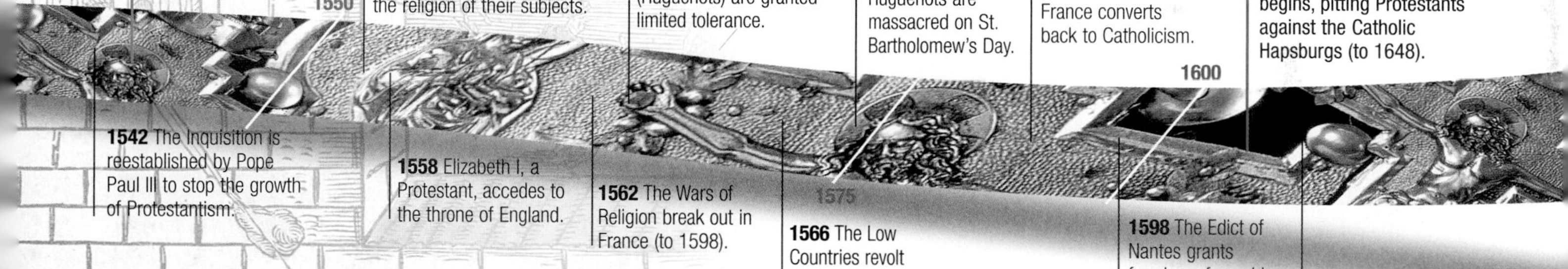

1542 The Inquisition is reestablished by Pope Paul III to stop the growth of Protestantism.

1545-63 The Council of Trent initiates the Counter-Reformation.

1555 In the Peace of Augsburg, Emperor Charles V permits the German princes to choose the religion of their subjects.

1558 Elizabeth I, a Protestant, accedes to the throne of England.

1562 The Wars of Religion break out in France (to 1598).

1563 French Protestants (Huguenots) are granted limited tolerance.

1566 The Low Countries revolt against their Spanish rulers (to 1609).

1572 About 30 000 Huguenots are massacred on St. Bartholomew's Day.

1593 Henry IV of France converts back to Catholicism.

1598 The Edict of Nantes grants freedom of worship to French Protestants.

1618 The Thirty Years' War begins, pitting Protestants against the Catholic Hapsburgs (to 1648).

1642-46 Civil wars break out in Britain, partly over religious disputes.

Wars of Religion

The religious turmoil of the Reformation boiled over into outright war on numerous occasions in the 16th and early 17th centuries. Among the major conflicts were:

- **French Wars of Religion** Religious differences gave rise to a series of wars in 1562-98 between the French houses of Bourbon and Guise. The Catholic Guise faction repeatedly attempted to destroy the Protestant Huguenots, many of whom fled to England, the Netherlands and Switzerland to escape.
- **The Dutch Revolt** The Protestant Dutch waged a long war against Spanish rule of the Low Countries (1566-1609).
- **Spanish Armada** In 1588, Philip II of Spain attempted to conquer and reconvert Protestant England. His large fleet (Armada) was driven into the North Sea and destroyed by storms off Scotland and Ireland.
- **Thirty Years' War** A series of religious wars devastated Germany from 1618 to 1648. The Catholic side was led by the Hapsburg emperors and their Spanish supporters; the Protestants were sustained by interventions from Christian IV of Denmark, Gustavus II Adolphus of Sweden and Cardinal Richelieu of France, who feared the power of the Hapsburgs and the Holy Roman Empire.

see also
166-67 **The Renaissance**
304-5 **Religions**

Louis XIV's declaration "L'état, c'est moi" (I am the State) expressed all the arrogance of an absolute king. Such power also gave some monarchs the confidence to grant certain liberties and to allow a new intellectual movement – the Enlightenment – to blossom. They prided themselves on their tolerant patronage of intellectual and cultural developments but were ruthless when free thinking began to look like revolutionary discontent.

Sun King Louis XIV's nickname reflected his absolute power, his sumptuous court (at Versailles from 1682), and his era of dazzling cultural achievements.

Anglo-Dutch Wars

Three wars were fought between Britain and the United Provinces of the Netherlands. The first hostilities were in 1652-54, when Britain closed its possessions to Dutch ships.The Dutch took control of the English Channel, but the English blockaded the Dutch coast and enforced a peace treaty. Continuing trade rivalry and the British seizure of New York provoked a second conflict in 1665-67. The Plague and Fire in London weakened British efforts, and the Dutch won trade concessions. War again broke out in 1672-74, after Charles II assisted Louis XIV against the Dutch before being repulsed at Texel (1673).

War of the Spanish Succession

Charles II of Spain died in 1700 with no heir; Philip of Anjou (Louis XIV's grandson) succeeded him. England, Austria, and others feared French ambitions and made an alliance. Philip gave the Spanish Netherlands to Louis, but in 1704-9, the Allies defeated France at **Blenheim** and in other battles. Then Charles of Austria (Philip's rival for the Spanish throne) became Holy Roman Emperor, giving him a claim to both Austria and Spain. The compromise **Treaty of Utrecht** (1713) confirmed Philip as king of Spain in return for renouncing claims to France; the Spanish Netherlands became Austrian. Charles refused at first but signed in 1714, establishing a balance of power in Europe.

1643 Louis XIV accedes to the throne of France at age 5.

1648 The Thirty Years' War ends; the Dutch win complete independence from Spain.

1649 Charles I of England is beheaded and the Commonwealth (republic) is established (to 1653).

1650

1652 The first Anglo-Dutch War breaks out.

1652

1660 The monarchy is restored in England with the accession of Charles II.

1666 Much of London is destroyed in the Great Fire.

1684 Isaac Newton proposes his theory of gravitation.

1685 Huguenots (French Protestants) are persecuted by Catholics and flee from France.

1688-9 William III (of Orange) and Mary II (daughter of James II) accede to the throne of England in the "Glorious Revolution."

1697 Eugène of Savoy ends Austria's war with the Turks by a victory at Zenta; the Hapsburgs recover Hungary.

1700

1700 Great Northern War between Sweden and Russia (to 1721).

1701 The War of the Spanish Succession begins (to 1714).

1701

1703 Peter the Great founds St. Petersburg; it becomes the Russian capital in 1712.

1704 The Allied victory at Blenheim curbs French expansion in Europe.

NEW IDEAS BLOSSOM

The Enlightenment was an intellectual movement driven by scientific discovery and skeptical inquiry. It freed thinking from Renaissance loyalty to classical wisdom and deeply questioned religion, society and politics. Enlightenment thinkers believed that a scientific approach could reveal a universal order, upon which to base government, morality and religion. This "Age of Reason" held out new prospects of equality and human progress. Key figures included:

- **Francis Bacon (1561-1626)** Bacon was an English lawyer, politician and thinker. He was an early advocate of the scientific approach to inquiry and a precursor of the Enlightenment.
- **Thomas Hobbes (1588-1679)** Hobbes was an English mathematician and philosopher, who maintained that natural life is "nasty, brutish and short."
- **René Descartes (1596-1650)** A French philosopher and mathematician, Descartes founded rationalism, the idea that all knowledge is derived from pure reason.
- **Benedict de Spinoza (1632-77)** Dutch philosopher Spinoza identified God with nature and believed that humans were subject to natural law. Overcoming personal desire was the basis of a good society.
- **John Locke (1632-1704)** A champion of freedom, English philosopher Locke argued that governments exist only by consent of the governed.
- **Baron de Montesquieu (1689-1755)** French philosopher Montesquieu proposed the separation of government powers (legislative, executive and judicial) to ensure freedom of the individual.
- **David Hume (1711-76)** Scottish antirationalist philosopher Hume held that knowledge comes from a kind of instinct based on perception, not from pure reason.
- **Jean-Jacques Rousseau (1712-78)** Rousseau's book *The Social Contract* argues that government exists to uphold justice, equality and freedom.
- **Denis Diderot (1713-84)** French philosopher and writer Diderot edited (with Jean d'Alembert) the 35-volume *Encyclopédie ou Dictionnaire Raisonné* (1751-80), the first general encyclopedia.
- **Adam Smith (1723-90)** Scottish philosopher Smith invented "laissez-faire" economics, arguing that free markets promoted prosperity throughout society.
- **Immanuel Kant (1724-1804)** German philosopher Kant argued that universal moral laws could be founded on reason rather than dogma and faith.

Outspoken radical In works such as *Candide* (1759), Voltaire (1694-1778) openly ridiculed the pretensions of philosophers, clergy, monarchy and nobility. He championed justice, tolerance and liberty, providing an intellectual foundation for the French Revolution.

Europe's empires, 1715

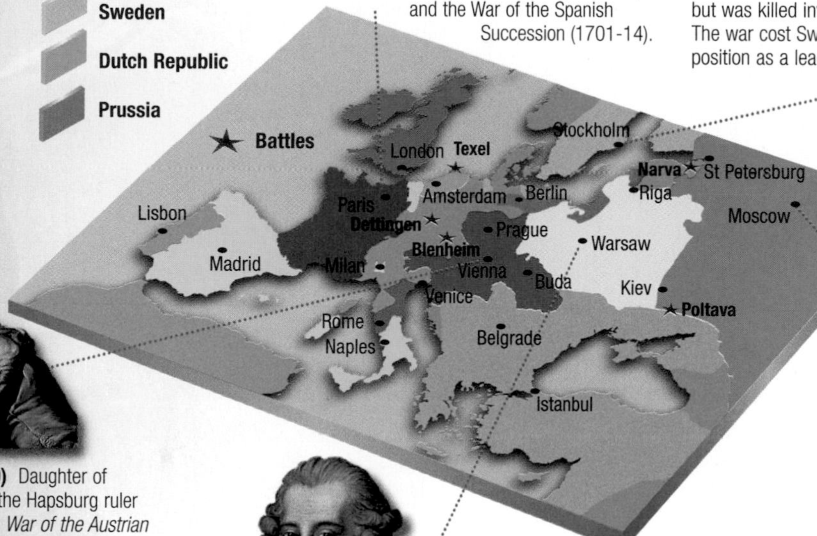

Louis XIV (1638-1715) Louis acceded to the throne at the age of five and was king of France from 1643 to 1715. He took full control of the state on the death of Cardinal Mazarin in 1661 and ruled with a firm belief in his own absolute power and the divine right of kings. He built up France's army and waged expansionist campaigns until checked by the War of the Grand Alliance (1688-97) and the War of the Spanish Succession (1701-14).

Charles XII (1682-1718) King of Sweden from 1697 to 1718, Charles defended Sweden from attack by Russia, Poland, Denmark and Saxony early in the Great Northern War (1700-21). He crushed the Russians at Narva (1700) and invaded Russia in 1709 but was defeated at Poltava. He resumed the war five years later but was killed invading Norway. The war cost Sweden its position as a leading power.

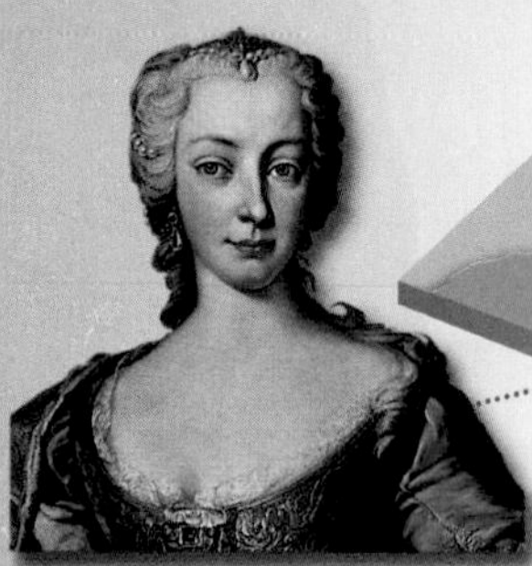

Maria Theresa (1717-80) Daughter of Charles VI, Maria became the Hapsburg ruler when she was just 23 (see *War of the Austrian Succession*). She ruled as an "enlightened despot," supporting the arts, introducing some reforms and reorganizing institutions such as the military. Her reign was fundamentally conservative and more radical change was accomplished only under her son Joseph II.

Frederick II "the Great" (1712-86) King of Prussia from 1740 to 1786, Frederick made his country a major power, winning Silesia from the Hapsburgs in the War of the Austrian Succession. He made an alliance with Russia to partition Poland (1772) and acquired Brandenburg and Pomerania. A brilliant soldier, he was a reformer and the patron of Voltaire but also an absolute ruler.

Peter I "the Great" (1672-1725) Peter ruled Russia from 1682 to 1725. He fought for Russian access to the Black Sea (Russo-Turkish Wars) and Baltic (Great Northern War), building up Russian military and naval strength beyond anything seen before. He founded St. Petersburg in 1703 and made it his capital. A tour of Europe in 1697-98 led to the modernization of Russian industry, society and bureaucracy. As emperor, his methods were often brutal, but he laid the foundations of modern Russia, making it a major power.

1707 The Act of Union unites England and Scotland.

1709 The Swedes are routed by the Russians at Poltava.

1720 J.S. Bach writes the Brandenburg Concertos.

1739 War between England and Spain over South American trade ("The War of Jenkins' Ear") begins (until 1748).

1740 Frederick II ("the Great") accedes to the throne of Prussia.

1740

1740 The War of the Austrian Succession begins (until 1748).

1745 A second Jacobite rebellion, which ends at Culloden (1746), fails to restore the Stuarts to the English throne.

1750

1755 An earthquake in Lisbon kills 60 000 people.

1756

1756 The Seven Years' War begins (until 1763). Wolfgang Amadeus Mozart is born.

1757 Robert Clive captures Calcutta to establish British dominance of India.

1759 British forces under James Wolfe capture Quebec from the French.

1761 Britain's supremacy in India and North America is recognized in the Peace of Paris.

1762 Catherine II "the Great" becomes sole ruler of Russia after the murder of her husband Peter III.

1772 Poland is partitioned by Prussia, Russia and Austria.

War of the Austrian Succession

A dispute over Austrian succession led to a war on three continents, involving six major powers and precipitating long-term shifts in European relations. Charles VI of Austria died in 1740 without an heir. He wanted the succession to pass via his daughter Maria Theresa, whose husband Francis would become Holy Roman Emperor. But Francis was opposed by Bavaria, Prussia and France. Spain contested Maria Theresa's claim to Italian land, and Britain challenged France over Indian and American territory. Austria lost Silesia to Prussia, and Spain was given three duchies in northern Italy.

Charles Albert of Bavaria became Holy Roman Emperor in 1743. Britain and Austria defeated France at Dettingen (1743) but France took British Madras (1746). Charles Albert died in 1745, and Francis became Holy Roman Emperor as originally planned. The war ended with the signing of peace at Aix-la-Chapelle (1748). Prussia was now a great power and the Anglo-French struggle over colonies had begun.

Seven Years' War

The Seven Years' War followed the War of the Austrian Succession. Austria, France, Russia, Saxony, Sweden and Spain fought against Prussia, Britain and Hanover; France and Britain also fought in North America – the war fought in North America is called the French and Indian War – and in India. The war began when Prussia invaded Saxony in 1756; Prussia faced defeat until Russia withdrew. Britain defeated France in 1759 at home and overseas. The war ended with Prussia in possession of Silesia and Britain gaining most French territory in eastern North America, control of India and several Caribbean islands.

see also

308-9 **Western thought**

476-79 **European leaders**

Europe in turmoil

From the French Revolution to Napoleon's defeat, 1789-1815

The violent contrast between gross social injustice and Enlightenment ideals of freedom and equality precipitated increasing instability in 18th-century France. As belief in the old order and absolute monarchy crumbled, calls for reform turned to riots, then rebellion, and then a revolution. Out of the chaos emerged one of modern history's most controversial giants, Napoleon Bonaparte.

CAUSES OF THE FRENCH REVOLUTION

1. **Government bankruptcy** The cost of wars meant Louis XVI had to summon the States-General (parliament) for the first time since 1614 to request funds. It demanded reforms in return.
2. **The Enlightenment** French intellectuals proposed new, egalitarian forms of government, leading to widespread discontent with existing social and political structures.
3. **Social inequality** The peasantry and urban poor had to pay the bulk of taxation, whereas the aristocracy were largely exempt.
4. **Revolution in America** French participants in the American Revolution (1775-83) saw liberty and democracy triumph. They returned with a passion for reform and change at home.
5. **Harvest failure** Failure of the 1788 harvest caused price rises, especially for bread. These added to the hardships of the poor, who still paid feudal dues and taxes to the state.
6. **Louis XVI's weakness** Louis was popular but indecisive and made repeated concessions that undermined royal prestige. His frivolous wife Marie-Antoinette was detested.

1775-83 The American Revolution brings independence to the US, largely on Enlightenment principles.

1787 Attempts to reform the French finances and tax system fail.

1789 Widespread riots in Paris lead to the storming of the Bastille prison on July 14. This is the start of the Revolution.

1790

1790 A new National Assembly abolishes the nobility in France.

1791 Louis XVI tries to flee Paris. He is forced to approve a new constitution ending the absolute monarchy in France.

1792 The French Republic is declared. The Revolutionary Wars begin as foreign powers intervene and last until 1802.

1793 French forces occupy the Austrian Netherlands (Belgium). Louis XVI is guillotined.

1793-94 Moderate deputies are expelled from the Convention, and the Reign of Terror, led by Robespierre, begins.

1793-96 A counterrevolution in the Vendée region of western France is suppressed.

1795-99 Revolutionary rule in France is formalized under the "Directory."

1796-97 French forces (led by Napoleon) defeat the Austrians in Italy.

1798 Napoleon attempts to conquer Egypt but is defeated by Nelson at the Battle of the Nile.

1799 A coup makes Napoleon First Consul, ending the Revolution.

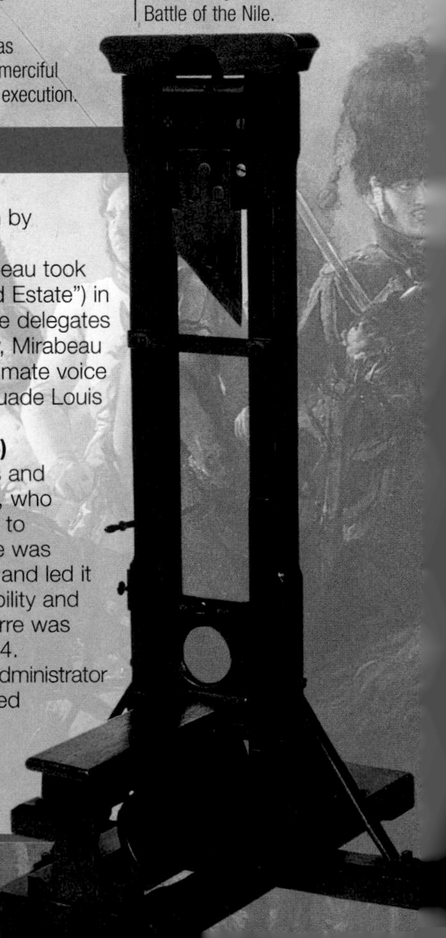

Great leveler The guillotine was introduced in 1792 as a quick, merciful and "democratic" instrument of execution.

Key figures of the Revolution

Georges Danton (1759-94) A lawyer and militant anti-Royalist, Danton was a member of the radical Jacobin group. He demanded the trial of Louis XVI and the creation of a republic. He was exiled in 1791-2 but returned as minister of justice, only to resign over the revolutionary council's harsh judgments. Danton led the government from April 1793 but opposed the Terror. Conflict with Robespierre led to his execution a year later.

Jean-Paul Marat (1743-93) A doctor and journalist, Marat joined the National Assembly in 1792. His popularity with the *sans-culottes* (the poor) alarmed the Girondins who saw him as a dangerous demagogue. He was murdered in the bath by Charlotte Corday, a Girondin supporter.

Comte de Mirabeau (1749-91) Mirabeau took part as a commoner (member of the "Third Estate") in the 1789 States-General. After Third-Estate delegates defiantly renamed it the National Assembly, Mirabeau helped force Louis to accept it as the legitimate voice of government. However, he failed to persuade Louis to form a constitutional monarchy.

Maximilien de Robespierre (1758-94) Robespierre led the revolutionary Jacobins and engineered the overthrow of the Girondins, who drew support from the provinces and tried to curb the powers of the Paris Assembly. He was elected to the Committee of Public Safety and led it after Danton. He was famed for incorruptibility and helped to orchestrate the Terror. Robespierre was arrested and executed after a coup in 1794.

Louis de Saint-Just (1767-94) As an administrator early in the Revolution, Saint-Just supported Robespierre. He was instrumental in the downfall of Danton and advocated the Terror. He was arrested and guillotined in the same coup as Robespierre.

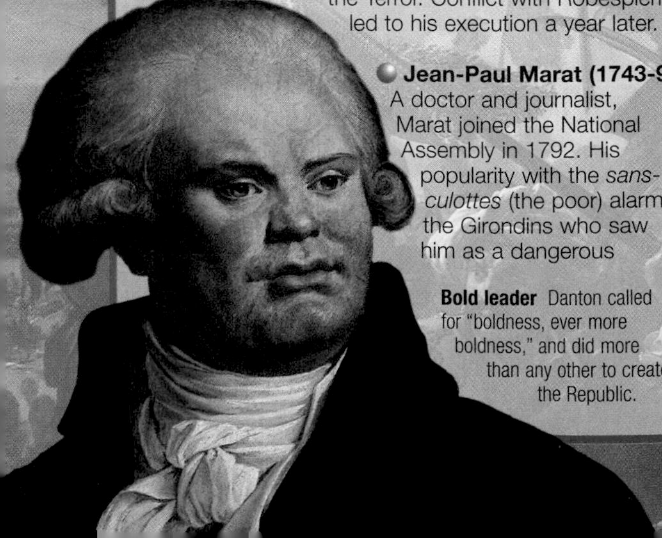

Bold leader Danton called for "boldness, ever more boldness," and did more than any other to create the Republic.

Napoleon's Europe At the height of his power, Napoleon directly or indirectly controlled half of Europe. He waged war from Spain to the outskirts of Moscow.

French empire, 1812

States dependent on France, 1812

French victories

French defeats

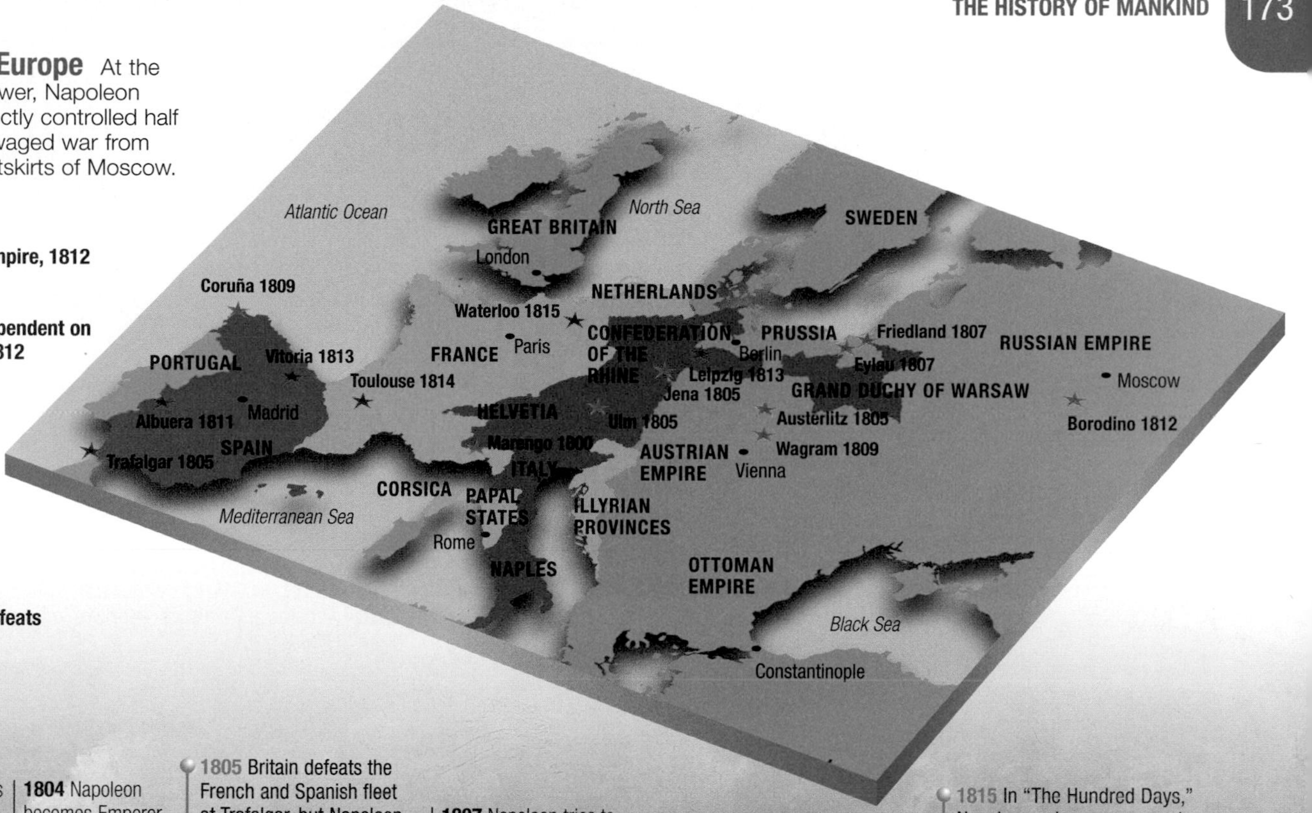

1800 Napoleon leads French forces to complete victory in Italy.

1802 Peace is agreed on between France and Britain in the Treaty of Amiens, but Britain resumes war in 1803.

1804 Napoleon becomes Emperor of France.

1805 Britain, with Austria, Sweden, Russia and Naples, organizes a new coalition against France.

1805 Britain defeats the French and Spanish fleet at Trafalgar, but Napoleon defeats Austria and Russia at Ulm and Austerlitz.

1806 Prussia joins war against France but is defeated at Jena.

1807 Napoleon tries to blockade British trade and invades Portugal through Spain.

1808-14 In the Peninsular War, Britain fights France in Spain and Portugal.

1810

1812 Napoleon invades Russia but is finally forced to retreat in winter with huge losses.

1813 French armies are defeated at Vitoria in Spain (June) and at Leipzig in Germany (October).

1814 Allied troops invade France; Napoleon is exiled.

1815 In "The Hundred Days," Napoleon seizes power again in France but is defeated at Waterloo (Belgium). The Congress of Vienna restores the European monarchies.

CONSEQUENCES OF THE FRENCH REVOLUTION

1. **Abolition of feudalism** The abolition of the last of the "feudal" ties binding peasants to their landlords brought France into line with Europe's most progressive states.
2. **Recognition of the Rights of Man** The Revolutionary concept of essential rights guaranteeing individual liberty is the foundation of modern human rights legislation.
3. **Destruction of the Church's power** The ending of the political power of the Church in France paved the way to a more secular society and liberated education.
4. **Two decades of war** The Revolution brought economic and political turmoil to Europe. French Revolutionary armies were often greeted as liberators but disillusion generally followed.
5. **A symbolic message** The Revolution sent shock waves through Europe's ruling classes. After the fall of Napoleon, many governments introduced repressive measures to quell liberalism and reform.
6. **Inspiration** As the first modern revolution attempting to transform the entire social and political fabric of a nation, the Revolution served as a model for liberation struggles in South America and Europe in the 19th and 20th centuries.

The "Little Corporal"

Napoleon Bonaparte (1769-1821), born in Corsica, rose rapidly to the rank of general in the Revolutionary Army. He was a leader of the 1799 coup and became First Consul. He crowned himself Emperor in 1804 and introduced popular reforms in government, the law and education. His wars were highly successful at first, and by 1812, he had created the largest European empire since Roman times. But the Peninsular War (1807-13) ended in defeat, and in 1812 he decided to invade Russia. After defeat at Leipzig (1813), he was deposed. He lost at Waterloo (1815).

see also

170-71 **Age of kings**
174-75 **Creation of the United States**
478-79 **European leaders**

Creation of the United States

Britain's prosperous North American colonies found their wealth attracting ever more taxation and control. Resentment against the distant ruler grew, finally spilling over into rebellion. The American Revolution brought freedom and an enlightened and democratic constitution. Over the following decades, the United States expanded across the entire continent, sparking the Indian Wars. But North and South were deeply divided, and the price of eventual unity was the bitter and costly Civil War.

Boston Tea Party Citizens dressed as Mohawk Indians board British ships and throw hated taxed tea into the Charles River.

Causes of the American Revolution

1. **Taxation** Britain tried to recoup the cost of the French and Indian War from the colonies but denied them a place in parliament. This "taxation without representation" was deeply resented.
2. **Colonial trade** Britain tried to restrict commerce between the North American states and other trading partners.
3. **A ban on expansion** The colonists resented a British prohibition on expanding into the West.
4. **Religious differences** Many colonists were dissenters who came to America to find religious freedom. The established position of the Anglican Church was seen as a threat.
5. **Propaganda** Pro-independence patriots influenced public opinion against British rule.

1607 The first permanent English settlement is established at Jamestown, Virginia.

1620 The Pilgrim Fathers found the Plymouth settlement in Massachusetts.

1664 England seizes New Amsterdam from the Dutch and renames it New York.

1700

1763 France cedes North American territories to Britain after the French and Indian War.

1764-65 The Sugar and Stamp Acts impose new taxes on the colonies, dividing the colonists into Loyalists and separatist Patriots.

1770 The Boston Massacre occurs when a mob provokes British soldiers. Five colonists are killed.

1773 The Boston Tea Party – protesting import taxes – occurs. The colonies agree to a provisional government at the First Continental Congress.

1775 British forces skirmish with colonial militias at Lexington and Concord.

1776 The Declaration of Independence is approved by the Second Continental Congress on July 4.

1777 British forces under Burgoyne surrender at Saratoga. France offers military help to the colonists.

1781 British forces under Cornwallis surrender at Yorktown, ending the war.

1783 Britain recognizes American independence with the Treaty of Paris.

Call to arms A statue of the Minutemen who fought the British at Concord.

Key figures of the American Revolution

John Adams (1735-1826) Adams was influential in drafting the Declaration of Independence and the Constitution. He later helped to negotiate the Treaty of Paris, and served as the second US president (1797-1801).

Marquis of Cornwallis (1738-1805) Cornwallis was the British commander in South Carolina. After initial successes, he moved north and was isolated and defeated at Yorktown in 1781.

Benjamin Franklin (1706-90) A printer, publisher, scientist and statesman, Franklin helped draft the Declaration of Independence. He enlisted French help for the colonists and negotiated the Treaty of Paris.

Thomas Jefferson (1743-1826) A wealthy Virginia planter and statesman, Jefferson was the main author of the Declaration of Independence. He was the third president of the US (1801-9).

Lord North (1732-92) North was British prime minister from 1770 to 1782. He tried to appease the colonists, but George III prevented him from compromising during the war.

Thomas Paine (1737-1809) Paine's pamphlet *Common Sense* (1776) turned American opinion towards independence. His *The Rights of Man* (1791) was a seminal text for revolutionaries.

Paul Revere (1735-1818) A Boston silversmith and printer, Revere warned of the British approach to Lexington and Concord in April 1775.

George Washington (1732-99) Washington commanded the Continental Armies, driving the British from Boston in 1776 and forcing their final surrender at Yorktown. He was elected to be first US president in 1789.

Consequences of the American Revolution

1. **A new constitution** The colonists drafted a constitution based on Enlightenment principles. By 1790, the United States was the most democratic nation in the world.
2. **Liberalization** The Anglican Church in America was separated from the state, and freedom of worship was guaranteed. Slavery was gradually abolished in the Northern states. Hereditary titles were forbidden.
3. **Expansion of the United States** US settlements gradually pushed west into Indian territory.
4. **Revolutionary ideas** The American experience showed for the first time in modern history that revolt against the old order could be successful – an idea that inspired revolutions in France (1789) and later in South America.

Growth of the United States

The modern United States grew out of the 13 British colonies on the East coast that declared independence in 1776. Over the following 100 years they expanded south and west by conquest, purchase and settlement. There are now 50 states; Hawaii was the last to join, in 1959.

- **pre-1750** (the 13 original British colonies)
- **1790** (including territories gained by Treaty of Paris)
- **1820** (including the Louisiana Purchase)
- **1855** (including territories won from Mexico 1846-48)
- **post-1850** (including territories settled after the Indian Wars)
- ★ battles

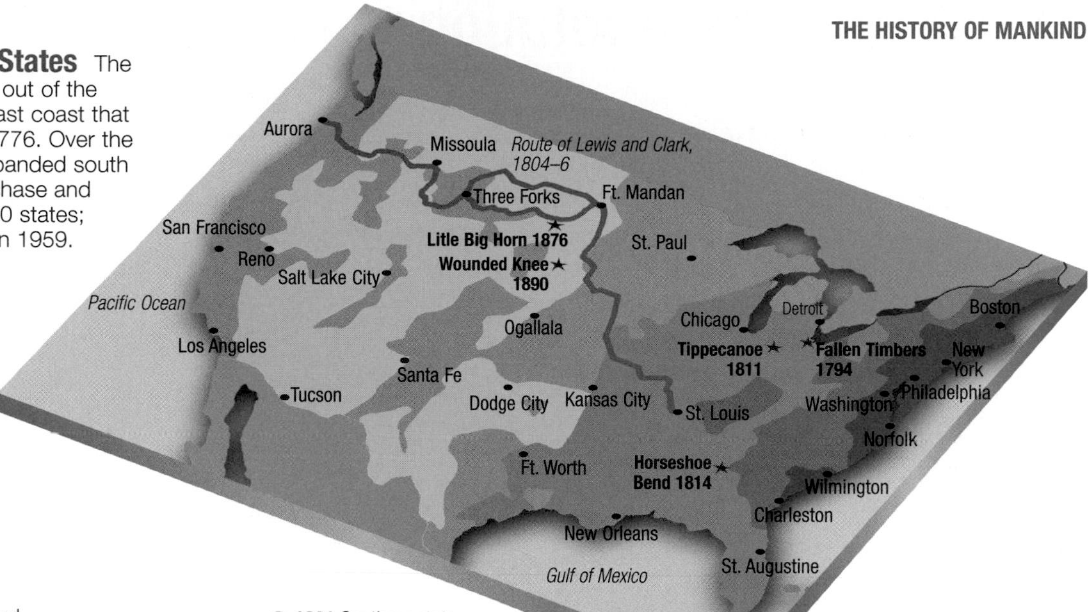

1787 The US Constitution is ratified by the states.

1789 George Washington becomes the first president (until 1797).

1800

1803 The US buys the huge Louisiana territory from France.

1804-6 Lewis and Clark pioneer an overland route to the West Coast.

1812-15 War of 1812 with Britain ends with a treaty.

1846-48 The Mexican–American War; the US gains Texas, New Mexico and California.

1848-49 The California gold rush encourages settlers to head West.

1850

1861 Southern states secede, forming the Confederate States of America. The resulting Civil War (lasting until 1865) begins badly for the North.

1863 President Lincoln emancipates all slaves in rebel territory.

1863 The Civil War turns against the South with Northern victories at Gettysburg and Vicksburg.

1865 The main Confederate Army surrenders at Appomattox Court House, Virginia. Lincoln is assassinated.

1867 The US buys Alaska from Russia for $7.2 million.

1869 The Union Pacific Railroad links the Atlantic and Pacific coasts.

1876 A US Cavalry detatchment under General Custer is wiped out by the Sioux at Little Bighorn.

1890 A massacre of the Sioux peoples at Wounded Knee ends the Indian Wars.

A house divided: the Civil War

As the United States expanded in the 1800s, rivalries and divisions became increasingly apparent. There were tensions between state and federal governments and between the interests of the industrializing and more populous North and the still agricultural South.

Slavery, though widely detested in the North, was the basis of Southern landowners' prosperity. A carefully contrived balance in Congress was threatened every time a new state joined the Union, and debate raged over whether to allow slavery in new states such as Kansas.

Hostility between North and South was exacerbated by two events. In 1859, **John Brown**, a militant abolitionist, staged a violent antislavery raid and was captured and hanged in Virginia. The following year, **Abraham Lincoln** was elected president. His pro-Union and antislavery views aroused Southern fears of a loss of power to the North.

In 1861 seven Southern (Confederate) states withdrew from the Union, and war with the North soon followed.

Jefferson Davis (1808-89) Davis became president of the Confederacy (South) in 1861. He tried to continue fighting after Lee's surrender at Appomattox but was captured and imprisoned.

Ulysses S. Grant (1822-85) In 1862, Grant became commander in chief of the Union armies; he won a series of victories, including Vicksburg in 1863, and brought about Lee's surrender in 1865 after a prolonged campaign at Richmond. He was elected president twice (1869-77).

Thomas "Stonewall" Jackson (1824-63) One of the Confederacy's most gifted generals, Jackson won his nickname after a heroic stand at Bull Run (1861). He was accidentally killed by his own men at Chancellorsville.

Robert E. Lee (1807-70) A brilliant, popular general, Lee commanded the Confederate Army of Northern Virginia and won victories at Fredericksburg and Chancellorsville. He was defeated at Gettysburg (1863) and surrendered at Appomattox in 1865.

Abraham Lincoln (1809-65) A self-taught lawyer and a congressman, Lincoln was elected president in 1860. His opposition to slavery provoked the secession of the Confederate states. The resulting Civil War brought four years of suffering and turmoil but saved the Union and put an end to slavery. After the war, Lincoln was assassinated by a Confederate sympathizer.

William T. Sherman (1820-91) Under Sherman's command in 1864, Union forces took Atlanta and laid waste the Georgia countryside – brutal but decisive inroads into Confederate heartlands.

Siege mortar The 32 cm (13 in.) Union mortar "Dictator," used at the siege of the Confederate city of Petersburg, Virginia.

see also
172-73 **Europe in turmoil**
198-99 **United States**
480-81 **Americans and world leaders**

The Industrial Revolution

From the steam engine to the production-line automobile

Largely spared from the wars and revolutions of continental Europe, Britain led the world in making the change from agriculture to an industrial economy in the 18th and 19th centuries. Demand for goods boomed, fueling mechanization and new ways of using water, coal and steam to drive production. The ripples spread outward to Europe, North America and eventually to every part of the globe as innovation followed innovation.

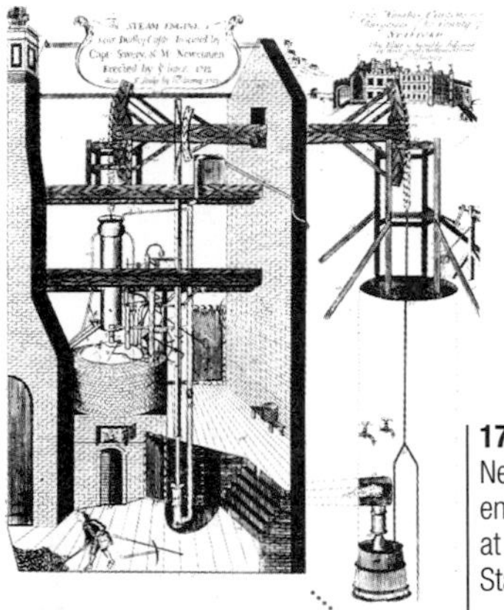

Revolutionary power Thomas Newcomen built the world's first successful steam engine in 1712. It was used to pump water from a coal mine.

Water-driven Richard Arkwright invented his spinning machine – powered by a water wheel and named a "water frame" – in around 1768. It made firm yarn for woven cloth.

1700

1701 The first practicable mechanical seed drill is invented by Jethro Tull of Berkshire, England.

Abraham Darby of Coalbrookdale, Shropshire, England, uses coked coal to produce cheaper iron.

1712 Thomas Newcomen's steam engine is installed at a coal mine in Staffordshire, England.

1733 John Kay's flying shuttle speeds the process of weaving.

1750

1761 The Bridgewater Canal, Britain's first entirely artificial waterway, is completed.

1765 James Watt's condenser makes steam engines much more efficient.

1767 James Hargreaves invents the spinning jenny.

1771 Richard Arkwright's textile mill at Cromford, Derbyshire, England, establishes the factory system.

1779 The world's first cast-iron bridge is completed by Abraham Darby at Ironbridge, Shropshire, England.

1785 The first power loom is patented by Edmund Cartwright.

1793 The cotton gin is introduced in Georgia by Eli Whitney

1800

1800 The first electric battery is built by Alessandro Volta in Italy.

1807 Gas street lighting is installed in Pall Mall, London.

1808 Richard Trevithick demonstrates a railroad locomotive in London.

WHY THE INDUSTRIAL REVOLUTION HAPPENED

1. **Wealth and resources** In the 18th century, Britain was the wealthiest country in Europe, with the most productive agriculture. It had the economic base, capital and market demand to shift from farming to manufactured products, and had the energy resources – in coal – to achieve this.
2. **Rapid population growth** In Britain, and then elsewhere, the population increased steeply in the 18th century, creating the need for more efficient farming. Agricultural mechanization improved the speed of production, reducing labor costs and making products cheaper – and increasing demand yet further.
3. **Increased demand** The growing need for cloth in particular could not be met by traditional production and inspired mechanical inventions such as the spinning jenny to speed the processing of imported American cotton. This set a precedent for the mechanization of industry.
4. **New energy sources** First water wheels and then coal and steam provided power to drive machinery and replaced the need for physical labor.
5. **New markets** The acquisition of foreign colonies and the growth of towns and cities at home opened up new opportunities for trade.
6. **Improved transportation** New transportation systems allowed the efficient movement of raw materials and distribution of manufactured goods, at first using canals (from the 1760s) and then railroads (from the 1830s).
7. **Political and economic changes** Land was no longer the sole source of wealth and power. Social change meant entrepreneurs could profit from their work, and it provided incentives to invest.

Mechanical separator Eli Whitney's cotton gin vastly speeded up the separation of seeds from cotton fibres, and helped to make the US the world's leading cotton producer.

FACT

The term "industrial revolution" was coined by French observers of the revolutionary changes taking place in 18th-century Britain.

Key Inventions

Spinning machines The hand-operated spinning jenny, invented by James Hargreaves in c. 1764, spun eight threads at a time. Richard Arkwright installed a water-powered spinning machine in his pioneering factory in 1771. Samuel Crompton's spinning mule (1779) enabled one worker to operate 1000 spindles. As a result, spinning kept abreast of increasingly mechanized weaving.

Weaving machines The flying shuttle, invented in 1733 by John Kay, increased the speed of broadloom weaving. Edmund Cartwright invented the steam-powered loom in 1785. French weaver Joseph-Marie Jacquard pioneered automation with his system of perforated cards to control the patterning of cloth on looms (1801).

Iron and steel In 1709, ironmaster Abraham Darby started using coke (coal residue) instead of expensive and scarce charcoal to smelt iron. This enabled the widespread use of iron for machinery, bridges and buildings. A century and a half later, in 1856, British engineer Henry Bessemer introduced the first method of mass-producing steel.

Steam power Devon blacksmith Thomas Newcomen built his first steam engine in 1712 as a colliery pump. Scottish engineer James Watt greatly improved its efficiency in 1764 by using a separate condenser. In 1781, he added a gearing system to produce a rotary motion so steam engines could power factory machines.

Fenced off Barbed wire, patented in the US in 1874, made it affordable for landowners to enclose their ranches.

The cotton gin In 1793, engineer Eli Whitney invented a machine to separate seeds from raw cotton 50 times faster than hand processing. He later developed mass-produced interchangeable parts for guns.

Canals and railroads Industrialization demanded new forms of transportation. In the 1790s, Britian embarked on a huge canal-building program, only to see it eclipsed shortly after by railroads. The first railroad opened in 1825; by 1850, rail was Britain's main form of transportation. Other countries followed suit.

The assembly line In the late 19th century, the US meat-packing industry was using powered chains to move animal carcasses through processing plants. Henry Ford adapted the system in 1913 to build his cars, revolutionizing factory production.

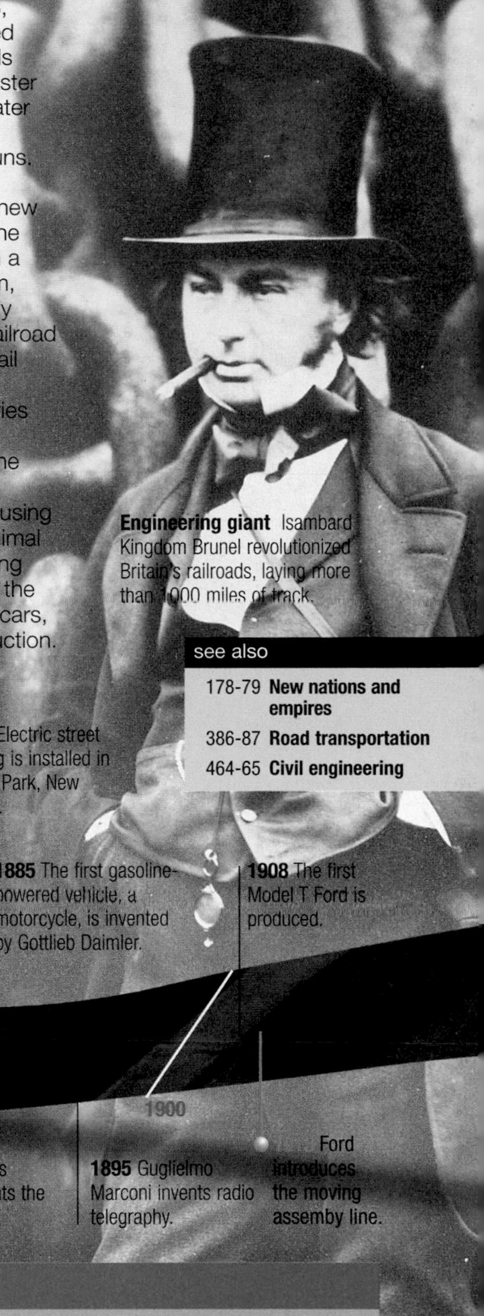

Engineering giant Isambard Kingdom Brunel revolutionized Britain's railroads, laying more than 1000 miles of track.

see also
178-79 **New nations and empires**
386-87 **Road transportation**
464-65 **Civil engineering**

1811-16 Luddites break up machinery in cotton and wool factories to protest unemployment.

1825 The first public railroad line, built by George Stephenson, opens between Stockton and Darlington, England.

1840 A penny post system is introduced in Britain.

1843 Cyrus Hall McCormick patents a mechanical reaper.

1848-49 Widespread social discontent leads to riots and rebellions across Europe.

1850

[illegible] Steel production is improved by the invention of the Bessemer process.

1865-66 A cable is laid across the Atlantic, linking Britain and the US for Morse code transmissions.

1869 The Suez Canal opens, cutting the journey from Europe to Asia by six weeks.

1874

1876 Alexander Graham Bell invents the telephone.

1877 Thomas Edison invents the phonograph.

1879 Electric street lighting is installed in Menlo Park, New Jersey.

1885 The first gasoline-powered vehicle, a motorcycle, is invented by Gottlieb Daimler.

1895 Guglielmo Marconi invents radio telegraphy.

1900

1908 The first Model T Ford is produced.

Ford introduces the moving assemby line.

Social conditions

Industrialization caused huge social upheaval as people left the land and flocked to towns and cities in search of work. The population rapidly concentrated around factories and mines, often in poor housing with little sanitation. Working conditions too were frequently abysmal, with long hours, risks to health and safety, a relentless machine-driven pace and low pay. Exploitation and child labor were common. Some enlightened industrialists did strive to improve the conditions of workers, but most advances were achieved only by changes in the law and by **trade union** action.

A few employers built **model settlements** for their workers. An early example was mill-owner **Robert Owen**, who created the community of New Lanark in Scotland in 1783. Others included Cadbury's garden city, **Bournville**, in England, and the communities established by the manufacturer **Krupp** in Essen, Germany.

Governments slowly began to take action to improve working and living conditions and eradicate the worst abuses. Britain's **Factory Act** of 1833 kept children under nine from working in textile mills, and the **Mines Act** of 1842 forbade women and children from going underground. In the United States, however, children worked in factories into the early 20th century. Governments also took increasing responsibility for social welfare. Britain passed a **Public Health Act** in 1875, and Germany's pioneering laws of the 1880s introduced insurance against illness, accidents and old age.

Trade associations struggled for better working conditions, but they were outlawed in much of Europe after the French Revolution. In Britain, unions were given limited rights after 1825, although strikes were illegal. The **"Tolpuddle Martyrs,"** six Dorset farm workers, were transported to Australia in 1834 for union activity, provoking a public outcry. Unions gradually won more rights and membership grew steadily through the 19th century.

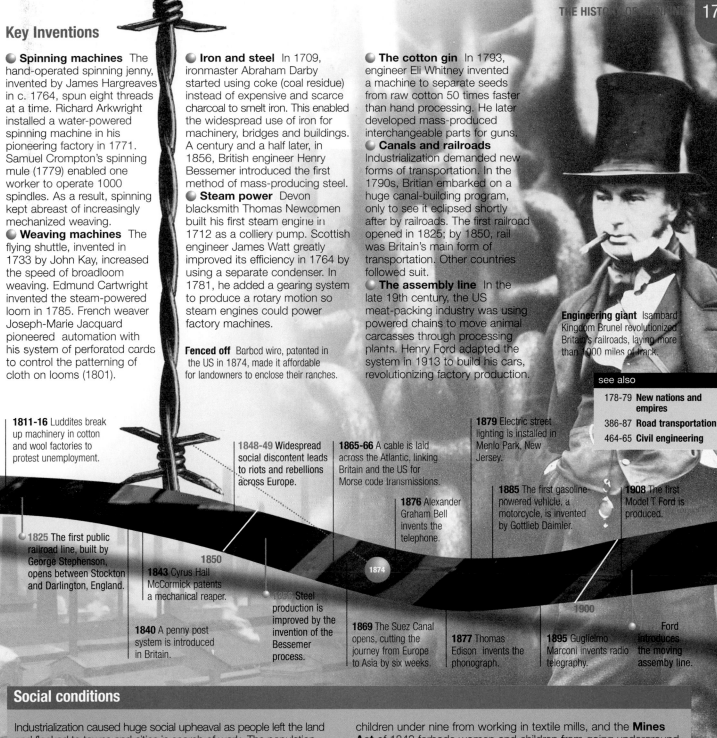

Child labor Boys as young as 13 and 14 were still working in mines in the United States into the early 20th century.

The French Revolution and the Napoleonic Wars reshaped Europe and changed the balance of power. The mighty Spanish and Ottoman empires faded, whereas Germany and Italy began a process of unification that turned them into world powers. Advanced nation–states such as Britain and France vied with one another to seize new territory, culminating in the 1880s "Scramble for Africa" that carved up a whole continent.

Explorers who opened the world

Heinrich Barth (1821-65) Barth was a German scholar who crossed the Sahara to West Africa in an 1849-55 British government expedition.

Sir Richard Burton (1821-90) Burton traveled in Arabia in 1853-54 disguised as a Muslim and reached Mecca. In 1857-59, he explored East Africa from Zanzibar looking for the source of the Nile.

René Caillié (1799-1838) In 1826-27 the French explorer Caillé became the first European to reach the fabled city of Timbuktu.

David Livingstone (1813-73) Livingstone was a British doctor and missionary who became the first European to cross Africa from the Atlantic coast to the Indian Ocean in 1853-56.

Sir Richard Burton

Mungo Park (1771-1806) Park was the first European to explore the River Niger in West Africa. He made one expedition in 1795-96 and a second in 1805-6.

John Hanning Speke (1827-64) Speke traveled with Burton in 1857-59 in search of the source of the Nile. He continued on his own to Lake Victoria, making a reutrn journey in 1860-62.

Henry Morton Stanley (1841-1904) Stanley was a British–American journalist who found the missing David Livingstone when he was lost in 1871. Stanley showed that Lake Victoria was the source of the Nile and crossed Africa via the Congo to the Atlantic coast.

The drive for colonies

By 1900, European colonial powers were racing to acquire territory across the globe.

BRITAIN'S COLONIAL WARS

Resistance by local populations led empire-building Britain into frequent conflicts.

Afghan Wars Britain went to war in 1838-42, 1878-80 and 1919 to gain control of Afghanistan and secure the northwest frontier of India. From 1880 to 1919, Britain controlled the Khyber Pass and influenced Afghan foreign policy.

Opium Wars Britain fought in 1839-42 and 1856-60 to protect its illegal trade in opium in China. The trade was damaging to Chinese society but British victories increased access to markets and brought possession of Hong Kong.

Indian Mutiny In 1857-58, widespread rebellion broke out against British rule, led by Indian soldiers of the East India Company. After the mutiny was crushed, the British government took over the rule of India.

Zulu War Britain attempted to annex Zululand in January 1879 but was resisted by the Zulus under King Cetshwayo, who almost wiped out a British column of 1700 troops at Isandhlwana. The British triumphed after a renewed campaign in March.

South African (Boer) Wars Britain attempted to annex the Boer (Afrikaner) republics in 1877. War followed in 1880-81, resulting in a Boer victory and an uneasy peace. War broke out again in 1899-1902. After initial defeats, Britain imposed colonial rule.

Ashanti Wars Britain fought a series of wars in the Gold Coast (Ghana), finally achieving the dissolution of the Ashanti confederation in 1896 and the seizure of their territories as a British protectorate.

Fighting spirit Ragtag Boers proved to be a match for the British army.

1783 Britain loses its American colonies at the end of the Revolutionary War.

1788 The first British convict ships arrive at Botany Bay, Australia.

1796-99 The British take control of Ceylon and southern India.

1800

1804 A slave revolt makes Haiti the first independent country in Latin America.

1806 The British occupy Cape Province of South Africa.

1819-26 Simón Bolívar leads South America to independence but fails to unite the new republics.

1821 Britain takes over the Gold Coast and Gambia in West Africa.

1826 Britain annexes Lower Burma and Assam.

1830 France conquers Algeria.

1831-36 Charles Darwin makes his around-the-world voyage in HMS *Beagle*.

1840 Britain annexes New Zealand, but colonization precipitates the first New Zealand ("Maori") War (1843-48).

1850

1853-56 Britain, France, Turkey and Piedmont defeat Russia in the Crimean War.

THE MAKING OF MODERN GERMANY

Unlike France and England, the Holy Roman Empire failed to develop a strong central power under a single strong monarchy in medieval times. Until the 17th century, Germany remained a mosaic of many states ruled by minor princes, each with its own borders, laws, customs duties and political structures. In the aftermath of the Thirty Years' War (1618-48), Prussia rose to prominence as the most powerful, but moves toward integration did not begin until the 19th century. Napoleon forcibly unified all the German-speaking states except Prussia and Austria in the **Confederation of the Rhine** (1806-13). In 1814-15 at the Congress of Vienna the conservative Prince **Clemens von Metternich** masterminded a 39-state **German Confederation** that included Austria and Prussia. Economic ties soon followed in the form of a **Zollverein** (Customs Union) led by Prussia. Political unification was pursued by the Prussian "Iron Chancellor" **Otto von Bismarck**. He established the **North German Confederation** after the Austro-Prussian War of 1866 and extended it after the Franco–Prussian War of 1870-71 to include southern Germany – a union known as the **Second Reich**. The king of Prussia, **Wilhelm I** (1797-1888), became the first Kaiser (Emperor) in 1871. Bismarck introduced social welfare legislation and a common currency but was dismissed by Kaiser **Wilhelm II** (reigned 1888-1918) in 1890. A period of colonial expansion then began under Bismarck's successor Leo von Caprivi (1890-94) and Wilhelm II.

Otto von Bismarck

see also

160-61 **Africa**

164-65 **The age of exploration**

180-81 **World War I**

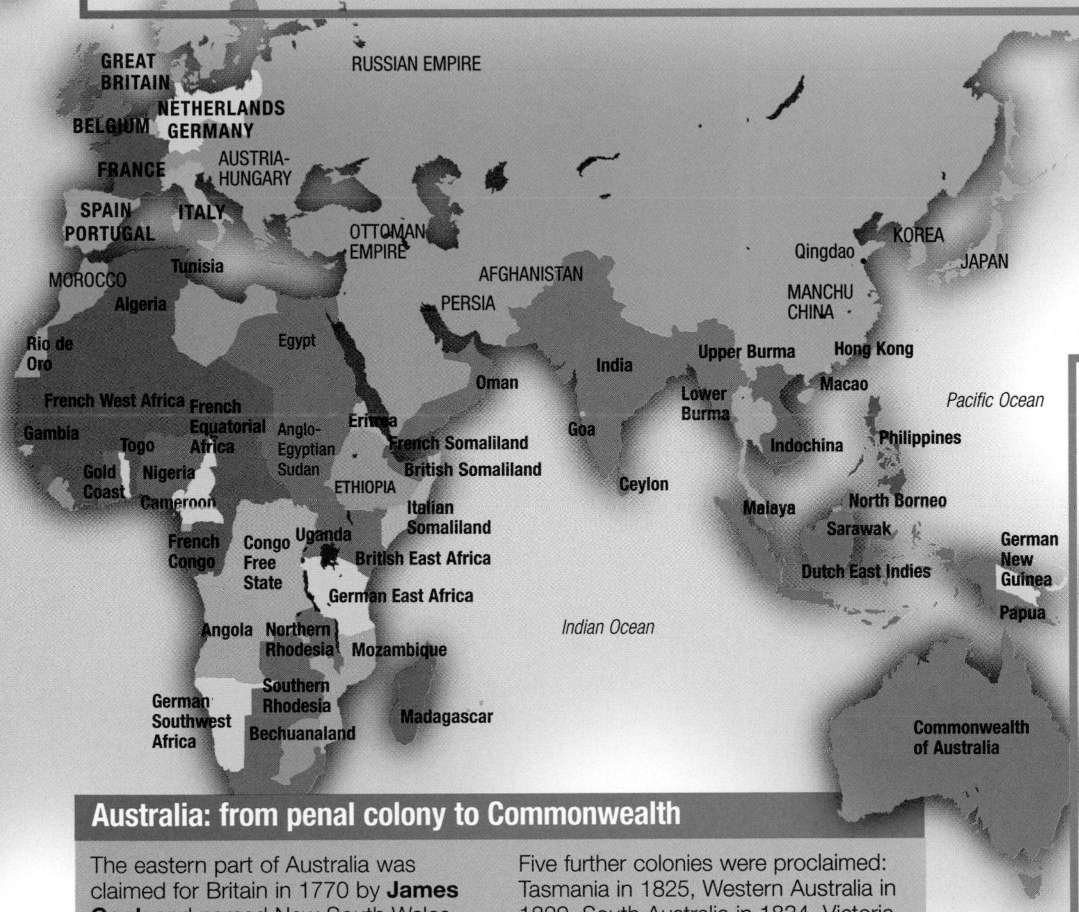

THE UNIFICATION OF ITALY

For more than 1000 years after the fall of Rome, Italy was a patchwork of city–states and small kingdoms and often under foreign rule. Hopes for unification grew after Napoleon's invasion in 1796-97 and a short-lived partial union followed. But by 1815, the country was again split into many states. Led by the radical nationalist, **Giuseppe Mazzini**, the **Risorgimento** ("resurrection") movement rapidly won support. In 1859, Italian and French forces drove the Austrians from Lombardy and then in 1861 **Giuseppe Garibaldi**'s volunteer "Red Shirts" toppled the Naples monarchy. **Victor Emmanuel II** of Piedmont–Sardinia became king of Italy. Full unification followed in 1870, when Venice and Papal Rome were annexed and Rome was made the national capital.

Australia: from penal colony to Commonwealth

The eastern part of Australia was claimed for Britain in 1770 by **James Cook** and named New South Wales. Britain used the new territory to settle transported convicts: The first **penal colony** was established in 1778. British government-assisted free settlement of Australia began in the 1830s, once the rich grasslands west of the Blue Mountains were opened to **sheep and wheat farming**. Five further colonies were proclaimed: Tasmania in 1825, Western Australia in 1829, South Australia in 1834, Victoria in 1851 and Queensland in 1859. **Gold rushes** in the 1850s and 1860s encouraged new waves of immigration from Europe, particularly to New South Wales and Victoria. The colonies were largely self-governing from the 1850s on and were federated as the Commonwealth of Australia in 1901.

1857-58 The Indian Mutiny against British rule in India breaks out.

1860-70 The Second New Zealand War pits Maoris against European settlers.

1862 France creates a protectorate in Indochina (Vietnam and Cambodia).

1867 Eastern Canada becomes a self-governing dominion within the British Empire.

1870-71 The Franco–Prussian War leads to the siege of Paris and the Commune. Germany is united under Prussia.

1877 Queen Victoria becomes Empress of India.

1882 The British occupy Egypt to protect their interests in the Suez Canal.

1883 Tunisia becomes a French protectorate.

1885 Leopold II of Belgium acquires the Congo as a personal fief.

1898 The US seizes Cuba, Puerto Rico, Guam and the Philippines in the Spanish–American War.

1899-1902 Britain eventually defeats the Boers in the South African War ("Boer War").

1900

1901 Australia becomes a self-governing Commonwealth.

The assassination of Archduke Franz Ferdinand of Austria–Hungary in Sarajevo plunged Europe into war. Mass armies were mobilized in the hope of a decisive victory, but the war turned into a bloody and horrific stalemate that lasted for four years and destroyed three empires.

FIVE CAUSES OF THE WAR

1. **German ambition** Germany's quest for world-power status led to clashes of interest with Britain, France and Russia.
2. **A naval arms race** The German attempt to build a world-class navy caused paranoia in Britain, the world's greatest sea power.
3. **The alliance system** Europe's system of alliances meant that any crisis could drag the whole continent into war.
4. **Mass mobilization** Germany's Schlieffen Plan made mobilization unstoppable and required the invasion of neutral Belgium, making a limited conflict impossible.
5. **Jingoistic nationalism** Powerful elements in several European governments sought a decisive war to focus patriotism and repress political discontent at home.

Western Front 1914-18

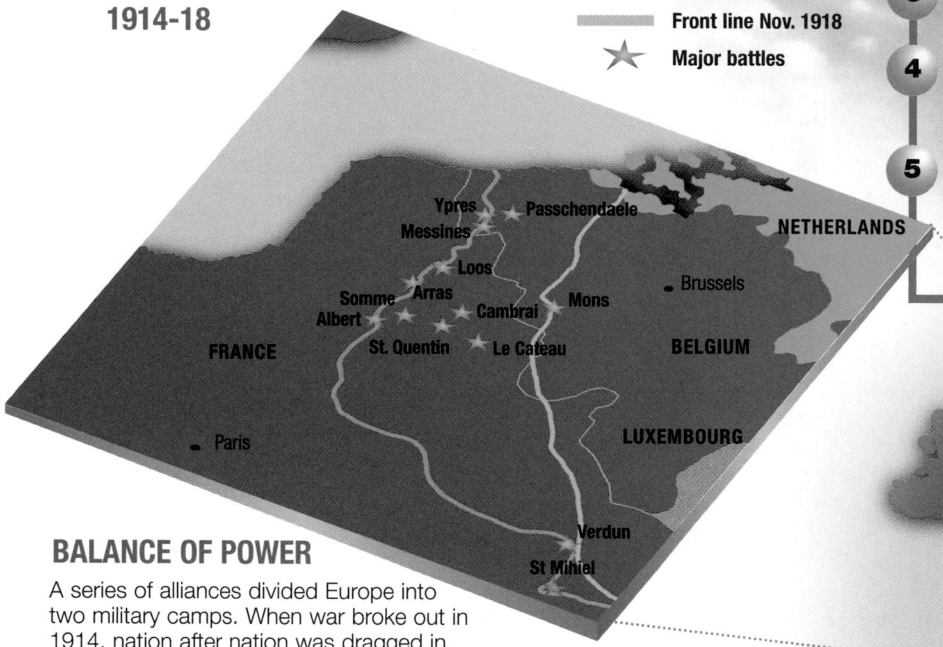

BALANCE OF POWER

A series of alliances divided Europe into two military camps. When war broke out in 1914, nation after nation was dragged in.

Central Powers
Germany, Austria–Hungary and Italy (Triple Alliance), plus the Ottoman Empire and Bulgaria.

Allied Powers
France, Russia and Great Britain (Triple Entente), plus Serbia, Belgium, Japan, Italy (in 1915), Portugal, Romania, Greece and the United States.

Neutral states

	Central Powers	Allied Powers
Armed manpower	7 710 000	11 330 000
Battleships	48	97
Submarines	37	37

1914

Tannenberg (30 AUG 1914) Two Russian armies are routed by a small German force.

First Marne (5-12 SEP 1914) German forces are driven back from Paris.

Masurian Lakes (15 SEP 1914) The Russians are heavily defeated.

First Ypres (30 OCT 1914) British troops hold off the German advance in Flanders.

Second Ypres (22 APR 1915) Germany uses poison gas.

Isonzo Front (23 JUN 1915) Italy's offensives against Austria–Hungary make minimal gains.

1916

Verdun (21 FEB 1916) Germany attempts to "bleed France white" in a battle of attrition.

June 28 Archduke Franz Ferdinand is assassinated; Austria–Hungary declares war on Serbia.

Aug. 1 Germany declares war on Russia; **Aug. 3** Germany declares war on France; **Aug. 4** Germany invades Belgium; Great Britain declares war on Germany.

1915

Feb. 19 The first Zeppelin raid hits England.

April 25 Allied troops land at Gallipoli.

May 7 *Lusitania* is sunk by a U-boat off Ireland.

Dec. 7 Turks trap the British at Kut in Mesopotamia. **Dec. 19** Allied troops evacuate the Dardanelles.

April 29 The Anglo–Indian garrison surrenders at Kut.

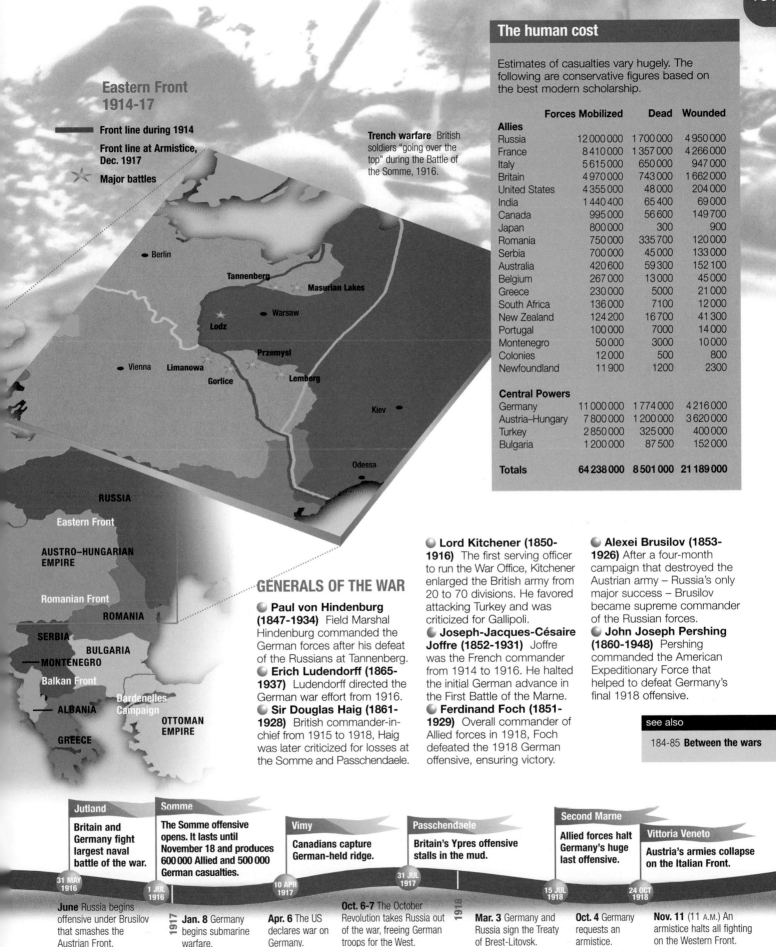

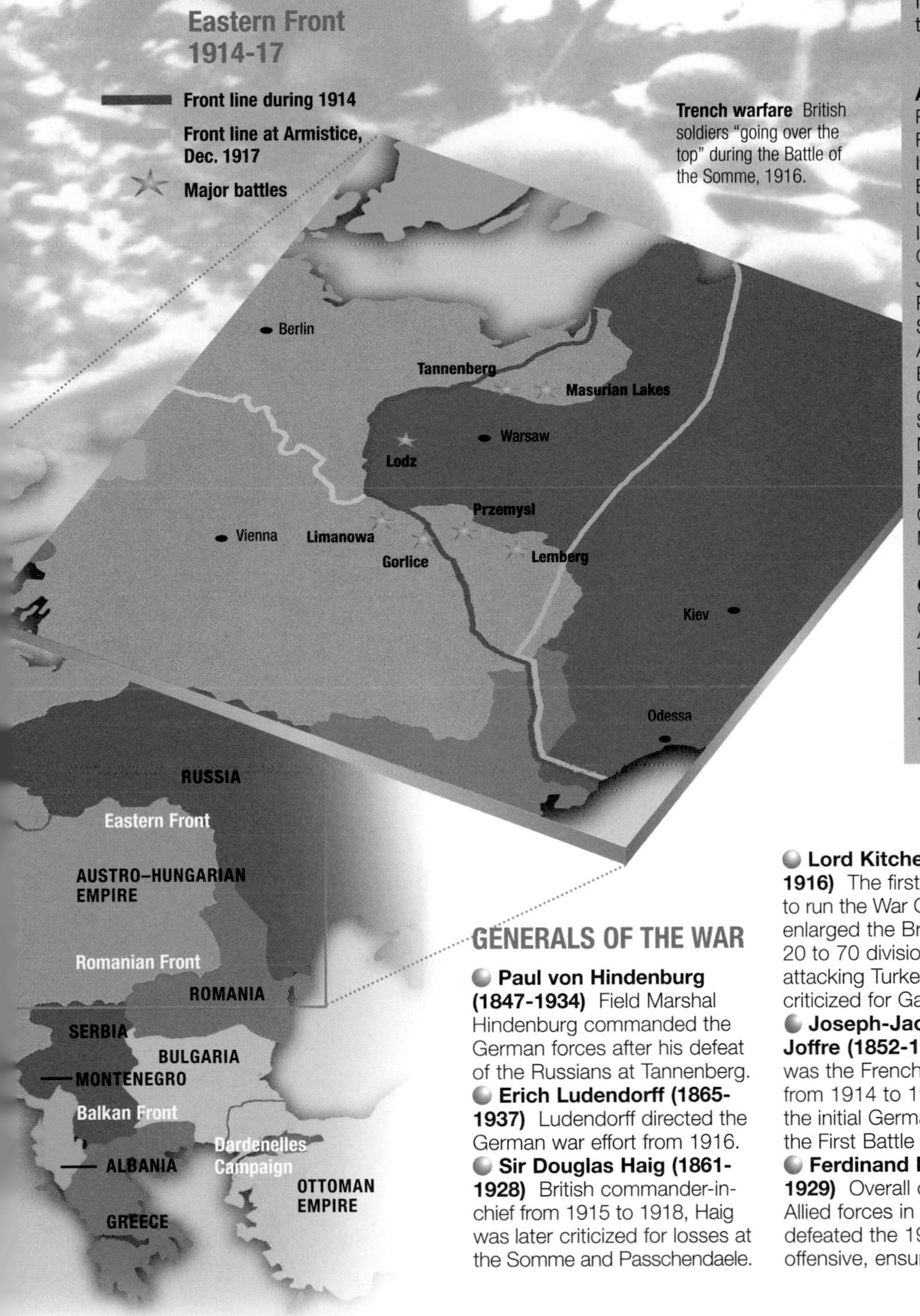

Trench warfare British soldiers "going over the top" during the Battle of the Somme, 1916.

The human cost

Estimates of casualties vary hugely. The following are conservative figures based on the best modern scholarship.

	Forces Mobilized	Dead	Wounded
Allies			
Russia	12 000 000	1 700 000	4 950 000
France	8 410 000	1 357 000	4 266 000
Italy	5 615 000	650 000	947 000
Britain	4 970 000	743 000	1 662 000
United States	4 355 000	48 000	204 000
India	1 440 400	65 400	69 000
Canada	995 000	56 600	149 700
Japan	800 000	300	900
Romania	750 000	335 700	120 000
Serbia	700 000	45 000	133 000
Australia	420 600	59 300	152 100
Belgium	267 000	13 000	45 000
Greece	230 000	5000	21 000
South Africa	136 000	7100	12 000
New Zealand	124 200	16 700	41 300
Portugal	100 000	7000	14 000
Montenegro	50 000	3000	10 000
Colonies	12 000	500	800
Newfoundland	11 900	1200	2300
Central Powers			
Germany	11 000 000	1 774 000	4 216 000
Austria–Hungary	7 800 000	1 200 000	3 620 000
Turkey	2 850 000	325 000	400 000
Bulgaria	1 200 000	87 500	152 000
Totals	**64 238 000**	**8 501 000**	**21 189 000**

GENERALS OF THE WAR

Paul von Hindenburg (1847-1934) Field Marshal Hindenburg commanded the German forces after his defeat of the Russians at Tannenberg.

Erich Ludendorff (1865-1937) Ludendorff directed the German war effort from 1916.

Sir Douglas Haig (1861-1928) British commander-in-chief from 1915 to 1918, Haig was later criticized for losses at the Somme and Passchendaele.

Lord Kitchener (1850-1916) The first serving officer to run the War Office, Kitchener enlarged the British army from 20 to 70 divisions. He favored attacking Turkey and was criticized for Gallipoli.

Joseph-Jacques-Césaire Joffre (1852-1931) Joffre was the French commander from 1914 to 1916. He halted the initial German advance in the First Battle of the Marne.

Ferdinand Foch (1851-1929) Overall commander of Allied forces in 1918, Foch defeated the 1918 German offensive, ensuring victory.

Alexei Brusilov (1853-1926) After a four-month campaign that destroyed the Austrian army – Russia's only major success – Brusilov became supreme commander of the Russian forces.

John Joseph Pershing (1860-1948) Pershing commanded the American Expeditionary Force that helped to defeat Germany's final 1918 offensive.

see also
184-85 **Between the wars**

Jutland — 31 MAY 1916 — Britain and Germany fight largest naval battle of the war.

Somme — 1 JUL 1916 — The Somme offensive opens. It lasts until November 18 and produces 600 000 Allied and 500 000 German casualties.

Vimy — 10 APR 1917 — Canadians capture German-held ridge.

Passchendaele — 31 JUL 1917 — Britain's Ypres offensive stalls in the mud.

Second Marne — 15 JUL 1918 — Allied forces halt Germany's huge last offensive.

Vittoria Veneto — 24 OCT 1918 — Austria's armies collapse on the Italian Front.

June Russia begins offensive under Brusilov that smashes the Austrian Front.

1917

Jan. 8 Germany begins submarine warfare.

Apr. 6 The US declares war on Germany.

Oct. 6-7 The October Revolution takes Russia out of the war, freeing German troops for the West.

1918

Mar. 3 Germany and Russia sign the Treaty of Brest-Litovsk.

Oct. 4 Germany requests an armistice.

Nov. 11 (11 A.M.) An armistice halts all fighting on the Western Front.

Russia entered the 20th century as an absolute monarchy ruled by Romanov tsars. Alongside the immense wealth of a few, millions lived in extreme poverty. Discontent was mounting, but calls for reform went unheeded, fueling radical movements and ideas. Revolution in 1905 forced Nicholas II to establish a parliament, and in 1917, he installed the world's first socialist government. By 1922, the USSR had come into being with Vladimir Ilych Lenin at its head.

FACT Germany helped Lenin return to Russia in 1917. He was thought so dangerous that his train was sealed until it crossed the border.

Fiery orator Lenin addresses Russian troops in 1920.

MAIN CAUSES OF THE REVOLUTION

1. **Liberal opposition** Liberals and intellectuals had long opposed tsarist autocracy. As early as 1825, moderates in the military tried to seize power and enforce reforms (the Decembrist revolt).
2. **Rapid economic change** Industrialization created an oppressed urban proletariat that became increasingly politicized.
3. **Repressive government** Harsh measures introduced by rulers such as Alexander III in the 1880s alienated public support and created a fertile breeding ground for revolutionary ideas.
4. **Weakness of Nicholas II** Nicholas II ignored calls for reform, and his reluctant creation of a powerless Duma (parliament) in 1905 did nothing to restore confidence. The influence of Rasputin on the tsarina seemed to symbolize the court's degeneracy.
5. **Military defeat** Russia's defeat by Japan in 1904-5 and disastrous failures in World War I (resulting in 7 million casualties) led to increasingly hostile public opinion.
6. **Food shortages** Inflation and food shortages caused by the war created suffering and hardship, especially in Russian cities.

NOTE: Russia abandoned the "Old Style" Julian calendar in February 1918. Old Style (OS) dates are given here where they are significant.

1861 Alexander II emancipates Russia's serfs.

1881 Alexander II is assassinated by revolutionaries and is succeeded by his son Alexander III.

1894 Nicholas II accedes to the Russian throne.

1900

1902-3 Strikes and civil unrest occur in Russian industrial centers.

1903 The Russian Social Democratic Workers' Party splits into Bolshevik and Menshevik factions.

1904-5 Russia is humiliated by defeat in the Russo-Japanese War.

1905 Revolution follows the massacre of protestors in St. Petersburg. Nicholas agrees to an elected Duma.

1914 Russia enters World War I against the Central Powers.

1915

March 8, 1917 (OS Feb. 23) Bread riots erupt in Petrograd (St. Petersburg).

March 12, 1917 (OS Feb. 27) The Petrograd garrison mutinies, turning a revolt into the Menshevik-led "February Revolution."

March 13-15, 1917 Soviets (councils) of workers, soldiers and peasants are set up across Russia.

March 15, 1917 Nicholas II abdicates; the Duma establishes a moderate, multiparty Provisional Government.

April 16, 1917 Lenin returns from Switzerland to Petrograd and calls for revolution against the Provisional Government.

May 3-4, 1917 (OS April 20-21) The "April Days" demonstrations against the government's failure to end Russia's part in the war occur.

The 1905 Revolution: the "dress rehearsal"

Strikes, heavy taxation and disgust with inept handling of the **Russo–Japanese War** boiled over in 1905. A demonstration in St Petersburg on January 22 (OS January 9), petitioned Tsar Nicholas II for reform, but Cossack troops opened fire on the unarmed crowds converging on the Winter Palace, killing between 50 and 1000 (estimates vary). Deep resentment at this **"Bloody Sunday"** resulted in strikes, assassinations and revolts in Poland, Latvia, Georgia and Finland. Nicholas ruled for 12 more years, but his people's devotion was fatally undermined. He was forced to introduce reforms and created an elected parliament, the Duma. A general strike led by Leon Trotsky and a mutiny on the battleship ***Potemkin*** won more concessions, including freedoms of conscience, speech and association. The moderates were satisfied and revolt died out, but 15 000 had died.

THE RUSSIAN CIVIL WAR (1918-20)

Many groups including nationalists, republicans, democrats and even radical Socialist Revolutionaries opposed the Bolsheviks after they seized power in 1917. A loose alliance – the **"White Army"** – was formed in opposition to the Bolshevik **"Red Army"** created by Trotsky in late 1917. Whites were united in opposing Lenin and the peace treaty with Germany but failed to coordinate. Fighting was widespread, from northern Russia to the Caucasus and Ukraine. Foreign powers including Britain, France, Japan and the United States aided the Whites but failed to hold territory against the Reds. White resistance weakened, crippled by internal divisions and the failure to develop a popular alternative to Bolshevism. In 1920, the White Army was defeated in the Crimea and later anti-Bolshevik uprisings were put down. Transcaucasian republics were crushed in 1922, which was followed by the creation of the USSR. The postrevolutionary turmoil was over, having cost 13 million lives.

Key figures

Alexander Kerensky (1881-1970) Kerensky headed the Provisional Government of July-October 1917. He failed to withdraw Russia from World War I or to introduce reforms.

Vladimir Ilych Lenin (1870-1924) A political theorist and revolutionary Marxist, Lenin devoted his life to establishing a Communist Russian state. He led the Bolshevik revolution of 1917, founded the Communist Party and became the first head of state of the USSR. A pragmatic leader, he permitted some capitalist reforms in his 1921 New Economic Policy.

Nicholas II (1868-1918) Nicholas was the last tsar, reigning from 1894 to 1917. He abdicated after the February Revolution and was executed.

Rasputin (1872-1916) Grigori Rasputin, a Siberian holy man, claimed to be able to alleviate the hemophilia of the tsar's son, Alexei. He briefly dominated state affairs through his influence over the tsarina but was murdered by monarchists.

Joseph Stalin (1879-1953) Stalin played a minor role in the October Revolution and led the Communist Party from 1922. He succeeded Lenin as head of state and turned the USSR into a world power. Stalin ruled as a dictator, eliminating rivals in a series of murderous "purges." His reign of terror and policy of forced collectivization cost an estimated 25 million lives.

Pyotr Stolypin (1862-1911) As prime minister of Russia after the 1905 revolution, Stolypin introduced reforms – notably in land ownership – but not fast enough to satisfy radicals. As a result, he was unpopular with both the left and the right. He resigned in March 1911 and was assassinated six months later.

Leon Trotsky (1879-1940) A Communist theorist, Trotsky met Lenin in London in 1902. He returned to Russia in 1905 and led the St. Petersburg Soviet (workers' council) in a strike that won major reforms. In 1917, he founded the Red Army, leading it throughout the Civil War. Trotsky was the obvious successor to Lenin but lost out to Stalin and was exiled in 1929. He continued to write and promote the cause of "world revolution" until he was murdered in Mexico on Stalin's orders.

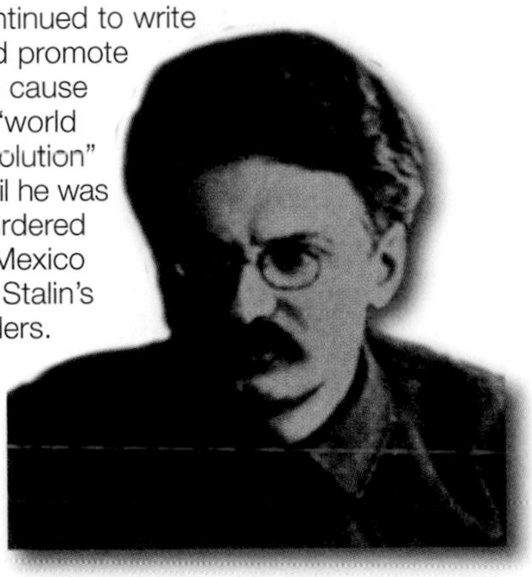
Trotsky (1879-1940)

Political forces in Russia

Narodniki ("Populists") The Narodniki were socialists who in the 1860s and 70s favored a republican, liberal government and Western technology. Some formed the People's Will terrorist movement, which assassinated Alexander II in 1881.

Octobrists Political moderates, the Octobrists were satisfied with the tsar's concessions of October 1905.

Kadets (Constitutional Democrats) The Kadets considered the 1905 changes inadequate. They wanted further reforms, including a limited monarchy. They dominated the first Duma but then declined in influence.

Black Hundreds (League of the Russian People) After the 1905 revolution, nationalists calling themselves Black Hundreds carried out attacks on revolutionaries and Jews.

Socialist Revolutionary Party Heirs to the Narodniki movement, the Socialist Revolutionaries sought revolution by mobilizing the peasantry using terrorism if necessary. They formed a majority in the Provisional Government but were disbanded after the Civil War.

Social Democratic Workers' Party A Marxist party founded by Georgi Plekhanov in 1898, the Social Democratic Workers' Party sought revolution led by industrial workers. In 1903, it split into Bolshevik and Menshevik factions.

Bolsheviks ("Majority") Led by Lenin, the Bolsheviks saw themselves as the vanguard of a popular socialist revolution. They supported the use of violence to overthrow the state and establish a "dictatorship of the proletariat."

Mensheviks ("Minority") The Mensheviks were moderate socialists who favored peaceful action through the Duma.

July 1917 The Bolshevik party is outlawed after mass armed demonstrations (the "July Days"); its leaders are arrested or go into hiding.

Sept. 8-12, 1917 An attempted counter-revolutionary coup by army commander General Kornilov fails.

Sept. 1917 Bolsheviks gain control of the Petrograd and Moscow Soviets.

Oct. 20, 1917 Lenin returns from hiding in Finland and urges armed revolution.

Nov. 6-7, 1917 (OS Oct. 24-25) The Bolsheviks overthrow the Provisional Government in the "October Revolution."

Dec. 1917 The Bolsheviks abolish private property, redistribute land, nationalize banks and put workers in control of industry.

March 3, 1918 The Bolshevik government signs a humiliating peace treaty with Germany. Civil war breaks out lasting until 1920.

July 1918 The royal family is executed.

Aug. 1918 An attempt to assassinate Lenin leads to the "Red Terror" – an attempt to crush all opposition to Bolshevism.

1920 The Whites fail to capture Moscow, and the Red Army defeats a Polish invasion.

1920

1921 Lenin introduces the New Economic Policy.

1922 Lenin proclaims the foundation of the Union of Soviet Socialist Republics (USSR).

1924 Lenin dies; by 1929, Stalin has outmaneuvered Trotsky and become leader of the USSR.

Fallen idol Children contemplate a dismantled statue of Alexander III in 1918. After the Revolution, many tsarist monuments were destroyed.

see also
180-81 **World War I**
184-85 **Between the wars**
240-41 **Russia**
310-11 **Western thought**

Aftershocks from World War I continued to rock Europe for two decades. The world economy fluctuated between boom and bust in the 1920s, and voters were tempted by radical ideas, particularly those of militaristic right-wing parties. In the late 1930s, the aggressive Nazi regime in Germany was mirrored in Japan and Italy, pushing the world toward another major war.

GERMANY'S FLASHPOINTS

The Treaty of Versailles (signed on June 28, 1919) not only burdened Germany with guilt for World War I and with heavy reparations payments but also redrew parts of the map of Europe. Austria–Hungary and the Russian and Ottoman Empires ceased to exist, and Germany lost territories as shown on the map. Many of these areas had long-established German populations and industrial centers; their occupation or seizure by other states caused bitter resentment in Germany, and this sense of injustice was exploited by the Nazis.

German territory ceded to other states

German speakers outside Germany

German territory occupied by Allied powers

Ruhr The Ruhr region was occupied by French and Belgian troops in 1923-25, after Germany defaulted on war reparations.

North Schleswig After a referendum in 1920, North Schleswig became Danish.

Polish corridor A large area of eastern Germany was granted to Poland at Versailles though its Polish majority was small.

Danzig (Gdansk) The former capital of West Prussia became a free city administered by the League of Nations.

Moresnet, Eupen and Malmedy Three cantons in western Germany were granted to Belgium under the Treaty of Versailles.

Alsace and Lorraine The disputed regions of Alsace and Lorraine (German since 1871) were granted to France at Versailles.

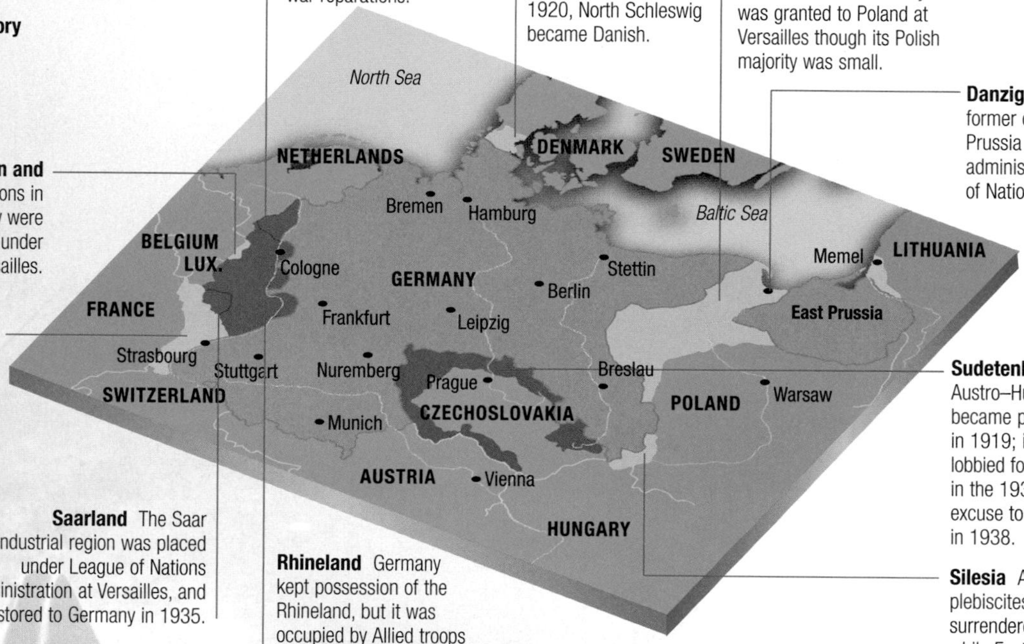

Sudetenland The former Austro-Hungarian Sudetenland became part of Czechoslovakia in 1919; its German population lobbied for union with Germany in the 1930s, giving Hitler the excuse to annex the region in 1938.

Saarland The Saar industrial region was placed under League of Nations administration at Versailles, and restored to Germany in 1935.

Rhineland Germany kept possession of the Rhineland, but it was occupied by Allied troops until 1927. German troops returned in 1936.

Silesia After a series of plebiscites, Upper Silesia was surrendered to Poland in 1919, while East Silesia became part of Czechoslovakia.

ECONOMIC CRISIS

World War I had a major impact on the world economy. Many economies had expanded artificially during the war, leading to a collapse in demand once the war was over. Most countries had also borrowed heavily and were unable to back their borrowings with gold reserves, causing a collapse of the **Gold Standard** and **devaluation**. In the United States, banks became overexposed in the speculative stockmarket boom of the late 1920s.

The US also suffered agricultural blight (the **"Dust Bowl"**) in the 1930s, caused by inflated farm prices and overworked land.

When the US stockmarket began to fall on **October 24, 1929**, panicked speculators tried to sell their stocks at any price, leading to a collapse that quickly spread around the world. By 1931, there were 8 million unemployed in the US, 5 million in Germany and 2.75 million in Britain.

Apart from increasing support for extremist politics, the Depression also prompted President Franklin Roosevelt to introduce his **New Deal**, a largely successful program of massive public works intended to create jobs. In Hitler's Germany, a huge **rearmament** program provided a similar boost to the economy (and those of Germany's rivals) – but the price was an arms race that hastened the drift toward war.

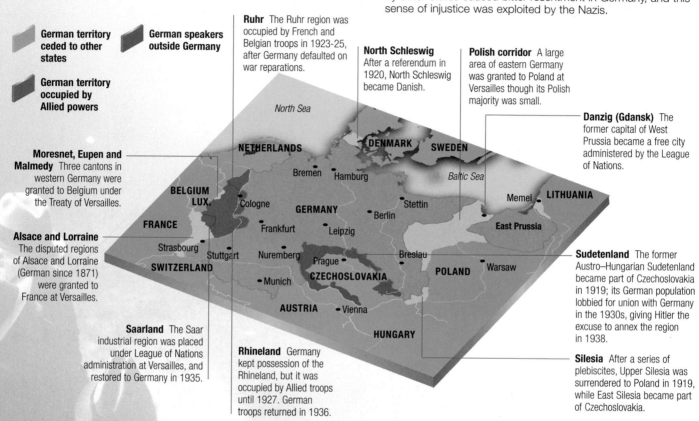

Dustbowl farmers Real hardship hit US farms during the Depression.

1918 World War I ends; the Peace Conference in Paris excludes Germany.

1919 The left-wing "Spartacist" uprising fails in Germany.

1920

1920 The League of Nations meets for the first time; the US refuses to join.

1921 German war reparations are set at 269 billion Marks ($10.4 million).

1922 Mussolini forms a Fascist government in Italy.

1923 France and Belgium occupy the Ruhr. German currency collapses.

1925

1925 Hitler publishes *Mein Kampf (My Struggle).*

1926 The General Strike in Britain lasts just nine days, though miners strike for six months.

1928 Trading volume on the New York Stock Exchange hits an all-time record.

1929 The Stock Market Crash sets off worldwide economic depression.

The rise of the dictators The period between the wars saw one-party dictatorships established across Europe. In the USSR, Stalin began a policy of systematically eliminating critics and rivals. In Germany, Hitler succeeded the Weimar Republic via the ballot box but then used his Nazi thugs to destroy political opponents. Mussolini dismantled Italy's democracy and used the Fascist Blackshirt militia to intimidate other politicians. Elsewhere, too, the 1920s and 30s saw the rise of authoritarian strongmen, from Horthy in Hungary (1920) and Salazar in Portugal (1928) to King Alexander in Yugoslavia (1929) and Franco in Spain (1939).

Joseph Stalin (1879-1953)
Born Joseph Dzhugashvili in Georgia, Stalin ("man of steel") became secretary-general of the Communist Party Central Committee in the USSR in 1922. He became head of state in 1927, presiding over a reign of terror in the 1930s that included show trials, purges, prison camps and the execution of 10 million people. From 1941, he led the Soviet Union's titanic struggle against Nazi Germany and dominated the postwar Allied settlement, imposing Soviet rule over Eastern Europe.

Benito Mussolini (1883-1945)
Mussolini was a journalist before he founded the National Fascist Party. He took over Italy in 1922, establishing himself as a dictator by 1926. He was initially widely supported for his economic reforms and for his annexation of Ethiopia in 1936 and Albania in 1939, but once war broke out Italy suffered a series of disastrous defeats. Mussolini was deposed in 1943 and executed by partisans in 1945.

Adolf Hitler (1889-1945)
Hitler was born in Austria, and served with distinction in World War I. He joined the National Socialist German Workers' Party (Nazis) in 1919 and became its leader in 1921. A failed coup in 1923 led to two years' imprisonment, during which he wrote his manifesto *Mein Kampf*. Hitler rallied militaristic support around the call to eliminate the Jews, to create a Greater Germany through eastern expansion, and to refute the Versailles Treaty. By 1933, the Nazis were the largest party in government, and Hitler became chancellor and then dictator *(Führer)*. Under his autocratic leadership in World War II, Germany suffered catastrophic defeat.

see also
180-81 **World War I**
186-87 **World War II**
378-79 **The principles of economics**

The Spanish Civil War (1936-39)

In 1931, a republic was declared in Spain, sparking a political crisis that became a testing ground for a wider European conflict between left and right. The **Republicans** included socialists, communists, anarchists and regional separatists. They were opposed by the **Nationalists** – monarchists, conservative Catholics and the fascist Falange Party. In 1936, a pro-Nationalist army uprising led by General Francisco Franco plunged Spain into civil war. Germany and Italy aided the Nationalists and the USSR helped the Republicans. Britain and France did not intervene, though many volunteers joined the pro-Republican **International Brigades**. The Republicans gradually lost ground, and in April 1939 Madrid fell. The Falange became the sole legal party, and Franco became the head of a fascist state until his death in 1975.

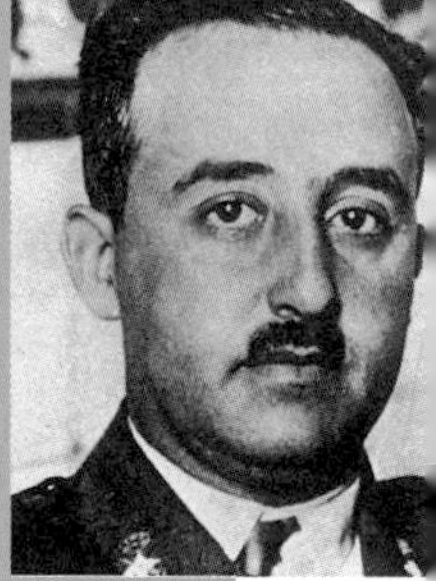

Francisco Franco

1930

1930 The Nazis win 100 seats in German elections.

1931 Spain is declared a republic.

1932 The Nazi Party becomes the largest political party in Germany after elections.

1933 Hitler becomes chancellor of Germany.

1934 Hitler arrests his SA rivals and other political opponents in the "Night of the Long Knives."

1935

1935 German Jews are stripped of their rights, and anti-Semitism is given legal sanction.

1936 Italy and Germany form a "Rome–Berlin Axis."

1936 Britain's King Edward VIII abdicates.

1936-39 Civil war devastates Spain.

1937 German bombers destroy the Republican Spanish town of Guernica.

1938 Germany occupies Austria and the Sudetenland. The Nazis attack Jews on the night of Nov. 9 – "Kristallnacht."

1939 German invasions of Czechoslovakia and Poland provoke world war.

World War II

From Hitler's invasion of Poland to the Hiroshima bomb

The costliest war in history engulfed more than three quarters of the world's people. Entire populations were targeted by aerial bombing, scorched-earth policies, concentration camps and genocide – many of which were justified by creeds of racial superiority. At its close – marked by the first, devastating use of atomic weapons – the Allied victors had to face a new world order, which included the demise of their old colonial empires and a hugely enhanced Soviet power.

FIVE CAUSES OF THE WAR

1. **Resentment at Versailles** The Versailles Treaty humiliated Germany, which had to forfeit territory and suffered prolonged economic hardship. Deeply felt resentment fueled extremist nationalist politics.
2. **Preoccupation with anti-Communism** Western powers tolerated extreme right-wing parties as a counterweight to Communism, not acknowledging the full implication of these parties' dictatorial ambitions.
3. **Territorial ambitions** The three Axis powers all sought new territories: Germany in Eastern Europe, Italy in Africa and the eastern Mediterranean, and Japan in Southeast Asia.
4. **An arms race** Rearmament stimulated the depressed 1930s economies, but it also created an arms race and growing mistrust among the European powers.
5. **The failure of internationalism** The League of Nations failed to keep aggression in check. Western leaders, haunted by the horror of World War I, preferred compromise and appeasement to confronting the aggressors.

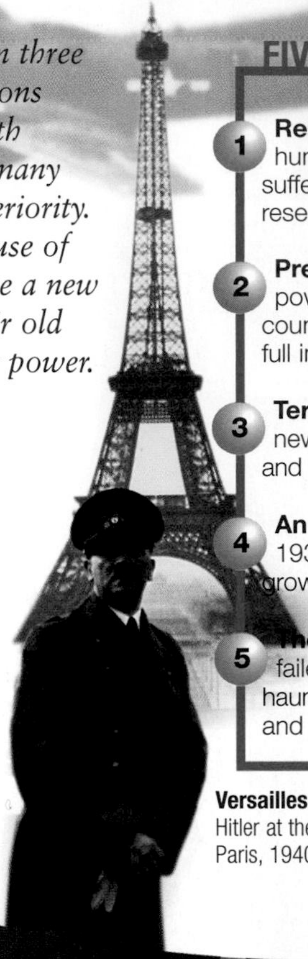

Versailles avenged Adolf Hitler at the Eiffel Tower in Paris, 1940.

1939

March 31 Britain and France promise to support Poland.

August 23 The Nazi–Soviet non-aggression pact frees Hitler to invade Poland.

September 1 Germany invades Poland.

September 3-10 Britain, France, Canada, Australia and New Zealand declare war on Germany.

1940

April 9 German troops invade Denmark and Norway.

May 10-14 Germany invades the Netherlands, Belgium, Luxembourg and France.

May 28-June 4 338 000 British and French troops are evacuated from Dunkirk, France.

July 10-October 31 In the Battle of Britain, British fighter planes resist German air attacks.

1941

April 17 Yugoslavia surrenders to German forces.

June 22 Germany launches its invasion of the USSR (Operation Barbarossa).

December 7 Japan launches a surprise attack on the US naval base at Pearl Harbor, Hawaii.

1942

February 15 Singapore falls to Japanese forces; 70 000 British and Commonwealth prisoners are taken.

THEATERS OF WAR

Europe Germany's victory over Poland (1939) was followed in summer 1940 by the occupation of Denmark, Norway, the Netherlands, Belgium and much of France. In early 1941, conquest of Yugoslavia and Greece completed German domination. The Allied counterattack began in Italy in 1943, followed by the D-Day landings in France in 1944. The Allied advance into Germany in 1944-45 was held up only at Arnhem (September 1944) and in the Ardennes.

North Africa Italian forces in North Africa suffered heavy defeats before the arrival of Rommel's Afrika Korps (February 1941). The Allies overcame Rommel only in late 1942 after defeating him at El Alamein and landing troops in French North Africa.

The Russian Front The war against Germany was won in the east by the Soviet Union. Despite initial victories, Germany found its forces drawn into an unwinnable war with a front at times 2700 km (1700 miles) long and an enemy who refused to surrender. Defeat at Stalingrad (1943) was a turning point, and the failure of the 1943 Kursk offensive was the beginning of the end.

The Pacific Japan needed to defeat the United States in the Pacific quickly, before US industrial production proved decisive. But Japan's stunning blow at Pearl Harbor (December 1941) was followed by the loss of its Japanese aircraft carriers at Midway (June 1942) and a US counteroffensive at Guadalcanal, Solomon Islands (August 1942). The remnants of the Japanese navy were destroyed at Leyte Gulf (October 1944), leaving Japan itself open to attack.

The Far East Coinciding with their attack on Pearl Harbor, the Japanese stormed European colonial possessions in the Far East and Southeast Asia: Hong Kong and Malaya (December 1941), the Dutch East Indies (January 1942) and the Philippines (December 1941). Japan occupied British-held Burma (January-March 1942) and threatened India. Their advance was finally halted at Imphal and Kohima, India (April 1944). Allied advances in Burma, China and Borneo in early 1945 ended Japan's Asian empire.

Pearl Harbor The surprise attack on the US fleet in 1941 was a tactical triumph but a political disaster for Japan. The US immediately entered the war with all its industrial might, and the battle for the Pacific began.

The war leaders

Winston Churchill 1874-1965 Churchill was a seasoned British politician, 64 years old at the outbreak of war. A long-term opponent of appeasement, he became prime minister of a coalition government in 1940. He inspired determined resistance to Hitler through stirring speeches, political resolve, a solid grasp of strategy and skilled diplomacy.

Douglas MacArthur 1880-1964 MacArthur was a retired US general who was recalled to defend the Philippines in 1941. Appointed Supreme Allied Commander in the Southwest Pacific, he oversaw the island-to-island campaign that led to Japan's defeat.

Franklin Delano Roosevelt 1882-1945 Roosevelt was in his third presidential term when the United States entered the war. He prepared the country for an anti-Japanese war in 1937 and led the national war effort. He died 26 days before the German surrender.

Bulldog spirit Winston Churchill's uncompromising stand against the Nazis united Britons through six years of war.

Tojo Hideki 1884-1948 Tojo was a professional soldier of samurai descent who rose to become the Japanese war minister (1940-44) and then prime minister (1941-44). He initiated the attack on Pearl Harbor and oversaw Japanese conquests in the Pacific, before military losses forced his resignation. He was hanged as a war criminal.

Bernard Montgomery 1887-1976 As commander of Britain's 8th Army in North Africa and Italy, Montgomery defeated Rommel in 1942 at El Alamein. He commanded Allied ground forces on D-Day.

Charles de Gaulle 1890-1970 A professional soldier with a distinguished record in World War I, de Gaulle led the French government in exile (Free French) during the war and inspired anti-German resistance in occupied France.

Dwight D. Eisenhower 1890-1969 Eisenhower was Supreme Commander of Allied forces in Europe (1942-45); he led the Allied "Torch" landings in North Africa in 1942 and in Italy in 1943. He then directed the 1944 D-Day landings.

Erwin Rommel 1891-1944 Rommel was a professional soldier with an outstanding record in World War I. He led a division in the German invasion of France. In 1941, he became commander of the Afrika Korps and won a series of victories until El Alamein. Implicated in a plot against Hitler in 1944, he committed suicide.

Hermann Göring 1893-1946 A World War I pilot, Göring became Minister of Interior and Air Minister in 1933. He rebuilt the Luftwaffe (air force) but was discredited after the Battle of Britain. Condemned in 1946 as a war criminal, he took poison before his execution.

Georgi Zhukov 1895-1974 Zhukov was a Tsarist conscript before joining the Red Army in 1918. He became the greatest Russian commander of the war. After the German invasion of the USSR, he supervised the defense of Leningrad and Moscow and was appointed commander-in-chief of Soviet troops. He won decisive victories at Stalingrad and Kursk in 1943 and led the Soviet advance on Berlin.

June 4-5 US planes sink four Japanese aircraft carriers in the Battle of Midway.

August 19 A raid on the French seaport of Dieppe claims 907 Canadian lives.

September 13 The Germans attack Stalingrad.

November 4 British and Commonwealth forces finally defeat Rommel's Afrika Korps at El Alamein, Egypt.

1943

January 31 Over 80 000 troops of the German Sixth Army surrender at Stalingrad.

July 5-17 The Kursk offensive leads to Germany's decisive defeat on the Russian Front.

July 10 British and American troops land in Sicily.

September 3 Italy surrenders as Allied forces advance north from Sicily.

1944

June 6 (D-Day) Allied forces land successfully in northwest France.

October 17-25 US forces destroy the remaining Japanese fleet at Leyte Gulf. This is the largest naval battle in history.

1945

May 8 VE Day (Victory in Europe): Germany surrenders unconditionally.

August 14 Japan surrenders unconditionally, following the destruction of Hiroshima (August 6) and Nagasaki (August 9) by US atomic bombs.

D-Day landing Allied troops land in Normandy, France (June 6, 1944) to open the "Second Front" against Germany.

Decisive weapon The atom bomb dropped on Hiroshima had more destructive power than all other armaments used up to that time put together.

The Holocaust

The term "The Holocaust" refers specifically to Nazi persecution of the Jews, although many others fell victim to the creed of racial purity, including gypsies, homosexuals and the mentally ill. State-sponsored persecution in the 1930s turned into outright genocide during the war and 6 million Jews died in the so-called "final solution."

Jewish Holocaust deaths (1939-45)

Austria	65 000	Italy	9000
Belgium	50 000	Latvia	8000
Czech.	277 000	Lithuania	135 000
France	83 000	Netherlands	106 000
Germany	180 000	Poland	3 000 000
Greece	71 000	Romania	370 000
Hungary	450 000	USSR	1 000 000

see also

184-85 **Between the wars**

The world map altered dramatically after World War II, as European colonial empires fell apart. Nationalist leaders emerged from local educated elites, and African soldiers returned from the war with raised expectations. The colonial powers, weakened by war, failed to reassert authority, and Russia and China offered alternative political visions. India won its freedom in 1947, setting a precedent for much of Asia and Africa.

Algeria

Algeria had been ruled by France since 1848. The Front de Libération Nationale (**FLN**) began a violent independence campaign in 1954, provoking a harsh French response. Settlers rioted to keep Algeria French, causing a political crisis in France and ushering in a new government (1958) under **de Gaulle**. Fighting in Algeria continued, and in April 1961, the antiindependence **OAS** group attempted a coup in France. Independence was granted on March 18, 1962, and the colonists were evacuated.

Coming of age Large areas of Africa and Asia became independent of their former colonial rulers after 1945. In the majority of cases, independence was granted peacefully, as shown.

Independence day Algeria celebrated when eight years of bloody conflict ended with independence from France in 1962.

Sub-Saharan Africa

In 1960, British prime minister Harold Macmillan made his **"winds of change"** speech to the South African parliament, acknowledging the rising tide of nationalist feeling developing in Africa. The transition to independence was at first peaceful.

In Britain's Gold Coast colony, radicals led by **Kwame Nkrumah** (1909-72) led a campaign of strikes, which won independence in March 1957, when the Gold Coast merged with British Togoland to form **Ghana**.

An independence movement grew in French **Senegal** after 1945, led by the poet and African Socialist **Léopold Senghor** (b. 1906). Senegal gained independence in 1960, with Senghor as president.

In the **Belgian Congo**, independence was hastily granted in 1960. Civil war erupted as the province of Katanga, led by **Moïse Tshombe** (1920-69), attempted secession from the regime of prime minister **Patrice Lumumba** (1925-61). UN forces intervened (1961-64), but the crisis was resolved only after a 1965 coup led by General **Mobutu Sésé Séko** (president 1970-97).

In the British colony of **Kenya**, the anticolonial **Mau Mau** rebellion (1952-57) cost 13 000 lives. Independence was granted in 1963, with the moderate leader **Jomo Kenyatta** (c. 1892-1978) as president.

1940

1940-41 Italy gives up Eritrea, Somalia and Ethiopia.

1945 Japan abandons its East Asian conquests.

1946 The Philippines become independent from the US.

1947 India and Pakistan become independent of Britain (August 15).

1948 Burma becomes independent of Britain.

1948-60 Malayan communists wage guerrilla war against Britain.

1949 Indonesia becomes independent of the Netherlands.

1950

1952-57 Mau Mau rebels in Kenya battle British colonial forces.

1954 Vietnamese forces defeat France at Dien Bien Phu.

1954-62 The Algerian war for independence brings France close to civil war.

1955-59 The EOKA pro-Greek terrorist campaign divides Cyprus.

1956 Britain and France intervene unsuccessfully in Egypt's Suez Crisis.

1957 Malaya and Ghana gain independence from Britain.

Israel

Jewish immigration to Palestine began in the Ottoman period and continued to 1918, inspired by **Zionism**, the political movement for a Jewish homeland. Immigration increased under the **British Mandate** (1923), leading to unrest between Jews and Palestinian Arabs. In 1947, after a Jewish **terrorist campaign**, the UN devised a plan to partition Palestine into separate Jewish and Arab states. The state of Israel was proclaimed on May 14, 1948 under **David Ben-Gurion** (1886-1973) and survived immediate attack by the **Arab League** (Egypt, Jordan, Syria, Iraq and Lebanon). Israel won further wars in 1967 (the **Six Day War**) and in 1973 (the **Yom Kippur War**).

Lost leader For a time, Sukarno was revered by the Indonesian people, but his adoption of Maoist ideas led to his downfall.

Indonesia

The Netherlands ruled the "East Indies" from the early 17th century on. The Partai Nasional Indonesia (PNI) was formed in 1927 by **Sukarno** (1901-70), under whom Indonesia gained quasi-independence in 1942, during the Japanese occupation. Sukarno declared full independence on the Japanese surrender in 1945. The returning Dutch faced a guerrilla war (1945-49) and granted independence to Indonesia in 1949, though they retained **Ambon** (until 1950) and **Western New Guinea** (until 1963). Sukarno's autocratic rule provoked a military coup in 1965 that effectively removed him from power.

East Timor was ruled by Portugal from 1702 on. After the Portuguese revolution in 1974, the **Fretilin** movement proclaimed independence, but East Timor was invaded by **Indonesia**. UN intervention in 1999 finally brought independence.

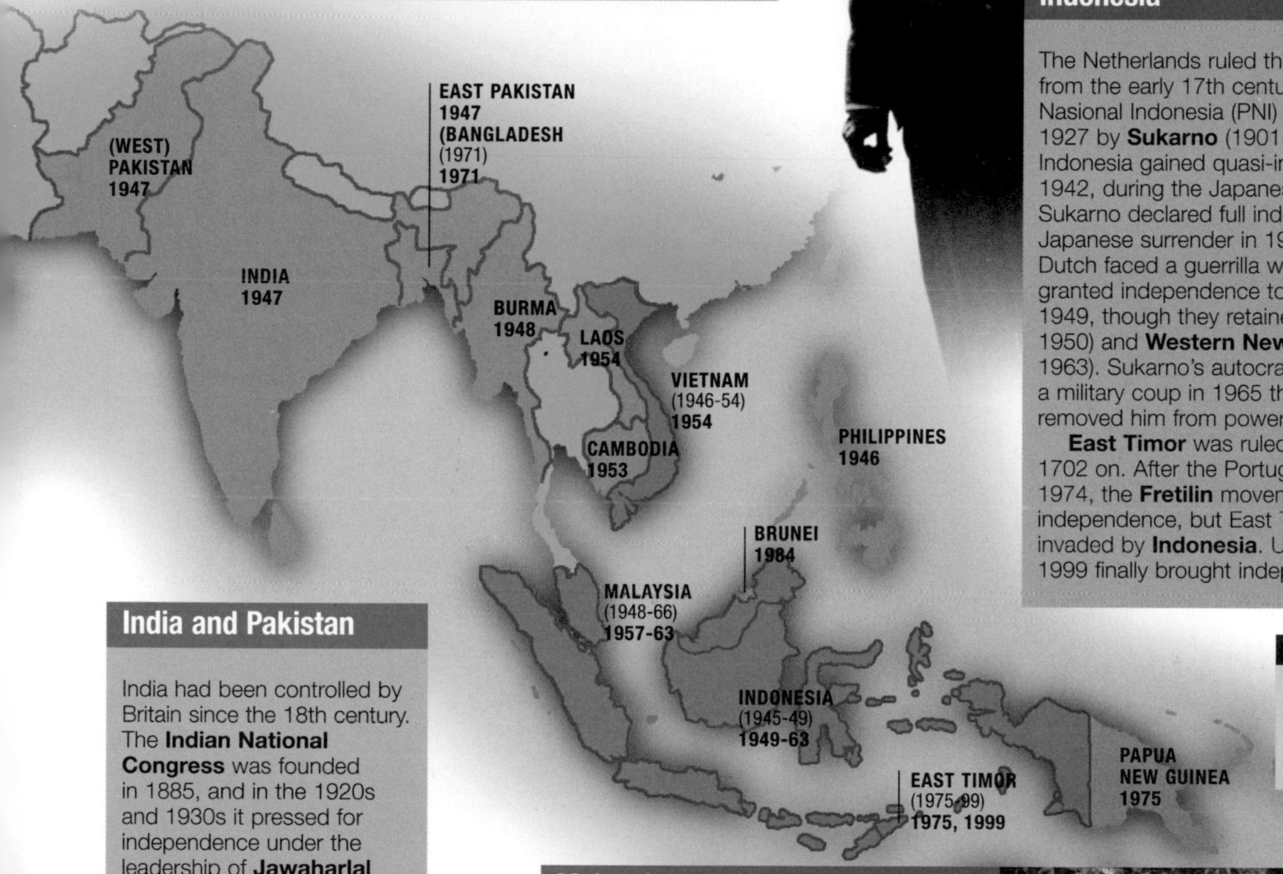

see also
186-87 World War II
190-91 The Cold War
192-93 New world order

India and Pakistan

India had been controlled by Britain since the 18th century. The **Indian National Congress** was founded in 1885, and in the 1920s and 1930s it pressed for independence under the leadership of **Jawaharlal Nehru** (1880-1964) and **Mohandas Gandhi** (1869-1948). Meanwhile, the **Muslim League** (founded in 1905) demanded a separate Muslim state (**Pakistan**). Amid escalating violence after 1945, Britain proposed two separate states; independence came into effect on August 15, 1947.

Malaysia

Malaya had been ruled by Britain since the early 19th century. In 1946, control was offered to the Malay sultans, but unrest and guerrilla war followed, led by the Communist Party (the **Malayan Emergency**, 1948-60). Independence was granted on August 31, 1957, but the war continued. **Malaysia** was formed in 1963 by Malaya, Sarawak, Sabah and Singapore which was ejected in 1965.

Malayan Emergency Every peasant became a communist suspect.

1960

1960 Cyprus gains independence from Britain.

1961 Indian forces seize Portugal's colonies of Goa, Daman and Diu.

1963 Indonesia seizes Western New Guinea (Irian Jaya) from the Dutch.

1964 Malta gains independence from Britain.

1965 Singapore becomes independent of Malaya.

1965-75 The US is drawn into the Vietnam War.

1967 Britain withdraws from Aden, a major strategic base.

1968 Britain announces the withdrawal of all forces east of Suez.

1970

1971 East Pakistan (Bangladesh) wins independence from Pakistan.

1974 A left-wing revolution in Portugal ends Portuguese colonialism.

1975 Indonesia seizes Portuguese East Timor.

1980

1980 Southern Rhodesia becomes independent as Zimbabwe

1990

1997 Britain returns Hong Kong to China.

1999 Portugal returns Macao to China.

The United States and the USSR emerged from World War II as the planet's superpowers. Their opposing ideologies shaped international politics for 45 years. The threat of nuclear destruction held both sides back from war; instead they maintained a nervous and uneasy truce, a "cold war" characterized by political posturing, spying and small proxy wars fought in other territories.

Behind the Iron Curtain

Winston Churchill used the term "Iron Curtain" at Fulton, Missouri, in 1946 to refer to the divide between the Soviet bloc (the USSR and its East European satellites) and the West. It became a physical reality when the East retreated behind closely guarded borders.

The **Berlin Airlift** was an early Cold War confrontation. Berlin consisted of four Allied zones, but the whole city lay within the Soviet bloc. In retaliation for currency reforms in West Germany, the USSR cut off all land links to West Berlin (June 1948). The Western Allies kept West Berlin supplied by an airlift, until the blockade was lifted in May 1949.

On the death of Stalin, some countries in Eastern Europe sought a more liberal communist policy.

In October 1956, the **Hungarian Uprising** occurred in support of the reformist government of **Imre Nagy** (1896-1958), who announced Hungary's withdrawal from the Warsaw Pact. Soviet troops invaded on November 4 and crushed the revolt.

In 1968, Czechoslovakia saw a period of liberalization (the **Prague Spring**) under premier **Alexander Dubcek**, who attempted to introduce "socialism with a human face." The USSR invaded on August 20 to crush the revolt. Dubcek was replaced in April 1969.

The military balance in the early 1960s

NATO
Founding members (1949): Belgium, Canada, Denmark, France (withdrew forces 1966), Iceland, Italy, Luxembourg, Netherlands, Norway, Portugal, UK and the US; plus Greece (1952), Turkey (1952), West Germany (1955) and Spain (1982)

Warsaw Treaty
(created 1955, disbanded 1991) USSR, Bulgaria, East Germany, Czechoslovakia, Hungary, Poland, Albania (until 1968) and Romania

	NATO	Warsaw Treaty
Ground forces	8 million	7.7 million
Battleships and aircraft carriers	76	
Submarines	nuclear 32 conventional 260	nuclear 12 conventional 495
Tanks	16 000	38 000
Bomber aircraft	2260	1600
Intercontinental and medium-range ballistic missiles	700	776

Korea

The former Japanese-occupied territory of Korea was divided in 1946 into (pro-Soviet) North Korea and (pro-Western) South Korea. In June 1950, South Korea was invaded by the North, leading to the intervention of a largely American **United Nations** force. A massive **Chinese** counteroffensive in support of the North (January 1951) resulted in a stalemate along the border. An **armistice** was signed in 1953, and the two Koreas remain strictly divided by a Demilitarized Zone (DMZ).

Cuba and the missile crisis

In 1959, a left-wing revolution led by **Fidel Castro** (1927-) ousted the corrupt regime of dictator **Fulgencio Batista** in Cuba. Castro was a lawyer who had previously been exiled to the United States and Mexico. The revolution was initially welcomed by the US, but relations soured as Castro nationalized American-owned property and declared himself a Marxist. His revolutionary comrade **Ernesto "Che" Guevara** (1928-67) began to transfer Cuba's economic ties from the US to the USSR.

After US-backed Cuban exiles mounted a failed invasion at the **Bay of Pigs** (1961), Castro turned increasingly to the USSR for political support. In 1962, he permitted the USSR to build **missile bases** in Cuba; these were detected by US aerial surveys (see right) on October 14. The US saw this as a direct threat and blockaded Cuba: President **John F. Kennedy** told the Soviet leader **Nikita Khrushchev** to withdraw the missiles or face nuclear attack. The world appeared to be on the brink of all-out conflict, but the USSR backed down on October 26 and removed the missiles. This was the most dangerous moment of the Cold War: Thereafter US and USSR began to seek **"peaceful coexistence."**

Castro's regime had a major influence on left-wing liberation movements in South America and Africa. Che Guevara was killed in Bolivia attempting to incite communist revolt. But the collapse of the USSR in 1990 left Cuba isolated.

1945 The Allied summit at Yalta divides Europe into postwar spheres of influence.

1946-49 Communist governments take over in Bulgaria, Hungary, Romania and Poland.

1948 Communists seize power in Czechoslovakia.

1948-49 The Soviet blockade of Berlin is broken by the "Berlin Airlift."

1949 Communists win the Chinese civil war; the USSR detonates its first atomic bomb.

1950 China supports North Korea against UN forces in the Korean War (to 1953).

1955 The Warsaw Pact treaty is signed by the USSR and its allies.

1956 Soviet troops crush a popular uprising in Hungary.

1959 Fidel Castro's leftist forces seize power in Cuba.

1962 The US and USSR come close to nuclear war in the Cuban Missile Crisis.

1964 The US intervenes militarily in Vietnam against communist forces.

Africa

Much of Africa was granted independence in the 1960s. The main theaters of conflict were the Portuguese colonies, which were denied independence until 1975.

Civil war occurred in **Angola** from 1974 between the leftist MPLA (backed by the USSR and Cuba) and UNITA (backed by South Africa and the USA). The MPLA took power in 1975, but sporadic fighting continues.

Mozambique's Marxist independence movement FRELIMO took power in 1975. South Africa supported the RENAMO guerrillas in a 16-year civil war that ended in 1992.

The socialist regime of **Gamal Abdul Nasser** (1918-70) of **Egypt** accepted Soviet aid after the Suez Crisis (1956). Nasser's successor **Anwar Sadat** (1918-81) cultivated US links from 1972.

Emperor Haile Selassie of **Ethiopia** was overthrown in 1974 in a socialist coup led by Colonel **Haile Mariam Mengistu** with Soviet backing. Mengistu's repressive rule lasted until 1991.

Indochina

Vietnam, Cambodia and Laos (**French Indochina**) were occupied by the **Japanese** during World War II. Each produced communist independence movements that resisted the return of French colonial rule after the war.

The communist **Vietnamese Republic** led by **Ho Chi Minh** (1890-1969) defeated the French at **Dien Bien Phu** (1954). The country was then divided into communist North Vietnam and noncommunist South Vietnam. US intervention to prevent reunification led to the full-scale **Vietnam War** (1964-73). North Vietnam overran South Vietnam in 1975.

In the parallel civil war in **Laos**, victory for the communist **Pathet Lao** also came in 1975.

In **Cambodia**, the victory of the communist **Khmer Rouge** in 1975 led to a regime of extreme brutality under which 2 million people died. Vietnam invaded in 1979 to depose the Khmer Rouge and finally withdrew in 1989.

see also

186-87 **World War II**
188-89 **End of empire**
192-93 **New world order**

Latin America

Under the Monroe Doctrine of 1823, the United States opposed all outside intervention in the Americas. After 1945, the doctrine came to mean resistance to communist regimes, even if they were supported by the local people.

Leftist reforms in **Guatemala** provoked a US-inspired military coup in 1954. The resulting guerrilla war (1960-96) saw the unleashing of right-wing death squads and terrorism.

A civil war (1980-92) in **El Salvador** between the US-backed government and the leftist FMLN guerrillas claimed 75 000 lives.

In **Nicaragua**, the corrupt US-backed Somoza regime was overthrown in 1979. The US then supported "Contra" rebels in a brutal ten-year civil war.

A communist government under **Salvador Allende** was elected in 1970 in **Chile**. A US-sponsored military coup under **Augusto Pinochet** led to repression and systematic elimination of political opponents.

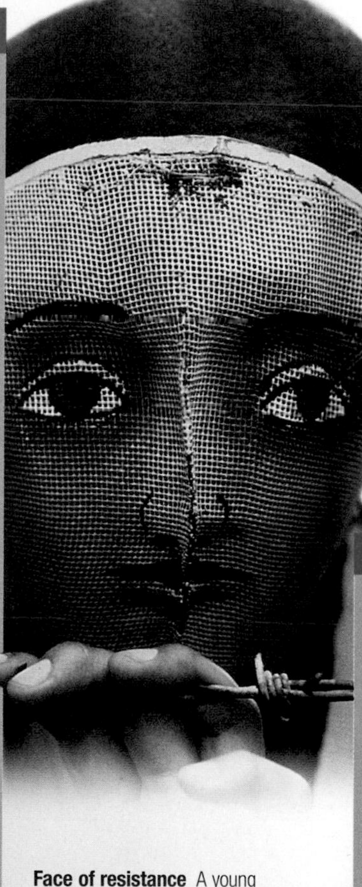

Face of resistance A young Sandinista guerrilla wears a mask to hide his identity. The popular left-wing movement took power in Nicaragua in 1979, provoking a violent US-financed backlash.

China

The Chinese communists led by **Mao Tse-tung** (1893-1976) emerged victorious from the civil war of 1946-9; the US-backed Nationalists retreated to **Taiwan**. The communists then began a series of campaigns, led by the **People's Liberation Army** (PLA) to purge China of "class enemies." These included the **Great Leap Forward** of 1958-60 (a program of land collectivization) and the disastrous **Cultural Revolution** (1965-76), which brought the country close to anarchy. China split with the USSR in the late 1950s over ideological and territorial disputes. A thaw in relations with the United States followed a visit by President **Richard Nixon** in 1972. Communist ideology softened after Mao's death, leading to a slow movement towards a **market economy**.

Mao Tse-tung

- **1968** The USSR crushes a reformist government in Czechoslovakia.
- 1970
- **1972** The US launches a policy of détente towards the USSR and China.
- **1975** Communist forces defeat the US-backed regime in South Vietnam.
- **1979** Soviet troops invade Afghanistan.
- 1980
- **1981** Martial law is imposed in Poland to curb the Solidarity trade union.
- **1983** The US announces its "Star Wars" satellite-based Strategic Defense Initiative.
- **1985** The reformist Mikhail Gorbachev comes to power in the USSR.
- **1987** The US and USSR remove intermediate-range nuclear weapons from Europe.
- **1989** Chinese troops crush a student protest in Tiananmen Square, Beijing.
- **1989** The communist regimes of Eastern Europe are overthrown.
- 1990
- **1990** The Cold War is declared ended.

In the final decades of the 20th century, the Cold War was replaced by an era of glasnost and perestroika (openness and reform) in the USSR followed by the collapse of Communism in Eastern Europe. Tensions eased and a "new world order" of cooperation seemed to beckon. But as the dust settled a more complex picture emerged. New nations struggled for stability, Islam became a political force and the United States sought a new role. A world of power blocs gave way to a mosaic of competing perspectives and ambitions.

Afghanistan

In 1973, Afghanistan's monarchy was overturned by the left-leaning general **Mohammed Daud Khan** in a military coup. Five years later, Daud was assassinated, and a Marxist regime was installed. In 1979, the USSR occupied the country.

Soviet troops faced a guerrilla war against US-supplied Islamic fighters (**mujaheddin**). About 14 000 Soviets died before Mikhail Gorbachev, under political pressure at home, finally withdrew his troops in 1988-9. Civil war ensued and ended when the **Taliban** took Kabul in 1996.

After the terrorist attacks in the US in 2001, the US declared war on terrorism and ousted the repressive Taliban government, establishing a more democratic government.

Middle East

Civil war between Christian and Muslim militias erupted in **Lebanon** in 1975-76. Israel invaded in 1978 and in 1982. Terrorist groups such as **Islamic Jihad** and **Hezbollah** organized the kidnapping of Western hostages in the late 1980s, and Israel finally withdrew from southern Lebanon in 2000.

Palestinian resentment within **Israel** erupted in December 1987 in open rebellion. The 1993 **Oslo Accords** established limited Palestinian self-rule, but extremist violence continued. In 1995, Israel's prime minister **Yitzhak Rabin** was assassinated by a Jewish radical. **Ehud Barak** (elected in 1999) offered Palestinians a generous settlement, but popular revolts continued and even intensified, provoking the election of the hardline **Ariel Sharon** as Israel's leader in 2001. Tension between the groups continues.

1979 The shah of Iran flees, ceding power to Ayatollah Khomeini's Islamic revolution.

1980

1980 The trade union Solidarity is founded in Poland.

1981 Ronald Reagan becomes president. He holds the position until 1988.

1982 Argentina invades the Falkland Islands, triggering war with Britain.

1983 The US's "Star Wars" initiative puts huge pressure on Soviet defense spending.

1985

1985 Mikhail Gorbachev becomes leader of the USSR.

1986 An explosion at the Chernobyl nuclear reactor in the USSR accelerates demands for government openness.

1987 The United States and USSR agree to cut intermediate nuclear missiles in Europe.

1988 The USSR begins troop withdrawals from Afghanistan (completed 1989).

1989 The Communist regimes in Eastern Europe are successively overthrown by their own citizens.

1990

1991 Boris Yeltsin becomes the first elected leader of the Russian Republic.

GULF WAR

By the end of the Iran–Iraq War, Iraq had amassed foreign debts of about $80 billion. Kuwait's refusal to give aid was the pretext for another war. In August 1990, Iraq invaded Kuwait and claimed it as an Iraqi province. A UN-sponsored international coalition, led by the US, liberated Kuwait with "Operation Desert Storm," a 39-day campaign of aerial bombardment that was followed by a ground campaign that lasted four days. In March 2003, the US and Britain undertook a second campaign to remove Saddam Hussein and his government.

Iran and Iraq

From the 1960s, **Muhammad Reza Shah Pahlavi** began a program of reform aimed at creating a modern secular state in Iran. However, inflation, corruption and the brutal suppression of opposition led to riots in 1977-78.

The shah fled in January 1979, and a fundamentalist Islamic republic headed by **Ayatollah Ruholla Khomeini** was set up. Hostility to the West led to the seizure of the US embassy in Tehran in 1979. In 1989, the moderate **Hashemi Rafsanjani** became secular president.

In 1980, President **Saddam Hussein** of Iraq took advantage of the turmoil in Iran to invade the country in retaliation for Iran's assistance to rebel Kurds in Iraq. This triggered the **Iran–Iraq War** (1980-88), fought mainly around the **Shatt al'Arab** waterway.

Although Iraq was supported by arms supplied by the West and the USSR, Iran held firm. There were over 1 million casualties before peace was reestablished in 1988. Just two years later, Iraq invaded Kuwait and was again at war (see *Gulf War*).

PERESTROIKA & GLASNOST

Mikhail **Gorbachev** became leader of the USSR in 1985 after a succession of aging, unreforming Soviet leaders had brought the country to a state of **economic stagnation**.

Gorbachev tried to modernize Soviet communism under the banners of **perestroika** (economic and social restructuring) and **glasnost** (government openness and accountability). But the introduction of limited democracy, press freedoms, free enterprise and the release of dissidents, led to an unstoppable drive to overturn Communist rule. As the USSR liberalized, the satellite states of East and Central Europe one by one voted in free elections for non-Communist governments (1989-90). Then Soviet states began to break away from the Union. By 1991, the USSR had ceased to exist, and instead a nominal **"Commonwealth of Independent States"** (CIS), came into being.

Mikhail Gorbachev
Gorbachev unleashed forces that led to the USSR's demise.

see also
188-89 **End of empire**
190-91 **The Cold War**

1991 The USSR is disbanded and Gorbachev resigns.

1992 Bosnia–Herzegovina declares independence from Yugoslavia; the resulting civil war lasts until 1995.

1994 Nelson Mandela becomes president of South Africa (until 1999). The UN fails to stop massacres in Rwanda.

1995

1995 UN troops fail to end a civil war in Somalia.

1996 Yasser Arafat becomes president of Palestine. The Taliban (Sunni fundamentalists) take over Afghanistan.

1997 President Mobutu of Zaire is ousted by opposition forces led by Laurent Kabila.

1998 Indonesia's President Suharto is forced from office after 30 years in power.

1999 Serb troops are driven out of Kosovo by a NATO bombing campaign.

2000

2000 Vladimir Putin is elected president of Russia; Israeli troops withdraw from Lebanon.

2001 George W. Bush takes office as president of the United States; Ariel Sharon is elected prime minister of Israel.

The collapse of Communism in Eastern Europe

Discontent with Communist rule, centered on the Gdansk shipyard where the **Solidarity** trade union was active, flared up in the early 1980s in **Poland**. Solidarity was banned in 1982, but the ban was lifted in April 1989, leading to a Solidarity victory in free elections in June and the first non-Communist government in the Soviet bloc. In September, **Hungary** opened its border with Austria and a mass exodus of East Germans heading for the West began. The Hungarian government declared a new republic, promising multiparty elections (held in 1990) and disbanding the Communist Party. Soon the spark of reform had become a blaze. By the end of 1989, **Erich Honecker** had resigned in East Germany and the **Berlin Wall** was down (below). In 1990 Czechoslovakia, Romania and some Yugoslav republics acquired non-Communist governments. States of the Soviet Union, starting with **Lithuania** and **Latvia**, pushed for independence, and in 1991, after an unsuccessful Communist coup, the USSR was dissolved. The new governments of Eastern Europe faced many problems. Centralized economies had to be restructured and new political institutions established. Germany battled with the massive task of reunification, and regional tensions revived in many places, spilling over into war in the Balkans and Chechnya.

South Africa

International pressure on South Africa to abandon its policy of **apartheid** (racial segregation weighted in favour of the white minority) increased in the 1980s. Trade sanctions and cultural and sporting bans were imposed by many countries, creating a sense of isolation and damaging the economy. In 1989, **P.W. Botha** resigned as leader of the ruling National Party, to be replaced by moderate and reforming **F.W. de Klerk**. In 1990, de Klerk lifted the ban on the **African National Congress** (ANC) – the main black political party – and released the ANC leader **Nelson Mandela** after 27 years of imprisonment. The remaining apartheid legislation was removed in July 1991. Nonracial **free elections** were held for the first time in South Africa in April 1994, giving an overwhelming victory to the ANC, and Nelson Mandela became president.

Nelson Mandela

Peoples and nations

Peoples and nations

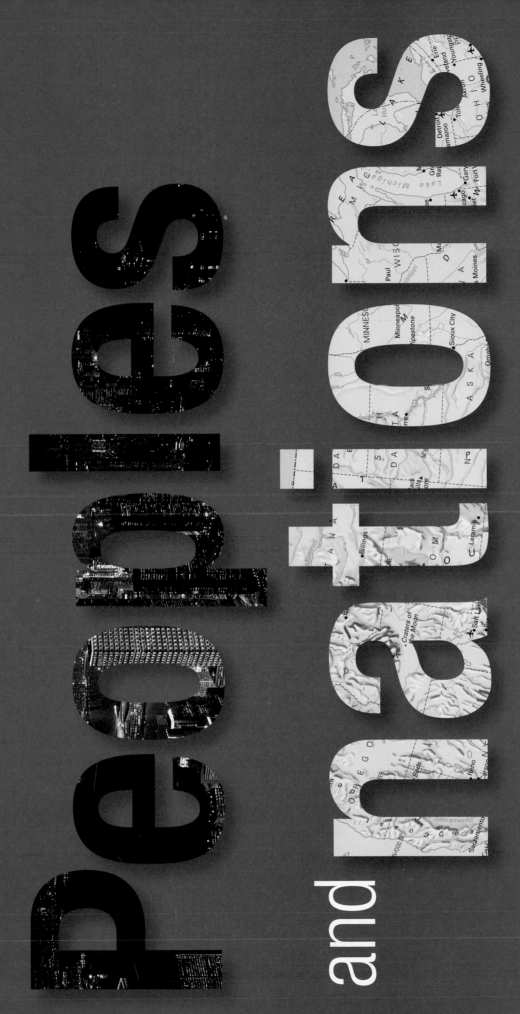

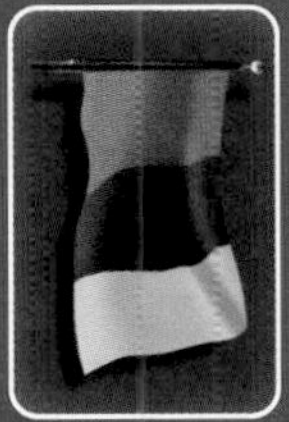

CANADA

OFFICIAL NAME
Canada

CAPITAL
Ottawa

Key dates

1497 John Cabot claims Canada for England.
1534-35 Jacques Cartier sails St. Lawrence River.
1604 French settlement; becomes "New France."
1663 New France made French "royal province."
1670 Hudson's Bay Co. sets up trading posts.
1713 Treaty of Utrecht: Britain acquires Nova Scotia, Newfoundland and Hudson Bay area.
1759 Battle of Quebec: British defeat French.
1760 British seize Montreal.
1763 All of New France becomes British.
1774 Quebec Act preserves French rights.
1791 Constitutional Act divides Quebec.
1867 Dominion (union) of Canada established.
1914-18 World War I: fights as one of Allies.
1931 Statute of Westminster gives full independence within British Commonwealth.
1939-45 World War II: fights as one of Allies.
1949 Newfoundland becomes tenth Canadian province.
1950-53 Korean War: troops join UN force.
1959 St. Lawrence Seaway links Great Lakes to the Atlantic.
1980 Quebec votes against secession.
1982 Canada Act ends last British legal control.
1990 Collapse of 1987 Meech Lake Agreement to protect Quebec's culture and language.
1994 North American Free Trade Agreement with US and Mexico.
1995 Quebec again rejects independence.
1999 Nunavut, self-governing territory, established in Canada's north.

Area 9 984 670 km² (3 855 382 sq miles)
Population 31 413 990
Population density 3 per km² (8 per sq mile)
Population growth rate 1.3%
Life expectancy 76 (m); 83 (f)
Languages English, French
Adult literacy rate 99%
Currency Canadian dollar (US $1 = 1.57 Canadian dollars)
GDP (US million $) 705 200
GDP per head (US $) 21 085

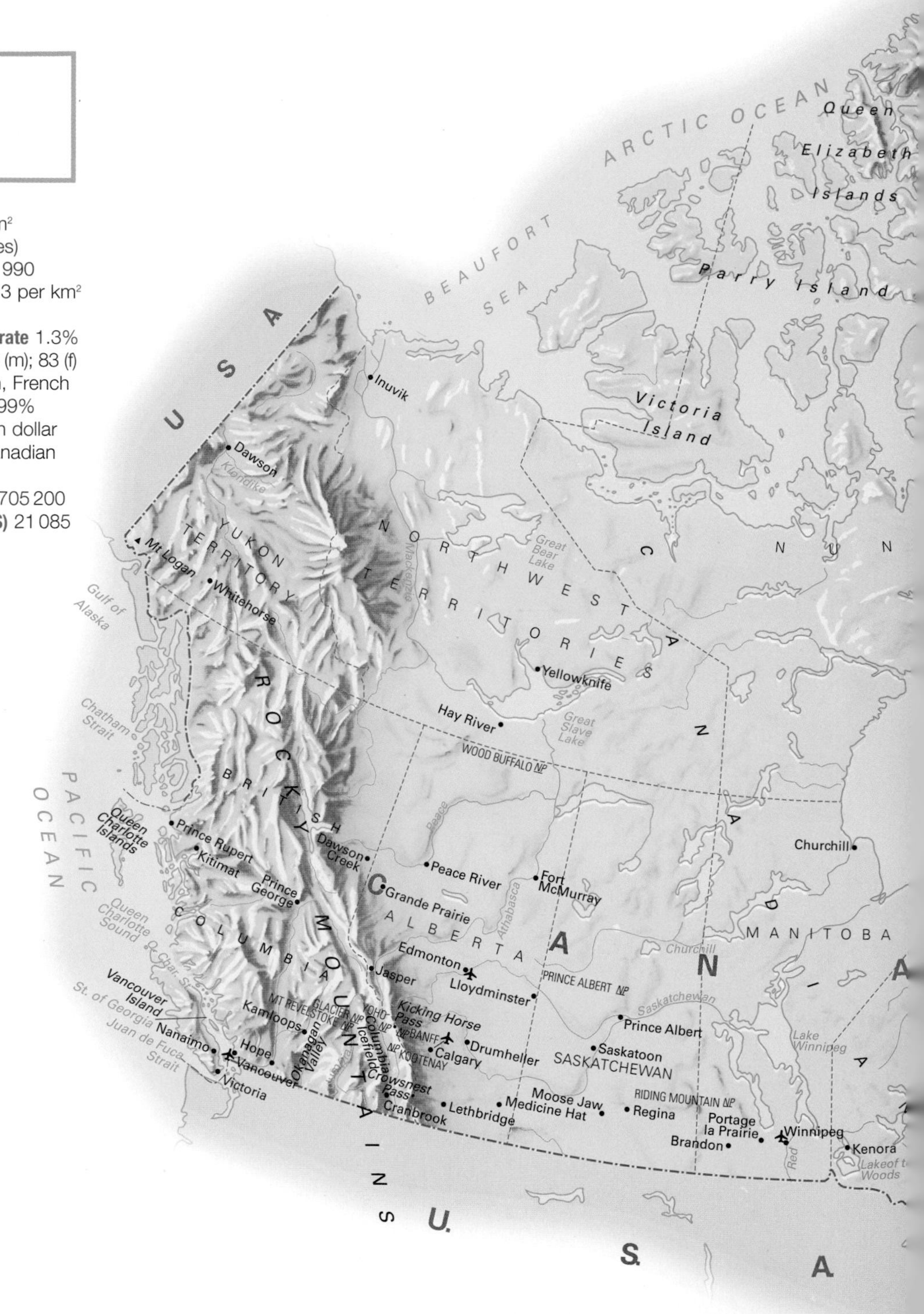

Provinces and Territories of Canada

Provinces	Capital	Admitted
Alberta	Edmonton	1905
British Columbia	Victoria	1871
Manitoba	Winnipeg	1870
New Brunswick	Fredericton	1867
Newfoundland	St. John's	1949
Nova Scotia	Halifax	1867
Ontario	Toronto	1867
Prince Edward Island	Charlottetown	1873
Quebec	Quebec City	1867
Saskatchewan	Regina	1905

Territories	Capital	Admitted
Northwest Territories	Yellowknife	1870
Nunavut	Iqaluit	1999
Yukon	Whitehorse	1898

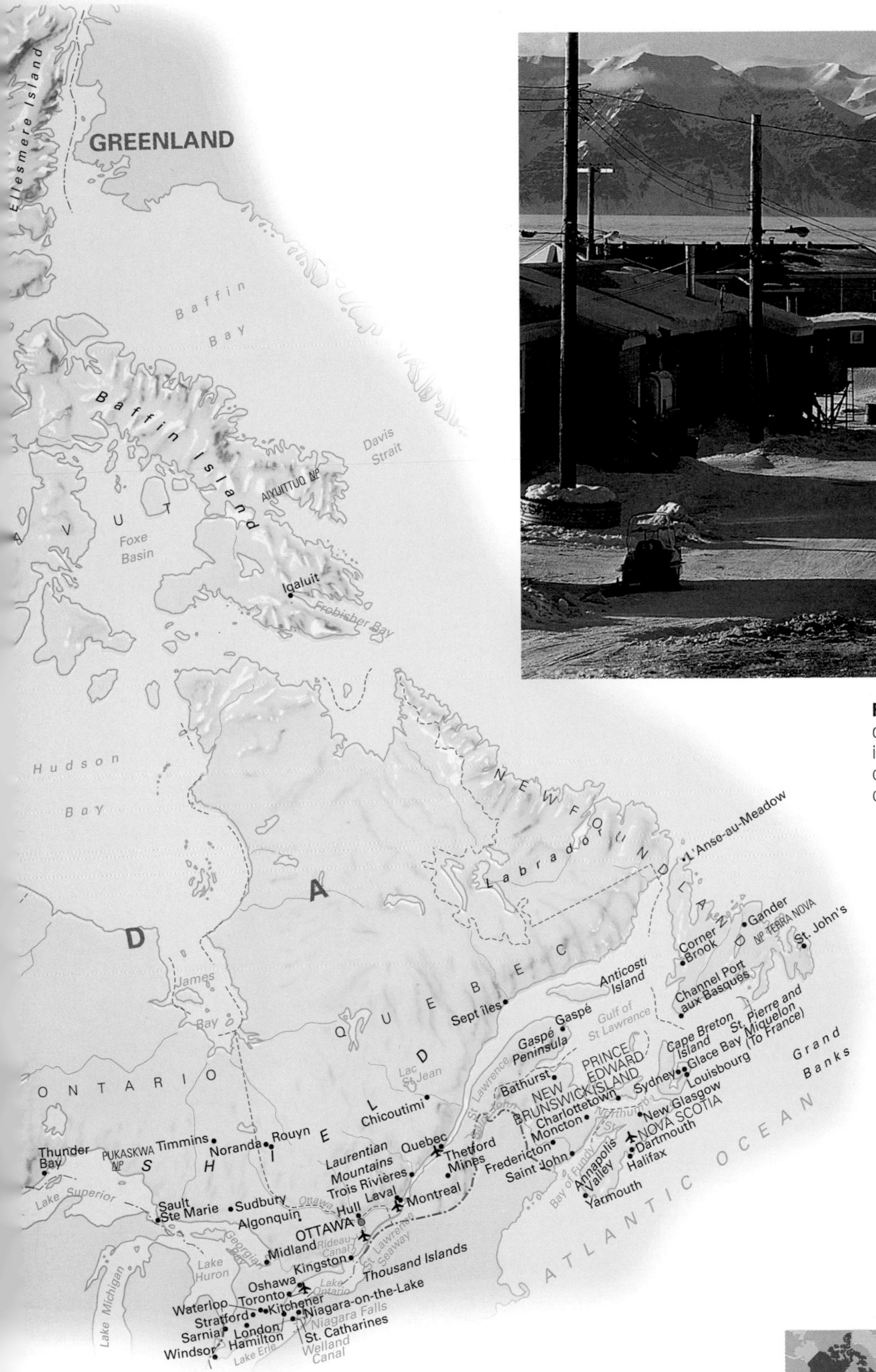

Frozen homeland Inuit people enjoy a relatively warm summer day in the town of Pond Inlet on Baffin Island, which is well inside the Arctic Circle. The Inuit – the indigenous inhabitants of the Canadian far north – achieved the long-held ambition of a self-governing homeland, called Nunavut, in 1999.

FACT

Canada and the United States share the world's longest frontier: a total of 8890 km (5525 miles).

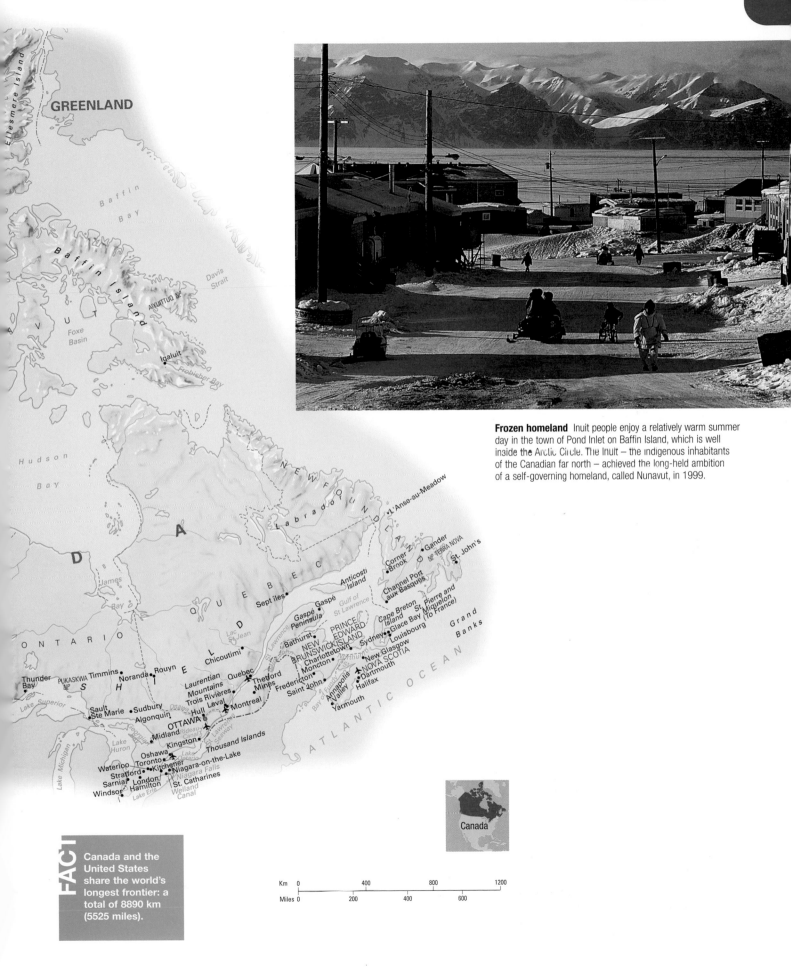

UNITED STATES

OFFICIAL NAME
The United States of America

CAPITAL
Washington, DC

Area 9 809 155 km² (3 787 319 sq miles)
Population 281 421 906
Population density 28 per km² (71 per sq mile)
Population growth rate 1%
Life expectancy 72 (m); 79 (f)
Languages English, Spanish and many immigrant and native languages
Adult literacy rate 95%
Currency US dollar
GDP (US million $) 9 178 000
GDP per head (US $) 33 922

Native culture A Cherokee artist from New Mexico stands beside a portrait of a warrior. The buffalo motifs emphasize the importance of the animal as a source of food and of hides for clothes and armor.

Linguistic legacy of the Native Americans

More than 200 native groups were encountered by the first Europeans settling in what is now the United States. Columbus (who thought he had reached the Indies or Southeast Asia) called them Indians. Their ancestors had crossed the Bering Strait from Siberia tens of thousands of years before. They looked vaguely similar to Asian peoples, but during the millennia of isolation they had developed distinct languages and cultures. As many as 15 million Native Americans lived in North America in 1492; today that figure has shrunk to about 2 million.

The Native Americans' strongest legacy has proven to be their many languages. Many words were adopted by early colonists from the more than 20 languages spoken by the Algonquian group of peoples. These include the names of native foods such as squash, succotash, pone (corn bread), pecan and persimmon, and of animals such as moose, raccoon, opossum, chipmunk, terrapin and woodchuck. Other familiar Native American words include caucus (a political meeting), podunk (a dull, small town), hickory, moccasin and toboggan, as well as the better-known powwow, tomahawk, teepee and totem.

The most obvious Native American names are those given to places – including 26 of the 50 states. For example, the name of Texas came from the Caddo language, meaning "friends" or "allies." Tennessee was named after a Cherokee village, and Ohio is an Iroquois word for "good river." The Massachusett was the name of a group living around Massachusetts Bay, and the name of Wyoming comes from Algonquian words meaning "on the great plain." Many cities, towns and rivers also trace their names to descriptive Native American words – for example, Chicago (Algonquian for "place of the onion") and Mississippi (Algonquian for "great river"). Among individuals immortalized are Black Warrior, a Choctaw chief, whose name in his own language was given to Tuscaloosa.

Very few Americans setting off for a vacation trip by mobile home know that Winnebago was the name of a plains group meaning "people of the muddy waters" – or that Winnipeg, in Canada, similarly means "dirty waters."

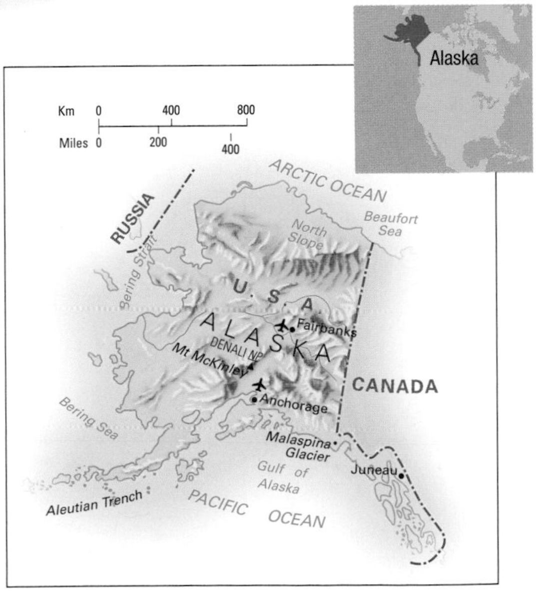

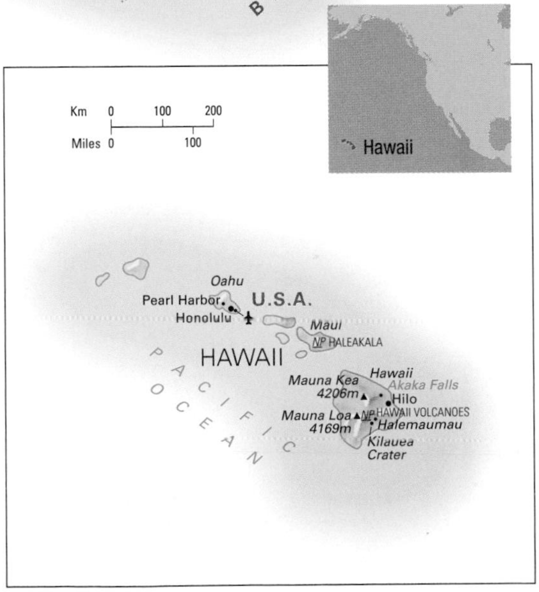

Key dates

16th c. Spanish, English and French explore North America.
1607 Chesapeake Bay colony established.
1620 "Pilgrims" found Plymouth Colony.
1624 Dutch settle in New York.
1682 French claim Mississippi valley.
1775-83 Revolution (War of Independence).
1776 Formal Declaration of Independence.
1783 Treaty recognizes US independence.
1803 Louisiana Purchase of western lands from France.
1846-48 Mexican War: US wins vast territories west of Rockies.
1861-65 Civil War: Union (North) fights secessionist Confederate (South) States.
1865 Slavery outlawed.
1917-19 Joins Allied side in World War I.
1929 Stock market crash leads to Depression.
1941 Japanese attack Pearl Harbor, Hawaii.
1941-45 Joins Allied side in World War II.
1950-53 Leads UN forces in Korean War.
1963 President Kennedy assassinated.
1964 Enters Vietnam War to assist South Vietnam against North.
1969 Neil Armstrong lands on Moon.
1973 Vietnam cease-fire; troops leave.
1974 President Nixon resigns over Watergate scandal.
1991 Leads international coalition in Gulf War.
1994 North American Free Trade Agreement with Canada and Mexico.
2001 Attacks kill nearly 3000 people, launching a "war on terrorism."

UNITED STATES

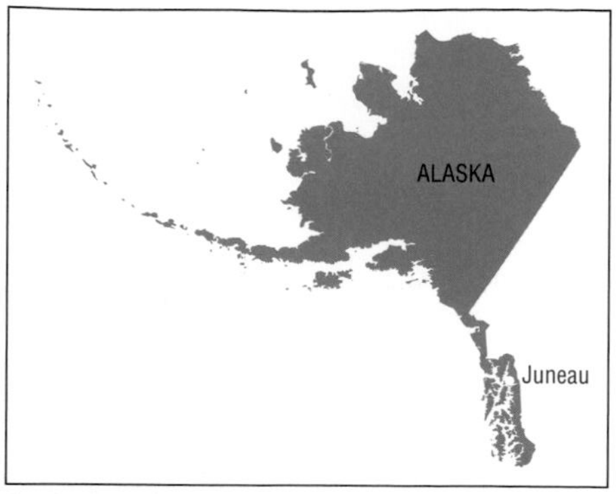

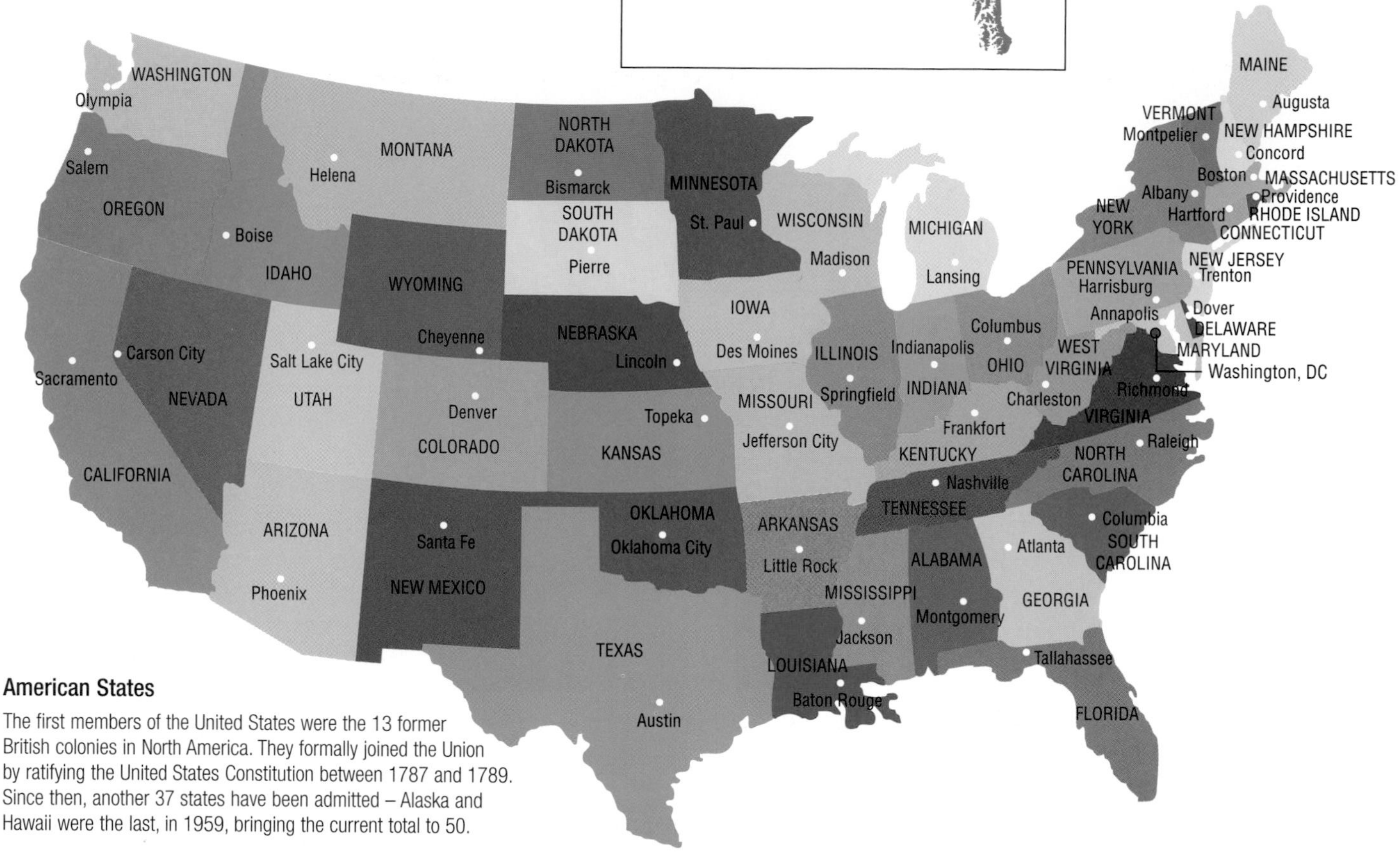

American States

The first members of the United States were the 13 former British colonies in North America. They formally joined the Union by ratifying the United States Constitution between 1787 and 1789. Since then, another 37 states have been admitted – Alaska and Hawaii were the last, in 1959, bringing the current total to 50.

States of the Union

Name	Nicknames	Capital	Admitted
Alabama	Heart of Dixie/Camellia State	Montgomery	1819
Alaska	Mainland State/The Last Frontier	Juneau	1959
Arizona	Grand Canyon State/Apache State	Phoenix	1912
Arkansas	Wonder State/Bear State/Land of Opportunity	Little Rock	1836
California	Golden State	Sacramento	1850
Colorado	Centennial State	Denver	1876
Connecticut	Constitution State/Nutmeg State	Hartford	1788
Delaware	First State/Diamond State	Dover	1787
Florida	Sunshine State/Everglade State	Tallahassee	1845
Georgia	Empire State of the South/Peach State	Atlanta	1788
Hawaii	Aloha State	Honolulu	1959
Idaho	Gem State	Boise	1890
Illinois	Inland Empire/Prairie State/Land of Lincoln	Springfield	1818
Indiana	Hoosier State	Indianapolis	1816
Iowa	Hawkeye State/Corn State	Des Moines	1846
Kansas	Sunflower State/Jayhawker State	Topeka	1861
Kentucky	Bluegrass State	Frankfort	1792
Louisiana	Pelican State/Sugar State/Creole State	Baton Rouge	1812
Maine	Pine Tree State	Augusta	1820
Maryland	Old Line State/Free State	Annapolis	1788
Massachusetts	Bay State/Old Colony	Boston	1788
Michigan	Great Lake State/Wolverine State	Lansing	1837
Minnesota	North Star State/Gopher State	St. Paul	1858
Mississippi	Magnolia State	Jackson	1817
Missouri	Show Me State/Bullion State	Jefferson City	1821
Montana	Treasure State/Big Sky Country	Helena	1889

Name	Nicknames	Capital	Admitted
Nebraska	Cornhusker State/Beef State	Lincoln	1867
Nevada	Sagebrush State/Silver State/Battleborn State	Carson City	1864
New Hampshire	Granite State	Concord	1788
New Jersey	Garden State	Trenton	1787
New Mexico	Land of Enchantment/Sunshine State	Santa Fe	1912
New York	Empire State	Albany	1788
North Carolina	Tar Heel State/Old North State	Raleigh	1789
North Dakota	Sioux State/Flickertail State	Bismarck	1889
Ohio	Buckeye State	Columbus	1803
Oklahoma	Sooner State	Oklahoma City	1907
Oregon	Beaver State/Sunset State	Salem	1859
Pennsylvania	Keystone State	Harrisburg	1787
Rhode Island	Little Rhody/Ocean State/Plantation State	Providence	1790
South Carolina	Palmetto State	Columbia	1788
South Dakota	Coyote State/Sunshine State	Pierre	1889
Tennessee	Volunteer State	Nashville	1796
Texas	Lone Star State	Austin	1845
Utah	Beehive State/Mormon State	Salt Lake City	1896
Vermont	Green Mountain State	Montpelier	1791
Virginia	Old Dominion State/Mother of Presidents	Richmond	1788
Washington	Evergreen State/Chinook State	Olympia	1889
West Virginia	Mountain State/Panhandle State	Charleston	1863
Wisconsin	Badger State/America's Dairyland	Madison	1848
Wyoming	Equality State	Cheyenne	1890

District of Columbia, site of Washington, DC, was established by Congress in 1790-91

MEXICO

OFFICIAL NAME
The United Mexican States

CAPITAL
Mexico City

Area 1 958 201 km^2 (756 066 sq miles)
Population 97 361 711
Population density 49 per km^2 (128 per sq mile)
Population growth rate 1.5%
Life expectancy 68 (m); 74 (f)

Languages Spanish and many local languages
Adult literacy rate 89.6%
Currency Mexican peso (US $1= 9.36 pesos)
GDP (US million $) 474 900
GDP per head (US $) 4926

Key dates

250-900 Mayan and other civilizations flourish.
10th-13th c. Toltec empire flourishes.
14th c. Aztecs found Tenochtitlán (Mexico City) and great empire.
1519-21 Cortés leads Spanish conquest.
1821 Independence from Spain.
1823 Becomes a republic.
1836 Loses Texas to the US.
1846-48 War with the US: much more territory lost.
1863-67 French troops occupy Mexico City.
1911 Revolution overthrows dictator Porfirio Diaz.
1917 New constitution introduces reforms.
1938 Nationalizes foreign oil companies.
1953 Women win vote.
1970s Huge oil discoveries.
1985 Earthquakes kill up to 10 000 people.
1994 North American Free Trade Agreement with US and Canada.

Fiesta! Children parade in the southern town of San Cristobal to celebrate Independence Day. This commemorates the September day in 1810 when Miguel Hildalgo, a priest, issued the first cry of defiance against Spanish rule and triggered the uprising that led to full independence 11 years later. Each year in the capital, Mexico's president reenacts Hidalgo's call to rebellion.

Northern Caribbean

CUBA

OFFICIAL NAME
The Republic of Cuba

CAPITAL
Havana

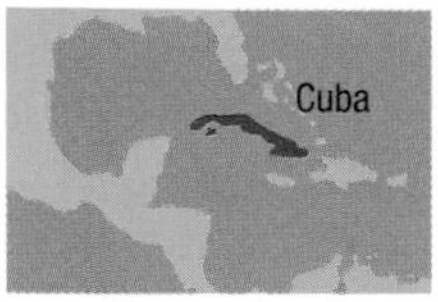

Area 110 860 km² (42 803 sq miles)
Population 11 160 000
Population density 100 per km² (260 per sq mile)
Population growth rate 0.9%
Life expectancy 74 (m); 77 (f)
Language Spanish
Adult literacy rate 95.7%
Currency Cuban peso (US $1 = 21 pesos)
GDP (US million $) 21 800
GDP per head (US $) 1960

Key dates

1492 Columbus lands and claims for Spain.
1898 US rule after Spanish-American War.
1902 Full independence.
1906-9 US occupation.
1933 Batista in power.
1959 Revolution: Fidel Castro deposes Batista.
1960 Pact with USSR. US companies seized; US trade embargo.
1961 CIA-backed Bay of Pigs invasion fails.
1962 US–USSR crisis over Soviet missiles in Cuba (later withdrawn).
1976 New constitution: socialist republic.
1987 Agreement with US on emigration.
1991 Soviet troops go.
1992 Tighter sanctions.

Tourism helps to beat the trade ban

The collapse of the Soviet empire in 1989 was a body blow to the Cuban economy. Soviet subsidies, including the payment of inflated prices for Cuban sugar, had amounted to $5 billion a year.

Cuba had turned to the USSR for aid and trade in the early 1960s, following a US trade embargo. This in turn was a response to a program of nationalization and land redistribution set up by Fidel Castro after he overthrew dictator Fulgencio Batista in 1959. Castro's revolution hurt US businesses in Cuba, and made it seem to the US that Communism was creeping into its backyard.

Relations further worsened after the failure of a US-backed invasion attempt at the Bay of Pigs in 1961 and during the missile crisis of 1962, when President Kennedy forced the USSR to withdraw its missiles from Cuban soil. The effectiveness of US trade sanctions can be seen today on the streets of Havana, where hundreds of ancient American cars are kept going by ingenuity and improvization.

But what the goods blockade has stopped, the tourist trade has, at least partially, replaced. By 1997, tourism was earning Cuba more than US $1 billion per year.

In 1997, a record 1.2 million foreigners visited Cuba. Significantly, 20 000 of them were American citizens. Relations between the two countries began to warm in 2000, and Castro looked forward to a further influx. "Let them come," he said. "We will treat them excellently."

A US $5 million seaside golf course at Varadero, which opened in 1998, may not have fit the image of an embattled communist society, but it brought in much-needed profits.

JAMAICA

OFFICIAL NAME
Jamaica

CAPITAL
Kingston

Area 10 991 km² (4244 sq miles)
Population 2 590 000
Population density 231 per km² (598 per sq mile)
Population growth rate 0.9%
Life expectancy 71 (m); 76 (f)
Languages English and local patois
Adult literacy rate 85%
Currency Jamaican dollar (US $1 = 45 Jamaican dollars)
GDP (US million $) 6700
GDP per head (US $) 2637

Key dates

1494 Columbus lands and claims for Spain.
1655 British rule begins.
1833 Slavery abolished.
1944 Representative parliament established.
1958-62 Part of West Indies Federation.
1959 Full internal self-government.
1962 Full independence within Commonwealth; joins UN.
1976 Takes half-ownership of Canadian and US bauxite mines.
1988 Hurricane Gilbert causes severe damage.

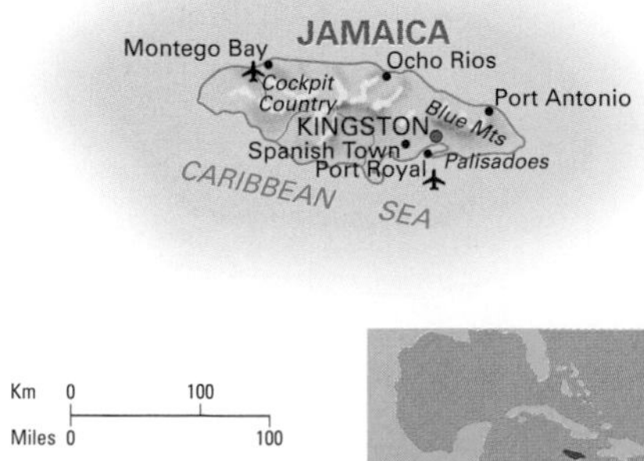

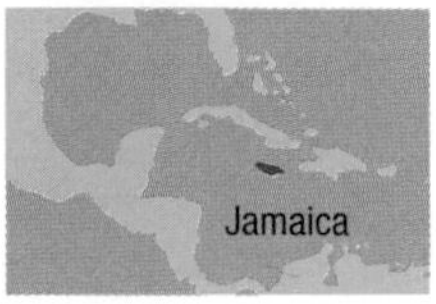

HAITI

OFFICIAL NAME
The Republic of Haiti

CAPITAL
Port-au-Prince

Area 27 750 km² (10 714 sq miles)
Population 7 803 000
Population density 276 per km² (714 per sq mile)
Population growth rate 2%
Life expectancy 52 (m); 56 (f)
Languages French, Creole
Adult literacy rate 45%
Currency gourde (US $1 = 24 gourdes)
GDP (US million $) 4300
GDP per head (US $) 562

Key dates

1492 Columbus lands.
1697 French control.
1804 Independence.
1915-34 US control.
1957 Dictator "Papa Doc" Duvalier takes power.
1971 "Baby Doc" Duvalier succeeds his father.
1986 Military coup ousts Baby Doc Duvalier.
1988-91 Series of elections and coups.
1994 US troops enforce civilian government.
1995 UN peacekeepers replace US troops.

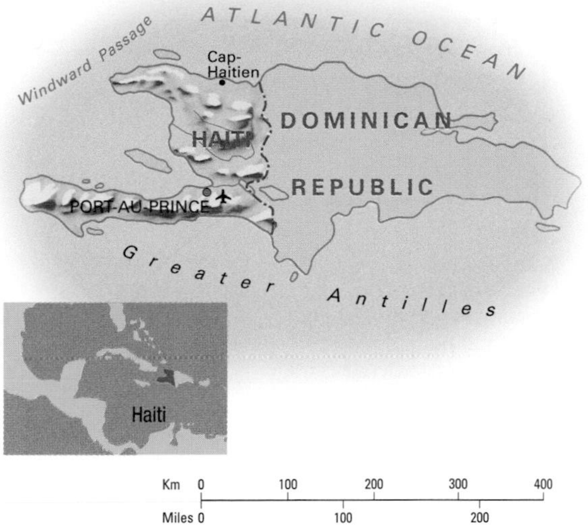

DOMINICAN REPUBLIC

OFFICIAL NAME
The Dominican Republic

CAPITAL
Santo Domingo

Area 48 422 km² (18 696 sq miles)
Population 8 348 000
Population density 167 per km² (434 per sq mile)
Population growth rate 2.1%
Life expectancy 68 (m); 72 (f)
Language Spanish
Adult literacy rate 82.1%
Currency Dominican Republic peso (US $1 = 16 pesos)
GDP (US million $) 16 900
GDP per head (US $) 2083

Key dates

1492 Columbus lands.
1496 Spanish colony.
1821 Independence, but Haiti invades.
1844 Full independence.
1916-24 US Marines occupy to keep peace.
1930-61 Trujillo rules as dictator.
1962 Free elections.
1963 Military coup.
1965 US Marines put down revolt.
1966 Constitutional government restored.
1979 Hurricane David causes severe damage.

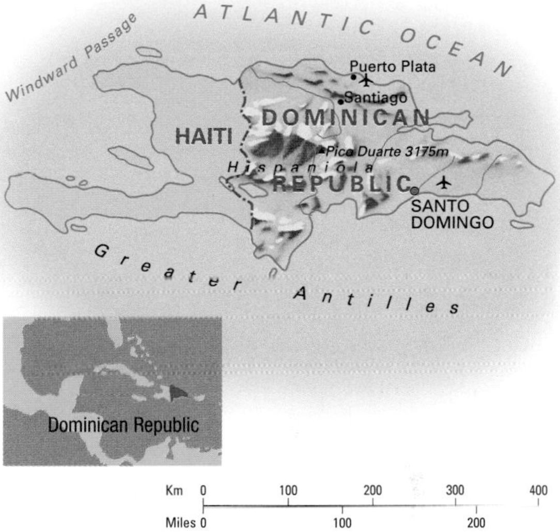

THE BAHAMAS

OFFICIAL NAME
The Commonwealth of The Bahamas

CAPITAL
Nassau, on New Providence

Area 13 939 km² (5382 sq miles)
Population 301 000
Population density 22 per km² (56 per sq mile)
Population growth rate 1.7%
Life expectancy 68 (m); 75 (f)
Language English
Adult literacy rate 98.2%
Currency Bahamian dollar (US $1 = 1 Bahamian dollar)
GDP (US million $) 3946
GDP per head (US $) 13 153

Key dates

1492 Columbus lands and claims for Spain.
17th c. British settle but Spanish forces attack.
1717 British colony.
1783 Spain gives up its claim.
1834 Slavery abolished.
1964 Internal self-government.
1973 Full independence within Commonwealth; joins UN.
1995 Refugees arrive from Cuba and Haiti.

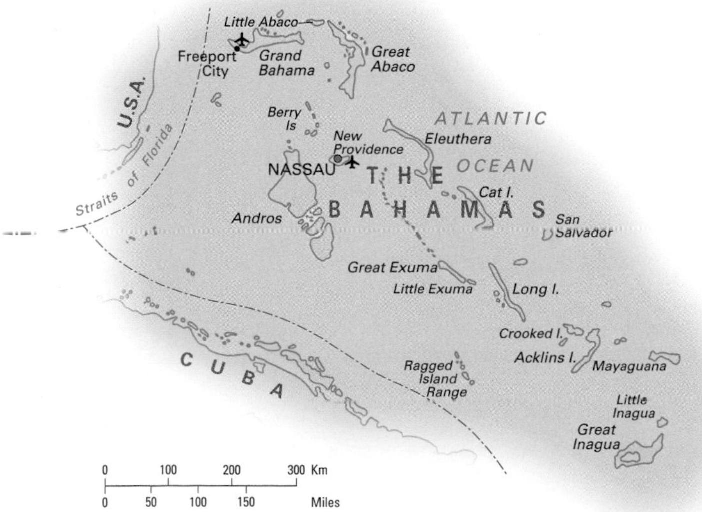

Southern Caribbean

ANTIGUA AND BARBUDA

OFFICIAL NAME
Antigua and Barbuda

CAPITAL
St. John's, on Antigua

Area 442 km² (170 sq miles)
Population 67 000
Population density 152 per km² (394 per sq mile)
Population growth rate 0.5%
Life expectancy 74 (m); 74 (f)
Languages English, English patois
Adult literacy rate 90%
Currency East Caribbean dollar (US $1 = 2.70 East Caribbean dollars)
GDP (US million $) 603
GDP per head (US $) 9000

Key dates

1632 British colony.
1834 Slavery abolished.
1967 Self-government.
1981 Full independence within Commonwealth.
1983 Joins US-led invasion of Grenada.
1995 Takes in refugees from Montserrat following volcano eruption.

ST. KITTS AND NEVIS

OFFICIAL NAME
The Federation of Saint Kitts and Nevis

CAPITAL
Basseterre, on St. Kitts

Area 261 km² (101 sq miles)
Population 41 000
Population density 157 per km² (406 per sq mile)
Population growth rate 0.5%
Life expectancy 67 (m); 70 (f)
Languages English
Adult literacy rate 97.3%
Currency East Caribbean dollar (US $1 = 2.70 East Caribbean dollars)
GDP (US million $) 264
GDP per head (US $) 6439

Key dates

1623 British settlement.
1834 Slavery abolished.
1967 Self-government.
1969 Anguilla becomes de facto British colony.
1980 Anguilla formally splits from St. Kitts and Nevis.
1983 Full independence within Commonwealth.
1998 Nevis referendum rejects secession.

PUERTO RICO

OFFICIAL NAME
Commonwealth of Puerto Rico

CAPITAL
San Juan

Status US commonwealth (dependency)
Area 9103 km² (3515 sq miles)
Population 3 522 000
Population density 387 per km² (1002 per sq mile)
Population growth rate 0.56%
Life expectancy 71 (m); 80 (f)
Languages Spanish, English
Adult literacy rate 89%
Currency US dollar
GDP (US million $) 34 700
GDP per head (US $) 9108

Key dates

1493 Columbus lands and claims for Spain.
1870 Slavery abolished.
1898 Under US rule after Spain loses Spanish–American War.
1917 Puerto Ricans given US citizenship.
1947 Gains right to elect own governor.
1952 Self-government as US dependency.
1989 Hurricane Hugo causes severe damage.
1998 Votes against independence and full statehood.

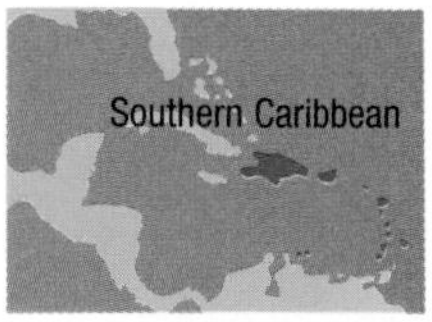

ST. LUCIA

OFFICIAL NAME
Saint Lucia

CAPITAL
Castries

Area 616 km² (238 sq miles)
Population 146 000
Population density 237 per km² (613 per sq mile)
Population growth rate 1.7%
Life expectancy 69 (m); 75 (f)
Languages English, French patois
Adult literacy rate 81.5%
Currency East Caribbean dollar (US $1 = 2.7 East Caribbean dollars)
GDP (US million $) 609
GDP per head (US $) 4171

Key dates

1650 French settlement after long resistance by native Carib peoples.
17th-18th c. France and Britain struggle for rule.
1814 Ceded to Britain.
1834 Slavery abolished.
1958-62 Part of West Indies Federation.
1967 Self-government.
1979 Full independence within Commonwealth.

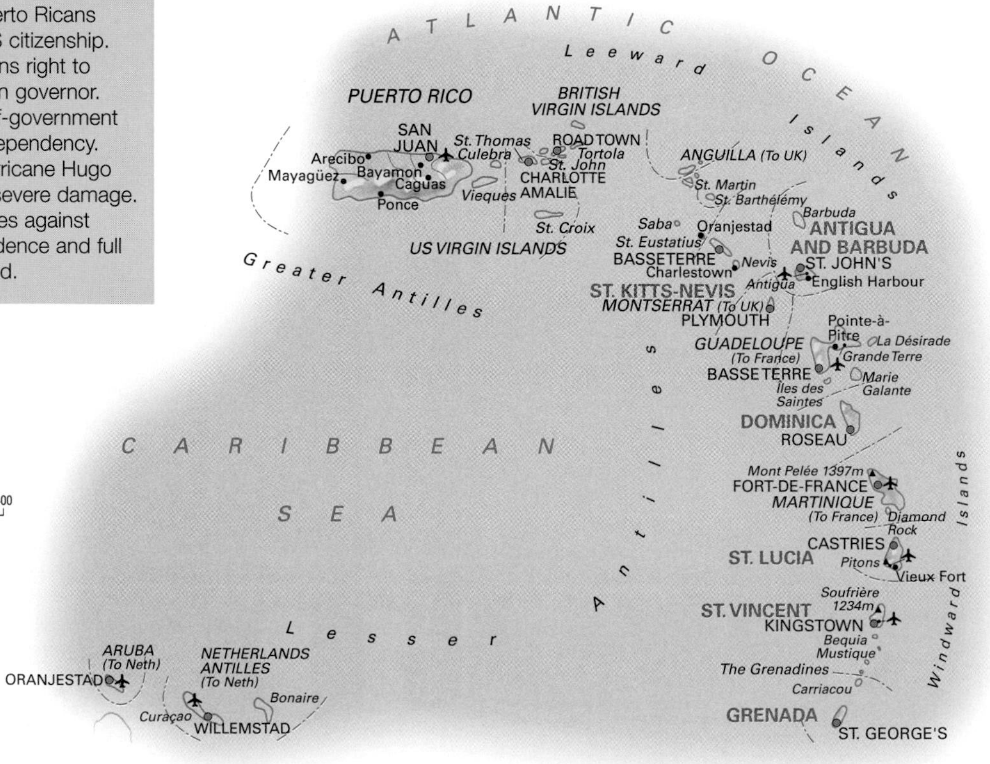

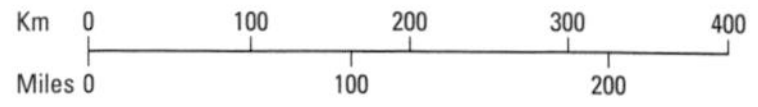

GRENADA

OFFICIAL NAME
Grenada

CAPITAL
St. George's

Area 344 km² (133 sq miles)
Population 93 000
Population density 270 per km² (699 per sq mile)
Population growth rate 0.2%
Life expectancy 71 (m); 71 (f)
Languages English, French patois
Adult literacy rate 90%
Currency East Caribbean dollar (US $1 = 2.7 East Caribbean dollars)
GDP (US million $) 333
GDP per head (US $) 3580

Key dates

1650 French settlement.
1793 British rule.
1834 Slavery abolished.
1967 Self-government.
1974 Full independence within Commonwealth.
1979 Bloodless coup.
1983 Marxist coup put down by US-led force.
1984 Elections restore democratic rule.

BARBADOS

OFFICIAL NAME
Barbados

CAPITAL
Bridgetown

Area 431 km² (166 sq miles)
Population 267 000
Population density 617 per km² (1598 per sq mile)
Population growth rate 0.55%
Life expectancy 70 (m); 76 (f)
Language English
Adult literacy rate 97%
Currency Barbados dollar (US $1 = 1.99 Barbados dollars)
GDP (US million $) 2393
GDP per head (US $) 8962

Key dates

1627 British colony.
1838 Slavery abolished.
1951 Introduction of universal suffrage.
1958-62 Part of West Indies Federation.
1966 Full independence within Commonwealth.
1983 Joins US-led invasion of Grenada.

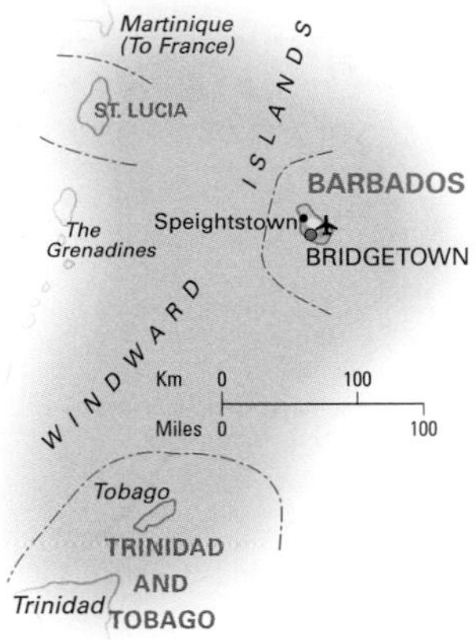

TRINIDAD AND TOBAGO

OFFICIAL NAME
The Republic of Trinidad and Tobago

CAPITAL
Port of Spain, on Trinidad

Area 5128 km² (1980 sq miles)
Population 1 289 000
Population density 250 per km² (646 per sq mile)
Population growth rate 1.2%
Life expectancy 72 (m); 72 (f)
Languages English, French, Spanish, Hindi, Chinese
Adult literacy rate 97.9%
Currency Trinidad and Tobago dollar (US $1 = 6.2 Trinidad and Tobago dollars)
GDP (US million $) 6700
GDP per head (US $) 5234

Key dates

1498 Columbus claims Trinidad for Spain.
1797 Britain captures Trinidad.
1814 Tobago ceded to Britain.
1958-62 Part of West Indies Federation.
1959 Self-government.
1962 Full independence within Commonwealth.
1976 Becomes republic.
1990 Coup attempt by Muslim extremists fails.

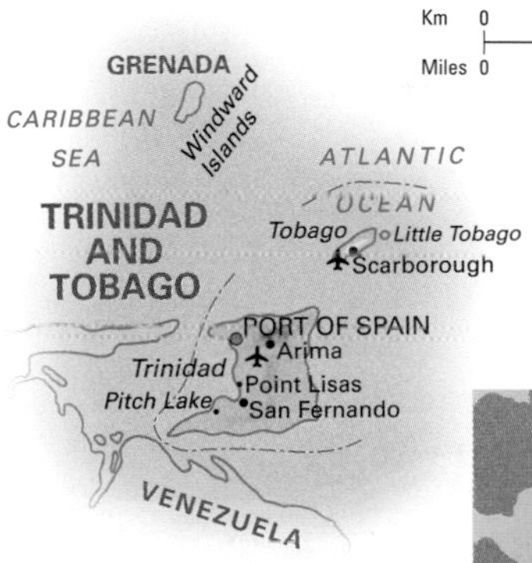

DOMINICA

OFFICIAL NAME
The Commonwealth of Dominica

CAPITAL
Roseau

Area 750 km² (290 sq miles)
Population 71 000
Population density 107 per km² (276 per sq mile)
Population growth rate 0.2%
Life expectancy 72 (m); 72 (f)
Languages English, French patois
Adult literacy rate 94.4%
Currency East Caribbean dollar (US $1 = 2.7 East Caribbean dollars)
GDP (US million $) 244
GDP per head (US $) 3050

Key dates

17th c. French and British settlements.
1805 British possession.
1834 Slavery abolished.
1967 Self-government.
1978 Full independence within Commonwealth.
1979 Severe hurricane.
1983 Joins US-led invasion of Grenada.

ST. VINCENT AND THE GRENADINES

OFFICIAL NAME
Saint Vincent and the Grenadines

CAPITAL
Kingstown, on St. Vincent

Area 389 km² (150 sq miles)
Population 112 000
Population density 288 per km² (747 per sq mile)
Population growth rate 0.9%
Life expectancy 72 (m); 72 (f)
Languages English, French
Adult literacy rate 82%
Currency East Caribbean dollar (US $1 = 2.7 East Caribbean dollars)
GDP (US million $) 300
GDP per head (US $) 2678

Key dates

1783 Becomes British colony.
1834 Slavery abolished.
1958-62 Part of West Indies Federation.
1969 Self-government.
1979 Full independence within Commonwealth.
1983 Joins US-led invasion of Grenada.

Central America

HONDURAS

OFFICIAL NAME
The Republic of Honduras

CAPITAL
Tegucigalpa

Area 112 088 km² (43 277 sq miles)
Population 6 385 000
Population density 55 per km² (143 per sq mile)
Population growth rate 3%
Life expectancy 65 (m); 70 (f)
Languages Spanish, English and local languages
Adult literacy rate 72.7%
Currency lempira (US $1 = 15.29 lempiras)
GDP (US million $) 5500
GDP per head (US $) 889

Key dates

1502 Columbus lands and claims for Spain.
1821 Independence as part of Central American Federation.
1838 Full independence.
1969 Expels Salvadoran immigrants; brief war.
1980s "Contra" guerrillas attack Nicaragua from bases in Honduras.
1992 Settles El Salvador border dispute.

BELIZE

OFFICIAL NAME
Belize

CAPITAL
Belmopan

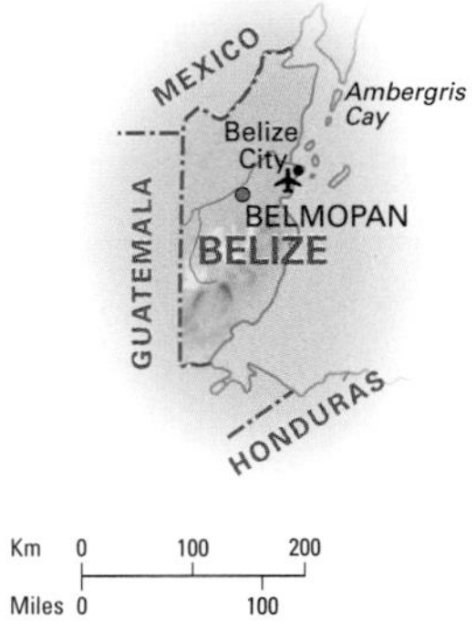

Area 22 965 km² (8867 sq miles)
Population 235 000
Population density 10 per km² (27 per sq mile)
Population growth rate 2.6%
Life expectancy 70 (m); 74 (f)
Languages English, Spanish, Creole, Garifuna, Maya, Ketchi, German
Adult literacy rate 90%
Currency Belizean dollar (US $1 = 1.97 Belizean dollars)
GDP (US million $) 646
GDP per head (US $) 2691

Key dates

1520s Spanish claim.
1862 Colony of British Honduras established.
1964 Self-government.
1973 Renamed Belize.
1975 British troops help defend border disputed by Guatemala.
1981 Full independence.
1991 Guatemala gives up claims to Belize.
1993 Border dispute with Guatemala ends.
1994 British troops leave.

COSTA RICA

OFFICIAL NAME
The Republic of Costa Rica

CAPITAL
San José

Area 51 100 km² (19 730 sq miles)
Population 3 589 000
Population density 69 per km² (179 per sq mile)
Population growth rate 1.5%
Life expectancy 73 (m); 78 (f)
Languages Spanish, English patois
Adult literacy rate 94.8%
Currency Costa Rican colón (US $1 = 323 colones)
GDP (US million $) 10 600
GDP per head (US $) 3002

Key dates

1502 Columbus lands and claims for Spain.
1821 Independence as part of Central American Federation.
1838 Full independence.
1948-49 Civil war follows disputed election.
1949 New constitution; army abolished.
1987 President Arias Sanchez wins Nobel Peace Prize.

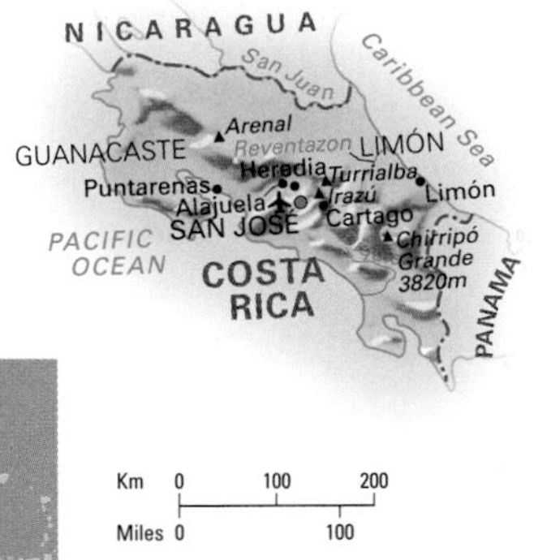

A respite in Central America's years of bloodshed

The 1980s and 90s brought an unexpected pause to the conflicts in troubled Central America and a Nobel Peace Prize for Costa Rica's President Arias Sanchez. He drew up a peace plan, which was signed in 1987 by El Salvador, Costa Rica, Guatemala and Nicaragua.

The Central American nations, after winning independence from Spain in 1821, had suffered more than 150 years of military coups, civil wars, border conflicts and guerrilla insurgencies.

In Nicaragua, Sandinista guerrillas had overthrown the dictatorship of the Somoza family in 1979, but their policy of land reform and nationalization alarmed the US, and they were attacked by right-wing Contras trained and funded by the CIA. With the country in severe recession, the Sandinistas lost the 1990 election. Clashes continued, but a cease-fire agreement was signed in 1994.

Guatemala, which had known little but disorder and death squads since a CIA-backed coup in 1954, made peace with left-wing rebels in 1996. In 1992, El Salvador and Honduras compromised on a long-standing border dispute. Arias's plan had set the mood for peace.

GUATEMALA

OFFICIAL NAME
The Republic of Guatemala

CAPITAL
Guatemala City

Area 108 889 km² (42 042 sq miles)
Population 11 088 000
Population density 99 per km² (257 per sq mile)
Population growth rate 2.9%
Life expectancy 62 (m); 67 (f)
Languages Spanish and many local languages
Adult literacy rate 55.6%
Currency quetzal (US $1 = 7.77 quetzales)
GDP (US million $) 18 100
GDP per head (US $) 1675

Key dates

1523 Spanish invasion.
1821 Independence as part of Central American Federation.
1839 Full independence.
1945 New constitution brings political reforms.
1952 Land reform starts.
1954 US backs military coup, bringing Carlos Castillo to power.
1985 New constitution restores civilian rule.
1991 Belize border dispute ends.
1993 Army removes dictatorial president.
1996 Peace agreement with left-wing rebels.

EL SALVADOR

OFFICIAL NAME
The Republic of El Salvador

CAPITAL
San Salvador

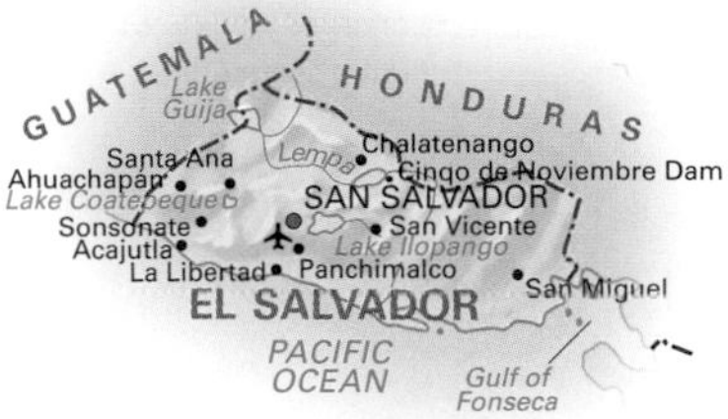

Area 21 041 km² (8124 sq miles)
Population 6 154 000
Population density 287 per km² (742 per sq mile)
Population growth rate 1.9%
Life expectancy 51 (m); 64 (f)
Languages Spanish and local languages
Adult literacy rate 71.5%
Currencies US dollar and Salvadorean colón (US $1 = 8.74 colones)
GDP (US million $) 12 000
GDP per head (US $) 1990

Key dates

1524 Spanish invasion.
1821 Independence as part of Central American Federation.
1840 Full independence.
1931 Military coup.
1969 Brief border war with Honduras.
1979 Fighting starts with left-wing guerrillas.
1980 Archbishop Romero assassinated.
1983 New constitution.
1992 Peace agreement with guerrillas.

NICARAGUA

OFFICIAL NAME
The Republic of Nicaragua

CAPITAL
Managua

Area 120 254 km² (46 430 sq miles)
Population 4 936 000
Population density 40 per km² (104 per sq mile)
Population growth rate 1.8%
Life expectancy 63 (m); 69 (f)
Languages Spanish, English and local languages
Adult literacy rate 65.6%
Currency gold cordoba (US $1 = 13.2 gold cordobas)
GDP (US million $) 2200
GDP per head (US $) 457

Key dates

1502 Columbus lands and claims for Spain.
1821 Independence as part of Central American Federation.
1838 Full independence.
1912-33 US occupation.
1937 Anastasio Somoza becomes dictator.
1956 Somoza killed; succeeded by son Luis.
1967 Luis Somoza dies; succeeded by brother Anastasio.
1979 Sandinistas win 17-year guerrilla war; Somoza flees. Supports rebels in El Salvador.
1982 "Contra" rebels begin guerrilla offensive.
1989 Peace talks fail.
1990 Sandinista defeat in elections. Peace agreed with Contras.
1998 Hurricane Mitch causes severe damage.

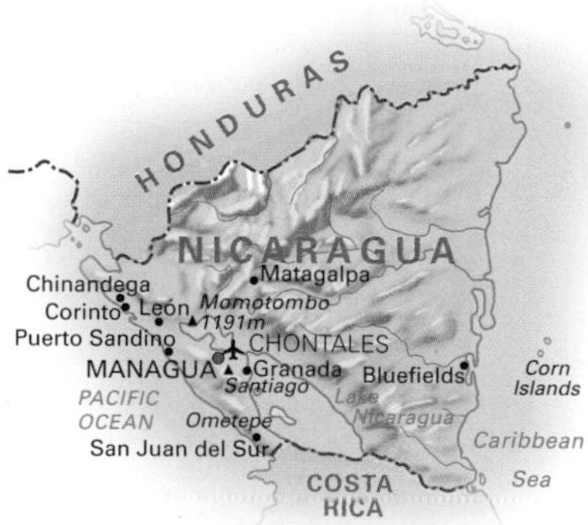

PANAMA

OFFICIAL NAME
The Republic of Panama

CAPITAL
Panama City

Area 75 517 km² (29 157 sq miles)
Population 2 809 000
Population density 37 per km² (95 per sq mile)
Population growth rate 1.3%
Life expectancy 71 (m); 76 (f)
Languages Spanish and local languages
Adult literacy rate 90.8%
Currencies US dollar and balboa (US $1 = 1 balboa)
GDP (US million $) 9500
GDP per head (US $) 3442

Key dates

1502 Columbus discovers.
1513 Balboa explores and claims for Spain.
1821 Independence as part of Colombia.
1855 Railway built across isthmus.
1903 Independence from Colombia won through US-supported revolt; US given control of Canal Zone.
1908-28 US supervises all elections.
1914 Canal completed.
1960s Dispute with US over Canal Zone treaty.
1968 Military coup.
1977 New Canal Zone treaty with US.
1979 Regains control of Canal Zone from US.
1983 General Noriega gains effective power.
1988 US courts indict Noriega for drug trafficking; US starts economic sanctions.
1989 National Assembly names Noriega head of government and declares state of war with US. US troops invade in order to arrest Noriega.
1990 Noriega surrenders.
1992 Noriega tried in US and sentenced to 40 years in prison.
1999 Panama gains operational control of canal; US retains defense rights.

Two oceans united

One British politician called it "the greatest liberty man has ever taken with nature." The Panama Canal linking the Atlantic and Pacific oceans took 40 000 men 10 years to complete. From 1904 to 1914, the US construction crew worked to move 315 million m³ (240 million cu yd) of earth: 6000 men died in the process. The US government thought the prize was worth it: The canal shortened sea journeys between New York and San Francisco by 13 000 km (8000 miles). By the end of the 20th century, it had revolutionized global economic development by boosting world trade and creating new markets. When the US turned control of the canal over to Panama in 1999, more than 700 000 vessels had completed the 24-hour passage, including 13 025 in 1998.

The first attempt to build a waterway through the Isthmus of Panama, made by a French company in the 1880s, cost 22 000 lives before the project ended in bankruptcy. Success came after President Theodore Roosevelt took up the challenge. Panama was then part of Colombia, which refused the US permission to build the canal. The US then backed a successful Panamanian revolt. With independent Panama's enthusiastic approval, Roosevelt spent $387 million and provided America's best engineers. He also sent his country's best medical officers – chief sanitary officer Dr. William C. Gorgas eliminated the twin threats of yellow fever and malaria by eradicating mosquitoes in the area.

Tight fit An ocean-going ship navigates Pedro Miguel Lock on the Panama Canal. There are three sets of locks on the canal – at its highest point, ships are 26 m (85 ft) above sea level.

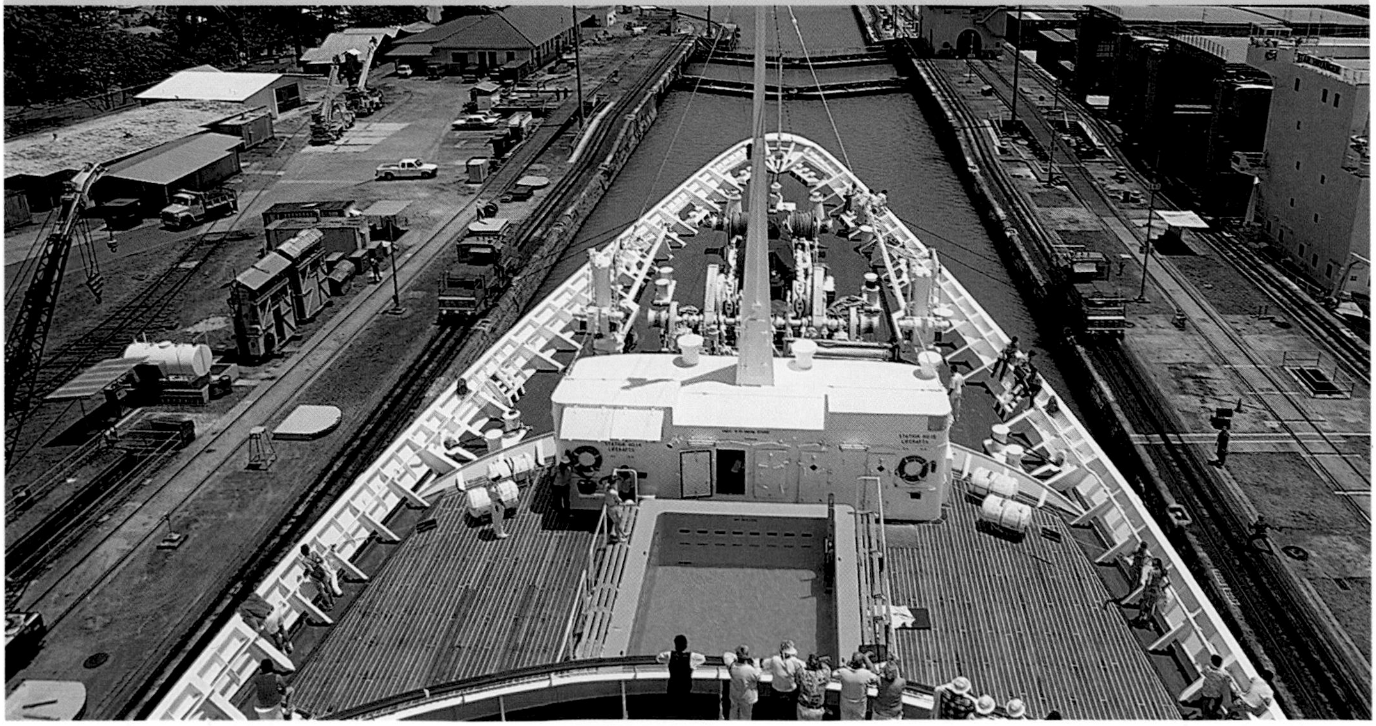

VENEZUELA

OFFICIAL NAME
The Republic of Venezuela

CAPITAL
Caracas

Area 912 050 km² (352 144 sq miles)
Population 23 706 000
Population density 25 per km² (66 per sq mile)
Population growth rate 1.7%
Life expectancy 69 (m); 75 (f)
Languages Spanish and local languages
Adult literacy rate 91.1%
Currency bolívar (US $1 = 710 bolívars)
GDP (US million $) 102 800
GDP per head (US $) 4423

Key dates

1498 Columbus claims for Spain.
1811-21 Liberated by Simón Bolívar; part of Greater Colombia.
1829 Full independence.
1917 Oil production begins.
1958 Violent protests force dictator Marcos Perez Jiménez to flee; democratic rule established.
1976 Nationalizes 21 oil companies.
1989 300 die in riots over price rises; martial law imposed.
1992 Two attempted military coups fail.
1994-95 Economic crisis; civil rights suspended.

COLOMBIA

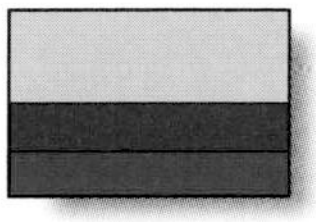

OFFICIAL NAME
The Republic of Colombia

CAPITAL
Bogotá

Area 1 141 748 km² (440 831 sq miles)
Population 41 589 000
Population density 36 per km² (93 per sq mile)
Population growth rate 1.5%
Life expectancy 66 (m); 72 (f)
Language Spanish
Adult literacy rate 91.3%
Currency Colombian peso (US $1 = 2328 pesos)
GDP (US million $) 77 100
GDP per head (US $) 1888

Key dates

1525 Spanish settle.
1538 Named New Kingdom of Granada.
1819 Liberated by Simón Bolívar; forms Greater Colombia.
1829-30 Venezuela and Ecuador break away.
1903 Loses Panama.
1948-62 "La Violencia": 200 000 die in political riots and rebellions.
1957-74 Coalition rule.
1978 Begins offensive against drug trade.
1989-90 Three presidential candidates assassinated.
1993 Police kill drug baron Pablo Escobar.
1996 Emergency to fight leftist guerrillas.

Chile, Bolivia, Ecuador and Peru

CHILE

OFFICIAL NAME
The Republic of Chile

CAPITAL
Santiago

Area 756 626 km² (292 135 sq miles)
Population 15 018 000
Population density 20 per km² (51 per sq mile)
Population growth rate 1.7%
Life expectancy 72 (m); 77 (f)
Languages Spanish, Araucanian
Adult literacy rate 95.2%
Currency Chilean peso (US $1 = 602 pesos)
GDP (US million $) 66 900
GDP per head (US $) 4514

Key dates

1541 Spaniards settle and found Santiago.
1818 Independence from Spain after eight-year struggle.
1879-83 Chile wins territory from Peru in War of the Pacific.
1891 Civil war – more than 10 000 killed.
1970 Marxist President Allende elected.
1973 Allende dies in US-backed military coup. Pinochet heads military junta.
1980 New constitution.
1989 Elections restore civilian government.
1998 Pinochet arrested in UK.
2000 UK government allows Pinochet to return home; charged in Chile with murder and kidnapping.

A CONTINENT'S SPINE

South America's Andes mountain range has always offered protection but has also created problems. People sought security from persecution in the inaccessible mountains even before the Incas built their great civilization on the high plateau of the Altiplano 800 years ago. Yet the physical barrier of the Andes range, running the length of the continent near the west coast, has blocked communications and held back modern civilization from villages away from the sea.

Transportation is difficult – pack animals are still used in some areas – and the obstacles to road and railroad construction hinder economic growth in countries such as Bolivia, Peru and Ecuador. (One railroad line, the Central, climbs to 4816 m [15 800 ft] – the highest standard-gauge track in the world.)

The Andes range – the world's longest at 7200 km (4475 miles) and second highest at over 6100 m (20 000 ft) – is the source of the Amazon and many other rivers. Its fertile soil is excellent for crops such as grain, corn, potatoes, coffee, tobacco and sugarcane, and the land yields mineral riches: oil in the foothills, gold and emeralds in Colombia, silver in Peru and Chile and tin in Bolivia.

The geologically young range is alive with tectonic activity. Its natural disasters have included an earthquake in Peru in 1970 that killed 50 000 people and the 1985 volcanic eruption in Colombia that cost 23 000 lives.

Young and restless The Andes are still growing as the Pacific floor pushes under South America. The result is frequent eathquakes and volcanic disasters along the entire range.

BOLIVIA

OFFICIAL NAME
The Republic of Bolivia

CAPITALS
La Paz and Sucre

Area 1 098 581 km² (424 164 sq miles)
Population 8 137 000
Population density 7 per km² (19 per sq mile)
Population growth rate 2.2%
Life expectancy 59 (m); 63 (f)
Languages Spanish, Quechua, Aymara
Adult literacy rate 83.1%
Currency boliviano (US $1 = 6.50 bolivianos)
GDP (US million $) 8400
GDP per head (US $) 1056

Key dates

15th c. Inca rule.
1534 Spanish conquest.
1825 Independence.
1879-83 War of Pacific: loses territory to Chile.
1932-35 Chaco War: loses territory to Paraguay.
1964-82 Military rulers.
1967 Defeat of revolt led by Che Guevara, who is captured and killed.
1980-83 US/European Community aid halted because of corruption.
1982 Civilian rule begins.

ECUADOR

OFFICIAL NAME
The Republic of Ecuador

CAPITAL
Quito

Area 272 045 km² (105 037 sq miles)
Population 12 411 000
Population density 45 per km² (116 per sq mile)
Population growth rate 2.3%
Life expectancy 67 (m); 72 (f)
Languages Spanish, Quechua and other local languages
Adult literacy rate 90.1%
Currency US dollar
GDP (US million $) 12 700
GDP per head (US $) 1043

Key dates

15th c. Inca rule.
1534 Spanish conquest.
1822 Independence as part of Colombia.
1830 Full independence.
1925-48 Many unstable governments.
1941 Border war with Peru: loses territory in Amazon Basin.
1963 Military coup.
1966 Civilian rule reestablished; new constitution adopted.
1972 Military coup.
1979 New democratic constitution.
1995 Fighting with Peru over disputed border.
1998 Emergency economic measures.
2000 Coup deposes president; protests over austerity measures.

A city for all seasons
Because of its location on the Equator and an altitude of 2775 m (9250 ft), Quito's climate can run the gamut of all four seasons in 24 hours.

PERU

OFFICIAL NAME
The Republic of Peru

CAPITAL
Lima

Area 1 285 216 km² (496 225 sq miles)
Population 25 232 000
Population density 19 per km² (50 per sq mile)
Population growth rate 2%
Life expectancy 66 (m); 70 (f)
Languages Spanish, Quechua, Aymara
Adult literacy rate 88.7%
Currency new sol (US $1 = 3.58 new sols)
GDP (US million $) 56 200
GDP per head (US $) 2266

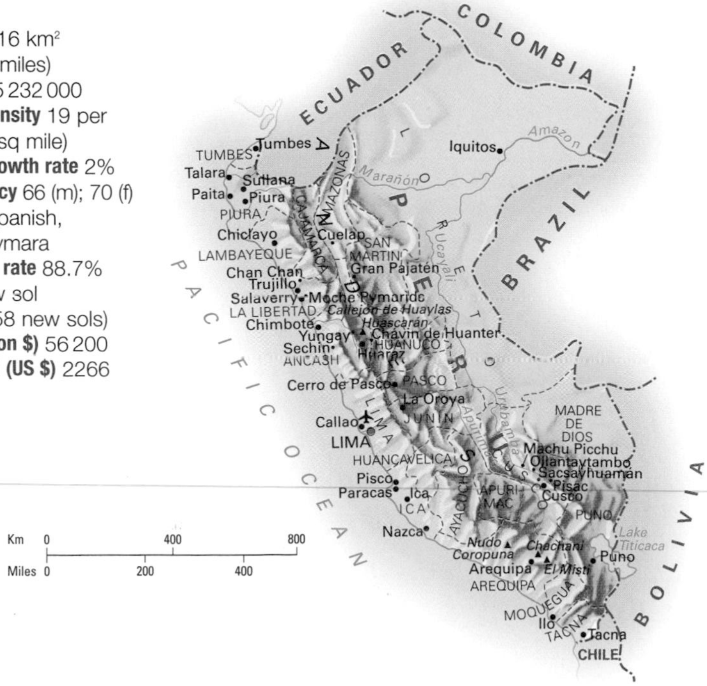

Key dates

c. 1200 Inca kingdom established.
1532-33 Conquest by Spanish under Pizarro.
1824 Independence after four-year war.
1879-83 War of Pacific: loses territory to Chile.
1930 Military coup leads to political repression.
1941 War with Ecuador: wins Amazon territory.
1945 Open elections.
1948 Military coup.
1963 Civilian rule; social reforms started.
1968 Military coup; industries nationalized.
1980 Elections. "Shining Path" communist guerrilla group active.
1992 "Shining Path" leader captured.
1995 Border fighting with Ecuador.
1996-97 Leftist Tupac Amaru guerrillas seize hostages; rescued by army; guerrillas killed.
2000 President Fujimori accused of corruption and forced to resign.

GUYANA

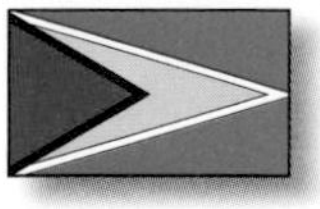

OFFICIAL NAME
The Cooperative Republic of Guyana

CAPITAL
Georgetown

Area 214 969 km² (83 000 sq miles)
Population 855 000
Population density 4 per km² (10 per sq mile)
Population growth rate 0.5%
Life expectancy 62 (m); 68 (f)
Languages English, Hindi, Urdu and local dialects

Adult literacy rate 98.1%
Currency Guyanese dollar (US $1 = 180 Guyanese dollars)
GDP (US million $) 690
GDP per head (US $) 811

FACT Guyanese speak English and play cricket for the West Indies – yet Guyana is a South American nation.

Key dates

1581 Dutch settlement.
1814 British control.
1831 Colony of British Guyana established.
1838 Last slaves freed; indentured laborers from India (East Indians) later brought in to replace slaves.
1961 Self-government.
1962-64 Political and racial violence between black and East Indian groups delays independence.
1964 People's National Congress (mainly black) wins election over Marxist-led People's Progressive Party (mainly East Indian).
1966 Full independence within Commonwealth; renamed Guyana.
1970 Becomes republic.
1978 "Jonestown massacre" – mass suicide and murder of 911 members of the People's Temple, an American religious cult.
1988 Economic reforms and privatization begin.

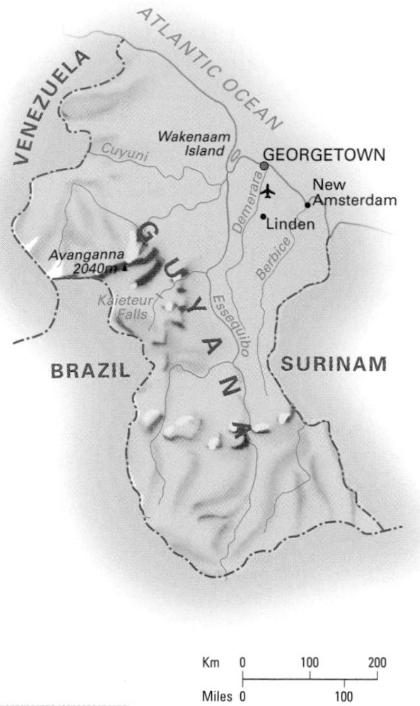

SURINAM

OFFICIAL NAME
The Republic of Surinam

CAPITAL
Paramaribo

Area 163 265 km² (63 037 sq miles)
Population 415 000
Population density 3 per km² (7 per sq mile)
Population growth rate 1.1%
Life expectancy 64 (m); 71 (f)
Languages Dutch, Hindi, Javanese, Sranang Tongo, Chinese, English

Adult literacy rate 93%
Currency Surinam guilder (US $1 = 981 guilders)
GDP (US million $) 842
GDP per head (US $) 2053

FACT Surinam is one of the most heavily forested countries in the world – 96 percent of its land is covered by trees.

Key dates

1651 British settlement.
1667 Dutch control in exchange for New York.
1863 Slavery abolished; indentured laborers later brought in from India and Indonesia to replace slaves.
1954 Dutch Guiana gains self-government.
1975 Full independence; about two fifths of population emigrate to Netherlands. Name changed to Surinam.
1980 Bloodless coup.
1982-87 National Military Council governs.
1987 Antigovernment rebels cause economic chaos.
1987 Three main parties unite and win elections; new constitution.
1990 Military coup forces resignation of civilian government.
1991 New elections.
1992 Peace treaty with guerrilla groups.

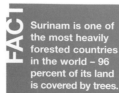

BRAZIL

OFFICIAL NAME
Federative Republic of Brazil

CAPITAL
Brasília

Area 8 511 996 km² (3 286 500 sq miles)
Population 165 371 000
Population density 19 per km² (49 per sq mile)
Population growth rate 1%
Life expectancy 64 (m); 70 (f)
Languages Portuguese and local languages
Adult literacy rate 85.2%
Currency real (US $1 = 2.22 reals)
GDP (US million $) 518 900
GDP per head (US $) 3207

Key dates

1500 Portuguese claim.
c. 1700 Gold and diamonds discovered.
1750 Treaty with Spain confirms Portuguese rule.
1808-21 Rio de Janeiro is capital of Portuguese empire after France invades Portugal.
1815 Declared kingdom.
1822 Independence declared; Pedro I crowned emperor.
1828 Loses Uruguay in war against Argentina.
1865-70 War against Paraguay; present borders established.
1888 Slavery abolished.
1889 Military coup deposes emperor; republic established.
1917-18 One of Allies in World War I.
1930 Coup; Vargas becomes president.
1934 New constitution; universal right to vote.
1937 Economic crisis; new constitution makes Vargas dictator.
1942-45 One of Allies in World War II.
1945 Military forces Vargas to resign.
1946 New constitution restores democracy.
1951 Vargas elected president.
1954 Military coup; Vargas kills himself.
1960 Capital moves to Brasília.
1964-85 Military rule.
1989 First direct election of president under new constitution.
1992 President Collor accused of corruption; resigns.
2002 Socialist Lula da Silva elected president amid financial turbulence.

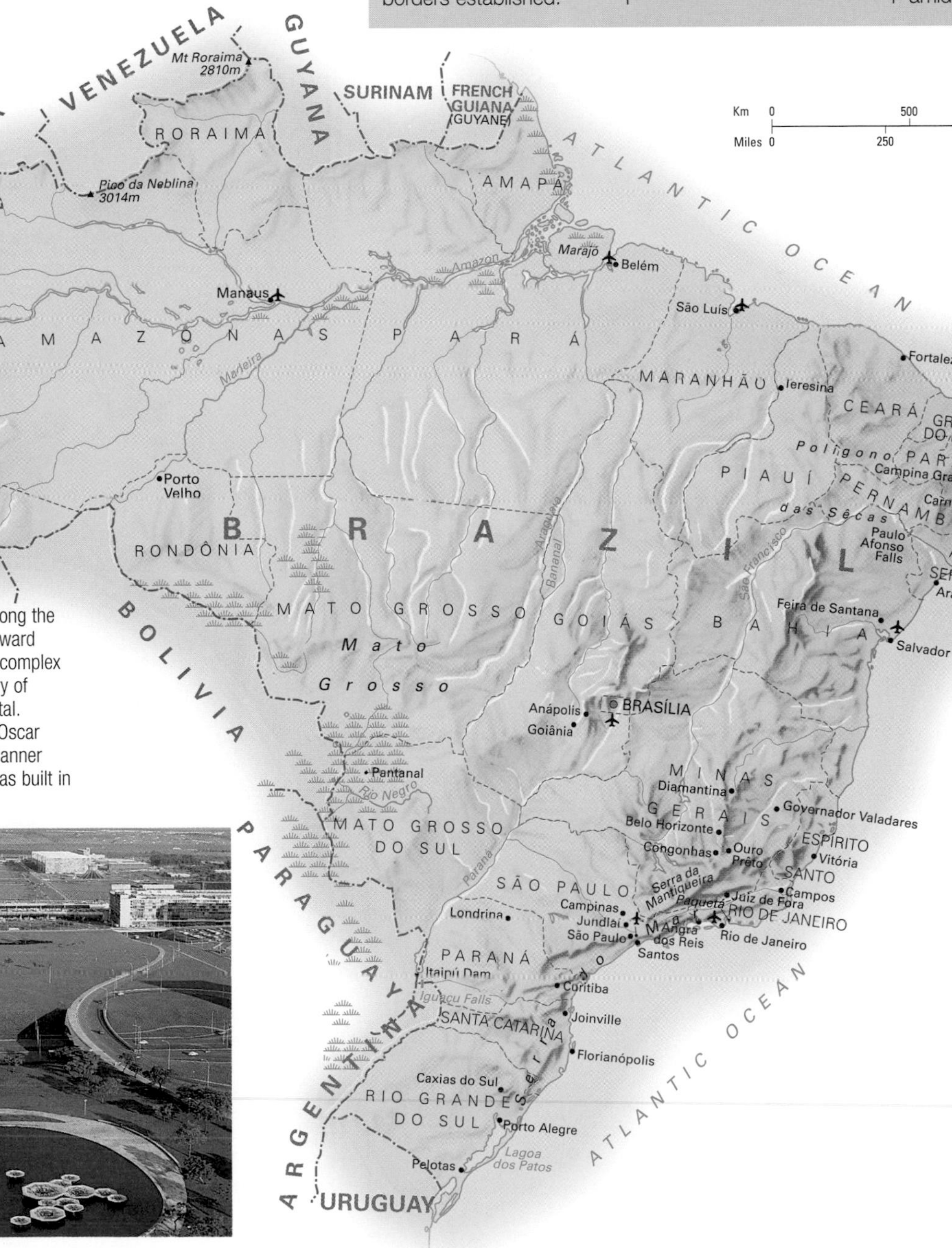

Urban plan A view along the main axis of Brasília toward the National Congress complex highlights the symmetry of Brazil's modernist capital. Designed by architect Oscar Niemeyer and urban planner Lúcio Costa, the city was built in just three years.

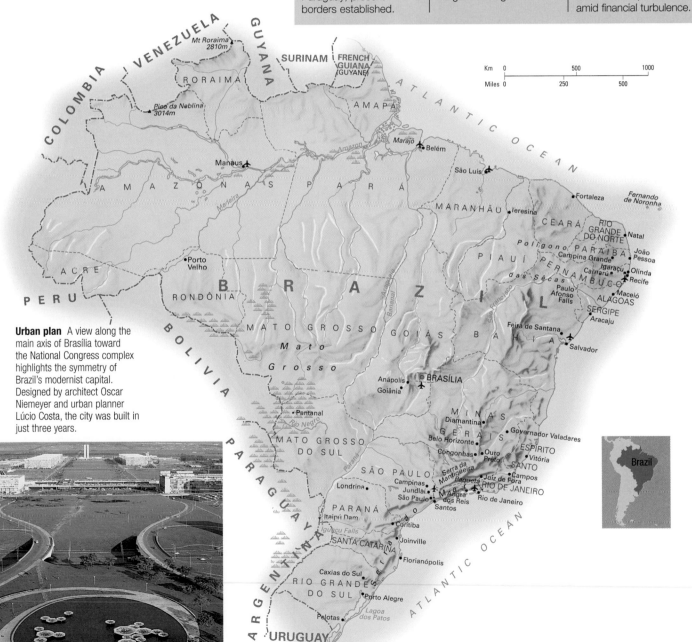

Paraguay, Uruguay and Argentina

PARAGUAY

OFFICIAL NAME
The Republic of Paraguay

CAPITAL
Asunción

Area 406 752 km² (157 048 sq miles)
Population 5 356 000
Population density 13 per km² (33 per sq mile)
Population growth rate 2.2%
Life expectancy 66 (m); 70 (f)
Languages Spanish, Guarani
Adult literacy rate 92.1%
Currency guarani (US $1 = 3805 guaranis)
GDP (US million $) 7600
GDP per head (US $) 1455

Key dates

1537 First Spanish settlement.
1588 Jesuits arrive; expelled 179 years later.
1811 Independence.
1865-70 War of the Triple Alliance: loses territory to Brazil, Argentina and Uruguay.
1932-35 Chaco War: gains territory in Gran Chaco from Bolivia.
1954 General Alfredo Stroessner seizes power.
1989 Coup overthrows Stroessner.
1992 New constitution.
1993 First democratic presidential election.

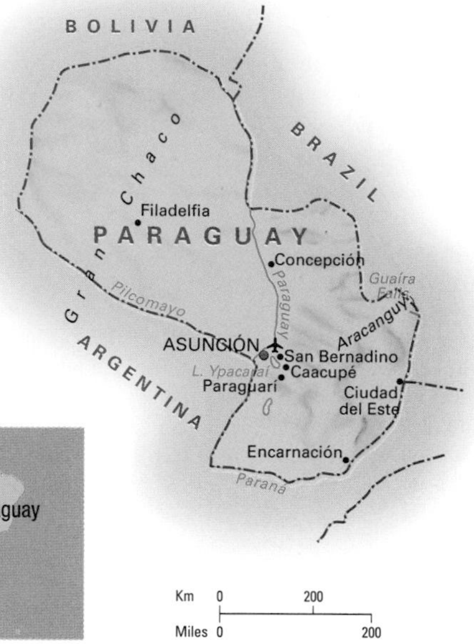

URUGUAY

OFFICIAL NAME
The Oriental Republic of Uruguay

CAPITAL
Montevideo

Area 176 215 km² (68 037 sq miles)
Population 3 313 000
Population density 19 per km² (48 per sq mile)
Population growth rate 0.6%
Life expectancy 68 (m); 74 (f)
Languages Spanish, Portuguese
Adult literacy rate 96.8%
Currency Uruguayan peso (US $1 = 12.9 pesos)
GDP (US million $) 19 400
GDP per head (US $) 5896

Key dates

1680 Portuguese settlement.
1726 Spanish found Montevideo.
1777 Spanish control.
1811-20 Struggle for independence with Spanish, Argentine and Portuguese forces ends in annexation to Brazil.
1825-28 Revolt (with UK and Argentine support) against Brazil wins full independence.
1836-52 Civil war between mainly rural Oribe and urban Colorado groups; won by Colorados.
1865-70 War of the Triple Alliance: supports Argentina and Brazil to defeat Paraguay.
1903 President Batlle begins reforms leading to stable democracy.
1942-45 Supports Allies in World War II.
1967 Tupamaro guerrilla group becomes active.
1972 State of internal war declared against Tupamaros; army stamps out their urban terrorism.
1973 Armed forces take control of government.
1976 Coup deposes repressive government.
1984 Democratic elections restore civilian government.

WEALTH OF THE PAMPAS

Despite the fact that its name translates as "Land of Silver," the true wealth of Argentina lies in its soil. The pampas, a huge expanse of grassland, stretches over 777 000 km² (300 000 sq miles) of central Argentina and into Uruguay. The Spanish introduced cattle and horses to these vast plains in the mid-16th century, and for centuries they roamed semiwild there. The pampas are home to a vast array of wildlife: ostrichlike rheas, deer, guanacos (which resemble llamas), giant anteaters and maned wolves, as well as livestock.

Only in the 19th century were the Pampas extensively settled by farmers, mainly from Europe, who established large *estancias* (cattle ranches) and farms. During those years, the hard-riding gauchos began to tame the wild horses and round up the wild cattle. Like the cowboys of North America's Wild West, they reveled in the freedom of wide open spaces. To city dwellers and later generations they became cultural symbols.

The Argentinians are great meat-eaters, consuming 70 kg (154 lb) per head per year. They are also prodigious meat-exporters, although it was not until the late 1800s, with the development of railroads and refrigerated steamships, that beef exports soared and Argentina began to amass wealth based on the products of the pampas. Its cattle business remains immense, but modern vehicles and machinery have consigned the gaucho into a hazy and legendary past.

ARGENTINA

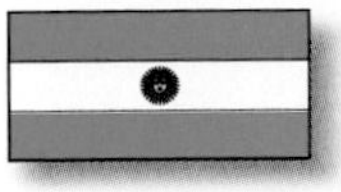

OFFICIAL NAME
The Argentine Republic

CAPITAL
Buenos Aires

Key dates

1516-26 Solis, Magellan and Cabot explore Rio de la Plata.
1536 Spanish settle briefly at Buenos Aires (refounded 1580).
1776 Separate Viceroyalty of La Plata.
1812-16 Jose de San Martin leads fight for independence; new state named United Provinces of La Plata.
1853 New constitution; Buenos Aires secedes.
1862 Buenos Aires rejoins as capital.
1916 First democratic elections.
1939-45 World War II: open sympathy with Germany, but declares war on Axis in 1945.
1943 Military coup.
1946 Colonel Juan Perón made president; assisted by wife Eva, reforms economy but represses freedoms.
1952 Eva Perón dies.
1955 Perón deposed; goes into exile in Spain.
1973 Perón returns from exile; wins election.
1974 Perón dies; third wife, María, becomes president.
1976 Military coup deposes María Perón.
1982 Invades Falkland Islands; Falklands War lost to Britain.
1983 Democratic elections; Perónist party suffers first defeat.
1985 Five former junta members judged guilty of murder and human rights abuses.
1909 Carlos Menem elected president.
1990 Relations with Britain restored. Military coup fails.
1994 New constitution.
2001 Economy falters; defaults on foreign debts.

Area 2 766 889 km^2 (1 068 302 sq miles)
Population 36 578 000
Population density 13 per km^2 (34 per sq mile)
Population growth rate 1.4%
Life expectancy 68 (m); 73 (f)
Languages Spanish, many other European languages and local languages
Adult literacy rate 96.2%
Currency Argentine peso (US $1 = 3.33 pesos)
GDP (US million $) 281 900
GDP per head (US $) 7804

A piece of Europe in South America

Argentina is the only country in South America whose population is predominantly European in origin. About 85 percent of its people trace their ancestry to Europe – mostly to Italy (35 percent) and Spain (25 percent). Others look back to Poland, France, Russia, Germany and the British Isles. Spanish is the official language, but German, English, French and Italian are often heard. A group of Welsh immigrants whose ancestors settled in Patagonia in the 1860s have never forgotten their roots. They still bring teachers across the Atlantic to keep Welsh a living language.

The same European origins are reflected in Argentina's culture. The capital's opera, the *teatro Colón*, was shipped stone by stone from Europe. Its opening performance, in 1908, was Verdi's *Aïda*. It was through contacts with the sports-loving British that Argentinians took up soccer, rugby, tennis and polo. But Europe is not the only influence. The tango, the best-known product of Argentina's popular culture, combines Cuban, Spanish, African and gaucho elements and is accompanied on the bandonéon, an instrument invented by a German.

The non-European 15 percent includes native Amerindians, people of black African origin, immigrants from the Middle East and Mestizos (people of mixed race).

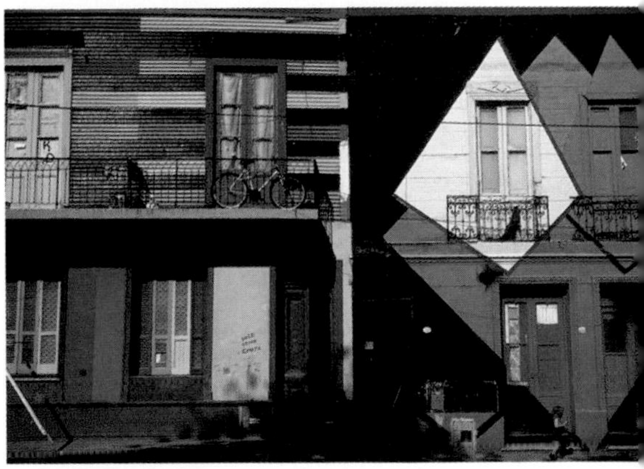

Bright barrio Not all the barrios of South America are shantytowns. The word simply means "neighborhood," and some, like La Boca in Buenos Aires, can be extremely stylish. Many of Argentina's Italian immigrants first settled in La Boca, and they provided the barrio with its brightly painted houses and restaurants.

Britain, Ireland and Iceland

ICELAND

OFFICIAL NAME
The Republic of Iceland

CAPITAL
Reykjavik

Area 103 000 km² (39 769 sq miles)
Population 279 000
Population density 3 per km² (7 per sq mile)
Population growth rate 1.1%
Life expectancy 76 (m); 80 (f)
Language Icelandic
Adult literacy rate 99%
Currency Icelandic krona (US $1 = 93 krona)
GDP (US million $) 8300
GDP per head (US $) 30 627

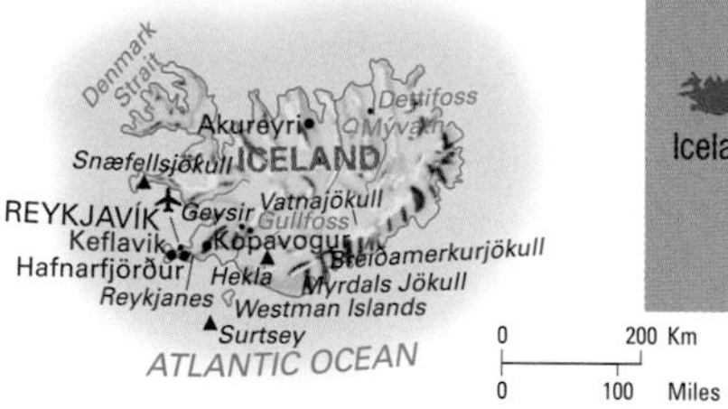

Key dates

c. 870 First Viking settlements.
930 Establishes Althing, world's first parliament.
1262 Althing accepts rule by king of Norway.
1380 Comes under Danish rule.
Late 18th c. Famine after volcanic eruptions destroy farmland.
1918 Independence under Danish crown.
1940-45 British and American garrison to prevent German invasion in World War II.
1944 Declares fully independent republic.
1976 "Cod war" with UK over fishing rights.

Centrally heated Iceland's capital, Reykjavik, is entirely heated by geothermal energy, which also provides much of the country's electric power.

IRELAND

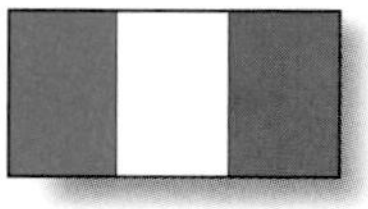

OFFICIAL NAME
The Republic of Ireland

CAPITAL
Dublin

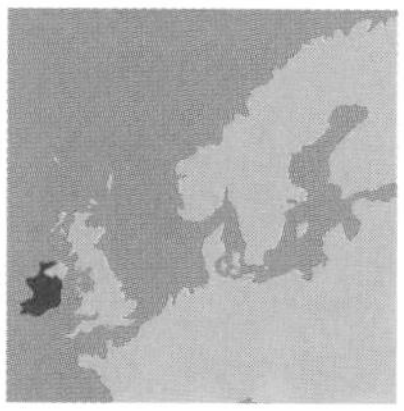

Area 70 285 km² (27 137 sq miles)
Population 3 745 000
Population density 53 per km² (136 per sq mile)
Population growth rate 0.6%
Life expectancy 72 (m); 78 (f)
Languages Irish, English
Adult literacy rate 99%
Currency euro (US $1 = 0.94 euros)
GDP (US million $) 86 900
GDP per head (US $) 23 486

FACT The Irish adopted the harp as their symbol after the occupying English banned them from playing bagpipes.

Key dates

1601 Battle of Kinsale establishes English rule.
1690 Battle of the Boyne leads to Protestant supremacy.
1801 All Ireland becomes part of United Kingdom.
1846-51 Famine kills 1 million; more than 1 million emigrate.
1916 British suppress Easter Rising in Dublin; 15 leaders executed.
1919 Nationalists form parliament (Dail) and Irish Republican Army.
1921 Anglo-Irish Treaty establishes Irish Free State (dominion under British crown); Northern Ireland remains British.
1937 Independent Eire established.
1949 Becomes republic.
1969-94 "Troubles" over Northern Ireland.
1973 Joins European Community.
1998 Good Friday peace agreement comes into force.

UNITED KINGDOM

OFFICIAL NAME
The United Kingdom of Great Britain and Northern Ireland

CAPITAL
London

Area 241 752 km² (93 341 sq miles)
Population 59 200 000
Population density 245 per km² (634 per sq mile)
Population growth rate 0.2%
Life expectancy 74 (m); 79 (f)
Languages English, Welsh
Adult literacy rate 99%
Currency pound sterling (£) (US $1 = £0.69)
GDP (US million $) 1 463 800
GDP per head (US $) 24 726

Key dates

A.D. 43 Roman invasion.
c. 410 Last Roman troops leave Britain.
1066 Norman invasion.
1215 Magna Carta limits power of king.
1337-1453 Hundred Years' War in France.
1588 Defeat of Spanish Armada.
1603 Union of English and Scottish kingdoms under James I and VI.
1642-51 English Civil Wars; king deposed.
1660 Crown restored.
1688 Parliament deposes James II in "Glorious Revolution."
1707 Act of Union joins England and Scotland as United Kingdom of Great Britain.
1801 Ireland made part of United Kingdom.
1815 Battle of Waterloo ends Napoleonic Wars.
1914-18 World War I.
1939-45 World War II.
1945-51 "Welfare state" created.
1960 Founding member of European Free Trade Association.
1973 Joins European Community.
1982 Falklands War.
1999 Scottish parliament and Welsh assembly established.

Norway, Denmark and Sweden

NORWAY

OFFICIAL NAME
The Kingdom of Norway

CAPITAL
Oslo

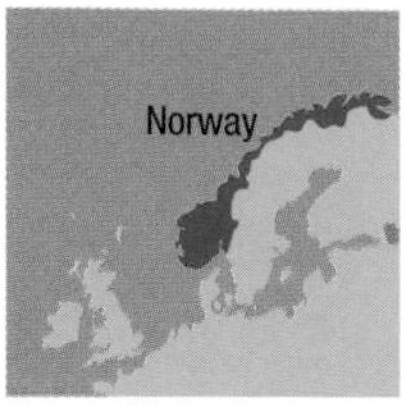

Area 323 877 km² (125 050 sq miles)
Population 4 462 000
Population density 14 per km² (35 per sq mile)
Population growth rate 0.4%
Life expectancy 74 (m); 80 (f)
Languages Norwegian, Lapp
Adult literacy rate 99%
Currency Norwegian krone (US $1 = 9.02 krone)
GDP (US million $) 152 200
GDP per head (US $) 34 356

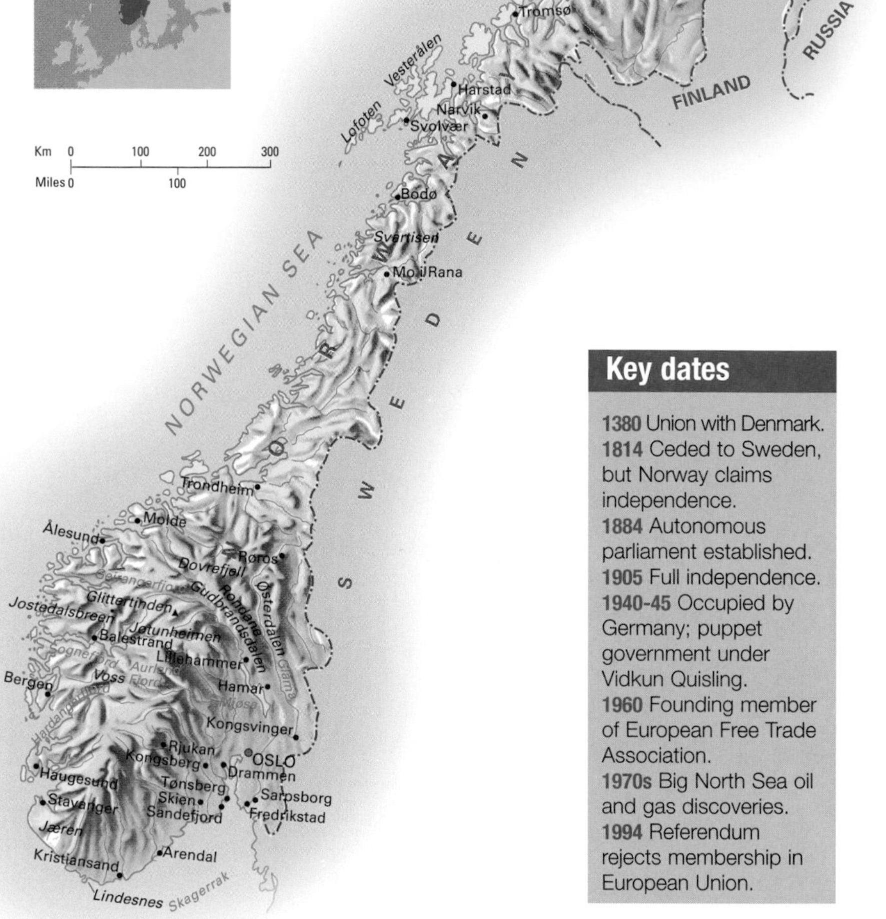

Nomads of the midnight sun

Life is changing for the Lapps living in the "Land of the Midnight Sun" in northern Norway, Sweden, Finland and Russia. They have long wandered the highlands with their reindeer herds, but about half are now settled in communities, farming, fishing, hunting, trapping and foresting. The outside world has also had an impact: The Chernobyl nuclear disaster in 1986 contaminated their reindeer, and mining and hydroelectric plans are changing their lands.

The Lapps (or Lapplanders), who call themselves "Saami," are among Europe's oldest peoples. They migrated from central Asia shortly after the last ice age. Today, about 60 000 Lapps live on about 388 500 km² (150 000 sq miles), mostly within the Arctic Circle and half in Norway. The various governments are trying to "normalize" Lapp society, but the Lapps remain independent and have their own parliaments in Norway, Finland and Sweden.

Key dates

1380 Union with Denmark.
1814 Ceded to Sweden, but Norway claims independence.
1884 Autonomous parliament established.
1905 Full independence.
1940-45 Occupied by Germany; puppet government under Vidkun Quisling.
1960 Founding member of European Free Trade Association.
1970s Big North Sea oil and gas discoveries.
1994 Referendum rejects membership in European Union.

DENMARK

OFFICIAL NAME
The Kingdom of Denmark

CAPITAL
Copenhagen

Area 43 094 km² (16 639 sq miles)
Population 5 327 000
Population density 123 per km² (319 per sq mile)
Population growth rate 0.1%
Life expectancy 72 (m); 77 (f)
Language Danish
Adult literacy rate 99%
Currency Danish krone (US $1 = 8.28 krone)
GDP (US million $) 180 100
GDP per head (US $) 33 981

Key dates

c. 950 Denmark united.
1380 Union with Norway.
1397 Union with Sweden.
1523 Cedes Sweden.
1814 Loses Norway.
1849 First democratic constitution.
1940-45 Neutral, but occupied by Germany.
1960 Founding member of European Free Trade Association.
1973 Joins European Community.

SWEDEN

OFFICIAL NAME
The Kingdom of Sweden

CAPITAL
Stockholm

Area 449 964 km² (173 732 sq miles)
Population 8 861 000
Population density 20 per km² (51 per sq mile)
Population growth rate 0.1%
Life expectancy 76 (m); 81 (f)
Languages Swedish, Finnish, Lapp
Adult literacy rate 99%
Currency Swedish krona (US $1 = 10.09 krona) Sweden will convert to the euro in 2005.
GDP (US million $) 243 700
GDP per head (US $) 27 536

Key dates

1397 Union of Sweden, Denmark and Norway.
1523 Independence from Denmark.
1809 Loses Finland to Russia.
1814 Acquires Norway in Napoleonic Wars.
1860-1900 Almost 1 million Swedes emigrate, most to North America.
1905 Loses Norway.
1914-18 Neutral in war.
1939-45 Neutral in war.
1960 Founding member of European Free Trade Association.
1995 Joins European Union.

Neighbors bridged Just over 600 years after the kingdoms of Sweden and Denmark were first politically united (and almost 500 years since they split apart again), a huge new bridge spans the Øresund Strait between the Swedish city of Malmö and the Danish capital Copenhagen. The bridge, which opened in July 2000, carries road traffic on the upper deck and trains on the lower deck. It stretches for 7.7 km (4.8 miles) and has a main span of 490 m (1608 ft).

GERMANY

OFFICIAL NAME
The Federal Republic of Germany

CAPITAL
Berlin

Area 356 974 km² (137 828 sq miles)
Population 82 087 000
Population density 230 per km² (595 per sq mile)
Population growth rate 0.1%
Life expectancy 72 (m); 79 (f)

Language German
Adult literacy rate 99%
Currency euro (US $1 = 0.94 euros)
GDP (US million $) 2 149 600
GDP per head (US $) 26 208

FACT The Ruhr region has the world's longest streetcar line; it connects eight cities along its 120 km (74 miles).

Key dates

800-43 Charlemagne's empire spans Germany.
942 Otto I crowned emperor; birth of Holy Roman Empire.
1438 Hapsburgs begin rule as Emperors.
1806 Napoleon ends Holy Roman Empire.
1815 Establishment of German Confederation.
1870-71 Franco-Prussian War; German Empire founded with Wilhelm I as Kaiser; Bismarck becomes chancellor.
1914-18 World War I fought and lost.
1919 Weimar Republic established.
1933 Adolf Hitler becomes chancellor.
1934 Hitler declares himself Führer; establishes Third Reich.
1939-45 World War II fought and lost; Germany divided into four occupation zones.
1948-49 Russians blockade Berlin.
1949 West Germany and East Germany formed.
1957 West Germany becomes founding member of European Economic Community.
1961 Berlin Wall built.
1989 Berlin Wall falls.
1990 East and West Germany reunified.
1999 Seat of government transferred from Bonn to Berlin.

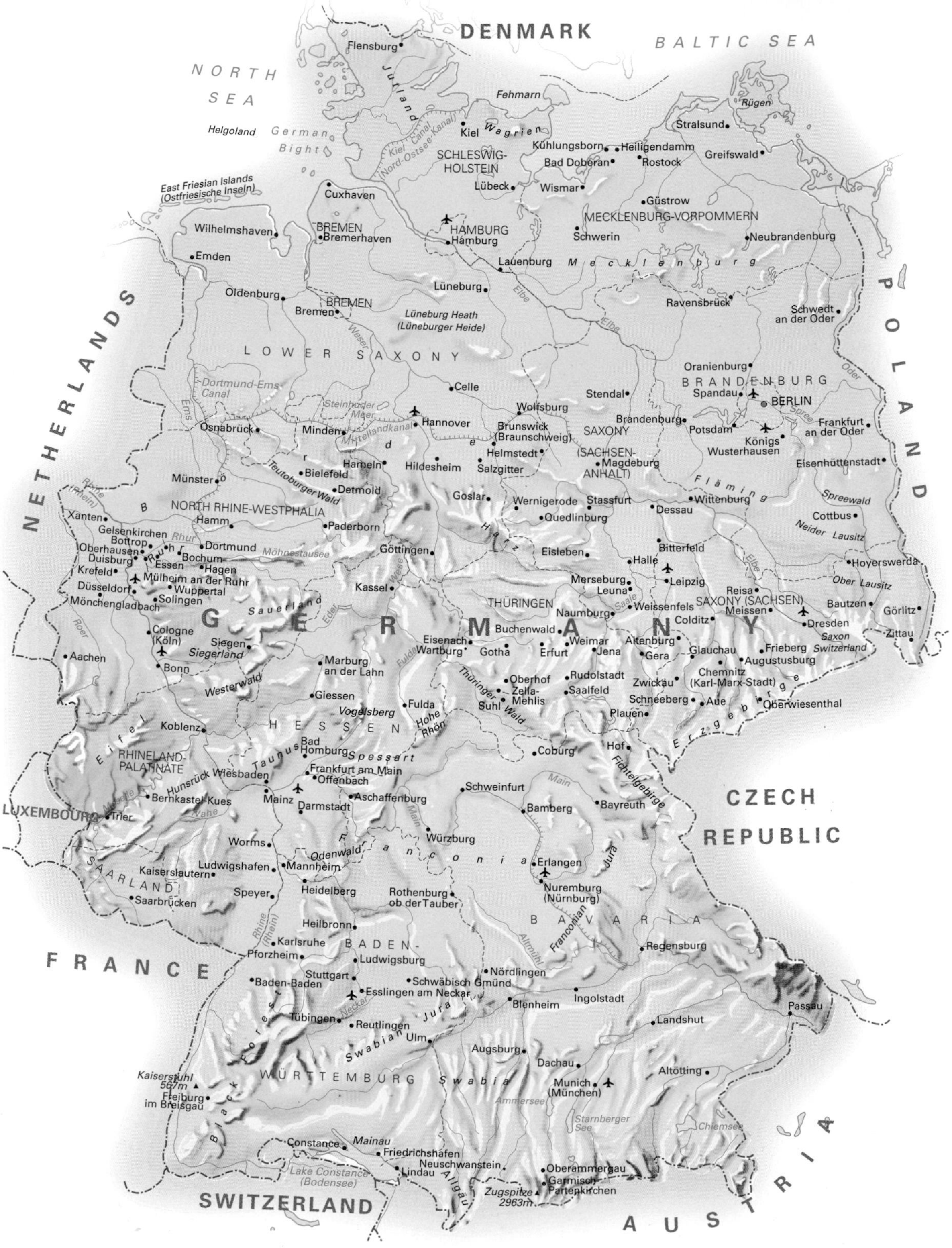

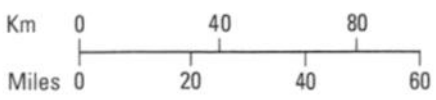

GDR – the other Germany

In 1949, both the Western Allies and the USSR declared a state in their zones of German occupation. In the west of the country, the Federal Republic came into being, and in the Soviet east, the German Democratic Republic was born.

The leadership of the new East German state, aware that it was in the front line of the ideological confrontation with the West, was ultra-loyal to the USSR. The concrete barrier, hurriedly constructed in 1961 around the western-controlled enclave of West Berlin, was officially called the "antifascist protection wall."

But the people of East Germany were never enthusiastic about Soviet socialism. In 1953, an uprising against Stalinism had been brutally suppressed, and a migration of qualified workers to the West had brought the economy close to collapse by 1960. This was the real purpose of the Wall: to keep valuable people from leaving.

The government strove to make life inside the country comfortable. By the 1970s, the standard of living was much higher in East Germany than in most socialist countries, but most people compared their lives with those of West Germans – whose affluence they experienced vicariously through television. Most GDR citizens were delighted when the reforming Soviet leader Mikhail Gorbachev ended support for their hardline regime in 1989. Within weeks, popular pressure in both Germanies brought down the Wall, and reunification soon followed.

NETHERLANDS

OFFICIAL NAME
The Kingdom of the Netherlands

CAPITAL
Amsterdam (gov't. at The Hague)

Area 33 939 km^2 (13 104 sq miles)
Population 15 810 000
Population density 463 per km^2 (1199 per sq mile)
Population growth rate 0.7%
Life expectancy 74 (m); 80 (f)
Language Dutch
Adult literacy rate 99%
Currency euro (US $1 = 0.94 euros)
GDP (US million $) 384 100
GDP per head (US $) 24 449

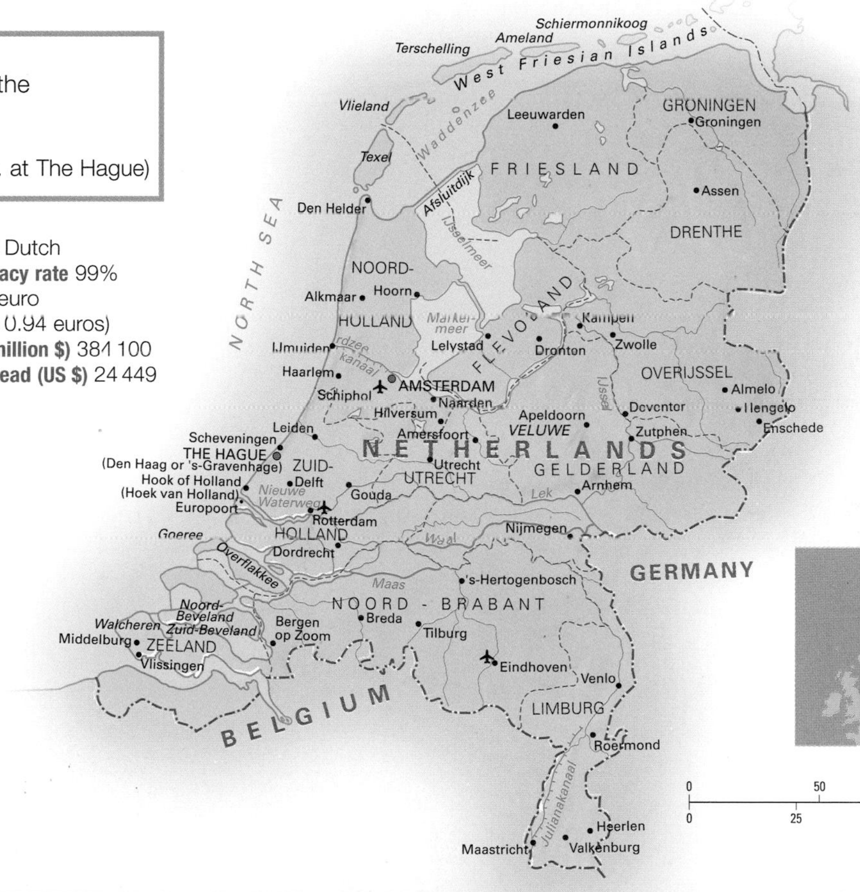

Key dates

14th-15th c. Dukes of Burgundy unite the Low Countries.
1516 Ruled by the Spanish monarchy.
1581 Dutch declare independence; recognized in 1648.
1652-74 Three naval wars against England.
1795-1813 French rule.
1815 Independent kingdom (with Belgium).
1830 Belgium breaks away to declare itself independent.
1940-45 Occupied by Germany despite neutrality.
1948 Joins Belgium and Luxembourg in Benelux customs union.
1949 Indonesia, its biggest colony, gains independence.
1957 Becomes founding member of European Economic Community.
1992 Hosts Maastricht conference that creates closer European union.

Wind against water This wind farm in the Polders is just the latest example of Dutch use of wind power. Almost half of the Netherlands lies below sea level, and wind-driven pumps have been used to drain it for more than 500 years.

France, Belgium and Luxembourg

FRANCE

OFFICIAL NAME
The French Republic

CAPITAL
Paris

Area 543 965 km^2 (210 026 sq miles)
Population 59 099 000
Population density 108 per km^2 (280 per sq mile)
Population growth rate 0.5%
Life expectancy 73 (m); 81 (f)
Languages French, Breton, Basque and several regional dialects
Adult literacy rate 95%
Currency euro (US $1 = 0.94 euros)
GDP (US million $) 1 445 000
GDP per head (US $) 24 553

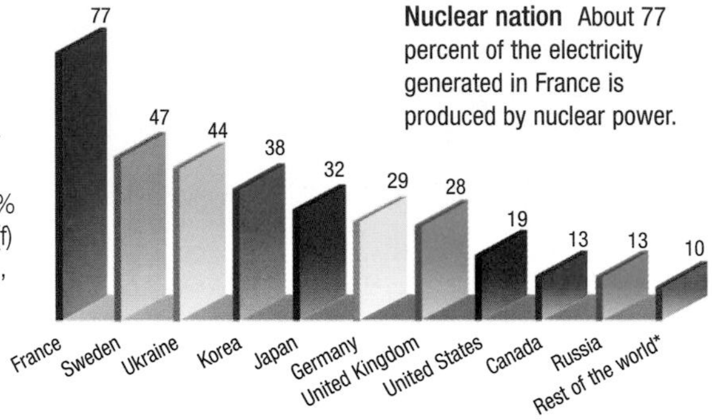

Nuclear nation About 77 percent of the electricity generated in France is produced by nuclear power.

Percentage of electricity produced by nuclear power, by country. *Denotes countries that have nuclear production facilities.

Key dates

486 Frankish king Clovis defeats the Romans.
1302 First States-General (parliament).
1337-1453 Hundred Years' War with England.
1789-99 Revolution establishes republic.
1799 Napoleon seizes power as emperor.
1815 Napoleon defeated; monarchy is restored.
1848 Second Republic.
1852 Second Empire under Louis Napoleon.
1870-71 Defeated in Franco-Prussian War.
1871 Third Republic.
1914-18 World War I fought mostly on French territory; 1.4 million French are killed.
1940-44 Defeat and occupation by Germany.
1946 Fourth Republic.
1946-54 Revolution in French Indochina.
1956 Independence for Morocco and Tunisia.
1957 Becomes founding member of European Economic Community.
1958 Fifth Republic; de Gaulle becomes president.
1962 Algeria wins independence.
1966 French troops withdrawn from NATO.
1968 Demonstrations for educational and political reforms.
1969 De Gaulle resigns.
1995-96 Renewed nuclear testing in the Pacific.

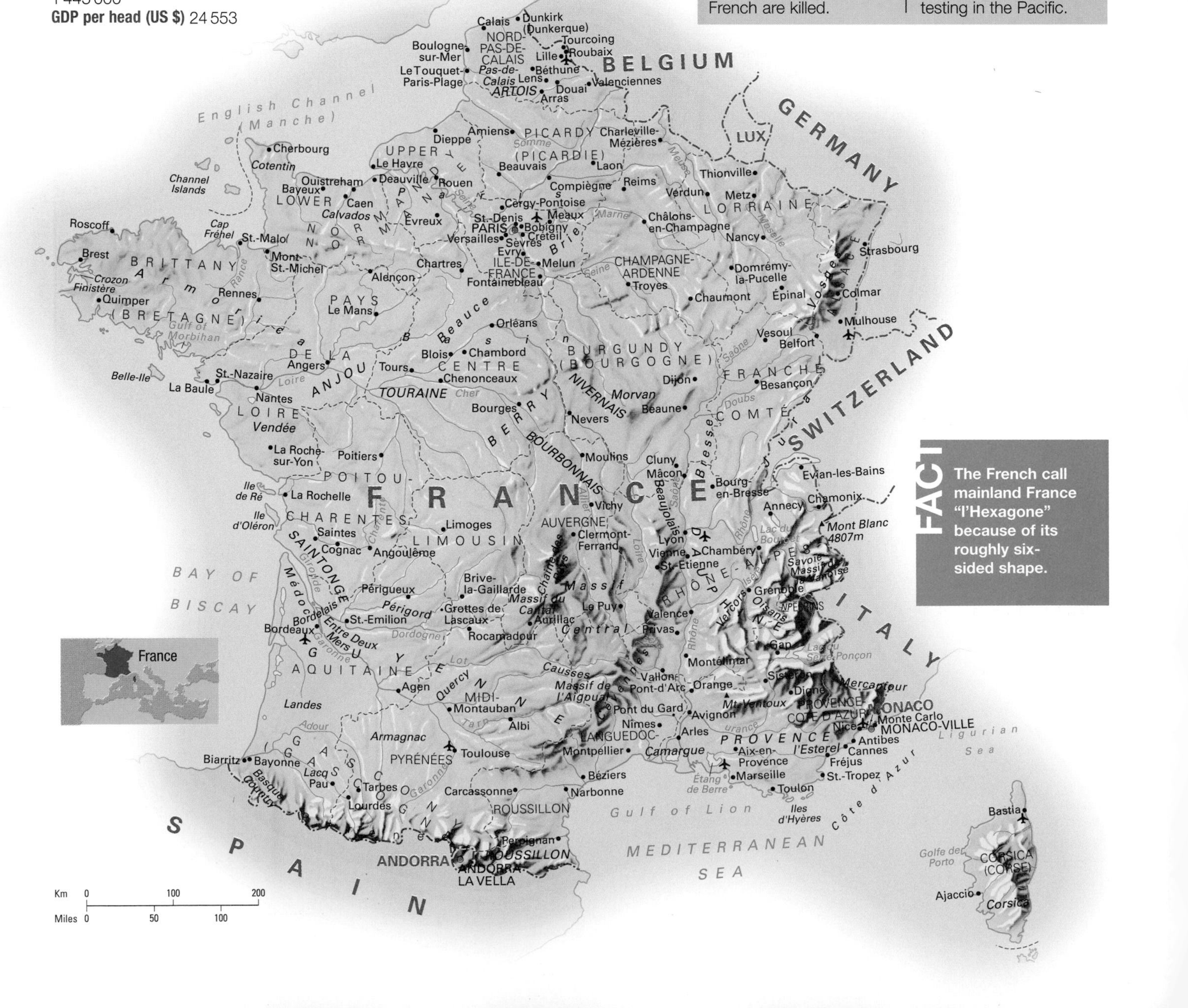

FACT

The French call mainland France "l'Hexagone" because of its roughly six-sided shape.

Alsace and Lorraine

For centuries, control of the provinces of Alsace and its larger western neighbor Lorraine vacillated between the rulers of France and Germany. The two nations contended for the region's rich iron, coal and potash resources. Alsace and Lorraine remain industrial, but traditional heavy industries are giving way to chemicals, textiles and electronics. The fertile land still supports the vineyards of Alsace and the orchards and grain fields of Lorraine.

Alsace and Lorraine were part of Roman Gaul and later of the medieval Holy Roman Empire. France acquired the territory during the 17th and 18th centuries. Germany annexed Alsace and part of Lorraine in 1871, after winning the Franco-Prussian War.

They were restored to France in 1919 at the end of World War I, and a movement began for autonomy. After Germany again annexed them during World War II – and about 20 000 of their citizens died in the German army on the Eastern Front – the two provinces were content to become French once again.

Today, Alsace and Lorraine have become a symbol of European unity. Their turbulent history has created a region where the two languages are spoken more or less equally and whose traditions, culture and architecture reflect both French and German influences.

As a gesture of reconciliation after the end of World War II, the Alsatian capital Strasbourg became the seat first of the Council of Europe and then of the European Parliament.

BELGIUM

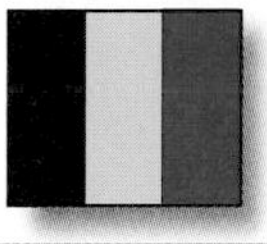

OFFICIAL NAME
The Kingdom of Belgium

CAPITAL
Brussels

Area 30 528 km² (11 787 sq miles)
Population 10 152 000
Population density 334 per km² (866 per sq mile)
Population growth rate 0.2%
Life expectancy 72 (m); 79 (f)
Languages Flemish, French, German
Adult literacy rate 99%
Currency euro (US $1 = 0.94 euros)
GDP (US million $) 244 200
GDP per head (US $) 23 917

Key dates

1830 Independence from the Netherlands.
1914-18 Neutral but occupied by Germany.
1940-45 Neutral but occupied by Germany.
1948 Joins Netherlands and Luxembourg in Benelux union.
1957 Becomes founding member of European Economic Community.
1993 Devolves power to three regions: Brussels, Flanders and Wallonia.

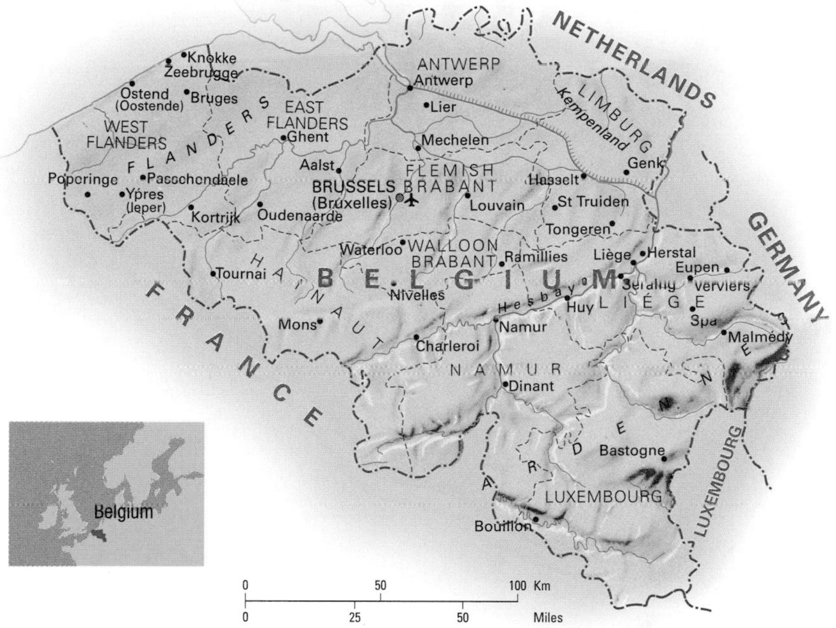

LUXEMBOURG

OFFICIAL NAME
The Grand Duchy of Luxembourg

CAPITAL
Luxembourg

Area 2587 km² (999 sq miles)
Population 429 000
Population density 166 per km² (430 per sq mile)
Population growth rate 1.5%
Life expectancy 70 (m); 77 (f)
Languages Letzeburgish (German-Moselle-Frankish dialect), French, German
Adult literacy rate 99%
Currency euro (US $1 = 0.94 euros)
GDP (US million $) 19 500
GDP per head (US $) 45 348

Key dates

1815 Grand Duchy under Dutch king.
1890 Independence from the Netherlands.
1914-18 Neutral but occupied by Germany.
1940-45 Neutral but occupied by Germany.
1948 Joins Belgium and Netherlands in Benelux customs union.
1952 Headquarters for European Coal and Steel Community.
1957 Becomes founding member of European Economic Community.

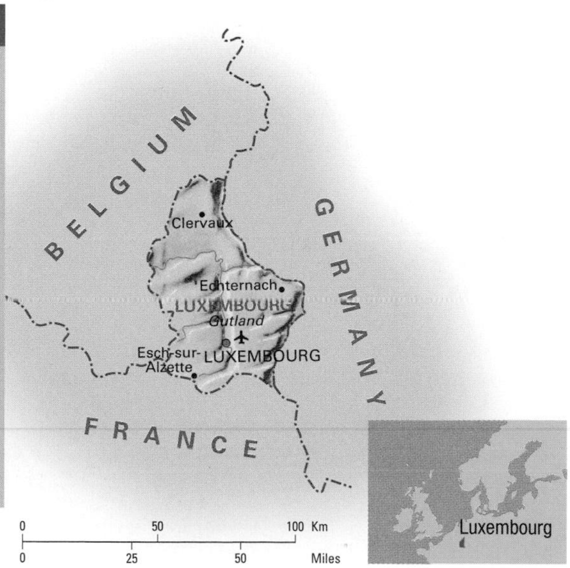

SPAIN

OFFICIAL NAME
The Kingdom of Spain

CAPITAL
Madrid

Area 504 782 km² (194 897 sq miles)
Population 39 418 000
Population density 78 per km² (202 per sq mile)
Population growth rate 0.1%
Life expectancy 73 (m); 80 (f)
Languages Spanish (Castilian), Catalan, Galician, Basque
Adult literacy rate 95.8%
Currency euro (US $1 = 0.94 euros)
GDP (US million $) 588 300
GDP per head (US $) 14 942

Building a new Spain The Guggenheim Museum in Bilbao, designed by the American architect Frank Gehry and opened in 1997, symbolizes the post-Franco regeneration of Spanish culture.

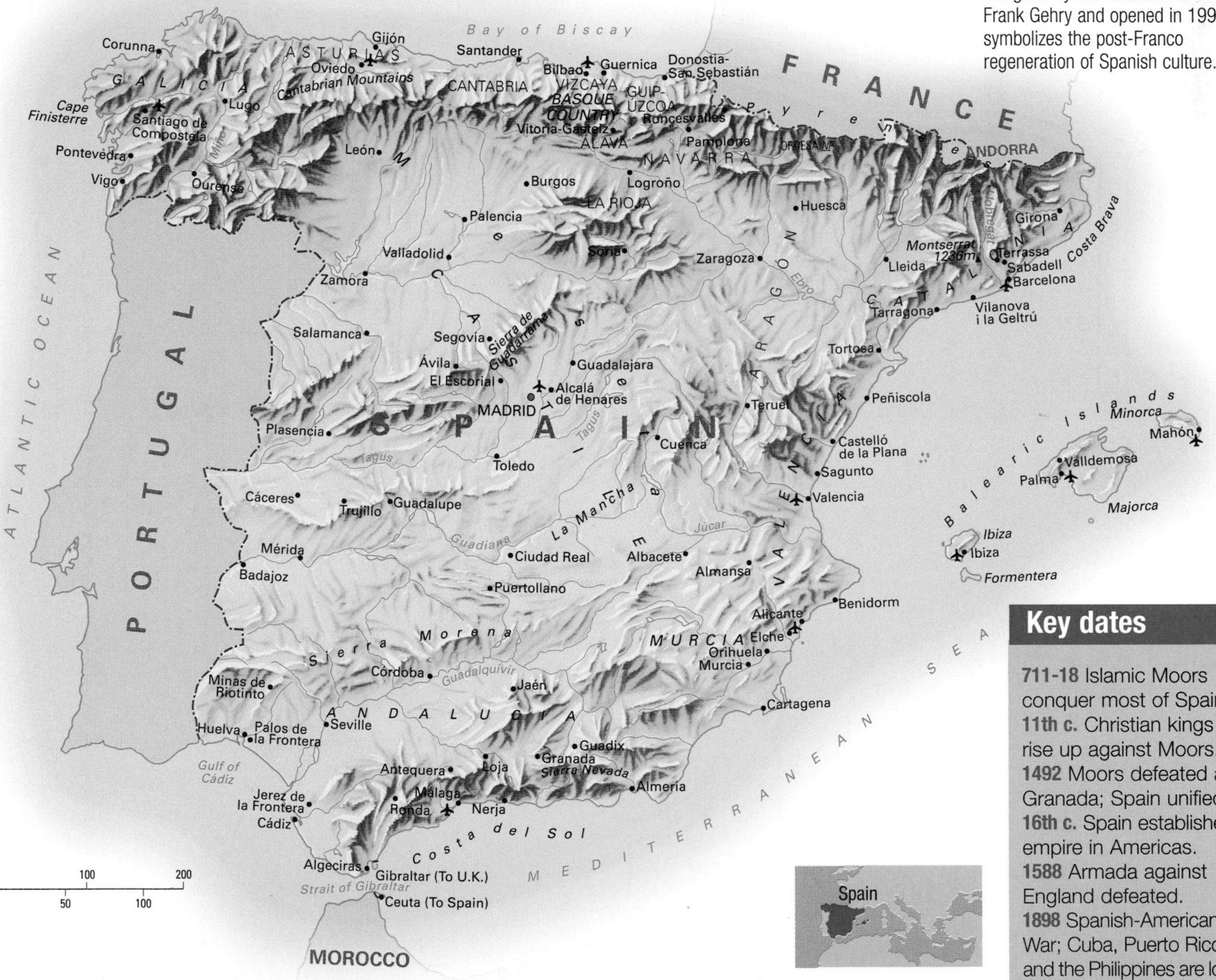

Spain's restless nationalities

Spain's two main ethnic minorities – the Basque and Catalan peoples – have long sought autonomy. Both were repressed during Franco's dictatorship, but in 1980 they gained regional autonomy, each with its own parliament. The Basque country straddles the western Pyrenees into France. Its three Spanish provinces have 620 000 people. The Basques speak a language unrelated to any other. A terrorist group, ETA (*Euzkadi ta Azkatasuna* – "Basque Homeland and Liberty"), has killed more than 800 people since 1968, with brief truces in 1989 and 1998-99.

The four northeastern provinces of Catalonia are home to 6 million people, many speaking Catalan, a distinct Romance language. Catalonia was independent from 1932 to 1939. Today it is Spain's main industrial area, and Barcelona, its capital, is one of Spain's most vibrant cities.

Key dates

711-18 Islamic Moors conquer most of Spain.
11th c. Christian kings rise up against Moors.
1492 Moors defeated at Granada; Spain unified.
16th c. Spain establishes empire in Americas.
1588 Armada against England defeated.
1898 Spanish-American War; Cuba, Puerto Rico and the Philippines are lost.
1936-39 Spanish Civil War; General Franco becomes dictator.
1968 Basque terrorist campaign begins.
1975 Franco dies; monarchy restored.
1980 Limited autonomy for Catalonia and Basque provinces.
1981 Military coup fails.
1986 Joins European Community.

PORTUGAL

OFFICIAL NAME
The Portuguese Republic

CAPITAL
Lisbon

Area 92 270 km² (35 626 sq miles)
Population 9 989 000
Population density 108 per km² (280 per sq mile)
Population growth rate 0.1%
Life expectancy 71 (m); 78 (f)
Language Portuguese
Adult literacy rate 85%
Currency euro (US $1 = 0.94 euros)
GDP (US million $) 108 900
GDP per head (US $) 10 922

Key dates

1143 Independent kingdom established.
1419 Overseas expansion begins.
1580 Spanish rule starts.
1640 Independence regained from Spain.
1822 Brazil declares independence.
1910 King deposed; republic proclaimed.
1916-18 Fights alongside Allies in World War I.
1926 Military coup begins dictatorship.
1928 Antonio Salazar becomes dictator.
1974 Military coup restores civil rights.
1974-76 Gives up most remaining colonies.
1976 Free elections.
1986 Joins European Community.

ANDORRA

OFFICIAL NAME
The Principality of Andorra

CAPITAL
Andorra la Vella

Area 468 km² (181 sq miles)
Population 80 000
Population density 158 per km² (409 per sq mile)
Population growth rate 3.3%
Life expectancy 79 (m); 79 (f)
Languages Catalan, French, Spanish
Adult literacy rate 99%
Currency euro (US $1 = 0.94 euros)
GDP (US million $) 1200
GDP per head (US $) 15 000

Key dates

819 Granted to Bishop of Urgel from Louis the Pious of Charlemagne.
1278-88 Joint rule by the (Spanish) bishop and French count (later king, then president) begins.
1970 Women gain vote.
1993 Parliamentary government begins.
1993 Joins UN.

MALTA

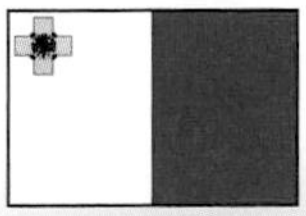

OFFICIAL NAME
The Republic of Malta

CAPITAL
Valletta

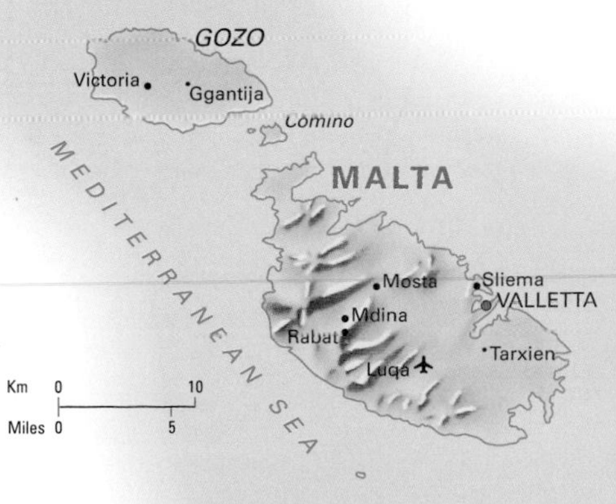

Area 316 km² (122 sq miles)
Population 386 000
Population density 1203 per km² (3115 per sq mile)
Population growth rate 1.1%
Life expectancy 75 (m); 79 (f)
Languages Maltese, English, Italian
Adult literacy rate 87.9%
Currency Maltese lira (US $1 = 0.45 Maltese lira)
GDP (US million $) 3400
GDP per head (US $) 8947

Key dates

1520 Becomes fiefdom of Order of St. John.
1798 Seized by France.
1800 Becomes British protectorate.
1814 Becomes British crown colony.
1947 New constitution gives self-government.
1956 Referendum in favor of full integration with Britain, but negotiations stall.
1964 Full independence under British crown.
1974 Establishes Republic of Malta.
1990 Applies for membership in European Community.

FACT
The UK awarded Malta the George Cross in 1942 for its people's courage under German bombardment.

Italy, Vatican City, San Marino and Monaco

ITALY

OFFICIAL NAME
The Italian Republic

CAPITAL
Rome

Area 301 323 km² (116 341 sq miles)
Population 57 343 000
Population density 191 per km² (495 per sq mile)
Population growth rate 0.1%
Life expectancy 74 (m); 80 (f)
Languages Italian, German, French, others
Adult literacy rate 97.1%
Currency euro (US $1 = 0.94 euros)
GDP (US million $) 1 176 400
GDP per head (US $) 20 427

Key dates

From c. 1000 City-states rise to power.
16th-18th c. Most Italian states under Spanish then Austrian control.
1796-1815 Most of Italy ruled by France.
1848 Revolutions in major Italian cities.
1861 Most of Italy united as kingdom.
1866 Acquires Mantua and Venetia after Austro-Prussian War.
1870 Rome is made the capital city.
1915-19 Joins with Allies in World War I.
1922 Fascist Mussolini named prime minister.
1925 Mussolini becomes dictator.
1929 Independence agreed for Vatican City.
1936 Seizes Ethiopia.
1939 Invades Albania.
1940-43 Joins with Axis in World War II.
1943 New government joins Allies and declares war on Germany.
1946 Republic declared.
1957 Becomes founding member of European Economic Community.
1997 Leads peacekeeping in Albania.

VATICAN CITY

OFFICIAL NAME
The State of the Vatican City

CAPITAL
Vatican City

Area 0.44 km² (0.17 sq mile)
Population 870
Population density 1977 per km² (5118 per sq mile)
Population growth rate 0%
Life expectancy 74 (m); 80 (f)
Languages Italian, Latin
Adult literacy rate 100%
Currency euro (US $1 = 0.94 euros)
GDP (US million $) 19
GDP per head (US $) 19 121

Key dates

756 First of Papal States established.
1377 Papal residence established in Rome.
1870 Papal States abolished.
1929 Italy recognizes pope's sovereignty over Vatican City.
1978 John Paul II elected first non-Italian pope in 456 years.

Tiny center of the Catholic world

Vatican City (Stato della Citta del Vaticano) is the world's smallest nation. The absolute ruler is the pope, who is elected for life; the population is fewer than 1000; Latin is an official language; it has a birthrate of zero; and there is no income tax. The city-state is less than a quarter the size of London's Hyde Park, yet it has its own diplomatic corps, flag, bank, broadcasting station and postage stamps. The country is protected by the Swiss Guard, a corps of papal bodyguards founded during the Renaissance.

Vatican City is the surviving remnant of the Papal States that once dominated much of central Italy; in 1859, just before Italian unification, papal territory covered about 44 000 km² (17 000 sq miles). The Papal States were abolished in 1870, but the Vatican's independence was guaranteed by Italian dictator Benito Mussolini in 1929. Located in the heart of Rome, on Vatican Hill near the bank of the Tiber, the state now covers only 44 ha (109 acres). Its buildings include St. Peter's basilica, the world's largest church, and the Vatican palace, the home of popes since 1377 and the world's largest residential palace. Its art masterpieces include Michelangelo's ceiling frescoes in the Sistine Chapel. Other buildings house art, manuscripts, maps, coins and medals.

Christian soldiers The papal Swiss Guards, founded in 1505, parade in uniforms said to have been designed by Michelangelo.

SAN MARINO

OFFICIAL NAME
The Republic of San Marino

CAPITAL
San Marino

Area 61 km² (24 sq miles)
Population 26 000
Population density 492 per km² (1250 per sq mile)
Population growth rate 1.5%
Life expectancy 73 (m); 79 (f)
Language Italian
Adult literacy rate 98.4%
Currency euro (US $1 = 0.94 euros)
GDP (US million $) 500
GDP per head (US $) 19 230

Key dates

4th c. The republic is founded by Marinus, a shepherd.
1631 Independence is recognized by the papacy.
1862 Treaty of friendship with Italy signed.
1960 Women given right to vote.
1992 Joins UN.

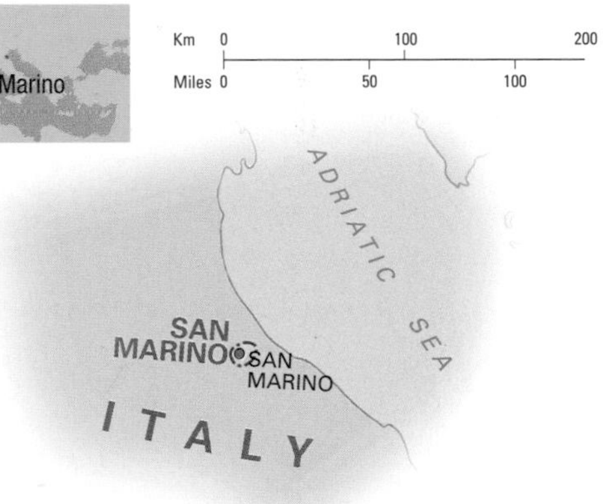

MONACO

OFFICIAL NAME
The Principality of Monaco

CAPITAL
Monaco

Area 1.95 km² (0.75 sq mile)
Population 33 000
Population density 16 410 per km² (42 667 per sq mile)
Population growth rate 0%
Life expectancy 78 (m); 78 (f)
Languages French, Monegasque, Italian, English
Adult literacy rate 99%
Currency euro (US $1 = 0.94 euros)
GDP (US million $) 847
GDP per head (US $) 26 470

Key dates

1297 Rule by Grimaldi family begins.
1798-1814 Ruled by France.
1848-61 Ruled by France.
1861 Independence.
1940-45 Occupation by Italy, then Germany.
1956 Prince Rainier III marries Grace Kelly.
1993 Monaco joins UN.

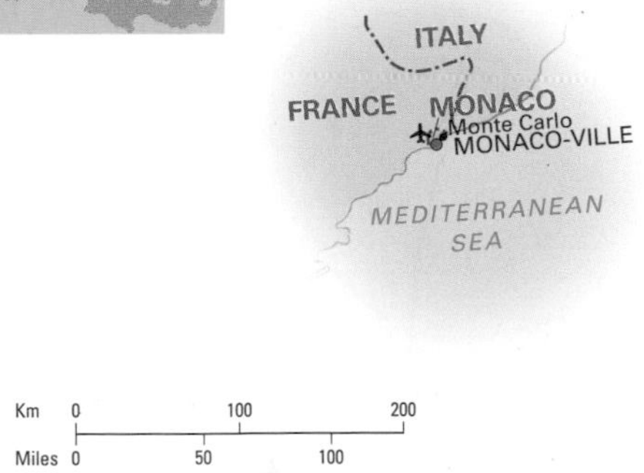

The Baltic Countries

ESTONIA

OFFICIAL NAME
The Republic of Estonia

CAPITAL
Tallinn

Area 45 227 km^2 (17 462 sq miles)
Population 1 370 500
Population density 32 per km^2 (83 per sq mile)
Population growth rate 0.6%
Life expectancy 62 (m); 73 (f)

Languages Estonian, Russian
Adult literacy rate 99.7%
Currency kroon (US $1 = 17.36 kroons)
GDP (US million $) 5400
GDP per head (US $) 3703

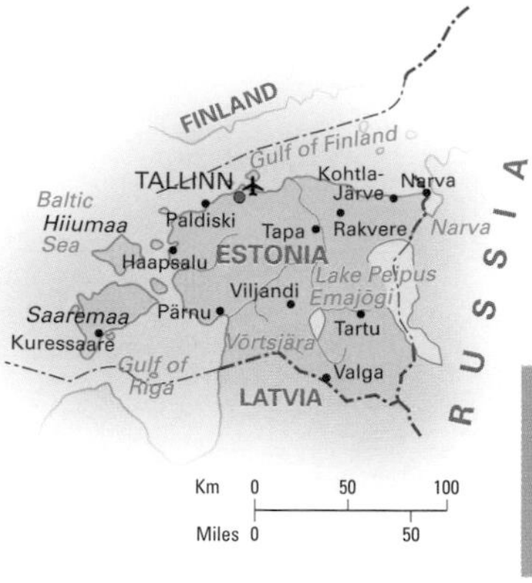

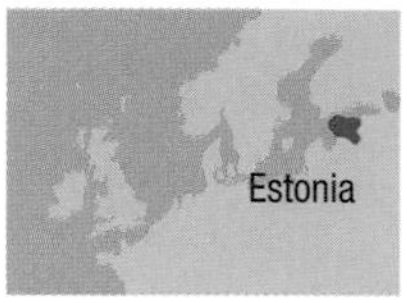

Key dates

1625 Swedish rule.
1721 Russian control.
1918 Independence proclaimed.
1940 Annexed to USSR.
1941-44 German occupation.
1990 Declares itself "occupied" by USSR.
1991 Independence declared; recognized by USSR. Joins UN.
1993 Soviet troops leave.

LATVIA

OFFICIAL NAME
The Republic of Latvia

CAPITAL
Riga

Area 64 589 km^2 (24 938 sq miles)
Population 2 432 000
Population density 38 per km^2 (98 per sq mile)
Population growth rate 0.1%
Life expectancy 60 (m); 73 (f)

Languages Latvian, Russian
Adult literacy rate 98%
Currency lats (US $1 = 0.62 lats)
GDP (US million $) 6568
GDP per head (US $) 2680

Key dates

1800 Russian control.
1918 Independence proclaimed.
1940 Annexed to USSR.
1941-44 German occupation.
1990 Claims independence from USSR.
1991 Independence recognized by USSR. Joins UN.
1993 Soviet troops leave.

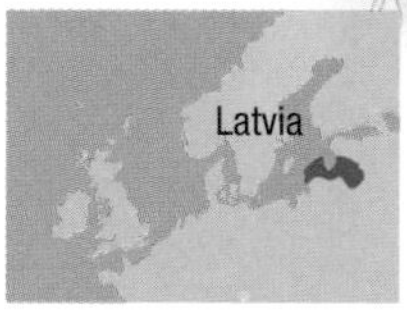

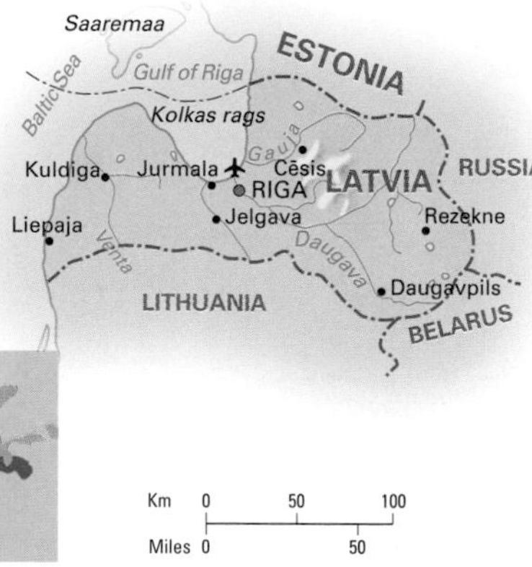

The long struggle for Baltic independence

Estonia, Latvia and Lithuania were the last states to join the USSR and the first to leave it. They were always unwilling members of the Soviet club. Independent between the world wars, all three were assigned to the Soviet sphere of influence under the terms of the secret protocol of the 1939 Nazi-Soviet nonaggression treaty. They were annexed in 1940 and subjected to a vicious purge of anti-Stalinists.

During the 50 years of Soviet rule, millions of ethnic Russians settled in the Baltic States. Few learned the local languages or integrated with the culture of the Baltic peoples, and this Russocentric insensitivity caused deep resentment. But throughout their Soviet years, the Baltic States served as a kind of ersatz-West: Life in well-kept cities such as Vilnius and Tallinn was comfortable, civilized, and always a few degrees more liberal than in the Russian heartland.

Independence movements sprang up in the Baltic States almost as soon as Gorbachev's policy of glasnost came into being. When Moscow allowed communist regimes in eastern Europe to collapse, independence campaigners claimed that their peoples had as much right to self-determination as the Czechs or Poles because they were also victims of Stalin's wartime land-grab. The logic was impeccable, but Gorbachev objected to the idea that a republic of the USSR might secede. In January 1991, independence demonstrators were attacked by Russian troops, and five were killed.

In spite of Gorbachev, independence came later that year. Russians in the Baltic States now found themselves unwelcome foreigners and were widely discriminated against. The new authorities saw contentious measures (such as a language qualification for citizenship) as vital to the salvation of their native culture. They also pressed ahead with the reconstruction of a free market economy. Estonia in particular was helped by Finland, its neighbor and ethnic cousin.

All three benefited from the facts that their peoples' entrepreneurial spark had not been entirely extinguished by Soviet economic planning and that the democratic interwar years were still well within living memory.

All three of the Baltic States have expressed a desire to join the European Union and the NATO defense alliance. Joining either would strengthen countries that over the past eight centuries, have experienced far more occupation than independence. In the 13th century, Estonia and Latvia were overrun by the Teutonic knights and the Livonian Brothers of the Sword, whose rule was later replaced by that of the Swedes and the Poles. In the 18th century, both countries fell under the dominion of Tsarist Russia. The collapse of Russia and Germany at the end of World War I opened the way to independence in 1918, but freedom did not last long: The Nazi-Soviet pact of 1939 placed all three Baltic countries under Soviet control. Lithuania, to protect itself against inroads by Teutonic knights and the Brothers of the Sword, formed alliances that grew into the Grand Duchy of Lithuania, an empire which, in the Middle Ages, stretched across Europe from the Baltic to the Black Sea. In the 18th century, Lithuania, as well as Estonia and Latvia, disappeared into the Tsarist embrace.

LITHUANIA

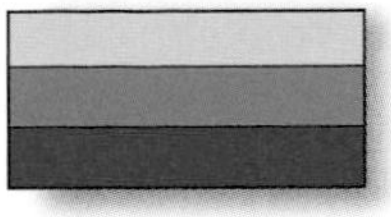

OFFICIAL NAME
The Republic of Lithuania

CAPITAL
Vilnius

Area 65 300 km² (25 212 sq miles)
Population 3 699 000
Population density 57 per km² (147 per sq mile)
Population growth rate 0.1%
Life expectancy 63 (m); 75 (f)
Languages Lithuanian, Russian, Polish
Adult literacy rate 98.4%
Currency litas (US $1 = 4 litas)
GDP (US million $) 10 472
GDP per head (US $) 2825

Flame of freedom A young Lithuanian conscript shows his distaste for the USSR by burning his Soviet military passport during 1990 independence demonstrations.

Key dates

c. 1200 Lithuania united as kingdom.
14th c. Great expansion.
1385 Union with Poland.
1795 Russian rule.
1919-20 Independence after war with Russia.
1926 Military coup.
1940 Annexed to USSR.
1941-44 German occupation.
1972 Anti-Soviet demonstrations.
1990 Declares formal independence.
1991 Independence recognized by USSR. Joins UN.
1993 Soviet troops leave.

FINLAND

OFFICIAL NAME
The Republic of Finland

CAPITAL
Helsinki

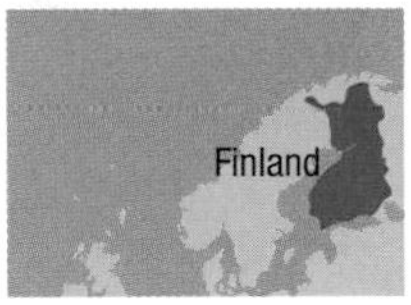

Area 338 144 km² (130 558 sq miles)
Population 5 165 000
Population density 15 per km² (39 per sq mile)
Population growth rate 0.4%
Life expectancy 72 (m); 80 (f)
Languages Finnish, Swedish, Lapp
Adult literacy rate 99%
Currency euro (US $1 = 0.94 euros)
GDP (US million $) 129 000
GDP per head (US $) 25 048

Key dates

13th c. Swedish rule.
1809 Russian rule after prolonged wars.
1917 Declares independence following the Russian Revolution.
1918 Civil war.
1919 Republic established.
1939-40 "Winter War" against USSR: defeat and loss of territory.
1941-44 Allied with Germany against USSR.
1944 Defeated; armistice with USSR.
1946 Declares neutrality.
1948 Signs treaty with USSR.
1955 Joins UN.
1992 New treaty with Russia.
1995 Joins European Union.

Russian influence Finland was ruled by Russia for most of the 19th century. Even today, their shared history is reflected in Finnish architecture.

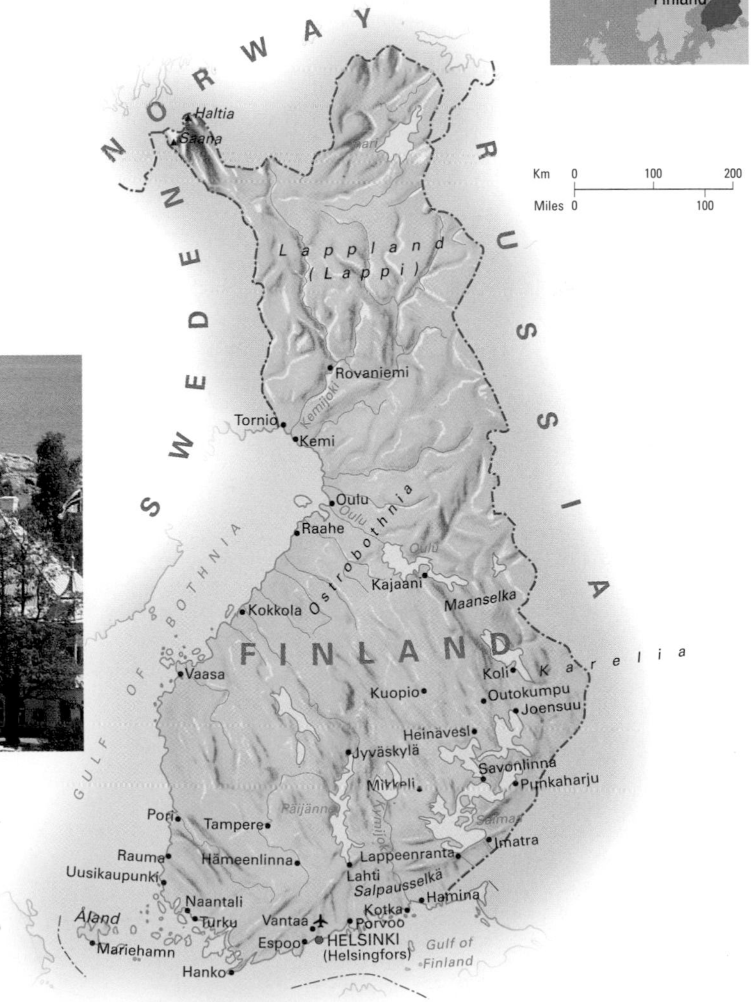

Poland, Czech Republic and Slovakia

POLAND

OFFICIAL NAME
The Republic of Poland

CAPITAL
Warsaw

Area 312 685 km² (120 728 sq miles)
Population 38 654 000
Population density 124 per km² (320 per sq mile)
Population growth rate 0.3%
Life expectancy 67 (m); 76 (f)
Languages Polish, German
Adult literacy rate 99%
Currency zloty (US $1 = 4 zlotys)
GDP (US million $) 155 400
GDP per head (US $) 4018

Key dates

966 Poland founded under King Mieszko I.
1385 Lithuanian union.
1772-95 Partitioned by Russia, Prussia, Austria.
1918 Independence gained.
1939 Germany invades.
1947 Communist government established.
1980 Solidarity trade union established.
1981 Martial law; Solidarity suspended.
1989 Open elections.
1990 Communist Party dissolved.
1997 New constitution.
1999 Joins NATO.

Poland's shifting history

Poland's frontiers have frequently shifted because its territories have been fought over by other nations. Yet a sense of national identity has remained, and Poland has always succeeded in reconstituting itself.

Territorially, the height of Poland's success came in the Middle Ages. Under the Jagiello dynasty, the Polish-Lithuanian empire stretched to the Black Sea. Most of that land was lost to Russia in later centuries. At the end of the 18th century, Poland was partitioned between Russia, Prussia and Austria, and disappeared from the map.

An independent Polish state with new boundaries was reestablished at the end of World War I. In 1920, a dispute with Soviet Russia over their border led to war, from which Poland emerged with a new swathe of land in the east. But this, and more besides, was lost in 1939. Germany invaded Poland from the west and the Soviet Union from the east. In 1941, with the German attack on the USSR, all of Poland came under Nazi control. Under occupation, the country was known by the bureaucratic formula "the General Government."

At the end of the war, the USSR reclaimed the lands it had seized in 1939. These were absorbed into the Soviet republics of Byelorussia and the Ukraine. Poland was awarded a band of German territory. In effect, the whole country was transposed 240 km (150 miles) to the west. After the Iron Curtain came down, the newly democratic Polish republic found itself at the heart of a Europe reborn.

Poland's shifting frontiers
During and after World War II the boundaries of Poland shifted westward.

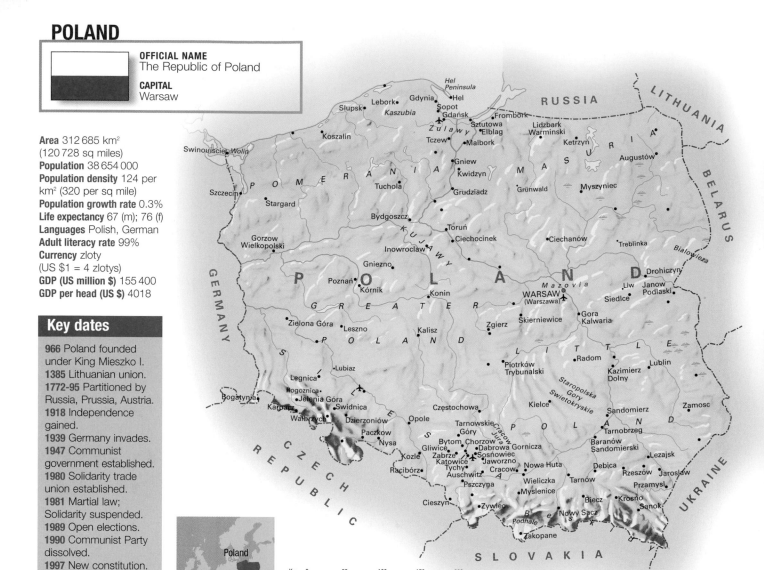

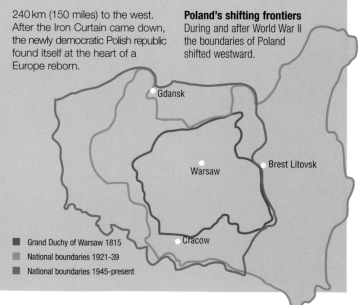

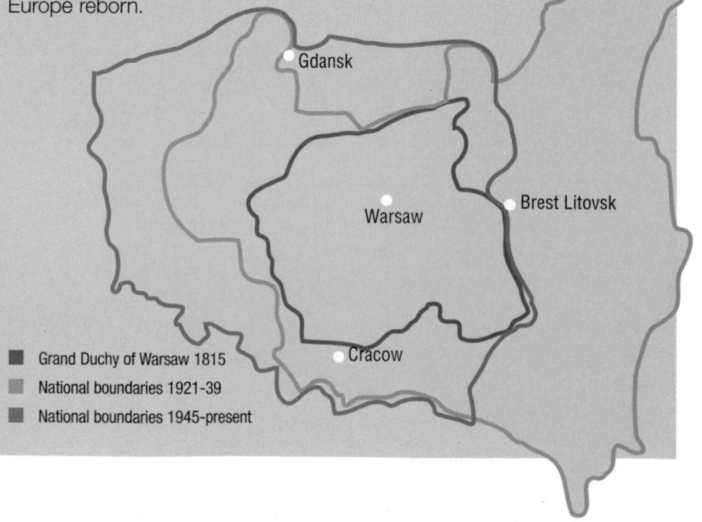

CZECH REPUBLIC

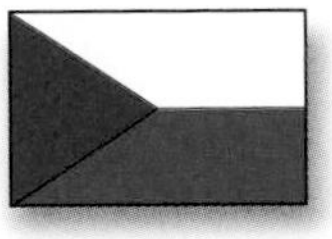

OFFICIAL NAME
The Czech Republic

CAPITAL
Prague

Area 78 864 km² (30 450 sq miles)
Population 10 283 000
Population density 130 per km² (338 per sq mile)
Population growth rate 0.1%
Life expectancy 70 (m); 77 (f)
Languages Czech, German and others
Adult literacy rate 99%
Currency Czech koruna (US $1 = 38 koruna)
GDP (US million $) 53 800
GDP per head (US $) 5228

Local brew A Prague man enjoys his pilsner beer. A strong, pale lager, pilsner, or pils, takes its name from the Czech town of Pilsen (Plzen), where it was originally brewed.

FACT "Good King Wenceslaus," the patron saint of the Czech Republic, was Duke of Bohemia from A.D. 925 to 929.

Key dates

10th c. Independent kingdom of Bohemia.
1212 Semi-independent kingdom within Holy Roman Empire.
1526 Hapsburg rule.
1867 Becomes part of Austro–Hungarian Empire.
1918 Independence; unites with Slovakia as Czechoslovakia.
1938 Nazi Germany annexes Sudetenland.
1939 German invasion. Czechoslovakia split.
1945 Reunion as Czechoslovakia.
1948 Communists seize power.
1968 "Prague Spring" liberalization is suppressed by a Soviet-led invasion.
1989 Pro-democracy demonstrations and strikes; Communist leaders resign.
1990 Multiparty elections; country officially renamed Czech and Slovak Federal Republic.
1993 Czech Republic peacefully divides from Slovakia. Joins UN.
1999 Joins NATO.

SLOVAKIA

OFFICIAL NAME
The Slovak Republic

CAPITAL
Bratislava

Area 49,036 km² (18 933 sq miles)
Population 5 395 000
Population density 110 per km² (285 per sq mile)
Population growth rate 0.4%
Life expectancy 68 (m); 76 (f)
Languages Slovak, Hungarian, Czech and others
Adult literacy rate 93%
Currency Slovak koruna (US $1 = 48 koruna)
GDP (US million $) 19 500
GDP per head (US $) 3617

Key dates

907-1867 Under Hungarian rule.
1867-1918 Exists as part of the Austro–Hungarian Empire.
1918 Establishment of Czechoslovakia.
1939-45 Independence from Czechoslovakia under Nazi control.
1945 Reunion as Czechoslovakia.
1992 Slovakia declares independence.
1993 Slovakia peacefully divides from Czech Republic; joins UN.

AUSTRIA

OFFICIAL NAME
The Republic of Austria

CAPITAL
Vienna

Area 83 858 km^2
(32 378 sq miles)
Population 8 177 000
Population density 96 per km^2 (250 per sq mile)
Population growth rate 0.5%
Life expectancy 73 (m); 80 (f)
Language German
Adult literacy rate 99%
Currency euro
(US $1 = 0.94 euros)
GDP (US million $) 215 300
GDP per head (US $) 26 646

FACT
In 1998, the Vienna Boys' Choir had its 500th anniversary. Both Schubert and Haydn once sang with the choir.

Key dates

955 German king Otto's rule begins.
962 Otto crowned Holy Roman Emperor.
1278 First Hapsburg emperor.
1806 Austrian Empire.
1867 Dual monarchy of Austria–Hungary set up.
1914 Invades Serbia, starting World War I; one of Central Powers.
1918 Defeat; empire ends; republic founded.
1938 Nazi occupation: union with Germany.
1939-45 Fights World War II as part of Axis.
1945 Allied occupation.
1955 Independence recognized; occupation forces leave; joins UN.
1995 Joins the European Union.

HUNGARY

OFFICIAL NAME
The Republic of Hungary

CAPITAL
Budapest

Key dates

9th c. Magyar invasion.
1000 Stephen becomes first king of Hungary.
1526 Ottoman rule.
c. 1700 Hapsburg rule.
1867 Dual monarchy of Austria–Hungary set up.
1914-18 Fights World War I as one of Central Powers; republic proclaimed after defeat.
1919 Admiral Horthy takes power as regent.
1941-44 Fights World War II on the side of Axis.
1944 Soviet occupation.
1947-49 Communists take power.
1956 Soviet troops crush government-backed anti-Soviet protests.
1968 Economic reforms.
1989 New constitution.
1990 Free elections.
1991 Soviet troops leave. Association pact with European Community.
1999 Joins NATO.

Area 93 030 km^2
(35 919 sq miles)
Population 10 068 000
Population density 109 per km^2 (281 per sq mile)
Population growth rate 0.4%
Life expectancy 65 (m); 74 (f)
Language Hungarian
Adult literacy rate 99%
Currency forint
(US $1 = 296 forints)
GDP (US million $) 48 500
GDP per head (US $) 4797

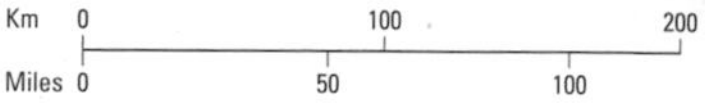

SWITZERLAND

OFFICIAL NAME
The Swiss Confederation

CAPITAL
Bern

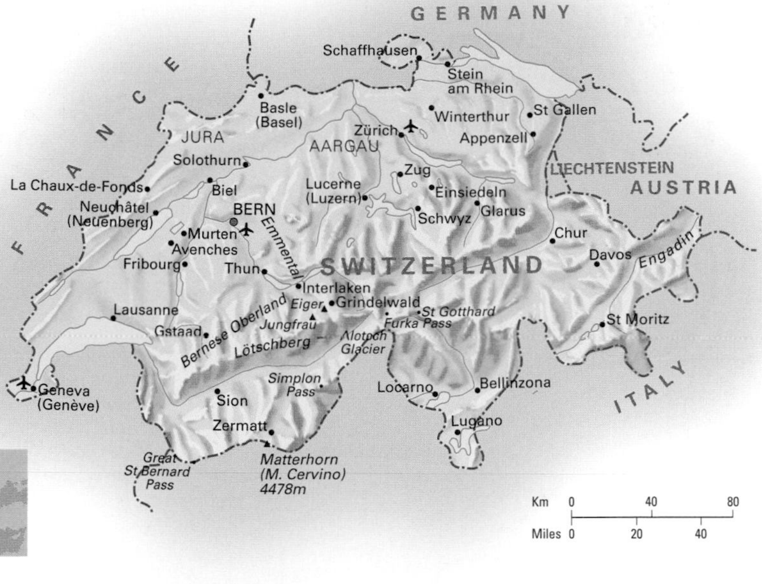

Area 41 284 km² (15 940 sq miles)
Population 7 140 000
Population density 172 per km² (446 per sq mile)
Population growth rate 0.3%
Life expectancy 75 (m); 82 (f)

Languages German, French, Italian and others
Adult literacy rate 99%
Currency Swiss franc (US $1 = 1.69 Swiss francs)
GDP (US million $) 261 400
GDP per head (US $) 37 428

Key dates

962 Becomes part of Holy Roman Empire.
1291 Founding of Swiss Confederation.
1499 Full independence.
1798-1815 French rule.
1848 New federal constitution.
1914-18 Neutral in War.
1920 League of Nations founded in Geneva.
1939-45 Neutral in war.
1960 Founding member of European Free Trade Association.
1963 Joins Council of Europe.
1971 Women gain vote.
1986 Voters reject UN membership.
1992 Voters reject closer ties to European Community.

FACT Switzerland has the world's highest rate of gun ownership but almost no firearms crime.

Switzerland's armed neutrality

About the only evidence of Switzerland's armed forces visible to the outside world has been the Swiss Army knife. The country's famed neutrality – first proclaimed in the 16th century – has been maintained by a countrywide militia. The militia keep arms, ammunition and uniforms at home, ready for speedy mobilization.

The army was strengthened during the two World Wars to guard the borders, and it remained on alert during the Cold War. Today, military spending accounts for as much as a third of the national budget. That pays for such hardware as the 400 modern jet aircraft flown by the Swiss Air Force, as well as equipment for the militia.

Switzerland's federal constitution says simply that "every Swiss male is liable for military service" and can be conscripted from the age of 20 to 42. Anyone unfit for military service must pay a military tax, but a civil service option is granted. Women can enlist, but not for combat duties. The cantons – the constituent regions of the Swiss Confederation – provide their local soldiers with physical training under federal government supervision; the defense department then gives regular military training.

All military personnel do regular target practice while off duty. They also perform "civil protection" duties in catastrophes or other emergencies.

At the beginning of the 21st century, Switzerland was preparing to ease its policy of "security through autonomy" and replace it with "security through cooperation" – prompted partly by events in the Balkans, less than an hour's flight away. It planned to cooperate with friendly nations in military training exercises and peace-support operations and would expand its participation in international security organizations.

Part-time soldiers Swiss reservists ride off on military exercises. Switzerland strongly defends its neutral status.

LIECHTENSTEIN

OFFICIAL NAME
The Principality of Liechtenstein

CAPITAL
Vaduz

Area 160 km² (61.8 sq miles)
Population 32 000
Population density 200 per km² (518 per sq mile)
Population growth rate 0%
Life expectancy 66 (m); 73 (f)
Language German (Alemannic dialect)
Adult literacy rate 95%
Currency Swiss franc (US $1 = 1.69 Swiss francs)
GDP (US million $) 1315
GDP per head (US $) 42 416

Key dates

Until 1719 Part of Holy Roman Empire.
1719 Full independence.
1815-66 Member of German Confederation.
1924 Economic union with Switzerland.
1984 Women gain vote.
1990 Joins UN.
1991 Joins European Free Trade Association.

SERBIA AND MONTENEGRO

OFFICIAL NAME
The State Union of Serbia and Montenegro

CAPITAL
Belgrade

Area 102 173 km² (39 449 sq miles)
Population 10 637 000
Population density 104 per km² (269 per sq mile)
Population growth rate 0.1%
Life expectancy 68 (m); 74 (f)
Language Serbo-Croat (Cyrillic script)
Adult literacy rate 89%
Currency Yugoslav new dinar (US $1 = 66.94 new dinars)
GDP (US million $) 15 243
GDP per head (US $) 1435

Key dates

1389 Ottoman rule.
1914 Austria–Hungary declares war on Serbia; start of World War I.
1918 Kingdom of Serbs, Croats and Slovenes established (renamed Yugoslavia in 1929).
1941-44 Nazi occupation.
1943 Belgrade liberated by Tito's partisans.
1945 Communist rule.
1980 Tito dies.
1990 Kosovo government dissolved.
1991 Slovenia, Croatia declare independence; war in Croatia.
1992 Macedonia and Bosnia–Herzegovina declare independence; war in Bosnia.
1995 Peace agreement.
1997-99 Kosovo war.
2000 Elections displace President Milosevic.

CROATIA

OFFICIAL NAME
The Republic of Croatia

CAPITAL
Zagreb

Area 56 610 km² (21 857 sq miles)
Population 4 554 000
Population density 81 per km² (209 per sq mile)
Population growth rate 0.7%
Life expectancy 68 (m); 76 (f)
Language Serbo-Croat (Roman script)
Adult literacy rate 93%
Currency kuna (US $1 = 8.39 kuna)
GDP (US million $) 20 100
GDP per head (US $) 4396

Key dates

1102 Hungarian rule.
1526-1699 Partial Ottoman rule.
1918 Kingdom of Serbs, Croats and Slovenes (later Yugoslavia).
1990 Elections won by nationalist Tudjman.
1991-92 Independence declared; civil war.
1992 Peace agreed; UN troops deployed.
1993-94 New fighting.
1996 Joins Council of Europe.
1998 Last Serb-held enclave retaken.

YUGOSLAVIA IN PIECES

Postwar Yugoslavia was a federation of six republics. Serbs were traditionally Orthodox, Croats and Slovenes were Catholic, and large Muslim communities lived in Macedonia, Montenegro and Bosnia. It was this religious and ethnic mix that led to the Balkan conflict of the 1990s. In 1991, Croatia and Slovenia declared independence, leading to war between Croats and the Serb-dominated Yugoslav army. In 1992, the war shifted to Bosnia, which had also declared independence. Two million Muslims were "ethnically cleansed." Meanwhile, Serb President Milosevic proclaimed a new Serb state. In 1995, NATO bombed Serb positions in Bosnia to force a peace. In 1998, conflict in Kosovo again brought NATO bombers into the fray. In 2000, the Serb people voted Milosevic out, but the Balkan tragedy is far from over.

Former Yugoslav republics

SLOVENIA

OFFICIAL NAME
The Republic of Slovenia

CAPITAL
Ljubljana

Area 20 253 km² (7820 sq miles)
Population 1 986 000
Population density 98 per km² (254 per sq mile)
Population growth rate 0.1%
Life expectancy 70 (m); 77 (f)
Languages Slovene, Serbo-Croat (Roman script), Hungarian, Italian
Adult literacy rate 99%
Currency tolar (US $1 = 240 tolars)
GDP (US million $) 19 700
GDP per head (US $) 9914

Key dates

1278 Hapsburg rule.
1809-15 French control.
1867 Part of Austro-Hungarian Empire.
1918 Becomes part of Kingdom of Serbs, Croats and Slovenes (later Yugoslavia).
1990 Nationalist coalition wins elections; vote for independence.
1991 Independence declared; fighting with Serb-dominated Yugoslav army ends with ceasefire.
1992 Joins UN.
1996 Applies to join European Union.

BOSNIA–HERZEGOVINA

OFFICIAL NAME
Bosnia and Herzegovina

CAPITAL
Sarajevo

Area 51 129 km² (19 741 sq miles)
Population 3 839 000
Population density 82 per km² (213 per sq mile)
Population growth rate 1.1%
Life expectancy 69 (m); 75 (f)
Languages Serbo-Croat (Muslims and Croats use Roman script; Serbs use Cyrillic)
Adult literacy rate 93%
Currency marka (US $1 = 2.17 marka)
GDP (US million $) 4200
GDP per head (US $) 997

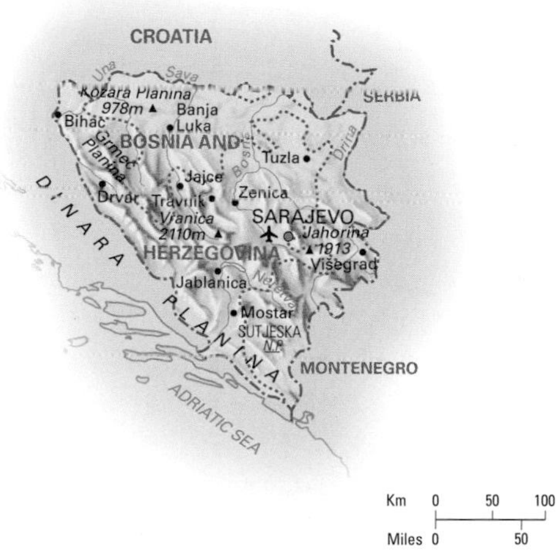

Key dates

1463 Ottoman rule.
1878 Austro–Hungarian control.
1918 Becomes part of Kingdom of Serbs, Croats and Slovenes (later Yugoslavia).
1992 Croats and Muslims vote for independence; Serbs boycott vote. Civil war starts; Serbs use "ethnic cleansing."
1995 NATO air strikes. Peace accord sets up two states with central government; policed by UN troops.
1996 Full relations with Yugoslavia.

MACEDONIA

OFFICIAL NAME
The Former Yugoslav Republic of Macedonia

CAPITAL
Skopje

Area 25 713 km² (9928 sq miles)
Population 2 011 000
Population density 78 per km² (201 per sq mile)
Population growth rate 1.5%
Life expectancy 69 (m); 73 (f)
Languages Macedonian, Albanian, Serbo-Croat (Cyrillic script)
Adult literacy rate 93%
Currency Macedonian denar (US $1 = 64.04 denars)
GDP (US million $) 3200
GDP per head (US $) 1600

Key dates

1371 Ottoman rule.
1912-13 Balkan Wars fought over Macedonia.
1918 Becomes part of Kingdom of Serbs, Croats and Slovenes (later Yugoslavia).
1991 Declares independence; dispute with Greece delays recognition.
1994 Continuing dispute leads to Greek trade embargo.
1995 New agreement with Greece; trade embargo lifted.
2000 Conflict with ethnic Albanian population.

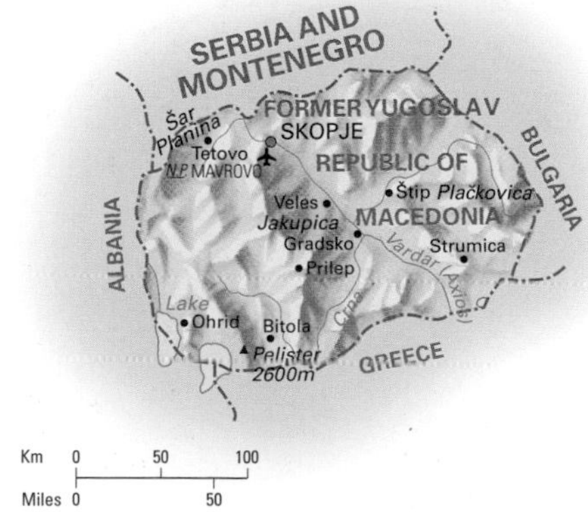

GREECE

OFFICIAL NAME
The Hellenic Republic

CAPITAL
Athens

Area 131 957 km² (50 949 sq miles)
Population 10 626 000
Population density 80 per km² (207 per sq mile)
Population growth rate 0.5%
Life expectancy 75 (m); 80 (f)
Language Greek (Demotiki, or modern Greek)
Adult literacy rate 95.2%
Currency euros (US $1 = 0.94 euros)
GDP (US million $) 123 400
GDP per head (US $) 11 727

Olympic origins
The temple of Hera at Olympia (left), 2600 years old, is the most ancient temple of the religious complex where the original Olympic games were held. The games were staged every four years from the 8th century B.C. to the end of the 4th century A.D.

Key dates

5th c. B.C. "Golden Age" of ancient Greece.
146 B.C. Roman rule begins.
1453 Conquest by Ottoman Empire.
1829 Independence.
1912-13 Balkan Wars: victory over Turkey and Bulgaria.
1924 Becomes republic.
1941-44 Occupied by Germany.
1946-49 Civil war: rebel communists defeated.
1949 Monarchy returns.
1967 Military coup; martial law imposed.
1973 Republic declared.
1974 Martial law ends; civilian government and free elections.
1981 Joins European Community.
1995 Normal relations with Macedonia.

FACT
Greece has about 2000 islands and almost 15 000 km (9300 miles) of coastline.

TURKEY

OFFICIAL NAME
The Republic of Turkey

CAPITAL
Ankara

Area 779 452 km² (300 948 sq miles)
Population 64 385 000
Population density 81 per km² (211 per sq mile)
Population growth rate 1.2%
Life expectancy 63 (m); 66 (f)
Languages Turkish, Kurdish

Adult literacy rate 82.3%
Currency Turkish lira (US $1 = 1 240 000 liras)
GDP (US million $) 209 200
GDP per head (US $) 3297

Key dates

1299 Birth of Ottoman Empire.
1912 First Balkan War against Greece: defeat and loss of territory.
1914-18 Fights World War I alongside Germany; defeated.
1923 Atatürk proclaims Republic of Turkey; starts modernization.
1960-61 Military rule.
1974 Invades northern Cyprus.
1980 Military coup.
1983 Civilian rule.
1984 Kurdish terrorist campaign begins.
1999 Kurdish leader Abdullah Ocalan sentenced to death.

CYPRUS

OFFICIAL NAME
The Republic of Cyprus

CAPITAL
Nicosia

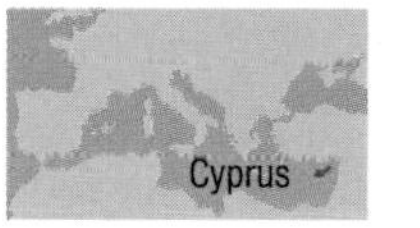

Key dates

1489 Venetian rule.
1570 Ottoman rule.
1878 British rule.
1950s Terrorist attacks on Britain and between Greeks and Turks.
1960 Independence.
1963 Fighting between Greeks and Turks.
1964 UN peacekeeping force arrives.
1974 Greek army coup; Turkey invades north.
1983 Turks proclaim Republic of Northern Cyprus (unrecognized).

Area 9251 km² (3572 sq miles)
Population 753 000
Population density 81 per km² (210 per sq mile)
Population growth rate 1.1%
Life expectancy 75 (m); 79 (f)

Languages Greek, Turkish
Adult literacy rate 94%
Currency Cyprus pound (US $1 = 0.64 Cyprus pound)
GDP (US million $) 9200
GDP per head (US $) 12 266

TENTATIVE CONTACTS ACROSS THE AEGEAN

It took violent earth tremors to bring about better relations between Turkey and Greece after centuries of enmity. When the suburbs of both Istanbul and Athens suffered serious damage in 1999, the shared human tragedy led to increased contact between the two nations.

Only two years before, they had agreed to find peaceful resolutions to future conflicts and in 2000 signed a series of accords pledging peace. These developments were warmly welcomed by the two nations' NATO allies because Turkey and Greece have a long history as uneasy neighbors.

The Ottoman Turks overthrew the Byzantine Empire in the 14th and 15th centuries and ruled all of Greece by 1460. A Greek national revival began in the late 18th century, but it was not until 1821 that a successful revolt occurred. Fighting back, the Turks massacred 25 000 people and sold 45 000 into slavery, provoking the British, Russians and French to help Greece finally to win its War of Independence in 1829.

Greece failed to gain disputed border areas in a disastrous war against the Ottomans in 1897, but victory in the Balkan Wars of 1912-13 led to Greek seizure of Crete and parts of Macedonia. In World War I, Greece reluctantly joined the Allies, but Turkey took Germany's side. As a result, Greece gained Thrace from the final collapse of the Ottoman Empire. In 1919, Greek forces invaded Izmir in Asia Minor but were driven out by troops led by Kemal Atatürk, the founder of modern Turkey, in 1922.

The last major conflict between the two countries was in Greek-dominated Cyprus in 1974, when Turkish forces invaded the north in response to a Greek-inspired military coup. The Turkish Cypriots declared their part of the island – about 40 percent of the total – independent in 1983. If the Greek–Turkish thaw continues, Cyprus may also find stability.

Central Europe

BULGARIA

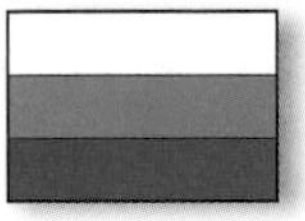

OFFICIAL NAME
The Republic of Bulgaria

CAPITAL
Sofia

Area 110 994 km² (42 855 sq miles)
Population 8 208 000
Population density 74 per km² (193 per sq mile)
Population growth rate 0.2%
Life expectancy 67 (m); 74 (f)
Languages Bulgarian, Turkish
Adult literacy rate 92%
Currency lev (US $1 = 2.16 levs)
GDP (US million $) 11 900
GDP per head (US $) 1442

Regulars and new arrivals The Black Sea coast of Bulgaria was a favorite destination for vacationers from all over Eastern Europe during the Communist era. It strove, with some success, to widen its appeal in the 1990s and is known today for having perhaps the best-run tourist industry in the former Soviet bloc.

Key dates

1018-1186 Part of Byzantine Empire.
1396 Ottoman rule.
1908 Full independence from Turkish rule.
1912-13 Balkan Wars.
1914-18 Fights World War I as German ally.
1939-44 Fights World War II as German ally.
1944 Soviet occupation after failure to make separate peace with Britain and US.
1946 Monarchy is abolished; government headed by Communists.
1948 Full Communist control.
1980s Ethnic Turks suppressed; many flee.
1990 Ethnic suppression reversed by reformist government.
1990 Free elections.
1991 New constitution; parliamentary republic.

MOLDOVA

OFFICIAL NAME
The Republic of Moldova

CAPITAL
Chisinau

Area 33 700 km² (13 010 sq miles)
Population 4 380 000
Population density 108 per km² (281 per sq mile)
Population growth rate 0.5%
Life expectancy 62 (m); 69 (f)
Languages Moldovan, Russian
Adult literacy rate 96.4%
Currency Moldovan leu (US $1 = 12.89 Moldovan leus)
GDP (US million $) 1049
GDP per head (US $) 287

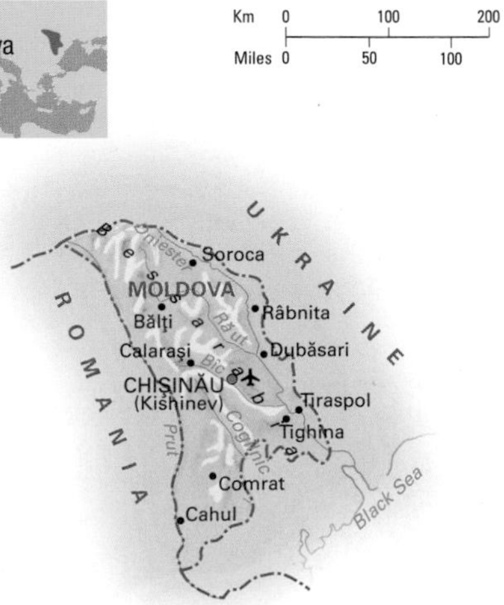

Key dates

16th c. Turkish rule.
1812 Russian control.
1918-40 Part of Romania.
1940 Becomes part of Soviet Union.
1990 Declares self-government; renamed Republic of Moldova.
1991 Full independence; joins Commonwealth of Independent States.
1992 Joins UN.
1992-93 Ethnic unrest.
1994 Free elections.

ROMANIA

OFFICIAL NAME
Romania

CAPITAL
Bucharest

Area 238 391 km² (92 043 sq miles)
Population 22 458 000
Population density 94 per km² (244 per sq mile)
Population growth rate -0.2%
Life expectancy 65 (m); 73 (f)
Languages Romanian, Hungarian, German and others
Adult literacy rate 96.7%
Currency Romanian leu (US $1 = 28 005 Romanian leus)
GDP (US million $) 32 400
GDP per head (US $) 1440

Key dates

15th c. Ottoman rule.
1829 Russian control.
1861 Romania united.
1878 Full independence.
1916-18 Ally of Britain in World War I; gains Transylvania.
1941-44 Ally of Germany in World War II.
1944 Joins Allies; Soviet occupation begins.
1947 Communist rule.
1989 President Nicolae Ceausescu overthrown.
1990 Free elections.

ALBANIA

OFFICIAL NAME
The Republic of Albania

CAPITAL
Tirana

Area 28 748 km² (11 100 sq miles)
Population 3 113 000
Population density 132 per km² (341 per sq mile)
Population growth rate 1.6%
Life expectancy 69 (m); 75 (f)
Languages Albanian (dialects: Gheg in north, Tosk in south)
Adult literacy rate 95%
Currency lek (US $1 = 144 leks)
GDP (US million $) 3555
GDP per head (US $) 937

FACT
Albania has Europe's highest infant mortality rate; 37 babies in every 1000 survive less than a month.

Key dates

15th c. Ottoman rule.
1912 First Balkan War: gains independence.
1914-20 Occupied by Italy in World War I.
1925 Becomes republic.
1928 President Zogu proclaimed King Zog.
1939-44 Occupied by Italy then Germany.
1944 Communist partisans seize power.
1961 Splits with USSR.
1991 Open elections.
1992 Reforms begin.
1997 Riots follow crash of investment funds.
1999 Influx of refugees from Kosovo.

Albania's long isolation

Most of Europe made rapid economic and social progress towards the end of the 20th century, but Albania, the smallest Balkan state, seemed to stand still. This was a legacy of the extreme Stalinist regime of 45 years, the longest-surviving in Europe. Today, with tight government controls, political instability and a weak infrastructure, Albania remains Europe's poorest and least developed country, although it has moved part-way towards democracy.

After World War II occupation by Italy and then (when Italy surrendered) Germany, Albania began independence in 1945 under the communism of former partisan leader Enver Hoxha. He headed a repressive government that imprisoned 200 000 people and executed 5000 from 1945 to 1985. His regime also banned all religions – and beards. Although he had been close to Stalin, Hoxha broke with the USSR in 1961 after Soviet leader Nikita Khrushchev denounced his predecessor. Hoxha switched allegiance to China, but that relationship failed in 1978 when China's post-Mao leadership introduced reforms.

After Hoxha died in 1985, his successor, Ramiz Alia, relaxed Albania's isolationism by establishing diplomatic relations with several countries. The regime also became less harsh in 1990, allowing religions and opposition parties; two years later, the Socialists (Communists) were defeated at the polls.

Economic reforms bore some fruits – there were more than 50 000 private businesses by 1993 – but troubles soon returned. Violence followed the collapse of pyramid investment schemes in 1997, and thousands fled to Italy. A year later, the Kosovo crisis caused thousands of ethnic Albanians to stream into the country.

Albania remains unstable and is plagued by widespread gangs. But its decades in the political wilderness are over. Its future looks set as a part of Europe rather than apart from it.

RUSSIA

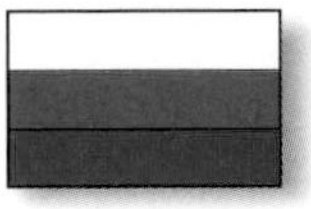

OFFICIAL NAME
The Russian Federation

CAPITAL
Moscow

Area 17 075 400 km² (6 592 850 sq miles)
Population 145 943 000
Population density 9 per km² (22 per sq mile)
Population growth rate –0.1%
Life expectancy 58 (m); 71 (f)
Languages Russian, Tatar, Yakut, Chuvash, Bashkir and others
Adult literacy rate 99%
Currency rouble (US \$1 = 28 roubles)
GDP (US million \$) 190 600
GDP per head (US \$) 1300

Mighty empire
The Soviet Union consisted of 15 republics totaling 22 402 194 km² (8 649 496 sq miles) with a total population in 1985 of nearly 300 million.

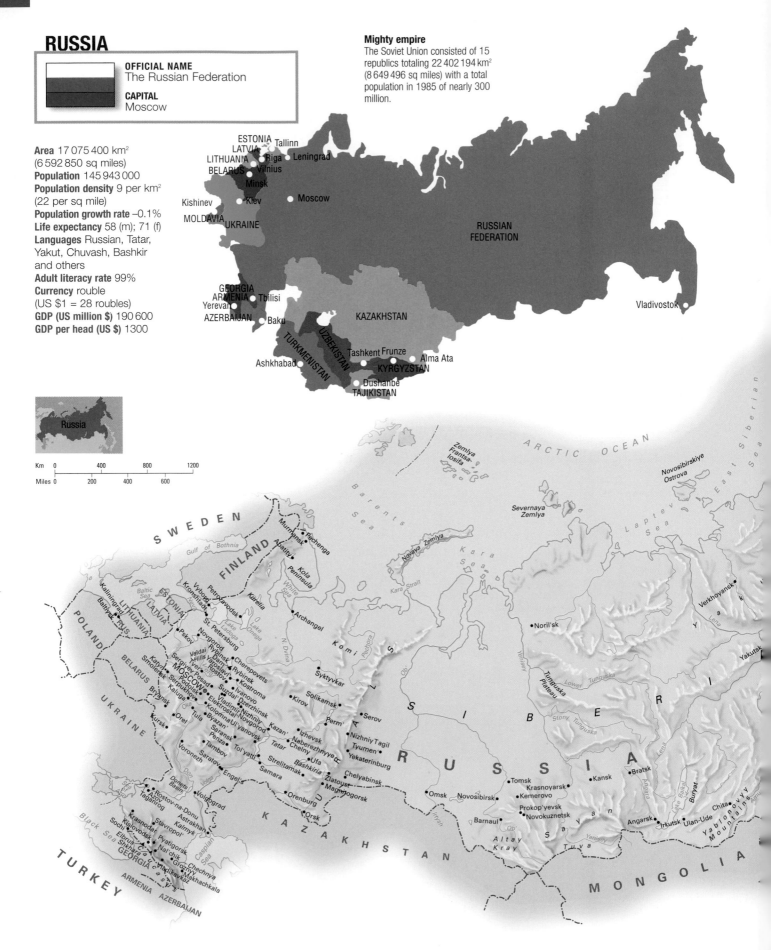

Russia's great upheaval

At the height of its success, between 1945 and 1985, Russia enjoyed enormous influence in the world. Moscow, the ancient heart of the Russian lands, was the capital of the largest country in the world. That country comprised 15 republics (of which the biggest was Russia itself, with about half the total Soviet population), and it commanded immense natural and industrial resources.

Russian influence extended beyond its borders into the hub of Europe. The Soviet Union also had three seats at the UN (one for the Ukraine, one for Belarus and a third for Russia and the remaining republics) and a vast military capacity. Russia, in its 20th-century Soviet incarnation, was stronger than at any time in its history and was feared or respected by the whole world. But Communist totalitarianism had frozen Russia's empire into one great ideological iceberg, and a long cold war with the West had almost bankrupted it.

Mikhail Gorbachev, appointed general secretary of the ruling Communist Party in 1985, introduced perestroika (restructuring) and glasnost (openness) to the USSR. These concessions encouraged the Soviet satellites and republics to demand independence, and drift away like ice floes: first the countries of eastern Europe, then the Baltic states, then the other 14 Soviet republics. Small-scale ethnic wars flared in several corners of the old Soviet state. The bloodiest was in Chechnya, in the Caucasus.

With the loss of the republics, Russia's stake in Europe was reduced to something less than it had been at the time of Catherine the Great in the 18th century. The Russian economy, exposed to the free market, went into steep decline, and Russia became dependent on Western aid. Millions of ordinary citizens were left bitter, destitute and nostalgic for the certainties of the Soviet past.

Since the collapse of the Communist empire in the early 1990s, Russia has been beset by violent crime and corruption, as well as economic problems. The bewildering loss of empire and prestige came about in the space of one short decade. It will take Russia much longer to recover from the trauma.

Key dates

9th c. State of Kievan Rus founded.
13th c. Mongol invasion.
1480 Mongol rule ends.
1905 Defeat by Japan; parliament established.
1914-17 Fights in World War I against Germany and Austria.
1917 Tsar overthrown in "February Revolution"; Bolsheviks seize power in "October Revolution."
1918-20 Communists win civil war.
1922 USSR established; Stalin rises to power.
1930s Industrialization; collective farms set up; Stalin purges rivals.
1939 Stalin and Hitler agree to divide Poland.
1941 German invasion.
1945 Beats Germany on Eastern Front; occupies eastern Europe. UN founding member.
1953 Stalin dies; Khrushchev becomes first secretary.
1956 Invades Hungary to suppress anti-Soviet demonstrations.
1958 Khrushchev becomes premier.
1962 Crisis with US over Soviet missiles based in Cuba.
1964 Brezhnev, Kosygin replace Khrushchev.
1968 Soviet forces invade Czechoslovakia to crush reforms.
1979-89 Invades and occupies Afghanistan.
1985 Gorbachev made general secretary; "glasnost" (openness) and "perestroika" (restructuring) begin.
1989 Open elections.
1991 USSR breaks up; Russia (led by Yeltsin) joins Commonwealth of Independent States.
1994-2000 Invasions of Chechnya.
2000 Putin president.

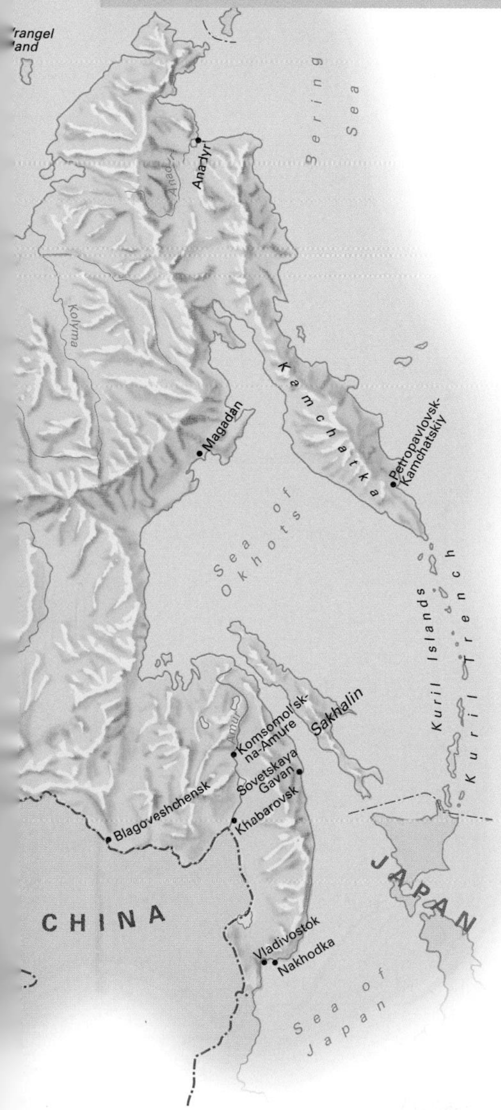

Tough fighters Chechen rebels (above) fought ferociously for independence from Russia in the 1990s. They held out against a far more powerful Russian army even after the Chechen capital Grozny was virtually destroyed.

Market economy When Communism collapsed in Russia, so did many state-run industries and shops. People were forced to trade at private-enterprise markets (right) or to barter for goods.

FACT The Trans-Siberian Railway, the world's longest, stretches 9438 km (5864 miles) east from Moscow.

UKRAINE

OFFICIAL NAME
The Republic of Ukraine

CAPITAL
Kiev

Area 603 700 km² (233 090 sq miles)
Population 50 106 000
Population density 84 per km² (217 per sq mile)
Population growth rate -0.6%
Life expectancy 62 (m); 73 (f)
Languages Ukrainian, Russian, Romanian, Hungarian, Polish
Adult literacy rate 96%
Currency hryvnya (US $1 = 5.41 hryvnyas)
GDP (US million $) 30 800
GDP per head (US $) 609

Key dates

9th c. State of Kievan Rus founded at Kiev.
14th c. Polish and Lithuanian rule.
1667-1790s Russian control.
1918 Ukraine proclaims independence.
1920 Russia invades.
1922 Founding republic of Soviet Union.
1941-44 World War II: occupied by Germany. Resistance to Germany and USSR.
1945 Becomes founding member of UN.
1954 Crimea transferred from Russia to Ukraine.
1986 Chernobyl nuclear disaster.
1990 Sovereignty over Soviet laws declared.
1991 Independence; joins Commonwealth of Independent States.
1992 Dispute starts over Crimean autonomy.
1995 Transfers nuclear warheads to Russia for destruction.

FACT Ukrainians claim that the world has more statues of their national poet Taras Shevchenko than of anyone else.

BELARUS

OFFICIAL NAME
The Republic of Belarus

CAPITAL
Minsk

Area 207 595 km² (80 153 sq miles)
Population 10 159 000
Population density 49 per km² (127 per sq mile)
Population growth rate 0.2%
Life expectancy 62 (m); 74 (f)
Languages Belarussian, Russian
Adult literacy rate 97.9%
Currency Belarussian rouble (US $1 = 1345.00 Belarussian roubles)
GDP (US million $) 11 991
GDP per head (US $) 1180

Key dates

13th c. Part of Lithuania.
1569 Part of Poland.
1772-95 Comes under Russian rule.
1918-19 Independence.
1919 Divided between Poland and Russia.
1922 Founding republic of Soviet Union.
1939 Polish-occupied areas retaken.
1941-44 Occupied by Germany.
1945 Becomes founding member of UN.
1990 Sovereignty over Soviet laws declared.
1991 Independence; joins Commonwealth of Independent States.
1996 Agrees to economic union with Russia.

FACT "Byelorussia" is the Russian form of the country's name. It was dropped upon independence.

GEORGIA

OFFICIAL NAME
Georgia

CAPITAL
Tbilisi

Area 69 700 km² (26 911 sq miles)
Population 5 399 000
Population density 73 per km² (188 per sq mile)
Population growth rate 1.3%
Life expectancy 68 (m); 76 (f)
Language Georgian
Adult literacy rate 99%
Currency lari (US $1 = 1.97 lari)
GDP (US million $) 4400
GDP per head (US $) 869

FACT Georgia's Black Sea coast is said to be the land of Colchis, from which Jason stole the Golden Fleece.

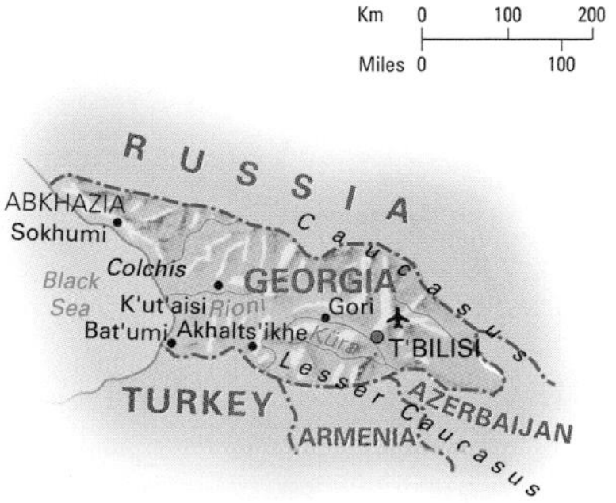

Key dates

c. 1800 Russian rule.
1918 Independence.
1921 Russia invades.
1922 Merged into USSR.
1936 Becomes separate republic within USSR.
1990 Open elections.
1991 Independence.
mid-1990s Ethnic civil wars after South Ossetia and Abkhazia declare independence.
1992 Joins UN.
1993 Joins Commonwealth of Independent States.
1994 Military pact with Russia.

ARMENIA

OFFICIAL NAME
The Republic of Armenia

CAPITAL
Yerevan

Area 29 800 km² (11 500 sq miles)
Population 3 795 000
Population density 119 per km² (308 per sq mile)
Population growth rate 1.1%
Life expectancy 67 (m); 74 (f)
Languages Armenian, Kurdish
Adult literacy rate 98.8%
Currency dram (US $1 = 548 drams)
GDP (US million $) 1880
GDP per head (US $) 531

FACT In the 4th century, Armenia was the first country in the world to adopt Christianity as its state religion.

Key dates

c. 100 Armenian empire.
1514 Ottoman control.
1639 Persians invade eastern Armenia.
1828 Russia annexes eastern Armenia.
1915 Turkey deports western Armenians; many are massacred.
1918 Independence.
1920 Russia invades.
1922 Merged into USSR.
1936 Becomes separate republic within USSR.
1989-94 Wars with Azerbaijan over enclave of Nagorno-Karabakh.
1991 Independence; joins Commonwealth of Independent States.

AZERBAIJAN

OFFICIAL NAME
The Azerbaijani Republic

CAPITAL
Baku

Area 86 600 km² (33 400 sq miles)
Population 7 983 000
Population density 88 per km² (229 per sq mile)
Population growth rate 0.4%
Life expectancy 65 (m); 74 (f)
Language Azerbaijani (Azeri)
Adult literacy rate 97.3%
Currency manat (US $1 = 4579 manats)
GDP (US million $) 3600
GDP per head (US $) 471

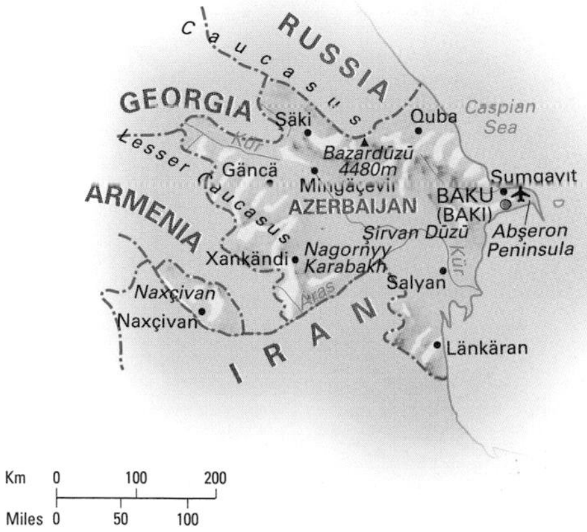

Key dates

16th-19th c. Alternate Persian and Ottoman Turkish control.
1813 Russian control begins.
1918 Independent state.
1920 Russia invades.
1922 Merged into USSR.
1936 Becomes separate republic within USSR.
1989-94 Wars with Armenia over enclave of Nagorno-Karabakh.
1991 Independence; joins Commonwealth of Independent States.
1992 Joins UN.
1994 Cease-fire in Nagorno-Karabakh.

Syria, Israel, Lebanon and Jordan

SYRIA

OFFICIAL NAME
The Syrian Arab Republic

CAPITAL
Damascus

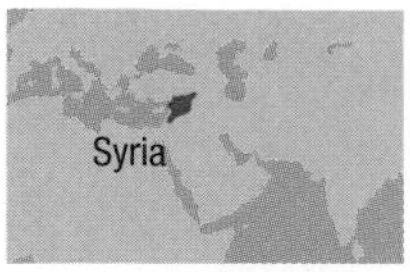

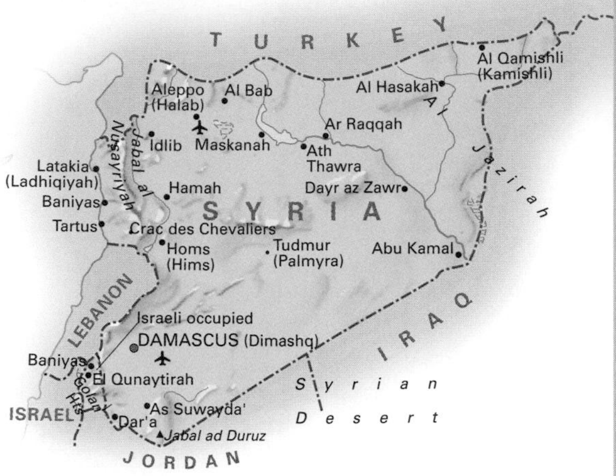

Area 185 180 km² (71 498 sq miles)
Population 16 110 000
Population density 87 per km² (225 per sq mile)
Population growth rate 2.5%
Life expectancy 64 (m); 68 (f)
Languages Arabic, Kurdish
Adult literacy rate 79.4%

Currency Syrian pound (US $1 = 52.5 Syrian pounds)
GDP (US million $) 16 500
GDP per head (US $) 1024

FACT
The Syrian capital, Damascus, is one of the world's oldest cities; it was founded about 5000 years ago.

Key dates

1516 Ottoman rule.
1920 League of Nations gives France control.
1946 Independence after French and British control in World War II.
1958-61 Joins Egypt in United Arab Republic.
1967 Golan Heights lost after defeat by Israel in Six-Day War.
1970 Military coup led by General Assad.
1971 Assad president.
1973 Yom Kippur War against Israel fails to regain Golan Heights.
1976 Peacekeeping force in Lebanon.
2000 Assad dies.

ISRAEL

OFFICIAL NAME
The State of Israel

CAPITAL
Jerusalem

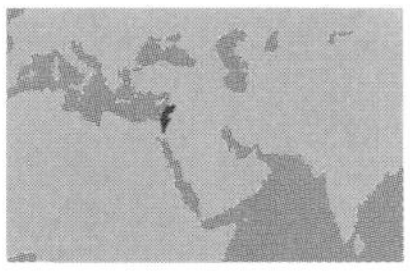

Area 21 946 km² (8473 sq miles)
Population 6 125 000
Population density 272 per km² (705 per sq mile)
Population growth rate 2.1%
Life expectancy 75 (m); 79 (f)
Languages Hebrew, Russian, Arabic, European languages

Adult literacy rate 95.6%
Currency new shekel (US $1 = 4.15 new shekels)
GDP (US million $) 95 400
GDP per head (US $) 15 979

Blustery frontier Wind generators built by an enterprising Jewish settler tower over abandoned Israeli trenches on the Golan Heights. United Nations troops man a border crossing between Israel and Syria a few hundred metres below.

Key dates

1517 Ottoman rule.
1920 League of Nations gives Britain control of Palestine (Israel and West Bank).
1948 Independent state declared; Arab allies invade unsuccessfully.
1956 Suez War: briefly occupies Sinai.
1967 Six-Day War: victory over Arab allies; occupies Gaza Strip, West Bank, Sinai, Golan Heights and Jerusalem.
1973 Yom Kippur War: attack by Egypt and Syria fails.
1978 Attacks PLO bases in Lebanon. Camp David Accords with Egypt.
1979 Israeli–Egyptian peace agreement.
1980 Capital moved to Jerusalem from Tel Aviv.
1982 Sinai withdrawal. Invades southern Lebanon to attack PLO.
1987 Arab uprising in Gaza and West Bank.
1993 Oslo accord: Israel recognized; some Palestinian self-rule.
1994 Peace accord with Jordan. Palestinian self-rule for Gaza Strip and Jericho; Arafat heads Palestinian government.
2000 Withdrawal from southern Lebanon; new intifada.

CONFLICT IN THE BIBLE LANDS

Conflict between the Israelis and Palestinian Arabs is one of the modern world's most intractable problems. Both peoples claim that much of modern Israeli territory was theirs in ancient times, and both demand jurisdiction in Jerusalem, where their holiest shrines are located.

Their modern conflict began with the UN's decision in 1947 to divide Palestine between Jewish and Arab territory. Palestine had been put under British supervision in 1920, and hundreds of thousands of Jews had migrated there, following Britain's 1917 "Balfour declaration" in favor of a Jewish "national home" in Palestine. Israel declared independence on May 14, 1948, and Arab forces invaded the next day in the first of several wars against the new state. The Palestine Liberation Organization (PLO) was formed in 1964 to reestablish independence for the Palestinian Arabs, and Yasser Arafat became its leader in 1969. In 1987, after Palestinians rioted in the Israeli-occupied Gaza Strip and West Bank, the PLO declared an independent Palestinian state. Two years later, Palestinians began a general uprising known as the intifada. In 1993, after secret talks in Oslo, Norway, an accord was signed by Israel and the PLO, formally recognizing each other's right to exist. Limited Palestinian self-rule was agreed upon, as well as a phased withdrawal of Israeli troops from the two Palestinian territories. Further agreements were signed, but extremists on both sides have extended the conflict into the 21st century.

LEBANON

OFFICIAL NAME
The Lebanese Republic

CAPITAL
Beirut

Area 10 452 km² (4036 sq miles)
Population 3 236 000
Population density 305 per km² (790 per sq mile)
Population growth rate 1.8%
Life expectancy 66 (m); 70 (f)
Languages Arabic, French, Kurdish, Armenian
Adult literacy rate 92.4%
Currency Lebanese pound (US $1 = 1514 Lebanese pounds)
GDP (US million $) 17 476
GDP per head (US $) 5478

Key dates

1516 Ottoman rule.
1920 League of Nations gives France control.
1943 Independence.
1975-76 Civil war.
1976 Syrian occupation.
1978 Israel invades to attack PLO bases; UN peacekeeping force.
1982 Israel again invades south.
1985-92 Shi'ite Muslim groups hold Western hostages.
1993 Israel attacks Hezbollah terrorists in south.
2000 Israel withdraws.

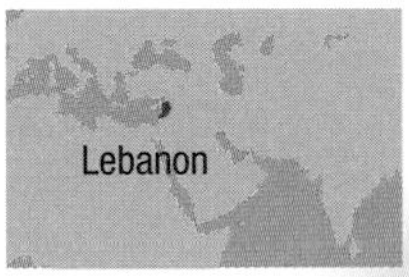

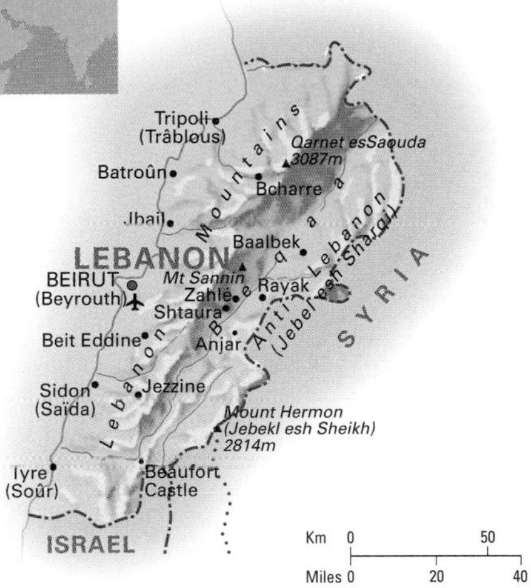

JORDAN

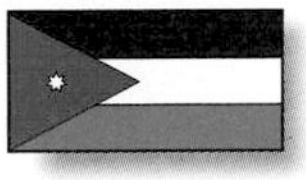

OFFICIAL NAME
The Hashemite Kingdom of Jordan

CAPITAL
Amman

Area 97 740 km² (37 738 sq miles)
Population 6 482 000
Population density 64 per km² (167 per sq mile)
Population growth rate 2.8%
Life expectancy 66 (m); 69 (f)
Language Arabic
Adult literacy rate 86.6%
Currency dinar (US $1 = 0.71 dinar)
GDP (US million $) 7500
GDP per head (US $) 1190

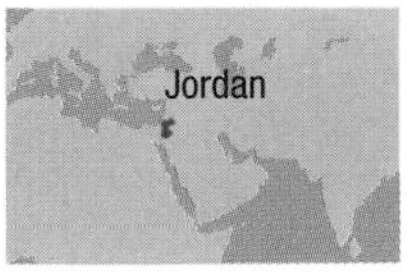

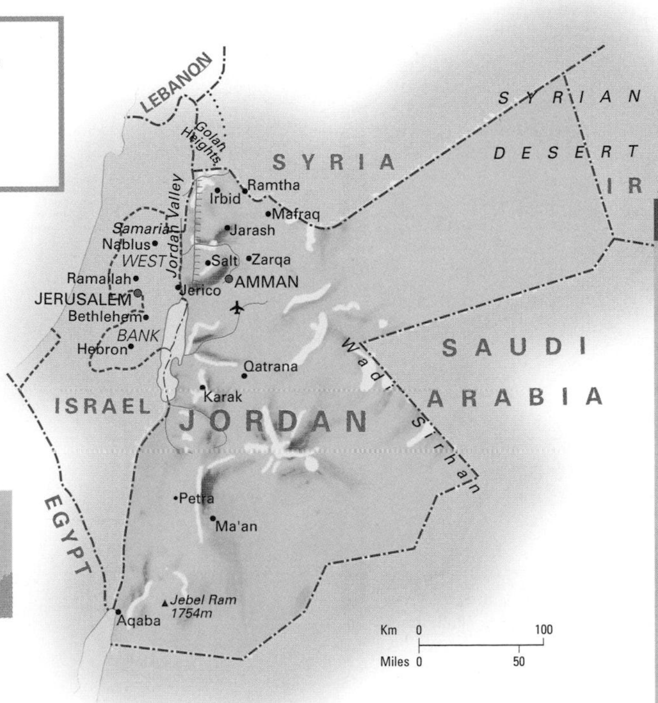

Key dates

1517 Ottoman rule.
1921 Partial self-rule (as Transjordan) under British control.
1946 Independence.
1948 War with Israel: gains West Bank and East Jerusalem.
1967 Six-Day War: loses West Bank and East Jerusalem to Israel.
1988 Cedes West Bank responsibility to PLO.
1994 Peace accord with Israel.
1999 King Hussein dies after reigning 46 years.

Iraq, Kuwait and Saudi Arabia

IRAQ

OFFICIAL NAME
The Republic of Iraq

CAPITAL
Baghdad

Area 438 317 km² (169 235 sq miles)
Population 22 450 000
Population density 50 per km² (129 per sq mile)
Population growth rate 2.1%
Life expectancy 77 (m); 78 (f)
Languages Arabic, Kurdish, Turkoman
Adult literacy rate 58%
Currency Iraqi dinar (US $1 = 0.312 dinars)
GDP (US million $) 26 700
GDP per head (US $) 1189

FACT

Several ancient civilizations grew up in present-day Iraq: Assyria, Sumer, Babylonia and Mesopotamia.

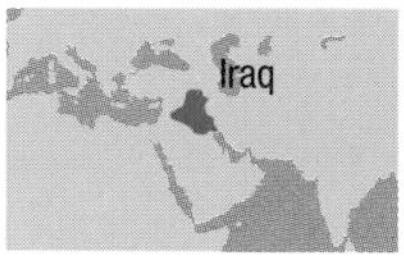

Key dates

539 B.C. Beginning of Persian rule.
A.D. 637 Arab conquest.
1534 Beginning of Ottoman rule.
1920 British control.
1932 Independence.
1945 Founding member of Arab League.
1958 Monarchy overthrown; republic.
1961-75 Kurdish revolt; intermittent fighting.
1979 Saddam Hussein becomes president.
1980-88 Inconclusive war after invading Iran.
1987-88 Poison gas used against Kurds.
1990 Invades Kuwait.
1991 Gulf War lost to US-led coalition. UN imposes sanctions and "safe zone" for Kurds.
1992 Allies impose no-fly zone in south to protect Shi'ite minority.
1996 US bombs military targets after Iraqi troops enter Kurdish territory.
2003 US-UK forces invade, overthrowing Saddam Hussein.

KUWAIT

OFFICIAL NAME
The State of Kuwait

CAPITAL
Kuwait City

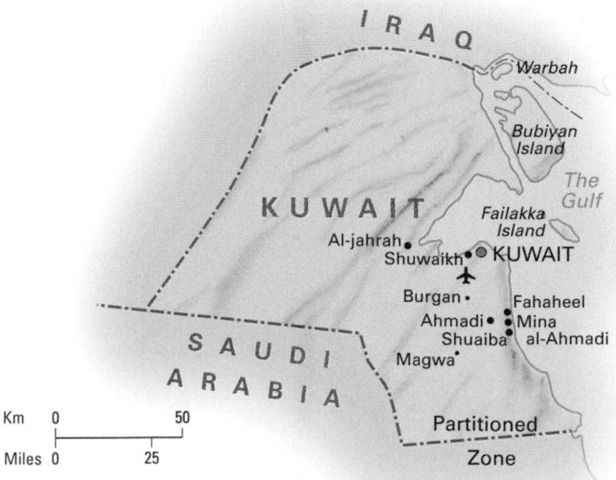

Area 17 818 km² (6880 sq miles)
Population 2 107 000
Population density 114 per km² (295 per sq mile)
Population growth rate 5%
Life expectancy 71 (m); 73 (f)
Languages Arabic, English
Adult literacy rate 78.6%
Currency Kuwaiti dinar (US $1 = 0.30 dinar)

GDP (US million $) 28 600
GDP per head (US $) 14 088

Legacy of war The Gulf War left Kuwait littered with wrecked and abandoned military hardware, such as this Iraqi tank. About 600 oil wells were set on fire by Iraqi troops before the conflict ended.

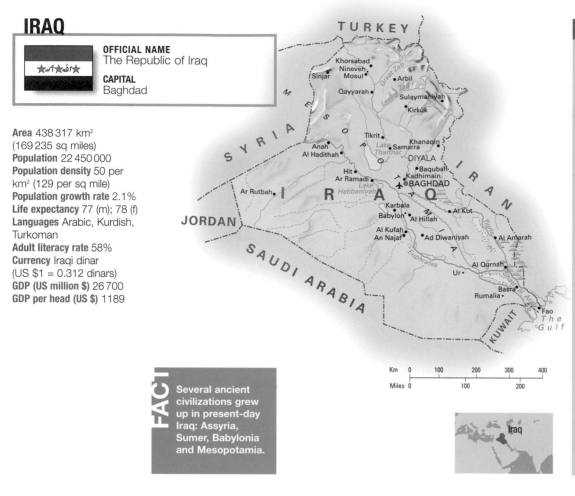

Key dates

1710 First Arab settlers.
1775 British mail depot.
1899 Self-governing British protectorate.
1934 Oil discovered.
1961 Full independence.
1973-74 Embargoes oil supplies to countries supporting Israel in Yom Kippur War.
1976-81, 1986 National assembly suspended.
1980s Supports Iraq during its war with Iran.
1981 Founding member of Gulf Cooperation Council.
1990 Invaded by Iraq; government goes into exile in Saudi Arabia.
1991 Gulf War: US-led coalition drives out Iraqi forces, who sabotage oil wells during retreat.
1992 National assembly revived; elections held.
1993 US-led air strikes repel Iraqi incursion.

SAUDI ARABIA

OFFICIAL NAME
The Kingdom of Saudi Arabia

CAPITAL
Riyadh

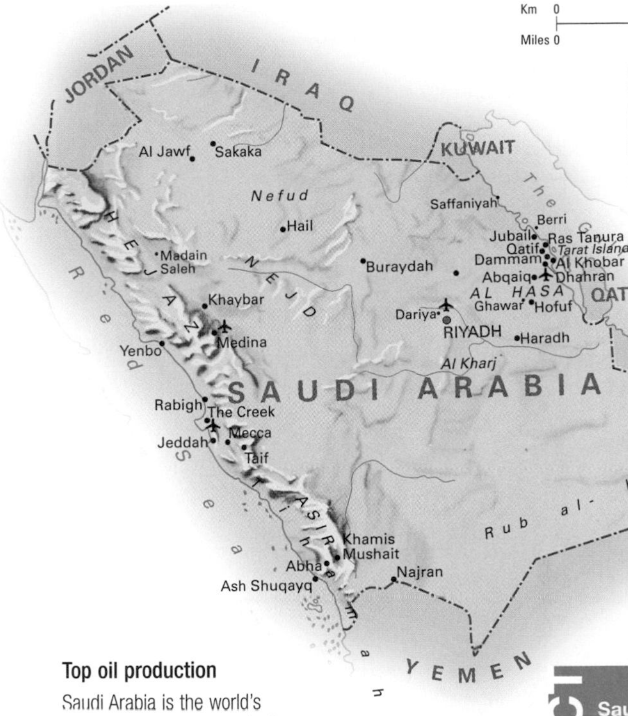

Area 2 240 000 km² (864 869 sq miles)
Population 19 895 000
Population density 9 per km² (23 per sq mile)
Population growth rate 2.7%
Life expectancy 68 (m); 71 (f)
Language Arabic
Adult literacy rate 63%
Currency riyal (US $1 = 3.75 riyals)
GDP (US million $) 132 900
GDP per head (US $) 6585

Key dates

1906-32 Ibn Saud unites Saudi Arabian kingdom.
1933 Oil discovered.
1945 Founding member of Arab League.
1948 War against Israel.
1973-74 Embargoes oil supplies to countries supporting Israel.
1975 King assassinated.
1981 Founding member of Gulf Cooperation Council.
1987 Breaks diplomatic relations with Iran.
1991 Joins US-led coalition in Gulf War.
1992 King establishes consultative council.
1996 Bomb kills 19 US troops at military base.

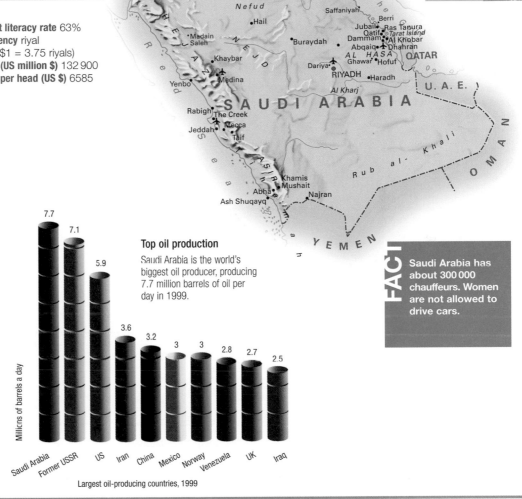

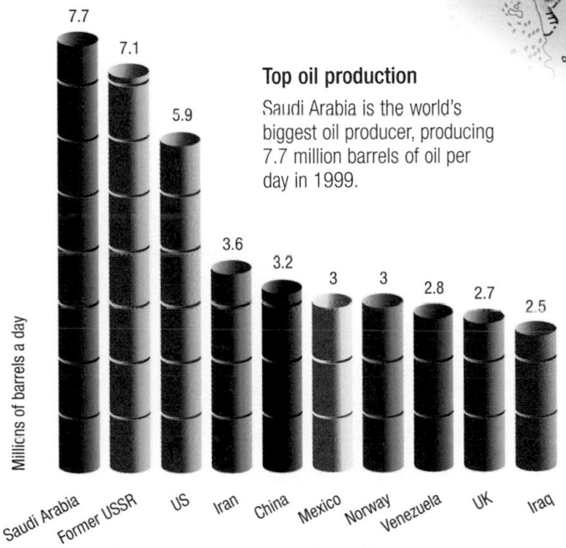

Top oil production
Saudi Arabia is the world's biggest oil producer, producing 7.7 million barrels of oil per day in 1999.

Largest oil-producing countries, 1999

FACT Saudi Arabia has about 300 000 chauffeurs. Women are not allowed to drive cars.

THE POLITICS OF OIL

Oil became both a source of conflict and a weapon in the 20th century. With the largest oil reserves located in the Middle East, that region became the focus of global economic and military rivalry.

The first oil to be discovered in the Middle East was in Persia (Iran) in 1908, followed by Iraq in 1927, then Bahrain, Kuwait, Saudi Arabia and Qatar in the 1930s. These nations were at first content to share in the profits of Western companies that had found and developed their vast resources. But they soon realized the advantages of ownership: Iran nationalized its oil industry in 1951, and Iraq did so in 1972. Saudi Arabia and its neighbors were becoming influential nations, and the final step was to turn oil into power as well as money.

The political power of oil was most clearly shown during five months in 1973-74, when the Arab-dominated Organization of Petroleum Exporting Countries (OPEC) created an oil crisis by banning exports to Western nations supporting Israel in the Yom Kippur War. Oil's strategic importance was also evident when Iraq invaded Kuwait in 1990, drawing a quick Western military response. The defeated Iraqis set 600 Kuwaiti oil wells on fire as they retreated. The subsequent international embargo on Iraqi oil exports showed that oil power can also be reversed.

The Middle East does not have a monopoly on crude oil supplies. After the OPEC crisis, the major Western nations accelerated their search for petroleum closer to home. Britain began to tap its North Sea oil fields in 1976. The US discovered extensive reserves in Alaska, and it boosted the development of offshore wells in the Gulf of Mexico. A desire for energy self-reliance and worries over the environmental impact of oil consumption have prompted a search for alternative energy. Even so, in 2000, a rise in oil prices after producers reduced output showed how powerful the oil weapon still is.

BAHRAIN

OFFICIAL NAME
The State of Bahrain

CAPITAL
Al Manamah

Area 695 km² (268 sq miles)
Population 666 000
Population density 921 per km² (2384 per sq mile)
Population growth rate 3.1%
Life expectancy 66 (m); 69 (f)
Languages Arabic, English
Adult literacy rate 85.2%
Currency Bahraini dinar (US $1 = 0.37 dinar)
GDP (US million $) 6800
GDP per head (US $) 10 625

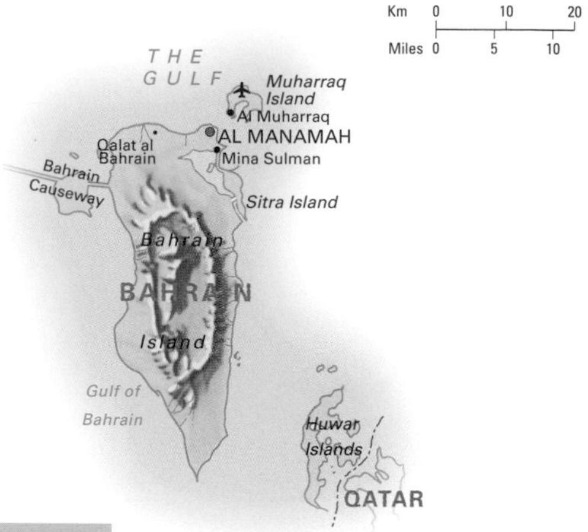

Key dates

17th c. Persian rule.
1782 Arab Al Khalifah clan displaces Persians.
1861 Becomes British protectorate.
1931 Oil discovered.
1971 Independence.
1973 National assembly elected.
1975 National assembly dissolved by emir. Buys controlling interest in oil companies.
1981 Founding member of Gulf Cooperation Council.
1991 Joins US-led coalition in Gulf War against Iraq.

QATAR

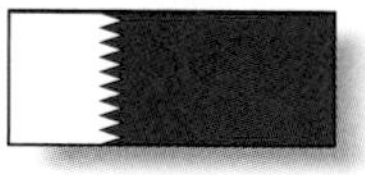

OFFICIAL NAME
The State of Qatar

CAPITAL
Doha

Area 11 437 km² (4416 sq miles)
Population 589 000
Population density 47 per km² (122 per sq mile)
Population growth rate 1.6%
Life expectancy 68 (m); 74 (f)
Languages Arabic, English
Adult literacy rate 79%
Currency Qatari rial (US $1 = 3.64 rials)
GDP (US million $) 10 100
GDP per head (US $) 18 703

Key dates

1872 Beginning of Ottoman rule.
1916 Becomes British protectorate.
1939 Oil discovered.
1971 Independence.
1972 Bloodless coup: Sheik Khalifa deposes cousin, Sheik Ahmad.
mid-1970s Oil industry nationalized.
1981 Founding member of Gulf Cooperation Council.
1991 Gulf War: joins US-led coalition against Iraq; provides air base.

UNITED ARAB EMIRATES

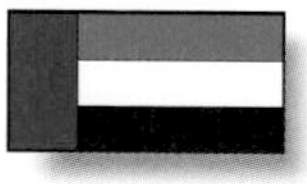

OFFICIAL NAME
The United Arab Emirates

CAPITAL
Abu Dhabi

Area 77 700 km² (30 000 sq miles)
Population 2 938 000
Population density 35 per km² (91 per sq mile)
Population growth rate 5.1%
Life expectancy 72 (m); 75 (f)
Languages Arabic, English
Adult literacy rate 79.2%
Currency dirham (US $1 = 3.67 dirhams)
GDP (US million $) 50 200
GDP per head (US $) 18 455

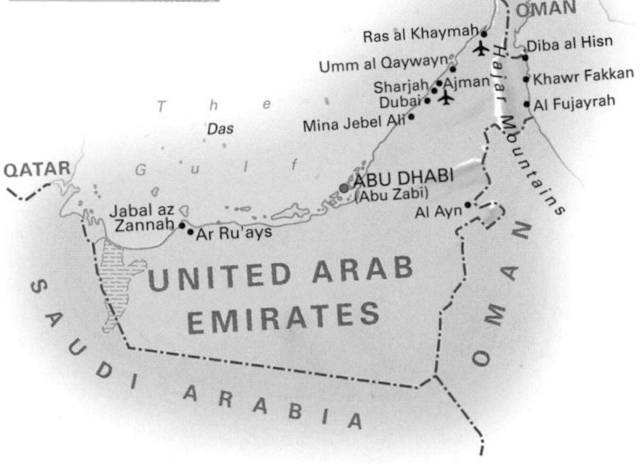

Key dates

7th c. Islamic Arab control established.
1820 Britain enforces truces between warring (Trucial) states. Becomes British protectorate.
1958 Oil discovered.
1971 Independence; six of the Trucial States, including Abu Dhabi and Dubai, form United Arab Emirates.
1972 Ras al Khaymah joins UAE.
1981 Founding member of Gulf Cooperation Council.
1991 Joins US-led coalition in Gulf War.

OMAN

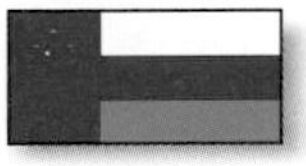

OFFICIAL NAME
The Sultanate of Oman

CAPITAL
Muscat

Area 309 500 km² (119 500 sq miles)
Population 2 460 000
Population density 7 per km² (19 per sq mile)
Population growth rate 2.3%
Life expectancy 67 (m); 71 (f)
Languages Arabic, English
Adult literacy rate 41%
Currency Omani rial (US $1 = 0.38 rials)
GDP (US million $) 14 500
GDP per head (US $) 6782

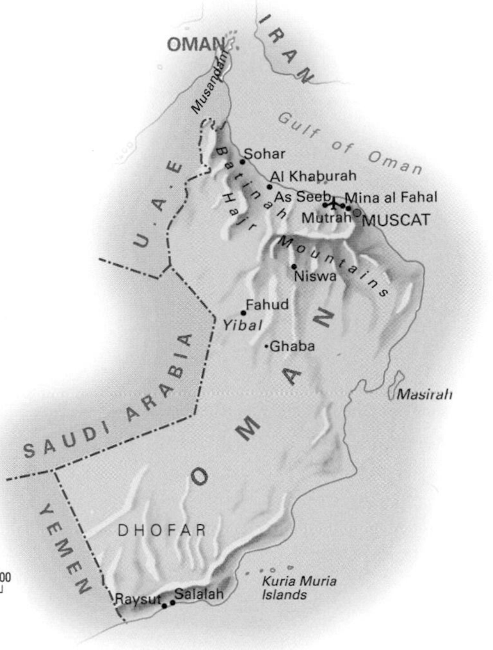

Key dates

7th c. Islamic conversion.
1507-1650 Portuguese control.
late 17th c. Sets up east African slaving posts.
1957 Britain helps defeat religious revolt.
1970 Modernization begins; name changed to Oman (from Muscat and Oman).
1981 Founding member of Gulf Cooperation Council.
1991 Joins US-led coalition in Gulf War against Iraq.
1992 Ends long border dispute with Yemen.

YEMEN

OFFICIAL NAME
The Republic of Yemen

CAPITAL
San'a

Area 527 968 km² (203 850 sq miles)
Population 17 676 000
Population density 32 per km² (82 per sq mile)
Population growth rate 2.9%
Life expectancy 55 (m); 56 (f)
Language Arabic
Adult literacy rate 38%
Currency Yemeni rial (US $1 = 166.4 rials)
GDP (US million $) 5200
GDP per head (US $) 304

Key dates

1839 UK takes Aden.
1918 North Yemen independent.
1968 Aden and South Yemen independent.
1971-72 War between North and South.
1978-79 War renewed.
1990 Union of North and South Yemen.
1994 Secession of South suppressed.

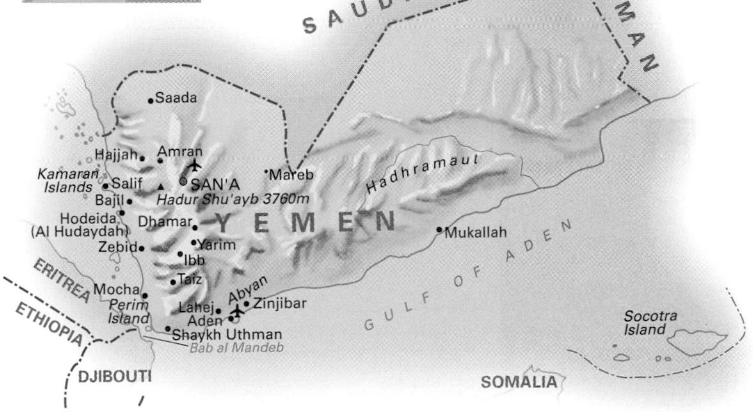

Desert capital San'a, the capital of unified Yemen at the edge of the "Empty Quarter," grew in importance in the Middle Ages as a trading post on the route through the Arabian peninsula to the port of Aden.

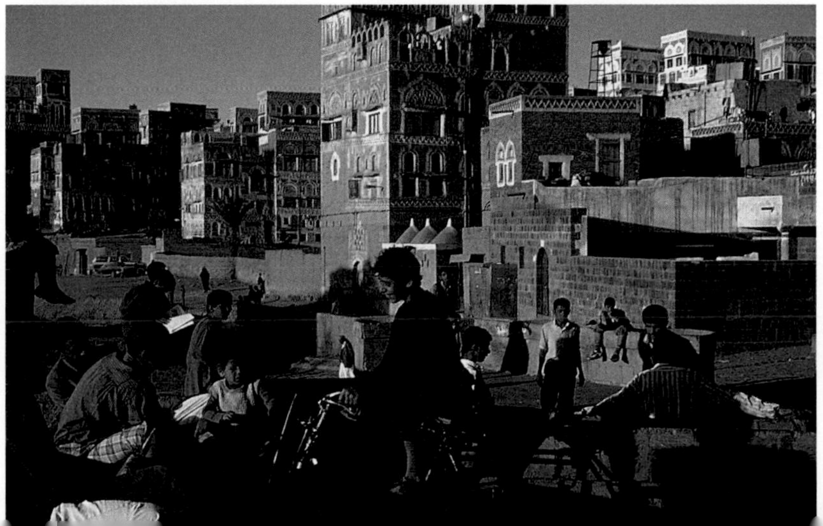

Iran, Pakistan and Afghanistan

IRAN

OFFICIAL NAME
The Islamic Republic of Iran

CAPITAL
Tehran (Teheran)

Area 1 648 000 km² (636 296 sq miles)
Population 62 746 000
Population density 38 per km² (97 per sq mile)
Population growth rate 1.2%
Life expectancy 58 (m); 59 (f)
Languages Farsi (Iranian), Turkic and other local languages
Adult literacy rate 72.3%
Currency Iranian rial (US $1 = 1747 rials)
GDP (US million $) 54 700
GDP per head (US $) 1207

Key dates

c. 550 B.C. Persian empire established.
7th c. A.D. Arab conquest.
1220 Mongol invasion.
1501 Savafid rule.
1826 Russian invasion.
1906 First constitution and parliament.
1908 Oil discovered.
1925 Army officer Reza Khan becomes shah.
1935 Renamed Iran (formerly Persia).
1941-45 British and Soviet occupation.
1951 Nationalizes oil industry.
1953 Boycott of Iranian oil. Shah briefly exiled.
1961 "White Revolution" starts modernization.
1979 Shah flees; Islamic republic set up, led by Ayatollah Khomeini. US hostages seized.
1980-88 Iraq invades; inconclusive war.
1981 Hostages freed.
1989 Khomeini dies.
1991 Kurdish refugees enter from Iraq.
1997 Moderate Khatami elected president.

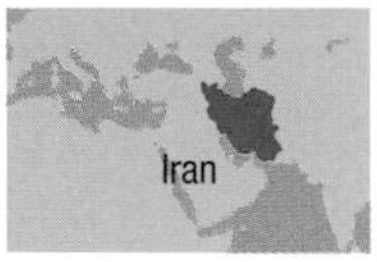

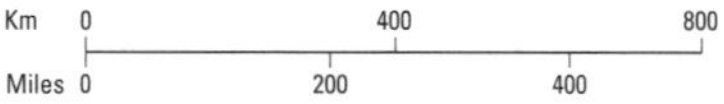

The Kurds and Kurdistan

The 20 million Kurds, who claim descent from Noah, are the world's largest distinct ethnic group with no state of their own. Most have turned from a traditional life of nomadic herding to become farmers but are fiercely loyal to their 3000-year-old culture and language. Kurdistan has never existed as a distinct state, yet the Kurds have played an important part in the history of western Asia since at least the 7th century.

After World War I, the Allies proposed a separate Kurdish state, but Turkey refused to cede territory. A Kurdish terrorist campaign against the Turkish government began in the 1980s. A Kurdish republic was established within Iran in 1946, but was abolished by the shah. Kurds in Iraq were victims of genocide in 1988-89.

After the 1991 Gulf War, Iraqi forces again assaulted Kurdish centers, and about 1.4 million refugees fled to Turkey and Iran. The UN has established Kurdish "safe havens" in northern Iraq, but today the Kurds remain isolated in pockets of their traditional territories, still without a recognized homeland.

Nowhere to go Kurdish refugees, having fled from ruthless attacks by Saddam Hussein's Iraqi army, gather in Siranbar refugee camp (left) in neighboring Iran in 1996. UN "safe havens" were not enough to give permanent protection.

Ghost homeland The area the Kurds want as their national home (above) extends over the territories of six countries. Despite widespread international support for the Kurds, not one of the six is prepared to yield land.

PAKISTAN

OFFICIAL NAME
The Islamic Republic of Pakistan

CAPITAL
Islamabad

Area 796 095 km² (307 374 sq miles)
Population 134 510 000
Population density 164 per km² (425 per sq mile)
Population growth rate 0.6%
Life expectancy 59 (m); 59 (f)
Languages Urdu, Punjabi, Pushto, Sindhi, Saraiki, English
Adult literacy rate 37.8%
Currency Pakistani rupee (US $1 = 61 rupees)
GDP (US million $) 66 000
GDP per head (US $) 500

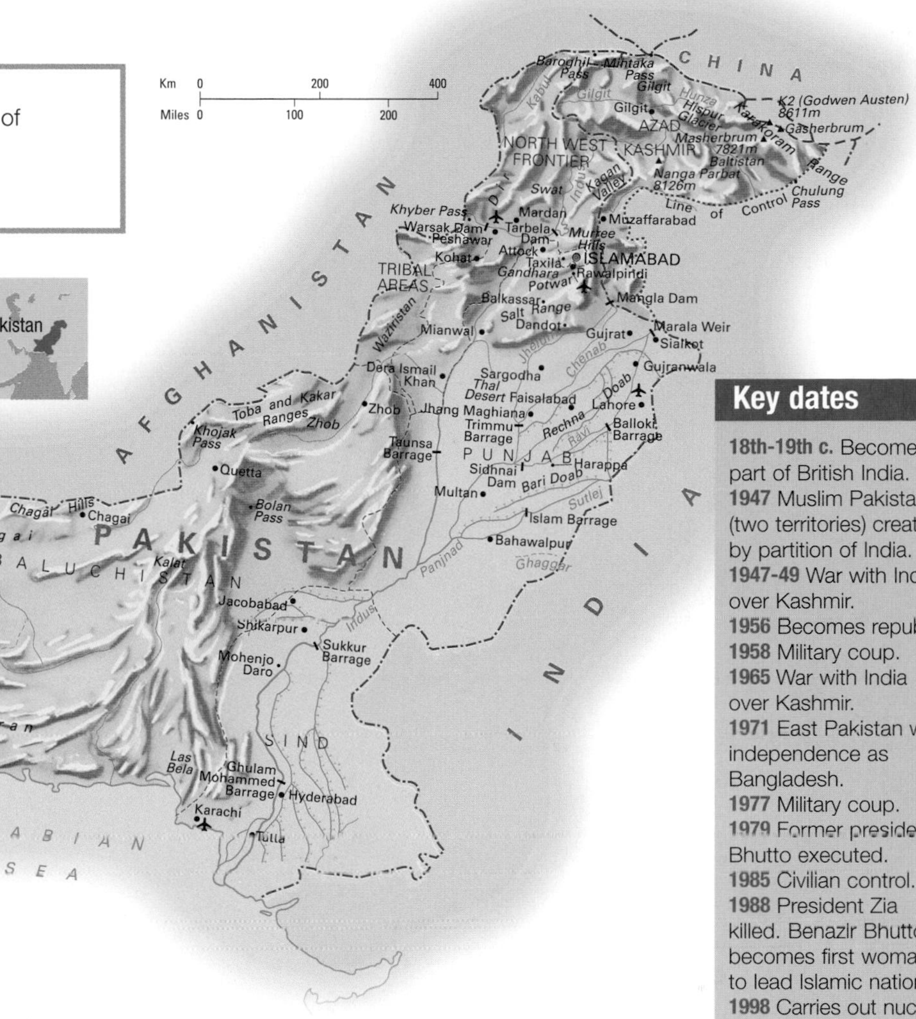

Key dates

18th-19th c. Becomes part of British India.
1947 Muslim Pakistan (two territories) created by partition of India.
1947-49 War with India over Kashmir.
1956 Becomes republic.
1958 Military coup.
1965 War with India over Kashmir.
1971 East Pakistan wins independence as Bangladesh.
1977 Military coup.
1979 Former president Bhutto executed.
1985 Civilian control.
1988 President Zia killed. Benazir Bhutto becomes first woman to lead Islamic nation.
1998 Carries out nuclear weapons tests.

AFGHANISTAN

OFFICIAL NAME
The Islamic State of Afghanistan

CAPITAL
Kabul

Area 652 225 km² (251 773 sq miles)
Population 18 800 000
Population density 29 per km² (75 per sq mile)
Population growth rate 1%
Life expectancy 43 (m); 44 (f)
Languages Pashto, Dari (dialect of Farsi or Iranian) and many local languages
Adult literacy rate 31.5%
Currency afghani (US $1 = 4750 afghanis)
GDP (US million $) 20 000
GDP per head (US $) 937

FACT
Afghanistan has the world's highest proportion of disabled people – more than 17 percent.

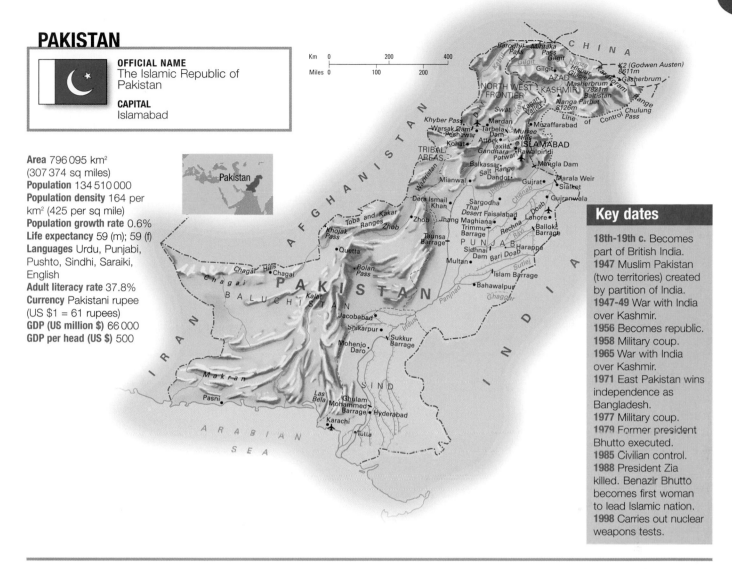

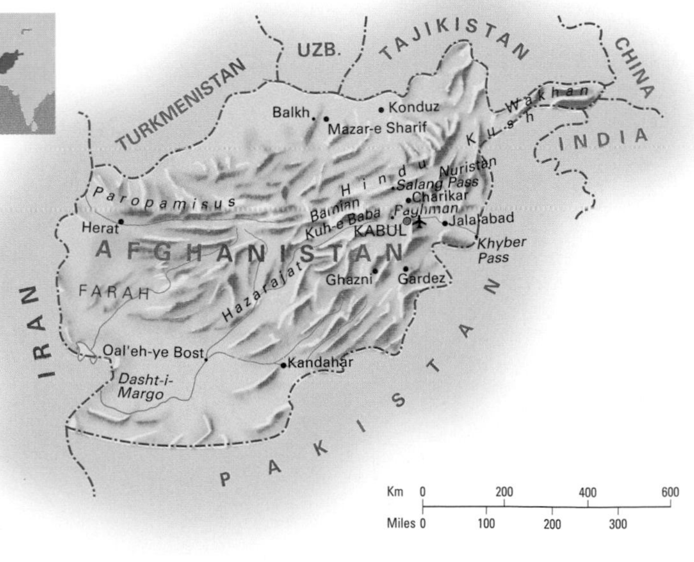

Key dates

19th c. Russia and UK struggle for control.
1880 UK protectorate.
1919 Independence.
1973 Military coup deposes monarchy.
1978 Pro-Soviet coup; war with Islamic rebels.
1979 Soviet invasion to shore up government.
1989 Soviet withdrawal.
1992 Islamic rebels take power; fighting continues.
1996 Fundamentalist Taliban faction in power.
2001 US-led forces overthrow Taliban; broad-based government formed.

KAZAKHSTAN

OFFICIAL NAME
The Republic of Kazakhstan

CAPITAL
Astana

Area 2 717 300 km² (1 049 150 sq miles)
Population 14 942 000
Population density 6 per km² (14 per sq mile)
Population growth rate 1.5%
Life expectancy 64 (m); 73 (f)
Languages Kazakh, Russian
Adult literacy rate 97.5%
Currency tenge (US $1 = 145 tenge)
GDP (US million $) 15 900
GDP per head (US $) 1055

FACT Dennis Tito, the world's first space tourist, took off from Kazakhstan's Baikonur launch pad in April 2001.

Key dates

13th c. Mongol control.
1731 Russian protectorate.
1920 Autonomous Communist republic.
1936 Becomes republic of Soviet Union.
1950s "Virgin Lands" project to cultivate the steppes.
1991 Independence; joins Commonwealth of Independent States.
1992 Joins UN.
1993 Approves Nuclear Non-Proliferation Treaty.
1998 Astana (formerly Akmola) declared capital in place of Almaty (Alma Ata).

KYRGYZSTAN

OFFICIAL NAME
The Kyrgyz Republic

CAPITAL
Bishkek

Area 198 500 km² (76 600 sq miles)
Population 4 822 938
Population density 24 per km² (61 per sq mile)
Population growth rate 1%
Life expectancy 61 (m); 70 (f)
Languages Kyrgyz (Cyrillic script; Latin script to be reintroduced), Russian
Adult literacy rate 97%
Currency som (US $1 = 49 soms)
GDP (US million $) 1200
GDP per head (US $) 255

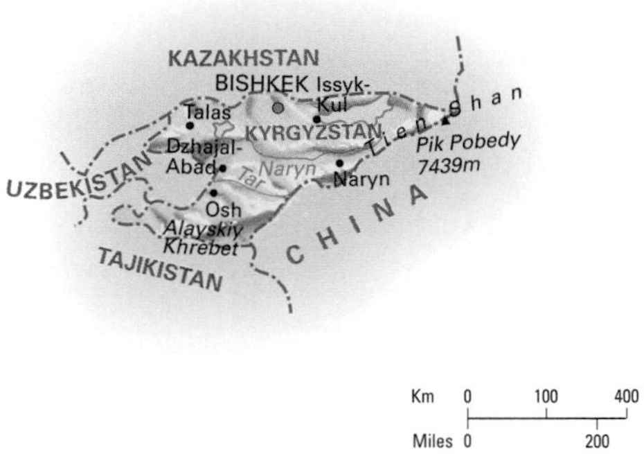

Key dates

13th c. Mongol rule.
17th c. Islam introduced.
1758 Chinese control begins.
1864 Russia replaces China as ruler.
1922 Merged into USSR.
1936 Becomes separate republic within USSR.
1990-95 Territorial dispute with Uzbeks.
1991 Independence; joins Commonwealth of Independent States.
1992 Joins UN.

TAJIKISTAN

OFFICIAL NAME
The Republic of Tajikistan

CAPITAL
Dushanbe

Area 143 100 km² (55 251 sq miles)
Population 6 237 000
Population density 43 per km² (110 per sq mile)
Population growth rate 1.2%
Life expectancy 65 (m); 71 (f)
Languages Tajik (Cyrillic script), Russian
Adult literacy rate 97.7%
Currency Tajik rouble (US $1 = 1260 Tajik roubles)
GDP (US million $) 1000
GDP per head (US $) 163

Key dates

13th c. Mongol rule.
14th-19th c. Uzbek rule.
late 19th c. Partly under Russian control.
1922 Merged into USSR.
1929 Becomes separate republic within USSR.
1991 Independence declared; joins Commonwealth of Independent States.
1992 Joins UN. Islamic rebels start civil war.
1997 Government achieves peace agreement with rebels.

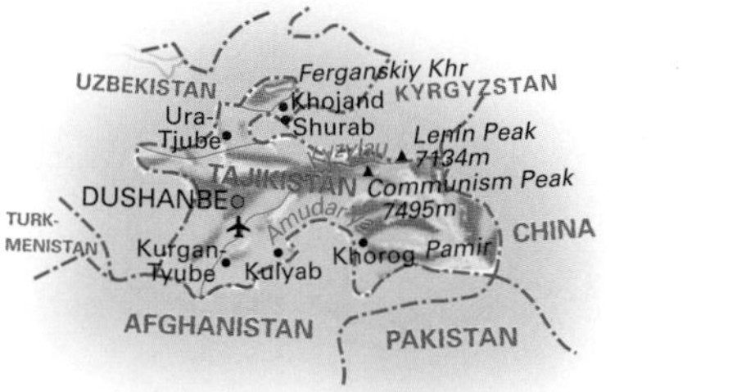

TURKMENISTAN

OFFICIAL NAME
The Republic of Turkmenistan

CAPITAL
Ashgabat

Area 488 100 km² (188 456 sq miles)
Population 4 384 000
Population density 10 per km² (26 per sq mile)
Population growth rate 2.5%
Life expectancy 62 (m); 68 (f)
Languages Turkmen (Latin-based script), Russian, Uzbek, Kazakh

Adult literacy rate 98%
Currency manat (US $1 = 5275 manats)
GDP (US million $) 3600
GDP per head (US $) 740

Key dates

10th c. Turkic settlement.
13th c. Mongol rule.
14th c. Islam introduced.
1885 Russian control.
1922 Becomes part of USSR.
1925 Becomes separate republic within USSR.
1991 Independence; joins Commonwealth of Independent States.
1992 Joins UN and Muslim Economic Cooperation Organization. New constitution; elections.
1997 Approves private ownership of land.

UZBEKISTAN

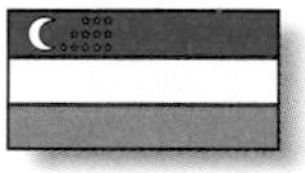

OFFICIAL NAME
The Republic of Uzbekistan

CAPITAL
Tashkent

Area 447 400 km² (172 740 sq miles)
Population 23 954 000
Population density 54 per km² (139 per sq mile)
Population growth rate 1.6%
Life expectancy 66 (m); 72 (f)
Languages Uzbek (Cyrillic script; reverting to Latin script), Russian, Kazakh

Adult literacy rate 97%
Currency som (US $1 = 337 som)
GDP (US million $) 11 400
GDP per head (US $) 474

Key dates

7th c. Arab conquest.
13th c. Mongol rule.
14th c. Tamerlane founds Mongol Empire's capital at Samarkand.
16th c. Uzbek invasion.
19th c. Russian control.
1924 Separate republic of Soviet Union.
1991 Independence; joins Commonwealth of Independent States.
1992 Joins UN.
1997 Law bars political parties from representing ethnic or religious groups.

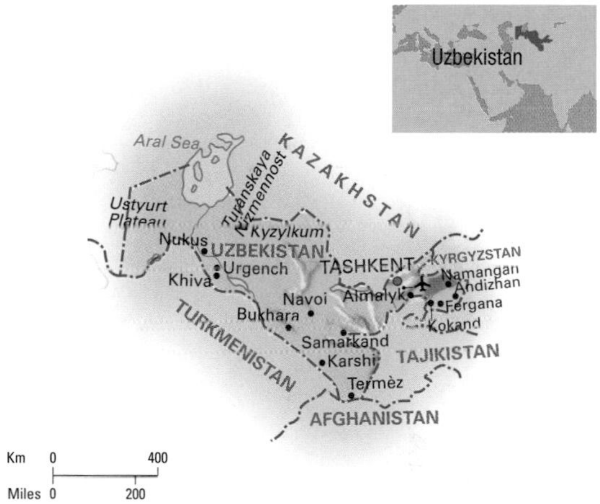

MONGOLIA

OFFICIAL NAME
Mongolia

CAPITAL
Ulan Bator

Area 1 566 500 km² (604 829 sq miles)
Population 2 382 525
Population density 2 per km² (4 per sq mile)
Population growth rate 2.8%
Life expectancy 62 (m); 65 (f)
Languages Khalkha Mongolian, Kazakh
Adult literacy rate 82.9%

Currency tugrik (US $1 = 1094 tugrik)
GDP (US million $) 953
GDP per head (US $) 397

Key dates

13th c. Genghis Khan creates Mongol Empire.
1680s Chinese rule.
1911 Chinese forces driven out.
1913 Self-rule by priest-king ("Living Buddha") under Russian control.
1924 "Living Buddha" dies; Communist republic established.
1961 Joins UN.
1966 Treaty with USSR; 60 000 Soviet troops stationed in Mongolia.
1989 USSR withdraws.
1990 Open elections.
1992 New constitution.
1996 US defense pact.

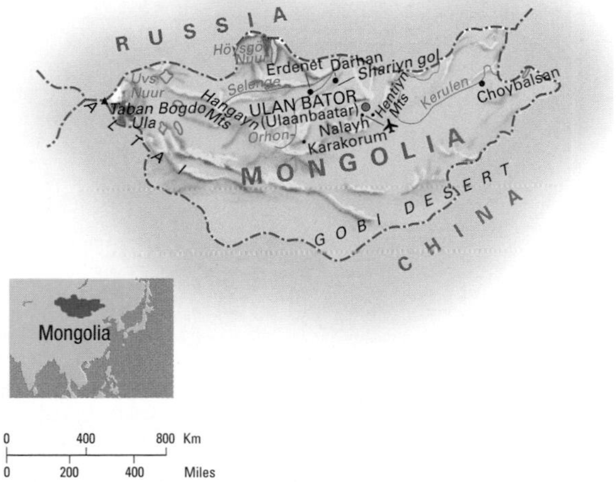

India, Sri Lanka and the Maldives

INDIA

OFFICIAL NAME
The Republic of India

CAPITAL
New Delhi

Area 3 287 263 km² (1 269 219 sq miles)
Population 1 030 000 000
Population density 295 per km² (765 per sq mile)
Population growth rate 1.4%
Life expectancy 57 (m); 58 (f)
Languages Hindi, English and many local languages
Adult literacy rate 52%
Currency rupee (US $1 = 46.8 rupees)
GDP (US million $) 468 300
GDP per head (US $) 482

Key dates

c. 3500 B.C. Indus Valley civilization.
c. 1500 B.C. Aryans settle.
530 B.C. Persian invasion.
326 B.C. Alexander the Great invades.
1526 Muslim Mogul Empire established.
1757 British East India Company wins Bengal.
1858 British government control after mutiny; Queen Victoria named Empress of India.
1885 Indian National Congress founded.
1906 Muslim League founded.
1920 Mahatma Gandhi starts peaceful campaign to end British rule.
1939-45 Fights World War II as one of Allies.
1947 Independence as India and Pakistan.
1947-49 War with Pakistan over Kashmir.
1948 Mahatma Gandhi assassinated.
1950 Becomes republic.
1962 Border fighting with China.
1965 War with Pakistan over Kashmir.
1975-77 Political crisis; state of emergency.
1984 More than 450 killed in attack on Sikh Golden Temple at Amritsar. Prime minister Indira Gandhi assassinated; replaced by her son Rajiv.
1990 Direct rule in Kashmir after riots. Ethnic riots in Punjab; more than 3500 killed.
1991 Rajiv Gandhi assassinated.
1992 Ayodhya mosque destroyed; more than 1200 die in riots.
1998 Conducts nuclear weapons tests; accepts Test Ban Treaty.

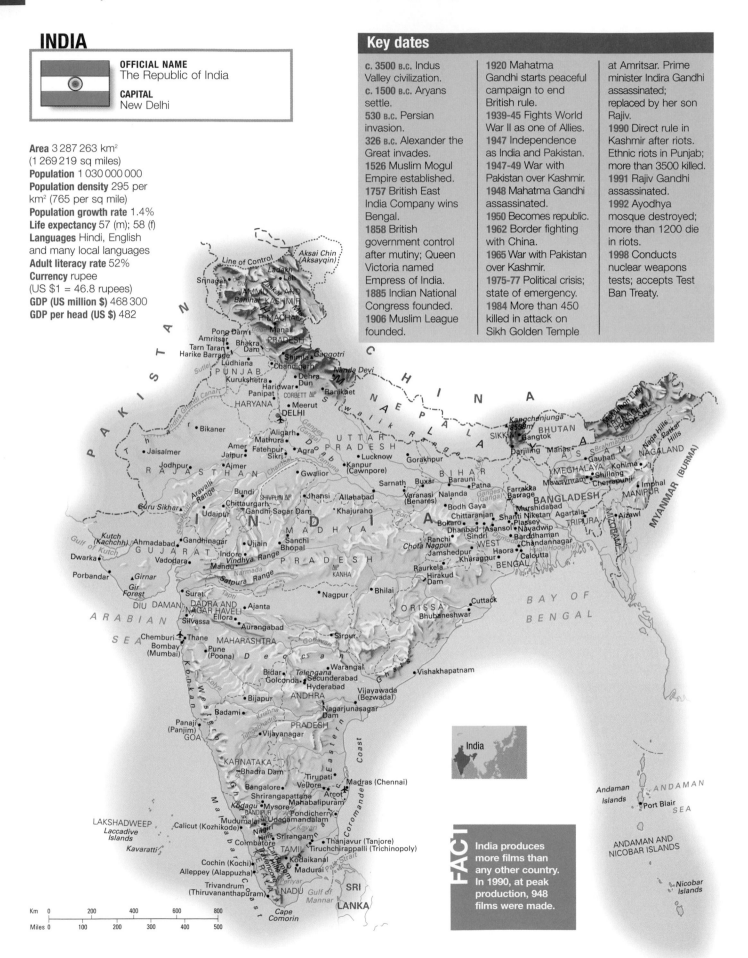

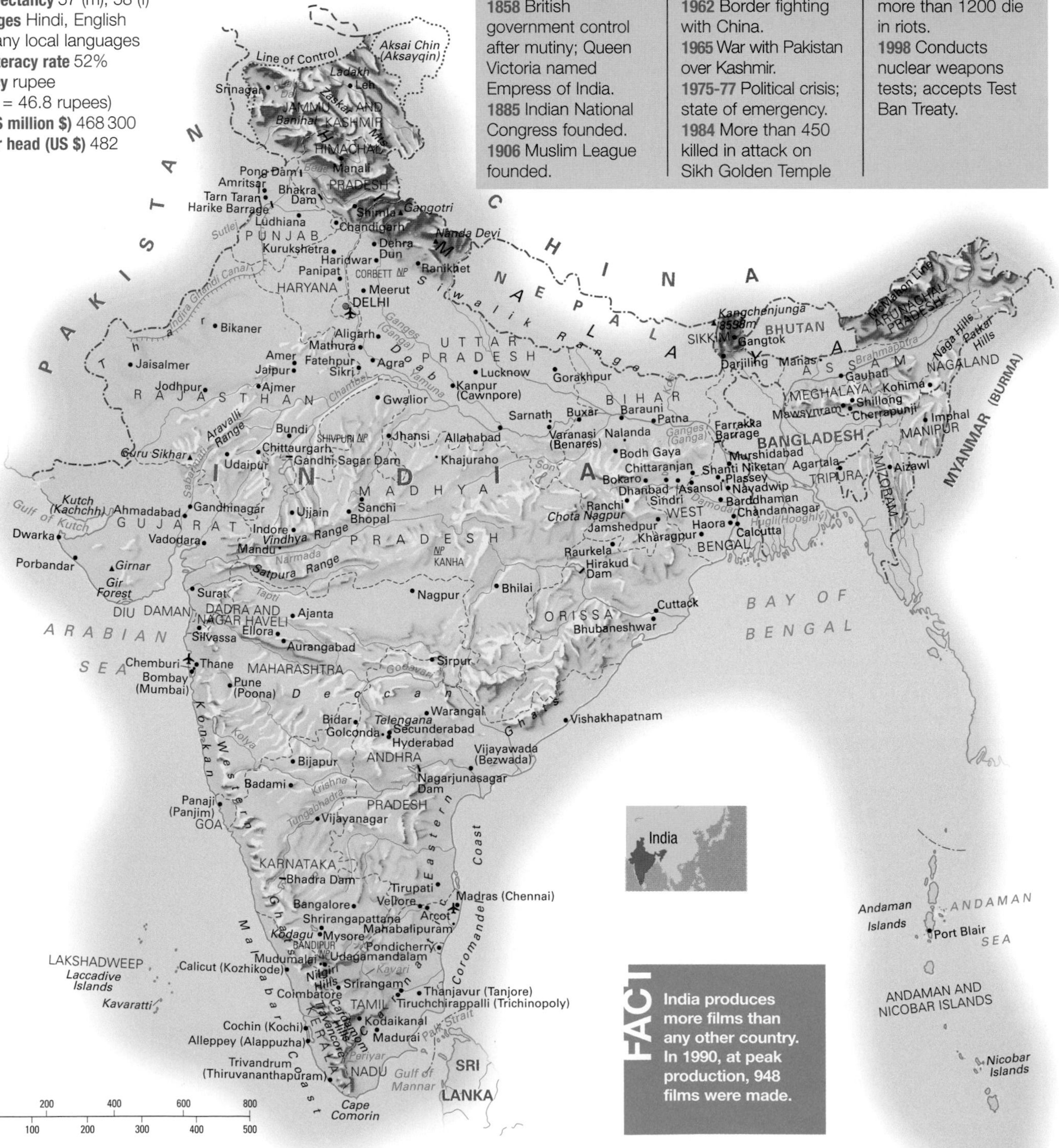

FACT
India produces more films than any other country. In 1990, at peak production, 948 films were made.

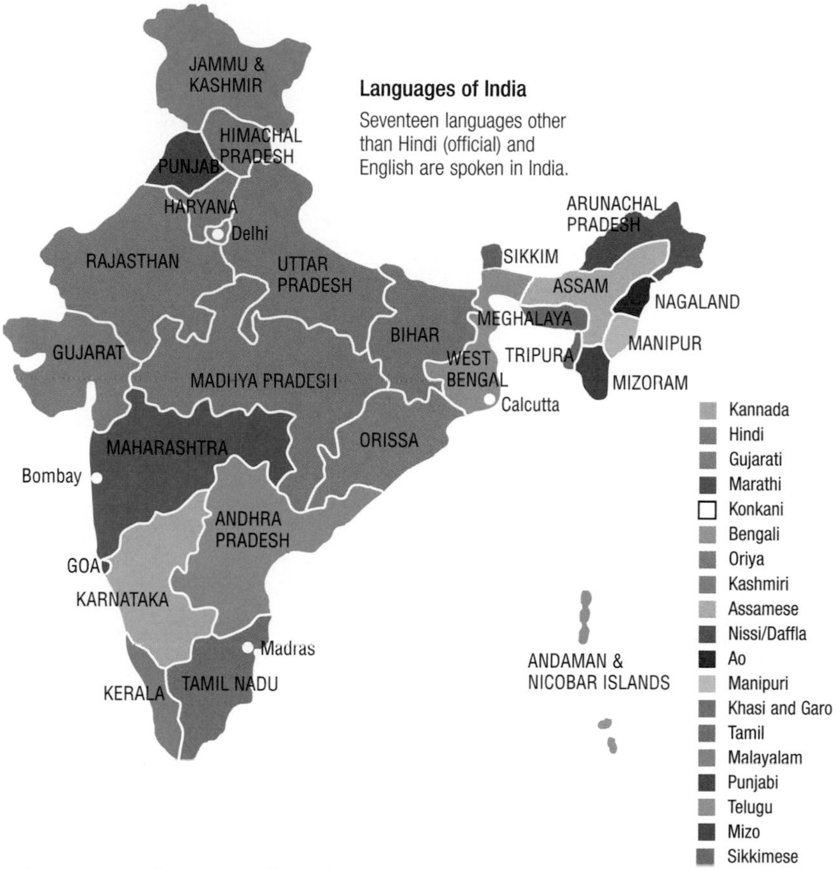

Languages of India

Seventeen languages other than Hindi (official) and English are spoken in India.

FLASHPOINT IN THE HIMALAYAS

When India and Pakistan tested nuclear weapons in 1998, it marked just the latest – if not the most dangerous – stage in a troubled 50-year relationship. Strife began as soon as British India was partitioned in 1947 into Muslim Pakistan and Hindu-dominated India. Then as now, the flashpoint was Kashmir.

The 222 236 km² (85 838 sq miles) of Kashmir's mountains and valleys are peopled largely by Muslims. But in 1947 Kashmir's ruler was a Hindu prince who, at independence, opted to join India. A two-year war was halted in 1949 by a UN cease-fire that divided Kashmir along today's border. Pakistan was left controlling a third of the region, home to 2 million of the 6 million Kashmiris. The rest forms the Indian state of Jammu and Kashmir.

Fighting between the two countries flared again in 1965-6 and in 1971. On the latter occasion, it focused mainly on East Pakistan, where India saw the chance to weaken its neighbor by helping East Pakistan to win independence.

India still keeps a large army in its part of Kashmir to suppress Islamic separatist violence that began in 1990. Cease-fires have regularly been violated; 100 were killed by shelling in 1998. However, negotiations begun in 1999 give some hope of eventual resolution to the dispute.

SRI LANKA

OFFICIAL NAME
Democratic Socialist Republic of Sri Lanka

CAPITAL
Colombo

Area 65 610 km² (25 332 sq miles)
Population 19 043 000
Population density 286 per km² (741 per sq mile)
Population growth rate 1.3%
Life expectancy 67 (m); 71 (f)
Languages Sinhala, Tamil, English
Adult literacy rate 90.2%
Currency Sri Lanka rupee (US $1 = 88 rupees)
GDP (US million $) 16 000
GDP per head (US $) 852

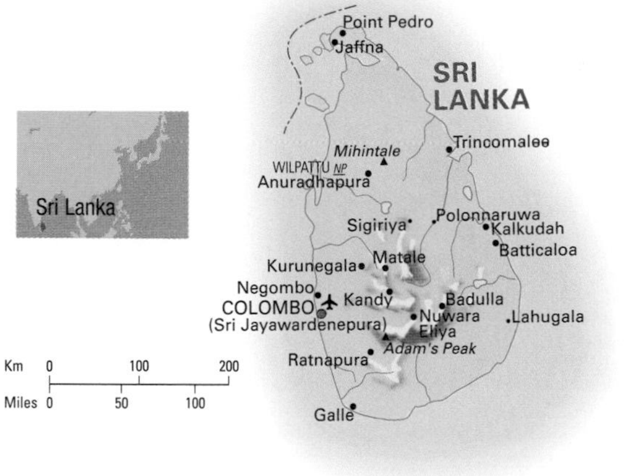

Key dates

1600-58 Portuguese rule.
1658-1795 Dutch rule.
1802-1948 British colony.
1948 Independence.
1959 Sinhalese extremist kills Prime Minister Solomon Bandaranaike.
1972 Changes name to Sri Lanka (from Ceylon).
1983 Guerrilla war starts with Tamil separatists; state of emergency.
1993 Tamil rebel kills President Ranasinghe Premadasa.

THE MALDIVES

OFFICIAL NAME
The Republic of Maldives

CAPITAL
Malé

Area 298 km² (115 sq miles)
Population 278 000
Population density 916 per km² (2374 per sq mile)
Population growth rate 3.2%
Life expectancy 67 (m); 67 (f)
Language Divehi (Maldivian, related to Sinhala)
Adult literacy rate 93.2%
Currency rufiyaa (US $1 = 11.77 rufiyaa)
GDP (US million $) 274
GDP per head (US $) 1079

Key dates

1558-73 Portuguese rule.
1573-1887 Rule by Islamic sultans.
1887 UK protectorate.
1965 Independence; leaves Commonwealth.
1968 Sultan deposed; republic established.
1982 Rejoins Commonwealth.
1988 Coup attempt by Sri Lankan mercenaries defeated by Indian army.

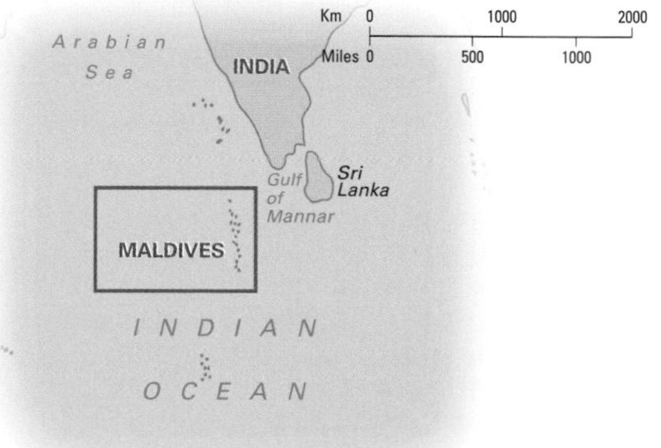

Nepal, Bhutan, Bangladesh and Myanmar

NEPAL

OFFICIAL NAME
The Kingdom of Nepal

CAPITAL
Kathmandu

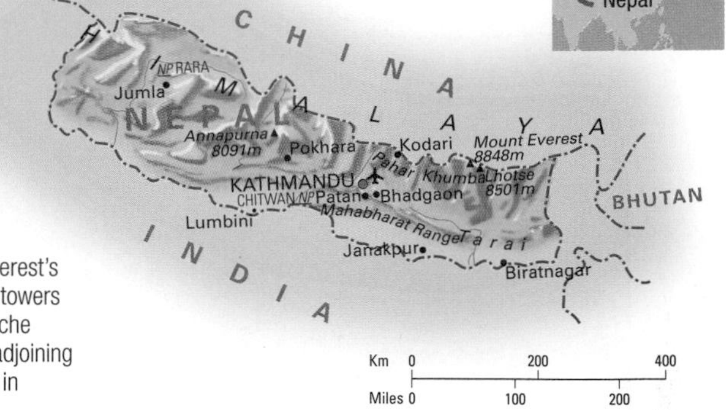

Area 147 181 km² (56 827 sq miles)
Population 22 367 000
Population density 148 per km² (384 per sq mile)
Population growth rate 1.9%
Life expectancy 50 (m); 48 (f)
Languages Napali, Maithir, Bhojpuri
Adult literacy rate 27.5%
Currency Nepalese rupee (US $1 = 74 rupees)
GDP (US million $) 4400
GDP per head (US $) 201

Heights of devotion Everest's 8848 m (29 028 ft) peak towers over the Buddhist Tengboche Gompa (monastery) and adjoining houses at Khumbu Himal in eastern Nepal.

Key dates

1769 King of Gurkha conquers Kathmandu.
1775 Nepal becomes unified kingdom.
1814-16 War with British after king tries to expand into India; becomes British protectorate.
1846 First Rana family member seizes power as prime minister.
1923 Independence.
1951 Revolution returns power to king.
1960 Political parties banned.
1962 New constitution; king still holds power.
1963 Abolishes caste system and polygamy.
1980 Pro-democracy riots; referendum; vote to retain status quo.
1990 Pro-democracy riots; new constitution; democratic monarchy.
1995 King dissolves parliament; overruled by Supreme Court.

BHUTAN

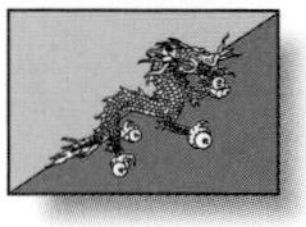

OFFICIAL NAME
The Kingdom of Bhutan

CAPITAL
Thimphu

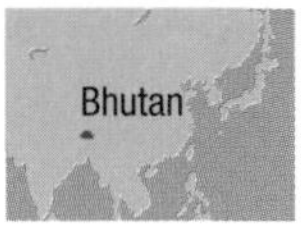

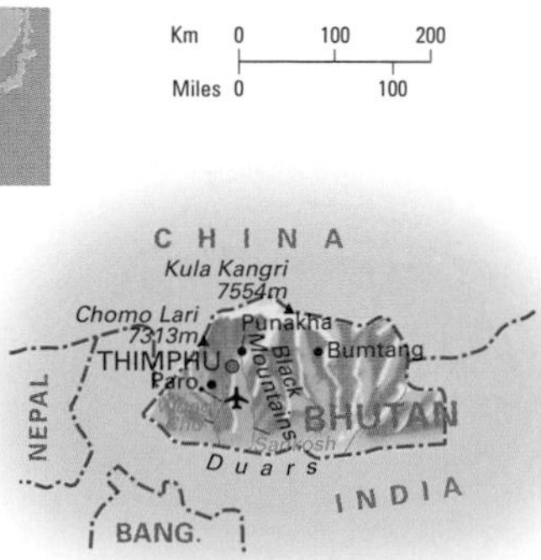

Area 46 500 km² (17 954 sq miles)
Population 2 064 000
Population density 43 per km² (111 per sq mile)
Population growth rate 2.2%
Life expectancy 49 (m); 52 (f)
Languages Dzongkha (Tibetan dialect), Nepali and others
Adult literacy rate 42.2%
Currency ngultrum (US $1 = 46.8 ngultrums)
GDP (US million $) 294
GDP per head (US $) 147

Key dates

c. 1630 Becomes separate state led by Tibetan lama.
1907 Monarchy formed.
1910 UK protectorate.
1949 Independence; receives aid from India.
1953 Establishes national assembly.
1959 Asylum for 4000 Tibetan refugees after China annexes Tibet.
1990 Demonstrations by Nepali-speakers after enforcement of Bhutanese customs.

BANGLADESH

OFFICIAL NAME
The People's Republic of Bangladesh

CAPITAL
Dhaka

Area 147 570 km² (56 977 sq miles)
Population 126 947 000
Population density 845 per km² (2190 per sq mile)
Population growth rate 1.2%
Life expectancy 57 (m); 56 (f)
Language Bengali
Adult literacy rate 38%
Currency taka (US $1 = 54 taka)
GDP (US million $) 36 400
GDP per head (US $) 291

Key dates

1858 British rule begins.
1947 British India partitioned; eastern Bengal independent as part of Pakistan.
1971 Wins war against West Pakistan (with Indian assistance); becomes independent as Bangladesh.
1975 Military coup; President Mujib killed.
1975-79 Martial law.
1979 Elections.
1981 President Zia killed by army rebels.
1982 Bloodless military coup.
1982-86 Martial law.
1986 Former military ruler Ershad elected president.
1990 Ershad charged with corruption; resigns.
1996 Elections marred by violence and alleged fraud.

MYANMAR

OFFICIAL NAME
The Union of Myanmar

CAPITAL
Yangon (Rangoon)

Area 676 553 km² (261 218 sq miles)
Population 45 059 000
Population density 71 per km² (184 per sq mile)
Population growth rate 2.1%
Life expectancy 57 (m); 63 (f)
Languages Myanmar (Burmese) and other local languages
Adult literacy rate 83.1%
Currency kyat (US $1 = 6.6 kyats)
GDP (US million $) 5916
GDP per head (US $) 122

Key dates

1886 British take control of Burma after three wars; becomes province of British India.
1937 Separated; partial self-government.
1942-45 Occupied by Japanese.
1948 Independence.
1962 Bloodless coup.
1974 New constitution.
1988 Military coup; many pro-democracy demonstrators killed.
1989 Changes name from Burma to Myanmar.
1990 Opposition leader Aung San Suu Kyi arrested; wins election landslide, but ruling junta refuses to recognize victory.
1991 Suu Kyi wins Nobel peace prize.
1997 Joins ASEAN.

FACT
Myanmar is the world's second-largest producer, after Afghanistan, of opium for the heroin trade.

CHINA

OFFICIAL NAME
The People's Republic of China

CAPITAL
Beijing

Area 9 571 300 km² (3 695 500 sq miles)
Population 1 274 115 000
Population density 132 per km² (342 per sq mile)
Population growth rate 1.4%
Life expectancy 66 (m); 70 (f)
Languages Northern Chinese (Mandarin or putonghua), Min, Wu, Yue (Cantonese) and others
Adult literacy rate 82.2%
Currency yuan, Hong Kong dollar and Macau pataca (US $1 = 8.27 yuan, HK $ 7.79 or 7.95 patacas)
GDP (US million $) 993 500
GDP per head (US $) 786

Key dates

c. 1766 B.C. Shang rule: first written records.
202 B.C.-A.D. 220 Strong empire under Hans.
1279-1368 Mongol rule.
1644-1912 Manchu rule.
1839-42 Opium War; UK wins Hong Kong.
1900-1 Western powers crush Boxer Rebellion.
1911 Republic declared.
1931 Japanese occupy Manchuria.
1937 Japanese invade.
1941-45 Joins Allies in World War II.
1946-49 Civil war.
1949 Mao Tse-tung Communists defeat Nationalists led by Chiang Kai-shek, who flee to Taiwan. People's Republic proclaimed.
1950-51 Takes over Tibet.
1959 Crushes revolt in Tibet; Dalai Lama flees.
1966 Mao instigates Cultural Revolution.
1969 Border clashes with USSR.
1971 Replaces Taiwan as member of UN.
1979 Economic reforms.
1989 Pro-democracy students massacred in Tiananmen Square, Beijing.
1997 UK returns Hong Kong to China.

China's ethnic diversity

The Chinese government has officially recognized 56 ethnic groups among the hundreds that live in its country. The Han people make up 91 percent of the total; the "national minorities" include Mongols, Manchus, Tatars, Tibetans, Koreans, Salars, Russians, Kazakhs and Qiangs. They live in every province and total 108 million out of China's 1.3 billion people.

Ethnic diversity has existed in China since the Qin dynasty in 221 B.C., but rivalries and tensions have never disappeared. The government proclaims equality, but minorities have suffered discrimination. In western provinces in particular in which ethnic minorities often correspond to religious groupings, the discrimination has led to civil disturbance. In 1993, police battled with rioting Muslims in Qinghai province. Beijing's stated policy is to crush any unrest, and officials were told to "wage an uncompromising struggle against separatists."

Religious diversity of China

About 31 percent of China's population follow one of the country's indigenous religions, Confucianism or Taoism, or one of the major world religions.

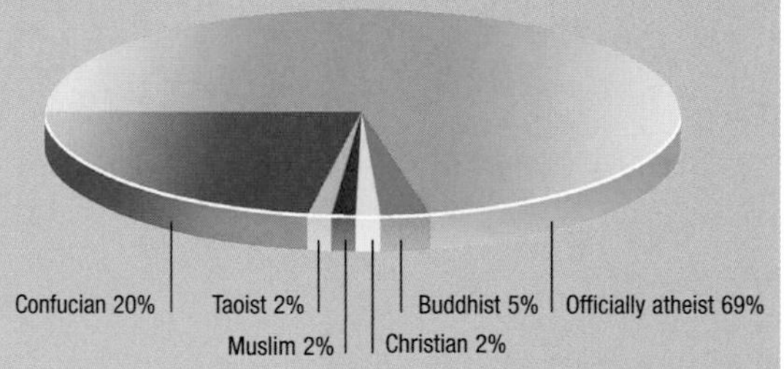

High living China is the world's most populous country, and Hong Kong (below) is its most crowded city. More people live in China today than inhabited the whole world 150 years ago. In parts of Hong Kong, population density exceeds 55 000 /km² (142 000 /sq mile).

RUSSIA
MONGOLIA
NEI MONGOL
CHINA
HEILONGJIANG
DONGBEI (MANCHURIA)
JILIN
LIAONING
HEBEI
SHANXI
SHAANXI
NINGXIA-HUI
QINGHAI
SHANDONG
HENAN
JIANGSU
ANHUI
HUBEI
SICHUAN
ZHEJIANG
HUNAN
JIANGXI
GUIZHOU
YUNNAN
FUJIAN
GUANGDONG
GUANGXI ZHUANG
NORTH KOREA
SOUTH KOREA
SEA OF JAPAN
YELLOW SEA
EAST CHINA SEA
SOUTH CHINA SEA
TAIWAN
VIETNAM
LAOS
MYANMAR (BURMA)
Amur (Heilong Jiang)
Wusuli Jiang (Ussuri)
Qiqihar
Daqing
Songhua Jiang
Harbin
Changchun
Fengman Dam
Siping
Liaoyuan
Shenyang
Fushun
Fuxin
Benxi
Liaoyang
Anshan
Yalu
Supung Dam
Chengde
Rehe Uplands
Liaodong Wan
Liaodong Peninsula
Bayan Obo
Yin Shan
Baotou
Hohhot
Zhangjiakou
Xuanhua
Shijingshan
BEIJING (Peking)
Qinhuangdao
Beidaihehaibin
Tangshan
Lugou Bridge
Datong
Tianjin
Xingang
Lüshun
Lüda
Korea Bay
Bo Hai
Dunhuang
Yumen
Qilian Shan
Pingluo
Yinchuan
Mu Us Shamo
Great Wall
Huang He
Shijiazhuang
Dazhai
Taiyuan
Yangquan
Taihang Shan
North China Plain
Qiu Xian
Handan
Fengfeng
Anyang
Jinan
Zibo
Shengli
Yidu
Weifang
Yantai
Weihai
Shandong Peninsula
Qingdao
Tai Shan
Qaidam Pendi
Qinghai Hu
Xining
Baiyin
Lanzhou
Yan'an
Xi Xian
Fen He
Loesslands of China
Jining
Da Yunhe (Grand Canal)
Sanmen Gorge
Luoyang
Kaifeng
Zhengzhou
Baoji
Xi'an
Wei He
Qin Ling
Pingdingshan
Shangtang
Huai He
Nanjing
Zhenjiang
Ma'anshan
Changzhou
Wuxi
Baoshan
Shanghai
Hefei
Yixing
Suzhou
Tai Hu
Huangpu Jiang
Zhoushan Archipelago
Daba Shan
Han Shui
Chang Jiang (Yangtse)
Chengdu
Emei Shan 3099m
Three Gorges Dam
Yichang
Shashi
Wuhan
Huangshi
Daye
Huang Shan
Hangzhou
Ningbo
Lu Shan
Jiujiang
Chongqing
Dongting Hu
Yueyang
Poyang Hu
Jingdezhen
Nanchang
Fuchun Jiang
Wenzhou
Qamdo
Salween (Nu Jiang)
Mekong (Lancang Jiang)
Changsha
Xiangtan
Shaoshan
Zhuzhou
Pingxiang
Zunyi
Wu Jiang
Hengyang
Xiang Jiang
Luoxiao Shan
Gan Jiang
Nanping
Fuzhou
Taiwan Strait
Yungui Plateau
Dongchuan
Guiyang
Huangguoshu
Dali
Er Hai
Kunming
Guilin
Yangshuo
Gui Jiang
Nan Ling
Luizhou
Xiamen
Shantou
Conghua
Guangzhou (Canton)
Zhu Jiang (Pearl River)
Bei Jiang
Xi Jiang
Foshan
Shenzhen
Jiangmen
Zhuhai
Macau (Aomen)
Hong Kong (Xianggang)
Gejiu
Red (Yuan Jiang)
Black (Babian Jiang)
Xishuangbanna
Nanning
Maoming
Zhanjiang
Leizhou Peninsula
Hainan Strait
Haikou
Gulf of Tongking
Hainan
Korea Strait
China
Km 0 200 400 600 800
Miles 0 200 400

JAPAN

OFFICIAL NAME
Japan

CAPITAL
Tokyo

Area 377 750 km² (145 850 sq miles)
Population 126 505 000
Population density 335 per km² (867 per sq mile)
Population growth rate 0.4%
Life expectancy 76 (m); 83 (f)
Language Japanese
Adult literacy rate 99%
Currency yen (US $1 = 122 yen)
GDP (US million $) 4 368 300
GDP per head (US $) 34 556

Key dates

645 First emperor.
710 First capital, at Nara.
794 Capital moved to Kyoto.
1192-1867 Shoguns (military leaders) rule.
1639-1853 Japan closed to outside world.
1867-68 Revolution restores emperor's rule; Edo renamed Tokyo and made capital.
1889 New constitution.
1904-5 War with Russia.
1910 Annexes Korea.
1914-18 Joins Allies in World War I; wins Pacific territories.
1931 Invades and occupies Manchuria.
1937 Attacks China.
1941 Enters World War II, attacking US fleet at Pearl Harbor.
1945 Atomic bombs destroy Hiroshima and Nagasaki; surrenders.
1946 New constitution: emperor becomes constitutional monarch.
1952 Occupation ends.
1956 Joins UN.
1972 Okinawa and other islands lost in World War II returned.
1990s Financial crisis.

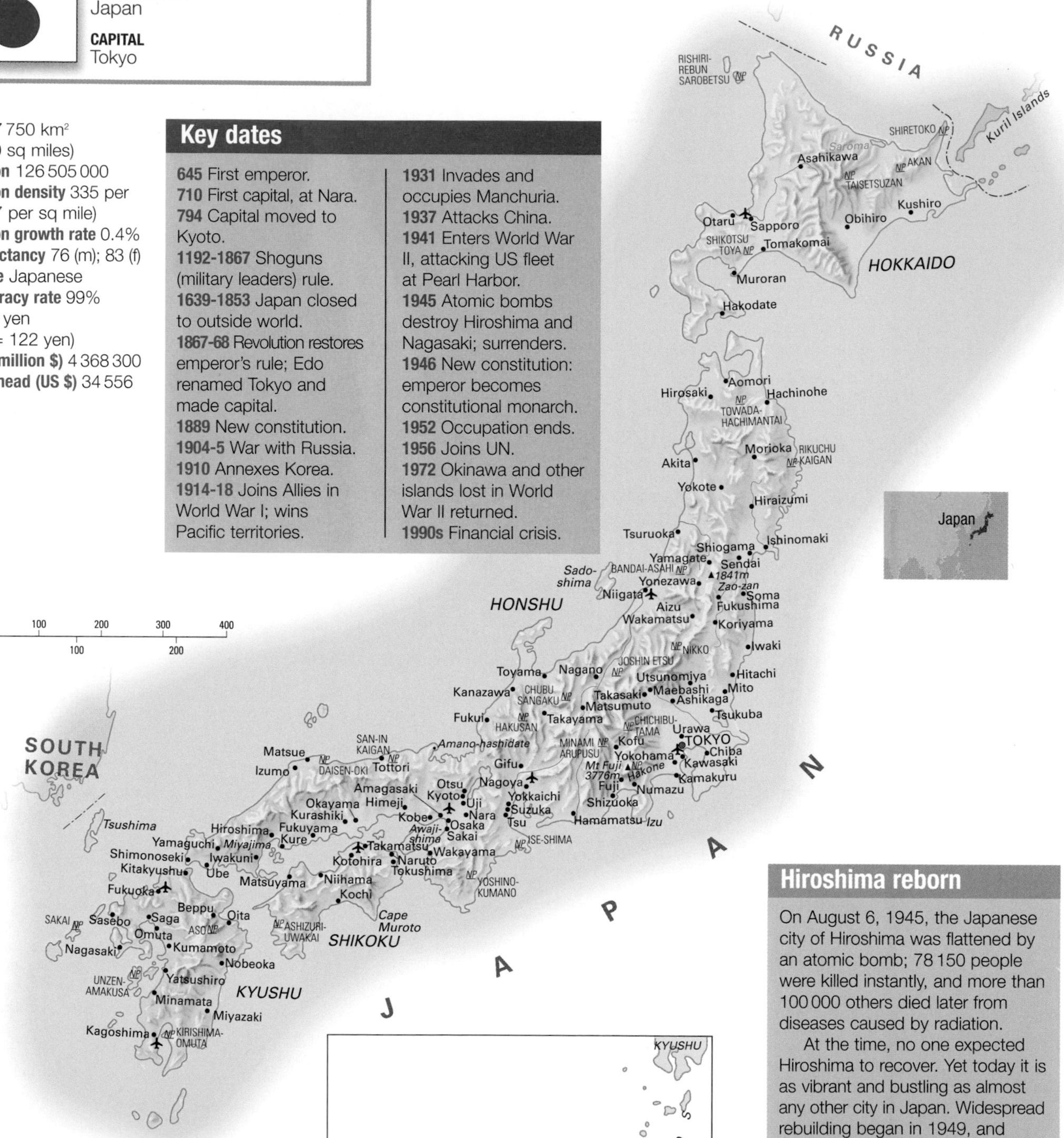

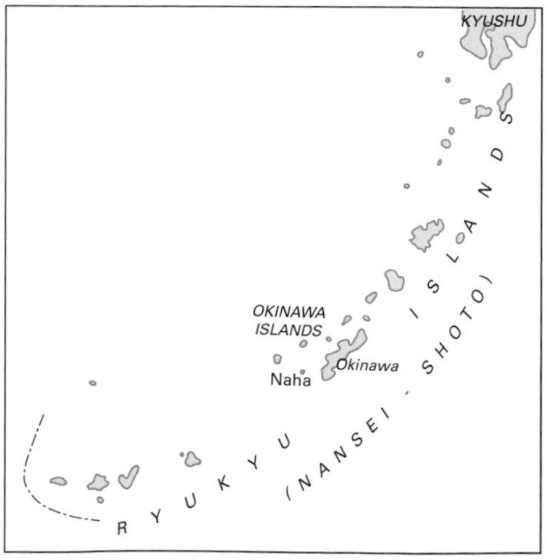

Hiroshima reborn

On August 6, 1945, the Japanese city of Hiroshima was flattened by an atomic bomb; 78 150 people were killed instantly, and more than 100 000 others died later from diseases caused by radiation.

At the time, no one expected Hiroshima to recover. Yet today it is as vibrant and bustling as almost any other city in Japan. Widespread rebuilding began in 1949, and Hiroshima is now home to more than 1 120 000 people. It processes food, builds ships and produces machinery, steel, motor vehicles and furniture.

Not that Hiroshima wants to forget its past. At the city's heart is a memorial: "Peace Park," with a gutted building left just as it was after the world's first nuclear attack. No amount of regeneration can erase the city's sad place in history.

KOREA'S LONG WAIT FOR RECONCILIATION

The first major conflict after World War II left Korea divided. But in August 2000, some South Koreans were finally able to embrace relatives cut off by the cease-fire line. A North Korean regime shaken by the breakup of the USSR, the death of its long-time dictator and the collapse of its economy, allowed two hundred to cross the heavily armed border. North and South Korean leaders had already met, and the construction of a rail link between the former enemies had begun. Asia's most dangerous border was beginning to open.

Half a century before, the Communist north had invaded the southern part of Korea. A US-led UN force drove the invaders back and then advanced almost to the Chinese border. China was drawn in, and its troops pushed the UN back. The three-year conflict saw the threat of nuclear war. A 1953 truce split the peninsula; despite the deaths of 37 000 GIs, this was America's first war without victory. But Communist expansion was blocked – the US had achieved its main objective, giving it the confidence to get involved in a similar war a decade later in Vietnam.

Tearful reunion Two family members separated by the division of Korea for 50 years greet each other during a brief border opening in August 2000.

NORTH KOREA

OFFICIAL NAME
Democratic People's Republic of Korea

CAPITAL
Pyongyang

Area 120 538 km²
(46 540 sq miles)
Population 23 702 000
Population density 194 per km² (502 per sq mile)
Population growth rate 1.8%
Life expectancy 68 (m); 74 (f)
Language Korean
Adult literacy rate 99%
Currency North Korean won
(US $1 = 2.20 won)
GDP (US million $) 4381
GDP per head (US $) 187

SOUTH KOREA

OFFICIAL NAME
The Republic of Korea

CAPITAL
Seoul

Area 99 392 km²
(38, 375 sq miles)
Population 46 858 000
Population density 467 per km² (1210 per sq mile)
Population growth rate 1%
Life expectancy 67 (m); 75 (f)
Language Korean
Adult literacy rate 98%
Currency South Korean won
(US $1 = 1313 won)
GDP (US million $) 395 300
GDP per head (US $) 8513

Key dates

1259-1368 Mongol rule.
1392-1910 Ruled by Yi dynasty of kings.
1910 Japan annexes.
1945 End of World War II: Soviet forces occupy northern Korea, US forces occupy southern Korea.
1948 Separate republics in north and south.
1950 North Korea invades South, starting Korean War; Chinese aid North Korea against US-led UN force.
1953 Cease-fire dividing North and South Korea.
1961 Military coup in South Korea.
1979 South Korean President Park killed.
1987 New constitution in South Korea after violent protests.
1991 Both join UN. Sign nonaggression pact.
1994 Kim Il Sung, North Korean leader, dies; succeeded by his son, Kim Jong Il.
2000 North-South summit; border opened for family reunions.

Thailand, Malaysia and Singapore

THAILAND

OFFICIAL NAME
The Kingdom of Thailand

CAPITAL
Bangkok

Area 513 115 km² (198 115 sq miles)
Population 60 606 947
Population density 119 per km² (309 per sq mile)
Population growth rate 0.8%
Life expectancy 64 (m); 69 (f)
Languages Thai, Chinese, Malay
Adult literacy rate 93.8%
Currency baht (US $1 = 45 baht)
GDP (US million $) 126 200
GDP per head (US $) 2062

Key dates

1238 Sukhotai kingdom.
1350 Ayutthaya kingdom established.
19th c. Treaties recognize Siam's independence.
1914-18 Supports Allies in World War I.
1932 Constitutional monarchy proclaimed.
1939 Changes name from Siam to Thailand.
1941-45 World War II: occupied by Japan; becomes unwilling ally.
1947 Military coup.
1965-72 Joins US-led forces in Vietnam War.
1973 Civilian rule.
1976-80 Military rule.
1991 Nonviolent military coup.

FACT Thailand is the only country in Southeast Asia never to have been colonized.

EAST ASIA'S "TIGER ECONOMIES"

Much of Southeast and eastern Asia experienced "miracle" economic growth in the 1980s only to see it halt in the mid-90s after several high-profile financial failures and stock market and exchange rate slumps. Leading the expansion were Thailand, Malaysia, Indonesia, Taiwan and South Korea – all at an early stage of development in the 1970s – as well as the well-established economies of Hong Kong and Singapore. They became known as the "tiger economies."

Thailand, for example, had a GNP growth rate of up to 10 percent per year – several times that of the US. Singapore became a clean, modern city and one of the world's great commercial and financial centers with Asia's second-highest standard of living (after Japan). Behind these powerhouses came China, a nation with the potential to outstrip them all.

The tiger economies' success was widely attributed to "Asian values": a combination of hard work, thrift and strong – even authoritarian – leadership. Many governments created sturdy financial markets by encouraging savings and promoting investment. They also intervened to support certain types of business through tax credits and subsidies.

Most of the "tigers" have improved the material situation of individual citizens, reducing gap between rich and poor. Between 1960 and 1990, the number of people living in poverty in Malaysia, for example, dropped from 37 percent of the population to less than 5 percent. Life expectancy increased from 56 to 71 between 1960 and 1990. But bust followed boom. The crisis began in 1997 and was triggered by a devaluation of the area's currencies. This caused loan defaults, because many debts were owed in foreign currencies. Land values dropped as fast as speculators had earlier sent them up. Authorities helped some troubled industries, but then the bubble burst and banks failed. As the 21st century began, international assistance was helping the region regain its confidence. But some economists warned of further trouble ahead.

Annual percentage growth rate in GNP

The GNP of the "tiger economies" grew much faster than the world average in 1980-89 (left) and 1990-98 (right).

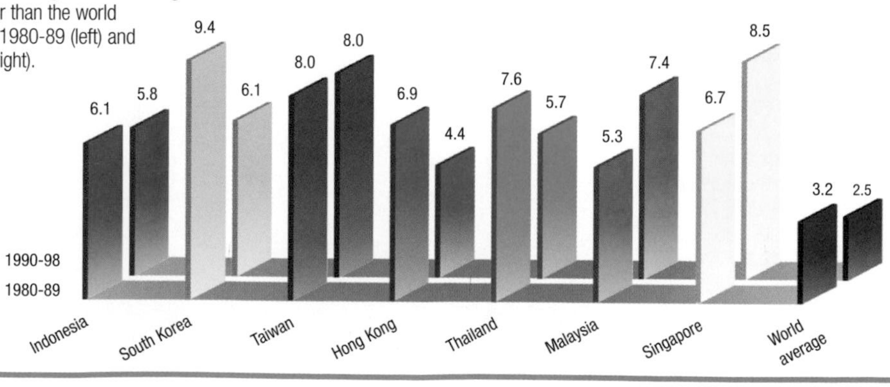

MALAYSIA

OFFICIAL NAME
Malaysia

CAPITAL
Kuala Lumpur

Area 329 758 km² (127 320 sq miles)
Population 22 712 000
Population density 67 per km² (174 per sq mile)
Population growth rate 2.5%
Life expectancy 68 (m); 73 (f)
Languages Malay (Bahasa Malaysia), English Chinese, Tamil, Iban
Adult literacy rate 83.5%
Currency ringgit (US $1 = 3.80 ringgits)
GDP (US million $) 81 700
GDP per head (US $) 3683

Key dates

16th-17th c. Portuguese, Dutch and British settle.
1867-on British colonial rule extended.
1941-45 Japanese occupation.
1948-54 Fighting against communist guerrillas.
1957 Malaya gains independence.
1963 Malaysia (Malaya, Sabah, Sarawak and Singapore) founded.
1963-65 "Confrontation" with Indonesia.
1965 Singapore secedes from Malaysia.
1967 Founding member of ASEAN.
1969 Anti-Chinese riots.
1987 Opposition activists arrested.

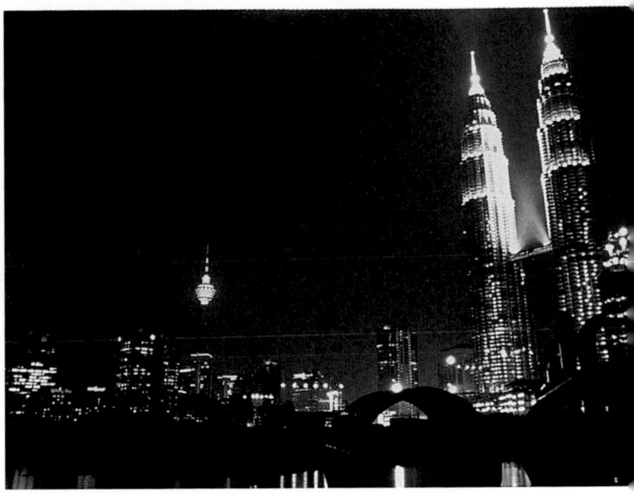

Standing tall Petronas Towers in Kuala Lumpur – the world's tallest office building in the year 2000 – symbolized Malaysia's rapid economic growth.

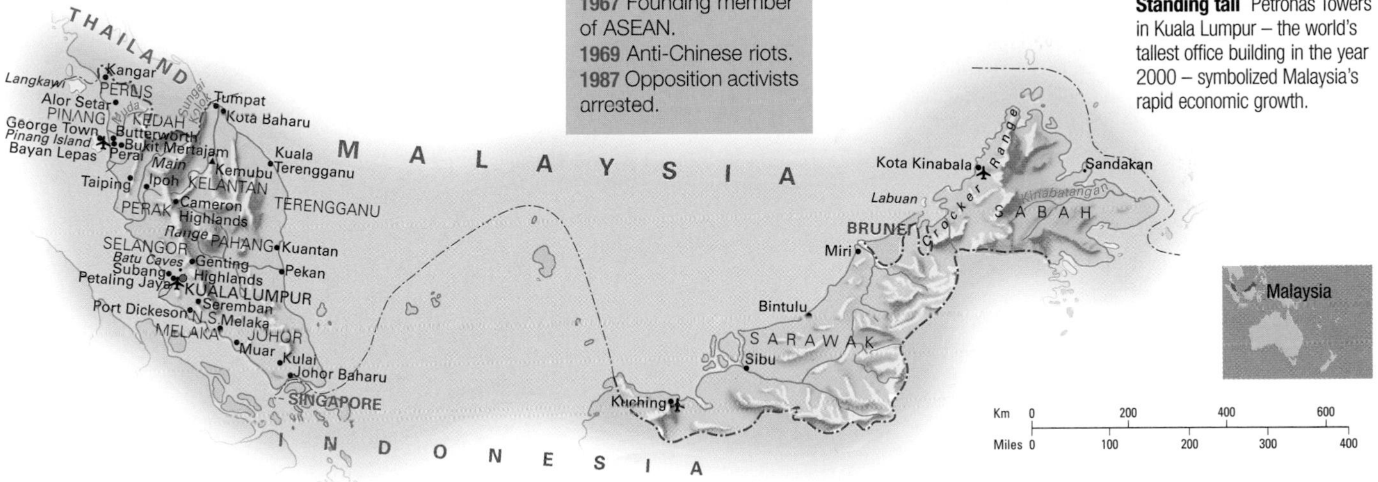

SINGAPORE

OFFICIAL NAME
The Republic of Singapore

CAPITAL
Singapore

Area 646 km² (249 sq miles)
Population 3 894 000
Population density 5991 per km² (15 511 per sq mile)
Population growth rate 3%
Life expectancy 74 (m); 78 (f)
Languages Malay, Chinese (Mandarin), Tamil, English
Adult literacy rate 91.1%
Currency Singapore dollar (US $1 = 1.81 Singapore dollars)
GDP (US million $) 91 800
GDP per head (US $) 23 720

Key dates

1819 Thomas S. Raffles founds Singapore.
1867 Straits Settlements become British colony.
1942-45 Japanese occupation.
1946 Separate colony.
1959 Self-government.
1963 Joins Malaya, Sarawak and Sabah to form Malaysia.
1965 Secedes from Malaysia; becomes independent republic.
1991 Powers of the presidency increased.
1993 First direct election for president.

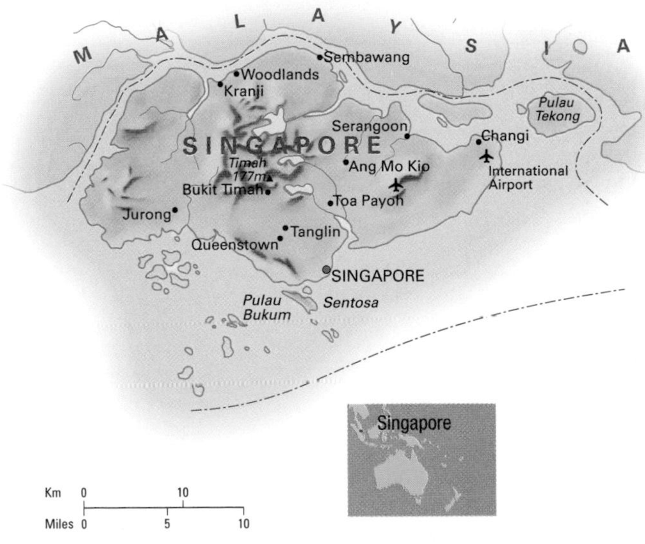

Vietnam, Cambodia, Laos and Taiwan

VIETNAM

OFFICIAL NAME
The Socialist Republic of Vietnam

CAPITAL
Hanoi

Area 331 114 km² (127 844 sq miles)
Population 76 324 753
Population density 234 per km² (607 per sq mile)
Population growth rate 1.3%
Life expectancy 63 (m); 67 (f)
Language Vietnamese and many local languages
Adult literacy rate 93.7%
Currency dông (US $1 = 14 561 dông)
GDP (US million $) 27 800
GDP per head (US $) 358

FACT
The Ho Chi Minh Trail, used to supply Vietcong forces, included over 300 km (200 miles) of tunnels.

Key dates

111 B.C. Chinese rule.
A.D. 939 Independence.
1858-83 French take control.
1941-45 World War II: Japanese control.
1945 Ho Chi Minh proclaims Democratic Republic of Vietnam.
1946 French begin to fight Vietminh forces.
1954 French defeated at Dien Bien Phu; Vietnam divided – communists control North Vietnam.
1957 Vietcong guerrillas attack South Vietnam.
1964 US starts air strikes against North.
1973 Cease-fire; US troops withdraw.
1975 Communists take Saigon; war ends.
1976 Socialist Republic of Vietnam proclaimed.
1978-79 Attacks Khmer Rouge in Cambodia.
1979 Border war with China.
1989 Withdraws from Cambodia.
1995 Diplomatic relations with US established.

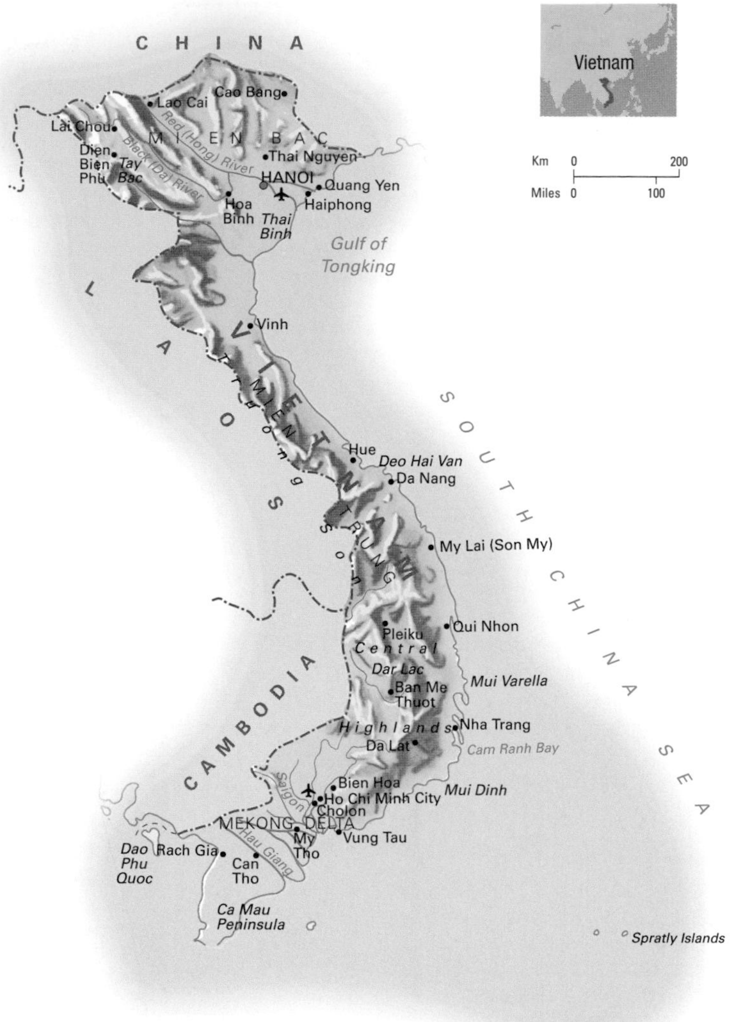

CAMBODIA

OFFICIAL NAME
The Kingdom of Cambodia

CAPITAL
Phnom Penh

Area 181 035 km² (69 898 sq miles)
Population 10 945 000
Population density 63 per km² (164 per sq mile)
Population growth rate 4.1%
Life expectancy 50 (m); 52 (f)
Language Khmer
Adult literacy rate 35%
Currency riel (US $1 = 3835 riels)
GDP (US million $) 3100
GDP per head (US $) 270

Key dates

7th c. Khmer Empire.
1863 French establish protectorate.
1941-45 World War II: Japanese control.
1953 Independence.
1970 Coup; monarchy abolished. Civil war.
1975 Khmer Rouge led by Pol Pot takes power.
1976-78 Khmer Rouge kills more than 2.5 million.
1978-79 Vietnam helps depose Khmer Rouge.
1992 Guerrilla war with Khmer Rouge begins.
1993 King restored.
1999 Joins ASEAN.

LAOS

OFFICIAL NAME
The Lao People's Democratic Republic

CAPITAL
Vientiane

Area 236 800 km² (91 400 sq miles)
Population 5 297 000
Population density 22 per km² (56 per sq mile)
Population growth rate 2.1%
Life expectancy 49 (m); 52 (f)
Languages Lao (Laotian), French and many local languages
Adult literacy rate 56.6%
Currency new kip (US $1 = 7600 new kips)
GDP (US million $) 1500
GDP per head (US $) 290

Key dates

1893 Becomes French protectorate.
1941-45 World War II: Japanese control.
1949 Self-government within French Union.
1954 Full independence.
1960-73 Intermittent civil war between communist and right-wing forces.
1975 Communists seize power; Vietnam sends troops in support.
1989 Open elections.
1991 New constitution.
1997 Joins ASEAN.

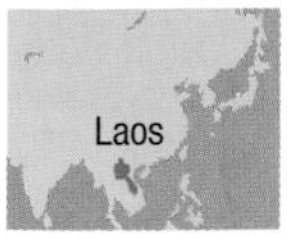

TAIWAN

OFFICIAL NAME
The Republic of China

CAPITAL
Taipei

Area 36 000 km² (13 900 sq miles)
Population 21 740 000
Population density 604 per km² (1564 per sq mile)
Population growth rate 1.2%
Life expectancy 72 (m); 78 (f)
Languages Northern Chinese (Mandarin), Taiwanese
Adult literacy rate 93.7%
Currency Taiwan dollar (US $1 = 32.8 Taiwan dollars)
GDP (US million $) 287 000
GDP per head (US $) 13 201

Key dates

1895-1945 Japanese control after Sino-Japanese War.
1949 Chiang Kai-shek's Nationalists arrive after mainland China falls to communists.
1954 US defense treaty.
1971 Expelled from UN.
1972 US forces leave.
1979 US ends treaty and official relations.
1987 Opposition political parties allowed.
1991 Ends state of civil war with China.
1991-92 Open elections.

SOUTHEAST ASIA'S ROAD TO PEACE

The former French Indochina was heavily scarred by war in the 20th century. Yet, as the new century began, the old colonies of Laos, Cambodia and Vietnam were enjoying peace and economic progress.

Cambodia and Laos moved toward democracy with multiparty elections. Vietnam turned its efforts to invigorating its economy, developing tourism and an oil industry. The United States helped by dropping its 30-year trade embargo in 1994, and the following year the two former enemies reestablished diplomatic relations.

The journey from colonial rule to prosperous independence was often violent for all three countries. After World War II, France's offer of autonomy for its Asian empire was accepted by Laos and Cambodia. But the Vietnamese wanted full independence and fought a successful war against the French only to see their country divided by an anticommunist movement in the South.

Civil wars led to communist victories in 1975 in all three former colonies. The North Vietnamese and Vietcong (South Vietnamese communist guerrillas) prevailed in the 18-year Vietnam War despite American intervention. In Laos, the communist Pathet Lao took power, but ten years later introduced political liberalization, a market economy and, in 1989, multiparty elections. In Cambodia, the extremist Khmer Rouge regime killed more than 2.5 million of its own people before it was removed by Vietnamese military intervention. Free elections were held in 1993, and the same year, a new constitution restored the monarchy.

The past behind him A statue of Ho Chi Minh overshadows Bill Clinton. His visit to Vietnam in 2000 was the first by a US president since the Vietnam War.

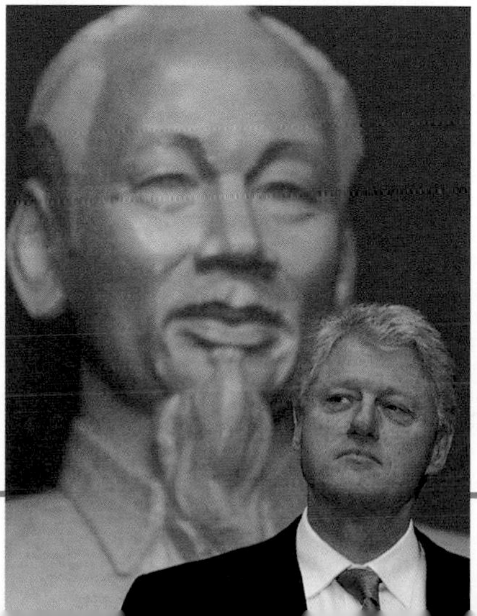

THE PHILIPPINES

OFFICIAL NAME
The Republic of the Philippines

CAPITAL
Manila

Area 300 000 km² (115 831 sq miles)
Population 82 842 000
Population density 276 per km² (715 per sq mile)
Population growth rate 1.9%
Life expectancy 63 (m); 67 (f)
Languages Filipino (based on Tagalog), English and many other local languages
Adult literacy rate 94.6%
Currency Philippine peso (US $1 = 50 pesos)
GDP (US million $) 77 500
GDP per head (US $) 1031

FACT

The Jeepney – a taxi converted from an army jeep – is a mainstay of Manila's public transport system.

Key dates

1521 Magellan lands.
1565 Becomes Spanish colony.
1898 Spanish-American war: ceded to US.
1942-45 Japanese occupation.
1946 Independence from US.
1967 Founding member of ASEAN.
1972-81 Martial law during fighting against Muslim separatist and communist guerrillas.
1983 Opposition leader Benigno Aquino killed.
1986 President Marcos deposed; Aquino's widow wins presidency.
1992 US forces leave.
1996 Peace treaty with Islamic separatists.
2000 Islamic separatists declare jihad (holy war); extremists take Filipino and Western hostages.
2001 President Estrada ousted; President Arroyo assumes power.

BRUNEI

OFFICIAL NAME
The Sultanate of Brunei

CAPITAL
Bandar Seri Begawan

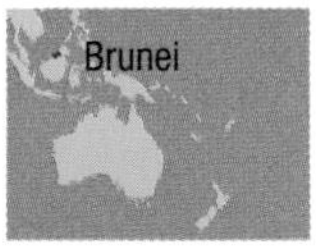

Area 5765 km² (2226 sq miles)
Population 344 000
Population density 60 per km² (154 per sq mile)
Population growth rate 1.8%
Life expectancy 70 (m); 73 (f)
Languages Malay, Chinese, English
Adult literacy rate 89%
Currency Brunei dollar (US $1 = 1.81 Brunei dollars)
GDP (US million $) 4850
GDP per head (US $) 15 645

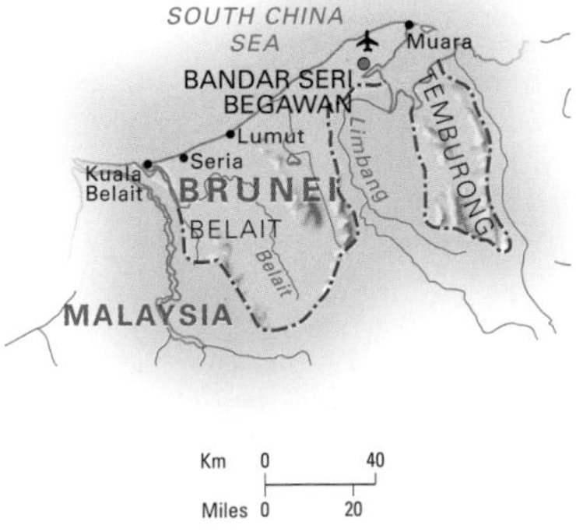

Key dates

15th c. First sultanate of Brunei established.
15th-16th c. Controls most of north Borneo and part of Philippines.
19th c. Loses much territory to Britain.
1888 Becomes British protectorate.
1929 Oil discovered.
1942-45 Japanese occupation.
1962 Abandons plans to join Malaysia.
1984 Full independence; joins ASEAN and UN.

FACT

The world's biggest residental palace – 1788 rooms, 257 bathrooms and garage space for 153 cars – belongs to the Sultan of Brunei.

INDONESIA

OFFICIAL NAME
The Republic of Indonesia

CAPITAL
Jakarta

Area 1 919 317 km² (741 053 sq miles)
Population 228 438 000
Population density 119 per km² (308 per sq mile)
Population growth rate 1.2%
Life expectancy 61 (m); 64 (f)
Languages Indonesian (Bahasa Indonesia, a form of Malay) and many local languages
Adult literacy rate 83.8%

Currency rupiah (US $1 = 11 775 rupiah)
GDP (US million $) 153 400
GDP per head (US $) 750

Key dates

16th-17th c. Portuguese, Dutch trading posts.
1799 Dutch rule.
1942-45 Japanese occupation.
1949 Independence.
1950 Joins UN.
1963 Dutch cede West New Guinea. Sukarno "president for life."
1963-65 "Confrontation" with Malaysia.
1965 Communist coup attempt; many killed. Suharto gains power.
1967 Suharto displaces Sukarno. Founding member of ASEAN.
1976 Takes East Timor.
1991 Sumatra rebellion; East Timor massacre.
1998 Riots in Jakarta; Suharto resigns.
1999 Quits East Timor.

After the fires A Borneo villager replants after forest fires caused widespread damage in the late 1990s. Smoke spread over much of Southeast Asia.

EAST TIMOR

OFFICIAL NAME
East Timor

CAPITAL
Dili

Area 14 604 km² (5637 sq miles)
Population 749 000
Population density 51 per km² (133 per sq mile)
Population growth rate 3.9%
Life expectancy 49 (m); 51 (f)
Languages Tetum, Portuguese, Bahasa Indonesia

Adult literacy rate Not available
Currency US dollar
GDP (US million $) Not available
GDP per head (US $) Not available

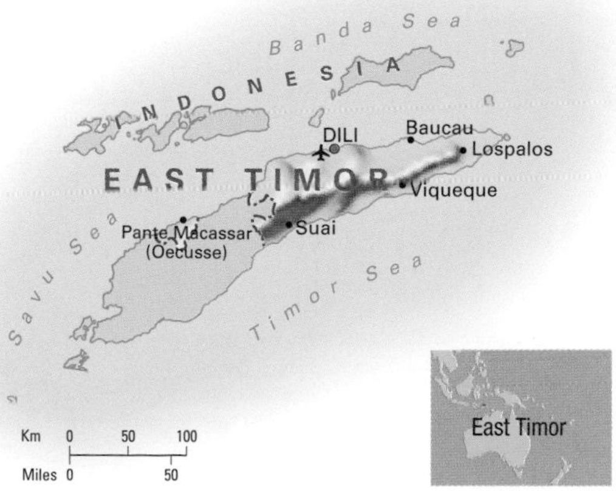

Key dates

16th c. Colonized by Portugal.
1975 Annexed by Indonesia; opposition suppressed.
1991 Indonesian troops open fire on protesters in Dili.
1999 Violence follows vote for independence; UN force restores order; Indonesia withdraws.
2001 Democratic elections.
2002 Full independence.

Australia and New Zealand

AUSTRALIA

OFFICIAL NAME
The Commonwealth of Australia

CAPITAL
Canberra

Area 7 682 300 km² (2 966 153 sq miles)
Population 18 967 000
Population density 2 per km² (6 per sq mile)
Population growth rate 0.8%
Life expectancy 75 (m); 80 (f)
Languages English, plus about 200 Aboriginal and many European and Asian languages
Adult literacy rate 95%
Currency Australian dollar (US $1 = 1.70 Australian dollars)
GDP (US million $) 389 800
GDP per head (US $) 20 811

Key dates

1770 Claimed by Britain.
1788 First penal colony.
1850-90 Six colonies gain self-government.
1870 Last convicts sent.
1901 Colonies unite as Commonwealth (federation) of Australia.
1902 Women win vote.
1914-18 One of Allies in World War I.
1927 Canberra becomes federal capital.
1939-45 One of Allies in World War II.
1942 Ratifies 1931 Statute of Westminster, giving independence within Commonwealth.
1951 Founds ANZUS security pact with New Zealand and US.
1965-72 Troops fight in Vietnam alongside US.
1967 Referendum gives Aborigines citizenship.
1986 Australia Act ends last British legal power.
1992 Land rights awarded to Aborigines.
1999 Referendum vote against republic.

The peopling of Australia

Proportion of Australians born overseas

One in five people living in Australia have moved there from another country. The figures are from 1996.

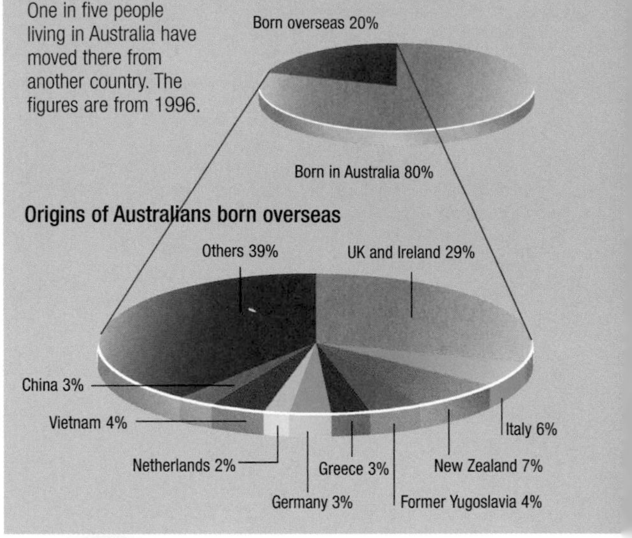

When the first British convict fleet landed at Sydney on January 26, 1788, Australia was considered *terra nullius* – unoccupied land. That definition of Australia remained fixed in law for more than 200 years.

The anniversary of the first convict landing has been celebrated every year since 1833; in 1931 it was named Australia Day. But as the bicentennial Australia Day approached in 1988, indigenous groups were proclaiming a quite different view of 1788. Far from being "unoccupied," they pointed out, Australia had a native population of at least 750 000 at the time of British settlement.

Australia's Aborigines declared 1988 "a year of mourning," and conducted their own protest march for "Freedom, Justice and Hope." Since then, Australia Day has been turned into a community day that celebrates the cultural diversity of the nation. In 1992, the Australian High Court overturned the concept of *terra nullius* and ruled that Aborigines could claim ownership of land.

Since World War II, waves of new settlers – at first only from Europe, but later from a wider pool – have led to a more diverse society. About 20 percent of today's Australians were born overseas. More than 100 languages are now spoken in addition to English. Added to those are about 200 indigenous languages spoken by the 386 000 Aboriginal and Torres Strait Islander people.

Australia used the 2000 Sydney Olympic Games to highlight its cultural diversity, and Canberra holds its own National Multicultural Festival each year. The country has also made moves to redress the historical injustices borne by indigenous people – ranging from massacres in the early years of the colony to the "theft" of Aboriginal children to be raised by foster parents in the mid-20th century. In 1996, a parliamentary statement made a commitment to reconciliation with Aboriginal and Torres Strait Islander people, "redressing their profound social and economic disadvantage."

The processes of ethnic integration and reconciliation have not always been smooth, and there has often been political opposition raised against them. But Stephen Fitzgerald, a former Australian ambassador to China, says, "We cannot clutch at . . . a white man's world now gone . . . We have to be Australian and not European."

NEW ZEALAND

OFFICIAL NAME
New Zealand

CAPITAL
Wellington

Area 270 534 km² (104 454 sq miles)
Population 3 811 000
Population density 14 per km² (36 per sq mile)
Population growth rate 0.9%
Life expectancy 73 (m); 79 (f)
Languages English, Maori
Adult literacy rate 99%
Currency New Zealand dollar (US $1 = 2.41 New Zealand dollars)
GDP (US million $) 52 400
GDP per head (US $) 13 825

Key dates

10th c. First Maori arrive from Pacific Islands.
1769 Capt Cook lands.
1840 Treaty of Waitangi: becomes British colony.
1852 Self-government.
1860-72 Wars over right to buy Maori land.
1893 Women gain vote.
1914-18 One of Allies in World War I.
1939-45 One of Allies in World War II.
1947 Ratifies 1931 Statute of Westminster, giving independence within Commonwealth.
1951 Founds ANZUS security pact with Australia and US.
1985 "Nuclear-free" policy introduced. French agents sink Greenpeace nuclear protest ship *Rainbow Warrior* at Auckland.
1988 Agrees to free trade pact with Australia.
1993 Referendum in favour of proportional representation.

FACT
About 75 percent of New Zealanders live on North Island, with almost a third clustered around Auckland.

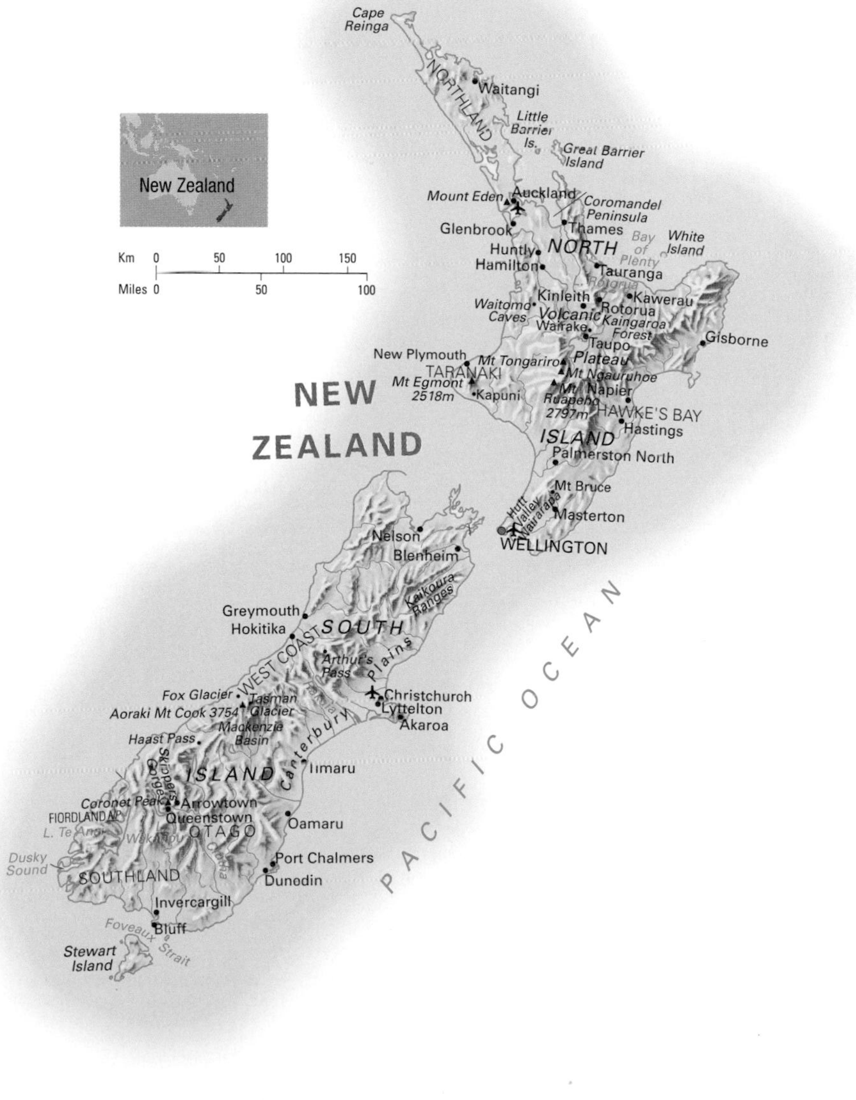

KIRIBATI

OFFICIAL NAME The Republic of Kiribati

CAPITAL Bairiki, on Tarawa

Independence 1979
Area 810 km² (313 sq miles)
Population 82 000
Population density 100 per km² (259 per sq mile)
Population growth rate 1.5%
Life expectancy 58 (m); 58 (f)
Languages I-Kiribati (Gilbertese), English
Adult literacy rate 90%
Currency Australian dollar (US $1 = 1.70 Australian dollars)
GDP (US million $) 51
GDP per head (US $) 654

MARSHALL ISLANDS

OFFICIAL NAME The Republic of the Marshall Islands

CAPITAL Dalap-Uliga-Darrit, on Majuro

Independence 1986
Area 180 km² (70 sq miles)
Population 61 000
Population density 339 per km² (871 per sq mile)
Population growth rate 3%
Life expectancy 64 (m); 68 (f)
Languages English, Marshallese, Japanese
Adult literacy rate 91%
Currency US dollar
GDP (US million $) 91
GDP per head (US $) 1649

FIJI

OFFICIAL NAME The Republic of Fiji Islands

CAPITAL Suva, on Viti Levu

Independence 1970
Area 18 376 km² (7095 sq miles)
Population 806 000
Population density 44 per km² (113 per sq mile)
Population growth rate 1.4%
Life expectancy 70 (m); 74 (f)
Languages Fijian, Hindi, English
Adult literacy rate 91.6%
Currency Fiji dollar (US $1 = 2.28 Fiji dollars)
GDP (US million $) 1808
GDP per head (US $) 2260

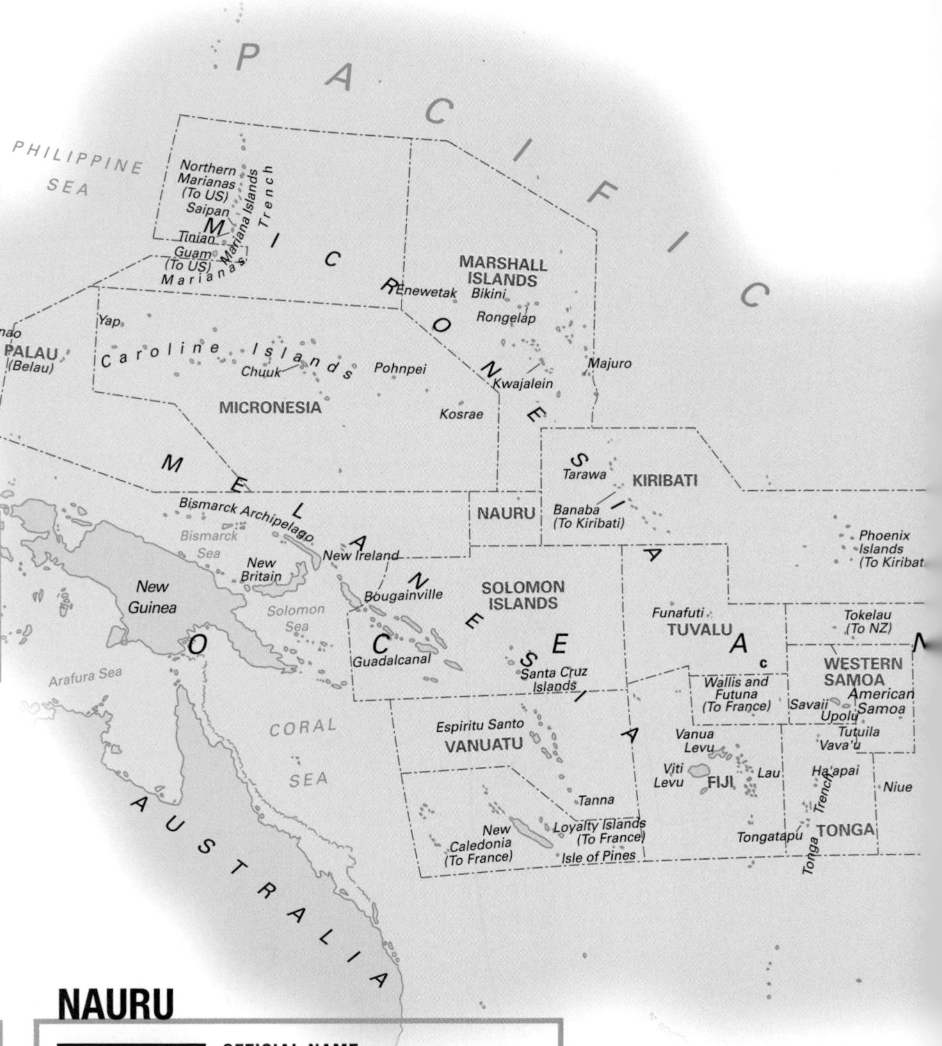

MICRONESIA

OFFICIAL NAME The Federated States of Micronesia

CAPITAL Palikir, on Pohnpei

Independence 1986
Area 700 km² (270 sq miles)
Population 116 000
Population density 157 per km² (407 per sq mile)
Population growth rate 1.8%
Life expectancy 71 (m); 71 (f)
Languages English, Trukese, Pohnpeian, Yapese
Adult literacy rate 90%
Currency US dollar
GDP (US million $) 259
GDP per head (US $) 2104

PALAU

OFFICIAL NAME The Republic of Palau

CAPITAL Koror, on Koror

Independence 1994
Area 508 km² (196 sq miles)
Population 18 000
Population density 39 per km² (102 per sq mile)
Population growth rate 2.1%
Life expectancy 60 (m); 63 (f)
Languages Palauan, English
Adult literacy rate 92%
Currency US dollar
GDP (US million $) 109
GDP per head (US $) 5450

NAURU

OFFICIAL NAME The Republic of Nauru

CAPITAL No official capital

Independence 1968
Area 21 km² (8 sq miles)
Population 11 000
Population density 516 per km² (1341 per sq mile)
Population growth rate 2.3%
Life expectancy 57 (m); 65 (f)
Languages Nauruan, English
Adult literacy rate 99%
Currency Australian dollar (US $1 = 1.70 Australian dollars)
GDP (US million $) 368
GDP per head (US $) 33 476

SAMOA

OFFICIAL NAME
The Independent State of Samoa

CAPITAL
Apia, on Upolu

Independence 1962
Area 2831 km² (1093 sq miles)
Population 169 000
Population density 59 per km² (154 per sq mile)
Population growth rate 0.5%
Life expectancy 64 (m); 70 (f)
Languages Samoan, English
Adult literacy rate 97%
Currency tala (Samoan dollar) (US $1 = 3.05 tala)
GDP (US million $) 179
GDP per head (US $) 1065

PAPUA NEW GUINEA

OFFICIAL NAME
The Independent State of Papua New Guinea

CAPITAL
Port Moresby

Independence 1975
Area 462 840 km² (178 704 sq miles)
Population 4 702 000
Population density 10 per km² (26 per sq mile)
Population growth rate 2.2%
Life expectancy 55 (m); 57 (f)
Languages Pidgin, English, Motu and many local languages
Adult literacy rate 72.2%
Currency kina (US $1 = 3.07 kina)
GDP (US million $) 3600
GDP per head (US $) 782

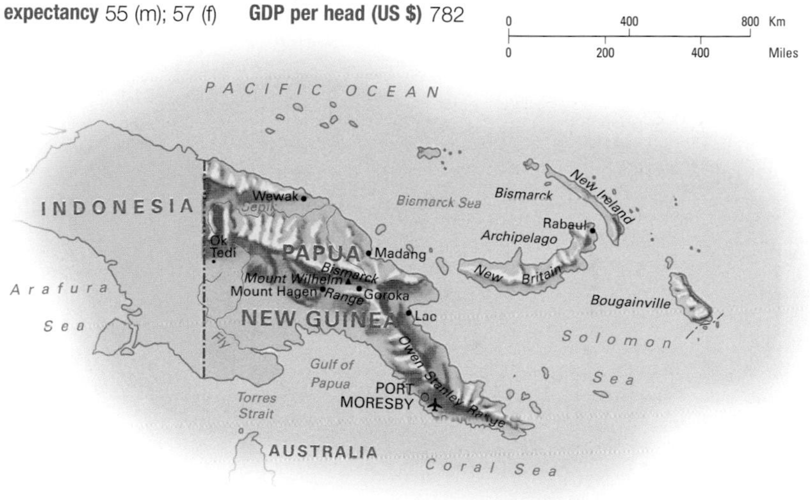

TUVALU

OFFICIAL NAME
Tuvalu

CAPITAL
Vaiaku, on Funafuti

Independence 1978
Area 26 km² (10 sq miles)
Population 11 000
Population density 385 per km² (1000 per sq mile)
Population growth rate 0%
Life expectancy 64 (m); 69 (f)
Languages Tuvaluan, English
Adult literacy rate 95%
Currency Australian dollar (US $1 = 1.70 Australian dollars)
GDP (US million $) 9
GDP per head (US $) 900

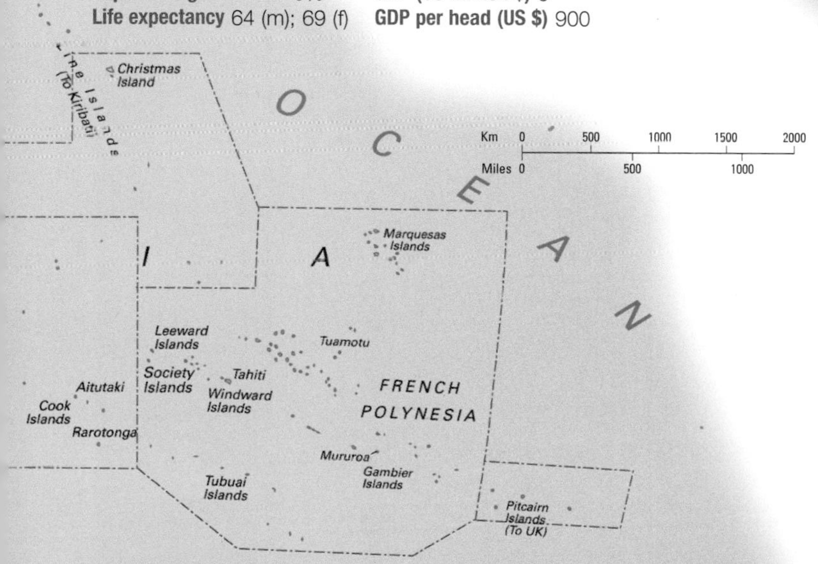

TONGA

OFFICIAL NAME
The Kingdom of Tonga

CAPITAL
Nuku'alofa, on Tongatapu

Independence 1970
Area 748 km² (289 sq miles)
Population 98 000
Population density 134 per km² (346 per sq mile)
Population growth rate 0.8%
Life expectancy 66 (m); 70 (f)
Languages Tongan, English
Adult literacy rate 93%
Currency pa'anga (Tongan dollar) (US $1 = 1.92 pa'anga)
GDP (US million $) 279
GDP per head (US $) 2790

VANUATU

OFFICIAL NAME
The Republic of Vanuatu

CAPITAL
Port Vila, on Efate

Independence 1980
Area 12 190 km² (4707 sq miles)
Population 186 000
Population density 15 per km² (38 per sq mile)
Population growth rate 2.5%
Life expectancy 63 (m); 67 (f)
Languages Bislama, English, French and many local languages
Adult literacy rate 53%
Currency vatu (US $1 = 146 vatu)
GDP (US million $) 245
GDP per head (US $) 1376

SOLOMON ISLANDS

OFFICIAL NAME
Solomon Islands

CAPITAL
Honiara, on Guadalcanal

Independence 1978
Area 27 556 km² (10 639 sq miles)
Population 430 000
Population density 15 per km² (39 per sq mile)
Population growth rate 3.4%
Life expectancy 68 (m); 73 (f)
Languages English, Melanesian, Pidgin and other local languages
Adult literacy rate 60%
Currency Solomon Islands dollar (US $1 = SI $5.27)
GDP (US million $) 319
GDP per head (US $) 759

Morocco, Algeria, Libya and Tunisia

MOROCCO

OFFICIAL NAME
The Kingdom of Morocco

CAPITAL
Rabat

Area 710 850 km² (274 461 sq miles)
Population 28 238 000
Population density 39 per km² (101 per sq mile)
Population growth rate 1.4%
Life expectancy 62 (m); 66 (f)
Languages Arabic, Berber, Spanish, French
Adult literacy rate 43.7%
Currency Moroccan dirham (US $1 = 10.86 dirhams)
GDP (US million $) 36 500
GDP per head (US $) 1313

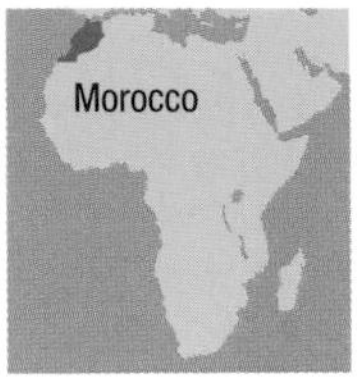

Key dates

680s Arab invasion.
19th c. France and Spain establish control.
1912 Divided between French and Spanish.
1953-55 Guerrilla liberation war.
1956 Independence from France (small Spanish enclaves remain).
1957 Sultan takes title of king.
1962 New constitution.
1965-70 State of emergency declared.
1975 Western Sahara ceded to Morocco and Mauritania but Polisario Front guerrillas claim full independence.
1979 Morocco occupies all of Western Sahara; Mauritania ends claim.
1991 Cease-fire in Western Sahara.
2001 Polisario Front threatens new war.

ALGERIA

OFFICIAL NAME
The Democratic and Popular Republic of Algeria

CAPITAL
Algiers

Area 2 381 741 km² (919 595 sq miles)
Population 30 774 000
Population density 13 per km² (32 per sq mile)
Population growth rate 1.6%
Life expectancy 65 (m); 66 (f)
Languages Arabic, French, Berber
Adult literacy rate 61.6%
Currency Algerian dinar (US $1 = 75 dinars)
GDP (US million $) 47 200
GDP per head (US $) 1583

Key dates

7th c. Arab invasion.
1518 Ottoman rule.
1830-1914 French extend colonial control.
1954 National Liberation Front (FLN) starts guerrilla liberation war.
1962 Independence from France.
1965 Military coup.
1967 Declares war on Israel; severs diplomatic relations with US.
1989 New multiparty constitution. Islamic Salvation Front (FIS) founded.
1991 FIS wins election.
1992 Military control; election nullified. FIS threatens holy war.
1996 New constitution.
1999 Terrorist amnesty, but violence continues.

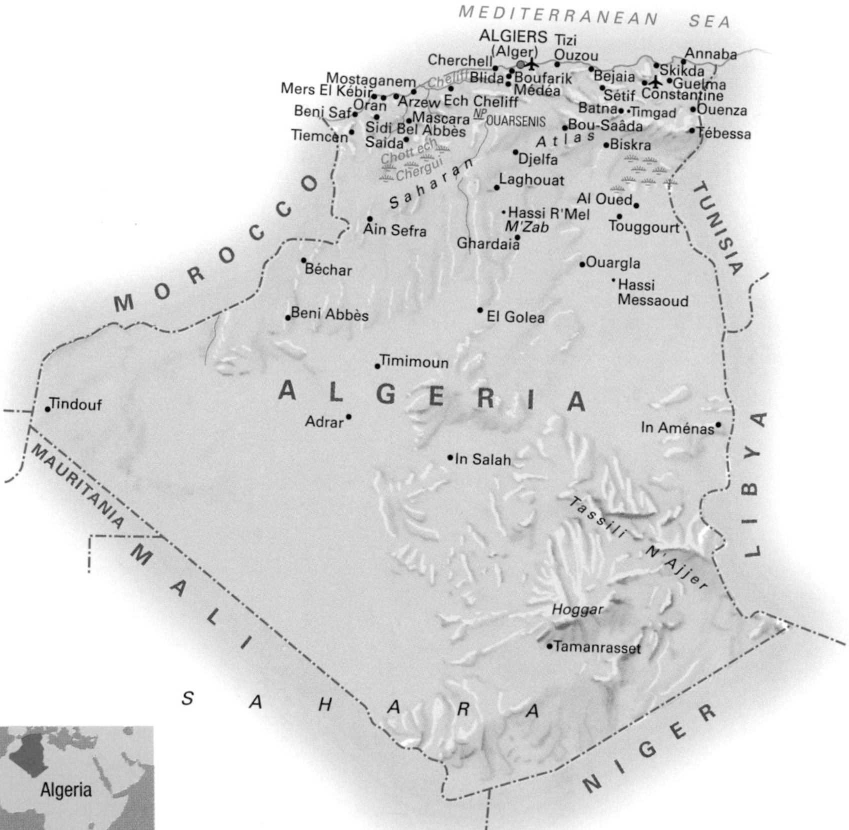

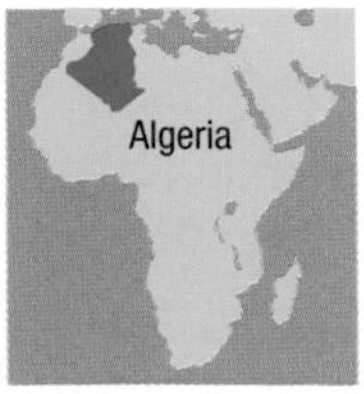

LIBYA

OFFICIAL NAME
The Great Socialist People's Libyan Arab Jamahiriya

CAPITAL
Tripoli

Area 1 775 500 km² (685 524 sq miles)
Population 5 471 000
Population density 3 per km² (8 per sq mile)
Population growth rate 3.6%
Life expectancy 62 (m); 65 (f)
Languages Arabic, English, Italian
Adult literacy rate 76.2%
Currency Libyan dinar (US $1 = 0.55 dinar)
GDP (US million $) 34 970
GDP per head (US $) 6393

Key dates

640s Arab invasion.
1551 Becomes part of Ottoman Empire.
1911 Italian invasion.
1951 Independence gained as kingdom.
1969 Military coup led by Colonel Gaddafi leads to formation of Arab Republic.
1977 Border war with Egypt.
1983 Invades Chad.
1986 Diplomatic ties cut by US because of support for terrorists. US attacks Libyan boats and bases.
1987 Chad troops force Libyan withdrawal.
1989 Further US attack.
1992 UN sanctions imposed when suspects alleged to have bombed US airliner over Scotland are not handed over.
1996 UN extends sanctions to countries investing in Libya.

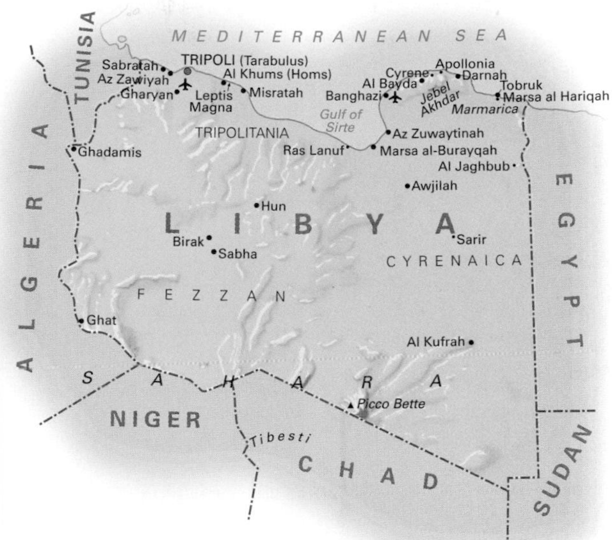

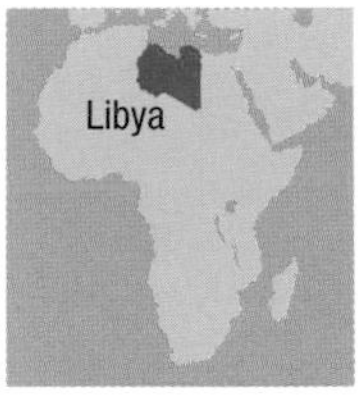

TUNISIA

OFFICIAL NAME
The Republic of Tunisia

CAPITAL
Tunis

Area 163 610 km² (63 170 sq miles)
Population 9 457 000
Population density 57 per km² (148 per sq mile)
Population growth rate 1.1%
Life expectancy 69 (m); 73 (f)
Languages Arabic, Berber, French
Adult literacy rate 66.7%
Currency Tunisian dinar (US $1 = 1.41 dinars)
GDP (US million $) 20 700
GDP per head (US $) 2218

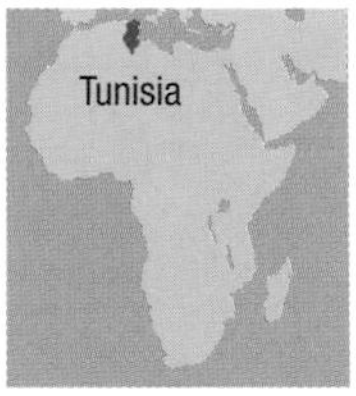

Key dates

7th c. Arab invasion.
1574 Becomes part of Ottoman Empire.
1881 French impose protectorate.
1955 Internal self-government.
1956 Full independence from France.
1957 Republic; Habib Bourguiba president.
1967 Joins Arab forces in Six-Day War against Israel.
1975 Bourguiba named president for life.
1985-88 Cuts diplomatic relations with Libya.
1987 Prime minister Ben Ali deposes Bourguiba.
1991 Measures against Islamic fundamentalism.
1995 Signs Association Agreement with European Union.

THE DESERT'S ADAPTABLE HERDERS

The Bedouin, nomadic herders of the Arabian, Sahara and Syrian deserts, have slowly adapted to modern life. Some still live in tents and roam traditional areas, breeding camels, horses, goats, sheep and cattle. Their tribes are still led by a sheikh and his council of elders, but modern governments want settled citizens, so most Bedouin have taken to a more sedentary lifestyle.

Although many urban Bedouin earn a living from handicrafts or manual labor, Bedouin families produce many doctors, lawyers, scientists and businessmen.

The Bedouin call themselves *Ahl-el-beit* (People of the Tent). They originated in Arabia but by the 7th century had spread to Syria and Egypt, then into Tunisia around 1050. They lived by trading in camels, offering protection along the caravan trade routes – and raiding their neighbors. From the 1920s on, motor transportation began to move commercial goods, and governments put an end to profitable theft.

The Bedouin have adjusted to change without surrendering their traditional values of honor, dignity, bravery and hospitality.

Egypt, Sudan, Eritrea, Ethiopia and Djibouti

EGYPT

OFFICIAL NAME
The Arab Republic of Egypt

CAPITAL
Cairo

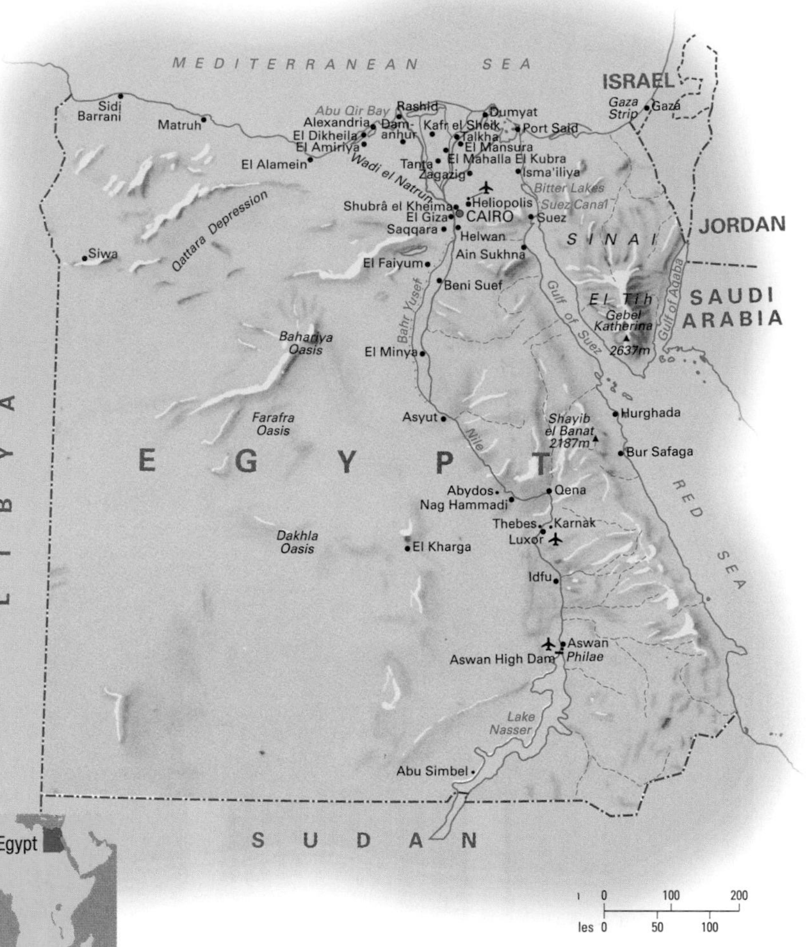

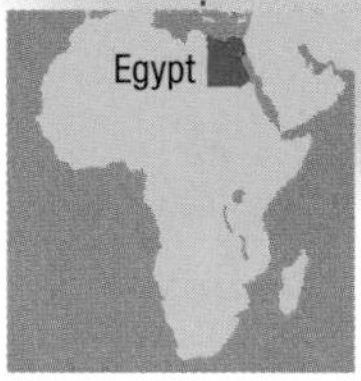

Area 997 738 km² (385 229 sq miles)
Population 67 226 000
Population density 66 per km² (171 per sq mile)
Population growth rate 3.4%
Life expectancy 63 (m); 66 (f)
Languages Arabic, English, French
Adult literacy rate 51.4%
Currency Egyptian pound (US $1 = 3.88 Egyptian pounds)
GDP (US million $) 89 400
GDP per head (US $) 1354

Key dates

c. 3100 B.C. First ancient Egyptian civilization.
A.D. 639 Arab invasion.
1517 Ottoman rule.
19th c. British control.
1869 Suez Canal built.
1914 UK protectorate.
1922 Independence from Britain.
1923 Monarchy formed under King Fu'ad I.
1948 War against Israel.
1952 Military coup; King Farouk forced out.
1956 Seizes Suez Canal; Britain, France and Israel invade.
1967 Defeat in Six-Day War with Israel.
1973 Defeat in Yom Kippur War with Israel.
1978 Signs Camp David Accord with Israel.
1979 Makes peace with Israel; expelled from Arab League (AL).
1981 Extremists kill President Sadat.
1982 Regains Sinai.
1989 Rejoins AL.
1991 Joins US-led coalition in Gulf War.
1997 Muslim extremists kill 58 foreign tourists.

SUDAN

OFFICIAL NAME
The Republic of Sudan

CAPITAL
Khartoum

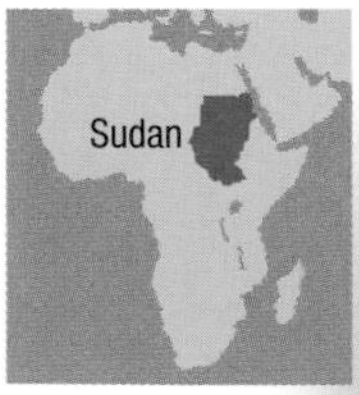

Area 2 505 813 km² (967 500 sq miles)
Population 28 883 000
Population density 12 per km² (30 per sq mile)
Population growth rate 0.1%
Life expectancy 49 (m); 52 (f)
Languages Arabic, English and local languages
Adult literacy rate 46.1%
Currency Sudanese dinar (US $1 = 258 Sudanese dinars)
GDP (US million $) 12 300
GDP per head (US $) 424

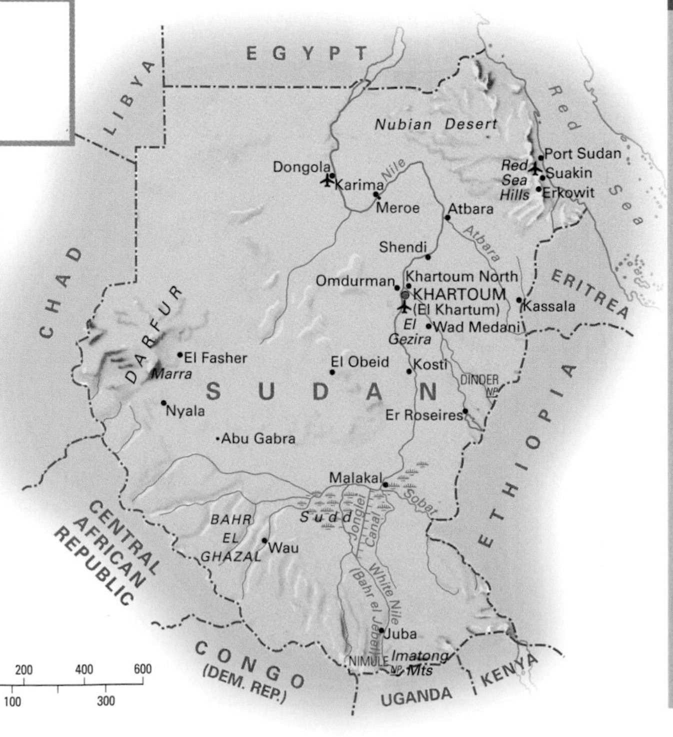

Key dates

14th c. Islamic control.
1821 Egypt invades.
1881 Mahdi's revolt.
1898 British-Egyptian victory at Omdurman.
1956 Independence from Britain.
1958 Military coup.
1973 One-party state.
1980s-90s Droughts cause severe famines.
1983 Imposes Islamic law; non-Muslim Sudan People's Liberation Army (SPLA) starts civil war in south.
1985 Military coup leads to multiparty system.
1986 Elections.
1989 Military coup; legislature replaced by military council.
1993 SPLA cease-fire.
1994 Renewed fighting.
1998 New Islamic constitution.

ERITREA

OFFICIAL NAME
The State of Eritrea

CAPITAL
Asmara

Area 121 144 km^2 (46 774 sq miles)
Population 3 719 000
Population density 31 per km^2 (81 per sq mile)
Population growth rate 2.7%
Life expectancy 48 (m); 51 (f)
Languages Arabic, Tigre, English
Adult literacy rate 20%
Currency nakfa (US $1 = 9.7 nakfa)
GDP (US million $) 800
GDP per head (US $) 215

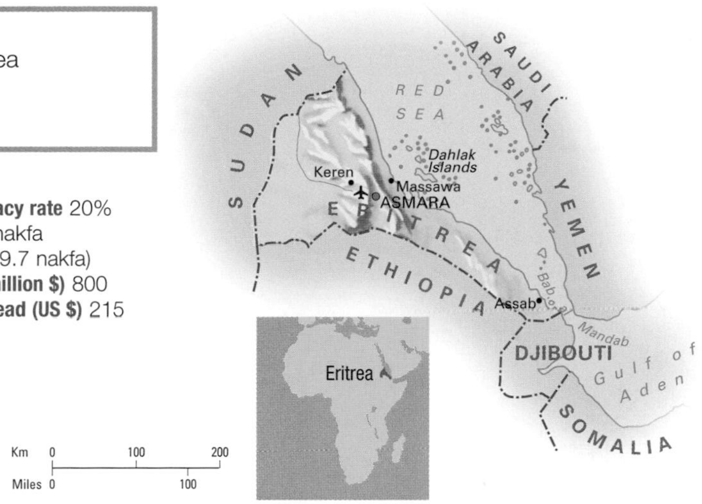

Key dates

7th c. Muslim control.
16th c. Ottoman rule.
1882-89 Italian conquest.
1941 Britain invades.
1952 Becomes a self-governing part of Ethiopia.
1961 Civil war started by rebel separatists.
1962 Annexed by Ethiopia.
1991 Eritrean rebels help overthrow Ethiopian government.
1993 Referendum; independent republic.
1998-2000 Border war with Ethiopia.

ETHIOPIA

OFFICIAL NAME
The Federal Democratic Republic of Ethiopia

CAPITAL
Addis Ababa

Area 1 133 380 km^2 (437 600 sq miles)
Population 61 672 000
Population density 53 per km^2 (137 per sq mile)
Population growth rate 2.9%
Life expectancy 46 (m); 49 (f)
Languages Amharic, English and many local languages
Adult literacy rate 35.5%
Currency birr (US $1 = 8.26 birrs)
GDP (US million $) 5675
GDP per head (US $) 94

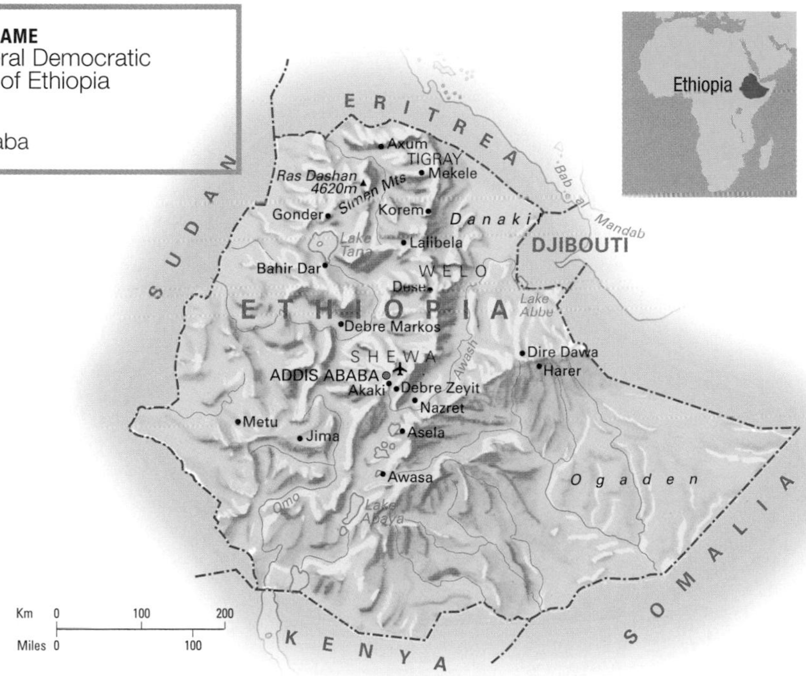

Key dates

1889 Ethiopian Empire united.
1930 Ras Tafari made emperor and takes title Haile Selassie I.
1935 Italian invasion.
1941 Liberated by British in World War II.
1962 Annexes Eritrea.
1974 Military coup ousts Emperor Haile Selassie. Start of land reform.
1977-78 War with Somalia in Ogaden.
1980s, -90s Severe droughts and famine.
1991 Government falls to Tigrean, Eritrean and other rebels.
1993 Eritrea secedes.
1995 Free elections in Ethiopia.
1998-2000 Border war with Eritrea.

DJIBOUTI

OFFICIAL NAME
The Republic of Djibouti

CAPITAL
Djibouti

Area 23 200 km^2 (8958 sq miles)
Population 629 000
Population density 27 per km^2 (69 per sq mile)
Population growth rate 4.1%
Life expectancy 47 (m); 50 (f)
Languages Arabic, French
Adult literacy rate 46.2%
Currency Djibouti franc (US $1 = 175 Djibouti francs)
GDP (US million $) 524
GDP per head (US $) 845

Key dates

9th c. Islamic conversion.
19th c. French control.
1967 Votes to keep French links; renamed Territory of the Afars and Issas.
1977 Independence; renamed Djibouti.
1979 Political parties unite to form People's Progress Assembly.
1992 Multiparty system.
1994 Peace accord with Afar rebels.

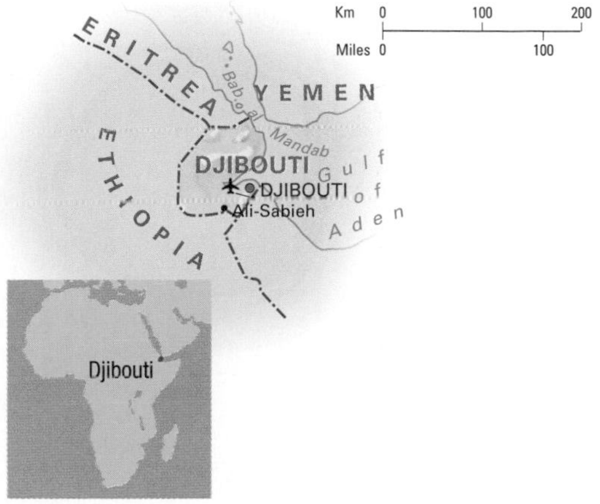

KENYA

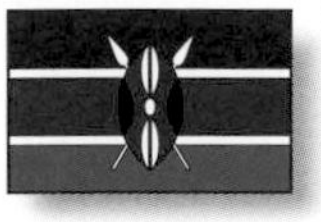

OFFICIAL NAME
The Republic of Kenya

CAPITAL
Nairobi

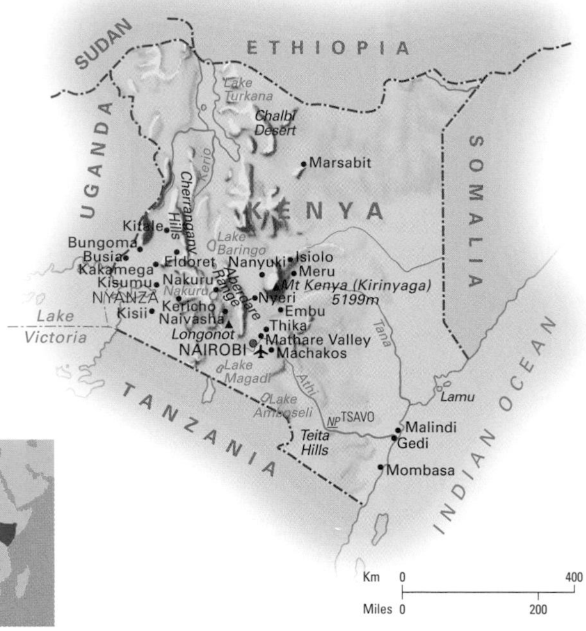

Area 580 367 km² (224 081 sq miles)
Population 29 549 000
Population density 50 per km² (129 per sq mile)
Population growth rate 2.9%
Life expectancy 57 (m); 61 (f)
Languages Swahili, English, Kikuyu, Luo
Adult literacy rate 78.1%
Currency Kenyan shilling (US $1 = 77.45 Kenyan shillings)
GDP (US million $) 9042
GDP per head (US $) 311

Key dates

1895 British control.
1952-60 Kikuyu terrorist group fights British rule.
1963 Independence from Britain.
1964 One-party state.
1990 Violent democracy demonstrations.
1991 Multiparty system established.
1992 First open elections.

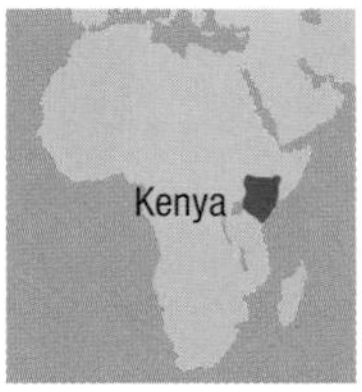

TANZANIA

OFFICIAL NAME
The United Republic of Tanzania

CAPITAL
Dodoma

Area 945 087 km² (364 900 sq miles)
Population 32 793 000
Population density 34 per km² (88 per sq mile)
Population growth rate 3.3%
Life expectancy 52 (m); 55 (f)
Languages Swahili, English and many local languages
Adult literacy rate 67.8%
Currency Tanzanian shilling (US $1 = 889 Tanzanian shillings)
GDP (US million $) 8500
GDP per head (US $) 264

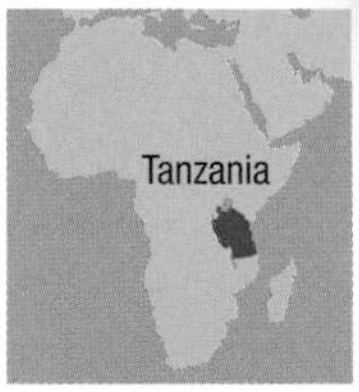

Key dates

1880s German control of mainland territory.
1890 Zanzibar becomes British protectorate.
1918 British control mainland (Tanganyika) after World War I.
1961 Tanganyika gains independence.
1962 Republic declared within Commonwealth.
1963 Zanzibar gains independence.
1964 Union of Zanzibar and Tanganyika creates Tanzania.
1979 Invades Uganda to depose Idi Amin.
1992 Multiparty system proposed.
1995 Democratic elections held.

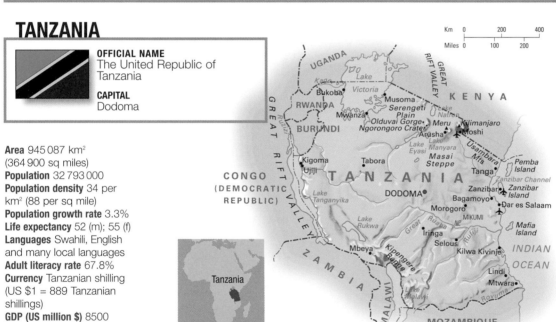

Happy grazing ground
Elephants wander in safety in Kenya's Amboseli National Park, with Kilimanjaro – Africa's highest peak – towering in the background. African elephants are still widely (and illegally) hunted for their ivory, but their power to attract tourists has led governments to give them greater protection in recent decades.

UGANDA

OFFICIAL NAME
The Republic of Uganda

CAPITAL
Kampala

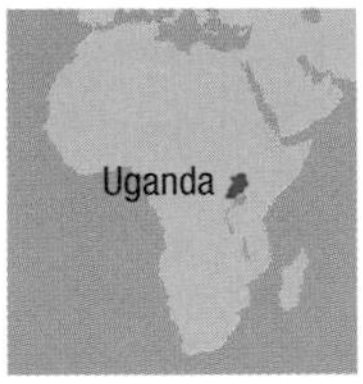

Area 241 139 km^2 (93 104 sq miles)
Population 21 620 000
Population density 87 per km^2 (226 per sq mile)
Population growth rate 2.8%
Life expectancy 40 (m); 42 (f)
Languages English, Luganda and other local languages
Adult literacy rate 61.8%
Currency Ugandan shilling (US $1 = 1785 Ugandan shillings)
GDP (US million $) 6000
GDP per head (US $) 285

Key dates

19th c. Powerful kingdom of Buganda.
1894 UK protectorate.
1962 Independence from Britain.
1963 Republic proclaimed; kabaka (king) elected president.
1967 Kabaka deposed.
1971 Idi Amin becomes dictator; kills more than 300 000 Ugandans and expels all Asians.
1979 Tanzanian troops and Ugandan exiles depose Amin.
1985 Military coup.
1986 Museveni made president; peace restored.
1995 New constitution.
1996 Free elections.

SOMALIA

OFFICIAL NAME
The Somali Democratic Republic

CAPITAL
Mogadishu

Area 637 657 km^2 (246 201 sq miles)
Population 9 240 000
Population density 14 per km^2 (38 per sq mile)
Population growth rate 2.9%
Life expectancy 45 (m); 49 (f)
Languages Somali, Arabic, English, Italian
Adult literacy rate 24.1%
Currency Somali shilling (US $1 = 2620 Somali shillings)
GDP (US million $) 6800
GDP per head (US $) 971

Key dates

1880s Britain and Italy establish colonies.
1960 Independence from Britain and Italy.
1969 Military coup leads to socialist republic.
1970s Severe drought.
1977-78 Invades Ogaden region of Ethiopia but troops driven back.
1991 Fighting between guerrilla groups. North claims independence as Somaliland (not recognized). Drought causes serious famine.
1992 Peacekeeping troops arrive to protect famine-relief effort.
1994-95 UN troops leave; rebels continue fighting.

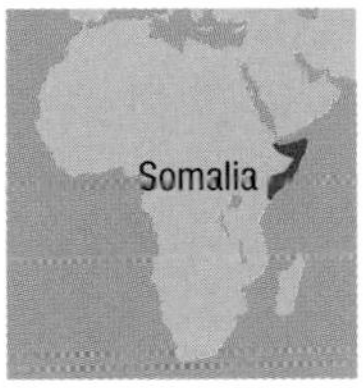

SEYCHELLES

OFFICIAL NAME
The Republic of Seychelles

CAPITAL
Victoria, on Mahé

Area 454 km^2 (175 sq miles)
Population 80 000
Population density 176 per km^2 (456 per sq mile)
Population growth rate 1.3%
Life expectancy 65 (m); 74 (f)
Languages Creole, English, French
Adult literacy rate 85%
Currency Seychelles rupee (US $1 = 6.05 rupees)
GDP (US million $) 579
GDP per head (US $) 7237

Key dates

16th c. Uninhabited islands discovered by Portuguese.
1770 French settlement.
1814 Ceded to Britain.
1976 Independence; becomes republic within Commonwealth.
1977 Socialist coup deposes first president.
1979 One-party state.
1993 New constitution: multiparty system.

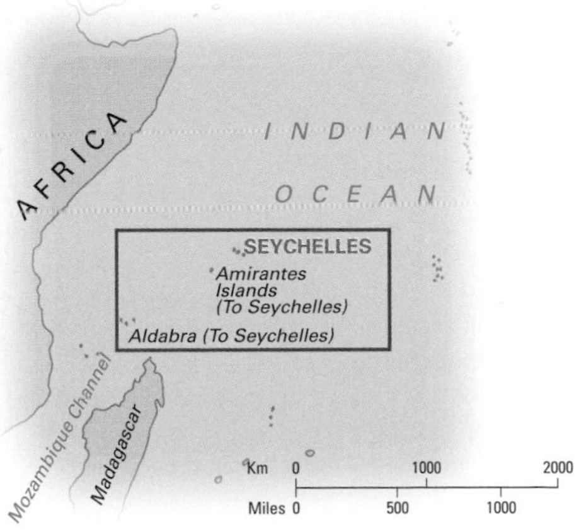

MALI

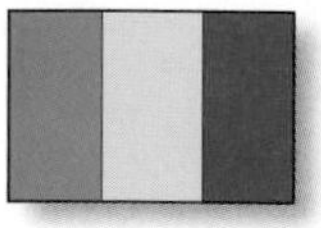

OFFICIAL NAME
The Republic of Mali

CAPITAL
Bamako

Area 1 240 192 km² (478 841 sq miles)
Population 10 960 000
Population density 9 per km² (22 per sq mile)
Population growth rate 2.8%
Life expectancy 55 (m); 58 (f)
Languages French and 12 other official languages
Adult literacy rate 31%
Currency CFA franc (US $1 = 727 CFA francs)
GDP (US million $) 2859
GDP per head (US $) 267

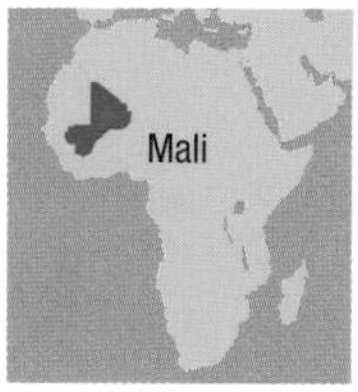

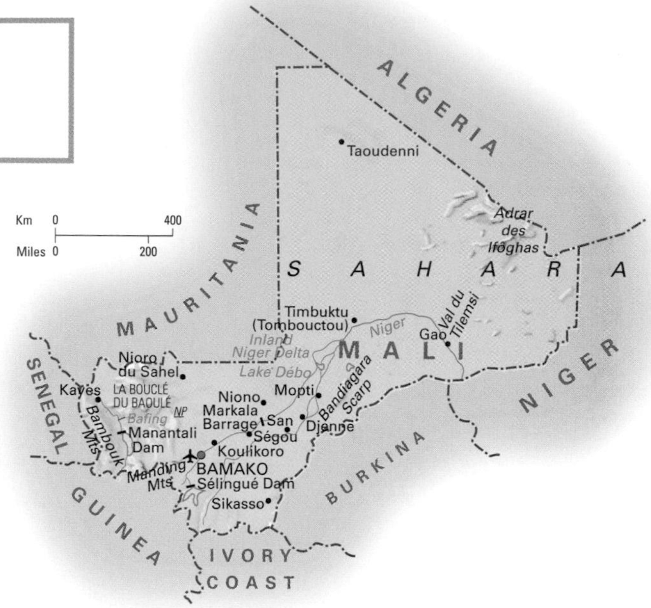

Key dates

4th-16th c. Part of Ghana, Mali and Songhai empires.
1895 French control.
1904 Becomes colony of French Sudan.
1958 Self-government under French rule.
1959 Joins Senegal in Mali Federation.
1960 Mali Federation breaks up; full independence gained as Republic of Mali.
1968 Coup overthrows socialist government.
1974 One-party state.
1991 Military coup.
1992 New constitution; multiparty elections.
1992 Peace accord with Tuareg guerrilla group.

SENEGAL

OFFICIAL NAME
The Republic of Senegal

CAPITAL
Dakar

Area 196 722 km² (75 955 sq miles)
Population 9 279 000
Population density 47 per km² (122 per sq mile)
Population growth rate 2.7%
Life expectancy 48 (m); 50 (f)
Languages French and many local languages
Adult literacy rate 33.1%
Currency CFA franc (US $1 = 727 CFA francs)
GDP (US million $) 5000
GDP per head (US $) 538

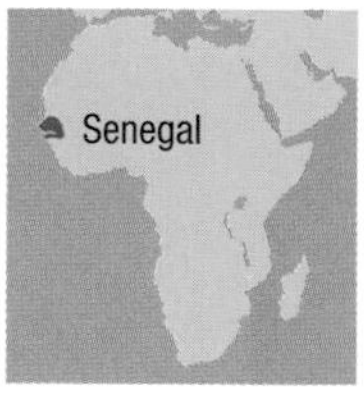

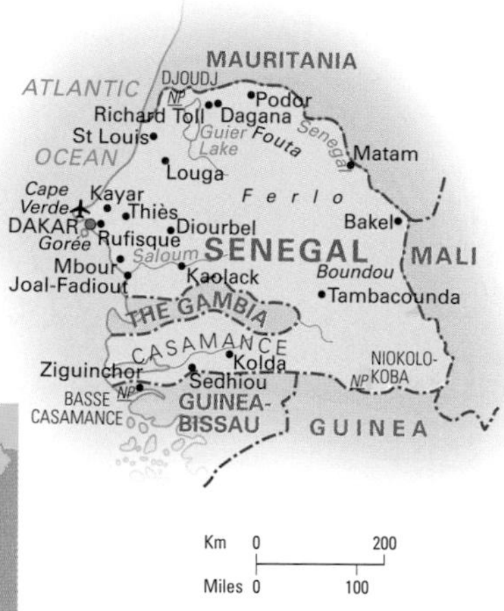

Key dates

4th-16th c. East forms part of Ghana, Mali and then Songhai empires.
17th c. European trading posts set up on coast.
1882 French colony.
1895 Dakar made capital of French West Africa.
1959 Senegal and Sudanese Republic form Mali Federation.
1960 Full independence.
1982-89 With Gambia, forms Confederation of Senegambia.
1998 Sends troops to help Guinea-Bissau to defeat army revolt.

THE GAMBIA

OFFICIAL NAME
The Republic of The Gambia

CAPITAL
Banjul

Area 11 295 km² (4361 sq miles)
Population 1 385 000
Population density 109 per km² (282 per sq mile)
Population growth rate 4.1%
Life expectancy 43 (m); 47 (f)
Languages English, Mandinka, Fula Wolof and other local languages
Adult literacy rate 38.6%
Currency dalasi (US $1 = 15.6 dalasi)
GDP (US million $) 375
GDP per head (US $) 304

Key dates

13th-15th c. Part of Mali Empire.
15th-18th c. European slaving posts set up.
19th c. British possession administered as part of Sierra Leone. Made separate colony in 1888.
1965 Independence.
1970 Republic within Commonwealth.
1982-89 Joins Senegal as part of Senegambia.
1994 Bloodless coup.
1996 New constitution.

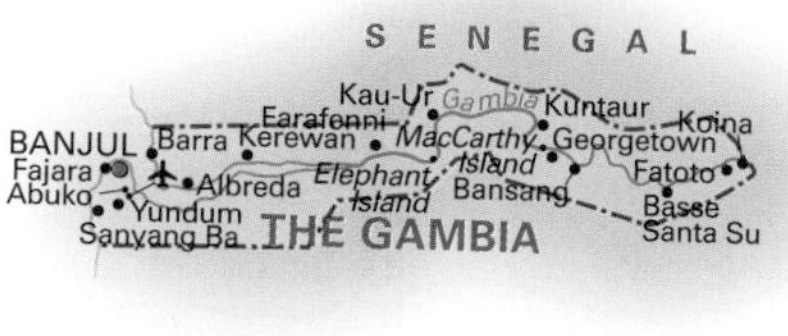

GUINEA-BISSAU

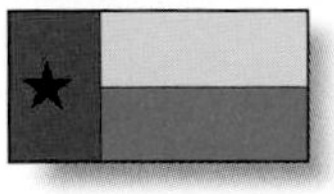

OFFICIAL NAME
The Republic of Guinea-Bissau

CAPITAL
Bissau

Area 36 125 km² (13 948 sq miles)
Population 1 187 000
Population density 32 per km² (83 per sq mile)
Population growth rate 1.1%
Life expectancy 41 (m); 44 (f)
Languages Portuguese, Creole
Adult literacy rate 54.9%
Currency CFA franc (US $1 = 727 CFA francs)
GDP (US million $) 205
GDP per head (US $) 176

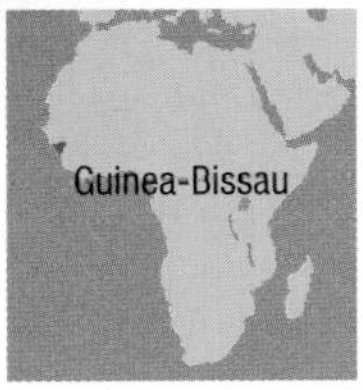

Key dates

17th-19th c. Portuguese slave-trading base.
1879 Becomes separate Portuguese colony.
1951 Made overseas province of Portugal.
1974 Independence after guerrilla war.
1980 Military coup.
1984 New constitution.
1994 Open elections.
1998 Army revolt defeated with help from Senegal and Guinea.

MAURITANIA

OFFICIAL NAME
The Islamic Republic of Mauritania

CAPITAL
Nouakchott

Area 1 030 700 km² (397 950 sq miles)
Population 2 598 000
Population density 2 per km² (6 per sq mile)
Population growth rate 2.5%
Life expectancy 50 (m); 53 (f)
Languages Arabic, French and many local languages
Adult literacy rate 37.7%
Currency ouguiya (US $1 = 252 ouguiyas)
GDP (US million $) 1825
GDP per head (US $) 721

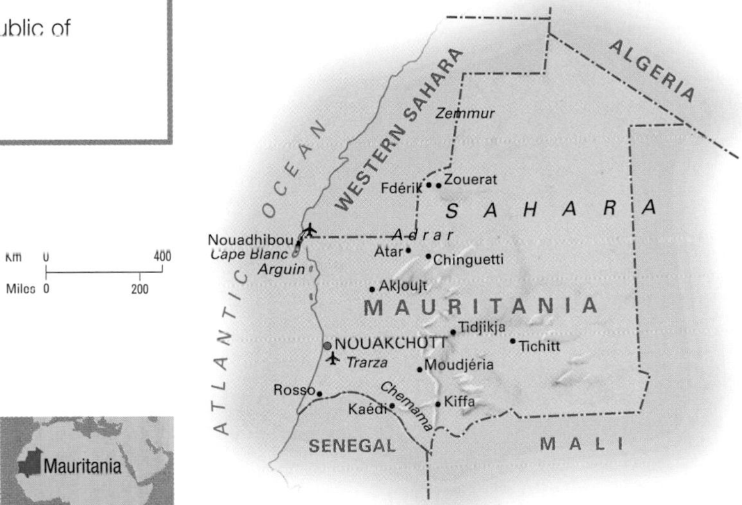

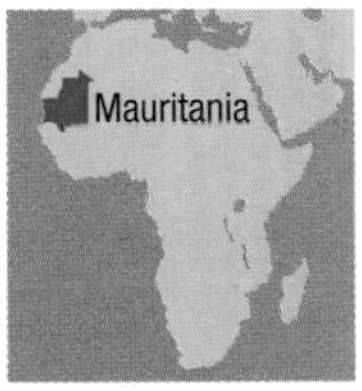

Key dates

4th-16th c. Areas form part of Ghana, Mali and then Songhai empires.
17th-18th c. European trading posts set up.
1903 French establish protectorate.
1958 Self-government.
1960 Independence; not recognized by Morocco.
1965 One-party state.
1970 Independence recognized by Morocco.
1975 Western Sahara ceded to Mauritania (south) and Morocco (north), but Polisario Front guerrillas resist.
1978 Military coup.
1979 Mauritania ends Western Sahara claims.
1996 Open elections.

CAPE VERDE

OFFICIAL NAME
The Republic of Cape Verde

CAPITAL
Praia

Area 4033 km² (1557 sq miles)
Population 418 000
Population density 104 per km² (270 per sq mile)
Population growth rate 2.3%
Life expectancy 64 (m); 71 (f)
Languages Portuguese, Creole
Adult literacy rate 71.6%
Currency Cape Verde escudo (US $1= 122 Cape Verde escudos)
GDP (US million $) 468
GDP per head (US $) 1114

Key dates

1460s Discovered and settled by Portuguese.
16th-17th c. Prospers as slave-trading post.
1879 Becomes separate Portuguese colony.
1975 Independence.
1981 Plans to unite with Guinea-Bissau ended.
1990 New constitution.
1991 Holds first multiparty elections.

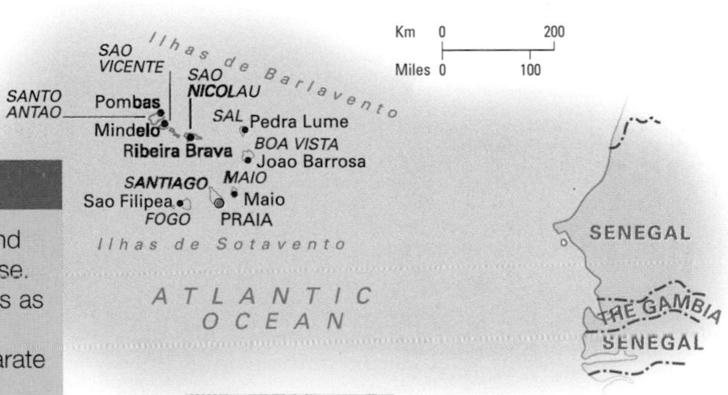

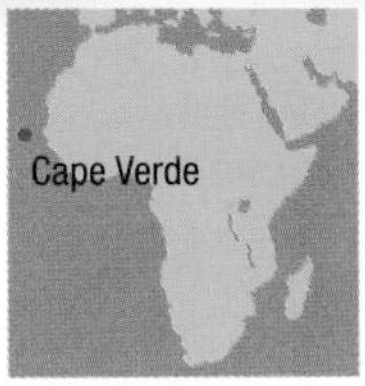

West Africa (South)

GUINEA

OFFICIAL NAME
The Republic of Guinea

CAPITAL
Conakry

Area 245 857 km² (94 926 sq miles)
Population 7 360 000
Population density 30 per km² (77 per sq mile)
Population growth rate 2.9%
Life expectancy 44 (m); 45 (f)
Languages French, Soussou, Manika and other local languages
Adult literacy rate 35.9%
Currency Guinean franc (US $1 = 1895 Guinean francs)
GDP (US million $) 3290
GDP per head (US $) 448

Key dates

13th-16th c. Part of Mali Empire.
1890 French colony.
1958 Independence; Sekou Touré leads one-party state.
1984 Bloodless coup after Touré's death.
1990 New constitution.
1993 Open elections.
1996 Government defeats revolt by rebels.

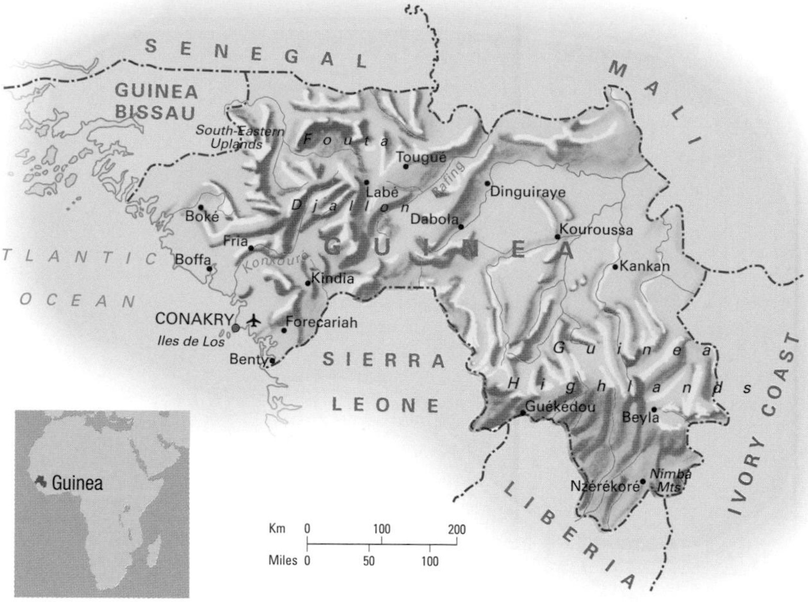

GHANA

OFFICIAL NAME
The Republic of Ghana

CAPITAL
Accra

Area 238 537 km² (92 100 sq miles)
Population 19 678 000
Population density 80 per km² (208 per sq mile)
Population growth rate 2.3%
Life expectancy 54 (m); 58 (f)
Languages English and many local languages
Adult literacy rate 64.5%
Currency cedi (US $1 = 7485 cedis)
GDP (US million $) 7885
GDP per head (US $) 411

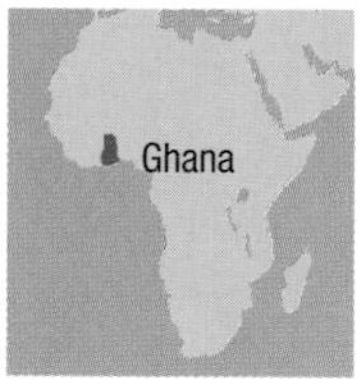

Key dates

15th c. Portuguese trade; named Gold Coast.
1642 Dutch control.
1874 British colony.
1954 Self-government.
1957 Independence (with British Togoland).
1960 Republic; Kwame Nkrumah president.
1964 One-party socialist state led by Nkrumah.
1966 Military coup.
1969 New constitution; civilian government.
1972-81 Four military coups.
1992 New constitution: multiparty system.
1993 Ethnic violence; more than 1000 killed.

SIERRA LEONE

OFFICIAL NAME
The Republic of Sierra Leone

CAPITAL
Freetown

Area 71 740 km² (27 699 sq miles)
Population 4 717 000
Population density 64 per km² (165 per sq mile)
Population growth rate 2.5%
Life expectancy 32 (m); 36 (f)
Languages English, Mende, Temne, Krio (Creole)
Adult literacy rate 31.4%
Currency leone (US $1 = 1894 leones)
GDP (US million $) 702
GDP per head (US $) 153

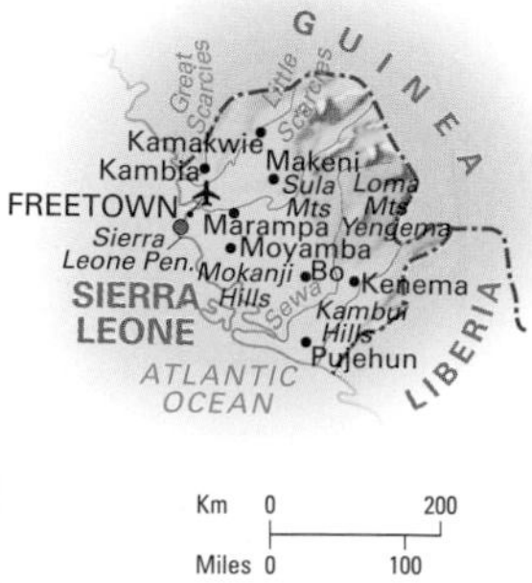

Key dates

1808 British colony.
1961 Independence.
1971 Becomes republic.
1978 One-party state.
1990s Series of military coups and civil war between rival groups.
1996 Ahmad Kabbah elected president.
1997 Military coup.
1998 Nigerian troops restore Kabbah.
1999-2000 UN force tries to restore peace.

LIBERIA

OFFICIAL NAME
The Republic of Liberia

CAPITAL
Monrovia

Area 97 754 km² (37 743 sq miles)
Population 2 930 000
Population density 27 per km² (71 per sq mile)
Population growth rate 1.1%
Life expectancy 54 (m); 57 (f)
Languages English and many local languages
Adult literacy rate 38.3%
Currency Liberian dollar (US $1 = 41.5 Liberian dollars)
GDP (US million $) 517
GDP per head (US $) 176

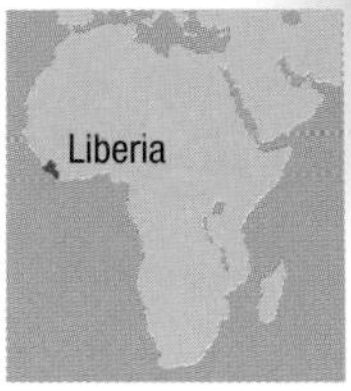

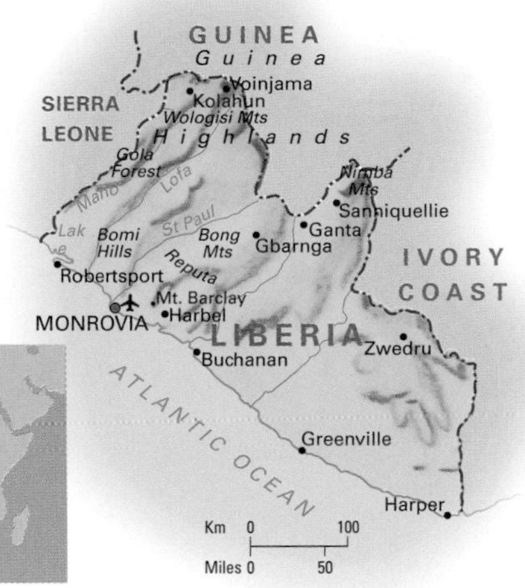

Key dates

1822 Founded by freed US slaves relocated by colonization societies.
1847 Independent republic; constitution modeled on US's.
1980 Military coup.
1989 Civil war begins between government and two rebel groups.
1990 President killed by rebels. Cease-fire.
1992 Renewed fighting.
1996 Peace agreement.
1997 Open elections.

IVORY COAST

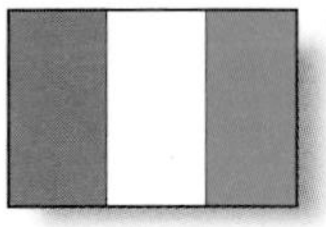

OFFICIAL NAME
The Republic of Côte d'Ivoire

CAPITAL
Yamoussoukro

Area 322 462 km² (124 503 sq miles)
Population 14 526 000
Population density 44 per km² (115 per sq mile)
Population growth rate 0.8%
Life expectancy 50 (m); 54 (f)
Languages French and many local languages
Adult literacy rate 40.1%
Currency CFA franc (US $1 = 727 CFA francs)
GDP (US million $) 11 411
GDP per head (US $) 798

Key dates

1842 French protectorate.
1893 French colony.
1958 Self-government.
1960 Independence; Felix Houphouet-Boigny leads one-party state.
1990 Protests lead to multiparty elections.
1993 Houphouet-Boigny dies in office.
1999 Military coup.

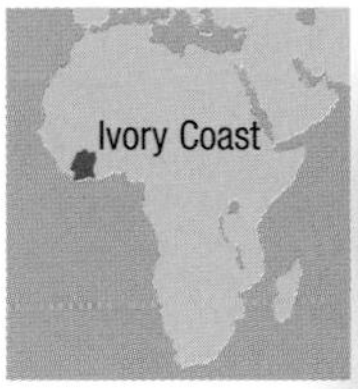

BURKINA FASO

OFFICIAL NAME
Burkina Faso

CAPITAL
Ouagadougou

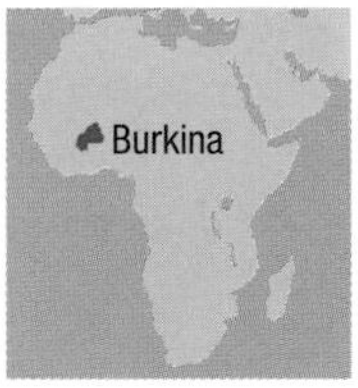

Area 274 200 km² (105 870 sq miles)
Population 11 616 000
Population density 39 per km² (101 per sq mile)
Population growth rate 1.5%
Life expectancy 45 (m); 47 (f)
Languages French, Mossi and many local languages
Adult literacy rate 19.2%
Currency CFA franc (US $1 = 727 CFA francs)
GDP (US million $) 2499
GDP per head (US $) 233

Key dates

14th c. Mossi kingdom established.
mid-15th c. Mossi capital at Ouagadougou.
1896 French capture Ouagadougou; set up protectorate.
1919 French colony of Upper Volta founded.
1932–47 Split among other French colonies.
1960 Independence.
1980 First of series of military coups.
1984 Changes name to Burkina Faso.
1991 New constitution; multiparty elections.

TOGO

OFFICIAL NAME
The Togolese Republic

CAPITAL
Lomé

Area 56 785 km² (21 925 sq miles)
Population 4 512 000
Population density 77 per km² (201 per sq mile)
Population growth rate 2.3%
Life expectancy 49 (m); 52 (f)
Languages French, Kabiye, Ewe and other local languages
Adult literacy rate 51.7%
Currency CFA franc (US $1 = 727 CFA francs)
GDP (US million $) 1464
GDP per head (US $) 332

Key dates

1884 German Togo protectorate set up.
1919 Divided between France and Britain.
1957 British Togoland merges with Ghana.
1960 French Togoland independent as Togo.
1967 Military coup.
1992 Multiparty elections approved.
1993 25 000 flee after violent demonstrations.
1994-98 Open elections.

BENIN

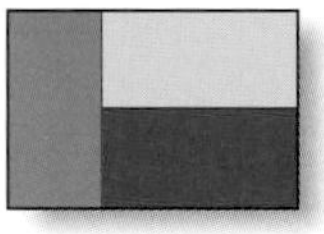

OFFICIAL NAME
The Republic of Benin

CAPITAL
Porto-Novo

Area 112 622 km² (43 484 sq miles)
Population 6 059 000
Population density 54 per km² (139 per sq mile)
Population growth rate 3%
Life expectancy 51 (m); 56 (f)
Languages French, Bariba, Fulani, Fon, Yoruba
Adult literacy rate 37%
Currency CFA franc (US $1 = 727 CFA francs)
GDP (US million $) 2261
GDP per head (US $) 374

Key dates

17th c. Kingdom of Dahomey flourishes, based on selling slaves.
1904 French colony of Dahomey established.
1958 Self-government.
1960 Full independence.
1972 Military coup.
1974 One-party Marxist state proclaimed.
1975 Changes name to Benin.
1978 New constitution reinstates civilian rule.
1991 First free elections.

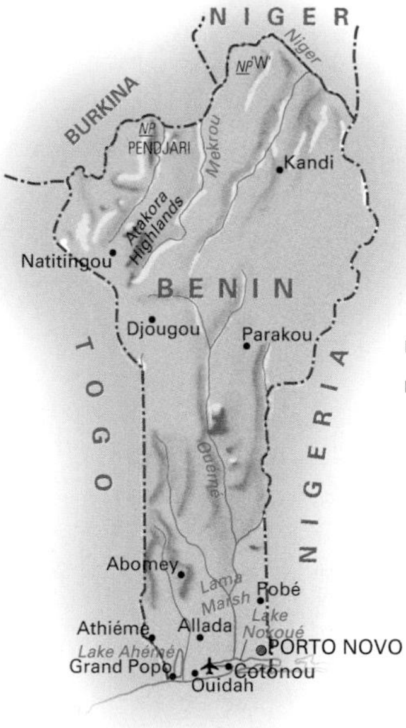

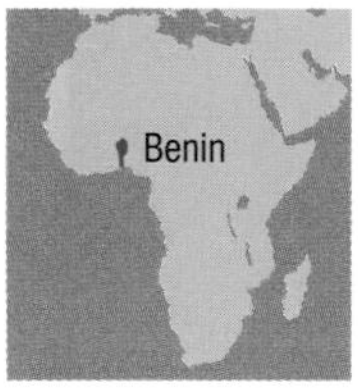

FACT Benin is named after an ancient kingdom, centered in Nigeria, which is renowned for its bronze sculptures.

NIGER

OFFICIAL NAME
The Republic of Niger

CAPITAL
Niamey

Area 1 267 000 km² (489 191 sq miles)
Population 10 400 000
Population density 8 per km² (21 per sq mile)
Population growth rate 3.2%
Life expectancy 45 (m); 48 (f)
Languages French and many local languages
Adult literacy rate 13.6%
Currency CFA franc (US $1 = 727 CFA francs)
GDP (US million $) 2000
GDP per head (US $) 198

FACT "W" National Park in Niger, Burkina Faso and Benin, is named after the shape of bends in the Niger River.

Key dates

11th-15th c. Tuareg people establish empire around Agadez.
16th c. Songhai Empire from Mali conquers Tuaregs.
1890s French gain control.
1922 French colony.
1960 Independence.
1960s-70s Severe drought causes food shortages.
1974 Military coup; suspends constitution.
1992 New constitution.
1993 Holds first democratic elections.
1996 Military coup.

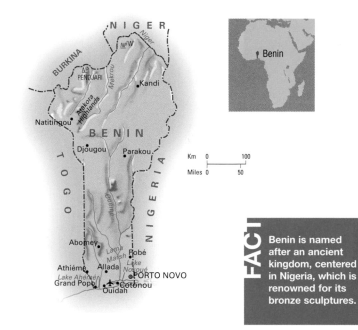

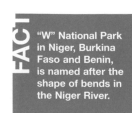

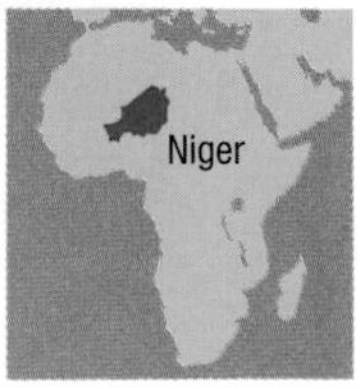

CHAD

OFFICIAL NAME
The Republic of Chad

CAPITAL
N'Djamena

Area 1 284 000 km² (495 800 sq miles)
Population 7 458 000
Population density 6 per km² (15 per sq mile)
Population growth rate 3.4%
Life expectancy 45 (m); 51 (f)
Languages French, Arabic and many local languages
Adult literacy rate 48.1%
Currency CFA franc (US $1 = 727 CFA francs)
GDP (US million $) 1743
GDP per head (US $) 239

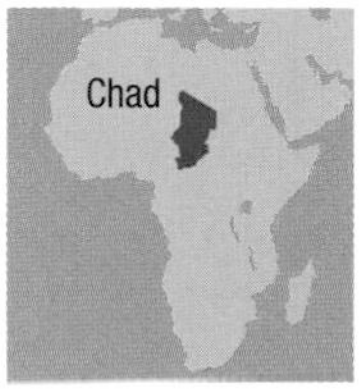

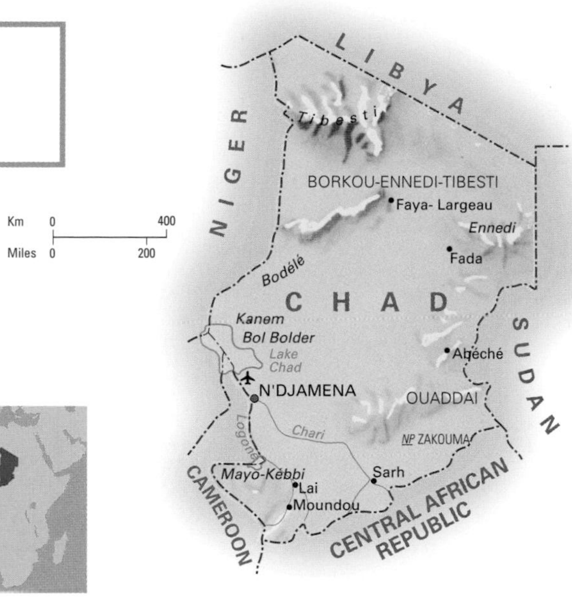

Key dates

8th-17th c. Powerful kingdoms develop on Sahara trade routes.
1880s French claim.
1920 French colony.
1960 Independence.
1966-86 Civil wars.
1975 Military coup.
1983 Libya occupies north; French troops support government.
1987 Rival Chad groups unite to drive out Libyan forces.
1989 Chad, Libya and France agree to cease-fire.
1990 Rebels overthrow government.
1996 New constitution.
1996-97 Presidential and legislative elections.

NIGERIA

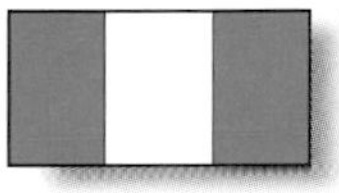

OFFICIAL NAME
The Federal Republic of Nigeria

CAPITAL
Abuja

Area 923 768 km² (356 669 sq miles)
Population 108 945 000
Population density 115 per km² (298 per sq mile)
Population growth rate 2%
Life expectancy 49 (m); 52 (f)
Languages English, Hausa, Yoruba, Ibo
Adult literacy rate 57.1%
Currency naira (US $1 = 124 naira)
GDP (US million $) 43 700
GDP per head (US $) 410

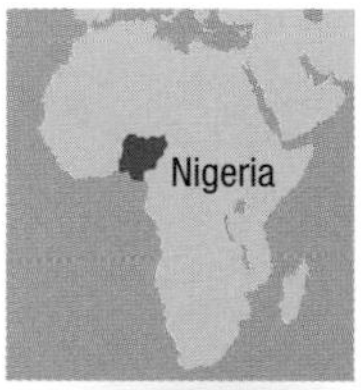

Key dates

14th-17th c. Kingdoms including Muslim Bornu in northeast and Benin in south, develop.
15th-18th c. European slaving posts set up.
early 19th c. Muslim Fulani defeat Hausa to control most of north.
1807 Britain outlaws slave trade.
1861 UK seizes Lagos.
1900-6 All of Nigeria made British colony and protectorate.
1954 Self-government in three-part federation.
1960 Independence within Commonwealth.
1960s Ethnic rivalries lead to civil war.
1966 Military coup; abolition of federal system leads to riots and countercoup.
1967 Four regions replaced by 12 states. Civil war after Ibo eastern region secedes as Biafra.
1970 Biafra defeated.
1976 Number of states increased to 19.
1979 Civilian rule.
1983 Military coup.
1991 Capital moved from Lagos to Abuja.
1993 Election followed by military coup.
1995 Execution of writer Ken Saro-Wiwa and other Ogoni protesters of environmental damage. Suspended from Commonwealth.
1998 Military ruler dies.
1999 Open presidential election; readmitted to Commonwealth.
2000 Introduction of Islamic law in north leads to ethnic tension.

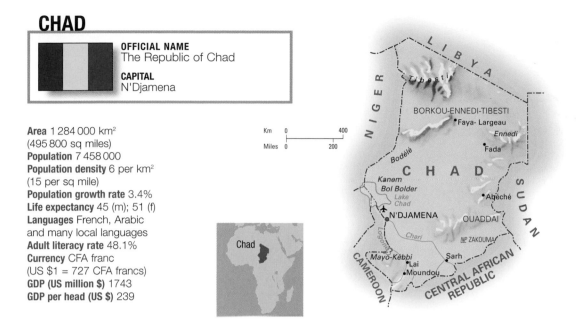

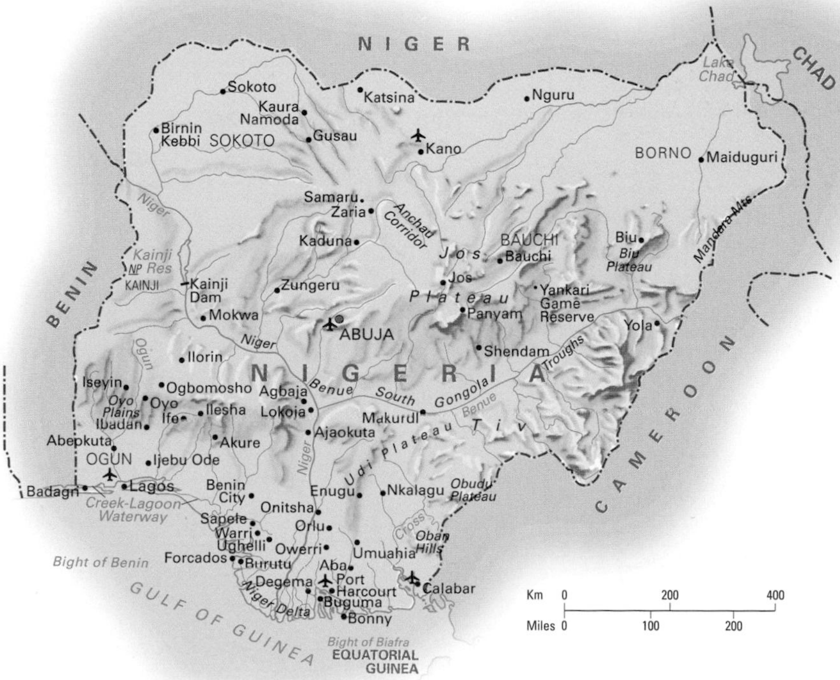

CAMEROON

OFFICIAL NAME
The Republic of Cameroon

CAPITAL
Yaoundé

Area 475 442 km² (183 569 sq miles)
Population 14 693 000
Population density 30 per km² (78 per sq mile)
Population growth rate 2.8%
Life expectancy 53 (m); 56 (f)
Languages English, French and many local languages
Adult literacy rate 63.4%
Currency CFA franc (US $1 = 727 CFA francs)
GDP (US million $) 9221
GDP per head (US $) 644

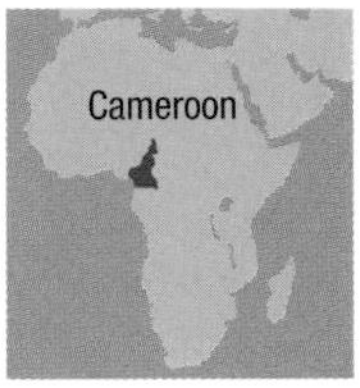

Key dates

15th c. First European slave-traders arrive.
1884 Becomes German protectorate.
1922 Divided between France and Britain.
1960 French Cameroon independent.
1961 British Cameroon independent; parts join Cameroon and Nigeria. Becomes federation.
1972 Two parts merged.
1992 Multiparty elections are held.
1995 New constitution; joins Commonwealth.

GABON

OFFICIAL NAME
The Gabonese Republic

CAPITAL
Libreville

Area 267 667 km² (103 347 sq miles)
Population 1 385 000
Population density 4 per km² (12 per sq mile)
Population growth rate 2.6%
Life expectancy 52 (m); 55 (f)
Languages French, Fang, Bantu dialects
Adult literacy rate 63.2%
Currency CFA franc (US $1 = 727 CFA francs)
GDP (US million $) 5086
GDP per head (US $) 4273

Key dates

15th c. First European slave-traders arrive.
1883 French colony.
1957 Self-government.
1960 Independence.
1964 Attempted coup.
1968 One-party state.
1990 New constitution: multiparty system.
1993 Election; riots after charges of vote fraud.
1995 New constitution.

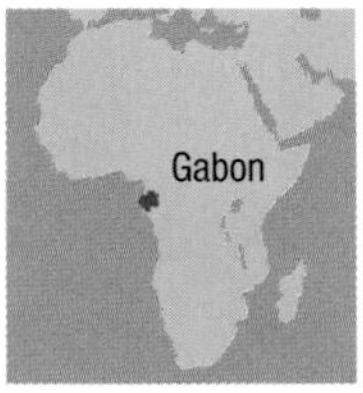

CENTRAL AFRICAN REPUBLIC

OFFICIAL NAME
The Central African Republic

CAPITAL
Bangui

Area 622 984 km² (240 535 sq miles)
Population 3 550 000
Population density 6 per km² (15 per sq mile)
Population growth rate 1.6%
Life expectancy 47 (m); 52 (f)
Languages French, Sango
Adult literacy rate 60%
Currency CFA franc (US $1 = 727 CFA francs)
GDP (US million $) 1128
GDP per head (US $) 323

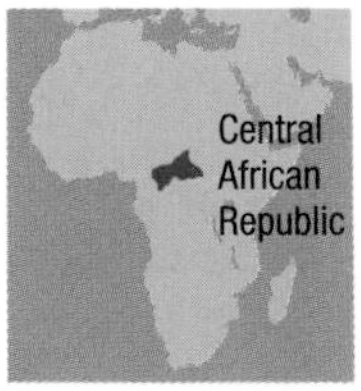

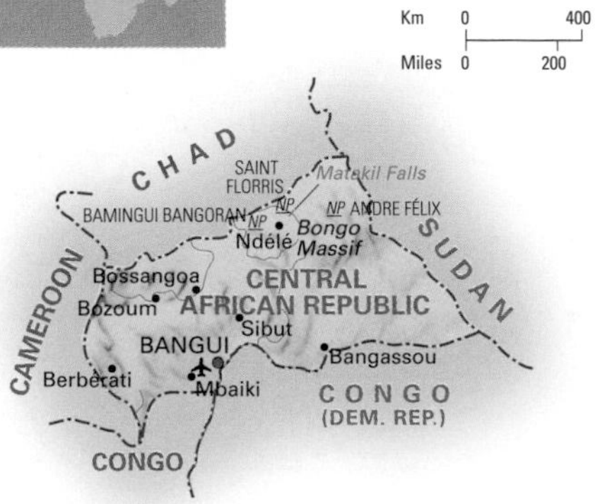

Key dates

1894 French establish colony of Ubangi-Shari.
1958 Self-government as Central African Republic.
1960 Independence.
1962 One-party state.
1966 Military coup; Jean-Bedel Bokassa becomes president.
1976 Bokassa declares himself emperor.
1979 Bloodless coup.
1993 Open elections; civilian government.
1996-97 French help crush military revolts.

EQUATORIAL GUINEA

OFFICIAL NAME
The Republic of Equatorial Guinea

CAPITAL
Malabo

Area 28 051 km² (10 830 sq miles)
Population 442 000
Population density 15 per km² (40 per sq mile)
Population growth rate 2.5%
Life expectancy 46 (m); 50 (f)
Languages Spanish, French, Fang and many local languages
Adult literacy rate 78.5%
Currency CFA franc (US $1 = 727 CFA francs)
GDP (US million $) 751
GDP per head (US $) 1746

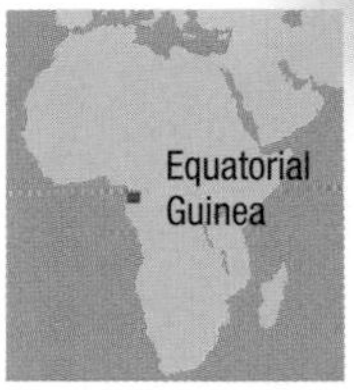

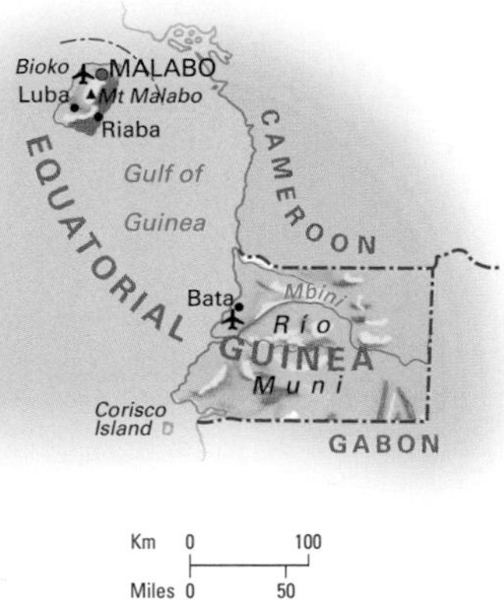

Key dates

1471 Portuguese explorers land; later claim territory.
19th c. Spanish control.
1959 Spanish colony.
1968 Independence from Spain. Macias Nguema seizes power.
1979 Military coup; Obiang Nguema Mbasogo president.
1991 New constitution.
1996-99 Elections marred by allegations of fraud.

SÃO TOMÉ & PRÍNCIPE

OFFICIAL NAME
The Democratic Republic of São Tomé & Príncipe

CAPITAL
São Tomé

Area 1001 km² (387 sq miles)
Population 144 000
Population density 140 per km² (362 per sq mile)
Population growth rate 2.1%
Life expectancy 67 (m); 67 (f)
Languages Portuguese and many local languages
Adult literacy rate 25%
Currency dobra (US $1 = 8203.5 dobras)
GDP (US million $) 35
GDP per head (US $) 250

Key dates

15th c. Portuguese explorers land.
1522 Becomes Portuguese province.
16th c. Becomes major center of slave trade.
1953 Portuguese troops kill protesting workers in "Batepa massacre."
1975 Independence.
1988 Coup attempt fails.
1991 Multiparty elections.
1995 Angolan mediation ends bloodless military coup after one week.

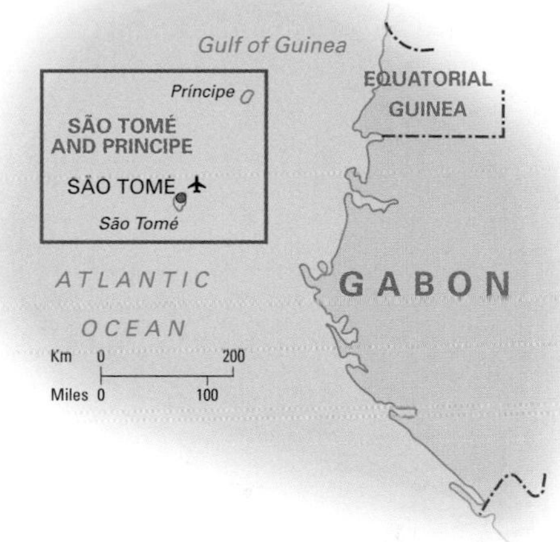

CONGO

OFFICIAL NAME
The Republic of the Congo

CAPITAL
Brazzaville

Area 342 000 km² (132 047 sq miles)
Population 2 864 000
Population density 8 per km² (21 per sq mile)
Population growth rate 3%
Life expectancy 48 (m); 54 (f)
Languages French, Kikongo, Lingala and other local languages
Adult literacy rate 74.9%
Currency CFA franc (US $1 = 727 CFA francs)
GDP (US million $) 3075
GDP per head (US $) 1102

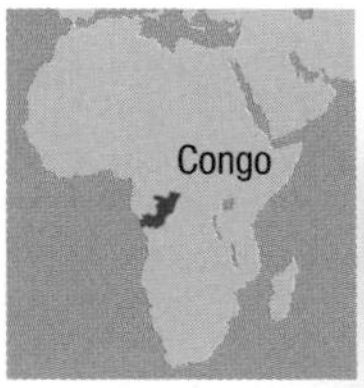

Key dates

15th-19th c. European traders buy slaves.
1880 Becomes French protectorate.
1903 French colony of Middle Congo.
1958 Self-government.
1960 Independence.
1969 Military coup.
1970 Marxist government renames country People's Republic of the Congo.
1990 Government abandons Marxism.
1992 New constitution; name reverts to Republic of the Congo. First multiparty presidential election.
1993 Legislative elections.
1997 Civil war restores former Marxist Sassou-Nguesso to presidency.

CONGO (DEMOCRATIC REPUBLIC)

OFFICIAL NAME
Democratic Republic of the Congo

CAPITAL
Kinshasa

Area 2 344 885 km² (905 365 sq miles)
Population 50 335 000
Population density 21 per km² (54 per sq mile)
Population growth rate 3%
Life expectancy 50 (m); 54 (f)
Languages French, Lingala, Kingwana, Tshiluba and other local languages
Adult literacy rate 77.3%
Currency Congolese franc (US $1 = 4.50 Congolese francs)
GDP (US million $) 926
GDP per head (US $) 18

Key dates

15th c. Kongo and other kingdoms established.
16th-19th c. Extensive slave-trading.
1885 Congo Free State established, directly ruled by Belgian king.
1908 Control taken by Belgian government.
1960 Independence. Copper-rich Katanga province secedes; civil war begins between rival groups.
1963 UN troops end Katanga secession.
1965 Military coup; Mobutu president.
1971 Renamed Zaire.
1977-78 Renewed war with Katanga exiles.
1996 Renewed civil war in east with rebels and Rwandan refugees.
1997 Rebels depose Mobutu; Laurent Kabila president. Name reverts to Democratic Republic of the Congo.
2001 Kabila killed; succeeded by his son.

RWANDA

OFFICIAL NAME
The Rwandan Republic

CAPITAL
Kigali

Area 26 338 km² (10 169 sq miles)
Population 7 235 000
Population density 251 per km² (649 per sq mile)
Population growth rate 2.7%
Life expectancy 45 (m); 48 (f)
Languages French, English, Kinyarwanda, Swahili
Adult literacy rate 60.5%
Currency Rwandan franc (US $1 = 431 Rwandan francs)
GDP (US million $) 2255
GDP per head (US $) 341

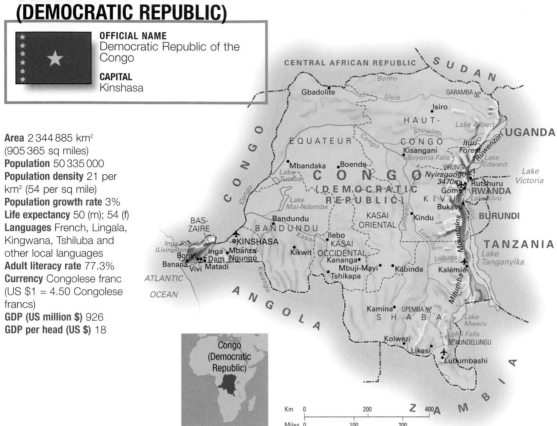

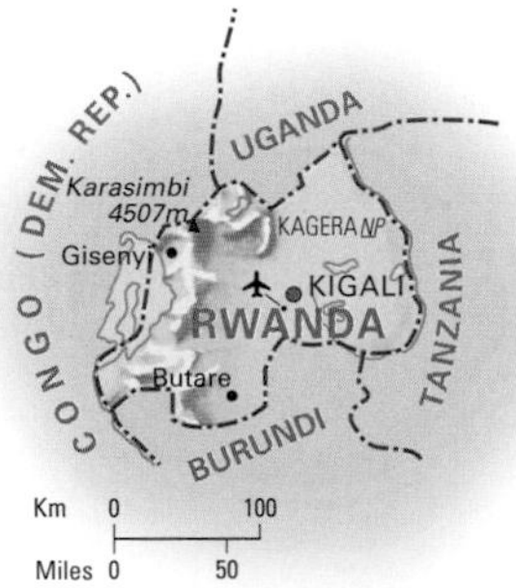

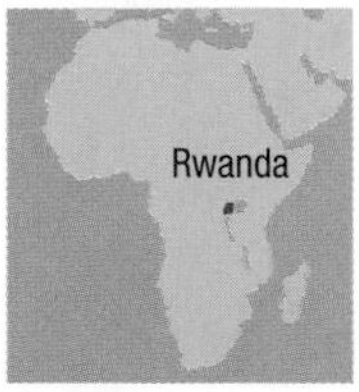

Key dates

1897 Becomes part of German East Africa.
1923 Administration by Belgium as part of Ruanda-Urundi.
1959 Hutus rebel against Tutsis; many killed or flee into exile.
1962 Independence under Hutu president.
1963 Tutsis massacred after failed coup.
1973 Military coup.
1990 Tutsi exiles begin attacks from Uganda.
1993 Peace treaty.
1994 President killed in plane crash. Hutu extremists start civil war; 500 000 (mainly Tutsi) massacred and 2 million Tutsis and Hutus flee to Zaire. Tutsi-led rebels defeat Hutus; establish government with Hutu president.
1995 Tutsi soldiers kill Hutu refugees.
1996 Many refugees flee back to Rwanda.

Ethnic violence in Central Africa

In 1994, the world was shocked by horrific images from Rwanda, as more than 450 000 Tutsis and moderate Hutus were massacred by gangs of Hutu extremists. The massacres were unleashed after the Hutu presidents of Rwanda and Burundi died when the aircraft in which they were traveling crashed under mysterious circumstances. But the conflict between Hutus and Tutsis, the major ethnic groups in both countries, dates back more than 500 years.The cattle-raising Tutsis moved into the region from Ethiopia in the 15th century and established their authority over the majority Hutu farmers.

Several Hutu uprisings in the 20th century led to mass killings on both sides. In 1994, more than a million Tutsis fled to Zaire, along with Hutus escaping reprisals, but the unsanitary refugee camps brought more deaths from disease and starvation. When more than a million refugees returned to Rwanda in 1996, Hutus found their farms occupied by Tutsis. Today Tutsis control both governments, and Hutu extremists wander their ravaged lands, attacking Tutsis and Western tourists alike.

BURUNDI

OFFICIAL NAME
The Republic of Burundi
CAPITAL
Bujumbura

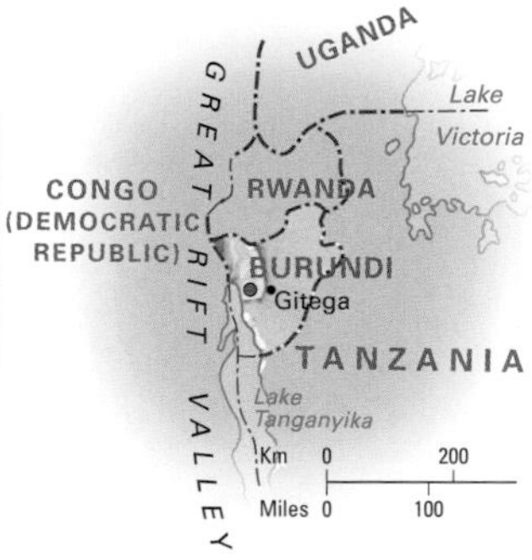

Area 27 834 km² (10 747 sq miles)
Population 6 483 000
Population density 226 per km² (586 per sq mile)
Population growth rate 1.4%
Life expectancy 43 (m); 46 (f)
Languages French, Kirundi, Swahili
Adult literacy rate 35.3%
Currency Burundi franc (US $1 = 806 Burundi francs)
GDP (US million $) 959
GDP per head (US $) 152

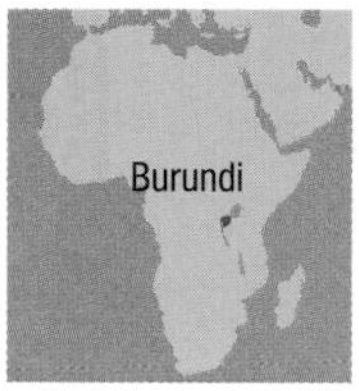

Key dates

1897 Becomes part of German East Africa.
1923 Administration by Belgium as part of Ruanda-Urundi.
1962 Independence under Tutsi control.
1972-73 Hutu revolt fails; 150 000 Hutus and 10 000 Tutsis killed.
1976 Military coup.
1981 New constitution.
1988 Army massacres thousands of Hutus.
1993 First multiparty presidential election: Hutu candidate wins but dies later in coup.
1993-96 About 150 000 die in ethnic clashes following 1993 coup.
1994 President (a Hutu) killed in plane crash; violent demonstrations.
1996 Tutsi-led military coup fails to halt ethnic violence.

ANGOLA

OFFICIAL NAME
The Republic of Angola
CAPITAL
Luanda

Area 1 246 700 km² (481 354 sq miles)
Population 12 479 000
Population density 10 per km² (25 per sq mile)
Population growth rate 3.2%
Life expectancy 45 (m); 48 (f)
Languages Portuguese, Umbundo, Kimbundo, Chokwe, Ganguela
Adult literacy rate 41.7%
Currency new kwanza (US $1 = 18.24 new kwanzas)
GDP (US million $) 4776
GDP per head (US $) 395

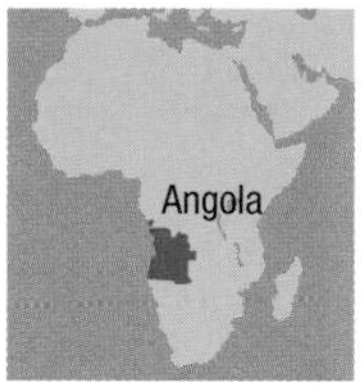

1 Cuanza Norte
2 Cuanza Sul
3 Benguela
4 Huambo

Key dates

1648 Portuguese win control; trade in slaves.
1961 War of liberation. Rival groups, including MPLA and UNITA, later start fighting each other.
1975 Independence from Portugal.
1976 Soviet-backed MPLA wins civil war.
1991 Peace treaty with West-backed UNITA.
1992 Elections. Fighting resumes after UNITA rejects results.
1994 UN-negotiated peace agreement.
1998 Civil war resumes.

ZAMBIA

OFFICIAL NAME
The Republic of Zambia
CAPITAL
Lusaka

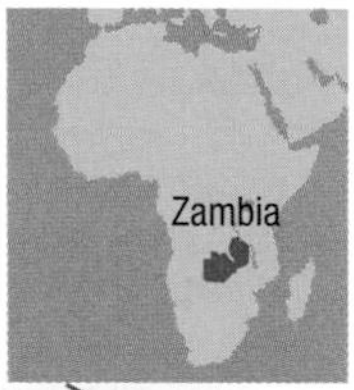

Key dates

1924 Becomes British protectorate of Northern Rhodesia.
1953 Federation formed with Southern Rhodesia and Nyasaland.
1964 Independence within Commonwealth as Zambia; Kenneth Kaunda president.
1970 Takes control of foreign-owned copper mines.
1972 One-party state.
1991 Multiparty elections reinstated; Kaunda defeated.
1997 Coup attempt fails.

Area 752 614 km² (290 584 sq miles)
Population 10 407 000
Population density 14 per km² (36 per sq mile)
Population growth rate 1.95%
Life expectancy 37 (m); 37 (f)
Languages English, Bemba, Kaonda, Lozi, Tonga and other local languages
Adult literacy rate 78.2%
Currency Zambian kwacha (US $1 = 3150 kwacha)
GDP (US million $) 3800
GDP per head (US $) 350

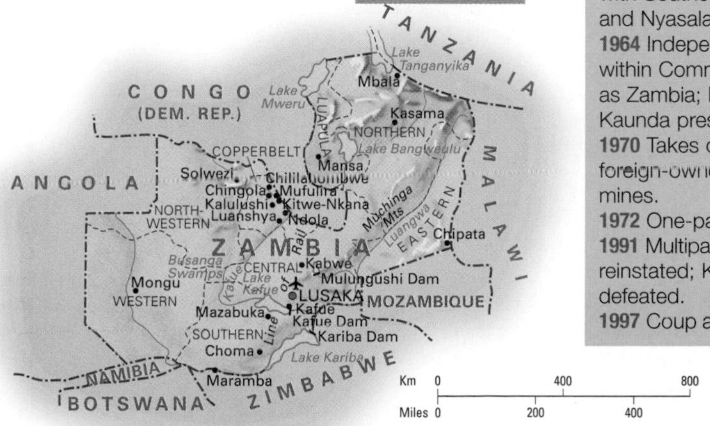

MALAWI

OFFICIAL NAME
The Republic of Malawi

CAPITAL
Lilongwe

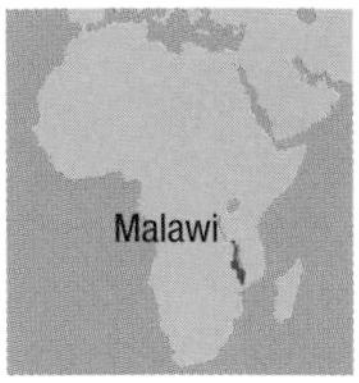

Area 118 484 km² (45 747 sq miles)
Population 10 640 000
Population density 87 per km² (226 per sq mile)
Population growth rate 1.8%
Life expectancy 43 (m); 46 (f)
Languages English, Chichewa and other local languages
Adult literacy rate 56.4%
Currency Malawian kwacha (US $1 = 79 kwacha)
GDP (US million $) 1792
GDP per head (US $) 173

Key dates

1891 Nyasaland made British protectorate.
1953 Federation formed with Northern and Southern Rhodesia.
1964 Independence as Malawi.
1966 One-party republic within Commonwealth.
1971 Hastings Banda made president for life.
1993 Multiparty system.
1994 Banda loses the first multiparty presidential election.

ZIMBABWE

OFFICIAL NAME
The Republic of Zimbabwe

CAPITAL
Harare

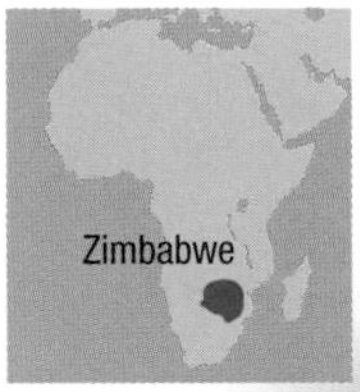

Area 390 759 km² (150 873 sq miles)
Population 13 079 000
Population density 32 per km² (84 per sq mile)
Population growth rate 3%
Life expectancy 58 (m); 62 (f)
Languages English, Chishona, Sindebele and other local languages
Adult literacy rate 85.1%
Currency Zimbabwe dollar (US $1 = 55 Zimbabwe dollars)
GDP (US million $) 5300
GDP per head (US $) 417

Key dates

1888 Cecil Rhodes gains mining rights.
1923 British colony of Southern Rhodesia.
1953 Federation formed with Northern Rhodesia and Nyasaland.
1961 New constitution restricts black vote.
1963 Federation ends.
1964 Named Rhodesia.
1964-74 Black activists imprisoned.
1965 Independence declared; unrecognized.
1966 UN sanctions.
1969 Constitution entrenches white rule.
1970s Black groups fight guerrilla war.
1979 Voting-rule change gives black-majority government. Cease-fire.
1980 Free elections; Robert Mugabe prime minister. Independence as Zimbabwe.
2000-1 Mugabe enforces land redistribution to black population.

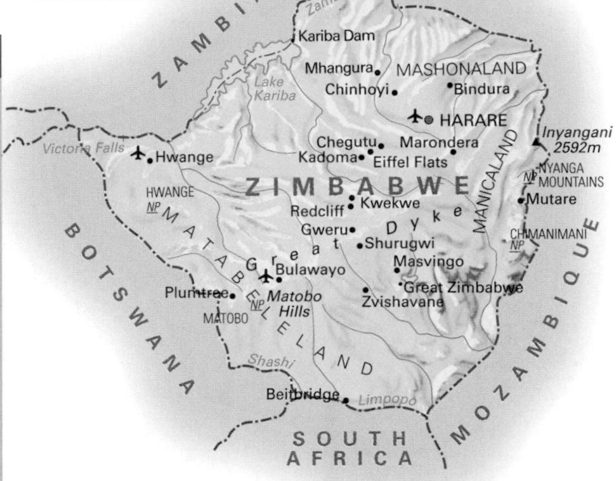

MOZAMBIQUE

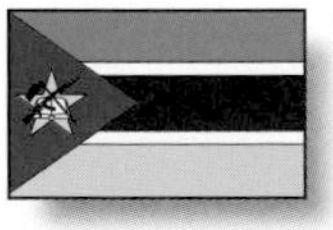

OFFICIAL NAME
The Republic of Mozambique

CAPITAL
Maputo

Key dates

1505 Portuguese slave-trading post set up.
1885 Portuguese colony recognized.
1960s Frelimo guerrillas start liberation war.
1974 Cease-fire; internal self-government.
1975 Independence as socialist republic.
1986 Plane crash kills President Machel.
1990 One-party rule ends.
1994 First multiparty elections.
1995 Joins the Commonwealth.
2000-1 Severe flooding.

Area 799 380 km² (308 641 sq miles)
Population 17 299 000
Population density 21 per km² (55 per sq mile)
Population growth rate 2%
Life expectancy 44 (m); 47 (f)
Languages Portuguese and many local languages
Adult literacy rate 40.1%
Currency metical (US $1 = 19 075 meticals)
GDP (US million $) 4037
GDP per head (US $) 238

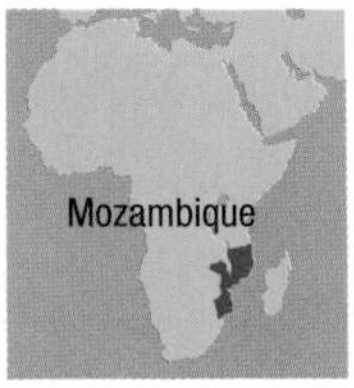

MADAGASCAR

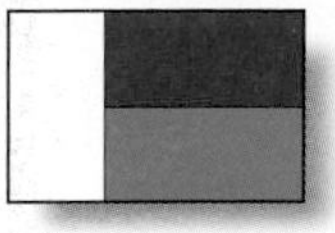

OFFICIAL NAME
The Republic of Madagascar

CAPITAL
Antananarivo

Area 587 041 km² (226 658 sq miles)
Population 15 497 000
Population density 26 per km² (66 per sq mile)
Population growth rate 2.6%
Life expectancy 55 (m); 58 (f)
Languages Malagasy, French, Hova and other local languages
Adult literacy rate 45.7%
Currency Malagasy franc (US $1 = 6320 Malagasy francs)
GDP (US million $) 3752
GDP per head (US $) 249

Key dates

17th-18th c. Center of piracy and slave trade.
1810 Merina kingdom outlaws slave trade.
1895 French colony.
1947-49 Armed guerrilla revolt against French.
1958 Self-government.
1960 Independence as Malagasy Republic.
1972 Military rule.
1975-80 Marxist state; renamed Madagascar.
1990 Multiparty system.
1992-93 Holds first democratic elections.
2000 Cyclone Eline causes severe damage.

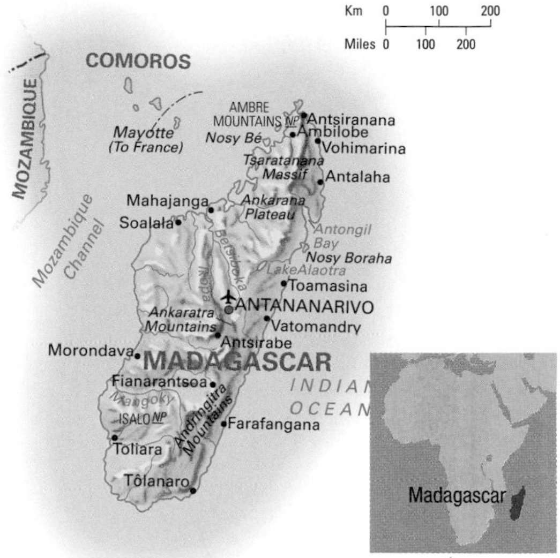

COMOROS

OFFICIAL NAME
The Federal Islamic Republic of the Comoros

CAPITAL
Moroni, on Grande Comore (Njazidja)

Area 1862 km² (719 sq miles)
Population 676 000
Population density 354 per km² (918 per sq mile)
Population growth rate 2.7%
Life expectancy 55 (m); 56 (f)
Languages Comorian (Swahili and Arabic), French, Arabic
Adult literacy rate 57.3%
Currency Comoros franc (US $1 = 546 Comoros francs)
GDP (US million $) 207
GDP per head (US $) 313

Key dates

15th c. Arab rule.
1843-86 French seize control.
1961 Self-government.
1974 Christian majority of Mayotte island votes to stay French; others vote to become independent.
1989 President Ahmed Abdallah assassinated.
1995 French troops invade to overthrow military coup.
1997 Anjouan (Nzwani) and Moheli (Mwali) declare secession.
1999 Military coup (19th coup or coup attempt since independence).

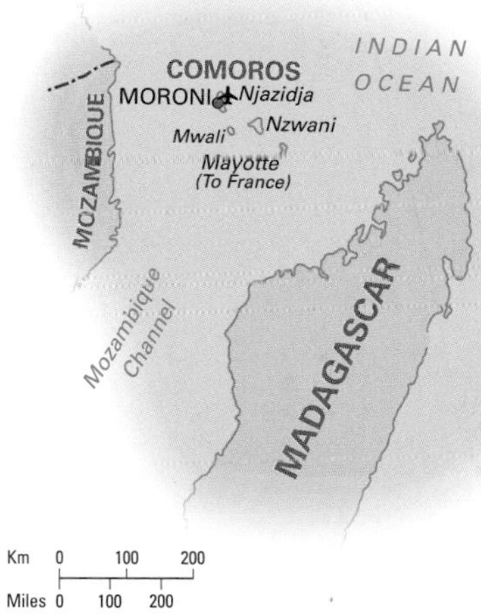

MAURITIUS

OFFICIAL NAME
The Republic of Mauritius

CAPITAL
Port Louis

Area 2040 km² (788 sq miles)
Population 1 174 000
Population density 569 per km² (1472 per sq mile)
Population growth rate 0.9%
Life expectancy 66 (m); 74 (f)
Languages English, Creole, French and several Indian and Chinese dialects
Adult literacy rate 82.9%
Currency Mauritian rupee (US $1 = 28 rupees)
GDP (US million $) 4574
GDP per head (US $) 3943

FACT
About 68 percent of Mauritians are descended from Indians who arrived there to work in the 1800s.

Key dates

1598 Dutch claim.
1715 French take possession.
1810 Captured by Britain.
1814 Becomes a British colony.
1833 Slavery abolished.
1965 Diego Garcia island separated to become part of British Indian Ocean Territory.
1967 Internal self-government.
1968 Becomes independent within the Commonwealth.
1992 Becomes republic.

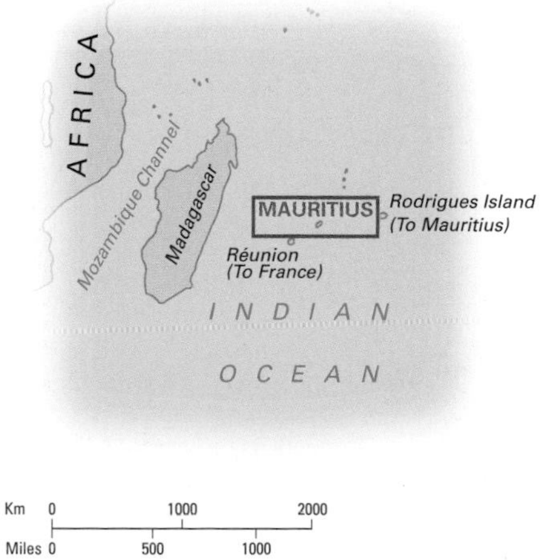

South Africa and Southern Africa

SOUTH AFRICA

OFFICIAL NAME
The Republic of South Africa

CAPITAL CITIES
Pretoria (administrative),
Cape Town (legislative),
Bloemfontein (judicial)

Area 1 219 080 km² (470 689 sq miles)
Population 43 054 000
Population density 35 per km² (90 per sq mile)
Population growth rate 2.4%
Life expectancy 60 (m); 66 (f)
Languages Afrikaans, English and nine African languages
Adult literacy rate 81.8%
Currency rand (US $1 = 8.15 rand)
GDP (US million $) 130 100
GDP per head (US $) 3085

Key dates

1652 Dutch settle Cape.
1814 Dutch transfer Cape Colony to Britain.
1836-38 Start of Boers' "Great Trek" to north; establish Natal.
1852-54 Boer colonies of Transvaal and Orange Free State recognized.
1868 Diamonds found.
1873-86 Gold found.
1877 Britain annexes Transvaal.
1879 Zulus defeated in Anglo-Zulu War.
1880-1902 Anglo-Boer wars lead to British rule.
1910 Union of South Africa formed from Boer and British colonies.
1912 African [Native] National Congress (ANC) founded.
1914-18 Fights World War I as one of Allies.
1931 Statute of Westminster gives independence within Commonwealth.
1939-45 Fights as one of Allies in World War II.
1948 Apartheid policy of racial division begins.
1960 Sharpeville massacre: 69 anti-apartheid protesters killed. ANC banned.
1961 Republic declared; leaves Commonwealth.
1962 ANC leader Nelson Mandela imprisoned.
1976 Soweto uprising against compulsory teaching of Afrikaans; police kill 600 black student demonstrators.
1986 International trade sanctions begin. South African forces attack ANC bases in Botswana, Zambia and Zimbabwe.
1990 ANC ban lifted; Mandela freed; reform negotiations start.
1991 Apartheid ends.
1993 Mandela and President F. W. de Klerk win Nobel Peace Prize. "Homelands" – semi-self-governing black territories – abolished.
1994 Mandela elected president in first multirace elections. Rejoins Commonwealth.
1995 Truth Commission set up to document human rights abuses.

FACT
The world's largest man-made hole is an old diamond mine at Kimberley, 500 m (1640 ft) across and 400 m (1310 ft) deep.

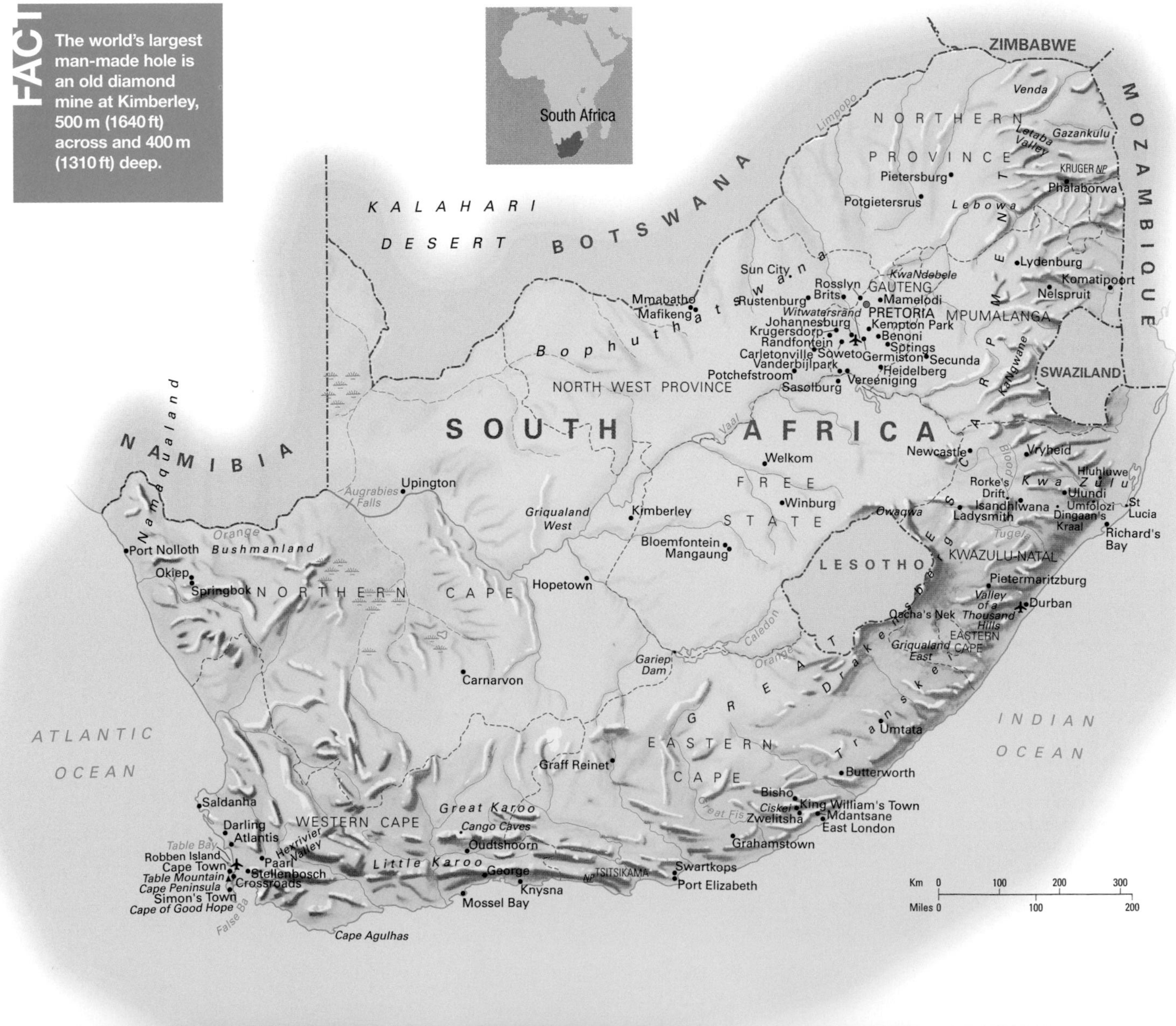

SWAZILAND

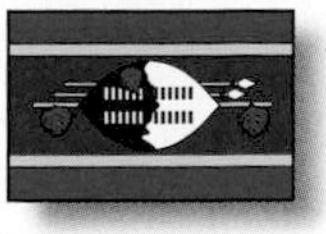

OFFICIAL NAME
The Kingdom of Swaziland

CAPITAL
Mbabane

Area 17 363 km² (6704 sq miles)
Population 980 000
Population density 55 per km² (142 per sq mile)
Population growth rate 1.5%
Life expectancy 55 (m); 60 (f)
Languages English, Siswati
Adult literacy rate 76.7%
Currency lilangeni (plural emalangeni; US $1 = 8.15 emalangeni)
GDP (US million $) 1206
GDP per head (US $) 1269

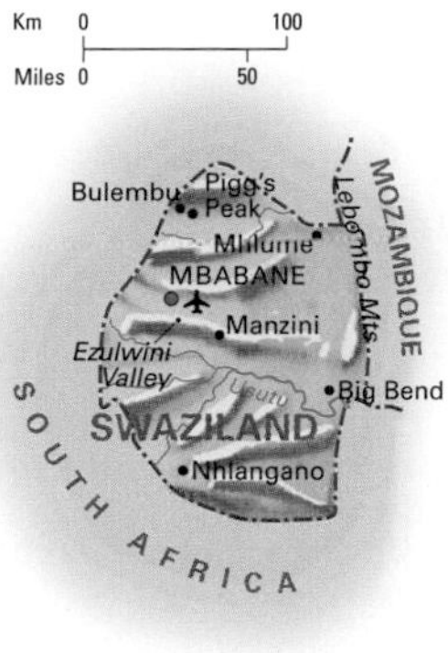

◀ Key dates

1902 British control.
1968 Independence within Commonwealth.
1973 King assumes absolute powers.
1978 Political parties banned.
1993 First free elections.

LESOTHO

OFFICIAL NAME
The Kingdom of Lesotho

CAPITAL
Maseru

Area 30 355 km² (11 720 sq miles)
Population 2 108 000
Population density 68 per km² (176 per sq mile)
Population growth rate 1.9%
Life expectancy 56 (m); 59 (f)
Languages English, Sesotho
Adult literacy rate 71.3%
Currency loti (plural maloti; US $1 = 8.15 maloti)
GDP (US million $) 983
GDP per head (US $) 477

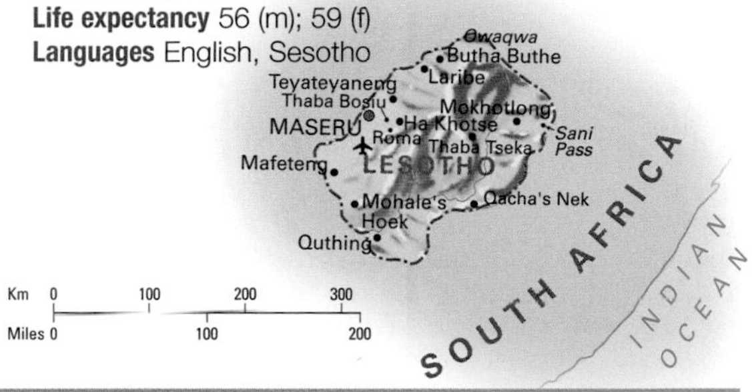

Key dates ▶

1868 Basutoland made British protectorate.
1966 Independence as Kingdom of Lesotho.
1986 South Africa blockades border against African National Congress guerrillas.
1991 Military coup.
1993 Free elections.

BOTSWANA

OFFICIAL NAME
The Republic of Botswana

CAPITAL
Gaborone

Area 581 730 km² (224 607 sq miles)
Population 1 611 000
Population density 3 per km² (7 per sq mile)
Population growth rate 2.1%
Life expectancy 56 (m); 62 (f)
Languages English, Setswana
Adult literacy rate 69.8%
Currency pula (US $1 = 5.68 pula)
GDP (US million $) 4700
GDP per head (US $) 2993

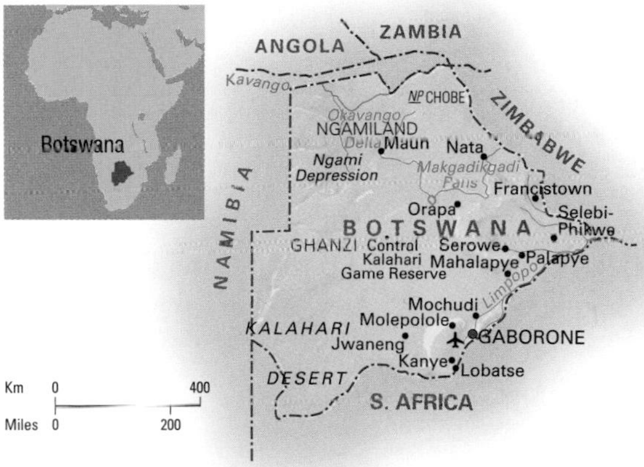

Key dates

1885 British protectorate of Bechuanaland.
1965 Self-government.
1966 Full independence as Botswana, within Commonwealth.
1985-86 South African troops raid African National Congress bases in Gaborone.
1994 South African relations normalized.

NAMIBIA

OFFICIAL NAME
The Republic of Namibia

CAPITAL
Windhoek

Area 824 292 km² (318 261 sq miles)
Population 1 695 000
Population density 2 per km² (5 per sq mile)
Population growth rate 2.7%
Life expectancy 54 (m); 57 (f)
Languages English, Afrikaans, German and local languages
Adult literacy rate 62%
Currency Namibian dollar (US $1 = 8.15 Namibian dollars)
GDP (US million $) 3000
GDP per head (US $) 1807

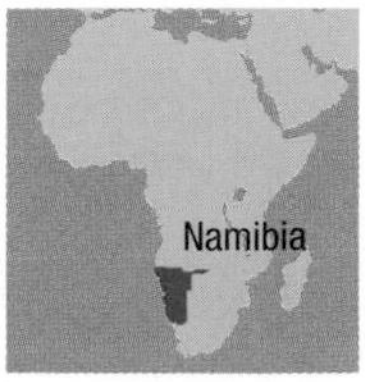

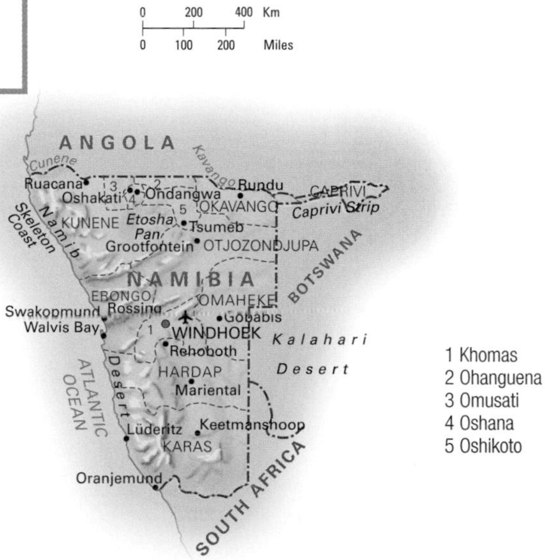

Key dates

1884 Germany annexes, as South-West Africa.
1915 World War I: South Africa invades.
1920 South Africa given mandate under League of Nations but takes total control.
1966 Southwest Africa People's Organization (SWAPO) starts guerrilla independence war.
1968 UN declares name change to Namibia.
1989 Agreement for cease-fire and end of South African rule.
1990 Full independence; joins Commonwealth.
1994 South Africa returns control of Walvis Bay port to Namibia.

International organizations

Since the 19th century, countries have increasingly recognized the benefits of international cooperation on economic, cultural, social, environmental and security matters. After the League of Nations failed to prevent World War II, much more effective international organizations have been set up.

The United Nations

The UN is the most important example of global collaboration. Since the end of World War II, it has been the main international forum for airing states' concerns and grievances, for maintaining peace and security (whether by diplomacy, arbitration, peacekeeping operations or direct military intervention) and for dealing with problems that challenge all of humanity (such as global warming).

The United Nations was established on October 24, 1945, by 51 states. Today nearly every country in the world is a member – a total of 191 at the beginning of 2003. It is not a world government, and it does not make laws. But member states agree to accept the obligations of the UN Charter, which sets out the basic "rules" governing international relations.

The UN system The United Nations has six main bodies (right). Five are based at its main headquarters in New York, and one – the International Court of Justice – is at The Hague, in the Netherlands. Specialized agencies (below) carry out numerous particular functions.

Security Council The UN body responsible for peace. Five of the 15 members (the US, the UK, France, Russia and China) are "permanent," with veto power.

General Assembly A forum for discussing world issues. All UN members are represented, each with one vote. Unlike the Security Council, it cannot enforce decisions.

Economic and Social Council Coordinates the UN's economic and social work, monitoring issues such as human rights, the status of women, drugs and the environment.

Trusteeship Council Supervised the running of UN Trust Territories (dependencies of states defeated in World War II), leading them to independence. This task was completed in 1994: The Council suspended operations, agreeing to meet again only if occasion required.

International Court of Justice The UN's main judicial organ, deciding legal disputes between states. It can only hear a case if the parties agree to it.

Secretariat The UN's administration center, carrying out day-to-day work and managing UN programs. Its head is the secretary-general, appointed by the General Assembly on the Security Council's recommendation.

UN secretaries-general

1946-52	**Trygve Lie** (Norway)
1953-61	**Dag Hammarskjöld** (Sweden)
1961-71	**U Thant** (Myanmar [Burma])
1972-81	**Kurt Waldheim** (Austria)
1982-91	**Javier Pérez de Cuéllar** (Peru)
1992-96	**Boutros Boutros-Ghali** (Egypt)
1997-	**Kofi Annan** (Ghana)

Autonomous organizations linked to the UN through special agreements

Name	Founded; headquarters	Principal activities/purposes
Food and Agriculture Organization (FAO)	1945 Rome	To improve agricultural productivity, food, security and the living standards of rural populations.
International Atomic Energy Agency (IEAE)	1957 Vienna	To promote the safe and peaceful use of atomic energy.
International Civil Aviation Organization (ICAO)	1947 Montreal	Setting international standards for the safety, security and efficiency of air transportation.
International Fund for Agricultural Development (IFAD)	1977 Rome	Organizing funding to raise food production and nutrition levels in developing countries.
International Labor Organization (ILO)	1919 Geneva	To set labor standards and draw up programs to improve working conditions around the world.
IMO **International Maritime Organization (IMO)**	1958 London	Improvement of international shipping procedures, raising of standards in maritime safety and reducing marine pollution.
IMF **International Monetary Fund (IMF)**	1947 Washington, DC	To promote monetary cooperation between nations, exchange-rate stability and expansion of trade.
International Telecommunication Union (ITU)	1865 Geneva	Cooperation to improve telecommunications and develop related technical facilities.
United Nations Educational, Scientific and Cultural Organization (UNESCO)	1946 Paris	International collaboration in science, communications, education and culture; protection of the world's natural and cultural heritage.
UNIDO **United Nations Industrial Development Organization (UNIDO)**	1966 Vienna	Advancement of industry in developing countries through technical assistance and advice.

Other key international organizations and alliances

Name	Founded; headquarters	Principal activities/purposes
Asia-Pacific Economic Cooperation (APEC)	1989 Singapore	Main regional body for promoting open trade and practical economic cooperation (21 members).
Association of Southeast Asian Nations (ASEAN)	1967 Jakarta	Promotion of regional economic development and trade between member countries (10 members).
CARICOM **Caribbean Community and Common Market (CARICOM)**	1973 Georgetown, Guyana	Coordination of economic and foreign policy (15 members; 3 associates).
Commonwealth	1931 London	Association of sovereign independent states (including the UK), nearly all British territories at one time (54 members).
League of Arab States (Arab League)	1945 Cairo	To promote closer ties among members and to coordinate economic, cultural and security policies (22 members).
North Atlantic Treaty Organisation (NATO)	1949 Brussels	Set up to defend Western Europe and North America; now has some central European members (19 members).
OECD **Organisation for Economic Cooperation and Development (OECD)**	1961 Paris	Organization of industrialized countries for cooperation on social and economic policies (29 members).
OAU **Organization of African Unity (OAU)**	1963 Addis Ababa, Ethiopia	To coordinate political, economic and defense policies, and eradicate colonialism in Africa (53 members).
Organization of American States (OAS)	1948 Washington, DC	To strengthen peace and security of the Americas, and promote economic development (35 members).
Organization of Petroleum Exporting Countries (OPEC)	1960 Vienna	To coordinate price and supply policies of major oil-producers (11 members).
Pacific Community	1947 New Caledonia	Regional cooperation and assistance (formerly South Pacific Commission; 27 member states and territories).

Name	Founded; headquarters	Principal activities/purposes
Universal Postal Union (UPU)	1875 Bern, Switzerland	Coordinating international collaboration by postal services.
WORLD BANK GROUP	Washington, DC	
International Bank for Reconstruction and Development (IBRD; World Bank)	1945	Providing loans and technical assistance to member governments.
International Development Association (IDA)	1960	Offering finance for development projects on interest-free terms to less-developed countries.
International Finance Corporation (IFC)	1956	Encouraging private enterprise in developing countries.
Multilateral Investment Guarantee Agency (MIGA)	1988	Promoting the flow of foreign direct investment to and among developing member countries.
World Health Organization (WHO)	1948 Geneva	To raise the standard of health of all peoples by promoting primary health care.
World Intellectual Property Organization (WIPO)	1970 Geneva	Protection of intellectual property, including copyrights, trademarks, industrial designs and patents.
World Meteorological Organization (WMO)	1950 Geneva	Global cooperation on weather observations and the rapid exchange of weather information.
World Trade Organizsation (WTO)	1995 Geneva	To ensure fair trade among countries (successor to the General Agreement on Tariffs and Trade [GATT]).

In addition, a number of UN offices, programs and funds (for example, the UN Development Program, UN Children's Fund, and World Food Program) work to improve the economic and social condition of people around the world. They are responsible to the UN General Assembly or to the UN Economic and Social Council.

Culture and entertainment

Culture and entertainment

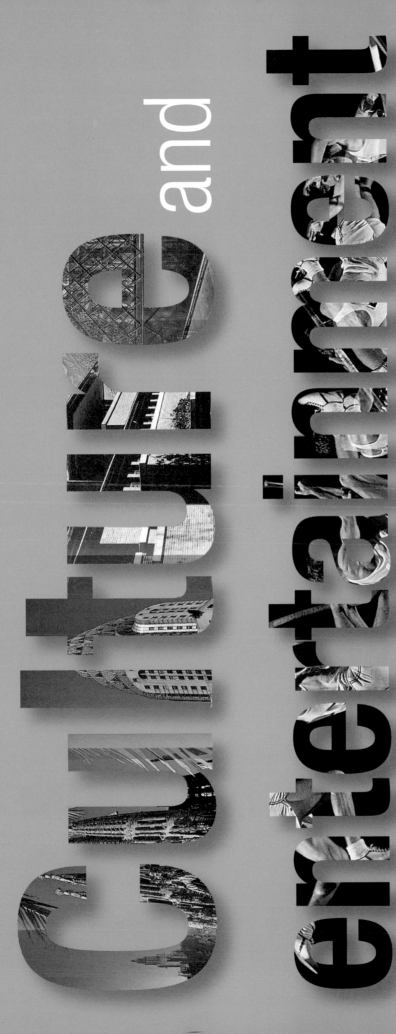

Although all animals communicate, only human beings possess the mental and physical faculties to use language that is capable of conveying complex ideas and knowledge – everything that makes civilization possible. It is likely that language and thought evolved together, stimulating each other. Scientists speculate that language first developed about 100 000 years ago, when the earliest human species, Homo sapiens, *first left Africa. Written forms appeared about 5000 years ago.*

LANGUAGE FAMILIES

Languages that appear to be historically related are grouped into families. All those in the same family are thought to have developed from a parent (proto) version of the language. They tend to have features in common, such as words with similar phonological characteristics describing similar concepts. For example, the Latin for father, *pater*, sounds similar to the equivalent word in many other languages – such as *padre* in Italian and Spanish, *père* in French and *fadar* in old German – suggesting that the languages all have a common ancestor.

At the end of the last Ice Age, 12 000 years ago, the rise in sea levels cut off many groups of people from each other, promoting the evolution of different languages and language families. Migration has led to further adaptations and amalgamations. Linguists now believe that tens of thousands of languages have existed, but few more than 5000 have been clearly identified.

DISTRIBUTION OF LANGUAGE FAMILIES

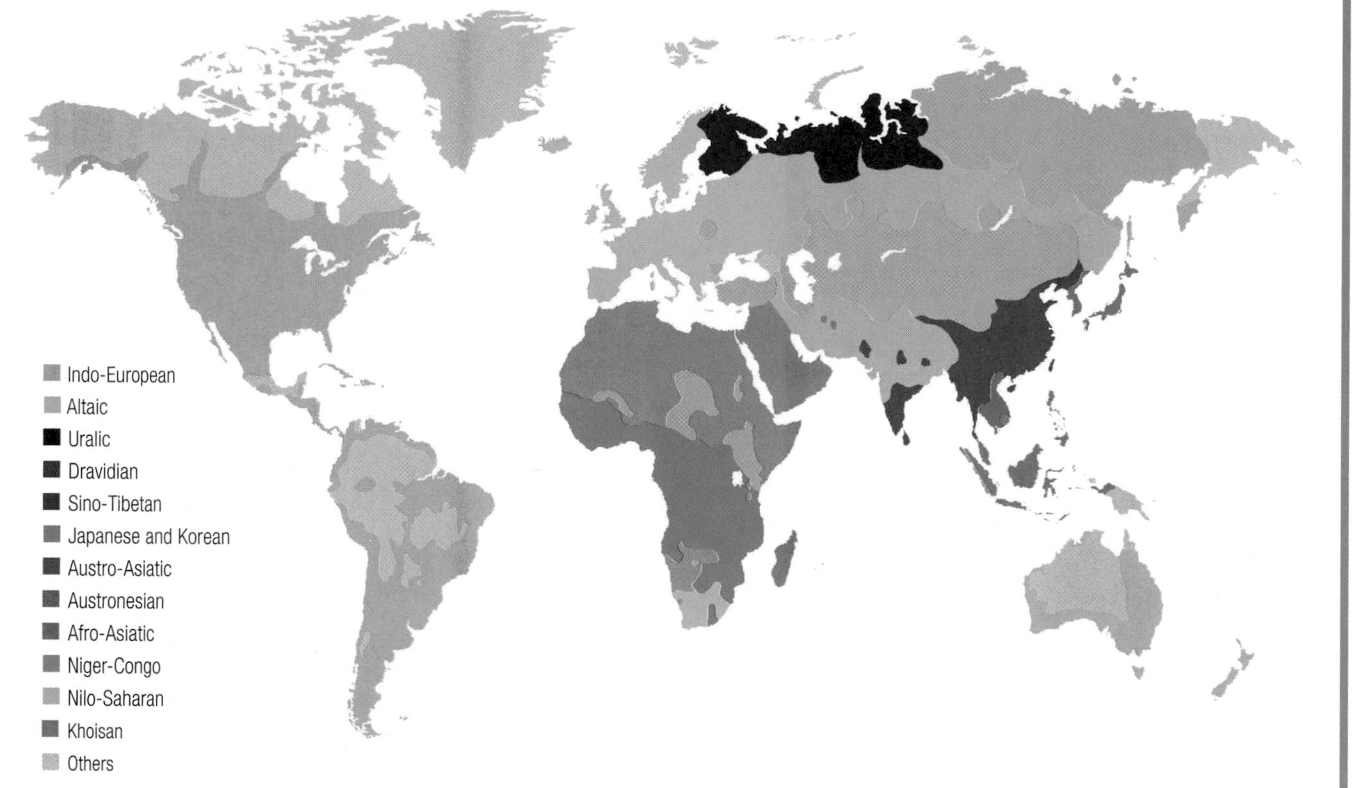

The families outlined below are groups of languages related by similarities in words, phrases and inflection.

Indo-European Spoken by about half the world's population (see opposite).
Altaic More than 50 languages, including Mongolian, Tungusian (Siberia/north China) and Turkish; spoken by 135 million people.
Uralic More than 20 languages, including Estonian, Finnish and Hungarian; spoken by about 24 million people.
Dravidian 24 languages, including Tamil and Teluga; spoken by 220 million people in southern India and Sri Lanka.
Sino-Tibetan More than 130 distinct languages spoken by about 1.2 billion people in China, Tibet and neighboring Far Eastern countries.
Japanese and Korean Languages with no obvious links to other families, with a total of about 200 million speakers.
Austro-Asiatic (Mon-Khmer) Vietnamese, Khmer (Cambodia) and the numerous Munda languages of India, with about 110 million speakers.
Austronesian (Malayo-Polynesian) More than 1000 languages, including Malay, Javanese, Hawaiian and Maori, with about 270 million speakers.
Afro-Asiatic A family of 371 (identified to date) languages, including Arabic, Hebrew, Berber, Hausa, and Amalhric, spoken by about 200 million people.
Niger-Congo About 1400 languages, of which Swahili, spoken by 35 million people in East Africa, is the most widely used.
Nilo-Saharan More than 30 languages spoken by 23 million people in East Africa.
Khoisan Southwestern African bushman languages, including Nama.
Others Little-studied families include the American Indian and southeast European Caucasian group, Thai and Laotian, and the 741 languages of Papua-New Guinea.

Indo-European family By far the most widely spoken family of languages is the Indo-European, to which a large range of European and Asian languages belong. By the dawn of the Christian era, speakers of its varied tongues stretched from Ireland to Bengal. Basque is the only extant European language that is not part of the Indo-European group.

Since the overseas expansion of European power began five centuries ago, four Indo-European languages – French, Portuguese, Spanish, and especially English – have become the main means of communication in many parts of the globe, often killing off native tongues. In fact, more people speak Indo-European languages outside Europe and Asia: North America has the largest English-speaking population, and South America has the most Spanish speakers.

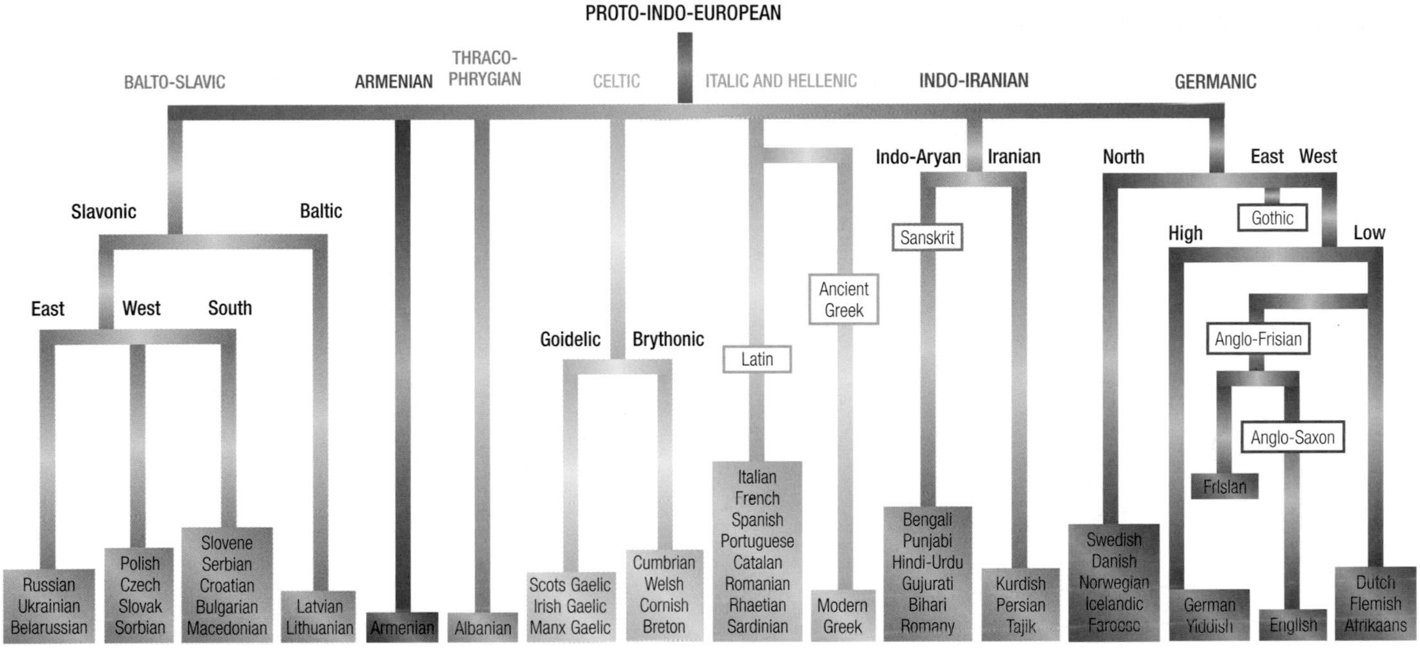

Major language speakers Of the estimated 6000 languages spoken in the world today, only about 200 have more than 1 million speakers, and only 23 have more than 50 million. Mandarin is spoken by more people than any other language, but English is the main vehicle of international communication.

- **Mandarin Chinese** Used in northern China and by Chinese minorities across Southeast Asia.
- **Spanish** Majority of speakers are in South and Central America.
- **English** The US has the greatest number of native speakers. English is the main language of science and diplomacy.
- **Hindi** Used in India and in Indian communities across the world.
- **Arabic** Used throughout the Arab world and as the sacred language of the Koran.
- **Bengali** Used in Bengal and Bangladesh and by Bengali communites worldwide.
- **Portuguese** Most speakers live in Brazil.
- **Russian** Widely used in the former republics of the USSR as well as in Russia.
- **Japanese** Majority of speakers are in Japan.
- **German** The official language in Germany, Austria, Liechtenstein and Switzerland, and widely used in Europe.
- **French** In addition to its use in Europe, it is a major language in Canada, the Caribbean and many former French colonies in Africa and Asia.

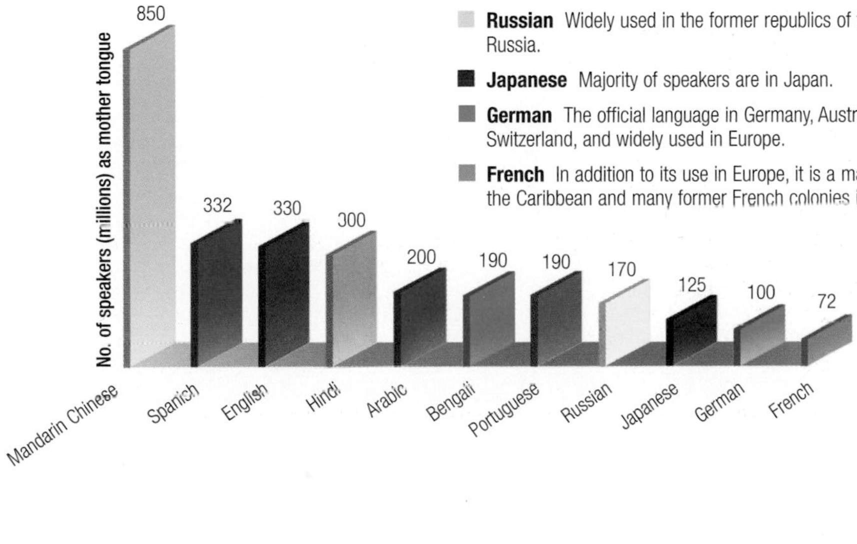

KEY TERMS

- **Cognates** Words in different languages that have the same root.
- **Etymology** The origin and development of words.
- **Phonetics** Study of how sounds are articulated, perceived and combined.
- **Phonology** Study of the sound system of a language.
- **Semantics** Study of the meaning of words.
- **Semiotics** Study of human communication, particularly the use of signs and symbols.
- **Syntax** Study of the structure of phrases and sentences.

see also
138-39 **The prehistoric world**
298-99 **Writing**

The oldest known writings are on clay disks from Mesopotamia, dating back to c. 8000 B.C. They are picture symbols, called pictograms, listing tallies of wine and oil, and reflect the commercial complexity of society in this area. Indeed, the invention of writing, allowing detailed records to be kept, was crucial to the growth of civilization.

ASIA

Indus Valley pictograms

c. 2500 B.C. Cities in the Indus Valley adapt Sumerian pictograms to create their own distinct writing system.

Chinese pictograms

1500 B.C. The Chinese develop their own pictogram script, which is written in columns running from right to left. Originally, simple pictograms, these develop into a vocabulary of about 4000 commonly used signs, known as characters.

MIDDLE EAST

Aramaic

c. 1000 B.C. A new alphabet develops in Aram (part of modern Syria). Aramaic script has no vowels and reads from right to left. Part of the Old Testament is written in it.

Sabean

c. 1000 B.C. The Sabean Arabs devise an alphabet, which spreads south into Africa.

Proto alphabet

Nabatean

c. 1000 B.C. The Nabateans of northern Arabia create their own distinct alphabet.

3500 B.C. The Sumerians develop a pictogram system, which spreads via trade to Egypt and the Indus Valley civilization in Pakistan.

2500 B.C. The Sumerians develop a system of signs with no apparent visual relation to objects. Written in wedge-shaped strokes, it is known as cuneiform, from the Latin *cuneus,* "wedge."

Sumerian pictograms

Cuneiform

2400 B.C. The Akkadians adopt and improve cuneiform.

AFRICA

Egyptian hieroglyphs

3400 B.C. Egyptian scribes improve pictograms to produce a script with about 2500 signs, or hieroglyphs, and are able to record whole sentences. This pictographic script remains in use for 36 centuries, longer than any other script has survived.

Hieratic script

c. 2000 B.C. Egyptian scribes develop the more abstract, free-flowing hieratic script.

Demotic script

c. 600 B.C. Demotic, a faster, more abbreviated form of hieratic, is the most commonly used Egyptian script.

Phoenician script

c. 1300 B.C. The Phoenicians create a 22-letter alphabet.

1500 B.C. The Mycenaean Greeks adapt cuneiform to their language.

EUROPE

Classical Greek

1000 B.C. The Phoenician alphabet spreads to "Dark Age" Greece, where writing had been forgotten after the collapse of Mycenae.

800 B.C. The Greeks add signs for vowels to the Phoenician alphabet. They also change the direction of writing to read from left to right. Colonization spreads Classical Greek script around the Mediterranean.

Etruscan

600 B.C. The Etruscans of central Italy adopt the Greek alphabet, which now has 24 letters: 17 consonants and seven vowels.

1750 B.C. Linear A ideograms are used on Crete.

1400 B.C. Linear B script is widely used in Minoan Greece.

THE DEVELOPMENT OF WRITING

The earliest written messages were conveyed using pictures, from which sprang systems of pictograms, or abstract representations of objects. These were gradually combined into ideograms, symbols for ideas, with exact meaning often linked to context. By the start of the third millennium B.C., the Sumerians were using a highly stylized system of ideograms, cuneiform script. Over the next thousand years, this evolved to represent sounds in the spoken language. But its hundreds of signs made mastery a lengthy business, and its use faded. A more concise set of phonetic symbols, from which all modern alphabets stem, was not invented until the second millennium B.C. by the Phoenicians.

3500 B.C. | 3000 B.C. | 2000 B.C. | 1500 B.C. | 1000 B.C. | 750 B.C. | 600 B.C.

Japanese — **Modern Japanese**

c. A.D. 800 The Japanese adopt Chinese characters for writing their spoken language.

Chinese logographic script — **Modern Chinese**

c. 200 B.C. Chinese logographic script brings uniformity to the use of characters.

Brahmi

c. 300 B.C. Brahmi, an alphabet with both vowels and consonants, is in use in northern India.

Sanskrit — **Modern Indian script**

A.D. 1000 Devanagari script develops from Brahmi and is used to record Sanskrit, the language of most Indian sacred texts.

Classical Hebrew — **Modern Hebrew**

c. A.D. 1 Hebrew square-letter script is now well developed. Like Aramaic, it records only consonants and reads from right to left. Most books of the Old Testament are written in it.

Ethiopic

c. 500 B.C. Ethiopic is the only independent script to emerge in sub-Saharan Africa.

Arabic — **Modern Arabic script**

c. A.D. 515 The first true Arabic script develops but only comes into widespread use after the Islamic holy book, the Koran, is transcribed into Arabic script in about A.D. 650. Like Hebrew, it is written from right to left.

Kufic script

c. A.D. 600 A variation on Arabic script – Kufic – develops around the town of Kufa, now in modern-day Iraq.

Cyrillic script — **Modern Russian alphabet**

A.D. 900 Greek missionaries, St. Cyril and St. Methodius, introduce a version of their alphabet to Russia. It consists of 24 Greek letters, plus 19 new ones appropriate to Russian.

1708 Letter forms are simplified and standardized.

1918 Alphabet is reduced to 33 letters.

Modern Greek alphabet

Classical Roman — **Modern Roman alphabet**

500 B.C. The Romans adapt the Greek alphabet. By about the third century B.C., it consists of 19 letters, and by the 1st century B.C., it has 23. Three more letters were later added to create the modern Roman alphabet of 26 letters.

Runic script

c. A.D. 250 Runic script is used in Scandinavia. Viking invaders later bring it to Britain. It has 24 characters, each with its own phonetic value.

see also
142-43 **Ancient Egypt**
144-45 **Ancient Greece**
146-47 **Ancient Rome**

500 B.C. | A.D. 1 | 500 | 1000 | 1500 | 2000

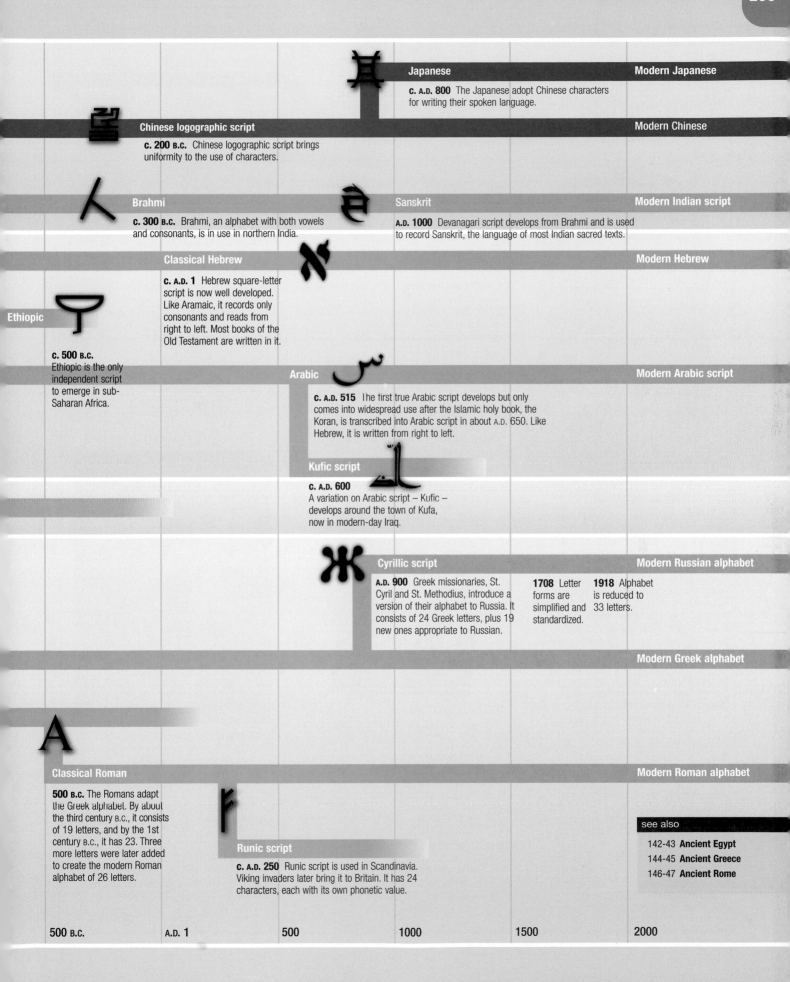

Greek mythology focuses primarily on the activities of 12 "sky gods," believed to live on top of Mount Olympus, the country's highest mountain. Many Greeks, however, continued worshipping older deities. When the Romans conquered Greece, in the 2nd century B.C., they adopted its gods wholesale, giving them Latin names.

The Greek pantheon The top line of gods in the diagram are brothers and sisters. Zeus, the supreme god, fathered lesser deities with his sister and consort, Hera, and with other goddesses and mortals.

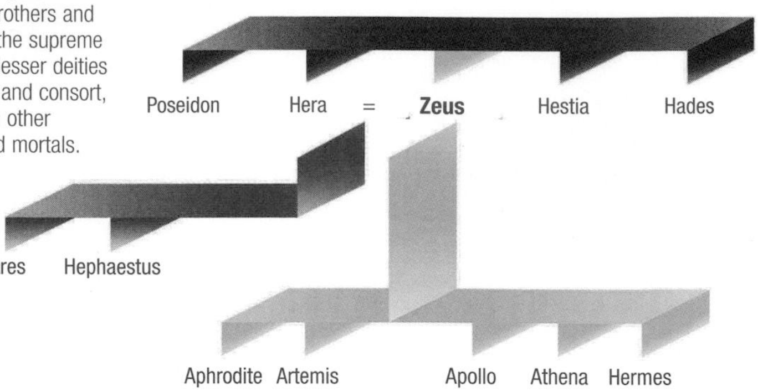

Divine inspiration Ancient Greek art, such as this 5th-century bronze of Zeus (above), depicts the gods – though immortal – as human in appearance.

THE TWELVE OLYMPIANS

Zeus/Jupiter King of the gods, lord of wind and thunder, and often depicted holding a thunderbolt. Zeus married his sister, **Hera**, but was unfaithful to her. He fathered many children, including the deities **Aphrodite**, **Apollo**, **Ares**, **Artemis**, **Athena**, **Hephaestus** and **Hermes**.

Hera/Juno Goddess of marriage and motherhood. Hera was jealous of **Zeus**' many lovers and devised ways to harm them and their offspring.

Poseidon/Neptune Ruler of the seas and usually depicted holding a trident, often with the gold chariot and white horses that he kept in his underwater palace. Poseidon was hot-tempered and constantly in conflict with his brother **Zeus**. His rages were thought to make the earth shake, causing earthquakes.

Apollo God of medicine, poetry and science, who could charm animals with the music of his lyre. He was the twin of **Artemis** and was also known as **Phoebus**, "the shining one."

Athena/Minerva Goddess of wisdom and patron of architects and sculptors. Athena was born fully formed from **Zeus'** head. She was a warrior goddess and is often depicted with a spear and shield.

Aphrodite/Venus Goddess of love born from the foam in the sea off the island of Cyprus. Aphrodite married **Hephaestus** but deceived him with Ares, Hermes and others. Her retinue included **Eros/Cupid** and the three **Graces**.

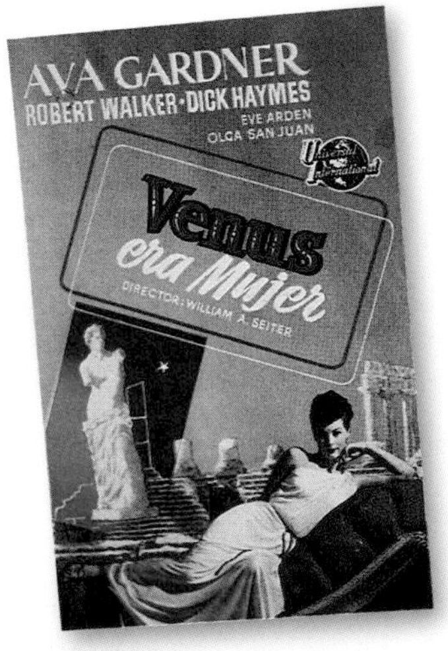

Screen goddess In the 20th century, the Roman deity Venus was still a symbol of love and beauty.

Hephaestus/Vulcan Blacksmith and patron of industry. Hephaestus was born lame. His mother, **Hera**, found him so ugly that she threw him to Earth, but he was later reinstated on Mount Olympus. He married **Aphrodite**. The Romans believed that his chief forge lay under Mount Etna in Sicily.

Hades/Pluto Ruler of the realm of the dead – the underworld – and brother of **Zeus**. Hades abducted **Persephone**, his niece, to be his consort.

Hermes/Mercury Quick-witted "messenger god," son of **Zeus** by the nymph **Maia**. Hermes is often depicted with winged sandals, taking messages from Heaven to Earth.

Artemis/Diana Virginal goddess of hunting and twin of **Apollo**. Artemis punished the mortal **Actaeon** for spying on her while she bathed by changing him into a stag so that his own hounds turned on him.

The huntress Artemis fiercely protected her chastity and punished suitors for approaching her.

Ares/Mars God of war, highly revered by the Romans as Mars. They regarded him as the father of **Romulus and Remus**, the founders of Rome. In early Roman religion, he was worshipped by farmers as a god of vegetation.

Hestia/Vesta Goddess of hearth and home and sister of **Zeus**. Hestia was chaste and retiring. The sacred flame in her temple in Rome was regarded as Rome's "hearth."

OTHER IMMORTALS

In addition to the Olympians, there were countless minor deities, many of whom were believed to share the Earth with man.

Dionysus/Bacchus God of theater, wine and ecstasy and son of **Zeus** by **Semele**, princess of Thebes. Dionysus grew up wild on Mount Nysa, where he learned to make wine. He was the focus of a major cult. Drunken female devotees were known as **bacchantes**.

Pan/Faunus or Silvanus Patron of shepherds and god of the woods. Pan is depicted with horns and goat's legs, playing reed pipes. He was fond of chasing nymphs such as **Syrinx**, who changed into a reed to escape him.

Prometheus and the Titans The 14 Titan deities deposed by **the Olympians**. When they challenged the new order, **Zeus** imprisoned them deep in the Earth. Prometheus remained loyal, so he was admitted to Olympus. He stole fire from the gods and gave it to humans. As punishment, he was chained to a rock, where an eagle tore out his liver, which regenerated every day.

Demeter/ Ceres Goddess of agriculture and fertility. When her daughter, **Persephone**, was abducted by **Hades**, Demeter kept crops from growing until Hades promised to return her. He agreed on the conditon that Persephone spend four months of the year with him in the underworld. These months became winter, when the Earth remains barren.

Satyrs Half-man, half-goat. Satyrs were fertility spirits who spent their time chasing nymphs through the forest and getting drunk.

Nymphs Beautiful spirits of the air, earth, trees and water, often loved by the gods. One nymph, **Echo**, fell in love with a mortal, **Narcissus**, who was obsessed with his own reflection.

Muses Nine goddesses of creative inspiration who accompanied **Apollo**.

Centaurs Half-man, half-horse. Centaurs were thought to possess both animal brutishness and human wisdom.

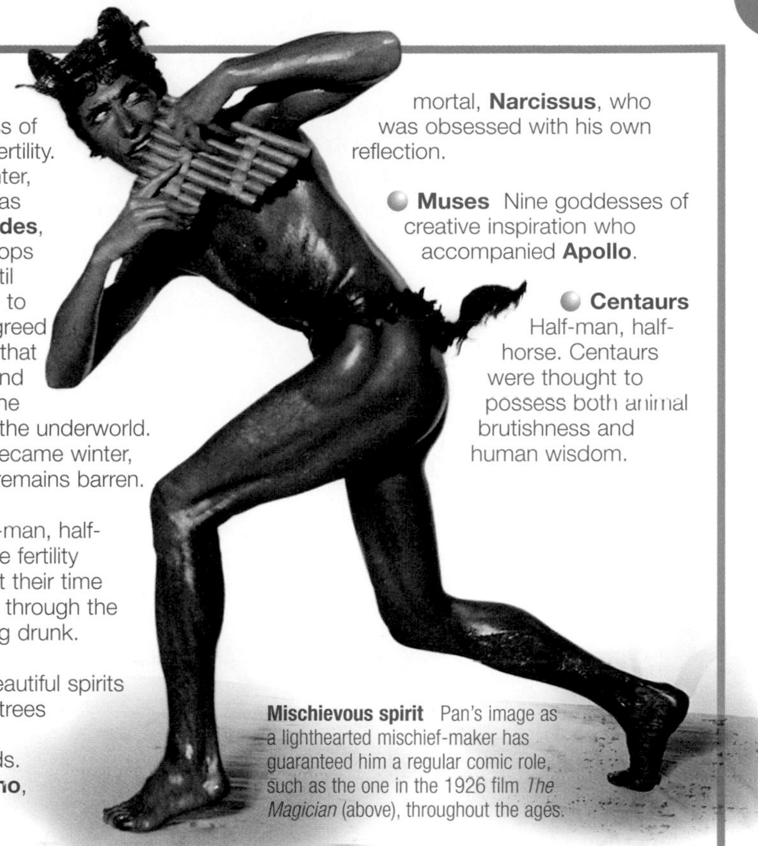

Mischievous spirit Pan's image as a lighthearted mischief-maker has guaranteed him a regular comic role, such as the one in the 1926 film *The Magician* (above), throughout the ages.

HEROES AND HEROINES

Heroes, though often half-divine in ancestry and superhuman in powers, were mortal.

Herakles/Hercules Son of **Zeus** by **Alcmene**, the Queen of Thebes. He was noted for his great strength. Driven mad by the jealous **Hera**, he killed his family. To atone for this, he undertook **12 labors**. These included capturing the man-eating horses of **Diomedes**, King of Argos; cleansing the **Augean stables**, home to 3000 oxen; and seizing **Cerberus**, the three-headed dog that guarded the underworld. He died from wearing a poisonous tunic made by the centaur **Nessus**. After his death, Zeus made him into a god.

Theseus and Ariadne Theseus, son of the Athenian king **Aegeus**, volunteered to be one of seven youths and maidens sent to Crete as an annual tribute to the **Minotaur**, a half-bull, half-human monster. Helped by the Cretan princess, Ariadne, Theseus entered the Minotaur's labyrinth and slew the beast. He then fled with Ariadne, but later abandoned her on Naxos, where **Dionysus** comforted her.

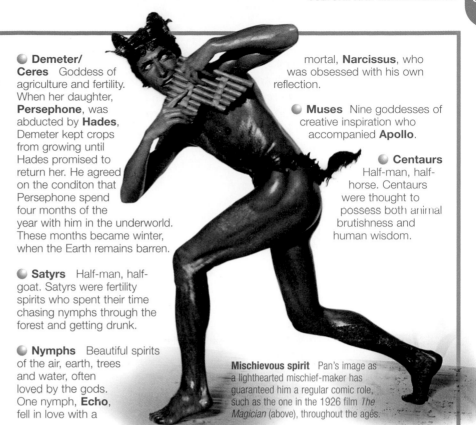

Favored by the gods Slaying the Minotaur (right) gave Theseus heroic status.

Jason and the Argonauts Given the task of obtaining the famed **Golden Fleece**, Jason set sail on his quest with a crew of heroes, including **Theseus**. At Colchis, Jason's destination, the king promised to surrender the Fleece if Jason could plow a field with wild bulls and sow it with dragon's teeth. As he did so, armed men sprang from the furrows to attack him, but he tricked them into fighting each other and won his prize.

Aeneas Son of **Aphrodite** and the Trojan **Anchises**. Aeneas escaped from the sacking of Troy (see right) and after many adventures, landed in Italy. There he married a princess, **Lavinia**, and built the city of **Lavinium**. Many noble Romans claimed him as their ancestor.

Romulus and Remus Twin sons of **Mars**. Romulus and Remus were suckled by a **she-wolf**. Legend states that they founded **Rome** in 753 B.C. The brothers quarrelled, and in a rage, Romulus killed his brother and became the city's first king.

The Trojan Horse

When the Greek queen, **Helen**, was abducted by the Trojan prince, **Paris**, Greece's armies assembled to avenge the insult. War raged for ten years, but the Greeks failed to capture the city of **Troy**. Eventually, the Trojans saw the Greeks sail away, leaving behind a huge **wooden horse**, apparently to placate the gods. Rejoicing, they dragged it inside their walls. That night, Greek soldiers hiding in the horse's belly, emerged to open the gates for their returning army, which then sacked the city.

see also

All cultures have a store of myths and legends relating to religious beliefs, but the uneven spread of methods of recording them and the development of later religions has meant that some mythologies are much better known today than others. In Europe, the German-Scandinavian and Celtic mythologies have survived alongside the well-documented stories of the Greeks and Romans. In the Americas, the related stories of the Aztec and Mayan gods remain among the best known.

Mythic opera German composer Wagner set Norse myths to music. Odin's daughter, Brunhild, appears in his *Der Ring Des Nibelungen* (above).

NORSE/TEUTONIC MYTHOLOGY

The Germanic and Norse peoples of the 5th-9th centuries had a common mythology. It has survived mainly in Norse sagas, because the Vikings who created them retained their pagan beliefs longer than their German neighbors did. Where German and Norse names differ, the Norse name is given first.

Odin/Wotan Chief of the **Vanir**, the Norse land and water gods, and creator of the world. Odin was the god of wisdom, war, art and culture. He was also a law-giver. Those who died heroically in battle would be welcomed by him to **Valhalla**, the great hall of immortality, or the feasting hall of **Asgard**, the home of the gods. Odin could change shape at will but was often depicted as a one-eyed wanderer in wide-brimmed hat and cloak.

Thor/Donar God of thunder, fertility and, to some extent, war. The hot-tempered but dull-witted Thor is usually depicted smashing his opponents with his magic hammer, known as **Mjollnir**. Vikings often wore small hammers as amulets, invoking Thor's protection and help in defeating enemies in battle.

Loki A malevolent joker-god who is found only in Norse myth. Loki was a trickster, fraud and thief and was regarded as the creator of chaos.

Baldur Son of **Odin** and **Frigga** and god of peace and light. Frigga made all things on Earth promise never to harm him, but she overlooked the mistletoe plant. The evil **Loki** gave a spear made of this to the blind god, **Holdur**, who was duped into hurling it at Baldur, killing him. His death signaled the coming of **Ragnarok**.

Freia The chief goddess among the Vanir. Freia (Lady) is associated with fertility and love. She is the twin sister or female aspect of the god **Frey**, bringer of peace and abundance.

Frigga The Queen of Heaven and wife of Odin. Frigga was, like **Freia**, associated with childbearing and marriage. She is the chief goddess of the Norse sky gods, known as the **Aesir**.

In pursuit of valor Some Valkyries were said to have the power to kill unworthy warriors and to protect those they favored. This 1865 painting depicts a Valkyrie riding to a battlefield.

The Valkyries Gold-haired warrior maidens with shining armor. The Valkyries served **Odin**. Some myths describe them as supernatural, but others suggest their mortality. They rode over land and sea to give victory to heroes chosen by Odin and took the fallen to **Valhalla**.

Asgard The heavenly home of the gods, built by giants and joined to Earth by a bridge called **Byfrost**, which is identified with rainbows or the Milky Way.

Ragnarok The name given to the final apocalypse, or "Twilight of the gods," in which all creation, including the gods, would perish. A new world order would then arise, which in later descriptions of Ragnarok includes a single deity. This probably represents the blending of Christianity into Norse myth. Christianity replaced the pagan religion in the 11th century.

Sigurd/Siegfried A descendant of **Odin**. Sigurd was persuaded by the smith **Regin** to kill the dragon **Fafnir** and win his hoard of gold. By bathing in the dragon's blood, Sigurd became invulnerable in all but one spot.

Beowulf The morality and monster-slaying of the 8th-century saga of Beowulf draws on Norse myth. The hero kills the monster **Grendel**, which has been attacking Denmark's royal court. He becomes king of the **Geats** and dies defending his people against a dragon.

CELTIC GODS AND LEGENDS

The Celts inhabited much of western Europe before the great Germanic migrations of 200 B.C. to A.D. 400. Elements of their culture have survived in Scotland, Wales, Cornwall and Brittany, but Ireland is the best source of Celtic myths because the Irish were never conquered by Rome and became Christians later than other Celts.

Tuatha dé Danaan The "Children of the goddess **Danu**" arrived in Ireland on a magic cloud and drove out the previous inhabitants, the **Fir Bolg**. They had four magic weapons: the **Stone of Destiny** (Lia Fail), which shrieked if a true king touched it; the **spear of Lug**; the **sword of Nuadu**; and a magic inexhaustible cauldron called **Dagda**. After being driven out by invaders called **"Milesians,"** they retired underground and became the **"Little People,"** the fairies.

Cuchulainn The leading figure in the epic ***Tain bo Cuilagne*** (the Cattle Raid of Cooley). Cuchulainn, son of the god **Lug**, was a superhuman warrior. At age five, he was able to fight off 150 other boys who were attacking him with spears. His fury in battle was said to be so great that it could make water boil. But he was a tragic figure. He killed his son **Conloach** in error and lost his powers by being tricked into eating dog, a taboo meat.

Tir nan Og An island of the dead in the far west or underworld. Tir nan Og was a blessed place of supreme happiness to which the gods invited select heroes. It has been identified with **Avalon**, "the island of apples," which was the final resting place of King **Arthur**.

Arthur The legend of Arthur was probably based on the life of an actual Romano-British leader. The son of King **Uther Pendragon**, he was educated by **Merlin**, and declared king after pulling the magic sword **Excalibur** from its stone. He held court in splendor at Camelot. His knights set out from there on the quest for the **Holy Grail**. His best friend, **Lancelot**, fell in love with his wife, **Guinevere**, and in his old age, his son **Mordred** led a rebellion against him. Arthur crushed it but was fatally wounded and ferried off to **Avalon**, where the "once and future king" was said to have been healed and from where he will one day return.

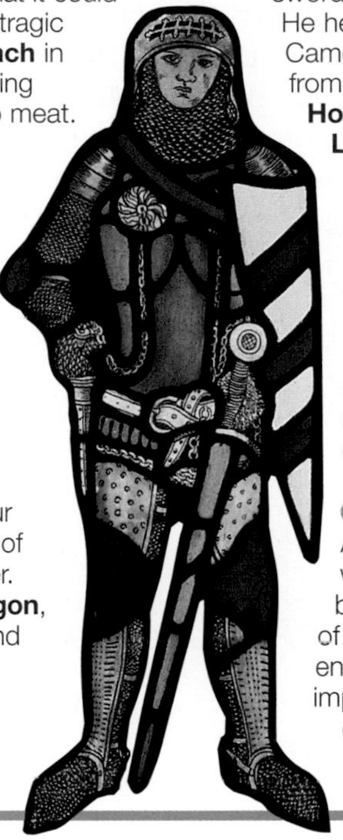

Arthurian romance The legend of Arthur inspired this stained-glass figure of Sir Lancelot by artist William Morris.

Merlin (Myrddin) A wise magician. Merlin was credited with helping build Stonehenge. In spite of his wisdom, he fell for the enchantress **Nimue**, who imprisoned him inside a crystal spiral.

AZTEC AND MAYA GODS AND LEGENDS

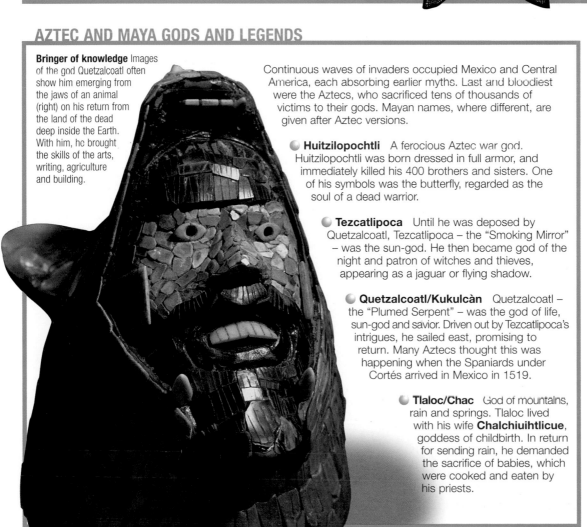

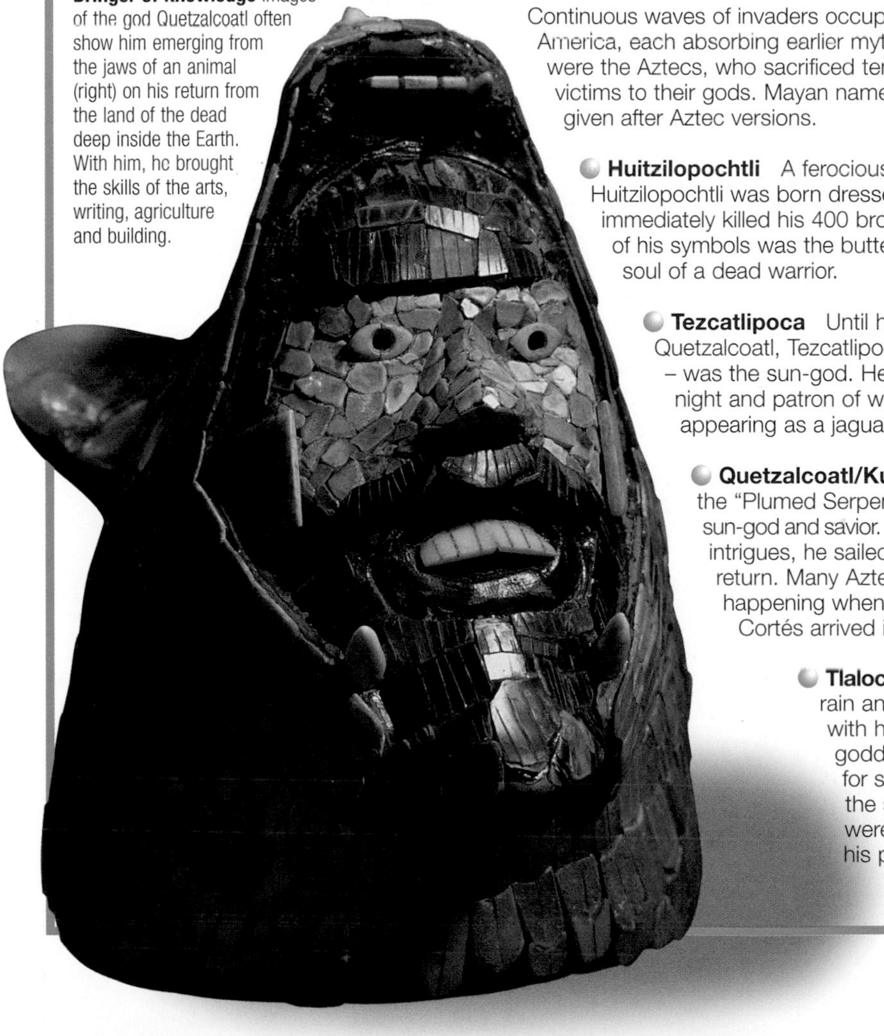

Bringer of knowledge Images of the god Quetzalcoatl often show him emerging from the jaws of an animal (right) on his return from the land of the dead deep inside the Earth. With him, he brought the skills of the arts, writing, agriculture and building.

Continuous waves of invaders occupied Mexico and Central America, each absorbing earlier myths. Last and bloodiest were the Aztecs, who sacrificed tens of thousands of victims to their gods. Mayan names, where different, are given after Aztec versions.

Huitzilopochtli A ferocious Aztec war god. Huitzilopochtli was born dressed in full armor, and immediately killed his 400 brothers and sisters. One of his symbols was the butterfly, regarded as the soul of a dead warrior.

Tezcatlipoca Until he was deposed by Quetzalcoatl, Tezcatlipoca – the "Smoking Mirror" – was the sun-god. He then became god of the night and patron of witches and thieves, appearing as a jaguar or flying shadow.

Quetzalcoatl/Kukulcàn Quetzalcoatl – the "Plumed Serpent" – was the god of life, sun-god and savior. Driven out by Tezcatlipoca's intrigues, he sailed east, promising to return. Many Aztecs thought this was happening when the Spaniards under Cortés arrived in Mexico in 1519.

Tlaloc/Chac God of mountains, rain and springs. Tlaloc lived with his wife **Chalchiuihtlicue**, goddess of childbirth. In return for sending rain, he demanded the sacrifice of babies, which were cooked and eaten by his priests.

Days of the week

The names of weekdays have roots in Norse and Roman myth.

Monday Norse "moon day," Latin *lunae dies* – giving *lundi* in French.

Tuesday The day of Tiu or Tyr, a Norse war god. Tyr's Roman form, Mars, is the root of the the French *mardi.*

Wednesday Wotan's day. The Roman's "day of Mercury" gives the French *mercredi*.

Thursday The day of Thor, or Donar, the root of Germany's *Donnerstag*. Rome's "day of Jupiter," which became France's *jeudi*.

Friday Frigga's day. Her Roman equivalent, Venus, is the root of *vendredi* in French.

Saturday Roman Saturn's day.

Sunday The pagan day of the Sun.

see also
148-49 **The making of Europe**
163-64 **Ancient America**
300-1 **Greek and Roman myths**
338-39 **Western literature**

Religion is one of mankind's oldest and most distinctive characteristics. Archaeologists have discovered in graves dating back 60 000 years artifacts that must have been intended for use in an afterlife, indicating a religious belief for which no other trace survives. Many cultures lacked cities or literacy or even the wheel, but none existed for long without some form of religion.

A family tree of religions

Most of the world's major religions can be placed in family groups, because they share common roots. For example, Judaism, Christianity and Islam, although now three very distinctive faiths, stem from the beliefs and rituals of people that lived in the ancient civilizations of the Middle East. Similarly, Buddhism and Jainism both spring from the teachings of men steeped in the tradition of Hinduism.

Some faiths, such as Confucianism, Taoism and Shintoism, have developed independently but show a great range of similarities, probably because they are all closely linked to the folklore of Southeast Asia. All three are usually practiced alongside Buddhism in their respective countries of origin.

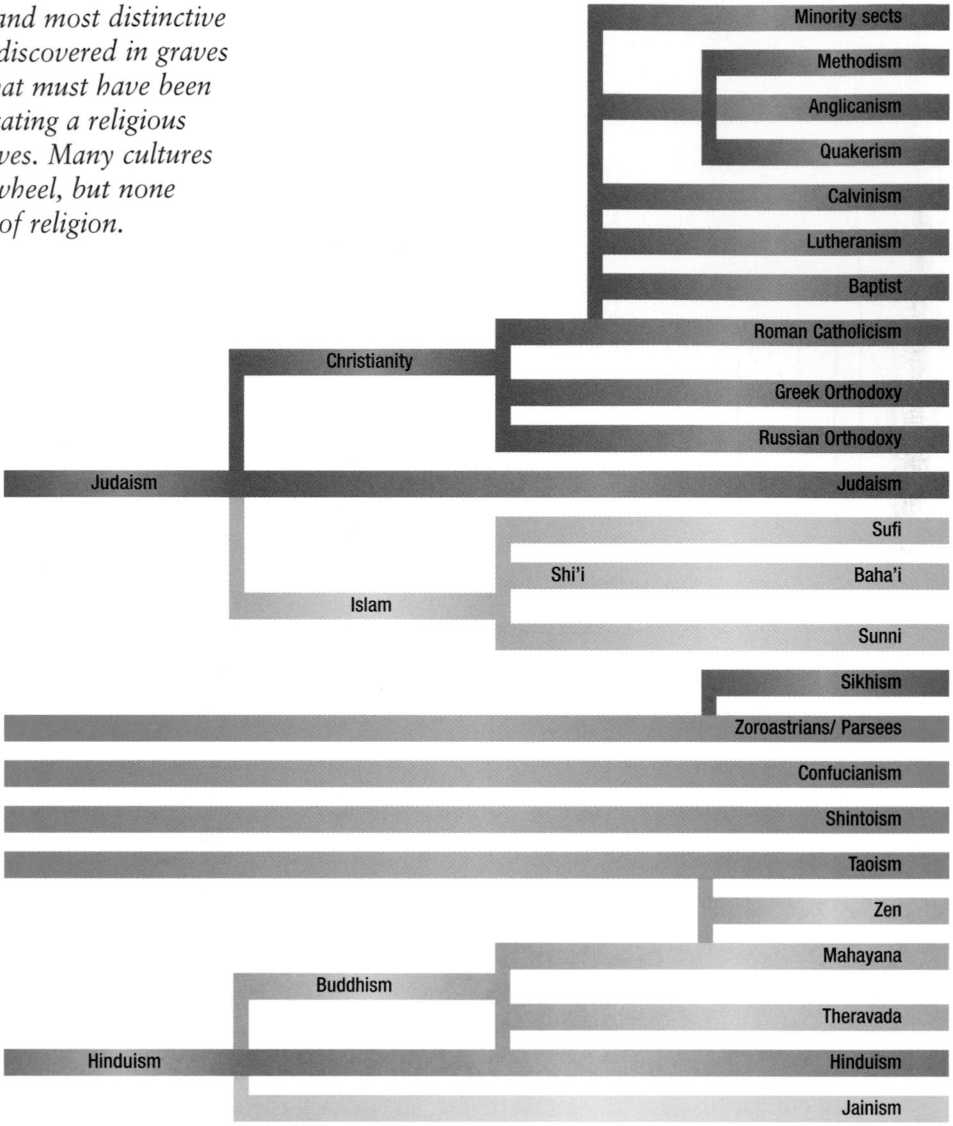

JUDAISM

First of the great monotheistic (worshipping one God) religions, Judaism emerged as a distinct faith under Moses, who is believed to have received the **Ten Commandments** from God on Mount Sinai around 1200 B.C. He united the Jewish people, and helped his successor, Joshua, conquer the promised land of Canaan, which the Jews renamed **Israel**. Revolt against Roman rule ended with the destruction of the Temple in Jerusalem in A.D. 70, and Judaism was spread around the globe by exiles.

Key beliefs Jews view the created world as essentially good and see God's divine plan in human history.

Worship Devout Jews attend the synagogue three times a day.

- In the morning and evening, they recite the basic affirmation of Judaism, the **Shema**, from the Torah (see below).
- The **Sabbath**, or day of rest, is the focal point of the week. It begins at sunset on Friday, when candles are lit, followed by prayers and a family meal.

Holy books The main holy book, the **Torah**, consists of the first five books of the Hebrew Bible, given to Moses on Mount Sinai. The basic laws of Jewish life are found in the Torah. A collection of scholarly commentaries on these, called the **Talmud**, is also considered sacred.

God's law The Torah, hand copied onto parchment scrolls, is read out at the synagogue. No human imagery appears on the richly decorated casing in obedience to the law not to make graven images.

see also
150-51 **Christianity**
168-69 **Clash of faiths**
308-9 **Western thought**
358-59 **Food**

CHRISTIANITY

Jesus Christ (c. 6 B.C.-A.D. 30), the founder of the religion that bears his name, was a Jew. His controversial teachings, along with his claim to speak with God's authority, brought him into conflict with the Jewish establishment. Eventually he was arrested and crucified in Jerusalem. After Emperor Constantine converted to Christianity in 311, it became the official faith of the Roman Empire. Followers have taken its message to the corners of the Earth, so that today, Christianity is the most widespread monotheistic religion (see map, left).

Roman Catholicism Roman Catholics acknowledge the authority of the pope, who is seen as being in direct succession from St. Peter, the first Bishop of Rome.

Eastern or Orthodox Church Challenges to the authority of the pope by the Orthodox Church, based in Constantinople, culminated in it breaking away in the Great Schism of 1054. Orthodoxy puts great emphasis on tradition, with icons playing a major role in worship. An icon is seen as a window to God, bringing the worshipper into the "real" presence of the subject depicted.

Protestantism In the 16th century, the authority of the Roman Catholic Church was challenged in a movement that became known as the **Reformation**.

Lutheranism dates from 1517, when Martin Luther attacked corruption in the Roman Catholic Church in Germany. Lutheranism stresses a personal relationship with God and study of the Bible as the route to salvation.

Protestantism took a more puritanical, authoritarian form in **Calvinism**, founded by John Calvin the 1540s. Followers believe their salvation is entirely in the hands of an all-knowing, all-powerful God.

Anglicanism, a flexible form of Protestantism, was finalized by the Elizabethan Settlement in England in 1559. It spread around the world with English-speaking peoples.

Anabaptist sects appeared in Germany in the early 16th century. They baptised only adults, as do their successors, the **Baptists**. In the 17th century, the **Quakers** sought a more direct path to God by dispensing with churches, liturgy and clergy. **Methodists** did not take such extreme measures when they split from the Church of England in 1729, but services were simplified to give the laity a bigger role.

Key beliefs All Christians believe in the divinity of Jesus Christ as the son of the three-in-one (triune) God. The third element in **the holy Trinity** is the Holy Spirit.

- Through his **crucifixion and resurrection**, Christ has shown humanity the path to eternal life.
- Most Christians believe that Christ will one day return to Earth to judge the living and the dead in **the Last Judgment**.

Worship The chief ritual, the **Eucharist** – also called the **Mass** (Roman Catholic) or **Holy Communion** (Anglican) – commemorates Jesus's Last Supper. Orthodox and Roman Catholic Christians believe that the bread in the Mass transforms into the "real presence" of Christ's body, but Protestants regard this as a symbolic act.

Holy books All Christians accept the Bible's **Old and New Testaments**; the latter records Christ's life.

Catholics and Orthodox Christians also accept the **teachings of the early Church Fathers**, such as Sts. Jerome and Augustine, but Protestants usually regard the Bible as the only holy script.

Atonement To Christians, Christ's death depicted right on an altarpiece by Rogier van der Weyden (1399-1464) – is his payment for the sins of man. By suffering, he opened up the path to salvation for all.

ISLAM

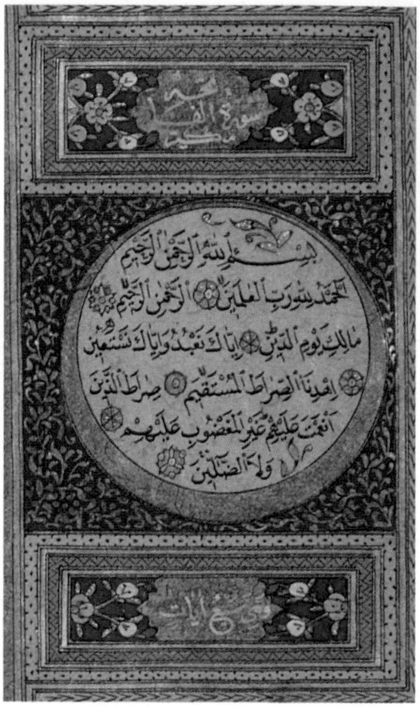

Act of devotion Muslim calligraphers produce copies of the Koran as a personal expression of faith.

Islam, meaning "submission to God," dates from A.D. 622, when the Prophet Muhammad fled from persecution in Mecca (now in Saudi Arabia) to Medina, an event known as the **Hegira**. By the time of his death in 632, all of Arabia had embraced the new religion. A century later, it had spread into Spain and Central Asia. Today, about 20 percent of the world is Muslim, and the faith is spreading faster than any other.

Islam divides into two branches: 80 percent of Muslims are **Sunni**; the minority are **Shia**. They differ in opinion over the correct line of descent from the Prophet.

Key beliefs Muslims regard this world as good and see or feel God's presence everywhere. However, they also view it only as a preparation for the next world.

- All Muslims believe in the oneness and omnipotence of God (**Allah**).
- Abraham, Moses and Jesus are Muhammad's divinely inspired precursors. Muslims reject Christ's divinity – like the other prophets, he is human. Muhammad is the final and greatest prophet.

Worship Islamic observance is based on performance of the **Five Pillars**, or duties:

- At least once in life, a Muslim must recite with complete conviction and understanding the profession of faith: "There is no God but Allah, and Muhammad is His Prophet."
- Muslims must pray five times a day: at dawn, noon, mid-afternoon, sunset and bedtime. They prostrate themselves facing Mecca, the site of the Prophet's tomb.
- Muslims should give alms – 2.5 percent of all their possessions – to the poor and needy every year.
- Muslims should observe the fast of **Ramadan**, the holy month, which commemorates the Hegira. No food, drink or smoke may pass their lips between dawn and sunset.
- Every Muslim who can should make a pilgrimage to Mecca at least once.

Holy book The **Koran** is believed to be the word of God revealed to the Prophet Muhammad. It contains 114 chapters (**suras**) giving detailed rules on every aspect of human life.

HINDUISM

Hinduism originated in northern India about 4000 years ago, and by the 11th century A.D. it had replaced Buddhism as the dominant religion in India.

Key beliefs Behind the countless Hindu gods and goddesses lies **Brahman**, the supreme reality – infinite, impersonal, uncreated, unnameable. Buried beneath layers of egotism at the core of every human lies the divine spark, **Atman**.

- The main Hindu gods – worshipped as manifestations of Brahman – are Brahma the Creator, Vishnu the Preserver and Shiva the Destroyer, who form the **Hindu trinity**, and Kali, goddess of death.
- The Hindu's goal is to unite Atman with Brahman by escaping the endless cycle of life, death and rebirth (**samsara**) through spiritual liberation (**moksha**). This is obtained by different paths, or **yogas**: spiritual knowledge through meditation (jnana yoga); the yoga of devotion to a particular god (bhakti yoga); and the yoga of good work (karma yoga).
- The Universe, both human and nonhuman, is governed by the laws of action (**karma**). Every action has its effect, good or bad, in this life or the next.
- Each person has an eternal soul that can be reborn millions of times and in millions of forms (**reincarnation**).

Worship This takes three forms.

- Daily worship, or **puja**, is carried out at home, at a shrine decorated with pictures of the gods.
- Worship also takes place in temples, led by a priest, or **brahmin**.
- Hindus make pilgrimages to sacred sites, such as the holy city of Varanasi (Benares) on the Ganges, where many bathe in the sacred waters or have their ashes scattered.

Holy books Hinduism has a variety of books considered holy: a collection of hymns, the **Vedas**; epic poems, the **Ramayana** and the **Mahabharata**, which includes the Bhagavad-Gita, a long account of Krishna, god of love; and philosophical writings, such as the **Upanishads**.

Elephant god Ganesh, one of the most popular Hindu gods, is revered as the Lord of Learning and Remover of Obstacles. His father, Shiva, cut off his head in error and then offered to replace it with the head of the first living thing he saw, which was an elephant.

BUDDHISM

Gautama, the Buddha or Enlightened One, was born about 560 B.C. in lowland Nepal. Breaking with his native Hindu tradition, he rejected the extremes of both asceticism and sensuality for the **Middle Way**, based on the Four Noble Truths (see below). Buddhism spread across India and as far as Japan and Indonesia.

Early in its history, Buddhism split into Theravada and Mahayana Buddhism.

Theravada Buddhism Theravada, the "Teaching of the Elders" (also known as Hinayana, the "Lesser Vehicle"), is dominant in Sri Lanka and Southeast Asia. It claims to be closest to the Buddha's original teachings and stresses the importance of meditation.

Mahayana Buddhism Mahayana, the "Greater Vehicle," found in China, Tibet, Korea and Japan, stresses devotion and compassion. It divides into distinct schools.

Tibetan Buddhism, or Lamaism, has elaborate rituals, scriptures and monastic orders. It is led by the Dalai Lama.

Zen or **Ch'an Buddhism** originated in China and Japan. Followers work toward enlightenment through meditation.

Pure Land Buddhism also originated in China and Japan. Devotees with true faith are believed to be reborn in paradise – the Pure Land or Realm.

Key beliefs Buddhism has no personal god. The Bodhisattvas of Mahayana Buddhism resemble Catholic saints or Hindu gods in effect being worshipped.

- **Bodhisattvas** are Buddhas – of which there are many – who have turned back to the world on the cusp of enlightenment in order to help others.
- Gautama preached **"Four Noble Truths,"** which are the basis of Buddhism:

1. All existence is suffering, or **dukkha** – meaning everything is wrong with life, not just pain but every frustration and grief.
2. The cause of suffering is craving, or wrong desire (**tanha**).
3. Ending craving leads to enlightenment.
4. The best way to enlightenment is the **Noble Eightfold Path**.

The Noble Eightfold Path consists of Right Views; Right Intentions; Right Speech; Right Conduct, including kindness; Right Livelihood (arms or drug-dealing are unacceptable); Right Effort, meaning willing one's way; Right Mindfulness, meaning understanding of life and oneself; and Right Contemplation, including meditation.

There are other aspects to Buddhist belief.

- Buddhists do not believe in an immortal soul but rather in no soul or no self (**anatta**); the idea of a separate "self" is illusory.
- Buddhists seek **nirvana** – the escape from the cycle of death and rebirth (**samsara**) by the snuffing out of individual existence and its desires and weaknesses.
- Gautama attained nirvana; others can and should follow his example.
- All Buddhists accept **five basic principles of life**: do not kill (Buddhists are vegetarian); do not steal; do not lie; be chaste; and do not take intoxicants.

Holy books Zen Buddhists reject all writing in favor of direct experience, but other forms of Buddhism have important scriptures.

The main text of Theravada Buddhism is the three-part **Pali Canon**, written 2000 years ago in the ancient Pali language of northern India. Mahayana Buddhism has many sacred documents in different languages. The two main ones are the **Chinese Canon** and the **Tibetan Canon**. Tibetan Buddhists study texts such as the **Lotus Sutra**.

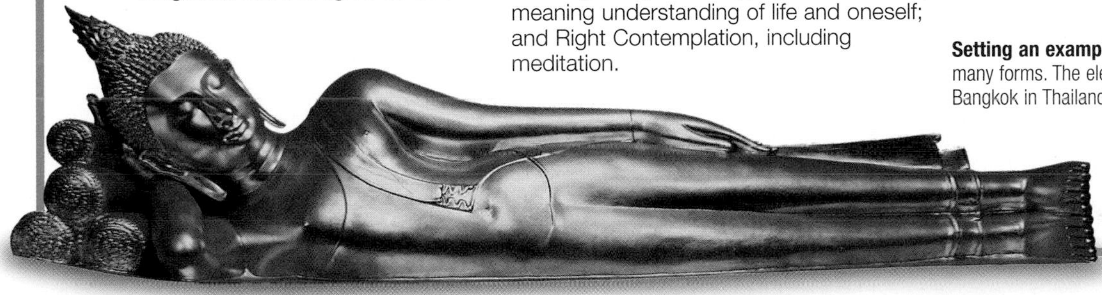

Setting an example Images of the Buddha take on many forms. The elegant reclining Buddha is from Bangkok in Thailand. Such representations serve as inspiration, because the aim of all Buddhists is to strive to become an enlightened one, or buddha, oneself.

SIKHISM

Sikhism originated in the 15th century A.D. amid conflicts between Muslims and Hindus in northern India. Offering a simple monotheism, it was intended as a peaceful middle way by its founder, Guru Nanak (1469-1539). But persecution by Muslims in the 17th century led to increasing militancy among the Sikhs.

Key beliefs Sikhs strive for union with God (**Satguru**) by adoring the Holy Name, through hard work and by being of service to others (**seva**), especially their own family.

- Sikhs believe in equality and give 10 percent of their income to the poor.
- There are no castes among the Sikhs, and men and women eat and work together.
- Sikhs should rise early, bathe and then meditate on God before going about their work.
- Sikhs avoid all intoxicants, including tobacco.
- Sikh men do not cut their hair but wear it concealed under a turban and are bearded. A dagger is carried on ceremonial occasions.
- All meat has to be killed in accordance with the **Jhatka law** of the "clean strike."

TAOISM

Taoism, the closest thing to a native religion in China, originally had no gods, temples or priests; it was essentially a philosophical system rather than a religion. It emphasized acceptance, in the form of a yielding and joyful attitude to life. Founded in the 6th century B.C. by the reclusive scholar and poet Lao Zi (Lao-Tzu) – supposedly author of its central text, the **Tao Te Ching** – it developed further under Chuang Tzu (Zhuang Zi) 200 years later, and rivaled Buddhism. Taoism is officially discouraged in China, but it survives in Taiwan and among overseas Chinese.

Leading the faith Taoist priests (above) play a leading role in communal events, such as festivals. They are called upon to perform harmonizing rites that will ensure the health, long life and prosperity of all.

see also

152-53 **The rise of Islam**
156-57 **India**
158-59 **China and Japan**
358-59 **Food**

Philosophy means "love of wisdom." Philosophers ask fundamental questions about the world and human life: Why do things happen the way they do? What can we know and how can we know it? How should we live our lives? They try to answer these questions using the power of reason rather than religious doctrines or scientific findings.

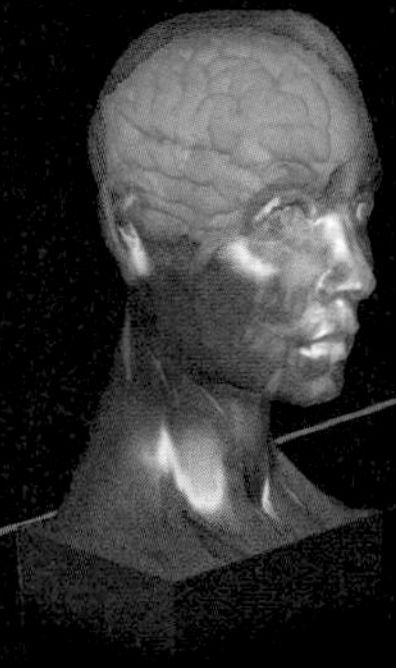

Socrates (c. 469-399 B.C.) Greek The ideas of Socrates are known to us entirely through the writings of his pupil Plato. He believed that true knowledge emerges through questioning and argument. He devised a method of teaching by systematic questioning – the "Socratic method" – a technique he used with his pupils.

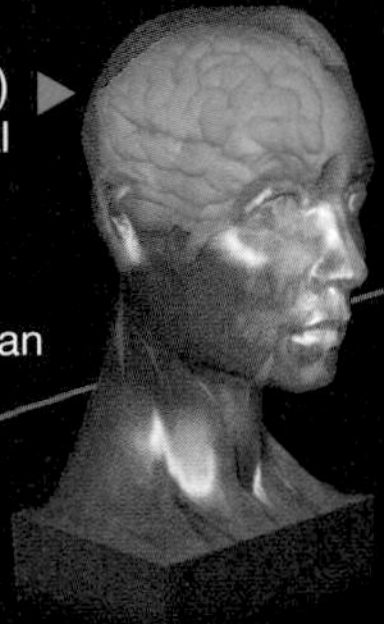

Plato (c. 427-347 B.C.) Greek Plato's central belief was that all objects in this world are copies of "Ideal Forms" that exist in an unchanging world beyond time and space. Knowledge of these is implanted in our minds at birth, and learning is a process of uncovering this knowledge. His ideas formed the basis of much subsequent philosophical debate.

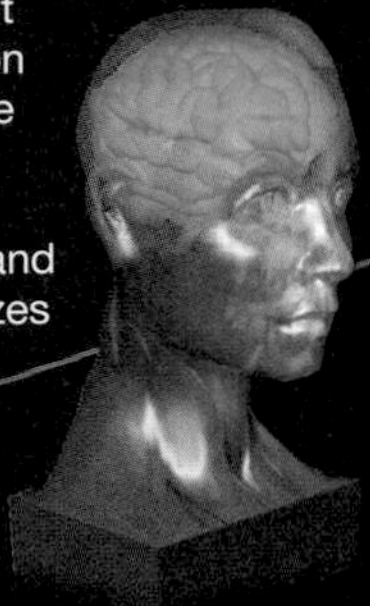

Aristotle (384-322 B.C.) Greek A pupil of Plato, Aristotle believed that the only world humans can be certain of is the one we live in and that we find out about it through observation and experience. He decided that all things have two qualities – matter and form. Form organizes matter into recognizable objects. God alone exists as "perfect form without matter."

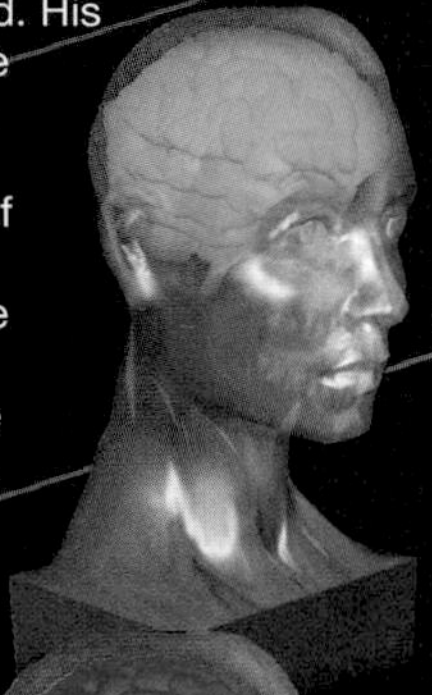

St. Augustine of Hippo (A.D. 354-430) North African St. Augustine fused ideas dominant in his time – including the idea that moral and intellectual discipline – with early Christian beliefs – brought people closer to God. His ideas laid the basis for the Christian philosophy of the Middle Ages and the Protestant beliefs of the Reformation.

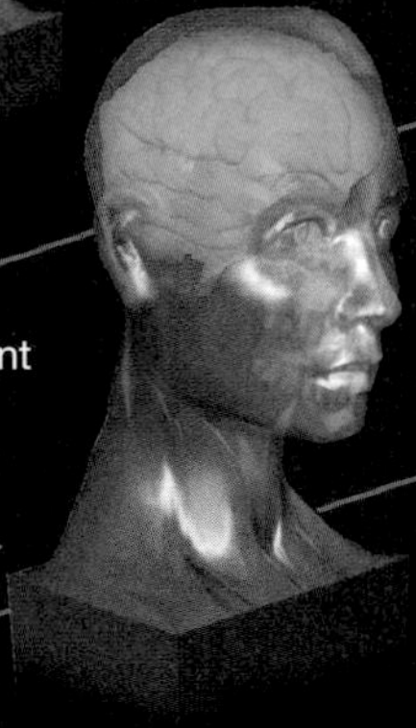

St. Thomas Aquinas (c. 1225-74) Italian Aquinas was inspired by the newly available translations of Aristotle's works. He believed that our senses provide our knowledge of reality. His fusion of Christianity and Aristotle's ideas is the basis for the Catholic doctrine that faith and reason are not incompatible.

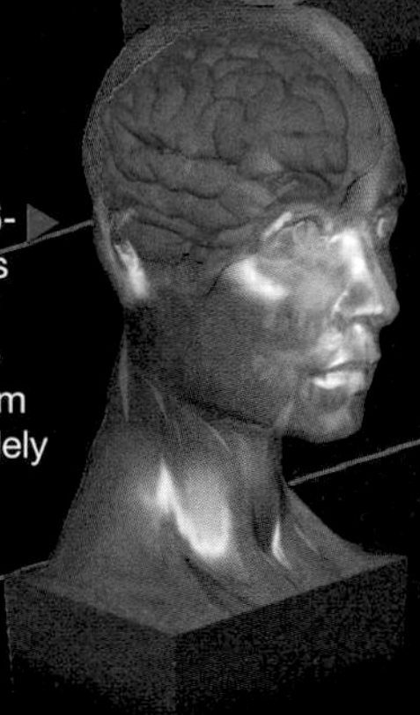

René Descartes (1596-1650) French Descartes marks the beginning of modern philosophy. He set out to build a system of knowledge based solely on his own powers of reasoning. Central to his thinking were his beliefs that mind and body are distinct substances – a theory known as dualism – and that God implants ideas that we can rediscover in our minds through reason.

KEY MOVEMENTS

School	Dates	Area	Key belief
Analytic philosophers	20th century	Europe	Problems can be clarified and solved by analyzing the language used to express them.
Cynics	4th century B.C.	Greece	The distinction between true and false values is all that matters.
Empiricists	18th century	Europe	Ideas are not innate; they are acquired through the senses and experience.
Epicureans	4th-3rd centuries B.C.	Greece	The avoidance of suffering is the prime good in life.
Existentialists	19th-20th centuries	Europe	In a world without fixed truths, we must invent and reinvent ourselves.
Postmodernists	20th century	Europe	The meanings of words and ideas can be found only by analyzing the beliefs and assumptions (structures of thought) that underlie what is being said.
Pragmatists	19th century	US	The truth of a belief depends on the usefulness of its practical application.
Rationalists	18th century	Europe	The only reliable truths are those that can be proven logically.
Skeptics	4th-2nd centuries B.C.	Greece	Our senses and reason are so misleading, we cannot be certain of anything.
Scholastics	Middle Ages	Europe	Aristotle's reasoning is not incompatible with Christian faith: In fact, reason demands faith in God.
Stoics	3rd c. B.C.-2nd c. A.D.	Greece and Rome	The world is governed by the laws of nature, and we must accept destiny.
Utilitarians	19th century	Britain	An action is morally right if it leads to greater happiness for the greater number of people.

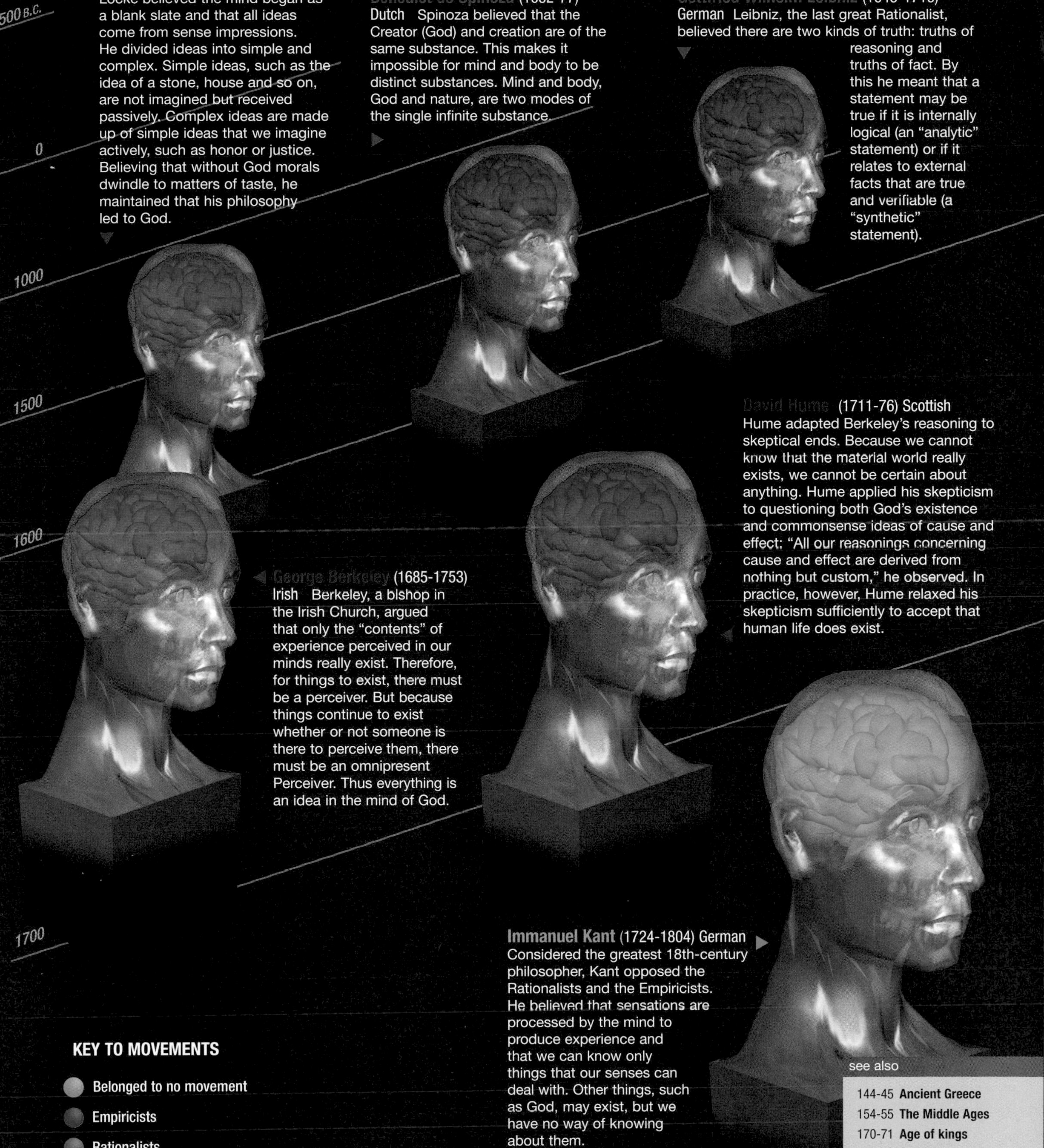

John Locke (1632-1704) English
Locke believed the mind began as a blank slate and that all ideas come from sense impressions. He divided ideas into simple and complex. Simple ideas, such as the idea of a stone, house and so on, are not imagined but received passively. Complex ideas are made up of simple ideas that we imagine actively, such as honor or justice. Believing that without God morals dwindle to matters of taste, he maintained that his philosophy led to God.

Benedict de Spinoza (1632-77) Dutch Spinoza believed that the Creator (God) and creation are of the same substance. This makes it impossible for mind and body to be distinct substances. Mind and body, God and nature, are two modes of the single infinite substance.

Gottfried Wilhelm Leibniz (1646-1716) German Leibniz, the last great Rationalist, believed there are two kinds of truth: truths of reasoning and truths of fact. By this he meant that a statement may be true if it is internally logical (an "analytic" statement) or if it relates to external facts that are true and verifiable (a "synthetic" statement).

George Berkeley (1685-1753) Irish Berkeley, a bishop in the Irish Church, argued that only the "contents" of experience perceived in our minds really exist. Therefore, for things to exist, there must be a perceiver. But because things continue to exist whether or not someone is there to perceive them, there must be an omnipresent Perceiver. Thus everything is an idea in the mind of God.

David Hume (1711-76) Scottish
Hume adapted Berkeley's reasoning to skeptical ends. Because we cannot know that the material world really exists, we cannot be certain about anything. Hume applied his skepticism to questioning both God's existence and commonsense ideas of cause and effect: "All our reasonings concerning cause and effect are derived from nothing but custom," he observed. In practice, however, Hume relaxed his skepticism sufficiently to accept that human life does exist.

Immanuel Kant (1724-1804) German
Considered the greatest 18th-century philosopher, Kant opposed the Rationalists and the Empiricists. He believed that sensations are processed by the mind to produce experience and that we can know only things that our senses can deal with. Other things, such as God, may exist, but we have no way of knowing about them.

KEY TO MOVEMENTS

- Belonged to no movement
- Empiricists
- Rationalists
- Scholastics

see also

144-45 **Ancient Greece**
154-55 **The Middle Ages**
170-71 **Age of kings**
304-5 **Religions**

Western thought 1800-present

By the mid 18th century, as scientific knowledge grew, philosophy became less focused on solving all the mysteries of the world. It was increasingly centered on analyzing the processes of human thought and reasoning, examining how our approach to the world colors our understanding of it and thus limits our powers of objectivity.

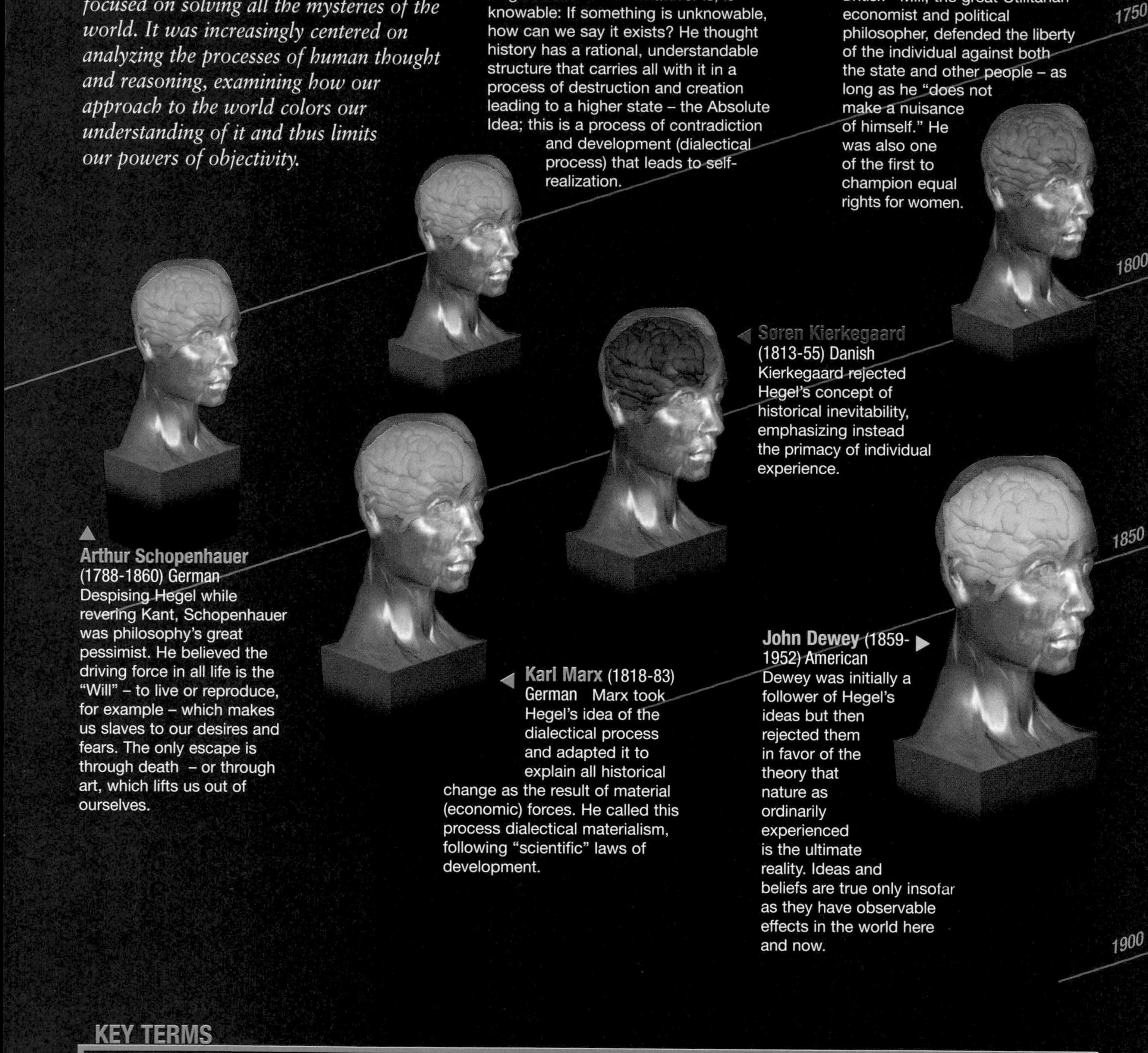

Georg Wilhelm Friedrich Hegel (1770-1831) German Reacting against Kant, Hegel believed that whatever is, is knowable: If something is unknowable, how can we say it exists? He thought history has a rational, understandable structure that carries all with it in a process of destruction and creation leading to a higher state – the Absolute Idea; this is a process of contradiction and development (dialectical process) that leads to self-realization.

John Stuart Mill (1806-73) British Mill, the great Utilitarian economist and political philosopher, defended the liberty of the individual against both the state and other people – as long as he "does not make a nuisance of himself." He was also one of the first to champion equal rights for women.

Arthur Schopenhauer (1788-1860) German Despising Hegel while revering Kant, Schopenhauer was philosophy's great pessimist. He believed the driving force in all life is the "Will" – to live or reproduce, for example – which makes us slaves to our desires and fears. The only escape is through death – or through art, which lifts us out of ourselves.

Søren Kierkegaard (1813-55) Danish Kierkegaard rejected Hegel's concept of historical inevitability, emphasizing instead the primacy of individual experience.

Karl Marx (1818-83) German Marx took Hegel's idea of the dialectical process and adapted it to explain all historical change as the result of material (economic) forces. He called this process dialectical materialism, following "scientific" laws of development.

John Dewey (1859-1952) American Dewey was initially a follower of Hegel's ideas but then rejected them in favor of the theory that nature as ordinarily experienced is the ultimate reality. Ideas and beliefs are true only insofar as they have observable effects in the world here and now.

KEY TERMS

Aesthetics The philosophical study of art and beauty.
A posteriori statement A statement that is validated by verification of the facts.
A priori statement A statement that is valid because of its internal logic, without reference to external facts or experience.
Dialectic Reasoning via question and answer, as used by Socrates; also the process identified by Hegel by which apparently contradictory aspects of knowledge and experience ("thesis" and "antithesis") can produce an inclusive whole ("synthesis").
Dialectical materialism Marx's application of Hegel's dialectic to the analysis of human history and politics.
Epistemology A branch of philosophy dealing with what we know and how we know it.
Ethics A branch of philosophy dealing with issues of right and wrong.
Logic A branch of philosophy that studies reasoned argument itself – its concepts, methods and rules.
Metaphysics An abstract branch of philosophy concerned with the ultimate nature of existence as seen from outside.
Ontology A branch of philosophy that asks what ultimately exists.
Synthetic statement A statement whose truth is determined by being tested against facts outside itself.

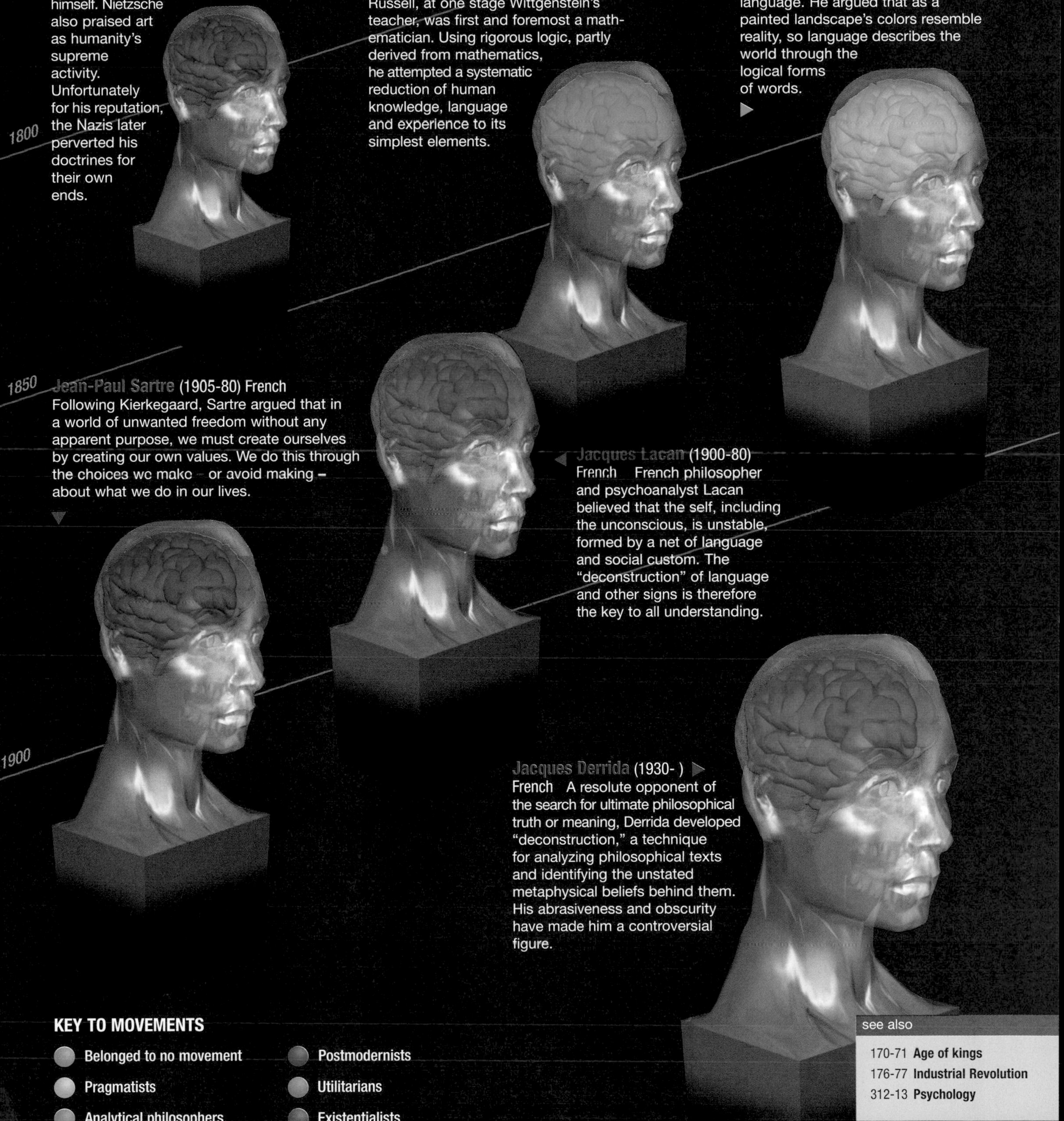

Friedrich Nietzsche (1844-1900) German Nietzsche rejected received values, especially Christian values, with his idea of the strong-willed Superman who could acknowledge that the Universe is meaningless – until given value by himself. Nietzsche also praised art as humanity's supreme activity. Unfortunately for his reputation, the Nazis later perverted his doctrines for their own ends.

Bertrand Russell (1872-1970) English Russell, at one stage Wittgenstein's teacher, was first and foremost a mathematician. Using rigorous logic, partly derived from mathematics, he attempted a systematic reduction of human knowledge, language and experience to its simplest elements.

Ludwig Wittgenstein (1889-1951) German Wittgenstein's early work aimed to complete the work of Kant and Schopenhauer by putting their ideas about the unknowable worlds on a logical basis through analysis of language. He argued that as a painted landscape's colors resemble reality, so language describes the world through the logical forms of words.

Jean-Paul Sartre (1905-80) French Following Kierkegaard, Sartre argued that in a world of unwanted freedom without any apparent purpose, we must create ourselves by creating our own values. We do this through the choices we make – or avoid making – about what we do in our lives.

Jacques Lacan (1900-80) French French philosopher and psychoanalyst Lacan believed that the self, including the unconscious, is unstable, formed by a net of language and social custom. The "deconstruction" of language and other signs is therefore the key to all understanding.

Jacques Derrida (1930-) French A resolute opponent of the search for ultimate philosophical truth or meaning, Derrida developed "deconstruction," a technique for analyzing philosophical texts and identifying the unstated metaphysical beliefs behind them. His abrasiveness and obscurity have made him a controversial figure.

KEY TO MOVEMENTS

- Belonged to no movement
- Pragmatists
- Analytical philosophers
- Postmodernists
- Utilitarians
- Existentialists

see also

170-71 **Age of kings**
176-77 **Industrial Revolution**
312-13 **Psychology**

Psychology is the study of the mind. It covers a very wide field of investigation, from learning and perception to behavioral aspects of business and education. The application of psychological ideas to illness is called psychiatry. Both psychology and psychiatry are relatively new disciplines. Before the 1880s, there was no concept that the processes of the mind could be observed and documented.

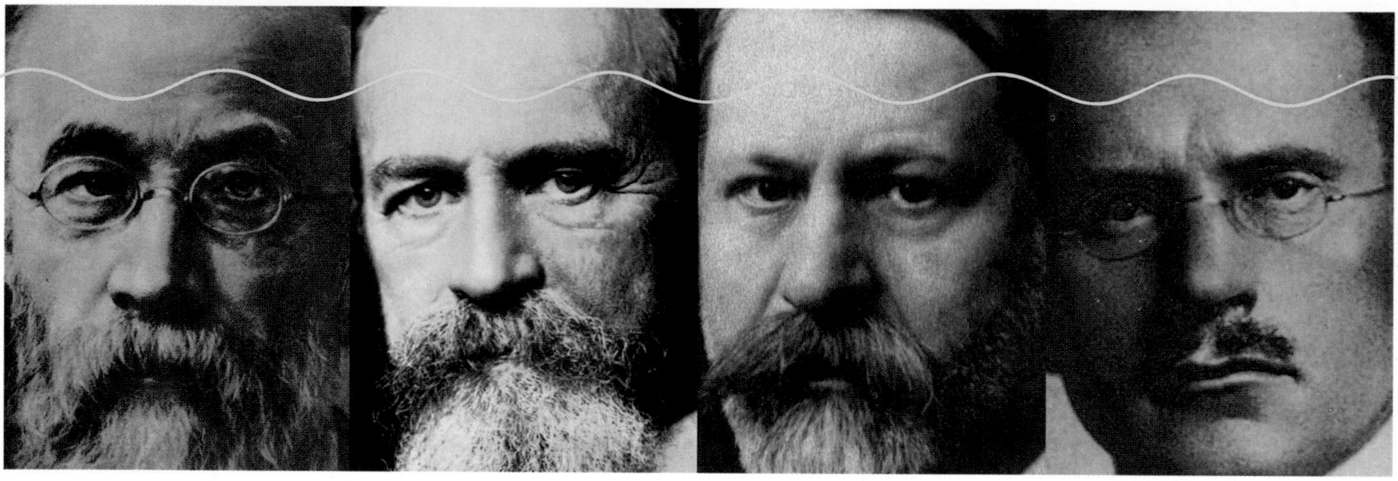

Wilhelm Wundt (1832-1920) German Wundt, a professor of physiology, established the first "laboratory for the mind" in Leipzig in 1879. He urged the practice of **"introspection,"** or self-analysis, along strict guidelines, recording and collating any findings. His book *Essentials of Physiological Psychology* (1874) helped to establish psychology as a science, and to link it closely with the study of workings of the human body.

William James (1842-1910) American James' *Principles of Psychology*, published in 1890, is the first and one of the greatest studies of the subject. He was the originator of the concept of **"stream of consciousness"** and was concerned with exploring the nature of individuality, choice and purpose. He also developed the theory that emotions are actually the sensation of physical changes in the body caused by exciting external events or perceptions.

Sigmund Freud (1856-1939) Austrian Freud, the inventor of **psychoanalysis** (see below), coined much of the terminology still used in psychology. His theory of the development of the psyche is based on the idea that alarming early memories are repressed, potentially causing neuroses in later life. He saw the psyche as composed of three impulses that frequently conflict: the primitive, instinctual **"id"**; the more rational **"ego"** (developing from about age two); and the **"superego,"** concerned with morality and other people.

Carl Jung (1875-1961) Swiss Breaking away from Freud, Jung stressed the importance of philosophical and religious as well as sexual experience. His concept of the human mind is based on the interaction between individual perception – the **"individual unconscious"** – and the shared pool of inherited memories, ideas, images and modes of thought – the **"collective unconscious."** Jung was also the first to analyze personalities on a scale from extrovert (social, impulsive and outwardly carefree) to introvert (solitary, reserved and preoccupied with the self).

Psychoanalysis

Psychoanalysis is the technique developed by Freud and his followers for the understanding and treatment of neuroses. The main technique used is analysis of what the patient says (or avoids saying) during the free association of ideas – that is, with the patient lying on a couch and speaking freely of whatever comes into his or her head. Interpreting dreams and other manifestations of the unconscious also plays a part. It is a lengthy process and is now quite rarely practiced. The aims are to uncover the memory of experiences – often from early childhood – that have been repressed, to resolve the feelings these generate, and in this way to remove the cause of the neurotic behavior. Resolution of any feelings exposed in this way generally occurs through the process of transference, in which emotional outbursts from the patient are directed at the analyst.

Other forms of therapy

Therapists and counselors use a wide range of techniques to resolve behavioral and psychological problems, but there are two dominant forms.

Cognitive-behavioral therapy emerged from the work of the Behaviorists (see Pavlov, above right). It is based on the principle that problems stem from faulty learning and can be treated by altering the way an individual perceives situations.

Client-centered therapy originated from the work of Carl Rogers. Clients are encouraged to solve their own problems through the therapist's use of three core skills:

- *congruence* – being genuine, open and honest in their responses to the client;
- *empathy* – seeing the world from the client's point of view;
- *unconditional positive regard* – treating the client with respect and maintaining a nonjudgmental attitude.

SPECIAL BRANCHES OF PSYCHOLOGY

Abnormal The study of unusual or deviant behavior or experiences.
Animal The use of psychological ideas to understand animal behavior.
Business The application of psychological ideas to management and advertising.
Clinical The study of health problems such as mental disorders.
Cognitive The study of processes such as learning, memory and the acquisition of language.
Developmental The study of psychological changes over a life span.
Educational The use of psychological ideas and techniques in educational assessment and advice.
Experimental The application of scientific experimental methods and analyses to the study of the mind.
Social The study of group behavior and human interaction.
Vocational The use of psychological techniques in assessing and developing career choices.

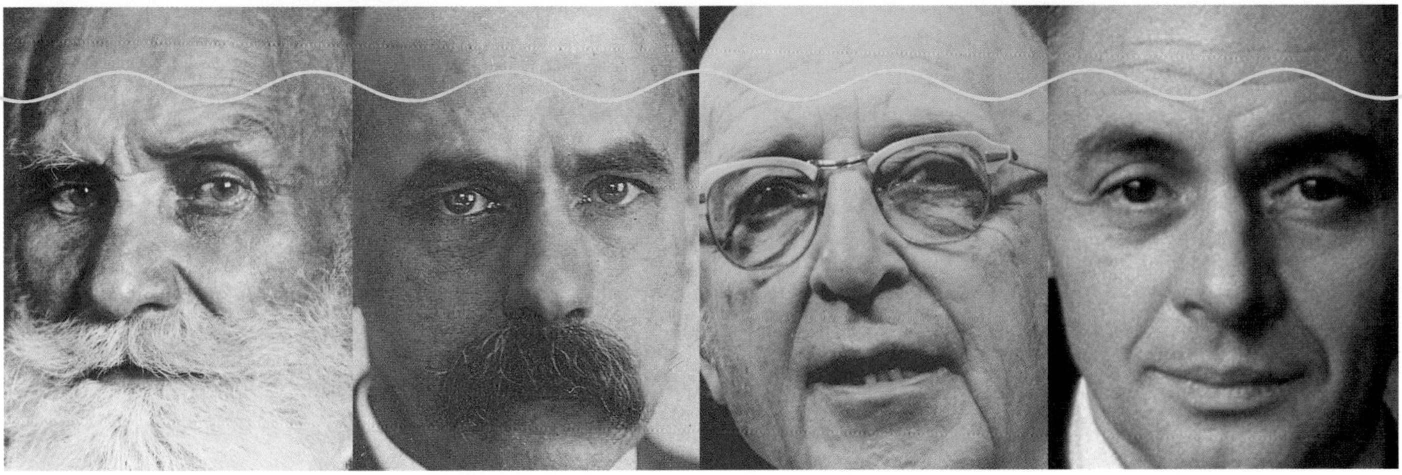

Ivan Pavlov (1849-1936) Russian Pavlov demonstrated that if a bell was rung just before dogs were fed, the dogs would soon begin to salivate (the **"response"**) at the sound of the bell alone (the **"stimulus"**). The discovery that a physical response can be evoked by a completely unconnected stimulus was called "conditioning." Later psychologists thought that conditioned responses on a far more complex level might hold the key to all human behavior. Pavlov rejected most of the claims of the so-called **Behaviorists**.

Max Wertheimer (1880-1943) Czech/German Wertheimer and his colleagues, Kurt Koffka and Wolfgang Köhler, argued against the Behaviorists, claiming that human perception involves the isolation of meaningful patterns of information from a chaotic mass of competing stimuli. In the 1950s, their ideas led to the emergence of **Gestalt** ("form" or "pattern") therapy. Gestalt therapists believe that in a healthy mind, input is organized into structures and that these provoke appropriate responses.

Carl Rogers (1902-87) American Rogers was the originator during the 1940s and 1950s of a **client-centered** approach to the practice of **psychotherapy**, which is now probably the style adopted by the majority of practitioners. He emphasized the importance of getting clients actively involved in the process and direction of their own therapy so that they would gain a sense of positively developing their potential rather than simply being offered a "cure."

R.D. Laing (1927-89) British Laing was a major figure in the 1960s and 1970s – with Thomas Szasz – in the **"antipsychiatry" movement**, which emphasized the role played by society in creating a great deal of so-called mental illness. Laing became one of the best-known therapists of his day, developing a number of highly accessible theories based upon the use of **personal "scripts"** and **interpersonal "games,"** as a means of understanding and resolving problems in human behavior.

KEY TERMS

- **Archetype** In Jungian psychology, the primal images or ideas that underlie our notions of gods, heroes or saints.
- **Complex** A cluster of emotionally charged ideas or perceptions that can affect behavior or health.
- **Ego** In Freudian terminology, the part of the psyche that consciously interacts with the outside world, conflicting with the id and the superego.
- **Id** In Freudian terminology, the instinctual libidinous feelings at the base of every human psyche that seek immediate satisfaction unfiltered by reason or morality.
- **Libido** In Freudian terminology, the innate sex drive; in other schools of psychology, a more general will to survive.
- **Masochism** Sexual pleasure or psychological relief derived from the experience of humiliation or physical pain.
- **Neurosis** A mental disturbance caused by nonphysical causes manifested in the form of anxiety, hysterical behavior or similar symptoms.
- **Oedipus complex** A Freudian theory – named from a Greek myth – of the unconscious enmity a son feels toward his father as a rival for his mother's affection; the female counterpart is known as an "Electra complex."
- **Oral/anal/phallic stages** According to Freud, stages of sexual focus through which children develop from birth to age six.
- **Paranoia** Delusions of persecution or, less often, of grandeur.
- **Repression** In Freudian and many later schools, the mechanism by which painful or embarrassing memories and ideas are suppressed in conscious memory while continuing to influence behavior through the unconscious.
- **Sadism** Sexual pleasure or psychological relief derived from inflicting pain or humiliation on others.
- **Superego** In Freudian terminology, the part of the psyche linked with higher feelings – altruism, ethics, conscience and guilt.

see also
310-11 Western thought
324-25 Western art
342-43 Western literature

Scientific thinkers

The search for a framework of knowledge about the world around us began with the theorizing of ancient philosophers. By the 17th century, experimentation and observation were the preferred tools of deduction. In both approaches, progress has relied on a few exceptionally creative thinkers.

Pythagoras Believed in the harmony of numbers.

MATHEMATICS

Five thousand years ago, Egyptians and Babylonians solved many problems in arithmetic and geometry, but the Greeks were the first to study pure mathematics systematically. **Thales** (c. 625-c. 546 B.C.) probably set out the first mathematical proofs based on deduction. **Pythagoras** (c. 580-c. 500 B.C.) believed numbers to be the essence of everything in nature. He or his followers devised the theorem of the right-angled triangle named after him by drawing on knowledge from Egypt and Babylon. **Euclid** (c. 300 B.C.) wrote one of the first comprehensive geometry texts, *The Elements*. Much of it summarized earlier work, but Euclid gave proofs of many geometric theorems. His work forms the basis of today's geometry.

The Indian **Brahmagupta** (598-670) was the first to treat zero as a number with arithmetical properties. Before him, no distinction could be made between, for example, 45 and 450. Arab scholar **Khwarizmi** (c. 800-c. 850) passed on Babylonian, Greek and Indian ideas in his treatises on arithmetic and algebra. The use of Arabic numerals spread to Europe through 11th-century translations of Khwarizmi's work.

The greatest mathematical advances in Europe began later, in the 17th century. **René Descartes** (1596-1650) invented analytical geometry; **Pierre de Fermat** (1601-65) founded modern number theory; and **Gottfried Leibnitz** (1646-1716) and **Isaac Newton** (1642-1727) independently invented the theory of calculus.

In the 19th century, **August Möbius** (1790-1868) helped establish topology, a branch of geometry that deals with the distortion of shapes; **George Boole** (1815-64) founded symbolic logic; and **Henri Poincaré** (1854-1912) in France explained how tiny variations in the initial conditions of an object, such as a planet or air mass, may affect its later behavior – this is the basis of chaos theory.

MATTER AND ENERGY

Greek philosophers **Leucippus** (5th c. B.C.) and **Democritus** (c. 460-c. 370 B.C.) believed that everything is made of minute, invisible, indivisible particles, or atoms. This philosophy – the basis of modern chemistry – was overshadowed for nearly 2000 years by **Aristotle's** (384-322 B.C.) view that matter is composed of four "elements": earth, air, fire and water.

There was little advance in the study of chemistry until 1803, when **John Dalton** (1766-1844) put forward an atomic theory to explain how chemical elements combine to form compounds in fixed proportions. In the 1860s, **Dmitri Mendeleyev** (1834-1907) related the chemical properties of elements to their relative atomic mass. He created the periodic table, which lists elements in ascending order of atomic weight.

In 1897 British physicist **J.J. Thomson** (1856-1940) found that atoms can be split by physical means and are built from even smaller particles. **Ernest Rutherford** (1871-1937) and **Niels Bohr** (1885-1962) explained in 1911-13 how atoms are built from subatomic particles. The work of all these scientists depended partly on the discovery of radioactivity by **Henri Becquerel** (1852-1908) in 1896.

Inside the atom Ernest Rutherford discovered the structure of the atom.

Meanwhile, German physicist **Max Planck** (1858-1947) founded quantum theory; the idea that atoms emit and absorb energy in discrete particle-like bundles called quanta.

In 1905, **Albert Einstein** (1879-1955) formulated his Special Theory of Relativity, which expresses the equivalence of matter and energy with the equation $E = mc^2$. The equation's significance was not realized until the late 1930s when experiments done by **Otto Hahn** (1879-1968) and **Fritz Strassmann** (1902-80) and interpreted by **Otto Frisch** (1904-79) and **Lise Meitner** (1878-1968) demonstrated nuclear fission (splitting the atom) and how it released energy.

EARTH SCIENCES

For many centuries, the biblical account of the Earth's creation was taken as the literal truth. The world was thought to be only about 6000 years old.

In 1830, Scottish geologist **Charles Lyell** (1797-1875), after studying fossils and gauging the speed that rocks change, concluded that the Earth is many millions of years old. He also argued that past geological events resulted from the same slow processes that occur today. On a larger scale, German geologist **Alfred Wegener** (1880-1930) saw how the coasts of Africa and South America fit together like jigsaw pieces. In 1912, he suggested that the continents were the fractured remains of one vast landmass – he called it Pangaea – that began to drift apart about 200 million years ago. His theory was ridiculed until the 1960s, when new evidence established an entirely new view of a dynamic Earth.

Environmental studies owe most to **Rachel Carson** (1907-64), who coined the term "ecosystem" and inspired the environmental movement with her book *Silent Spring*, and **James Lovelock** (1919-), whose 1972 "Gaia hypothesis" proposed that the Earth and its creatures and plants operate as a single organism.

COSMOLOGY

Ancient philosophers watched the stars move across the sky and assumed that the Earth was the center of the Universe, with other heavenly bodies moving around it. This belief, set out by Greek astronomer **Claudius Ptolemy** (c. A.D. 90-c. 168), influenced European astronomers for almost 1500 years. But some Greeks – notably **Heraclides of Pontus** (4th c. B.C.) and **Aristarchus of Samos** (3rd c. B.C.) – insisted correcty that the planets revolve around the Sun, not the Earth.

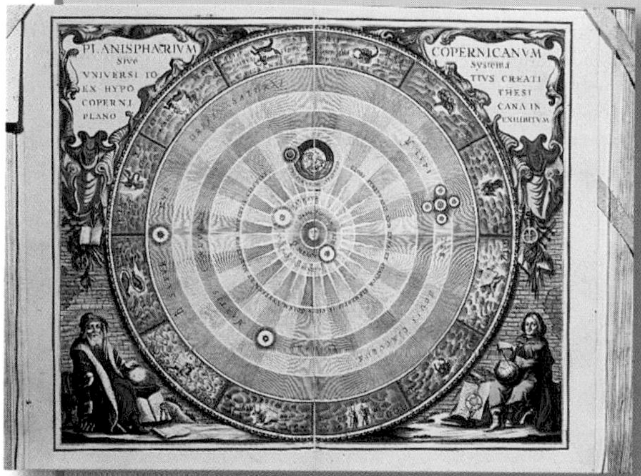

Revolutionary text Pages from Copernicus's book show the orbits of the planets around the Sun.

Nicholas Copernicus (1473-1543) was the first European astronomer to hold this view, believing that the Earth's orbit and spin are responsible for the way the planets and stars appear to move. His book *Concerning the Revolutions of the Heavenly Spheres* was published in the year he died. His ideas were suppressed by the Roman Catholic Church for more than a century.

Galileo Galilei (1564-1642) used an early telescope to observe sunspots, the moons of Jupiter and other astronomical phenomena. He saw that Venus shows phases just like the Moon, proving that it orbits the Sun, as Copernicus said. But Galileo's *Dialogues* (1632) was also banned by the Church, and the Inquisition made him recant his ideas.

Even before Galileo, German astronomer **Johannes Kepler** (1571-1630) had worked out the physical laws governing the paths of planets about the Sun. An early believer in Copernicus, he at first thought that the planets move in circular orbits, but he later refined his theories to show that the orbits are elliptical. He said there must be a force between the Sun and planets to hold them in orbit – an early description of gravity.

By far the greatest advances in cosmology were made by **Isaac Newton** (1642-1727). Apart from his discoveries about optics and his invention of calculus (see opposite), Newton devised laws of motion and gravitation that remained unchallenged for 230 years. His book *Principia* (1687) set out three laws of motion explaining the properties of forces and the relationship among force, mass and acceleration, and also the properties of gravity. His insights at last explained the movement of the planets and other heavenly bodies and formed the cornerstone of "classical" physics. They have enabled us to predict the motion of all kinds of bodies, from galaxies to bicycles.

Newton's laws were only superceded when **Albert Einstein** (1879-1955) published his General Theory of Relativity in 1916. This extended Special Relativity (see opposite) to cover acceleration, including the effect of gravity. Einstein concluded that time and space must be distorted around massive objects – that they are not constant in all situations. This knocked the bottom out of Newtonian physics, even though the difference predicted by Newton's and Einstein's equations is minute, except at the very smallest (atomic) or largest (cosmic) scale, or at speeds close to that of light.

Scientists did not realize the true size of the Universe until 1925, when American astronomer **Edwin Hubble** (1889-1953) discovered galaxies beyond ours. By measuring the color shift of the light in their spectra, he realized that stars are moving away from us and from each other – the farther away the star, the faster it was moving. He inferred that the Universe is expanding and must have begun at a specific point in the past – the "big bang." This formed the foundation of modern cosmology.

The greatest contribution to the field since the work of Einstein has been made by British physicist **Stephen Hawking** (1942-). Hawking examined the concept of the big bang and tried to combine quantum mechanics and relativity theory into a single theory explaining the nature and origins of the Universe.

Space eye The Hubble Space Telescope, named after Edwin Hubble, has found evidence of black holes and other strange cosmic objects.

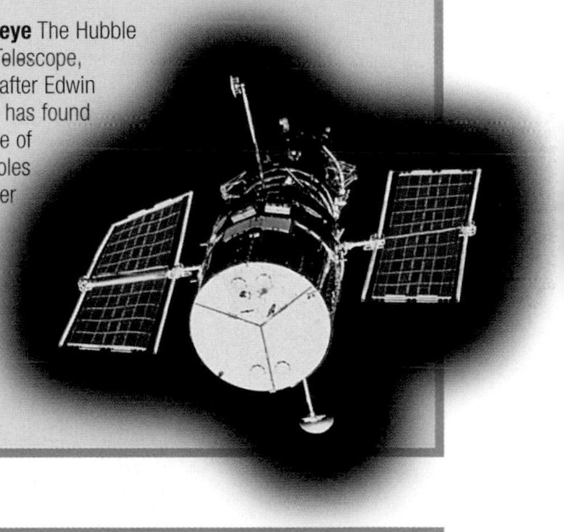

LIFE SCIENCES

The biblical account of the Creation – in which living things had existed unchanged for all time – dominated biology as much as geology. A first step toward radical change was made by Swedish botanist **Carolus Linnaeus** (1707-78), the first person to classify all living things systematically, founding the science of taxonomy.

In the late 18th century, French naturalist **Jean Lamarck** (1744-1829) developed ideas of how organisms might evolve. But in 1858 British naturalist **Charles Darwin** (1809-82) revolutionized biology – and ideas about mankind's place in creation – when he proposed a mechanism for evolution through natural selection. His plant and animal studies showed that the characteristics that help individuals survive in a particular habitat get passed on and eventually become the basis for a new species or variety.

Further biological principles were discovered through working with individual organisms. **Gregor Mendel** (1823-84) began the study of heredity by experimenting with pea plants. He traced how size, color and other traits are passed down intact from generation to generation, regardless of the environment in which the plants were reared. Sixty years later, American biologist **Thomas Hunt Morgan** (1866-1945) proved that genes – the units of heredity – are carried on minute structures, called chromosomes, inside living cells. This marked the start of the modern science of genetics.

In 1953, **James Watson** (1928-) and **Francis Crick** (1916-) looked inside chromosomes. They studied x-ray diffraction images created by **Rosalind Franklin** (1920-58) showing genetic material – molecules of DNA – and discovered the molecules' precise double-helix structure. They worked out how DNA molecules could copy themselves and pass on genetic information using chemical sequences. This theory was later confirmed with experiments and opened the way to genetic engineering, DNA profiling, and other advances.

see also
10-11 **Planet Earth**
152-53 **The Rise of Islam**
418-19 **Mechanics**
428-29 **Relativity**

Since prehistoric times, the human form has been a central inspiration for many artists. It was the ancient Greeks who first raised sculpture to a transcendent level. The first marble figures from Greece date from c. 2500-1400 B.C. Their simple, abstract forms are still appealing today. By the 5th century B.C., Greek art had taken on a new sophistication, which was to influence artists into the 15th century and beyond.

Hellenistic and Roman In the 3rd century B.C., sculptors of the Hellenistic world mostly copied earlier masters. The Romans collected Greek art, but also developed genres of their own: the accurate portrait bust, the narrative relief sculpture (as in the military campaign recorded on Trajan's Column) and the mosaic. Roman painting is known only from 1st-century B.C. murals found at Pompeii and Herculaneum, which include vivid decorative frescoes depicting landscapes and fake architectural features.

Roman art Wall paintings in Pompeii included portraits.

500 B.C. | 0 | 250 | 500 | 750 | 1000

Classical Around 480 B.C., Greek sculptors developed a new, realistic way of portraying the human body, keeping true to its form (naturalism). Classical sculptors adhered to strict aesthetic standards – their balanced, well-defined statues epitomize the Greek ideal of beauty and strength. The style first emerges in the *Apollo* of Piombino (of about 490 B.C.) and a majestic bronze god (probably Zeus) by an unknown sculptor. The male nude was perfected by two sculptors, **Polyclitus** and **Phidias**, but only clumsy Roman copies of their works survive. In the 4th century B.C., the softer forms of the female nude were used as a subject. **Praxiteles** created the first full-size female nude, the *Aphrodite* of Cnidus. Rivaling him was **Lysippus**, who "modeled bronze as if it were wax." The Classical style waned after the death of Alexander the Great in 323 B.C., as art moved into the Hellenistic period.

Classical symmetry The bronze *Apollo* of Piombino displays the balance and beauty of the Greek ideal.

SCULPTURE KEY TERMS

- **Cameo** Carving on gemstone, glass or ceramic in which the background is cut away so that the design emerges in relief. The term is also often used for a portrait cut on a gemstone.
- **Chryselephantine** Statues where the flesh is covered in gold and the draperies in ivory.
- **Frieze** Horizontal band on the upper part of a wall, often decorated with carvings.
- **Intaglio** Figure or design cut into and below the surface of a metal or stone block.
- **Mobile** Sculpture consisting of individual parts suspended on wires and moved by air currents or, more recently, by motors.
- **Relief** Sculpture in which the forms project from a background. In **low relief** (bas-relief), forms project by less than half their depth; in **high relief**, by more than half.

Gothic height Tall statues with fine drapery depict *The Visitation* (c. 1220) at Chartres Cathedral.

Byzantine and medieval Roman mosaic work was further developed in the Byzantine Empire in the 5th century A.D. The technique added color and splendor to the great religious buildings. Naturalism gave way to simplified or "stylized," images of religious icons and complex decorative patterns. In Western Europe, the main art forms that survived are book illumination and relief sculpture in churches. From the 12th century on, northern European cathedrals were decorated with stained glass, along with carvings of unnaturally tall figures in a new style known as Gothic, which stressed spirituality in its reach toward heaven.

Gothic iconography The elegant figures of the *Wilton Diptych* represent the presentation of England's Richard II to the Virgin.

International Gothic

The elaborate, graceful work of Sienese artists such as **Simone Martini** created a new style that combined the detail of Italian naturalism with the elegance of northern European Gothic forms. The style proved popular with northern courts such as that of the Duc de Berry, where the **Limbourg** brothers produced richly colored miniature paintings. One of the greatest paintings in the style is the *Wilton Diptych* now in the National Gallery in London. The typically medieval anonymity of its creator further distinguishes the work from true Renaissance art.

1200 1300 1350

Early Renaissance

The Renaissance is usually said to have begun in Italy with painter **Giotto** in the late 13th century. Renaissance artists returned to the naturalist style of Classical art in the hope of reproducing its grandeur and beauty. Painters experimented with light and shadow to bring realistic depth to their work, and a mathematical system was invented for creating the illusion of three-dimensional space (linear perspective); **Masaccio** was the first to use perspective successfully. Italian artists of the time used tempera paint, but Flemish painter **van Eyck** pioneered the use of oil paint, which better captured effects of light and texture.

Classical influence was also felt by Italian sculptors. In the late 13th century, Nicola **Pisano** and his son Giovanni studied Greek and Roman sculptural forms while working on Gothic religious buildings and created images of Christian saints with the naturalism of Classical times. **Donatello**'s *David* (1430-32), the first free-standing male nude since Roman times, captured a realism and vitality that was entirely new.

New depth *St. Francis Honored by a Simple Man* (1296-97) shows Giotto's ability to suggest three-dimensional form.

Sculpture facts and figures

- Michelangelo's acclaimed sculpture of Moses on the gigantic tomb of Pope Julius II was originally intended to be one of 40 monumental figures carved by the artist. Lack of finance ruined plans for the other 39.
- The world's most controversial sculpture is the surviving 75 m (247 ft) of a 160 m (524 ft) frieze from Parthenon in Athens and dates from the 5th century B.C. In 1805, Lord Elgin, British ambassador to Constantinople, shipped it to England. The Greek government is campaigning for its return.
- An ongoing sculpture of Sioux hero Chief Crazy Horse being carved into Thunderhead Mountain, South Dakota, will eventually be the tallest statue on Earth. The finished figure will measure 172 m (563 ft) high by 195 m (641 ft) across.

Artists A-C

The major figures in Western art are acclaimed for their vision, skill and innovation, and the influence they exercised on other artists.
■ Refers to a key work.

Gianlorenzo Bernini (1598-1680) Italian
A series of life-sized statues (1618-25) assured Bernini a reputation as the leading Italian Baroque artist. In 1623, he became architect of St. Peter's Basilica in Rome.
■ Sculpture *The Ecstasy of St. Teresa*

Josef Beuys (1921-86) German
Beuys became a major influence in 1960s conceptual art through his opposition to formalism and professionalism. His work ranged from assemblages of garbage to perfomance pieces.
■ Performance *How to Explain Pictures to a Dead Hare*

Sandro Botticelli (1445-1510) Italian
Botticelli painted the first female nudes for 1000 years. In 1481-82 he worked on the ceiling of the Sistine Chapel. His paintings depicting religious and mythological scenes influenced later Pre-Raphaelite and Art Nouveau styles.
■ *Spring; Birth of Venus*

Louise Bourgeois (1911-) French-American
The disturbing, mostly abstract works of Bourgeois explore the anguish of human relationships. Bourgeois' one-woman show in New York in 1982 established her as a leading contemporary sculptor.
■ *Here I Am, Here I Stay*

Constantin Brancusi (1876-1957) Romanian
The elegant, geometric sculptures of Brancusi were created from pure, simple shapes, mostly in marble or bronze. His work contributed to the evolution of abstract sculpture.
■ *The Kiss*

Georges Braque (1882-1963) French
Braque's landscapes of 1908, influenced by Picasso, gave rise to the term "Cubism." His later, less angular still life paintings received worldwide acclaim.
■ *The Portuguese*

Pieter Bruegel the Elder (1525-69) Flemish
Bruegel was one of the first painters to focus on landscapes and village scenes, combining close observation with fantasy.
■ *Country Wedding; Hunters in the Snow*

Caravaggio (1571-1610) Italian
Caravaggio shocked his Baroque contemporaries with the revolutionary realism he brought to paintings of sacred themes. His use of sharp contrasts of light and shade to create drama influenced painters across Europe: Many traveled to Rome to see his work.
■ *Conversion of St. Paul*

Benvenuto Cellini (1500-71) Italian
Cellini was a leading sculptor of the Mannerist tradition – a Renaissance style defined by grace and sophistication. His elegant bronzes and delicate, highly wrought metalwork epitomized the luxury of Italian courtly life.
■ *Perseus*

Paul Cézanne (1839-1906) French
Cézanne wanted to capture structure and intensity rather than subjective sensations in his paintings. His Postimpressionist approach made him a leading contributor to the development of Cubism and abstract art.
■ *Card Players; Mont Sainte-Victoire*

see also
144-45 **Ancient Greece**
146-47 **Ancient Rome**
154-55 **The Middle Ages**
166-67 **The Renaissance**

In the 16th century, a rejection of the Greek ideals of balance and naturalism resulted in Mannerism, characterized by crowded scenes, overdramatic gestures and poor perspective. Balance and elegance survived into the 17th century in Baroque and Classicism, and soon, Dutch artists turned away from the human form to a new subject – landscape.

Baroque In the early 17th century, artists turned away from the exaggerations of Mannerism to more realistic representations of the world. The style can be seen in the "living" feel and dramatic movement in sculptural figures by **Bernini**. In painting, Baroque is represented by grand unity – overall balance rather than focusing on a particular aspect of a scene – and the strong diagonals, curves and tonal contrasts exemplified by the work of **Caravaggio**. The uncluttered, elegant portraits of the period by **Rubens**, **Van Dyck** and **Velázquez** influenced later portrait artists such as Gainsborough.

Velázquez Portrait of the Infanta Dona Margarita of Austria.

1500

1600

High Renaissance Two centuries of experiments with ways of depicting the human figure, perspective and oil paints culminated in the High Renaissance, which is conventionally dated 1500-20. The major figures were **Leonardo da Vinci**, **Michelangelo** and **Raphael**. All produced large-scale, ambitious, complex works. Most painting was done on wooden panels or directly onto walls and ceilings, but **Giorgione** and **Titian** introduced the practice of painting on canvas. Italian Renaissance ideas began to influence German and Dutch artists, including **Dürer**.

In Italy, some artists began to depart from the established Renaissance ideas of balance and naturalism, striving instead for dramatic effects. This "Mannerist" style also extended to the work of sculptors such as **Bellini**.

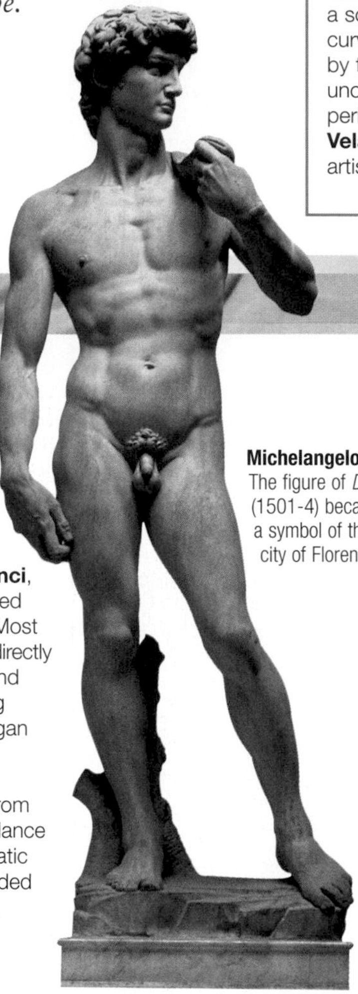

Michelangelo The figure of *David* (1501-4) became a symbol of the city of Florence.

Caravaggio Tonal contrast adds drama to *The Supper at Emmaus* (1601). Caravaggio used real people from the streets of Rome as his models.

PAINTING SUBJECTS

Religion In the Middle Ages, religious stories were artists' chief subjects. After 1800, religious commissions and works became rare. One exception to this rule is the work of Matisse, who in the 1950s designed murals and stained glass for the Chapel at Vence in southern France.

History and myth Scenes of uplifting courage, self-sacrifice or generosity, based on ancient history and myths, were once regarded as the highest art. Some offered a cloak for erotic art, using nude women painted as goddesses. Twentieth-century artists such as Picasso have at times depicted minotaurs and other creatures from their own private mythologies.

Portraits Individual portraiture emerged in the Renaissance. Leonardo da Vinci was the first portraitist of genius, but Raphael's portrait of Pope Leo X set new standards of realism, showing the pensive face of his patron in fine detail. The self-portraits of Rembrandt are honest paintings, "warts and all," a style echoed by modern portraitist Lucian Freud.

Still life The first realistic paintings of inanimate objects appeared in 17th-century Spain, often in kitchen scenes *(bodegones)*. The 18th-century still lifes of Chardin inspired the Impressionists, Cézanne and the Cubists.

Genre These often small-scale works depict everyday life and surroundings. The Venetian Jacopo Bassano painted animals in this style in the 16th century, but in 17th-century Holland a genre movement arose. Painters often specialized in particular themes – for example, tavern or kitchen scenes or musical parties. In the 18th century, Chardin and Hogarth painted famous genre scenes.

Landscape Painting landscapes was long regarded as inferior to historical or religious painting. It started to win favor in 17th-century Holland thanks to works by Hobbema, Vermeer and Ruisdael. They influenced English landscapists such as Gainsborough and Constable, who in turn influenced the French Impressionists.

Abstract art Shape and color are used rather than recognizable forms. The style arose in the 1920s, led by painters such as Wassily Kandinsky, and diversified over the next 30 years, when Ben Nicholson created reliefs from geometric shapes and Jackson Pollock created "action" paintings with drips of color.

Classicism In the 16th and early 17th centuries, a family of three Bolognese painters called the **Carracci** looked to Michelangelo and Raphael in an attempt to revive the harmony and balance of the High Renaissance style. They influenced two French painters in 17th-century Rome, **Nicolas Poussin** and Claude Lorraine (usually known as **Claude**). Poussin founded French Classicism with austere, geometrically planned versions of classical myths. Claude painted subjects from ancient mythology set in idealized landscapes.

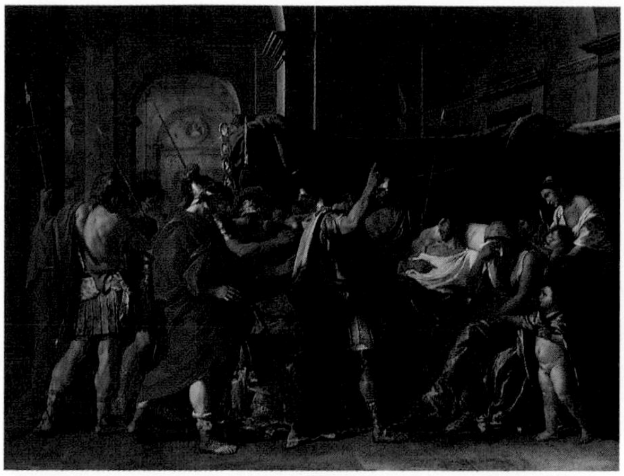

Poussin Nicolas Poussin painted *The Death of Germanicus* (1627) in Rome, where he spent 17 years developing his classical style.

1700

17th-century Dutch painting Painting in the Protestant Dutch Republic of the 17th century developed chiefly from the earlier Flemish realism, but was also influenced by Caravaggio's Baroque style. The Republic had no royal courts or churches to provide patronage for grand works of art – its artists painted ordinary people and everyday life. **Rembrandt**, who became Amsterdam's leading portrait painter, also recorded the progress of his own life with great perception in a series of self-portraits. **Frans Hals** portrayed Dutch dignitaries. **Vermeer** created calm interiors, and **Ruisdael**, **Cuyp** and **Hobbema** pioneered a new art form: unadorned landscape.

Hobbema *The Avenue at Middelharnis* (1689), Meindert Hobbema's best-known work, helped to popularize the landscape genre among English travelers.

Painting facts and figures

- The largest painting in the world is the 600 m² (6450 sq ft) ceiling fresco in the Bishop's Palace in Würzburg, Germany. It depicts the Four Continents and was painted in 1750-51 by Gianbattista Tiepolo, a Venetian.
- Pablo Picasso (1881-1973) was the most versatile and prolific artist of the 20th century. He produced 13 500 paintings, 100 000 prints, 34 000 illustrations and 300 sculptures.
- The most expensive painting ever sold at auction is van Gogh's *Portrait of Dr. Gachet* (1890) – Gachet was his patron – which reached a price of $82.5 million in May 1990 at Christie's in New York.
- The world's most valuable painting is assumed to be Leonardo da Vinci's *Mona Lisa* (c. 1504), kept in the Louvre in Paris. In 1960, when the painting was exhibited in the US, it was valued for insurance purposes at $100 million.

Artists C-E

Jean-Baptiste-Siméon Chardin (1699-1779) French
Expertise with color and skilled composition made Chardin the most successful genre and still life painter in France.
■ *Saying Grace; Breakfast Table*

Claude Lorraine (c. 1600-82) French
From his home in Rome, Claude specialized in works illustrating ancient myths. But it was the settings for these scenes – huge, formalized Roman landscapes, rich in light, shade and mood – that influenced later landscape artists such as Turner.
■ *Cephalus and Procris*

John Constable (1776-1837) British
Constable's observations of changing light and atmosphere in the English countryside influenced other Romantic painters and the 19th-century Impressionists.
■ *The Hay Wain*

Salvador Dali (1904-89) Spanish
Dali was a leading exponent of Surrealism, which drew images from the unconscious mind. He described his hallucinatory pictures as "hand-painted dream photographs."
■ *Birth of Liquid Desires*

Jacques-Louis David (1748-1825) French
The heroic subjects chosen by David, a central figure in the Neoclassical movement, expressed a self-sacrifice and devotion to duty that captured the atmosphere of revolutionary France.
■ *Oath of the Horatii; Coronation of Napoleon*

Edgar Degas (1834-1917) French
Degas stood out among the Impressionists for his portrayal of indoor subjects, such as ballet and theater, rather than landscape. His paintings of human figures capture a feeling of movement.
■ *Absinthe; Rehearsal in the Opera Foyer*

Eugene Delacroix (1798-1863) French
The works of Delacroix were notorious for their violence and exoticism, inspired by a visit to Morocco. His subject matter and dramatic use of color made him one of the most influential Romantic painters.
■ *Death of Sardanapulus; Algerian Women*

Donatello (1386-1466) Italian
Donatello played a key role in creating the Early Renaissance style in Florence. His sculptures worked independently of their surroundings – a quality not seen since classical times.
■ *St. George*

Marcel Duchamp (1887-1968) French
Though he produced little work, Duchamp, as the first "anti-artist," helped to change perceptions of what art is through acts such as exhibiting a urinal.
■ *Nude Descending Staircase*

Albrecht Dürer (1471-1528) German
Dürer visited Italy to learn about Renaissance perspective and how to draw nudes. His sense of color and proportion, and his engraving technique in particular, made him the greatest northern European artist of his day.
■ *Self-portrait; Knight*

Sir Jacob Epstein (1880-1959) American-British
Epstein's sculptures – primitive-looking, distorted nudes – were criticized for offensiveness. His later naturalistic portrait busts are considered the best in the modern genre.
■ *The Rock Drill*

see also
166-67 **The Renaissance**
168-69 **Clash of faiths**
300-1 **Greek and Roman myths**

Rococo and Romanticism moved art away from the mythological, historical and religious themes of earlier centuries. Though a strain of Greek influence still remained among the Neoclassicists, other artists began looking to contemporary literature and poetry – and to "real life" – for their inspiration, rejecting the idealism of earlier artistic movements.

Neoclassicism From the 1760s, Europe began discovering what ancient Greek and Roman art had really looked like. Information came from the excavations at Pompeii and from travelers' tales of Greece. This led to the rejection of Rococo in favor of a simple but grand style, again modeled on Classical sculpture. French painters such as **David** and his followers **Gérard**, **Gros** and **Ingres** produced works glorifying the French Revolution. Italian artist **Canova**, whose works include the tomb of Pope Clement XIV, was the leading Neoclassical sculptor.

Canova The balanced beauty of the *Three Graces* (1813-16) echoes ancient Classical ideals.

1700

1750

Rococo Early 18th-century high society grew bored with the historical and noble themes of Baroque. Wealthy patrons began to welcome the intimate, pleasure-loving art of **Watteau**, who painted scenes of people in contemporary dress enjoying themselves. The new Rococo style – elegant, sensual and ornamental – soon spread throughout Europe. Only the serious and dignified genre scenes of **Chardin** stood apart from the new style.

Fragonard *The Swing* (c. 1766), a frothy, light-hearted painting, epitomizes the Rococo style.

Romanticism The Romantics rejected Neoclassicism's intellectual approach in favor of the direct expression of feelings and individual experience. German artist **Friedrich** believed that landscape should express the artist's spiritual state, and Romantic landscapes often contained symbolic features such as ruins and twisted trees. **Delacroix** produced huge canvases often inspired by literature. Romantic painters also experimented with looser brushwork and more varied ways of applying paint. For **Turner** as for **Constable**, Dutch landscapes offered early models, but Turner soon outstripped earlier artists to pioneer an almost abstract treatment of light, color and space.

Turner In *Rain, Steam and Speed* (1844), hazy, smudged tones give a feeling of momentum.

PAINTING KEY TERMS

- **Alla prima** Oil-painting method in which oils are applied without underpainting.
- **Cartoon** Full-size design for a painting.
- **Chiaroscuro** Strongly contrasting light and shade.
- **Diptych** Oil painting in two panels hinged together; a **triptych** has three parts, and a **polyptych** has four or more.
- **Foreshortening** Perspective applied to a single object, such as an arm pointing directly at the observer.
- **Fresco** Painting executed on plaster.
- **Gesso** Mix of chalky pigment and glue used to prepare canvas or panel.
- **Golden section** Proportion of a line or rectangle divided so that smaller part is to larger as larger is to whole. Once thought to possess aesthetic power.
- **Grisaille** Painting done entirely in shades of gray.
- **Ground** "Support" on which a painting is made, such as primer on canvas.
- **Hatching** Use of fine parallel lines to suggest shading.
- **Icon** Image of a saint or holy person created as an object of veneration or religious comtemplation.
- **Impasto** Thickly applied paint retaining marks of brush or other implement.
- **Pentimento** The top layer of an oil painting becomes transparent with age, showing the artist's underpainting.
- **Picture plane** Imaginary plane occupied by the physical surface of the painting. Perspective lines appear to recede from it.
- ***Pietà*** Painting or sculpture of the Virgin Mary holding the dead Christ on her lap.
- **Primitive** Originally applied to medieval Italian painters, and now applied to artists who paint with childish simplicity.
- **Sanguine** Reddish brown chalk used for coloring.
- **Scumbling** Brushing an opaque color lightly over a previous layer.
- ***Trompe l'oeil*** Painting that tricks the viewer into thinking that the objects exist in three dimensions.

Realism The rejection of both Neoclassicism and Romanticism in favor of the direct observation of real life was the key aim of Realism. **Courbet** believed that "painting is essentially a concrete art and must be applied to real things." His canvases portrayed everyday scenes, often on an epic scale. *Burial at Ornans*, showing ordinary villagers at a graveside, shocked the established art world with its "vulgarity." There was no recognized Realist school, but Courbet's determined rejection of established authority had a powerful influence on later art movements, from Impressionism to Cubism and beyond.

Courbet Critics disliked *Burial at Ornans* (1849-50) because it moved away from the artistic tradition of idealizing life.

1800 1850

Pre-Raphaelites and Symbolism The Pre-Raphaelite Brotherhood was formed of young painters obsessed with Romantic poetry who wanted to return to what they saw as art's simplicity before Raphael. They included **Rossetti**, **Millais** and **Holman Hunt**. The romantic medieval style of **Burne-Jones** became associated with the movement through its similarity to Rossetti's later work. In the 1880s, the Symbolists also drew on literary sources. Inspired by poets Baudelaire and Mallarmé, **Moreau**, **Puvis de Chavannes** and **Redon** chose their subjects from mythology and fantasy. Symbolists used light and distortion to produce a psychological impact.

Burne-Jones *Laus Veneris* (1873-75) depicts German knight Tannhäuser discovering the home of Venus, goddess of love.

Types of paint

Acrylic A synthetic paint invented in the 1960s. Soluble in water and quick-drying, acrylics can be used as thin washes or as thick opaque impasto.

Gouache An opaque watercolor also known as body color or poster paint.

Oil Paint pigment is mixed with a drying oil, normally linseed. Oil paints, developed in Flanders around 1420, permit greater depth, subtlety and richness of color than other media and allow many different textures, from rough impasto to silky smoothness. Titian was the first master to exploit oil's potential fully in the 1500s, radically reworking and changing pictures as he went along.

Pastel The powdered pigment is mixed with gum or resin to bind it, and formed into sticks. Pastel was a favored medium of the Impressionists.

Tempera The paint pigment is dissolved in water and mixed, or tempered, in egg yolk. Tempera dries very fast, so it does not allow changes of the original design to be made.

Watercolor Pigments bound with a water-soluble medium (usually gum). Lighter tones are created by thinning the paint with water so that the white of the paper shows through. Watercolors are popular with landscapists because they are convenient for outdoor use.

Artists G-K

Paul Gauguin (1848-1903) French
The Postimpressionist paintings of Gauguin show the primitive influences of Tahiti, where he spent much of his later life. His use of patterns of color to provoke the imagination made him an influential Symbolist artist.
Tahitian Women; Ia Orana Maria

Giotto di Bondone (1267-1337) Italian
Giotto introduced depth and drama to painting with his sense of perspective and realistic, expressive human figures. He was the first artist to break free from two-dimensional medieval art.
Frescoes, Arena Chapel, Padua, Italy

Francisco de Goya (1746-1828) Spanish
Goya was a penetrating portraitist who painted his sitters in sometimes unflattering detail. He was also an early Romantic visionary whose depictions of the evils of war are unsurpassed.
Family of Charles IV; 3 May 1808

Barbara Hepworth (1903-75) British
This leading British abstract sculptor of the 20th century explored the relationship between space and form. Hepworth based her work on the shapes of naturally weathered objects.
Single Form

David Hockney (1937-) British
In the 1960s, Hockney emerged as a Pop Artist – a label he always rejected. Since his mid-twenties, the quality of his work – from painting and fine line drawing to collage and graphic art – has earned him critical acclaim.
A Bigger Splash

William Hogarth (1697-1764) British
Hogarth's brilliant satirical engravings and his accomplished, informal portraits made him the first great British artist.
The Rake's Progress

Hans Holbein the Younger (c. 1497-1543) German
The startling realism of Holbein's style helped him become the leading northern Renaissance portraitist. He settled in England and became court painter to Henry VIII.
The Ambassadors

Edward Hopper (1882-1967) American
Hopper's paintings and etchings present an atmospheric vision of city life, depicting urban US interiors with lonely human figures. He is considered a master etcher and an outstanding figurative painter.
Nighthawks

Jean-Auguste-Dominique Ingres (1780-1867) French
Superb draftsmanship made Ingres the supreme exponent of French Neoclassicism. He was devoted to depicting grand mythological themes but is better known for his nudes and portraits.
Bather; Madame Rivière

Wassily Kandinsky (1866-1944) Russian-German
Kandinsky was the most influential early abstract theorist and painter. He believed that art should reflect inner feelings and that color and shape alone could create an emotional response.
Sketch for Composition IV

Paul Klee (1879-1940) Swiss
Klee's original, inventive style made him a unique 20th-century artist. His poetic form of abstract art is sometimes described as resembling doodles.
Before the Gates of Kairouan

see also
144-45 **Ancient Greece**
172-73 **Europe in turmoil**
176-77 **Industrial Revolution**
340-41 **Western literature**

Western art 1850-1930

The switch from the subjective, atmospheric visions of the Impressionists to the objective, structured compositions of the Postimpressionists signaled the beginnings of modern art. The intense, unrealistic colors of the Expressionists and the distorted forms of Cubism and Surrealism freed art from its traditional restraints.

Postimpressionism By the 1880s, some artists felt that the Impressionists' faithful rendering of nature restricted their freedom of expression and that form and color could be used in different ways. **Seurat** placed colors as dots so they would "mix" in the eye of the viewer – a technique known as pointillism; **Gauguin** used flattened forms and unrealistic colors; **van Gogh** used bold, vibrant colors and thick paint; and **Cézanne** created vivid, carefully structured landscapes, still lifes and figure paintings. **Rodin** restored heroic seriousness to sculpture but with exceptional passion and realism. His life's work, the bronze *The Gates of Hell* (started 1880), is crowded with nearly 200 dramatic figures.

Rodin *The Kiss* (1888) originated from a concept designed for *The Gates of Hell.*

1850 1875 1900

Impressionism The Impressionists rejected Romanticism's exotic subject matter and emotionalism, wanting instead to capture immediate visual "impressions" of their subjects, and suggesting forms through fleeting effects of light. **Monet**, **Pissarro** and **Sisley** painted the same landscapes repeatedly in changing light. **Manet** and **Degas** normally painted urban or indoor scenes, as did **Berthe Morisot** and **Mary Cassatt**. The official "Salon" rejected the Impressionists' work, so the group organized eight exhibitions of their own from 1874 to 1886, after which they broke up.

Monet After creating a water garden at his house in Giverny in 1890, Monet spent 20 years painting its shimmering colors.

Fauvism At an exhibition in Paris in 1905, the wild energy, simplified forms and jarring combinations of intense colors in pictures by **Matisse**, **Vlaminck**, **Derain**, **Rouault** and **Dufy** led an art critic to dismiss the artists as *fauves* – "wild beasts." The movement lasted only three years, but it deeply influenced the Expressionists and Abstract Expressionists.

PICASSO: ARTIST OF THE 20TH CENTURY

No 20th-century artist can rival Spanish-born Picasso for fame, versatility, influence or number of works. His early work is often categorized into the "Blue Period" – paintings of social outcasts in elegiac blue tones – and the "Rose Period," depicting dancers and acrobats in warmer pinks. His studies of Cézanne and African sculpture led to the first Cubist painting, *Les Demoiselles d'Avignon* (1907), which overturned Western ideas about form and beauty with its distorted bodies and masklike faces. Picasso later turned to sculpture, and was one of the first artists to create three-dimensional works by combining miscellaneous items in ingenious ways, rather than by carving or modeling. He constructed *Head of a Bull, Metamorphosis* (1943) from bicycle parts. Though many of Picasso's works display emotional force through images of despair, his contrasting playful style and eclecticism opened up the possibilities of modern art.

***Guernica* (1937)** Picasso's emotional response to the German bombing of the Basque capital, Guernica, during the Spanish Civil War, expresses the horror of armed conflict.

Franz Marc *The Fate of the Animals* (1913) expresses Marc's feeling for what he called the "inner spiritual side of nature."

Expressionism Any work that uses distortion to reflect the state of mind of the artist can be labeled "expressionist." The central aim is the communication of subjective emotions through strong colors and dynamic or fantastical forms. The style underwent intense development among artists such as **Kirchner**, **Klee**, **Macke** and **Marc** in Germany between 1905 and 1930.

Cubism Cubist painters of the early 1900s sought to depict three-dimensional objects without illusory perspective or even distinct colours. In this, Cubism marked a radical break from the idea, dating from the Renaissance, that art should reflect nature. Cubism had two phases. In Analytic Cubism an object's different aspects – sides, top and base – could all be shown at once, and the process was pushed almost to the point of total abstraction. In Synthetic Cubism, elements such as textured materials and lettering were combined (synthesized) with painting – a new technique which became known as collage.

1920

1930

Futurism An Italian movement originating around 1909, Futurism jettisoned as much of Italy's overwhelming artistic past as it could, inspired by contemporary life's speed and machinery. The style copied the repeating geometric planes used by Cubists to portray motion and speed. Painter and sculptor **Boccioni** was Futurism's outstanding artist, creating paintings blurred with movement and sculptures of dynamic, striding figures. Futurism died with World War I, but it had an important influence on subsequent art in Britain and Russia and on the Dadaists.

Salvador Dali *The Metamorphosis of Narcissus* (1937) juxtaposes mundane and incongruous objects. Dali claimed that deliberately cultivated paranoia was a source of creativity.

Giacomo Balla *Velocity of Cars and Light* (1913) portrays motion with pure line and tone. Balla was a contemporary of Boccioni.

Dada and Surrealism In 1915, an art movement was founded that rejected everything in life and in art. Its nihilism, humor and urgent desire to shock appealed to postwar disillusionment. Dada's key tenet, espoused by its most influential figure, Marcel **Duchamp**, was that art was whatever the artist said it was. After Duchamp, any object in any material was potentially a work of art. Surrealism, the fundamental aim of which was to create art direct from the unconscious, emerged in Paris in the 1920s. Surrealist artists, such as **Magritte** and **Dali**, typically used obsessively detailed images or objects in dreamlike and disturbing ways.

FACT

Five of the top ten most expensive paintings ever sold at auction were painted by Pablo Picasso.

Artists K-P

Jeff Koons
(1955-) American
Koons turns banal subject matter into large, iconographic objects, often by commissioning traditional manufacturers working in materials such as metal or porcelain. His art helped to establish the term Neo-Geometricism (or "Neo-Geo"), which refers to its unemotional, impersonal content.
■ *Puppy*

Leonardo da Vinci
(1452-1519) Italian
Leonardo is often described as the artistic and scientific genius of the Renaissance. In his paintings, oil paint subtly models light and shade, creating pictures with mysterious landscapes and beautiful, expressive human figures.
■ *Mona Lisa*

Roy Lichtenstein
(1923-97) American
A founder and leading proponent of Pop Art, Lichtenstein uses images inspired by comic strips to create original, well-composed paintings.
■ *Wham!*

Edouard Manet
(1832-83) French
This first Impressionist (though he never exhibited with other Impressionists) is also known as the "first modern painter" for his choice of subjects. He painted contemporary life rather than basing his work on traditional or moral themes.
■ *Déjeuner sur L'Herbe; Olympia*

Henri Matisse
(1869-1954) French
The French Riviera provided a rich source of color for Matisse, who built an international reputation as a modern painter equaled only by Picasso. His use of pure, vivid tones rather than natural shades inspired Fauvism.
■ *L'Escargot*

Michelangelo
(1475-1564) Italian
By his early twenties, Michelangelo had already displayed technical mastery in his sculptures of the human figure. The composition and emotional expressiveness of his statues, frescoes and architecture raised the profile of art as a profession.
■ Sistine Chapel ceiling

Piet Mondrian
(1872-1944) Dutch
Mondrian's rigorously abstract art, with compositions of primary colors enclosed by lines, influenced graphic art and industrial design as well as later abstract art.
■ *Composition with Red, Black, Blue and Grey*

Claude Monet
(1840-1926) French
It was Monet's painting *Impression: Sunrise* that gave the Impressionists their name. He specialized in depicting variations of light and atmosphere.
■ *The Gare St. Lazare; Rouen Cathedral*

Henry Moore
(1898-1986) British
The main works of the best-known sculptor of the 20th century represent the human form in a bold, semiabstract style and often on a huge scale. The figures reflect the curving shapes of the landscape.
■ *King and Queen*

Piero della Francesca
(c. 1415-92) Italian
Renaissance painter Piero della Francesca combined solemn grandeur with pure color and used classical architecture to emphasize mathematical perspective. Though influential in his own era, the level of his skill was largely recognized retrospectively, in the 20th century.
■ *Legend of the True Cross* fresco cycle; *The Baptism of Christ*

see also
166-67 **The Renaissance**
312-13 **Psychology**

As the 20th century progressed, simplicity and minimalism became key elements in painting and sculpture. Definitions of art expanded to include video recordings, staged events and assemblages of natural objects. The act of creation is now as important as the artwork it creates.

Abstract Expressionism

Dating from the 1940s, Abstract Expressionism is the first American movement not to be influenced by European painting, although it drew on Surrealist ideas of artistic creation. Abstract Expressionists aimed for spontaneous expression at the expense of representational design. **Jackson Pollock** developed a technique of throwing or dripping paint onto a canvas known as gestural or action painting. **Mark Rothko**'s shimmering expanses of color are known as color-field painting. Other leading exponents include **Willem de Kooning** and **Barnett Newman**.

Pollock The forms within *Blue Poles: Number II* (1952) raise images from the observer's unconscious mind.

1930 1940 1950 1960

Brancusi The head of *Mademoiselle Pogany III* (1933) is formed by a few simple curves.

Modernism

In painting, the term sums up a variety of styles from the 1920s to the 1960s, characterized by abstraction, flat colors and an emphasis on the canvas as an artificial surface. The most purely Modernist painter is **Piet Mondrian**. In sculpture, Modernism was a distinct movement, experimenting with form and structure. **Constantin Brancusi**, considered one of the 20th century's greatest sculptors, reduced his forms to near-abstract simplicity. **Henry Moore** rejected classical ideals of beauty for more vital, rougher forms based on natural shapes such as human figures, shells, bones. **Barbara Hepworth** also looked to nature but in a wholly abstract way. **Anthony Caro**'s Modernism owes more to the ideas of Pop Art in using standard industrial parts such as steel plates or aluminium tubing welded together and brightly painted.

Conceptualism

Conceptualists assert that the creative act is more important than the object created; at its most extreme, it might consist of no more than an idea for a work of art. The movement includes Performance Art (events staged by the artist), Body Art (the artist's expression of ideas – often confrontational – using his or her body), and Land Art (the creation of artworks through the interaction of the artist and the environment).

Koons *Puppy* (first made in 1992) is a 13 m (44 ft) high conceptual sculpture made of living plants.

Pop Art

"Transient, low-cost, mass-produced, young . . . sexy, gimmicky," said **Richard Hamilton** of the movement he helped create. Influenced by Dada, Pop Art took emblems of the modern world – such as comics and advertisements – and used their ideas and images to create original art. Chief proponents were **Warhol** and **Lichtenstein** in the US and Hamilton, **Peter Blake** and **Allen Jones** in Britain.

Lichtenstein *In the Car* (1963) expresses tension between two characters in a simple, graphic image.

WHAT IS AN INSTALLATION?

Installations are works of art created in harmony with or as part of their setting or environment – usually a gallery. They arose in the 1960s from the belief that the context in which a work of art is viewed is as important as its content. Installation artists either totally reconstruct a room (as in the work of Russian **Ilya Kabakov**) or compose a work of art with various objects using the room as a "canvas" (a method exemplified by British artist **Cornelia Parker**).

Parker *Cold, Dark Matter – An Exploded View* (1991) was created by suspending pieces of wood between the floor and the ceiling.

VIDEO

Since the 1960s, artists have exploited the expressive potential of video technology, including instant replay, continuous repetition, slow motion, large-scale and multiscreen projection, and soundtracks. Artists such as **Bill Viola** and **Sam Taylor Wood** produce work about human behavior, relationships and identity that has an intimate, intense and sometimes disturbing effect.

Figurative painting Despite radical developments in the accepted notions of art and artworks, art representing animal or human figures (figurative art) continues to thrive – though usually in modified forms. Alongside **Francis Bacon**, **Lucian Freud** and **David Hockney**, figurative painting since the 1970s has included the Postmodernist so-called "Neo-Expressionists," such as **Anselm Kiefer** and **Julian Schnabel**.

Hockney *American Collector* (1968) displays Hockney's draftsmanship, and his ability to convey human personality in an uncluttered, graphic style.

1970 1980 1990 2000

Minimalism Some artists reacted against Abstract Expressionism's emotiveness, believing in letting raw materials set in geometric configurations "speak" directly to observers. This did not always work: In 1976, **Carl Andre**'s *Equivalent VIII* – 120 bricks arranged in a rectangle – attracted derision and was vandalized while on display at London's Tate Gallery.

Contemporary Art By the late 1980s, art had reached the logical conclusion of Duchamp's Dada philosophy, becoming whatever the artist wanted it to be. **Rachel Whiteread** achieved instant fame in 1992 with *Untitled (House)*, a cast of the inside of a Victorian terraced house. Much of her work concentrates on the spaces between objects, which she captures by filling them with plaster or wax to reveal something like a photographic negative of the original space. **Damien Hirst** has displayed dead animals preserved in tanks of formaldehyde to explore the themes of life and death. New technology has also stimulated developments: video recordings, films and computer-generated images have now become acceptable as artistic media.

Hirst Much of Hirst's work, including *The Physical Impossibility of Death in the Mind of Someone Living* (1991; right), is intended to tap in to "people's worst fears."

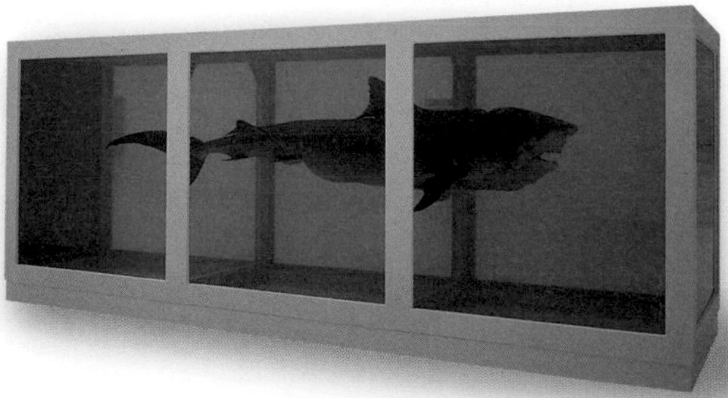

Land Art

Some Land Art projects involve digging out and rearranging quantities of earth and rock. American **Robert Smithson**'s *Spiral Jetty* was a 457.2 m (1500 ft) long spiral of rock and salt crystals on the edge of Great Salt Lake in Utah. British artist **Andy Goldsworthy** creates patterns and forms from materials such as leaves, pebbles and ice to express the power and transcience of nature.

Goldsworthy Stone cairn constructed on Kangaroo Island, Australia.

Artists P–Z

Jackson Pollock
(1912-56) American
This leading abstract Expressionist aimed for the direct expression of his unconscious. His paintings hint at gestures or forms among their colored drips or trails.
■ *Number 14*

Raphael
(1483-1520) Italian
The limpid colors, graceful figures and symmetrical architectural backgrounds of Raphael's paintings made him a leading artist of the High Renaissance. His work inspired all of the later classical painters.
■ *The School of Athens; Madonna della Sedia*

Rembrandt (1606-69) Dutch
The most highly regarded of the Dutch painters – a master of technique in painting and etching. Rembrandt was the first to establish a profoundly perceptive, expressive style of portraiture.
■ *The Anatomy Lesson of Dr. Tulp; Self Portrait (1658)*

Auguste Rodin
(1840-1917) French
Rodin's expressive natural forms revived the popularity of sculpture among the public and secured his reputation as the leading French Postimpressionist sculptor.
■ *The Thinker*

Peter Paul Rubens
(1577-1640) Flemish
The "father of High Baroque style" was known for his huge, dramatic canvases painted for courts across Europe.
■ *Self Portrait with Isabella Brant; Arrival of the Queen at Marseilles*

Titian
(c. 1483-1576) Italian
One of the greatest Renaissance artists. Titian's bold brushwork revolutionized oil painting techniques. His style influenced many later painters, including Rubens and Velázquez.
■ *Pietà*

J.M.W. Turner
(1775-1851) English
Romantic painter Turner developed an almost abstract style. His use of pure light and color prefigured the work of the Impressionists.
■ *Steamer in a Snowstorm*

Jan van Eyck
(1390-1441) Flemish
Early Renaissance painter van Eyck was the first to demonstrate technical prowess with oil paint. His works show fine detail and rich colors.
■ *The Arnolfini Marriage*

Vincent van Gogh
(1853-90) Dutch
Postimpressionist van Gogh strove to convey his inner vision through swirling colors and brushwork. His style laid the foundations of Expressionism.
■ *Cornfield and Cypress Trees; Sunflowers*

Diego Velázquez
(1599-1660) Spanish
Baroque court portraitist Velázquez eliminated props and allegory to concentrate on his sitters. His techniques influenced later painters such as Goya and Manet.
■ *Maids of Honor*

Jan Vermeer (1632-75) Dutch
Vermeer became the leading Dutch genre painter through his expert compositional skills and use of light and shade in domestic scenes.
■ *Girl Reading; The Kitchen Maid*

Andy Warhol (1928-87) American
From his "Factory" studio, Warhol produced emotionless, graphic likenesses that became part of American iconography.
■ *Gold Marilyn Monroe*

see also
166-67 **The Renaissance**
312-13 **Psychology**

Architecture 600 B.C.-A.D. 1600

Buildings are the most visible and often the most durable of human creations – the largest scale of all artistic works – and they reveal much about the culture in which they were created. Architecture, like any other art form, is subject to fashion. The style of a building may derive from a specific architect or group or from the characteristic building techniques of a particular era and culture.

Romanesque (1000-1100) Also known as Norman, this was the second medieval style chronologically, following the Byzantine style (450-600) of the Eastern Roman Empire. It used Classical elements such as round arches in heavy-walled buildings. The massive solidity of Romanesque walls and columns was necessary to support the roofs – which were at first supported by tunnel vaults and later by rib vaulting. Romanesque churches were lavishly decorated with religious carvings.

Temple Concordia, Parthenon, Greece Built by Ictinus and Callicrates, 447-432 B.C.

The Colosseum, Rome The first free-standing amphitheater, A.D. 70-72; architects unknown.

San Vitale, Ravenna, Italy 6th-century Byzantine church.

Chartres cathedral, France c. 1194-1260.

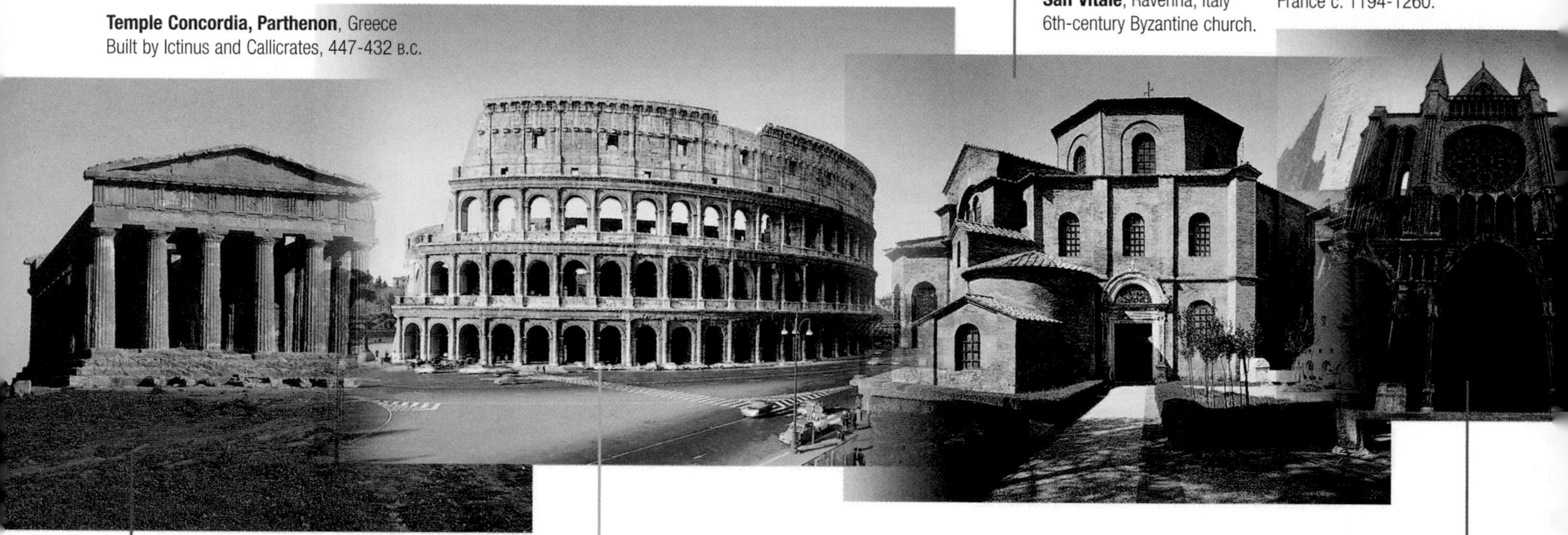

Classical Greek (c. 600-300 B.C.) The Greeks aimed to create an ideal beauty in the design of their large public buildings. They originally built in wood but began using stone in about 600 B.C. Even early temples have a perfect symmetry derived from strict mathematical proportion. By 490 B.C., the Greeks were building in marble and were gilding temples or painting them vivid red and blue. Greek architecture reached its zenith with buildings such as the Parthenon in Athens, in which many apparently straight lines are in fact precise curves designed to counter optical distortion. The Greeks also pioneered the building of huge semicircular open-air theaters.

Roman (c. 200 B.C.-A.D. 400) Roman architects borrowed many techniques – domes from the Persians, arches from the Etruscans and various architectural motifs from the Greeks. They developed new types of buildings: amphitheaters, basilicas and aqueducts. They invented concrete, with which they erected vast domes and vaults, turning architecture into a form of engineering rather than art. The Colosseum (built A.D. 72-82), the biggest Roman amphitheater, seated 55 000 people on tiers. Large flat-roofed buildings called basilicas were used for public meetings. Aqueducts, such as the 47 m (155 ft) Pont du Gard (built A.D. 14) near Nîmes, France, carried water on raised tiers of arches.

Gothic (1150-1500) Gothic, the third medieval style, arose in northern France and possibly was influenced by arches built by the Moors in Spain. Its distinguishing feature is the pointed arch, which allows higher roofs and windows. Solid or arched "flying" buttresses transmit the roof's weight – and particularly the sideways forces caused by the pointed arch – to the ground. It quickly became a recognizable international style, with particularly fine examples in Germany (e.g., Cologne cathedral) and Britain.

THE FIVE ORDERS

Classical Greek and Roman architects worked to set standard relationships between various elements – particularly the base, structural supports (columns) and entablature (beams) they carried. These styles are known as orders and include precise rules for decoration and other elements. The three Greek orders are the Doric, Ionic and Corinthian. The Romans adapted these styles and added two of their own: the Tuscan and Composite.

Tuscan **Doric** **Ionic** **Corinthian** **Composite**

Gothic arches and windows

The pointed arch and window were key characteristics in Gothic architecture and were made possible by flying buttress, another Gothic innovation. Essentially a form of permanent external scaffolding, flying buttresses carried the weight of the roof directly to the ground. This allowed architects to reduce wall thickness and to increase the height and size of arches and windows correspondingly.

The most extreme example of the Gothic window can be seen in the Sainte-Chappelle, the chapel built by Louis IX in Paris, completed in 1248. The walls are no more than frames around huge stained-glass windows, creating an airy, diaphanous building flooded with light.

In general, the lighter and higher the roof of a Gothic cathedral and the bigger its windows, the later it was built.

Florence cathedral, Italy The dome was designed by Brunelleschi, c. 1420.

Villa Rotunda, Vicenza House designed by Palladio, 1550-51.

Renaissance (1400-1600) During the Renaissance, the plentiful Roman ruins in Italy inspired architects to create a style based largely on a revival of Greek and Roman principles. There was a renewed emphasis on geometric proportion, light, and authentic Classical decoration. Round arches and domes returned, as did the five orders (see left). For the first time since the Roman period, architects undertook large-scale urban planning.

Palladian (1550-1750) Architect Andrea **Palladio** created a simplified Renaissance style emphasizing harmonious proportions and symmetry and restrained decoration. He was the first to use a columned temple design as a frontage – the most imitated aspect of his style. His influence in England, Ireland and North America continued into the 19th century.

Key terms

Architrave In Classical architecture, the ledge or lintel resting on the columns.
Barrel vault Arched semicircular vaulting resting on supporting walls.
Buttress A structure built against a wall to give extra support or to transmit the outward thrust of a vault or arch.
Clerestory A windowed wall stretching above the main roof level to allow extra light into a building.
Cornice The projecting upper part of an entablature (see opposite); or a moulded horizontal projection at the top of a wall.
Cupola A small dome on a roof or turret.
Entasis The slight bulge in a column to counter the optical illusion that it is thinner in the middle.
Flying buttress A buttress in the form of a half-arch.
Gable The triangular end of a roof.
Keystone The central wedge-shaped stone at the top of an arch.
Lintel A beam or slab above an opening.
Mullion A vertical window divider.
Pediment The triangular structure above a doorway or peristyle of a Classical or Renaissance building.
Peristyle A row of columns.
Pilaster A rectangular column, with base and capital, attached to a wall.
Spandrel The triangular space between two arches or an arch, ceiling and wall.
Stucco A mortar coating imitating stone.
Tracery The decorative stone framework of a large, usually Gothic, window.
Transom A horizontal window divider.
Tympanum The space between a lintel and the arch above it.

Architects A-H

This list covers the most successful, innovative and influential architects from the past 600 years of mainstream Western architecture.
■ Refers to a key work.

Leon Battista Alberti (1404-72) Italian
Important in spreading knowledge of Classical architecture he was an early proponent of the idea that beauty in architecture derives from harmony and proportion.
■ Malatesta Chapel, Rimini, Italy

Gian Lorenzo Bernini (1598-1680) Italian
He transformed much of Rome, building palaces, churches and squares in the Baroque style on a huge and dynamic scale. He also influenced large-scale city planning across Europe.
■ Baldacchino, St. Peter's, Rome

Donato Bramanto (1444-1514) Italian
The leading architect of the High Renaissance in Rome, he favored simple, elegant forms in a sober, Classical style. He began the rebuilding of St. Peter's.
■ Church of San Pietro in Montorio, Rome

Filippo Brunelleschi (1377-1446) Italian
Regarded as the founder of the Italian Renaissance style, his dome for Florence cathedral (the Duomo) was a triumph of engineering. His later buildings were more purely Classical.
■ Florence cathedral dome

Norman Foster (1935-) British
His High Tech Postmodernist buildings make use of precision engineering and the latest technology. Many are built from modular components.
■ Hong Kong Airport

Ange-Jacques Gabriel (1698-1782) French
Influenced by Palladio, his work was typical of the measured and sober grandeur of French Classicism – for example, the Place de la Concorde, Paris (begun 1757).
■ Petit Trianon, Versailles, France

Antoní Gaudí (1852-1926) Spanish (Catalan)
Highly individual and original, he pioneered the use of fluid, organic forms in buildings in the Art Nouveau style. His influence still grows.
■ Church of the Sagrada Familia (begun 1874), Barcelona, Spain

Frank Gehry (1929-) American
His bold, original, often huge, Postmodernist buildings defy almost every architectural convention. He has made use of a wide variety of building materials.
■ Guggenheim Museum, Bilbao, Spain

Walter Gropius (1883-1969) German
Head of the Bauhaus school of architecture and design 1919-20, he emigrated to the US in 1937. He argued for the arts to be unified, and for the use of modern materials and forms. He had a huge influence on the growth of Modernism through his teaching.
■ Fagus Works, Alfeld-an-der-Leine, Germany

Jules Hardouin-Mansart (1646-1708) French
His strong sense of visual drama and splendor made him the most successful architect of Lous XIV's reign. In his early career, he worked in the Baroque style. Toward the end of his life, he adopted a lighter style that represented the first step towards Rococo.
■ Hall of Mirrors, Versailles, France

see also
144-45 **Ancient Greece**
146-47 **Ancient Rome**
166-67 **The Renaissance**
462-63 **Building**

During the 17th century, the purity of the Renaissance began to give way to the more ornate Baroque and Rococo styles. After revivals of the Classical and Gothic styles during the 19th century, architects in the late 19th and 20th centuries began using a range of new technologies and materials to create entirely new styles of buildings.

Romanticism/Historicism (1800-1900) New influences from Egypt (brought back by French scholars with Napoleon's army) and Asia and popular interest in the medieval "Gothic" past led to a movement of imitative architecture directly opposed to the pure style of Neoclassicism. Partly covered by the term "Gothic Revival," it had strong Romantic and religious undertones. Characteristic features include pointed arches, battlements and finials, and elaborate surface decoration.

Art Deco (1918-1940) Art Deco (or Style Moderne) architecture is characterized by the streamlined, mechanical shapes and repetitive geometric decoration seen in New York's Rockefeller Center (especially the interiors), Chrysler Building and Empire State Building. Many features were constructed from chrome, enamel or glass.

St. Peter's Colonnade, Rome Bernini's novel freestanding colonnades provide a backdrop to the piazza before St. Peter's.

Nash terrace, Regent's Park, London John Nash was a leading exponent of Neoclassicism.

Houses of Parliament, London Charles Barry designed this in the Gothic Revival style.

Church of the Sagrada Familia, Barcelona Gaudí used concrete to mold organic shapes.

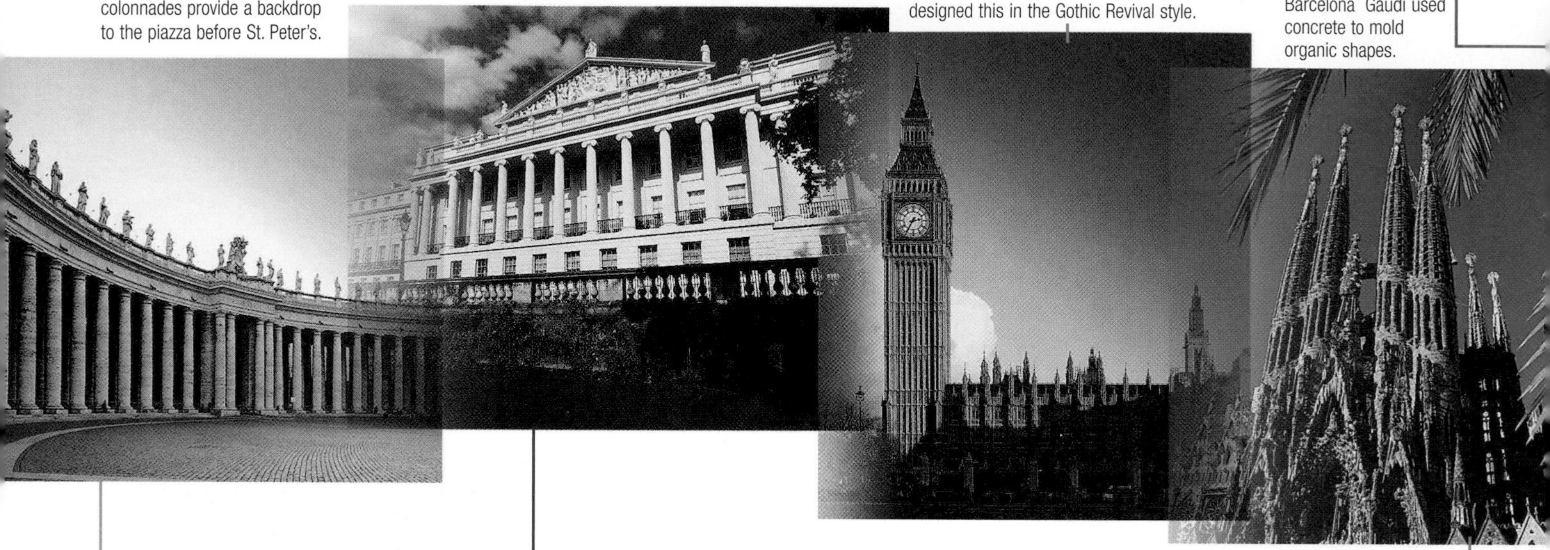

Baroque and Rococo (1600-1760) Italian architect and sculptor **Bernini** established the theatrical style, elaborate surface detail and vivid wall paintings of Baroque, which became popular across Europe. In the 18th century, when an influx of wealth from colonial expansion and a growing demand for civic rather than religious buildings gave architects more freedom, a light-hearted variant of Baroque evolved in the form of Rococo. Flowing lines and elaborate, elegant decorative schemes were combined with light interiors created by including more windows.

Neoclassicism (1750-1850) Partly as a reaction to Baroque excess, European architects such as Claude **Ledoux** looked back to Roman and Greek architecture for a "pure" Classical style. Inspiration came from archaeological excavations, such as those at Pompeii (1748). The new movement sought to recreate Classical grandeur using simple, geometric layouts and tall Classical columns, and it copied Greek or Roman decoration.

Art Nouveau (1890-1914) Art Nouveau extended well beyond architecture, most notably into furnishings and interior design. Its roots lay in a revival of interest in the sinuous, flowing shapes of Celtic design. Technological developments in metalwork and poured concrete made possible the use of such motifs in architecture in the early 20th century. Outstanding examples are Hector **Guimard**'s Paris Métro station entrances and the organic-looking buildings of Antonî **Gaudí** in Barcelona, Spain.

Details and decoration

Arabesque A decoration using flowing curved lines, spirals and plant tendrils, often in a repeating pattern.
Cartouche A panel in the form of a curling piece of paper or a scroll, usually bearing an inscription.
Checkerwork A pattern of squares in alternating colors or materials, such as stone and brick, to produce a chessboard effect. It is used on walls and floors.
Chevron A repeating pattern of V shapes or zigzags common in Romanesque architecture and revived in Art Deco.
Festoon A carved garland of fruit or flowers, often including a ribbon or bow.
Finial A carved or molded object at the apex of a gable or pinnacle.
Fretwork Straight horizontal and vertical lines used to create a repeating geometric pattern.
Frieze A band of decorative carving near the top of a wall.
Gargoyle A water spout at roof level often in the form of a grotesque figure.
Grotesque A decoration in which human, animal and plant forms are combined.
Mosaic Small pieces of glass or stone, called tesserae, are set in mastic to form geometric patterns or representational pictures. They can be used on floors or walls and were a particular feature of Roman and Byzantine buildings.
Pendant A sculptural ornament suspended from the central point of a vault or ceiling and common in Late Gothic vaulting.
Rosette A disk decorated with roses, common in Neoclassical architecture.
Running dog A repeating wave pattern, often used in a frieze and common in Classical architecture.
Scallop A carved or molded shell.
Scroll A partly rolled scroll in relief molding, often used in a repeating pattern and seen on Classical columns and in Gothic vaults.

International modernism (1920-1975) Modernism rejected ornament and links with past styles, stripping away everything except what was functionally necessary. Its main influence can be seen in commercial and industrial buildings. The Bauhaus design school, founded by **Walter Gropius** in Germany, became a center of Modernist design. **Le Corbusier**'s principles included the "free plan" (walls independent of the structural frame) and "free façade" (windows positioned independently of the stucture).

Pluralism (1975-) A mixture of styles, often described by the umbrella term "Postmodernism," arose from a dissatisfaction with mainstream Modernist design. Two major schools currently exist. In the **High Tech** school, elements from previous styles are reused in new combinations made possible by technological advances. In the **Deconstruction** school, the emphasis is on movement and disorientation – fragmenting or expanding spaces through the unconventional treatment of basic elements such as floors and walls.

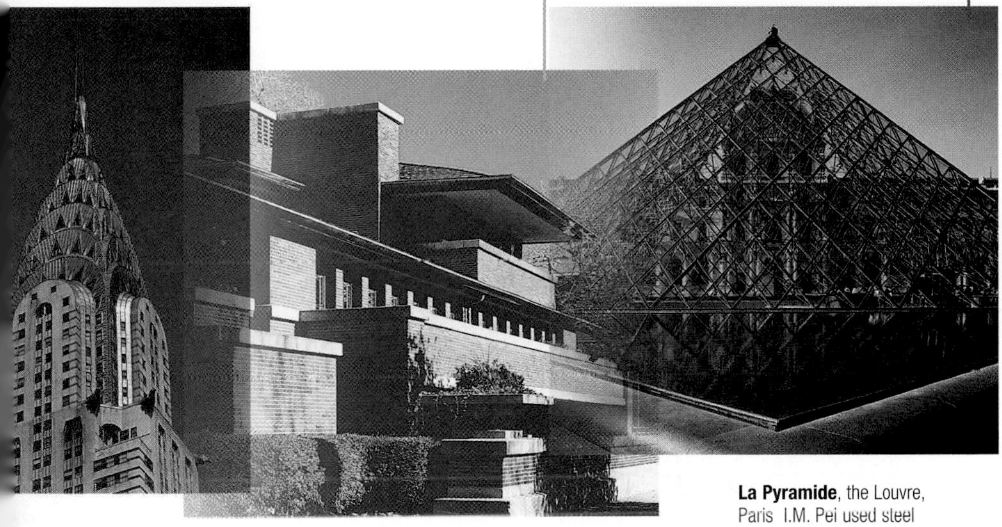

Chrysler Building, New York William Van Alen's fan-shaped tiers are typical of Art Deco decoration.

Robie House, Chicago Frank Lloyd Wright's first "prairie house" has a sculptural simplicity.

La Pyramide, the Louvre, Paris I.M. Pei used steel struts and more than 900 pieces of glass to create a modern pyramid.

TODAY'S ARCHITECTURE

Early 21st-century architecture shares the 20th-century belief that the function of a building should dictate the technology and materials used to build it.

Two themes dominate. One is that in an era of permanent and ever more rapid change, architecture must be flexible and responsive, never constrained by theory. Dutch architect **Rem Koolhaas** epitomizes this approach. His buildings consist of abstract forms, sometimes two or more that appear to be unrelated, but in which the internal layout is entirely logical and functional.

The second theme in contemporary architecture is to fuse conservation and innovation – to use architecture in urban regeneration and to safeguard the environment. American **Frank Gehry**'s startlingly original Guggenheim Museum in Bilbao succeeded in breathing life into a decaying industrial city as well as housing works of art. His plans for the new Guggenheim Museum in New York continue this theme on an even more dramatic scale. Similarly, Swiss architect **Jacques Herzog**'s Tate Modern gallery, built out of London's derelict Bankside power station, dovetails culture and urban renewal. And **Norman Foster**'s Reichstag (Parliament) in Berlin uses 94 percent less energy than its 19th-century predecessor. His planned Greater London Authority Headquarters promises a virtually nonpolluting building.

Experience Music Project, Seattle (Gehry)

Architects L-Z

Le Corbusier
(1887-1975)
Swiss/French Born Charles-Edouard Jeanneret, le Corbusier was a champion of Modernism. Early in his career, he designed influential cube-shaped white houses. Later he pioneered a more sculptural and expressive style based on abstract shapes realized in concrete.
■ Villa Savoie, Poissy, France

Louis Le Vau
(1612-70) French
The first of the great French Baroque architects and the original architect of Versailles his most impressive work was that done on the grand scale.
■ Château de Vaux-le-Vicomte, near Melun, France

Adolf Loos
(1870-1933) Austrian
One of the first Modernists, he built bold, square buildings – many of them simple cubes – with no ornament, often using reinforced concrete.
■ Steiner House, Vienna

Michelangelo [Buonarroti]
(1475-1564) Italian
He rejected Classical notions of proportion and harmony in favor of complex and unsettling spatial effects. He used features such as columns and architraves for their visual effect as much as for structural support. His dynamic spaces influenced 17th-century architects, especially Bernini.
■ Major contribution to St. Peter's Basilica, Rome

Ludwig Mies van der Rohe
(1886-1969)
German/American
A proponent of the International Modernist style, he created elegant buildings using materials such as glass and steel. He emphasized simplicity of design, good craftsmanship and immaculate finishes, and his style has been imitated around the world.
■ Lever House, New York

Andrea Palladio
(1508-80) Italian In a series of villas, palaces and churches, he combined Classical ideas of symmetry and harmonious proportions with simplicity of layout and minimal decoration. His contemporaries considered his buildings to be unsurpassable, and his influence spread throughout Europe with the publication of his *Four Books on Architecture* (1570).
■ Church of San Giorgio Maggiore, Venice

Richard Rogers
(1933-) British/Italian
He exploits modern technology, selecting techniques and materials that best suit a building's function. His particular concern has been for urban renewal and the use of energy-efficient techniques.
■ Lloyd's Building, London

Christopher Wren
(1632-1723) English
Working in a Baroque-influenced Classical style, he built more than 50 churches in London after the Great Fire of 1666. He also designed a series of palaces. He was equally skilled on a small or giant scale.
■ St. Paul's Cathedral, London

Frank Lloyd Wright
(1867-1959) American
The leading American Modernist of the early 20th century, he created elegant, flowing spaces rather than the harsh geometry of his European contemporaries.
■ Robie House, Chicago

see also
462-63 **Building**

Classical music 800-1800

The early Christian Church absorbed and adapted the pagan music of antiquity and the East. Yet the development of Western church music led, in turn, to new realms of expression and technique in secular music over the next centuries. These reached a pinnacle with the works of Mozart in the 18th-century "Classical" period.

Middle Ages The earliest medieval church music was a chant called plainsong sung alternately by priest and choir. Most music had a single melodic line (monophony), but from about the 9th century, music with two or more melodies sung simultaneously (polyphony) developed. By 1100, a system for writing down music had been devised (it was previously passed on orally).

Renaissance In the Renaissance, instrumental music emerged as a separate style from vocal music, and music was written specifically for particular instruments. The northern European tradition of elaborate polyphony merged with the southern (mainly Italian) taste for chords and harmonies. The madrigal, a form of secular song in five or six parts, was invented in about 1530 in the Netherlands and Italy. It became popular in Elizabethan England and increased the trend toward secular music.

Early Baroque The Baroque style emerged in Italy during the early 1600s. It rejected Renaissance serenity for dramatic contrasts in tone, volume and pace. A new style of religious music developed – oratorio – written for solo voices, chorus and orchestra. New instrumental forms also emerged: the sonata (for solo instruments) and the concerto (for a solo instrument with orchestra). Instrumental music gained in popularity through the widespread use of the harpsichord and organ. The most celebrated violins and cellos ever made were produced during this period by Nicolo Amati of Cremona in Italy, whose pupils included Antonio Stradivari.

Medieval troubadours From a 14th-century German manuscript.

Italian viola Made by Gaspar da Salo c. 1600.

800

840-50 Earliest treatise on Gregorian chant is written.
c. 1100 Troubadours (wandering poet composers) first appear in southern France.

1200

12th century Hildegard of Bingen publishes 77 musical poems.
Early 14th century Composer Philippe de Vitry publishes *Ars Nova* ("New Art") outlining new forms of musical harmony.

1500

1570 Palestrina's *Missa Brevis* is first performed.
1573 Thomas Tallis composes *Spem in alium*, a motet for 40 voices.
1592-95 William Byrd composes his three Masses.

1600

1607 Monteverdi's opera *L'Orfeo* produced in Mantua.

KEY TERMS

Alto An abbreviation of contralto.
Aria An extended vocal solo, often with orchestral accompaniment, in opera, oratorios and cantatas.
Bagatelle A short, light instrumental piece, often for piano.
Baritone Middle-range male singing voice, between tenor and bass.
Bass Lowest male singing voice.
Cantata Vocal music with an orchestral accompaniment.
Chamber music Music written for a small group of performers, usually three to eight players. The term originally meant music for performance in a private salon or room.
Continuo An abbreviation for "basso continuo," denoting a continuous bass part usually on keyboard running through a piece. It is common in Baroque work.
Contralto Lowest female singing voice.
Countertenor High male singing voice at alto pitch.
Duet A piece of music written for two performers or two instruments.
Fantasia Piece in an improvisatory style.
Fugue A piece of music with several lines of melody built up in sequence and then repeated, overlapping one another.
Gregorian chant Plainsong named after Pope Gregory the Great, who organized a review of church music in the 6th century.
Impromptu A short improvised piece.
Libretto The text of an opera or oratorio.
Lieder German "songs," especially 19th-century solo and piano songs.
Madrigal Unaccompanied song for four or five voices with secular text.
Mezzo-soprano A female singing voice between soprano and contralto.
Movement Symphonies and concertos are divided into sections, or movements, each with its own pace, theme and mood.
Nocturne A dreamy musical piece, often for piano, that evokes the night.
Pitch The highness or lowness of a note.
Prelude Short instrumental piece.
Quartet A group of four musicians or a piece written for four instruments.
Quintet A group of five musicians or a piece written for five instruments.
Requiem A Mass for the dead.
Septet A group of seven musicians or a piece written for seven instruments.
Sextet A group of six musicians or a piece written for six instruments.
Soprano Highest female singing voice.
Symphony A major orchestral piece, normally in three or four movements.
Syncopation Stressing of normally unstressed beats of meter.
Tenor Highest normal male singing voice.
Toccata A keyboard piece that shows the player's touch and dexterity.
Treble Soprano-like singing voice.
Trio A group of three musicians or a piece written for three instruments.

Late Baroque Baroque music reached its finest expression during the late 1600s and early 1700s, in the work of **Bach** and **Handel**. Bach wrote mainly church music (particularly Passions, religious cantatas and organ pieces) whereas Handel's work was mostly dramatic (opera, oratorios and secular cantatas). Both composers brought the twin traditions of polyphonic melody and harmonic chords together in a highly sophisticated way. Both also helped develop a clear and formal system of key changes and scales that gave music a new technical precision.

Classical During the 1700s and early 1800s, music retained much of the formality of Baroque music. It was emotionally restrained, with a new emphasis on a single tuneful melody in place of Baroque polyphony. The symphony became the most important orchestral form; the sonata emerged as the most important form in instrumental music as a whole. The sonata reached perfection in late-18th-century Vienna – by then the world's music capital – in the work of **Haydn**, **Mozart**, **Gluck** and the young **Beethoven**.

Baroque style 17th-century music wove around base lines played on a keyboard such as this organ of c. 1627.

Mozart From the age of four, Mozart performed as a pianist. He began composing at five.

1650

1674 Jean-Baptiste Lully's opera *Alceste* is first performed.
1689 Henry Purcell's opera *Dido and Aeneas* is written.

1700

1721 J.S. Bach's *Brandenburg Concertos* are first performed.
1721 Vivaldi's *Four Seasons* is published.
1742 Handel's *Messiah* premieres.
1791 Mozart's *The Magic Flute* is first performed in the year of the composer's death.

NOTATION GLOSSARY

Musical notes symbolize the duration of a sound, and the five-line stave denotes the sound's pitch (its level on the musical scale). Key signatures are symbols on the stave at the beginning of a piece of music that alter its tone, while keeping the sounds of the notes complementary to one another.

Whole note (semibreve; 4 counts)
= **Two half notes** (minims)
= **Four quarter notes** (crotchets)
= **Eight eighth notes** (quavers)
= **Sixteen sixteenth notes** (semiquavers)
♭ flat (1/2 tone lower)
♯ sharp (1/2 tone higher)

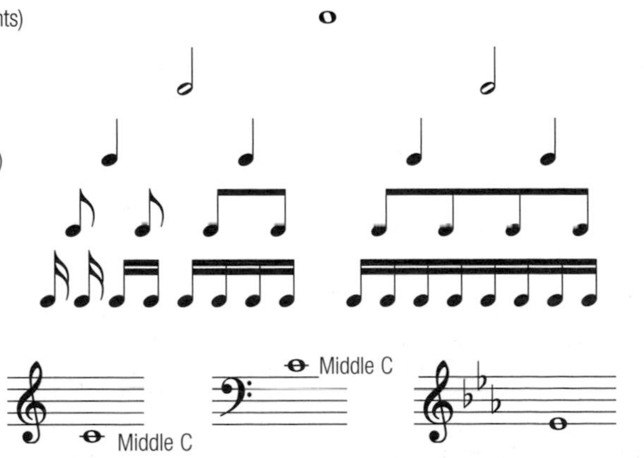

Treble clef **Bass clef** **Key signature** E flat major

Composers A-H

The following A-Z is a guide to the principal classical composers.
■ Refers to a key work.

J.S. Bach
(1685-1750) German
An outstanding organist, Bach had a great command of counterpoint (combining melodies), a characteristic of the Late Baroque era. Among his works are fugues and preludes for the organ and church cantatas.
■ *Brandenburg Concertos; B Minor Mass*

Ludwig van Beethoven
(1770-1827) German
Beethoven's compositions progressed from classical works to passionate music that shocked his contemporaries and bridged the Classical-Romantic divide. He is known for symphonies, concertos and sonatas. Many of his masterpieces were written after he became deaf.
■ *Symphony No. 3* (Eroica), *Piano Sonata No. 14* (Moonlight)

Johannes Brahms
(1833-97) German
Brahms is known for his original rhythms and counterpoint. He composed symphonies, concertos, piano and chamber music and many songs. He also wrote the world's most famous lullaby, *Wiegenlied.*
■ *Clarinet Quintet*

Benjamin Britten
(1913-76) English
Britten's Modernist music often uses discordant sounds to create moods, as in his operas, but he also wrote church music. He cocreated the annual Aldeburgh Festival.
■ *Peter Grimes*

Frédéric Chopin
(1810-49) Polish
He was a Romantic who combined exceptional piano technique with creative harmonies and beautiful melodies. Chopin wrote many short pieces, including the "Minute Waltz," nocturnes, preludes and mazurkas.
■ *Nocturnes*

Aaron Copland
(1900-90) American
Copeland's compositions were inspired by jazz, cowboy songs and US folk music. Besides symphonies and piano works, he wrote music for ballets and Hollywood films.
■ *Appalachian Spring*

Antonin Dvořak
(1841-1904) Czech
A Romantic known for joyous melodies, Dvořak used folk tunes in many works, including the *New World Symphony.* He also wrote operas, concertos and piano music.
■ *Slavonic Dances*

Edward Elgar
(1857-1934) English
A Late Romantic, Elgar developed a heroic "national" style in his five *Pomp and Circumstance* marches. His melodic music created different moods in symphonies, oratorios, concertos and sonatas.
■ *Enigma Variations*

George Frideric Handel
(1685-1759) German/English
Handel is best known for the *Messiah* and other religious oratorios in the British choral tradition. He also wrote opera, coronation anthems and inspirational music in many forms.
■ *Water Music*

Joseph Haydn
(1732-1809) Austrian
Haydn greatly advanced the forms of the symphony and string quartet during the Classical era. His music often humorously imitated everyday sounds such as a clock, hen and donkey.
■ "Paris Symphonies" Nos. 82-87

see also
154-55 **The Middle Ages**
166-67 **The Renaissance**
338-39 **Western literature**
454-55 **Recorded sound**

The formal beauty of 18th-century compositions gave way to the "Romantic" period, in which emotional expression was paramount. The symphony came into its own, and some of the finest operas were written. In the 20th century, music has developed in a wealth of ways – the 12-tone scale, folk influences, electronic sound and even Orthodox church music have played significant roles.

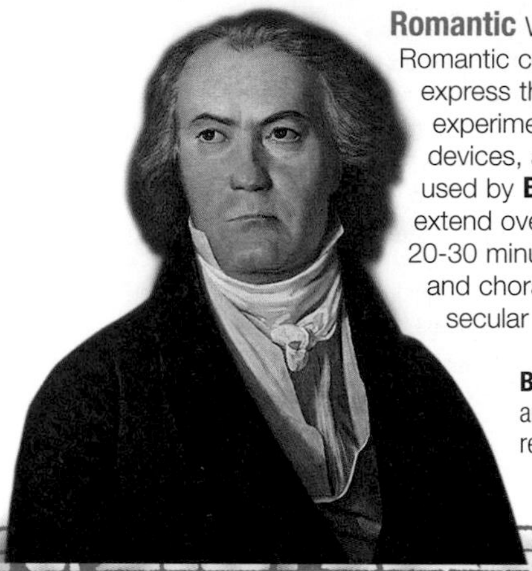

Romantic Working during the early to mid 1800s, Romantic composers sought dramatic ways to express their feelings. Rhythmic energy and experimentation became important expressive devices, as did the unusual, dissonant chords used by **Beethoven**. Symphonies began to extend over an hour in length, in contrast to the 20-30 minutes of the Classical period. Chamber and choral music declined in importance, but secular song remained popular.

Beethoven The forward-looking compositions and wide influence of Beethoven secured him a reputation as the greatest composer of all time.

Late Romantic As the 19th century drew to a close, Romantic composers wrote for increasingly large orchestras and experimented with new kinds of expressive effects. Whereas previous composers had used dramatic key changes and dissonant chords for expressive effect, **Wagner** used them continuously to create emotional weight and tension. **Debussy** and **Ravel** introduced new rhythm patterns and new types of harmony, some based on unconventional scales. Nationalism had a major impact. Folk melodies and popular song inspired the music of **Sibelius**, **Dvořak**, **Elgar** and **Richard Strauss**.

Strauss Distinctive compositions such as *The Blue Danube* (1867) earned Johann Strauss the nickname "the waltz king."

1800

1800 The Romantic style is introduced with Beethoven's *Symphony No. 1*.
1816 Rossini's *The Barber of Seville* premieres.
1830 Berlioz composes the *Symphonie Fantastique*; Chopin writes his first mazurka.

1850

1853 Verdi's opera *Rigoletto* is first performed.
1859 Wagner premieres *Tristan und Isolde*.
1871 Verdi's *Aida* is first performed.
1892 Tchaikovsky's *The Nutcracker* premieres.

A GUIDE TO THE ORCHESTRA

The musicians in a full orchestra are always seated by instrument in a standard arrangement. The treble instruments are generally to the left, and bass instruments are to the right. The exact seating arrangements depend on the piece being performed. Sometimes, for example, percussion might occupy more space.

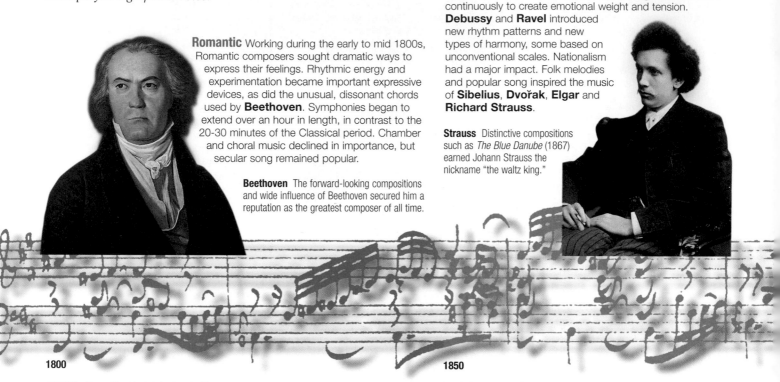

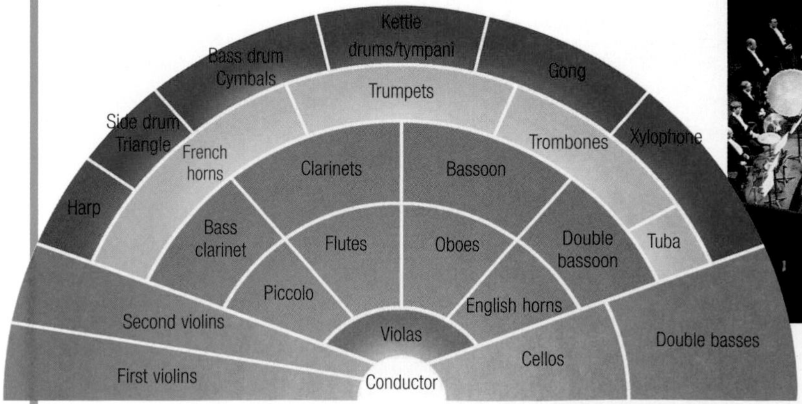

Making music Modern symphony orchestras are seated in a schematic arrangement to ensure a full, balanced sound.

Modernism In 1913, *The Rite of Spring* by **Stravinsky** caused a riot at its Paris premiere because it rejected all traditional rhythm, instead juxtaposing discordant "blocks" of music. Other composers, such as **Schoenberg**, adopted the 12-tone scale for whole pieces rather than short sections. Or, like **Bartók** or **Gershwin**, they added influences from folk music or jazz. After 1945, **Stockhausen** and others carried this Modernist experimentation to new levels, with music composed from a wide variety of electronic and mechanical sounds completely unrelated to conventional musical instruments.

Postmodernism In the late 20th century, some composers returned to writing more accessible, harmonic music. Current music includes a range of approaches, from the trance-like minimalism of **Glass** or **Reich** to the Postmodernist revival of older musical forms, such as the Orthodox church music used by **Tavener**.

Stravinsky Russian ballets such as *The Firebird* (1910) made Stravinsky's modern style popular.

Tavener Stravinsky's music and Russian Orthodoxy inspired John Tavener's later compositions, such as *The Protecting Veil* (1989) and *Mary of Egypt* (1992).

1900

1913 Stravinsky's *The Rite of Spring* is first performed.
1921 Arnold Schoenberg formulates the 12-tone scale, to be adopted later by Berg and Webern.
1924 George Gershwin's *Rhapsody in Blue* premieres.

1960

1961 Britten's *War Requiem* premieres.
1984 Philip Glass's opera *Akhnaten* premieres.
1988 Steve Reich composes *Different Trains.*
1989 John Tavener's *The Protecting Veil* premieres.
1992 Henryk Górecki's *Symphony No. 3* is first performed.

Opera

Opera is generally said to have originated about 400 years ago with Monteverdi. In the 18th century, Handel developed the genre with superb solo arias, and Gluck's *Orfeo* showed how a libretto's musical and dramatic possibilities could be fully exploited. Haydn's operas were eclipsed by Mozart's later works of genius.

The two greatest opera composers of the 19th century were Verdi and Wagner. Verdi's genius emerged in *Rigoletto*, *La Traviata*, *Il Trovatore* and *Aida*. After a 16-year gap, he produced *Otello* (1887), with its varied, dynamic and tragic score.

Wagner strove for transcendent "music-drama" rooted in Nordic myth. The four operas of *The Ring* (1850-74) are considered by some as the greatest work in Western music. In France, Berlioz wrote a grandiose Romantic opera, *The Trojans* (1856-58). In 1875 came Bizet's popular, passionate opera *Carmen*, Johann Strauss's archetypal Viennese operetta *Die Fledermaus* (The Bat), and the social satire of English operetta *HMS Pinafore* by Gilbert and Sullivan. At the turn of the century, Puccini dominated Italian opera with the popular works *La Bohème* (1896) and *Tosca* (1900).

Singing opera The voice of tenor Luciano Pavarotti is acclaimed for its purity of tone.

Composers L-Z

Franz Liszt
(1811-86) Hungarian
Liszt invented the symphonic poem, or tone poem, an orchestral composition inspired by subject matter such as literature or poetry and intended to evoke mental pictures. A great pianist, his works include 20 Hungarian Rhapsodies inspired by gypsy music.
■ *Transcendental Studies*

Felix Mendelssohn
(1809-47) German
Mendelssohn's music combines Romantic passion with Classical form. He created melodies for overtures, including the Scottish-inspired *Fingal's Cave*, symphonies, concertos, sonatas and other forms.
■ *Italian Symphony*

Wolfgang Amadeus Mozart
(1756-91) Austrian
A musical prodigy, Mozart developed the concerto form and wrote jubilant operas such as *The Magic Flute*. His emotional music enriched many other musical forms – he was the only composer to write in every musical genre of his day.
■ *Piano Concerto No. 21 in C* (Elvira Madigan), *The Marriage of Figaro*

Giacomo Puccini
(1858-1924) Italian
An opera composer renowned for his flowing and dramatic melodies, Puccini based his emotionally charged music on stories of love, tragedy and violence in such operas as *Madame Butterfly.*
■ *La Bohème*

Franz Schubert
(1797-1828) German
Schubert composed more than 600 songs, which are noted for their memorable melodies. His other works included many symphonies, such as the "Unfinished Symphony," piano sonatas, chamber music and overtures.
■ *Quintet in C*

Richard Strauss
(1864-1949) German
A conductor and Late Romantic composer influenced by Wagner, Strauss was known for his dramatic operas. He advanced the symphonic poem form and composed songs.
■ *Der Rosenkavalier*

Igor Stravinsky
(1882-1971) Russian
Stravinsky was a Modernist who used innovations of harmony and rhythm for ballet music. His dramatic dissonant compositions created a completely new musical style.
■ *The Firebird*

Peter Tchaikovsky
(1840-93) Russian
Melodic, emotional music made Tchaikovsky renowned for ballets such as *Swan Lake*. His *Piano Concerto No. 1* is the world's most popular and most recorded concerto.
■ *Romeo and Juliet*

Giuseppe Verdi
(1813-1901) Italian
Verdi's powerful Romantic operas mix memorable arias with dramatic Italian moods. His "Chorus of the Hebrew Slaves" in *Nabucco* became an anthem for Italian independence.
■ *La Traviata*

Richard Wagner
(1813-83) German
The theories of composer and conductor Wagner influenced the harmony, orchestration and structure of future opera. He united music, drama and other arts to create what he described as "music-drama" – a term he preferred to opera.
■ *Der Ring des Nibelungen.*

see also
302-3 **World mythology**
454-55 **Recorded sound**

At the turn of the 20th century, popular music existed in the form of light opera, or "operetta," and in the theatrical entertainment prevailing in British music halls and in vaudeville in the US, which attracted large and enthusiastic audiences. Fifty years later, the Western world's teenagers bopped to rock'n'roll. The catalyst for this transformation came when the descendants of west African slaves introduced the US to the rhythm of jazz.

1900-1919

The new century opened in the heyday of **music hall** and **vaudeville**. In 1907, Viennese operetta reached a high point when Franz Lehár's The Merry Widow opened in London, and in New York, Florenz Ziegfeld staged the first of his revues, the Ziegfeld Follies. The wealth of shows created a demand for new songs, and the popular music business began in New York's Tin Pan Alley, a street named for the constant pounding of pianos by songwriters demonstrating their work to publishers.

Singing minstrel Lithuanian-born actor and singer Al Jolson built his reputation in vaudeville. His 1919 version of George Gershwin's composition "Swanee" sold more than 2 million copies.

At the same time, a craze for **ragtime** gripped the US. The "ragged time" (syncopated) tunes were influenced by folk tradition, minstrel shows and marching bands. Scott Joplin's "Maple Leaf Rag" (written in 1899) sold more than a million copies as sheet music. In 1911, songwriter Irving Berlin's long career began with the hit "Alexander's Ragtime Band."

Behind the scenes, rhythms brought to the US by African slaves could be heard in New Orleans' brothels, where black musicians entertained the clients, and elsewhere. Their improvised music, influenced by blues and ragtime, became known as **jazz**. Jazz didn't remain behind closed doors – a group of white southerners formed The Original Dixieland Jazz Band in 1912 and entertained the rest of the city. The jazz sound drifted north, played by bands on Mississippi riverboats, and when the New Orleans' red light district closed in 1917, the Dixieland band traveled to New York.

Soon, Dixieland jazz became known across the US. In 1922, the Cotton Club jazz venue opened in New York, making the new sound fashionable. US troops took jazz across the Atlantic to Europe during World War I.

1920-1929

Musical comedy continued to develop alongside jazz. Broadway, the Manhattan theater district, enjoyed its heyday in the 1920s. Memorable songs caught the public imagination in light entertainment shows such as Lady Be Good (1924) – **George Gershwin**'s first major musical. Gershwin's music fused classical music, popular music and jazz to create a new, distinctively American sound. In the same year, US bandleader Paul Whiteman commissioned Gershwin to write his most famous piece of music, "Rhapsody in Blue." By 1925, Broadway had 80 theaters, and between 1927 and 1928, 280 new productions opened, including **Jerome Kern**'s Show Boat, with plotting and characterization that set new standards for the stage musical.

By the twenties, the center of the jazz world had shifted from New Orleans to the speakeasies of Prohibition-era Chicago, where **Louis Armstrong**, **Bix Beiderbecke** and **Jelly Roll Morton** became the new giants of jazz. A new style of solo improvisation earned trumpeter, cornet player and gravelly voiced singer Armstrong worldwide acclaim. Vocalist **Bessie Smith** made a series of recordings with the top musicians of the decade, including Armstrong, which earned her the nickname "Empress of the Blues." In 1927, **Al Jolson** starred in the first "talkie," The Jazz Singer, and Bix Beiderbecke recorded the jazz classic "Singin' the Blues." Standards of musicianship reached a pinnacle, and the decade as a whole became known as the "jazz age." As the jazz craze spread across the US, a new type of music crept onto the radio in the South and Midwest US – **country music**. The nostalgic rural songs, rooted in the folk tradition of English, Scottish and Irish settlers, told moral tales, accompanied by guitars and fiddles.

In 1925, the country music showcase Grand Ole Opry was first broadcast from Nashville, Tennessee. The show proved a hit with the burgeoning radio audience and would establish country music as a new American genre.

Talking jazz Singer, trumpeter and cornet player Louis "Satchmo" Armstrong created "scat" – a vocal style that imitated musical instruments.

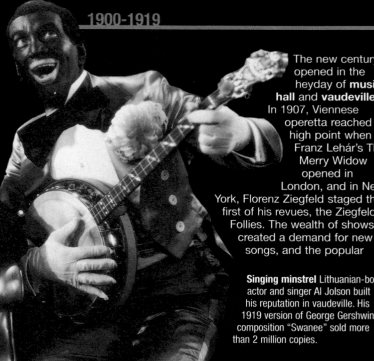

1930-39

Musicals now moved onto the big screen in lavish Hollywood productions. Radio star **Bing Crosby** introduced his smooth looks and crooning voice in King of Jazz (1930). The Gay Divorcee (1934), based on a **Cole Porter** story, and Top Hat (1935) by **Irving Berlin** entertained with pure escapism. In 1935, Gershwin's "folk opera," Porgy and Bess – a mixture of operatic style, popular music and jazz – opened on Broadway.

The end of Prohibition in 1933 forced many musicians out of the illegal drinking clubs and into the open. Jazz adapted its style for wider appeal, tailoring itself to the dance hall in the form of big bands and swing. Bandleaders **Count Basie**, **Duke Ellington** and **Paul Whiteman** led the change. Vocalist **Billie Holiday** dominated the decade with her jazz interpretations of popular songs, recording with saxophonist **Lester Young**, whose light tone influenced soloists such as Charlie Parker. In 1934, **Fats Waller** introduced his humorous vocal jazz style, and three years later, **Glenn Miller** began leading orchestras in his distinctive style of swing.

Big-band leader Trombonist Glenn Miller put the swing into dance orchestras with his innovative arrangements.

1940-49

Hollywood continued to create star vocalists such as **Ella Fitzgerald** and **Frank Sinatra**. In 1942, Irving Berlin's genius for melody produced the song "White Christmas"; Bing Crosby's version has sold more than 30 million copies.

The smoothness of swing provoked a jazz rebellion in the form of **bebop**, or "hot jazz" – an experimental form with complex rhythms and harmonies, led by saxophonist **Charlie Parker**, trumpeter **Dizzy Gillespie** and guitarist **Charlie Christian** – the first to use electrical amplification. At the same time, **Woody Guthrie**'s songs, such as "This Land is Your Land," caused a quiet revolution in folk music, expressing popular sentiments about the Great Depression and the suffering of the poor. His writing was to influence Bob Dylan and a host of folk singers 20 years later.

The mixing of musical styles opened up new avenues. Under the influence of swing, country music was transformed: **Western swing** emerged, with amplified guitars and strong dance rhythms, and **honky tonk** developed in the hands of singers such as **Hank Williams**.

In 1949, Billboard magazine christened a new fusion of blues, boogie-woogie, jazz and mainstream pop music: **rhythm and blues**.

Ol' Blue Eyes Frank Sinatra recorded his first hit, "All or Nothing at All," in 1943. He remained a top concert performer into the 1990s.

1950-59

Rhythm and blues, characterized by the rolling guitar rhythms of **Jackie Wilson** and the laid-back style of **B.B. King**, became big business in the US in the early 1950s. Country music also became increasingly commercial. **Johnny Cash** began recording in 1955, and in 1957, **Patsy Cline** won the talent competition that launched her career.

A mixture of black rhythm and blues and white country music produced the dominant style of the new decade – **rock'n'roll**. The regular beat and young lyrics appealed to teenagers, and the first music charts, which appeared in the US in the late 1940s and in Britain in 1952, confirmed its popularity. In 1955, **Bill Haley**'s "Rock Around the Clock" reached Number 1 – sales eventually topped 22 million. In the same year, the manic piano style and outrageous clothes of **Little Richard** made "Tutti Frutti" a hit, and **Chuck Berry** made his debut with "Maybellene." The rock'n'roll of Berry and the rhythm and blues of B.B. King became two of the most important influences on the popular music of the 1960s.

In 1956, **Elvis Presley** released "Heartbreak Hotel." Because he was white and sounded black, he captured the spirit of rock'n'roll and became the biggest-selling artist in the history of popular music. In 1957, **Jerry Lee Lewis** released the classic rock'n'roll tracks "Whole Lotta Shakin" and "Great Balls of Fire." In the same year, **Buddy Holly** and The Crickets, using a line-up of two guitarists, a bassist and a drummer, and studio techniques such as double-tracking, set trends that still persist in popular music with the release of "Peggy Sue."

Just one year after Buddy Holly's death in a plane crash in 1959, popular music began to take a new direction.

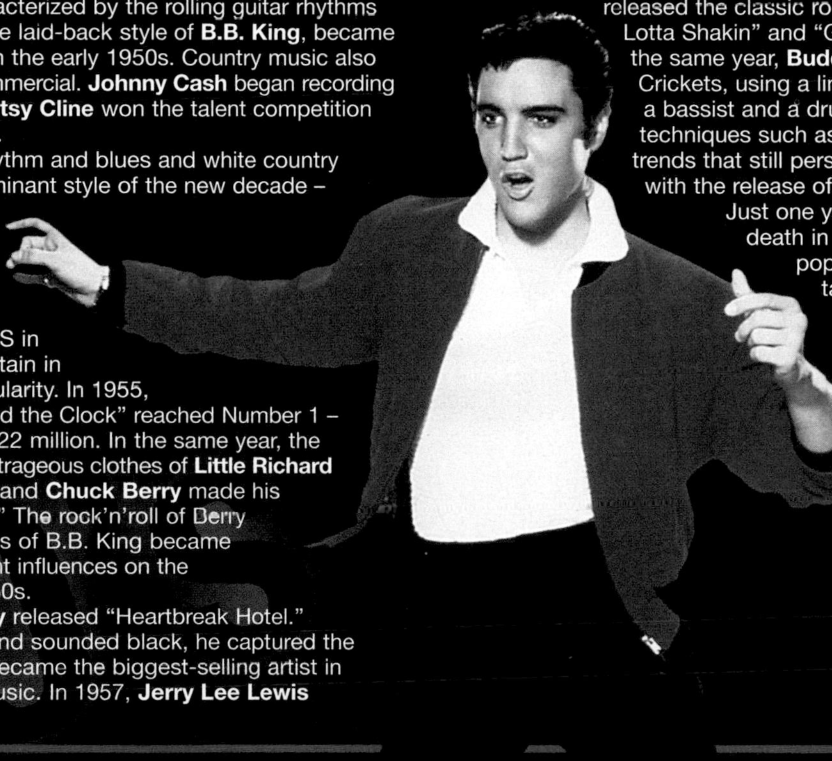

American dream Elvis Presley produced 14 consecutive million-selling records before he was conscripted into the army in 1958.

see also

348-53 **Cinema**
400-1 **Information economy**
454-55 **Recorded sound**

In the 1960s, the folk tradition gave pop music a new focus by introducing a social conscience into modern lyrics. In combination with teenage angst, this led to the rebelliousness of punk and heavy rock in the 1970s. Reacting against such intensity, disco and later electronic pop had wide appeal. By the end of the 20th century, a huge variety of musical styles catered to every taste and cultural niche.

1960-1969

In the US, rock'n'roll gave way to a revival of **folk** and pure **rhythm and blues**, styles more suited to a decade of political protest. Singers **Bob Dylan** and **Joan Baez** led the movement. Dylan's "Blowin' in the Wind" (1962) became a civil rights anthem.

By the middle of the decade, the rise of the small Motown record label in Detroit led to its name becoming a byword for **soul** music – a new singing style with its roots in the gospel tradition. **Stevie Wonder**, the **Supremes**, **Marvin Gaye** and **Gladys Knight** popularized the Motown sound.

In Britain, **The Beatles** created their own musical style with a blend of clear melodies and complex rhythms. Their 1963 single "From Me to You" began an unbroken run of UK number one hits that dominated the decade, lasting until 1967. Paul McCartney and John Lennon were the group's chief lyricists. Their compositions included "Please Please Me" and "Hey Jude." The Beatles stopped performing as a band in 1969.

Rock music continued to develop in Britain, where **Jimi Hendrix** worked on his experimental guitar technique, and the **Rolling Stones** created a mix of rhythm and blues and rock'n'roll. In 1968, a heavier rock style began to emerge in the music of **Led Zeppelin**.

Voice of a generation Bob Dylan's songwriting was heavily influenced by the socially-conscious style of 1940s singer Woody Guthrie.

The fab four The Beatles created the first "concept" album, *Sgt. Pepper's Lonely Hearts Club Band* (1967) – a collection of songs connected by a narrative thread.

1970-1979

The Led Zeppelin rock style became known as **heavy metal**, and throughout the 1970s, new groups such as **Van Halen** (formed in 1974) and **Def Leppard** [redacted] adopted the sound. A mixture of [redacted] and melodic pop, with flamboyant stage costumes and make-up, produced the **glam rock** of **Elton John** and **David Bowie**.

In contrast, disco music became an international force, with a pop beat designed for dancing and an emphasis on slick studio production. The well-produced vocal harmonies of Swedish group **ABBA** made them a Europe-wide success with sing-along hits such as "Dancing Queen" (1976).

West Indian rhythms fused black disco with soul to create **reggae**, which has a strong off-beat and heavy bass line. Jamaican musician **Bob Marley** popularized the sound worldwide with hits including "Get Up, Stand Up" (1973) and "No Woman No Cry" (1975).

[redacted] Meanwhile, musicals were brought up [redacted] date with Jesus Christ Superstar, which opened in London in 1973.

In the second half of the decade, the spirit of youth rebellion arose again, this time in the form of aggressive, thrashing **punk** rock. Leading the new genre, the **Sex Pistols** attacked contemporary Britain in the lyrics of "Anarchy in the UK" (1976) and "God Save the Queen" (1977).

Reggae star Bob Marley made his first record at the age of 19. In 1965, he formed his group, The Wailers, with "Bunny" Livingstone and Peter Tosh.

1980-1989

Punk survived into the 1980s in Britain, metamorphosing into fast, distorted, uncommercial hardcore rock, but a backlash soon began in the London clubs. **Spandau Ballet** and **Duran Duran** drew on glam rock and elaborate clothes and make-up to perform the melodic pop of the **New Romantics**. Thrashing guitars were abandoned for synthesizers by **Depeche Mode**, and computer-based German band **Kraftwerk** enjoyed a new popularity.

In the US, vocal soloists took the lead. **Madonna**'s debut album (Madonna, 1983) produced five US hit singles, including "Holiday" and "Lucky Star" (1984). Only two other vocalists could compete: **Prince**, who had number ones with "Let's Go Crazy" (1984) and "When Doves Cry" (1985), and **Michael Jackson**, whose Thriller (1982) became the most successful album of all time, selling 42 million copies by the early 1990s.

Into the groove Madonna became known for her extravagant costumes and provocative personae during the 1990 Blonde Ambition tour. The 1991 film *In Bed With Madonna* recorded behind-the-scenes footage of the tour.

In New York, **rap**, rhythmic chanting of streetwise lyrics over a heavy, rhythmic backing track emerged. Its distinctive style spawned a host of pop subcultures, including **hip-hop**, which took its percussive effect from "scratching" (manually rotating) vinyl records – extracting ("sampling") musical phrases to create new tracks, set to an electronic drum beat.

Digital sampling using computer technology opened up new forms of dance music. In Chicago, a mix of black disco and pop, using studio sampling and dubbing, became known as **house** music, named after the dance club Warehouse.

From Chicago house music, **acid house** evolved, stripping away vocals and melodies and replacing them with the distinctive acid sound of the synthesizer.

In the late 1980s, New York club Paradise Garage brought a new sound to dance music – the rhythmic but soulful **garage**.

1990-1999

In the early 1990s in Seattle, heavy rock and punk combined to create **grunge** – fast, thrashing rock with melodic overtones. The sound brought commercial success for **Nirvana**, and their album Nevermind (1991) popularized grunge worldwide.

[illegible] British pop musicians reacted against grunge with the distinctive sound of **Britpop**. Beatles-influenced groups **Oasis** and **Blur** – influenced by earlier British bands Madness and The Kinks – competed for the top chart position. By 1997, US influences had diluted the style.

[illegible] Dance music and rap continued to develop derivative styles. As the 1980s ended, the minimalist electronic sound of **techno** jumped from its birthplace in Detroit to Europe. There, beefed up with stronger beats and bass lines, it evolved into **hardcore** and, by the mid-1990s, **jungle** music. Rap evolved into **ragga** – rapping in Jamaican patois.

In the pop charts, mainstream solo vocalists and "teen" bands dominated. **Madonna**'s sound matured with her Ray of Light album (1998), an introspective though "danceable" selection of tracks.

[illegible] Canadian singer, **Celine Dion**, recorded "Because You Loved Me" (1996), the highest-selling adult contemporary single ever, and a year later she could be heard on radio stations the world over singing "My Heart Will Go On," the theme tune to the film Titanic.

In Britain, a female quintet, the **Spice Girls**, eclipsed the success of popular boybands such as **Take That** when sales of their albums Spice (1996) and Spiceworld (1997) made them the most commercially successful UK pop artists of the decade.

Reach for the stars S-Club 7 is an example of the carefully constructed, expertly marketed, clean-cut boy and girl band of the late 1990s.

see also

348-53 **Cinema**
400-1 **Information economy**
454-55 **Recorded sound**

Western literature 800 B.C.-A.D. 1700

The earliest literature of many cultures includes founding myths that were collected together into epic narratives – the Iliad *(ancient Greece), the* Aeneid *(ancient Rome),* Beowulf *(England), the* Poema del Cid *(Spain), the* Chanson de Roland *(France) and the* Nibelungenlied *(Germany). Other forms of poetry also evolved as did prose narrative and nonfiction. In the 14th century, European writers began to rediscover the literature of the classical Greeks and Romans, and used it as their model.*

How the novel evolved Prose writing emerged in ancient Greece, but the novel took much longer to evolve as an art form. Many strands contributed to the emergence of the novel in 16th-century Europe. Writers drew on the traditions of sagas and romances, biographical sketches and diaries and journals. The term novel comes from the Italian *novella,* meaning "story" or "piece of news." It came to be used to describe stories about everyday life, sometimes based on contemporary incidents or events, distinguishing them from romances, which were set in the past.

800 B.C. — **19 B.C.** — **A.D. 900** — **1300**

- **c. 800 B.C.** Homer compiles the *Iliad* and the *Odyssey,* the greatest Greek epic poems and cornerstones of later Western literature.
- **c. 450 B.C.** Herodotus writes the first major Greek prose, a history of the Persian Wars.
- **c. 300 B.C.** Poet Theocritus invents the pastoral, a country idyll based on a fantasy world peopled by shepherds and shepherdesses.
- **19 B.C.** Virgil dies just before completing his epic masterpiece the *Aeneid.*
- **8 B.C.** Horace, noted for his *Odes* and *Satires,* dies. Ovid is exiled, possibly for his scandalous love poetry, *Ars Amatoria.* He dies in A.D. 18.
- **c. A.D. 900** The Old English epic *Beowulf* is written down. It probably dates back to c. 750.
- **c. 1120** *The Chanson de Roland,* one of the earliest French romances appears. As for much work of this period, the author is unknown.
- **1307** Dante begins the *Divine Comedy,* the first great epic poem in Italian.
- **1387** Chaucer starts the *Canterbury Tales,* one of the first poems written in English.

Classical literature Ancient Greece produced some of the earliest poetry of any note, largely in the form of the *Iliad* and the *Odyssey,* two epic works by **Homer** that explored themes of love, honor, vengeance and death. Later poets focused on shorter lyric verse, such as the pastoral fantasies of **Theocritus**.

The *Odyssey* Homer's epic recounted Odysseus's escape from the Cyclops.

The Greeks were also responsible for the first history and scientific texts. **Herodotus**, considered the "father of history," was a masterly writer of prose.

Rome aimed to rival the Greek output. This was largely achieved by the poets **Virgil**, **Horace** and **Ovid** under the patronage of the Emperor Augustus (27 B.C.-A.D.14). Virgil is recognized as Rome's greatest poet, but Horace is the finest stylist, and, with Ovid, he influenced 18th-century English poetry.

The Romans, too, wrote prose histories. **Caesar** described his own exploits in *The Gallic Wars*. **Tacitus** and **Suetonius** chronicled the emperors, and **Cicero**, the master of oratory, provided sharply observed social commentary in his letters.

Medieval romances and epics Sagas, prose narratives about the exploits of well-known kings and warriors, were popular in medieval Iceland and Scandinavia. Until the 12th century, they existed only in oral form.

Romances, long poetic tales of knightly valor, first appeared in France and Germany in the 12th century. Although written to entertain, they also have moral lessons. Some of the best known are the *Chanson de Roland* and the allegorical *The Romance of the Rose*, with its theme of idealized "courtly love," a central topic of much 12th-century poetry. English romances appeared in the 13th century and included the chivalric *Sir Gawain and the Green Knight*. By the 15th century, romances were being written in prose.

Narrative poetry was widely written and culminated in the work of **Dante** and **Chaucer**, who were also among the first poets to write lyric poetry to be read rather than sung. In 14th-century Italy, there was a fashion for the prose short story, or **novella**. These were often published in collections, such as **Boccaccio**'s *Decameron.*

Pseudonyms

Anthony Burgess John Wilson, forbidden to write while in the British colonial service, became famous as Anthony Burgess for *A Clockwork Orange*, *Enderby* and *Earthly Powers*.

Izak Dinesen Karen Blixen wrote *Gothic Tales* as Izak Dinesen in order to escape the name of a husband she loathed.

George Eliot Mary Ann Evans masked her gender with a male pseudonym to help to secure publication of her novels. Sales fell briefly when her identity was revealed.

George Orwell Eric Blair chose the surname Orwell because "O" seemed to him to be the best initial for catching a buyer's attention.

George Sand Armandine Dudevant took a man's name so that she would be taken seriously when she began writing romantic novels in the 1830s.

Stendhal Henri Beyle, author of *The Scarlet and Black*, adopted his *nom de plume* when he was serving as a French consul in Italy.

William Shakespeare

1400 · 1500 · 1600

c. 1477 William Caxton sets up a printing press in London. He publishes many of his own translations of French works, which strongly influence 15th-century English prose.

1579 *Euphues, the Anatomy of Wit* by John Lyly, the first English picaresque novel, is published.

1590 Sir Philip Sidney's *Arcadia* and the first three books of Edmund Spenser's the *Faerie Queene* are published.

1605 The first part of *Don Quixote* by Cervantes appears.

1609 The complete *Sonnets* of William Shakespeare are published. They form the longest sonnet cycle in English.

1667 Milton finishes *Paradise Lost*, his great religious epic.

Dante's *Inferno* One of the punishments described by Dante, illustrated by William Blake.

The Renaissance The rediscovery of classical literature began in 14th-century Italy and resulted in a different world view from that of medieval feudalism. Classical culture emphasized the importance of the individual, which contributed to an introspective approach to writing. Lyric poetry, including songs and religious and mystical poems, flourished, as did the love poem in sonnet form. The sonnet was developed in the 14th century by **Petrarch** in Italy and **Ronsard** in France and was perfected by **Shakespeare**. **Spenser**'s *The Faerie Queene* brought the chivalric epic tradition to an end.

An early form of the novel, known as the picaresque, appeared in 16th-century Spain. In the picaresque, a roguish hero romps through a series of self-contained adventures. **Cervantes**' romance *Don Quixote* is the best example.

In the 17th century, English poets **Donne**, **Marvell** and **Herbert** wrote verse focused on analysis of the heightened emotions aroused by love and religion. The group later became known as the Metaphysical Poets. **Milton** revived the epic with *Paradise Lost*.

Writers A-G

The following poets and novelists helped to shape the course of Western literature.

■ Refers to a major work.

Jane Austen
(1775-1817) British
In her concentration on ordinary characters in everyday situations, Austen created a microcosm of the larger world.
■ *Pride and Prejudice*

Emily Brontë
(1818-48) British
She wrote poetry and one novel, in which she showed a deep love of nature and understanding of human passion. She was one of the first novelists to refrain from judging the behavior of her characters.
■ *Wuthering Heights*

Lord Byron
(1788-1824) British A Romantic poet whose verse melodramas caught the imagination of Europe, his work influenced Romanticism in poetry, music and painting.
■ *Don Juan*

Miguel de Cervantes
(1547-1616) Spanish
In *Don Quixote*, Cervantes ridiculed the chivalric code and the whole romance tradition. It is the most translated book after the Bible. He also wrote plays and poems.
■ *Don Quixote*

Geoffrey Chaucer
(1343-1400) English
Considered one of the finest poets in English literature, he was the first English poet to develop the use of the ten-syllable line, which evolved into the heroic couplet.
■ *Canterbury Tales*

Dante Alighieri
(1265-1321) Italian
The first major author to write in Italian rather than Latin. He wrote one of the greatest of all narrative poems, and influenced Chaucer among others.
■ *Divine Comedy*

Charles Dickens
(1812-70) British
In novels that move between high farce and grim reality, Dickens created a model of society in his time.
■ *Oliver Twist*

Fyodor Dostoyevsky
(1821-81) Russian
One of the first novelists to explore the ambiguities of the human psyche. His novels deal with universal themes of sin, suffering, guilt, conscience and the search for faith.
■ *Crime and Punishment*

George Eliot (Mary Ann Evans) (1819-80) British
Eliot introduced several plot strands and a variety of characters, and developed the psychological analysis of characters. She also used her work to discuss moral and social problems in Victorian England.
■ *Middlemarch*

Thomas Stearns (T.S.) Eliot (1888-1965)
American/British
A founding Modernist poet and dramatist, Eliot revolutionized poetry through his insistence on the use of new forms and rhythms, and modern subject matter, such as the industrial city.
■ *The Waste Land*

Gustave Flaubert
(1821-80) French
A perfectionist who spent hours on every sentence, Flaubert's psychological insight and piling up of precise detail – based on extensive research and observation – made him an influential early realist.
■ *Madame Bovary*

Gabriel García Márquez
(1928-) Colombian
Through short stories and novels set in his native Colombia, García Márquez became a leading practitioner of magic realism.
■ *One Hundred Years of Solitude*

see also

146-47 **Ancient Rome**
166-67 **The Renaissance**
302-3 **World mythology**
344-47 **Drama**

Eighteenth-century writers were influenced by Classicism, drawn to the order, harmony and moral sense that they found in early Roman models. The novel took shape in its modern form. Toward the end of the century there was a reaction against the discipline of Classicism as writers produced work which emphasized the importance of imagination.

Forms of poetry

Allegory A story in verse or prose in which characters and incidents have one or more symbolic meanings in addition to the literal meaning.
Dramatic monologue A poem in which a speaker reveals his or her inner thoughts and ideas to an audience.
Elegy A reflective poem usually dealing with death and mortality.
Epic A long narrative poem often celebrating the feats of heroes and often about the founding of a race or nation. Homer's *Iliad* and Virgil's *Aeneid* are ancient epics; Tolstoy's *War and Peace* is an epic in novel form.
Epigram A short poem ending with a witty saying.
Free verse A verse without meter or rhyme.
Lyric Originally, a poem sung to a lyre; now a nonnarrative poem expressing an individual's ideas and feelings.
Soliloquy An interior monologue in which a character examines his or her thoughts and feelings.
Sonnet A poem of 14 lines usually in iambic pentameter.

Voltaire　Jane Austen

1700

1719 Daniel Defoe's *Robinson Crusoe* appears.

1726 *Gulliver's Travels*, Jonathan Swift's satirical masterpiece, is published.

1731 Abbé Prévost's *Manon Lescaut* establishes the novel in France.

1740 Henry Fielding's novel *Joseph Andrews* is published, followed by *Tom Jones* in 1749.

1747 Samuel Richardson produces *Clarissa*, considered his finest work.

1755 Samuel Johnson finishes his *Dictionary of the English Language*.

1759 The first instalments of Laurence Sterne's *Tristram Shandy* appear.

1774 Goethe's *Sorrows of Young Werther* introduces the first romantically morbid young hero.

1789 *The Power of Sympathy* by William Hill Brown is the first American novel.

Classicism Literature, particularly in England and France in the late 17th and 18th century, was characterized by a passion for clarity of form and a strong sense of reason and order. Styles followed those of the ancient Greeks and Romans, who were much admired. In England, poets such as **Dryden** and **Pope** produced satirical verse in heroic couplets modeled on the poetry of Virgil and Ovid. French classical scholar and poet **la Fontaine** drew on classical forms and sources for many of his *Fables*.

Satire was a common element in literature of this time. In addition to verse, there was a large body of satirical prose, such as **la Bruyère**'s *The Characters, or the Manner of the Age* and **Swift**'s *Gulliver's Travels*. Prose in general flourished. Many modern forms, including the novel, biography, travel writing and journalism, developed.

The essay was popular and owed much to the growth of journalism, with the increasing number of periodicals offering opportunity for publication. **Samuel Johnson**, a leading satirist and prose stylist, was noted for his *Rambler* and *Idler* essays.

The rise of the novel The novel became established in its modern form, largely in England and France in the 18th century. **Defoe** and **Richardson** set the format in England, and **Fielding** took it further, with more complex plots and greater realism. **Sterne**'s *Tristram Shandy* dispensed with a chronological framework to present life as a jumble of unrelated events. The early 19th century brought **Austen**'s ironic dissections of human motivation and folly.

Psychological insight was already a noted quality of some of the earliest French novels, such as those of **Madame de la Fayette**, written in the late 17th and early 18th centuries. **Abbé Prévost**'s *Manon Lescaut*, published in 1731, foreshadowed Romanticism. By the mid 18th century, political and philosophical writers like **Voltaire** and **Rousseau** were using fictional situations as a vehicle for their ideas on the importance of emotions and individualism.

Tristram Shandy An illustration from 1786.

Children's classics

Books written specifically for children first appeared in the 18th century. During the 19th century, the major genres were established. F.R. Marryat pioneered the boys' adventure story with *Masterman Ready* (1841), followed by R.M. Ballantyne's *The Coral Island* (1857). In 1857, Thomas Hughes's *Tom Brown's Schooldays* established the vogue for school stories. C.M. Yonge's *The Daisy Chain* (1856) and Louisa May Alcott's *Little Women* (1868) brought in the family saga. Anna Sewell's *Black Beauty* (1877) provided a model for animal stories.

In the early 20th century, Kenneth Grahame's *Wind in the Willows* (1908), A.A. Milne's *Winnie the Pooh* (1926) and Arthur Ransome's *Swallows and Amazons* (1930) became classics. Fantasy was established as a leading genre by J.R.R. Tolkien with *The Hobbit* (1937) and *Lord of the Rings* (1954-55). C.S. Lewis combined fantasy with adventure and allegory in *The Chronicles of Narnia* (1950-54).

At the beginning of the 20th century, Helen Bannerman and Beatrix Potter successfully championed the idea of books in which text and illustrations are equally important.

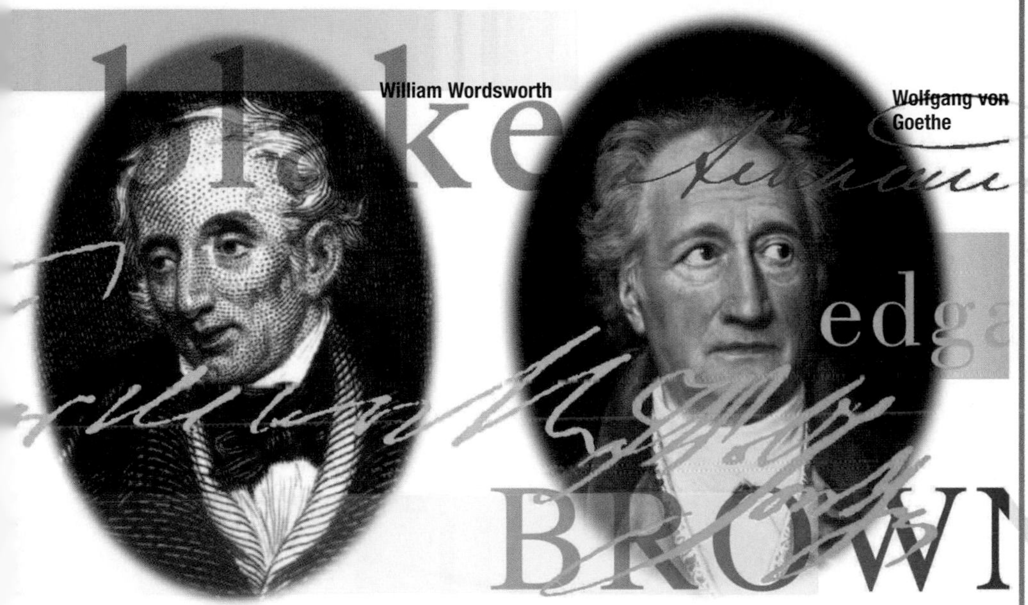

1800

1820

1798 The publication of *Lyrical Ballads*, by William Wordsworth and Samuel Taylor Coleridge, launches English Romanticism.

1811 *Sense and Sensibility*, Jane Austen's first major work, is published.

1812 Lord Byron's *Childe Harold* triggers a new phase of English Romanticism.

1818 Mary Shelley publishes her Gothic novel *Frankenstein.*

1821 The first great American novel, James Fenimore Cooper's *The Spy*, appears.

1823 Alexander Pushkin begins the verse novel *Eugene Onegin.*

Romanticism Romanticism represented a backlash against the formality of the Classicists. It idealized "nature," and stressed the importance of individual experience. Lyric poetry was revived throughout Europe: Short verses were the perfect vehicle for poets who wanted to present delicate sketches of fleeting emotion. German poets such as **Hölderlin** and **Goethe** led the way. The first major English Romantics – **Blake**, **Coleridge** and **Wordsworth** – followed, inspiring a second generation, including **Byron**, **Shelley** and **Keats**. **Hugo** was the main influence in France.

Idealization of the past led to a vogue for historical fiction: **Scott**'s novels and poems were an influence on the great Russian poet **Pushkin**. An obsession with darker emotions fueled the Gothic novel, such as those of **Shelley** in England and **Poe** in the US.

By 1830, Romanticism was shaping the work of some of the first American literary giants. **Thoreau**, **Hawthorne** and **Melville** treated the natural world as symbolic of the spiritual world, and came to be known as Romantic symbolists.

Childe Harold's Pilgrimage Byron's poem provided a model for the romantic hero.

Writers G-N

Wolfgang von Goethe
(1749-1832) German
A poet, dramatist and novelist, Goethe was a leading figure in the German Romantic movement, although his dramatic and lyrical verse transcended any Romantic/Classical divide. He transformed German poetry, raising it to among the world's greatest.
▪ *The Sorrows of Young Werther*

Nathaniel Hawthorne
(1804-64) American
One of the finest early American novelists, Hawthorne was preoccupied with themes of sin, conscience and ancestral guilt. His classical style and use of allegory influenced other American writers such as Melville and Henry James.
▪ *The Scarlet Letter*

Seamus Heaney
(1939-) Irish
Heaney's earlier poetry drew on rural Ireland and expresses a strong sense of physical environment. His later works deal increasingly with Ireland's political problems.
▪ *Selected Poems 1966-87*

Ernest Hemingway
(1899-1961) American
A writer of novels and short stories, Hemingway's economic style, terse dialogue and characterizations have made him one of the most influential and imitated writers of his time.
▪ *A Farewell to Arms*

Homer
(c. 800 B.C.) Greek
The stories in Homer's epics had been told many times, but he transformed his source material through poetic power and the development of character. The Greeks admired him above all other poets.
▪ *Odyssey*

Victor Hugo
(1802-85) French
A central figure in the Romantic movement and often considered France's greatest lyric poet, Hugo experimented with language and rhythm in his poetry, and his novels have an epic sweep.
▪ *Les Misérables*

Henry James
(1843-1916) American
In his novels, short stories and plays, James explored the clash between the American and European characters and the impact of old and new cultures on each other. He explored characters' inner selves confronted with difficult moral choices.
▪ *The Portrait of a Lady*

James Joyce
(1882-1941) Irish
A Modernist who revolutionized the structure of the novel and pushed language to the limits of communication, Joyce's use of the "stream of consciousness" technique influenced many writers, including Virginia Woolf and William Faulkner.
▪ *Ulysses*

Thomas Mann
(1875-1955) German
A Modern novelist, Mann chronicled the decline of the German bourgeoisie, the creative anguish of artists and the perils of Nazism.
▪ *The Magic Mountain*

Herman Melville
(1819-91) American
Melville created the mixed-genre Romantic/symbolic novel, and increased the scope and stylistic range of American fiction.
▪ *Moby Dick*

John Milton
(1608-74) English
He wrote poetry in a variety of forms, including sonnets and a masque. His greatest achievement was producing the finest postclassical epic poem. His work mixes passion with self-discipline, and was an influence on the Romantics.
▪ *Paradise Lost*

see also
170-71 **Age of kings**
344-47 **Drama**

In an era of rapid industrialization, Romanticism seemed too escapist. Nineteenth-century novelists wanted to describe the real world and the social forces at work in it. This trend was overturned in the early 20th century by writers who wanted to make a complete break with the past. At the end of the century, poets and novelists experimented with a range of approaches, including parody, pastiche and a mixture of traditions.

Key terms

Alliteration A repetition of consonants in nearby words, especially at the start of words: "...rifles rapid rattle..."
Assonance Two or more nearby words that contain a similar vowel sound: "...swimmers into cleanness leaping..."
Blank verse Verse that does not rhyme but has meter.
Foot A group of two to four syllables making up a unit of rhythm in verse.
Hexameter Verse with a six-foot line.
Iambic A foot consisting of two syllables in a short-long combination.
Irony Language expressing a meaning other than the literal: "big deal."
Metaphor A figure of speech in which one object is described in the terms of another: "A river of men poured across the bridge."
Meter Sound patterns formed by stressed and unstressed syllables. Meter underlies rhythm and with it most poetry.
Pentameter A five-foot line.
Simile A figure of speech in which a comparison is used to intensify an image: "The moon hung like a cheap earring."

Leo Tolstoy

James Joyce

Virginia Woolf

1830

1837 The first installments of *Oliver Twist* appear, confirming Charles Dickens as the century's most popular writer.

1850

1855 The first edition of Walt Whitman's *Leaves of Grass* pioneers free verse.

1857 Gustave Flaubert's *Madame Bovary* outrages public morals by its nonjudgmental analysis of the heroine's adultery.

1859 Charles Darwin publishes his radical theory of evolution in *The Origin of Species*, precipitating the loss of old religious certainties.

1863 The first episodes of Leo Tolstoy's epic novel *War and Peace* appear.

1872 George Eliot completes *Middlemarch*, considered by some the greatest English novel of its time.

1900

1915 D.H. Lawrence's novel *The Rainbow* is seized by police for obscenity.

1922 T.S. Eliot's *The Waste Land* and James Joyce's *Ulysses* are published. Marcel Proust finishes *Remembrance of Things Past*.

1926 Ernest Hemingway's *The Sun Also Rises* captures the disillusion of the postwar generation.

Realism Around 1830, many writers, particularly novelists in England, France and the US, began to look to ordinary people and daily life – usually middle and lower-class – for their subject matter. Some aimed at reform by exposing social ills.

Dickens' work focuses sharply on contemporary society. But it was **George Eliot**, and later **Hardy**, who gave a more objective portrait of mid-19th-century England, as **Balzac** and **Flaubert** did for France. Many, like **Twain** in the US, highlighted the comic and absurd.

By the late 19th century, **James** and **Dostoyevsky** were enriching the strong characterization central to Realist work with deep psychological analysis. In France, the more documentary style of **Zola** and **de Maupassant** heralded a new movement known as Naturalism.

Great Expectations Pip speaks to Miss Haversham in the novel by Dickens.

Modernism World War I brought sweeping social and cultural change and a sense of anger. Modernists rejected tradition in favor of experimental techniques and contemporary subjects.

Proust and **Conrad** broke free of chronological sequence in the plots of their novels. **Joyce** and **Woolf** portrayed their characters through the "stream of consciousness" technique – the unedited flow of thoughts and feelings running through a character's mind.

Poets such as **Pound** and **Eliot** cast aside traditional meter. **William Carlos Williams**, writing in prose and verse, emerged as a leading Modernist in the US.

The Museyroom A scene from Joyce's *Finnegan's Wake* illustrated by John Glashan.

Travel writing

Ever since an unknown Egyptian wrote *The Journeying of the Master of the Captains of Egypt* in the 14th century B.C., authors, explorers and scientists have recorded their travels. Early examples include the *History* of Herodotus (c. 485-425 B.C.) describing Egypt and Africa, and *Description of Hellas* (2nd century A.D.) by Greek writer Pausanias.

Merchant Marco Polo published an account of his 24 years traveling in China and India in the 13th century. European explorers in the 16th century recorded their voyages. Hakluyt's *Principall Navigations, Voiages and Discoveries of the English Nation* (1598) is a large collection of these accounts.

Nineteenth-century German explorer and scientist Alexander von Humboldt published 35 volumes of his travels and scientific reports, *Voyage aux régions equinoxiales du Nouveau Continent*. It is the largest body of travel writing produced by one person. In 1872, Francis Galton published the first survival guide, *Art of Travel; or Shifts and Contrivances Available in Wild Countries*.

Notable travel writers of the 20th century include Freya Stark, Wilfred Thesiger, Thor Heyerdahl and Eric Newby.

Saul Bellow

1930

1937 *Spain*, W.H. Auden's poem about the Spanish Civil War, speaks for a generation about the rise of fascism.

1949 Orwell publishes *1984*, a political satire awakening the West to the evils of Stalinism.

1950

1955 The pedophile hero of Vladimir Nabokov's *Lolita* creates scandal.

1957 Patrick White emerges as a major novelist with *Voss*, his heroic tale of life in Australia's outback.

1968 *One Hundred Years of Solitude by* Gabriel García Márquez signals the emergence of magic realism.

1980

1981 Salman Rushdie's *Midnight's Children* marks the arrival of Postmodernism in Anglo-Indian fiction.

20th century Although the effects of Modernism were far-reaching, many novelists continued with more traditional forms. In the US, **Dreiser** wrote naturalistic novels based on documentary evidence such as newspaper reports and official archives. **D.H. Lawrence** analyzed the mood of self-destruction of his times. **Fitzgerald** expressed the disillusion felt by the generation that had been through World War I.

In the 1930s, poet **W.H. Auden** reacted against Modernism, seeing it as academic, elitist and difficult to understand. His work addressed political and social issues, and he used traditional poetic forms, meter and rhythms to make his work intelligible to as wide an audience as possible.

The trend toward intelligibility in poetry continued in the following decades, in the Neoromanticism of **Dylan Thomas** in the 1940s and the protests of the Beat Poets in the 1960s. **Frost** became the unofficial poet laureate in the US.

In the 1950s, the antihero and the nonhero first appeared in the novels of American authors **Bellow**, **Roth** and **Updike**.

In France, the ***nouveau roman*** (the new novel or antinovel) appeared. Influenced by Modernism, authors such as **Duras** and **Mauriac** strove for a kaleidoscope of impressions in an attempt to imitate the way we experience life.

In the 1980s, the name **magic realism** was given to a type of fiction in which the real is mixed with the fantastic, dreamlike and inexplicable. **García Márquez** is a leading exponent, and **Angela Carter**, **Grass** and **Rushdie** have all used its techniques.

Writers O-Z

George Orwell
(1903-50) British
His early work included semi-autobiographical and comic novels, but he is best known for his later political novels and for his journalism.
■ *1984*

Ezra Pound
(1885-1972) American
Through his poetry, criticism, and championing of contemporaries such as Eliot and Joyce, he helped create the Modernist revolution. His translations of the poetry of ancient civilizations such as Greece and China revived interest in these cultures.
■ *Cantos*

Marcel Proust
(1871-1922) French
A prolific writer of short stories and novels, his nonlinear treatment of time, detailed analysis of characters' observations and thought processes, and original style were major influences on 20th-century writers.
■ *Remembrance of Things Past*

Alexander Pushkin
(1799-1837) Russian
Although he was influenced by Western models, Pushkin forged a distinctly Russian style. His poetry established Russian as a literary language, so he is often seen as the founder of Russian literature.
■ *Eugene Onegin*

Salman Rushdie
(1947-) Indian/British
Among the most celebrated and controversial of contemporary writers, Rushdie draws on Indian memories, legends and Muslim theology.
■ *Midnight's Children*

William Shakespeare
(1564-1616) English
Considered the world's greatest dramatist, Shakespeare was also a true Renaissance poet. His output included long narrative poems based on classical myths, and a 156-sonnet cycle.
■ *Hamlet*

Alexander Solzhenitsyn
(1918-) Russian
In novels and histories that chronicle life in Stalinist Russia, Solzhenitsyn sought to make literature a weapon against oppression.
■ *The Gulag Archipelago*

Leo Tolstoy
(1828-1910) Russian
He wrote novels, short stories, plays and essays. Tolstoy's major novels – great, gaudy portraits of Russian society – are considered among the greatest ever written.
■ *War and Peace*

Virgil
(70 B.C.-19 B.C.) Roman
The greatest Latin poet, Virgil created for the new Roman Empire a national epic to rival Homer's. His pastoral poetry has often appealed more to later generations.
■ *The Art of Husbandry*

Walt Whitman
(1819-92) American
Whitman's vigorous poetry is marked by its pioneering free verse and unabashed celebration of sexuality. His style was a strong influence on Modernist poets.
■ *Leaves of Grass*

William Wordsworth
(1770-1850) British
Cofounder of English Romanticism with Coleridge, Wordsworth created a simple poetry based on language as it is used in everyday speech.
■ *The Prelude*

William Butler Yeats
(1865-1939) Irish
Yeats moved from romantic themes in his early work to subjects as diverse as Irish folklore, political themes and the occult, which he treated in diction and rhythms close to common speech.
■ *The Winding Stair*

see also
176-77 **The Industrial Revolution**
312-13 **Psychology**
344-47 **Drama**

Drama began with the ancient Greeks as plays performed by individual actors. Early Greek drama evolved from religious festivals at which choruses of masked male actors recited or sang stories about the misfortunes of the heroes of myth and history. Around 550 B.C., a Greek poet called Thespis stepped forward from the chorus to recite speeches, becoming the first actor. He also exchanged lines with the leader of the chorus, creating the first instances of stage dialogue.

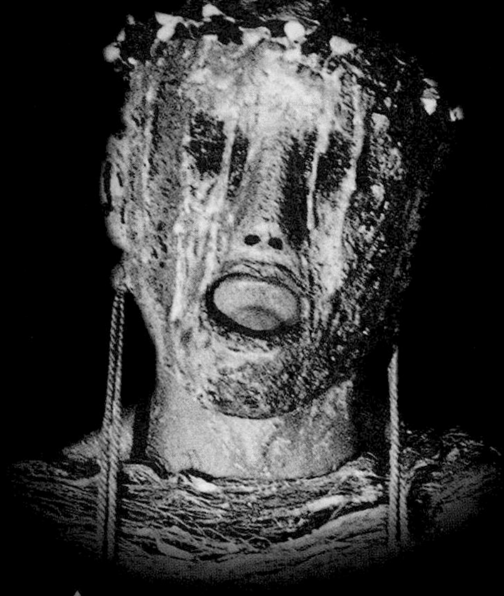

Roman The Romans built fine theaters, but their drama was derived from the Greeks. **Plautus** is known for topical comedies. Philosopher and politician **Seneca** wrote nine tragedies. They were never staged at the time but were used as models by Renaissance dramatists. What pleased the Roman public most – apart from gladiatorial combat – was "pantomime," a mixture of farce, song and mime.

Classical Greek Ancient Greek theater took three forms: tragedy, satire and comedy. Tragedy involved a hero pitted against the forces of fate, such as in **Sophocles**'s Oedipus plays. It explored themes of divine law, free will, fate, justice and retribution. **Aeschylus** and **Euripides** explored the use of character and experimented with the chorus. Satire, then as now, ridiculed and criticized public figures, as in the work of dramatists such as **Aristophanes**. **Menander** was the first prominent writer of comedy, in which stock character types representing human follies were set against each other in order to make fun of them.

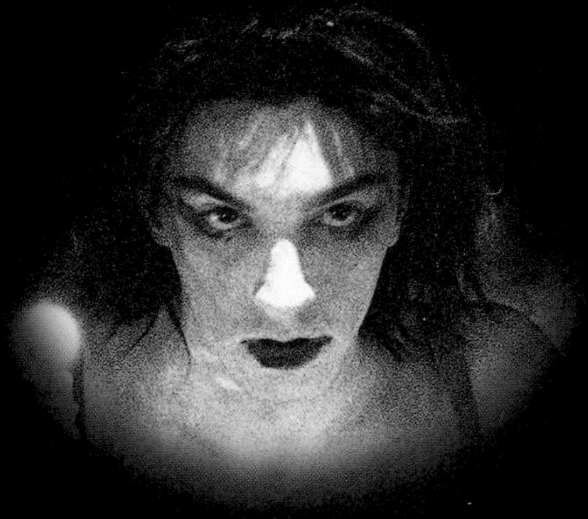

Medieval (11th-14th century) From 1100, new forms of drama developed in Europe. Plays based on Bible stories – called mystery or miracle plays – were performed, first as tableaux in churches and then outdoors. In some places these were collected into cycles of plays, such as the York Cycle in England. Plays portraying Christ's crucifixion were known as passion plays. The Oberammergau Passion Play (1634) is still performed. Along with these emerged plays in which virtues and vices were personified in order to teach a moral lesson, known as morality plays.

Theater design – stage and audience

The ancient Greek amphitheater Large open-air amphitheater provided a model for later theater design.

Elizabethan theater Separated players from the ground-level standing audience using a raised stage, and created a backdrop.

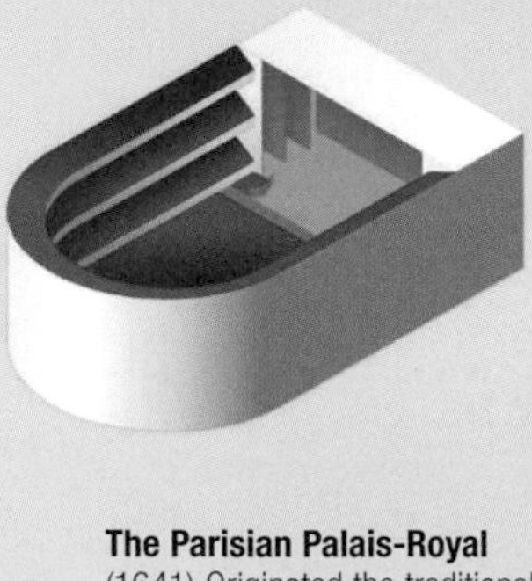

The Parisian Palais-Royal (1641) Originated the traditional design of a proscenium to frame the action and movable scenery.

Theater-in-the-round In use since the 1930s, this allows a close rapport between audience and performers.

Elizabethan (16th-17th century) In England, a strong theater tradition grew out of a revived interest in classical, especially Roman, drama combined with the medieval tradition of miracle and morality plays. Several major playwrights emerged from a large and diverse group of dramatists. **Christopher Marlowe** revolutionized theater by probing his tragic heroes' inner conflicts and showing the expressive versatility of blank verse. **William Shakespeare**'s poeticism gave his plays atmosphere and emotional force. He broke the rules of classical drama by interweaving plots with subplots, moving the action from place to place and introducing comic elements into tragedies. His rival **Ben Jonson** followed the classical tradition more closely, using satirical comedies to attack vices such as greed and hypocrisy. In the early 17th century, "revenge" tragedy became popular, seen in Shakespeare's later tragedies and the plays of **John Webster**.

▼

see also

144-45 **Ancient Greece**
146-47 **Ancient Rome**
166-67 **The Renaissance**
338-43 **Western literature**

Restoration (17th-18th century) After the English monarchy returned, playwrights such as **William Wycherley** and **William Congreve** wrote comedies that caricatured the morals and behavior of upper-class society. This type of comedy became known as comedy of manners. In the 18th century, **Richard Sheridan** and **Oliver Goldsmith** continued this tradition. Tragedy took the form of "heroic drama" – plays written in rhyming couplets, with emphasis on spectacle, extreme passions and violent exchanges between characters. **John Dryden** was the leading proponent.

▼

▲

French golden age (17th century) Theater in 17th-century France modeled itself closely on classical drama. Tragedy pointed out the consequences of people's follies, and comedy ridiculed them. Plays also followed Aristotle's rules of unity of action, time and place – the action must be based on one incident (no subplots) and take place in one setting and in the space of one day. **Pierre Corneille** established the French classical tradition but was eclipsed by **Jean Racine**, whose tragedies were written in formal verse. **Molière** wrote satirical comedy, such as Tartuffe, in which he attacked religious hypocrisy.

SHAKESPEARE

William Shakespeare (1564-1616) produced 37 plays, some in collaboration with others, between 1590 and 1616. He drew on a range of sources – the plays of Seneca and Plautus, medieval morality plays, Italian commedia dell'arte, historical chronicles and folk traditions. From these styles, which influenced his plots, characterization and use of rhetorical and theatrical devices, he produced highly original drama.

Early comedies
- The Two Gentlemen of Verona (1590-91)
- The Taming of the Shrew (1593)
- The Comedy of Errors (1594)
- Love's Labor's Lost (1594-95)

Histories
- Henry VI, Parts I, II and III (1592)
- Richard III (1592-93)
- King John (1595)
- Richard II (1595)
- Henry IV, Parts I and II (1596-97)
- Henry V (1598)

Later comedies
- A Midsummer Night's Dream (1595-96)
- The Merchant of Venice (1596-97)
- The Merry Wives of Windsor (1597-98)
- Much Ado About Nothing (1598)
- As You Like It (1599)
- Twelfth Night (1601)
- Troilus and Cressida (1602)
- Measure for Measure (1603)
- All's Well That Ends Well (1604-5)

Tragedies
- Titus Andronicus (1592)
- Romeo and Juliet (1595)
- Julius Caesar (1599)
- Antony and Cleopatra (1606)
- Coriolanus (1608)
- Hamlet (1600-1)
- Othello (1603-4)
- Timon of Athens (1605)
- King Lear (1605-6)
- Macbeth (1606)

Late plays
- Pericles (1607)
- The Winter's Tale (1609)
- Cymbeline (1610)
- The Tempest (1611)
- Henry VIII (1613)

The conventions of the classical age survived into the 19th century, but 20th-century theater broke away from traditional forms to explore ways of making drama represent real life more closely. The emphasis moved away from clever plotting toward the expression of inner feelings or satirical social and political commentary. By the end of the century, a broad range of alternative theater groups existed alongside the mainstream.

Japanese Noh plays (17th-19th century) Noh plays originated in Japanese courtly circles in the 14th century and flourished from the 17th to 19th centuries. The subjects were taken from classical Japanese literature, with stately dances performed to an accompaniment of drums and flute. Language was sonorous and honorable for all characters.

Romanticism (mid 18th-19th century) Dramatists reacted against the virtues of reason and respect for convention of the classical age. In Germany, **Johann Wolfgang von Goethe** and **Friedrich Schiller** produced work that promoted feelings and imagination. In Britain and the US, this trend produced a shift from tragedy to melodrama, plays with simple plots and strong emotional appeal, with a musical accompaniment to heighten the mood. Toward the end of the century, the satirical comedies of **Oscar Wilde** and **Arthur Pinero** became popular.

Social realism (late 19th-early 20th century) Dramatists turned their attention to the ills of society in plays that were true to life but selective in presenting only what was essential – a style known as realism. **Henrik Ibsen**, **George Bernard Shaw**, **John Synge** and **Eugene O'Neill** wrote realist drama. **Chekhov** took realism further in plays that presented life as it is in every detail and in which atmosphere and the inner lives of characters are more important than plot -- known as naturalism. Another related style, seen in some of **Strindberg's** plays, was symbolism, in which truth is presented through allegorical means.

KEY DRAMATISTS

Since the expansion of theatrical forms during the 17th century, several playwrights have stood out for their skills of dramatic interpretation and their ability to reflect contemporary concerns.

Samuel Beckett (1906-89) Irish The plays of Beckett are characterized by their themes – the failure of human communication and the pointlessness of human endeavor – and well-honed prose. ■ Waiting for Godot

Anton Chekhov (1860-1904) Russian Collaboration with Stanislavsky in 1898 brought Chekhov his first successes. His emphasis on atmosphere rather than action influenced later playwrights such as Pinter. ■ The Cherry Orchard

Wolfgang von Goethe (1749-1832) German Goethe was a supreme dramatist, whether reworking ancient tragedies or compiling his Romantic masterpiece. ■ Faust

Maxim Gorky (1868-1936) Russian Political activist Gorky wrote about social outcasts. He was exiled for his revolutionary fervor. ■ The Lower Depths

Henrik Ibsen (1828-1906) Norwegian The controversial subject matter and uncomfortable endings of Ibsen's plays

The actor's role
John Gielgud and Ralph Richardson bring David Storey's characters to life in *Home*.

Theater of the Absurd In Paris in the 1950s, a type of drama developed in which motiveless characters and nonexistent plots were used to express life's final futility. The leading playwrights were Irish writer **Samuel Beckett** and Romanian-born **Eugene Ionesco**. Other playwrights linked to the Theater of the Absurd are **Harold Pinter**, **Edward Albee** and **Tom Stoppard**. Eastern European dramatists such as **Vaclav Havel** used the style of Theater of the Absurd to satirize society under communist rule and the struggle of the individual against bureaucracy.

Political satire (early 20th century) After World War I, European chaos was mirrored in theater. **Bertolt Brecht** emerged as the leading German playwright. He introduced epic theater, in which the audience is encouraged to watch a play without becoming emotionally involved so that they can think about its themes objectively. Devices such as songs, banners and masks create a distancing or "alienation" effect that reminds the audience that the action in front of them is a performance rather than reality. In prerevolutionary Russia, **Maxim Gorky** depicted social misery in The Lower Depths. In Soviet Russia, **Mikhail Bulgakov** produced satirical plays such as The Day of the Turbins. In Paris, **Alfred Jarry** attacked bourgeois conventions in his satirical farce King Ubu.

Since 1950 **Arthur Miller** and **Tennessee Williams** emerged as the leading playwrights in 1950s America. Both portrayed a society that was decadent and obsessed with power. In Britain, **John Osborne**'s plays challenged the established social order. During the 1970s and 1980s, the theme of disillusionment continued in the work of **David Mamet** in the United States and **David Hare** in Britain. **Neil Simon** (American) and **Alan Ayckbourn** (British) produced domestic comedies about deteriorating relationships. During the 1960s, small alternative or fringe theater companies emerged in response to rising production costs and the competition from television. They used alternative venues such as cafes and pubs, and many tackled social and political issues. Minorities such as ethnic groups and AIDS campaigners used theater to fight discrimination.

were unique in European drama. Ibsen is the father of modern realist theater, although his later work became increasingly symbolist. ■ A Doll House

Arthur Miller (1915-) American Miller explores human relationships through the themes of guilt and of responsibility to self and society. ■ Death of a Salesman

Molière (1622-73) French Molière's depictions of human follies raised comedy to the same level as tragedy. ■ Tartuffe

Eugene O'Neill (1888-1953) American The down-to-earth dramas of O'Neill were the antithesis of contemporary Broadway's melodrama and romanticism. ■ Long Day's Journey into Night

Harold Pinter (1930-) British Pinter uses everyday language and silences to convey his characters' thoughts. His plays explore the problems of identity and communication. ■ The Caretaker

Jean Racine (1639-99) French The tragedies of Racine were based on historical and classical subjects. ■ Phèdre

August Strindberg (1849-1912) Swedish Strindberg experimented with a variety of theatrical styles, including naturalism. His later works centered around religion and symbolism. ■ Miss Julie

see also
176-77 **Industrial Revolution**
185-86 **Between the wars**
338-43 **Western literature**

Cinema 1890-1940

The early days of the motion picture

The story of filmmaking is one of rapid technical change and of the supremacy of Hollywood: Within 20 years of the invention of the motion picture, the industry had become a huge business with Hollywood at its heart. By the 1920s, film had become the most important new medium of the 20th century.

Swashbuckling hero Douglas Fairbanks, Sr., whose graceful athleticism in films such as *The Mark of Zorro* (1920; left) made him a heartthrob, was one of the earliest stars to experience public interest in his personal life.

1893 Thomas Edison patents the peephole Kinetoscope and makes the world's first moving picture (of a man sneezing).
1895 Louis and Auguste Lumière open a cinema in Paris.
1897 Georges Méliès opens a film studio in Paris and goes on to make 500 short films.

1903 *The Great Train Robbery* establishes scripted narrative film in 12 minutes and 14 scenes.
1905 A permanent cinema opens in Pittsburgh.
1908 D.W. Griffith, the "father of film," joins Biograph studio as a director.
1909 Studios create the "star system" by exploiting the popularity of actors and actresses to attract film audiences.
1911 Film studios are set up in Hollywood; among the earliest is Keystone Pictures, founded by directors Cecil B. DeMille, D.W. Griffith and Mack Sennett.
1914 *The Squaw*, the first Hollywood feature-length Western, opens.
1915 Griffith's epic *Birth of a Nation* and Charlie Chaplin's *The Tramp* are released.
1917 Chaplin signs the first $1million film contract.
1919 Chaplin, Mary Pickford and Douglas Fairbanks, Sr. found United Artists studio: Film stars become superstars.

1890

1900

1920

Birth of the cinema The Lumière brothers' Cinematograph (left) could both record and project moving images. Their first film (1895) showed workers leaving the Lumière factory.

1920 *The Mark of Zorro* starts a trend for swash-buckling epics.
1921 *The Four Horsemen of the Apocalypse* makes a worldwide romantic idol of Rudolph Valentino. His early death in 1926 brings mass hysteria to the US.
1923 *The Covered Wagon* establishes the Western as a staple genre: Until the mid-1950s, a quarter of Hollywood films are Westerns. The Hollywood studio system is founded with the opening of Warner Bros.
1924 New studios Columbia and MGM are established.
1925 Chaplin directs and stars in *The Gold Rush*. King Vidor's antiwar film *The Big Parade* opens. Sergei Eisenstein pioneers new framing and editing techniques in *Battleship Potemkin*.
1927 "Talkies" are born with *The Jazz Singer*.
1928 Mickey Mouse makes his debut in *Steamboat Willie*, the first cartoon with sound.
1929 *Wings* wins the first Academy Award (Oscar) for best film.

FACT Charlie Chaplin's trademark bowler hat and walking cane were sold for $73,000 at auction in 1995.

Global celebrity Charlie Chaplin directed many of the films he starred in, including *The Gold Rush* (left) in 1925. Chaplin went to Hollywood in 1914; by 1916 he had made more than 50 silent films. The silent genre, understood across the world, made Chaplin the first international movie star.

DIRECTION

Most 1920s and 1930s film directors were no more than glorified technicians employed by studios to create showcases for star performers, but a few exceptional talents began to establish the artistic importance of film direction.

D.W. Griffith, with his epics *The Birth of a Nation* (1915) and *Intolerance* (1916), established the basic "language" of film: long scenic shots, close-ups, fading in and out at the beginning and end of scenes, and crosscutting (editing together) scenes from different locations. **Cecil B. DeMille**, best known for directing biblical epics such as *The Ten Commandments* (1923), produced and wrote his films, as did French director **Jean Renoir** (*La Grande Illusion*, 1937).

Russian director **Sergei Eisenstein** borrowed ideas from modernist art and music to create "montage" – editing a series of different shots together into "conceptual" scenes, the themes of which are perceived in the mind of the viewer. The technique was used to its greatest effect to dramatize a massacre at Odessa in the Russian Revolution propaganda film *Battleship Potemkin* (1925).

In 1929, **Alfred Hitchcock** explored the use of sound for dramatic effect in *Blackmail*, Britain's first "talkie," in which a woman's thoughts are heard by the audience.

By the late 1950s, directors were acknowledged as a creative force, each with a recognizable personal style as well as technical mastery. Hitchcock became known for moments of suspense, and **John Cassavetes** used low-budget techniques such as hand-held cameras and grainy prints. **François Truffaut** filmed on location, abandoning smooth narratives for disconnected scenes (*Jules et Jim*, 1962). In Italy, **Federico Fellini** excelled in subversive fantasy (*La Dolce Vita*, 1960).

In contemporary cinema, the name of the director indicates the style of a film and helps ensure a level of success at the box office. **Steven Spielberg**, the most commercially successful contemporary director, is best known for his blend of sentiment and adventure (*E.T. The Extra Terrestrial*, 1982; *Jurassic Park*, 1993).

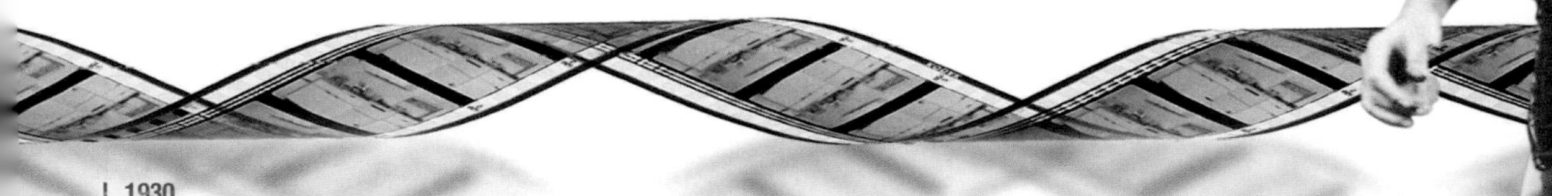

1930

1930 The golden age of Hollywood and the studio system begins: Movies become the world's favorite entertainment. Greta Garbo utters her first screen words *(Anna Christie)*. Marlene Dietrich debuts *(The Blue Angel)*. Gangster films premiere with *Little Caesar*, starring Edward G. Robinson. John Wayne stars for the first time, in *The Big Trail*.

1931 Horror films are established with *Dracula*, starring Bela Lugosi, and *Frankenstein*, starring Boris Karloff.

1932 The Tarzan series begins with Johnny Weissmuller in *Tarzan the Ape Man*.

1933 *Flying Down to Rio* introduces the first of ten Ginger Rogers/Fred Astaire films. *King Kong* sets new standards in special effects. The Marx Brothers' *Duck Soup* opens.

1934 French director Jean Vigo establishes an international reputation with *L'Atalante*. Six-year-old Shirley Temple stars in *Stand Up and Cheer*.

1935 Color feature films are introduced with *Becky Sharp*. Alfred Hitchcock's spy thriller *The 39 Steps* opens.

1937 Jean Renoir directs one of the definitive French masterpieces, *La Grande Illusion*.

1939 *Gone with the Wind*, *Stagecoach* and *The Wizard of Oz* are released.

Romantic lead Errol Flynn was chosen over contender James Cagney for the role of Robin in the popular 1938 version of *The Adventures of Robin Hood*.

Who's who – stars' stage names

Stage name	Real name	Stage name	Real name
Joan Crawford	Lucille Le Sueur	**Groucho Marx**	Adolph Marx
Tony Curtis	Bernard Schwarz	**Marilyn Monroe**	Norma Jean Baker
Marlene Dietrich	Marie Losch	**Mary Pickford**	Gladys Smith
Diana Dors	Diana Fluck	**Ginger Rogers**	Virginia McMath
Kirk Douglas	Yussur Demsky	**Mickey Rooney**	Joe Yule
Douglas Fairbanks	Julius Ullman	**Barbara Stanwyck**	Ruby Stevens
Greta Garbo	Greta Gustafsson	**Robert Taylor**	Spangler Brough
Cary Grant	Archibald Leach	**John Wayne**	Marion Morrison
Rita Hayworth	Margarita Cansino	**Loretta Young**	Gretchen Belzer
Carole Lombard	Jane Peters		

see also

334-37 **Popular music**
400-1 **Information economy**

Cinema 1940-70

From the darkness of wartime to the licentiousness of the 1960s

Throughout the 1950s, Technicolor epics and technical advances such as 3-D, Cinerama and Cinemascope expanded the possibilities of film. The following decade marked the end of the studio system and the rise of independent film-makers and brought the first explorations of sex and violence to the big screen.

1940 *The Grapes of Wrath* reflects on the Depression. Bing Crosby and Bob Hope make *The Road to Singapore*, the first of seven "Road" films.
1941 In *Citizen Kane*, director Orson Welles uses innovative overlapping dialogue, multiple character viewpoints and flashbacks to create a dark mood.
1942 *Casablanca* opens.
1945 The French historical epic *Les Enfants du Paradis* is released.
1946 Postwar American realism begins with the hope-in-despair themes of *The Best Years of Our Lives* and *It's a Wonderful Life*. *Great Expectations* and *Brief Encounter* inaugurate a golden age of British filmmaking.
1947 In the US, the hunt for Communist influences in Hollywood ends many careers.
1949 The first of the classic Ealing comedies are made in London: *Passport to Pimlico*, *Kind Hearts and Coronets* and *Whisky Galore!*

1950 Melodrama and black humor come together in *Sunset Boulevard*. Marilyn Monroe has her first big role in *All About Eve*.
1951 Marlon Brando makes a huge impact in *Streetcar Named Desire*.
1952 A high point of the Hollywood musical is reached with *Singin' in the Rain*, starring Gene Kelly. The Western matures with *High Noon*.
1953 In the Japanese film *Tokyo Story*, director Yasujiro Ozu abandons camera movements such as panning and keeps every frame still to record family relationships in close detail.
1955 James Dean appears in *East of Eden* and *Rebel Without a Cause*.
1956 The sci-fi boom begins with *Invasion of the Body Snatchers*. DeMille directs his second version of *The Ten Commandments*.
1958 *Carry On Sergeant* is released, the first of 30 Carry Ons made over the next 34 years.
1959 French "nouvelle vague" (new wave) is launched by François Truffaut's *Les Quatre Cent Coups*.

Hollywood icon Death at a young age made Marilyn Monroe a symbol of Hollywood's exploitation of physical beauty.

1940

1950

East meets West Japanese director Akira Kurosawa's *The Seven Samurai* (1954) blended skilfully executed action sequences with portrayals of peasant life. In 1960, John Sturges remade the film as *The Magnificent Seven*.

FILM ACTING

In the earliest days of the cinema, stage acting techniques were transferred wholesale to the screen. But the grand theatrical gesture is rarely convincing on film, and as a result, the trend in screen acting has consistently been toward greater naturalism – performers "react" rather than "act."

This ability to appear natural in front of the camera – to project a personality that the audience identifies with and warms to – has been the hallmark of almost all the great film stars. From **Buster Keaton**'s silent comedies to **John Wayne**'s action heroes, the best film actors have been able to conjure up an unmistakable screen presence. **Greta Garbo** was undistinguished as a stage performer in her native Sweden, but on the screen, she had a magnetic persona.

In the 1920s, German cinema led a reaction against naturalistic acting, using exaggerated body and facial gestures, deliberately emphasized by camera angles. The technique was later used by Russian director Sergei Eisenstein in *Ivan The Terrible* (1944).

In the early 1950s, many film actors were influenced by "Method," a technique based on the theories of the Russian theatre director Konstantin Stanislavsky. The Method required actors to recall emotions and reactions from their past experiences and to use them in their performances; in short, to bring even greater realism to the screen.

Method acting's leading model was **Marlon Brando**, whose seemingly halting performances in films such as *On the Waterfront* (1954) and *The Godfather* (1972) were in fact the product of rigorous training by Polish-born Lee Strasberg, founder of the Actors Studio in New York. The idea was to "fake" as little as possible. This pursuit of realism was taken further in later years by **Robert De Niro** (also trained by Strasberg) who, in preparation for his Oscar-winning role as a dissolute boxer in *Raging Bull* (1980), put on nearly 27 kg (60 lb) in weight.

The close-up intimacy of film and the public interest in celebrities' private lives has often meant that established stars bring their personal stamp, or image, to a part. For some, this results in typecasting – for example, John Wayne was repeatedly cast as a solitary cowboy, **Arnold Schwarzenegger** is mainly associated with action-adventure movies and **Jim Carrey** often appears in zany, slapstick comedies.

The film actor's task has always been hampered by the peculiar demands of the medium. On stage, a performance is concentrated into a few hours. On film, it is assembled piece by piece, often over several months and in a sequence different from the progression of the story. Creating a convincing character in these disjointed circumstances is the unique challenge facing any film actor.

1960

1960 Hitchcock releases *Psycho.*
1961 *West Side Story* is the first modern musical.
1962 Sean Connery stars in the first Bond film, *Dr. No.* The epic returns with *Lawrence of Arabia.*
1963 The $44 million *Cleopatra* almost bankrupts Fox studios.
1965 *The Sound of Music*, the biggest grossing musical of all time, opens.
1966 The licentiousness of the 1960s is epitomized in *Blow-Up* and the following year in *The Graduate.*
1967 The trend toward violence as glamour begins with *Bonnie and Clyde.*
1968 A new film classification system introduces the X-rated film.
1969 Cinema meets the counterculture in *Easy Rider.*

Spaghetti Western Clint Eastwood's edgy, justice-dispensing character in *The Good, the Bad and the Ugly* (1966) became a model for later fictional cowboys and private detectives.

Artistic control François Truffaut argued that the director should be the main creative force behind a film – a concept labelled *nouvelle vague* (new wave). He used flowing camera movements and voice-over narrative to capture feelings in *Jules et Jim* (1962).

see also

334-37 **Popular music**
400-1 **Information economy**

From the 1970s, levels of explicit, gritty screen violence, sex and horror rose continually, and they have become leading themes in contemporary cinema. Today, digital technology has turned the adventure story into a high-tech blockbuster spectacular.

1970 *Airport* launches the disaster movie.
1971 Woody Allen's *Bananas* is released. The violence in *Dirty Harry*, *The French Connection*, *Straw Dogs* and *Clockwork Orange* shocks audiences.
1977 *Star Wars* introduces the high-tech sci-fi spectacular.
1979 *Apocalypse Now* explores the trauma of the Vietnam War.

1981 Steven Spielberg collaborates with George Lucas (as producer) to make the adventure film *Raiders of the Lost Ark*.
1984 Big-budget violence and special effects reach new heights in *The Terminator* (James Cameron).
1985 Independent film company Merchant Ivory begins a series of classic literary adaptations with E.M. Forster's *A Room With a View*. Digital technology is first used in *Young Sherlock Holmes* to create a sword-wielding knight made of stained glass.
1989 In *The Abyss* (James Cameron), new digital techniques are used to conjure up a creature out of sea water.

Big-budget thrills
Terminator 2: Judgement Day (1991), starring Arnold Schwarzenegger (right), was the first $100-million budget film. Sci-fi special effects are less expensive than the water-based effects used in films such as *Titanic*.

1992 Quentin Tarantino uses violence as a central theme in *Reservoir Dogs*.
1993 Digital technology creates realistic dinosaurs and mixes them with live action in Steven Spielberg's *Jurassic Park*.
1995 *Toy Story* is the first digitally animated full-length feature film.
1996 Comedian Jim Carrey commands the first $20 million salary, for *The Cable Guy*.
1997 *Titanic* (James Cameron) becomes the most expensive film ever made ($200 million).
1999 *Star Wars Episode 1 – The Phantom Menace* breaks the film sequel tradition to provide a prequel to the classic 1970s sci-fi epic.

2000 The epic picture in the style of *Ben-Hur* is revived by Ridley Scott in *Gladiator*. Ang Lee's *Crouching Tiger, Hidden Dragon* creates a new form of martial arts film: The central characters are strong women, and the film has an emotional depth lacking in other "action" pictures.

1970 1980 1990

Digital effects In *Gladiator* (2000), computer technology was used to build up images, as in this scene where the actors fight a tiger with digitally enhanced movements.

FILM GENRES

There is no definitive list of film genres, and the boundaries between them are often blurred. Listed here are films that broke new ground and spawned imitators.

Action-thrillers Fast-paced, violent and often sexually explicit, the action-thriller is a relatively recent phenomenon, largely launched by the James Bond series in the early 1960s.
Goldfinger (1964)
Deliverance (1972)
Die Hard (1988)
Terminator 2 (1991)
Speed (1994)

Adventure The improbable adventures of dashing characters were a mainstay of 1930s Hollywood. The genre was reinvigorated in the 1980s by the Indiana Jones trilogy.
The Black Pirate (1926)
Mutiny on the Bounty (1935)
The Prisoner of Zenda (1937)
The Adventures of Robin Hood (1939)
Raiders of the Lost Ark (1981)

Adventure Harrison Ford in *Raiders of the Lost Ark.*

Cartoons and animation Walt Disney's *Snow White and the Seven Dwarfs*, made in the face of great skepticism, showed the potential of animation.
Snow White and the Seven Dwarfs (1937)
Who Framed Roger Rabbit? (1988)
Toy Story (1995)
Chicken Run (2000)

Comedy Silent movies lent themselves naturally to visual comedy, but the coming of sound in the late 1920s changed the emphasis to dialogue.
The General (1927)
Bringing Up Baby (1938)
Some Like It Hot (1959)
Annie Hall (1977)
Four Weddings and a Funeral (1994)

Cult This category covers films with limited commercial appeal, often dealing with bizarre or freakish subjects.
Freaks (1932)
The Valley of the Dolls (1967)
Pink Flamingos (1984)

Drama As a genre, drama films are those that deal seriously and more or less realistically with serious, normally adult issues. Drama is, for the most part, the single largest category of film, and contains some of the most memorable movies ever made.
Grand Hotel (1932)
La Règle du Jeu (1939)
Citizen Kane (1941)
The Misfits (1961)
Schindler's List (1993)

Fantasy Fantasy films are those in which the laws of reality have been suspended and anything can happen (with special effects well represented). They have mostly tended to be children's films.
King Kong (1933)
The Wizard of Oz (1939)
E.T. The Extra-Terrestrial (1982)
Batman (1989)
Jurassic Park (1993)

Gangster Gangster films and their offshoots – detective and crime films – began to emerge in the 1930s, largely in response to the lawlessness of American Prohibition. They rival the Western as the definitive American film form. In the 1940s, many gangster movies also epitomized the stark, pared-down style of *film noir*.
Scarface (1932)
Double Indemnity (1944)
The Big Sleep (1946)
The Godfather (1972)
L.A. Confidential (1997)

Horror As a visual medium, film is particularly suited to horror. Some of the most arresting horror films could be called psychological thrillers, but recent trends have been toward increasingly explicit levels of horror and violence.
Nosferatu (1922)
Psycho (1960)
The Exorcist (1973)
Halloween (1978)
The Silence of the Lambs (1991)

Musicals Sound was introduced in 1927 with *The Jazz Singer*, a silent film with several musical numbers sung by Al Jolson. It was an immediate sensation. The film musical built on a rich stage tradition to include lavish dance sequences.
42nd Street (1933)
Top Hat (1935)
Yankee Doodle Dandy (1942)
Singin' in the Rain (1952)
The Sound of Music (1965)

Period and history films These overlap with drama and, frequently, with fantasy films, but a recurring element is the epic: lavish, spectacular and not always historically accurate.
The Birth of a Nation (1915)
Anna Karenina (1935)
Ben-Hur (1959)
Lawrence of Arabia (1962)
Shakespeare in Love (1998)

Romance Romance is a central element of many films, but surprisingly few are exclusively (or almost exclusively) love films.
Wuthering Heights (1939)
Waterloo Bridge (1940)
Brief Encounter (1946)
When Harry Met Sally (1989)
The Bridges of Madison County (1995)

Science fiction In the late 1960s, sci-fi moved up from B-movie status thanks to the increasing sophistication of special effects.
Planet of the Apes (1967)
2001: A Space Odyssey (1968)
Star Wars (1977)
Blade Runner (1982)
Independence Day (1996)

War After World War I, war became a frequent subject for the movies.
All Quiet on the Western Front (1930)
La Grande Illusion (1937)
Apocalypse Now (1979)
Das Boot (1981)
Saving Private Ryan (1998)

Western The Western rapidly became the definitive form of American film. Its golden age ended in the 1960s.
Stagecoach (1939)
High Noon (1952)
The Searchers (1959)
A Fistful of Dollars (1964)
Unforgiven (1992)

Horror Linda Blair in *The Exorcist*, still considered one of the most frightening films ever made.

Televisions are found in 98.1 percent of US homes; 35 percent own two sets and 41 percent own three or more. In 2000, about 33 000 television stations worldwide produced 48 million hours of programs. TV sets are already offering the Internet and email, and the near future will usher in interactive television.

Television records

Longest-running program *Meet the Press*, US (1947).
Longest-running soap opera *Guiding Light*, US (1952); it began on radio in 1937.
Longest-running children's program The BBC's *Blue Peter*, UK (1958).
Longest-serving presenter Patrick Moore, with the BBC's *The Sky at Night* (1957).
Biggest audience for a series *Baywatch*; more than 1.1 billion viewers weekly in 142 countries.
Most episodes broadcast *Bozo the Clown*; over 150 000 shown on US TV since 1949.
Most money won on a game show £1 million on *Who Wants to be a Millionaire* (2000) in UK.
Biggest contract Oprah Winfrey, $150 million for 4 years of work.

Coronation of George VI In 1937, the BBC makes one of the earliest outdoor broadcasts.

Truth or Consequences NBC's show becomes the world's first sponsored TV progam, in 1941. Advertisers include Adam Hats, Bulova Watches, Botany Worsted and Ivory Soap.

I Love Lucy Within six months of its debut, the comedy series was watched in more than 10 million US homes.

Man on the Moon A world audience estimated at 500 million watch as the Apollo 11 spacecraft lands on the Moon in 1969, and astronaut Neil Armstrong takes the first lunar walk.

1925 Scottish engineer and inventor John Logie Baird transmits a television picture (of office boy William Taynton).
1928 In the US, General Electric begins regularly scheduled TV programs (a half-hour three times a week) at its radio station WGY in Schenectady, New York. The BBC begins daily TV transmissions in the UK.
1936 The BBC begins regular public television service.
1938 The US has about 100 television sets in use; US company NBC broadcasts a feature film *(The Scarlet Pimpernel)*.
1939 Television is demonstrated to millions for the first time, at the New York World's Fair.

1940 Experimental color broadcasts are made by CBS from New York's Chrysler Building.
1941 NBC and CBS begin regular television transmission.
1944 A television soap opera, *Painted Dreams*, begins in the US; it was also radio's first soap in 1930.
1949 In the US, network television linking stations around the country is launched and cable television is introduced.

1953 About 1 million TV sets are bought by the British to watch the coronation of Elizabeth II.
Richard Nixon's popularity is boosted after 60 million Americans watch him saying that his only personal political gift was his dog, Checkers.
1954 Joseph McCarthy's televised claims of Communist infiltration of the US Army are shown to be based on falsified evidence.
1955 Commercial television begins in the UK with ITV; Gibbs SR Toothpaste is the first commercial.

1962 The first transatlantic satellite transmission of television programs is made by Telstar communication satellite built by AT&T.
1963 Millions around the world follow the aftermath of the assassination and the funeral of President John F. Kennedy, and millions of Americans see a murder on live TV as Lee Harvey Oswald, Kennedy's suspected assassin, is shot by Jack Ruby.
1964 About 73 million Americans watch The Beatles' first US television appearance, on the *Ed Sullivan Show*.
1967 BBC2 begins a scheduled color TV service, Europe's first.
About 400 million people worldwide watch the first global satellite TV program, *Our World*, featuring The Beatles playing "All You Need Is Love" in England.
1969 Television records astronaut Neil Armstrong taking the first steps on the Moon.

Drama

Early dramas consisted of filmed versions of theatrical productions, such as the 1937 BBC version of George Bernard Shaw's *How She Lied to Her Husband*. The 1960s saw the introduction of drama series and more action. Today, drama generally encompasses any fiction series.

1961 *The Avengers* adventure-drama series begins.
1963 *Doctor Who* popularizes science fiction; *Star Trek* begins in the US in 1966.
1965 *I Spy* debuts in the US, introducing the first black hero.
1970 *The Six Wives of Henry VIII* is the first historical drama.
1971 *Upstairs, Downstairs* reflects on changes in British society. The series, which finished in 1975, was watched by 300 million viewers in 50 countries. Unlike earlier costume drama series, it was written specifically for TV.
1972 The 26-part *War and Peace* establishes a new way of showing literary works.
1978 *Dallas* is first shown in the US. It runs for another 13 years and is broadcast in more than 130 countries.
1998 The first ever 60-second sitcom, or blipcom, airs on the US network TV Land.

Documentaries

Documentaries began as films in the 1930s. In the 1950s, television began to use them to expose political and social problems, as well as to entertain and educate.

1951 Edward R. Murrow and Fred Friendly start the CBS series *See It Now*, laying the groundwork for the American documentary tradition.
1960 *Primary* follows political candidates for the first time and features new, more intimate camera techniques.
1961-62 Each of the three major networks carries a documentary series.
1971 The CBS documentary *The Selling of the Pentagon* results in a Congressional investigation into charges of unethical journalism.
1983 PBS premieres FRONTLINE and the 13-hour *Vietnam: A Television History*.
1994 Ken Burns' 18½-hour *Baseball* attracts 45 million viewers, making it PBS' highest rated series ever.

Sports

Sports have been a staple of television since its early days. Today, the impact of every major sporting event can be measured by the size of its television audience (800 million people worldwide watched the 2003 Super Bowl and 1.6 billion watched the 2002 World Cup finals).

1931 The Derby from Epsom, England, is the world's first broadcast sporting event.
1936 The Berlin Olympics are televised throughout Germany.
1939 The first televised sporting event in the US is a college baseball game between Columbia and Princeton.
1947 The 1947 World Series is the first World Series to be telecast. An estimated 4 million people watch – the first mass audience for a television broadcast.
1948 Professional wrestling debuts on network television.
1958 *Grandstand*, the world's longest-running sports show, debuts on the BBC.
1963 Instant replay is first used in the Army-Navy football game.
1964 NBC broadcasts the opening ceremonies of the 1964 Tokyo Olympics live – the first live color program transmitted to the US by satellite.
1970 Monday Night Football debuts on ABC.
1979 ESPN, the first all-sports television network, is launched in the US.
1995 A 30-second commercial during Super Bowl XXIV costs up to $1.3 million.
Late 1990s New technology and cable television systems allow broadcasting of almost all sporting events – professional, amateur and college.

see also
400-1 **Information technology**
452-53 **Digital communications**

Vietnam War In the early 1970s, daily US news coverage of American casualties and pictures of the fighting in South Vietnam led to widespread public pressure to end the military effort. In January 1973, a cease-fire ended 12 years of war.

1972 The events of a Palestinian terrorist attack on Israeli athletes at the Munich Olympics are broadcast around the world.
A videodisk is demonstrated in Germany.
Home Box Office (HBO) is the world's first subscription cable television service.
Ceefax teletext information is introduced by the BBC.
1973 Americans watch the Senate hearings on the Watergate political scandal that would force president Richard Nixon to resign on live television the following year.
Also in the US, the 12-hour slavery saga *Roots* (shown in regular episodes) attracts audiences of 130 million.

Royal wedding The 1981 wedding of Prince Charles and Lady Diana Spencer in London is viewed around the world by 700 million people.

1980 Cable News Network (CNN) begins 24 hour newscasts in the US.
1983 More than 107 million people in the US watch the final episode of the comedy series *M*A*S*H*, still a US record for a single program.
1984 The Live Aid charity rock concerts, linking London and Boston by TV satellite, are seen live by about 1.8 billion people worldwide, raising approximately $50 million for famine relief in Africa.
1985 Cable television shopping channels begin in the US.
1989 Sky TV, the first UK satellite television channel, is launched.

Interactive television In 1999, Sky TV launched services that viewers could control through their handsets. Email through the television is now also available.

1991 The Gulf War, covered mainly by CNN, is the first war followed live worldwide.
1997 The funeral of Diana, Princess of Wales, is seen by an estimated 2.5 billion people around the world.
1998 Digital television is introduced, with potential for hundreds of new channels.

New millennium
Fireworks ring in the New Year 2000 in Sydney, Australia, as part of celebrations that are broadcast worldwide.

The oldest known written news reports – ancient Rome's Acta Diurna *("Daily Events") – were hung in prominent places for all citizens to read. After the Roman Empire disintegrated, it took more than 1200 years before written news reached the general public again.*

Top newspaper and magazine circulation by country

Country	Largest magazine	Circulation	Largest newspaper	Circulation
Brazil	*Veja*	1.12 million weekly	*Folha de Sao Paolo*	449 000
Canada	*Reader's Digest*	1.01 million monthly	*Toronto Star*	460 000
France	*Télé 7 Jours*	2.56 million weekly	*Ouest France*	758 000
Germany	*TV Movie*	2.59 million bimonthly	*Bild*	4.23 million
Italy	*L'Espresso*	388 000 weekly	*Corriere della Sera*	1.08 million
Japan	*Young Jump*	1.96 million weekly	*Yomiuri Shimbun*	10.22 million
Spain	*Hola*	760 000 weekly	*El Pais*	410 000
UK	*What's on TV*	1.74 million weekly	*News of the World*	4.07 million
US	*AARP The Magazine*	21.5 million monthly	*Wall Street Journal*	1.86 million

NEWSPAPERS AND MAGAZINES

In the 16th century, news became widely available in pamphlets covering current events. During the following century, newspapers, magazines and illustrated narrative strips became well established. From 1618, the Dutch pioneered weekly newspapers with *corantos* ("current news") translated into English and French and circulated widely through trading links. Broadsheets appeared independently at about the same time in Japan. The first British newspaper was the *Weekley Newes* (1622), and the first in North America was *Publick Occurrences* (1690).

Gallic style *Paris Match* introduced photojournalism to France more than 50 years ago, and it is still a best-selling magazine.

Reading for leisure Intellectual journals published in England, France, Germany and Italy in the 1660s marked the beginning of the magazine industry. The first entertainment magazine, *Le Mercure Galant*, with court news, anecdotes and poetry, appeared in France in 1672. By the end of the century, England had produced periodicals such as the *Gentleman's Journal* (1692) and the *Ladies' Mercury* (1693). *The Gentleman's Magazine* followed in 1731. North America's first, the *American Magazine* (1741), lasted just three months, but by the turn of the century there were more than 100 titles in the US.

Man of influence
William Randolph Hearst's sensationalist treatment of Cuba's struggle for independence helped provoke the Spanish–American War.

The age of the press barons By 1855 all of today's leading British quality dailies – *The Times*, *The Observer*, *The Guardian* and *The Daily Telegraph* – had been established. In the US, the reputations of the *New York Times* and *The Washington Post* were growing. By the end of the century, modern journalism began to evolve, shaped by a handful of powerful businessmen. The faltering *New York World* owed its revitalization to Joseph Pulitzer. Under his management, the newspaper produced the world's first color supplement (1893) and regular comic strip (1895). Pulitzer's competition came in the form of William Randolph Hearst and his *Morning Journal*. Hearst introduced sensational stories with banner headlines and lavish pictures, a style of news reporting that came to be known as "yellow journalism."

In Britain, Lord Northcliffe (Alfred Harmsworth) introduced the small-format US-style tabloid, the *Daily Mail* (1896) – the first paper in the world to reach a circulation of more than 1 million copies per day, and the *Daily Mirror* (1903), also selling a million copies per day by 1914. Lord Beaverbrook (Max Aitken) took over the competing *Daily Express* in 1919 and raised its circulation to a record-breaking 2.25 million copies a day. Today's largest circulation figures belong to the tabloid *News of the World* (founded in 1843), which sells just over 4 million copies a week.

The rise of photojournalism
Photojournalism took off in the 1920s with the appearance of *Time* (1923), the *New Yorker* (1925) and *Life* (1936) in the US and *Picture Post* (1938) in Britain. Postwar depression was lifted in Germany with *Stern* magazine (1948), and France began *Paris-Match* (1949).

Breaking news In 1972, *The Washington Post*'s investigation into a break-in at the Democratic Party's Watergate headquarters implicated the Republicans, forcing President Nixon to resign.

Newspaper launch dates

Date	Newspaper	Country
1785	*The Times*	UK
1791	*The Observer*	UK
1821	*The Guardian*	UK
1838	*Bombay Times*	India
1851	*The New York Times*	US
1855	*The Daily Telegraph*	UK
1874	*Yomiuri Shimbun*	Japan
1876	*Corriere della Sera*	Italy
1877	*The Washington Post*	US
1888	*Financial Times*	UK
1889	*The Wall Street Journal*	US
1918	*Pravda*	Russia
1923	*Hindustan Times*	India

COMIC CHARACTERS

Character	Cartoonist	Date	Country
Little Orphan Annie	Harold Gray	1924	US
Blondie	Chic Young	1929	US
Popeye	Elzie C. Segar	1929	US
Tintin	Hergé	1929	Belgium
Dick Tracy	Chester Gould	1931	US
Li'l Abner	Al Capp	1934	US
Peanuts	Charles Schulz	1950	US
Andy Capp	Reg Smythe	1957	UK
Astérix	Albert Uderzo	1959	France
Doonesbury	Garry Trudeau	1970	US
Garfield	Jim Davis	1978	US
Dilbert	Scott Adams	1988	US

Press records

- **The country with the largest number of newspapers** is India, which has 4235 mostly regional titles.
- **The world's best-selling magazine** is *Reader's Digest*, which sells 27 million copies per month in 18 languages. The US edition alone sells 15 million copies per month.
- **The oldest surviving daily newspaper** is Austria's *Wiener Zeitung*, established in 1703.
- **The oldest surviving weekly newspaper** is Sweden's *Post-och Inrikes Tidningar*.

see also
342-43 **Western literature**
354-55 **Television**
400-1 **Information economy**

ILLUSTRATORS AND CARTOONISTS

Illustrating publications for widespread circulation required a broad range of artists with many different skills. The 19th-century newspaper industry needed factual illustrations and sent reporters such as Thomas Nast out into the field to capture real events in pen and ink. Illustration for entertainment began even earlier, with the caricatures drawn by Arthur Pond for Britain's *London Magazine* in the 1740s. Their broad appeal created a market for satirical magazines such as *Punch* (1841). By 1865, the comic strip had arrived with the German pictorial narrative *Max und Moritz*, drawn by Wilhelm Busch.

Comic-strip hero Tintin and his dog Milou (known as Snowy in the UK and US) first set out on their adventures in 1929. Since then, 25 million copies of the comic-strip stories have been sold.

Leading illustrators

- **George Cruikshank** (1792-1878) British
Great technical facility and robust satire made Cruikshank the leading political cartoonist of his day. He also illustrated more than 850 books and is well known as the illustrator of Charles Dickens' *Sketches by Boz.*
- **Hergé (Georges Remi)** (1907-83) Belgian
The writer and illustrator who created Tintin and his moral adventure stories, Hergé is widely credited as the finest creator of the *bande dessinée* (comic strip).
- **Thomas Nast** (1840-1902) German (naturalized American)
This political cartoonist created the donkey symbol for the Democratic political party and the elephant for the Republicans. His caricatures helped expose political corruption in the New York administration.
- **Frederic Remington** (1861-1909) American
Remington is the best known illustrator of the American West, whose drawings of soldiers, cowboys and Native Americans shaped popular views of the West for decades.
- **Norman Rockwell** (1894-1978) American
This chronicler of middle America, whose covers for *The Saturday Evening Post* magazine, drawn over a period of 47 years, became an American institution.
- **Charles Schulz** (1922-2000) American
Schulz is the creator and cartoonist of *Peanuts*, the world's most popular comic strip.
- **James Thurber** (1894-1961) American
This writer and illustrator is famous for his cartoons of the frustrated day-dreaming urban man.

Small-town style Norman Rockwell sold his first cover to *The Saturday Evening Post* in 1916. He went on to draw another 316 covers.

Food long ago evolved beyond the basic function of sustaining life. It defines social groups, reflects religious attitudes and moral beliefs governing what can be eaten, and in the rituals of meal times promotes social cohesion. History, culture and technology have profoundly affected how we obtain, prepare and consume food.

Food and major religions

Buddhism The killing of animals is not permitted. Buddhists are vegetarian.
Christianity No overall rules, but some avoid meat on Fridays, especially Good Friday, when Christ was crucified.
Hinduism Beef is forbidden because cattle are held to be sacred. Many sects are fully vegetarian.
Islam Pork, alcohol and the flesh of any animal found dead are forbidden; other meat must be *halal* – from animals killed in a prescribed manner.
Judaism Strict laws govern *kosher* (permitted "pure") food. Meat must be from cloven-hoofed animals that chew the cud and have been killed by a *shohet* (trained ritual slaughterer). Shellfish and fish without skins and scales are forbidden. Meat and dairy foods must not be mixed.

Cuisines of the world Each of the world's societies has its own distinctive cuisine, based on climate, available food resources and culture.

Western Europe's cuisine reflects the distribution of olive trees. To the south, the main cooking fat is olive oil; in the north, butter and other animal fats are used. Other defining features are available vegetables: Root vegetables are used in the north, often in hearty stews; garlic and tomatoes are used in the south.

Central Europe still shows the influence of the former Austro-Hungarian Empire in its cuisine, including variations of paprika-laden goulash. Austria's link to Germany is seen in such dishes as *Apfelstrudel*, sausages and *Wienerschnitzel*. Coffee reached Continental Europe from Turkey through this region.

The Middle East and North Africa derive their cuisine from the Ottoman Empire. Lamb dishes predominate, and olives, yogurt, nuts, vine leaves, couscous and rice are some of the common local ingredients. Sweets are extremely sweet – as in *halva*, which combines sugar, sesame seeds and almonds.

India is well known for its use of spices to produce a wide range of subtly flavored dishes; the taste tends to be hottest in the south. Chicken and lamb are favorite ingredients, but poverty and religion restrict meat-eating: Strict Buddhists and many Hindus eat no meat, and Muslims eat no pork. Milk and curds are widely used.

FAST FOOD

The first "fast food" was the sandwich, reputedly invented 250 years ago by the 4th Earl of Sandwich, who put a slice of beef between two pieces of bread in order to avoid losing time at the gaming table. Today's fast food is a 20th-century American invention.

The first hamburger chain, White Castle, began selling 5-cent square hamburgers in 1921; it still sells 500 million a year. Many fast-food chains had small beginnings. Colonel Harland Sanders opened his first fried chicken shop, using his $105 social security check, in Corbin, Kentucky, in 1952, when he was 65. Twelve years later he sold the company for $2 million. In 2000, KFC was serving more than 2 billion chicken meals annually in 82 countries.

In a similar way, two college students, Frank and Dan Carney, borrowed $600 from their mother to begin Pizza Hut in Witchita, Kansas, in 1958. By 2000, Pizza Hut had 12 000 outlets worldwide and was selling 1.7 million pizzas a day.

The two biggest hamburger chains also began in the 1950s: Burger King in Miami in 1954, and McDonald's in 1955 in San Bernadino, California. In 2000, Burger King's 11 340 restaurants around the world were visited by 15 million customers a day and sold a total of 2.6 billion hamburgers. In 1999, McDonald's served 15 billion customers – 43 million people a day – in more than 29 000 restaurants worldwide. The busiest McDonald's is in Pushkin Square in Moscow, which serves more than 40 000 customers per day.

Key dates

600s Forks are used in the Middle East.
1589 Forks are first used at the French court.
1609 Tea from China is shipped to Europe.
1650 Tea is introduced into England. First English coffee house opens.
1809 Nicolas Appert (France) preserves food in heat-sterilized bottles; canning is patented in England.
1840 Afternoon tea is established in England.
1851 First refrigerated railroad car (US).
1868 First "Pullman" railroad dining car.
1880 Canned fruits and meats go on sale.
1890 First cafeterias and diners in US.
1908 First tea bags are introduced in US.
1930 Birdseye introduces frozen foods.
1936 First in-flight meals (American Airlines). Food blender introduced.
1937 Instant coffee is invented in Switzerland.
1953 US has about 17 000 supermarkets.
1954 Frozen "TV dinners" launched in US.
1990 UK approves first genetically modified food item, a variety of yeast.
1994 First genetically modified tomato is produced in US.

Sealed in a can The advent of canned food added variety to the daily diet.

China and Japan share rice and noodles as staples, but China is so vast that it has many regional cuisines. The emphasis is on balance – the principles of yin and yang – with the right mix of staples and vegetables and meat for health. Japan's formal culture means that the presentation of food is as important as its taste.

Southeast Asia is noted for its fish and seafood, rice and noodle dishes and for such local and introduced spices as ginger, galangal, lemongrass and chili. Chinese cooking has influenced dishes in much of Southeast Asia, as has French cooking in Indochina. Fermented fish sauce is widely used as a flavoring.

North America uses local ingredients such as corn, but there are few truly native recipes. Immigrants have created the world's most varied cuisine, including Cajun, Tex-Mex and "fusion" cooking. Many "ethnic" dishes such as chop suey and deep-dish pizza are unknown in their supposed countries of origin.

Central and South America have combined the inherited cuisines of Spain, Portugal and other European nations with such local ingredients as beans, corn, chili peppers and plantains, and with indigenous cooking methods. Seafood is plentiful in the Caribbean, as are beef and lamb in South America.

FOOD AND EXPLORATION

Throughout history, people have transplanted foods from one place to another. As a result, many foods are now grown thousands of miles from their place of origin.

For example, Alexander the Great introduced apricots to Greece from Asia in about 300 B.C., and Europeans took radishes to China in about A.D. 700. The Romans systematically took foods to lands they conquered, such as orange trees from India to plant in North Africa in the 1st century. The Moors of North Africa then took orange trees to Spain by about the 8th century (along with olives and spinach), and by 1493, Columbus had shipped Spanish oranges to the West Indies.

Columbus was a keen collector of exotic foods, shipping home corn, pineapples and beans. The Spanish found the Aztecs using chocolate in about 1500 and took that home. The French introduced large-fruited North American strawberries to Europe in 1624.

English explorer Francis Drake took sassafras (and tobacco) from Virginia to England. Captain William Bligh's purpose, during the voyage that ended in the *Bounty* mutiny, was to introduce breadfruit trees from Tahiti to the West Indies to feed plantation slaves.

Some foods made a two-way trip. The turkey was taken home from Mexico by Spanish conquistadors about 1519, and English colonists later shipped it to their North American colonies. The Spanish introduced the potato to Europe from South America in the 16th century, and it returned west with the English to North America as a "new" crop. Italian explorers shipped tomatoes grown by the Incas and Aztecs to Italy in about 1550; Europeans took them to the US in the late 18th century.

see also
164-65 **Age of exploration**
304-7 **Religions**

Football

Football evolved from rugby in the 1800s. Today, it is run by the National Football League (NFL). As well as being the US's most popular professional sport, it is played in over 650 American colleges, which compete yearly for the national title.

The aim of the game Football is played between two teams of up to 45 players (including substitutes). Only 11 players from each team are on the field ("gridiron") at any one time. The object is for players to gain ground up the field and score points, either by carrying or catching the oblong ball over the opponents' goal line for a touchdown or by kicking the ball over the crossbar between the goalposts.

The sequence of play The game is divided into four 15-minute quarters, with a half-time interval. Each quarter starts with one team kicking the ball to the other team, which is then allowed four attempts (downs) to advance 10 yd (9 m) or more up the field with the ball. If they succeed, they get four more downs; if they fail, their opponents win possession of the ball. A down ends when a player with the ball is stopped by opposing players or goes out of bounds, or if a pass is thrown and missed.

The roles of different players Each team has three separate groups of players.

- **Offense** When a team wins possession, it puts its offense on the field. The offense's job is to move the ball forward, either by running with it or by one player throwing it and another catching it. The 11 men in the offense are led by the quarterback, who is the playmaker and throwing specialist. He is supported by three receivers, whose job it is to run into space upfield and catch the ball. The quarterback is protected from the front by a line of five players (the center, the right and left tackles, and the right and left guards) and from behind by two players; the fullback and tailback (also known as running backs). Sometimes the quarterback will opt to give the ball to the running backs to run with rather than to attempt to throw it.
- **Defense** The job of the defense is to prevent the opposition's offense from moving the ball forward. This is done most effectively by tackling ("sacking") the quarterback before he can make a throw or pass.
- **Special teams** This group comes onto the field for kicking situations: to start or restart play; to kick a field goal; or to gain ground by punting the ball upfield.

Super Bowl winners

Begun in 1967, this game between the champions of the professional American and National Football Conferences (the AFC and NFC, which together comprise the NFL) is now the US's biggest sporting event.

Year	Champion
1967-68	Green Bay Packers
1969	New York Jets
1970	Kansas City Chiefs
1971	Baltimore Colts
1972	Dallas Cowboys
1973-74	Miami Dolphins
1975-76	Pittsburgh Steelers
1977	Oakland Raiders
1978	Dallas Cowboys
1979-80	Pittsburgh Steelers
1981	Oakland Raiders
1982	San Francisco 49ers
1983	Washington Redskins
1984	Los Angeles Raiders
1985	San Francisco 49ers
1986	Chicago Bears
1987	New York Giants
1988	Washington Redskins
1989-90	San Francisco 49ers
1991	New York Giants
1992	Washington Redskins
1993-94	Dallas Cowboys
1995	San Francisco 49ers
1996	Dallas Cowboys
1997	Green Bay Packers
1998-99	Denver Broncos
2000	St. Louis Rams
2001	Baltimore Ravens
2002	New England Patriots
2003	Tampa Bay Buccaneers

Most Super Bowl wins	
Dallas Cowboys	5
San Francisco 49ers	5
Pittsburgh Steelers	4
Green Bay Packers	3
Washington Redskins	3

LEGENDS

Joe Namath

(1943-) American

Namath is acknowledged as one of the best passers in the game. As quarterback, he led the New York Jets to the 1969 Super Bowl championship, after which he was named the game's most valuable player, and made 173 touchdowns in a career lasting 23 years.

Body armor All football players wear helmets, and protective pads on their thighs, hips, knees, groin, ribs, arms and shoulders. Some also wear padded fingerless gloves.

The playing area

The American football field, or gridiron, is covered by grass or an artificial alternative called AstroTurf. It is measured in yards and is 100 yd (91 m) long by $53\frac{1}{2}$ yd (49 m) wide.

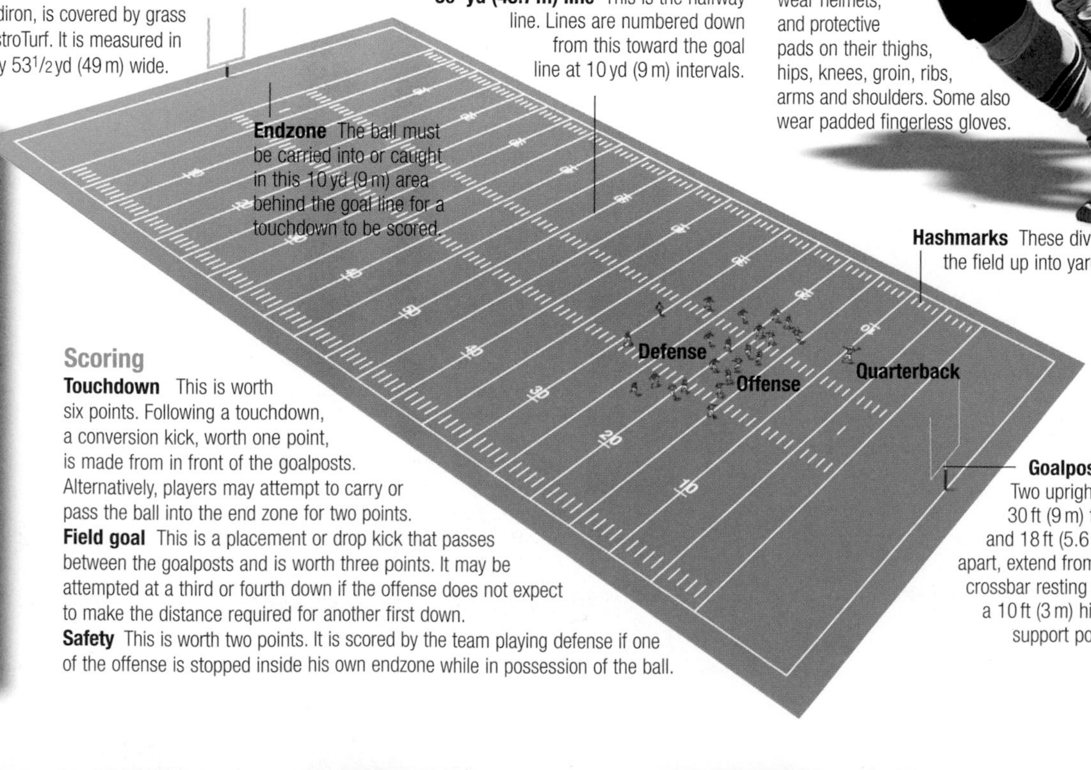

50-yd (45.7 m) line This is the halfway line. Lines are numbered down from this toward the goal line at 10 yd (9 m) intervals.

Endzone The ball must be carried into or caught in this 10 yd (9 m) area behind the goal line for a touchdown to be scored.

Hashmarks These divide the field up into yards.

Goalposts Two uprights, 30 ft (9 m) tall and 18 ft (5.6 m) apart, extend from a crossbar resting on a 10 ft (3 m) high support pole.

Scoring

Touchdown This is worth six points. Following a touchdown, a conversion kick, worth one point, is made from in front of the goalposts. Alternatively, players may attempt to carry or pass the ball into the end zone for two points.

Field goal This is a placement or drop kick that passes between the goalposts and is worth three points. It may be attempted at a third or fourth down if the offense does not expect to make the distance required for another first down.

Safety This is worth two points. It is scored by the team playing defense if one of the offense is stopped inside his own endzone while in possession of the ball.

LEGENDS

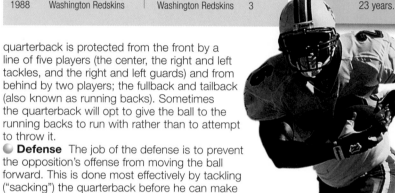

Joe Montana

(1956-) American

This quarterback played for San Francisco 49ers and Kansas City Chiefs between 1979 and 1994. He led the 49ers to four Super Bowl championships, in one of which he orchestrated a 92 yd (84 m) winning drive in the closing seconds.

Baseball

Considered the US's national sport, baseball developed from the old English game of rounders, which arrived in the 18th century with the first settlers. Baseball's most prestigious tournament, the World Series, began in 1903. It is played at the end of the season between two teams, the winners of the National and American League championships.

World Series champions

Year	Champion	Year	Champion	Year	Champion
1970	Baltimore Orioles	1983	Baltimore Orioles	1997	Florida Marlins
1971	Pittsburgh Pirates	1984	Detroit Tigers	1998	NY Yankees
1972	Oakland A's	1985	K'sas City Royals	1999	NY Yankees
1973	Oakland A's	1986	NY Mets	2000	NY Yankees
1974	Oakland A's	1987	Minnesota Twins	2001	Arizona Diamondbacks
1975	Cincinnati Reds	1988	LA Dodgers	2002	Anaheim Angels
1976	Cincinnati Reds	1989	Oakland A's		
1977	NY Yankees	1990	Cincinnati Reds		
1978	NY Yankees	1991	Minnesota Twins		
1979	Pittsburgh Pirates	1992	Toronto Blue Jays		
1980	P'delphia Phillies	1993	Toronto Blue Jays		
1981	LA Dodgers	1994	No series		
1982	St. Louis Cardinals	1995	Atlanta Braves		
		1996	NY Yankees		

Most Series won since the tournament began

NY Yankees	26 wins
St. Louis Cardinals	9 wins
Phil/KC/Oakland A's	9 wins
Br'klyn/LA Dodgers	6 wins

The aim of the game

Baseball is played by two teams of nine players, each batting and fielding in turn. Balls are thrown or "pitched" by a pitcher to the opposing batter. Batters attempt to hit the ball into the field and run round a series of "bases," touching each on the way, to score a run. The team that scores the most runs wins.

How baseball is played

The pitcher throws the ball toward the batter, who stands next to home base. The pitcher aims at the area over home base, at a height between the batter's armpits and knees. This area is known as the strike zone.

- If the ball is pitched outside the strike zone and the batter does not swing at it, the pitch is declared a "ball"; after four balls, the batter advances to first base. If the ball is pitched within the strike zone, but the batter either does not swing at it, swings at it but misses or hits it beyond the foul lines the pitch is declared a "strike." After three strikes, the batter is out.
- Batters who hit a ball inside the field can start running to first base, or farther if they have time before the ball is fielded. Batters who have reached a base can proceed to the next base when a subsequent batter hits the ball. Only one runner can occupy a base at one time. Batters who hit the ball far enough to run around all four bases at once score a home run. A home run is always scored if a batter hits the ball outside the field.
- In addition to the "three strikes" out, a batter can also be out if the ball is caught before it touches the ground or if a fielder in possession of the ball touches (tags) him or first base before he can reach it. Base runners making their way around the bases can also be put out by being tagged by a fielder.
- The game is divided into nine periods of play known as innings. Each innings is divided into two halves, with one team batting and the other fielding in turn. To end their half of the inning, the fielding side must get three players of the batting team out.

LEGENDS

Joe DiMaggio
(1914-99) American

"Joltin' Joe" played with just one team, the New York Yankees (1936-51). In 1941, he set a record by getting hits in 56 consecutive games. During his career, he hit 361 home runs. He was also an outstanding center fielder.

Equipment

Ball A cork core in rubber casing, wound with yarn and covered with leather. It weighs 142-156 g (5-5 1/2 oz) and is 7.3 cm (2 7/8 in.) in diameter.

Bat A smooth, round, solid wooden (or aluminium) stick, not more than 107 cm (42 in.) long and 6.9 cm (2 3/4 in.) in diameter at the thickest part.

Protective gear Fielders wear padded leather gloves for catching the ball; the larger glove worn by catchers and first basemen is known as a mitt. Catchers and batters wear helmets and other special protective gear.

Playing area The playing area covers about 2 acres. It is made up of an infield, or "diamond," 27 m (90 ft) square and an outfield. The outfield is split in two by an arc called the grass line, running 29 m (95 ft) from the pitcher's plate.

Field positions Three fielders stand in an arc beyond the grass line and are known as the right fielder, center fielder and left fielder.

Bases The four corners of the diamond are named counterclockwise as home base, first base, second base and third base; home base is a slab of white rubber, the other bases are marked by white canvas bags. The distance between bases is 27 m (90 ft).

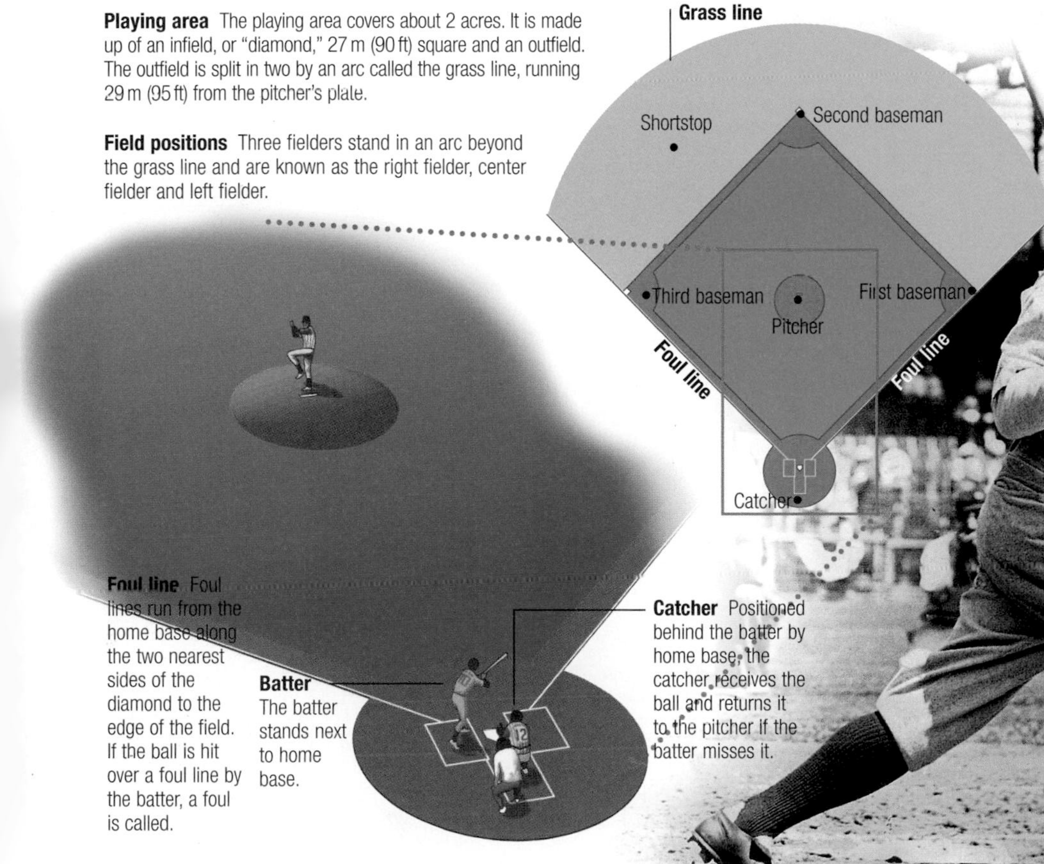

Foul line Foul lines run from the home base along the two nearest sides of the diamond to the edge of the field. If the ball is hit over a foul line by the batter, a foul is called.

Batter The batter stands next to home base.

Catcher Positioned behind the batter by home base, the catcher receives the ball and returns it to the pitcher if the batter misses it.

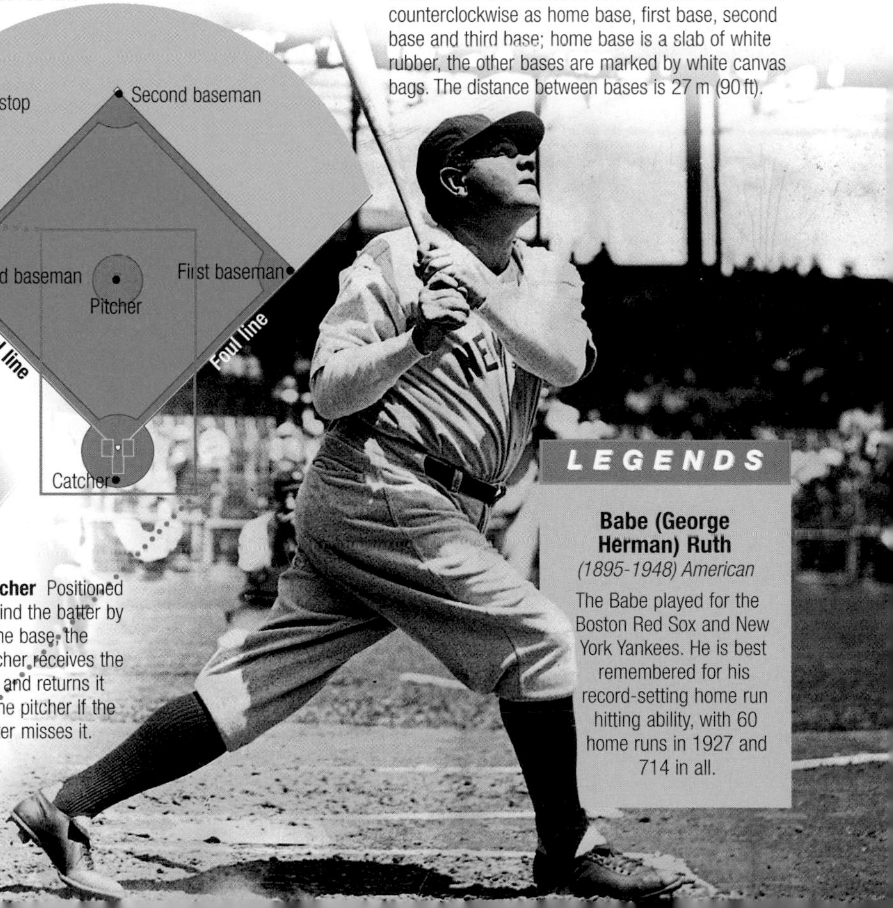

LEGENDS

Babe (George Herman) Ruth
(1895-1948) American

The Babe played for the Boston Red Sox and New York Yankees. He is best remembered for his record-setting home run hitting ability, with 60 home runs in 1927 and 714 in all.

Basketball

Games similar to basketball have been played for centuries; the oldest known version, called Pok-ta-Pok, was played by the Olmecs of Mexico 3000 years ago. The modern game was invented in 1891 by a Canadian – Dr. James Naismith – at the YMCA Training School in Massachussets. His aim was to revive his pupils' interest in sports.

The ball Round, with an outer surface of leather, rubber or synthetic material. It weighs 567-650 g (20-23 oz) and is 24-25 cm (9 1/2-9 3/4 in.) wide.

High and mighty Apart from skill, height is a basketball player's most important attribute. Few of today's professionals are under 1.8 m (6 ft) tall.

The aim of the game

In basketball, two teams try to score points by throwing the ball into their opponents' basket while stopping the other side from scoring. Players can throw, bounce ("dribble") and pass the ball, but cannot carry or kick it. Basketball is a noncontact sport, and players have a "personal" space that others may not violate deliberately.

How basketball is played

The referee starts the game by tossing the ball into the center circle, between the two opposing centers (jump ball). The team that gets the ball tries to advance it toward their opponent's basket. Goals, known as "baskets," are scored for throwing a ball into a basket. They are worth two or three points depending on the player's distance from the basket. A basket from a free throw (awarded for fouls) is worth one point. After a basket is scored, play is restarted by the defending team from behind its end line.

Olympic men's champions

Men's basketball was introduced to the Olympics in 1936. In 1980, the US boycotted the Moscow games. Professional players were first admitted in 1992.

Year	Nation	Year	Nation
1936	US	1972	USSR
1948	US	1976	US
1952	US	1980	Yugoslavia
1956	US	1984	US
1960	US	1988	USSR
1964	US	1992	US
1968	US	1996	US
		2000	US

Duration, teams and time rules

Amateur basketball games comprise two halves of 20 minutes each; professional games have four periods of 12 minutes each. If a game ends in a draw, 5-minute periods may be played until there is a winner. There are two teams of ten for amateur games; 12 players are on professional teams. Only five players from each team are allowed on the court at any time: two forwards, a center (usually the tallest player) and two guards. There are three time rules.

- **30-second rule** A team must shoot at the basket within 30 seconds of gaining possession of the ball.
- **10-second rule** A team gaining possession of the ball in its half of the court (back court) must get it into the other side (front court) within 10 seconds.
- **3-second rule** A player in possession of the ball may not be in the opposing side's restricted area for more than 3 seconds.

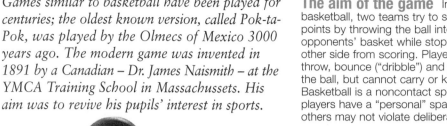

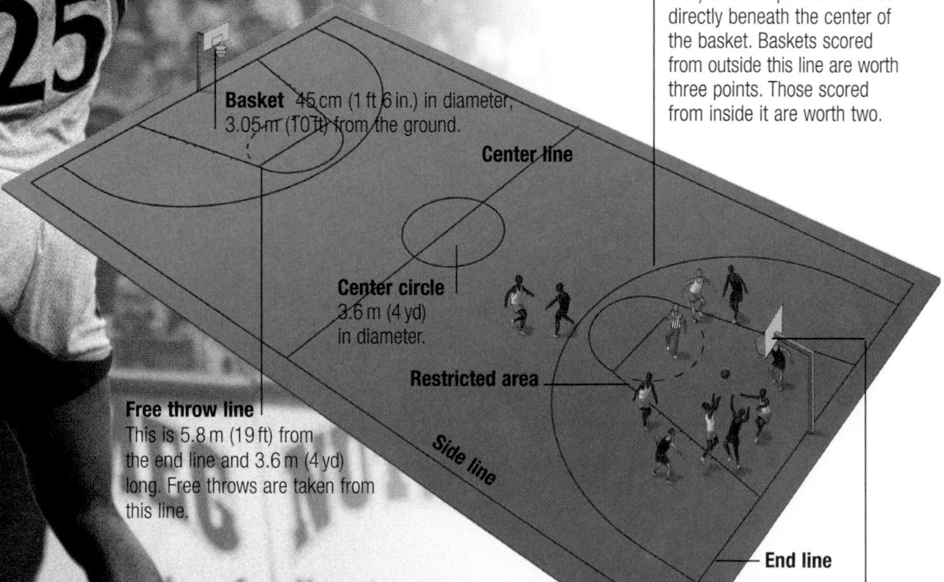

Basketball court dimensions 28 x 15 m (31 x 16 yd)

Three point line Semicircle with a radius of 6.25 m (20 ft 6 in.) from the point on the floor directly beneath the center of the basket. Baskets scored from outside this line are worth three points. Those scored from inside it are worth two.

Basket 45 cm (1 ft 6 in.) in diameter, 3.05 m (10 ft) from the ground.

Center circle 3.6 m (4 yd) in diameter.

Free throw line This is 5.8 m (19 ft) from the end line and 3.6 m (4 yd) long. Free throws are taken from this line.

Fouls There are two types of foul; personal fouls (illegal body contact) and technical fouls (for example, bad sportsmanship). Fouls are penalized by free throws. Players committing five (amateur) or six (professional) personal fouls are sent off for the rest of the game.

Backboard Positioned at the center of each back line. It is 1.8 m (5 ft 11 in.) long and 1.2 m (3 ft 11 in.) high, with its lower edge 2.9 m (9 ft 6 in.) from the floor.

LEGENDS

Michael Jordan
(1963-) American

In his 13 seasons with the Chicago Bulls, Jordan led the team to six National Basketball Association (NBA) championships (1991-93 and 1996-98). His career average of 31.5 points per game is the best in NBA history.

Hockey

Ice hockey was invented in the 1850s in Canada, where it is now the national game. It is the fastest team sport of all – players can reach speeds of more than 48 km/h (30 mph), and the puck may travel at up to 190 km/h (118 mph).

The aim of the game Ice hockey developed from field hockey and shares the same basic objective: to score more goals than the opposition. Beyond that, ice hockey differs in a number of ways. It is a contact sport, in which "checking" an opponent to take him out of play is a legitimate tactic. The offside rule is different, and infringements are penalized differently. Ice hockey teams have up to 18 members, but no more than six may be on the ice at any time. These are the goaltender, right and left defense, center, right wing and left wing. A game lasts for an hour, which is split into three 20 minute periods.

Officials and rules The officials are a referee, two linesmen and goal judges, a scorer, game timekeeper and penalty timekeeper. Infringements include

- **Icing** This occurs when one team shoots the puck from its defensive zone over the other team's goal line.
- **Offside** A player is offside if he takes a pass that has crossed both blue lines (or the center line and one blue line in Canadian and professional games). A player who enters the attacking zone ahead of the puck is also offside. Offsides are penalized with a face-off – the puck is dropped between two players, who then compete for it. Face-offs also penalize icing and restart the game after a goal.
- **Fouls** These include elbowing, charging and "high-sticking." The offending player is sent off for 2 minutes.

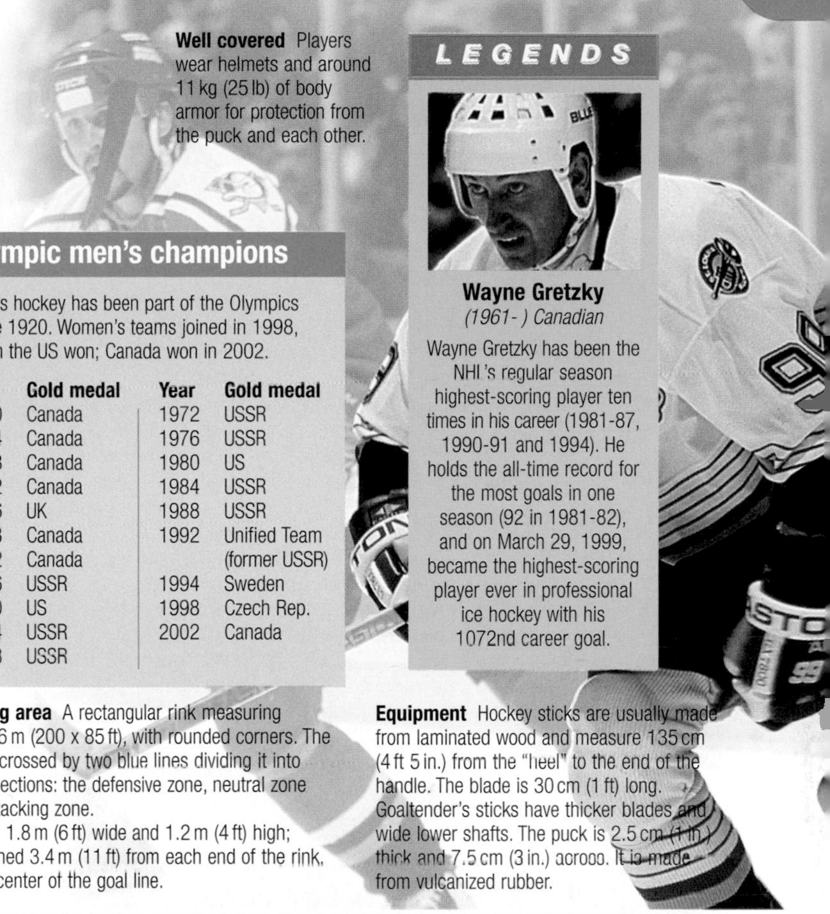

Well covered Players wear helmets and around 11 kg (25 lb) of body armor for protection from the puck and each other.

Olympic men's champions

Men's hockey has been part of the Olympics since 1920. Women's teams joined in 1998, when the US won; Canada won in 2002.

Year	Gold medal	Year	Gold medal
1920	Canada	1972	USSR
1924	Canada	1976	USSR
1928	Canada	1980	US
1932	Canada	1984	USSR
1936	UK	1988	USSR
1948	Canada	1992	Unified Team (former USSR)
1952	Canada		
1956	USSR	1994	Sweden
1960	US	1998	Czech Rep.
1964	USSR	2002	Canada
1968	USSR		

LEGENDS

Wayne Gretzky
(1961-) Canadian

Wayne Gretzky has been the NHL's regular season highest-scoring player ten times in his career (1981-87, 1990-91 and 1994). He holds the all-time record for the most goals in one season (92 in 1981-82), and on March 29, 1999, became the highest-scoring player ever in professional ice hockey with his 1072nd career goal.

Playing area A rectangular rink measuring 61 x 26 m (200 x 85 ft), with rounded corners. The rink is crossed by two blue lines dividing it into three sections: the defensive zone, neutral zone and attacking zone.

Goals 1.8 m (6 ft) wide and 1.2 m (4 ft) high; positioned 3.4 m (11 ft) from each end of the rink, in the center of the goal line.

Equipment Hockey sticks are usually made from laminated wood and measure 135 cm (4 ft 5 in.) from the "heel" to the end of the handle. The blade is 30 cm (1 ft) long. Goaltender's sticks have thicker blades and wide lower shafts. The puck is 2.5 cm (1 in.) thick and 7.5 cm (3 in.) across. It is made from vulcanized rubber.

Stanley Cup champions and finalists

The Stanley Cup is awarded to the team that wins the final round of the National Hockey League best-of-seven playoffs.

	Winning team	Finalist		Winning team	Finalist
1927	Ottawa Senators	Boston Bruins	1965	Montreal Canadiens	Chicago Blackhawks
1928	New York Rangers	Montreal Maroons	1966	Montreal Canadiens	Detroit Red Wings
1929	Boston Bruins	New York Rangers	1967	Toronto Maple Leafs	Montreal Canadiens
1930	Montreal Canadiens	Boston Bruins	1968	Montreal Canadiens	St. Louis Blues
1931	Montreal Canadiens	Chicago Black Hawks	1969	Montreal Canadiens	St. Louis Blues
1932	Toronto Maple Leafs	New York Rangers	1970	Boston Bruins	St. Louis Blues
1933	New York Rangers	Toronto Maple Leafs	1971	Montreal Canadiens	Chicago Blackhawks
1934	Chicagio Blackhawks	Detroit Red Wings	1972	Boston Bruins	New York Rangers
1935	Montreal Maroons	Toronto Maple Leafs	1973	Montreal Canadiens	Chicago Blackhawks
1936	Detroit Red Wings	Toronto Maple Leafs	1974	Philadelphia Flyers	Boston Bruins
1937	Detroit Red Wings	New York Rangers	1975	Philadelphia Flyers	Buffalo Sabres
1938	Chicago Blackhawks	Toronto Maple Leafs	1976	Montreal Canadiens	Philadelphia Flyers
1939	Boston Bruins	Toronto Maple Leafs	1977	Montreal Canadiens	Boston Bruins
1940	New York Rangers	Toronto Maple Leafs	1978	Montreal Canadiens	Boston Bruins
1941	Boston Bruins	Detroit Red Wings	1979	Montreal Canadiens	New York Rangers
1942	Toronto Maple Leafs	Detroit Red Wings	1980	New York Islanders	Philadelphia Flyers
1943	Detroit Red Wings	Boston Bruins	1981	New York Islanders	Minnesota North Stars
1944	Montreal Canadiens	Chicago Blackhawks	1982	New York Islanders	Vancouver Canucks
1945	Toronto Maple Leafs	Detroit Red Wings	1983	New York Islanders	Edmonton Oilers
1946	Montreal Canadiens	Boston Bruins	1984	Edmonton Oilers	New York Islanders
1947	Toronto Maple Leafs	Montreal Canadiens	1985	Edmonton Oilers	Philadelphia Flyers
1948	Toronto Maple Leafs	Detroit Red Wings	1986	Montreal Canadiens	Calgary Flames
1949	Toronto Maple Leafs	Detroit Red Wings	1987	Edmonton Oilers	Philadelphia Flyers
1950	Detroit Red Wings	New York Rangers	1988	Edmonton Oilers	Boston Bruins
1951	Toronto Maple Leafs	Montreal Canadiens	1989	Calgary Flames	Montreal Canadiens
1952	Detroit Red Wings	Montreal Canadiens	1990	Edmonton Oilers	Boston Bruins
1953	Montreal Canadiens	Boston Bruins	1991	Pittsburgh Penguins	Minnesota North Stars
1954	Detroit Red Wings	Montreal Canadiens	1992	Pittsburgh Penguins	Chicago Blackhawks
1955	Detroit Red Wings	Montreal Canadiens	1993	Montreal Canadiens	Los Angeles Kings
1956	Montreal Canadiens	Detroit Red Wings	1994	New York Rangers	Vancouver Canucks
1957	Montreal Canadiens	Boston Bruins	1995	New Jersey Devils	Detroit Red Wings
1958	Montreal Canadiens	Boston Bruins	1996	Colorado Avalanche	Florida Panthers
1959	Montreal Canadiens	Toronto Maple Leafs	1997	Detroit Red Wings	Philadelphia Flyers
1960	Montreal Canadiens	Toronto Maple Leafs	1998	Detroit Red Wings	Washington Capitals
1961	Chicago Blackhawks	Detroit Red Wings	1999	Dallas Stars	Buffalo Sabres
1962	Toronto Maple Leafs	Chicago Blackhawks	2000	New Jersey Devils	Dallas Stars
1963	Toronto Maple Leafs	Detroit Red Wings	2001	Colorado Avalanche	New Jersey Devils
1964	Toronto Maple Leafs	Detroit Red Wings	2002	Detroit Red Wings	Carolina Hurricanes

Soccer

Soccer, called football outside the United States, is the most popular team sport in the world. In 1904 the game's governing body FIFA (Fédération Internationale de Football Association) was founded by seven countries – today it boasts more than 200 member nations.

The aim of the game Two teams compete to score goals; a goal is scored by a player kicking, heading or otherwise deflecting the ball with any part of his body other than his hands or arms over the goal line between the posts and under the crossbar. There are 11 players on each team: one goalkeeper and ten outfield players (with attacking, midfield or defensive roles). During the game, players can be replaced by substitute players; each team can use up to three substitutes. A player who has been replaced takes no further part in the game. Teams change ends at halftime.

Duration and extra time Most soccer games last for 90 minutes (two 45 minute halves, with an interval). If at the end of that time the score is even, the game is declared a tie. In knock-out competition, however, if the score is even at the end of play, extra time may be played, generally for 30 minutes. A further stalemate can lead to a replay or a "penalty shoot-out": Each team gets five penalty shots at goal. If the score is still even at the end of the shoot-out, the first team to miss a penalty shot loses. Sometimes the first goal scored in extra time (the so-called "golden goal") is used to settle a match.

Officials and sanctions A soccer game is controlled by a referee, two assistant referees who patrol the touchlines and a fourth official. The main sanctions issued by the referee are:

- **Yellow card** A "caution" given to a player for flouting the rules or for dissent. Too many yellow cards over time can lead to suspension by soccer authorities.
- **Red card** This is issued to a player for two yellow card offenses in the same game or for a particularly serious or violent infringement; the player is sent off the field and suspended.

Foul play, whether deserving of a card or not, is penalized by a free kick being given to the opposition from the point where the infringement was made. The opposition must retreat 9 m (10 yd) from the ball. If a foul is committed inside the penalty box, the opposition is awarded a penalty kick, which is taken from the penalty spot directly in front of the goal.

LEGENDS

Stanley Matthews
(1915-2000) English

An attacking player with exceptional ball control skills, Matthews played 54 times for England. His last first-class game was in 1965, when he was 50.

World Cup holders

The World Cup is held every four years. Japan and South Korea will host it in 2002 and Germany in 2006.

Year	Result of the final
1930	Uruguay 4-2 Argentina
1934	Italy 2-1 Czechoslovakia
1938	Italy 4-2 Hungary
1950	Uruguay 2-1 Brazil
1954	W. Germany 3-2 Hungary
1958	Brazil 5-2 Sweden
1962	Brazil 3-1 Czechoslovakia
1966	England 4-2 W Germany
1970	Brazil 4-1 Italy
1974	W. Germany 2-1 Holland
1978	Argentina 3-1 Holland
1982	Italy 3-1 W. Germany
1986	Argentina 3-2 W. Germany
1990	W. Germany 1-0 Argentina
1994	Brazil 0-0 Italy (3-2 pen)
1998	France 3-0 Brazil
2002	Brazil 2-0 Germany

Team formations Today's favored options for the deployment of players include a formation using four defenders, four midfield players and two attackers, known as 4-4-2, and other structures such as 4-2-4, 4-3-3, or 3-5-2 (using defenders as backup attackers, called "wing backs"). The choice depends on the attributes of the players available and the assessment of the opposition.

Fouls

Handball Other than goalkeepers, players are not allowed to touch the ball with their hands or arms, except for "throw-ins" after the ball has gone over the touchline. A goalkeeper may not handle the ball outside the penalty area or if it has been kicked (rather than headed) back by a teammate.

Offside A player is offside if, while he is in the opponents' half, a pass is made to him from a colleague when there is only one defending player (which may be the goalkeeper) between himself and the goal line. He is not offside if there is a second defender in line with or in front of him at the moment the passing player hits the ball.

Reckless tackling This is judged by the referee, whose decision is final.

The playing area

Almost all soccer pitches (fields) are made of turf. Sizes vary but those used for international matches must be 100-110 m x 64-75 m (110-120 yd x 70-80 yd).

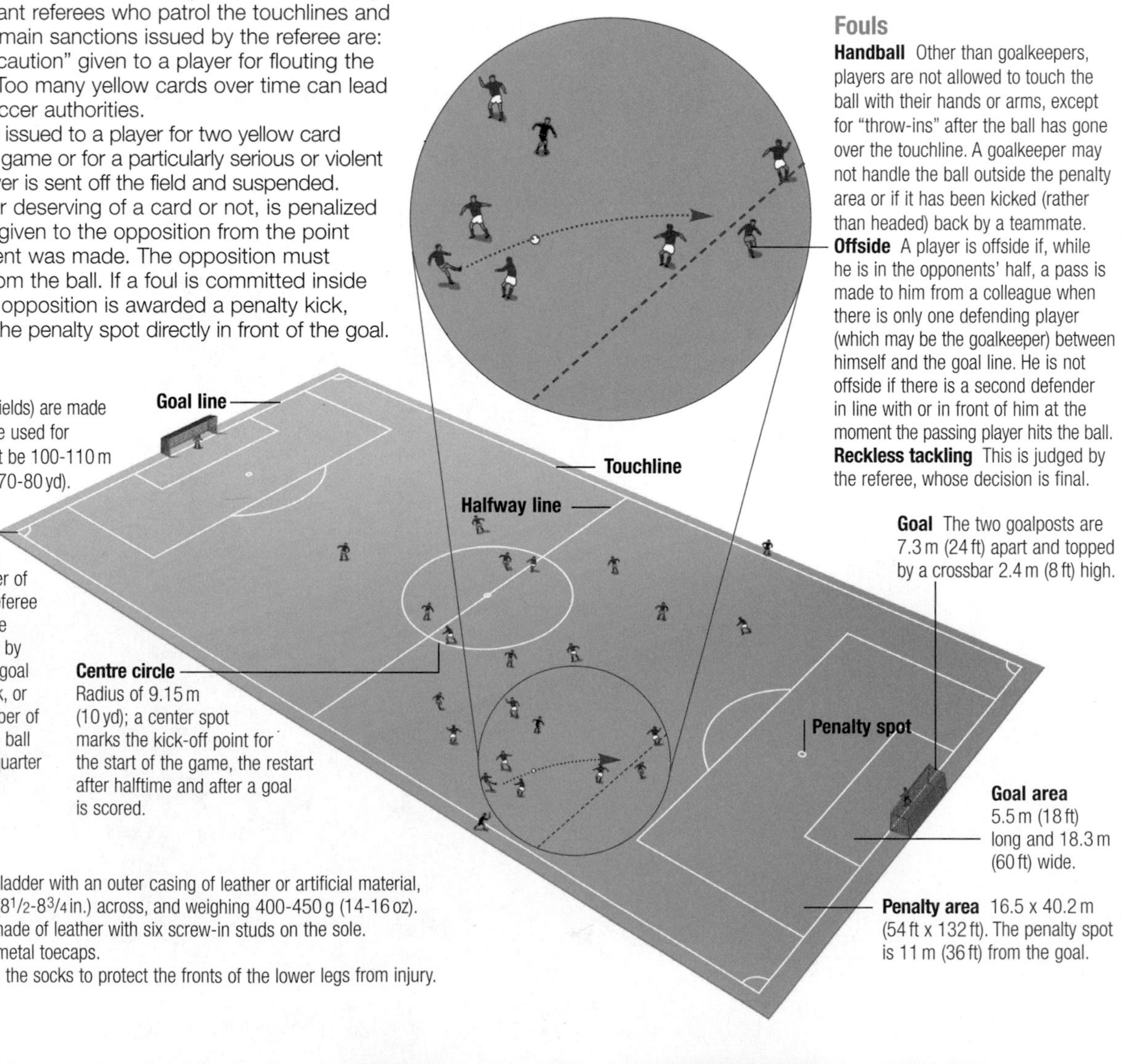

Corner If the ball is knocked over the goal line outside the goal by a player of the defending team, the referee calls for a corner kick to be taken (if it is knocked over by an attacking player, it is a goal kick instead). A corner kick, or corner, is taken by a member of the attacking side with the ball placed inside the marked quarter circle (radius 90 cm [3 ft]).

Centre circle Radius of 9.15 m (10 yd); a center spot marks the kick-off point for the start of the game, the restart after halftime and after a goal is scored.

Goal The two goalposts are 7.3 m (24 ft) apart and topped by a crossbar 2.4 m (8 ft) high.

Goal area 5.5 m (18 ft) long and 18.3 m (60 ft) wide.

Penalty area 16.5 x 40.2 m (54 ft x 132 ft). The penalty spot is 11 m (36 ft) from the goal.

Equipment

Ball An air-filled rubber bladder with an outer casing of leather or artificial material, measuring 21.5-22.5 cm ($8\frac{1}{2}$-$8\frac{3}{4}$ in.) across, and weighing 400-450 g (14-16 oz).
Cleats Lightweight and made of leather with six screw-in studs on the sole. Some soccer cleats have metal toecaps.
Shin pads Worn beneath the socks to protect the fronts of the lower legs from injury.

Summer Olympics

Games were not held during the two World Wars. Soccer was not a medal sport at the 1896 and 1932 Olympics.

Year	Gold	Silver	Bronze
1900	England	France	Belgium
1904	Canada	US I	US II
1908	England	Denmark	Netherlands
1912	England	Denmark	Netherlands
1920	Belgium	Spain	Netherlands
1924	Uruguay	Switzerland	Sweden
1928	Uruguay	Argentina	Italy
1936	Italy	Austria	Norway
1948	Sweden	Yugoslavia	Denmark
1952	Hungary	Yugoslavia	Sweden
1956	USSR	Yugoslavia	Bulgaria
1960	Yugoslavia	Denmark	Hungary
1964	Hungary	Czechoslovakia	Germany
1968	Hungary	Bulgaria	Japan
1972	Poland	Hungary	East Germany and USSR
1976	East Germany	Poland	USSR
1980	Czechoslovakia	East Germany	USSR
1984	France	Brazil	Yugoslavia
1988	USSR	Brazil	West Germany
1992	Spain	Poland	Ghana
1996	Nigeria	Argentina	Brazil
2000	Cameroon	Spain	Chile

US Major League Soccer (MLS) Cup

Year	Result of the final
1996	D.C. United 3-2 Los Angeles Galaxy
1997	D.C. United 2-1 Colorado Rapids
1998	Chicago Fire 2-0 D.C. United
1999	D.C. United 2-0 Los Angeles Galaxy
2000	K.C. Wizards 1-0 Chicago Fire
2001	San Jose Earthquakes 2-1 Los Angeles Galaxy
2002	Los Angeles Galaxy 1-0 New England Revolution

European championships

Year	Result of the final
1960	USSR 2-1 Yugoslavia
1964	Spain 2-1 USSR
1968	Italy 2-0 Yugoslavia
1972	W. Germany 3-0 USSR
1976	Czechoslovakia 2-2 W. Germany
1980	W. Germany 2-1 Belgium
1984	France 2-0 Spain
1988	Netherlands 2-0 USSR
1992	Denmark 2-0 Germany
1996	Germany 2-1 Czech Republic
2000	France 2-1 Italy

LEGENDS

Diego Maradona

(1960-) Argentinian

Acknowledged as the world's best player by the mid-1980s, Maradona created controversy during the 1986 World Cup in which Argentina defeated England when he apparently used his hand to score a goal – an action he later ascribed to "the Hand of God."

Euro stars Frenchman Lilian Thuram (right) tackles Italian Roberto Baggio. Tackles are fair if the referee judges that the player is not careless, reckless or excessively forceful.

LEGENDS

Pelé (Edson Arantes do Nascimento)

(1940-) Brazilian

Widely considered the greatest attacking player ever, Pelé became the first player to score 1000 goals in first-class games in 1969, and scored 1283 in total.

LEGENDS

Alfredo Di Stéfano

(1926-) Argentinian

Alfredo Di Stéfano is best remembered for his goal-scoring achievements for Real Madrid in the 1950s. "The Blond Arrow," as he was nicknamed, took the team to five consecutive European Cup wins. A combination of injury, nationality issues and sheer bad luck meant that he never got to play in the World Cup.

Golf

Golf probably originated in Scotland – there is documentary evidence of its being banned there in 1457 and later of its being played by Scottish royalty, including King James IV and Queen Mary. The rules of the modern game are kept by the Royal and Ancient Golf Club of St. Andrews in Scotland, which is considered by most countries to be the sport's governing body.

The aim of the game Golf is played by individual competitors on a large outdoor course, usually made up of 18 sections, called holes. The object is to hit the ball, using specialized clubs, from the starting point (tee) of a section into the hole, or cup, at the end. Players are scored by the number of hits (strokes) that they take to complete each hole; the fewer the better. There are two ways of deciding the winner of a game. The method most often used in professional tournaments takes the winner to be the person who played the fewest strokes in total over the 18 holes. The second method – called match play – awards the game to the player who wins the most holes overall (a hole is won by the player that completes it in the fewest strokes).

The golf course The holes that comprise a golf course are divided into three sections (tee, fairway and green) and dotted with various hazards.

US Open

First played in 1895.

Year	Winner
1970	Tony Jacklin
1971	Lee Trevino
1972	Jack Nicklaus
1973	Johnny Miller
1974	Hale Irwin
1975	Lou Graham
1976	Jerry Pate
1977	Hubert Green
1978	Andy North
1979	Hale Irwin
1980	Jack Nicklaus
1981	David Graham
1982	Tom Watson
1983	Larry Nelson
1984	Fuzzy Zoeller
1985	Andy North
1986	Raymond Floyd
1987	Scott Simpson
1988	Curtis Strange
1989	Curtis Strange
1990	Hale Irwin
1991	Payne Stewart
1992	Tom Kite
1993	Lee Janzen
1994	Ernie Els
1995	Corey Pavin
1996	Steve Jones
1997	Ernie Els
1998	Lee Janzen
1999	Payne Stewart
2000	Tiger Woods
2001	Retief Goosen
2002	Tiger Woods

LEGENDS

Gary Player
(1936-) South African

Winner of more than 100 tournaments in the 1960s and 1970s, including all four major championships: the US Masters (1961, 1974, 1978); US PGA (1962, 1972); US Open (1965); and British Open (1959, 1968, 1974). He is best remembered for the phrase: "The more I practice, the luckier I get."

Tee The tee is the area marking the starting place for the hole to be played (in this picture it is obscured by trees); the first play for a hole is known as the tee shot. "Tee" is also the word used for the small peg on which the ball is placed for the tee shot.

Fairway This area of mown grass between the tee and the green varies in length. If the green cannot be reached in one shot, this is where golfers aim to play.

Green The green is a closely mown and carefully tended area around the hole. The hole is 11 cm ($4^1/_4$ in.) wide, 10 cm (4 in.) deep and marked with a flag known as the pin. The green is usually roughly circular in shape but rarely level, increasing the difficulty of getting the ball in the hole.

Hazards Various obstacles are positioned to catch wayward shots and to make it difficult for players to proceed. The most common are sand traps, or "bunkers," rough surrounding ground ("rough") and water obstacles such as ponds and streams.

Playing terms

- **Par** The number of strokes that golfers of high ability should take to complete the hole. The hole above is a par four – a good golfer should take four shots from tee to getting the ball in the cup.
- **Bogey** The term for a hole completed in one stroke over par – in this case, five shots. The player's first drive goes into the rough and the third into a bunker.
- **Birdie** The term for a hole completed in one stroke under par – in this case, three shots.
- **Eagle** A hole completed in two under par – in this case two shots. The player makes a very long and well-positioned first drive and the second shot lands in the hole.

Handicap An advantage or compensation given according to a golfer's ability or experience to even the chances of winning. A handicap is determined by the number of strokes the golfer takes to complete a round: For example, players who take a par 70 course in 80 strokes have a handicap of 10. Players with a higher handicap than their opponents receive an allowance of shots equal to the difference.

The perfect drive To hit the ball hard (drive), the golf player swings the club back around the body and then swings forward to strike the ball and follow through in one smooth action, transferring weight to the front foot and unwinding the hips as the club swings all the way round to end up down the back.

LEGENDS

Jack Nicklaus
(1940-) American

The "Golden Bear," as he is known, is considered to be the most talented golfer of the 20th century. Between 1962 and 1986, he set a record by winning 18 titles at professional golf's premier events or Major championships.

British Open

Begun in 1860, the British Open Championship is the oldest major tournament.

Year	Winner
1970	Jack Nicklaus
1971	Lee Trevino
1972	Lee Trevino
1973	Tom Weiskopf
1974	Gary Player
1975	Tom Watson
1976	Johnny Miller
1977	Tom Watson
1978	Jack Nicklaus
1979	Seve Ballesteros
1980	Tom Watson
1981	Bill Rogers
1982	Tom Watson
1983	Tom Watson
1984	Seve Ballesteros
1985	Sandy Lyle
1986	Greg Norman
1987	Nick Faldo
1988	Seve Ballesteros
1989	Mark Calcavecchia
1990	Nick Faldo
1991	Ian Baker-Finch
1992	Nick Faldo
1993	Greg Norman
1994	Nick Price
1995	John Daly
1996	Tom Lehman
1997	Justin Leonard
1998	Mark O'Meara
1999	Paul Lawrie
2000	Tiger Woods
2001	David Duval
2002	Ernie Els

US Masters

First played in 1934.

Year	Winner
1970	Billy Casper
1971	Charles Coody
1972	Jack Nicklaus
1973	Tommy Aaron
1974	Gary Player
1975	Jack Nicklaus
1976	Raymond Floyd
1977	Tom Watson
1978	Gary Player
1979	Fuzzy Zoeller
1980	Seve Ballesteros
1981	Tom Watson
1982	Craig Stadler
1983	Seve Ballesteros
1984	Ben Crenshaw
1985	Bernhard Langer
1986	Jack Nicklaus
1987	Larry Mize
1988	Sandy Lyle
1989	Nick Faldo
1990	Nick Faldo
1991	Ian Woosnam
1992	Fred Couples
1993	Bernhard Langer
1994	José María Olázabal
1995	Ben Crenshaw
1996	Nick Faldo
1997	Tiger Woods
1998	Mark O'Meara
1999	José María Olázabal
2000	Vijay Singh
2001	Tiger Woods
2002	Tiger Woods

Clubs

Players carry a range of clubs, each designed for different types of stroke. There are three main types of golf club.

- **Woods** Generally used for power shots, and, in spite of their name, usually made of metal. They have large heads and longer shafts than other clubs, and are numbered 1 to 5. No. 1, or the "driver," is used for the tee shot; any wood, including the driver, may be used for distance shots off the tee.
- **Irons** Numbered 1 to 9 and used for shorter precision shots. A no. 1 iron hits the ball lower and farther than a no. 2, which hits lower and farther than a no. 3, and so on. There are two other clubs known as wedges. They are the sand wedge for getting balls out of bunkers and the pitching wedge for chipping the ball up onto the green.
- **Putters** Used on the green for hitting the ball along the ground (putting) toward the hole. They are not numbered but there are many different designs.

Players can take a maximum of 14 clubs on a round (usually three or four woods, nine or ten irons and a putter). Clubs are carried by an assistant called a caddie.

LEGENDS

Tiger Woods
(1975-) American

Tiger Woods turned professional in 1996. In June 2000, he won the US Open by 15 strokes, the biggest margin ever in a Major tournament. In July of the same year, he won the US PGA Championship, making him the youngest player ever to have won all four of professional golf's Major championships.

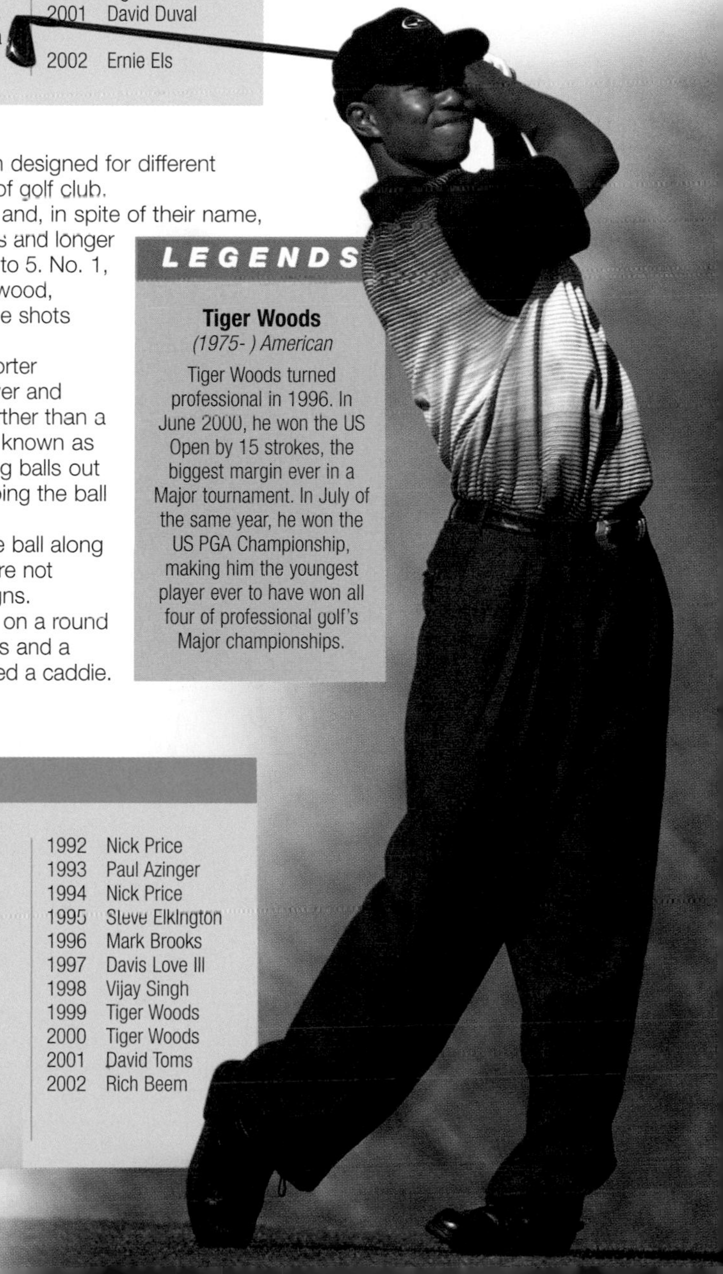

US PGA Championship

The first championship was held in 1916.

Year	Winner
1970	Dave Stockton
1971	Jack Nicklaus
1972	Gary Player
1973	Jack Nicklaus
1974	Lee Trevino
1975	Jack Nicklaus
1976	Dave Stockton
1977	Lanny Wadkins
1978	John Mahaffey
1979	David Graham
1980	Jack Nicklaus
1981	Larry Nelson
1982	Raymond Floyd
1983	Hal Sutton
1984	Lee Trevino
1985	Hubert Green
1986	Bob Tway
1987	Larry Nelson
1988	Jeff Sluman
1989	Payne Stewart
1990	Wayne Grady
1991	John Daly
1992	Nick Price
1993	Paul Azinger
1994	Nick Price
1995	Steve Elkington
1996	Mark Brooks
1997	Davis Love III
1998	Vijay Singh
1999	Tiger Woods
2000	Tiger Woods
2001	David Toms
2002	Rich Beem

Tennis

Tennis originated in the monasteries of 11th-century France, where the indoor game now known as real tennis was first played. The modern game of lawn tennis was not created until 1873 in England; its first championships were held at Wimbledon in 1877. The first international lawn tennis competition was the Davis Cup tournament, which started in 1900 and is played between national teams.

The aim of the game Tennis is played with a racket and a ball on an indoor or outdoor court between two opponents (singles) or two pairs (doubles). Points are scored by hitting the ball over the net into the receiving player's half of the court in such a way that it cannot be successfully returned.

Service The game begins with one player serving. He or she stands behind the baseline, tosses the ball into the air and strikes it into the receiver's side of the court. Servers have two chances to make a valid serve; if they fail, they lose the point – a double fault. Service alternates between players with each game.

Let If a serve touches the net before landing in the receiver's court, a let is called and the serve is replayed.

Strokes These include the forehand, backhand, lob, overhead smash (hit like a serve), drop shot and volley.

Scoring A game is played to four points, designated by the terms 15, 30, 40 and game. A player who does not score a point remains at zero or "love." If the score becomes 40-all, a "deuce" is called. A game must be won by two clear points, so play continues from deuce until one player leads by that margin.

Set and match Games are grouped into sets. To win a set, a player must have won six games and lead by at least two. If the score reaches six games each, a tiebreaker game may be played to determine the winner of a set. Each match has a maximum of five sets for men and three for women and mixed doubles.

Officials An umpire, referee, and line judges decide whether or not a ball is out of play. In professional tournaments, electronic devices may also be employed for this purpose.

Grand Slam title holders

A Grand Slam is achieved by holding all four Major titles – the Australian Open, French Open, Wimbledon and the US Open – at the same time.

Men's Singles	
Donald Budge	1938
Rod Laver	1962, 1969
Women's Singles	
Maureen Connolly	1953
Margaret Court	1970
Martina Navratilova	1983/4
Steffi Graf	1988, 1993/4

LEGENDS

Rod Laver

(1938-) Australian

Rod Laver won his first major title, the Australian open, in 1960. The following year, he won Wimbledon, then, two years later, became only the second male player ever to win a Grand Slam. He repeated the feat in 1969.

Wimbledon singles champions

Year	Men	Ladies
1950	Budge Patty	Louise Brough
1951	Dick Savitt	Doris Hart
1952	Frank Sedgman	Maureen Connolly
1953	Vic Seixas	Maureen Connolly
1954	Jaroslav Drobny	Maureen Connolly
1955	Tony Trabert	Louise Brough
1956	Lew Hoad	Shirley Fry
1957	Lew Hoad	Althea Gibson
1958	Ashley Cooper	Althea Gibson
1959	Alex Olmedo	Maria Bueno
1960	Neale Fraser	Maria Bueno
1961	Rod Laver	Angela Mortimer
1962	Rod Laver	Karen Hantze-Susman
1963	Chuck McKinley	Margaret Smith
1964	Roy Emerson	Maria Bueno
1965	Roy Emerson	Margaret Smith
1966	Manuel Santana	Billie Jean King
1967	John Newcombe	Billie Jean King
1968	Rod Laver	Billie Jean King
1969	Rod Laver	Ann Haydon-Jones
1970	John Newcombe	Margaret Smith Court
1971	John Newcombe	Evonne Goolagong
1972	Stan Smith	Billie Jean King
1973	Jan Kodes	Billie Jean King
1974	Jimmy Connors	Chris Evert
1975	Arthur Ashe	Billie Jean King
1976	Bjorn Borg	Chris Evert
1977	Bjorn Borg	Virginia Wade
1978	Bjorn Borg	Martina Navratilova
1979	Bjorn Borg	Martina Navratilova
1980	Bjorn Borg	Evonne Goolagong Cawley
1981	John McEnroe	Chris Evert Lloyd
1982	Jimmy Connors	Martina Navratilova
1983	John McEnroe	Martina Navratilova
1984	John McEnroe	Martina Navratilova
1985	Boris Becker	Martina Navratilova
1986	Boris Becker	Martina Navratilova
1987	Pat Cash	Martina Navratilova
1988	Stefan Edberg	Steffi Graf
1989	Boris Becker	Steffi Graf
1990	Stefan Edberg	Martina Navratilova
1991	Michael Stich	Steffi Graf
1992	André Agassi	Steffi Graf
1993	Pete Sampras	Steffi Graf
1994	Pete Sampras	Conchita Martinez
1995	Pete Sampras	Steffi Graf
1996	Richard Krajicek	Steffi Graf
1997	Pete Sampras	Martina Hingis
1998	Pete Sampras	Jana Novotna
1999	Pete Sampras	Lindsay Davenport
2000	Pete Sampras	Venus Williams
2001	Goran Ivanisevic	Venus Williams
2002	Lleyton Hewitt	Serena Williams

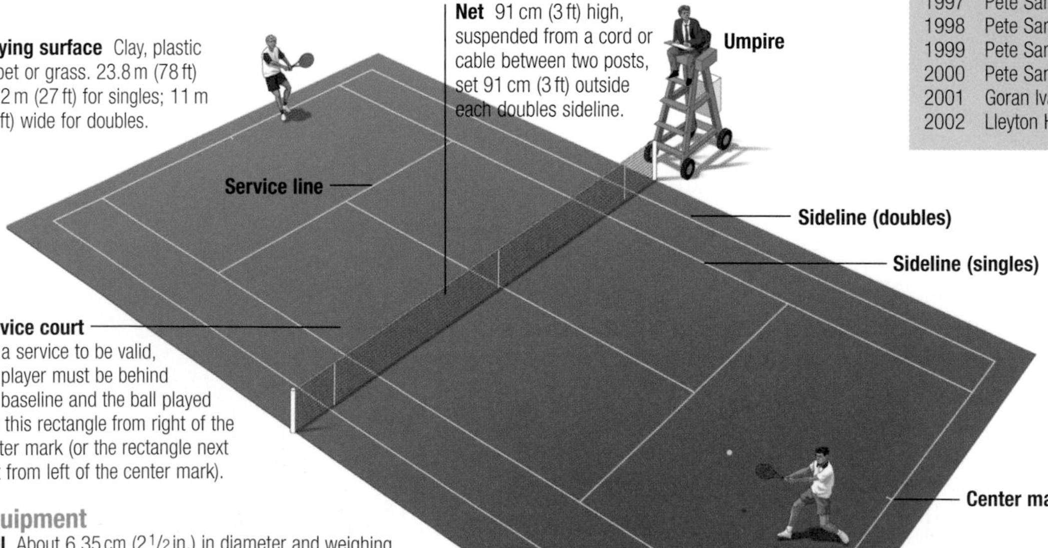

Playing surface Clay, plastic carpet or grass. 23.8 m (78 ft) x 8.2 m (27 ft) for singles; 11 m (36 ft) wide for doubles.
Net 91 cm (3 ft) high, suspended from a cord or cable between two posts, set 91 cm (3 ft) outside each doubles sideline.
Umpire
Service line
Sideline (doubles)
Sideline (singles)
Service court For a service to be valid, the player must be behind the baseline and the ball played into this rectangle from right of the center mark (or the rectangle next to it from left of the center mark).
Center mark
Baseline

Equipment

Ball About 6.35 cm (2 1/2 in.) in diameter and weighing approximately 56.7 g (2 oz), it is hollow, with a cover of wool and man-made fiber over inflated rubber.

Racket With a maximum length of 81.5 cm (32 in.), the oval head must not be more than 39.4 cm (15 1/2 in.) and 29.2 cm (11 1/2 in.) wide. It is usually strung with sheep gut or a synthetic material, such as nylon.

LEGENDS

Martina Navratilova

(1956-) Czech (American from 1978)

Martina Navratilova was the outstanding female player of the 1980s. Her power and athleticism were unprecedented in women's tennis. In all, Navratilova won 18 Grand Slam titles and 149 other singles titles during her career.

LEGENDS

Pete Sampras

(1971-) American

Pete Sampras is the most successful player in recent years. His victory in the 2000 Wimbledon men's singles was not only his seventh in that tournament, but also his 13th Major tournament title – an all-time men's record.

High-tech rackets

Graphite, titanium and glass fiber frames make modern tennis rackets much stronger than the wooden and metal ones they replaced. As a result, today's rackets can be strung much tighter, greatly increasing the speed of the ball.

Davis Cup

Year	Winning team
1970	United States
1971	United States
1972	United States
1973	Australia
1974	South Africa
1975	Sweden
1976	Italy
1977	Australia
1978	United States
1979	United States
1980	Czechoslovakia
1981	United States
1982	United States
1983	Australia
1984	Sweden
1985	Sweden
1986	Australia
1987	Sweden
1988	W. Germany
1989	W. Germany
1990	United States
1991	France
1992	United States
1993	Germany
1994	Sweden
1995	United States
1996	France
1997	Sweden
1998	Sweden
1999	Australia
2000	Spain
2001	France
2002	Russia

Squash

Squash was created at Harrow School, England, in the mid-19th century, and by the early 1900s, it was a favorite school game. The modern rules were not set until after World War I. Its popularity grew rapidly in the 1920s, when formal competitions were established.

Squash is played in an enclosed court between two players. One serves against the front wall and the other tries to return before the ball can bounce twice. Shots may be glanced off the back and side walls, as long as the ball reaches the front wall without first touching the ground or going above the front, side or back wall lines. Only the server wins points, the receiver having to win a rally to gain service.

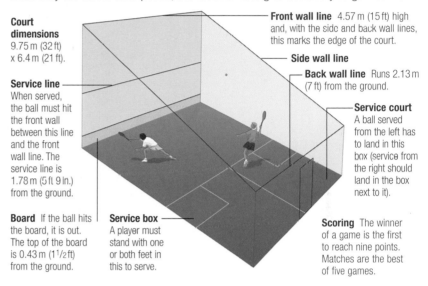

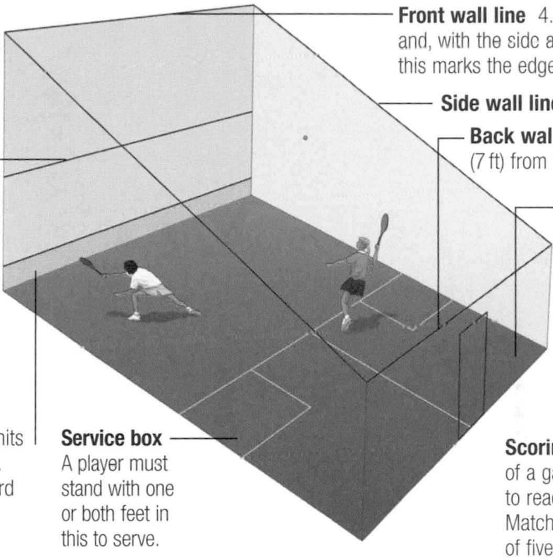
Court dimensions 9.75 m (32 ft) x 6.4 m (21 ft).
Front wall line 4.57 m (15 ft) high and, with the side and back wall lines, this marks the edge of the court.
Side wall line
Back wall line Runs 2.13 m (7 ft) from the ground.
Service line When served, the ball must hit the front wall between this line and the front wall line. The service line is 1.78 m (5 ft 9 in.) from the ground.
Service court A ball served from the left has to land in this box (service from the right should land in the box next to it).
Board If the ball hits the board, it is out. The top of the board is 0.43 m ($1^1/_2$ ft) from the ground.
Service box A player must stand with one or both feet in this to serve.
Scoring The winner of a game is the first to reach nine points. Matches are the best of five games.

Badminton

Badminton is a singles or doubles game played on an indoor court with rackets and a shuttlecock, or birdie. The object is to strike the birdie over the raised net and score points by grounding it in the opponents' half of the court or by forcing an error. As in squash, only the server can score points.

Equipment

Shuttlecock A half-sphere of cork or plastic, with a feather or nylon skirt.
Racket 66 cm (26 in.) long, and 21 cm ($8^1/_2$ in.) at the broadest point of the head.

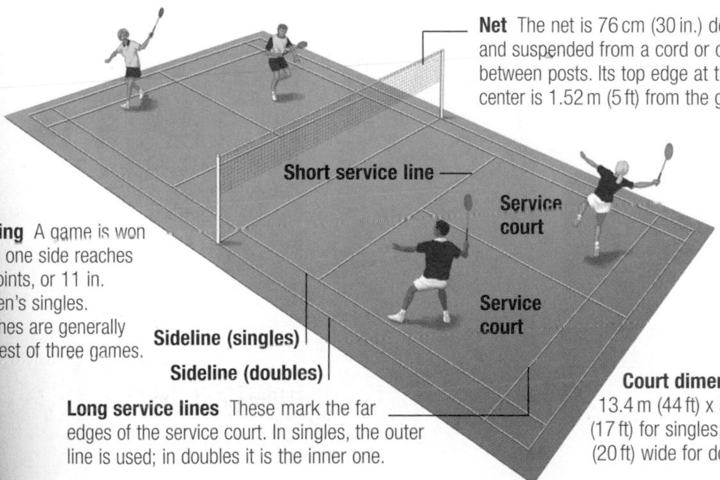
Net The net is 76 cm (30 in.) deep and suspended from a cord or cable between posts. Its top edge at the center is 1.52 m (5 ft) from the ground.
Short service line
Service court
Service court
Scoring A game is won when one side reaches 15 points, or 11 in women's singles. Matches are generally the best of three games.
Sideline (singles)
Sideline (doubles)
Long service lines These mark the far edges of the service court. In singles, the outer line is used; in doubles it is the inner one.
Court dimensions 13.4 m (44 ft) x 5.18 m (17 ft) for singles; 6.1 m (20 ft) wide for doubles.

The modern Olympics have been held every four years since 1896, except during the two World Wars. Here are highlights from the popular Summer Olympics.

1896 Athens

245 men from 14 nations competed. The **modern marathon** was born. **American students** dominated track and field.

Most medals
Gymnast **Hermann Weingärtner** (Germany) won three golds, two silvers and a bronze.

Local hero The first modern marathon was won, appropriately, by a Greek, Spiridon Louis.

1900 Paris

1319 people from 22 countries entered. The Games were eclipsed by the Great Exhibition. **Women competed** for the first time.

Most medals
Irving Baxter (US) won two golds and three silvers in track and field.

1904 St. Louis

687 competitors from 13 nations took part. 525 of the competitors were from the US and **some events included only Americans**.

Most medals
Anton Heida (US) won five golds and a silver in men's gymnastics.

1908 London

2035 men and women from 22 countries took part. The Games were marred by allegations of **bias by the British judges**, particularly against the American track and field team, which at one point threatened to withdraw.

Memorable event
Dorando Pietri, a sweetshop owner from Capri, Italy, collapsed four times just yards from the finish of the marathon and was helped over the line to win. Despite protests, he was disqualified.

Most medals
Mel Sheppard (US) won golds in three of the men's track and field events.

1912 Stockholm

2547 competitors from 28 countries took part. **Swimming and modern pentathlon** were included for the first time, and **gymnastics** became popular as a spectator sport, with 1000 competitors from 13 countries entering those events. **Electronic timing devices** were used for the first time.

Memorable event
Jim Thorpe (US) won gold in the pentathlon and decathlon, but was ordered to return his medals six months later when it transpired that he had been paid a small sum for playing baseball years before.

Most medals
Hannes Kolehmainen (Finland) won three gold medals, for the 5000 m, 10 000 m and the 8000 m cross-country.

1920 Antwerp

2669 competitors from 29 nations entered. Antwerp was chosen in honor of the Belgian people, who had lived under enemy occupation for four years of the First World War. **Germany, Austria, Bulgaria, Hungary and Turkey** were not invited.

Memorable event
Oscar Swahn (Sweden) became the **oldest Olympic medalist ever** when he won a silver in the running deer team shooting event (since discontinued) at age 72. Four years earlier, he had won gold in the same event, making him the **oldest Olympic gold medalist** as well. Both records still stand.

Most medals
Willis Lee (US) won five golds, one silver and one bronze in the shooting events.

1924 Paris

3092 people from 44 countries competed. The **Olympic motto** *citius, altius, fortius* ("faster, higher, stronger") was coined. French fans caused outrage by booing other countries' national anthems.

Memorable event
Swimmer **Johnny Weissmuller** (US) won gold medals in the 100 m and 400 m freestyle and 4 x 200 m freestyle relay events. He went on to win two more golds in the 1928 Amsterdam Olympics before achieving even greater fame as Hollywood's best-known Tarzan.

Most medals
Ville Ritola (Finland) won four golds and two silvers in distance running events. His teammate, **Paavo Nurmi**, won five golds.

1928 Amsterdam

3014 competitors from 46 countries took part. This was the first year that **women competed in track and field** events, although they had previously featured in tennis, golf, swimming, archery, fencing and yachting. **Germany** was invited to the Games for the first time since World War I.

Memorable event
Center-forward **Dhyan Chand** brought gold to the Indian men's field hockey team for the first time. Chand went on to win golds in 1932 and 1936; over the course of the three Olympics, his team scored 102 goals and conceded just three.

Most medals
Swiss gymnast **Georges Miéz** won three golds and one silver.

1932 Los Angeles

Just 1408 people from 37 nations competed as a result of the Great Depression. **Automatic timing devices** and the **photo-finish camera** were introduced, as were **podiums** for award ceremonies and the playing of **winners' national anthems**. The 50 km walk marked the entry of **walking** as an Olympic sport.

Memorable event
Mildred (Babe) Didrikson (US) was the star of the Games, winning gold in the javelin and 80 m hurdles and silver in the high jump. She later became one of the finest women golfers of all time and, in 1950, was voted the best woman athlete of the half-century.

Most medals
Male gymnast **István Pelle** (Hungary) won two golds and two silvers.

1936 Berlin

3738 competitors from 49 nations entered. The Berlin Games were the **first to be televised**.

Memorable event
Adolf Hitler tried to turn the Games into a Nazi propaganda event but was thwarted by the success of non-Aryan athletes. African-Americans took gold medals in every track event from 100 m to 800 m.

Most medals
Jesse Owens (US) won golds in the 100 m, 200 m, long jump and sprint relay.

Olympic flame Berlin's Games were the first to be preceded by the torch relay.

1948 London

4099 people from 59 countries took part. **Germany and Japan** were not invited, and the **USSR** did not send a team. Communist countries were involved for the first time and the London Games had the first **defections of participants**.

Memorable event
The moving **opening ceremony**, in which the teams of all 59 nations marched one after the other, did much to heal the wounds of war, particularly because the 1940 and 1944 games had been canceled because of the war.

Most medals
Thirty-year-old Dutch mother of two **Fanny Blankers-Koen** won golds in the 100 m and 200 m sprints, 80 m hurdles and 4 x 100 m sprint relay.

1952 Helsinki

4925 athletes from 69 nations entered. The **USSR** competed for the first time and, despite fears that there would be problems, Soviet and American athletes got along well. The Games were **superbly organized**, leading some commentators to suggest that they should always be held in Scandinavia.

Memorable event
Czech runner **Emil Zatopek** completed an incredible triple, taking gold in the 5000 m, 10 000 m and marathon. His wife, Dana, won a gold medal in the javelin.

Most medals
Gymnast **Maria Gorokhovskaya** (USSR) won seven medals (two golds and five silvers), the most ever won by a woman in a single Games.

1956 Melbourne

3342 competitors from 72 nations entered. This was the **first Olympics held in the Southern Hemisphere**. The **equestrian events** took place in Stockholm because of Australian quarantine laws.

Most medals
Gymnasts **Viktor Chukarin** (USSR) and **Ågnes Keleti** (Hungary) each won four golds and two silvers.

Dawn Fraser The Australian swimmer began her Olympic career by winning two golds and a silver.

1960
Rome

5348 athletes from 83 nations participated. Some events were held in **brand-new facilities**, others in **ancient stadia**. The wrestling, for instance, took place in the Basilica of Maxentius, where Romans had held similar contests 2000 years before. This was the last Games to which **South Africa** was invited for 32 years. It was followed by the first **Paralympics**.

Memorable event
Cassius Clay won boxing gold in the light-heavyweight division for the US. He changed his name to Muhammad Ali in 1964.

Most medals
Gymnast **Boris Shaklin** (USSR) won four golds, two silvers and a bronze.

1964
Tokyo

5140 competitors from 93 countries took part. These were the **first Games held in Asia**. Two new sports, **judo and volleyball**, were introduced, and three competitors received their **third successive Olympic golds**: swimmer Dawn Fraser (Australia), showjumper Hans Winkler (Germany) and sculler Vyacheslav Ivanov (USSR). **Don Schollander** (US) won four swimming golds.

Memorable event
The **Japanese** used the Games to **put the war behind them**. A student born near Hiroshima on the day the atomic bomb fell lit the flame.

Most medals
Larissa Latynina (USSR) won two golds, two silvers and two bronzes in the women's gymnastic events.

1968
Mexico City

5531 people from 112 nations competed. The choice of Mexico City was controversial because of the **high altitude**. The low air density meant that **world records in sprint events** tumbled, but distance running became more difficult. Sprinters John Carlos and Tommie Smith gave **black power salutes** on the podium.

Memorable event
Bob Beamon (US) beat the world long jump record by 55.25 cm (21 3/4 in.). Upon realizing what he had achieved, he suffered a seizure and collapsed but later recovered to claim his gold medal.

Most medals
Gymnast **Mikhail Voronin** (USSR) won two golds, four silvers and a bronze.

1972
Munich

7123 competitors from 121 countries entered. Full-scale **drug testing began**. The US lost the basketball final for the first time, to the USSR.

Hostage crisis Eleven members of the Israeli team were murdered by Palestinian terrorists.

Memorable event
Olga Korbut (USSR) charmed television audiences around the world on her way towards winning three gymnastics gold medals.

Most medals
American Swimmer **Mark Spitz** won seven golds – the most won by one person in a single Olympic Games.

1976
Montreal

6028 athletes from 82 countries entered. The Games were **boycotted by African nations** in protest of the International Olympic Committee's refusal to bar New Zealand, after a rugby tour of South Africa by its All Blacks team. Poor planning and corruption meant that the Games were a **financial disaster**.

Memorable event
Caribbean men took gold in the sprint events and 800 m. The 100 m was won by Hasely Crawford (Jamaica), the 200 m by Don Quarrie (Trinidad and Tobago) and the 400 m and 800 m by Alberto Juantorena (Cuba).

Most medals
Gymnast **Nikolai Andrianov** (USSR) won four golds, two silvers and a bronze.

1980
Moscow

5217 people from 80 countries competed. The **US, Canada, West Germany and Japan boycotted** the Games in protest at the Soviet invasion of Afghanistan. Despite this, more world records were set than in 1976. **East German women** won 11 golds on the running track, setting seven world records in the process.

Memorable event
British runners **Steve Ovett and Sebastian Coe** battled it out in the middle-distance finals. Ovett took gold and Coe silver in the 800 m before the honors were reversed in the 1500 m.

Most medals
Gymnast **Aleksandr Dityatin** (USSR) won eight medals (three golds, four silvers and a bronze), the most by any man in a single Games.

1984
Los Angeles

6797 athletes from 140 nations took part. There was a **boycott by the USSR** as revenge for the Moscow boycott four years earlier. The Games took place in the same stadium as in 1932. **Daley Thompson** (UK) won gold in the decathlon for the second Olympics in succession.

Memorable event
American athlete **Carl Lewis** delighted home fans by taking gold medals in four events; the 100 m, 200 m, long jump and 4 x 100 m relay.

Most medals
Male gymnast **Li Ning** (China) won three golds, two silvers and a bronze.

1988
Seoul

8465 people from 159 nations competed. **Florence Griffith-Joyner (Flo Jo)** won three golds and a silver for the US.

Fallen hero Canadian Ben Johnson won the 100 m in a world record time but was stripped of his gold three days later after testing positive for steroids.

Most medals
Swimmer **Matt Biondi** (US) won five golds, a silver and a bronze. Another swimmer, **Kristin Otto** (Germany), won six golds – the most by any woman in a single Olympics.

1992
Barcelona

9364 competitors from 169 countries took part. Former Soviet republics competed as the **Unified Team** under the Olympic flag, and came top of the medal table. A **united German team** took part, and **South Africa** returned to Olympic competition following the ending of apartheid.

Memorable event
Cyclist Chris Boardman (UK) unveiled a controversial **bicycle design**. Made from carbon fiber, titanium and aluminium, and with a one-piece frame and disc wheels, it was more aerodynamic than the traditional bicycles used by other competitors.

Most medals
Male gymnast **Vitaly Shcherbo** won six golds for the Unified Team.

1996
Atlanta

10 744 competitors from 197 countries entered. **Michelle Smith** (Ireland) became the first Irish multiple medal winner, with three swimming golds.

Memorable event
A **bomb** went off in the Centennial Olympic Park killing one person.

Most medals
Russian gymnast **Alexei Nemov** won two golds,

Michael Johnson
Completed an unprecedented double by winning the 200 m and 400 m sprints. He finished the 200 m final in a world record time.

2000
Sydney

10 651 athletes from 199 nations took part. The **triathlon** was held for the first time and **tae-kwon-do**, which had been a demonstration sport in the 1988 and 1992 Olympics, was first fought for medals. Aboriginal Australian **Cathy Freeman** thrilled the home crowd by winning the 400 m.

Memorable event
British rower **Steve Redgrave** became the first competitor to collect five consecutive Olympic gold medals.

Most medals
Alexei Nemov topped the tables again, matching his 1996 total of two golds, a silver and three bronzes.

2004
Athens

In 2004, the Olympics will return to the city of their birth. 296 events in 28 sports will be held (at the 1896 Games there were just 43 events in nine sports), and more than 11 000 athletes from 199 nations are expected to enter. The Games will run from **August 13 to 29** in facilities that will include a newly renovated Panathenaic Stadium – the place where the first modern Olympics were held.

see also

362 **Basketball**
363 **Hockey**
364-65 **Soccer**
373 **Skiing and Ice Skating**

Skiing

There are three basic kinds of skiing: Alpine (downhill and slalom racing), Nordic (cross-country skiing and ski jumping), and freestyle, which focuses on acrobatics.

Nordic skiing

Skiing originated in Scandinavia as a way of getting around in snow-covered landscapes. The modern sport of cross-country skiing developed from this tradition. The other Nordic skiing sport is ski jumping.

Cross-country skiing Competitors race on lightweight, narrow skis over distances of 10-50 km (6.2-31 miles), propelling themselves with the aid of poles. Events are contested in two disciplines: classical, in which skiers must push the toe ends of their skis almost diagonally outwards as they stride, and freestyle, in which no restriction is placed on the type of stride used.

Ski jumping In this sport, competitors glide down a prepared steep incline to a takeoff point up to 90 m (295 ft) high. They are judged on the length of their jump, style of execution, coordination and balance. Jumps of more than 150 m (490 ft) can be achieved. Ski-jumping skis are about 244 cm (8 ft) long, making them the longest variety of all. They are also wider and heavier than any other skis.

FREESTYLE SKIING

Freestyle skiing developed in the 1960s. There are three events: moguls, in which skiers race down a course with large bumps of hard-packed snow; aerials, in which they perform acrobatic jumps; and ballet, which takes place on smooth slopes to music. Mogul and aerial skiing are Olympic events.

LEGENDS

Jean-Claude Killy

(1944-) French

After winning the first World Cup for men in 1967 (and retaining the title the following year), Killy went on to duplicate Anton Sailer's achievement, winning all three skiing events at the 1968 Winter Olympics.

Pole position Jean-Claude Killy races for gold in the slalom event of the 1968 Grenoble Winter Olympics.

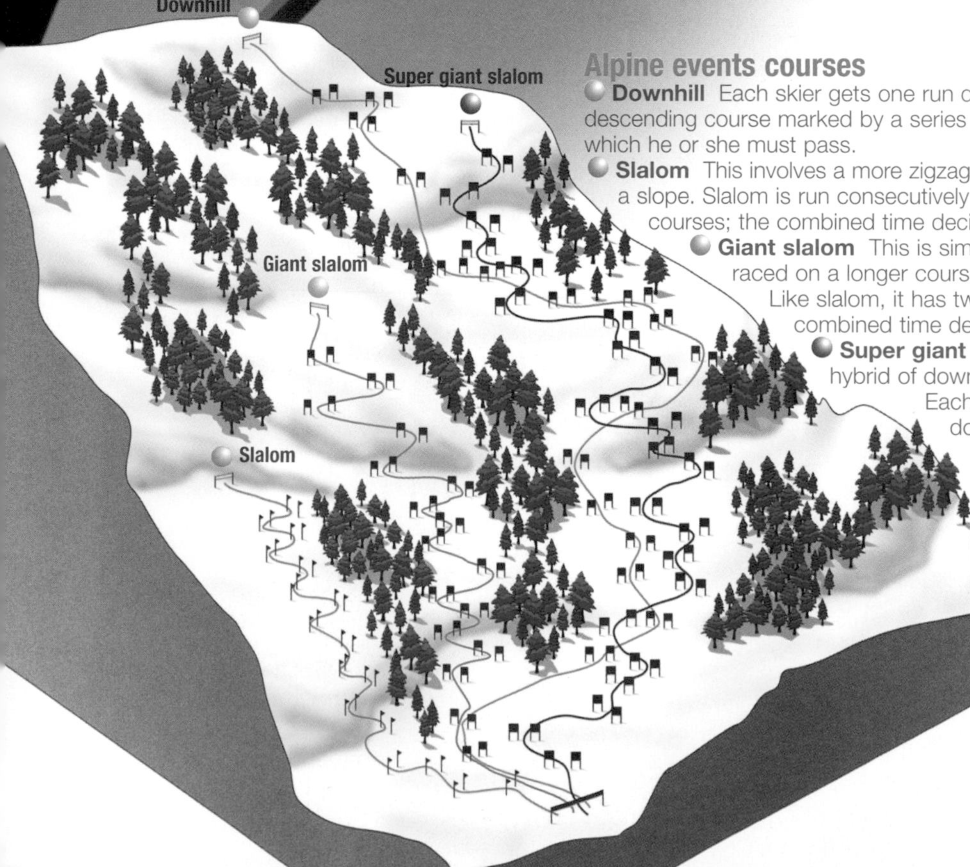

Alpine events courses

Downhill Each skier gets one run down a sharply descending course marked by a series of "gates" through which he or she must pass.

Slalom This involves a more zigzagging progression down a slope. Slalom is run consecutively over two different courses; the combined time decides the winner.

Giant slalom This is similar to slalom but is raced on a longer course with shallower turns. Like slalom, it has two runs. The best combined time determines the winner.

Super giant slalom This is a hybrid of downhill and giant slalom. Each skier gets one run down the course.

LEGENDS

Anton Sailer

(1935-) Austrian

At the 1956 Winter Olympics, 21-year-old Sailer became not only the youngest skier ever to win a gold medal in men's Alpine skiing but also the first to win all the Olympic Alpine skiing titles (downhill, slalom and giant slalom). By the end of the 1958 season, he had won seven world titles.

2002 Winter Olympics

Men's Alpine skiing

Event	Gold medalist	Nation	Time
Downhill	Fritz Strodl	Austria	1:39.13
Super giant slalom	Kjetil Andre Aamodt	Norway	1:21.58
Giant slalom	Stephan Eberharter	Austria	2:23.28
Slalom	Jean-Pierre Vidal	France	1:41.06
Combined	Kjetil Andre Aamodt	Norway	2:25.67

Women's Alpine skiing

Downhill	Carole Montillet	France	1:39.56
Super giant slalom	Daniela Ceccarelli	Italy	1:13.59
Giant slalom	Janica Kostelic	Croatia	2:30.01
Slalom	Janica Kostelic	Croatia	1:46.10
Combined	Janica Kostelic	Croatia	2:43.28

Ski jumping

Individual	Gold medalist	Nation	Points
70 m (K90)	Simon Ammann	Switzerland	133.5
90 m (K120)	Simon Ammann	Switzerland	281.4

Team

Large hill		Germany	974.1

BOBSLED

A crew of two or four take a running start with a sleigh and then sit in it and slide down an ice chute with banked walls, using steering and the distribution of their weight to help guide the sled in bends. Braking is against the rules. It is allowed only to stop the sled at the end of a run or to correct skids. The number of runs in a competition varies; the winning team is the one with the lowest combined time at the end. Courses are typically 1.2-1.5 km (0.75-1 mile) long.

LUGE

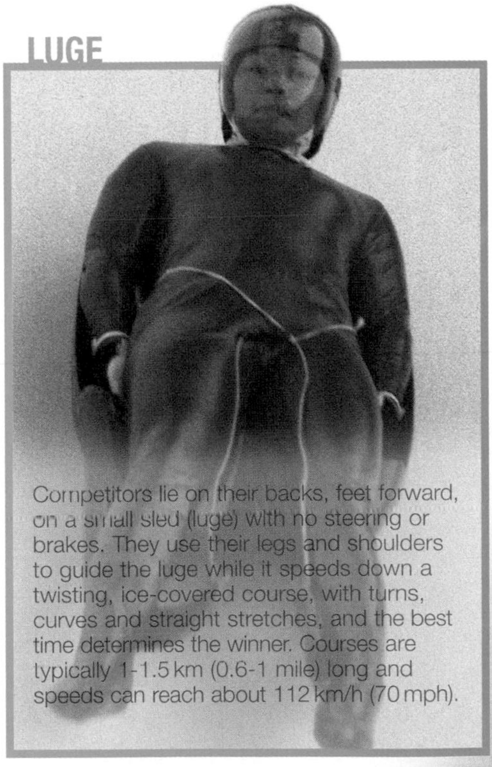

Competitors lie on their backs, feet forward, on a small sled (luge) with no steering or brakes. They use their legs and shoulders to guide the luge while it speeds down a twisting, ice-covered course, with turns, curves and straight stretches, and the best time determines the winner. Courses are typically 1-1.5 km (0.6-1 mile) long and speeds can reach about 112 km/h (70 mph).

Figure skating originated in Britain in the early 1700s, and speed skating appeared in the Netherlands at about the same time. The first ice-skating club was formed in Edinburgh, Scotland, around 1742. Artificial rinks did not appear until 100 years later.

Figure skating and ice dancing

Competiton is on rinks of 60 m x 30 m (196 ft x 98 ft).

Figure skating In Olympic competition, the men's, women's and pairs events each consist of a short program, during which skaters must perform eight different prescribed elements made up of jumps, spins, step sequences, spirals and linking movements, and a free-skating program, in which they select their own elements. The short program makes up a third of their final score; the free-skating program is two-thirds of it.

Ice dancing This pairs event has four parts, all set to music. Competitors must perform two compulsory dances (the rhythm and tempo of which are defined), one original dance (also to a prescribed rhythm) and one free dance (to music chosen by the pair). The free dance accounts for half of the final score.

Skating moves

There are several moves. The most common ones are

Axel A flying spin in which the skater skates forward into the takeoff (in all other flying spins the skater skates backward into the takeoff).

Lutz A flying spin with the takeoff from the back of one skate and the landing on the back of the other.

Camel spin A spin on one leg, with the other at a right angle to the ice.

Death spiral The man spins, holding his partner's hands as she glides on one skate in an almost horizontal position.

Speed skating

This racing on ice takes place over courses ranging from 500 m (546 yd) to 10 000 m (6.2 miles) in length. Speed skates have longer blades than figure or ice-dancing skates.

LEGENDS

Irina Rodnina *(1949-)* and **Aleksandr Zaitsev** *(1952-) Russian*

Rodnina and Zaitsev won Olympic gold in the figure-skating pairs twice, in 1976 and 1980, and topped the World Championships every year from 1973 to 1978. Rodnina also won an Olympic gold for the figure-skating pairs in 1972 with Alexei Ulyanov, and held the World Championship title with him from 1969 to 1972.

Winter Olympics

Figure skating 2002

Event	Gold medalist(s)	Nation
Men's singles	Alexei Yagudin	Russia
Women's singles	Sarah Hughes	US
Pairs	Jamie Salé & David Pelletier	Canada
	Elena Berezhnaya & Anton Sikharulidze	Russia
Ice dancing	Marina Anissina & Gwendal Peizerat	France

LEGENDS

Jayne Torvill *(1957-)* and **Christopher Dean** *(1958-) British*

This ice dancing pair won the World Championship four times in a row (1981-84), and the European championship in 1981, 1982, 1984 and 1994. In 1984, they won gold at the Olympics with an unprecedented perfect score of six for artistic impression from every judge.

Perfect start Torvill and Dean begin their gold-medal-winning performance at the 1984 Winter Olympics in Sarajevo.

The global economy

The global economy

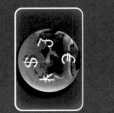

Money and markets

The evolution of currency and its trade in financial markets

Money evolved as a more convenient way of exchanging goods than barter. Early coins were valued for their precious-metal content. Today's currency is worth little in itself, but it is accepted as a means of payment by government order. New methods of payment led to the growth of the money markets, which trade items of monetary value, from currency and gold to shares in companies and bonds – certificates of debt.

Changing faces Since the Middle Ages, money has progressed from pure gold to plastic. A 16th-century Spanish doubloon contrasts with a Diner's Club card – the world's first credit card. In 1951, the Diner's Club issued the card to 200 customers, who could use it to pay at 27 restaurants in New York.

WHAT IS MONEY?

Money is a universally accepted medium of exchange for goods and services. It is quicker and easier to use than bartering. Barter is inefficient because it involves finding someone who is selling what you want and who wants what you have for sale. It also requires the creation of a complex system of comparative values among different types of goods.

Metal coins have endured as a medium of exchange since the 8th century B.C. because they have many convenient characteristics.

- Metal can be shaped into small denominations, making coins portable and suitable for small transactions.
- The precious metals originally used in coin manufacture gave them a high intrinsic value relative to their size and weight.
- Coins are durable, and recyclable – they can be melted down and recast.
- Branded metal disks are difficult to counterfeit.

For larger transactions, the exchange of paper money proved more convenient. Paper notes represented a promise by the issuer to pay the bearer a certain value in gold or silver and became widespread in the 18th century.

The link between hard currency and precious metal began to disappear after World War I. Gold exports had been restricted during the war, and natural resources were dwindling. Many bank clients did not require access to gold, and it became unnecessary for banks to maintain huge reserves to back up their currency. The "promise to pay" is no longer valid – most modern currency is not backed by precious metal. It derives its value from a fiat – a government order that declares it legal tender – and is known as fiat money.

Today, the purchase of goods and services does not rely on hard currency. Checks, originating from 17th-century banker's orders, and credit cards, a 20th-century invention, have made payment without cash easy and efficient.

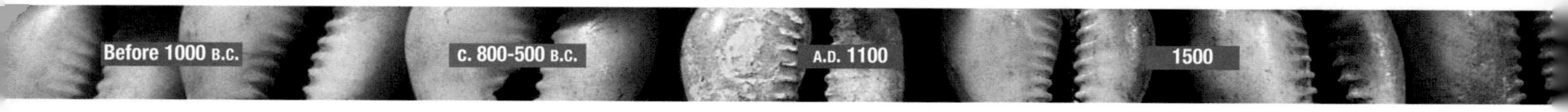

Before 1000 B.C.

Early money
Decorative tools and weapons and objects of religious and ceremonial significance are widely accepted as payment.

In Europe, metal rings and spirals are exchanged between traders.

In India, China and the Middle East, cowrie shells are exchanged as a form of payment. As trade develops, the use of cowrie shells circulates around Asia, Africa and the Pacific Islands.

c. 800-500 B.C.

Metal money
The first coins with values fixed by their country of issue appear. Chinese traders exchange copper disks. In Lydia (modern Turkey), merchants strike high-value coins from electrum, a gold-silver alloy.

7th century B.C. Aegean city–states issue precious-metal coins bearing state emblems.

6th century B.C. The first pure gold and silver coins, each with a guaranteed weight and stamped with the insignia of King Croesus, are produced in Lydia.

A.D. 1100

International systems
Bills of exchange – written promises to pay at a future date – are issued by merchants and banks to provide credit for trade. In France, bills of exchange are traded, a practice that contributes to the later emergence of the stock exchange.

1252 The city of Florence mints *fiorini d'oro* (gold flowers) – gold coins bearing the image of a lily. Their use in international trade makes them valuable across Europe. Outside Italy, they are known as florins.

1500

Capital markets
Joint-stock companies appear when multiple owners subscribe capital to fund a new business. The companies are chartered by European heads of state to explore and colonize new territory.

1555 English merchants trading in Russia form the first joint-stock company, The Muscovy Company. Each merchant owns a share of the company's assets and profits.

1600 The joint-stock East India Company is formed to trade in East and Southeast Asia.

The Big Mac index

In the 1980s, the *Economist* magazine launched the Big Mac index as a way of comparing the purchasing power of the world's currencies. A Big Mac is one of the few products that is identical the world over. In the US in April 2001, a McDonald's Big Mac cost $2.54. In Switzerland, the same burger cost the equivalent of $3.65; in Malaysia, it cost just $1.19. In other words, you could buy more for your dollar in Malaysia than in the US or Switzerland. If a currency has a higher purchasing power in its own country than elsewhere (making a Big Mac cheap), it is said to be undervalued: you need to spend more of it to buy the same thing in other countries. If the currency buys less in its own country than elsewhere (making a Big Mac expensive), it is overvalued.

The price of a Big Mac, April 2001
Showing percentage under or overvalued against US$

	US$	%
United States	*2.54*	*0*
Australia	1.52	–40
Canada	2.14	–16
China	1.20	–53
Denmark	2.93	+15
Euro area	2.27	–11
Japan	2.38	–6
Malaysia	1.19	–53
Russia	1.21	–52
Switzerland	3.65	+44
United Kingdom	2.85	+12

MONEY MARKETS

Institutions that buy and sell currency and short-term finance are known as money markets. Market dealers trade in gold bullion, foreign currency and short-term securities – documents that guarantee the later repayment of a debt or claim, such as bonds or stocks and shares.

Gold bullion market Bars or ingots of gold are mainly traded for use in the manufacture of coins, industrial components and jewelery. The major bullion markets are in Hong Kong, London and New York.

Foreign exchange market Foreign exchange dealers buy and sell currencies. The US dollar is the main medium of exchange: Currencies are exchanged for dollars, which are then exchanged for another currency.

Securities market The buying and selling of securities takes place in **stock exchanges**. Deals are administered by brokers, who buy and sell on behalf of clients and charge a commission for their services. The world's largest stock exchanges are in London, New York and Tokyo.

On-screen trading In 1983, the Toronto stock exchange introduced electronic trading, giving members instant access to trade information on computer screens. By 1985, Toronto had forged trading links across North America. The system was adopted worldwide, accelerating trade and widening its scope.

Key terms

- **Bonds** Certificates of government or corporate debt that will be repaid at a fixed interest rate after a fixed period of time.
- **Stocks and shares** Shares are portions of capital subscribed in return for part ownership of a company. Stocks are groups of shares; in Britain, the term can refer specifically to fixed interest loans made to companies, local authorities or governments.

FACT

The first stock exchanges appeared in Antwerp (1531), Hamburg (1558) and Amsterdam (1611). The London stock exchange opened in 1773, and New York's opened in 1817.

Valueless money In the 1920s, the German government printed money in an effort to fulfill wartime reparation payments. As the country's stock of currency rose, so did prices. In 1923, inflation reached a peak of 332 percent per month, rendering the German currency worthless.

see also
378-79 **Principles of economics**

1657

Banking and paper money
The Bank of Stockholm begins operating – the first bank to be founded with a lending department. In 1661, it issues Europe's first banknotes. In 1664, bad debts drive the bank into insolvency.

1668 The demise of the Bank of Stockholm leads to the formation of the world's first central bank – the state-owned Bank of Sweden.

1694 The Bank of England is founded and helps to establish the City of London as a center of global financial activity.

1700

Bursting bubble
Lack of regulation encourages French and British joint-stock companies to engineer wild speculation in their shares by promising rich rewards to investors.

1720 Britain's South Sea Company offers shares to the public. The company encourages rumors of enormous future profit, bribing politicians to promote the business. The share price rises from £128 in January to £1000 in August. In September, investors lose confidence in the deal – the bubble bursts and share prices crash.

1920s

Market crash
Easy credit in the US in the 1920s drives investors to borrow to buy stocks. Share values climb steeply.

1929 The US's central banking regulator, the Federal Reserve, brings the financial speculation to an end by tightening credit.

October 24, 1929: Black Thursday Investors lose confidence and begin selling shares; the following Tuesday, the market collapses. The US calls in its international loans, and European banks close, unable to fulfil their obligations. Private investors withdraw their savings, leading to a worldwide economic crisis.

1975

Deregulation
May 1 1975: May Day The New York stock exchange abolishes fixed commission charges for brokers, allowing them to negotiate competitive rates.

October 1986: Big Bang The London stock exchange abolishes fixed charges for brokers. Its unique system of jobbers (who buy and sell shares) and brokers (who liaise between jobbers and the public) ends when the two jobs are merged. This allows brokers to deal directly in shares, and promotes market growth.

Gold standard

Until 1937, the monetary systems of many countries followed a common standard, under which the basic unit of currency was equal to a fixed weight of gold. Each coin or banknote in circulation had to be backed by an equivalent value of gold kept in the vaults of the central bank. Gold had a common value in all countries, making the exchange of payments easier.

Britain introduced the gold standard in 1821. By 1900, most of the world's leading economies had joined. It was suspended during World War I and gradually abandoned after the Great Depression of 1929.

Economics investigates the production, distribution and consumption of wealth. Microeconomics looks at individuals, groups of consumers, companies and industries, and macroeconomics operates on a larger scale, studying the global economy and the complex internal and external interaction of countries or communities of states with common economic policies, such as the European Union.

The basic economic problems

At the heart of economics is the idea that economic resources (land, skilled workers, fuel supplies and so on) are finite, but people's wants are infinite. Moreover, the availability of some resources is uneven, so while populations in developed countries have plentiful food supplies, the people in many developing countries starve.

Supply and demand The allocation of scarce resources takes place largely in the market, which is not so much a place as an arrangement between people wanting to sell goods or services and those who want to buy them and who have an agreed means of exchange, such as money. The market is governed by the laws of supply and demand. Supply is the amount of a commodity that producers will supply at a certain price, and demand is the amount people are willing to buy at a given price. Producers can put an accurate price on the goods they sell by analyzing supply and demand.

Where supply meets demand The example below shows the supply and demand data for a motor company producing a new vehicle. Analysis of supply shows that at a price of $5000 each, the company can viably produce 400 000 vehicles; at a price of only $2000, the number of vehicles goes down to 100 000. Analysis of demand, by contrast, shows that a price of $5000 will attract only 200 000 customers, whereas a price of $2000 will attract 400 000. There is just one "equilibrium price": At $4000, the number of vehicles the company can economically produce at that price equals the number of vehicles customers are willing to buy at the same price.

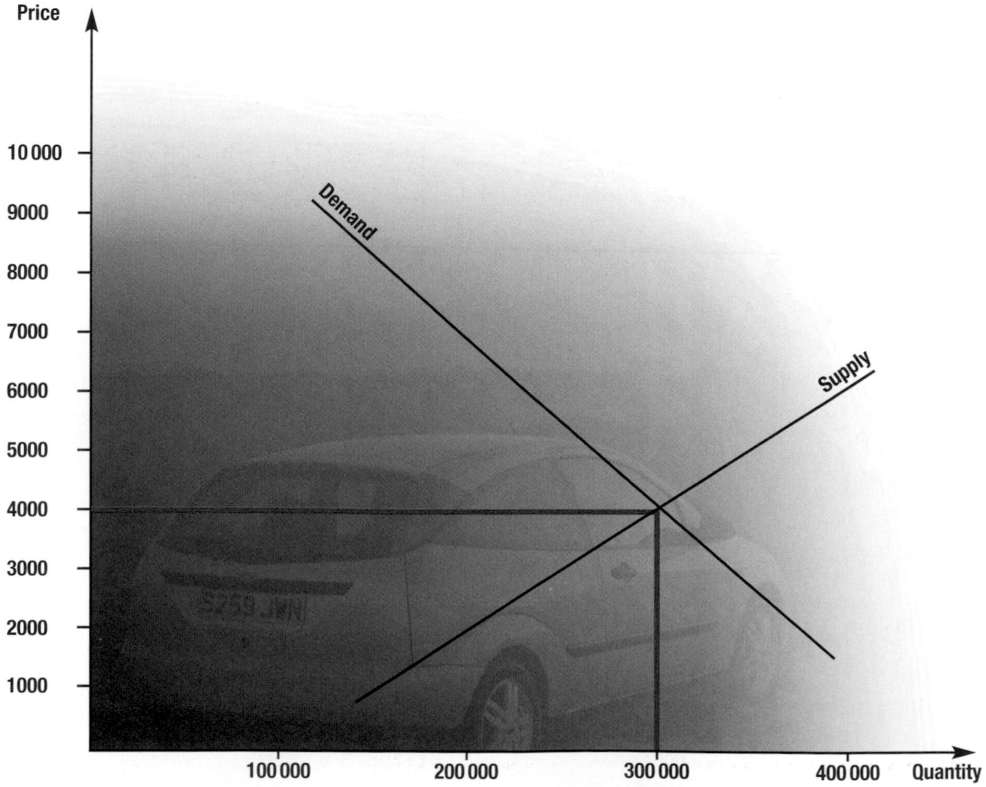

BOOM AND SLUMP

Free market economies experience fluctuations known as booms and slumps in economic activity. These often shadow each other in countries with similar economic systems. A boom is a long period of expansion – in which goods and services produced (the gross domestic product, GDP) increase – combined with a rise in employment, which raises the demand for goods. There are usually also increases in interest rates. The downside of a boom may be

- **Inflation** This is a general rise in prices over a long period, which may be caused by increased demand or by a rise in costs of the raw materials and labor. Typically, it would be followed by…
- **Deflation** If demand falls because it is satisfied or interrupted by some outside event, there may be a sustained fall in prices, which causes output to fall and unemployment to rise.
- **Stagflation** Employment may stagnate or fall while prices are rising. This occurred in Western economies during the 1970s.
- **Recession** This is a sudden, shortlived decline in economic activity. There may be a sharp fall in production and a rise in unemployment.
- **Depression** This is a more prolonged version of the latter, the most notable example of which was during the 1930s.

Fluctuations in GDP in the United States

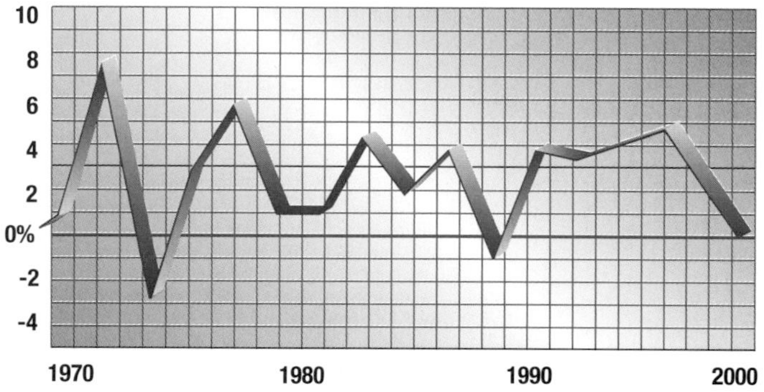

KEY TERMS

- **Capital** Any material wealth that can be used to produce further wealth (profit). Capital may exist in the form of money or property. Farms, factories, machinery, buildings and exchangeable notes and coins are all forms of capital.
- **Land** All natural resources owned by an individual, partnership, company or nation, including any part of the sea or outer space.
- **Money supply** An economy's stock of assets that can be exchanged for goods and services, including notes, coins, and bank deposits and accounts.
- **National income** The incomes of all residents of an economy added together.
- **Reserves** The total amount of foreign currency and gold kept by a country for the settlement of foreign debts in the eventuality of them being called in.

Key economic theories

Economic theorists do two things – analyze the system, like scientists, and come up with ways of changing and improving it, like politicians. The story of economic thought is a story of that process of observation and intervention. Some economists do one or the other, while some try to do both.

Mercantilism
Key idea: Government should intervene in economic activity to increase national wealth.

Laissez-faire
Key idea: The economy is self-regulating and government should leave it alone.

Malthusian economics
Key idea: Population increases faster than the increase in the output of food supplies.

Classical economics
Key idea: Knowledge of manufacturing and the role of labor are the key to understanding how society will develop.

Economic determinism
Key idea: The free market system is merely a stage in the process of economic development.

Macroeconomics
Key idea: Putting a figure on the output of all factories, industries and other work units can help decision-making by government.

Technostructure
Key idea: Modern economies produce ever larger corporations that operate as monopolistic power systems.

Monetarism
Key idea: An increase in the supply of money is a major cause of inflation.

Gerard Malines
(1586-1641)
English merchant and government official. Published *The Centre of the Circle of Commerce* (1623).
His arguments:
- Import tariffs should be raised and gold bullion exports banned.
- Government should control foreign currency dealing.

Adam Smith
(1723-90)
Scottish professor of philosophy. Published *An Inquiry into the Wealth of Nations* (1776).
His arguments:
- The self-interest of ordinary people can contribute to the wealth of the economy.
- Division of labor: Productivity is increased by specialization.

Thomas Malthus
(1766-1834)
English parson and mathematician. Published *Essay on the Principle of Population* (1798).
His arguments:
- An exploding population will result in mass starvation.
- Individual restraint on the size of families is the only way to avert catastrophe.

David Ricardo
(1772-1823)
European financial market trader. Published *Principles of Political Economy and Taxation* (1817).
His arguments:
- The value of all goods derives from the effort put into producing them.
- A theoretical model of the economy needs to be built in order to study it.

Karl Marx
(1818-83)
German journalist and philosopher. Published *Das Kapital (Capital)* (1867).
His arguments:
- Industrialization concentrates capital in the hands of fewer and larger firms.
- Workers are not paid; they choose to sell their services to an employer.

John Maynard Keynes
(1883-1946)
English mathematician. Published *A General Theory of Employment, Interest and Money* (1936).
His arguments:
- There is no inherent tendency for unemployment to fall.
- Spending on public works can generate an economic upturn.

John Kenneth Galbraith
(1908-)
American economist. Published *American Capitalism* (1952).
His arguments:
- Large companies become preoccupied with their own survival.
- Advanced economies create false demands.

Milton Friedman
(1912-)
American economist. Published *Inflation, Causes and Consequence* (1963).
His arguments:
- Control of the money supply is needed to control inflation.
- High pay is industry's reward to risk-takers.

see also
376-77 **Money and markets**

TYPES OF ECONOMIC SYSTEM

Economies are classified according to whether a free market economy operates or whether there is state intervention. In practice, most countries' economies have a degree of both.

- **Free market economy** Minimal government control. The laws of supply and demand determine how the country's resources are allocated and to whom. This system is also called "capitalism" because capital may be owned and controlled by any individual.
- **Mixed economy** An active private sector coexists with a degree of central planning. Entrepreneurs produce and sell goods according to the laws of supply and demand and may own capital and employ workers. The state also owns capital and may own and operate industries or sectors, such as transportation, education or the health system.
- **Planned economy** All economic resources – land, property, and capital – are owned by the state. The government plans how these resources, including labor, will be allocated, what farmers and factories will produce, and how and to whom the goods they produce will be distributed. This type of economy is called "communist" because all capital is communally owned.

Estimated state intervention, percent

Economic activities

People produce wealth by selling goods or services. Economists group economic activities into three sectors (below). Most developing economies rely heavily on one primary-sector activity, but advanced economies range across all three.

Primary sector	Agriculture Fishing Mining and quarrying
Secondary sector	Manufacturing Construction Energy and water
Tertiary sector	Services (insurance, distribution, transportation, education, health care)

The world produces enough food for everyone to receive an adequate supply, but food shortages and famines still occur. The main causes include overpopulation, particularly in India and China; drought, which has repeatedly occurred in sub-Saharan Africa; and war. Famines induced by human conflict have provoked international action to alleviate hunger, made possible by new agricultural practices and improvements in global communication.

THE GREEN REVOLUTION

Hunger became a global issue in the wake of the World Wars. International armed conflict disrupted food supplies, highlighting the need for an agency to ensure that every country could meet its food requirements. In 1945, the United Nations' Food and Agriculture Organization (FAO) was established with the intention of raising levels of food production and nutrition worldwide.

A new initiative

An acceleration in population growth after World War II reached its peak in the early 1960s. In 1963, the FAO launched the Green Revolution, aiming to provide enough food to accommodate future population expansion. They developed higher-yielding varieties (HYVs) of grains such as rice, wheat and corn through selective breeding (interbreeding different varieties to encourage desirable qualities). HYVs produced three crops annually on the same land. Farmers were also encouraged to use high levels of fertilizers and pesticides to improve yields.

By the 1980s, wheat and rice yields had increased dramatically; some developing countries produced surpluses for the first time. The increased income led to the mechanization of more farms, further increasing yields. Agrochemical companies making fertilizers and pesticides grew into large businesses.

Human intervention Cross-fertilizing strains of rice improves the crop's yield and disease resistance.

The disadvantages

Overall, wealthier farmers benefited from the initiative more than poorer ones, who were unable to afford the new HYV seeds, fertilizers and pesticides. Mechanization led to unemployment, and repeated cropping damaged the soil. Chemical fertilizers and pesticides were found to be toxic to workers and caused pollution. Some authorities believe the answer to world food shortages now lies in a new revolution based on genetically modified (GM) crops.

Genetically modified crops

Advances in biotechnology have made it possible to alter the genes of a plant so that it exhibits a particular characteristic. The desired gene is taken from one organism and inserted into another organism. For example, a gene conferring resistance to an insect pest can be transferred from a bacterium to corn.

Advantages

- Disease-resistant and pest-resistant GM crops reduce the need for chemical sprays.
- Crops are more productive, and the produce has a longer shelflife.

Disadvantages

- The long-term effects on humans and the environment are unknown.
- The developing world, which would benefit the most from GM crops, cannot afford them.
- GM crops decrease biodiversity.

Natural adaptation Several natural varieties of Andean corn (below) arose from the plant's adaptations to the diverse climates of the region, providing a rich resource for selective breeding.

Global Calorie consumption

According to the United Nations, an average adult should consume a minimum of 2400 Calories per day to lead a healthy, active life. Those who are more active or live in colder climates require more Calories than those who are less active or live in the tropics. In countries where the average daily consumption is 2000 Calories or less (2000 Calories is equivalent to 2.2 kg/5 lb of potatoes or 1.4 kg/3 lb of rice), the majority of the population is chronically malnourished. About 800 million people in the developing world do not get enough to eat. In the developed world, about 34 million people have poor diets and unreliable food supplies.

Calories consumed per day per person

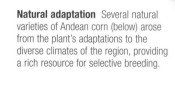

Worst famines of the 20th century

Most of the worst famines of the last century had man-made causes. Although crop failure and distribution problems were contributing factors, lack of food has usually been connected to the disruptions to agriculture caused by unsuccessful government policies or war.

1921-23	**Russia**	The effects of a drought are exacerbated by the Bolshevik government, which orders the surrender of rural grain supplies for consumption in the cities. Poverty and food shortages lead to the deaths of 6 million peasants.
1933-38	**Russia**	From 1929 to 1933, Stalin orders small farms to group into collectives, which are forced to supply grain to the government at low prices. Famine follows, resulting in 5 million deaths in the Caucasus and Ukraine.
1943	**Bengal**	As a result of wartime food shortages after the Japanese conquest of Burma,1.5 million people die.
Late 1940s	**China**	Drought coupled with the disruptions caused by civil war between the Communists and Nationalists kills about 5 million people.
1958-61	**China**	About 20 million die as a result of Mao Tse-Tung's "Great Leap Forward," in which nationalization of all farms and experimental systems for planting crops fail to produce results.
1967-70	**Nigeria**	A million people starve to death during civil war in the province of Biafra.
1984	**Ethiopia**	Since 1975, when the state took over all land ownership, peasants have been forced to sell grain to the government at below market prices. Harvests decline, and drought finally brings famine, killing nearly a million.

Organic farming

Organic farming aims to produce food without the use of agrochemicals and with minimal damage to the environment. Soil is fertilized with manure or organic compost. Crop rotation techniques and natural pest-eating predators are used to minimize plant diseases and pest damage.

Advantages
- Improves soil structure
- Reduces pollution
- Benefits wildlife

Disadvantages
- Crop yields are lower than those of conventional farms
- Produce is expensive
- Natural pest control is not effective in tropical climates

see also
382-83 **Fruits of the earth**
384-85 **Breeding and rearing**
438-39 **Inherited characteristics**

Fruits of the earth ▶ The crops that feed the world

Plants have been cultivated as food for about 10 000 years. Until recently, however, the diet of a particular region was more or less based on what grew under local climate and soil conditions. In the 20th century, science, along with a revolution in communications and transportation, has created a lucrative global market in fruit and vegetables. Almost anything is now available anywhere at any time – for a price.

Roots

The swollen, starchy roots, or tubers, of potato, sweet potato and yam plants play a major role both as cash crops in the world economy and in providing basic nourishment for growing populations.

Weights are in metric tons.

Potatoes First cultivated by the people of the Andes in South America, they were brought to Europe in the 16th century. By the 19th century, they had become a staple food from Ireland to Siberia.

World production, 2000:
308.2 million metric tons

Sweet potatoes A native of tropical America, they are a food staple in the southern United States, where they are also fed to livestock. In Japan they are used to make alcohol.

World production, 2000:
141.1 million metric tons

Yams The edible tubers of various tropical vines belonging to the genus *Dioscorea*, they are eaten as vegetables in the tropics. In eastern Asia, they are used for medicinal purposes, such as helping digestion.

World production, 2000:
37.8 million metric tons

Fruit

Fruit is cultivated commercially in most climate zones, from tropical to cool temperate. It is an important source of vitamins and minerals.

Weights are in metric tons.

Apples Originally from Afghanistan, apples are now grown in most temperate regions of the world. A large part of the European crop is used for making cider.

World production, 2000:
60 million metric tons

Bananas Now grown in tropical climates from Africa to the West Indies to Taiwan, bananas probably originated in Southeast Asia. Plants bear up to 200 fruits.They are harvested while still green and ripen later.

World production, 2000:
58.7 million metric tons

Tomatoes Native to South America, tomatoes were once thought to be poisonous and until the 18th century, were grown only for decoration. They are now cultivated worldwide, often under glass.

World production, 2000:
100.8 million metric tons

Grains

Grains have been cultivated as a staple food since prehistoric times, with stalks and straw used for fodder. They are largely grown in temperate zones with moderate rainfall.

Weights are in metric tons.

Wheat The cultivation of wheat can be traced back to ancient Egypt. The soft grains are used to make flour for bread, and flour from the harder, glutinous grains makes pasta, semolina and breakfast foods.

World production, 2000:
580 million metric tons

Rice For about half the world's population, rice is the main source of nourishment. This native of Southeast Asia needs warm, wet conditions.

World production, 2000:
597.2 million metric tons

Corn Corn is native to North America. It needs a sunny growing climate. It can be eaten as a vegetable, used for oil and ground to make cornstarch.

World production, 2000:
589.3 million metric tons

Legumes

Legumes are the edible seeds of leguminous plants, one of the historic staple foods in Asia. They are increasingly used worldwide as part of a vegetarian diet because of their high protein content.

Weights are in metric tons.

Lentils Native to southern Asia, lentils are one of the oldest known foods. Archaeologists have found them discarded at Bronze Age sites. They are widely used in African, Indian and Middle Eastern cooking.

World production, 2000:
3.2 million metric tons

Peas The small, round, green seeds of the pea plant are grown throughout the temperate regions of the world. There are a number of varieties, some of which have edible pods.

World production, 2000:
17.9 million metric tons

Beans An important source of protein, some, such as green beans, have edible pods; others, such as kidney and fava beans, have edible seeds. Many are preserved by drying.

World production, 2000:
23.4 million metric tons

Other major crops

In addition to the main staples mentioned above, there is an array of other important crops that are vital to the economies of the various countries that cultivate them.

Weights are in metric tons.

Coconuts The milk contained in the coconut shell is used in cooking and as a drink, and the flesh is eaten. Coir, used in matting, comes from the husk, and chopped shell is used as a soil cover by gardeners.

World production, 2000:
58.4 million metric tons

Sugar The world's major source of sugar is sugar cane, a giant tropical grass. The tuberous sugar beet is the main native source of sugar in colder, temperate climates.

World production, 2000:
1531.7 million metric tons

Cocoa beans The seeds of the tropical cacao tree are roasted and ground to make cocoa powder, from which chocolate is made. The Aztecs introduced it to the Spanish in the 16th century.

World production, 2000:
3.1 million metric tons

Top producers

The figures given below are for the year 2000 and include crops for both home consumption and export. Many third-world countries are concentrating increasingly on exports. This often means that the best land is reserved for growing high-priced "luxury" produce to sell to the West. Hopefully, this should generate a healthy profit plus sufficient money to buy any necessary staples that can no longer be homegrown. Frequently, however, the focus on cash crops leads to a deterioration in the local diet.

Coffee (million metric tons)		Corn (million metric tons)		Rice (million metric tons)		Sugar (million metric tons)		Tea (million metric tons)		Wheat (million metric tons)	
Brazil	2.1	US	253.2	China	198.7	Brazil	19.2	India	0.9	China	109.7
Colombia	0.6	Brazil	32.0	India	129.0	EU	17.9	China	0.7	EU	103.8
Indonesia	0.5	Mexico	18.8	Indonesia	50.8	India	14.3	Kenya	0.3	US	69.4
Vietnam	0.4	France	16.4	Vietnam	30.5	China	8.9	Sri Lanka	0.3	India	65.9
Mexico	0.3	Argentina	16.0	Bangladesh	29.8	US	7.2	Turkey	0.2	Russia	27.0

Grapes The green and purple berries of *Vitis vinifera* have been cultivated in the warmer parts of southern Europe and the Middle East for thousands of years. The bulk of the crop is used in making wine.

World production, 2000:
62.3 million metric tons

Oranges Originating in Southeast Asia, oranges first came to Europe in the Middle Ages. They grow well in the tropical and subtropical regions of the Americas, the Mediterranean, Australia and South Africa.

World production, 2000:
66.1 million metric tons

Olives Prized for their fruit and oil, olives have been grown in the eastern Mediterranean region for at least 3000 years. The countries around the Mediterranean are still the leading producers.

World production, 2000:
13.7 million metric tons

Oats Higher in fat and protein than other grains, oats grow well in the cool regions of Russia and North America. They are used for breakfast cereals and as an ingredient in processed foods, such as peanut butter.

World production, 2000:
26 million metric tons

Barley First grown in ancient Egypt, barley is now mostly grown in Europe. It is one of the most hardy of grains. It is a basic ingredient of malting and brewing: Over 10 percent of the world's output is used in this way.

World production, 2000:
132.9 million metric tons

Rye A cold-resistant grain, rye is native to northern Europe, where it is grown as animal fodder. It is also used to make "black" breads, flakes for breakfast cereal and with barley to make rye whiskey.

World production, 2000:
20 million metric tons

see also

384 85 **Breeding and rearing**

Soy beans These versatile beans have a high protein content. They can be eaten as a vegetable; used to produce cooking oil, flour, soy "milk" or meat-substitute, or fermented for soy sauce.

World production, 2000:
161 million metric tons

Peanuts Also known as groundnuts, peanuts are native to tropical South America, and are a concentrated source of fat, protein and calories. The largest producers are the US, India, China and West Africa.

World production, 2000:
34.5 million metric tons

Chickpeas Native to Asia, but now widely grown elsewhere, chickpeas are also known as gram or garbanzo. They are usually sold in dried form. Chickpeas can also be ground and made into flour.

World production, 2000:
8.8 million metric tons

FACT In Brazil, a motor fuel called bagasse is derived from sugar.

Coffee Seeds from trees of the *Coffea* species are roasted to make coffee beans. Coffee drinking originated in Arabia and was introduced into Europe in the 17th century.

World production, 2000:
7.1 million metric tons

Tea The drink is made from the dried leaves of the *Camellia sinensis* shrub, widely cultivated in eastern Asia. The drink was introduced into Europe from China in the 17th century.

World production, 2000:
2.9 million metric tons

Pepper Pepper grows on a climbing vine native to India's Malabar coast. From classical times, it was traded with Europe, where its value was so great that it was used as a medium of exchange.

World production, 2000:
248 570 metric tons

Vanilla Used for flavoring, vanilla extract comes from the pods of tropical climbing orchids, native to Central America. The Spanish brought it to Europe from Mexico.

World production, 2000:
5312 metric tons

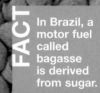

Livestock provides mankind with food, clothing and muscle power. Scientific breeding and advances in veterinary medicine are now helping to create more profitable animals, but there can be an unforeseen price to pay for this in the form of poorer quality meat and the spread of deadly disease across species.

Cattle

Beef cattle Because beef cattle are bred for meat production, they have heavy, well-developed muscle tissue and need large bones to support it. They are particularly big around the loins and hindquarters, where the meat of greatest financial value is found.

- **Aberdeen Angus** The black, heavily built Aberdeen Angus breed originated in Scotland. It is widely reared for its high quality meat.
- **Beefmaster** A Brahman-Hereford-Shorthorn crossbreed, the Beefmaster was first bred in Texas in 1908. Red, often with white markings, it is hardy, fertile and gives low-fat meat.
- **Brahman** Mainly farmed for cross-breeding. Brahman cattle are sacred to Hindus, who use them only for milk.
- **Brangus** A Brahman-Aberdeen Angus crossbreed, the Brangus was bred to be fertile and hardy by the United States Department of Agriculture in 1932. It is black and has no horns.
- **Charolais** The French Charolais breed is frequently used for crossbreeding. Most are white or pale cream, with an occasional black marking.
- **Chianina** Originally bred as draft animals in Tuscany, Chianina are particularly good meat producers. They are white or light gray.
- **Hereford** Being hardy and quick to mature makes the Hereford a popular breed. It is red and white.
- **Simmenthal** Red with white markings, the Swiss Simmenthal breed is used extensively for crossbreeding.

Dairy cows These produce 10-15 liters (2.2-3.3 gallons) of milk each day for about ten months after the birth of a calf. Unlike beef cattle, they are tall and fine-boned with large udders.

- **Ayrshire** The heavy-set Scottish Ayrshire has a very high milk yield. It is red or brown with white markings.
- **Brown Swiss** Only classified as a dairy breed in the US, the Brown Swiss cow is reared elsewhere for its rich, dense meat. It ranges from milky to dark, dusky brown.
- **Holstein** Usually with black and white markings, the Holstein is a native of the Netherlands. It gives high yields of milk and butterfat.
- **Guernsey** Fawn with white markings, the Guernsey cow produces milk that is especially high in butterfat.
- **Jersey** Milk from Jersey cows contains 50 percent more cream than that from other breeds. Coloring ranges from light grey to dark fawn.

Milk and meat Some breeds of cattle are good for both meat and milk. In some cases, they give high milk yields when reared in one part of the world, but are better at developing muscle for beef under different conditions.

- **Milking Shorthorn** Red with a few white markings, Milking Shorthorns are highly fertile and long-lived.
- **Red Poll** Red or cream-colored with no horns, the Red Poll was first bred in England in the 1860s.

The versatile cow Although cattle are reared primarily for food, there are a number of valuable by-products.

- **Beef tallow** provides glycerine for lipstick and hand creams and is an ingredient of shampoos, other cleaning agents and antifreeze.
- **Bonemeal,** made of ground up bones and hooves, is no longer used as fodder in most countries but can be used as a fertilizer by gardeners on their own property, for example.
- **Casein** is the main protein in milk, and the chief ingredient in cheese. It is also used in cosmetics, paint and glue and as a protein supplement to treat malnutrition. When mixed with rennin, an enzyme, it can be used to make plastic objects such as buttons.
- **Gelatin,** made from hide and bone, is used as a setting agent in cooking, such as in preparing mousses, gelatin molds or jam. Photographic film also contains gelatin, and pills and capsules are often coated with it.
- **Glue** is made from collagen, a mixture of bone and tissue.
- **Leather** includes soft, fine calfskin and the tougher hides, which are used to make durable goods such as the soles of shoes.

Beef facts

Biggest beef producers (1999)

		thousand metric tons
1	US	12050
2	European Union	7609
3	Brazil	6182
4	China	4674
5	Argentina	2650

Biggest beef exporters (1999)

		thousand metric tons
1	Australia	1289
2	US	1141
3	Brazil	615
4	European Union	600
5	Canada	540

Dairy facts

Biggest dairy product producers (1999)

		thousand metric tons
1	European Union	121078
2	US	77773
3	India	37750
4	Russia	32415
5	Brazil	22604

Biggest consumers of milk (1999)

		gallons per capita
1	South Africa	180
2	Finland	48
3	Canada	47
4	Ireland	38
5	Sweden	35

Sheep

It is estimated that there are about 1.2 billion sheep worldwide. In Australia, they outnumber humans by about ten to one. Breeds are classified according to whether they have fine, medium or coarse wool.

- **Cheviot** Large, with a white face and black muzzle, the Cheviot is a Scottish breed. It produces prime quality lamb and especially strong wool, which is often blended with other yarns for durability.
- **Columbia** Originally from the US, Columbia sheep are a Rambouillet-Lincoln crossbreed. They have large frames and white faces. Their fleece can weigh up to 7 kg (16 lb).
- **Hampshire** The large-framed, white-faced Hampshire breed is mainly reared for its meat and for crossbreeding.
- **Karakul** A native of Asia, Karakuls produce quality meat and coarse, brown or gray wool used in carpets.
- **Lincoln** With the longest hair of any sheep breed, the fleece from a Lincoln can weigh over 9 kg (20 lb). But the wool is coarse and only suitable for making carpets.
- **Merino** First bred in Spain in the 12th century, Merino sheep produce fine wool fibers of very high quality. The white fleece can weigh up to 5 kg (11 lb).
- **Rambouillet** Largest of the fine wool breeds of sheep, the Rambouillet originated in France. The soft, white fleece can weigh up to 8 kg (18 lb).
- **Southdown** Small, with brown markings on the face and legs, Southdown sheep were first bred in England. They mature early, producing fleeces that can weigh up to 3 kg (7 lb).

Lamb and wool facts

Biggest lamb producers (1999)

		thousand metric tons
1	China	1250
2	European Union	1 058
3	Australia	608
4	New Zealand	498
5	Pakistan	301

Biggest wool producers (1998)

		thousand metric tons
1	Australia	700
2	China	277
3	New Zealand	261
4	Uruguay	78
5	Argentina	68

Pigs

Pigs are farmed in almost all parts of the world but not in Muslim or Jewish communities.

- **Berkshire** An English breed, the medium-sized Berkshire is black with a white face, tail tip and feet. Its meat is sold as pork and processed into bacon.
- **Duroc** Originally bred in the US in the late 19th century, the hardy Duroc gives high quality pork and lard. Coloring varies from light yellow to dark red.
- **Hampshire** Black with a white "belt" across its forelegs and shoulders, the medium-weight Hampshire has a distinctive long body.
- **Yorkshire or Large White** A large, pale animal, sometimes with dark markings, the Yorkshire is an English-Chinese crossbreed. It is a major provider of pork and bacon and is frequently used for crossbreeding.

The profitable pig
Pigs grow quickly and provide a wide range of meat and other products.

- **Bacon** is fatty meat from the back and sides that is salted and often smoked.
- **Bristles** are used to make paint brushes.
- **Lard**, a soft, white fat, is widely used for cooking.
- **Pigskin** is used for high quality leather goods.

Pig facts

Biggest pork producers (1999)

		thousand metric tons
1	China	39 858
2	US	8 785
3	Germany	3 940
4	Spain	2 900
5	Brazil	1 752

Biggest pork exporters (1999)

		thousand metric tons
1	Denmark	1230
2	Netherlands	1164
3	Belg/Lux	647
4	France	570
5	Canada	502

Chickens

The recognized types are American, English, Mediterranean, and Asiatic; all the common breeds are variations of these four. There are more than 5 billion commercially kept chickens worldwide, the majority of which are reared for meat production.

- **Cornish** The Cornish breed is often used in crossbreeding to produce meaty birds.
- **Leghorn** The Italian Leghorn breed is one of the most prolific egg-layers.
- **New Hampshire** A meaty bird, the New Hampshire is also a good producer of eggs.
- **Rhode Island Red** This North American breed is one of the best-known chickens, valued for its high-quality meat.

see also
382-83 **Fruits of the earth**

The development of motorized road transportation was one of the defining features of the 20th century. It brought unprecedented mobility to millions and created a huge industry out of the inventions of workshop pioneers. The first internal combustion engines were built to power factory machines. When they were fitted to a bicycle and to a four-wheeled carriage, the results were the first motorcycle and the "horseless carriage" – the first automobile.

THE AUTOMOBILE MATURES

The automobile was not a single development but the sum total of hundreds – even thousands – of individual inventions. The key ones, however, were the compact gas-powered internal combustion engine and the pneumatic (air-filled) tire. Although these were both invented in 19th-century Europe and first brought together in Germany and France, the United States took the lead in car manufacturing and use early in the 20th century. Public demand for fast, easy and cheap personal transportation was met by mass-production techniques first introduced there, and the opening up of oil fields made cheap fuel available to power the new freedom of the road.

A century later, cars were far more sophisticated machines (see page 388), but they were well on the way to becoming victims of their own success. The 20 000 cars on the world's roads in 1900 had grown to more than 230 million by 2000. Dwindling world oil reserves and fears about pollution and global warming are forcing manufacturers to seek viable alternatives to the gas engine while trying to cut fuel consumption and pollution from existing designs. Meanwhile, in developing countries, car ownership remains a distant dream for large numbers of people.

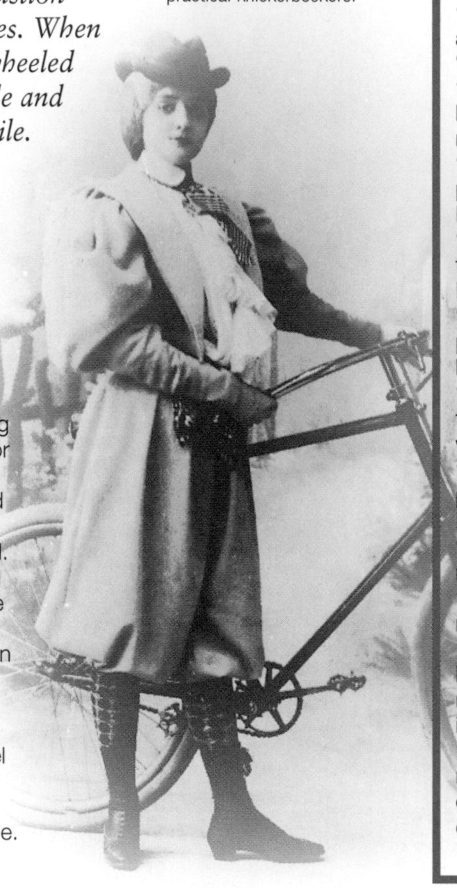

Liberating cycle The bicycle brought women new freedom in the late 19th century. They dressed accordingly, abandoning long skirts for the more practical knickerbockers.

Evolution of the bicycle

1790 The French "Celerifère." Looking like a wooden scooter, it has a fixed front wheel and no seat or pedals.
1818 Baron Karl von Drais adds a seat and steerable front wheel to make the "Draisienne," or hobbyhorse.
1839 Scotsman Kirkpatrick Macmillan builds a cycle with pedals, connecting rods and cranks to turn the rear wheel.
1861 Frenchman Pierre Michaux adds pedals linked to the front wheel of a Draisienne. He calls it the "Vélocipède."
1870 The Vélocipède is developed into the "high" bicycle, or "penny-farthing." Its large front wheel increases speed.
1879 Englishman Henry Lawson patents the "Bicyclette," a chain-driven bicycle with same-sized wheels.
1885 In Britain, J.K. Starley produces the first successful "safety bicycle," with simple gears and suspension.
1888 Scottish inventor John Dunlop patents the pneumatic tire for bicycles. It is used for automobiles from 1895 on.
1909 Dérailleur gears are introduced, moving the driving chain on sprockets.
1938 Epicyclic gears, contained in the rear wheel hub, are introduced.
1973 The "mountain bike" – with a large number of gears and heavily ridged tires suitable for rough terrain – is introduced.
1980s Professional racing bicycles make use of lightweight carbon-fiber composites, later incorporated into the design of leisure bicycles.

Horseless carriage This 1886 Daimler, the first four-wheeled gas-powered carriage, had its engine suspended at the back. It was capable of going 19 km/h (12 mph).

Putting the world on wheels More than 15 million Model T Fords were built in the 20 years the car was in production.

Beetling to success Although developed before World War II, the Volkswagen Beetle did not go into mass production until after the war.

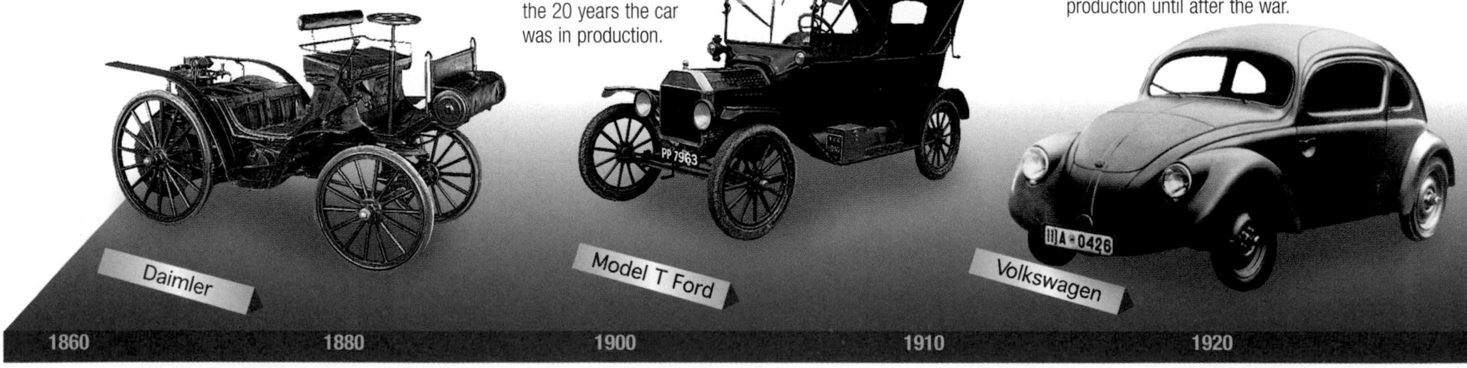

1860 Etienne Lenoir of France builds the first practical internal combustion engine; a stationary industrial gas engine, it has limited commercial success.

1876 Nikolaus Otto of Germany develops the four-stroke internal combustion gas engine, the basis of the modern car engine.

1883–85 In Germany, engineers Gottlieb Daimler (with Wilhelm Maybach) and Karl Benz develop the first gas engines.

1890 René Panhard and Emile Levassor of France build the first specially designed gas engine car.

1892 German engineer Rudolf Diesel patents the compression-ignition engine.

1901 Gottlieb Daimler's son Paul builds the first Mercedes. Its steel chassis makes it the forerunner of the modern steel-bodied car.

1901–6 American Ransom E. Olds builds 18 000 Oldsmobiles by mass-production methods, using prefabricated components.

1908 Henry Ford introduces the mass-produced Model T.

1911 The Studebaker Company in the United States offers deferred payment plans for car purchases.

1913 Henry Ford revolutionizes car-manufacturing with his moving production line for Model Ts. Production increases to over 240 000 cars per year; the price drops from $850 to $260 by 1925.

1920s Buses and trucks are made with diesel engines.

1922 Low-pressure "balloon" tires bring greater comfort.

1928 The last Model T Ford is produced.

1935 In Germany, Ferdinand Porsche unveils the rear-engine Volkswagen ("people's car").

Horse-drawn carriages

By the late 19th century, horse-drawn carriages had evolved from crude wagons to become highly sophisticated vehicles in a variety of designs for special purposes. Some showed signifiicant technical innovations. The brougham of 1838, for example, had no separate chassis. Instead, the rear axle, suspension and front undercarriage were mounted directly on the body – a principle used in many modern cars.

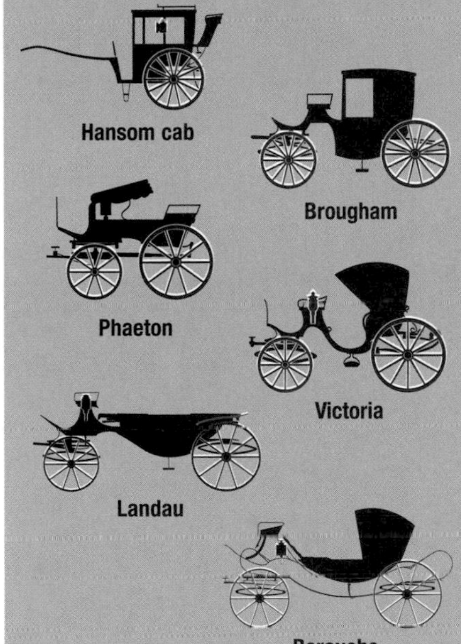

Brief history of the motorcycle

Just as the car developed from the motorized "horseless carriage," the motorcycle was born from the combination of the bicycle with a particularly compact version of the internal combustion gas engine.

1885 Gottlieb Daimler produces the world's first motorcycle by mounting a gas-powered internal combustion engine on a wooden-framed bicycle. Independently, Karl Benz installs a gas engine on a tricycle.

1894 The Hildebrand brothers and Alois Wolfmüller manufacture a two-cylinder, four-stroke motorcycle capable of going 39 km/h (24 mph).

1895 The compact French-developed de Dion-Bouton engine sets the standard for four-stroke motorcycle engines.

1903 The Honold-Bosch high-tension magneto provides much-improved fuel ignition.

1907 Harley-Davidson builds the first two-cylinder V-twin motorcycle engine.

1911 Variable-speed gears and clutch are introduced.

1913 A motorcycle is timed for the first time at more than 160 km/h (100 mph).

1914 The first production motorcycle with an electric starter – the Indian Hendee Special – is introduced.

1914 Drum (internal expanding) brakes are introduced for motorcycles.

1947 The first motor scooters – Vespa and Lambretta – with small wheels, low-powered enclosed engines, and open frames and running boards, are launched.

1959 Japanese manufacturers start to dominate the world motorcycle market.

1968 The first production motorcycle with disk brakes – the Honda CB750 appears.

1980s High-performance motorcycles with turbocharged engines are introduced.

1990s Fuel Injection is introduced for some motorcycle engines.

Poor man's car The motorcycle and sidecar, such as this BSA from 1922 with its own hood, provided transportation for families who could not afford cars.

see also
388-89 **The modern car**
390-91 **Trains**
402-3 **Fossil fuels**

All fins and chrome Cadillac stylist Harley Earl introduced large tail-fins in 1948. This 1959 Eldorado was one of the last models to bear his hallmark so prominently.

Mini Minor The Mini started a trend for front-wheel-drive compact cars. Among its revolutionary features were a space-saving transverse (sideways-mounted) engine and rubber suspension.

People carrier The Renault Espace created a new kind of large family car – part station wagon, part minibus.

1948 New tire designs improve car performance and road handling. The French company Michelin introduces safer and longer-lasting radial tires. In the United States, the Goodyear company introduces the convenient tubeless tire.

1951 Dunlop introduces disk brakes. Pads operated by hydraulics grip each side of a disk attached to the wheels.

1959 The British Motor Corporation unveils the revolutionary Austin-Morris Mini, designed by Greek-born engineer Alec Issigonis.

1965 Lawyer Ralph Nader publishes his book *Unsafe at Any Speed* criticizing car safety standards. It leads to much stricter safety regulations governing car design and to the use of seat belts and airbags.

1970 Federal laws require big cuts in car exhaust pollution, leading to the introduction of catalytic converters to clean up exhaust gases.

Mid 1970s World fuel crises slow down the growth of the car industry and give a new impetus to small, fuel-efficient cars.

1980 Japanese car output exceeds that of the United States for the first time.

1980 Renault of France launches the Espace, setting a new trend for "people carriers."

1997 Mercedes-Benz's A-class is the first small runabout from an upscale car manufacturer.

1997 Toyota and Honda introduce highly fuel-efficient "hybrid" gas-electric cars.

The modern car ▶

Complex systems to make cars safer, more comfortable and less polluting

Over 500 million cars use the world's roads, and problems of pollution and threatened fuel shortages face car manufacturers and users alike. There is constant pressure on makers to devise ways to engineer safer, cleaner and more economical cars and to include designs and gadgets with customer appeal.

Car systems Today's cars are recognizable descendants of Panhard and Levassor's 1890 vehicle, though they generally have a one-piece "monocoque" body with no separate chassis, and the individual systems are vastly more complex than they were in 1890. Most medium or large cars have engines in the front driving the rear wheels, but small and medium-sized cars generally have front-wheel drive. In some cars and all-terrain vehicles, transfer gearboxes divide power among all four wheels. Safety systems are of major importance: Side-impact bars, crumple zones, collapsing steering columns, airbags and anti-lock brakes all help protect car users.

FOUR-STROKE ENGINE CYCLE

Most gas-powered cars have four-stroke engines. The power stroke, which provides the driving force, occurs once every two complete turns of the crankshaft. For smooth, continuous power delivery, most engines have four, six, eight or even more cylinders that fire in turn.

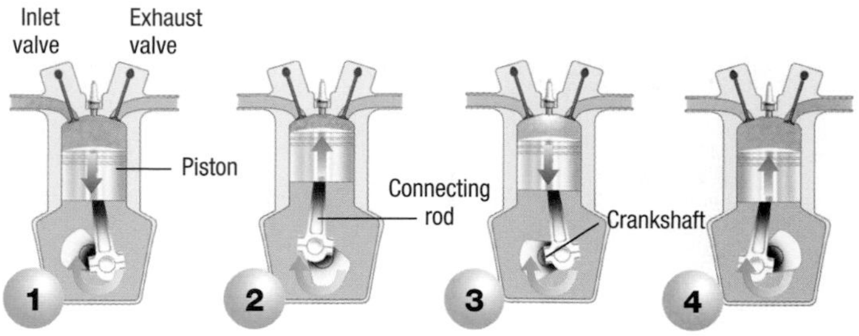

Intake or induction Inlet valve is open. Exhaust valve is closed. Piston moves down. Gas-air mixture is drawn in.

Compression Inlet and exhaust valves are closed. Piston moves up. Gas-air mixture is compressed.

Power Inlet and exhaust valves are closed. Spark plug ignites gas-air mixture. Piston is driven down by expanding burning gases.

Exhaust Inlet valve is closed. Exhaust valve is open. Piston moves up. Exhaust gases are driven out.

Fuel system The fuel pump draws fuel from the tank. Fuel and air are then mixed in the correct proportions and fed into the engine. Fuel injection is generally used now; this squirts a measured amount of fuel directly into the air stream entering the engine.

Engine Chains, belts or gear shafts operate the inlet and exhaust valves and time the delivery of electric current to the spark plugs.

Electrical system The battery supplies power when the car is not running. Once the engine is started, the alternator generates enough electricity to run all the electrical systems and accessories and to keep the battery fully charged.

Exhaust system An arrangement of pipes takes burned exhaust gases from the engine. One or more silencers smooth the flow to reduce noise. In most new cars, a catalytic converter chemically changes some of the gases to less-polluting carbon dioxide and water.

Starter motor This electric motor turns the engine's flywheel through its cycle until the engine starts to turn on its own.

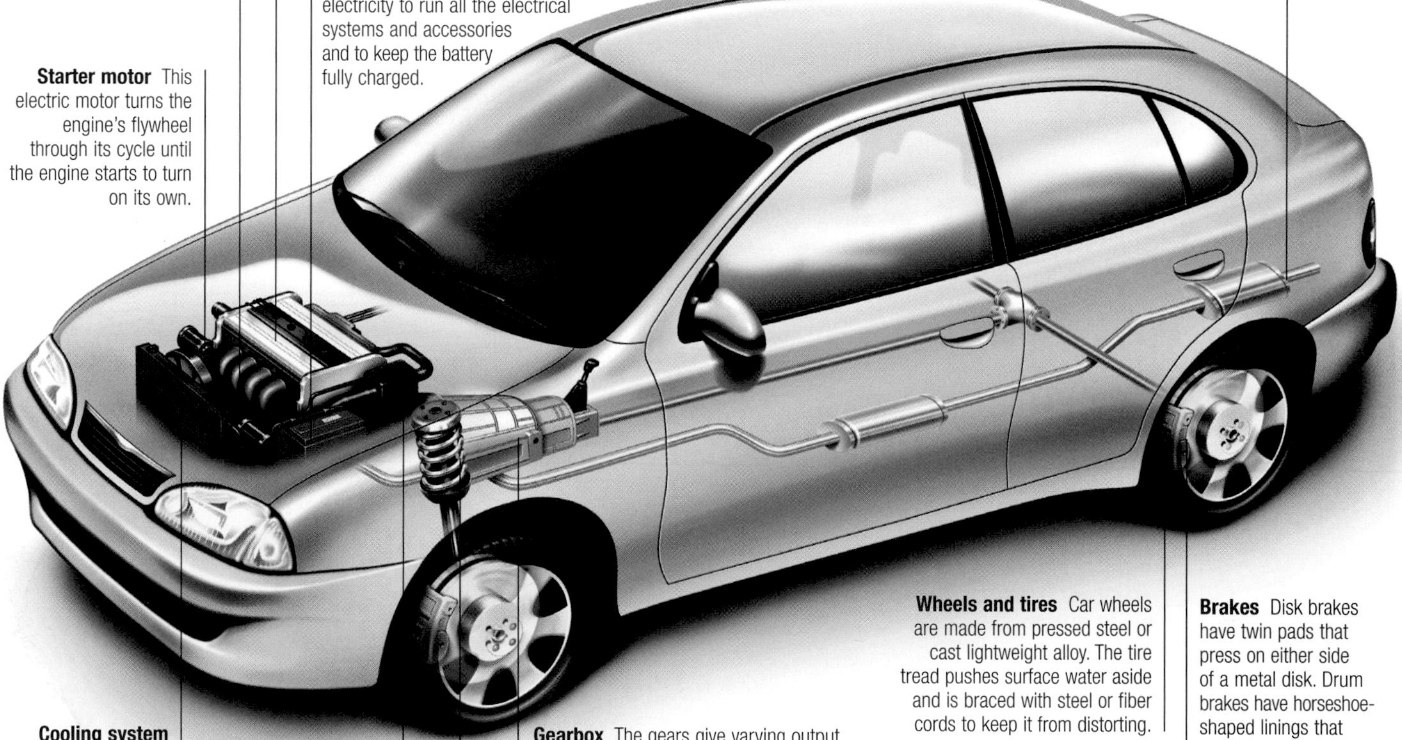

Wheels and tires Car wheels are made from pressed steel or cast lightweight alloy. The tire tread pushes surface water aside and is braced with steel or fiber cords to keep it from distorting.

Brakes Disk brakes have twin pads that press on either side of a metal disk. Drum brakes have horseshoe-shaped linings that press outward onto the inner surface of the brake drum; these are more efficient for parking and are often fitted in the rear.

Cooling system Some car engines are air-cooled, but usually, water circulates through channels in the engine and then through the radiator, where air blown by a fan dissipates the excess heat.

Ignition system The engine needs carefully timed sparks to ignite the fuel-air mixture. This used to be done with a coil and distributor, but most new cars have electronic ignition.

Gearbox The gears give varying output speeds for a given engine speed. An automatic transmission automatically changes the gear ratio, according to road speed and engine load, usually under electronic control.

Suspension and steering Springs and shock absorbers attach each wheel to the body and keep it stable as the car travels over uneven surfaces. Many cars have power-assisted steering to reduce effort.

Alternative power for vehicles

Dwindling oil reserves and the need to reduce the emissions of carbon dioxide and other "greenhouse" gases are forcing car manufacturers to seek alternatives to the traditional internal combustion engine. One approach is to develop efficient "lean-burn" engines; another is to use wholly new fuels or technologies – or both.

Electric vehicles (EV)
EVs are powered by an electric motor driven by electricity from batteries.

Pros:
- No greenhouse gases emitted
- Can be refueled (recharged) at home

Cons:
- Limited range
- Lengthy daily recharging needed
- Generating power to recharge batteries may produce greenhouse gases

Hybrid electric vehicles (HEV)
A battery-powered electric motor drives the car at low speed, or, when necessary, assists a small internal combustion engine – which also recharges batteries.

Pros:
- Reduced fuel consumption
- Good range

Cons:
- Some emissions from the internal combustion engine
- Complex

Liquefied petroleum gas (LPG)
This by-product of the petroleum industry is used to power internal combustion engines.

Pros:
- Reduced fuel costs
- Reduced greenhouse gas emissions

Cons:
- LPG is a fossil fuel with finite reserves
- Needs a special pressurized fuel tank

Fuel cell
Hydrogen from the electrolysis (electrical splitting) of water is combined with oxygen from air to generate electricity to power a motor.

Pros:
- No carbon dioxide emitted (only by-product is water)
- Good fuel economy and range
- Almost silent

Cons:
- Hydrogen is currently more expensive than gasoline

Ethanol
Used on its own or mixed with gas to power internal combustion engines, ethanol (ethyl alcohol) is a renewable fuel made from corn and other crops.

Pros:
- Made from a renewable resource
- Reduced greenhouse gas emissions

Cons:
- Limited public refueling sites

see also
386-87 **Road transportation**
390-91 **Trains**
402-3 **Fossil fuels**

The world's biggest vehicle manufacturers

	Group	Units sold 1998 (millions)	Turnover $ (billions)	Major brands
1	**General Motors**	8.1	126	Buick, Cadillac, Chevrolet, Opel, Saab, Vauxhall
2	**Ford**	6.8	119	Ford, Jaguar, Land Rover, Lincoln, Mazda, Volvo
3	**Toyota**	5.2	109	Daihatsu, Lexus, Toyota
4	**Volkswagen**	4.6	62	Audi, Bentley, Seat, Skoda, Volkswagen
5	**Daimler Chrysler**	4.5	111	Chrysler, Dodge, Jeep, Mercedes, Smart
6	**Nissan**	2.5	58	Infiniti, Nissan
7	**Honda**	2.3	45	Acura, Honda
8	**PSA Peugeot Citroën**	2.3	29	Citroën, Dacia, Peugeot
9	**Renault**	2.1	35	Alpine, Renault
10	**Mitsubishi**	1.8	32	Mitsubishi

The world's busiest road networks

		thousand km traveled per year per km of road
1	Indonesia	8134
2	Hong Kong	6071
3	Bahrain	2808
4	Mongolia	2169
5	Israel	2096
6	Thailand	1546
7	Portugal	1297
8	UK	1089
9	Belgium	1074
10	Germany	889

Car ownership The United States is by far the world leader in car ownership, with more than 130 million cars on its roads. However, a number of smaller countries have more cars per thousand population, as shown below.

The world's longest road networks

		thousand km			thousand km
1	United States	6348	6	Australia	913
2	India	3320	7	Canada	902
3	Brazil	1980	8	France	893
4	China	1210	9	Germany	656
5	Japan	1152	10	Italy	655

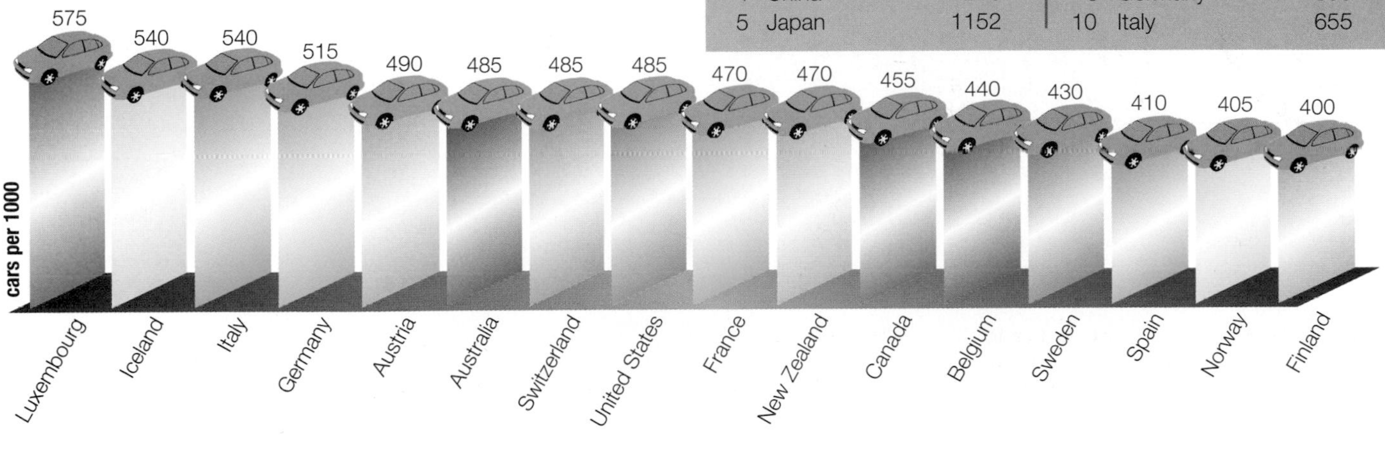

The train was the first truly mass means of transportation. Hundreds of thousands of miles of track were built on almost every continent during the 19th century, opening up many remote areas and driving economic development. Despite competition from road and air transportation, railroads still thrive in hauling heavy cross-country freight, in transporting millions of commuters and in linking cities up to 1000 km (600 miles) apart at high speed.

Steep climb San Francisco's cable cars make light work of the city's hills. The carriage clamps onto a moving cable driven from a central engine house.

Trolleys, streetcars and light trains

The first horse-drawn trolley service started in New York City in 1852. The trolley ran along rails set into the road. Almost 20 years later cable cars – pulled by a continuously moving cable housed in a trough in the road – were introduced in San Francisco.

City transportation evolved in the late 19th century with such innovations as steam trolleys, battery-powered electric trolleys and trolleys powered from overhead electric cables – with power transmitted to the trolley via a "trolley," a pole topped with a metal wheel that ran along the cable – hence the name trolley car or trolley. An electric "trolley bus" service started in British cities in 1911, running until the introduction of diesel-engined buses in the late 1940s.

In these days of traffic congestion and pollution, cities worldwide have modernized, extended or reintroduced their trolley systems in an effort to improve urban environments. In other cities, futuristic-looking overhead railroad systems, such as London's Docklands Light Railway and the SkyTrain in Vancouver, provide the answer.

1800

1801 Richard Trevithick builds the first steam locomotive, able to pull a 10-metric-ton load at 8 km/h (5 mph).

1825 British engineer George Stephenson runs the first public steam train, using his engine *Locomotion*. Passengers travel at up to 24 km/h (15 mph) between Stockton and Darlington in northern England.

1829 Stephenson and his son Robert build the *Rocket*, which reaches the astonishing speed of 38 km/h (24 mph).

1830 The Liverpool and Manchester Railway opens, using Stephenson's *Rocket* – this is the true birth of the railroads.

The Baltimore and Ohio Railroad is the first railroad in the United States. It uses the locomotive *Tom Thumb*.

Iron horse The railroad opened up the American West.

1850

1850 The US has 14 500 km (9000 miles) of railroad track; Britain has more than 9600 km (6000 miles).

1863 The world's first subway opens in London.

1869 The first transcontinental railroad is created when the Union Pacific and Central Pacific railroads link up in Utah.

Inventor George Westinghouse patents the pneumatic (air) brake for trains.

1890 The world's first deep-level electric subway – nicknamed the "Tube" – starts operating in London.

1896-97 The first subway in continental Europe opens in Budapest, Hungary. The first in the US, opens in Boston.

1900

1900 The *Métropolitain* (or "Métro") subway opens in Paris.

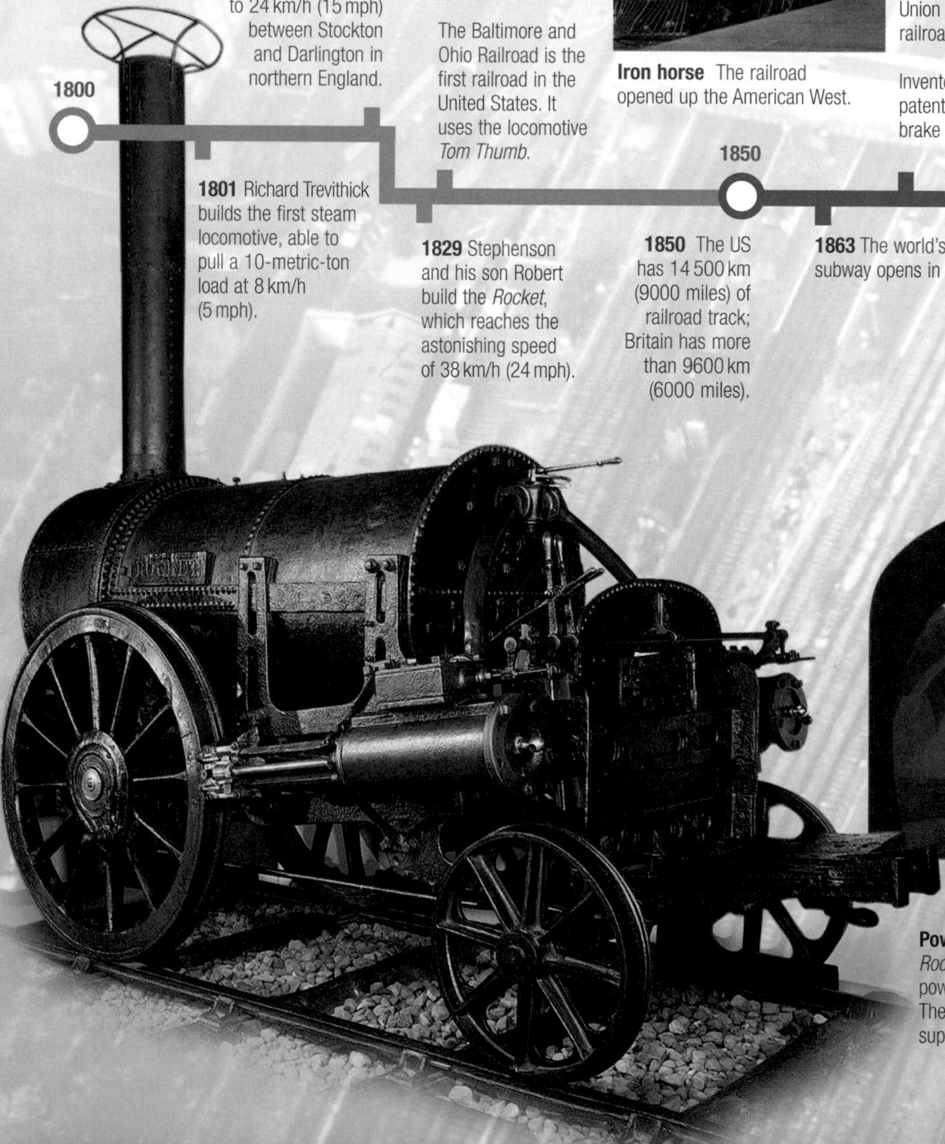

Power on wheels Stephenson's *Rocket* was the fastest and most powerful locomotive of its day. The Stephensons went on to supply many European railroads.

Smoky journey London's subway – the first in the world – used coal-fueled steam engines.

Modern train technologies

Magnetic levitation trains "Maglev" trains can travel at more than 500 km/h (310 mph). The trains "float" 1-10 cm (1/2-4 in.) above a guideway, kept aloft by a powerful magnetic field. Speed is regulated by means of an alternating current fed to magnets placed along the guideway, so that the magnetic field "travels" along the track. These trains are still experimental.

Tilting trains The overall speed of conventional trains is limited by their ability to negotiate curves. They can reach 235 km/h (145 mph), but are limited to 145 km/h (90 mph) on many bends. A tilting train can travel around corners 25-40 percent faster. The train's undercarriage is fitted with a computerized device that controls pistons to adjust the angle at which the carriages tilt.

Monorail Monorail train systems, such as those in Tokyo and Sydney, are electrically powered and run at relatively low speeds. Some systems use an overhead rail from which the train is suspended, and others use a single undercarriage rail with guidewheels to stabilize the carriages.

Automatic light railroad This is well suited to city environments because it minimizes disruption during construction: The Docklands Light Railway in London connects the City and Docklands business districts. The driverless trains are operated from a central control room by a computerized system.

High-speed trains The Japanese "Bullet," French TGV and other high-speed trains have powerful electric engines at each end and run on special tracks with gentle curves. Signaling data are transmitted to the train via computers. TGV carriages are linked by four-wheel "trucks" instead of having separate sets of bogies, aiding stability.

Tilting train This Swedish X-2000 train, like the innovative Italian Pendolino, senses curves in the track ahead, and a computer causes the carriages to tilt accordingly.

1900

1901 The first monorail system opens in Wuppertal, Germany.

1916 After 25 years' work, the Trans-Siberian Railway across Russia is completed.

1928 Union Limited and Union Express launch a railroad service using bright-blue luxury carriages between Cape Town and Johannesburg. The service is officially renamed the Blue Train in 1946.

1930s The first lightweight, high-speed diesel trains enter service in Germany and the United States.

1940 In the US, the Santa Fe Railroad opens the first regular diesel-electric freight service.

1950

1964 Japan introduces the Shinkansen ("Bullet") train, capable of traveling at 209 km/h (130 mph).

1983 The French TGV (*Train à Grande Vitesse*) service starts running between Paris and Lyon. The trains attain an average speed of 360 km/h (186 mph).

1988 The Pendolino high-speed train enters service in Italy. It is the first commercially successful tilting train that is able to reach high speeds on standard track.

1994 The 50-km (31 mile) Channel Tunnel rail link connects Britain with France, carrying high-speed passenger-, car- and truck-transporting trains.

2000

2000 By the turn of the century, there are more than 1.2 million km (750 000 miles) of rail track around the world.

Rail safety

Safe train operation depends on effective signaling. Most systems use red, yellow and green signals, like traffic lights, but they rely on drivers remaining alert and responding to the signals. Automatic protection systems help reduce the risk of human error.

Automatic Warning System (AWS) Passing a yellow or red signal activates a buzzer in the driver's cab. If the driver fails to cancel the warning sound, the brakes are automatically applied.

Train Protection and Warning System (TPWS) Unlike AWS, TPWS cannot be overridden by the driver. It initiates automatic braking of the train if it is about to pass a red signal or exceed the speed limit on a curve.

Automatic Train Protection (ATP) This is the most effective and expensive system. Equipment along the tracks monitors the speed of the train and transmits a calculated "safe" speed to a display in the cab. If the driver exceeds this speed, automatic braking is applied.

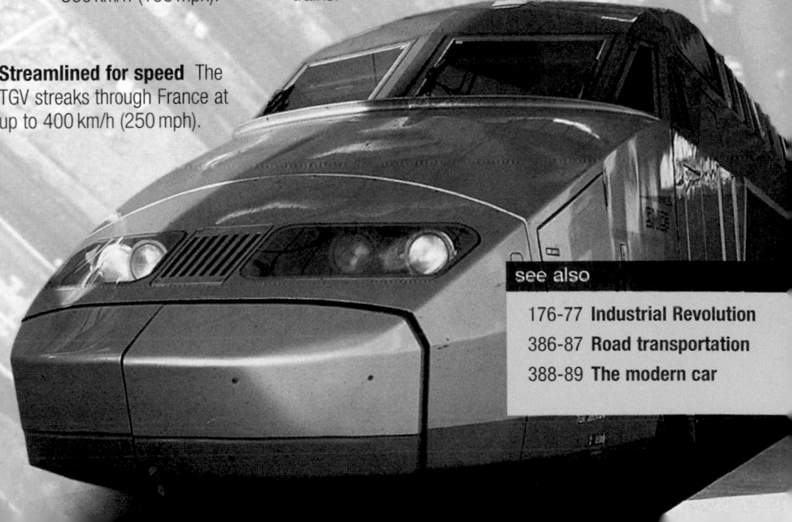

Streamlined for speed The TGV streaks through France at up to 400 km/h (250 mph).

TRAIN FACTS

The world steam speed record, 203 km/h (126 mph), was set in Britain in 1938 by the engine *Mallard* (above).

The fastest trains in regular service are the French TGVs, which consistently average speeds of 300 km/h (186 mph).

The world speed record for a maglev train was set in Japan in 1999. The five-coach train reached 552 km/h (343 mph) while traveling on an 18 km (11 mile) test track.

The world's longest railway line, the Trans-Siberian Railway, runs about 9300 km (5780 miles) from Moscow to Vladivostok.

The longest stretch of straight track, across the Nullarbor Plain in Australia, runs 478 km (297 miles) without a bend.

The world's longest railway tunnel, the Seikan, links the Japanese islands of Honshu and Hokkaido. It is 53.9 km (31.1 miles) long; its lowest point lies 240 m (787 ft) below sea level.

see also

176-77 **Industrial Revolution**
386-87 **Road transportation**
388-89 **The modern car**

Steamships to hydrofoils ▶

Technology keeps an ancient form of transportation competitive

Even in this age of mass air travel, shipping carries the bulk of the world's trade. At the same time, demand for vacations at sea has led to the building of huge cruise liners that are able to carry more than 3000 passengers and are equipped with a vast range of entertainment facilities. The desire for speedy travel has been satisfied by high-tech vessels such as hovercraft, multihulled ships and hydrofoils. Nor has air power made the world's navies obsolete, although fast patrol boats, aircraft carriers and submarines have replaced heavily armored "dreadnoughts" (battleships).

Plimsoll line These lines painted on a ship's hull show the maximum depth it can safely ride in the water when loaded. Ships sit higher in cold salt water than in warm or fresh water, so the Plimsoll line shows a series of depths.

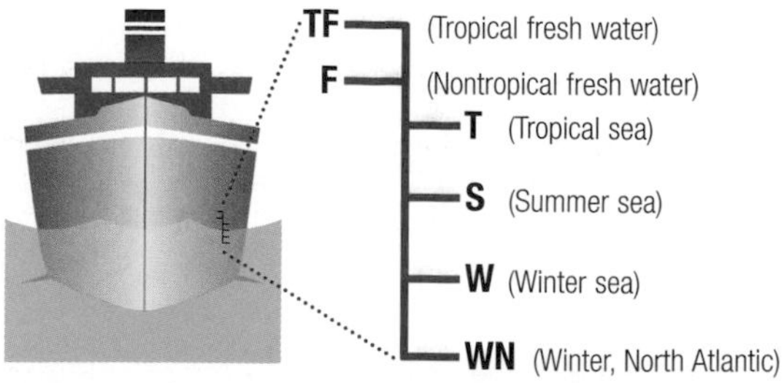

The Blue Riband

A group of transatlantic shipping companies introduced the Blue Riband award in 1833 – before the days of steamships – for liners making the fastest crossings between Europe and North America. Modern rules state that the vessels must be real passenger ships, not small boats, in order to rule out specially built competitors.

Blue Riband holders since 1900 *(in order of speed; route lengths varied)*

Ship	Line	Year	Duration (days:hrs:mins)	Speed (knots)
Deutschland	Hamburg America	1900	5:15:46	22.42
Kaiser Wilhelm II	North German Lloyd	1904	5:12:44	23.12
Lusitania	Cunard	1907	4:19:52	23.99
Mauritania	Cunard	1908	4:20:15	24.86
Bremen	North German Lloyd	1929	4:17:42	27.83
Europa	North German Lloyd	1930	4:17:06	27.91
Rex	Italian Line	1933	4:13:58	28.92
Normandie	French Line	1935	4:03:02	29.98
Queen Mary	Cunard White Star	1936	4:00:27	30.14
United States	United States Line	1952	3:12:12	34.51
Hoverspeed Great Britain	Hoverspeed	1990	3:07:54	36.60
Cat-Link V	Scandlines	1998	2:20:09	41.28

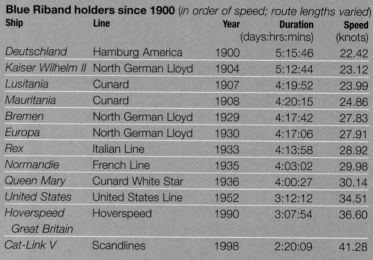

Atlantic queen Launched in 1934, the *Queen Mary* (above in New York harbor) won the Blue Riband two years later and kept it for 16 years.

Key measurements

Deadweight tonnage (dwt) A ship's total carrying capacity, including crew, passengers, supplies, fuel and spare parts as well as cargo. Measured in metric tons, it is used for tankers and cargo ships.
Displacement tonnage The weight of the water a ship displaces, measured in metric tons. It is used mostly for naval ships.
Gross tonnage (grt) A measure of the volume of the space within a commercial ship's hull. It has nothing to do with weight. One grt equals 100 cu ft, or about 3 m³.
Nautical mile Still used both at sea and in the air, it equals 1852 m (6076 ft or about 1.15 land miles). A **knot** is a speed of one nautical mile per hour.
Net tonnage A measurement of volume similar to gross tonnage, this is based on passenger and cargo space only, excluding the engine room and fuel store. It is used when calculating harbor fees and taxes.

1900 | 1910 | 1930 | 1940 | 1950

1902 Germany launches the *Preussen*, still the biggest sailing ship ever built. It is 132 m (433 ft) long, with five masts and a steel hull.

1906 The first full-sized self-propelled hydrofoil is successfully tested by Italian engineer Enrico Forlanini.

1908 Britain launches the first diesel-powered submarine.

1914-18 During World War I, Germany proves the effectiveness of naval submarines by sinking many Allied ships.

1916 The British Navy commissions HMS *Argus*, the first aircraft carrier. It is converted from a passenger liner.

1937 The first commercial hydrofoil service starts in Germany.

1939-45 World War II proves the importance of submarines and aircraft carriers in naval warfare.

The world's biggest merchant fleets

Number of vessels over 100 grt (1999)

1	Japan	8462
2	Panama	6143
3	United States	5642
4	Russia	4694
5	China	3285

1954 The United States launches the world's first nuclear-powered ship – the submarine *Nautilus* – which sets new underwater speed and endurance records.

1959 British inventor Christopher Cockerell builds a full-sized hovercraft – the first truly amphibious craft.

HOVERCRAFT

Hovercraft ride on a cushion of air, which allows them to travel over water, swamps, beaches or fairly level land. Powerful fans, driven by gas turbine or lightweight diesel engines, pump air into a hollow chamber formed by the flexible skirt around the craft. The air escapes from there into the wider space between the hull and the ground or water, forming the air cushion on which the craft rides. Propellers above the stern push it forward, and rudders in the airflow steer. Top speeds may approach 70 knots (130 km/h). For extra maneuverability there are swiveling air nozzles, known as thrusters, on each side of the bow. Like hydrofoils, hovercraft are used as military patrol craft as well as short-distance car and passenger ferries.

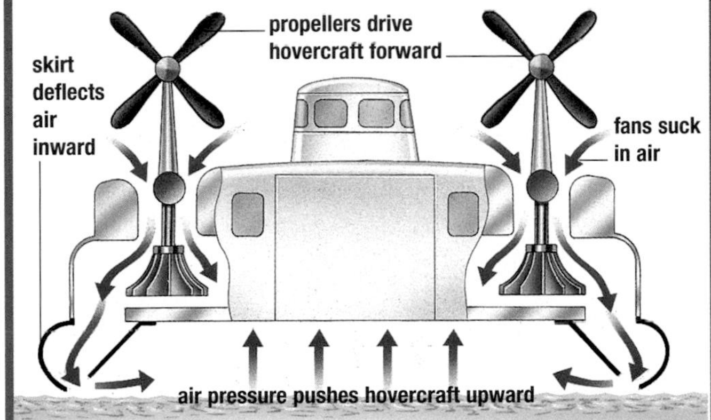

Supercarrier The two nuclear reactors on board the *Nimitz*-class USS *John C. Stennis* will power it for about a million nautical miles (1.85 million km) before refueling. The ship cruises at more than 30 knots (34.5 mph) and is operated by a crew of 6250. The flight deck covers an area of 1.8 ha (4.5 acres). The carrier was commissioned in 1995.

How a hydrofoil works
A hydrofoil uses the same principle as an aircraft. It has a foil or "wing" mounted underneath the hull, which "flies" through the water, creating lift. When there is enough lift to raise the main hull above the water level, drag is greatly reduced and cruising speeds of 55 knots (100 km/h) are possible in calm waters. Powered by diesel or gas turbine engines and mostly used as short-distance passenger ferries, hydrofoils are also used as ocean-going military patrol boats and for carrying guided missiles. A hydrofoil with fully submerged foils and an automatic stabilizing system to keep it level can operate in rougher water than the conventional surface-piercing type with V-shaped foils, shown here.

1970 1980 1990 2000

1970s to 90s The United States Navy launches its *Nimitz*-class aircraft carriers. At 100 000 metric tons, these vessels are the world's biggest warships.

1976 The largest ship afloat, the supertanker *Seawise Giant*, is launched; it is enlarged and renamed *Jahre Viking* in 1980. Its deck covers more than 30 000 m² (320 000 sq ft) – equal to more than six and a half football fields – and it has a deadweight tonnage of 564 763 metric tons. When fully laden, it draws too much water to pass through the English Channel.

1980 Japanese coastal vessels fitted with computer-controlled rigid vertical sails, or foils, save up to 50 percent of fuel.

1985 The ROV (remotely operated vehicle) *Argo* discovers the wreck of the liner *Titanic* (which sank in 1912) 3738 m (12 263 ft) deep, on the Atlantic seabed.

1999 The *Voyager of the Seas* is launched. As the world's biggest passenger ship, it has berths for 3800 passengers.

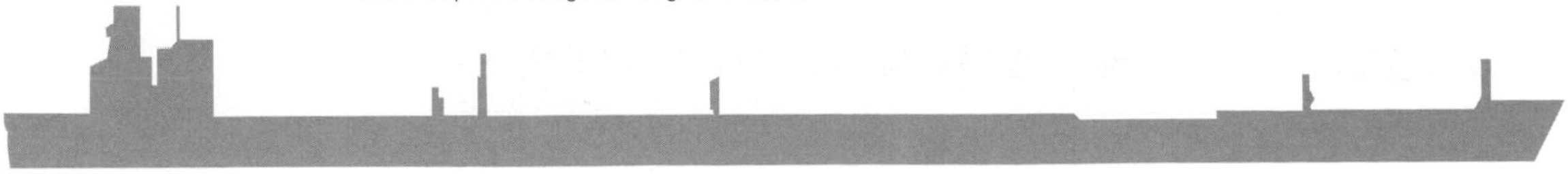

Jahre Viking At 458.5 m (1504 ft), it is as long as 43 buses in a row.

Aviation

The 200-year journey from hot-air balloons to supersonic flight

In 1999, 1.6 billion people flew on scheduled flights worldwide. A little over 200 years earlier, aviation history began when two Frenchmen drifted just a few miles in a hot air balloon. The following years produced aircraft as diverse as the tiny microlight (little more than a giant kite fitted with an engine) airliners that carry hundreds of passengers and jet fighters capable of speeds of more than 3200 km/h (2000 mph).

Ferdinand, Count von Zeppelin (1838–1917)

German
Zeppelin, a general in the German army, retired early in order to devote himself to designing and building the rigid-framed dirigible airships that would come to bear his name. His vast cigar-shaped craft – first flown in 1900 – were the first commercially viable airships. German military Zeppelins bombed London during World War I.

George Cayley (1773-1857)

British
Cayley was a Yorkshire baronet who was passionate about flight. Today, he is widely recognized as the father of the science of aerodynamics. He worked out the main principles of flying and wrote about parachutes and helicopters. But the engines of his day were not capable of getting a craft airborne. He built a number of gliders, one of which in 1853 carried his coachman a distance of some 400 m (1300 ft), but it had no flight controls.

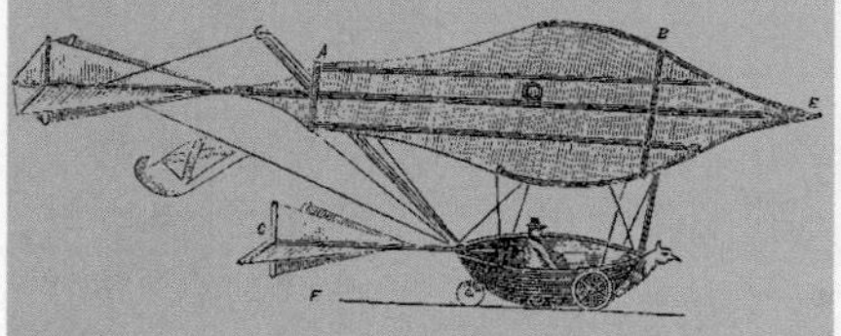

Louis Blériot (1872-1936)

French
Blériot's hop from Calais to Dover in 1909 was the first international airplane flight over water. His craft were among the first successful monoplanes, and in 1908 he introduced flap-type ailerons for flight control.

Junkers J1
Germany, 1915
The J1 was the first all-metal airplane with cantilevered wings entirely supported by an internal framework rather than by external struts or cables.

Fokker EI/III
Germany, 1915
"Flying Dutchman" A.H.G. Fokker's pioneer fighter planes enabled the pilot to fire a machine gun ahead without hitting the propeller blades.

1750 — **1800** — **1900** — **1925**

October 15, 1783
In Paris, the first manned flight takes place. Jean-François Pilâtre de Rozier rises 25 m (80 ft) in a tethered hot air balloon built by the Montgolfier brothers.

November 21, 1783
Again in Paris, the first manned free (untethered) flight takes place in a Montgolfier balloon as before. The passengers, Pilâtre de Rozier and François-Laurent, marquis d'Arlandes, spend 25 minutes in the air.

December 1, 1783
Frenchmen Jacques Charles and Nicolas Robert make the first manned flight in a hydrogen-filled balloon, which they designed and built.

1799
In Britain, Sir George Cayley produces the first designs for a winged aircraft powered by propellers.

1849
An unmanned Austrian balloon makes the first aerial bombing raid in history against Venice.

1853
Frenchman Henri Giffard makes the first powered flight, in a steam-powered dirigible (steerable airship).

Sir George Cayley's coachman makes the first manned but uncontrolled flight by a winged glider.

1891-96
German engineer Otto Lilienthal makes several controlled glider flights.

1900
In Germany, a Zeppelin airship takes its first flight.

December 17, 1903
In the US, the Wright brothers make the first powered manned flight.

1909
Frenchman Louis Blériot flies an airplane across the Channel from France.

The Zeppelin *Deutschland* enters commercial service.

1914
The world's first regular passenger airplane goes into service, flying across Tampa Bay, Florida.

1914-18
During World War I, rapid technological advances result from the extensive use of fighters, bombers and reconnaissance planes, as well as from bombing and reconnaissance balloons and airships.

1919
The British *R34* makes the first transatlantic crossing by an airship.

British aviators John Alcock and Arthur Whitten Brown make the first nonstop transatlantic flight by airplane.

1927
American aviator Charles Lindbergh makes the first solo nonstop transatlantic flight by airplane.

Wright brothers

Wilbur (1867-1912) and Orville (1871-1948); American
The Wright brothers' first successful controlled flight in a powered heavier-than-air craft, in 1903, was the culmination of years of preparation. They had experimented extensively with wings and rudder controls and built their own lightweight gas engine. They set up their own aircraft-manufacturing company in 1909.

Wright brothers' *Flyer* (1903)

Concorde
Britain/France, 1976
The first supersonic airliner has a cruising speed of 2330 km/h (1450 mph). Its high cost, along with environmental problems, limited production to 16 aircraft. A fatal accident in 2000 grounded the entire fleet for more than a year.

see also
396-97 **First steps in space**
398-99 **Cooperation in space**

Douglas DC3 ("Dakota")
United States, 1936
The twin-engine 21-seater DC3 airliner (also called the Dakota) became one of the most widely used transport aircraft in the world. Some DC3s are still in service today.

de Havilland Comet
Britain, 1952
The Comet was the first jet airliner. A series of accidents caused by metal fatigue grounded the first model, but an improved version was rolled out in 1958.

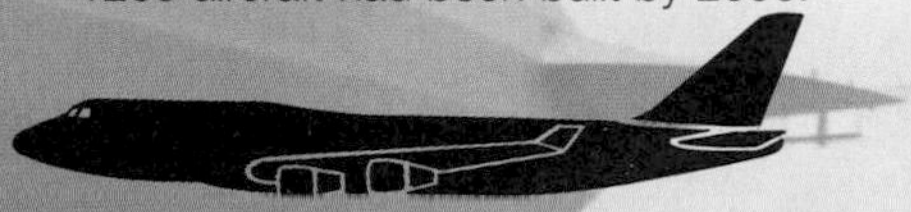

Boeing 747
United States, 1970
The 747 was the first commercial jumbo-jet airliner, able to carry almost 500 passengers and powered by large-diameter turbofan engines. More than 1200 aircraft had been built by 2000.

F-100 ("Super Sabre")
United States,1953
The F-100 fighter made history as the first supersonic production aircraft.

Boeing 247
United States, 1933
The first modern airliner, the Boeing 247 was a twin-engined all-metal monoplane carrying ten passengers at 300 km/h (185 mph).

Hawker Siddeley Harrier
Britain, 1966
This was the first operational V/STOL (vertical/short takeoff and landing) military aircraft, widely flown from land and aircraft carriers.

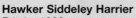

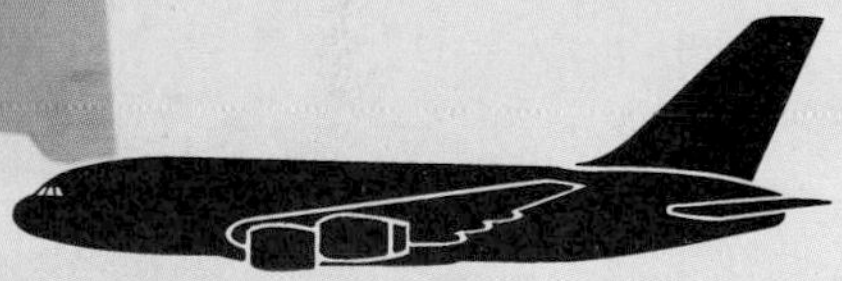

Airbus A380
Britain/France/Germany/Spain, 2006 (scheduled)
The European consortium's double-deck "superjumbo" will seat up to 1000 and may provide restaurants, shops, a gym and sleeper cabins.

1950 1975 2000

1930
British engineer Frank Whittle patents his gas turbine (jet) engine design.

1935
A French-built Breguet-Dorand craft makes the first controlled flight by a helicopter.

1937
The hydrogen-filled German airship *Hindenburg* explodes in the United States, and passenger-carrying airships cease service.

1939
Russian-born American engineer Igor Sikorsky builds and flies the first single-rotor helicopter.

The Heinkel He-178, built in Germany, becomes the first successful jet aircraft.

1939-45
Advances during World War II include the first jet fighter, airborne radar and naval air power.

1947
American Chuck Yeager breaks the sound barrier in a Bell X-1 rocket plane.

1952
The British de Havilland Comet launches the first jet airliner service.

1959
The Boeing 707 jet starts services in North America and across the Atlantic.

1960s
The development of highly efficient turbofan engines makes it possible to build wide-bodied "jumbo-jet" airliners, heralding the era of low-cost mass air travel.

1976
Air France and British Airways start operating supersonic passenger services using Concorde, which crosses the Atlantic in just 3½ hours.

1999
Bertrand Piccard of Switzerland and Brian Jones of England succeed in making the first nonstop around-the-world flight in a balloon, the Breitling Orbiter 3.

Air speed records

Pilots have pushed aircraft to the limits of speed ever since the earliest days of flying, and in the process they have stimulated far-ranging design and engineering improvements. Most of the records set here (over a timed, measured course) were achieved in military aircraft.

			km/h	(mph)
1905	W. Wright	United States	61.2	(38.0)
1912	J. Vedrines	France	174.1	(108.18)
1922	W. Mitchell	United States	358.84	(222.97)
1932	J.H. Doolittle	United States	473.76	(294.38)
1933	J. Wedell	United States	490.82	(304.98)
1939	F. Wendel	Germany	755.14	(469.22)
1945	H.J. Wilson	Britain	975.66	(606.25)
1948	R.L. Johnson	United States	1079.84	(670.98)
1952	J.S. Nash	United States	1124.13	(698.5)
1953	F.K. Everest Jr	United States	1215.28	(755.14)
1955	H.A. Hanes	United States	1323.3	(822.26)
1956	L.P. Twiss	Britain	1821.99	(1132.13)
1957	A.E. Drew	United States	1943.44	(1207.6)
1958	W.W. Irwin	United States	2259.66	(1404.09)
1959	G. Mosolov	Soviet Union	2388.03	(1483.85)
1959	J.W. Rogers	United States	2455.79	(1525.96)
1961	R.B. Robinson	United States	2585.12	(1606.32)
1962	G. Mosolov	Soviet Union	2680.99	(1665.89)
1965	R.L. Stephens	United States	3331.5	(2070.1)
1976	E.W. Joersz	United States	3529.56	(2193.16)

Much of the early impetus for space travel came from Cold War political rivalry between the United States and the Soviet Union. The Russians took the lead when they put the first man in space in 1961. This prompted President Kennedy to commit the US to a program to land men on the Moon within the decade. American industrial resources enabled the US to overtake its rival, and the Soviet focus shifted to long-term space stations.

Spin-offs from space

The space program created thousands of technological problems, needing new materials, new miniaturized sensors and new electronic systems. Many of these technologies have now become a part of everyday life. Despite common belief, they did not include nonstick pans. They do include:

- **bar codes** These are based on NASA systems for keeping track of the millions of spacecraft parts.
- **quartz watches** They were first used on Apollo flights.
- **miniature artificial heart** This was developed from fuel-pump technology used in the space shuttle.
- **charge-coupled devices** Based on satellite sensors, these are used in video cameras and to detect cancers.
- **water-cooled suits** Originally used by astronauts, they are now available for medical and other applications.
- **fire-retardant metallic materials** Now used to protect firefighters, they were first used in space.
- **pressurized ball-point pens** These pens, which can write when upside-down, were first used by Apollo astronauts.
- **cordless electric drills** They were first used by Apollo astronauts to gather moon rocks.

Konstantin Tsiolkovsky
(1857-1935)
Russian physicist and teacher
In 1903, Tsiolkovsky published a theoretical paper on rocketry. He later forecast space travel and suggested the use of liquid fuels and multistage rockets.

Robert Goddard
(1882-1945)
American physicist
Goddard experimented with solid and liquid-fueled rockets, developing propellant pumps and gyroscopic controls. He launched his first 1.2 m (4 ft) liquid-fueled rocket to a height of 56 m (184 ft) in 1926. His achievements were only appreciated after his death.

Wernher von Braun
(1912-77)
German engineer
Von Braun led the team that built the V2 rocket, used against Allied cities in the last year of World War II. Von Braun surrendered to the United States Army at the end of the war and later led the NASA team that developed the Saturn rockets that took the first men to the Moon.

Yuri Gagarin
(1934-68)
Soviet cosmonaut
Soviet Air Force pilot Gagarin (above) made history when he piloted his Vostok 1 spacecraft into Earth's orbit on April 12, 1961, becoming the first person in space. He remained in orbit for just over 89 minutes, traveling at a speed of about 27 400 km/h (over 17 000 mph). The whole mission lasted 1 hour 48 minutes from start to finish. Gagarin died in an aircraft crash while training for another space mission.

John Glenn
(1921-)
American astronaut
Glenn was the first American to orbit the Earth (which he did three times in about four hours), in the Mercury capsule Friendship 7 on February 20, 1962. Glenn left the astronaut program in 1964 and later became a US senator. He returned to space at age 77, in 1998, on board the space shuttle Discovery, becoming the oldest man in space.

Saturn V rocket with Apollo spacecraft

Neil Armstrong
(1930-)
American astronaut
Armstrong was the first man to set foot on the Moon. A United States Navy pilot and civilian test pilot before he became an astronaut, Armstrong and a co-astronaut performed the first successful space docking maneuver in 1966. Three years later, Armstrong commanded the Apollo 11 lunar landing mission. Armstrong did not go into space again after this.

1805
English artillery officer William Congreve builds the first modern military rockets, measuring 100 cm (40 in.) long, with a range of 1800 m (5900 ft). They are used with limited success at the Battle of Waterloo in 1815.

October 4, 1957
The "space age" begins with the launch of the first artificial satellite, the Soviet's 85 kg (185 lb) *Sputnik 1*.

1960

May 5, 1961
Alan Shepard is the first American in space. His suborbital flight reaches a height of 100 km (62 miles) above the Earth's surface.

May 25, 1961
In an address to Congress, President Kennedy sets his country the challenge of landing a man on the Moon and returning him safely to Earth before the end of the 1960s.

June 16, 1963
Russian Valentina Tereshkova becomes the first woman in space.

1965

March 18, 1965
Russian Alexei Leonov makes the first "space walk" from *Voskhod 2* orbiting 2500 km (300 miles) above Earth.

July 14, 1965
Mariner 4, an unmanned American spacecraft, flies by Mars and sends back photographs.

February 3, 1966
The Soviet Luna 9 probe makes the first soft landing on the Moon.

January 27, 1967
Fire on board an Apollo capsule during launch-pad tests kills three astronauts. The Apollo program is delayed while parts of the capsule are redesigned.

December 21, 1968
The Apollo 8 mission is the first manned mission to orbit the Moon. After ten orbits and six days, it splashes down in the Pacific, within 5 km (3 miles) of its target.

July 20/21, 1969
Americans Neil Armstrong and "Buzz" Aldrin are the first humans to set foot on the Moon, during the Apollo 11 mission.

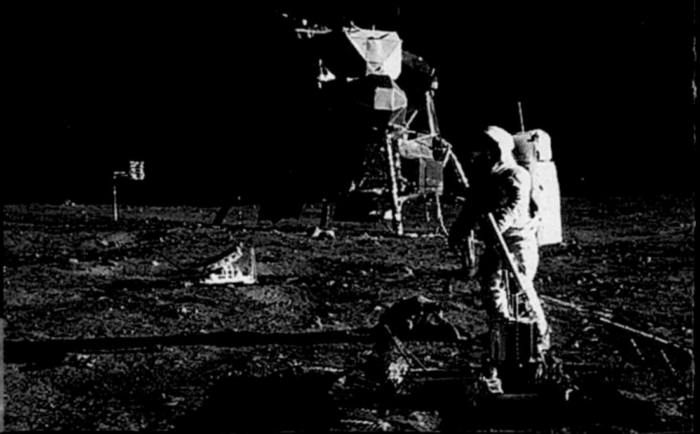

Moonwalking Apollo astronauts explore the Moon at last in July 1969.

Manned Apollo flights

Between May 1964 and April 1968, there were nine unmanned suborbital and orbital flights around the Earth that tested various components of the Apollo system. On January 27, 1967, a fire in the command module (probably caused by a spark in the pure-oxygen atmosphere) killed the crew, Virgil (Gus) Grissom, Edward White and Roger Chaffee. They were training for the first planned manned Apollo Earth-orbit flight, mission AS-204, scheduled for February 21, 1967. Resulting modifications to electrical and air-supply systems delayed the Apollo program for over a year.

Mission	Dates	Crew	Destination	Notes
Apollo 7	October 11-22, 1968	Walter Schirra, Donn Eisele, Walter Cunningham	Earth orbit	First manned Apollo test flight. Delayed over a year by January 1967 fire.
Apollo 8	December 21-27, 1968	Frank Borman, James Lovell, William Anders	Lunar orbit	First manned lunar flight, using command/service module only.
Apollo 9	March 3-13, 1969	James McDivitt, David Scott, Russell Schweickart	Earth orbit	First flight test, including separation and redocking, of lunar module (the module that will be used for landing on the Moon).
Apollo 10	May 18-26, 1969	Thomas Stafford, John Young, Eugene Cernan	Lunar orbit	First flight test of lunar module in lunar orbit.
Apollo 11	July 16-24, 1969	Neil Armstrong, Michael Collins*, Edwin ("Buzz") Aldrin	Sea of Tranquility	First lunar landing.
Apollo 12	November 14-24, 1969	Charles Conrad, Richard Gordon*, Alan Bean	Ocean of Storms	Second lunar landing. Brought back parts of old *Surveyor 3* probe.
Apollo 13	April 11-17, 1970	James Lovell, John Swigert, Fred Haise	(Lunar swingby)	Lunar landing cancelled after explosion in fuel cell severely damaged craft.
Apollo 14	January 31-February 9, 1971	Alan Shepard, Stuart Roosa*, Edgar Mitchell	Fra Mauro	Third lunar landing. Hand-pulled "lunar cart" used.
Apollo 15	July 26-August 7, 1971	David Scott, Alfred Worden*, James Irwin	Hadley Rille	Fourth lunar landing. Powered Lunar Rover used. Lunar subsatellite released.
Apollo 16	April 16-27, 1972	John Young, Thomas Mattingly*, Charles Duke	Descartes	Fifth lunar landing. Lunar Rover used. Lunar subsatellite released
Apollo 17	December 7-19, 1972	Eugene Cernan, Ronald Evans*, Harrison Schmitt	Taurus-Littrow	Final lunar landing. Lunar Rover used. Schmitt was the first professional geologist on the Moon.

*Command module pilot – remained in lunar orbit while other crew members landed; in all crew lists, the mission commander is named first.

Contact in space A commemorative United States stamp marks the 1975 docking of the Apollo and Soyuz spacecrafts.

see also
22-23 **The Moon**
398-99 **Cooperation in space**

1970-72
Three unmanned Soviet lunar probes return soil samples to Earth. Two of them use remote-controlled rover vehicles.

1970

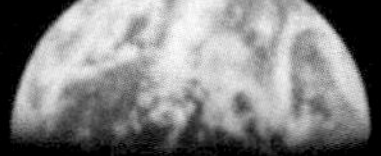

1971-82
A series of Soviet Salyut space stations are launched, to operate for up to five years. Crews spend up to eight months on board.

April 19, 1971
The Soviet Union launches the first Earth-orbiting space station, Salyut 1.

June 7, 1971
Three Soviet cosmonauts are killed when air leaks from their Soyuz 11 during reentry.

November 13, 1971
The American probe *Mariner 9* orbits Mars and transmits data and images of the planet and its moons for 11 months.

May 14, 1973
The first American space station, Skylab, is launched but is damaged. Repairs are successfully carried out in orbit.

December 3, 1973
After a 21 month flight, the American probe *Pioneer 10* passes by Jupiter. It is followed in 1974 by *Pioneer 11*.

February 5, 1974
The American probe *Mariner 10* flies past Venus on its way to a rendezvous with Mercury, which it reaches on March 29.

1975

July 17, 1975
An American Apollo capsule successfully docks with a Soviet Soyuz craft. This is the first step toward international space stations.

October 21, 1975
The Soviet *Venera 9* lander sends the first images of the surface of Venus.

July 20, 1976
NASA launches *Viking 1* and, six weeks later, *Viking 2* to land on Mars. They send back images and data but report no signs of life.

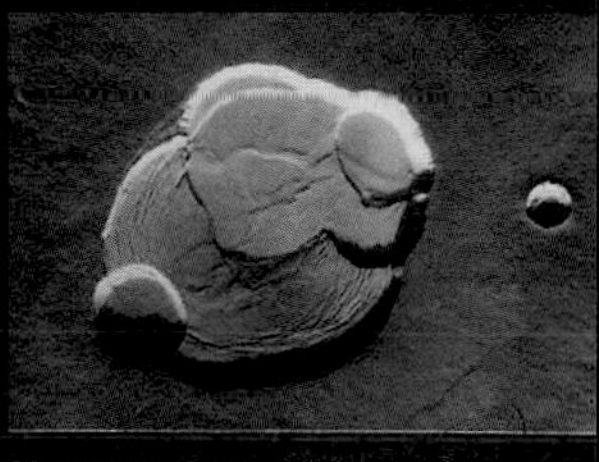

Olympus Mons Viking took a stunning image of the crater on Mars' highest mountain.

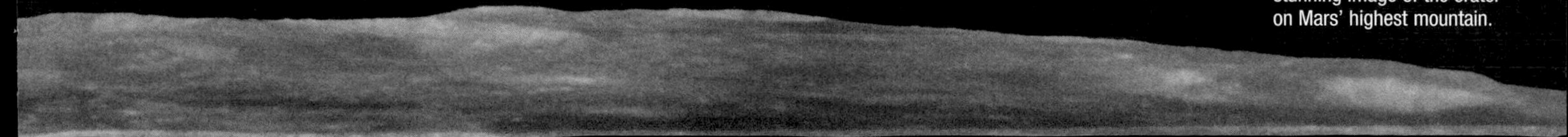

Space exploration continues, but it is marked by increasing international cooperation rather than the old Cold War rivalries. After Apollo's success, it was time to develop a reusable craft to bring down the enormous costs of space travel. At the same time, closer investigations of other planets continued, and increasingly sophisticated telescopes and other instruments were sent into space.

The space shuttle

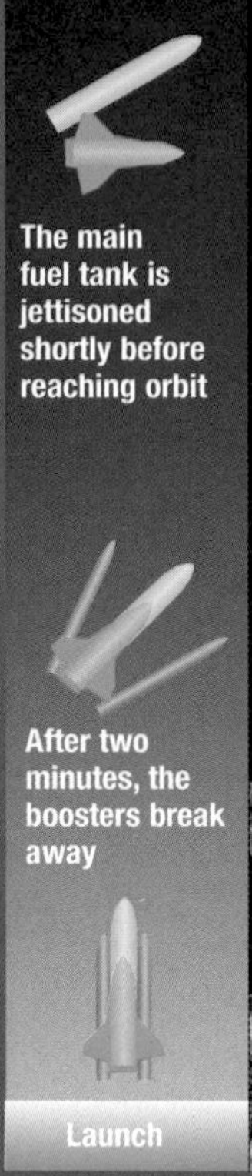

The main fuel tank is jettisoned shortly before reaching orbit
After two minutes, the boosters break away
Launch

The space shuttle, first launched in 1981, made history as the first reusable spacecraft. A cross between a rocket and a glider, its proper name is the Space Transportation System (STS).

On liftoff, the main craft is dwarfed by the huge external fuel tank, which supplies the three main engines; it is discarded just before reaching orbit. The craft also has two external solid-fuel booster engines that are ditched soon after liftoff. The shuttle's own tanks contain enough fuel for maneuvering in orbit and for reentry.

The craft has a large payload bay for carrying satellites and space probes to be launched from orbit. This is also where the crew repair satellites that have been retrieved by a robot arm. The shuttle was designed for launching and servicing military satellites as well as for civilian use.

The craft reenters the Earth's atmosphere belly-first (protected by a ceramic tile heat shield), then glides down to land like an aircraft.

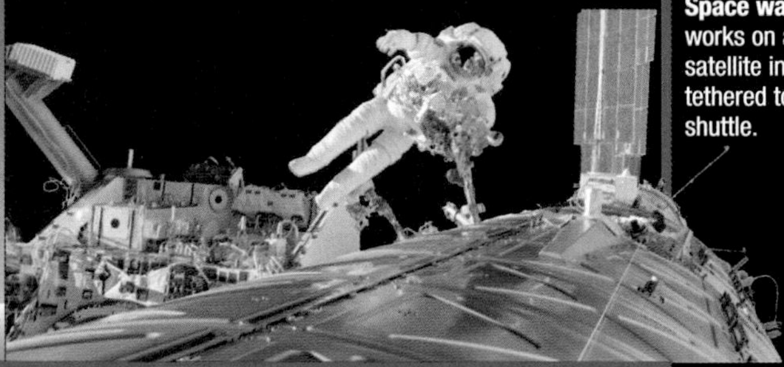

Space walk An astronaut works on a retrieved satellite in orbit while tethered to the space shuttle.

Orbiters and landers to Mars and beyond

Galileo Launch date: October 1989
Galileo has been orbiting Jupiter since December 1995 and continues to send images and data.

Mars Observer Launch date: September 1992
Mars Observer was scheduled to start orbiting Mars in the late summer of 1993, but communication was lost just three days before it was due to enter orbit.

Mars Global Surveyor Launch date: November 1996
Global Surveyor went into orbit around Mars on September 11, 1997. It continues to provide maps of the surface of Mars, showing the distribution of minerals.

Mars Pathfinder Launch date: December 1996
Pathfinder landed on Mars on July 4, 1997. It took photographs of the site and released a six-wheeled, 63 cm (25 in.) Sojourner vehicle equipped to analyze rocks.

Cassini-Huygens Launch date: October 1997
The Cassini orbiter is due to go into Saturn's orbit in July 2004 and to send the European-built Huygens probe into the atmosphere of Saturn's moon Titan four months later.

Mars Odyssey Launch date: April 2001
Mars Odyssey's mission is to map the surface of Mars, to assess it for hazards for any future human exploration and to establish evidence of potential water resources.

Mars Exploration Rovers Launch date: summer 2003
The two powerful Exploration Rovers should reach the surface of Mars in January or February 2004. The identical craft will land in different regions and carry out analysis of soil and rocks, searching for evidence of liquid water.

1977
The United States makes test glides and landings of the space shuttle *Enterprise*, launching it from an aircraft.

1977
The US launches two deep-space *Voyager* probes. *Voyager 1* uses a rare alignment of four outer planets and their gravity to act as a sling-shot moving it from one planet to the next.

1979-89
The *Voyager* space probes send back detailed images of Jupiter, Saturn, Uranus and Neptune.

1980

April 12, 1981
The United States space shuttle *Columbia* makes its first 54-hour space flight. Many more flights follow, for civilian and military purposes, including the launch and repair of satellites.

January 28, 1986
The explosion of the space shuttle *Challenger*, 73 seconds after its tenth lift-off, kills all seven crew. It is caused by a fuel leakage.

February 20, 1986
The first part of the Soviet space station Mir is launched; it will last for 15 years.

1990

April 24, 1990
The United States and the European Space Agency launch the Hubble Space Telescope. Results are disappointing. The mirror is found to have a tiny inaccuracy and the images are not as clear as expected.

August 10, 1990
The United States probe *Magellan* enters the orbit of Venus and begins a radar survey of the planet's surface.

October 6, 1990
The European probe *Ulysses* goes to study the Sun's poles.

December 1993
Orbiting American astronauts carry out repairs to the Hubble Space Telescope, correcting the fault in the mirror.

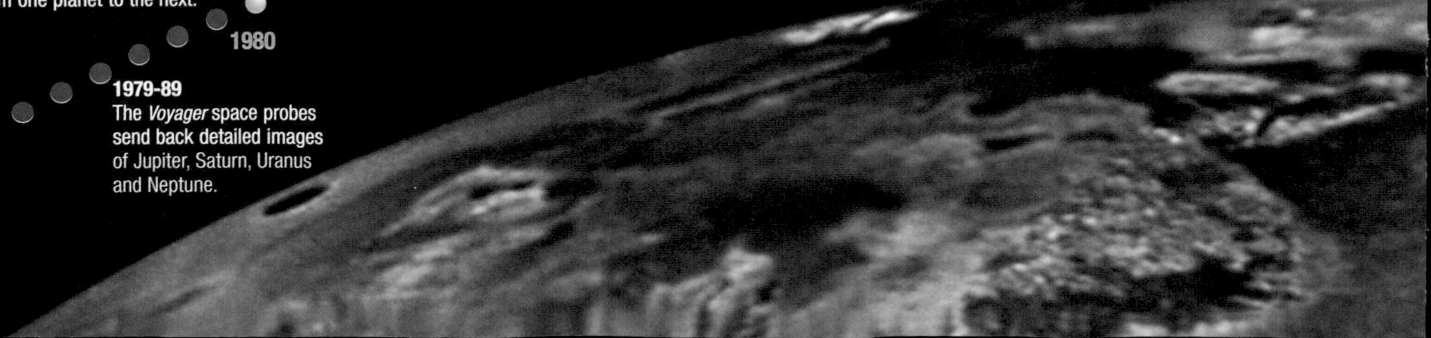

The International Space Station

A Russian rocket launched in November 1999 carried into space the first part of what will be the biggest space structure ever built – the International Space Station (ISS), also known as space station Alpha. When completed in about 2005, it will be as big as a football field, orbiting at an altitude of about 350 km (220 miles). It will have 6500 m^2 (70 000 sq ft) of power-generating solar panels and will be a bright moving object in the night sky.

Collaborators from a number of countries are building various laboratory, control and living modules, which will be attached to a central girder-like truss. Up to seven specialists at a time will be able to conduct research in a wide range of fields. Floating "personal satellite assistants" – spherical electronic robots 15 cm (6 in.) across – will aid crew communications.

American space shuttles and Russian Soyuz spacecraft are the initial means of getting to and from the station, but a new highly efficient shuttle, the X-38, is being developed in the United States. It will dramatically reduce the cost of launching each metric ton of payload into space and will also act as a "lifeboat" in case of emergency.

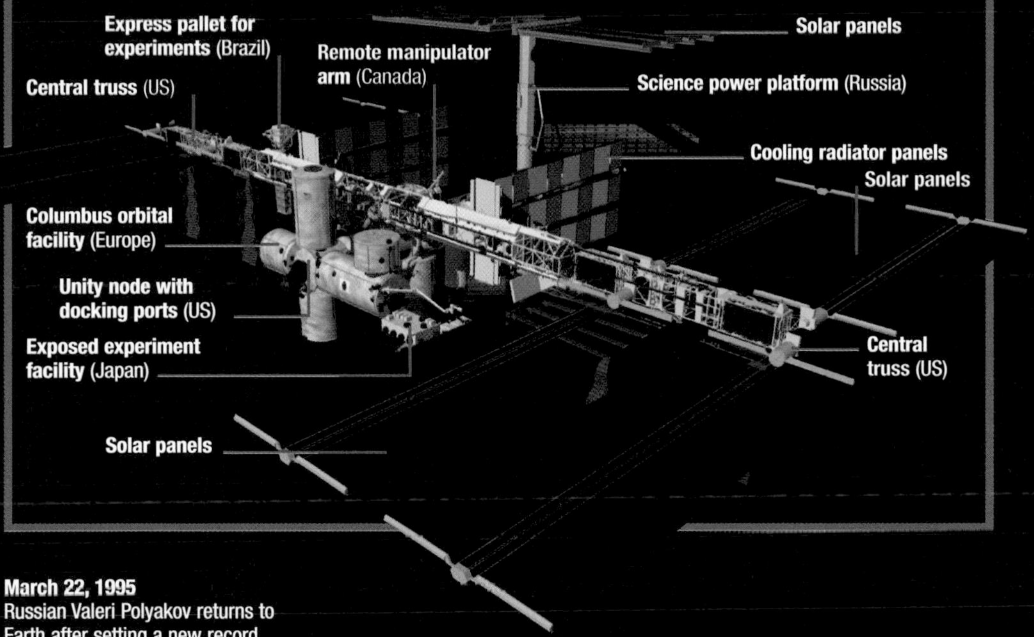

March 22, 1995
Russian Valeri Polyakov returns to Earth after setting a new record for manned space flight with more than 14 months aboard Mir.

December 7, 1995
The American probe *Galileo*, launched on October 18, 1989, reaches Jupiter. One section goes into orbit and the other enters the planet's atmosphere. It transmits data for more than an hour as it descends. The orbiter goes on to send detailed images of Jupiter and its moons.

1995

June 25, 1997
An unmanned supply craft collides with Mir, damaging the space station's power supply, disabling its computer and endangering the crew's lives. Later repairs allow Mir to continue orbiting until 2001.

October 15, 1997
The American *Cassini* probe, with the European *Huygens* lander, is launched on a flight to Saturn. It is expected to go into orbit around Saturn in 2004.

July 4, 1997
The United States *Pathfinder* lands on Mars and explores the site with the tiny Sojourner rover.

February 18, 1998
Voyager 1 becomes the most distant space probe, overtaking *Pioneer 10*. By the year 2000, it is more than 12 billion km (7.5 billion miles) away.

October 29-November 7, 1998
John Glenn, the first American in orbit, joins a space shuttle flight, becoming the oldest person to go into space.

November 20, 1998
A Russian rocket launches the first section of the International Space Station (ISS). Three weeks later, Americans launch the next.

January 3, 2000
Galileo passes close to Jupiter's moon Europa. Its radar detects evidence of salty water below Europa's frozen surface.

November 2, 2000
An American astronaut and two Russians begin the first full-scale mission on board the International Space Station.

2000

February 1, 2003
US space shuttle *Columbia* breaks apart on re-entry, killing crew of seven.

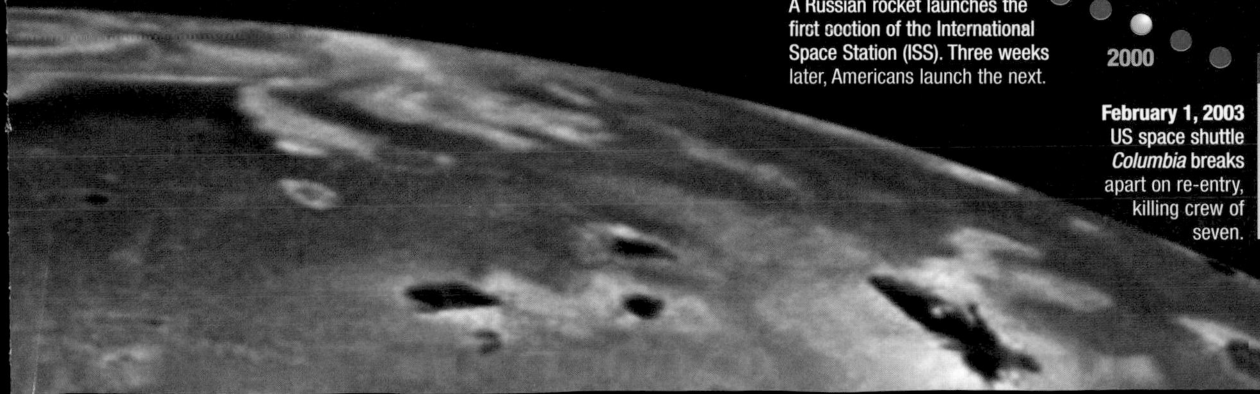

SPACE FACTS

Mountains of the Moon American astronaut John Young's six trips into space are a record. He also reached the highest lunar altitude when he stood with Charles Duke at 7830 m (25 688 ft) on the Descartes Highlands.

"Sling-shot" effect If a space vehicle approaches a planet at the correct angle and distance, the planet's gravitational pull not only changes the craft's direction, but also speeds it up. The planet slows down a tiny amount in compensation. This "sling-shot" effect has been used a number of times – notably with *Voyager 1*, which passed four planets in 1979-89.

Space feud Cosmonauts Valentin Lebedev and Anatoly Berezovoi got on each other's nerves on board Mir in 1982. They hardly spoke to each other for 211 days.

Heat of entry A spacecraft entering Earth's atmosphere compresses and heats the air in front of it, rather like a giant meteor. The space shuttle uses a protective shield of heat-resistant tiles made of silica fibers, but most earlier spacecraft had layers of "ablative" coatings that simply burned off slowly.

Space junk About 300 satellites orbit the Earth, but they share space with more than 20 000 identified pieces of space junk. These include satellite and rocket parts, lost tools, paint flecks and even discarded human waste.

see also

20-21 **The planets**
22-23 **The Moon**
396-97 **First steps in space**
472-73 **The night sky**

Information, and the technologies involved in processing and transmitting it, are a major source of economic power. Virtually every business depends on communication technology, from telephones to computers and the Internet. Corporations that own and sell information and entertainment – media businesses – have become richer and more powerful than many small nations, and their spread is increasingly global.

THE RISE AND RISE OF THE MEDIA

Three factors fed the rising importance of the information and entertainment industries during the 20th century:

- a rising demand from consumers with increasing spare time;
- a growth in the amount of information (from academic research to pure entertainment) being created; and
- technological advances in the delivery of the information.

The technological factor became overwhelming with the development of personal computers and particularly with the Internet in the 1980s and 1990s, leading to a vast growth in the accessibility of information – the so-called "information revolution."

Creating a global marketplace

One important effect of new technology was the blurring of the distinction between different media, which encouraged large-scale mergers of media and entertainment businesses (see below). Some forecasters predict a future in which television and radio programs and movies are distributed over a superfast version of the Internet, newspapers and magazines are delivered in the same way, and "e-books" replace the printed version. The Internet has also begun to affect traditional methods of selling – millions now shop online for goods as varied as cars, computers and groceries. In 1999 alone, new "dot.com" businesses fueled stock markets by several trillion dollars – only to see a slump the next year when investors realized how long it might take for such firms to make a profit.

The Web explosion

In the seven years between 1993 and 2000, the number of sites on the World Wide Web grew from a few hundred to nearly 25 million, and the number of individual Web pages to more than 1 billion. In the same period, the number of "host" computers on the Internet – those with a registered Internet address – grew from just over a million to almost 100 million.

There were an estimated 300 million Internet users in 2000. Nearly half were American, but the medium has circled the globe, with an estimated 9 million people on-line in China and almost 2 million in Africa. A record 5.8 million "surfers" logged on to CNN's Web site the day after the 2000 US presidential elections.

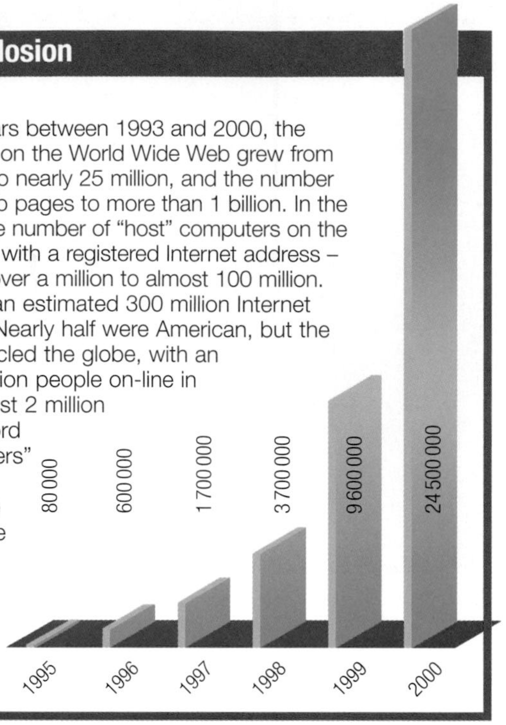

GLOBAL MEDIA GIANTS

The trend toward mergers that began in the 1980s has created several giant media firms that are not always profitable. The six biggest span a wide range of media, in areas such as publishing, music and TV.

Viacom

Viacom, a US company, acquired the Hollywood studio Paramount and the video retailer Blockbuster in 1994. In 2000, it completed a $50 billion merger with CBS Corporation. Businesses include
Film: Paramount Pictures; United Cinemas International (partly owned)
Broadcasting: CBS Television, with 39 stations and more than 200 affiliates; cable networks MTV, Nickelodeon, Showtime, BET and VH1; Infinity Broadcasting, with 180 radio stations
Book publishing: Simon & Schuster; Pocket Books
Other: Paramount theme parks; Blockbuster video stores; the largest outdoor advertising sites in North America
Worth: In 2001, Viacom and CBS together had revenues of $23 billion and losses of $223 million.

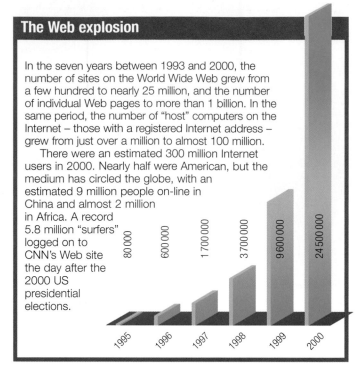

Vivendi Universal

This company was created in 2000 by the merger of French firms Vivendi (with businesses ranging from telecommunications to water supply) and Canal Plus (television) with Seagram of Canada. Businesses include
Films: Universal Studios; Canal Plus; Studio Canal
Broadcasting: Universal Television; Canal Plus; Canal Satellite; USA network; Sci-Fi Channel; Trio
Music: Universal Music Group, including MCA, Polydor, Island Records, Motown, Decca
Book publishing: Havas (France), with 60 imprints
Internet: Vivendi Universal Net, including MP3.com (music site) and Education.com (education site)
Other: Universal Studios theme parks; Cetegal Group; mobile and other telecommunications networks; Spencer Gifts
Worth: The combined company has revenues of $51 billion. In 2001, Vivendi posted losses of $12 billion.

Bertelsmann

A German company, Bertelsmann owns the world's largest book-publishing group and Europe's biggest broadcasting corporation. Businesses include
Broadcasting: Television channels RTL (Germany), M6 (France) and part of Channel 5 (Britain); 14 radio stations
Music: More than 200 music labels, including RCA and Arista (US) and Ariola (Germany)
Magazines and newspapers: Gruner & Jahr, with more than 80 magazines; 11 newspapers in Germany and Eastern Europe, including *Berliner Zeitung*
Book publishing: Random House and Transworld groups (US and UK), including Knopf, Crown, Bantam, Doubleday, Dell, Jonathan Cape, Century, Hutchinson, Ebury Press and Corgi; Berlin Verlag, Goldmann, and Siedler Verlag (Germany); Plaza & Janés (Spain); Sudamericana (Argentina); book clubs in many countries; Internet stores BOL.com and Barnes&Noble.com
Internet: Comundo (Internet access); Lycos (search engine)
Worth: In 2001, Bertelsmann had revenues of $17.9 billion, assets of $10.4 billion and profits of $701 million.

LEADERS IN THE INFORMATION ECONOMY

The degree to which a nation participates in the information technology revolution is measured by the Information Society Index – a measure of people's "information wealth." The index is based on four main factors:

- Computer infrastructure, including the number of computers in homes, schools and businesses.
- Information access, including television, radio, telephones and fax machines.
- Internet access, including the use of e-commerce
- Social factors such as levels of school enrollment, press freedom and civil liberties

1999 rank	2000 rank	Country	2000 score
1	**1**	Sweden	6496
4	**2**	Norway	6112
3	**3**	Finland	5953
2	**4**	United States	5850
5	**5**	Denmark	5837
12	**6**	United Kingdom	5662
8	**7**	Switzerland	5528
9	**8**	Australia	5382
11	**9**	Singapore	5269
7	**10**	The Netherlands	5238
10	**11**	Japan	5182
6	**12**	Canada	5126
13	**13**	Germany	4937
16	**14**	Austria	4868
14	**15**	Hong Kong	4745
17	**16**	New Zealand	4483
15	**17**	Belgium	4439
18	**18**	Taiwan	4296

Silicon Valley

The information technology (IT) industry has created several economic boom areas, most famously Silicon Valley, near San Francisco, California. It began in 1953, when Stanford University leased some of its land in Palo Alto for a high-tech industrial park. Soon companies such as Hewlett-Packard and IBM had bases there; more quickly followed, attracted by the facilities and highly skilled manpower available, the proximity of advanced research centers and the opportunity to do business with each other.

The Silicon Valley name, derived from the material used for microchips, was coined by journalist Don Hoefler in 1971. Today, 4000 IT companies are based between San Francisco and San José, accounting for 40 percent of California's export trade. Similar areas soon grew in New York City (nicknamed "Silicon Alley"), Scotland ("Silicon Glen") and Bangalore, India ("Silicon Plateau").

see also
348-53 **Cinema**
354-55 **Television**
356-57 **Newspapers**
456-57 **The Internet**

Media mogul Rupert Murdoch (1931-) inherited the *Melbourne News* in 1952 and started to build a media empire. He took over often weak newspapers in Britain, the US and elsewhere and made them successful. Buying 20th Century Fox in 1985 took him into film and television, and in 1989 he began building a global satellite TV network.

Media and sports Ted Turner, founder, of CNN bought the Atlanta Hawks in 1977.

News Corporation

Headed by Rupert Murdoch and based in Australia, News Corp. is the world's leading publisher of English-language newspapers, printing 40 million copies a week of more than 175 titles. It is also a major television filmmaker and book publisher. Businesses include

Films: 20th Century Fox; Fox Searchlight
Broadcasting: Fox Network, with more than 25 television stations; FX (US); British Sky Broadcasting (BSkyB); STAR (Asia); Foxtel (Australia)
Newspapers and magazines: *The Australian* and *Daily Telegraph* and *Sunday Telegraph* (Australia); *The Times*, *Sunday Times*, *The Sun* and *News of the World* (UK); *New York Post* (US); numerous newspapers in Pacific region; *TV Guide* (US, partly owned)
Book publishing: HarperCollins (US, Canada, Australia, and UK); Zondervan (US)
Sports: Los Angeles Dodgers (baseball); National Rugby League (Australia)
Worth: In 2001, News Corporation had revenues of $13.7 billion, assets of $43.2 billion and losses of $401 million.

AOL Time Warner

This media giant was created in 2001 by the merger of Internet firm America Online (AOL) with Time Warner, the world's largest media company. Businesses include

Films: Warner Bros.; Hanna-Barbera; Castle Rock
Broadcasting: Cable News Network (CNN); Cartoon Network; Home Box Office (HBO); Turner Broadcasting System (TBS); Turner Network Television (TNT); Time Warner Cable network; The WB
Music: Warner Bros.; Atlantic; Elektra; Rhino
Magazines: *Time*; *People*; *Sports Illustrated*; *Fortune*; many others
Book publishing: Little, Brown and Company; Warner Books
Sports: Atlanta Braves (baseball); Atlanta Hawks (basketball); Goodwill Games
Internet: America Online (AOL); CompuServe; Netscape
Other: Theme parks; Warner Bros. studio stores in 30 countries
Worth: In 2001, the company had revenues of $38 billion, but posted an almost $5 billion loss.

Disney

As well as the entertainment businesses usually associated with the Disney name, this US company also makes CDs and audio cassettes and produces musicals. Businesses include

Films: Walt Disney; Miramax; Touchstone; Buena Vista
Broadcasting: Radio and television stations including ABC network; Disney Channel; ESPN (sports); SoapNet
Music: Buena Vista Music Group; Walt Disney Records
Internet: Part of Infoseek (search engine); other Internet sites
Other: Disney and Disney-MGM theme parks; Walt Disney Theatrical Productions
Worth: In 2001, Disney's revenues were $25.3 billion, with losses of $158 million.

Shakespeare in Love Miramax's 1998 blockbuster.

Almost 80 percent of the energy consumed globally is produced by burning fossil fuels – coal, oil (petroleum) and natural gas. Fossil fuels are the remains of living organisms that have been buried in the Earth for millions of years. They are the cheapest and most effective way of producing energy, but resources are finite and are steadily being used up.

Carbon dioxide levels

Burning fossil fuels releases carbon dioxide, which contributes to global warming by trapping infrared radiation in the atmosphere – known as the "greenhouse effect." China, the Middle East and the former USSR produce the largest amounts of carbon dioxide in relation to the amount of energy they create.

Production of CO_2 in metric tons of CO_2 per metric ton of oil equivalent, 1998

North Korea	3.63	South Africa	3.19	Israel	3.00	Morocco	2.86
Macedonia	3.40	Estonia	3.17	Gibraltar	2.98	Lebanon	2.84
Poland	3.32	Libya	3.11	Czech Republic	2.94	Iraq	2.83
Kazakhstan	3.23	Greece	3.06	Ireland	2.90	China	2.77

How a refinery works

Oil refineries separate the chemical components, or fractions, of crude oil. Each fraction vaporizes (boils) at a different temperature. Crude oil is heated until it begins to vaporize and then is fed into the bottom of a distillation tower. Oil vapor rises up the tower as it cools, condensing into different liquids at different levels and remaining gaseous at the top. Each fraction forms a different end product.

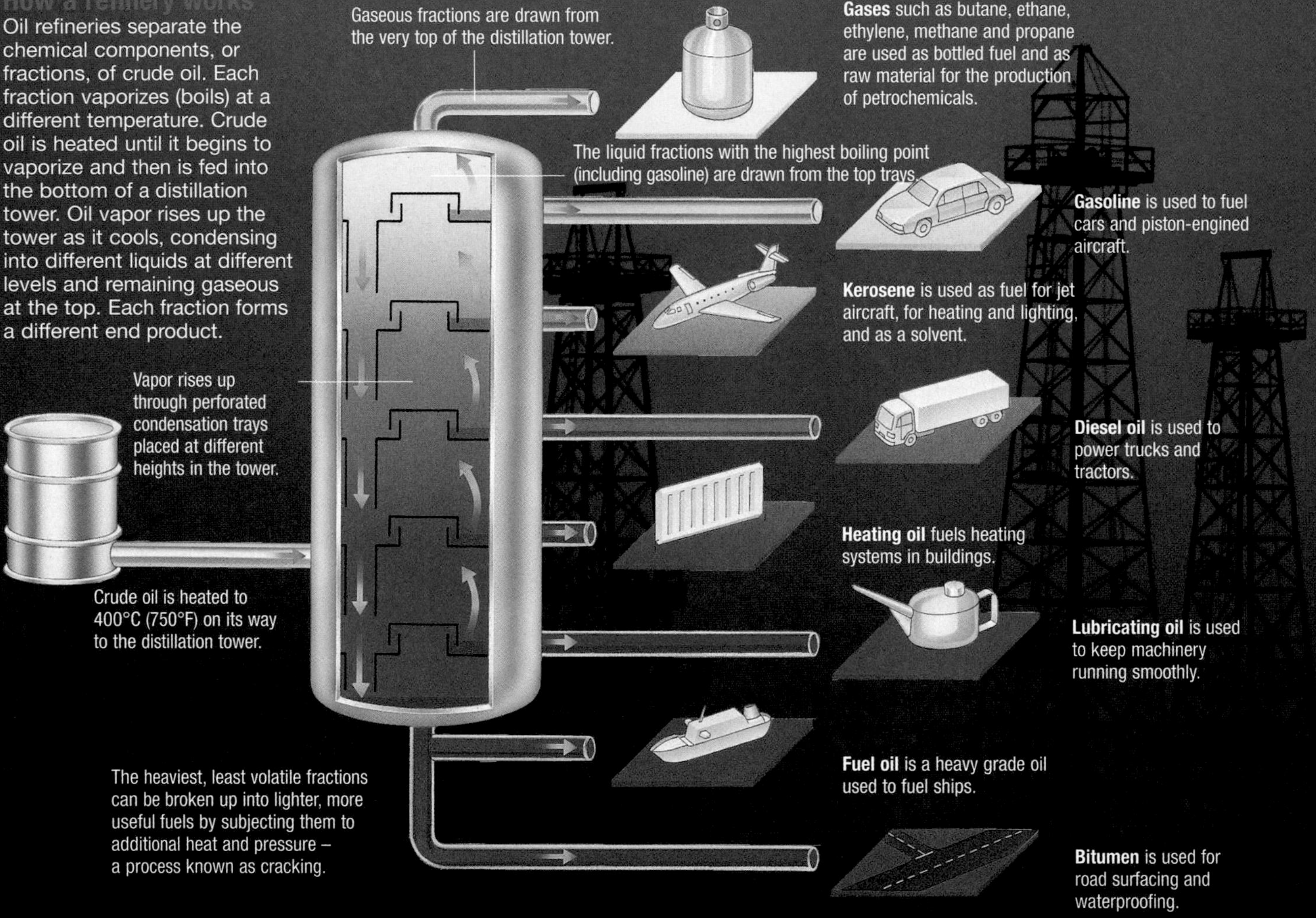

Gaseous fractions are drawn from the very top of the distillation tower.
Gases such as butane, ethane, ethylene, methane and propane are used as bottled fuel and as raw material for the production of petrochemicals.
The liquid fractions with the highest boiling point (including gasoline) are drawn from the top trays.
Gasoline is used to fuel cars and piston-engined aircraft.
Kerosene is used as fuel for jet aircraft, for heating and lighting, and as a solvent.
Vapor rises up through perforated condensation trays placed at different heights in the tower.
Diesel oil is used to power trucks and tractors.
Heating oil fuels heating systems in buildings.
Crude oil is heated to 400°C (750°F) on its way to the distillation tower.
Lubricating oil is used to keep machinery running smoothly.
Fuel oil is a heavy grade oil used to fuel ships.
The heaviest, least volatile fractions can be broken up into lighter, more useful fuels by subjecting them to additional heat and pressure – a process known as cracking.
Bitumen is used for road surfacing and waterproofing.

400 B.C. 0 1200s 1500s 1600s 1700s 1800s

370 B.C. Coal first used as a fuel in China.

13th century The first commercial coal mines go into operation in England and Belgium.

Before 16th century Native Americans use oil from pools and wells as fuel.

Early 17th century Coal overtakes wood and charcoal as the most-used industrial fuel in England.

1765 In England, coal gas is used to light the offices of a mine near Whitehaven, Cumberland.

Late 18th century In Britain, American scientist Benjamin Thompson invents efficient coal grates, stoves and chimneys.

1815 British scientist Humphrey Davy invents the safety lamp, making coal mining safer.

1821 William Hart digs the first natural gas well, 8 m (26 ft) deep, at Fredonia, New York.

c. 1850 Processes are developed for distilling kerosene from oil shale, tar and oil.

1855 Robert Bunsen, a German chemist, invents an efficient gas burner for use in ovens and heaters.

1859 Edwin Drake drills the first oil well, at Oil Creek, Pennsylvania.

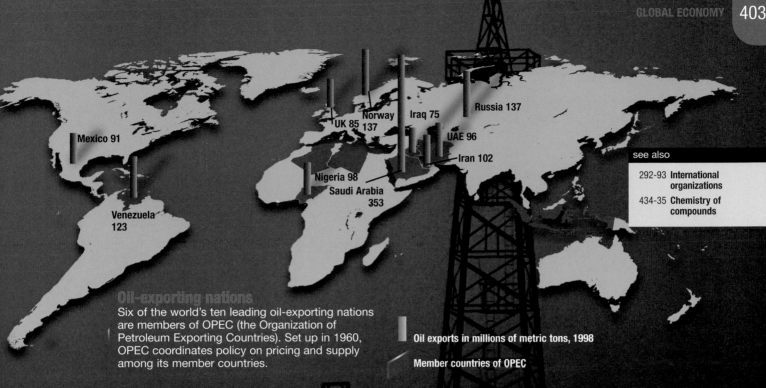

see also
292-93 International organizations
434-35 Chemistry of compounds

Oil-exporting nations

Six of the world's ten leading oil-exporting nations are members of OPEC (the Organization of Petroleum Exporting Countries). Set up in 1960, OPEC coordinates policy on pricing and supply among its member countries.

Oil exports in millions of metric tons, 1998

Member countries of OPEC

Oil

About 95 percent of the world's oil has been produced by 5 percent of its oil fields. Two thirds of the largest fields have been found in the Middle East. Scientists estimate that reserves will run out before 2060.

	Top producers, 1996 (million barrels per day)			Top consumers, 1996 (million barrels per day)	
1	Saudi Arabia	9.23	1	US	17.81
2	US	8.00	2	Japan	5.55
3	Russia	6.17	3	China	4.11
4	Iran	3.80	4	Germany	2.92
5	Mexico	3.50	5	Russia	2.46
6	Venezuela	3.34	6	South Korea	2.02
7	Norway	3.22	7	France	2.01
8	China	3.21	8	Italy	1.98
9	UK	2.80	9	India	1.82
10	UAE	2.71	10	Canada	1.82

Natural gas

Russia and the Middle East originally contained the world's largest natural gas reserves. Only 14 percent of global reserves have been used up, but it is estimated that remaining reserves are likely to run out before 2115.

	Top producers, 1996 (billion m^3)			Top consumers, 1996 (billion m^3)	
1	Russia	551.3	1	US	612.4
2	US	543.8	2	Russia	364.7
3	Canada	160.4	3	UK	88.7
4	UK	90.3	4	Germany	79.5
5	Algeria	72.8	5	Canada	70.3
6	Indonesia	68.4	6	Japan	69.5
7	Netherlands	63.6	7	Ukraine	68.8
8	Uzbekistan	51.1	8	Italy	57.2
9	Iran	50.0	9	Iran	51.7
10	Saudi Arabia	46.0	10	Uzbekistan	47.0

Coal

Coal reserves exist in every continent, including Antarctica, but technology and economics will only allow the recovery of 7 percent. Estimates of when reserves will run out range from 2250 to around 3400.

	Top producers, 1996 (million metric tons)			Top consumers, 1996 (million metric tons)	
1	China	625.7	1	China	615.4
2	US	589.6	2	US	533.7
3	India	147.8	3	India	153.6
4	Australia	147.5	4	Russia	102.8
5	South Africa	118.3	5	Japan	88.4
6	Russia	104.6	6	South Africa	87.9
7	Poland	76.3	7	Germany	84.7
8	Germany	61.3	8	Poland	60.9
9	Canada	41.1	9	Australia	45.8
10	Ukraine	39.6	10	UK	40.7

1872 The first natural gas pipelines are constructed in Pennsylvania and New York.

1882 Thomas Edison builds the world's first large-scale electricity generating station in New York.

1890 The process for making smokeless fuel from coal is patented.

1900s

1908 The first big discovery of oil is made in the Middle East, in Persia (Iran).

1913 The invention of thermal cracking (see How an oil refinery works, opposite) boosts the output of gasoline from each barrel of crude oil.

1940s Cracking is used to boost the output of aviation fuel in World War II.

1948 The Al-Ghawar oil field is discovered in Saudi Arabia. It later proves to be the world's largest oil field, containing 82 billion barrels.

1970s The 5470 km (3400 mile) Northern Lights gas pipeline is built from the Arctic Circle to Europe.

1973 The Arab-Israeli war provokes a world energy crisis when Arab nations stop exporting oil to the US, Israel's ally.

1974 The Organization of Petroleum Exporting Countries quadruples oil prices. Global economic recession follows.

1991 Iraq releases almost a million metric tons of crude oil into the sea during the Gulf War – the biggest-ever oil spill.

1990s Asia, Europe and the US research Clean Coal Technologies (CCTs) to reduce emissions and increase efficiency.

2000

Nuclear power is generated by the fission, or splitting apart, of atoms of uranium or plutonium. The process releases huge amounts of energy using small amounts of raw material: The fission of 1 kg (2.2 lb) of uranium releases as much energy as burning 2000 metric tons of coal or 8000 barrels of oil.

Creating power: the chain reaction

Atoms are composed of electrons surrounding a nucleus which contains protons and neutrons. Bombarding an atom with neutrons splits the nucleus into two parts. This process, called fission, releases energy (as heat) and radioactivity, and it frees up more neutrons. The neutrons can be captured and used to bombard further atoms, continuing the process in a chain reaction. Fission is regulated by substances known as moderators (usually water or metal) which slow the neutrons down to improve their chances of hitting nuclei. If the energy is contained and controlled, it provides a source of power; if it is not contained, it causes a huge "atomic" explosion.

Types of nuclear reactor

Pressurized water reactor (PWR) The most common design for nuclear reactors (also known as light water reactors) uses high-pressure water as a coolant. The coolant removes heat from the reactor's core and channels it into a heat exchanger, which produces steam. The steam spins turbines to generate electricity.

Boiling water reactor (BWR) This is another type of light water reactor. The coolant passes through the core and is allowed to boil, producing steam.

Pressurised heavy water reactor (PHWR) The coolant is "heavy water," processed water with a higher molecular weight than ordinary water.

Light water graphite reactor (LWGR) LWGR fuel rods are contained in individual pressure tubes surrounded by water (the coolant) and graphite (the moderator, which slows the neutrons and thus speeds up the process of fission).

Gas-cooled reactor (GCR) GCRs use pressurized carbon dioxide instead of water as a coolant.

Advanced gas-cooled reactor (AGR) Advanced GCRs work in the same way as ordinary GCRs, but they use chemically manufactured enriched uranium as fuel. Enriched uranium is about five times more concentrated than natural uranium.

Fast breeder reactor (FBR) Breeder reactors produce more fuel (in the form of plutonium) than they consume. FBRs do not use a moderator, so the neutrons are able to travel faster. The original fuel is a type of uranium that becomes unstable when bombarded by fast neutrons and decays into plutonium.

PRESSURIZED WATER REACTOR

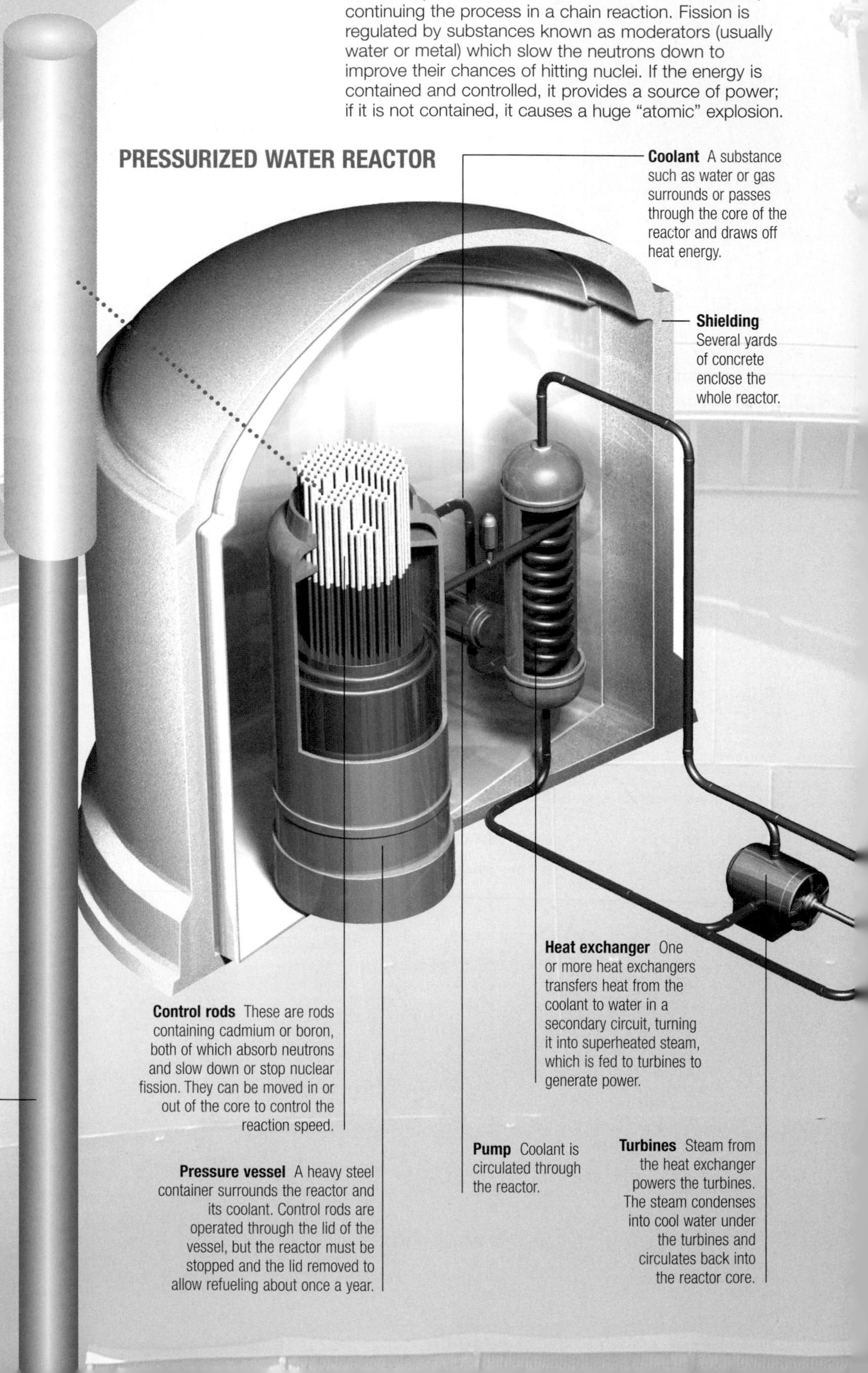

Coolant A substance such as water or gas surrounds or passes through the core of the reactor and draws off heat energy.

Shielding Several yards of concrete enclose the whole reactor.

Heat exchanger One or more heat exchangers transfers heat from the coolant to water in a secondary circuit, turning it into superheated steam, which is fed to turbines to generate power.

Control rods These are rods containing cadmium or boron, both of which absorb neutrons and slow down or stop nuclear fission. They can be moved in or out of the core to control the reaction speed.

Fuel rods Nuclear fuel – usually uranium oxide pellets – is contained in rods about 4 m (13 ft) long by 1 cm (1/2 in.) in diameter. These are surrounded by a moderator substance that slows down the neutrons (fast-moving neutrons bounce off uranium atoms instead of penetrating them).

Pressure vessel A heavy steel container surrounds the reactor and its coolant. Control rods are operated through the lid of the vessel, but the reactor must be stopped and the lid removed to allow refueling about once a year.

Pump Coolant is circulated through the reactor.

Turbines Steam from the heat exchanger powers the turbines. The steam condenses into cool water under the turbines and circulates back into the reactor core.

Leading producers of nuclear power

Percentage of domestic electricity supplied by nuclear power, 1998

1	France	77	7	UK	28
2	Sweden	47	8	US	19
3	Ukraine	44	9 (tie)	Canada	13
4	South Korea	38	9 (tie)	Russia	13
5	Japan	32		Rest of the world	10
6	Germany	29		*World total*	*17*

The most common types of power reactor used by leading producers

Overall, the pressurized water reactor is the most widely used around the world. France, the second largest producer of nuclear power, and Russia have the only fast breeder reactors.

	Country	PWR	BWR	GCR	PHWR	LWGR	AGR	FBR	Production in million MW hrs
1	US	69	34						714
2	France	58						1	388
3	Japan	23	27						332
4	Germany	14	6						162
5	Russia	13				15	14	1	104
6	UK	1		20					100
7	South Korea	12			4				90
8	Ukraine	13				1			75

FOR AND AGAINST

Pros

- Nuclear power uses less raw material than fossil fuel.
- It does not release uncontrolled harmful emissions into the atmosphere, unlike fossil fuels. In one year, one nuclear reactor at 80% capacity can generate 7 billion kwh, enough to power 650,000 homes.

Cons

- Nuclear power stations are expensive to build.
- Public concern has led to protests over the storage of highly radioactive waste and the danger it poses to human health. The exposure of humans to radiation as a result of malfunctions at power stations has provoked calls for the closure of all nuclear plants.
- The gathering of raw material for nuclear power production risks the possibility of its appropriation for the unlicensed manufacture of nuclear weapons.

Key dates

1905 Albert Einstein's Special Theory of Relativity suggests that mass (matter) can be converted into energy.

1938 German scientists Otto Hahn and Fritz Strassmann split uranium atoms by bombarding them with neutrons. The process involves the loss of mass, which is converted into energy, confirming Einstein's theory.

1942 A team led by Enrico Fermi at the University of Chicago builds a nuclear reactor and creates the first man-made uranium chain reaction. This is the birth of the nuclear age.

1943-45 Reactors are built in Hanford, Washington, to manufacture plutonium for use in atomic bombs.

1952 An experimental dual-purpose breeder reactor is built in Idaho – it produces both electricity and plutonium fuel.

1956 The first full-scale nuclear power station opens near Sellafield in Britain. The following year, a reactor overheats, setting the core on fire and releasing radioactivity into the local area.

1957 A chemical explosion in radioactive waste tanks at a plant near Chelyabinsk, USSR, contaminates a wide area in the Urals.

1979 Malfunction and operator error cause the loss of coolant in a reactor at Three Mile Island in Pennsylvania, leading to the overheating and partial meltdown of its core.

1986 A reactor explodes at Chernobyl, Ukraine, killing 32 people and spreading radioactivity as far as France and Italy. Radiation sickness later kills many more people in the surrounding area.

1999 Operator error causes an uncontrolled chain reaction at the Tokaimura processing plant in Japan. Three workers are irradiated: two later die; hundreds more are exposed.

Dealing with the waste

Levels of radioactivity deplete over time. The toxic radioactive waste produced by nuclear fission is categorized as low, intermediate or high-level, depending on how long it is likely to remain dangerous. Low and intermediate-level waste includes items such as discarded protective clothing and the sludge and resin produced by the reaction process. Low-level waste is incinerated, compressed and stored underground. Intermediate-level waste is shielded in drums and placed inside a concrete or bitumen chamber.

High-level waste includes dangerous isotopes (see page 426), whose radioactivity lasts in some cases for hundreds or even thousands of years. These are currently stored in liquid form in stainless-steel tanks at specialized waste disposal sites. The liquid continues to emit heat, and has to be cooled continually.

Long-term plans have been made to store high-level waste inside solid glass blocks and keep it above ground for 50 years before disposal. This will allow its radioactivity to decay to lower levels. It could then be stored in the same way as intermediate-level waste.

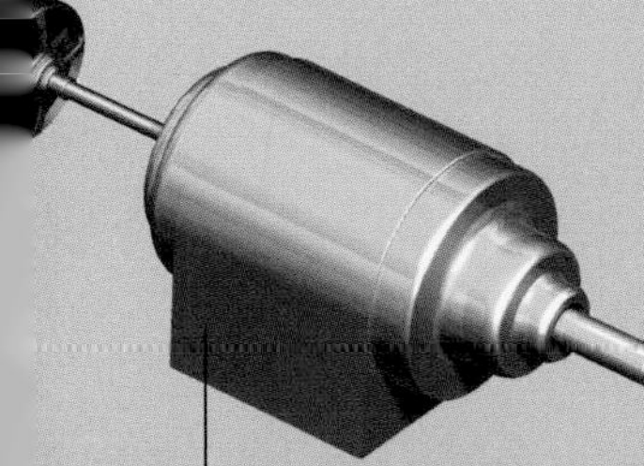

Generator The electricity generated provides a local or national supply. The output of a typical commercial nuclear power station is usually between 600 and 1000 megawatts.

Geiger counting Radiation levels are periodically checked at disposal sites such as this low-level waste site in Hanford, WA.

see also

426-27 **Radioactivity**
428-29 **Relativity**

The unrelenting global demand for energy and the knowledge that fossil fuel reserves will not last forever have led to a hunt for renewable resources. The use of hydroelectricity is well established. In countries such as Norway and Brazil, it accounts for more than 90 percent of domestic electricity generation. The oil crisis of the 1970s created renewed interest in wind power, a field now led by Germany, the US, Denmark and India.

A.D. 1000 — 1800

915 Windmills are used to grind grain in Seistan, Persia.

12th century Windmills become common in Europe, particularly in the Netherlands, where they are used for draining marshes.

1891 An experimental hydroelectric power plant is built in Germany.

1893 The world's first major hydroelectric plant is built at Niagara Falls on the US-Canadian border.

HYDROELECTRICITY

Hydroelectric power stations use the power of falling water to drive a turbine coupled to an electric generator. Stations are built at natural waterfalls, such as Niagara Falls on the US-Canadian border, or by constructing a dam across a river and controlling the water flow through artificial channels.

In areas where the demand for electricity varies throughout the day, pumped-storage hydroelectric plants are used. In periods of low demand, surplus power generated by the plant is used to reverse the water flow and fill an artificial reservoir behind the dam. The stored water is released at times of peak demand to provide extra power.

- **Pros** Running costs are low and hydroelectric plants do not produce harmful emissions. Constructing dams helps to regulate seasonal flooding and provides water for irrigation.
- **Cons** Construction costs are high. Dams may flood large areas of land, upsetting the local ecological balance.
- **Biggest plants** The Itaipú plant on the Paraná River (Brazil-Paraguay border) has a capacity of 12 600 megawatts. The Three Gorges project on the Yangtze River in China, due for completion in 2009, will have a capacity of 18 200 megawatts.

A river of energy The 7744 m (25 500 ft) stretch of dams that make up the Itaipú complex on the Brazil-Paraguay border are connected to 18 generating units with a capacity of 700 MW each. The energy captured from the Paraná River supplies 25 percent of Brazil's power and 78 percent of Paraguay's power.

Leading producers of hydroelectricity for domestic use, 1998

Total production of hydroelectricity in million megawatt hours
World total: 2643

Percentage of domestic power generation provided by hydroelectricity
World total: 18.4 percent

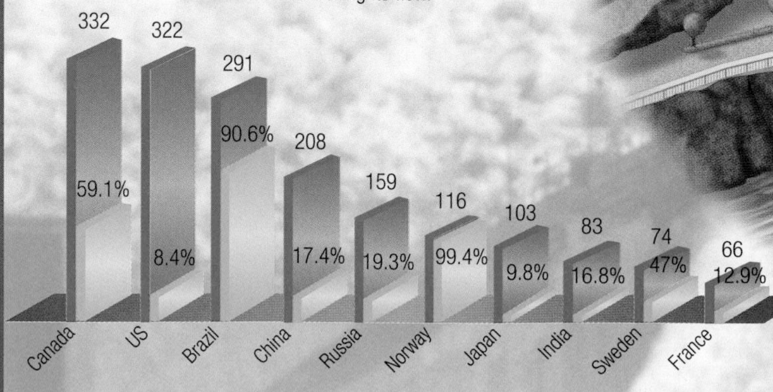

Generating power A hydroelectric plant (right) creates energy by trapping a river behind a dam and controlling its flow.

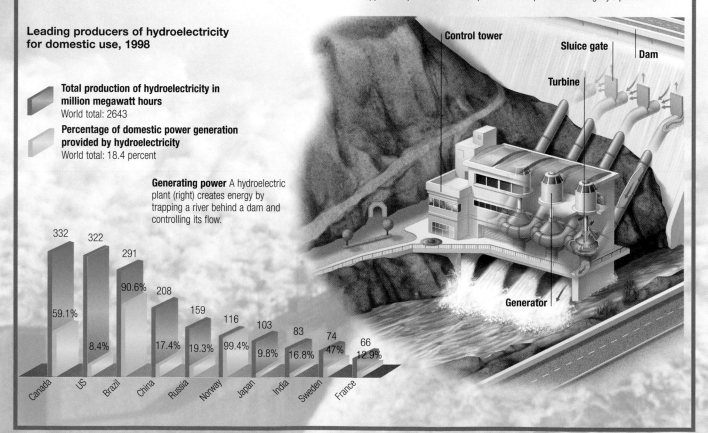

1900 1940 1960 1980

1904 The world's first geothermal power plant opens at Larderello, Italy, with a generating capacity of 250 kW.

1941 The first modern wind turbine generating 1250 kW is built in Vermont.

1960 The first thermal power plant using solar energy is built in the Soviet republic of Turkmenistan.

1967 Construction of the first major tidal power plant is completed in the Rance estuary, near St. Malo, France.

1982 The 10-MW Solar One power plant begins operating in the Mojave Desert in California. By the 1990s, another eight solar plants have been built in the Mojave.

see also

22-23 **The Moon**

48-49 **Weather**

TIDAL AND WAVE POWER

Specialized hydroelectric plants harness the power of tides using dams constructed across river estuaries. During the flood tide, sluice gates are opened, allowing water to flow through the dam. At high tide, the gates are shut, trapping the water, which is released in a controlled flow as the tide ebbs.

Power plants have also been designed to harness the energy in the rise and fall of sea waves on ocean coasts. The movement of the waves compresses air inside covered chambers, pushing and pulling the air through reversible turbines. This technology is currently experimental, but its global energy potential is estimated at 2-3 million megawatts.

Pros Tidal and wave power plants do not produce harmful emissions, and offer a vast, sustainable resource.

Cons Tidal power is suitable only where the tidal range (the difference between high and low tide) is 6 m (20 ft) or more. Energy output varies because tides vary in height from day to day and season to season. Wave power energy output is also inconsistent because the size of waves varies. Power plants may cause ecological harm to the shoreline by altering tidal levels in estuaries and along coastlines. Ring-shaped offshore "tidal lagoon" plants are currently being planned, which may solve this problem.

Biggest plants The Rance estuary, near St. Malo, France, is the world's largest working tidal plant, with 24 turbines and a total capacity of 240 megawatts. The Azores, Portugal, have the world's largest wave installation, with a total power capacity of 1 megawatt.

Capturing the tides Reversible turbines capture energy during both ebb and flood tides.

WIND POWER

Most modern wind turbines have three-bladed propellers up to 100 m (330 ft) across attached to a generator. Computer control keeps the propeller facing the wind and adjusts its direction according to the wind strength. Generators can have a capacity of up to 4 megawatts each, but 250-500 kilowatts is more common. They are often grouped together offshore or in "wind farms" on windy ridges, plains or coasts.

The total worldwide energy capacity of wind turbines has increased by more than 25 percent per year since 1997. In 2000, it was estimated at more than 10 000 megawatts – ten times the capacity of 1990 – and rapidly increasing.

Pros The cost of running wind farms is competitive with the best coal or gas-powered generating stations, and wind turbines do not create harmful emissions.

Cons Power output varies depending upon the strength of the wind. The turbine blades and their mechanical gearboxes are noisy. The turbines also take up a great deal of space and are often considered unsightly. They can pose a threat to birds.

Biggest plants The largest wind farms – about 5000 turbines each – are in Altamount Pass and Tehachapi Pass, California. In combination with smaller California wind farms in San Gorgonio Pass, Pacheco Pass and Solano, they generate 30 per cent of the world's wind power. In 1995, California's wind power capacity reached 2.9 billion kilowatt hours of electricity a year – enough to supply 500 000 homes.

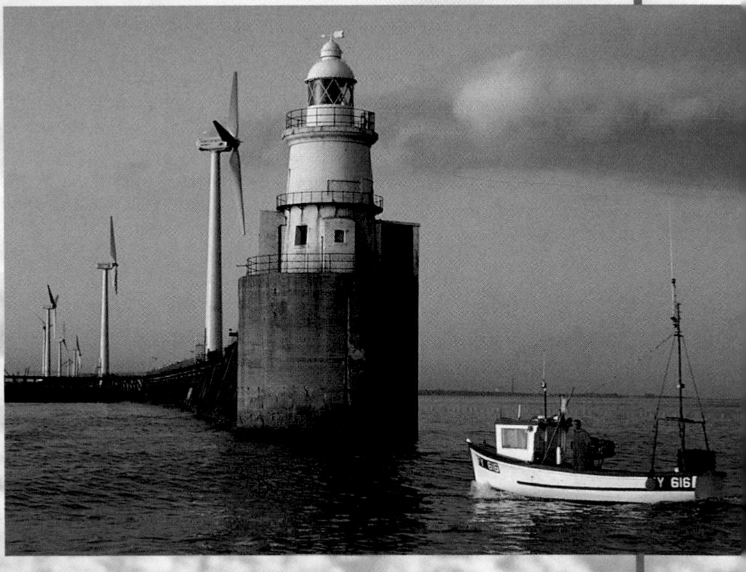

Coastal power Nine 300 kW turbines began operating at Blythe Harbour in the UK, in 1993. In 2000, two 2 MW turbines were built half a mile offshore. The Blythe turbines capture enough energy to supply 5000 homes.

By the end of the 20th century, several viable alternatives to fossil fuels had emerged. Solar power heats water in more than a million homes in Greece. Iceland capitalizes on its natural geothermal resources to heat 85 percent of its houses. Biomass energy, produced by the burning or chemical processing of organic matter, provides 15 percent of domestic power in Scandinavia and is the main energy source for millions of villagers in China and India.

SOLAR POWER

Two solar technologies are being developed. *Solar thermal* employs mirrors to focus the Sun's rays onto a heat collector, which boils water directly or heats an intermediate fluid such as oil, which is then used to generate steam to drive a turbine.

Solar electric exploits the principle that combinations of certain dissimilar materials, such as silicon and boron, create an electric charge when light is applied to them. This photoelectric effect, which can convert sunlight directly into electricity, is used for household energy supplies and to power calculators, satellite phones and experimental cars.

- **Advantages** Solar energy is an endlessly sustainable power source that causes no pollution.
- **Disadvantages** Large power plants cover huge expanses of land; generators produce power only during daylight hours and are only usable in areas with plentiful sunshine.
- **Biggest plant** A series of nine solar-power plants in the Mojave Desert in California, with computer-controlled parabolic mirrors, covers 400 hectares (1000 acres). It has a total output of 354 megawatts – enough to supply power to 500 000 people.

Under the African sun A reliance on wood for fuel has led to deforestation and inadequate energy supplies in the Sudan. In the 1990s, relief agencies and the United Nations Environment Programme began installing solar panels in Sudanese villages to power essentials such as lighting, refrigeration and water pumps.

Concentrated energy A giant parabolic reflector, built in 1969 in the Pyrenees mountains at Odeillo, France, directs the sun's rays to a single focal point, where a receiver collects the energy. The parabola receives sunlight from 63 heliostats (computer-controlled mirrors that move to reflect sunlight at a constant angle) positioned on an opposite hillside. Temperatures usually reach between 800°C (1472°F) and 2500°C (4532°F), providing a maximum power of 1000 kW.

GEOTHERMAL POWER

In regions with high levels of volcanic activity, the heat of rocks and underground water is used to produce electricity. Any naturally occurring steam is transported in pipes to the surface, where it drives turbines, which generate electricity. Holes are also drilled down to hot rocks and then water is run across them to produce steam. In 1998, the worldwide capacity of geothermal power reached 8240 megawatts.

- **Advantages** Geothermal power uses less land area per megawatt than almost any other kind of power plant and supplies energy 24 hours a day.
- **Disadvantages** Natural sources of steam are quite rare, and the energy they supply is not a truly renewable resource – natural hot spots can cool and take thousands of years to regenerate; power plants can be noisy, and their pipes often become corroded by waterborne minerals.
- **Biggest plant** The world's largest developed geothermal field, The Geysers in California, is capable of generating up to 1900 megawatts, but there are restrictions on energy production in order to prolong the life of the plant.

Leading geothermal power producers, 1998
Capacity in megawatts

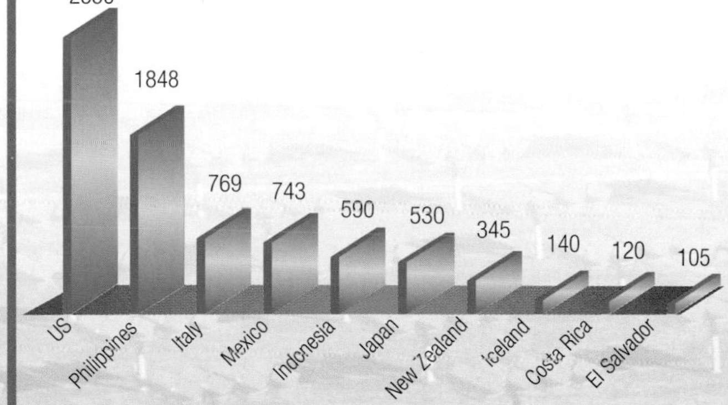

Steam power Planning for the Wairakei geothermal energy plant on New Zealand's North Island began in 1947, after sustained dry weather led to a hydroelectricity shortage. The Wairakei plant began operating in 1958; 40 years later, its operating capacity reached just over 160 megawatts.

BIOMASS

Power is generated from decaying organic matter and waste, such as plants, wood, straw, manure and household garbage. These are known collectively as biomass. Techniques for converting biomass into energy include

Tapping biogas Decaying animal waste and buried rubbish give off methane gas, which is collected and burned as fuel in specially designed biogas digesters.

Combustion Burning household garbage, rather than dumping it can contribute to a city's energy supply. Each metric ton of refuse can produce up to 400 m^3 (14 000 cu ft) of methane.

Alcohol fermentation During fermentation, enzymes break down plant starches into simpler compounds, eventually producing ethanol, a high-octane fuel. A small quantity of ethanol is frequently blended into the gasoline used in cars.

Plant oil processing Removing glycerine from vegetable oil leaves a clear liquid, known as biodiesel. This is burned as diesel fuel.

- **Advantages** Resources are endlessly renewable. Combustion reduces waste, and biofuels reduce pollution.
- **Disadvantages** Combustion creates gases that pollute the environment; if released, methane collected through biogas digesters also contributes to global warming.
- **Leading producers** The US has 70 biogas sites. The largest – in the Puente Hills in California – generates 46 megawatts. Most of the world's 350 combustion plants are in Europe and Japan: Germany burns about 5.5 million metric tons of refuse a year; Japan burns about half a million. Brazil produces about 3 billion gallons of liquid biofuel (ethanol and diesel) a year; the US produces about 1 billion gallons.

Recycling success More than 2.5 million household biogas plants have been installed in India since 1980. In many communities, biogas digesters attached to toilets use human waste to create energy for lighting and cooking. This helps improve hygiene, and frees up animal manure for use as fertilizer.

see also
404-5 **Nuclear power**
406-7 **Renewable energy**

Science and invention

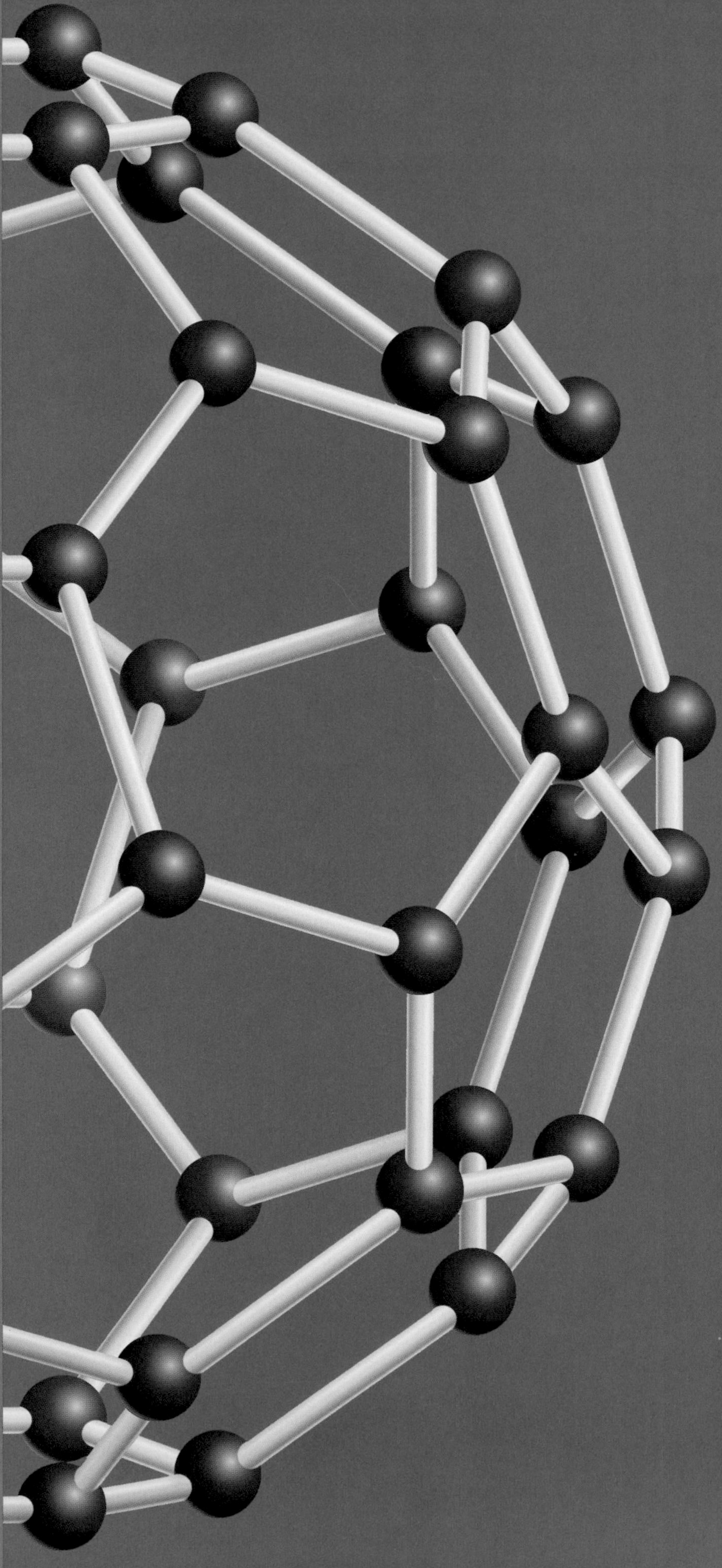

Science and invention

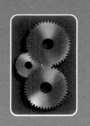

Numbers and sequences

Mathematics is the study of numbers, shapes and quantities. It forms a part of other disciplines, from physics, chemistry and biology to computing, economics and management theory and is an essential tool for understanding the world. It even extends into aesthetics through concepts such as the "golden ratio," creating pleasing proportions in art and architecture.

Branches of mathematics

Mathematics is divided into two major areas: pure and applied.

- **Pure mathematics** is the study of mathematical theory without considering any particular practical applications.
- **Applied mathematics** is the use of mathematics in other activities, including scientific disciplines such as physics, chemistry or biology.

The main branches of pure and applied mathematics are

- **Arithmetic** The study of numbers and the relationships among them, including addition, subtraction, multiplication and division.
- **Algebra** The use of letters or symbols in calculations as substitutes for any unknown numbers.
- **Calculus** The study of continuous change, such as curving lines on graphs, using algebra.
- **Geometry** The study of points, lines, angles, surfaces and solids and the relationships among them.
- **Probability** The study of random events and ways of calculating the likelihood of their happening.
- **Set theory** The study of sets. A set is any group of specified elements – for example, all people over age 50 – in which there is a rule determining whether or not an element is a member of the set.
- **Statistics** The collection, organization and interpretation of numerical data.
- **Trigonometry** The study of angles and triangles and their application to problems in geometry and other areas.

Pi (π)

An irrational, or inexact, number (see below), π or *pi* is defined as the ratio of the circumference of a circle to its diameter.

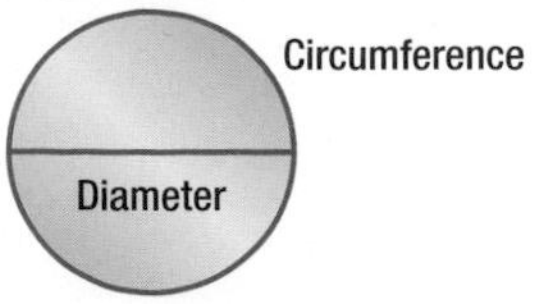

- It is one of the most important numbers in mathematics, used to calculate the lengths of curves, the areas of curved surfaces and the volumes of solids. It even appears in formulas describing the vibration of strings and the motion of pendulums.
- As an irrational number, it cannot be represented as a fraction, although the improper fraction $^{22}/_{7}$ is sometimes used to show its approximate value.
- To the first **120** decimal places, its numerical value is:
3.141592653589793238462643383279502884197169399375105820974944592307816406286208998628034825342117067982148086513282306647

NUMBERS OF DIFFERENT KINDS

The simplest numbers are **natural (or whole) numbers**, used for counting things in whole amounts. They are the first numbers that children learn – **1, 2, 3, 4, 5, 6, 7** and so on.

- **Integers** A refinement on natural numbers, integers are numbers used for counting whole steps backward or forward, up or down.
  An integer consists of a natural number with a plus or minus sign in front of it: **–7, –6, –5, –4, –3, –2, –1, 0, +1, +2, +3, +4, +5, +6, +7**. In practice, of course, positive integers are normally written without the plus sign.

- **Real numbers** All the numbers that exist, not just integers, but also the limitless supply of other numbers that lie in between each pair of integers, are described as real numbers These are expressed as fractions or decimals: **6.989, 5$^{5}/_{8}$** and so on.

- **Prime numbers** A whole number that can only be divided exactly by itself and by 1 is known as a prime number.
  Example: The first 20 prime numbers are **2, 3, 5, 7, 11, 13, 17, 19, 23, 29, 31, 37, 41, 43, 47, 53, 59, 61, 67, and 71.**

- **Factors** A factor is any number that divides exactly into another number.
  Example: The factors of **12** are **1, 2, 3, 4, 6** and **12**.
  A factor that is also a prime number is called a prime factor.
  Example: **2** and **3** are prime factors of **12**.

- **Perfect numbers** Natural numbers that equal the sum of all their factors are called perfect numbers.
  Example: **28** is a perfect number because **1, 2, 4, 7** and **14** are its factors, and **1 + 2 + 4 + 7 + 14 = 28.**
  The first six perfect numbers are: **6, 28, 496, 8128, 33550336, 8589869065.**

- **Infinity** The number that is too large to count, found at the theoretical end of the line of real numbers, is infinity. It is represented by the symbol ∞.

- **Irrational numbers** Most numbers (known as rational numbers) can be expressed exactly, using decimals or fractions, but a few have precise values that can never be written down in this way. These are irrational numbers.
  Example: The square root of **2** is irrational. An approximate value is **1.4142135623730950488016887242097.**
  You could keep adding more and more digits to this number and still never write it down exactly.

- **Repeating decimal** Expressed as decimals, some rational numbers have an infinite expansion – the numbers after the decimal point do not end.
  Example: **$^{1}/_{2}$ = 0.5**, but **$^{1}/_{6}$ = 0.1666666666666** repeating.
  Sometimes a group of digits is repeated.
  Example: **$^{3}/_{7}$ = 0.42857142857 142857142 . . .**

- **Golden ratio** Also called the golden section, the golden mean and the divine proportion, the golden ratio is an irrational number with the value of $(1 + \sqrt{5})/2$ or approximately **1.618034**.
  It can be calculated using the Fibonacci sequence (see opposite). If each number in the Fibonacci sequence is divided by the number preceding it, it produces a ratio that eventually stabilizes at about **1.618034**.

Number line The numbers on the line below are integers and are used to count whole steps. The line of real numbers would be impossible to depict, because it would have to include the literally countless numbers that lie between integers.

-5 -4 -3 -2 -1 0 1 2 3 4 5

NUMBER PATTERNS

Number patterns – sometimes known as sequences – are ordered sets of consecutive numbers that are governed by a rule.

A simple sequence is shown by the natural numbers: **1, 2, 3, 4, 5, 6, 7, 8, 9, 10, 11**. These are connected by the rule "add one to the previous number."

Two common types of sequences are arithmetic progressions and geometric progressions.

Arithmetic progressions In an arithmetic progression, the difference between successive numbers – the *common difference* – never varies.
Example: The sequence **4, 6.5, 9, 11.5, 14, 16.5, 19** is an increasing sequence with a common difference of **2.5**.

The sequence **176, 150, 124, 98, 72, 46, 20** is a decreasing sequence with a common difference of **26.**

If you know the common difference (**d**) and the first number (**a**) of an arithmetic progression, you can work out what any successive number in the sequence will be. To calculate the **nth** number (usually called a "term") in the sequence, multiply **d** by **n–1** and then add **a**.
Formula: The value of the **nth** term **= a + (n–1)d.**
Example: What is the value of the **11th** term of this sequence:
6, 10, 14, 18, 22, 26 . . .?
a = 6 and **d = 4**
The value of the **11th** term
= 6 + (11–1) x 4
= 6 + 10 x 4 = 46

Geometric progressions Each number in a geometric progression is multiplied by a particular, fixed amount – the *common multiple* – to get the next number in the sequence.
Example: The sequence **2, 4, 8, 16, 32, 64, 128, 256** is a geometric progression where the common multiple is **2**:
2 x 2 = 4, 2 x 4 = 8, 2 x 8 = 16, and so on.

To work out the **nth** number, or term, in a geometric progression, calculate the value of the common multiple (**m**) to the power of **n–1**, then multiply the result by **a** (the first number in the sequence).
Formula: The value of the **nth** term **= $am^{(n-1)}$.**
Example: What is the value of the **8th** term of this sequence:
3, 6, 12, 24, 48, 96 . . . ?
a = 3 and **m = 2**
The value of the **8th** term
= $3 \times 2^{(8-1)}$
= 3×2^7 (that is, 2 multiplied by itself seven times)
= 3 x 128 = 384

0 1 1 2 3 5 8 13 21 34 55

The Fibonacci sequence

In the sequence above, each succeeding number, or term, is made by adding the previous two – **0 + 1 = 1, 1 + 1 = 2, 1 + 2 = 3, 2 + 3 = 5**, and so on.

The sequence was discovered by the mathematician Leonardo of Pisa or Leonardo Fibonacci (c. 1170-1240). In the centuries since then, it has been found to have many interesting properties related not only to mathematics but also to nature, art and architecture. It is also closely connected with the golden ratio (see opposite).

Rectangles and spirals The Fibonacci sequence can be expressed not just as numbers, but also as a series of rectangles and as a spiral drawn using the rectangles. It is in this form that it most often occurs in nature and art.

Fibonacci rectangles are constructed as follows.

- Draw two small squares, each measuring **1 unit x 1 unit**. Overall, they produce a rectangle measuring **1 x 2**.
- Draw a **2 x 2** square under this rectangle. Overall, this produces a **2 x 3** rectangle.
- Draw a new **3 x 3** square, with one of its sides as the right-hand side of the previous rectangle. This produces a **3 x 5** rectangle.
- Draw a new **5 x 5** square, with one of its sides as the top side of the previous square. This produces a **5 x 8** rectangle.

(This process can be carried on indefinitely.)

To create the spiral, draw a quarter circle in each square, starting with the first. The resulting spiral is very similar to those found in the shells of certain mollusks, including snails and *Nautilus* shells.

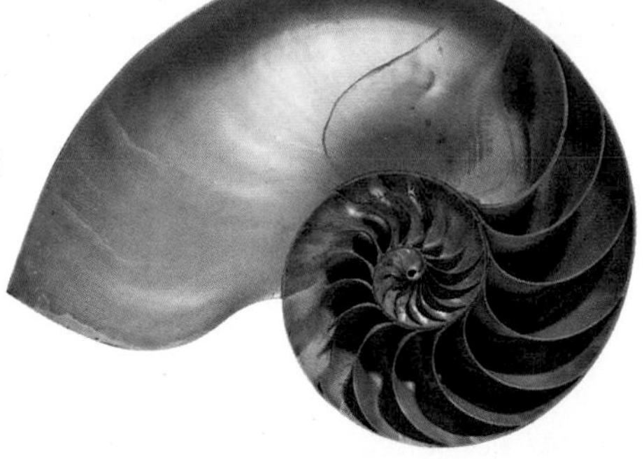

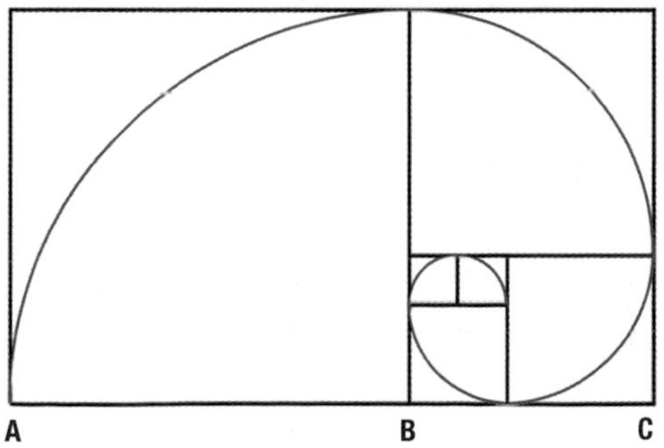

Fibonacci and the golden ratio Fibonacci rectangles have several odd properties. Each, for example, has sides that are two successive Fibonacci numbers long. The rectangles also involve the golden ratio. Take the rectangle measuring **5 x 8**: **8 ÷ 5 = 1.6**. The next rectangle after that would measure **8 x 13**: **13 ÷ 8 = 1.625**. The more rectangles added, the closer the ratio comes to the golden ratio – roughly **1.618034**.

These proportions are found in many of the things we find pleasing or beautiful. The ancient Greeks were aware of this, as is often revealed in their architecture. The front of the Parthenon in Athens, for example, is a Fibonacci rectangle, about **1.6** times wider than it is tall. Also, the dimensions of paintings frequently conform to the golden ratio and have their focus of interest at the point where Fibonacci rectangles meet.

Fibonacci in nature and art
A *Nautilus* shell (above left) forms a Fibonacci spiral. In the rectangles (left), the distance from A to C (13 units) divided by that from A to B (8 units) equals 1.625 – roughly the golden ratio. In the painting by J.M.W. Turner (above), the focal point, the locomotive, lies on the same axis.

see also
414-17 **Geometry**
482-83 **Scales and measurements**

Fundamentals of geometry

Geometry is the branch of mathematics that studies the nature of lines, points, surfaces and solids. Definitions of the different kinds of angles and shapes, some of which were laid down by ancient Greek mathematicians as early as the sixth century B.C., are fundamental to understanding it. They established many principles that are still in use today. Until recently, most of the geometry taught in schools was that described by Euclid in the third century B.C.

LINES

A **line** connects two or more points. It has only one dimension – length – and can be straight or curved.

A **point** is a position in space. It has no dimensions – neither length, width nor depth.

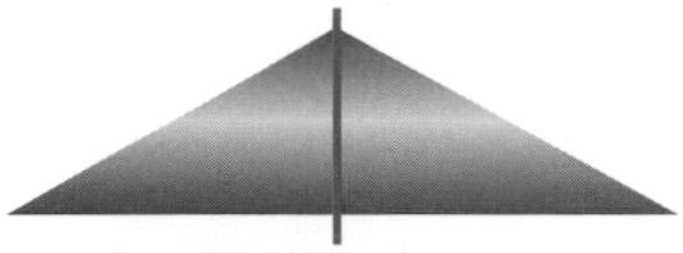

Axis or line of symmetry A line dividing a symmetrical shape (an isosceles triangle, for example) into two reflecting (mirror) halves is called a line of symmetry.

Perpendicular A straight line that meets a second straight line at a right angle (90°) is said to be perpendicular to the second line.

Parallel Two or more lines that are the same distance apart everywhere along their lengths are parallel. By convention, parallel lines are indicated by arrowlike marks.

Tangent A straight line that touches a curve at one point only, but does not cross it, is a tangent.

ANGLES

An angle is the space between two lines that meet or intersect. The point at which they meet is called a vertex. Angles are measured in degrees (°). There are six basic types of angle.

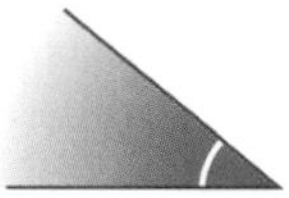

Acute angle An angle of less than 90°.

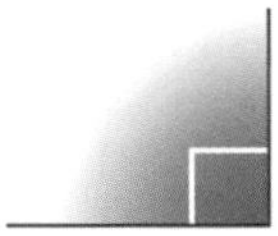

Right angle An angle of exactly 90°, indicated by a small square in diagrams.

Obtuse angle An angle of more than 90° and less than 180°.

Straight angle An angle of exactly 180°.

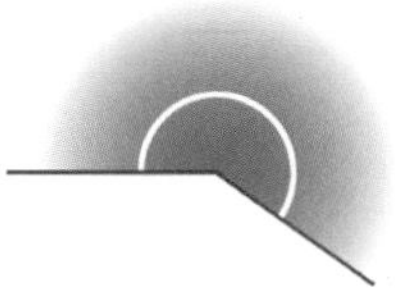

Reflex angle An angle of more than 180° and less than 360°.

Round angle An angle of exactly 360°.

TRIANGLES

A triangle has three vertices and three sides. The sum of the three internal angles in a triangle is always 180° (see diagram right). There are six basic types of triangle.

Sum of the angles As the internal angles of a triangle always add up to 180°, it is possible to work out the missing angle a: **180 – 80 – 40 = 60**. The external angles (**140 + 120 + 100**) add up to **360°**.

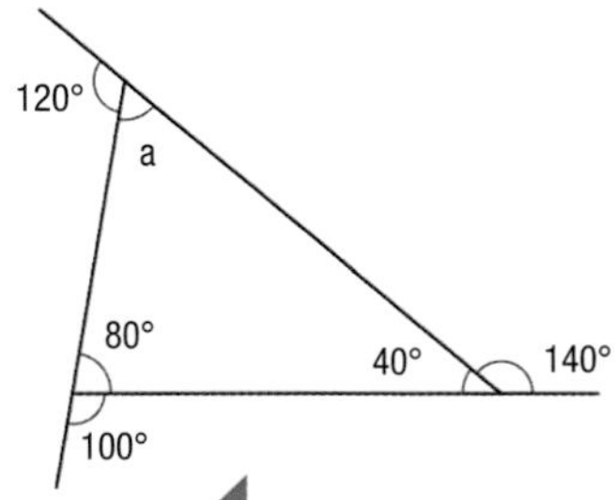

Equilateral triangle All three sides have the same length, and all three internal angles measure 60°. There are three axes of symmetry.

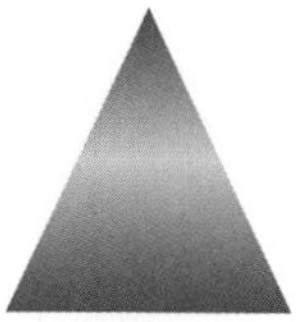

Isosceles triangle At least two sides have the same length, and at least two of the angles are the same. There is one axis of symmetry.

Scalene triangle All three sides are different lengths, and all three angles are different. There are no axes of symmetry.

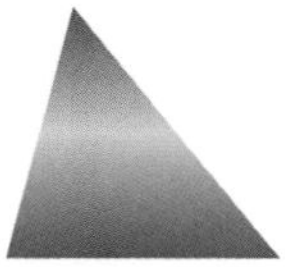

Acute triangle All three angles are acute (less than 90°).

Right triangle One angle is exactly 90° – a right angle. The side opposite the right angle (the longest side) is called the hypotenuse.

Obtuse triangle One angle of the triangle is an obtuse angle (greater than 90° and less than 180°).

QUADRILATERALS

A quadrilateral is a plane shape enclosed by four sides (also described as a four-sided polygon). The sum of the four internal angles of a quadrilateral is always 360°. There are six basic types of quadrilateral.

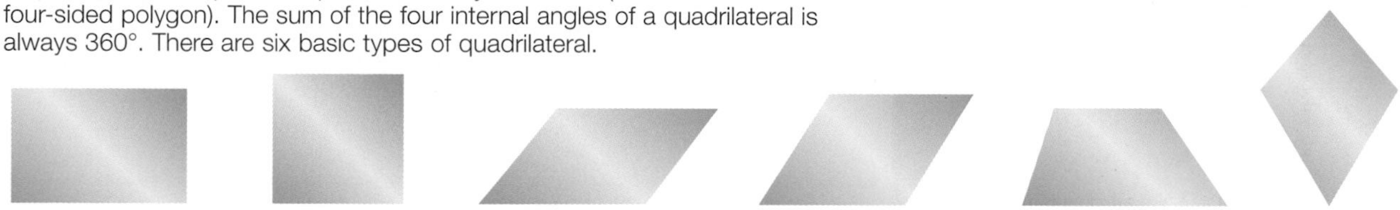

Rectangle All internal angles are right angles. Opposite sides are parallel and the same length.

Square An equal-sided rectangle. All four angles are right angles and all sides are the same length.

Parallelogram Opposite sides are parallel and equal in length. Opposite angles are equal.

Rhombus An equal-sided parallelogram. Opposite sides are parallel. Opposite angles are equal. All sides are the same length.

Trapezoid Two sides are parallel but have different lengths. If the other two, nonparallel sides have the same length, it is known as an isosceles trapezoid.

Diamond Two pairs of adjacent sides have the same length. Opposite angles are equal.

CIRCLES AND CURVES

Geometry is also concerned with curved lines and the shapes, both plane (for example, circles) and solid (for example, spheres), that are enclosed by them. The following terms describe curved shapes and their features.

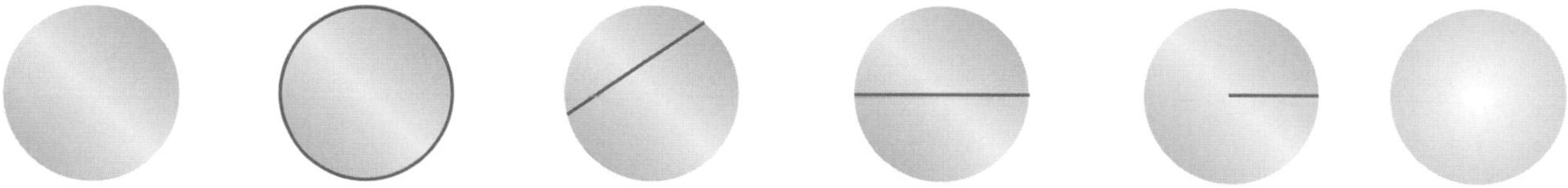

Circle A flat shape enclosed by one curved line. All points on the curved line are equally distant from the circle's center.

Circumference The line that marks the perimeter (boundary) of a circle. The term is also used to describe the distance around the perimeter.

Chord A straight line that joins any two points on the circumference.

Diameter A chord that passes through the center of a circle. The term is also used to describe the length of that chord.

Radius A straight line joining the center of a circle to any point on its circumference. It is also used to describe the length of that line.

Sphere A solid shape, enclosed by a single curved surface. All points on the curved surface are equally distant from the sphere's center.

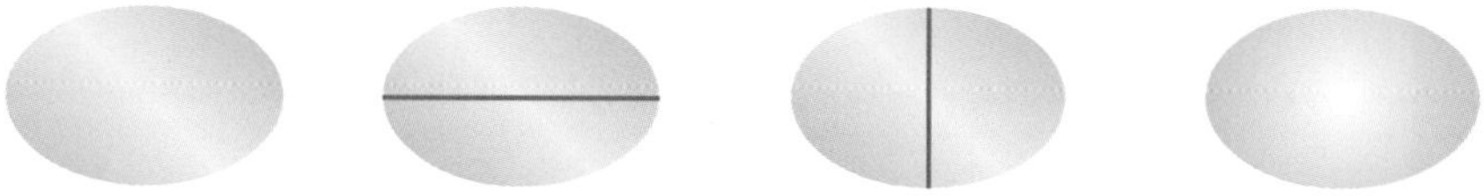

Ellipse Also known as an oval. Mathematically, an ellipse is a cross section of a cone (see right) that does not pass through the base of the cone and is not parallel to it.

Major axis The long axis of an ellipse. This is a straight line that passes through the center of an ellipse, divides it into two equal halves and joins the two opposite points on its circumference that are farthest apart.

Minor axis The short axis of an ellipse. It is a straight line that passes through the center – at a right angle to the major axis – and joins the two opposite points on the circumference that are closest to each other.

Ellipsoid Also known as an "ovoid." A solid shape in which cross sections are all either ellipses or circles.

Cylinder A tubular solid shape that has straight sides and is circular in cross section.

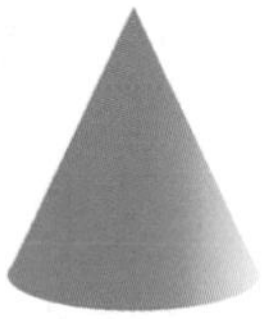

Cone A solid shape that has a circle for its base and straight sides that taper to a point at the apex (top).

Polygons

A polygon is any plane shape enclosed by three or more straight lines. A regular polygon, such as a square (regular quadrilateral), has sides of equal length and all of its internal angles are the same size; an irregular polygon, such as a trapezoid (irregular quadrilateral), has sides and angles of different sizes.

Polygons are named according to the number of sides they have. The more sides they have, the greater the sum of their internal angles. The sum of a polygon's external angles (see Triangles, opposite), however, is always 360°.

Name	Number of sides	Sum of internal angles
Triangle	Three	180°
Quadrilateral	Four	360°
Pentagon	Five	540°
Hexagon	Six	720°
Heptagon	Seven	900°
Octagon	Eight	1080°
Nonagon	Nine	1260°
Decagon	Ten	1440°

see also
412-13 **Numbers and sequences**
482-83 **Scales and measurements**

The geometry of Euclid and his predecessors has many practical applications. Trigonometry, the science of measuring triangles, based on a 2500-year-old theorem by Pythagoras, has been used for centuries by engineers, surveyors and navigators to determine heights, angles and distances. In addition, there are numerous useful ancient Greek formulas for calculating the areas and volumes of circles and spheres, for example.

PYTHAGOREAN THEOREM

Pythagoras (c. 572-497 B.C.) famously formulated a theorem for calculating the length of the long side – known as the hypotenuse – of a right triangle. It states that the square of the length of the hypotenuse is equal to the sum of the squares of the other two sides. The ability to establish the length of a third side by knowing the length of the other two is the basis for trigonometry (see below).

To do the calculations that are described here, you will need a calculator with a square root (√) key.

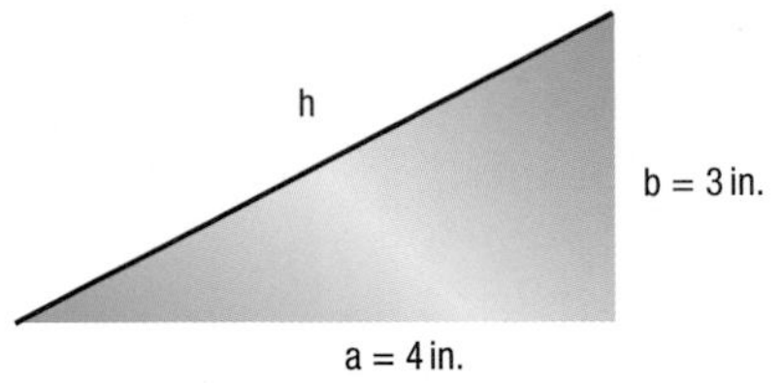

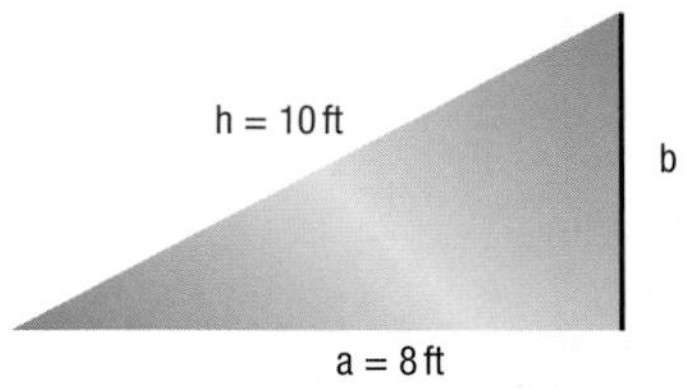

You know	the length of the two shorter sides (a and b), in this case 4 in. and 3 in.	the length of the hypotenuse (h) and one shorter side (a), in this case 10 ft and 8 ft
You need	the length of hypotenuse (h)	the length of the other shorter side (b)
Formula	$h = \sqrt{(a^2 + b^2)}$	$b = \sqrt{(h^2 - a^2)}$
Method	Take the length of side a (4 in.)	Take the length of the hypotenuse (10 ft)
	Find its square (4 x 4 = 16)	Find its square (10 x 10 = 100)
	Take the length of side b (3 in.)	Take the length of side a (8 ft)
	Find its square (3 x 3 = 9)	Find its square (8 x 8 = 64)
	Add the two squares together ($a^2 + b^2 = 16 + 9 = 25$)	Take the smaller square away from the bigger ($h^2 - a^2 = 100 - 64 = 36$)
	Find the square root of the sum ($h = \sqrt{25} = 5$), so the length of the hypotenuse is 5 in.	Find the square root of the result ($b = \sqrt{36} = 6$), so the length of side b is 6 ft.

THE USES OF TRIGONOMETRY

Tangent, sine and cosine – known as trigonometric ratios – relate to the proportions of right triangles. If you know the length of one side of a right triangle and the size of one of the two acute angles, you can use these ratios to work out the length of the other two sides and the size of the other acute angle.

Naming the sides In trigonometry, each side of a right triangle is named in relation to the known acute angle x:

- the **hypotenuse** is the longest side, opposite the right angle.
- the **opposite** side is facing angle x.
- the **adjacent** side is the remaining side, next to angle x.

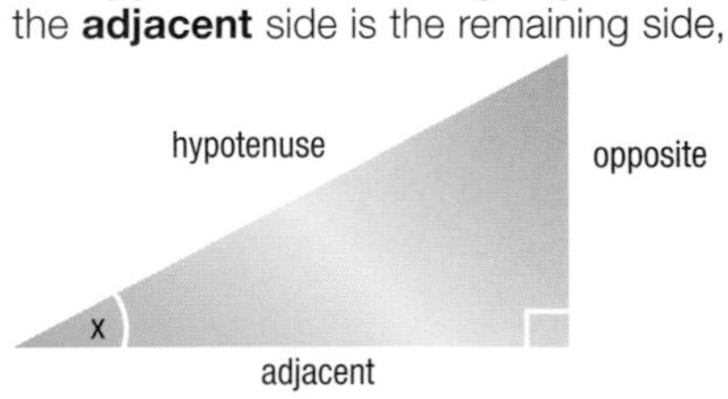

Tangent, sine and cosine Each of the three trigonometric ratios – known as tangent, sine and cosine – relates the size of angle x to the length of two of the sides.

For example, the tangent (tan) of angle x is the ratio of the length of the opposite side to the length of adjacent side. Put mathematically, the **tangent of angle x = the length of the opposite side ÷ the length of the adjacent side.**

Or:

$\tan x = \frac{\text{opposite}}{\text{adjacent}}$ $\sin x = \frac{\text{opposite}}{\text{hypotenuse}}$ $\cos x = \frac{\text{adjacent}}{\text{hypotenuse}}$

Example A surveyor stands **450 ft** from the base of a tower and has to look up at an angle of **40°** to the ground to see its top. How high is the tower? A scientific calculator provides values for tan, sin and cos.

Angle x = **40°**
The length of the adjacent side = **450 ft**
The unknown is the opposite side.
If tan x = opposite ÷ adjacent
tan 40° = height ÷ 450
therefore,
height = **450 x tan 40°**
= **450 x 0.839 = 377.6 ft**

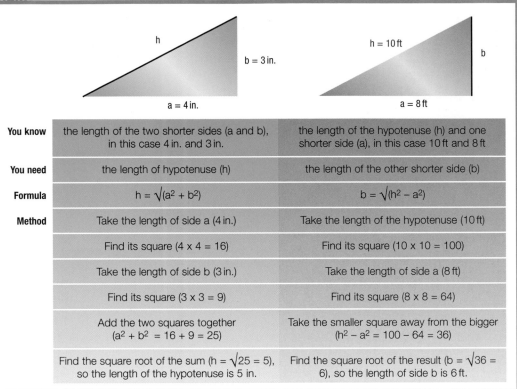

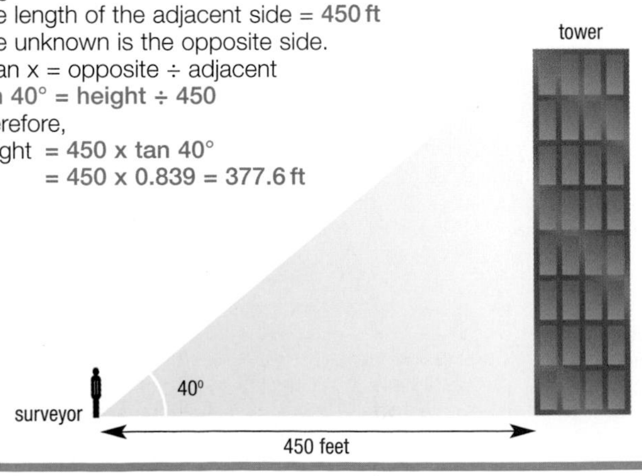

CALCULATING AREA AND VOLUME

The shapes described by geometry include plane (two-dimensional) shapes and solid (three-dimensional) shapes.

The formulas for calculating the area or volume of these different shapes are broken down here into a series of steps.

If your calculator does not have a pi (π) key, 3.14159 should be taken as the value of pi in these calculations.

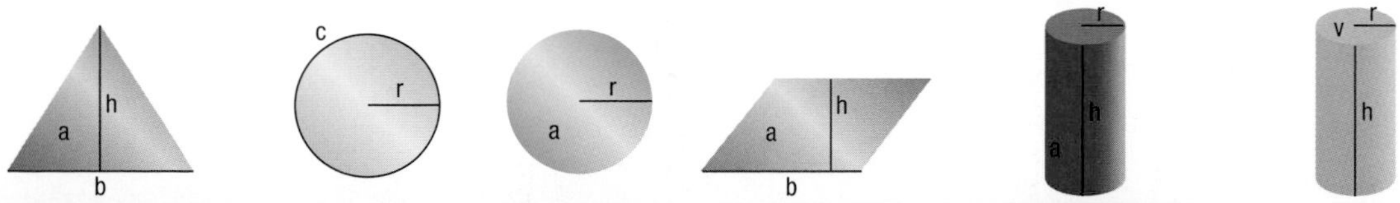

Shape	Triangle	Circle	Circle	Parallelogram	Cylinder	Cylinder
You know	length of base (b) and perpendicular height (h)	radius (r)	radius	length of base (b) and height (h)	radius (r) and height (h)	radius (r) and height (h)
You need	area (a)	circumference (c)	area (a)	area (a)	surface area (a)	volume (v)
Formula	$a = \frac{bh}{2}$	$c = 2\pi r$	$a = \pi r^2$	$a = bh$	$a = 2\pi r(r + h)$	$v = \pi r^2 h$
Method	Measure the length of the base (for example, 7 cm)	Measure the radius (for example, 6 cm)	Measure the radius (for example, 6 cm)	Measure the length of the base (for example, 9 cm)	Measure the radius (for example, 5 cm) and the height (for example, 9 cm)	Measure the radius (for example, 5 cm) and the height (for example, 9 cm)
	Measure the perpendicular height (for example, 12 cm)	Multiply by 2 (6 x 2 = 12)	Find its square (6 x 6 = 36)	Measure the height (for example, 5 cm)	Add the radius and the height together (5 + 9 = 14)	Find the square of the radius (5 x 5 = 25)
	Multiply the two together (7 x 12 = 84)				Multiply by 2 (14 x 2 = 28)	Multiply by the height (25 x 9 = 225)
					Multiply by the radius (28 x 5 = 140)	
	Divide by two (a = 84 ÷ 2 = 42 cm²)	Multiply by π (c = 12 x π = 37.7 cm)	Multiply by π (a = 36 x π = 113.1 cm²)	Multiply the two together (a = 9 x 5 = 45 cm²)	Multiply by π (a = 140 x π = 439.8 cm²)	Multiply by π (v = 225 x π = 706.9 cm³)

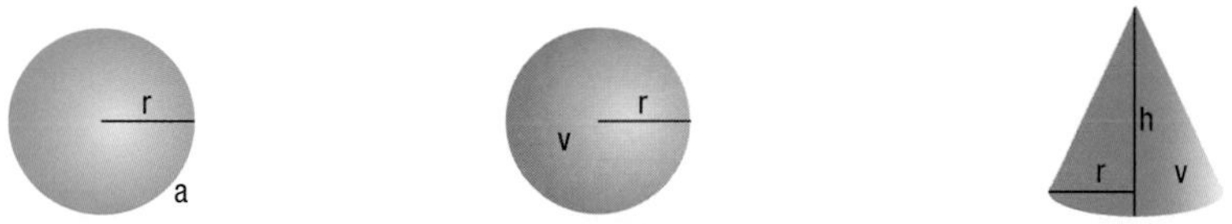

Shape	Sphere	Sphere	Cone
You know	radius (r)	radius (r)	height (h) and radius of base (r)
You need	surface area (a)	volume (v)	volume (v)
Formula	$a = 4\pi r^2$	$v = \frac{4\pi r^3}{3}$	$v = \frac{\pi r^2 h}{3}$
Method	Measure the radius (for example, 5 cm)	Measure the radius (for example 5 cm)	Measure the radius (for example, 3 cm) and the height (for example, 8 cm)
	Find its square (5 x 5 = 25)	Find its cube (5 x 5 x 5 = 125)	Find the square of the radius (3 x 3 = 9)
	Multiply by 4 (25 x 4 = 100)	Multiply by 4 (125 x 4 = 500)	Multiply by the height (9 x 8 = 72)
		Divide by 3 (500 ÷ 3 = 166.66)	Multiply by π (72 x π = 226.2)
	Multiply by π (a = 100 x π = 314.2 cm²)	Multiply by π (v = 166.66 x π = 523.6 cm³)	Divide by 3 (v = 226.2 ÷ 3 = 75.4 cm³)

see also
412-13 **Numbers and sequences**
482-83 **Scales and measurements**

The branch of physics that describes the effects of forces – pushes and pulls – on objects is called mechanics. It governs many aspects of life, from weighing a bag of potatoes to the trajectory of a space rocket. It is often divided into two fields: statics, dealing with mass, weight and gravity; and dynamics, dealing with moving, accelerating and colliding objects.

MASS, WEIGHT AND GRAVITY

The terms "mass" and "weight" are often used interchangeably, to mean how "heavy" an object is. Yet each has its own distinct scientific meaning and units of measurement. The link between them is gravity.

- **Mass** is the amount of matter in an object – how much "stuff" it contains. It is measured in grams (g), kilograms (kg) or metric tons (t) – or, in the traditional system, ounces (oz), pounds (lb) and tons (t). The mass of an object remains the same wherever it is. A golfer, for example, would have the same mass on Earth and on the Moon – and so would his golf ball (see below).

- **Weight** is the force experienced by an object when gravity pulls it down. It is measured in newtons (N) and depends on both the mass of the object and the pull of gravity.

Confusion arises because the weight of, for example, a supermarket bag of potatoes is quoted in kilograms (or pounds), not newtons. For everyday nonscientific usage, this does not matter because the weight of an object with a mass of 1 kg is the same at sea level everywhere on Earth. On the Moon, however, the pull of gravity is one-sixth that on Earth, so the object would have one-sixth its terrestrial weight.

Weight is calculated by applying Newton's second law of motion (see right):

If the mass of an object = 1 kg
Acceleration due to Earth's gravity = 9.8 m/s^2
The weight of the object (that is, the force exerted by gravity) = mass x acceleration
= 1 kg x 9.8 m/s^2 = 9.8 N

- **Gravity** is generally thought of as the force that pulls on objects and makes them fall to the Earth's surface. For example, it keeps the feet of a juggler firmly on the ground and makes the pins he has thrown into the air drop back to his hands. On Earth, gravity accelerates everything toward the ground at 9.8 m/s^2.

In fact, a force of gravity exists between *all* objects – even between the juggler and his pins – and depends on the mass of the objects and the distance between them. However, it is usually too weak to measure unless one or both objects has a large mass. The Earth's gravitational pull keeps the Moon in orbit around it. The Moon also exerts a gravitational pull on the Earth, although its mass – and, therefore, its gravitational pull – is only one-sixth that of Earth's mass. The theory of relativity explains gravity in terms of a curvature of space (see pages 428 and 429).

FACT
The Earth's gravitational pull accelerates a 1-g falling leaf at exactly the same rate as a 1-ton rock.

Newton's laws of motion

English physicist and mathematician Isaac Newton (1642-1727) formulated his three laws of motion to describe how objects move when acted upon by forces.

1 First law of motion
An object will either stay still or keep moving in a straight line at a steady speed unless it is pushed or pulled by a force. This tendency to stay still or keep moving is referred to as the object's inertia (see opposite). A golf ball remains stationary unless hit by a club. Once in motion, it continues but is slowed by two forces – gravity and friction (air resistance).

2 Second law of motion
When a force acts on an object, the object will either start to move, speed up, slow down, stop or change direction. The size of a force, the acceleration it produces and the mass of the object are closely related.

The force that accelerates the object (N) equals the mass of object (kg) multiplied by the acceleration produced (m/s^2). (For units of acceleration, see box "Measuring motion" opposite.) The greater the force, the greater the change of movement. A golf ball tapped with a putter will accelerate far less than one hit at full force with a driver.

3 Third law of motion
If one object exerts a force – a push or pull – on another, the second object will pull or push to an equal and opposite extent. This means that forces always act in pairs – actions and reactions. For example, the force that propels a shell out of a gun barrel (action) is accompanied by the equal and opposite force (reaction) of the gun recoiling or moving backward.

Golf on Earth

Golfer's mass is 80 kg (176 lb).
Downward acceleration due to gravity is 9.8 m/s^2, so **golfer's weight** is 80 x 9.8 = 784 N.
Golf ball's mass is 0.045 kg; **ball's weight** is about 0.44N.

When the golfer hits the ball on Earth, he makes it travel about 100 m (109 yd). Gravity pulls the ball back to Earth, and air resistance also helps to slow down the ball.

Golf on the Moon

Golfer's mass is 80 kg (176 lb).
Downward acceleration due to gravity is 1.6 m/s^2, so **golfer's weight** is 80 x 1.6 = 128 N.
Golf ball's mass is 0.045 kg; **ball's weight** is about 0.072N.

On the Moon, the same swing would make the ball go about 600 m (656 yd) because the Moon's gravitational pull on the ball is one-sixth that on Earth. Also, there is no air resistance to slow the ball down.

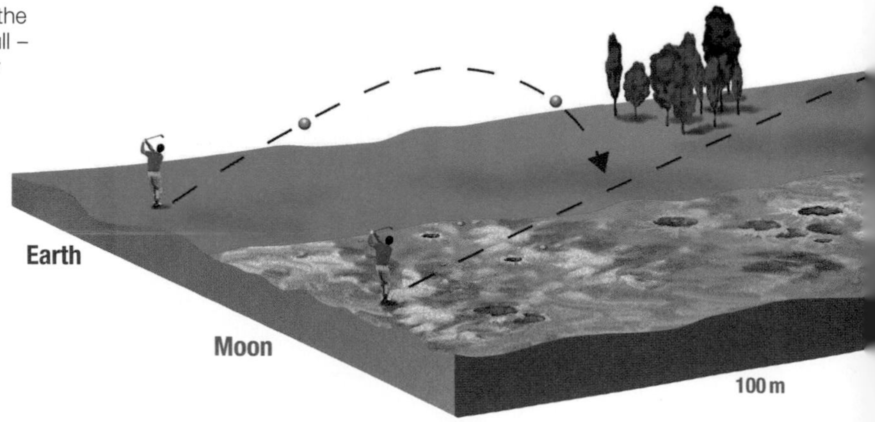

FORCE AND MOTION

A force is an invisible push or pull, the effects of which can be seen or felt. Forces cause objects that are free to move to start or stop moving or to change their direction or speed. They cause objects that are not free to move to stretch, bend, twist or change shape. A steadily moving or stationary object will continue in that state until and unless a force is applied to it.

Inertia

The tendency of an object to resist any change in its steady motion or stationary state is called inertia. Even assuming no friction, it takes a hard push to make a stalled car roll forward because it resists any change in its state of motion. But once it moves, the car's inertia will try to keep it moving in a straight line. The greater the mass of the object, the greater its inertia.

Momentum

This is a measure of a moving object's tendency to keep moving and the force needed to alter it. All moving objects have momentum, which is equal to mass multiplied by velocity; therefore the more massive and the faster the object, the greater its momentum. It is a vector quantity (see right).

When two objects collide, momentum is transferred. An important law of physics says that the total momentum of the objects is the same before and after the collision.

Friction

Friction is a force that opposes the motion of an object and reduces its momentum. It exists wherever the surfaces of two objects – however smooth they may appear – rub together. As they slide over each other, surface projections catch on each other and – however tiny these may be – slow down movement. That is why dragging a heavy object along the ground is such hard work. The rougher the surfaces, the greater the friction. Oil and other lubricants reduce friction by keeping the projections apart so that they do not catch.

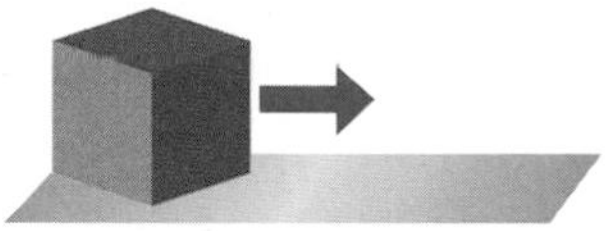

Friction between a sliding block and the surface soon slows the block down.

With a ball, the area in contact with the surface is much less, so much less friction is generated.

Air resistance is friction between moving objects and air molecules. Objects with a large surface area are usually in contact with more air than those with a small surface, so they produce more air resistance.

MEASURING MOTION

As in all scientific fields, mechanical measurements are made in International System (SI) units, based on the meter (m) for distance, kilogram (kg) for mass and second (s) for time.

Distance and displacement Distance is simply the length of a straight line between two places. It can indicate how far apart two objects are, or how far an object has traveled from its starting point.

The displacement of an object moving from one point to another, on the other hand, includes direction of movement as well as the straight-line distance it moves. For example, a billiard ball might be displaced 2 m (7 ft) to the southwest.

Displacement is known as a **vector quantity** because it has both magnitude and direction; distance, which has magnitude but no particular direction, is a **scalar quantity**.

Speed and velocity Speed describes how fast an object is traveling by stating the distance it travels in a certain amount of time. For example, if a car travels 400 km (250 miles) in 5 hours, its average speed (allowing for variations during the journey) = 400 km ÷ 5 h = 80 km/h (50 mph).

Velocity is a measure not only of how fast an object is moving but also of the direction of movement. So a car traveling 400 km north in 5 hours has a northward velocity of 80 km/h. The velocity of a moving object changes if either its speed or its direction alters. If the car traveling at 80 km/h turns a corner without changing its speed, its velocity still changes because it is changing direction. In other words, speed, like distance, is a scalar quantity, but velocity, like displacement, is a vector quantity.

Acceleration Acceleration measures the rate of change in the velocity of an object – that is, how quickly the object is speeding up in a particular direction. Acceleration equals the change in velocity (m/s) divided by the time taken for this change (s); it is measured in meters per second per second (m/s/s or m/s^2). Acceleration is always a vector quantity.

Suppose this racing car accelerates from a standing start to a velocity of 180 km/h (50 m/s) in 5 seconds. Its acceleration = 50 m/s ÷ 5 s = 10 m/s^2. If the driver then applies the brakes and takes 4 seconds to stop, its acceleration = –50 m/s ÷ 4 s = –12.5 m/s^2.

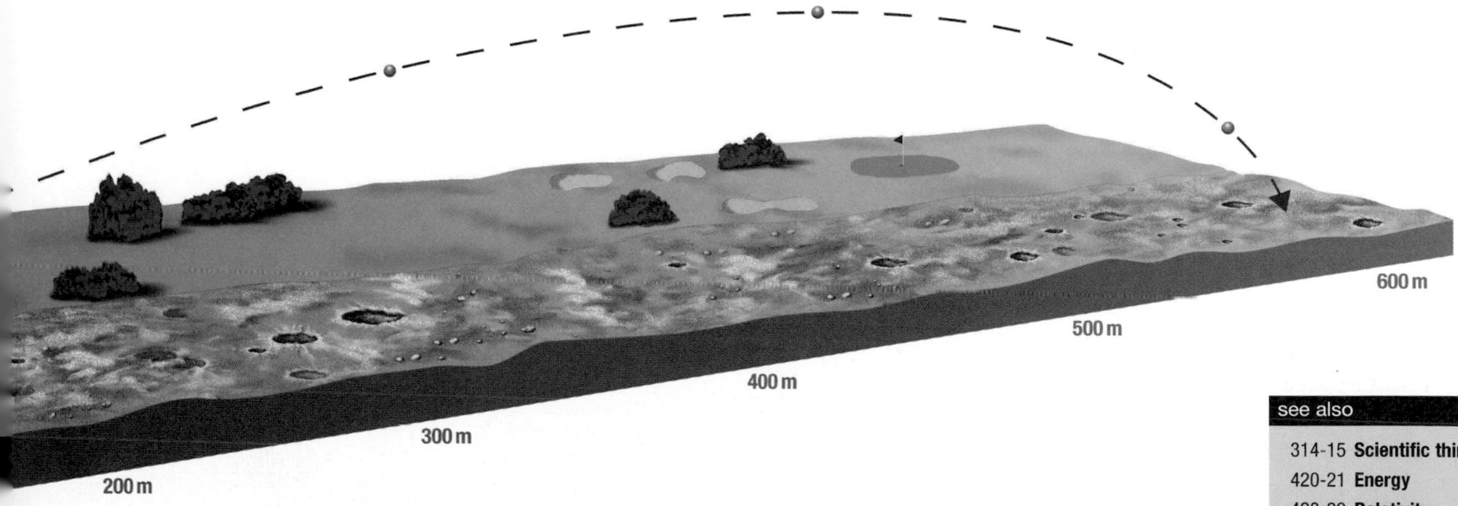

see also

314-15 **Scientific thinkers**
420-21 **Energy**
428-29 **Relativity**

Every change in the Universe, from the whisper of a breeze to the explosion of a supernova, involves the expenditure or transfer of energy. The Universe itself was created in a huge burst of energy – the big bang – and 15 billion years later this energy still keeps the Universe in action. The meaning of the term in physics is more precise than in general usage: Energy is the capacity to do work. Much of technology is concerned with changing energy from one form into another.

Potential energy
This is stored energy that an object has because of its position or shape. An aircraft gains potential energy as it rises against the force of gravity; if it goes into a dive, this potential energy is released and converted into kinetic energy. In a similar way, a squeezed ball or a stretched bowstring also holds potential energy that is unlocked when it is released.

Kinetic energy
This is the energy of movement. A moving aircraft, like every moving object, has kinetic energy, which returns to zero when it comes to rest. An important formula states that $E = mv^2$, where E is the kinetic energy of a moving object, m is its mass, and v its velocity, or speed. So, at the same speed, energy is proportional to mass, but doubling speed quadruples kinetic energy.

TYPES OF ENERGY

Energy exists in many different forms, and any physical change involves one form of energy changing into another. The process through which an aircraft takes off, for example, illustrates almost every form of energy known to physics. Energy is never created or destroyed; it only changes form. This principle is known as the conservation of energy (see box opposite).

Nuclear energy
Nuclear energy is locked in the nuclei of atoms, in the forces that hold their component parts – subatomic particles – together. It is released as heat and electromagnetic energy by nuclear reactions, such as those in the Sun, and in nuclear reactors and explosions. Such reactions involve the annihilation of mass and its conversion into energy.

Chemical energy
This is the energy stored in chemical compounds, such as the fuel in an aircraft's tanks – which originated when sunlight produced sugars in fossil plants by photosynthesis. When an aircraft takes off, chemical energy is converted into heat by burning fuel, and that energy is converted into the kinetic energy of movement, the potential energy of height, plus sound energy.

Electrical energy
Electricity powers the lighting and runs many systems on an aircraft. Electrical energy, or electricity, is the movement of tiny charged subatomic particles called electrons. When electric current flows through a wire, electrons jump from atom to atom. Electricity is one of the most useful forms of energy, because it is easily transported and converted into other forms.

Light energy
Light, which can be detected by the eyes, is the best-known form of electromagnetic energy, which also includes infrared (the radiant form of heat). The Sun is Earth's primary source of light. Other sources of light energy include electricity (in light bulbs and fluorescent tubes) and burning (the conversion of chemical energy into heat and light energy).

Conservation of energy and mass

A basic principle of classical mechanics – the physics of the everyday world as set out by Newton (see page 418) – is the law of the conservation of energy. This states that energy is never created or destroyed; it only changes form. Similarly, physical and chemical activities always conserve mass (matter).

But the theory of relativity (page 428) showed that mass and energy are equivalents linked by the equation $E = mc^2$. In ordinary mechanical systems, the mass change accompanying energy transfer cannot be measured, but it is significant in nuclear reactions. The new law of conservation of mass energy says that mass and energy together can never be created or destroyed.

Heat energy
This is the energy every object in the Universe possesses because of the vibration or movement of the atoms and molecules that make it up. The faster these particles move, the more heat energy the object has and the hotter it is. Heat is generated in a jet engine by burning fuel, causing gases to expand and to shoot from the rear of the engine, which propels the aircraft.

Sound energy
Sound energy takes the form of pressure waves that pass through the air. They are produced by vibrations at the sound source, the gases shooting from an aircraft engine. When these sound waves reach the ear, they are turned into electrical impulses by sensors, which travel to the brain where they are "heard" as sounds.

HEAT

Heat represents the kinetic (movement) energy of an object's constantly moving atoms and molecules. If something warms up, "fixed" molecules, such as those in a solid, vibrate more rapidly; those in a gas move around faster. It is possible to get close to absolute zero (–273.15°C), the temperature at which all atomic and molecular movement would cease, but it is impossible to actually reach it.

Temperature, measured using a thermometer, is not the same as heat. The more heat energy a particular object contains, the higher its temperature is, but different materials require different amounts of heat energy to raise their temperature by the same amount (measured in degrees). The heat needed to increase the temperature of 1 g of a substance by 1°C is called its specific heat.

Heat always flows from warmer places to cooler ones. It travels in three ways. **Conduction** is the transfer of heat through a substance, by hotter, faster-moving molecules colliding with their neighbors, so that they vibrate or move faster. **Convection** is the flow of moving currents of heat through a liquid or a gas. When part of a liquid or gas is heated, the molecules move further apart, so it becomes less dense or lighter than any surrounding colder material. As a result, it rises, creating a circulating "convection current" that transfers heat energy. **Radiation** is the flow of heat in the form of infrared rays from one object to another.

An important form of heat transfer takes place when a solid melts or a liquid evaporates: Heat energy – called latent heat – is taken in without the substance changing temperature. Conversely, when a gas condenses into a liquid or a liquid freezes into a solid, latent heat is given out.

LIGHT

Light, like all forms of electromagnetic radiation (see page 424), travels through empty space at 299 792 km/s – the fastest anything can move. It takes just over 8 minutes for light to travel from the Sun to Earth. It moves more slowly in other transparent media – at about three-quarters its normal speed in water and two-thirds in glass.

Light rays travel in straight lines but bounce off most surfaces; this is called **reflection**. Light surfaces reflect more light than dark ones. Light rays are reflected from a polished surface, such as a mirror, at the same angle as they strike it, but rough surfaces scatter light in all directions.

When light rays enter glass or water from air, the slowing-down makes them bend toward the vertical. This bending is called **refraction**. Prisms refract light rays in this way, and lenses act by refracting rays so that they focus an image.

SOUND

Sound waves consist of waves of high pressure (compression) and low pressure (rarefaction) following each other and traveling outwards from the sound source. How loud a sound is depends on the difference between the high and low-pressure regions. The sound's pitch (low or high) depends on how quickly one wave follows another – the frequency. It is measured in hertz (Hz), or waves per second. People with good hearing can hear sounds from a lowest pitch of about 20 Hz to a high of 20 000 Hz (20 kHz).

Sound, unlike light, cannot travel through a vacuum. Its speed depends on the nature of the medium carrying it. Sound moves at about 340 m/s in air at sea level, more slowly at high altitudes; it travels five times faster in water.

Energy, work and power

- **Energy** is defined as the capacity to do work, or make things happen – moving something, heating it, or changing it in some way. It is measured in units called joules (J) and kilojoules (kJ, thousands of joules) – kJ are often used instead of calories to quantify the energy content of foods. Gas and electricity bills often use kilowatt-hours (kWh); 1 kWh = 3.6 million joules.
- **Work** is what energy "makes happen"; it is the end result of energy being converted from one form into another. They are so closely related that, like energy, work is measured in joules.

  In the case of movement, work is done when a force acts on an object, moving the object in the direction of the force. For example, a forklift does work by lifting crates against gravity, converting chemical energy (fuel) into potential energy (lift). If the crates have a mass of 300 kg, they weigh 2940 newtons (N). Suppose they are lifted vertically a distance of 2 m. Work done (J) = force (N) x distance moved (m) = 2940 N x 2 m = 5880 J (or 5.88 kJ).
- **Power** measures how quickly work is done – in other words, the rate at which energy is converted from one form to another. It is measured in watts (W); 1 W is the conversion of 1 J in one second. Suppose the forklift above lifts the crates in 6 seconds. Power (W) = work (J) ÷ time (s) = 5880 J ÷ 6 s = 980 W.

  The power of an electrical appliance measures how quickly it "consumes" electricity – that is, converts it into another form of energy. A 1000 W (1 kW) iron, for example, converts electricity into heat at a rate of 1000 J per second. In an hour, it uses 1 kWh of electricity.

see also
418-19 **Mechanics**
422-23 **Electricity and magnetism**

Electricity and magnetism are closely linked; both are caused by charged subatomic particles called electrons. Electricity can be generated using magnetism, and a magnetic field can be created with electricity. Their partnership results in one of the most useful inventions in history: the electric motor. In fact, the two forces are different aspects of the same fundamental force of nature: the electromagnetic force that helps to hold all matter together.

WHAT IS ELECTRICITY?

Electrons have a negative electrical charge. If a surplus of electrons builds up on an object – for example, by friction (rubbing) – it acquires an overall negative charge. An object with a deficit of electrons is positively charged. This kind of electricity is described as static – electricity that normally does not move or flow. A high enough charge may cause a spark as electrons jump to a point of lower or opposite charge. Electrical charges have two other properties:

- **Attraction and repulsion** Objects with the same ("like") charges – both positive or both negative – repel each other, but opposite charges attract.

- **Induction** A charged object induces an opposite charge in another nearby object – positive induces negative, and vice versa.

Current electricity Atoms of some substances, such as metals, have loosely attached electrons that can easily move from atom to atom. The moving electrons constitute an electric current. Because like charges repel each other, the movement of one negatively charged electron repels an electron in the next atom, which knocks on the next electron in line, and so on. No single electron moves far, but the overall electrical disturbance travels along the conductor through a domino effect.

- **Current and voltage** The size of an electric current is a measure of how many electrons pass a given point every second. It is measured in ampères, or amps (A). One amp is equivalent to the flow of 6 million trillion electrons per second.

The force that pushes electrons along is called electromotive force. It may be created by a battery or a generator. Electromotive force is measured in volts (V) and is often referred to as voltage.

- **Resistance** How much any material opposes an electric current's flow is called resistance. It is caused by random collisions of atoms and electrons, which slow down electron flow. It is measured in ohms (Ω).

The relationship among voltage, current and resistance is given in Ohm's law. This states that voltage (V) equals current (I) multiplied by resistance (R):

$V = I \times R$

Or, current equals voltage divided by resistance:

$I = V \div R$

Electrical circuits

There are two kinds of electrical circuit:

- **Series circuit** The components and electrical source are linked one after the other in a series circuit. The same current flows through all of them in turn, but the increased resistance means the current is smaller. So, two light bulbs in series will glow less brightly than just one. A break in any part of a series circuit stops the whole current flowing.

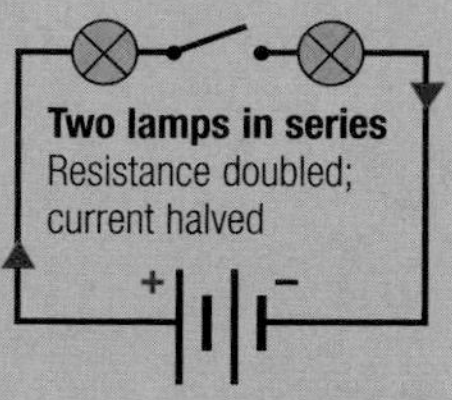

- **Parallel circuit** A circuit split into branches, with components side by side, is described as parallel. Each branch receives the full current because, in effect, each is connected directly to the source. This means that two bulbs in parallel glow brighter than the same two in series. Also, a break in one branch of a parallel circuit only stops current flow in that branch.

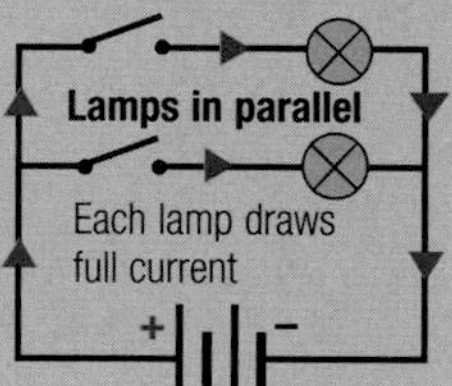

Electrical conductivity

Materials differ in their ability to conduct an electric current – their conductivity. There are four groups:

- **Insulators** are materials such as plastics, rubber and ceramics that have a high resistance to the flow of electricity because they lack free electrons.
- **Conductors** have plenty of free electrons and conduct electricity well. They include most metals (silver and copper are best) and carbon a nonmetal.
- **Semiconductors**, such as silicon, have conductivity in between that of insulators and conductors.
- **Superconductors** offer no resistance at all to current flow. Most metals become superconductors near absolute zero (–273.16°C).

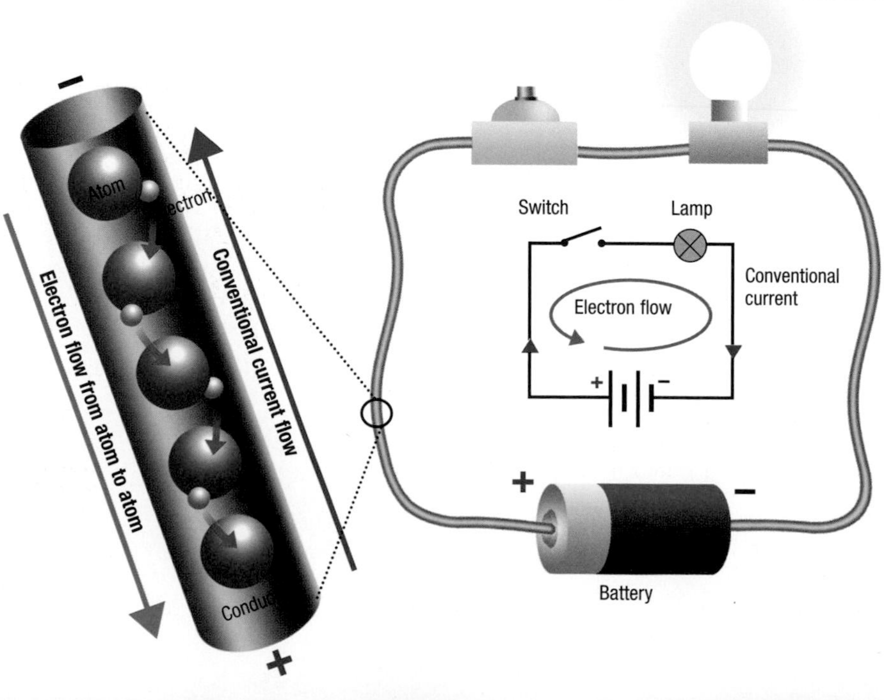

Current confusion The basic laws governing electric charges and currents were worked out long before the electron was discovered. It was decided arbitrarily that electric current flowed from the positive pole of a battery to the negative. When the electron was discovered, it was realized that electron flow is actually in the opposite direction, but the direction of "conventional" current flow was retained.

Showing circuits Electrical circuits are represented by circuit diagrams, which use internationally recognized symbols for the various components. The circuit on the left consists of a battery linked with wires to a switch and a light bulb. Chemical reactions inside the battery cause an electron buildup at its negative terminal. The electrons travel along the wire to the positive terminal. On the way, they pass through a wire filament inside the light bulb. This heats the filament, causing it to glow, releasing light and heat energy. Opening the switch breaks the circuit, so electrons can no longer flow.

WHAT IS MAGNETISM?

Like electricity, magnetism is a force produced by the movement of electrons inside atoms. All materials are magnetic, but some – notably iron, steel, cobalt, nickel and some ceramics – are far more magnetic than others; they are called ferromagnetic materials.

The spinning electrons inside atoms create minute magnetic fields – areas in which a magnetic force acts. In ferromagnetic materials, the fields of many atoms reinforce each other in small areas known as domains to form mini-magnets. Normally, the domains are arranged randomly and their magnetic fields cancel out. But if the domains are all aligned in the same direction, a familiar bar magnet is created. This will attract – that is, exert a pulling force on – other ferromagnetic materials and will attract or repel other magnets, depending on how they are aligned.

A permanent magnet, such as a bar magnet, is always magnetic. A temporary magnet, such as an electromagnet (see below), can gain and lose its magnetic force.

Magnetic poles Every magnet has two poles – north and south – at opposite ends. The Earth is magnetic, and a magnet's north pole is so called because it is attracted to the Earth's North Pole; its south pole is south-seeking. As with electrical charges, opposite magnetic poles attract each other, and like poles repel. If a magnet's north pole is near the south pole of another, the two snap together, but two north poles push each other apart.

Lines of force A magnetic field has direction; it acts along invisible lines called lines of force, or flux. These loop around a magnet from pole to pole and can be seen if iron filings are sprinkled around a bar magnet. The filings cluster around the poles, where the flux lines are closest and the magnetic force is strongest.

Induction Just as an electric charge induces an opposite charge, a magnet induces magnetism in a nearby ferromagnetic material. A north pole induces a south pole and vice versa. This is why magnets attract unmagnetized ferromagnetic materials, such as iron filings or a pin.

The magnetic compass

The Earth has a magnetic field produced by the movement of molten iron in its core and behaves like a giant bar magnet. A compass is a lightweight magnet that can swing freely to detect this field. The compass's north pole points to magnetic north, which is close to but not the same as, geographic north. Confusingly, the compass's north pole is attracted north because what we call magnetic north pole is, in fact, the south pole of Earth's magnet.

Magnetic fields Iron filings sprinkled on a sheet of paper laid over magnets will show the direction and strength of the magnetic fields around them: (1) nearby north and south poles are attracted, and (2) two nearby south poles repel each other.

see also
26-27 **Structure of the Earth**
424-25 **Electromagnetic spectrum**
432-33 **The periodic table**

Electromagnetism

The relationship of electricity and magnetism – electromagnetism – is the basis of electric motors and is used widely in industry.

Magnetism from electricity When electricity flows through a wire, it produces a weak magnetic field. The field is reinforced by winding the wire into a coil, so that fields produced by all the loops of wire add together. An iron core inside the coil concentrates the field even more. A coil like this is called an electromagnet; its magnetic field disappears as soon as the current is switched off.

Electric motors In its simplest form, an electric motor consists of a coil of wire pivoted in the magnetic field between the poles of a permanent magnet or an electromagnet. A current flowing through the coil creates its own magnetic field, with forces of attraction and repulsion between it and the magnetic field around it. These forces lead to movement: The coil spins, driving a shaft.

Current is fed to the coil through carbon rods called brushes. A device called a commutator links the brushes to the coil. It ensures that the direction of the current in the coil reverses every half-turn, so that the coil is always pushed up on one side and pulled down on the other. This creates a continuous rotary movement.

Electricity from magnetism Moving a wire or coil though a magnetic field generates an electric current inside the wire or coil. This is known as electromagnetic induction and is how electricity is generated in a power station or – on a much smaller scale – a bicycle generator. If the turning coil of a generator has a commutator (as in an electric motor), the connection will be reversed each half-turn, so the current produced will always flow in the same direction; this is called direct current (DC). Without a commutator, the current reverses direction each half-turn; this is called alternating current (AC).

A transformer combines the electromagnetic effect with induction. AC electricity is fed to a coil, which creates a continually reversing magnetic field. This magnetic field, in turn, induces electricity at a different voltage in another coil on the same core.

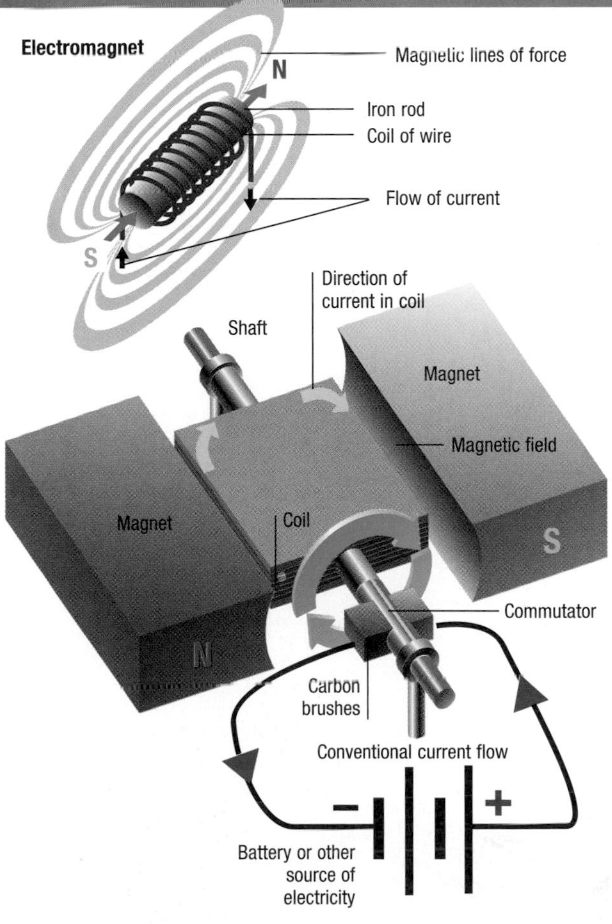

The electromagnetic spectrum

The Universe is permeated with the energy of electromagnetic radiation. Of the many ways in which this radiation manifests itself, only visible light and infrared, or radiant heat, can be perceived by the senses. Other types range from radio waves to X-rays and the gamma rays produced by nuclear explosions. All, however, are made up of patterns of electrical and magnetic energy that move through the vacuum of space at the same constant speed – the speed of light.

WHAT ARE ELECTROMAGNETIC WAVES?

Any kind of electromagnetic radiation can be thought of as waves of energy, which are generated by oscillating electric and magnetic fields (see pages 422-23).

Radio waves, for example, are a form of electromagnetic radiation that can be created by oscillating electric currents in a wire. The negatively charged subatomic particles called electrons flowing along the wire create a zone (or field) of electrical influence around themselves; they also create a magnetic field. If the electrons are made to move rapidly backwards and forwards – that is, oscillate – the associated electric and magnetic fields change in unison, creating radio waves.

Frequency and wavelength Differences in frequency and wavelength are largely what distinguish the various kinds of radiation.

- **Frequency** is the number of times per second the electrical and magnetic fields reach their maximum strength – that is, the number of complete oscillations or vibrations per second. It is measured in hertz (Hz).
- **Wavelength** is the distance a wave travels in the time it takes to complete one oscillation. It is measured in meters (m).

The higher the frequency, the shorter the wavelength, and vice versa. Mathematically, wavelength equals the speed of light divided by frequency. For example, a radio station broadcasting at 100 megahertz (100 000 000 Hz) has a wavelength (in meters) of 299 792 000 (m/s) ÷ 100 000 000 (Hz) = 2.99792 m.

The energy of electromagnetic waves depends on wavelength. Radio waves, microwaves and infrared have longer wavelengths (lower frequency) than visible light, and they carry less energy. Ultraviolet, X-rays and gamma rays have shorter wavelengths (higher frequency) than visible light and carry more energy. In fact, they carry sufficient energy to penetrate some solid material, such as flesh.

Waves or particles?

In most ways, electromagnetic radiation acts like waves, but sometimes it can be more like a stream of discrete particles. Particles of electromagnetic radiation are called quanta – or photons, in the case of light particles.

- **Wave effects** Radiation shows wavelike behavior when it is reflected from certain surfaces. Light, for example, is reflected from a mirror, while radio waves bounce off aircraft to be detected on radar screens.
- **Particle effects** Radiation demonstrates particle-like properties when it reacts with something to bring about physical or chemical change. For example, light particles or photons falling on a solar cell are converted into an electric current. This is called the photoelectric effect.

The way in which electromagnetic waves combine the properties of both waves and particles is known as wave-particle duality and is the fundamental principle in quantum physics. This describes how the amount of energy in each quantum of electromagnetic radiation, depends on the frequency of the radiation.

TYPES OF RADIATION	Radio	Microwave
Frequency	Up to 3000 MHz	3000 MHz to 3000 GHz
Wavelength	More than 10^{-1} m (more than 10 cm)	10^{-1} to 10^{-4} m (10 cm to 0.1 mm)
Sources	Oscillating electric currents, sparks, cosmic sources	Magnetron, maser, cosmic sources
Detectors	Electronic circuits, including radio and television sets	Electronic circuits
General effects	Induces matching small oscillating electric currents in conductors	Induces matching small oscillating electric currents in conductors; heating effect if frequency matches natural vibration frequency of molecules
Applications	Radio and television broadcasting and telecommunications; also radio telescopes, "cordless" phones, and "wireless" computer network systems	Telephone and other telecommunications links; cellular telephones; radar; heating and cooking food; also microwave telescopes for astronomy
Uses in action	The use of radio frequencies is regulated by international and national bodies in order to avoid interference. Various "bands" are reserved for particular uses, such as broadcasting, police and emergency services, other mobile communications.	In a microwave oven, water molecules in food absorb the waves and get hot; plastic and ceramics absorb no microwaves. Radar works by sending out a narrow beam of microwaves and detecting the time it takes for their "echo" to return from objects. Cellular phones use weak microwaves. Cosmic microwaves can indicate age of Universe.

Seeing colors

Light is detected by sensors in the retina, the inner lining of the eye. White light is a mixture of colors, with wavelengths ranging from red (longest) through orange, yellow, green and blue, to violet (shortest).

Our eyes cannot tell the difference between "pure" colors of the true wavelengths and mixtures of certain other colors. For example, a mixture of red and green light looks yellow. This is because our eyes have only three types of color sensors, which respond to red, green and blue. Our brains interpret the signals from these sensors as all the subtle colors we perceive.

see also
420-21 **Energy**
422-23 **Electricity and magnetism**
428-29 **Relativity**

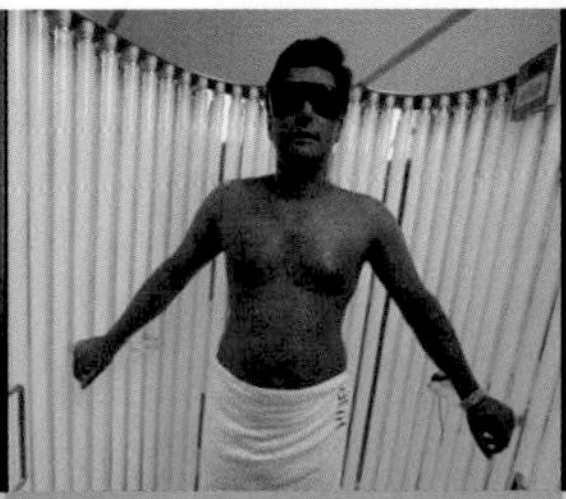
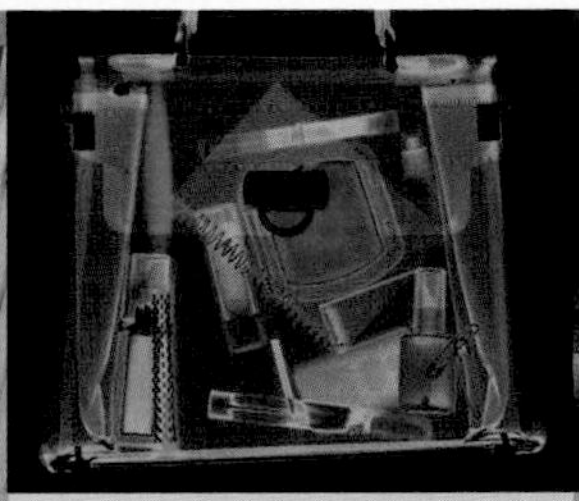

Infrared	Visible light	Ultraviolet	X-rays	Gamma rays
3000 GHz to 430 THz	430 to 750 THz	750 THz to 300 PHz	300 PHz to 30 EHz	More than 30 EHz
10^{-4} to 7×10^{-7} m (0.1 mm to 700 millionths of a millimeter)	7×10^{-7} to 4×10^{-7} m (700 to 400 millionths of a millimeter)	4×10^{-7} to 10^{-9} m (400 millionths to 1 millionth of a millimeter)	10^{-9} to 10^{-11} m (1 millionth to 10 billionths of a millimeter)	Less than 10^{-11} m (less than 10 billionths of a millimeter)
Warm and hot objects including light bulb with special filter; infrared laser	Hot or burning objects, including the Sun and stars; fluorescent materials; electrical discharge; lasers; some chemical reactions	Extremely hot objects, including the Sun and stars; some fluorescent materials; electrical discharge; ultraviolet laser	Fast electron bombardment of metal target; the Sun, stars and other cosmic sources	Nuclear reactions, including radioactive decay, nuclear reactor or explosion; stars and other cosmic sources
Thermopile (heat sensor); thermal imaging sensor; special photographic film	Eyes; photographic film; charge-coupled device; photoelectric cell	Fluorescent materials; photographic film; insects' eyes; electronic devices	Fluorescent materials; photographic film; indirectly, by detecting any ionization they cause	Fluorescent materials; photographic film; indirectly by detecting any ionization they cause
Causes warming when radiation is absorbed	Triggers certain chemical reactions; triggers sensors in eyes of animals; powers photosynthesis when absorbed by chloroplasts in plant cells	Tans, then burns skin and may cause cancers; at high levels can cause blindness; kills bacteria and viruses, and damages or destroys plant life	Pass through many solid materials; can cause genetic mutations and cancers; can damage delicate electronic equipment	Pass through all but very thick or heavy solid materials; cause mutations and damage to cells, leading to "radiation sickness" and often death
Radiant heaters; electric stoves and toasters; television remote controls; some night-vision devices and thermal-imaging cameras; infrared astronomy; aerial surveying	Vision; photography, cinematography and television; bleaching; power generation (using photocells); entertainment and communications (with lasers and fiber-optics)	Vision in insects (to detect some "invisible" patterns on flowers); optical brighteners in laundry detergent; sterilization in hospitals; some night-vision cameras	Observing bones and other internal body structures (densest parts are opaque to X-rays); checking metal joints and welds; destroying cancerous cells	Checking dense structures, such as aircraft bearings, for cracks and other flaws; destroying cancerous cells
Infrared aerial and satellite images can show crop ripening by detecting heat from crops; also used for spotting forest fires.	The many colors that we see consist of light of different wavelengths; red light has the longest wavelength, violet light has the shortest.	Many flowers have patterns visible only in ultraviolet light. These patterns help insects find nectar and pollen. Most of the Sun's intense ultraviolet rays are absorbed by the "ozone layer," a thin zone high in the stratosphere. This stops too much ultraviolet light from reaching Earth, where it can harm living things.	Many stars produce X-rays; the Sun emits its most powerful X-rays during bursts of intense activity called "solar flares." These X-rays can damage satellite equipment in Earth's orbit and may also penetrate the Earth's atmosphere and damage delicate electrical equipment on the surface.	Gamma rays, although dangerous, do not cause as great tissue damage as some other types of nuclear radiation, such as alpha particles (see page 426). An extremely thick concrete shell is needed to shield people from gamma rays produced in nuclear reactors – or, in a fallout shelter, from a nuclear explosion.

Radioactivity

Natural and man-made radiation that can harm and heal

Long before the structure of the atom was fully understood, mysterious radiation – some of which could pass through solid objects – was found to be emitted by certain natural elements. The phenomenon was called radioactivity. The radiation was found to consist of three main types of ray, and study of the rays helped elucidate the structure of matter. It is now understood that radioactivity is a property of unstable atomic nuclei. It may occur naturally or be induced by bombarding unstable nuclei with subatomic particles from cosmic rays, radioactive materials or a nuclear reaction or explosion.

WHAT IS RADIOACTIVITY?

Radioactivity occurs when unstable atomic nuclei emit high-energy subatomic particles or radiation. There are three types of radiation, each with different properties. Their discoverers called them alpha (α), beta (β) and gamma (γ) rays according to how far they could penetrate various materials.

Alpha and beta rays proved to be streams of subatomic particles so they are now usually known as alpha and beta particles rather than rays. Emission of either from a nucleus changes its structure and the structure of its atom, so that it becomes an atom of a different element. This change is called decay or transformation. Gamma rays are like very powerful X-rays. Their emission does not involve nuclear decay but is simply the shedding of excess nuclear energy. They often accompany or follow the emission of alpha particles, beta particles, or both.

All three types of radiation can be harmful to the human body. In energy terms (and thus in penetrating power), alpha particles are the weakest, and gamma rays are the strongest. However, the power of radiation to destroy cells can be harnessed to treat cancers.

Alpha particles

Each alpha particle consists of two protons and two neutrons packed together and is in fact identical to the nucleus of a helium atom. Alpha particles have a positive charge. They are ejected as the nucleus of a radioactive atom decays. Alpha particles are too heavy to be knocked off course by molecules in air, so they move in a straight path.

Penetration Alpha particles are stopped by a thin sheet of paper.

Effect Alpha particles cannot penetrate skin and enter the body only if radioactive matter is consumed or inhaled. Inside the body, even a single alpha particle can cause harm by altering the make-up of a living cell, thus triggering cancer.

Example Uranium-238 emits alpha particles as it decays to form thorium-234.

Beta particles

A beta particle is a fast-moving electron emitted by a nucleus when an excess neutron (which is neutral) changes into a positively charged proton. This increases the atom's atomic number by one; the beta particle carries away the excess negative charge. Beta particles have very little mass, travel at around half the speed of light, and can be knocked off course by air molecules.

Penetration Beta particles are stopped by a (.2 in.) thick sheet of aluminium.

Effect Some beta particles can pass through the skin but are most likely to cause damage if a beta-emitter is inhaled or eaten. If this contaminates the bones, for example, it may trigger leukemia.

Example Strontium-90 emits beta particles when it decays to form yttrium-90.

Gamma rays

A form of electromagnetic radiation (see page 425), gamma rays are similar to X-rays but with a shorter wavelength. Like X-rays, they can penetrate most materials. Gamma rays have no mass and travel in a straight path at the speed of light. They are produced when (or very shortly after) nuclei break down as are any emissions of alpha or beta particles or both.

Penetration A sheet of lead (1.6 in.) thick reduces gamma ray intensity by about 90 percent. Very thick concrete is needed to shield people completely.

Effect Gamma rays penetrate the body. They are dangerous mainly because they create ions (charged atoms), which damage living tissues.

Example Radium-226 emits gamma rays when it decays to form radon-222.

Differing versions of the same element

Almost all elements can exist in several chemically identical versions that have small physical differences at the atomic level; they are called isotopes. Their atoms share the same atomic number, but they differ in atomic mass.

Atomic number The atoms that make up a particular element are defined by their atomic number – the number of protons in each nucleus. For example, if an atom has six protons, it must be carbon; if it has 92 protons, it is uranium.

Atomic mass The atomic mass of an atom, on the other hand, depends on the numbers of both protons and neutrons in its nucleus. Isotopes differ in atomic mass because they differ in the number of neutrons in their nuclei. Take the case of two isotopes of carbon, for example.

Carbon-12
Atomic number 6; atomic mass 12
Nucleus contains 6 protons and 6 neutrons

Carbon-14
Atomic number 6; atomic mass 14
Nucleus contains 6 protons and 8 neutrons

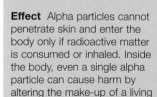

Radio-isotopes
Isotopes with unstable nuclei (including carbon-14) are likely to decay. They are known as radioisotopes – that is, radioactive isotopes. About 1500 radio-isotopes have been found. Sixty of them exist in nature; the rest have been made during nuclear reactions or particle physics experiments.

Chain of decay

Some radioactive isotopes decay in several steps (emitting various particles at each step) before they reach a stable state. A series of isotopes, often with widely differing half-lives for each part, formed by the decay of one element into another is called a radioactive series. Thorium-232, for example, goes through ten transformations to become lead.

ALL IN HALF-LIVES

The half-life of an isotope is a measure of the rate at which it decays. The decay of any single nucleus is unpredictable, but in any collection of atoms, half will decay over a certain period; this is the half-life. Over the half-life period, radioactivity reduces by half. In the following same half-life period, half the remaining nuclei (not half the original number) decay, and the radioactivity falls to a quarter of the original level, and so on. The half-life of any given radio-isotope can vary from a fraction of a second to many millions of years.

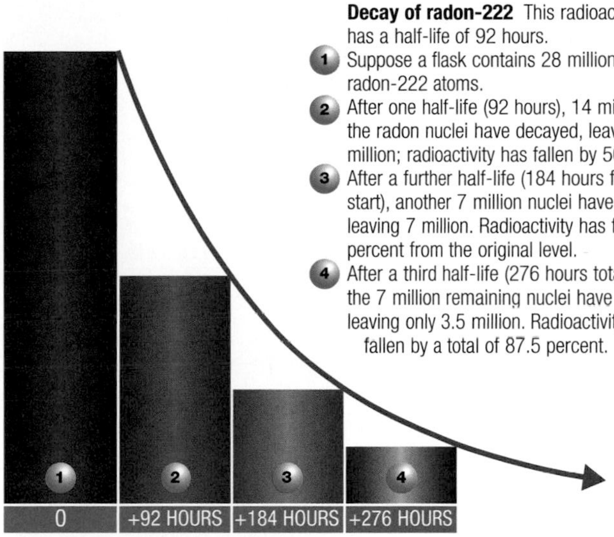

Decay of radon-222 This radioactive gas has a half-life of 92 hours.

1. Suppose a flask contains 28 million radon-222 atoms.
2. After one half-life (92 hours), 14 million of the radon nuclei have decayed, leaving 14 million; radioactivity has fallen by 50 percent.
3. After a further half-life (184 hours from the start), another 7 million nuclei have decayed, leaving 7 million. Radioactivity has fallen 75 percent from the original level.
4. After a third half-life (276 hours total), half the 7 million remaining nuclei have decayed, leaving only 3.5 million. Radioactivity has fallen by a total of 87.5 percent.

Natural radioactivity

Natural radioisotopes occur widely on Earth in rocks and minerals. They produce low levels of radioactivity known as "background radiation." In most places, this radiation is harmless, but in some areas radon gas leaks from rocks and can be harmful if it is trapped in cellars of houses. There are two groups of natural radioisotopes:

Primordial Created in the earliest days of the Universe, primordial radioisotopes are billions of years older than Earth itself. They have very long half-lives – about 4.5 billion years for uranium-238, for example.

Cosmogenic Created when cosmic rays bombard atoms in the upper atmosphere, cosmogenic radioisotopes have much shorter half-lives but are constantly replenished. For example, carbon-14 has a half-life of 5730 years. It is taken up by living organisms, so its decay can be used to estimate when they died.

Nuclear fission and fusion

Nuclear reactors and nuclear weapons make use of the fact, established by the theory of relativity (see page 428), that mass and energy are two aspects of the same thing. Matter – mass – is annihilated and converted into energy, either by nuclear fission (the splitting of heavy nuclei) or by nuclear fusion (the joining of light nuclei). In either case, the mass of the fission or fusion products – including any subatomic particles emitted – is less than that of the initial nuclei. The "lost" mass is turned into a burst of energy.

Fission Nuclear fission relies on the fact that the nuclei of some isotopes, such as uranium-235 and plutonium-239, become highly unstable if they capture a neutron. They instantly split into two lighter nuclei plus additional neutrons – which can then split more nuclei in a chain reaction (see right). Energy is released as gamma rays and other radiation and as the kinetic energy of the fission products, creating a great deal of heat. In a bomb, the chain reaction builds up in millionths of a second, and the energy release is explosive. In a reactor, control rods ensure that there are just enough neutrons to maintain a steady reaction.

Fusion Nuclear fusion uses the heat of a fission reaction. This makes the nuclei of hydrogen or its isotopes deuterium and tritium fuse to form helium nuclei. There is again a loss of mass and a huge release of energy. Fusion fuels the Sun, but no one has yet built a reliable fusion reactor for power generation.

Chain reaction Each time a neutron causes a uranium-235 (U-235) nucleus to split, surplus neutrons are produced. If there is a "critical mass" of U-235 present, these neutrons cause more nuclei to split, and so on in a chain reaction. But if there is not enough U-235, too many neutrons escape and the reaction fizzles out.

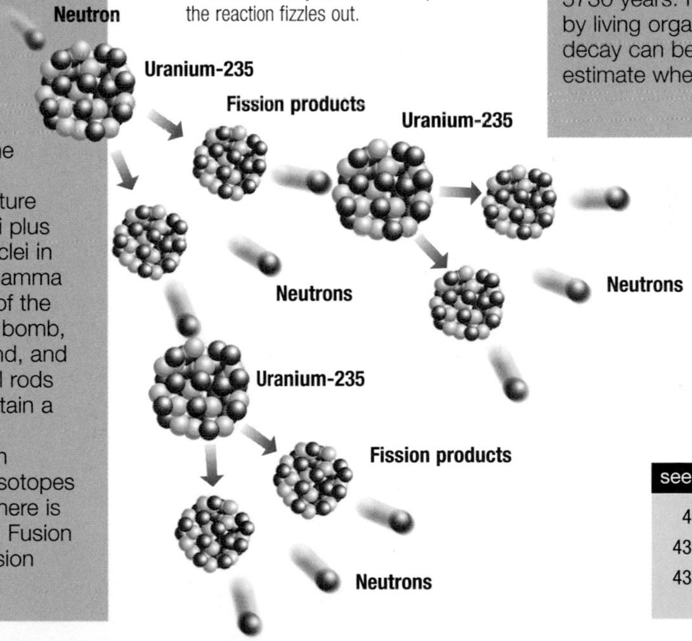

see also

404-5 **Nuclear power**
430-31 **Atoms and molecules**
432-33 **The periodic table**

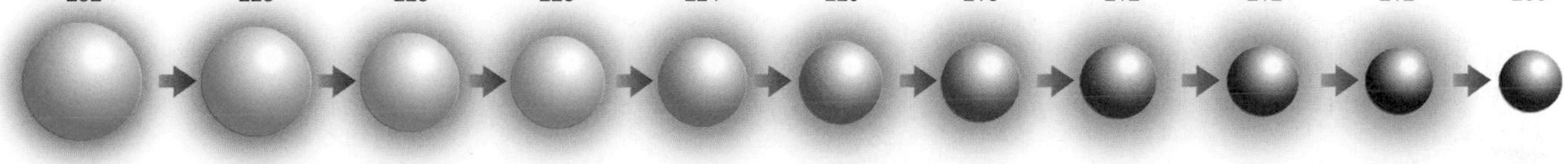

Isotope	Thorium-232	Radium-228	Actinium-228	Thorium-228	Radium 224	Radon-220	Polonium-216	Lead-212	Bismuth-212	Polonium-212	Lead-208
Emission	α, γ	β, γ	β, γ	α, γ	α, γ	α	α	β, γ	β	α	
Half-life	14×10^9 years	5.8 years	6.1 hours	1.9 years	3.6 days	55 seconds	0.15 seconds	11 hours	61 minutes	300×10^{-9} seconds	stable

Albert Einstein's two theories of relativity are an attempt to explain the true nature of motion, mass, energy and gravity. His thinking superseded many of the concepts enshrined in the classical tradition of Newtonian physics. The General Theory deals with gravity; the Special Theory makes predictions about how objects behave at near-light speeds.

WHAT IS RELATIVITY?

At the heart of relativity lies an insight into how we measure space and time. Imagine a man sitting on a train reading a book. According to the man, his book is stationary – which, indeed, it is, within his particular **frame of reference**. Now imagine a woman standing on a railway platform seeing the man and his book through the window of the passing train. The train is traveling at 100 km/h so, for the woman, the book is moving forward at 100 km/h. Next, imagine a girl sitting in a train going in the opposite direction at 20 km/h. She too sees the man and his book, as her train passes his. According to her, the book is traveling backward at 120 km/h. Finally, imagine astronauts in space. From their point of view, the book is spinning around the Sun at many thousands of kilometers per hour.

No fixed point Everything depends on the frame of reference. Using different frames of reference, totally different measurements emerge, all legitimate in their different ways. Relativity, then, makes this key point: There is no such thing as an absolute measurement of space. No object is completely at rest in space. Consequently, no fixed point exists from which to make absolute measurements.

The speed of light One absolute does exist: The speed of light. Imagine a car traveling toward you at 30 m/s (108 km/h). Common sense might tell you that because the car is moving toward you, light from the headlights is traveling at 30 m/s faster than the speed of light – that is, $c + 30$ m/s (where c is the speed of light). But common sense would be wrong. Regardless of how much or how fast an observer may move relative to a source of light, the speed of light remains the same. Unlike anything else in the Universe, the speed of light is independent of any frame of reference. But speed is distance over time. For the speed of light to be constant, distance and – crucially – time must be subject to change depending on the point of view of the observer. This is Einstein's greatest insight: Time is not constant; it passes more quickly for some observers than others, depending on their circumstances.

A lot of energy from a little mass

Newtonian physics sees mass and energy as distinct. The Special Theory, however, removes the distinction: In relativity, mass is "frozen" energy. And according to the equation $E = mc^2$, the energy locked up in mass is immense. Since c^2 – the square of the speed of light – is 90 000 000 000 000 000, for every unit of mass (m) the energy locked up in it is 90 000 000 000 000 000 times that amount.

It was this insight that paved the way for the exploitation of energy from matter by the splitting of the atom (more precisely, the atomic nucleus). In a nuclear reactor, the amount of energy that can, in theory, be extracted from just 100 g (3½ oz) of fuel is enough to keep a million 100 watt lightbulbs lit for three years. A nuclear bomb can produce an equally large amount of energy from 100 g (3½ oz) of fuel. This is why a warhead small enough to sit on a kitchen table can explode with enough force to destroy a city.

SPECIAL THEORY OF RELATIVITY

The Special Theory (published in 1905) deals with the behavior of objects moving in the "special," gravity-free environment of empty space.

Working from the basic insights about frame of reference and the speed of light, it makes a series of often startling predictions about mass, energy and time. Among other things, it states

- that mass and energy are equivalent and can be converted into one another. This leads to the famous equation $E = mc^2$. In other words, the energy **(*E*)** of an object at rest equals its mass **(*m*)** multiplied by the speed of light **(*c*)** squared.
- that as a body accelerates, its energy and mass increase and its length decreases in the direction of travel. Were an object able to reach the speed of light, it would have infinite mass and zero length. This means that the speed of light is the speed limit of the Universe.
- that when an object is moving, time seems to run more slowly to an "outside" observer, although it seems to run "normally" to the person moving. This discrepancy is noticeable only near light speeds. It means that measurements of time, like those of space, are relative, not absolute.

GENERAL THEORY OF RELATIVITY

Isaac Newton's law of gravitation published in 1687 states that gravity is a force that exists between two bodies of matter, and its size depends on their mass and the distance between them.

It suggests that the gravitational pull the Sun exerts on the planets of the Solar System, for example, takes place instantaneously over millions of kilometers. But this is incompatible with the concept put forward in the Special Theory of Relativity that nothing can travel faster than the speed of light.

- **Explaining gravity by relativity** In 1915, Einstein proposed a General Theory that explained gravity. According to the General Theory, gravity is a property of space, time and mass, not a force of attraction between bodies. The presence of a gravitational field is the result of the space-time continuum (see opposite) becoming curved around a body, whereas the lack of a gravitational field leaves it flat.

This is easier to understand if the space-time continuum is imagined as a stretched rubber sheet. If a heavy ball is placed on the sheet, it creates an indentation. A smaller ball rolled across the sheet will be affected by that hollow and roll toward the heavy ball.

- **The Sun and planets** Newtonian physics explains the curved orbit of a planet around the Sun by saying that the planet is attracted by the force of gravity to the Sun. The General Theory says that the planet's path is curved because the Sun – with its great mass – distorts and curves the space-time continuum around it.

In the General Theory's distorted space, a curve is the shortest distance between two points and is therefore the path followed by the planet. This also applies to light, which is "bent" by the curve in the space-time continuum.

Time and relativity

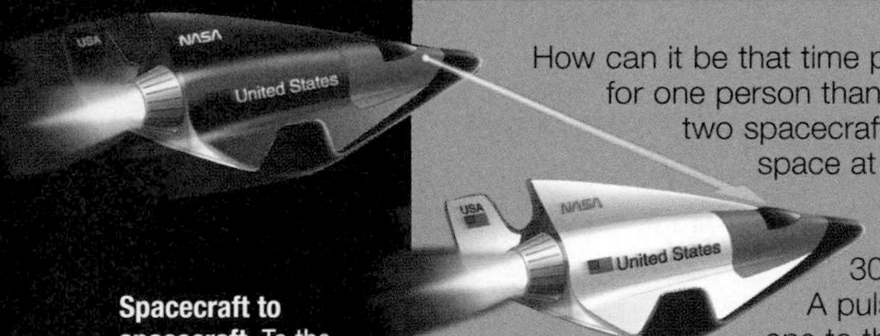

Spacecraft to spacecraft To the astronauts on board, the pulse of light travels in a straight line and takes 1 second because it is traveling near the speed of light.

How can it be that time passes at a different rate for one person than for another? Consider two spacecraft travelling through space at 99 percent of the speed of light at a fixed distance of 300 000 000 m apart. A pulse of light is sent from one to the other. To astronauts on board, this pulse travels in a straight line because the two craft are stationary relative to one another and it takes 1 second (see left).

An observer on Earth, however, viewing the spacecraft through a telescope, sees the light beam follow a diagonal path (see below). This path is obviously longer than the straight line observed by the astronauts, and the light takes longer, from this point of view, to travel from one craft to the other.

Both the astronauts and the Earth observer have witnessed the same event but from different frames of reference. The Earth observer sees the beam taking seven times longer to travel between the spacecraft than the astronauts do. Yet the speed of light is constant – it is the only constant in the Universe. So the only explanation for the light seeming to take longer for the observer on Earth is that time itself was moving more slowly for him relative to the astronauts on the spacecraft. Time does not pass at the same rate for the astronauts and the observer. Time, like space, is related to the frame of reference in which it is being measured.

Seven-second beam With the spacecraft travelling at 99 percent of the speed of light, the beam (watched from Earth) takes 7 seconds to pass from one craft to the other.

Seen from Earth For the observer on Earth, the beam takes a diagonal path because the second craft has moved on by the time the beam reaches it.

Space-time

The General Theory proposes a concept of the space-time continuum. In physics, space embodies the idea of distance and has three dimensions at right angles to each other. An object can move in three dimensions to reach a certain point: forward or backward, right or left, down or up.

Movement also involves a fourth dimension, namely time. Time and the three dimensions of space can be combined in a four-dimensional system of space-time, or a space-time continuum. According to the General Theory, space-time, mass and gravity are interdependent.

Relativity: the evidence

Since Einstein put forward his ideas of relativity, many of them have been tested experimentally and proven to be correct.

- Atomic clocks on spacecraft have been shown to be fractionally slower than atomic clocks left on Earth.
- Particle physics has shown that subatomic particles traveling at high speed gain mass by exactly the amount Einstein predicted.
- Light from stars has been shown to be "bent" by the Sun, providing evidence for the distortion of space-time by a large mass.
- Particles in cosmic rays should only last a fraction of a second when they reach the Earth's atmosphere. They exist significantly longer (long enough for detection) because they are traveling through space at the speed of light, so time slows down for them.

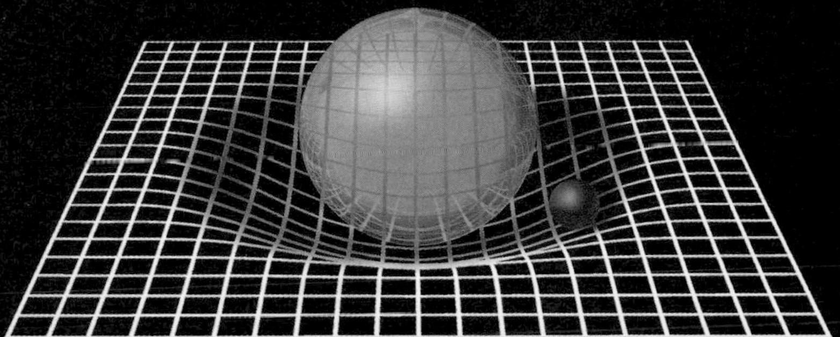

What is gravity? If space-time is seen as a rubber sheet, it is easy to see how a larger object distorts it more than a smaller one. The smaller object then "falls" towards the larger – the effect known as gravity.

see also

12-13 **The Universe**
404-5 **Nuclear power**
418-19 **Mechanics**
426-27 **Radioactivity**

Every substance on Earth is made up of the atoms of one or more elements. To understand why a substance appears as it does and why it behaves in a certain way under particular circumstances, chemists study the properties of the atoms of the many different elements and of the compounds the atoms combine to form. From their findings, they devise laws that help describe the nature of matter.

WHAT IS AN ATOM?

An atom is the smallest particle of any element that can take part in a chemical reaction. It is composed of a positively charged central core – the nucleus (see below) – surrounded by orbiting, negatively charged electrons.

Carbon atom with 6 protons and 6 neutrons in its nucleus

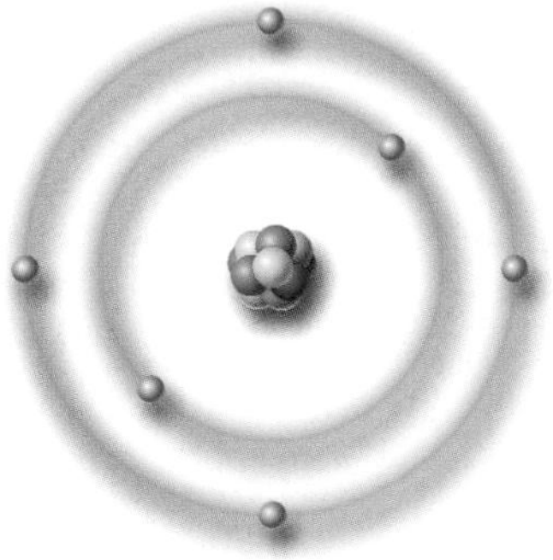

Orbiting electrons
2 in inner shell
4 in outer shell

Sulfur atom with 16 protons and 16 neutrons in its nucleus

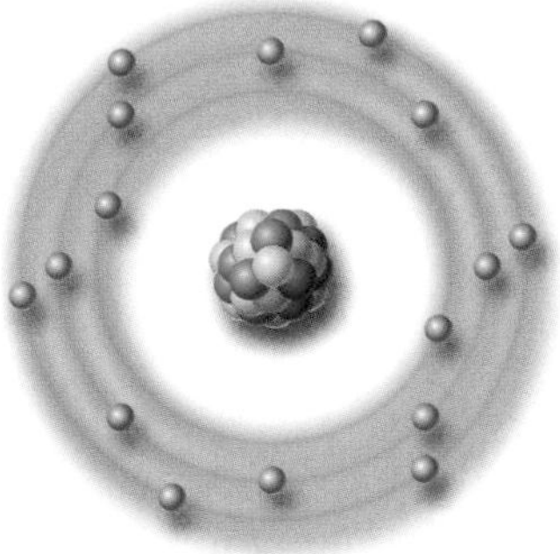

Orbiting electrons
2 in inner shell
8 in middle shell
6 in outer shell

Electron shells Electrons orbit the nucleus in layers or shells. The innermost shell can carry up to two electrons, and the next shell can carry up to eight and the third shell can carry up to 18 electrons. The chemical characteristics of an atom are determined by the degree to which its outermost electron shell is filled.

The nucleus Almost the entire mass of an atom resides in its nucleus, which is composed of protons and neutrons. Protons are positively charged; neutrons are electrically neutral. Any element is defined by the number of protons in the nucleus of each atom, known as its atomic number. Carbon, for example, has six protons in the nucleus of each atom, so its atomic number is six.

The electrons The nucleus is surrounded by orbiting electrons – tiny, negatively charged particles. For a neutral atom of any element, the number of orbiting electrons equals the number of protons. The orbiting electrons determine the chemical behavior of an atom, because atoms combine, or bond, by either sharing or transferring electrons (see page 434). The electrons are arranged in layers (shells) at different distances from the nucleus. Each shell can contain a certain maximum number of electrons.

Ions An ion is an electrically charged atom or group of atoms. Normally, the charge on an atom is neutral, but during chemical reactions, electrons can move from atom to atom, so that the atoms gain an overall positive or negative charge, producing positive or negative ions. Positively charged ions are known as cations, and negatively charged ions are called anions.

Branches of chemistry

The study of chemistry is divided into a number of distinct disciplines.

- **Analytical chemistry** develops and uses techniques to determine precisely what elements are present in a substance and in what proportions.
- **Applied chemistry** is the practical application of chemical knowledge and techniques to agriculture, industry, medicine and other commercial areas.
- **Biochemistry** is the study of the chemical processes that take place in living organisms.
- **Inorganic chemistry** is the study of the properties of the elements and all their compounds, except for those of carbon.
- **Organic chemistry** is the study of the numerous compounds of carbon. All living organisms are based on carbon molecules – this is why the discipline is termed organic chemistry.
- **Physical chemistry** is concerned with the physical effects of chemical structures, particularly energy changes and reaction rates.
- **Polymer chemistry** is the study of compounds made from long repeating chains of molecules. Organic examples include DNA and proteins, and the majority of plastics are synthetic polymers.
- **Structural chemistry** is the study of how atoms are arranged in molecules and the types of bonds between them.

WHAT IS A MOLECULE?

Many substances are made up of molecules, which consist of two or more atoms of the same or different elements joined together. The bonds linking atoms in a molecule are formed by electrons being "shared" (see page 434). A molecule is the smallest part of such a substance that can exist on its own.

A water molecule, for example, is made up of one oxygen atom bonded to two hydrogen atoms; if it were to be broken up into its constituent atoms, it would no longer have the properties we associate with water.

Any substance may be represented by its chemical formula. This shows the proportions of the atoms of the different elements in it. The formula H_2O tells you that you need two hydrogen atoms for every oxygen atom to make water. Similarly, the formula for sulfuric acid, H_2SO_4, tells you that sulfuric acid contains hydrogen, sulfur and oxygen in the ratio of 2:1:4.

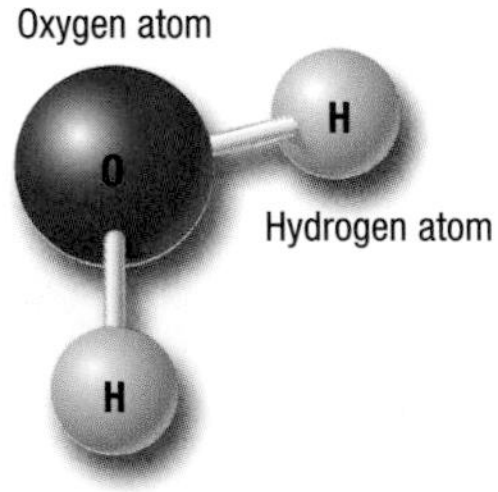

Water molecule, H_2O

Sulfuric acid molecule, H_2SO_4

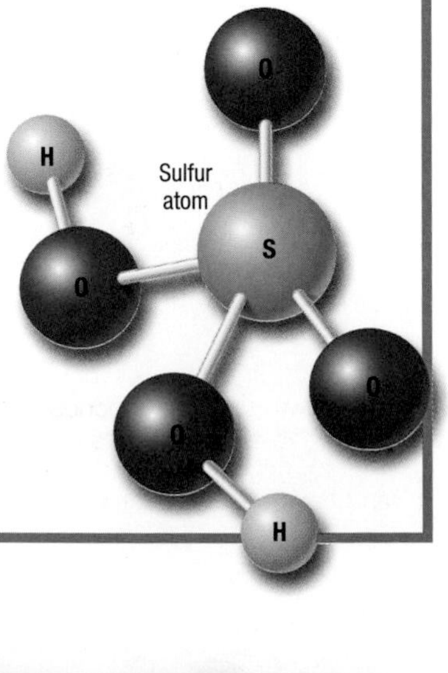

Naming an element

In chemistry, the basic substances are called elements. Any pure element consists of atoms that are chemically identical. A pure sample of the element gold, for example, will contain only gold atoms.

For convenience, chemists have given each element a specific name and symbol. The **symbol** for an element consists of one or two letters – usually a shortened version of its full name. These symbols have been agreed upon by scientists internationally.

The vast majority of the elements that are known today were discovered in the last two to three hundred years. Many of these have been given names that refer to their identifying characteristics as perceived by their discoverer. Oxygen, for example, means "acid-former," from the 18th-century theory that all acids contain oxygen; the name for chlorine – a greenish gas – is derived from the word *khloros*, a Greek term for yellow-green.

Some of the elements, however, have been known and used since antiquity. They usually have names that are derived from Latin or Ancient Greek:

Element	Latin	Symbol
Copper	Cuprum	Cu
Gold	Aurum	Au
Iron	Ferrum	Fe
Lead	Plumbum	Pb
Mercury	Hydrargyrum	Hg
Potassium	Kalium	K
Silver	Argentum	Ag

More recently, the convention has been to name elements in honor of famous scientists:

Curium (Marie Curie)
Nobelium (Alfred Nobel)
Fermium (Enrico Fermi)

This honor has also been extended to names of places:

Californium (California)
Americium (America)
Francium (France)
Polonium (Poland)

There is a new proposal to name the elements according to the Latin for their **atomic number** (see The nucleus, opposite). The transactinides (atomic numbers 104 and over) are already being named in this way – see the periodic table, pages 432-33.

EXISTING IN DIFFERENT FORMS

Some elements exist in more than one form of molecule or crystal. These different forms are called allotropes.

- **Allotropic gases** differ in their molecular structure. For example, a molecule of ordinary oxygen gas (O_2) is made of two oxygen atoms, but a molecule of the allotrope ozone (O_3) is made of three oxygen atoms. Their physical properties also differ: Ordinary oxygen is odorless, but ozone has a sharp smell.
- **Solid allotropes** have different crystal structures. For example, carbon has three allotropes – diamond, graphite and fullerene – each of which has different physical properties. The different structures arise from the way the carbon atoms are linked together.

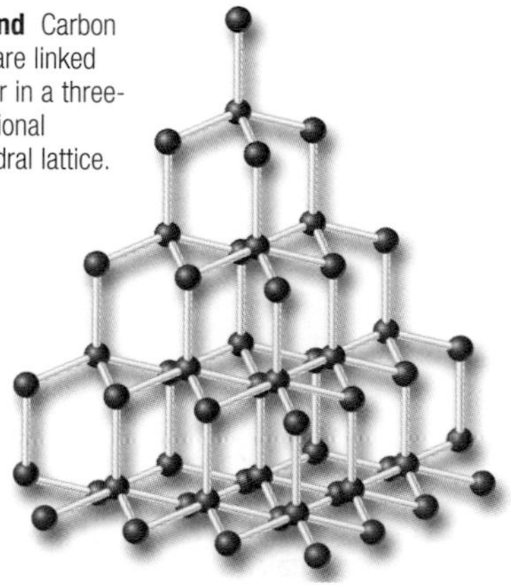

Diamond Carbon atoms are linked together in a three-dimensional tetrahedral lattice.

- **Diamond** Strong bonds extend in all directions throughout the entire transparent diamond crystal, making it extremely inflexible and hard – it is the hardest known substance.

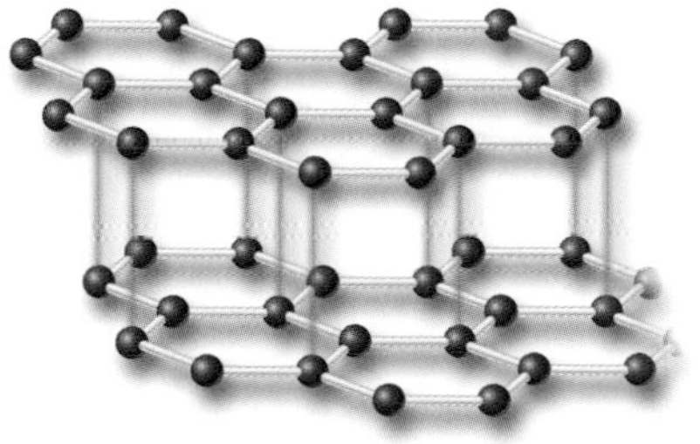

Graphite Sheets of strongly bonded carbon atoms are linked together by much weaker bonds, so they can easily slide over each other.

- **Graphite** The weak bonds between the layers of atoms make graphite slippery and soft and therefore a good lubricant. Being black, it is also used as a drawing medium.

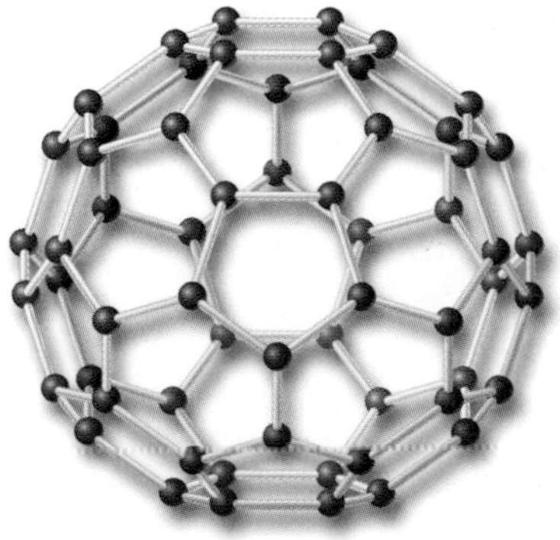

Fullerene Each molecule consists of a ball-shaped cluster of 60 carbon atoms.

- **Fullerene** Soft, heat-resistant fullerene crystals were discovered in 1985, when a high-powered laser was aimed at graphite. It is sometimes known as buckminsterfullerene.

KEY TERMS

- **Atom** The smallest part of an element that can take part in a chemical reaction.
- **Atomic number** The number of protons in the nucleus of an atom. All atoms of the same element have the same atomic number.
- **Molecule** Two or more atoms that are chemically bonded. With compounds, it is the smallest amount that can take part in a chemical reaction.
- **Ion** An atom or group of atoms that carries an electrical charge.
- **Element** A substance that consists entirely of chemically identical atoms.
- **Compound** A substance containing atoms of two or more different elements that are combined chemically.
- **Chemical reaction** A process involving two or more substances that results in a chemical change.
- **Catalyst** A substance that markedly alters the speed of a chemical reaction without itself undergoing any permanent chemical change.
- **Combustion** A chemical reaction in which a substance reacts rapidly with oxygen, giving off heat and light in the form of a flame.
- **Oxidation** The addition of oxygen to an element or compound during a chemical reaction. Oxidation is also said to occur if hydrogen is removed.
- **Reduction** The addition of hydrogen to an element or compound during a chemical reaction. Reduction is also said to occur if oxygen is removed.
- **pH** A measure of acidity or alkalinity. A pH of 7 is neutral, and substances with lower pHs are acidic, and those with a higher number are alkaline.

see also
432-33 **The periodic table**
434-35 **Chemistry of compounds**

The periodic table was created by the Russian chemist Dmitri Mendeleyev in 1869. He arranged all the elements according to atomic number and the patterns he observed in their chemical properties. Although more elements are now known, the table remains basically the same and is used by chemists to predict how elements might react together.

Reading the periodic table

Each box in the periodic table gives four pieces of information:

Box	
1	the atomic number of the element
H	its symbol
Hydrogen	its name
1.00	its relative atomic mass

I	II					
1 **H** Hydrogen 1.00						
3 **Li** Lithium 6.9	4 **Be** Beryllium 9.01					
11 **Na** Sodium 23.0	12 **Mg** Magnesium 24.5					
19 **K** Potassium 39.1	20 **Ca** Calcium 40.1	21 **Sc** Scandium 44.96	22 **Ti** Titanium 47.88	23 **V** Vanadium 50.94	24 **Cr** Chromium 51.00	25 **Mn** Manganese 54.94
37 **Rb** Rubidium 85.5	38 **Sr** Strontium 87.6	39 **Y** Yttrium 88.91	40 **Z** Zirconium 91.22	41 **Nb** Niobium 92.91	42 **Mo** Molybdenum 95.94	43 **Tc** Technetium 98
55 **Cs** Cesium 132.9	56 **Ba** Barium 137.4	57-71 Lanthanide series	72 **Hf** Hafnium 178.49	73 **Ta** Tantalum 180.95	74 **W** Tungsten 183.85	75 **Re** Rhenium 186.21
87 **Fr** Francium 223.0	88 **Ra** Radium 226.0	89-103 Actinide series	104 **Unq** Unnilquadium (261)	105 **Unp** Unnilpentium (262)	106 **Unh** Unnilhexium (263)	107 **Uns** Unnilseptium (264)

57 **La** Lanthanum 138.91	58 **Ce** Cerium 140.12	59 **Pr** Praseodymium 140.91	60 **Nd** Neodymium 144.24
89 **Ac** Actinium 227	90 **Th** Thorium 232.04	91 **Pa** Proctanium 231.04	92 **U** Uranium 238.03

Key:

- metals
- nonmetals
- metalloids
- transition elements

Groups

Eight vertical columns of elements, labeled I-VIII, are arranged down the left and right side of the periodic table. These are called groups. Each group contains elements that tend to react chemically in similar ways because they all have atoms in which the arrangement of electrons around the nucleus is similar. As well as a number, each group of elements has a name:

Group I	the alkali metals
Group II	the alkaline-earth metals
Group III	the boron elements
Group IV	the carbon elements
Group V	the nitrogen elements
Group VI	the oxygen elements
Group VII	the halogen elements
Group VIII	the noble gases

- The alkali metals (group I) have just one electron in their outermost shells. This is easily lost, making these elements very reactive.
- Similarly, the halogen elements (group VII) are very reactive; they lack just one electron to form a complete outer shell.
- In contrast, the noble gases (group VIII) have complete outer shells and are unreactive.
- Moving down each group, certain features of the elements change: The diameter of their atoms increases; atoms lose their outermost electrons more easily; and the density increases.

Periods

Each horizontal row in the table is called a "period." Reading across a period from left to right, the number of electrons in the outer shell or subshell of the elements increases. There are two other trends:

- The elements change from being metallic to nonmetallic in nature.
- The melting point of the elements gradually increases to a maximum in group IV (the carbon elements), decreasing again toward group VIII (the noble gases).

Transition elements

In the middle of the periodic table – from scandium to zinc, from yttrium to cadmium, and from hafnium to mercury – are the transition metals. These elements are similar in that their unfilled electron subshells are not in the outermost shell (unlike the elements in the left and right-hand blocks of the table). The subshells in the outer shells are filled and some of the "places" in the inner shells are vacant. These elements are known for high density and are good conductors of heat and electricity.

The sequence of transition metals is interrupted by the lanthanide (57-71) and actinide (89-103) series.

Since the 1960s, a number of extremely heavy elements – the trans-actinides (104 and above) have been created. These are all "artificial," meaning that they can be produced only in a nuclear reactor or particle accelerator, in which atoms of lighter elements collide at high speed, merging briefly to form an atom of a new element.

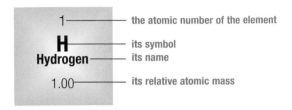

Sheet copper Like many of the transition metals, copper is a good conductor of heat.

ATOMIC NUMBER AND MASS

Atomic number The number of protons in the nucleus (see page 430) of each atom of an element is known as the atomic number of that element.

Relative atomic mass How heavy an atom of a particular element is relative to one atom of any other element is expressed as relative atomic mass. Each pair of protons and neutrons is approximately equal to one atomic mass unit. Carbon, with six neutrons and six protons in the nucleus of its atoms, has a relative atomic mass of 12.

Sometimes an atom of a particular element contains extra neutrons in its nucleus and is known as an isotope. An element may have several isotopes with varying atomic masses because of the extra neutrons. In this case, the atomic mass shown in the table is the average for the isotopes found in a typical sample of the element.

Native silver Like its periodic table neighbors copper and gold, silver conducts electricity well and so is widely used in electrical circuits.

					III	IV	V	VI	VII	VIII
										2 **He** Helium 4
					5 **B** Boron 10.81	6 **C** Carbon 12.00	7 **N** Nitrogen 14.01	8 **O** Oxygen 16.00	9 **F** Fluorine 19.00	10 **Ne** Neon 20.18
					13 **Al** Aluminium 26.98	14 **Si** Silicon 28.09	15 **P** Phosphorus 30.97	16 **S** Sulfur 32.06	17 **Cl** Chlorine 35.45	18 **Ar** Argon 39.94
26 **Fe** Iron 55.85	27 **Co** Cobalt 58.93	28 **Ni** Nickel 58.69	29 **Cu** Copper 63.55	30 **Zn** Zinc 65.38	31 **Ga** Gallium 69.72	32 **Ge** Germanium 72.6	33 **As** Arsenic 74.92	34 **Se** Selenium 78.96	35 **Br** Bromine 79.90	36 **Kr** Krypton 83.80
44 **Ru** Ruthenium 101.07	45 **Rh** Rhodium 102.91	46 **Pd** Palladium 106.42	47 **Ag** Silver 107.87	48 **Cd** Cadmium 112.41	49 **In** Indium 114.82	50 **Sn** Tin 118.69	51 **Sb** Antimony 121.7	52 **Te** Tellurium 127.60	53 **I** Iodine 126.90	54 **Xe** Xenon 131.29
76 **Os** Osmium 190.2	77 **Ir** Iridium 192.22	78 **Pt** Platinum 195.08	79 **Au** Gold 196.97	80 **Hg** Mercury 200.59	81 **Tl** Thallium 204.38	82 **Pb** Lead 207.2	83 **Bi** Bismuth 208.98	84 **Po** Polonium 209	85 **At** Astatine 210	86 **Rn** Radon 222
108 **Uno** Unniloctium (265)	109 **Une** Unnilenium (266)	110 **Uun** Ununnilium (369)	111 **Uuu** Unununium (266)							

61 **Pm** Promethium 145	62 **Sm** Samarium 150.36	63 **Eu** Europium 151.96	64 **Gd** Gadolinium 157	65 **Tb** Terbium 158.93	66 **Dy** Dysprosium 162.50	67 **Ho** Holmium 164.93	68 **Er** Erbium 167.26	69 **Tm** Thulium 168.93	70 **Yb** Ytterbium 173.04	71 **Lu** Lutetium 174.97
93 **Np** Neptunium 237.05	94 **Pu** Plutonium 244	95 **Am** Americium 243	96 **Cm** Curium 247	97 **Bk** Berkelium 247	98 **Cf** Californium 251	99 **Es** Einsteinium 252	100 **Fm** Fermium 257	101 **Md** Mendelevium 258	102 **No** Nobelium 259	103 **Lw** Lawrencium 260

Metals, nonmetals and metalloids

The periodic table is made up of metals, nonmetals, metalloids and transition elements.

Metals Most metals exhibit these properties:
- Solid at room temperature.
- Opaque except in extremely thin films.
- Good conductors of heat and electricity.
- A lustrous sheen when polished.
- Crystalline in structure when solid.

Nonmetals A typical nonmetallic element will be a gas at room temperature and is a poor conductor of heat and electricity.

Metalloids Metalloids, or semimetals, have some of the properties of metals and some of the properties of nonmetals.

Transition elements See opposite page.

see also

426-27 **Radioactivity**
430-31 **Atoms and molecules**
434-35 **Chemistry of compounds**

When two or more atoms of different elements combine, they form a compound. Because there are many different elements, the potential for creating different compounds is enormous. The atoms in a compound are held together by bonds, which can be very strong, such as metallic bonding, or relatively weak, as in covalent bonding. The types of bonds holding a compound together determine its physical properties, such as its melting and boiling points.

How atoms bond Atoms of different elements bond with each other to form compounds. They do this by gaining, losing or sharing electrons in their outer electron shells (see page 430).

Ionic bonding Electrons are transferred between atoms, turning each atom into a positively or negatively charged ion (see page 430). An example of an ionic compound is table salt, sodium chloride (NaCl). Each sodium atom has lost an electron from its outer shell to form a positively charged sodium ion (Na^+); each chlorine atom has received an electron to form a negatively charged chloride ion (Cl^-).

With opposite charges, the ions are strongly attracted to one another. They arrange themselves in a lattice (see below), in which each ion is surrounded by as many of the opposite charge as possible. It takes a lot of energy to break the forces between them. As a result, most ionic compounds are solid at room temperature.

Ionic bonding in sodium chloride (NaCl)

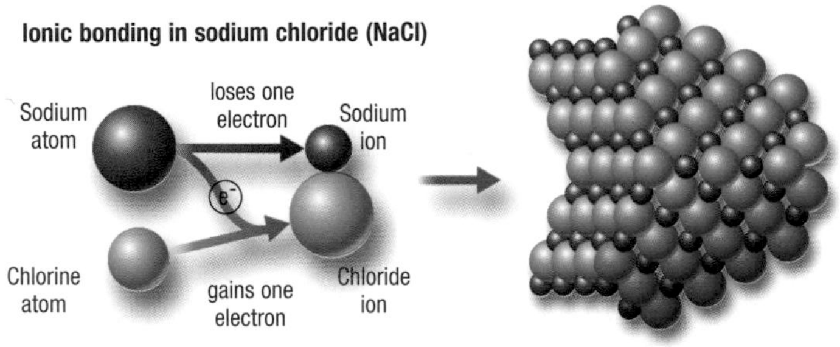

Covalent bonding A single covalent bond forms between two atoms when they share a pair of electrons. Each contributes one of the electrons. Double and triple bonds can also form. Water (H_2O) is an example of a covalent compound, in which one hydrogen atom shares electrons with two oxygen atoms.

Although each molecule in a covalent compound is held together by strong bonds, the electrostatic attraction between the molecules is weak. Consequently, the melting points of covalent compounds are usually lower than for ionic compounds: Most are liquids and gases at room temperature.

Covalent bonding in water (H_20)

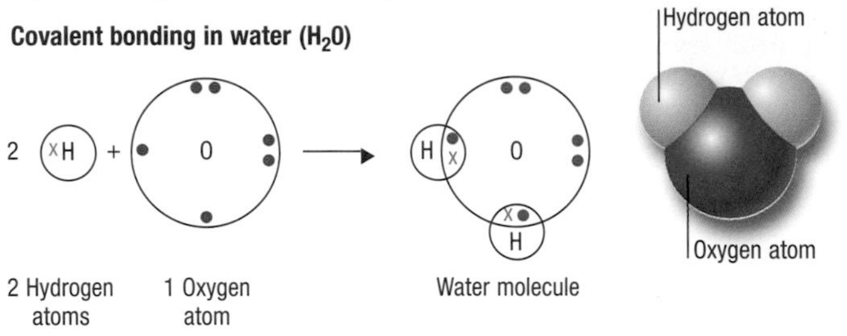

Metallic bonding In a metal, each atom has comparatively few electrons in its outer shell. As a result, the atoms readily lose their outer electrons, becoming positively charged ions. The "lost" electrons then form a "sea" of shared electrons flowing between the ions. This acts like a strong electrostatic "glue," because of the powerful attraction between the oppositely charged ions and electrons. This is why metals are generally strong and have high melting points.

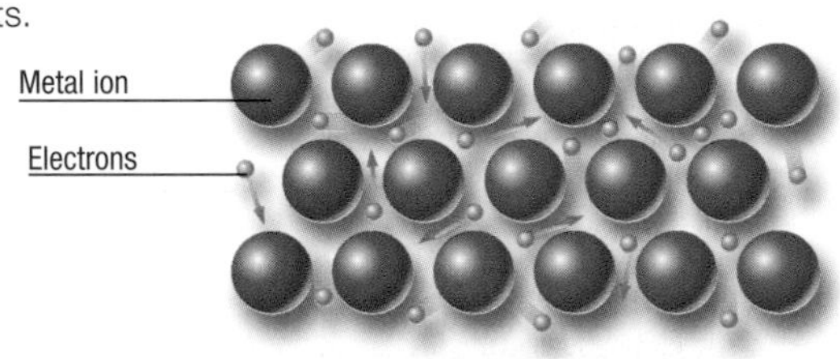

Understanding chemical reactions

Chemical reactions occur when elements or compounds react together to form different substances. The substances present before the reaction are called the reactants (or reagents), and those at the end are called the products.

Rates of reaction How fast a reaction occurs – or whether it occurs at all – depends not only on the reactants but also on prevailing conditions. For example, heating reactants can speed up a reaction.

Catalysts are often used in industry to speed up chemical reactions or to help to make them take place. Metals and metal oxides, for example, can speed up a reaction between gases by providing a surface that absorbs the reactant molecules, bringing them closer together. A catalyst takes part in a reaction, but – unlike the reactants – it remains unchanged and is not used up.

Changes in energy In any chemical reaction, energy is either given out or taken in. Energy is taken in to break bonds between atoms; it is given out when bonds are formed. A reaction in which energy is taken in is called an endothermic reaction; when energy is given out it is called an exothermic reaction.

Burning fuels is an exothermic reaction: Energy is given out. Forming hydrogen and oxygen gas from water is an endothermic reaction: Energy is taken in to break down the bonds between the hydrogen (H) and oxygen (O) atoms that water molecules (H_2O) are composed of.

Balanced equations

All chemical reactions can be described by means of equations. For example, the reaction between sodium and water could be written as follows:

sodium + water → sodium hydroxide + hydrogen

However, this equation tells us only what substances are involved in the reaction. If it is written using their chemical formulas, it reveals what is happening to the atoms and molecules involved:

$$Na + H_2O \longrightarrow NaOH + H_2$$

This equation is not balanced: There are more hydrogen atoms on the right-hand side than on the left-hand side. All chemical reactions obey a simple law – the law of conservation of mass. This states that the total mass of all the products of a reaction equals the total mass of all the reactants, so there must be the same number of atoms on either side of an equation for it to represent a reaction accurately:

$$2Na + 2H_2O \longrightarrow 2NaOH + H_2$$

It is now clear that when sodium reacts with water, two atoms of sodium combine with two molecules of water to produce two molecules of sodium hydroxide and one of hydrogen.

ACIDS AND BASES

All substances are either acidic, basic or neutral. The exact degree can be measured using what is known as the pH (potential of hydrogen) scale. Neutral substances have a pH of 7, acids have a pH less than 7, and bases have a pH greater than 7.

Acids An acid dissolves in water to produce hydrogen ions. Hydrogen atoms in the molecules of the compound separate from the other atoms to become positively charged ions (H^+), which move freely in solution.

For example, if the gas hydrogen chloride (HCl) is dissolved in water, the hydrogen and chlorine atoms separate to become positively charged hydrogen ions (H^+) and negatively charged chlorine atoms (Cl^-) held in solution – hydrochloric acid.

The proportion of an acid's molecules that "dissociate" in this way determines its strength. A common strong acid is nitric acid (HNO_3), used in fertilizers and explosives. Weak acids include acetic (or ethanoic) acid (CH_3CO_2H), found in vinegar, and citric acid ($C_6H_8O_7$), which gives lemons, grapefruits and other citrus fruits their distinctive taste.

Bases Bases can be seen as the "opposite" of acids. They form a group of compounds, all of which react with the hydrogen ions produced by acids and neutralize them. If a base is water-soluble, it is called an alkali.

When an acid is neutralized by a base, the products are a salt (a type of ionic compound – see opposite) and water. For example, mixing hydrochloric acid (HCl) with potassium hydroxide (KOH) produces the salt potassium chloride and water:

$$KOH + HCl \blacktriangleright KCl + H_2O$$

Alkalis An alkali is a base that will dissolve in water to produce hydroxide ions (OH^-). An example is sodium hydroxide (NaOH), or caustic soda, which is used in making soap and paper. When it is dissolved in water, its molecules break up to form positively charged sodium ions (Na^+) and negatively charged hydroxide ions (OH^-), which are held in solution. The strength of an alkali is determined by how many of its molecules "dissociate" in this way to give off hydroxide ions.

One of the properties of alkalis is that they convert oil and grease into soluble soaps that are easily washed away. They are therefore used in various cleaning agents. Ammonium hydroxide (NH_4OH), for example, is a common ingredient in household cleansers.

see also

402-3 **Fossil fuels**
430-31 **Atoms and molecules**
432-33 **The periodic table**

ORGANIC COMPOUNDS

Carbon is unique in that its atoms can link up into long chains and rings. This often results in compounds with very large molecules. Many of these compounds were first discovered in living organisms, so study of them is known as organic chemistry. A number of industrial products – fuels, plastics, and man-made fibers – are also classified as organic because they, too, have molecules that are based on a ring or chain of carbon atoms.

Hydrocarbons The most basic organic compounds are hydrocarbons, which contain only carbon and hydrogen atoms. They are largely used as fuels and as raw material for plastics, fibers, rubbers and industrial chemicals.

Aliphatic compounds Organic compounds in which carbon atoms are joined in a chain are called aliphatic. They are grouped into classes according to the structure of their molecules:

- **Alkanes** have single bonds between the carbon atoms. The simplest is methane (CH_4) – natural gas is 99 percent methane. Others are also fuels: ethane (C_2H_6), propane (C_3H_8) and butane (C_4H_{10}).

Propane molecule

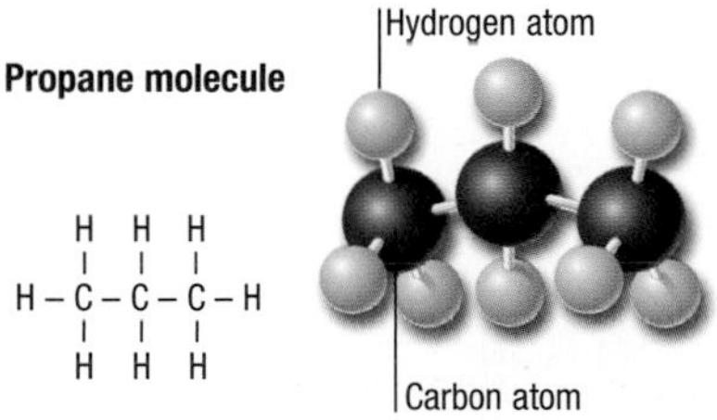

- **Alkenes** have at least one double bond (see Covalent bonding, opposite) between the carbon atoms. They include ethene (C_2H_4), propene (C_3H_6) and butene (C_4H_8).

In a process known as polymerization, the double bonds in alkene molecules can be broken. This allows a number of the molecules to link together as one huge molecule. Many plastics are made in this way. Polyethylene, for example, is a polymerized version of ethene.

Ethene molecule

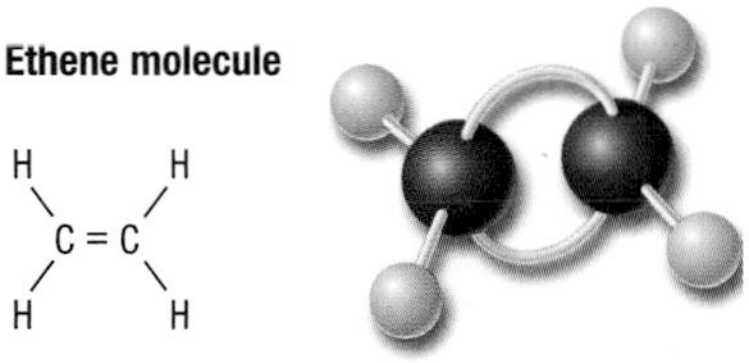

- **Alcohols** contain one or more hydroxide group (OH^-). They include ethanol (C_2H_5OH), which is the alcohol in alcoholic drinks. It is produced when yeasts ferment. It is also used as a solvent in products ranging from paints to glues and perfumes.

Ethanol molecule

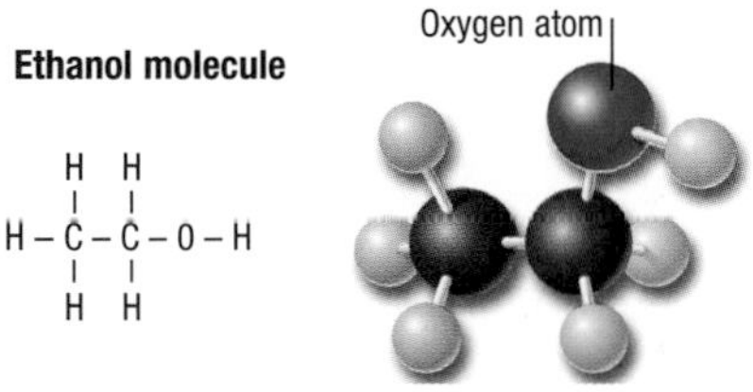

Aromatic compounds Organic compounds with molecules containing a group of six carbon atoms linked in a ring are called "aromatic." This is because a group of these compounds isolated from coal tar around 1860 had very strong and distinctive smells.

The simplest aromatic hydrocarbon is benzene; its molecular structure is known as the benzene ring (C_6H_6). In some aromatic compounds, other atoms or chemical groups replace the hydrogen atoms in the benzene ring. For example, phenol (C_6H_5OH) – also known as carbolic acid and used in disinfectants and plastics – is formed when a hydroxide group (OH^-) replaces one of the hydrogen atoms.

Benzene molecule

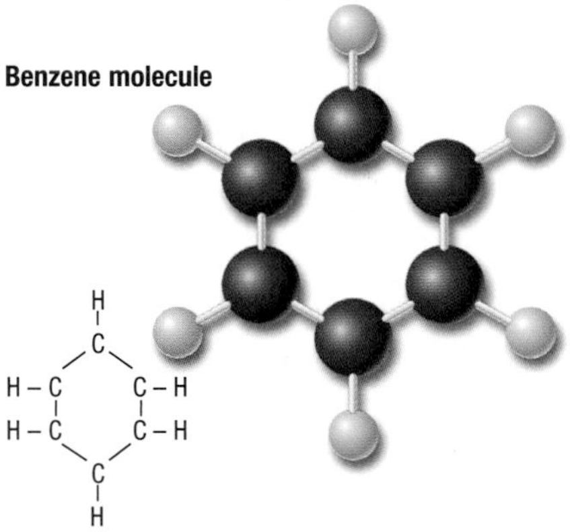

Cracking Long-chained hydrocarbon molecules are often converted into shorter ones – usually to create more useful compounds – using a process known as cracking. For example, crude oil obtained from oil fields contains many unusable hydrocarbons, such as decane. This is "cracked" by heating to 500-900°C in the absence of oxygen, usually with a catalyst (see page 431), to produce octane – used in petrol – and ethene, another fuel.

Living organisms come in myriad shapes and forms, yet at their most fundamental level they are all remarkably similar. The basic structural unit of every living thing is the cell. Cells with particular functions group together to form tissues, which in turn make up a plant's or animal's organs.

FACT Robert Hooke coined the term "cell" in 1665. He likened the cells he saw in bark to the monastic cells of monks.

CELLS, TISSUES AND ORGANS

Cells are the tiny building blocks from which organisms are made. Most cells are invisible unless viewed under a microscope: As a rule, only egg cells are large enough to be seen with the naked eye.

Many types of microscopic organisms, such as bacteria and amoebas, are just a single cell. Larger organisms consist of many cells joined together. Simple multicellular organisms, such as sponges, are made of large numbers of just a few types of cell arranged randomly. But most plants and animals have specialized types of cells organized into tissues.

The cells in tissues are all of the same kind and have a particular function. Animal tissues include muscle – made of cells that have the ability to contract – and nervous tissue, which is formed from cells that can transmit electrical (nervous) impulses. The tissues of plants are less commonly known but include xylem and phloem (see page 76).

In most plants and animals, tissues are organized into organs. A few organs are composed almost entirely of one kind of tissue; the heart, for example, is made of cardiac muscle and very little else. Most organs, however, incorporate several tissue types. Organs may be combined and work together in organ systems.

Cell structure All living cells have four features in common. They are:

- A cell membrane, which separates the contents of the cell from the outside world.
- Cytoplasm, a jellylike substance that fills the cell.
- Protein-building bodies called ribosomes.
- DNA – the list of instructions that enables the cell to function and replicate itself.

Living organisms are divided by biologists into two groups – those that have cells with nuclei and those that do not. The only organisms that lack cell nuclei are bacteria and cyanobacteria (commonly known as blue-green algae). They are the Earth's most primitive life forms and have their own kingdom in biological classification, the Monera.

All members of the other four kingdoms – Protista (which includes amoebas), Fungi, Plantae and Animalia – have nuclei in their cells that contain their DNA. They also share a range of other internal cell structures called organelles, which (apart from ribosomes) are absent from bacteria and cyanobacteria. Organelles carry out various functions in the cell.

TYPES OF CELL

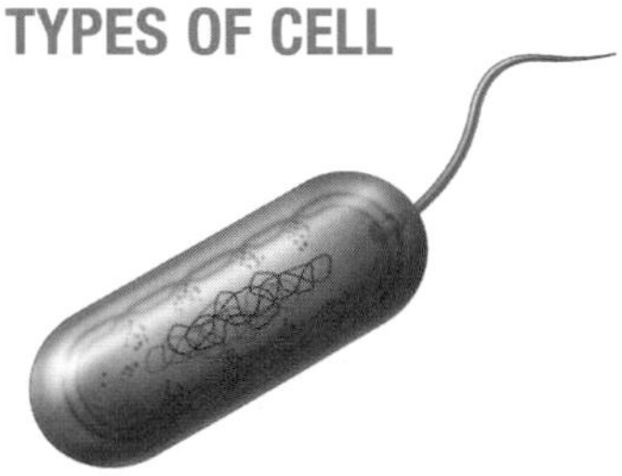

Bacterial cell Bacteria have no nuclei or other obvious internal structures; the genetic material is a simple DNA strand.

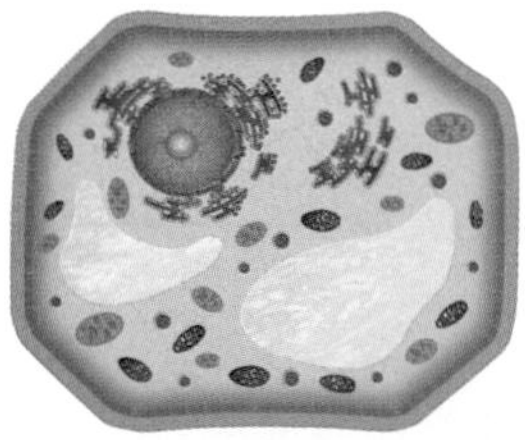

Plant cell Green plant cells are unique in having chloroplasts, tough cell walls and usually a fluid-filled central vacuole.

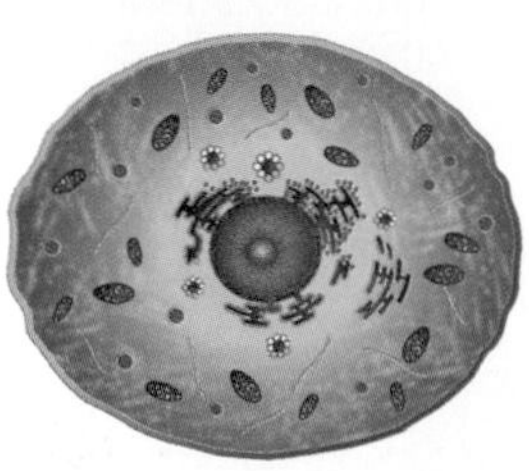

Animal cell With no rigid wall or vacuole, an animal cell has an irregular shape; no chloroplasts means it cannot make sugars.

Parts of a typical cell

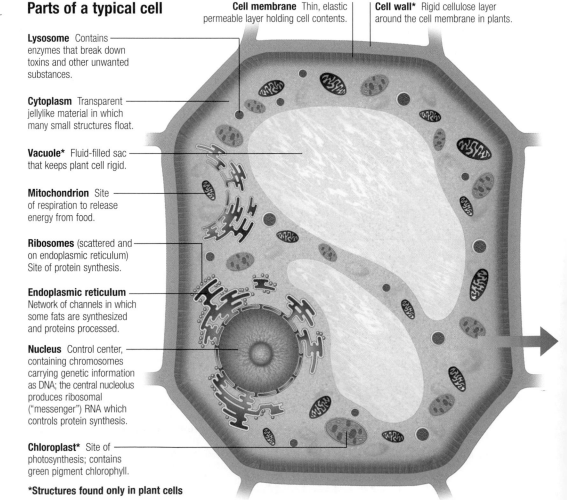

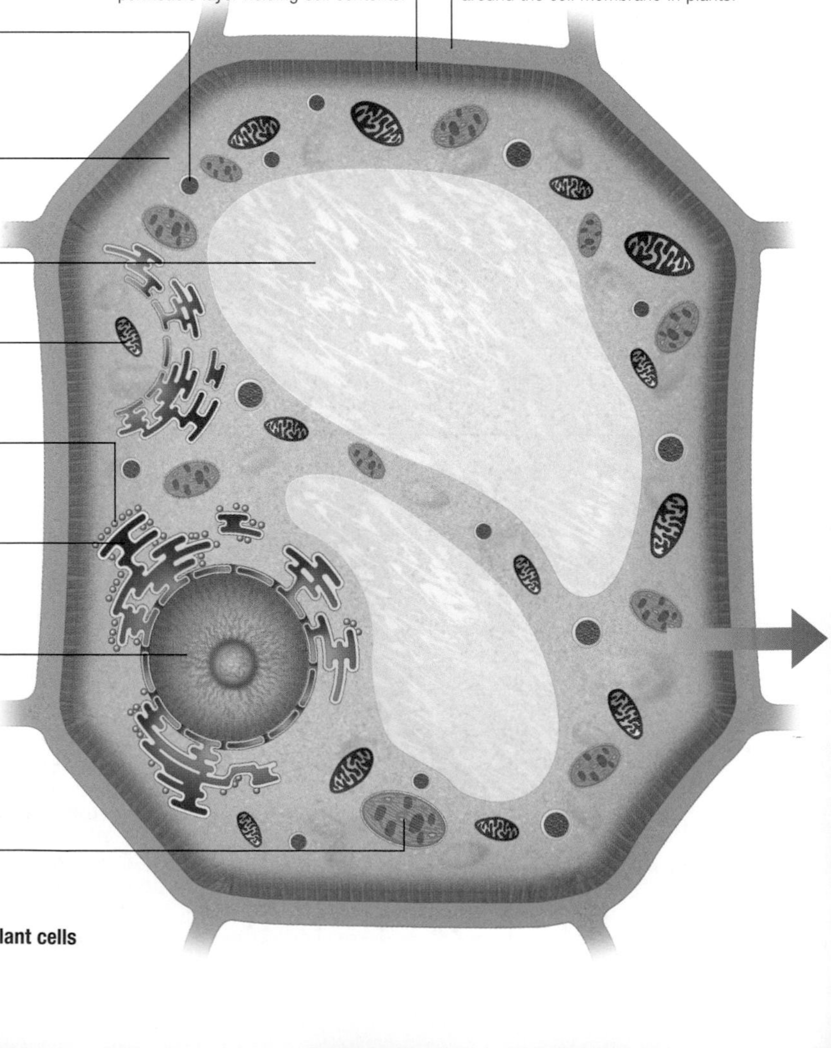

Cell membrane Thin, elastic permeable layer holding cell contents.

Cell wall* Rigid cellulose layer around the cell membrane in plants.

Lysosome Contains enzymes that break down toxins and other unwanted substances.

Cytoplasm Transparent jellylike material in which many small structures float.

Vacuole* Fluid-filled sac that keeps plant cell rigid.

Mitochondrion Site of respiration to release energy from food.

Ribosomes (scattered and on endoplasmic reticulum) Site of protein synthesis.

Endoplasmic reticulum Network of channels in which some fats are synthesized and proteins processed.

Nucleus Control center, containing chromosomes carrying genetic information as DNA; the central nucleolus produces ribosomal ("messenger") RNA which controls protein synthesis.

Chloroplast* Site of photosynthesis; contains green pigment chlorophyll.

***Structures found only in plant cells**

THE CHEMICAL BASIS OF LIFE

A typical animal's body is about 60 percent water by weight; in a plant, that figure may be higher. Other than water, the main types of chemicals found in all living things are nucleic acids (the components of DNA and RNA; see pages 130-31), proteins, carbohydrates and lipids.

Proteins These form most of the structural materials in animals' bodies and also make up the enzymes that control all biochemical activity in cells.

Proteins consist of chains of small molecules called amino acids. About 100 different amino acids exist in nature, but the proteins in animals' bodies are made out of just 20 types. Amino acids are classified as essential or nonessential. Nonessential amino acids can be synthesized from other proteins, but essential amino acids cannot and must therefore be obtained through food.

Enzymes are specialized proteins made from between 100 and 1000 amino acids. The chain of amino acids in an enzyme folds into a unique shape that allows it to catalyze (speed up) a specific chemical reaction.

Every change that takes place inside a living cell is facilitated by enzymes. There are thousands of different types. A single-celled bacterium, for example, has about 1000 different enzymes floating around in its cytoplasm.

Carbohydrates The principal role of carbohydrates in living organisms is supplying energy. However, one type – cellulose – forms the cell walls of plants and is their main structural material.

All carbohydrate molecules are made up of carbon, hydrogen and oxygen atoms. Generally speaking, they contain twice as many hydrogen atoms as they do carbon or oxygen atoms.

Carbohydrates fall into three main groups: monosaccharides, disaccharides and polysaccharides.

Monosaccharides are simple sugars with up to ten carbon atoms in each molecule. Examples include glucose, which is involved in energy release in cells (see below).

Disaccharides, such as sucrose (cane sugar), consist of two monosaccharide molecules joined together. They must be broken down into monosaccharides before cells can release their energy.

Polysaccharides are also known as complex carbohydrates and are made up of many monosaccharides joined together. The most important polysaccharides are starch and cellulose. Starch is the main food storage material of plants.

Lipids Lipids contain carbon, hydrogen and oxygen but have far fewer oxygen atoms than carbohydrates do. Lipids include fats, oils, waxes, phospholipids (which form cell membranes) and steroids (which include some hormones and other important substances). Lipids dissolve poorly in water, but store more than twice as much energy per gram as carbohydrates. Fats are animals' main energy storage materials.

ENERGY FROM RESPIRATION

Through the biochemical process known as respiration (not to be confused with breathing), cells combine oxygen with glucose to produce carbon dioxide, water and energy. The energy produced drives all life-sustaining processes.

$$C_6H_{12}O_6 + 6O_2 \rightarrow 6CO_2 + 6H_2O + \text{energy}$$

glucose + oxygen → carbon dioxide + water + energy

Respiration occurs in all living things. If oxygen is available, it is an extremely efficient process, releasing 37 percent of the total energy in glucose for use by the organism. If oxygen is not available, respiration becomes less efficient. It may still occur in a simplified form, however, with glucose split to produce two molecules of lactic or pyruvic acid.

Dead cells and cell products

A living organism does not consist solely of living cells. Cells are constantly dying (and most are replaced as they do), but many dead cells form important structures in their own right. An animal's skin, hair, feathers, scales, nails and claws are all formed from dead cells. So is the protective bark of a tree and the woody material of its trunk and branches (only the thin cambium layer beneath the bark is alive). Many other important biological materials, including bone and shell, are inert matter secreted by the organism's cells.

Tissues (below) consist of groups of cells with a specific function.

The cell (left) is the basic unit that can display all the functions of a living thing – although that does not necessarily mean that it can survive on its own.

An organ (such as a leaf) is a functional unit made up of various tissues.

Oak tree An entire organism may have many organs and specialized tissues and consist of trillions of cells. Alternatively, it may be just one cell, as in the case of most microorganisms.

60-61 **How plants live**
438-39 **Inherited characteristics**

Inherited characteristics

The appearance of organisms is determined by their genes, which are passed down to them from their parents. The rules that govern this process were established in the second half of the 19th century and were found to apply to all living things. This discovery marked the birth of a new discipline, genetics, which is the fastest-growing branch of the biological sciences.

HOW TRAITS ARE PASSED ON

For thousands of years, farmers have encouraged desirable attributes in plants and animals through selective breeding. It was a rather hit-and-miss process, because no one understood the mechanisms that govern heredity. In the 1860s, Gregor Mendel (1822-84) worked out how characteristics are passed on from one generation to the next, using a series of experiments on peas.

Mendel wondered why peas have either purple flowers or white flowers and never shades in between. He noticed that when he crossed a pure-bred strain of purple-flowered peas with a white-flowered strain, the offspring (known as the f1 generation) always had purple flowers. But if he went on to fertilize one of the f1 plants with pollen from another, the second-generation (f2) offspring had white- and purple-flowered plants, in a ratio of 1:3. From these results, he worked out that the inheritance of each characteristic is determined by paired factors (now called genes). Although an individual may inherit two different forms (alleles) of a gene – one from each parent – for a trait, only one of the forms will be expressed. Both can be passed on to the next generation.

The explanation is that some alleles are dominant – that is, they cause a visible characteristic even if another, so-called recessive, allele is also present. The f1 pea plants each carried a dominant allele for purple flowers (called P) and a recessive allele for white flowers (w); their genotype (genetic pattern) was Pw (see below). In the f2 generation, when Pw peas were self-pollinated, the result was peas with genotypes PP, Pw, wP and ww. Only the pea plants with two recessive alleles (ww) had white flowers; the rest were purple.

Mendel also crossed plants with yellow and green seeds and ones with wrinkled and smooth seeds. He found that these characteristics follow the same rules. It is now known that some features (such as people's hair color) are governed by a number of genes, and the pattern of heredity is not so clear-cut.

Mendel's peas This diagram shows the stages in Mendel's experiments in cross-breeding pea plants (see story above). Dominant forms of genes (alleles) are traditionally annotated with a capital letter, recessive ones with a letter in lower case. Here, the dominant allele is that for purple flowers (P) and the recessive one that for white flowers (w).

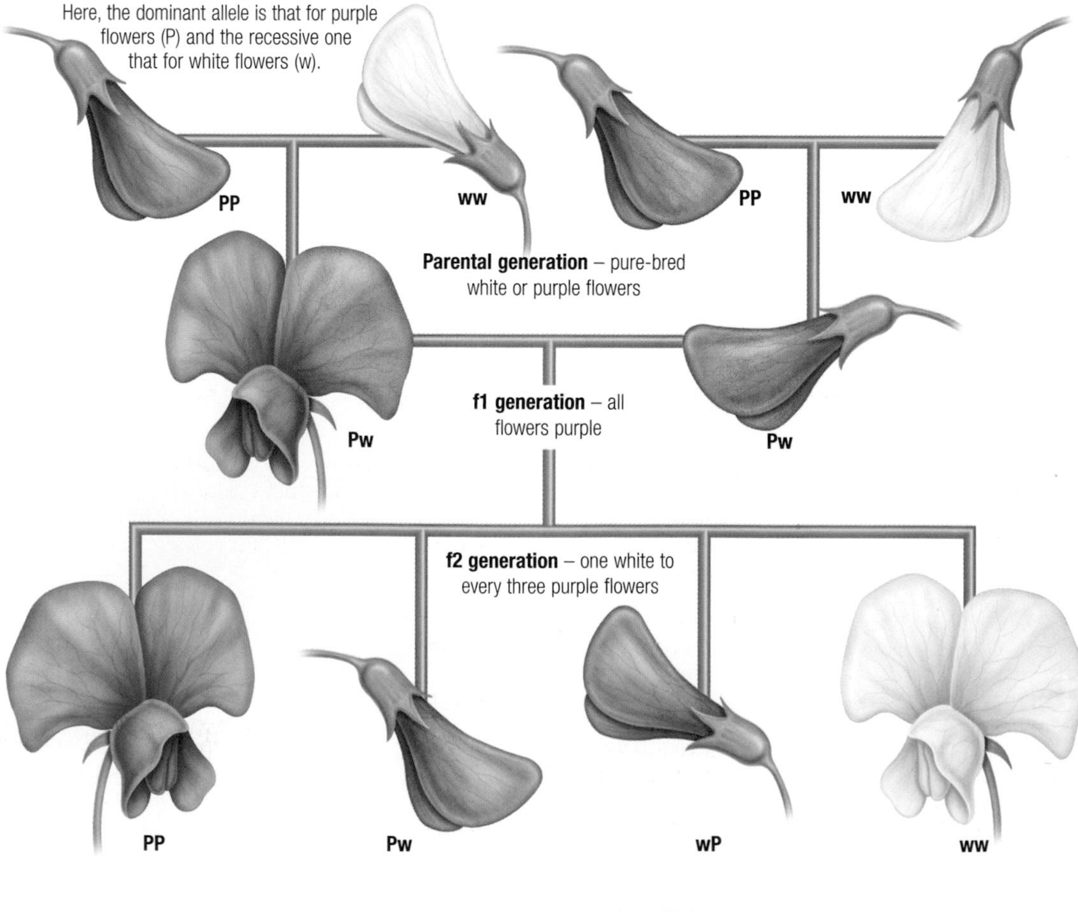

WHAT MAKES AN INDIVIDUAL?

Every cell in a living organism contains enough information to make a complete copy of that organism. The information is stored inside the nucleus of the cell in its chromosomes.

Chromosomes occur in pairs usually of the same size and shape. In each pair, one chromosome came originally from the male parent, the other from the female. This fact is what makes people look similar to their parents but not exactly like either of them. Different organisms have different numbers of chromosomes in each cell. For example, humans have 23 pairs of chromosomes, chickens have 18 pairs, peas have 7 pairs and fruit flies have only 4 pairs.

Chromosomes are primarily made up of DNA (see pages 130-31), which is itself a combination of four chemical units called bases. Genes, which govern bodily characteristics, correspond to specific sections of the DNA – specific sequences of the bases. They are like instructions written in a four-letter chemical "alphabet." The genes in chromosomes are mixed up whenever new eggs or sperm are created (see opposite), and this is the reason that every one of us looks unique – except, of course, identical twins (see pages 130-31).

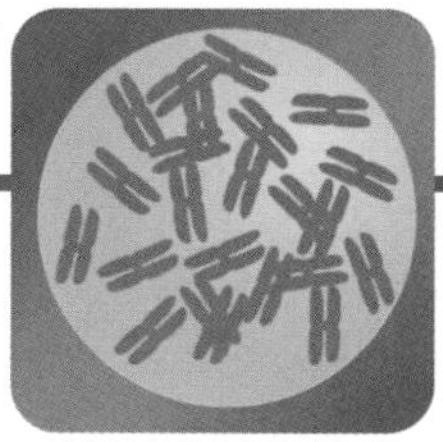

Male or female?

The gender of an organism is determined by its sex chromosomes. In most species, there are two types of sex chromosome, X and Y. Females have two X chromosomes in each of their body cells, but the cells of males have an X and a Y. (In some insects, males have just one X and no Y; they are referred to as "XO.")

All eggs contain a single X chromosome (see How sex cells divide, opposite). Half of a male's sperm carry an X chromosome and half carry a Y (or no sex chromosome at all in an XO insect). If an "X" sperm fertilizes an egg, the result is "XX" – a female offspring. If a "Y" (or "O") sperm fertilizes it, the result is "XY" (or "XO") – a male.

HOW CELLS DIVIDE FOR GROWTH

Growth involves an increase in the number of cells in an organism. The process by which cells divide to form new cells during growth is called mitosis. The parent cell divides into two daughter cells that are identical to each other and to the parent cell in every respect – including the number of chromosomes in the nucleus. In fact, every nonsex cell in an organism carries an identical genetic "blueprint." The nucleus always divides before the rest of the cell after passing through a series of changes.

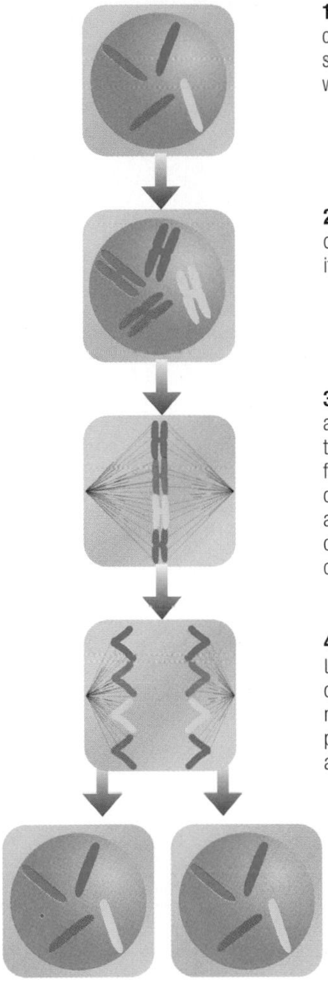

1 Just before cell division, the chromosomes in the nucleus get shorter and fatter and can be seen with a microscope.

2 Each chromosome makes a copy of itself. The original chromosome and its copy are joined near the middle.

3 The joined chromosome copies arrange themselves near the center of the cell. A structure called a spindle forms, with fibers spanning the length of the cell. The chromosome copies attach themselves to the spindle; it contracts, pulling the originals and copies to opposite ends of the cell.

4 A new nuclear membrane begins to form around the two groups of chromosomes. A new cell membrane – known as the cell plate (not shown) – begins to form across the middle of the cell.

5 The cell plate eventually cuts the cell entirely in half to form two new cells. Once this has happened, the chromosomes begin to unwind, becoming long and slender again until eventually they can no longer be seen.

The new cells are identical to each other and to the parent cell. The whole process of mitosis takes from about 15-20 minutes in bacteria to 18-20 hours in most animal and plant cells. The cells now grow to full size before dividing again.

HOW SEX CELLS DIVIDE

Genes are passed from parents to offspring through their sex cells or gametes – sperm and eggs. These specialized cells contain only half the normal number of chromosomes, but they carry an assortment of characteristics inherited from the previous generation. They are produced by a special type of cell division called meiosis, which takes place in humans in the ovaries or testes.

1 In the initial stage of meiosis, pairs of chromosomes move toward each other and match up against each other along their whole lengths.

2 The chromosomes now each divide in two lengthways to form twin threads joined at the middle. These double chromosomes cross over one another and exchange genetic material with their partners.

3 The double pairs with their newly shuffled genes now begin to separate and are pulled towards opposite ends of the cell. A nucleus then forms at each end and the cell divides in two.

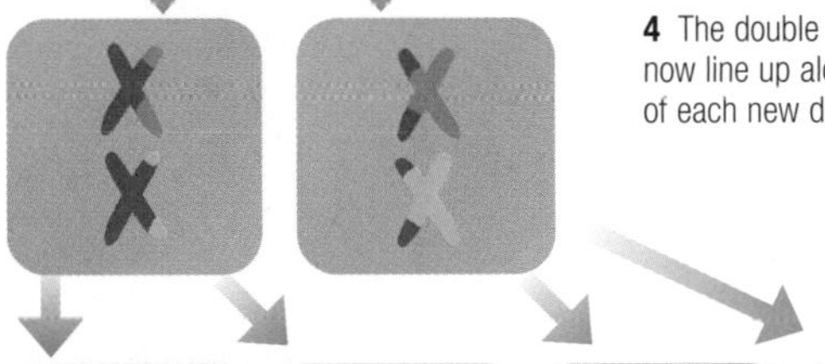

4 The double chromosomes now line up along the center of each new daughter cell.

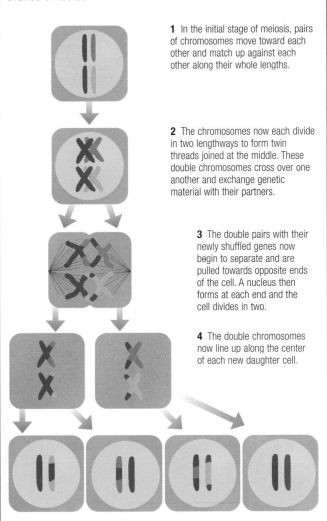

5 Finally these double chromosomes separate, and each daughter cell again divides in two, as in mitosis. This results in four daughter cells, each with half the number of chromosomes, with some genetic material from each original parent.

Key terms in genetics

Allele One of two or more alternative forms of a gene.
Base One of the chemical building blocks that make up DNA (see page 151).
Dominance An allele is said to be dominant with respect to an alternative allele if – when both alleles are present in an organism – the physical trait it encodes for is expressed and that which the other allele encodes for is not.
Genes The genetic material that determines all inherited characteristics. Genes operate by controlling the structure of particular proteins.
Genome The sequence of bases in all of the DNA, including the genes, of an organism's chromosomes.
Heterozygote An organism that received unlike alleles for a particular characteristic from each of its two parents.
Homozygote An organism that received similar alleles for a particular characteristic from both of its two parents.
Meiosis The process of cell division that creates sex cells, in which the chromosome number is halved.
Mitosis The process of cell division for growth, in which the daughter cells have the same number of chromosomes as the parent cell.
Phenotype The visible effects of the expression of a gene.
Recessive An allele is said to be recessive if it produces an effect only in individuals that inherit similar alleles from both parents. A recessive allele is not expressed in organisms that inherit unlike alleles from their two parents but can be passed on to future generations.

see also
130-31 **Cells and DNA**
436-37 **Structure of living things**

The archaeologist's job is to piece together knowledge about vanished cultures from the material objects left behind – from buildings and boats to tools, clothes, weapons and household items. Many different sciences are involved in finding, interpreting and dating remains, and new techniques and technologies are continually advancing the discipline.

Archaeologists at work

Work on an archaeological site happens in a series of stages. First, the area is identified and surveyed. Then excavation begins. Buildings, temples and tombs are uncovered, and their contents are revealed. Finally, individual objects are taken away and analyzed in detail. These two pages take you through the process at one of the great finds of recent times – the pyramids of Sipán in Peru, where excavations began in 1987.

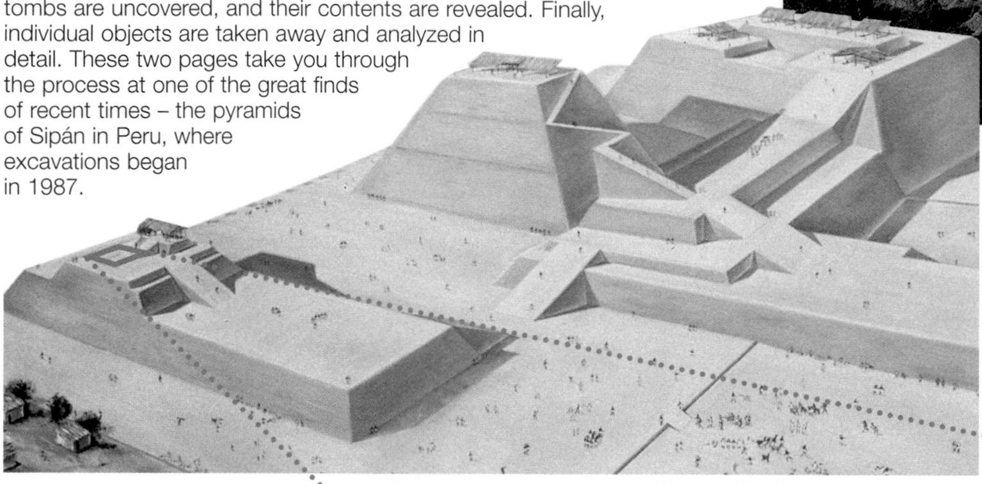

1 Locating the site

The pyramids of Sipán (above) were well known as an ancient site but remained unexcavated until recently. In 1987, looters found a royal tomb full of treasures from the 1st to 3rd century A.D. Moche civilization. An informer told the police, and as news leaked out excavations were hastily begun to protect the site from more raids.

2 Doing a survey

A contour map of Sipán (above) helped to create a picture of how the site looked in ancient times. This was the start of the next stage of discovery – the survey. Surveying involves drawing an outline map, which records any relevant surrounding features such as rivers or ancient roads. A grid is placed on the map so that points can be precisely located and finds can be accurately recorded. After the survey any artifacts on the surface of the site are recorded and removed so that excavation can begin.

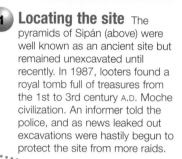

3 Excavating the site

Excavation is an extremely slow process – it took several years at Sipán. The exact location and nature of each item has to be recorded before it is removed for further analysis. Tiny fragments of pottery, for example, may be recovered only by filtering soil through a sieve. The soil itself may be subjected to microscopic analysis. Tools range from a simple paintbrush, used to remove soil around the most delicate artifacts, to a mechanical digger for removing topsoil and cutting sections through a site.

Dating by tree rings

The science of dating wood from patterns of tree growth, known as dendrochronology, can often help archaeologists determine the age of the site they are working on. Each year that a tree grows, it adds a new ring to its girth. The thickness of the ring is determined by environmental conditions such as temperature and rainfall. Over time, patterns that are common to all the trees of the same species in the same area form among the rings. The rings can be counted to show the age of the tree at death; the pattern of the rings can also be compared with those of other trees of the same species to find out when the tree died.

To date an object made from a tree – a ship's mast, for instance – the pattern of rings is compared with those of wood from similar trees whose year of death is known in order to search for matching growth patterns. By matching the patterns, it is possible to calculate the year in which the tree died or was cut down.

Because the growth rings and their patterns vary according to environmental conditions, wood can be used to date natural events such as droughts or glaciation, as well as man-made artifacts. Certain tree species are particularly useful to dendrochronologists because of their longevity. The American bristlecone pine, for example, lives for over 4500 years and can give clues to conditions long before recorded history.

Measuring decay

Radiocarbon dating
Radiocarbon dating (also known as carbon dating) has been used to date specimens as old as 35 000 years.

It is based on the principle that throughout life all living matter absorbs a radioactive form of carbon known as carbon-14. When a plant or animal dies, it stops absorbing carbon-14 and the carbon-14 it contains gradually decays to form nitrogen-14.

Scientists can detect the presence of carbon-14, and they know the rate at which it decays. They can measure the level of carbon-14 in the remains of a once-living object, such as the wooden mast of a ship. This can be compared with the carbon-14 in a living tree, revealing how long ago the tree died and giving a clue to the age of the mast.

Luminescence dating
For specimens that are more than 40 000 years old, archaeologists may resort to techniques such as luminescence dating. This can be used for specimens that contain minerals such as quartz.

- As a result of exposure to natural radiation in the form of heat or light, the mineral acquires a degree of latent "luminescence."
- When scientists reexpose an artifact containing minerals to heat or light, this luminescence is released and can be measured using a device known as a photomultiplier tube.
- It is possible to work out when the object was last exposed to heat or light and to estimate its approximate age from the amount of luminescence released.

Royal tomb, Sipán An artist's impression shows how this royal figure would have looked when buried. His ear ornaments were of gold and turquoise.

4 Analysis Special skills come into their own at this stage. A physical anthropologist examined a Sipán skeleton and was able to tell that the man had probably suffered from arthritis but since his teeth were in good condition, it is likely he had a healthy diet. He was between 35 and 45 when he died – a decent age for a Moche. Many complex techniques are used for such analysis, including powerful DNA testing. A procedure called the polymerase chain reaction (PCR) is carried out on tissue samples. This can amplify even the tiniest trace of DNA, helping to reveal details such as genetic defects and the cause of death.

FACT
Clues from Homer's epic poem the *Iliad* helped Heinrich Schliemann find the lost city of Troy in 1870.

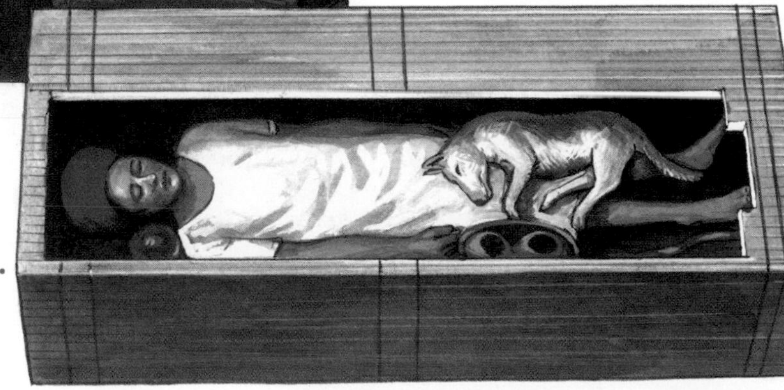

Faithful unto death At the feet of the main figure the archaeologists found the coffin of a child buried with his pet dog.

see also
138-39 **The prehistoric world**
426-27 **Radioactivity**

Everyday inventions 1850-1920

The 70 years between 1850 and 1920 saw a revolution in devices for helping to make home life and some of its associated chores less tedious and more hygienic. Some inventions, such as the automatic washing machine, were electrically powered versions of older hand-cranked models, and other inventions were brand-new household tools, from the toaster and vacuum cleaner to the food processor and refrigerator.

Mechanical clothes washer

In 1858, American inventor Hamilton Smith patented a hand-cranked mechanical washing machine – a wooden drum fitted with a dolly (a set of paddles fixed to a long handle). The drum had to be filled and emptied by hand. Automatic machines were not possible until hot and cold running water and domestic electricity became widely available in the early 20th century.

Hand power Hamilton Smith's mechanical washer did little to alleviate the physical effort involved in washing.

Sewing machine

Massachusetts factory worker Elias Howe provoked little public interest when he patented a hand-powered sewing machine in 1846. In 1851, while Howe searched for backers in England, another American, Isaac Singer, produced a foot-powered machine which violated the patent. Howe took legal action, reestablished his patent in 1854 and began receiving royalties, but Singer's version became the earliest mass-produced domestic appliance.

1850

1851 Gas oven

1860

1870

1876 Telephone

1877 Phonograph

1880

1880 Food mincer, perforated toilet paper

1882 Electric iron

1888 Record player

1889 Electric oven

1890

Electric light

In 1878, British physicist Joseph Swan passed an electric current through a carbon filament sealed inside a glass tube, creating the first electric light, which burned for a few hours. Thomas Edison based his longer-lasting bulb of 1879 on Swan's idea.

The world's most prolific inventor

When Ohio-born Thomas Alva Edison left school in 1859, the few electrical devices in existence ran on low-powered batteries. By the time of his death in 1931, as a result of his inventive genius and entrepreneurship, a network of generators and power cables supplied the electricity demands of every large city in the United States.

Edison's work as an inventor began in earnest in 1876, when he set up the world's first commercial laboratory in Menlo Park, New Jersey. During a lifetime of work on electricity and communications, he took out patents on a record-breaking 1093 inventions, including:

1870 A high-speed stock ticker – a machine that recorded transactions at the stock exchange in Wall Street.
1872 The electric typewriter.
1874 The quadruplex telegraph, which simultaneously sent four messages along a single telegraph line.
1877 The tinfoil phonograph, which reproduced sound using a stylus and foil cylinder.
1878 The carbon transmitter for telephones and microphones.
1879 An electric light bulb with a carbon filament. Durability was increased by improving the vacuum inside the bulb.
1880 An electric trolley.
1891 The "Kinetoscope," which projected the first moving pictures from celluloid film.
1900 The nickel-alkaline battery.

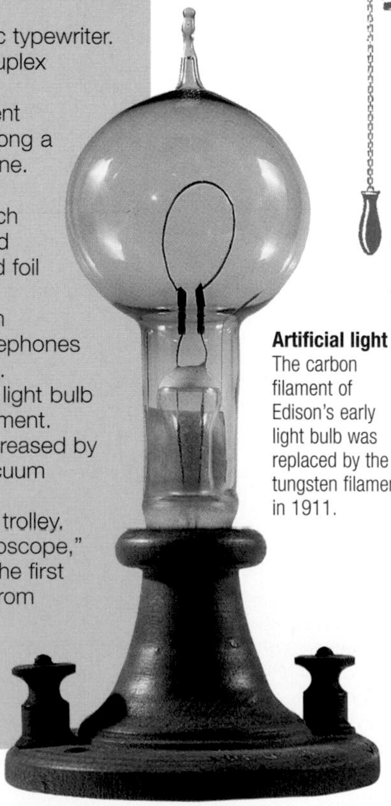

Artificial light The carbon filament of Edison's early light bulb was replaced by the tungsten filament in 1911.

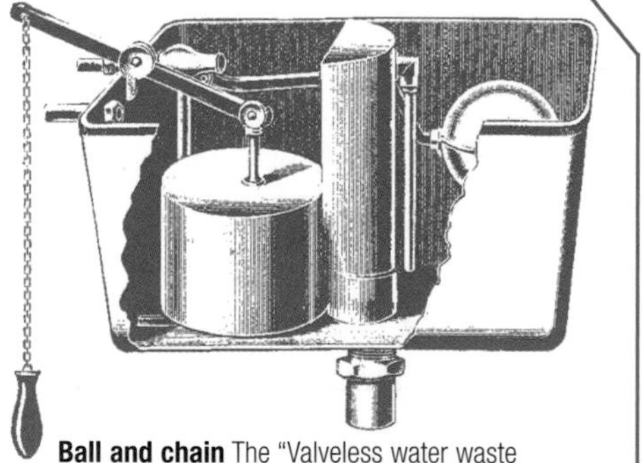

Ball and chain The "Valveless water waste preventer," a design often credited to Englishman Thomas Crapper, was first patented by Albert Giblin.

Valveless water cistern

A toilet flushed by water from a cistern, invented by Thomas Brightfield, was first used in London in 1449. In 1775, Englishman Alexander Cummings introduced the S-bend pipe, which trapped water in the closet and reduced unpleasant smells. A domestic flush toilet remained impractical until the widespread installation of public sewerage in the 19th century. Thomas Twyford designed the first one-piece china toilet in 1885.

Vacuum flask

In 1892, Scottish physicist James Dewar developed a way of keeping liquid gases at low temperatures while in storage. He created a vacuum within the double walls of a glass bottle, which reduced heat transference to a minimum. The German Reinhold Burger marketed the technique for domestic use in 1902 as the Thermos flask.

Cold store The Kelvinator corporation produced some of the earliest electric refrigerators, such as this 1926 model.

Refrigerator

German engineer Karl von Linde developed the first domestic refrigerator in 1879. His device used a steam pump to circulate ammonia, a coolant used in industrial refrigeration since the late 1850s. In 1923, Swedish engineers Carl Munters and Balzer von Platen created the first electric refrigerator, the Electrolux, using a motor instead of a steam pump. In the same decade, scientists developed synthetic refrigerants such as Freon to replace the toxic ammonia.

Dewar flask James Dewar devised this flask to store liquid oxygen and nitrogen for experiments.

Food processors

The earliest electric whisk, produced in the US in 1910, was low powered and unreliable. In 1919, Troy Metal Products released the KitchenAid, the first mixer with a stand and bowl. In 1950, the Kenwood Chef appeared in Britain, with multiple attachments enabling everything from whisking to can opening.

Formica

Americans Daniel O'Conor and Herbert Faber patented Formica as an insulation material for electric wiring in 1913. In the mid-1920s, they marketed it as a furniture laminate. The wipe-clean, heatproof qualities of Formica made it a popular material for cabinet surfaces in the new fitted kitchens of the following decade.

Vacuum cleaner

The first vacuum cleaner, operated from the street via a long hose, was invented in England in 1901 by Hubert Cecil Booth. Six years later, American businessman William Hoover developed a lightweight, upright version for ease of use inside the home.

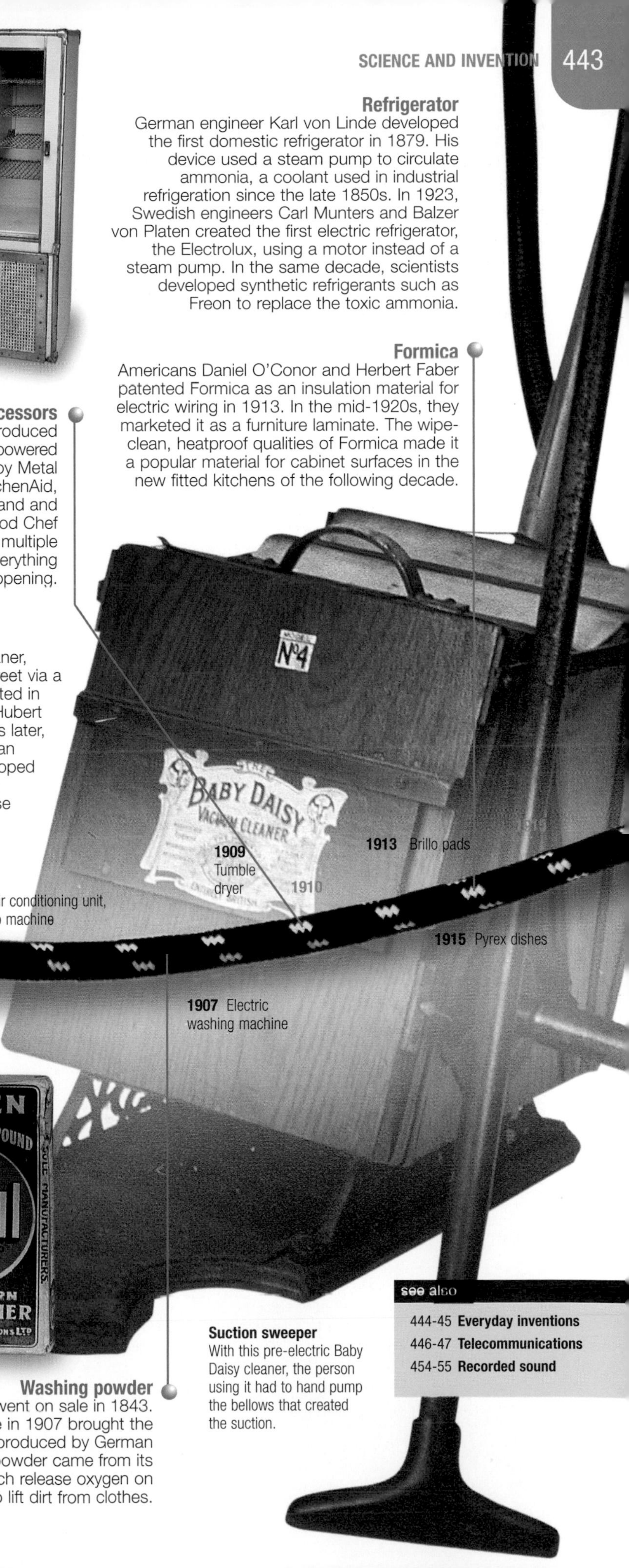

1890

1893 Spring-loaded clothes pin

1899 Electric hairdryer

1900

1900 Brownie box camera

1902 Air conditioning unit, espresso machine

1907 Electric washing machine

1909 Tumble dryer

1910

1913 Brillo pads

1915 Pyrex dishes

Toaster

The electric toaster has changed little since its introduction by Crompton, a British company, in 1893. Crompton's device – "The Eclipse" – toasted bread one side at a time. The spring-loaded mechanism that ejects toasted bread originated in Minnesota in 1927. Three years later, thermostatic controls were added to trigger springing when the toast was ready.

Washing powder

Babbitt's Best Soap, the earliest soap powder, went on sale in 1843. The arrival of the automatic washing machine in 1907 brought the first modern washing powder – Persil – produced by German company Henkel & Cie. The name of the powder came from its active ingredients, perborate and silicate, which release oxygen on contact with water, helping to lift dirt from clothes.

Suction sweeper With this pre-electric Baby Daisy cleaner, the person using it had to hand pump the bellows that created the suction.

see also

444-45 **Everyday inventions**
446-47 **Telecommunications**
454-55 **Recorded sound**

Everyday inventions 1920-present

In the 20th century, advances in electronics paved the way for the miniaturization of items such as the radio and the introduction of the mobile phone. Man-made fibers and other synthetic products brought us nylon stockings, adhesive tape, nonstick cooking pans and magnetic tape for video recording.

Adhesive tape

Adhesive tape was a development of waterproof Cellophane first produced by the DuPont company in 1927. This tape, adhesive only at the edges, was used in automobile spray-painting shops to guard windows and fittings. In 1934, fully coated adhesive tape became available and people started to use it in the home.

Can opener

It took nearly 130 years after the invention of the can for the can opener to come along in 1931. At first, people had to open the cans with a hammer and chisel. Fixed openers appeared in the late 1850s and cutting wheels in the 1870s, but it was another 60 years before these developments were combined into a single device.

Microwave oven

During World War II, British physicists John Randall and Henry Boot were working on radar defenses. There was anecdotal evidence that the microwaves generated by their radar system were killing birds. The microwaves were causing water molecules in the birds' bodies to rotate, which created friction. The heat generated "cooked" the birds. This is how all microwaved food is cooked, and it explains why an object without water molecules stays cool in a microwave oven. The microwave oven was patented in 1945 but did not become a popular feature in homes until the 1980s, when miniaturization and economies of scale made it commercially viable.

ISBN 0-276-42434-4

9 780276 424342 >

Bar code

In 1949, American Bernard Silver and former fellow student Norman Woodland developed a code of thick and thin black stripes or bars. It was not until the 1960s that two key advances – a laser beam to scan the bars and a microchip to process the information – made bar codes a practical possibility. The establishment by the US Department of Defense of an industry standard paved the way for the bar code to be widely adopted.

1920

1921 Electric kettle

1922 Dishwasher

1927 Refrigerator

1928 Television

1930

1934 Laundromat

1935 Tape recorder

1938 Tupperware

1940

1948 Vinyl LP records

1950

1950 Rubber gloves

Portable valve radio

The first portable radio was portable in name only: It weighed about 4.5 kg (10 lb). It was designed by American J. McWilliams Stone in 1922. At the time, all radios were heavy because of the large transformers needed to deliver the high voltages demanded by valve circuits. The small, lightweight, low-powered and more reliable transistor was invented in 1947 and by 1955 was being used in truly portable radios.

Big brown box Bulky valves and vacuum tubes meant bulky radios, even portable ones such as this Pye from 1929.

Nylon

Joseph Swan, the inventor of the light bulb, also developed the first man-made fiber in 1883. He was going to use it as a filament in his light bulb, but it proved unsuitable. Several other attempts were made to produce man-made fibers, but these met with little practical success. American company DuPont produced the first successful synthetic fiber – nylon – in 1938. Originally used for toothbrush bristles, the new fiber was adapted for use in stockings in 1940. In the 1950s, the principles involved in producing nylon were applied to make other synthetic materials, such as acrylic (1950), Dacron (1953) and Polyester (1953).

Seamed nylons Stretchable and yet tough, nylon was an ideal material for products ranging from bristles to stockings to parachutes.

VCR

The first video recordings on magnetic tape were demonstrated in 1951. Video recorders for domestic use appeared in 1963 but did not become practical and affordable until the middle of the 1970s. At first there were eight different operating systems, none of them compatible with each other, until the industry finally settled on VHS (Video Home System) for domestic use.

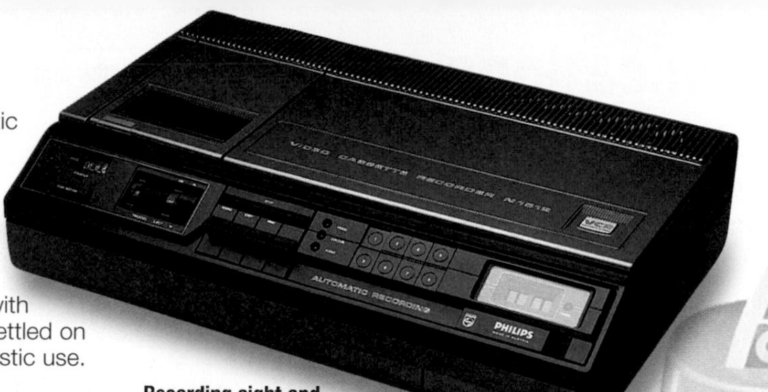

Recording sight and sound An early Philips video recorder, from 1974.

On the move Early mobile phones were the size of a small brick; now miniaturization is limited only by the size of the keypad.

Mobile phone

Radio-telephone systems were first introduced in the 1940s on an experimental basis. They suffered from radio interference. In 1947, Bell Laboratories found a solution by establishing a network of small areas or "cells," each with its own low power and frequency. As the telephone passed from one cell to another, it was "switched" to the next transmitter. In 1978, the Illinois Bell company introduced this cellular system to the public. The experiment proved to be a success, and mobile networks were soon established across the United States and Europe.

see also

396-97 **First steps in space**
442-43 **Everyday inventions**
446-47 **Telecommunications**
454-55 **Recorded sound**

1955 1960 1970 1980 1990 2000

1955 Superglue, transistor radio

1961 Electric toothbrush

1968 The Jacuzzi

1975 Home computer

1979 Walkman

1982 CD player, camcorder

1996 DVD player, digital camera

Nonstick kitchenware

Teflon – its trade name – is a tough synthetic resin. It was first developed by the DuPont company in 1938. Marc Grégoire of France founded the Tefal company in 1955 to use the material in the production of his range of nonstick kitchenware.

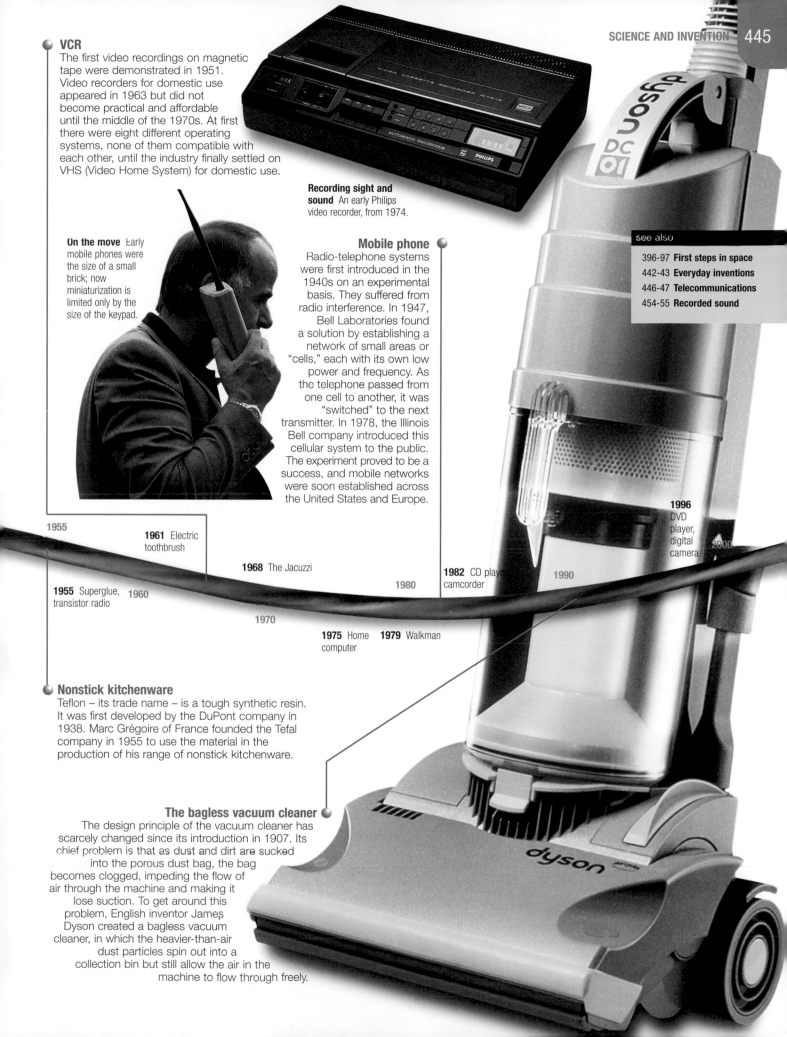

The bagless vacuum cleaner

The design principle of the vacuum cleaner has scarcely changed since its introduction in 1907. Its chief problem is that as dust and dirt are sucked into the porous dust bag, the bag becomes clogged, impeding the flow of air through the machine and making it lose suction. To get around this problem, English inventor James Dyson created a bagless vacuum cleaner, in which the heavier-than-air dust particles spin out into a collection bin but still allow the air in the machine to flow through freely.

Long-distance communication began in the 1840s with telegraph messages sent by cable between cities, and, later, between continents. Then came telephones, which transmitted the human voice as a sound wave. Radio opened up "wireless" communication, and microchips made instruments portable. With the advent of the modem, it became possible to plug computers and other digital devices into a telephone line. New technologies cut costs and increased volume, but the demand for more communication continues to grow unabated.

Alexander Graham Bell (1847-1922) Bell was a teacher of the deaf, and his work on the telephone grew out of attempts to create and transmit voice sounds electrically. He worked on his telephone apparatus with Thomas Watson in Boston, and the first words transmitted were, "Mr. Watson, come here – I want you." Bell demonstrated his invention widely and set up the Bell Telephone Company in 1877 to exploit it. He played little part in developing the business. Later in life he worked on other electrical inventions and for the welfare of the deaf.

Exporting talent Bell was born in Scotland but moved to Canada for health reasons, and then to the US. He did most of his work at Boston University, where he was Professor of Vocal Physiology.

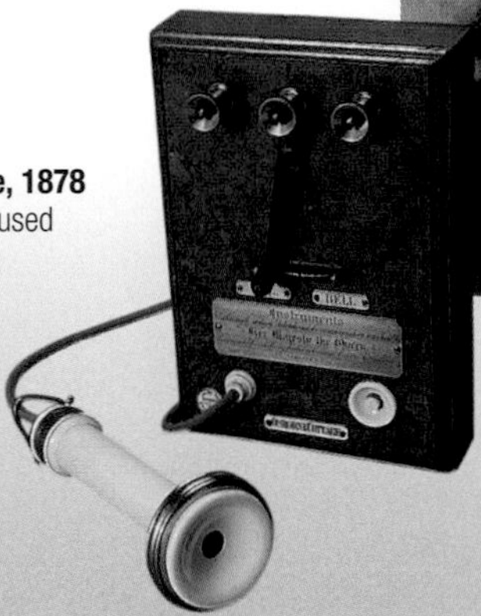

Bell telephone, 1878 Queen Victoria used this instrument.

1837 British scientists Charles Wheatstone and William Cooke patent an electromagnetic telegraph system.
1840 American inventor Samuel Morse patents his own electromagnetic telegraph.
1843 British clockmaker Alexander Bain invents a device for sending exact copies – the first facsimile (fax) machine.
1844 The first long-distance telegraph cable is laid, between Baltimore and Washington DC.

The first telegraph The message was converted into code on a strip of ticker tape.

1830

1850-55 The first teleprinters are developed.
1861 In the United States, the Transcontinental Telegraph links California with Missouri and the east coast.
1866 The first permanent transatlantic telegraph cable links Ireland and Newfoundland.

1860

1869 Thomas Edison invents the ticker tape machine for transmitting Wall Street stock prices.
1872-76 Inventors including Thomas Edison devise systems for sending two, four, and five "multiplexed" telegraph messages along one line simultaneously.

1870

1876 Scottish-born American inventor Alexander Graham Bell is granted the first patent for the electric telephone.
1878 Edison invents the carbon-granule telephone microphone, which gives much clearer speech.
1889 American Almon Strowger invents the automatic telephone exchange.
1895 Italian Guglielmo Marconi first demonstrates wireless (radio) telegraphy.

1900

1901 Marconi sends the first transatlantic wireless telegraph signal, from Cornwall to Newfoundland.
1902 German Arthur Korn invents the photoelectric scanning of images. By 1910, this is regularly used to transmit newspaper pictures. The first trans-pacific telegraph cable is laid between Canada and New Zealand.

THE TELEPHONE NETWORK

The telephone system was built to carry soundwaves – the human voice. Nowadays, fax machines, computers and cell phones all link into the system, sending enormous quantities of data in digital form (as opposed to analog – see page 452). To cope with the need for ever increasing capacity, most exchanges are now electronic and the links between them are generally digital, using fiber-optic, microwave and satellite technology. The weak point of the system is the connection to the user. For many businesses and homes, the "last mile" is still just a pair of copper wires – placing a severe limit on speed and capacity.

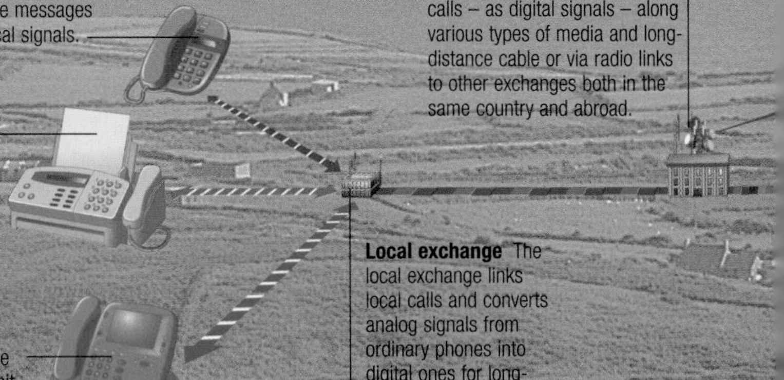

Ordinary phone This sends and receives voice messages as analog electrical signals.

Fax machine A fax machine sends and receives signals via a modem that converts analog signals into digital ones.

Digital phone Used in some offices, digital phones transmit digital signals directly to the exchange using an ISDN (Integrated Services Digital Network) link.

Main exchange This routes calls – as digital signals – along various types of media and long-distance cable or via radio links to other exchanges both in the same country and abroad.

Local exchange The local exchange links local calls and converts analog signals from ordinary phones into digital ones for long-distance transmission to a main exchange.

Biggest telephone users

Telephone lines Land lines per 100 people (2001)		Cellular phones Subscribers per 100 people (2001)	
1 Bermuda	87.15	1 Taiwan	96.88
2 Luxembourg	78.30	2 Luxembourg	96.73
3 Sweden	73.91	3 Hong Kong	85.90
4 Denmark	72.33	4 Italy	83.94
5 Norway	72.01	5 Norway	82.53
6 Switzerland	71.79	6 Iceland	82.02
7 United States	66.45	7 Israel	80.82
8 Iceland	66.39	8 Austria	80.66
9 Canada	65.51	9 Sweden	79.03
10 Cyprus	64.25	10 Finland	77.84
11 Germany	63.48	11 Portugal	77.43
12 Netherlands	62.11	12 UK	77.04
13 Japan	59.69	13 Netherlands	76.70
14 UK	58.80	14 Slovenia	75.98
15 Hong Kong	57.66	15 Greece	75.14

1960 The first communications satellite, Echo 1, is launched.
1962 PCM digital signals are used for the first time to make telephone transmissions.
1965 Early Bird (Intelsat 1) is the first geostationary commercial communications satellite. It can transmit 240 phone calls at any one time.

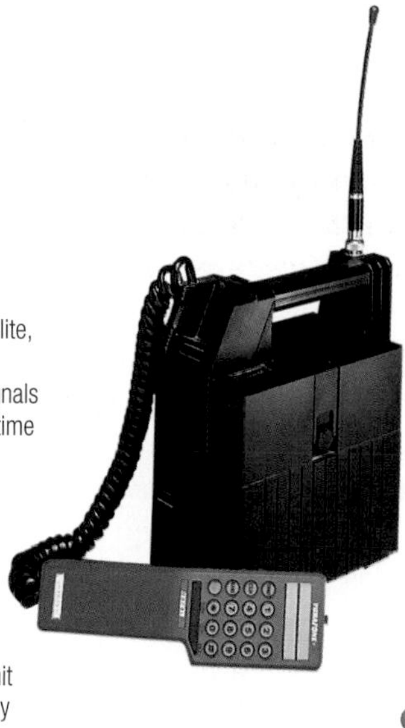

"Transportable" telephone, 1985 True portability did not come until the miniaturization revolution of the 1990s.

1980s Cheap, compact and fast fax machines appear. They take off first in Japan, where pictographic writing makes telegraphy difficult.
1981 Europe's first cellular phone system is established in Scandinavia.
1988 The first transatlantic fiber-optic cable is laid. It can carry 40 000 simultaneous telephone calls.
1990s Digital cellular phone systems are introduced.
1999 Morse Code is abandoned in favor of international signals with the growth of satellite communications.

1970 The first successful low-loss optical fiber, able to carry thousands of simultaneous signals over long distances, is demonstrated. For the first time, ordinary customers are able to make direct-dialed transatlantic telephone calls.
1978 The first operational cellular phone system is set up in Chicago.

1920s Glass rods suggested as a communications medium – the principle behind fiber optics.
1921 Detroit police introduce first two-way mobile radios.
1931 The first telex (public teleprinter) exchange is set up in London.

1947 Bell Laboratories devises a cellular mobile phone system.
1956 The first transatlantic telephone cable is laid.
1958 The modem is invented. Computers can communicate over telephone lines.

| 1920 | 1950 | 1960 | 1970 | 1980 | 2000 |

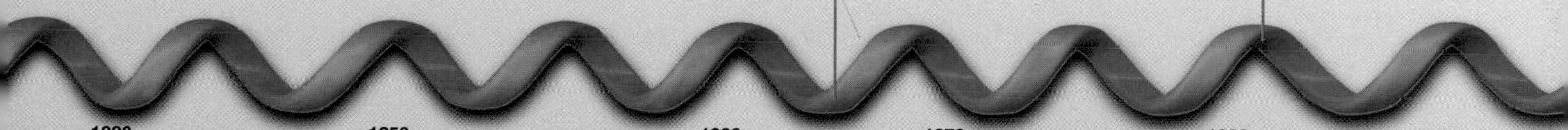

1937 American H.A. Reeves invents PCM (Pulse Code Modulation), a radio wave that transmits in coded pulses as a way of sending signals digitally.

1958-59 The development of the first microchip leads to further miniaturization, making digital communication possible.

Communications satellite Satellites relay signals where no cables exist (including to and from ships) or where cables are overloaded.

Network exchange This handles calls to and from subscribers' cell phones.

Repeater This boosts signals at intervals along long-distance cables.

Terrestrial microwave link These are often used to link local and main exchanges. Dish aerials send and receive the microwave signals in a narrow beam along a line of sight.

Telephone

Fax machine

Telephone

Fiber-optic cable Many of these cables cross land and sea, carrying thousands of simultaneous messages.

Telephone

Cell phone When switched on, the phone transmits continuous signals that allow computers at the base stations to keep track of it.

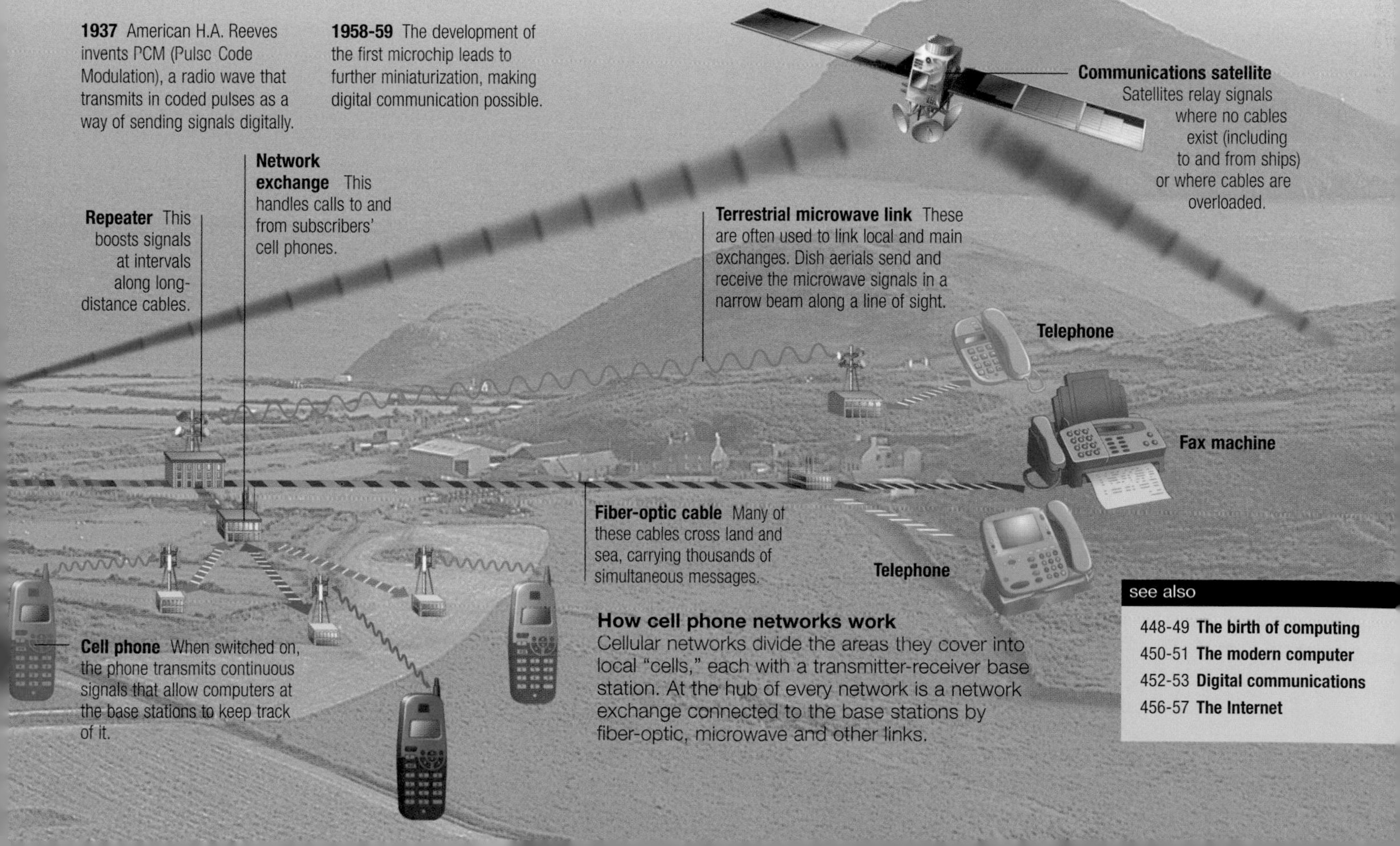

How cell phone networks work
Cellular networks divide the areas they cover into local "cells," each with a transmitter-receiver base station. At the hub of every network is a network exchange connected to the base stations by fiber-optic, microwave and other links.

As early as the 1830s, there were machines – or plans for machines – that embodied many of the principles of modern computing. But their mechanism was too complex for 19th-century engineering, and the leap from theory to practice had to await the development of electronics – especially transistors and integrated circuits – over a century later.

Inventing the computer The first computer was Charles Babbage's design for an "analytical engine" (see below). It was a true computer because it could be programmed not only to follow a series of logical steps but also to take into account the results of previous steps in the program. Not until World War II, however, was it possible to build fully functioning electromechanical and finally electronic computers.

Electronic components work faster than mechanical ones and are relatively small. They can act as electronic switches, which represent the 0s and 1s of binary numbers, and be arranged in so-called logic circuits to carry out mathematical operations. Complex calculations, however, involve many such operations, and many components are needed. The first machines used valves that generated a lot of heat; these computers filled whole rooms and needed cooling. Transistors made smaller, more powerful computers possible. The final step was the integrated circuit that combined tiny components into a single unit and led to the development of the PC (personal computer).

Manchester's marvel The Mark 1 built at Manchester University achieved a record-breaking error-free run of nine hours on the night of June 16-17, 1949.

1642 French mathematician Blaise Pascal invents the first mechanical calculator.

1801 French engineer Joseph-Marie Jacquard builds a loom controlled by punch cards.

1888 American Herman Hollerith invents a punch-card tabulating machine. His company becomes the International Business Machines (IBM) Corporation.

1943 "Colossus," a computer for breaking German codes, is built at Bletchley Park, England.
1946 ENIAC (Electronic Numerical Integrator and Computer) is unveiled at the University of Pennsylvania.

1947 John Bardeen, Walter H. Brattain and William B. Shockley invent the transistor while working at Bell Laboratories.

1949 Manchester Mark I, the first stored-program computer, with random-access memory and magnetic drum storage, is built in Manchester.

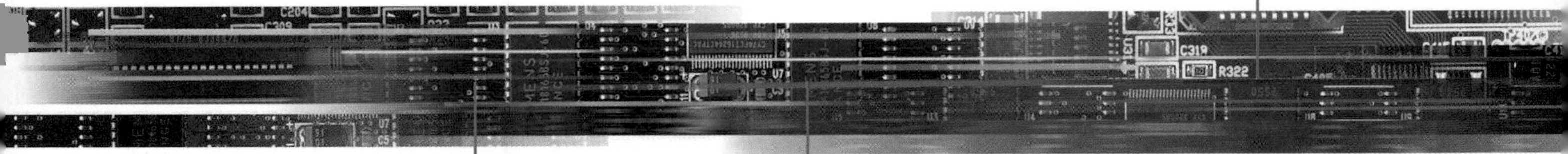

1600 **1800** **1940**

Charles Babbage (1791-1871)
English mathematician Charles Babbage designed calculating machines that contained many key elements of modern computers – but he could not complete any of them. His "difference engines" were intended to automate the calculation and printing of mathematical tables. His "analytical engine" was designed to be programmed with punch cards to perform arithmetical operations in any order and even to follow programmed logic. It included separate "mill" (processing) and "store" (memory) units and other elements of modern computers. Babbage was hindered by engineering and financial problems, but London's Science Museum built a working difference engine in 1991.

Computing machine A section of the "mill" (central processor) of Charles Babbage's "analytical engine" was one of the few parts completed at the time of his death.

Alan Turing (1912-54)
British mathematician and logician Turing developed the logical processes by which computers operate. His paper *On Computable Numbers* (1937) described a theoretical "universal machine" that could, in principle, carry out any calculation. The machine would respond to sequential commands by reading or scanning a tape. Turing proved that this could, in theory, imitate logical human thought.

During World War II, Turing played an important part in cracking the German military "Enigma" codes. He later contributed to the development of the Manchester Mark 1 and the Ferranti Mark 1. He was also a pioneer in artificial intelligence, predicting that computers would one day match human intelligence. His "Turing test" was designed as an objective measure of what was to count as achieving this status.

Software: programming computers

Early computer programs were written in "machine code" – a tedious and time-consuming process in which strings of binary numbers were generated to control the mechanism directly. In 1952, American scientist Grace Murray Hopper had the idea of writing programs in a higher-level, symbolic form, which would then be translated automatically into machine code. This was the start of the programming languages that revolutionized computing from the 1950s on. But programs still had to be custom-made for each computer and each new task; only with the arrival of program "packages" – usable on a range of computers to handle standardized jobs such as accounting and word processing – did computers become simple enough for almost anyone to use.

Software pioneer Hopper was both a research scientist and a reserve naval officer.

The first personal computer The Altair 8800, from the New Mexico-based company MITS Inc., started the personal computer revolution. It was the first commercially available microcomputer, launched in kit form in 1975 for $395. There was no software available for the machine, and users had to program it to perform calculations by flipping a row of switches; the output was read (in binary code) from a row of light-emitting diodes (LEDs). But now hobbyists could afford their own computers (at a time when commercial computers cost many thousands of dollars), and thousands bought them. Among them was the Harvard student Bill Gates, who saw an opportunity and wrote a version of the BASIC programming language for the 8800, making the machine much easier to program and launching a new software industry.

All in a box The Altair 8800 had no keyboard, no video screen, no tape or disk drive, and no more than 256 bytes of memory.

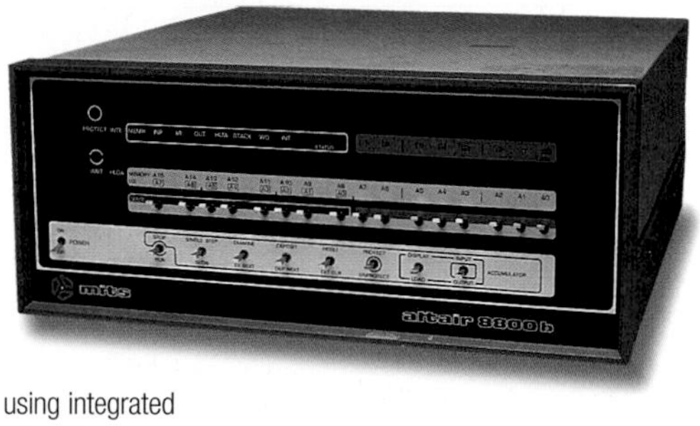

1951 The Ferranti Mark 1, the first commercially produced computer, is launched. Eight are eventually sold.
1958 Americans Jack Kilby of Texas Instruments and Robert Noyce of Fairchild make integrated circuits by placing two transistors on a single piece of silicon.
1958 The "second generation" computers, using transistors instead of valves, are produced. Computers start to become tools of business, not just of governments and universities.

1963 DEC (Digital Equipment Corporation) introduces the first minicomputer.
1964 BASIC (Beginner's All-purpose Symbolic Instruction Code) is invented, making programming easier.
1968 Alan Shugart of IBM launches the 8 in. (20 cm) floppy magnetic disk.
1968 Doug Engelbart demonstrates the use of a computer mouse for the first time.
1969 Gary Starkweather of Xerox invents the laser printer.

1970 The first computers using integrated circuit control chips are produced.
1971 Ted Hoff of Intel develops the first microprocessor – "a computer on a chip" – the 4004.
1973 IBM launches the first hard disk drive.
1974 IBM produces the first super-fast computer, using parallel processing.
1979 The VisiCalc spreadsheet – the first major PC business program – is launched.

1980 Microsoft licenses QDOS from Seattle Computer Products, adapts it, and wins the contract to supply the operating system for IBM's new PC.
1980 The first miniature 5.25 in. "Winchester" hard-disk drive is launched.
1981 IBM introduces its first personal computer.

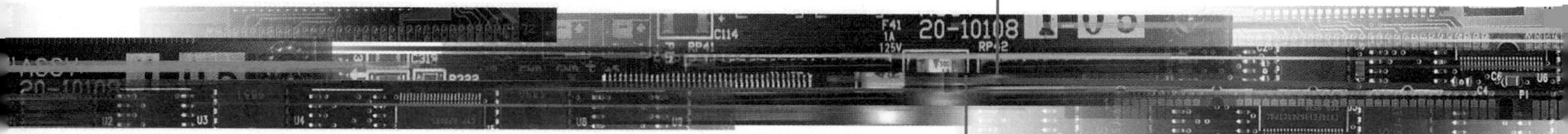

1950 1960 1970 1980

The transistor

Computers work by controlling the flow of electrical current, so that it is sometimes on and sometimes off. At first they did this by means of valves and were huge, costly, unreliable and power-hungry. After World War II transistors were developed. Their small size, reliability, low power needs and ability to function as an amplifier, oscillator and electronic switch were ideal in a wide range of electronic applications – but particularly computers, which use mainly the switching function. Integrated circuits (see page 451) with millions of tiny transistors have now largely replaced individual components.

Breakthrough The first transistor was developed in 1947 and stood 10 cm (4 in.) tall. Their modern descendants are far too small to be seen with the naked eye.

Steve Jobs (1955-)
Steve Wozniak (1950-)
Apple Computers' joint founders were Wozniak, an engineer, and Jobs, who had worked on video games and had a passion for technology. They built their first computer in the Jobs family garage in 1976. They sold 600 of this first Apple and then in 1977 launched the Apple II – a huge success thanks partly to its built-in color graphics software. It appealed to businesses and schools alike, and for five years was the world's best-selling computer. In 1984, the Apple Macintosh was the first successful graphical computer (see *The gooey revolution*, page 450). However, management clashes led to both founders leaving the company in 1985. Jobs founded a new company, NeXT, but returned to lead Apple in 1997.

Apple growers School friends Jobs (right) and Wozniak joined forces to develop and market the Apple I, originally designed by Wozniak.

see also
314-15 **Scientific thinkers**
450-51 **The modern computer**
452-53 **Digital communications**

The 1980s and 90s were a revolutionary era in computing. Speed and power increased dramatically, and size and price diminished. Desktop machines appeared in offices, homes and schools, with new kinds of software for the new users. Powerful databases enabled organizations to store and process vast quantities of information, while network technology connected machines, allowing data and software to be shared as never before.

Moore's Law in action

The speed at which microprocessors work, their "clock speed," is measured in megahertz. The figures below are for processors at the time they were introduced.

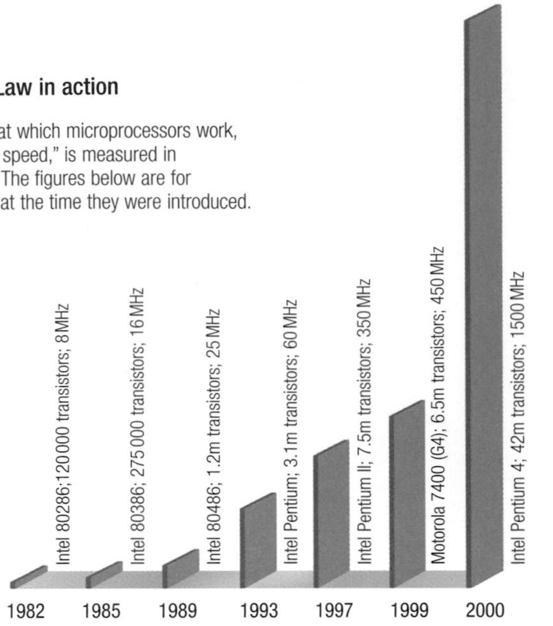

Processing power The microprocessor is the "brain" of the computer, the microchip that processes data at high speed according to programmed instructions – see opposite. Moore's Law, named after the Intel executive Gordon Moore, predicts a doubling in complexity and power of microprocessors every two years. So far, Moore's prediction has been easily met, at least for Intel processors. The Intel Pentium 4 microchip, for example, introduced in 2000, is more than 23 times faster than the first Pentium, introduced just seven years earlier in 1993.

1981 IBM launches its first personal computer. In the same year, the $17 000 Xerox Star computer is equipped with the WIMP (Windows, Icons, Menus, Pointer) system – forerunner of the modern "click and drag" GUI. The Star flops.

1982 Compaq launches the first IBM compatible computer.
1983 The Apple Lisa computer uses GUI.
1984 The Apple Macintosh, using GUI extensively, is the first successful graphical computer.

1985 The first desktop-publishing software is put on the market. In the same year, Microsoft launches the first version of Windows.
1989 NEC launches the first portable computer with a color liquid-crystal diode (LCD) screen.

1990 Microsoft produces Windows 3, the first really successful version of Windows. The company's annual sales top $1 billion.
1994 Apple launches its Power Macintosh.
1995 Microsoft comes out with the Macintosh-like Windows 95 GUI.

1998 Microsoft becomes world's most valuable company, valued on the US stock market at $261 billion. Apple launches the iMac, a low-price version of the Power Macintosh with all-in-one case.

2000 The "Lovebug" virus disables emails in the US Congress and British Parliament.

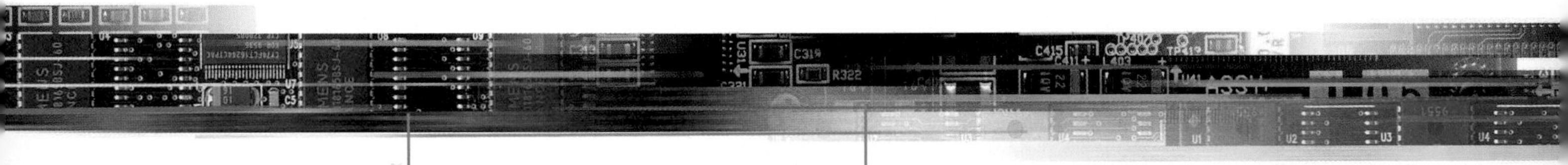

1980 — 1990 — 2000

The gooey revolution In the beginning, the only way to get a computer to do something was to type instructions in code or to press the "function" keys. Programmers learned code like a foreign language, and no one could use a computer without special training. The graphical user interface, or GUI (sometimes pronounced "gooey") changed all that. The idea of the GUI was to use visual images (or "icons") on the screen to represent commands – an approach that many users found more intuitive. Xerox developed the original GUI at its Palo Alto Research Center (PARC) in California in the 1960s. They spent more than $100 million on the project but never made a commercially successful product. Apple was the first to realize the true potential of GUI with the Macintosh computer, launched in 1984. The metaphor of the screen as a "desktop" that could be controlled by a "drag and drop" system proved hugely popular, and the following year Microsoft launched a similar system for IBM-compatible machines – Windows. Despite taking ten years to catch up with many features of the Apple system, Windows now runs on the great majority of the world's PCs.

Little Mac Apple's first attempt to introduce a personal computer using a GUI was the Lisa, introduced in 1983. It was slow and expensive, and it flopped commercially. The much cheaper Macintosh (left), launched the following year, had a profound impact as Microsoft rushed to follow the trend with its GUI operating system Windows.

Bill Gates (1955-) Gates started programming at 13, and by the age of 32 was the world's richest man. As a schoolboy, he and a friend, Paul Allen, hacked into the security system of a local firm's computer and were then asked to look for its weaknesses. At Harvard, he developed a version of the BASIC computer language for the Altair (see page 449), and then dropped out to form Micro-soft (the hyphen was later dropped) with Allen in 1975. They had a vision of computers as a useful tool for everyone. Their big break was a contract with IBM for an operating system for IBM's new personal computer. In the 1980s and 90s, Microsoft developed and made a huge success of its Windows GUI, but its business practices brought accusations of monopoly tactics.

WHAT IS SOFTWARE?

The instructions, or programs, that tell a computer what to do are known as software. Software is written in code, using languages such as BASIC, C or Pascal. These commands are then converted by other programs into simpler binary code (consisting of 1s and 0s) that directly operates the machine. In much modern software, users do not see the code or need to know how to program. Instead they issue commands by using graphic devices such as visual icons, "buttons" or pull-down "menus."

There are four main types of software:
Operating system (OS) The OS controls the computer by performing everyday tasks such as receiving data from the keyboard, displaying information on screen, or storing it in memory or on a hard-disk drive. It works the whole time a computer is switched on. Users normally interact with the OS through a graphical user interface (GUI) and keyboard.
Applications Programs created to perform specific tasks are known as applications. They include word processing (WP); database management (for storing details of a company's stock and customers, for example); desktop publishing (DTP); and spreadsheets for financial calculations such as budgets.
Peripherals software Scanners, digital cameras, printers and other devices all need software to connect to a computer.
Utilities "Housekeeping" tasks such as screening data files for viruses, repairing damage to the hard disk and ensuring efficient data storage are handled by programs called utilities.

MAIN PARTS OF A MICROCOMPUTER

Most of the components in a computer fall into one of two categories: memory, or storage, components that hold data, and processing components that perform operations on the data.

RAM chips Microchips that store data and programs in use. Data in RAM is lost when power is extinguished.

Floppy, CD-ROM and/or DVD-ROM drives Various types of data storage devices that use removable disks – varying in capacity from 1.4 megabytes for a floppy disk to several thousand megabytes for a DVD-ROM.

Power-supply unit (PSU) It converts mains-voltage power to steady low-voltage direct current (DC) to power the various components.

Hard drive The main permanent store of data and programs. It stores data as magnetic signals in binary code on metal disks. The data are "read" from and "written" to the disks, as they spin at high speed, by small magnetic heads like those of a tape recorder.

Central processing unit (CPU) or microprocessor The microchip that processes data and coordinates input, output and storage devices. It generates a lot of heat, so it usually has a cooling fan.

Motherboard The main circuit board – a printed circuit whose wires link the main components.

BIOS A chip that stores vital data even when the computer is switched off. It includes instructions for "booting up" (starting) the computer.

Expansion slots Connectors into which expansion cards that add special functions can be slotted.

Controller chips Specialized chips run functions such as graphics and control components such as hard drives.

KEY TERMS

- **Binary** Number system based solely on 0s and 1s.
- **BIOS** *Basic input-output system*. A chip that controls basic computer functions.
- **Bit** *Binary digit*. The smallest unit of information.
- **Buffer** Temporary memory that holds data ready for use.
- **Bus** Main communicating wires on the motherboard.
- **Byte** A group of eight bits; it represents – in binary – a number from 0 to 255 or a symbol.
- **CD-ROM** *Compact disc read-only memory*. A CD that stores data or a program.
- **Clock speed** The speed at which a processor works.
- **DVD** *Digital versatile disc*. A very high-capacity disc for storing data or software.
- **File** A piece of code or set of data kept together as a unit.
- **Hardware** The physical components of a computer.
- **Modem** *Modulator-demodulator*. A device linking a computer to a phone line.
- **Motherboard** The printed circuit board that carries a computer's main microchips.
- **Network** Two or more computers linked together.
- **RAM** *Random-access memory*. Computer memory that can be changed by "overwriting" it with new data.
- **ROM** *Read-only memory*. Nonerasable memory.
- **Virus** A damaging, self-replicating program.

Microchips for everything

Microchips – also called silicon chips or simply "chips" – consist of miniature electrical components connected together on a circuit board. They form part of all modern computers and most other electronic devices. Each chip has thousands or even millions of components such as tiny diodes and transistors etched on its surface by a photographic process. The components are linked by metal tracks less than a micron (one-thousandth of a millimeter) wide that carry electrical signals between them. At the core of a computer is the microprocessor chip, or central processing unit (CPU), which is responsible for most of the computational work. The smaller and more densely packed the components on a chip, the more complex and faster its operations. Scientists are now trying to develop even faster microchips based on optical, chemical or "quantum" (single-electron) activity rather than electric current.

see also
400-1 **Information economy**
448-49 **The birth of computing**
452-53 **Digital communications**
456-57 **The Internet**

Digital communications

Digital simply means numerical, and digital communications reduce everything – from the music of Beethoven to a Botticelli painting – to a series of numbers. The result is faster reproduction that is more easily stored and free from distortion. It was only with computer technology's ability to calculate and manipulate numbers that digital communications became possible.

Analog and digital signals In nature, we get most of our information in the form of sound and light, which travel as waves of continuously varying quantities. Man-made communication systems, however, may use either continuous signals or discrete signals.

Systems that use continuous signals are known as analog, because they construct fluctuating electrical currents or voltages that are analogs of the original continuous sound or light wave.

A microphone, for example, converts the air pressure fluctuations of sound waves into a continuously varying electrical current that mimics the shape of the original sound waves.

Digital communication systems, on the other hand, measure the original waves and describe them as a series of discrete numbers. The numbers are converted into binary, a number system based on the digits 1 and 0. The binary numbers are used to generate a stream of electrical pulses, the digit 1 corresponding to "on" and the digit 0 to "off." When the pulses are received, a digital-analog converter (DAC) changes them back into sound or light, allowing us to hear a sound or see an image that was sent to us as nothing more than a long stream of 1s and 0s.

The benefits of digital

Digital transmission has many advantages over analog. Because it is numerical, errors can be detected and corrected, and by identifying patterns in the numbers, the information can be compressed for faster transmission. In addition, digital devices can communicate with one another because they all use information in the same, numerical form. This is why you can, for example, plug a digital camera into a computer, download music files from the Internet or send a photograph by email.

1 Analog signal This consists of a varying electrical voltage or current. It may come, for example, from a microphone, representing a sound wave, or from a video camera, representing the varying brightness of a scene.

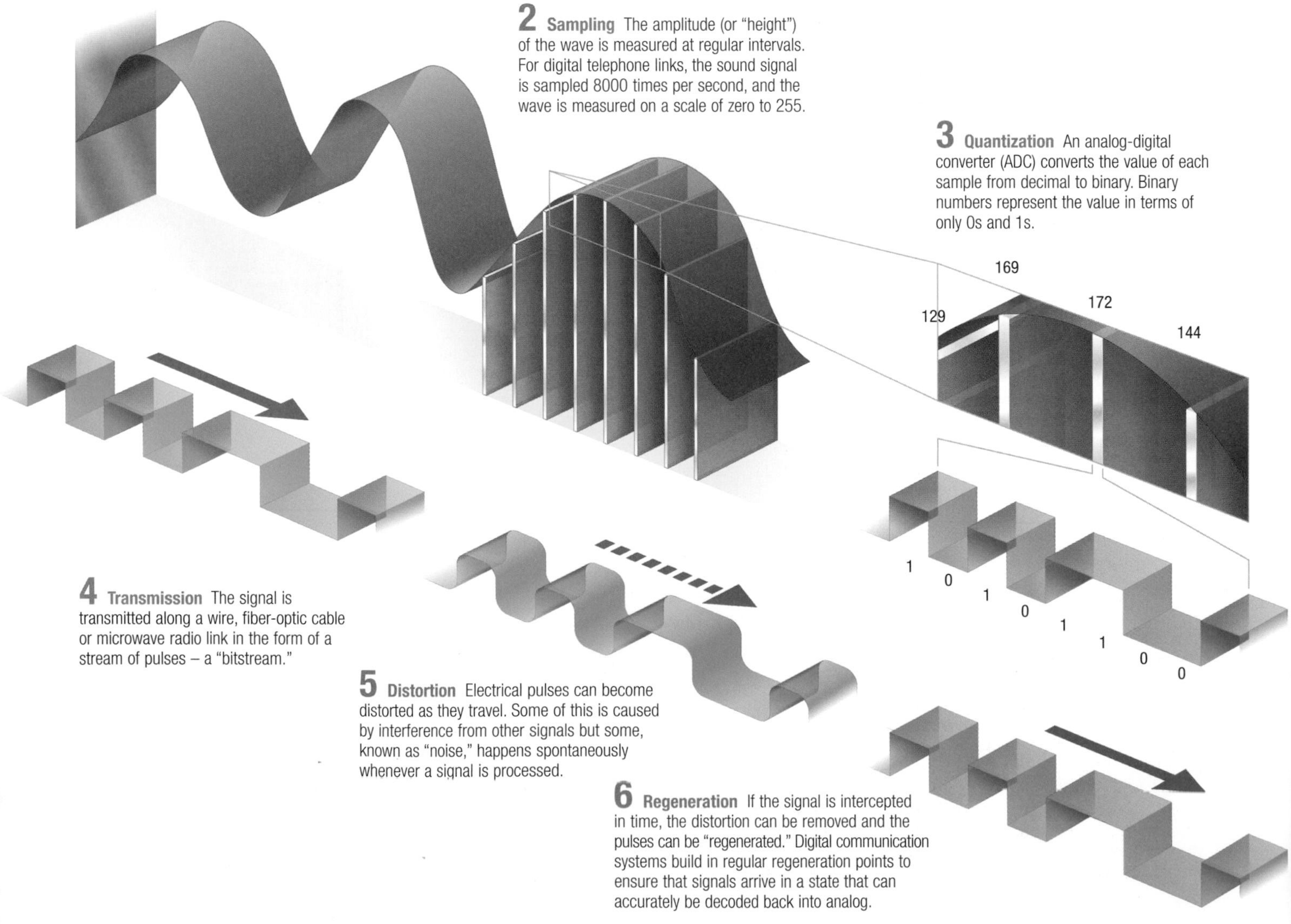

2 Sampling The amplitude (or "height") of the wave is measured at regular intervals. For digital telephone links, the sound signal is sampled 8000 times per second, and the wave is measured on a scale of zero to 255.

3 Quantization An analog-digital converter (ADC) converts the value of each sample from decimal to binary. Binary numbers represent the value in terms of only 0s and 1s.

4 Transmission The signal is transmitted along a wire, fiber-optic cable or microwave radio link in the form of a stream of pulses – a "bitstream."

5 Distortion Electrical pulses can become distorted as they travel. Some of this is caused by interference from other signals but some, known as "noise," happens spontaneously whenever a signal is processed.

6 Regeneration If the signal is intercepted in time, the distortion can be removed and the pulses can be "regenerated." Digital communication systems build in regular regeneration points to ensure that signals arrive in a state that can accurately be decoded back into analog.

DIGITAL TYPE

All computers use binary numbers to represent letters, figures and written symbols. These computer "codes" were first standardized with the American Standard Code for Information Interchange (ASCII), also known as the machine code, in 1963.

ASCII, now used by all personal computers in countries that use the Roman alphabet, employs a string of eight binary digits (or "bits") to represent 128 characters. This is enough to encode small and capital letters, numerals, punctuation marks, and 32 special "control characters" to govern computer functions – with another 128 "extended" characters, such as accented and non-Latin letters and graphics symbols.

Examples of ASCII codes include:

Binary number	Decimal equivalent	Character encoded
00010010	36	$
01000001	65	A
01101011	107	k
10100100	164	ñ

The letter "k," for example, is encoded by the number 107. When the "k" key is pressed, the machine code 107 is generated and is then converted into the equivalnet binary number (01101011). The binary code signal can then be processed by the computer, and the letter "k" will appear on the screen in front of you – and all this happens in microseconds.

Languages such as Chinese and Japanese have many more distinct characters, however, and have to be represented by 16 binary digits.

FACT A single CD-ROM can store 112 million words of digital text – about twice as much as the *Encyclopedia Britannica*.

DIGITAL SOUND

The first use of digital sound was in transmitting telephone conversations. When a sound is converted from analog to digital, it is measured ("sampled") at regular intervals. The quality of the signal that results depends both on the accuracy with which it is measured (the fineness of the scale) and the rate of sampling (the number of samples per second).

Two main types of sampling are used, 8-bit and 16-bit, but sampling technology is rapidly developing, allowing the development of higher and higher quality sound reproduction.

8-bit sampling Digital telephone links use 8-bit sampling, because the human voice does not have a very wide range of frequencies. In 8-bit sampling, sound wave frequencies are measured as an eight-digit binary number. Each sample is assigned one of 256 different values, 256 being the highest number that can be represented by eight digits in binary. This yields reasonably clear speech but is not suitable for music, for example. Digital telephones sample at a rate of 8000 times per second – or 8000 kHz. A rate of 10 000 samples per second – 10 000 kHz – is enough for speech recording.

16-bit sampling An audio CD uses 16-bit sampling – giving a scale with a possible 65 536 different levels – and samples are taken at the rate of 44 100 times per second (44 100 kHz) in each of two stereo channels. The result is much higher-fidelity sound than the low-frequency, 8-bit sampling used for the telephone. New systems such as DVD-Audio, however, now offer 24-bit sampling (almost 17 million levels).

DIGITAL IMAGES

All electronic imaging systems work by scanning an image in narrow strips. Each strip is in turn divided into squares called pixels ("picture elements"). For color reproduction, each pixel is coded according to the levels of red, green and blue that it contains – the three primary colors of light.

The brightness of each color is measured for each pixel, and, as in other digital systems, converted into a binary number. The result is a so-called "bitmap" of the image that can be transmitted, recorded and reproduced on a TV screen, computer monitor or other digital device.

The clarity and accuracy of the image depends on several factors, including the number of pixels in a given area, how frequently they are scanned and the "color depth" – the number of levels (as for sound) against which the brightness of each color in each pixel is measured. High-quality color images, such as those used in printing, are usually scanned at 12 bits per primary color (4096 different levels of brightness) and 22 500 pixels per square inch – about eight times the number on a television or computer screen.

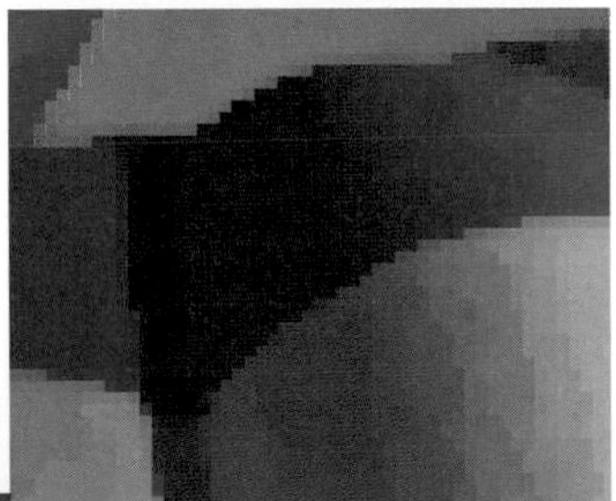

Patchwork picture The detail shows how each pixel interprets the color values inside its own little square.

see also
354-55 **Television**
412-13 **Numbers and sequences**
448-51 **Computers**
454-55 **Recorded sound**

Life today would be unthinkable without recorded music, voice and sound. Yet the technology is little more than 100 years old. Sound recording began in the late 19th century with the cylinder phonograph. Film soundtracks, tape, stereo, the LP and the videocassette followed, joined in the digital era by a series of high-tech devices, from the CD in 1982 to MiniDisc, DVD and MP3 in the 1990s.

Wurlitzer

Music machine Jukeboxes arrived in the 1930s on a wave of enthusiasm for swing music.

1877 American inventor Thomas Edison develops the cylinder phonograph for recording and playing back sound.
1887 German-American inventor Emile Berliner develops the gramophone.
1890 A coin-operated cylinder phonograph with four listening tubes – an early forerunner of the jukebox – is installed in a San Francisco saloon.

1902 Double-sided disks are pioneered by South American Ademor Petit, who discovers that liquid shellac will spread more evenly if grooves are being impressed on both sides.
1927 The first successful sound films have soundtracks recorded on 50 cm (20 in.) disks, turning at 33⅓ rpm.
1927 The first all-electric jukebox is produced.
1927 British inventor John Logie Baird produces the first video recordings, capturing short TV programs on disks made of wax and magnetic steel. He calls the technique Phonovision.

1931 British inventor Alan Blumlein patents Binaural (stereo) recording.
1934 The Wurlitzer multiple-selection jukebox is introduced.

1870 | 1900 | 1930 | 1940 | 1950

From phonograph to gramophone Edison's phonograph used a rotating metal cylinder wrapped with tinfoil; a stylus attached to a diaphragm vibrated according to the sound created and made indentations on the foil, recording the sounds. Later, he used wax-coated cardboard. The first words Edison recorded were "Mary had a little lamb." Although successful at first, Edison's phonograph was eventually displaced by Berliner's disk gramophone. This used hard rubber (later shellac) disks turning at 30 rpm, soon increasing to 60 and later to 78 rpm (the increased speed gave better-quality sound). Berliner was also the first to mass-produce disks by pressing them from a metal master disk.

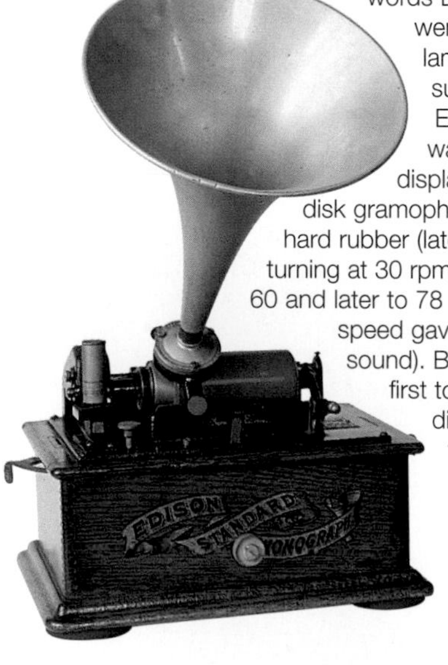
Edison Standard Phonograph

Edison phonograph, 1890s

1935 German engineers give a public demonstration of the Magnetophon tape recorder, manufactured by BASF and AEG.

1941 Stereo sound is used for the first time in the cinema.
1948 Birth of the LP: the 30 cm (12 in.) long-playing 33⅓ rpm vinyl disc is launched. It is able to play for about 46 minutes.

1956 The first practicable professional videotape recorder is demonstrated in the United States.
1958 The first stereo LP discs are issued.

HOW A VINYL RECORD WORKS

A conventional gramophone disk carries sound information in the form of an oscillating spiral groove leading from the outside edge of the record almost to the middle. When the record turns, the pickup stylus (needle) follows the oscillations of the groove, which correspond to the peaks and troughs of the sound waves, converting them into a tiny electric current that is amplified and converted back into sound in the loudspeakers. In mono recordings, the stylus simply oscillates from side to side. In a stereo record, the left- and right-hand channels are recorded as separate variations in the two walls of the groove.

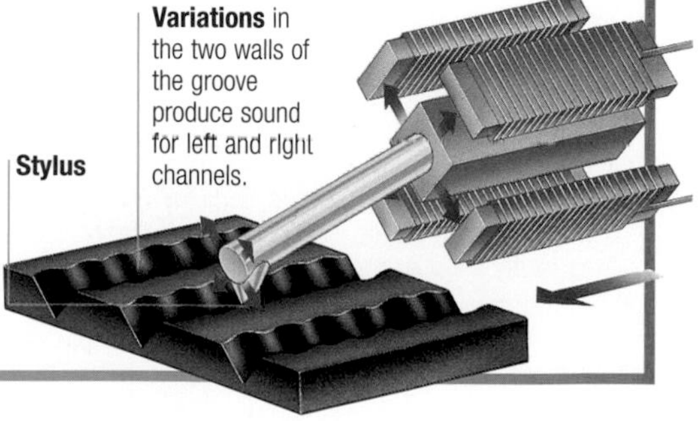
Stylus
Variations in the two walls of the groove produce sound for left and right channels.

Dolby sound systems

The Dolby noise-reduction system involves boosting the recording level of high-pitched sound frequencies and then reducing the level on playback, which greatly reduces tape hiss. Dolby later developed digital and surround-sound systems for cinemas and home entertainment systems. They record up to six channels of digital sound coded on one soundtrack, with normal stereo music speakers, a central front speaker for dialog, and mono rear speakers for surround effects.

see also

334-37 **Popular music**
400-1 **Information economy**
452-53 **Digital communications**
468 **Movies**

Akio Morita (1921-99) Akio Morita and the Japanese company he cofounded have been responsible for many of the most important innovations in home recording. It was Morita who pioneered the Walkman (originally Soundabout) personal cassette player – against the advice of many of his colleagues. By the time of his death, 100 million Walkmans had been sold in the United States alone. His company also pioneered the videocassette recorder, the camcorder, the MiniDisc and (jointly with Philips) the Compact Disc (CD) and Digital Audio Tape (DAT).

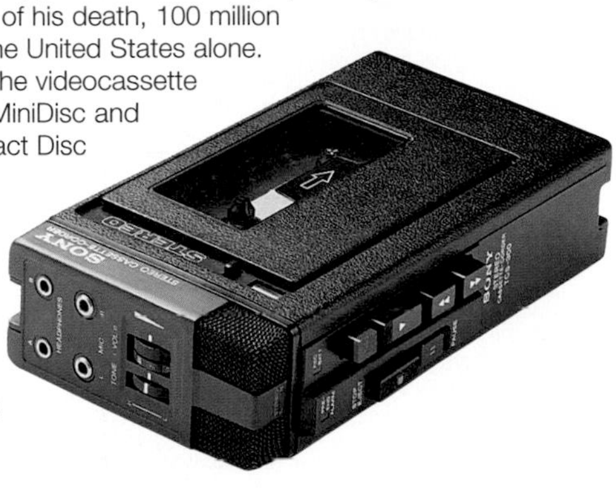

Sony Walkman, 1979 Akio Morita is said personally to have inspired the Walkman. He wanted a small, portable device to listen to music while on the golf course.

1992 The digital rerecordable MiniDisc (MD) is launched. It measures 6 cm (2½ in.) across and can record up to 80 minutes.
1996 In Japan, Digital Versatile Discs (DVDs) are launched. They are the same size as CDs but can store 25 times the data.

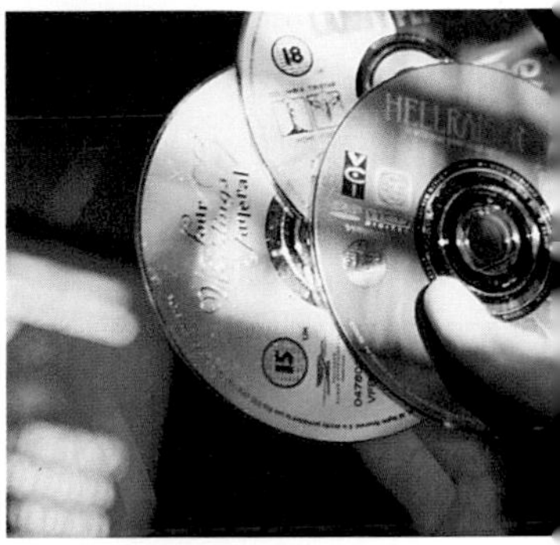

DVDs These disks can store the huge amount of data needed to display a full-length feature film. The digital picture quality is superior to that of video.

1960 | 1970 | 1980 | 1990 | 2000

1963 The compact tape cassette is introduced.
1965 Sony produces the first consumer videotape recorder.
1969 American electronics engineer Ray M. Dolby invents a system of noise reduction for tape recordings.

1970 The first domestic videocassette recorders appear.
1975 Sony brings out the Betamax domestic videocassette.
1976 Sony launches the VHS (JVC) videocassette format, which overtakes its Betamax.

1980 The first domestic video camcorder is produced.
1982 The CD is launched. Measuring 12 cm (4 1/2 in.) across, it is able to record 74 minutes. It is the first commercially successful digital recording medium.

1997 The MP3 compressed digital recording system is launched, allowing high-quality sound transmission on the Internet.

2001 Domestic DVD-R (recordable DVD) video recorders are launched.

RECORDING ON MAGNETIC TAPE

Magnetic tape is a thin plastic ribbon coated on one side with a magnetic material. During recording, the head magnetizes the coating. The strength of the magnetization corresponds to the amplitude of the sound input signal. During playback, the tape moving past the tape head causes a small varying electric signal that is amplified and fed to the loudspeakers. With video tape images, the varying brightness of the three primary colors (red, green and blue) is recorded as variations in the strength of magnetization.

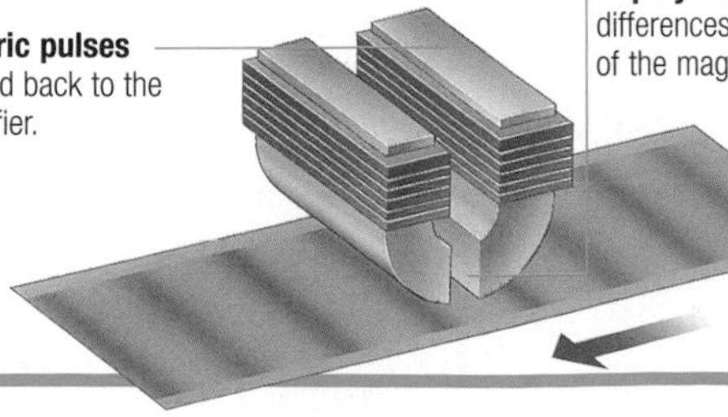

Electric pulses are fed back to the amplifier.

Replay head picks up differences in the strength of the magnetization.

SOUND FROM A DIGITAL DISK

Digital data are stored on CDs, DVDs and MiniDisks in the form of microscopically small "pits" (that absorb light), separated by flat "lands" (that reflect it). They are arranged in a spiral from the inside of the disk toward the outer edge. During playback, a laser beam shines on the spinning disk. A photocell responds to variations in the light reflected from the pits and lands, creating a succession of on/off electrical signals. A digital-analog converter (DAC) translates these digital signals to produce analog electrical signals representing sounds or colors.

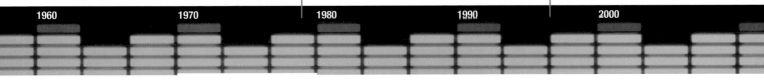

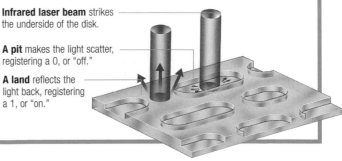

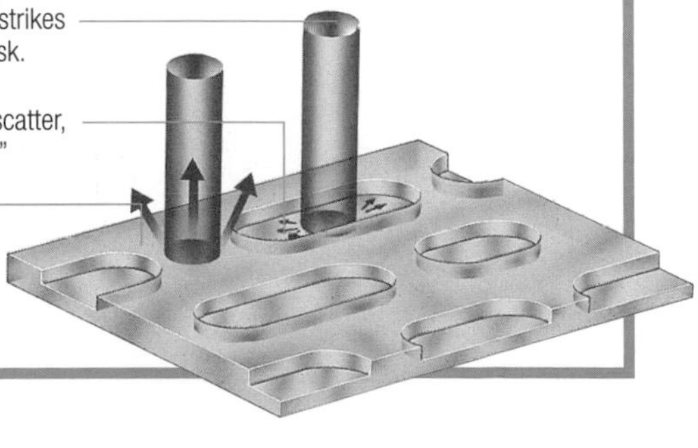

Infrared laser beam strikes the underside of the disk.

A pit makes the light scatter, registering a 0, or "off."

A land reflects the light back, registering a 1, or "on."

The Internet

How a network of computer networks is changing the world

Computer networks began as a way of connecting massive mainframes in research laboratories and universities to increase their power and allow scientists to share data. Then came conventions called protocols that permitted exchanges across networks – literally internetwork communication. In the 1980s, a system of unique addresses was developed, allowing any computer to contact any other – the Internet as we know it. As personal computing put machines into offices and homes across the world, applications such as the World Wide Web, e-commerce and email began to change the way we live, work and do business.

WHAT IS THE INTERNET?

The heart of the Internet consists of computers known as routers, connected by high-speed backbone links using fiber-optic and other cable and satellite links. The routers are, in turn, connected with thousands of smaller networks and millions of individual computers.

Large companies, government and academic institutions and some homes often have direct Internet access via computers called Internet servers that are always connected. Other users dial in by telephone line from time to time, linking to a server at their Internet service provider.

Data are sent around the Internet by means of "packet switching." Whether it takes the form of email, web pages or computer files, the information is split up into small "packets,"

Early 1960s In the United States, the Rand Corporation begins studies into secure military communications networks. The results of this research were later used in developing the Internet.

Early 1970s Email and newsgroup systems grow rapidly on the Arpanet. The network's controllers take the first steps to link separate networks in a network of networks – later known as the Internet. Key to this development is the transmission-control protocol (TCP) for communication between networks, devised by American scientist Vint Cerf.

1969 American military and academic researchers establish the Arpanet network, based on systems devised by Paul Baran. Initially, the Arpanet links just four mainframe computers. By 1971 there are 23 computers in the network.

Vinton G. (Vint) Cerf (1943-)
Vint Cerf was the co-designer (with Robert E. Kahn) of the TCP/IP Internet protocol. He and Kahn were awarded the US National Medal of Technology in 1997 for their work.

1982 The term "Internet" is first used by Vint Cerf and Bob Kahn.

1984 The system of domain names (Internet addresses) is introduced.

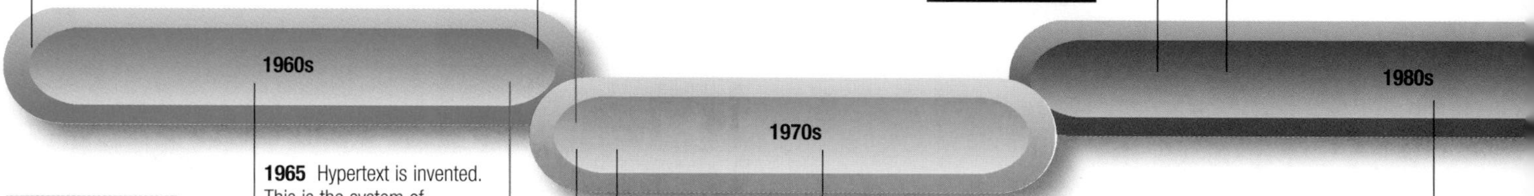

1965 Hypertext is invented. This is the system of clickable text later used to link web pages.

Paul Baran (1926-)
In 1962, Paul Baran at Rand proposes packet switching – a method of breaking messages into separate chunks that can travel across a network to the same destination following different routes.

1974 Telnet, the first commercial version of Arpanet, is set up.

1973 The first transatlantic Arpanet links are established.

1975 Dial-up online bulletin boards and information services, including CompuServe and America Online (AOL), are established.

1988 The number of "host" computers on the Internet reaches 60 000. Host computers are permanently connected data-holding computers. They store vast amounts of data but access to them is difficult.

1984 Canadian writer William Gibson coins the term "cyberspace" in his novel *Neuromancer.*

1990 The original Arpanet is disbanded, leaving the Internet in its place.

THE LANGUAGE OF INTERNET ADDRESSES

Every computer connected to the Internet has to have a unique "address" so that when information is requested, other machines know where to send a response and so that they in turn can request information from it. Many users on personal computers do not have their own Internet addresses but rather connect through a service provider, using a temporarily assigned address.

Internet addresses take the form of four sets of numbers separated by dots – for example, 123.4567.89.1011. There is also often a verbal name (called a domain name) associated with the numerical address to make it easier to remember. Powerful computers called domain-name servers (DNSs) store every address on the Internet and automatically translate domain names into numerical Internet addresses.

Computers that host websites generally have domain names that start "www," followed by a dot, one or more words separated by dots, and a suffix such as ".com" or ".edu" identifying the type of organization – commercial or educational in this case.

Uniform resource locators (URLs) Web sites also have unique addresses known as URLs. These start with "http://," which identifies the protocol by which web information is transmitted. Then comes the domain name of the host computer on which the site is stored and, for particular pages or files within a website, a slash (/) and a file name, often with a suffix such as .html.

each of which is digitally "labeled" with its destination address. A succession of routers send it by the quickest available path until it reaches its target. Once there, the packets are reassembled into the right order to make the complete file. Because Internet traffic is constantly in flux and there are many paths between routers, each packet may – and often does – follow a different route.

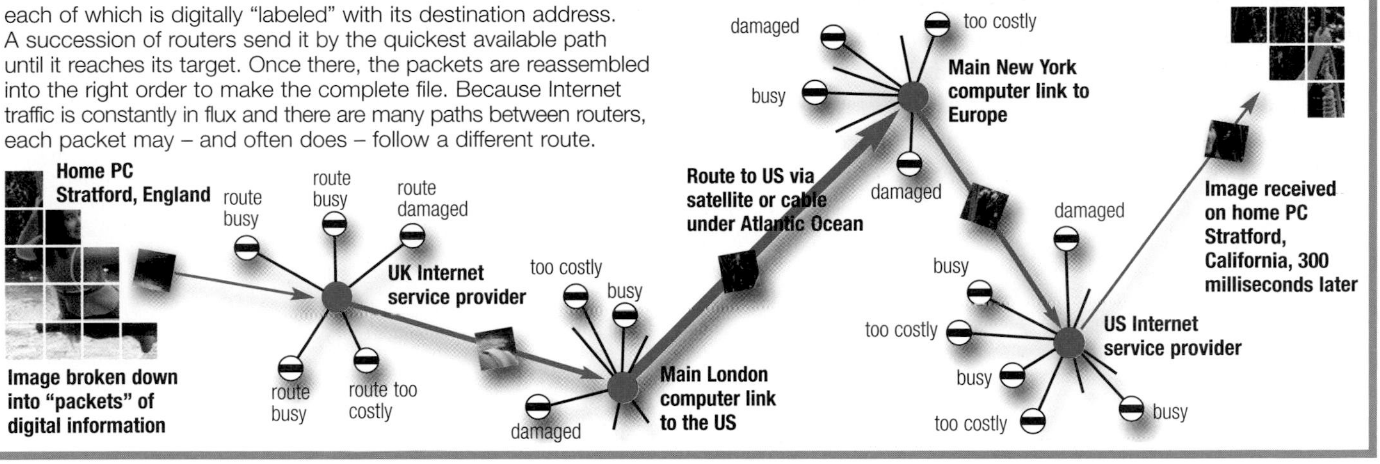

Tim Berners-Lee (1955-) an English scientist working at the European nuclear research center in Geneva, develops the World Wide Web (WWW) and its URL, HTML and HTTP standards.

1994 Netscape Navigator, a commercial version of Mosaic and the first mass-market web browser, is launched.

The first web radio stations and first online bank are established.

1995 The Java programming language enables more complex web pages.

The first search engines – online programs for finding information on the web – are created.

2000 The Internet has about 95 million host computers, about 25 million web-sites and more than 1 billion web pages.

1990s

2000s

1991 The Internet is fully opened to commercial traffic.

The number of Internet host computers reaches 1 million.

The first Internet service providers (ISPs) offer inexpensive public Internet access via the telephone network.

Marc Andreessen (1971-) In 1993, Marc Andreessen and Eric Bina develop the Mosaic browser to display web pages.

1990s Web traffic multiplies by about 3500 annually.

1996 The number of host computers on the Internet reaches 10 million.

1999 Internet 2, or Abilene, a high-power research network, is launched.

1995 Online bookseller Amazon.com is founded. It makes no money but leads the way for e-commerce.

see also

400-1 **The information economy**
446-47 **Telecommunications**
448-51 **Computing**
452-53 **Digital communications**

Email – or electronic mail – uses the Internet to transmit messages between users with unique addresses. Messages are created and routed between computers with special software until they reach the correct address.

Newsgroups People with a common interest sign up and gain access to a dedicated Internet location. There they can post and read messages on an electronic "bulletin board," make contact and enter into discussions.

KEY TERMS

GIF Graphic Interchange Format – a compressed format used for the rapid transmission of graphics.

HTML HyperText Markup Language – the main programming language used to construct web pages.

HTTP HyperText Transfer Protocol – the system for moving hypertext files (that is, web pages) across the Internet.

ISP Internet Service Provider – an organization through which subscribers connect to the Internet.

JPEG Joint Photographic Experts Group – a compressed format used for the rapid transmission of graphics.

Log on/off Connect to (using a digital password) and disconnect from the Internet or a particular web server.

Modem Modulator-Demodulator – a device for converting digital data into analog and back again, allowing a computer to use ordinary telephone lines.

MPEG Moving Pictures Experts Group – a compressed format used for transmitting video files.

MP3 A compressed file format for music.

POP Point of Presence – a telephone number from which a subscriber can dial in to an ISP's system and thus connect to the Internet.

Server Computer or program giving services (such as access or storage of web files or the forwarding of emails).

TCP/IP Transmission Control Protocol/Internet Protocol – the system that moves data around the Internet.

URL Uniform Resource Locator – the official name for a web address.

WAP Wireless Application Protocol – method of accessing web pages on mobile phones; likely to be superseded by third generation (3G) mobile phones.

The foundations of medical science were laid early. Anatomy (the structure and form of the body) and physiology (the study of the body's functions) were taught in medical schools founded as early as 300 B.C. in Alexandria, Egypt. Over the next 2000 years, physicians gradually uncovered rational explanations for illnesses and developed treatments for them.

Surgical pioneer Indian surgeon Sushruta is credited with having written the first version of a medical textbook, called the *Sushruta-samhita*, in the 8th century B.C. This outlines a number of surgical techniques and medicinal remedies. The Hindu religion forbade him to dissect dead bodies in order to learn more about human anatomy. Instead, he immersed the bodies in water for several days and then simply pulled them apart without the need for cutting. He administered alcohol as a sedative during operations and used a combination of hot oils and tar to staunch bleeding. He pioneered the basic techniques of skin grafting and plastic surgery, as well as treating cataracts by the removal of the lens of the eye.

The spread of disease

In the second half of the 19th century it became apparent how infectious diseases spread. Until then, doctors believed that infection arose from noxious gases, or miasmas, produced by rotting matter and stagnant water.

The development of the microscope in the 17th century revealed the existence of microorganisms that were invisible to the naked eye. It was not until the 1860s that the French microbiologist Louis Pasteur (1822-95) demonstrated that some of these microorganisms caused disease. In 1882, a German doctor, Robert Koch (1843-1910), was the first to identify a germ responsible for a particular ailment: the tubercle bacillus that leads to tuberculosis.

c. 8000 B.C. Trepanning – the technique of boring a hole in the skull – is practiced by Neolithic people, probably to release "evil spirits."

c. 1000 B.C. *The Treatise of Medical Diagnosis and Prognosis*, describing symptoms for 3000 illnesses, is written on clay tablets in Babylon.

c. A.D. 170 Greek physician Galen proves that arteries and veins carry blood, not air. He uses bloodletting to restore the body's fluids to "perfect balance," and carries out some of the first scientific dissections.

1510 Ambroise Paré, the "father of modern surgery," is born. Rather than cauterizing wounds, he applied soothing lotions, helping to cut death rates.

1543 Belgian anatomist Andreas Vesalius uses dissection to prove that many of Galen's ideas were wrong.

1604 Italian physician Hieronymus Fabricius publishes *De formato foetu*, a landmark in the study of embryology.

1628 English physician William Harvey outlines the circulation of blood in his *Anatomical Study of the Motion of the Heart and of the Blood in Animals.*

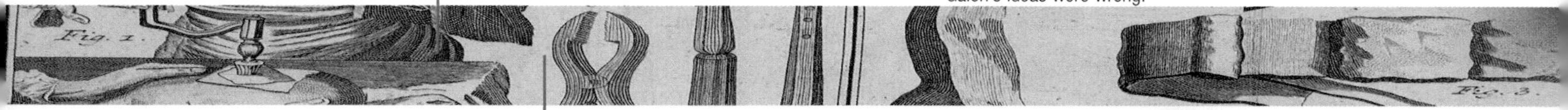

8000 B.C. | 1000 B.C. | 0 | A.D. 170 | 1500 | 1600

3000 B.C. The Chinese *Ne'i ching* makes the first reference to the circulation of blood. In Egypt, physician Imhotep records his remedies.

2000 B.C. *The Vedas*, a sacred medical text on the treatment of diseases and casting out of devils, is written in India.

384 B.C. Greek philosopher Aristotle is born. His writings on biology, particularly on subjects such as comparative anatomy and embryology, would have great influence on the science and practice of medicine for nearly 2000 years.

Father of medicine Greek physician Hippocrates (c. 460-c. 370 B.C.) used observation and deductive reasoning to lay the foundation of a scientific approach to medicine. He also taught that diet, hygiene and environment can influence a person's health. There is no evidence that he formulated the Hippocratic oath of medical ethics, still taken by many medical school graduates.

1674 By using a crude microscope, Dutch scientist Anton van Leeuwenhoek becomes the first person to observe bacteria.

Exploring a secret world Leeuwenhoek's pioneering microscope (above) could magnify up to 300 times.

HUMORS AND BLOODLETTING

From the time of the ancient Greeks until the 18th century, it was believed that everything was made of four elements – air, water, fire and earth – and that these elements were mirrored in the body by four humors: blood, phlegm, choler (yellow bile) and black bile, respectively. Illness resulted when the natural balance of these humors was disturbed. Treatment involved drawing off excess or poisonous humors to restore the balance. This was usually done by bloodletting, either cutting open a vein or applying bloodsucking leeches. In the 19th century, the humor theory fell into disrepute.

Split personality The balance of the four humors was believed to affect mental as well as physical health. Each humor was linked with a distinct personality type (right): sanguine, melancholy, choleric or phlegmatic.

Antiseptics

Infection following surgery was a common cause of death until the late 19th century. Doctors routinely operated in blood-caked clothes and in dirty rooms with dirty hands and instruments.

In the 1840s, Hungarian obstetrician Ignaz Semmelweis demonstrated that if doctors just washed their hands, the death rate of mothers after childbirth fell dramatically. The main breakthrough came in 1865, when British surgeon Joseph Lister began spraying carbolic acid on wounds to kill bacteria, using antiseptic dressings and improving general hygiene.

HOSPITALS AND NURSING

Many public hospitals were founded in the 18th and 19th centuries, but the standard of care was often abysmal. In 1854, during the Crimean War, Englishwoman Florence Nightingale (1820-1910) took 38 nurses to Scutari, where she turned a dirty, rat-infested hospital into a clean, bright area where wounded men could receive medical attention and adequate food. The death rate dropped from 40 to 2 percent; Nightingale earned the nickname "the lady of the lamp." In 1860, she opened the first of many nurse training schools at St. Thomas' Hospital, London, which transformed the status of nursing.

Bestseller *Notes on Nursing* (1860) by Florence Nightingale (left) was published widely and in many languages.

Tribute The sum of £50 000 was raised to start Nightingale's nursing school.

Inoculation Edward Jenner (1749-1823), a country doctor, noted that dairymaids who had contracted cowpox appeared to be immune to the deadlier smallpox. To test his theory, in 1796, Jenner deliberately infected an eight-year-old boy, James Phipps, with cowpox through two scratches on his arm. A few weeks later he inoculated him with smallpox, which proved harmless. He named the practice "vaccination" after the Latin *vaccina* (cowpox). Parliament awarded Jenner grants totaling £30 000 for his discovery.

International recognition Napoleon had a medal struck to honor Edward Jenner (right).

1864 French scientist Louis Pasteur introduces the "germ theory of disease."
1865 Joseph Lister pioneers antiseptic surgery.
1866 Austrian monk Gregor Mendel experiments with crossbreeding pea plants. His results are the basis of genetics.
1867 Uncontrolled cell division is seen as the cause of cancer.

1892 Russian embryologist and immunologist Elie Metchnikoff identifies white blood cells.
1897 English physician Ronald Ross proves that mosquitoes are responsible for spreading the microscopic parasite that causes malaria.
1899 German chemists Felix Hoffman and Heinrich Dreser prepare aspirin from salicylic acid found in willow bark.

1700 — 1800 — 1850 — 1860 — 1890

1753 Scottish naval surgeon James Lind records the benefits of citrus fruit in treating scurvy. Vitamins in food – in this case vitamin C – were not recognized as vital to life until 1906.
1816 French physician René Laënnec invents the stethoscope.

1847 Hungarian obstetrician Ignaz Semmelweis introduces the practice of cleansing the hands and instruments with a solution of chloride of lime before carrying out surgery.
1851 German physicist Hermann von Helmholtz invents the ophthalmoscope to observe the interior of the eye.

1853 French surgeon Charles Gabriel Pravaz and Scottish physician Alexander Wood independently invent the hypodermic syringe.
1854 British physician John Snow discovers that cholera is communicated via contaminated water.

X-rays While experimenting with electric current flow in a cathode ray tube, Wilhelm Röntgen (1845-1923) noticed that, although he could see no light going towards it, a nearby piece of the substance barium platinocyanide glowed whenever the tube was switched on. He found that this "new" form of light – actually a part of the electromagnetic spectrum that is invisible to the naked eye – was able to penetrate most materials and leave an impression on a photographic plate. Armed with this information, he took the first X-ray (of his wife's hand) in 1895. In 1901, he was awarded the first Nobel prize for physics.

Visionary Wilhelm Röntgen's discovery of X-ray photography revolutionized medical diagnosis.

Anesthetics

Until the mid-19th century, surgery was an agonizing process. There were no satisfactory methods of numbing the pain, although various plant extracts and drugs such as opium and cocaine were used to reduce the effects. In many cases, terrified patients were held or tied down while the surgeon speedily wielded his scalpel. In 1846, at Massachusetts General Hospital, dentist William Morgan successfully used inhaled ether vapor to render a patient unconscious while surgeon John Warren painlessly removed a tumor from the patient's neck.

The following year, Scottish doctor James Young Simpson employed chloroform as an anesthetic, and it soon replaced the more unpredictable ether. In 1853, Queen Victoria made anesthetics publicly acceptable when she allowed her physician to give her chloroform during the birth of her eighth child.

In the years that followed, both ether and chloroform were superseded by safer, more controllable anesthetics, some inhaled, others injected, that allowed surgeons the time to carry out longer and more complex operations.

see also
424-25 **Electromagnetism**
460-61 **Modern medicine**

In the 20th century, the approach to the treatment of disease became increasingly scientific. Drugs were created to combat a wide range of complaints by manipulating the molecules of synthetic chemicals. Toward the end of the century, a flourishing biotechnology industry was offering genetic engineering as a means of tackling disease even before it manifested itself. Technological advances made the successful replacement of body parts common.

At the dentist's

Modern technology has brought new, preventative and "painless" techniques to dentistry.

- **Fluoride** Since the mid-1940s, when it was proven that fluoride helped prevent tooth decay, it has been added to drinking water and toothpaste and used to coat children's teeth.
- **Air abrasion** Rather than drilling decay, dentists can now blow it away gently without the need for an anesthetic. The resulting cavity is plugged with safe, long-lasting filler, which is dried and cured (hardened) using ultraviolet light.
- **Ultrasound** Tartar buildup, often the cause of decay, was once removed by scraping. Now ultrasound can break down tartar without damaging the teeth.
- **Camera close-ups** The intra-oral camera, connected to a monitor, gives instant close-up detail of the mouth.

  The Panorex camera produces panoramic views of the teeth and gums, providing information about existing dental work, supporting bone and any signs of infection.
- **Digital radiography** allows immediate X-rays without the wait for X-ray plates to develop.

1901 Austrian physician Karl Landsteiner discovers and names the four blood groups – A, B, O and AB.
1903 Dutch physiologist Willem Einthoven develops the electrocardiogram (EKG). It records the heart's electrical impulses, allowing detection of irregularities in heartbeat.
1906 German surgeon Eduard Zirm is first to transplant a cornea successfully.
1921 Johnson & Johnson start selling the Band-Aid.

1931 German engineer Ernst Ruska designs the first electron microscope. Its level of magnification and detail allow the observation of viruses.
1938 British surgeon John Wiles performs the first artificial hip replacement.

1943 Streptomycin, a cure for tuberculosis and meningitis, is discovered.
1944 American surgeon Alfred Blalock performs the first open-heart operation.

1953 American surgeon John H. Gibbon is the first to use a mechanical heart and blood purifier during surgery.
1953 Cambridge scientists James Watson and Francis Crick, with Rosalind Franklin and Maurice Wilkins, discover the double-helix structure of DNA.

1900 | 1930 | 1940 | 1950

1924 German psychiatrist Hans Berger develops the electroencephalogram (EEG) for recording the electrical activity of the brain through the skull. It is helpful in diagnosing brain disorders.

Alexander Fleming (1881-1955) In 1928, Fleming, a bacteriologist at St. Mary's Hospital in London, noticed an unusual mold on a neglected culture dish in his laboratory. It appeared to be inhibiting the growth of bacteria, so he decided to investigate. He obtained a crude sample of the antibacterial agent in the mold, which he called penicillin.

Fleming's discovery, however, raised little interest. It was 1941 before two biochemists, Howard Florey and Ernst Chain, processed penicillin to create the first antibiotic drug. In 1945, they and Fleming shared the Nobel prize for medicine.

Lifesaver Alexander Fleming in his laboratory in St. Mary's Hospital London.

1954 American physician Jonas Salk develops a polio vaccine.
1957 Scottish obstetrician Ian Donald uses ultrasound scanning to detect problems in an unborn child.

Replacement body parts

Artificial replacements for missing or damaged eyes and limbs have been in existence for at least 1000 years, but until the mid 20th century they were often cumbersome and of limited use. Sophisticated medical technology has brought a range of very effective, high-tech devices.

It is now possible, for example, to restore eyesight using retinal implants. A microchip is placed in the retina and the patient issued with a pair of glasses fitted with a charge-coupled device (CCD) that is able to form images electronically.

Precision grip Touch sensors in the thumb and fingers of artificial hands can monitor how firmly an object is held.

Images collected by the CCD are fired to the microchip via a laser. The microchip interprets them and converts them into a series of electrical pulses, which stimulate the nerve cells behind the retina.

Complex and lightweight artificial legs can mimic the movement characteristics of real legs. This is achieved with the aid of motion detectors linked to pneumatic devices that act in place of the leg muscles to create a natural flowing movement.

Sensors in artificial arms and hands can pick up nerve impulses from the body and use them to trigger movement in the artificial limb.

DRUG DELIVERY SYSTEMS

Until recently, drugs were administered either through the mouth (orally) or by injection. Advances in the development of drug delivery systems mean that this no longer has to be.

- **Slow-release patches** These consist of a thin membrane containing a dose of the drug – usually in the form of a gel – and a protective coating. They are held next to the skin by adhesive. The drug passes through the membrane at a steady rate and is released into the patient's body through the skin. The rate of absorption is determined by the nature of the membrane.
- **Slow-release capsule** The capsule, which is sheathed in a thin, permeable membrane, is inserted under the skin. The drug, which is usually suspended in a gel, gradually passes through the membrane and into the bloodstream.
- **Injection gun** This uses a microcylinder of compressed helium to eject a drug at a speed such that it passes through the outer skin layers and into the bloodstream without puncturing. Unlike hypodermic needles, a single injection gun can be used on any number of people with no risk of transmitting disease.

Computer-designed drugs

Computers allow scientists to design a drug using a mathematical model of its molecular structure and of the chemicals it has to react with in the body. The computer-designed molecules will "fit" into the hollow receptor regions of the body's natural chemicals. Once a fit has been found, the drug is synthesized and then tested on living tissue before use.

On-screen treatment By the end of the 20th century, new drugs were being developed by scientists using complex computer software.

1961 American physician Albert Sabin develops a polio vaccine that can be administered orally.

1967 British electrical engineer Godfrey Hounsfield develops the computerized axial tomography (CAT) scanner.

1973 American biochemists Herbert Boyer and Stanley Cohen develop a technique for the cloning of DNA.

1974 American physician Raymond Damadian invents the MRI (magnetic resonance imaging) scanner.

1995 A patent is issued for a blood substitute that increases oxygen levels in the brain during cardiac surgery.

2000 Drugs are routinely designed by computer.

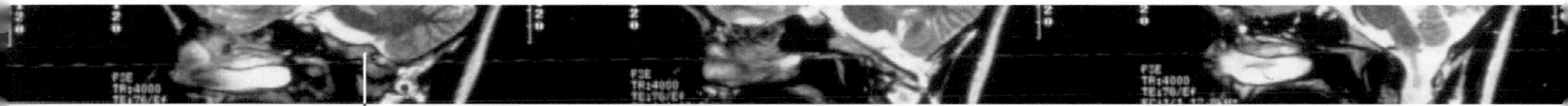

1960 1970 1990 2000

Christiaan Barnard (1922-2001) The first human heart transplant took place at Cape Town's Groote Schuur Hospital on December 3, 1967. Cardiac surgeon Christiaan Barnard transferred the heart of a 25-year-old woman into the body of 55-year-old Louis Washkansky. The patient survived for 18 days.

Undeterred, Barnard carried out a second transplant on January 2, 1968. This time the recipient lived for 563 days after the operation.

New techniques have increased success rates dramatically. By 2000, there had been over 50 000 transplants, with patients leading active lives more than ten years after surgery.

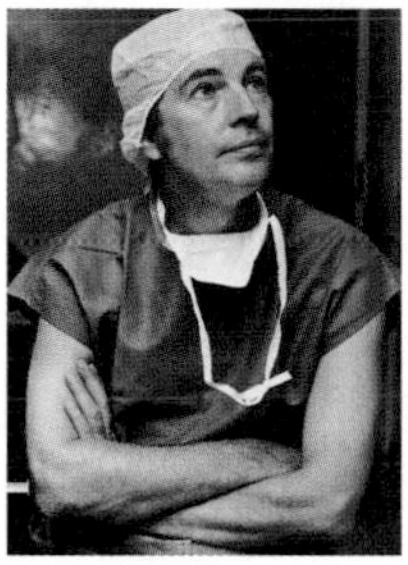

Pioneer The charismatic, good-looking Barnard won worldwide fame.

Minimal invasion

Some surgery can be performed via a tube called an endoscope, without making large cuts into the body. It is inserted into a tiny "keyhole" incision or a natural orifice.

The endoscopic tube contains control wires and a set of optical fibers, which relay images to a monitor.

Surgery is carried out using specially adapted miniature tools that are passed down a central channel in the endoscope.

The bronchoscope (for chest and throat operations), arthroscope (for joints) and laparoscope (for abdomen) are all forms of endoscope.

LASER SURGERY

The laser is replacing the scalpel in many areas of surgery, particularly in optical surgery, in which absolute precision is required. Unlike a scalpel, which tears through flesh leaving blood vessels exposed and leaking, the laser minimizes bleeding.

- The laser cuts by generating heat in body tissues.
- This heat is sufficient to seal (cauterize) severed blood vessels and so keeps bleeding to a minimum.
- In addition to acting as a scalpel, the heat from the laser can also be used to "weld" delicate body parts, such as detached retinas, back together.

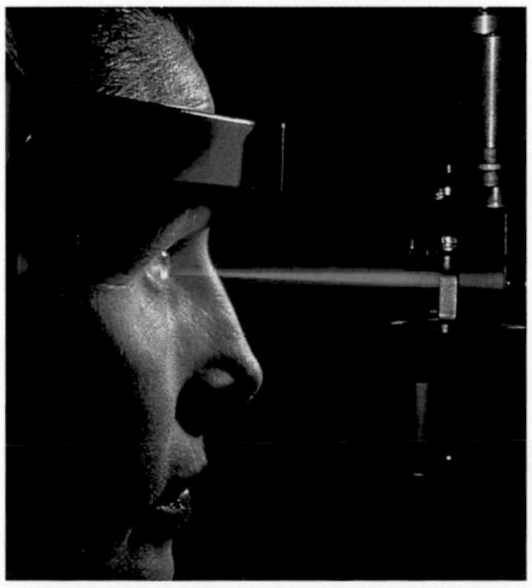

Painless Using a laser to perform eye surgery is quick and safe and requires no anesthetic.

see also
448-51 **Computers**
458-59 **Origins of medicine**

 From the pyramids of Egypt to the soaring structures of the 20th century

The earliest buildings used naturally occurring materials such as timber, mud and stone. The introduction of man-made bricks, terracotta and – in Roman times – durable cement and concrete enabled builders to become far more inventive. Concrete was rediscovered less than 250 years ago, and was combined with steel for strength in the 19th century. The development of high-tech materials in the 20th century allowed for even taller and wider buildings.

SPANNING THE GAP

Architects have developed a range of building methods to produce wide interior spaces uncluttered by supports.

- **Cantilever** This is a beam or girder supported at one end only. It relies on the intrinsic rigidity of materials such as reinforced and prestressed concrete.
- **Dome** A dome can be either hemispherical or pointed. If the base is not circular, triangular corner sections (pendentives) are needed.
- **Geodesic dome** Interlocking lightweight metal or plastic tubes form a rigid, geometric framework.
- **Gothic arch** The pointed Gothic arch can span much wider spaces than the round arch. Its form is such that great lateral (sideways) forces from the weight of the arch must be braced with external buttresses. These were solid at first, but later, flying (hollowed) buttresses were developed.
- **Post and lintel** A horizontal beam (lintel) rests on vertical columns (posts). Only a limited space can be spanned by this method without the need for intermediate columns. Timber and steel-framed construction are modern versions of the system.
- **Ridgepole and rafters** A ridgepole is the timber along the ridge of a roof to which the rafters are attached. Together, they form a tent-like pitched roof.
- **Round arch** The earliest true arch is made of stone or concrete and built on a timber framework that is later removed. The load is transferred to columns strong enough to resist sideways forces.

c. 6000 B.C. Sun-dried bricks are used for building in the Middle East.

c. 3500 B.C. Fired bricks are first used in the Middle East.

c. 2650-2500 B.C. The pyramids are built in Egypt. The earliest is the Step Pyramid of Djoser (above) at Saqqara.

From c. 1500 B.C. The post-and-lintel system is used for building huge Egyptian temples.

5th century B.C. The Royal Palace in Persepolis (Persia) and the Parthenon (Athens) are the world's largest post-and-lintel buildings.

4th century B.C. The Romans first use the rounded masonry arch.

3rd-2nd centuries B.C. The Romans extend the round arch to form barrel vaulting.

3rd century B.C. The Romans make hydraulic cement from volcanic silica dust (pozzolana) and lime.

c. 250 B.C. The Pharos (lighthouse) of Alexandria, Egypt, is built. It may have stood over 122 m (400 ft) high.

121 B.C. The platform of the Roman temple of Concord is built using concrete. It survives to this day and is the oldest known Roman concrete structure.

118-28 A.D. Concrete is used to build the dome of the Pantheon in Rome, which has a diameter of 43 m (141 ft).

7000 B.C. · 6000 B.C. · 5000 B.C. · 4000 B.C. · 3000 B.C. · 2000 B.C. · 1000 B.C. · 600 B.C. · 550 B.C. · 500 B.C. · 450 B.C. · 400 B.C. · 350 B.C. · 300 B.C. · 250 B.C. · 150 B.C. · 100 B.C. · 50 B.C. · 0 · 50 A.D. · 100 A.D.

WAYS TO BUILD HIGH

With increasing desire to build taller and taller buildings, architects have had to devise new methods of construction. Traditional load-bearing external walls have been replaced by metal frames and concrete cores.

- **Skeleton frame** The oldest and best-known structure for a tall building comprises a frame made from steel girders, reinforced concrete, or steel tubes. These support the floors and "curtain" walling, which is hung around the frame. Sometimes diagonal cross-bracing girders are used to strengthen the structure.
- **Cable-hung** This modern innovation comprises a concrete core (containing lifts and other services) and floor slabs. Each floor is supported by the core and by cables hanging from floor to floor around the perimeter. The slabs may be cast at ground level and hoisted into position.
- A hybrid version may use a **tubular steel frame** with triangular steel trusses placed at regular intervals, from which "hangers" are suspended to support the floors.

The Pantheon The dome of Rome's temple to the gods is based on a sphere: The height of the walls is equal to the radius of the dome.

Great Pyramid Giza's Great Pyramid stands 137 m (450 ft) high and contains about 2.3 million blocks of stone.

The Parthenon Athens' great temple was the supreme example of the simple Doric style in Greek architecture.

Hagia Sophia Istanbul's Hagia Sophia took just six years to build. The dome is 30 m (100 ft) in diameter.

On solid foundations

Foundations have to support a building's entire weight – which may run to many millions of metric tons. The design depends on the size of the building and the nature of the ground.

Footings (slabs of reinforced concrete) are placed beyond the building's perimeter to spread the load. Cylindrical piers are used to transmit the load to solid bedrock; in softer ground, steel or concrete piles may be driven down to find firm soil or rock.

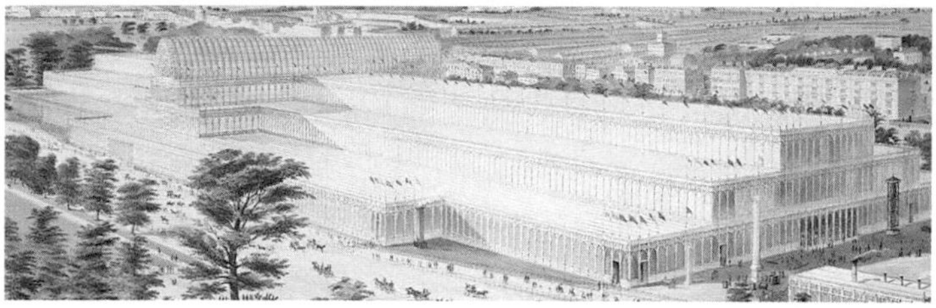

Palace of industry Sir Joseph Paxton's Crystal Palace (1851) was the first example of prefabrication: The parts were factory-made and assembled on site.

Scaling new heights Chicago's metal-framed Home Insurance building set the style for high-rise building.

532-37 Hagla Sophia in Constantinople (Istanbul) is built. The dome has a square base with triangular vaulted corners, known as pendentives.

1418-36 The Duomo – the dome of Florence Cathedral – is constructed.

1845 A reliable process is developed for producing Portland cement.

c. 1850 French gardener Joseph Monier invents reinforced concrete with steel rods inserted for strength.

1885 The first steel-framed skyscraper, the ten-story Home Insurance Building in Chicago, is constructed.

1889 The Eiffel Tower is erected in Paris. At 300 m (984 ft), it is the tallest structure in the world.

1973 The World Trade Center, at 411 m (1349 ft), overtakes the Empire State Building.

1974 Chicago's Sears Tower sets a new height record: 443 m (1454 ft).

1976 The 553 m (1815 ft) CN Tower in Toronto (left) tops the world's buildings. Glass-fronted elevators transport visitors to the viewing platforms.

200 500 1000 1400 1600 1700 1750 1800 1825 1850 1875 1900 1910 1920 1930 1940 1950 1960 1970 1980 1990 2000

1144 In France, the abbey of Saint-Denis is the first building in the Gothic style, with pointed arches and buttresses.

c. 1175 Flying buttresses are first used to support Gothic arches.

1653 The Taj Mahal is built in Agra, India.

1756 English engineer John Smeaton rediscovers hydraulic cement, first invented by the Romans.

1851 Made from prefabricated iron and glass, the vast Crystal Palace is built for the Great Exhibition in London.

1852 In the US, Elisha Otis invents the passenger lift, making skyscrapers feasible.

1855 The pneumatic Bessemer process dramatically increases steel production.

1922 German engineer Walter Bauersfeld invents the geodesic dome. It is later developed and popularized by Buckminster Fuller in the US.

1931 The Empire State Building is constructed in New York. It remained the world's tallest building for more than 40 years rising to 381 m (1250 ft).

1996 The 452 m (1483 ft) twin Petronas Towers in Kuala Lumpur, Malaysia, overtake the Sears Tower as the world's tallest inhabited building.

1999 The Millennium Dome is completed in London. With a diameter of 320 m (1050 ft), it is the world's biggest dome.

2001 A devastating terrorist attack on the World Trade Center takes place on 11th September. The subsequent collapse of the twin towers, the world's 3rd tallest inhabited building, changes the Manhattan skyline forever.

Spreading the light

Large modern buildings are designed with systems that channel natural light to the interior. This saves energy as well as improving the quality of the environment within the building.

One method uses mirrored "sun scoops," which reflect light inward toward ceiling reflectors on the side walls. A more sophisticated version uses a computer-controlled heliostat that tracks the Sun and reflects its light down a light guide in a central service shaft.

Mirrors and specially designed light extractors channel the light to where it is wanted. Light extractors are plastic tubes with a molded "microprism" on the outside, rather like the prismatic diffusers commonly used in fluorescent-tube lights.

Eden Project This geodesic conservatory, completed in 2001, was built in a former china clay pit in Cornwall, England. It is 200 m (650 ft) long and 45 m (145 ft) high.

CN Tower Built to transmit TV and radio signals, the CN Tower still tops the world's highest inhabited buildings.

The Eiffel Tower The world-famous Parisian landmark was built from 7620 metric tons of iron.

The Petronas Towers The record-breaking Malaysian towers will be topped when the Shanghai World Financial Center is completed in 2004.

see also

326-27 **Architecture**

464-65 **Civil engineering**

Technological advances and new materials have allowed increasingly ambitious structures. These include Japan's Akashi-Kaikyo Bridge, the world's longest suspension bridge, with a span of nearly 2 km (1¼ miles), and the Channel Tunnel, fulfilling a centuries-old dream of linking Britain with mainland Europe. They are two milestones along a road that began with the ancient Egyptians, the first people to show civil engineering skills with the building of a dam across the Nile in 3000 B.C.

TUNNELING

A fire lit against a tunnel face would be enough to crack any solid rock and allow progress in short stages. Later, holes were drilled and packed with explosives to break up the rock. A major advance for tunnelling through soft earth or rock came in 1815 with the invention of the tunneling shield. It consisted of a protective tubular metal structure pushed forward by jacks. As it was moved, a tunnel lining – originally bricks or cast-iron sections, later reinforced concrete – was installed behind it.

The same basic system is used today, such as for the Channel Tunnel project (left), but the digging is done by a tunnel-boring machine, which looks like a giant drill with a rotating cutter head and hard tungsten carbide teeth. Other types of automatic equipment remove the spoil, and install lining segments.

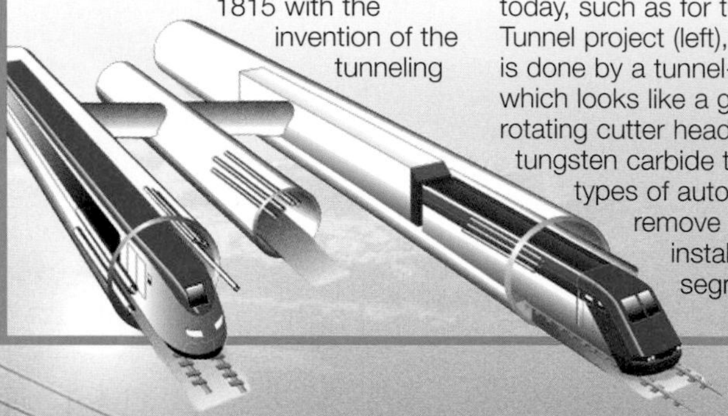

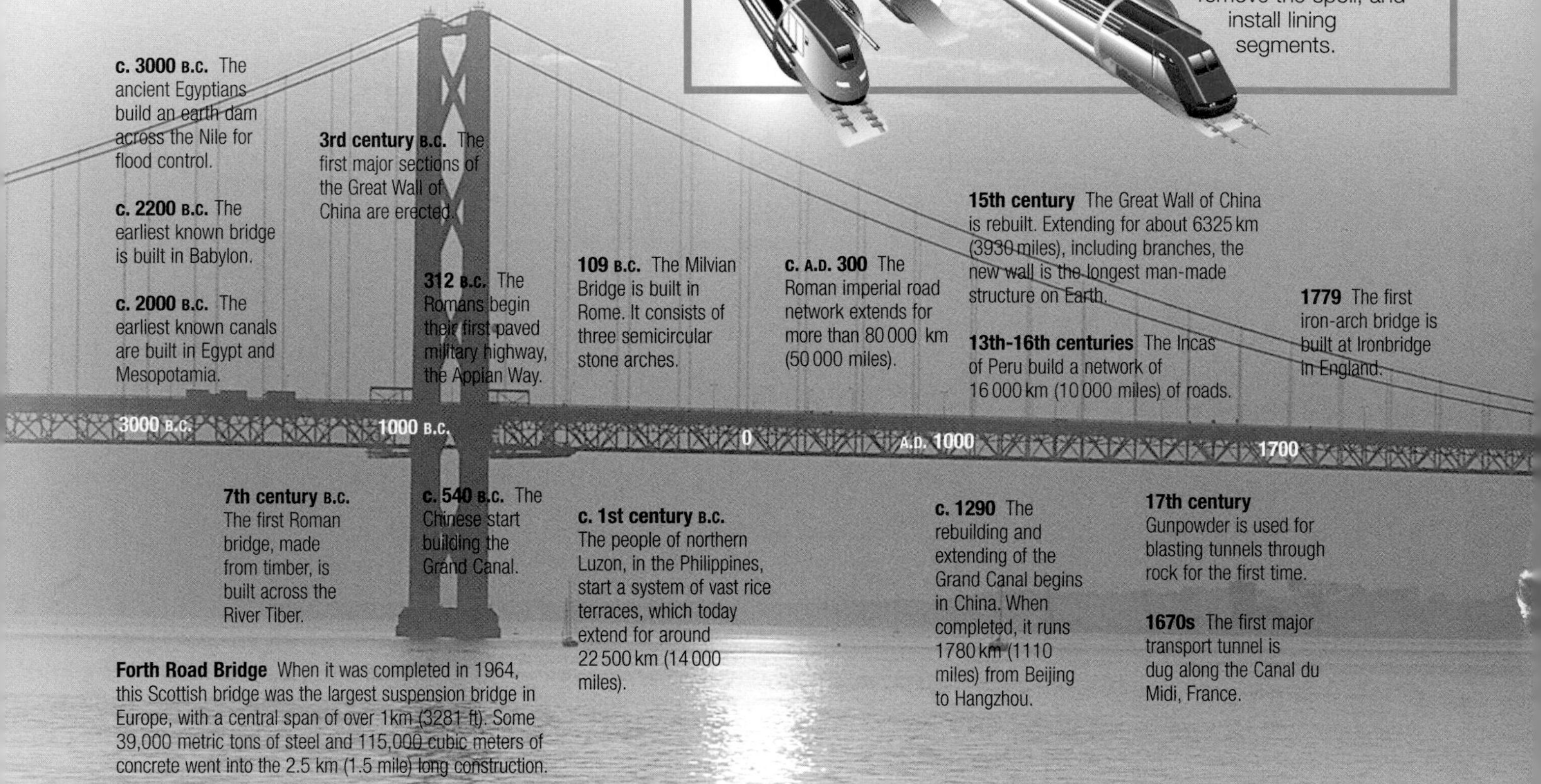

c. 3000 B.C. The ancient Egyptians build an earth dam across the Nile for flood control.

c. 2200 B.C. The earliest known bridge is built in Babylon.

c. 2000 B.C. The earliest known canals are built in Egypt and Mesopotamia.

7th century B.C. The first Roman bridge, made from timber, is built across the River Tiber.

3rd century B.C. The first major sections of the Great Wall of China are erected.

312 B.C. The Romans begin their first paved military highway, the Appian Way.

c. 540 B.C. The Chinese start building the Grand Canal.

109 B.C. The Milvian Bridge is built in Rome. It consists of three semicircular stone arches.

c. 1st century B.C. The people of northern Luzon, in the Philippines, start a system of vast rice terraces, which today extend for around 22 500 km (14 000 miles).

c. A.D. 300 The Roman imperial road network extends for more than 80 000 km (50 000 miles).

15th century The Great Wall of China is rebuilt. Extending for about 6325 km (3930 miles), including branches, the new wall is the longest man-made structure on Earth.

13th-16th centuries The Incas of Peru build a network of 16 000 km (10 000 miles) of roads.

c. 1290 The rebuilding and extending of the Grand Canal begins in China. When completed, it runs 1780 km (1110 miles) from Beijing to Hangzhou.

17th century Gunpowder is used for blasting tunnels through rock for the first time.

1670s The first major transport tunnel is dug along the Canal du Midi, France.

1779 The first iron-arch bridge is built at Ironbridge in England.

Forth Road Bridge When it was completed in 1964, this Scottish bridge was the largest suspension bridge in Europe, with a central span of over 1 km (3281 ft). Some 39,000 metric tons of steel and 115,000 cubic meters of concrete went into the 2.5 km (1.5 mile) long construction.

Building materials

Concrete and steel are the materials that, above all others, have made possible large-scale modern civil engineering works. Concrete is strongest in compression, and steel is strongest under tension. Combining them in reinforced concrete has the advantages of both. In prestressed concrete, stretched steel cables embedded in the wet concrete are released after setting. Other materials used to reinforce concrete include glass or fibers embedded in it to add strength and plastic reinforcing rods used in place of steel.

DAMS AND BARRIERS

Most big dams have a compacted core of stones or earth, usually faced with concrete and stabilized by their own great weight. Sometimes they are buttressed on the downstream side to help to withstand the weight of the water.

Smaller ones may be built of solid concrete with steel reinforcing rods or cables. In a narrow canyon, a dam is curved outwards on the upstream side, arched against the pressure of the water. The curvature pushes much of the water pressure away from the dam itself and onto the canyon walls.

A variation is the temporary dam, or barrier, such as the one across the Thames in London (below), which, at 520 m (1705 ft), is the world's longest movable tidal barrier. Underwater gates can be raised to deal with any sudden surges of water from the sea and then lowered again to allow ships to pass.

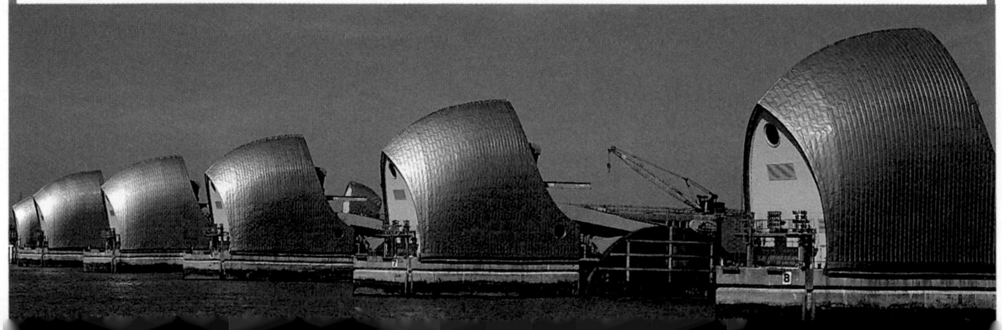

Road construction

Roman roads were built primarily for infantry, not vehicles, and often used layers of rammed earth and gravel, with a top layer of flat stones to give the soldiers a firm footing.

The next major advance came 1500 years later with French engineer Pierre Trésaguet and Scottish engineers John McAdam and Thomas Telford. They used layers of compacted graded stones, with a camber (curved surface) to aid drainage. Telford preferred a surface of flat stones, but McAdam's compacted small broken stones proved best – particularly when he later bonded them with tar to make tarmacadam, or "tarmac."

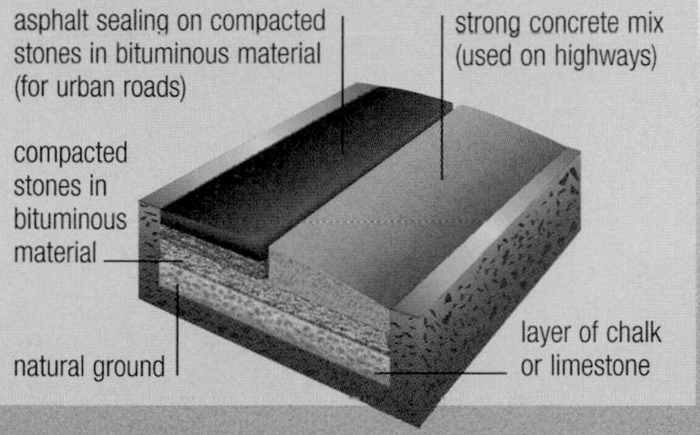

Airport on water
Runway space is at a premium in a densely populated mountainous country such as Japan. One solution is to build island airports, such as Nagasaki airport, opened in 1975 and built on an artificially enlarged island.

see also

386-95 **Transportation**
406-9 **Renewable energy**
462-63 **Building**
474 **Signs and wonders**

c. 1815 Scottish engineers John McAdam and Thomas Telford devise methods for building durable roads.

1826 Thomas Telford builds the first iron suspension bridge across the Menai Straits in Wales.

1800

1825-43 French-born engineer Marc Brunel invents the tunneling shield, used to dig the first rail tunnel under the River Thames.

1869 The Suez Canal opens. It is 190 km (118 miles) in length.

1874 The first steel-arch bridge is built at St. Louis, Missouri.

1850

1883 The Brooklyn Bridge, the first suspension bridge using steel cables, is built in New York.

1892 Frenchman François Hennebique invents prestressed concrete.

1906-32 The Dutch build a 32 km (20 mile) dyke as part of a plan to drain the Zuider Zee.

1914 The Panama Canal is opened. It is 82 km (51 miles) long and has 12 locks to traverse the mountains.

1932 The Sydney Harbour Bridge is built.

1936 The Hoover Dam on the border of Arizona and Nevada is built.

1900

1937 The Golden Gate Bridge is built in San Francisco. Its main span is 1280 m (4200 ft).

1962 The Grand Dixence Dam is built in Switzerland. It becomes the world's highest concrete dam.

1964 The Volga-Baltic Canal is constructed in Russia; it is 850 km (528 miles) long.

1969 The second Lake Pontchartrain Causeway in Louisiana becomes the longest multispan bridge in the world, at 38 km (24 miles).

1950

1984 The Thames Flood Barrier is built in London.

1988 The Seikan railroad tunnel in Japan is completed. It is the world's longest at 54 km (34 miles).

1994 The Channel Tunnel between France and Britain is completed. It is the world's longest underwater tunnel at 50 km (31 miles).

1998 The Akashi-Kaikyo Bridge in Japan becomes the world's longest suspension bridge, with a main span of 1990 m (6529 ft).

2000

2000 The Øresund Bridge, a double-decker road and rail link joining Denmark and Sweden, becomes the world's longest cable-stayed bridge at 1092 m (3583 ft) long.

Bridge construction

Arch bridge

Trussed arch bridge

Cantilever bridge

Suspension bridge

Bridge design has to take into account such factors as the gap to be spanned, the nature of the land underneath and on either side, and the type and amount of traffic it is intended to carry. There are seven main types:

Beam This is the simplest of all bridge designs, in which the deck rests on piers at either end. Nowadays, the beam is made of reinforced concrete or steel girders.

Arch On an arch bridge, a deck formed of a rigid beam rests on a curved arch.

Bowstring arch An arch, usually made of steel girders, rises above the deck beam, part or all of which is supported by hangers extending down from the arch.

Trussed arch bridge On a trussed arch bridge, the deck beam is supported by a framework of bars that are arranged in a crisscross pattern for rigidity.

Cantilever This is a more complex version of a trussed bridge. There are usually two diamond-shaped rigid trusses. Each is supported at its center on a pier and anchored to the shore at one end. Their other ends are linked by a short beam.

Suspension This type of bridge can span longer distances than any other – up to 2000 m (7000 ft). The piers are extended upward to form towers. Heavy, multistrand suspension cables, anchored firmly to the banks and passing over the top of the towers, support the deck with vertical hangers.

Cable-stayed This is similar to the suspension bridge, except that regularly spaced individual steel cables run directly from the towers to the deck.

Ready reference

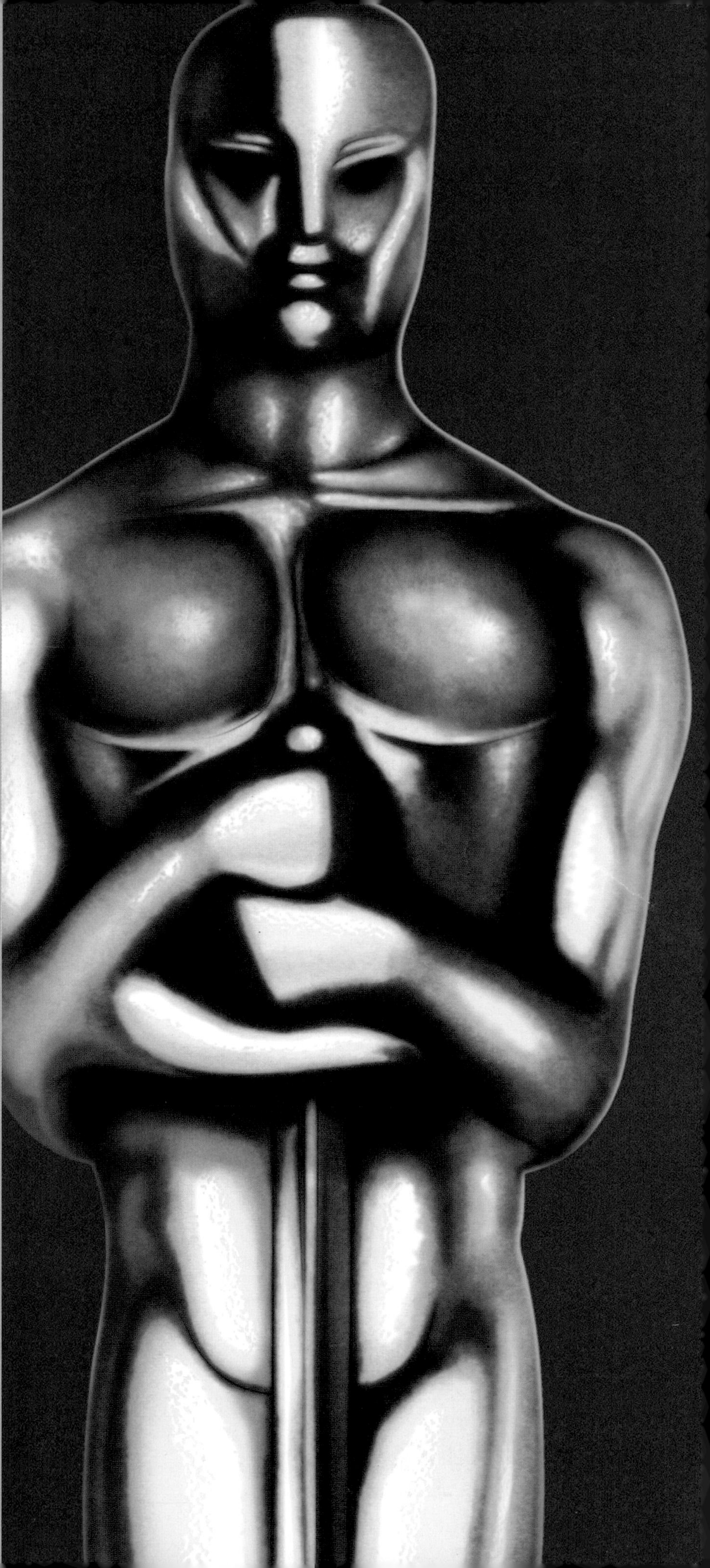

Ready reference

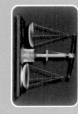

The Academy Awards (Oscars)

The Academy of Motion Picture Arts and Sciences first presented awards in 1929. Awards are given in March for movies released in the previous year. The year given is when the movie was released, not when it won the award.

Best picture

1927-28 *Wings*
1928-29 *Broadway Melody*
1929-30 *All Quiet on the Western Front*
1930-31 *Cimarron*
1931-32 *Grand Hotel*
1932-33 *Cavalcade*
1934 *It Happened One Night*
1935 *Mutiny on the Bounty*
1936 *The Great Ziegfeld*
1937 *The Life of Emile Zola*
1938 *You Can't Take It With You*
1939 *Gone With the Wind*
1940 *Rebecca*
1941 *How Green Was My Valley*
1942 *Mrs. Miniver*
1943 *Casablanca*
1944 *Going My Way*
1945 *The Lost Weekend*
1946 *The Best Years of Our Lives*
1947 *Gentlemen's Agreement*
1948 *Hamlet*
1949 *All the King's Men*
1950 *All About Eve*
1951 *An American in Paris*
1952 *The Greatest Show on Earth*
1953 *From Here to Eternity*
1954 *On the Waterfront*
1955 *Marty*
1956 *Around the World in 80 Days*
1957 *The Bridge on the River Kwai*
1958 *Gigi*
1959 *Ben Hur*
1960 *The Apartment*
1961 *West Side Story*
1962 *Lawrence of Arabia*
1963 *Tom Jones*
1964 *My Fair Lady*
1965 *The Sound of Music*
1966 *A Man for All Seasons*
1967 *In the Heat of the Night*
1968 *Oliver!*
1969 *Midnight Cowboy*
1970 *Patton*
1971 *The French Connection*
1972 *The Godfather*
1973 *The Sting*
1974 *The Godfather: Part II*
1975 *One Flew Over the Cuckoo's Nest*
1976 *Rocky*
1977 *Annie Hall*
1978 *The Deer Hunter*
1979 *Kramer vs Kramer*
1980 *Ordinary People*
1981 *Chariots of Fire*
1982 *Gandhi*
1983 *Terms of Endearment*
1984 *Amadeus*
1985 *Out of Africa*
1986 *Platoon*
1987 *The Last Emperor*
1988 *Rain Man*
1989 *Driving Miss Daisy*
1990 *Dances With Wolves*
1991 *The Silence of the Lambs*
1992 *Unforgiven*
1993 *Schindler's List*
1994 *Forrest Gump*
1995 *Braveheart*
1996 *The English Patient*
1997 *Titanic*
1998 *Shakespeare in Love*
1999 *American Beauty*
2000 *Gladiator*
2001 *A Beautiful Mind*
2002 *Chicago*

Best actor

1927-28 Emil Jannings *(The Last Command)*
1928-29 Warner Baxter *(In Old Arizona)*
1929-30 George Arliss *(Disraeli)*
1930-31 Lionel Barrymore *(A Free Soul)*
Fredric March *(The Royal Family of Broadway)*
1931-32 Wallace Beery *(The Champ)*
Fredric March *(Dr. Jekyll and Mr. Hyde)*
1932-33 Charles Laughton *(The Private Life of Henry VIII)*
1934 Clark Gable *(It Happened One Night)*
1935 Victor McLaglen *(The Informer)*
1936 Paul Muni *(The Story of Louis Pasteur)*
1937 Spencer Tracy *(Captain Courageous)*
1938 Spencer Tracy *(Boys' Town)*
1939 Robert Donat *(Goodbye, Mr. Chips)*
1940 James Stewart *(The Philadelphia Story)*
1941 Gary Cooper *(Sergeant York)*
1942 James Cagney *(Yankee Doodle Dandy)*
1943 Paul Lucas *(Watch on the Rhine)*
1944 Bing Crosby *(Going My Way)*
1945 Ray Milland *(The Lost Weekend)*
1946 Fredric March *(The Best Years of Our Lives)*
1947 Ronald Colman *(A Double Life)*
1948 Laurence Olivier *(Hamlet)*
1949 Broderick Crawford *(All the King's Men)*
1950 Jose Ferrar *(Cyrano de Bergerac)*
1951 Humphrey Bogart *(The African Queen)*
1952 Gary Cooper *(High Noon)*
1953 William Holden *(Stalag 17)*
1954 Marlon Brando *(On the Waterfront)*
1955 Ernest Borgnine *(Marty)*
1956 Yul Brynner *(The King and I)*
1957 Alec Guinness *(The Bridge on the River Kwai)*
1958 David Niven *(Separate Tables)*
1959 Charlton Heston *(Ben Hur)*
1960 Burt Lancaster *(Elmer Gantry)*
1961 Maximilian Schell *(Judgment at Nuremberg)*
1962 Gregory Peck *(To Kill a Mockingbird)*
1963 Sydney Poitier *(Lilies of the Field)*
1964 Rex Harrison *(My Fair Lady)*
1965 Lee Marvin *(Cat Ballou)*
1966 Paul Scofield *(A Man for All Seasons)*
1967 Rod Steiger *(In the Heat of the Night)*
1968 Cliff Robertson *(Charly)*
1969 John Wayne *(True Grit)*
1970 George C. Scott *(Patton)*
1971 Gene Hackman *(The French Connection)*
1972 Marlon Brando *(The Godfather)*
1973 Jack Lemmon *(Save the Tiger)*
1974 Art Carney *(Harry and Tonto)*
1975 Jack Nicholson *(One Flew Over the Cuckoo's Nest)*
1976 Peter Finch *(Network)*
1977 Richard Dreyfuss *(The Goodbye Girl)*
1978 Jon Voight *(Coming Home)*
1979 Dustin Hoffman *(Kramer vs Kramer)*
1980 Robert De Niro *(Raging Bull)*
1981 Henry Fonda *(On Golden Pond)*
1982 Ben Kingsley *(Gandhi)*
1983 Robert Duvall *(Tender Mercies)*
1984 F. Murray Abraham *(Amadeus)*
1985 William Hurt *(Kiss of the Spider Woman)*
1986 Paul Newman *(The Color of Money)*
1987 Michael Douglas *(Wall Street)*
1988 Dustin Hoffman *(Rain Man)*
1989 Daniel Day Lewis *(My Left Foot)*
1990 Jeremy Irons *(Reversal of Fortune)*
1991 Anthony Hopkins *(The Silence of the Lambs)*
1992 Al Pacino *(Scent of a Woman)*
1993 Tom Hanks *(Philadelphia)*
1994 Tom Hanks *(Forrest Gump)*
1995 Nicholas Cage *(Leaving Las Vegas)*
1996 Geoffrey Rush *(Shine)*
1997 Jack Nicholson *(As Good As It Gets)*
1998 Roberto Benigni *(Life is Beautiful)*
1999 Kevin Spacey *(American Beauty)*
2000 Russell Crowe *(Gladiator)*
2001 Denzel Washington *(Training Day)*
2002 Adrien Brody *(The Pianist)*

Best actress

1927-28 Janet Gaynor *(Seventh Heaven)*
1928-29 Mary Pickford *(Coquette)*
1929-30 Norma Shearer *(The Divorcee)*
1930-31 Marie Dressler *(Min and Bill)*
1931-32 Helen Hayes *(The Sin of Madelon Claudet)*
1932-33 Katharine Hepburn *(Morning Glory)*
1934 Claudette Colbert *(It Happened One Night)*
1935 Bette Davis *(Dangerous)*
1936 Luise Rainer *(The Great Ziegfeld)*
1937 Luise Rainer *(The Good Earth)*
1938 Bette Davis *(Jezebel)*
1939 Vivien Leigh *(Gone With the Wind)*
1940 Ginger Rogers *(Kitty Foyle)*
1941 Joan Fontaine *(Suspicion)*
1942 Greer Garson *(Mrs. Miniver)*
1943 Jennifer Jones *(The Song of Bernadette)*
1944 Ingrid Bergman *(Gaslight)*
1945 Joan Crawford *(Mildred Pierce)*
1946 Olivia de Havilland *(To Each His Own)*
1947 Loretta Young *(The Farmer's Daughter)*
1948 Jane Wyman *(Johnny Belinda)*
1949 Olivia de Havilland *(The Heiress)*
1950 Judy Holliday *(Born Yesterday)*
1951 Vivien Leigh *(A Streetcar Named Desire)*
1952 Shirley Booth *(Come Back, Little Sheba)*
1953 Audrey Hepburn *(Roman Holiday)*
1954 Grace Kelly *(The Country Girl)*
1955 Anna Magnani *(The Rose Tattoo)*
1956 Ingrid Bergman *(Anastasia)*
1957 Joanne Woodward *(The Three Faces of Eve)*
1958 Susan Hayward *(I Want to Live)*
1959 Simone Signoret *(Room at the Top)*
1960 Elizabeth Taylor *(Butterfield 8)*
1961 Sophia Loren *(Two Women)*
1962 Anne Bancroft *(The Miracle Worker)*
1963 Patricia Neal *(Hud)*
1964 Julie Andrews *(Mary Poppins)*
1965 Julie Christie *(Darling)*
1966 Elizabeth Taylor *(Who's Afraid of Virginia Wolf?)*
1967 Katharine Hepburn *(Guess Who's Coming to Dinner)*
1968 Katharine Hepburn *(The Lion in Winter)*
1969 Maggie Smith *(The Prime of Miss Jean Brodie)*
1970 Glenda Jackson *(Women in Love)*
1971 Jane Fonda *(Klute)*
1972 Liza Minnelli *(Cabaret)*
1973 Glenda Jackson *(A Touch of Class)*
1974 Ellen Burstyn *(Alice Doesn't Live Here Anymore)*
1975 Louise Fletcher *(One Flew Over the Cuckoo's Nest)*
1976 Faye Dunaway *(Network)*
1977 Diane Keaton *(Annie Hall)*
1978 Jane Fonda *(Coming Home)*
1979 Sally Field *(Norma Rae)*
1980 Sissy Spacek *(Coal Miner's Daughter)*
1981 Katharine Hepburn *(On Golden Pond)*
1982 Meryl Streep *(Sophie's Choice)*
1983 Shirley MacLaine *(Terms of Endearment)*
1984 Sally Field *(Places in the Heart)*
1985 Geraldine Page *(The Trip to Bountiful)*
1986 Marlee Matlin *(Children of a Lesser God)*
1987 Cher *(Moonstruck)*
1988 Jodie Foster *(The Accused)*
1989 Jessica Tandy *(Driving Miss Daisy)*
1990 Kathy Bates *(Misery)*
1991 Jodie Foster *(The Silence of the Lambs)*
1992 Emma Thompson *(Howard's End)*
1993 Holly Hunter *(The Piano)*
1994 Jessica Lange *(Blue Sky)*
1995 Susan Sarandon *(Dead Man Walking)*
1996 Frances McDormand *(Fargo)*
1997 Helen Hunt *(As Good As It Gets)*
1998 Gwyneth Paltrow *(Shakespeare in Love)*
1999 Hilary Swank *(Boys Don't Cry)*
2000 Julia Roberts *(Erin Brockovich)*
2001 Halle Berry *(Monster's Ball)*
2002 Nicole Kidman *(The Hours)*

The prizes for peace and literature

Alfred Nobel, the Swedish inventor of dynamite, left most of his fortune to found the Nobel prizes. These are awarded to those who have "conferred the greatest benefit on mankind" and for a body of work rather than a single work. There are six categories: physics, chemistry, economics, physiology or medicine, literature and peace. The awards are presented each December; the peace prize in Oslo, Norway and the rest in Stockholm, Sweden. The prizes are worth about $1 million apiece.

Nobel Peace Prize

1901 Jean Henri Dunant *(Switzerland)*
Frederic Passy *(France)*
1902 Elie Ducommun *(Switzerland)*
Charles Albert Gobat *(Switzerland)*
1903 Sir William Randal Cremer *(UK)*
1904 Institut de Droit International *(Belgium)*
1905 Baroness Bertha von Suttner *(Austria)*
1906 Theodore Roosevelt *(US)*
1907 Ernesto Moneta *(Italy)*
Louis Renault *(France)*
1908 Klas Arnoldson *(Sweden)*
Fredrik Bajer *(Denmark)*
1909 Auguste Beernaert *(Belgium)*
Paul d'Estournelles de Constant *(France)*
1910 Bureau International Permanent de la Paix *(Switzerland)*
1911 Tobias Asser *(Netherlands)*
Alfred Fried *(Austria)*
1912 No award
1913 Elihu Root *(US)*
Henri la Fontaine *(Belgium)*
1914-16 No award
1917 Comité International de la Croix-Rouge (Red Cross; *Switzerland)*
1918 No award
1919 Woodrow Wilson *(US)*
1920 Leon Bourgeois *(France)*
1921 Karl Branting *(Sweden)*
Christian Lange *(Norway)*
1922 Fridtjof Nansen *(Norway)*
1923-24 No award
1925 Joseph Chamberlain *(UK)*
Charles Dawes *(US)*
1926 Aristide Briand *(France)*
Gustav Stresemann *(Germany)*
1927 Ferdinand Buisson *(France)*
Ludwig Quidde *(Germany)*
1928 No award
1929 Frank Kellogg *(US)*
1930 Lars Söderblom *(Sweden)*
1931 Jane Addams *(US)*
Nicholas Murray Butler *(US)*
1932 No award
1933 Sir Norman Angell *(UK)*
1934 Arthur Henderson *(UK)*
1935 Carl von Ossietzky *(Germany)*
1936 Carlos Saavedra Lamas *(Argentina)*
1937 Viscount Cecil of Chelwood *(UK)*
1938 Office International Nansen pour les Refugiés *(Switzerland)*
1939-43 No award
1944 Comité International de la Croix-Rouge (Red Cross; *Switzerland)*
1945 Cordell Hull *(US)*
1946 Emily Greene Balch *(US)*
John Raleigh Mott *(US)*
1947 The Friends Service Council *(UK)*
The American Friends Service Committee *(US)*
1948 No award
1949 Lord Boyd Orr of Brechin *(UK)*
1950 Ralph Bunche *(US)*
1951 Léon Jouhaux *(France)*
1952 Albert Schweitzer *(France)*
1953 George Marshall *(US)*
1954 Office of the United Nations High Commissioner for Refugees
1955-56 No award
1957 Lester Bowles Pearson *(Canada)*
1958 Georges Pire *(Belgium)*
1959 Philip Noel-Baker *(UK)*
1960 Albert Lutuli *(South Africa)*
1961 Dag Hammarskjöld *(Sweden)*
1962 Linus Pauling *(US)*
1963 Comité International de la Croix-Rouge (Red Cross; *Switzerland)*
Ligue des Sociétés de la Croix-Rouge *(Switzerland)*
1964 Martin Luther King, Jr. *(US)*
1965 United Nations Children's Fund *(UNICEF)*
1966-67 No award
1968 René Cassin *(France)*
1969 International Labour Organization *(Switzerland)*
1970 Norman Borlaug *(US)*
1971 Willy Brandt *(West Germany)*
1972 No award
1973 Henry Kissinger *(US)*
Le Duc Tho *(Vietnam, declined)*
1974 Seán MacBride *(Republic of Ireland)*
Sato Eisaku *(Japan)*
1975 Andrei Sakharov *(USSR)*
1976 Betty Williams *(UK)*
Mairead Corrigan *(UK)*
1977 Amnesty International *(UK)*
1978 Anwar el Sadat *(Egypt)*
Menachem Begin *(Israel)*
1979 Mother Teresa *(Yugoslavia)*
1980 Adolfo Perez Esquivel *(Argentina)*
1981 Office of the United Nations High Commissioner for Refugees
1982 Alva Myrdal *(Sweden)*
Alfonso Garcia Robles *(Mexico)*
1983 Lech Walesa *(Poland)*
1984 Desmond Mpilo Tutu *(South Africa)*
1985 International Physicians for the Prevention of Nuclear War, Inc. *(US)*
1986 Elie Wiesel *(US)*
1987 Oscar Arias Sanchez *(Costa Rica)*
1988 UN Peace-keeping Forces
1989 Dalai Lama (Tenzin Gyatso; *Tibet)*
1990 Mikhail Gorbachev *(USSR)*
1991 Aung San Suu Kyi *(Myanmar)*
1992 Rigoberta Menchú Tum *(Guatemala)*
1993 Nelson Mandela *(South Africa)*
Frederik Willem de Klerk *(South Africa)*
1994 Yasser Arafat *(PLO)*
Shimon Peres *(Israel)*
Yitzhak Rabin *(Israel)*
1995 Joseph Rotblat *(UK)*
Pugwash Conference on Science and World Affairs *(Canada)*
1996 Carlos Filipe Ximenese Belo *(East Timor)*
José Ramos-Horta *(East Timor)*
1997 International Campaign to Ban Landmines *(US)*
Jody Williams *(US)*
1998 John Hume *(Northern Ireland)*
David Trimble *(Northern Ireland)*
1999 Médecins Sans Frontières *(France)*
2000 Kim Dae Jung *(South Korea)*
2001 Kofi Annan *(Ghana)*
2002 Jimmy Carter *(US)*

Nobel Prize for literature

1901 Sully Prudhomme *(France)*
1902 Theodor Mommsen *(Germany)*
1903 Bjornstjerne Bjornson *(Norway)*
1904 Frederic Mistral *(France)*
Jose Eizaguirre *(Spain)*
1905 Henryk Sienkiewicz *(Poland)*
1906 Giosue Carducci *(Italy)*
1907 Rudyard Kipling *(UK)*
1908 Rudolf Eucken *(Germany)*
1909 Selma Lagerlöf *(Sweden)*
1910 Paul von Heyse *(Germany)*
1911 Maurice Maeterlinck *(Belgium)*
1912 Gerhart Hauptmann *(Germany)*
1913 Rabindranath Tagore *(India)*
1914 No award
1915 Romain Rolland *(France)*
1916 Verner von Heidenstam *(Sweden)*
1917 Karl Gjellerup *(Denmark)*
Henrik Pontoppidan *(Denmark)*
1918 No award
1919 Carl Spitteler *(Switzerland)*
1920 Knut Hamsun *(Norway)*
1921 Anatole France *(France)*
1922 Jacinto Martinez *(Spain)*
1923 W.B. Yeats *(Ireland)*
1924 Wladyslaw Stanislaw Reymont *(Poland)*
1925 George Bernard Shaw *(UK)*
1926 Grazia Deledda *(Italy)*
1927 Henri Louis Bergson *(France)*
1928 Sigrid Undset *(Norway)*
1929 Thomas Mann *(Germany)*
1930 Sinclair Lewis *(US)*
1931 Erik Axel Karlfeldt *(Sweden)*
1932 John Galsworthy *(UK)*
1933 Ivan Bunin *(Russian, domiciled France)*
1934 Luigi Pirandello *(Italy)*
1935 No award
1936 Eugene O'Neill *(US)*
1937 Roger Martin Du Gard *(France)*
1938 Pearl S. Buck *(US)*
1939 Frans Eemil Sillanpaa *(Finland)*
1940-43 No award
1944 Johannes V. Jensen *(Denmark)*
1945 Gabriela Mistral *(Chile)*
1946 Hermann Hesse *(Switzerland)*
1947 André Gide *(France)*
1948 T.S. Eliot *(UK)*
1949 No award
1950 William Faulkner *(US)*
Bertrand Russell *(UK)*
1951 Pär Lagerkvist *(Sweden)*
1952 François Mauriac *(France)*
1953 Winston Churchill *(UK)*
1954 Ernest Hemingway *(US)*
1955 Halldor Kiljan Laxness *(Iceland)*
1956 Juan Ramón Jiménez *(Spain)*
1957 Albert Camus *(France)*
1958 Boris Pasternak *(USSR)*
1959 Salvatore Quasimodo *(Italy)*
1960 Saint-John Perse *(France)*
1961 Ivo Andric *(Yugoslavia)*
1962 John Steinbeck *(US)*
1963 George Seferis *(Greece)*
1964 Jean-Paul Sartre *(France)*
1965 Mikhail Sholokhov *(USSR)*
1966 S.Y. Agnon *(Israel)*
Nelly Sachs *(Sweden)*
1967 Miguel Angel Asturias *(Guatemala)*
1968 Yasunari Kawabata *(Japan)*
1969 Samuel Beckett *(Ireland)*
1970 Alexander Solzhenitsyn *(USSR)*
1971 Pablo Neruda *(Chile)*
1972 Heinrich Böll *(West Germany)*
1973 Patrick White *(Australia)*
1974 Harry Martinson *(Sweden)*
Eyind Johnson *(Sweden)*
1975 Eugenio Montale *(Italy)*
1976 Saul Bellow *(US)*
1977 Vicente Aleixandre *(Spain)*
1978 Isaac Bashevis Singer *(US)*
1979 Odysseus Elytis *(Greece)*
1980 Czeslaw Milosz *(US/Poland)*
1981 Elias Canetti *(UK)*
1982 Gabriel García Márquez *(Colombia)*
1983 William Golding *(UK)*
1984 Jaroslav Seifert *(Czechoslovakia)*
1985 Claude Simon *(France)*
1986 Wole Soyinka *(Nigeria)*
1987 Joseph Brodsky *(US)*
1988 Naguib Mahfouz *(Egypt)*
1989 Camilo José Cela *(Spain)*
1990 Octavio Paz *(Mexico)*
1991 Nadine Gordimer *(South Africa)*
1992 Derek Walcott *(St. Lucia)*
1993 Toni Morrison *(US)*
1994 Kenzaburo Oe *(Japan)*
1995 Seamus Heaney *(Ireland)*
1996 Wislawa Szymborska *(Poland)*
1997 Dario Fo *(Italy)*
1998 José Saramago *(Portugal)*
1999 Günter Grass *(Germany)*
2000 Gao Xingjian *(China)*
2001 V.S. Naipul *(UK)*
2002 Imre Kertész *(Hungary)*

Greek

The Greek alphabet developed from the Phoenician system in the 9th century B.C., but unlike the Phoenicians, the Greeks created separate symbols for vowels and for upper case (capital) and lower case letters. Until about 500 B.C., it was written from right to left. Several variations existed until the Ionian form became the official Athenian alphabet in 403 B.C. The modern Greek alphabet is used, almost unchanged, in the Greek-speaking world.

Letter	Name	Transliteration (sound)
Α, α	alpha	a
Β, β	beta	b
Γ, γ	gamma	g
Δ, δ	delta	d
Ε, ε	epsilon	e (short)
Ζ, ζ	zeta	z
Η, η	eta	e (long *ee*)
Θ, θ	theta	th (soft)
Ι, ι	iota	i
Κ, κ	kappa	k
Λ, λ	lambda	l
Μ, μ	mu	m
Ν, ν	nu	n
Ξ, ξ	xi	x
Ο, ο	omicron	o (short)
Π, π	pi	p
Ρ, ρ	rho	r
Σ, σ	sigma	s
Τ, τ	tau	t
Υ, υ	upsilon	y
Φ, φ	phi	f
Χ, χ	chi	ch (as in *loch*)
Ψ, ψ	psi	ps
Ω, ω	omega	o (long *oh*)

Cyrillic

The Cyrillic alphabet, an offshoot of Greek, was created in the 9th century A.D., reputedly by the Greek missionaries St. Cyril and St. Methodius. It became the script of the Russian, Ukrainian, Bulgarian, Serbian and Belarussian peoples. The alphabet originally had 43 letters, but modern versions have about 30, with national variations. There is no universally agreed transliteration system, but the equivalents shown here are widely used to go from Russian to English.

Letter	Transliteration (sound)
А, а	a
Б, б	b
В, в	v
Г, г	g
Д, д	d
Е, е	ye
Ё, ё	yo
Ж, ж	zh
З, з	z
И, и	i
Й, й	i
К, к	k
Л, л	l
М, м	m
Н, н	n
О, о	o
П, п	p
Р, р	r
С, с	s
Т, т	t
У, у	u
Ф, ф	f
Х, х	kh
Ц, ц	ts
Ч, ч	ch
Ш, ш	sh
Щ, щ	shch
Ъ, ъ	(hard sign)
Ы, ы	y
Ь, ь	(soft sign)
Э, э	e
Ю, ю	yu
Я, я	ya

Hebrew

The Hebrew alphabet was standardized in about the 1st century A.D. and has remained almost unchanged. It is used to write the various forms of Hebrew, as well as Yiddish, a language derived from southern German dialects that is spoken by eastern European Jewish communities. It is written from right to left, and only the consonants are represented by letters. Vowels are indicated by marks placed below or to the left of a consonant; some marks, shown in the list below, also change the pronunciation of consonants. There is no universally agreed transliteration system for the Hebrew alphabet, but the one given here is widely used for transliterating into English.

Symbol	Name	Transliteration (sound)
א	alef	(silent)
ב	bet	b, v
ג	gimmel	g, j
ד	dalet	d
ה	he	h (pronounced only with vowel marks)
ו	vav	v, w
ז	zayin	z
ח	khet	strong *h* as in *loch*
ט	tet	t
י	yod	y
כ	kaf	kh
ך (as final letter)	kaf	kh
ל	lamed	l
מ	mem	m
ם (as final letter)	mem	m
נ	nun	n
ן (as final letter)	nun	n
ס	samekh	s
ע	ayin	(silent)
פ	pe	p, f
ף (as final letter)	pe	p, f
צ	tzade	ts
ץ (as final letter)	tzade	ts
ק	qof	k
ר	resh	r
ש	shin	sh, s
ת	tav	t

Arabic

The Arabic alphabet developed around the 5th century A.D. Today's alphabet is descended from the 10th-century Nashki form. It is written from right to left and consists of consonant letters with vowels indicated by marks (vowel marks are usually omitted, except in children's books and the Koran). Letters are written differently according to whether they appear on their own (isolated), at the start of a word (initial), in the middle (medial) or at the end (final).

Name	Transliteration	Isolated	Final	Initial	Medial
alif	'	أ	ـا	أ	ـا
ba	b	ب	ـب	بـ	ـبـ
ta	t	ت	ـت	تـ	ـتـ
tha	th	ث	ـث	ثـ	ـثـ
jim	j	ج	ـج	جـ	ـجـ
ha	h	ح	ـح	حـ	ـحـ
kha	kh	خ	ـخ	خـ	ـخـ
dal	d	د	ـد	د	ـد
dha	dh	ذ	ـذ	ذ	ـذ
ra	r	ر	ـر	ر	ـر
za	z	ز	ـز	ز	ـز
sin	s	س	ـس	سـ	ـسـ
shin	sh	ش	ـش	شـ	ـشـ
sad	s	ص	ـص	صـ	ـصـ
dad	d	ض	ـض	ضـ	ـضـ
ta	t	ط	ـط	طـ	ـطـ
za	z	ظ	ـظ	ظـ	ـظـ
ain	'	ع	ـع	عـ	ـعـ
ghain	gh	غ	ـغ	غـ	ـغـ
fa	f	ف	ـف	فـ	ـفـ
qaf	q	ق	ـق	قـ	ـقـ
kaf	k	ك	ـك	كـ	ـكـ
lam	l	ل	ـل	لـ	ـلـ
mim	m	م	ـم	مـ	ـمـ
nun	n	ن	ـن	نـ	ـنـ
ha	h	ه	ـه	هـ	ـهـ
waw	w	و	ـو	و	ـو
ya	y	ى	ـى	يـ	ـيـ

Roman numerals

The Romans developed a numerical system based on seven letters representing seven numbers: I (1), V (5), X (10), L (50), C (100), D (500), and M (1000). All other numbers are derived by adding letters together (III represents 3) – except when a smaller letter is followed by a larger one, in which case the smaller is subtracted from the larger (IV represents 4). Calculations using Roman numerals were clumsy and difficult, which is why Arabic numerals triumphed.

I	1
II	2
III	3
IV	4
V	5
VI	6
VII	7
VIII	8
IX	9
X	10
XI	11
XIV	14
XV	15
XVI	16
XIX	19
XX	20
XXIX	29
XXX	30
XL	40
IL	49
L	50
LIX	59
LX	60

LXVIII	68
LXIX	69
XC	90
IC	99
C	100
CIC	199
CC	200
CD	400
D	500
DC	600
CM	900
M	1000
MCMLXXXIX	1989

Braille

In the Braille system of writing and printing for the blind, letters and numbers are represented by combinations of raised dots that are then read by touch. It was invented in France in 1829 by Louis Braille, who became blind at the age of three. Each character, or "cell," consists of six dots, arranged vertically in two columns of three dots; there are two different sizes of dots, small and large. Both hands are used in reading: The right hand identifies the letters, and the left picks out the beginning of the next line.

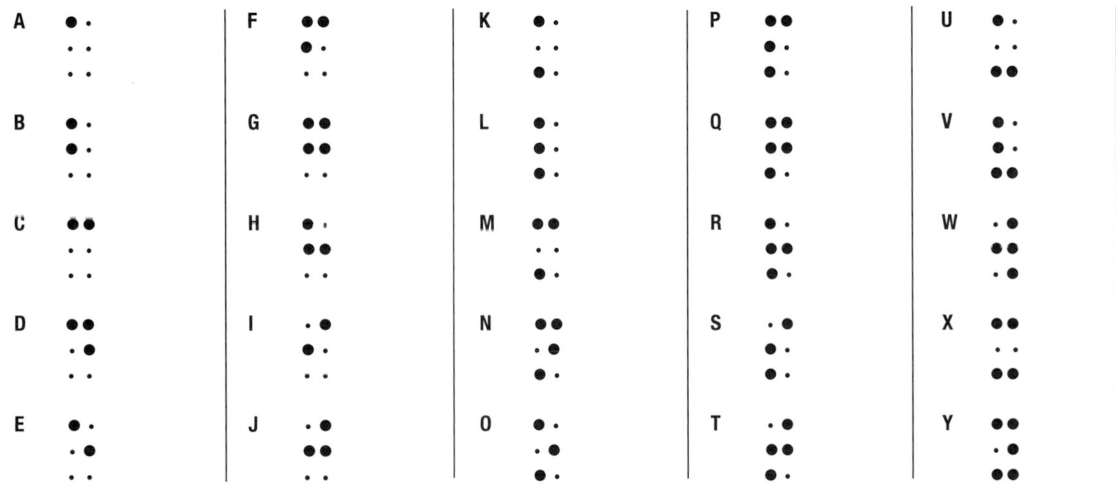

Numbers: The "cell" shown below indicates that a number follows. The numbers are indicated by the letters A-J.

Astronomers have divided the sky around the Earth into 88 areas, each of which contains a grouping of stars, or constellation. Many constellations were named after people and creatures in classical mythology, such as the flying horse Pegasus. In the 17th and 18th centuries, many constellations of the Southern Hemisphere were named after scientific instruments, such as the telescope.

The North Star

Polaris is the star closest to the north celestial pole; it lies at the end of the "handle" of Ursa Minor. It is actually a triple star system made up of two stars in orbit around one another and a single star. Because the Earth wobbles on its axis, the North Star varies over time: In 12 000 years it will be Vega in the constellation Lyra.

The northern sky

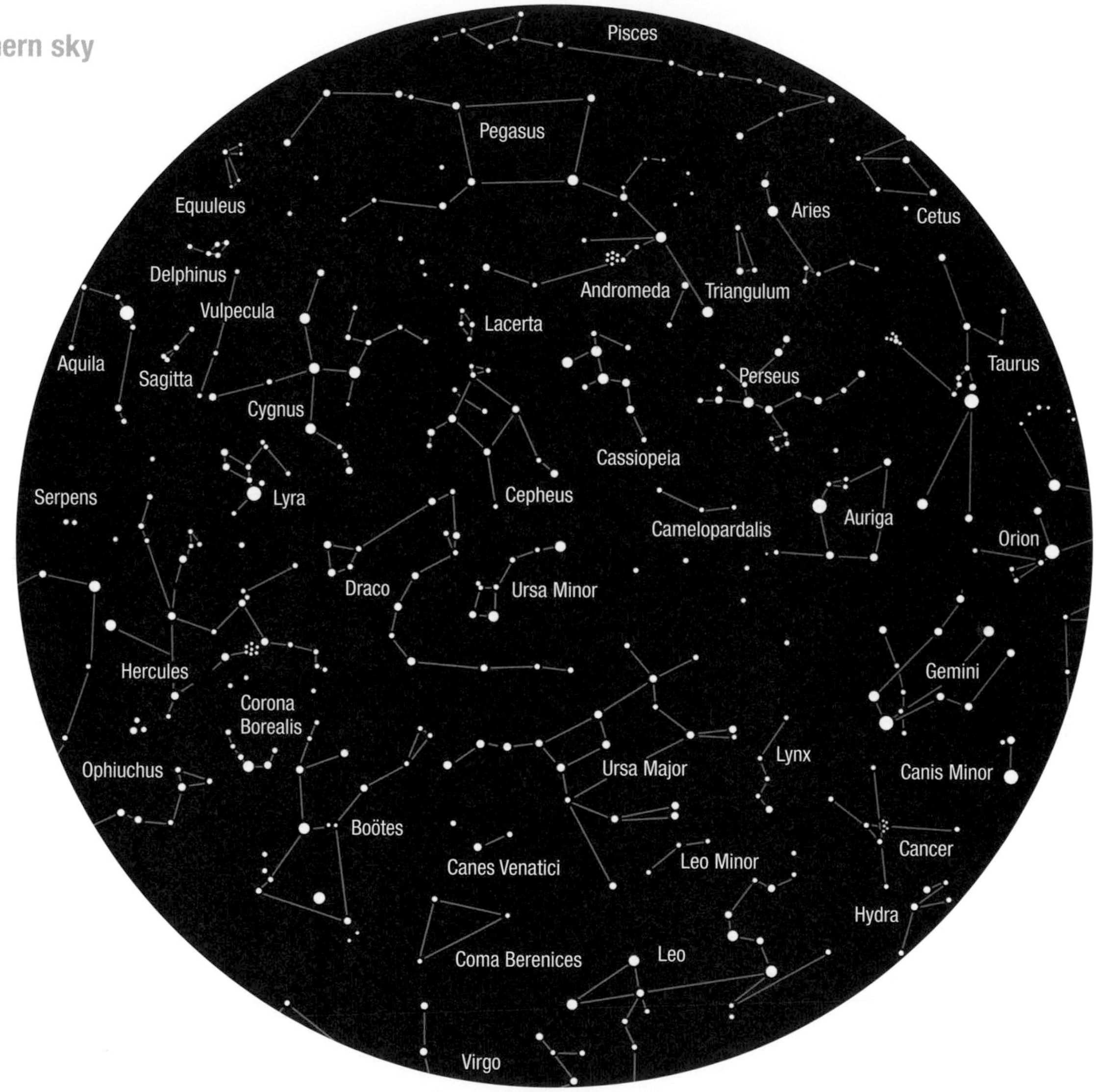

Latin name	English name
Andromeda	Andromeda
Aquila	The Eagle
Aries	The Ram
Auriga	The Charioteer
Boötes	The Herdsman
Camelopardalis	The Giraffe
Cancer	The Crab
Canes Venatici	The Hunting Dogs
Canis Minor	The Little Dog
Cassiopeia	Cassiopeia
Cepheus	Cepheus
Cetus	The Whale
Coma Berenices	Berenice's Hair
Corona Borealis	The Northern Crown
Cygnus	The Swan
Delphinus	The Dolphin
Draco	The Dragon
Equuleus	The Little Horse or Foal
Gemini	The Twins
Hercules	Hercules
Hydra	The Water Snake
Lacerta	The Lizard
Leo	The Lion
Leo Minor	The Little Lion
Lynx	The Lynx
Lyra	The Lyre
Ophiuchus	The Serpent Bearer
Orion	The Hunter
Pegasus	The Flying Horse
Perseus	Perseus
Pisces	The Fishes
Sagitta	The Arrow
Serpens	The Serpent
Sextans	The Sextant
Taurus	The Bull
Triangulum	The Triangle
Ursa Major	The Great Bear
Ursa Minor	The Little Bear
Virgo	The Virgin
Vulpecula	The Fox

Mapping the celestial sphere

From our vantage point on the Earth, the constellations appear to be laid out on the inside of a hollow sphere, which rotates around the Earth in an east–west direction once every 24 hours. Astronomers call this the celestial sphere, and the stars maps on these pages are convenient ways of laying out the two halves of this theoretical sphere on paper.

The part of the celestial sphere that is visible depends on the observer's position on the Earth's surface and on the Earth's position in its orbit. For both maps, the stars on the edge are visible at certain seasons in the other hemisphere – Canis Major, for example, can be seen in the Northern Hemisphere in winter. Those in the center are always invisible or very low in the sky in the other hemisphere.

The southern sky

Latin name	English name
Antlia	The Air Pump
Apus	The Bee
Aquarius	The Water Bearer
Ara	The Altar
Caelum	The Engraving Tool
Canis Major	The Great Dog
Capricornus	The Sea Goat
Carina	The Keel
Centaurus	The Centaur
Chamaeleon	The Chameleon
Circinus	The Pair of Compasses
Columba	The Dove
Corona Australis	The Southern Crown
Corvus	The Crow
Crater	The Cup
Crux Australis	The Southern Cross
Dorado	The Swordfish
Eridanus	The River
Fornax	The Furnace
Grus	The Crane
Horologium	The Clock
Hydrus	The Little Snake
Indus	The Indian
Lepus	The Hare
Libra	The Scales
Lupus	The Wolf
Mensa	The Table
Microscopium	The Microscope
Monoceros	The Unicorn
Musca	The Fly
Norma	The Rule
Octans	The Octant
Pavo	The Peacock
Phoenix	The Phoenix
Pictor	The Painter
Piscis Austrinus	The Southern Fish
Puppis	The Poop or Stern
Pyxis	The Mariner's Compass
Reticulum	The Net
Sagittarius	The Archer
Scorpius	The Scorpion
Sculptor	The Sculptor
Scutum	The Shield
Telescopium	The Telescope
Triangulum Australe	The Southern Triangle
Tucana	The Toucan
Vela	The Sail
Volans	The Flying Fish

Seven Wonders of the World

From the 2nd century B.C., various lists record seven great monuments as wonders of human accomplishment:

The Pyramids at Giza, Egypt (the only one still standing).
The Hanging Gardens of Babylon (near modern-day Baghdad, in Iraq), step pyramids planted with trees and lush vegetation.
The tomb of King Mausolus at Halicarnassus (modern-day Bodrum, in Turkey); the magnificent monument is the origin of the word "mausoleum."
The Temple of Artemis at Ephesus, Turkey.
The Colossus of Rhodes, a huge bronze statue by the entrance to the harbor of the Greek island.
The statue of Zeus at Olympia, Greece, made of gold and ivory.
The Pharos of Alexandria, Egypt, a lighthouse.*
**Some lists feature the walls of Babylon, or the palace of King Cyrus, instead of the Pharos of Alexandria.*

Anniversaries

In many countries, wedding anniversaries and other commemorative celebrations are associated with particular materials. Traditionally, gifts should be made of the corresponding material.

1st	Paper	13th	Lace
2nd	Cotton	14th	Ivory
3rd	Leather	15th	Crystal
4th	Fruit, flowers, linen	20th	China
5th	Wood	25th	Silver
6th	Iron, sugar	30th	Pearl
7th	Copper, wool	35th	Coral
8th	Bronze, pottery	40th	Ruby
9th	Pottery, willow	50th	Gold
10th	Tin	55th	Emerald
11th	Steel	60th	Diamond
12th	Silk, linen	70th	Platinum

Birthstones

In folklore, gems are associated with a specific month. They are thought to bring good luck to a person born in that month.

January	Garnet	July	Ruby or onyx
February	Amethyst	August	Carnelian or peridot
March	Bloodstone or aquamarine	September	Chrysolite or sapphire
April	Diamond	October	Aquamarine, tourmaline or opal
May	Agate or emerald	November	Topaz
June	Pearl or moonstone	December	Turquoise or zircon

Signs of the zodiac

The zodiac was the name given by the ancient Greeks to the band of the celestial sphere containing the paths of the Sun, the Moon and the principal planets. In Western astrology, this band is divided into 12 equal parts. Each part bears the name of a constellation for which it was originally named, but because of the slow shift of the Earth on its axis, constellations do not now cover the same areas of sky as the zodiacal signs of the same name.

Sign	English name	Dates*	Sign	English name	Dates*
Aries	The Ram	Mar. 21-Apr. 19	Libra	The Scales	Sept. 23-Oct. 23
Taurus	The Bull	Apr. 20-May 20	Scorpio	The Scorpion	Oct. 24-Nov. 21
Gemini	The Twins	May 21-June 21	Sagittarius	The Archer	Nov. 22-Dec. 21
Cancer	The Crab	June 22-July 22	Capricorn	The Sea Goat	Dec. 22-Jan. 19
Leo	The Lion	July 23-Aug. 22	Aquarius	The Water Bearer	Jan. 20-Feb. 18
Virgo	The Virgin	Aug. 23-Sept. 22	Pisces	The Fishes	Feb. 19-Mar. 20

**Dates may differ from year to year by one or two days.*

The world's longest tunnels

Name	Country	Year	Purpose	Length
1 Seikan	Japan	1985	Underwater, rail	53.9 km (33 miles)
2 Channel	England/France	1994	Underwater, rail	49.9 km (31 miles)
3 Moscow underground	Russia	1990	Railroad	37.9 km (23 miles)
4 London underground	UK	1939	Railroad	27.8 km (17 miles)
5 Laerdal	Norway	2000	Highway	24.5 km (15 miles)
6 Dai-shimizu	Japan	1979	Underwater, rail	22.5 km (14 miles)
7 Kanmon	Japan	1975	Railroad	19.3 km (12 miles)
Simplon I	Switzerland	1906	Railroad	19.3 km (12 miles)
Simplon II	Italy	1922	Railroad	19.3 km (12 miles)
8 Apennine	Italy	1934	Railroad	17.7 km (11 miles)
9 St. Gotthard	Switzerland	1980	Road	16.3 km (10 miles)
10 Rokko	Japan	1972	Railroad	16 km (10 miles)

The world's tallest buildings

The world's tallest structures are telecommunications towers; the CN Tower, in Toronto, Canada, holds the record at 555 m (1821 ft). Below are the world's tallest habitable buildings.

Name	Location	Year	Height
Petronas Towers	Kuala Lumpur, Malaysia	1996	452 m (1482 ft)
Sears Tower (with spires)	Chicago	1974	443 m (1454 ft) (520 m/1707 ft)
World Finance Center	Hong Kong	2001	400 m (1312 ft)
Jin Mao Building (with spire)	Shanghai, China	1997	382 m (1255 ft) (420 m/1378 ft)
Empire State Building (with spire)	New York	1931	381 m (1250 ft) (449 m/1472 ft)
Central Plaza	Hong Kong	1992	374m (1227 ft)
Bank of China Tower	Hong Kong	1989	369 m (1209 ft)
T&C Tower	Kao-shiung, Taiwan	1997	348 m (1142 ft)
Amoco Building	Chicago	1973	346 m (1136 ft)
John Hancock Center (with spires)	Chicago	1969	343 m (1127 ft) (449 m/1470 ft)

The world's longest bridges

Name	Country	Year	Length of main span
Suspension bridges			
1 Akashi-Kaikyo	Japan	1998	1990 m (6529 ft)
2 Great Belt East	Denmark	1997	1624 m (5328 ft)
3 Humber	England	1981	1410 m (4626 ft)
4 Jiangyin	China	1998	1385 m (4544 ft)
5 Tsing Ma	Hong Kong	1997	1377 m (4518 ft)
Cable-stayed bridges			
1 Øresund	Denmark/Sweden	2000	1092m (3583 ft)
2 Tatara	Japan	1999	890 m (2920 ft)
3 Pont de Normandie	France	1994	856 m (2808 ft)
4 Qinghzhou Minjiang	China	1996	605 m (1985 ft)
5 Yang Pu	China	1993	602 m (1975 ft)
Cantilever bridges			
1 Pont de Québec	Canada	1917	549 m (1800 ft)
2 Forth Rail Bridge	Scotland	1890	521 m (1710 ft)
3 Minato	Japan	1974	510 m (1673 ft)
4 Commodore John Barry	US	1974	494 m (1622 ft)
5 Greater New Orleans, 1 and 2	US	1958, 1998	both 480 m (1575 ft)
Steel arch bridges			
1 New River Gorge	US	1977	518 m (1700 ft)
2 Bayonne (Kill Van Kull)	US	1931	504 m (1654 ft)
3 Sydney Harbour	Australia	1932	503 m (1650 ft)
4 Fremont	US	1973	383 m (1257 ft)
5 Port Mann	Canada	1964	366 m (1200 ft)

Dynasties of ancient Egypt

Period	Dynasty	Dates
Early period	First Dynasty	c. 3100-2905 B.C.
	Second Dynasty	c. 2905-2700 B.C.
Old Kingdom	Third Dynasty	c. 2700-2680 B.C.
	Fourth Dynasty	c. 2680-2544 B.C.
	Fifth Dynasty	c. 2544-2407 B.C.
	Sixth Dynasty	c. 2407-2200 B.C.
First Intermediate Period	Seventh to Tenth Dynasties	c. 2200-2100 B.C.
Middle Kingdom	Eleventh Dynasty	c. 2100-1991 B.C.
	Twelfth Dynasty	c. 1991-1786 B.C.
Second Intermediate Period	Thirteenth to Seventeenth Dynasties	c. 1786-1570 B.C.
New Kingdom	Eighteenth Dynasty	c. 1570-1293 B.C.
	Nineteenth Dynasty	c. 1293-1185 B.C.
	Twentieth Dynasty	c. 1185-1100 B.C.
Third Intermediate Period	Twenty-first to Twenty-sixth Dynasties	c. 1100-525 B.C.
Late Dynastic Period	Twenty-seventh to Twenty-first Dynasties	c. 525-332 B.C.

Roman emperors

The Julio-Claudian emperors

Augustus	27 B.C.-A.D. 14
Tiberius	14-37
Caligula	37-41
Claudius	41-54
Nero	54-68
Galba	68-69
Otho	69
Vitellius	69

The Flavian emperors

Vespasian	69-79
Titus	79-81
Domitian	81-96

The Antonine emperors

Nerva	97-98
Trajan	98-117
Hadrian	117-38
Antoninus Pius	138-61
Marcus Aurelius[1]	161-80
Lucius Verus[1]	161-69
Commodus	180-92
Pertinax	193
Didius Julianus	193

[1] *Joint emperors.*

The Severi

Septimius Severus	193-211
Caracalla[2]	211-17
Geta[2]	211-12
Macrinus	217-18
Elagabalus	218-22
Severus Alexander	222-35

[2] *Joint emperors.*

The soldier emperors

Maximinus the Thracian	235-38
Gordian I[3]	238
Gordian II[3]	238
Balbinus[4]	238
Pupienus[4]	238
Gordian III	238-44
Philip the Arabian	244-49
Decius	249-51
Trebonianus Gallus	251-53
Aemilianus	253
Valerian[5]	253-60
Gallienus[5]	253-68

[3] *Joint emperors.* [4] *Joint emperors.*
[5] *Joint emperors.*

The Illyrian emperors

Claudius II Gothicus	268-70
Quintilus	270
Aurelian	270-75
Tacitus	275-76
Probus	276-82
Carus	282-83
Numerian[6]	283-84
Carinus[6]	283-84

[6] *Joint emperors.*

Diocletian and the Tetrarchy

Under the tetrarchy, four emperors ruled jointly, each with responsibility for a different sector of the empire.

Diocletian	284-305
Maximian	286-305
Constantius I Chlorus	293-306
Galerius	293-311
Severus	305-7
Maximinus	305-13
Maxentius	306-12
Licinius	308-24

Dynasty of Constantine

Constantine I the Great[7]	306-37
Constantine II[8]	337-40
Constans[8]	337-50
Constantius II[8]	337-61
Julian the Apostate	361-63
Jovian	363-64

[7] *Sole emperor: 324-37.*
[8] *Joint emperors.*

Western empire

Valentinian split the empire into western and eastern halves, making his brother Valens ruler of the eastern empire.

Valentinian I	364-75
Gratian	375-83
Valentinian II	375-92
Maximus[9]	383-88
Eugenius[9]	392-94
Honorius	395-423
Constantine III[9]	409-11
Valentinian III	423-55
Petronius Maximus	455
Avitus	455-56
Majorian	457-61
Libius Severus	461-65
Anthemius	467-72
Olybrius	472
Glycerius	473-74
Julius Nepos	474-80
Romulus Augustulus	475-76[10]

[9] *Usurpers.*
[10] *End of the Roman Empire in the west.*

Eastern empire

Valens	364-78
Theodosius I the Great	379-95
Arcadius	395-408
Theodosius II	408-50
Marcian	450-57
Leo	457-74
Zeno	474-91

The eastern empire survived until the fall of its capital Constantinople (modern Istanbul) to the Ottoman Turks in 1453.

Caliphs

The caliph was the leader of the Muslim world. The title comes from the Arabic phrase for "successor of the Messenger of God." It was adopted by successors of the Prophet Muhammad after his death in A.D. 632. The first caliph was Muhammad's father-in-law Abu Bakr, who set in motion the Arab conquests of Persia, Iraq and the Middle East. Abu Bakr and his three successors are known as the "perfect" or "rightly guided" (*al-rashidun*) caliphs.

Orthodox caliphate

Abu Bakr	632-34
Umar I	634-44
Uthman	644-56
Ali	656-61

Islam splits: The Shiites insist that only descendants of Ali should hold authority among Muslims; other Muslims accept the Umayyad dynasty of Damascus.

Umayyad caliphate

Mu'awiyah I	661-80
Yazid	680-83
Mu'awiyah II	683-84
Marwan	684-85
Abd al-Malik	685-705
al-Walid	705-15
Sulayman	715-17
'Umar II	717-20
Yazid II	720-24
Hisham	724-43
al-Walid II	743-44
Yazid III	744
Ibrahim	744
Marwan II	744-50

Abbasid caliphate

as-Saffah	749-54
al-Mansur	754-75
al-Mahdi	775-85
al-Hadi	785-86
Harun ar-Rashid	786-809
al-Amin	809-13
al-Ma'mun	813-33
al-Mutasim	833-42
al-Wathiq	842-47
al-Mutawwkkil	847-61
al-Muntasir	861-62
al-Mustain	862-66
al-Mu'tazz	866-69
al-Muhtadi	869-70
al-Mu'tamid	870-92
al-Mu'tazid	892-902
al-Muktafi	902-8
al-Muqtadir	908-32
al-Qahir	932-34
ar-Razi	934-40
al-Muttaqi	940-44
al-Mustagfi	944-45
al-Muti'	945-74
at-Tai'	974-94
al-Qadir	994-1031
al-Qaim	1031-75
al-Muqtad	1075-94
al-Mustazhir	1094-1118
al-Mustarshid	1118-35
ar-Rashid	1135-36
al-Muqtafi	1136-60
al-Mustanjid	1160-70
al-Mustaz	1170-80
an-Nasir	1180-1225
az-Zahir	1225-26
al-Mustansir	1226-42
al-Musta'sim	1242-58

A puppet caliphate of Abbasid descent existed in Cairo until ousted by the Ottomans in 1517. The title was then borne by Ottoman sultans until 1922 and was abolished by the Turkish republic in 1924.

Holy Roman Emperors

Beginning with the coronation of the Frankish king Charlemagne in A.D. 800, the Holy Roman Emperor was recognized by the Catholic Church as the secular ruler of Christendom. The empire was based in Germany, and the emperor was also usually the German king, elected by the leading German princes. Occasional clashes between Holy Roman Emperors and the papacy and among claimants to the throne led to periods in which the title was claimed by more than one person. The title was abolished in 1806.

Carolingian House	
Charles I the Great (Charlemagne)	800-14
Louis I the Pious	814-40
Lothair I	840-55
Louis II	855-75
Charles II the Bald	875-77
Charles III the Fat	877-87
Arnulf of Carinthia	887-98
Louis III the Child	899-911
House of Franconia	
Conrad I	911-18
House of Saxony	
Henry I the Fowler	919-36
Otto I the Great	936-73
Otto II	973-83
Otto III	983-1002
Henry II	1002-24
Salian House	
Conrad II	1024-39
Henry III	1039-56
Henry IV	1056-1105
Henry V	1105-25
House of Supplinburg	
Lothair II of Saxony	1125-37
House of Hohenstaufen	
Conrad III	1138-52
Frederick I Barbarossa	1152-90
Henry VI	1190-97
Philip of Swabia	1198-1208
House of Welf	
Otto IV of Brunswick[1]	1208-15
House of Hohenstaufen	
Frederick II[2]	1212-50
Henry Raspe of Thuringia (rival)	1246-47
William of Holland (rival)	1247-56
Conrad IV[3]	1237-54
Interregnum	1254-73
Richard of Cornwall (rival)	
Alfonso X of Castile (rival)	
House of Hapsburg	
Rudolf I	1273-91
House of Nassau	
Adolf	1292-98
House of Hapsburg	
Albert I of Austria	1298-1308
House of Luxembourg	
Henry VII	1308-13
House of Wittelsbach	
Louis IV of Bavaria	1314-46
Frederick of Austria (rival)	1314-30
House of Luxembourg	
Charles IV	1346-78
Günther of Schwarzburg (rival)	1349
Wenceslas	1378-1400
House of Wittelsbach	
Rupert of the Palatinate	1400-10
House of Luxembourg	
Sigismund	1410-37
Jobst of Moravia (rival)	1410-11
House of Hapsburg	
Albert II of Austria	1438-39
Frederick III	1440-93
Maximilian I	1493-1519
Charles V	1519-56
Ferdinand I	1556-64
Maximilian II	1564-76
Rudolf II	1576-1612
Matthias	1612-19
Ferdinand II	1619-37
Ferdinand III	1637-57
Leopold I	1658-1705
Joseph I	1705-11
Charles VI	1711-40
House of Wittelsbach	
Charles VII of Bavaria	1742-45
House of Hapsburg-Lorraine	
Francis I of Lorraine	1745-65
Joseph II	1765-90
Leopold II	1790-92
Francis II	1792-1806

[1] *German king 1208-12, Emperor 1209-15*

[2] *German king 1212-20, Emperor 1220-50*

[3] *German king only*

Popes

The papacy traces itself back to St. Peter in the 1st century A.D. Listed here are the popes starting from 1417, when the papacy moved back to Rome after being based at Avignon, France, for nearly 70 years.

Martin V (Oddone Colonna)	1417-31
Eugenius IV (Gabriele Condulmer)	1431-47
Nicholas V (Tommaso Parentucelli)	1447-55
Calixtus III (Alfonso de Borgia)	1455-58
Pius II (Aeneas Silvius Piccolomini)	1458-64
Paul II (Pietro Barbo)	1464-71
Sixtus IV (Francesco della Rovere)	1471-84
Innocent VIII (Giovanni Battista Cibo)	1484-92
Alexander VI (Rodrigo Borgia)	1492-1503
Pius III (Francesco Todeschini Piccolomini)	1503
Julius II (Giuliano della Rovere)	1503-13
Leo X (Giovanni de Medici)	1513-22
Adrian VI (Adrian Dedel)	1522-23
Clement VII (Giulio de Medici)	1523-34
Paul III (Alessandro Farnese)	1534-50
Julius III (Gianmaria del Monte)	1550-55
Marcellus II (Marcello Cervini)	1555
Paul IV (Giovanni Pietro Caraffa)	1555-59
Pius IV (Giovanni Angelo de Medici)	1559-66
Pius V (Michele Ghislieri)	1566-72
Gregory XIII (Ugo Buoncompagni)	1572-85
Sixtus V (Felice Peretti)	1585-90
Urban VII (Gianbattista Castagna)	1590
Gregory XIV (Niccolo Sfondrati)	1590-91
Innocent IX (Gian Antonio Facchinetti)	1591-92
Clement VIII (Ippolito Aldobrandini)	1592-1605
Leo XI (Alessandro de Medici-Ottaiano)	1605
Paul V (Camillo Borghese)	1605-21
Gregory XV (Alessandro Ludovisi)	1621-23
Urban VIII (Maffeo Barberini)	1623-44
Innocent X (Giambattista Pamfili)	1644-55
Alexander VII (Fabio Chigi)	1655-67
Clement IX (Giulio Rospigliosi)	1667-70
Clement X (Emilio Altieri)	1670-76
Innocent XI (Benedetto Odescalchi)	1676-89
Alexander VIII (Pietro Vito Ottoboni)	1689-91
Innocent XII (Antonio Pignatelli)	1691-1700
Clement XI (Gian Francesco Albani)	1700-21
Innocent XIII (Michelangelo dei Conti)	1721-24
Benedict XIII (Pietro Francesco Orsini)	1724-30
Clement XII (Lorenzo Corsini)	1730-40
Benedict XIV (Propero Lambertini)	1740-58
Clement XIII (Carlo Rezzonico)	1758-69
Clement XIV (Lorenzo Ganganelli)	1769-75
Pius VI (Giovani Angelo Braschi)	1775-1800
Pius VII (Barnaba Chiaramonti)	1800-23
Leo XII (Annibale della Genga)	1823-29
Pius VIII (Francesco Saveno Castiglioni)	1829-31
Gregory XVI (Bartolomeo Alberto Cappellari)	1831-46
Pius IX (Giovanni Maria Mastai Ferretti)	1846-78
Leo XIII (Vincenzo Gioacchino Pecci)	1878-1903
Pius X (Giuseppe Sarto)	1903-14
Benedict XV (Giacomo della Chiesa)	1914-22
Pius XI (Achille Ratti)	1922-39
Pius XII (Eugenio Pacelli)	1939-58
John XXIII (Angelo Giuseppe Roncali)	1958-63
Paul VI (Giovanni Battista Montini)	1963-78
John Paul I (Albino Luciani)	1978
John Paul II (Karol Jozef Wojtyla)	1978-

Kings and queens of England and the United Kingdom

Saxon line

Egbert	802-39
Ethelwulf	839-55
Ethelbald	855-60
Ethelbert	860-66
Ethelred I	866-71
Alfred the Great	871-99
Edward the Elder	899-924
Athelstan	924-39
Edmund I	939-46
Eadred	946-55
Eadwig	955-59
Edgar	959-75
Edward the Martyr	975-78
Ethelred II the Unready	978-1016
Edmund II Ironside	1016 (Apr.-Nov.)

Danish line

Canute	1016-35
Harold I	1035-40
Hardicanute	1040-42

Saxon line

Edward the Confessor	1042-66
Harold II	1066 (Jan.-Oct.)

Norman line

William I the Conqueror	1066-87
William II Rufus	1087-1100
Henry I	1100-35
Stephen	1135-54

House of Plantagenet

Henry II	1154-89
Richard the Lionheart	1189-99
John	1199-1216
Henry III	1216-72
Edward I	1272-1307
Edward II	1307-1327
Edward III	1327-77
Richard II	1377-99

House of Lancaster

Henry IV	1399-1413
Henry V	1413-22
Henry VI	1422-61, 1470-71

House of York

Edward IV	1461-70, 1471-83
Edward V	1483 (April-June)
Richard III	1483-85

House of Tudor

Henry VII	1485-1509
Henry VIII	1509-47
Edward VI	1547-53
Lady Jane Grey	1553 (July 10-19)
Mary I	1553-58
Elizabeth I	1558-1603

House of Stuart

James I (James VI of Scotland)	1603-25
Charles I	1625-49
Commonwealth	1649-60
Charles II	1660-85
James II	1685-88
William III and Mary II	1689-94
William III	1694-1702
Anne	1702-14

House of Hanover

George I	1714-27
George II	1727-60
George III	1760-1820
George IV	1820-30
William IV	1830-37
Victoria	1837-1901

House of Saxe-Coburg-Gotha

Edward VII	1901-10

House of Windsor

George V	1910-36
Edward VIII	1936
George VI	1936-52
Elizabeth II	1952-

Kings and queens of Scotland

Kenneth I Macalpin	843-58
Donald I	858-62
Constantine I	862-77
Aed	877-88
Giric and Eochaid	878-89
Donald II	889-900
Constantine II	900-43
Malcolm I	943-54
Indulf	954-62
Dubh	962-66
Culen	966-71
Kenneth II	971-95
Constantine III	995-97
Kenneth III	997-1005
Malcolm II	1005-34
Duncan I	1034-40
Macbeth	1040-57
Lulach	1057-58
Malcolm III	1058-93
Donald III	1093-94
Duncan II	1094
Donald III (restored)	1094-97
Edgar	1097-1107
Alexander I	1107-24
David I	1124-53
Malcolm IV	1153-65
William the Lion	1165-1214
Alexander II	1214-49
Alexander III	1249-86
Margaret Maid of Norway	1286-90
Interregnum	1290-92

House of Balliol

John Balliol	1292-96
Interregnum	1296-1306

House of Bruce

Robert Bruce	1306-29
David II	1329-71

House of Stewart (Stuart)

Robert II	1371-90
Robert III	1390-1406
James I	1406-37
James II	1437-60
James III	1460-88
James IV	1488-1513
James V	1513-42
Mary, Queen of Scots	1542-67
James VI	1567-1625

(King of England and Scotland after 1603)

British prime ministers

Name	Term	Party
Sir Robert Walpole	1721-42	Whig
Earl of Wilmington	1742-43	Whig
Henry Pelham	1743-54	Whig
Duke of Newcastle	1754-56	Whig
Duke of Devonshire	1756-57	Whig
Duke of Newcastle	1757-62	Whig
Earl of Bute	1762-63	Tory
George Grenville	1763-65	Whig
Marquess of Rockingham	1765-66	Whig
Earl of Chatham	1766-68	Whig
Duke of Grafton	1768-70	Whig
Lord North	1770-82	Tory
Marquess of Rockingham	1782	Whig
Earl of Shelburne	1782-83	Whig
Duke of Portland	1783	Coalition
William Pitt the Younger	1783-1801	Tory
Henry Addington	1801-4	Tory
William Pitt the Younger	1804-6	Tory
Lord Grenville	1806-7	Coalition
Duke of Portland	1807-9	Tory
Spencer Perceval	1809-12	Tory
Earl of Liverpool	1812-27	Tory
George Canning	1827	Coalition
Viscount Goderich	1827-28	Tory
Duke of Wellington	1828-30	Tory
Earl Grey	1830-34	Tory
Viscount Melbourne	1834	Whig
Sir Robert Peel	1834-35	Whig
Viscount Melbourne	1835-41	Whig
Sir Robert Peel	1841-46	Conservative
Lord John Russell	1846-52	Liberal
Earl of Derby	1852	Conservative
Lord Aberdeen	1852-55	Peelite
Viscount Palmerston	1855-58	Liberal
Earl of Derby	1858-59	Conservative
Viscount Palmerston	1859-65	Liberal
Lord John Russell	1865-66	Liberal
Early of Derby	1866-68	Conservative
Benjamin Disraeli	1868	Conservative
W.E. Gladstone	1868-74	Liberal
Benjamin Disraeli	1874-80	Conservative
W.E. Gladstone	1880-85	Liberal
Marquess of Salisbury	1885-86	Conservative
W.E. Gladstone	1886	Liberal
Marquess of Salisbury	1886-92	Conservative
W.E. Gladstone	1892-94	Liberal
Earl of Rosebery	1894-95	Liberal
Marquess of Salisbury	1895-1902	Conservative
Arthur James Balfour	1902-5	Conservative
Sir Henry Campbell-Bannerman	1905-8	Liberal
H.H. Asquith	1908-15	Liberal
	1915-16	Coalition
David Lloyd George	1916-22	Coalition
Andrew Bonar Law	1922-23	Conservative
Stanley Baldwin	1923-24	Conservative
Ramsay MacDonald	1924	Labour
Stanley Baldwin	1924-29	Conservative
Ramsay MacDonald	1929-31	Labour
	1931-35	Coalition
Stanley Baldwin	1935-37	Coalition
Neville Chamberlain	1937-40	Coalition
Winston Churchill	1940-45	Coalition
Clement Attlee	1945-51	Labour
Sir Winston Churchill	1951-55	Conservative
Sir Anthony Eden	1955-57	Conservative
Harold Macmillan	1957-63	Conservative
Sir Alec Douglas-Home	1963-64	Conservative
Harold Wilson	1964-70	Labour
Edward Heath	1970-74	Conservative
Harold Wilson	1974-76	Labour
James Callaghan	1976-79	Labour
Margaret Thatcher	1979-90	Conservative
John Major	1990-97	Conservative
Tony Blair	1997-	Labour

France

France emerged as a unified state at the end of the 15th century. The absolute rule of French kings came to an end with the French Revolution (1789-99).

Carolingian House	
Pepin the Short	751-68
Carloman	768-71
Charles the Great (Charlemagne)	768-814
Louis I the Pious	814-40
Charles I the Bald	840-77
Louis II the Stammerer	877-79
Louis III	879-82
Carloman	882-84
Charles II the Fat	884-88
Robertian House	
Eudes	888-98
Carolingian House	
Charles III the Simple	893-922
Robertian House	
Robert I	922-23
Rudolf	923-36
Carolingian House	
Louis IV d'Outremer	936-54
Lothair	954-86
Louis V the Sluggard	986-87
Capetian House	
Hugh Capet	987-96
Robert II the Pious	996-1031
Henry I	1031-60
Philip I	1060-1108
Louis VI the Fat	1108-37
Louis VII the Younger	1137-80
Philip II Augustus	1180-1223
Louis VIII the Lion	1223-26
Louis IX	1226-70
Philip III the Bold	1270-85
Philip IV the Fair	1285-1314
Louis X the Stubborn	1314-16
John I	1316
Philip V the Tall	1316-22
Charles IV the Fair	1322-28
House of Valois	
Philip VI	1328-50
John II the Good	1350-64
Charles V the Wise	1364-80
Charles VI the Mad	1380-1422
Charles VII the Victorious	1422-61
Louis XI	1461-83
Charles VIII	1483-98
Line of Orléans	
Louis XII	1498-1515
Line of Angoulême	
Francis I	1515-47
Henry II	1547-59
Francis II	1559-60
Charles IX	1560-74
Henry III	1574-89
House of Bourbon	
Henry IV	1589-1610
Louis XIII	1610-43
Louis XIV	1643-1715
Louis XV	1715-74
Louis XVI	1774-92
Louis XVII	1793-95
First Republic	
National Convention	1792-95
Directory	1795-99
Consulate:	
Napoleon Bonaparte, First Consul	1799-1804
House of Bonaparte, First Empire	
Napoleon I	1804-14, 1815
Napoleon II	1815
House of Bourbon	
Louis XVIII	1815-24
Charles X	1824-30
Line of Orléans	
Louis Philippe I	1830-48
Second Republic	
Louis Napoleon Bonaparte, President	1848-52
House of Bonaparte, Second Empire	
Napoleon III	1852-70
Third Republic: presidents	
Louis Adolphe Thiers	1871-73
Marie Edmé de MacMahon	1873-79
Jules Grévy	1879-87
Sadi Carnot	1887-94
Jean Paul Pierre Casimir-Périer	1894-95
François Félix Faure	1895-99
Émile Loubet	1899-1906
Armand Fallières	1906-13
Raymond Poincaré	1913-20
Paul Deschanel	1920
Alexandre Millerand	1920-24
Gaston Dourmergue	1924-31
Paul Doumer	1931-32
Albert Lebrun	1932-40
Fourth Republic: presidents	
Vincent Auriol	1947-54
René Coty	1954-58
Fifth Republic: presidents	
Charles de Gaulle	1958-69
Georges Pompidou	1969-74
Valéry Giscard d'Estaing	1974-81
François Mitterrand	1981-95
Jacques Chirac	1995-

Ireland

In 1921, the Anglo-Irish Treaty created the Irish Free State. A new constitution in 1937 established Ireland (Eire) as a sovereign state.

Presidents	
Douglas Hyde	1938-45
Sean Thomas O'Kelly	1945-59
Eamon de Valera	1959-73
Erskine H. Childers	1973-74
Cearbhall O'Dalaigh	1974-76
Patrick J. Hillery	1976-90
Mary Robinson	1990-97
Mary McAleese	1997-
Prime ministers (taoiseachs)	
Eamon de Valera	1921
Arthur Griffith	1922
William Cosgrave	1922-32
Eamon de Valera	1932-48
John Aloysius Costello	1948-51
Eamon de Valera	1951-54
John Aloysius Costello	1954-57
Eamon de Valera	1957-59
Sean Lemass	1959-66
John Lynch	1966-73
Liam Cosgrave	1973-77
John Lynch	1977-79
Charles Haughey	1979-81
Garret Fitzgerald	1981-82
Charles Haughey	1982
Garret Fitzgerald	1982-87
Charles Haughey	1987-92
Albert Reynolds	1992-94
John Bruton	1994-97
Bertie Ahern	1997-

Spain

Muslim Moors conquered most of Spain in the 8th century. Christian reconquest began in the 11th century; in 1492, Ferdinand II of Aragon and Isabella of Castile unified Spain.

House of Hapsburg	
Charles I*	1516-56
Philip II	1556-98
Philip III	1598-1621
Philip IV	1621-65
Charles II	1665-1700

Charles I of Spain is better known to history as the Holy Roman Emperor Charles V – see page 476.

House of Bourbon	
Philip V	1700-46
Ferdinand VI	1746-59
Charles III	1759-88
Charles IV	1788-1808
Ferdinand VII	1808
House of Bonaparte	
Joseph Napoleon	1808-1813
House of Bourbon	
Ferdinand VII	1813-33
Isabella II	1833-68
House of Savoy	
Amadeus	1870-73
First Republic	1873-74
Five presidents in just under two years.	
House of Bourbon	
Alfonso XII	1874-85
Alfonso XIII	1886-1931
Second Republic: presidents	
Niceta Alcalá Zamora	1931-36
Manuel Azana	1936-39
Dictatorship: Caudillo (leader)	
Francisco Franco y Bahamonde	1936-75
House of Bourbon	
Juan Carlos I	1975-
Prime ministers since 1976	
Adolfo Suárez González	1976-81
Leopoldo Calvo Sotelo y Bustelo	1981-82
Felipe González Marquez	1982-96
José Maria Aznar	1996-

Italy

In 1861, Vittorio Emanuele II of Piedmont became king of the newly united Italy. Benito Mussolini, prime minister from 1922 to 1943, held dictatorial powers from 1928 on.

House of Savoy

Vittorio Emanuele II	1861-78
Umberto I	1878-1900
Vittorio Emanuele III	1900-46
Umberto II	1946

Republic: presidents

Enrico da Nicola	1946-48
Luigi Einaudi	1948-55
Giovanni Gronchi	1955-62
Antonio Segni	1962-64
Giuseppe Saragat	1964-71
Giovanni Leone	1971-78
Sandro Pertini	1978-85
Francesco Cossiga	1985-92
Oscar Luigi Scalfaro	1992-99
Carlo Azeglio Ciampi	1999-

Prime ministers from 1945

Ferruccio Parri	1945
Alcide De Gasperi	1945-53
Giuseppe Pella	1953-54
Amintore Fanfani	1954
Mario Scelba	1954-55
Antonio Segni	1955-57
Adone Zoli	1957-58
Amintore Fanfani	1958-59
Antonio Segni	1959-60
Fernando Tambroni-Armaroli	1960
Amintore Fanfani	1960-63
Giovanni Leone	1963
Aldo Moro	1963-68
Giovanni Leone	1968
Mariano Rumor	1968-70
Emilio Colombo	1970-72
Giulio Andreotti	1972-73
Mariano Rumor	1973-74
Aldo Moro	1974-76
Giulio Andreotti	1976-79
Francesco Cossiga	1979-80
Arnaldo Forlani	1980-81
Giovanni Spadolini	1981-82
Amintore Fanfani	1982-83
Bettino Craxi	1983-87
Amintore Fanfani	1987
Giovanni Goria	1987-88
Ciriaco De Mita	1988-89
Giulio Andreotti	1989-92
Giuliano Amato	1992-93
Carlo Azeglio Ciampi	1993-94
Silvio Berlusconi	1994-95
Lamberto Dini	1995-96
Romano Prodi	1996-98
Massimo D'Alema	1998-2000
Giuliano Amato	2000-1
Silvio Berlusconi	2001-

Prussia and Germany

Kings of Prussia

Friedrich I	1701-13
Friedrich Wilhelm I the Soldier King	1713-40
Friedrich II the Great	1740-86
Friedrich Wilhelm II	1786-97
Friedrich Wilhelm III	1797-1840
Friedrich Wilhelm IV	1840-61
Wilhelm I	1861-71

Emperors (Kaisers) of Germany

Wilhelm I	1871-88
Friedrich III	1888
Wilhelm II	1888-1918

Weimar Republic: presidents

Friedrich Ebert	1919-25
Paul von Hindenburg	1925-34

Third Reich: Führer

Adolf Hitler	1934-45

Federal Republic: presidents

Theodore Heuss	1949-59
Heinrich Lübke	1959-69
Gustav Heinemann	1969-74
Walter Scheel	1974-79
Karl Carstens	1979-84
Richard von Weizsäcker	1984-94
Roman Herzog	1994-99
Johannes Rau	1999-

Chancellors

Otto von Bismarck	1871-90
Leo von Caprivi	1890-94
Chlodwig Karl Victor	1894-1900
Bernhard von Bülow	1900-9
Theobald von Bethmann-Holweg	1909-17
Georg Michaelis	1917
Georg von Hertling	1917
Max von Baden	1918
Friedrich Ebert	1918
Philipp Scheidemann	1919
Gustav Bauer	1919
Hermann Müller	1920
Konstantin Fehrenbach	1920
Karl Josef Wirth	1921
Wilhelm Cuno	1922
Gustaf Streseman	1923
Wilhelm Marx	1923
Hans Luther	1925-26
Wilhelm Marx	1926-28
Heinrich Brüning	1929-32
Franz von Papen	1932
Kurt von Schleicher	1932-33
Adolf Hitler	1933-34*
Konrad Adenauer	1949-63
Ludwig Ehrhard	1963-66
Kurt Georg Kiesinger	1966-69
Willy Brandt	1969-74
Helmut Schmidt	1974-82
Helmut Kohl	1982-98
Gerhard Schröder	1998-

** In 1934, Hitler combined the posts of president and chancellor into the role of Führer (leader).*

German Democratic Republic (East Germany)

The GDR was created from the Soviet-occupied zone in postwar Germany. With German reunification in 1990, it was absorbed into the Federal Republic of Germany.

President

Wilhelm Pieck	1949-60

Chairmen of the Council of State

Walter Ulbricht	1960-73
Willi Stoph	1973-76
Erich Honecker	1976-89
Egon Krenz	1989
Gregor Gysi	1989-90

Russia

Rurik dynasty

Ivan III the Great	1472-1505
Vasily III	1505-33
Ivan IV the Terrible	1533-84
Boris Godunov	1598-1605

Romanov dynasty

Mikhail	1613-45
Alexei	1645-76
Fyodor III	1676-82
Peter I the Great	1682-1725
Catherine I	1725-27
Peter II	1727-30
Anna	1730-40
Ivan VI	1740-41
Elizabeth	1741-62
Peter III	1762
Catherine II the Great	1762-96
Paul I	1796-1800
Alexander I	1800-25
Nicholas I	1825-55
Alexander II	1855-81
Alexander III	1881-94
Nicholas II	1894-1917

Head of provisional government

Alexander Kerensky	March-October 1917

Soviet Union:

General secretaries of the Communist Party

Vladimir Lenin	1917-24
Joseph Stalin	1924-53
Nikita Khrushchev	1953-64
Leonid Brezhnev	1964-82
Yuri Andropov	1983-84
Konstantin Chernenko	1984-85
Mikhail Gorbachev	1985-91

Russian Federation: presidents

Boris Yeltsin	1991-99
Vladimir Putin	1999-

The Americas

The United States

Presidents

George Washington	1789-97	Federalist
John Adams	1797-1801	Federalist
Thomas Jefferson	1801-9	Democratic-Republican
James Madison	1809-17	Dem-Rep
James Monroe	1817-25	Dem-Rep
John Quincy Adams	1825-29	Independent
Andrew Jackson	1829-37	Democrat
Martin Van Buren	1837-41	Democrat
William H. Harrison	1841	Whig
John Tyler	1841-45	Whig, then Democrat
James K. Polk	1845-49	Democrat
Zachary Taylor	1849-50	Whig
Millard Fillmore	1850-53	Whig
Franklin Pierce	1853-57	Democrat
James Buchanan	1857-61	Democrat
Abraham Lincoln	1861-65	Republican
Andrew Johnson	1865-69	Democrat
Ulysses S. Grant	1869-77	Republican
Rutherford B. Hayes	1877-81	Republican
James A. Garfield	1881	Republican
Chester A. Arthur	1881-85	Republican
Grover Cleveland	1885-89	Democrat
Benjamin Harrison	1889-93	Republican
Grover Cleveland	1893-97	Democrat
William McKinley	1897-1901	Republican
Theodore Roosevelt	1901-9	Republican
William H. Taft	1909-13	Republican
Woodrow Wilson	1913-21	Democrat
Warren G. Harding	1921-23	Republican
Calvin Coolidge	1923-29	Republican
Herbert Hoover	1929-33	Republican
Franklin D. Roosevelt	1933-45	Democrat
Harry S Truman	1945-53	Democrat
Dwight D. Eisenhower	1953-61	Republican
John F. Kennedy	1961-63	Democrat
Lyndon B. Johnson	1963-69	Democrat
Richard M. Nixon	1969-74	Republican
Gerald R. Ford	1974-77	Republican
James Earl Carter	1977-81	Democrat
Ronald W. Reagan	1981-89	Republican
George H.W. Bush	1989-93	Republican
William J. Clinton	1993-2001	Democrat
George W. Bush	2001-	Republican

Canada

Prime ministers

John A. Macdonald	1867-73
Alexander Mackenzie	1873-78
John A. Macdonald	1878-91
John J.C. Abbott	1891-92
John S.D. Thompson	1892-94
Mackenzie Bowell	1894-96
Charles Tupper	1896
Wilfrid Laurier	1896-1911
Robert L. Borden	1911-20
Arthur Meighen	1920-21
W.L. Mackenzie King	1921-26
Arthur Meighen	1926
W.L. Mackenzie King	1926-30
Richard B. Bennett	1930-35
W.L. Mackenzie King	1935-48
Louis Stephen St. Laurent	1948-57
John George Diefenbaker	1957-63
Lester B. Pearson	1963-68
Pierre Elliott Trudeau	1968-79
Joe Clark	1979-80
Pierre Elliott Trudeau	1980-84
John Turner	1984
Brian Mulroney	1984-93
Kim Campbell	1993
Jean Chrétien	1993-

Mexico

Presidents

Benito Juárez	1867-72
Sebastián Lerdo de Tejada y Corral	1872-76
Juan Méndez	1876-77
Porfirio Díaz	1877-80
Manuel González	1880-84
Porfirio Díaz	1884-1911
Francisco León de la Barra	1911
Francisco Indalecio Madero	1911-13
Victoriano Huerta	1913-14
Francisco Carvajal	1914
Venustiano Carranza	1914
Antonio Villarreal González	1914
Eulalio Martín Gutiérrez Ortiz	1914-15
Roque González Garza	1915
Francisco Lagos Cházaro	1915
Venustiano Carranza	1915-20
Adolfo de la Huerta	1920
Alvaro Obregón	1920-24
Plutarco Elías Calles	1924-28
Emilio Portes Gil	1928-30
Pascual Ortiz Rubio	1930-32
Abelardo Luján Rodríguez	1932-34
Lázaro Cárdenas	1934-40
Manuel Avila Camacho	1940-46
Miguel Alemán Valdés	1946-52
Adolfo Ruiz Cortines	1952-58
Adolfo López Mateos	1958-64
Gustavo Díaz Ordaz	1964-70
Luís Echeverría Alvarez	1970-76
José López Portillo y Pacheco	1976-82
Miguel de la Madrid Hurtado	1982-88
Carlos Salinas de Gortari	1988-94
Ernesto Zedillo Ponce de Leon	1994-2000
Vicente Fox Quesada	2000-

Africa and The Middle East

Israel

Prime ministers

David Ben-Gurion	1948-53
Moshe Sharett	1953-55
David Ben-Gurion	1955-63
Levi Eshkol	1963-69
Golda Meir	1969-74
Yitzhak Rabin	1974-77
Menachem Begin	1977-83
Yitzhak Shamir	1983-84
Shimon Peres	1984-86
Yitzhak Shamir	1986-92
Yitzhak Rabin	1992-95
Shimon Peres	1995-96
Benjamin Netanyahu	1996-99
Ehud Barak	1999-2001
Ariel Sharon	2001-

Turkey

Presidents

Mustafa Kemal Pasha (Atatürk from 1934)	1923-38
Ismet Inönü	1938-50
Celal Bayar	1950-60
Cemal Gürsel	1960-66
Cevdet Sunay	1966-73
Fahri Korutürk	1973-80
Kenan Evren	1980-89
Turgut Özal	1989-93
Süleyman Demirel	1993-2000
Ahmet Necdet Sezer	2000-

Egypt

Presidents

Gamal Abd al-Nasser	1953-70
Anwar Sadat	1970-81
Mohammed Hosni Mubarak	1981-

Saudi Arabia

Kings

Abdul Aziz (ibn Saud)	1932-53
Saud (ibn Abd al-Aziz)	1953-64
Faisal (ibn Abd al-Aziz)	1964-75
Khalid (ibn Abd Al-Aziz)	1975-82
Fahd (ibn Abd Al-Aziz)	1982-

South Africa

Prime ministers

Louis Botha	1910-19
Jan Smuts	1919-24
James Hertzog	1924-39
Jan Smuts	1939-48
Daniel Malan	1948-54
Johannes Strijdon	1954-58
Hendrik Verwoerd	1958-66
Balthazar Johannes Vorster	1966-78
Pieter Botha	1978-84*

**Post abolished in 1984.*

Presidents

Pieter Botha	1984-89
Frederik Willem de Klerk	1989-94
Nelson Mandela	1994-89
Thabo Mbeki	1999-

Asia and the Pacific

China

Dynasties and regimes

Five Emperors	2250-2140 B.C.
Xia	2140-1711 B.C.
Shang or Yin	1711-1066 B.C.
Zhou	1066-256 B.C.
Qin (Ch'in)	221-206 B.C.
Han	206 B.C.-A.D. 220
Three Kingdoms (San-kuo)	220-80
Tsin	265-420
South and North Dynasties	420-589
Sui	581-618
Tang	618-906
Five Dynasties	906-60
Song (Sung)	960-1279
Yuan	1279-1368
Ming	1368-1644
Qing (Ch'ing)	1644-1911
Republic	1912-49
People's Republic	1949-

People's Republic: Chairmen or General Secretaries of the Communist Party

Mao Tse-tung	1949-76
Hua Guofeng	1976-81*
Hu Yaobang	1982-87
Zhao Ziyang	1987-89
Jiang Zemin	1989-

** From 1978 to 1997, China's effective ruler, or "Paramount leader," was Deng Xiaoping.*

Presidents*

Li Xiannian	1983-88
Yang Shangkun	1988-93
Jiang Zemin	1993-

** The post of president, abolished in the late 1960s, was re-created in 1982.*

Japan

Emperors

According to tradition, Japan's first *tenno* or emperor was Jimmu (660-585 B.C.), a descendant of the sun goddess Amaterasu. He was the ancestor of all later emperors and empresses. Listed here are the emperors and empresses from the start of the Heian period.

Heian period

Kammu	781-806
Heizei	806-9
Saga	809-23
Junna	823-33
Nimmyo	833-50
Montoku	850-58
Seiwa	858-76
Yozei	877-84
Koko	884-87
Uda	887-97
Daigo	897-930
Suzaku	930-46
Murakami	946-67
Reizei	967-69
Enyu	969-84
Kazan	984-86
Ichijo	986-1011
Sanjo	1011-16
Ichijo II	1016-36
Suzaku II	1036-45
Reizei II	1045-68
Sanjo II	1068-72
Shirakawa	1072-86
Horikawa	1086-1107
Toba	1107-23
Sutoku	1123-41
Konoye	1141-55
Shirakawa II	1155-58
Nijo	1159-65
Rokujo	1166-68
Takakura	1169-80
Antoku	1181-83

Kamakura period

Toba II	1184-98
Tsuchimikado	1199-1210
Juntoku	1211-21
Chukyo	1221
Horikawa II	1222-32
Shijo	1233-42
Saga II	1243-46
Fukakusa II	1247-59
Kameyama	1260-74
Uda II	1275-87
Fushimi I	1288-98
Fushimi II	1299-1301
Nijo II	1302-8
Hanazono	1309-18
Daigo II	1319-38

Nambokucho period

For over 50 years from the 1330s, two different branches of the imperial family ruled at rival courts in the north and south.

Southern emperors

Murakami II	1339-68
Chokei	1369-72
Kameyama II	1373-92

Northern emperors

Kogon	1331-33
Komyo	1336-48
Suko	1349-52
Kogon II	1353-71
Enyu II	1372-82

Muromachi period

Komatsu II	1383-1412
Shoko	1413-28
Hanazono II	1429-64
Tsuchimikado II	1465-1500
Kashiwabara II	1501-26
Nara II	1527-57
Okimachi	1558-86

Azuchi-Momoyama period

Yozei II	1587-1611

Edo period

Mizunoo II	1611-29
Meisho	1630-43
Komyo II	1644-54
Saiin II	1655-62
Reigen	1663-86
Higashiyama	1687-1709
Nakamikado	1710-35
Sakuramachi	1736-46
Momozono	1746-62
Sakuramachi II	1763-70
Momozono II	1771-79
Kokaku	1780-1816
Ninko	1817-46
Komei	1847-66

Modern period

Mutsuhito	1866-1912
Yoshihito	1912-26
Hirohito	1926-89*
Akihito	1989-

** Regent from 1921*

India

Emperors

Mughal dynasty

Babur	1526-30
Humayun	1530-40

Sur dynasty

Sher Shah	1540-45
Islam Shah	1545-53
Muhammad Adil	1554-55

Mogul dynasty

Humayun	1555-56
Akbar I the Great	1556-1605
Jahangir	1605-27
Shah Jahan I	1627-58
Aurangzeb Alamgir I	1658-1707
Bahadur Shah I	1707-12
Jahandar Shah	1712-13
Farrukhsiyar	1713-19
Rafi al-Darajat	1719
Shah Jahan II	1719
Muhammad Shah	1719-48
Ahmad Shah	1748-54
Alamgir II	1754-59
Shah Alam	1759-1806
Akbar II	1806-37
Bahadur Shah II	1837-58

After the British sent the last emperor into exile, Queen Victoria assumed the title of Empress of India.

Prime ministers since independence

Jawaharlal Nehru	1947-64
Lal Bahadur Shastri	1964-66
Indira Gandhi	1966-77
Moraji Desai	1977-79
Charan Singh	1979-80
Indira Gandhi	1980-84
Rajiv Gandhi	1984-89
Viswanath Pratap Singh	1989-90
Chandra Shekhar	1990-91
P.V. Narsimha Rao	1991-96
Atal Behari Vajpayee	1996
H.D. Deve Gowda	1996-97
Inder Kumar Gujral	1997-98
Atal Behari Vajpayee	1998-

Australia

Prime ministers

Edmund Barton	1901-3
Alfred Deakin	1903-4
John C. Watson	1904
George Houstoun Reid	1904-5
Alfred Deakin	1905-8
Andrew Fisher	1908-9
Alfred Deakin	1909-10
Andrew Fisher	1910-13
Joseph Cook	1913-14
Andrew Fisher	1914-15
William M. Hughes	1915-23
Stanley M. Bruce	1923-29
James H. Sculin	1929-31
Joseph A. Lyons	1932-39
Robert Gordon Menzies	1939-41
Arthur William Fadden	1941
John Curtin	1941-45
Joseph Benedict Chifley	1945-49
Robert Gordon Menzies	1949-66
Harold Edward Holt	1966-67
John Grey Gorton	1968-71
William McMahon	1971-72
Gough Whitlam	1972-75
J. Malcolm Fraser	1975-83
Robert J.L. Hawke	1983-91
Paul Keating	1991-96
John Howard	1996-

New Zealand

Prime ministers

Henry Sewell	1856
William Fox	1856
Edward William Stafford	1856-61
William Fox	1861-62
Alfred Domett	1862-63
Frederick Whitaker	1863-64
Frederick Aloysius Weld	1864-65
Edward William Stafford	1865-69
William Fox	1869-72
Edward William Stafford	1872
George M. Waterhouse	1872-73
William Fox	1873
Julius Vogel	1873-75
Daniel Pollen	1875-76
Julius Vogel	1876
Harry Albert Atkinson	1876-77
George Grey	1877-79
John Hall	1879-82
Frederick Whitaker	1882-83
Harry Albert Atkinson	1883-84
Robert Stout	1884
Harry Albert Atkinson	1884
Robert Stout	1884-87
Harry Albert Atkinson	1887-91
John Ballance	1891-93
Richard John Seddon	1893-1906
William Hall Jones	1906
Joseph George Ward	1906-12
Thomas Mackenzie	1912
William Ferguson Massey	1912-25
Francis Henry Dillion Bell	1925
Joseph Gordon Coates	1925-28
Joseph George Ward	1928-30
George William Forbes	1930-35
Michael J. Savage	1935-40
Peter Fraser	1940-49
Sidney J. Holland	1949-57
Keith J. Holyoake	1957
Walter Nash	1957-60
Keith J. Holyoake	1960-72
John R. Marshall	1972
Norman Kirk	1972-74
Wallace Rowling	1974-75
Robert D. Muldoon	1975-84
David Lange	1984-89
Geoffrey Palmer	1989-90
Michael Moore	1990
James Bolger	1990-97
Jenny Shipley	1997-99
Helen Clark	1999-

Metric system

The metric unit of length, the meter, was first defined in France in 1799. All other lengths were derived from it in multiples of ten. This decimal system applies to all metric weights and measures.

Length	
1 mm	1 millimeter (mm)
10 mm	1 centimeter (cm)
10 cm	1 decimeter (dm)
100 cm/10 dm	1 meter (m)
1000 m	1 kilometer (km)

Area	
1 mm^2	1 sq millimeter (mm^2)
100 mm^2	1 sq centimeter (cm^2)
100 cm^2	1 sq decimeter (dm^2)
10 000 cm^2	1 sq meter (m^2)
10 000 m^2	1 hectare (ha)
1 million m^2/100 ha	1 sq kilometer (km^2)

Weight	
1 g	1 gram (g)
1000 g	1 kilogram (kg)
1000 kg	1 metric ton (t)

Volume (solid)	
1 cm^3	1 cubic centimeter (cm^3)
1000 cm^3	1 cubic decimeter (dm^3)
1000 dm^3	1 cubic meter (m^3)

Volume (liquid)	
1 ml	1 milliliter (ml)
10 ml	1 centiliter (cl)
10 cl	1 deciliter (dl)
100 cl/10 dl	1 liter (l)
100 l	1 hectoliter (hl)

SI units

The Système International d'Unités (SI), or International System of Units, is a modernized form of the metric system, which was internationally agreed upon in 1960.

	SI unit	Symbol
absorbed radiation dose	gray	Gy
amount of substance	mole	mol
electric capacitance	farad	F
electric charge	coulomb	C
electric conductance	siemens	S
electric current	ampere	A
energy or work	joule	J
force	newton	N
frequency	hertz	Hz
illuminance	lux	lx
inductance	henry	H
length	metre	m
luminous flux	lumen	lm
luminous intensity	candela	cd
magnetic flux	weber	Wb
magnetic flux density	tesla	T
mass	kilogram	kg
plane angle	radian	rad
potential difference	volt	V
power	watt	W
pressure	pascal	Pa
radiation dose equivalent	sievert	Sv
radiation exposure	roentgen	r
radioactivity	becquerel	Bq
resistance	ohm	Ω
solid angle	steradian	sr
sound intensity	decibel	dB
temperature	degree Celsius	°C
temperature, thermodynamic	kelvin	K
time	second	s

SI prefixes

Multiples	Prefix	Symbol	Example
10	deca	da	darad (decaradian)
100 (10^2)	hecto	h	hW (hectowatt)
1000 (10^3)	kilo	k	km (kilometer)
1 000 000 (10^6)	mega	M	MHz (megahertz)
1 000 000 000 (10^9)	giga	G	GJ (gigajoule)
1 000 000 000 000 (10^{12})	tera	T	TV (teravolt)
1 000 000 000 000 000 (10^{15})	peta	P	PPa (petapascal)
1 000 000 000 000 000 000 (10^{18})	exa	E	Elx (exalux)
1/10 (10^{-1})	deci	d	dSv (decisievert)
1/100 (10^{-2})	centi	c	cN (centinewton)
1/1000 (10^{-3})	milli	m	mA (milliampere)
1/1 000 000 (10^{-6})	micro	µ	µBq (microbecequerel)
1/1 000 000 000 (10^{-9})	nano	n	ns (nanosecond)
1/1 000 000 000 000 (10^{-12})	pico	p	pF (picofarad)
1/1 000 000 000 000 000 (10^{-15})	femto	f	fr (froentogen)
1/1 000 000 000 000 000 000 (10^{-18})	atto	a	aT (attotesla)

Feet, pounds and quarts

The traditional system of weights and measures used in Britain and the US evolved from a mix of Roman, old northern European and improvised units. The current length of the mile and weight of the pound were set in the late 1500s; the length of the inch, foot and yard were set in 1855.

Length	
1 in.	1 inch
12 in.	1 foot (ft)
3 ft	1 yard (yd)
5 1/2 yd	1 rod
22 yd/4 rods	1 chain
220 yd/10 chains	1 furlong
5280 ft/1760 yd/8 furlongs	1 mile

Length, nautical	
6 ft	1 fathom
100 fathoms	1 cable length
6080 ft	1 nautical mile

Area	
1 sq in.	square inch
144 sq in.	1 square foot (sq ft)
9 sq ft	1 square yard (sq yd)
304 1/4 sq yd	1 square rod
40 sq rods	1 rood
4840 sq yd/4 roods	1 acre
640 acres	1 square mile

Weight	
1 oz	1 ounce
16 oz	1 pound (lb)
14 lb	1 stone (UK)
8 stones (UK)	1 hundred-weight (cwt)
2000 lb	1 short ton
2240 lb/20 cwt	1 long ton

Volume (solid)	
1 cu in.	1 cubic inch
1728 cu in.	1 cubic foot (cu ft)
27 cu ft	1 cubic yard (cu yd)

Volume (liquid)	
1 fl oz (US)	1 fluid ounce (29.6 cm^3)
16 fl oz (US)	1 pint (US)
2 pints (US, UK)	1 quart (US, UK)
4 quarts (US, UK)	1 gallon (US, UK)
1 fl oz (UK)	(=28.41 cm^3)
20 fl oz (UK)	1 pint (UK)

Temperature scales

The Celsius (or centigrade) temperature scale was devised by the 18th-century Swedish astronomer Anders Celsius. In the Celsius scale, water freezes at 0° and boils at 100°; each degree is one hundredth part of the range between the two.

The Fahrenheit temperature scale was also devised in the 18th century, by German instrument-maker Gabriel Fahrenheit. In it, water freezes at 32° and boils at 212°.

A third scale is the Kelvin scale, whose zero point (0K) is absolute zero, approximately –273.15°C.

How to convert Fahrenheit to Celsius F° = (C° x 1.8) + 32

How to convert Celsius to Fahrenheit C° = (F° – 32) ÷ 1.8

°C	°F	°C	°F
100	212	30	86
95	203	25	77
90	194	20	68
85	185	15	59
80	176	10	50
75	167	5	41
70	158	0	32
65	149	–5	23
60	140	–10	14
55	131	–15	5
50	122	–20	–4
45	113	–25	–13
40	104	–30	–22
35	95		

How to convert metric to traditional

To convert	into	multiply by
Length		
millimeters	inches	0.0394
centimeters	inches	0.3937
meters	feet	3.2808
meters	yards	1.0936
kilometers	miles	0.6214
Area		
square centimeters	square inches	0.155
square meters	square feet	10.764
square meters	square yards	1.196
hectares	acres	2.471
square kilometers	square miles	0.386
Volume		
cubic centimeters	cubic inches	0.061
cubic meters	cubic feet	35.315
cubic meters	cubic yards	1.308
liters	pints	1.760
liters	gallons	0.220
Weight		
grams	ounces	0.0352
kilograms	pounds	2.2046
metric tons	long tons	0.9842

How to convert traditional to metric

To convert	into	multiply by
Length		
inches	millimeters	25.4
inches	centimeters	2.54
feet	meters	0.3048
yards	meters	0.9144
miles	kilometers	1.6093
Area		
square inches	square centimeters	6.4516
square feet	square meters	0.093
square yards	square meters	0.836
acres	hectares	0.405
square miles	square kilometers	2.58999
Volume		
cubic inches	cubic centimeters	16.387
cubic feet	cubic meters	0.0283
cubic yards	cubic meters	0.7646
fluid ounces	milliliters	28.41
pints	liters	0.568
gallons	liters	4.55
Weight		
ounces	grams	28.35
pounds	kilograms	0.45359
(long) tons	metric tons	1.016

Decibel scale

The decibel (dB) is used to compare loudness or density of sound. An increase of ten decibels is equivalent to a ten-fold increase in the density of sound.

Decibels	Sound level
0	Faintest audible sound
10	Low whisper
20	Average whisper
20-50	Quiet conversation
50	Normal speech
50 65	Loud conversation
65-70	Traffic on busy street
65-90	Train
75-80	Factory (light to medium work)
90	Highway traffic or other heavy traffic
90-100	Thunder
110-140	Jet aircraft taking off
130	Threshold of pain in the ear
140-190	Space rocket lifting off

Time zones

The Earth's surface is divided into 24 time zones. Each is 15 degrees of longitude wide, with local variations – for example, most of Western Europe keeps to time zone A, even though physically it straddles zones Z and A.

The zones begin at the Greenwich meridian (0° longitude). For every zone to the west of the Greenwich meridian, the clock time is one hour earlier; for every zone to the east, the time is one hour later. Some countries create daylight-saving hours by setting clocks one hour or more ahead of standard time for part of the year. The calendar date moves one day forward to the west of the International Date Line.

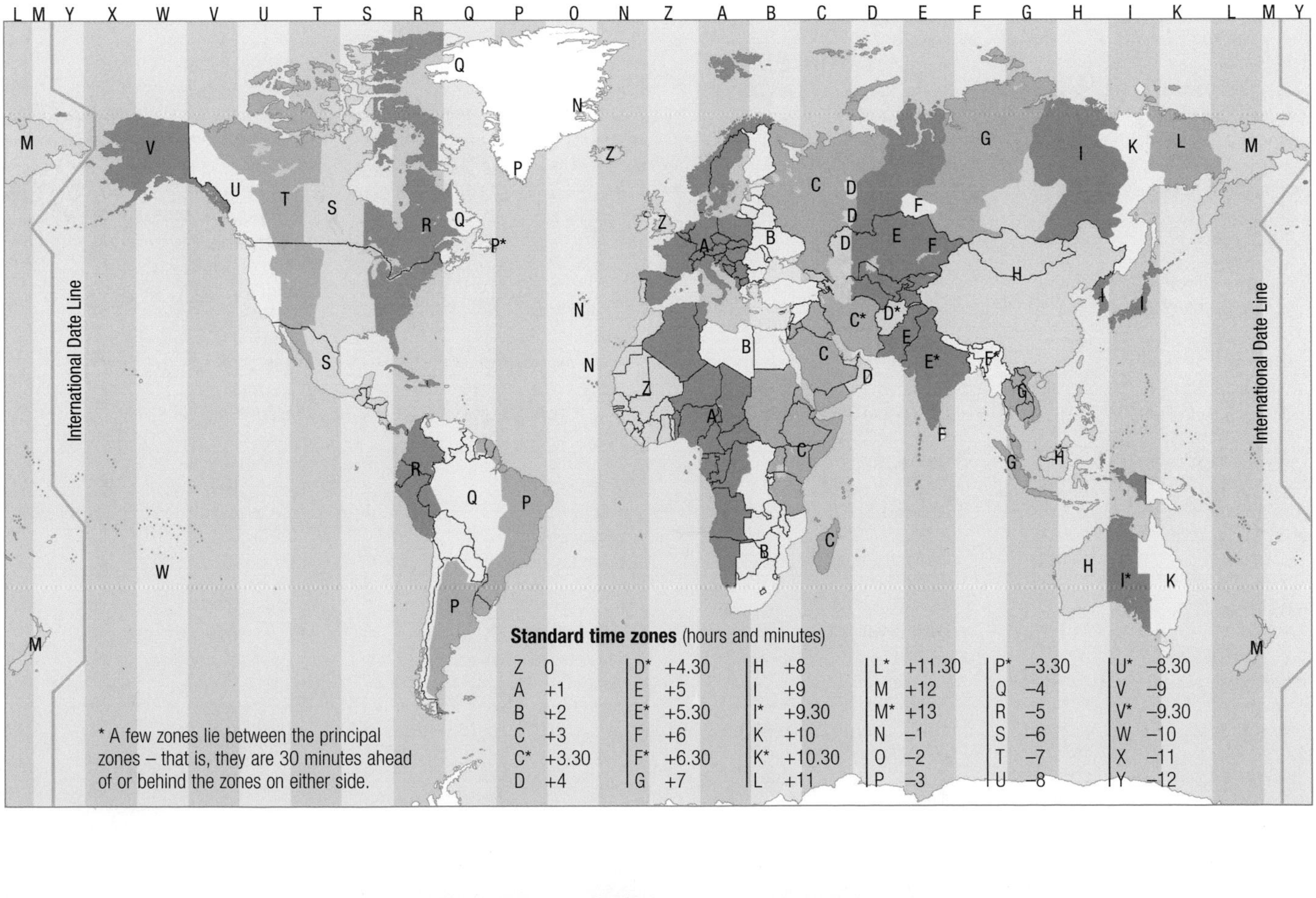

Page numbers in **bold** indicate main entries; those in *italics* indicate information in captions and/or illustrations only.

This index should be used in conjunction with the cross-referencing system in the text of the book.

A

B

C

D

E

F

H

M

N

Q

R

S

U

V

W

X

Y

Z

Acknowledgments

Abbreviations:
T=Top; M=Middle; B=Bottom;
R=Right; L=Left

BBCNHU – BBC Natural History Unit Picture Library
DRK – DRK Photos
OSF – Oxford Scientific Films
SPL – Science Photo Library

Timelines: Bradbury & Williams. **2-7** © PhotoDisc Europe Ltd; © Digital Vision Ltd; Martin Woodward; Image Quest 3–D; Mirashade. **9** Julian Baker Illustrations. **10** Julian Baker Illustrations, TR; Michael Robinson, B. **11** B. & C. Alexander, TR; Julian Baker Illustrations, ML; SPL/PLI, BR. **12-13** Julian Baker Illustrations. **14** Galaxy Picture Library/ESO, T; SPL/Royal Observatory, Edinburgh, M; SPL/T. & D. Hallas, B. **14-15** Tom Stack & Associates/B. & S. Fletcher. **16-17** Julian Baker Illustrations. **18** SPL/NASA, ML; Julian Baker Illustrations. **19** Galaxy Picture Library/TRACE-1/Stanford-Lockheed Institute for Space Research, T; Galaxy Picture Library/KPNO/T.Rinmele, M.Hanna/AURA/NOAO/NSF, B. **20** SPL/US Geology Survey, TL; NASA/JPL, TM; Genesis/NASA, TR; Artworks Ian Atkinson. **21** NASA/JPL; Genesis/NASA TM; SPL/STScI/NASA, TR; Artworks Ian Atkinson. **22** Galaxy Picture Library, ML; **22-23** SPL/NASA. **23** Michael Robinson, TR; DRK/S. Nielsen, MR. **24** Julian Baker Illustrations, ML; Michael Robinson, B. **25** Galaxy Picture Library/Roger Lynds/AURA/NOAO/NSF, T; Auscape/Jean-Paul Ferrero, B. **26** Julian Baker Illustrations. **27** Michael Robinson; map, Bradbury & Williams/Mountain High. **28** Auscape/Jean-Paul Ferrero, TR; DRK/Jeff Foott, BM; Michael Robinson. **29** Robert Harding Picture Library/Tony Gervis, TM; Natural History Museum, London, BR; Artworks Michael Robinson. **30-31** Artworks Michael Robinson; Colorific/Greg Girard/Contact. **32** Minden/Frans Lanting, T; DRK/C.C. Lockwood, ML; Ardea/D. Parer & E. Parer-Cook, MM; Ardea/François Gohier, MR; Artworks Michael Robinson. **33** OSF/Hjalmar R. Bardarson. **34-35** Mountain High/Bradbury & Williams. **35** Michael Robinson, BR. **36** SPL/Earth Satellite Corporation, TR; Bradbury & Williams, MR; **36-37** DRK/Kim Heacox. **37** Woodfall Wild Images/David Woodfall, T. **38** Michael Robinson, T; Katz Pictures/JD, BR. **39** FLPA/T. & P. Gardner, BL; John Cleare Mountain Camera, BR. **40** Digital Vision, T; Hutchison Library/Christina Dodwell, BL; NHPA/B. Jones & M. Shimlock, BR. **41** SPL/WorldSat International & J. Knighton/Earth Satellite Corporation/WorldSat Productions/NRSC/Tom Van Sant, Geosphere Project/Planetary Visions. **42** Bradbury & Williams, T; Julian Baker Illustrations, B. **42-43** Woodfall Wild Images/David Woodfall. **44** Michael Robinson, TR; Bradbury & Williams, M. **44-45** Woodfall Wild Images/David Woodfall. **45** Bradbury & Williams/Mountain High, TR; Woodfall Wild Images/David Woodfall, ML; Ardea/François Gohier, BL. **46** Julian Baker Illustrations. **47** DRK/Johnny Johnson, TR; Michael Robinson, MR; SPL/NASA/Goddard Space Flight Centre, BL. **48** Michael Robinson, ML. **48-49** SPL/Larry Miller. **49** Artwork Michael Robinson; Woodfall Wild Images/Ashley Cooper, T; DRK/Tom Bean, ML; Tom Stack & Associates/Mark Allen Stack, MM; Corbis/George Lepp, ML; Corbis/Richard Hamilton Smith, B. **51** Bruce Coleman/Jorg & Petra Wegner; Wildlife Art Ltd. **52** SPL/PH. Plailly/Eurelios, TL; Wildlife Art Ltd, TR; Bedrock Studios Ltd, BR. **53** SPL/Sinlair Stammers, TR; Wildlife Art Ltd, TL, MM; Bedrock Studios Ltd, BR. **54** Ardea/J.L. Mason, TM, TR; WildLife Art, B. **55** Auscape/Nicholas Birks, TR; DRK/Jeremy Woodhouse, MR. **56-57** Wildlife Art Ltd. **57** SPL/PH.Plailly/Eurelios, TL; Bradbury & Williams, TR; BBCNHU/Bruce Davison, BL. **58** Wildlife Art Ltd. **59** Auscape/Mark Spencer, TL; NHPA/Michael Tweedie, MM; OSF/Deni Bown, BL; Ardea/François Gohier, MM; DRK/Fred Bruemmer, BR. **60** Wildlife Art Ltd, TR; Lee Peters, BL. **61** Wildlife Art Ltd, TL, BL; SPL/Dr Jeremy Burgess, MM; DRK/Jeff Foott, BR. **62** Wildlife Art Ltd, MR. **63** SPL/Sinclair Stammers, TM; Wildlife Art Ltd, ML; Natural History Museum, London, MR. **64-65** Artworks Wildlife Art Ltd; SPL/D. Roberts. **66** Tom Stack Associates/ David Young, TR; Reproduced by kind permission of the Director, British Geological Survey, NERC copyright reserved, MM. **67** Wildlife Art Ltd, TL,BR; Bradbury & Williams, BL. **68** Ardea/François Gohier, TR; Bedrock Studios Ltd/Bradbury & Williams, BM. **68-69** Bedrock Studios Ltd. **70** Tom Stack & Associates/Tom & Therisa Stack, TM. **70-71** Bedrock Studios Ltd. **72-73** Wildlife Art Ltd. **73** Bradbury & Williams, TR. **74** Ardea/François Gohier, TR; Wildlife Art Ltd, B. **75** Digital Vision Ltd, BR. **76** NHPA J & M Bain, MM; Artwork Wildlife Art Ltd, MM; Digital Vision Ltd, BL. **77** Bradbury & Williams, T; Wildlife Art Ltd, BM, BR. **78** Digital Vision Ltd, TL; Bruce Coleman Collection/Kim Taylor, MM; Artwork Wildlife Art Ltd, MM. **79** Bradbury & Williams, T; Wildlife Art Ltd, BM. **80** Wildlife Art Ltd, TL, TM, TR; Bruce Coleman Collection/Pacific Stock, B. **81** Bradbury & Williams, T; Wildlife Art Ltd, MM, BL; Minden Pictures/Frans Lanting, BR. **82** Bradbury & Williams, T; Dorling Kindersley Ltd/Frank Greenaway, BL; Wildlife Art Ltd, MM, BR. **83** Bradbury & Williams, T; Wildlife Art Ltd, ML, MR, BL, BR. **84** Wildlife Art Ltd, TL; Bruce Coleman Collection/Kim Taylor, MM; Wildlife Art Ltd, MM; DRK/Michael Fogden, BR. **85** Bradbury & Williams, T; NHPA/Stephen Dalton, ML; Wildlife Art Ltd, BR. **86** Minden Pictures/Frans Lanting, MM; Wildlife Art Ltd, MM. **87** Bradbury & Williams, T; Wildlife Art Ltd, MM, BR; NHPA/Stephen Dalton, BL. **88** Wildlife Art Ltd, ML; Bruce Coleman Collection/Kim Taylor, MM; Wildlife Art Ltd, MM. **89** Bradbury & Williams, T; Wildlife Art Ltd, MM, BR; Ardea/Masahiro Iijima, BL. **90** Bradbury & Williams, T; Artworks Wildlife Art Ltd. **91** Bradbury & Williams, T; Wildlife Art Ltd, BL; Tom Stack & Associates/Dave Watts, BR. **92** Bradbury & Williams, T; Wildlife Art Ltd, ML, MR, BL. **93** Bradbury & Williams, T; Wildlife Art Ltd, ML, MR; DRK/Jeff Foott, BM. **94** Bradbury & Williams, T; Wildlife Art Ltd, ML, MR; Ardea/Zdenek Tunka, MM; DRK/Wayne Lankinen, BL. **95** Wildlife Art Ltd. **96** DRK/Don & Pat Valenti, TR. OSF/Robert Tyrell, BL. **97** Bruce Coleman Collection/Jorg & Petra Wegner. **98** DRK/Anup Shah. **99** Bradbury & Williams, T; Still Pictures/Roland Seitre, ML; Wildlife Art Ltd, MR; Minden Pictures/Mitsuaki Iwago, BR. **100** Bradbury & Williams, T; NHPA/Stephen Dalton, BL; DRK/M. Harvey, BR. **101** Bradbury & Williams, T; DRK/Michael Fogden, ML; Minden Pictures/Frans Lanting, MM; Bradbury & Williams, MR; DRK/Tom Brakefield, BL; Wildlife Art Ltd, BR. **102** Bradbury & Williams, T, ML; Wildlife Art Ltd, MR, BR. **103** Bradbury & Williams, T, MR; Wildlife Art Ltd, ML, MM, BR. **104** Gerald Cubitt, TR; Don Stephens & Associates, ML; BBCNHU/Michael & Patricia Fogden, BL; DRK/Marty Cordano, BR. **105** Natural History Museum, London, TL, TR; Mary Evans Picture Library, TM; Doug Perrine/Innerspace Visions, BL; NHPA/Stephen Dalton, BR. **106** Bradbury & Williams, TR, background, MM; Wildlife Art Ltd, MM, BR. **107** Bradbury & Williams, TR, background, MM; Wildlife Art Ltd, MM. **108** Bradbury & Williams, TR, background, MM, BL, BM, BR; Wildlife Art Ltd, MM. **109** SPL/John Reader, TL; © Adrie & Alfons Kennis, MM; Bottom left-right DRK, Peter D. Pickford; Ardea/Jean-Paul Ferrero; DRK/Stephen J. Krasemann; DRK/Barbara Cushman Rowell. **111** Mirashade. **112** Antbits, BL; Mirashade, R. **113** Mirashade, L, TR; Antbits, MR. **114** Mirashade, L; Mirashade/Antbits, R. **115** Mirashade, T; Martin Woodward, B. **116** Mirashade, L; Mirashade/Antbits, R. **117** Antbits. **118** Mirashade. **119** Antbits, L; Mirashade/Antbits, R. **120** Martin Woodward, L; Mirashade, R. **121** Martin Woodward, ML, MM, BM; Mirashade, R. **122** Antbits, L; SPL/Quest, R. **123** SPL/H. Raguet, TM; SPL/John Burbidge, TR; Bradbury & Williams, BR. **124** Martin Woodward, TL; Mirashade/Martin Woodward, R; Ishihara Plates/Kanchara Shuppan Co Ltd, BL. **125** Martin Woodward, ML; Mirashade/Antbits, R; Allsport USA/Mike Powell, BL. **126** Martin Woodward. **127** Martin Woodward, L; SPL/Prof. P. Motta, ML; Mirashade, MR; NHPA/Stephen Dalton, R. **128** SPL/Dr. Yorgos Nikas, TR, BR. **129** Amanda Williams. SPL/James Stevenson, BM. **130** SPL/Juergen Berger, BL; SPL/Quest, BM; SPL/CNRI, BR. **130-31** Martin Woodward. **131** SPL/J.C. Revy, TR. **132** Centre for Brain & Cognitive Development, Birkbeck College, BL; Bradbury & Williams/Kanizsa Square, BM; background, photography Jane Sackville West. **133** Bubbles/Angela Hampton, TM; Katz Pictures/Karen Kasmanski, BM; background, photography John Meek. **135** AKG; Bradbury & Williams. **136** Maps Bradbury & Williams; Roger Stewart, TM, MR; **137** Maps Bradbury & Williams; Roger Stewart, TL, ML, MR, BR. **138** Auscape/Ferrero-Labat, TR; AKG/Erich Lessing/Natural History Museum, Vienna, BL; AKG/Erich Lessing/Natural History Museum, Vienna, BR. **139** Museum of Antiquities, University of Newcastle, TL; British Museum, London, TR; Bradbury & Williams/Mountain High, B. **140** Bradbury & Williams/Mountain High, TR; Michael Holford/British Museum, BL; AKG/Erich Lessing/Department of Oriental Antiquities, Louvre, Paris, BM. **141** Michael Holford/ British Museum, TL; The Art Archive/ Aleppo Museum, Syria/Dagli Orti, TM; Bridgeman Art Library/Louvre, Paris, TR; map Bradbury & Williams/ Mountain High. **142** Robert Harding/ Simon Harris, TL; Michael Holford/ British Museum, TR, BL. **142-43** Artwork Digital Wisdom. **143** AKG/Erich Lessing, BR. **144** Michael Holford, TR; Michael Holford/British Museum, BL; Bradbury & Williams/Mountain High, BR. **145** AKG/Erich Lessing/Musée Vivenel Compiégne, TL; AKG/Erich Lessing, TM; Michael Holford/British Museum, TR; AKG/Erich Lessing/National Museum of Archaeology, Naples, BL; Bradbury & Williams, BR. **146** Michael Holford, TL; Bridgeman Art Library, BR. **146-47** Map Bradbury & Williams/Mountain High. **148** Michael Holford/British Museum, TR; AKG/Erich Lessing/Louvre, Paris; Bradbury & Williams/Mountain High, BR. **149** Bradbury & Williams/Mountain High, TL; Werner Forman Archive/Viking Ship Museum, Bygdoy, TR; Bridgeman Art Library/Louvre, Paris, BL. **150-51** Map Bradbury & Williams/Mountain High. **151** Roger Stewart, TR. **152** Roy Williams, ML. **152-53** Map Bradbury & Williams/Mountain High. **153** The Art Archive/Dagli Orti, TR. **154-55** Map, Bradbury & Williams/Mountain High. **155** Werner Forman Archive/University Library, Prague, TM; Bridgeman Art Library/British Library, London, BR. **156** Bradbury & Williams, TR, BL; AKG/Jean-Louis Nou, BM. **156-57** Corbis/© Ric Ergenbright. **157** Bridgeman Art Library/National Museum of India, New Delhi, TR; Bradbury & Williams, TL, BR; Michael Holford/Victoria & Albert Museum, London, BL. **158** Bridgeman Art Library, TR; The Art Archive/Victoria & Albert Museum, London, MR;

Michael Holford/Victoria & Albert Museum, London, BL. **159** AKG/Erich Lessing/Musée Guimet, Paris, MR; The Art Archive/Gunshots, BL. **160** Werner Forman Archive/Courtesy Entwistle Gallery, London, BL. **160-61** Map Bradbury & Williams/Mountain High. **161** Michael Holford/ British Museum, TR; Werner Forman Archive/Private Collection, New York, MM. **162** Werner Forman Archive/Anthropology Museum, Veracruz University, Jalapa, TR; Werner Forman Archive, ML; Bradbury & Williams/Mountain High, MR; Werner Forman Archive/Museum für Volkerkunde, Vienna, BL; The Art Archive/Honduras Institute, Tegucigalpa/Dagli Orti, BM. **163** Map Bradbury & Williams/Mountain High; Werner Forman Archive/Musuem für Volkerkunde, Berlin, MM. **164** Jean-Loup Charmet, MM; Bildarchiv Preussischer Kulturbesitz, MR. **164-65** Map Bradbury & Williams/ Mountain High. **165** Jean-Loup Charmet, TM; Bridgeman Art Library, BM. **166** *The Arnolfini Portrait*, 1434, oil on panel by Jan van Eyck, National Gallery, London/AKG/Erich Lessing, MM. **166-67** Michael Holford. **167** *The Flagellation*, *c.*1458, on panel by Piero della Francesca, Galleria Nazionale delle Marche, Urbino/AKG. **168** Bildarchiv Preussischer Kulturbesitz/ Kunstverein, Winterthur, TR; Bildarchiv Preussischer Kulturbesitz/ Kubstmuseum, Basel, BL. **168-69** Background, *The St Bartholomew's Day Massacre*, 1572, 16th-century woodcut, German, Bibliotheque de Protestantisme, Paris/Bridgeman Art Library. **169** Corbis/© Elio Ciol, MR. **170** *Louis XIV*, 1701, oil on canvas by Hyacinthe Rigaud, Louvre, Paris/AKG/ Erich Lessing; *Voltaire*, marble bust by Jean-Antoine Houdon, Louvre, Paris, BM. **171** The Art Archive/Musée de Versailles/Dagli Orti, TR; Bradbury & Williams/Mountain High, TM; Bildarchiv Preussischer Kulturbesitz/Uffizi Gallery, Florence, ML; AKG, MM; *Peter the Great*, 1717, oil on canvas by Jena-Marc Nattier, Hermitage, St Petersburg/Bridgeman Art Library, MR. **172** The Art Archive/Musée Carnavalet, Paris/Dagli Orti, BL; Bridgeman Art Library/Musée Carnavalet, Paris, BR. **172-73** Background, *The Battle of Austerlitz*, 1829, oil on canvas by François Gerard, Gallerie de Batailles, Versailles/AKG. **173** Bradbury & Williams/Mountain High. **174** Bridgeman Art Library/Private Collection, TR; Corbis/© Kevin Fleming, BL. **175** Bradbury & Williams/Mountain High, TR; Hulton Getty, BR. **176** Science & Society Picture Library, TL; Michael Holford/Science Museum, London, TR; Michael Holford/Science Museum, London, BR. **176-77** Background, Bildarchiv Preussischer Kulturbesitz. **177** State Library of New South Wales, Sydney, Australia, TL; Bridgeman Art Library/Stapleton Collection, TR; Corbis/Lewis Hine, BM. **178** The Art Archive/Richard Borough Council/ Eileen Tweedy, MM; Corbis/© Paul Almasy, BL. **178-79** Map, Bradbury & Williams/Mountain High. **179** AKG/ Archiv für Kunst & Geschichte, Berlin, TR. **180-81** Popperfoto, T; Maps, Bradbury & Williams/Mountain High. **182-83** David King Collection. **184** Bradbury & Williams/Mountain High, MM; Hulton Getty, BR; background, *Unemployed in the San Francisco Job Center*, 1938, photograph by Dorothea Lange/AKG. **185** Hulton Getty, TR, BL; AKG, MM, BR. **186** Corbis, TM; The Art Archive/ National Archives, BR. **186-87** AKG. **187** The Art Archive/Imperial War Museum, TM; © Magnum/Robert Capa, BL; Hulton Getty, BR. **188** ©Magnum/Nicolas Tikomiroff, ML. **188-89** Map, Bradbury & Williams/ Mountain High. **189** Hulton Getty, TR, BR. **190** Hulton Getty, BR. **190-91** © Bettmann/Corbis. **191** © Magnum/ Susan Meiselas, ML; © Magnum/Philip Jones Griffiths, MR; AKG, BR. **192** © Bettmann/Corbis, TR; Corbis/ © David & Peter Turnley, BR. **192-93** © Magnum/Jean Gaumy. **193** Corbis/ © David & Peter Turnley, TR; Frank Spooner Pictures/Patrick Piel, BL; Corbis/© David & Peter Turnley, BR. **195** Esto/Tim Griffiths. **197** B. & C. Alexander, TR. **198** South American Pictures/Charlotte Lipson, ML. **216-22** Maps © Readers Digest/revised and updated by Bradbury & Williams. **216** View/Dennis Gilbert. **219** Scanpix. **221** Environmental Images/Martin Bond. **222** Bradbury & Williams, TL. **224** Esto © Ralph Richter. **227** Katz Pictures/ Tommaso Bonaventura/Contrasto. **228** Bradbury & Williams, BR. **229** Katz Pictures/Jeremy Nicholl, TR; Corbis/ © Layne Kennedy, BL. **230** Colin Woodman, BR. **231** Corbis/Reuters NewMedia Inc. **233** © Magnum/A. Venzago, MR. **234** Colin Woodman, BR. **236** Sonia Halliday Photographs, TL; The Art Archive/Archaeological Museum, Naples/Dagli Orti, TR. **238** Trip/M. Barlow. **240** Colin Woodman, TR. **241** Trip/T. Noorits, MM; Katz Pictures/Visum/Gerd Ludwig,BR. **244** Popperfoto. **246** Katz Pictures/Ben Gibson, BR. **247** Bradbury & Williams, MM. **249** © Magnum/Harry Gruyaert, BM. **250** Frank Spooner Pictures/ Peterson, BL; Colin Woodman, BR. **255** Bradbury & Williams, TL. **256** Robert Harding Picture Library/James Green, MM. **258** Bradbury & Williams, MM; Esto/© Tim Griffiths, B. **261** Frank Spooner Pictures/Gamma, TR. **262** Bradbury & Williams, B. **263** © Magnum/Stuart Franklin, TR. **265** Popperfoto, BR. **266** Bradbury & Williams, ML; Popperfoto, BL. **267** Environmental Images/Mark Fallander, TR. **268** Bradbury & Williams, TR. **200** Colin Woodman. **201** Katz Pictures/ Tomasz Tomaszewski, BL. **208** Trip/ Ben Belbin, B. **210** DRK/Jeff Foott, ML. **211** Trip/B. Gadsby, TR. **213** South American Pictures/© Tony Morrison, BL. **215** © Magnum/Stuart Franklin, BR. **276** OSF/Martyn Colbeck, BL. **292-93** The World Bank Group (WB): The International Bank for Reconstruction and Development (IBRD), International Development Association (IDA),International Finance Corporation (IFC), Multilateral Investment Guarantee Agency (MIGA); APEC; NATO; OECD. **295** Robert Harding Picture Library; Angelo Hornak Library; Arcaid/Richard Bryant. **296** Colin Woodman. **297-99** Bradbury & Williams. **300** Bradbury & Williams, TR; Bridgeman Art Library/National Archaeological Museum, Athens, ML; Ronald Grant Archive, MM; Bridgeman Art Library, MR. **301** Ronald Grant Archive, TR; Bridgeman Art Library/ Pergamon Museum, Berlin, BM. **302** Ronald Grant Archive, TR; Bridgeman Art Library/National Museum, Stockholm, BM. **303** Bridgeman Art Library/Bradford Art Galleries and Museums, TR; Werner Forman Archive/National Museum of Anthropology, Mexico, BL. **304** Colin Woodman. **305** Corbis/Richard T. Nowitz, TR; Bridgeman Art Library/ Koninklijk Museum voor Schone Kunsten, Antwerp, BR. **306** Bridgeman Art Library/Musée Condé, Chantilly, BR. **307** Michael Freeman, ML; © Magnum/Fred Mayer, BR. **308-11** Mirashade. **312** AKG, TL, TR; Bettmann/Corbis. **313** Left-right: Bettmann/Corbis; Topham Picturepoint; Corbis/Roger Messmeyer; Corbis/David Reed. **314** Bridgeman Art Library/Pinacoteca Capitolina Palazzo Conferratori, Rome, TR; Popperfoto, BM. **315** Bridgeman Art Library/British Library, London, TL; SPL/NASA, MR. **316** SCALA/Museo Nazionale, Napoli, TR; *The Visitation*, column statues from east portal of north trancept, c.1220, stone, Chartres Cathedral/Bridgeman Art Library/Peter Willi, MR; *The Apollo of Piombino*, Greek bronze, 1st century BC, Louvre, Paris/Bridgeman Art Library/Peter Willi, BL. **317** *The Wilton Diptych: Richard II presented to the Virgin and Child by his Patron Saint John the Baptist and Saints Edward and Edmund*, 1395-9, anonymous, tempera on panel, National Gallery, London, TR; *St Francis Honoured by a Simple Man*, 1296-7, fresco by Giotto di Bondone, San Francesco, Upper Church, Assisi/Bridgeman Art Library, BR. **318** *The Infanta Doña Margarita of Austria*, c.1660, oil on canvas by Diego Velázquez de Silva, Museo Nacional Del Prado, Madrid/Collection of Philip IV, TR; *David*, 1501-4, marble by Michelangelo Buonarroti, Galleria dell'Accademia, Florence/Bridgeman Art Library, ML; *The Supper At Emmaus*, 1601, oil and tempera on canvas by Michelangelo Merisi da Caravaggio, National Gallery, London, MR. **319** *The Death of Germanicus*, 1627, oil on canvas by Nicholas Poussin, The Minneapolis Institute of Arts/The William Hood Dunwoody Fund, TM; *The Avenue at Middelharnis*, 1689, oil on canvas by Meindert Hobbema, National Gallery, London, MM. **320** *Three Graces*, marble by Antonio Canova, V&A Picture Library, TR; *The Swing*, 1767, oil on canvas by Jean-Honoré Fragonard, Wallace Collection, London/Bridgeman Art Library, ML; *Rain, Steam, and Speed – The Great Western Railway*, oil on canvas by Joseph Mallord William Turner, National Gallery, London, MR. **321** *Burial at Ornans*, 1849-50, oil on canvas by Gustave Courbet, Musée d'Orsay, Paris/Bridgeman Art Library, TM; *Las Veneris*, 1873-75, oil and gold paint on canvas by Sir Edward Burne-Jones, Laing Art Gallery, Newcastle-upon-Tyne, Tyne & Wear/Bridgeman Art Gallery, ML. **322** *The Kiss*,1886, marble by Auguste Rodin, Musée Rodin, Paris/Bridgeman Art Library, TR; *The Waterlily Pond with the Japanese Bridge*, 1899, oil on canvas by Claude Monet, Private Collection/Bridgeman Art Library/Peter Willi, MM; *Guernica*, 1937, oil on canvas by Pablo Picasso, Museo Nacional Centro de Arte Reine Sofia, Madrid/Bridgeman Art Library/ D.A.C.S., BR. **323** *The Fate of the Animals*, 1913, oil on canvas by Franz Marc, Oeffentliche Kunstsammlung Basel, Kunstmuseum/Photography Martin Bühler, TL; *Metamorphosis of Narcissus*, 1937, oil on canvas by Salvador Dali, © Tate, London 2001, MR; *Velocity of Cars and Light*, 1913, oil on card by Giacomo Balla, Moderna Museet, Stockholm/ Bridgeman Art Library/Peter Willi/ D.A.C.S., BL. **324** *Blue Poles: Number II*, 1952, enamel and aluminium painted on glass by Jackson Pollock, Australian National Gallery, Camberra/ Bridgeman Art Library/D.A.C.S., TR; *Mademoiselle Pogany III*, 1933, plaster by Constartine Brancusi, Musée National d'Art Moderne, Paris/ Bridgeman Art Library/Peter Willi, TL; *Puppy*, 1992, by Jeff Koons, Guggenheim Museum, Bilbao/© Jeff Koons Productions, MM; *In the Car*, 1963, magna on canvas by Roy Lichtenstein, Scottish National Gallery of Modern Art, Edinburgh/Bridgeman Art Library/D.A.C.S., MR; *Cold Dark Matter: An Exploded View*, 1956, mixed media by Cornelia Parker, © Tate, London 2001/© Cornelia Parker, BL. **325** *American Collectors (Fred and Marcia Weisman)*, 1968, acrylic on canvas by David Hockney/ © David Hockney, TM; *The Physical Impossibility of Death in the Mind of Someone Living*, 1991, tiger shark, glass, steel, 5% formaldehyde solution, by Damien Hirst, Saatchi Gallery, London/© Damien Hirst/photograph courtesy Science, MM; *Kangaroo Island, South Australia 26 February 1992* by Andy Goldsworthy/© Andy Goldsworthy, BL; **326-27** Middle left-right: Scala, 1, 2, 3, 5; Corbis/Ruggero Vanni, 5; Angelo Hornak, 6. **327** Martin Woodward, BM. **328-29** Middle left-right: Angelo Hornak, 1, 5, 7; View/ © Andrew Holt, 2; View/© Nick Hulton, 3; Robert Harding Picture Library, 4; Arcaid/© Richard Bryant, 6; Arcaid/

© John Edward Linden, BR. **330** The Art Archive/University of Heidelberg/ Dagli Orti, TL; Christie's Images, TR; **331** V&A Picture Library, TL; AKG, TR; Bradbury & Williams, BM. **332** AKG/ Breitkopf & Haertel Archive, Leipzig, TL; Lebrecht Collection, TR; Bradbury & Williams, BL; Lebrecht Collection/ Robin Del Mar, BR. **333** AKG/Archiv für Kunst und Geschichte, Berlin, TL; Lebrecht Collection/George Newson, TR; Zoë Dominic Collection/ © Catherine Ashmore, BL. **330-33** Timeline, *Prelude and Fugue in B minor for Organ*, handwritten score, Leipzig, *c.*1740 by J.S. Bach/Lebrecht Collection. **334** Brown Brothers, TL, BR. **335** © Bettmann/Corbis TR, ML; London Features. Redferns/© Michael Ochs Archives, TL, BR; © Bettmann/ Corbis, TR. **337** Corbis/© Matthew Mendelsogn, TL; London Features, BR. **338** Bridgeman Art Library/Museo Archaelogico Nazionale, Naples, TL; Dante reading from the Divine Comedy, 1465 panel by Domenico di Michelino, Duomo, Florence, TM; *Portrait of Chaucer, from the Ellesmere Manuscript of Canterbury Tales by Chaucer* (facsimile edition), 1911/Bridgeman Art Library/Private Collection, TR; Mary Evans Picture Library, BL. **339** Bridgeman Art Library/British Library/Portrait engraving by Droeshurt, 1623, TM; *The Simoniac Pope*, pen, ink and watercolour, 1824-7 by William Blake, © Tate, London 2001, BL. **340** Bridgeman Art Library/Private Collection/Portrait by Nicholas de Largilliére, TL; Bridgeman Art Library/Private Collection, TR; Bridgeman Art Library/Private Collection/watercolour by John Nixon, BR; *John Milton's Signature*/Hulton Getty. **341** Bridgeman Art Library/Private Collection/Portrait engraving by C. Rolls, TL; Bridgeman Art Library/Neue Pinakothek, Munich/Portrait by Joseph Carl Stieler, TR; Mary Evans Picture Library/H. Richter, engraved by Staines, BR; *Pushkin's Signature*/© Novosti, London; *Goethe's Signature*/AKG. **342** © Novosti, London, TL; Bridgeman Art Library/Private Collection, TM; Hulton Getty, TR; Mary Evans Picture Library/Engraving by Marcus Stone, BL; © John Glashan/from *Things*, edited by Tony & Carol Burgess (Ward Lock Educational), BR; *Tolstoy's Signature* and *Dostoevsky's Signature*/© Novosti, London. **343** © Bettmann/Corbis. **344** © Allan Titmuss/*The Oedipus Plays* by Sophocles, TL; Mander & Mitchenson Theatre Collection/*The York Cycle of Mystery Plays*, TR; © Catherine Ashmore/*Thyestes* by Seneca, MM; Martin Woodward, B. **345** © Simon Annand/*The Miser* by Moliere, TM; © Zoë Dominic/*King Lear* by William Shakespeare, ML; © Zoë Dominic/*The School For Scandal* by Richard Sheridan, MR. **346** © Mander & Mitchenson The, TM; Haga Library Inc. Tokyo/© Toshiro Morita/Noh play *Othello*, ML; © Mark Drouet/Arena Images/*Uncle Vanya* by Chekhov, MR; © John Haynes/*Home* by David Storey, BR. **347** © John Haynes/*Schweyk In The Second World War* by Bertolt Brecht, TL; © Zoë Dominic/ *Inadmissible Evidence* by John Osborne, TR; © Zoë Dominic/*Happy Days* by Samuel Beckett, MM. **348** Ronald Grant Archive, TR, ML; Joel Finler Collection, BM. **350** Joel Finler Collection, TR; Ronald Grant Archive, B. **351** Ronald Grant Archive, BL; Pictorial Press Limited, BR. **352** © Carolco/Kobal, TM; Rex Features, B. **353** © Lucas Film Ltd/Paramount/ Kobal, ML; Ronald Grant Archive, BR. **348-52** Timeline, Ronald Grant Archive. **354-55** Timeline left-right: © BBC, 1; © Globe Photos Inc, 2; Culver Pictures, 3; SPL/NASA, 4; Rex Features, 5; © Sky News, 7; Popperfoto, 6, 8. **356** Paris Match Magazine, ML; John Frost Newspaper Collection, MR; Popperfoto, BL. **357** Hergé/Moulinsart 2001, BL; Printed by permission of the Norman Rockwell Family Trust Copyright © 1958 the Norman Rockwell Family Trust/AKG, BR. **358-59** Middle left right: Robert Harding Picture Library/© Roy Rainford, 1; Corbis/© Adam Woolfitt, 2; Corbis/© Jonathan Blair; Robert Harding Picture/© M. Joseph, 4; Corbis/© Richard T. Nowitz, 5; Corbis/© Catherine Karnow, 6; Corbis/© Diego Lezama Orezzoli, 7; Corbis/© Ted Spiegel, 8. **358** The Anthony Blake Photo Library/© RDL, BR. **359** Robert Opie Collection, TR. **360** Brown Brothers, TR; Allsport/Andy Lyone, MR; Colorsport, BL; Roger Stewart, BM. **361** Culver Pictures, MR,BR; Roger Stewart, BL. **362** © Bettmann/Corbis/David Tulis, ML; Allsport/Jonathan Daniel, BL; Roger Stewart, BR. **363** Colorsport, T; Allsport/ Glenn Gratty, BR. **364** Allsport, TM; Corbis/© Reuters NewMedia Inc, TR; Roger Stewart, BM. **365** Popperfoto, TR; Allsport/Hulton Collection, BL; www.sporting-heroes.net, BM; Colorsport/Olympia, BR. **366** Colorsport, TR; www.sporting-heroes.net, B; **367** Allsport/David Cannon, T; Corbis/© Tony Roberts, ML; Corbis/© Tony Roberts, BR. **368** www.sporting-heroes.net, TM; Roger Stewart, BM. **369** Corbis/© Jerome Prevost, TL; www.sporting-heroes.net, BL; Roger Stewart, TR, BR. **370** AKG/Albert Meyer, TL; Popperfoto, BL; Hulton-Getty, BR. **370-71** Background, Corbis/© Karl Weatherly. **371** Popperfoto, TM; Allsport/Gray Mortimore, ML; Allsport/Mike Hewitt, BR. **372** Corbis/© TempSport, TL; © Bettmann/ Corbis, MR; Roger Stewart, BL; © Bettmann/Corbis, BR. **373** Colorsport, TR; Corbis, BL; Popperfoto, BR. **375** Bradbury & Williams/Mountain High; Rex Features. **376** Diner's Club UK, TM; © Archivo Iconografico, S.A./Corbis, TR; Timeline, The Art Archive/Private Collection/Dagli Orti; Werner Forman Archive, BL; SCALA, BR. **377** © Archivo Iconografico, S.A./Corbis, MM; Timeline, Rex Features/Simon Walker; Corbis/© Charles O'Rear, BR. **378** Background, © Ford, BL; Artworks, Stefan Morris. **379** Top left-right: © Bettmann/Corbis, 2; Mary Evans Picture Library, 3; AKG, 4; © Hulton-Deutsch Collection/Corbis, 5; © Bettmann/Corbis, 6, 7; Corbis/© Roger Ressmeyer, 8; Artwork, Bradbury & Williams, T; Stefan Morris, BL **380** Panos Pictures/Duncan Simpson, MM; Corbis/Ted Spiegel, BM. **380-81** Map, Bradbury & Williams/Mountain High. **381** Background, Panos Pictures/Chris Sattlberger. **382-83** Top-bottom, SPL/Astrid & Hanns-Friedler Michler, 1; SPL/Ed Young, 2; Still Pictures/Michel Breuil, 3; SPL/BSIP JOLYOT, 4; Still Pictures/Sophie Boussamba, 4. **384** SPL/Jeremy Walker. **385** SPL/Time David, TL; SPL/Cyril Ruosso, TR; Robert Harding Picture Library, BR. **386** Brown Brothers, TM; Science & Society Picture Library, BL, BM; © Volkswagen, BR. **387** Roger Stewart, TL; Science & Society Picture Library, TR; LAT, BL; Neill Bruce, BM; Alvey & Towers, BR. **388** Matthew White. **389** Bradbury & Williams. **390** © Bettmann/Corbis,TM; © Hulton-Deutsch Collection/Corbis, MM; Science & Society Picture Library, BL, BR. **390-91** Background, Rex Features. SPL/Martin Bond, TM; © Hulton-Deutsch Collection, TR; SPL/François Sauze, BR. **392** Stefan Morris, TR; Brown Brothers, ML. **392-93** Background, TRH Pictures; Artwork, Stefan Morris. **393** Mark Franklin, TL; TRH Pictures, TR; Bradbury & Williams, B. **394** Science & Society Picture Library, ML, BR; **394-95** Background, The Flight Collection; Artwork, Mark Franklin. **395** The Flight Collection, TL; Aviation Photographs International, TR. **396** SPL/Novosti, TL; NASA, BR. **396-97** Background, NASA. **397** Toucan Books, MR; SPL/US Geological Survey, BR. **398** Bradbury & Williams, ML; NASA, MM. **398-99** Background, SPL/NASA. **399** NASA. **400** Bradbury & Williams, TR; John Meek, BL. **401** Frank Spooner Pictures/Pace, ML; Allsport/Al Bello, MR; Kobal Collection/Miramax Films/Universal Pictures, BR. **403-4** Background, Corbis/© Bill Ross; Artwork, Mark Franklin; Timeline, Stefan Morris; Map, Bradbury & Williams/Mountain High. **404-5** Artwork, Matthew White; background, Corbis/© Charles E. Rotkin. **405** Corbis/© Roger Ressmeyer, BR **406** Still Pictures/Julio Etchart, TR; Stefan Morris, BL; Matthew White, BR. **406-7** Background, Still Pictures/Julio Etchart; Timeline, Stefan Morris. **407** Matthew White, BL; Still Pictures/ Mike Jackson, BR. **408** Still Pictures/ Hartnut Schwarzbach, TR; Corbis/© Paul Almasy, BL. **408-9** Background, Corbis/© Roger Ressmeyer. **409** Bradbury & Williams, TL; Corbis/ © Ecoscene, BL; Panos Pictures, BR. **411** Martin Woodward; Bradbury & Williams. **413** Natural History Museum, London, MM; *Rain, Steam, and Speed – The Great Western Railway*, oil on canvas by Joseph Mallord William Turner, National Gallery, London, BR; Artwork, Bradbury & Williams, BM. **414-17** Artwork, Bradbury & Williams. **418** © Bettmann/Corbis, TR. **418-19** Artwork, Roger Stewart. **419** Bradbury & Williams, ML; Roy Williams, MR. **420-29** Background, Corbis/© George Hall. **422** Bradbury & Williams. **423** Dorling Kindersley Ltd, TR; Roger Stewart, BR. **424-25** Top left-right: Rex Features, 1; John Meek, 2; SPL/NASA, 3; Woodfall Wild Images/Jeremy Moore, 4; Corbis/© Leif Skoogfors, 5; SPL/Hugh Turvey, 6; SPL/US Air Force, 7. **426-27** Bradbury & Williams, **428** AKG. **429** Matthew White, TL; MM; Bradbury & Williams, BL. **430-31** Martin Woodward. **432-33** Natural History Museum, London. **434-35** Martin Woodward. **436** Martin Woodward. **437** Martin Wooward, BL; Woodfall Wild Images/Niel Hicks, BM; BBCNHU/Chris O'Reilly, BR. **438** Antbits, BL; Bradbury & Williams, MR. **439** Bradbury & Williams. **440** Bill Ballenberg/NGS Image Collection, TR; Painting, Alberto Gutiérrez/photograph Guillermo Hare, ML; Christopher Donnan/© Walter Ava/Bruning Museum, BR. **441** Artwork by Roger Stewart adapted from the painting of the Burial Chamber of Tomb 2 by Percy Fiestas, BL; Christopher Donnan/© Walter Ava/Bruning Museum, BR. **442** Brown Brothers, TR; Michael Holford/Science Museum, BM; Science & Society Picture Library, BR. **443** Science & Society Picture Library, TM; Michael Holford/Royal Institution, London, ML; Robert Opie Collection, MR, BM. **444** © Reader's Digest, TR; Science & Society Picture Library, BL; Robert Opie Collection, BR. **445** Science & Society Picture Library, TM; SPL/ Adam Hart-Davis, ML; Trip/Dyson, R. **446** Rex Features, TL; Science & Society Picture Library, TM; SPL/Library of Congress, TR. **446-47** Background, Woodfall Wild Images/ David Woodfall; Artwork, Martin Woodward. **447** Science & Society Picture Library, TR; Science & Society Picture Library/NASA, MM. **448** Science & Society Picture Library, TR, BL; SPL, BR. **449** © Bettmann/ Corbis, TL; Science & Society Picture Library, TR, BL; Frank Spooner Pictures, BR. **450** Bradbury & Williams, TR; Science & Society Picture Library, BL. **451** © Steve McDonough, MM; Intel Corporation, BR. **452** Martin Woodward. **453** Digital Vision, BR. **454** Sotheby's Picture Library, TR; Robert Opie Collection, BL; Mark Franklin, BR. **455** © Sony, TL; Science & Society Picture Library, TM; Rex Features/Adrian Denis; Mark Franklin, BL, BR. **456** Paul Baran, ML; © Vint Cerf, MR. **457** Bradbury & Williams, T; Frank Spooner Pictures/Carolina

Salguero-FB, ML; Frank Spooner Pictures, MR. **458** Timeline, Science & Society Picture Library, MR; SPL/Jean-Loup Charmet, BM. **459** SPL/Stanley B. Burns, MD/The Burns Archive, New York, TL; SPL/George Bernard, TR; SPL, MM; Popperfoto, MR; Timeline, Science & Society Picture Library/ NMP/RMD. **460** Timeline, SPL/BSIP Boucharlet; SPL/St Mary's Hospital Medical School, MM; SPL/James King-Holmes, BL. **461** SPL/Geoff Tompkinson, TR; Timeline, SPL/James King-Holmes; AKG, MM; SPL/National Institutes of Health, BM. **462** The Art Archive/Dagli Orti, TL; © Magnum/ Fred Mayer, BR. **462-63** Background, Mark Franklin. **463** The Art Archive/ Eileen Tweedy, TL; Frank Spooner Pictures/ Gamma/Roger Viollet, TM; © Magnum/Stuart Franklin, BM. **464** Darren R. Awuah, TR; Trip/B. Gibbs, BR. **464-65** Background, Collections/ B. Shuel. **465** Stefan Morris, TL; Corbis/© Michael S. Yamashita, TR; Mark Franklin, BL. **467** Bradbury & Williams. **472-73** Bradbury & Williams. **469** Bradbury & Williams. **483** Colin Woodman.

Covers: © PhotoDisc, Inc.